PROUST'S DUCHESS

PROUST'S DUCHESS

HOW THREE CELEBRATED WOMEN CAPTURED THE IMAGINATION OF FIN-DE-SIÈCLE PARIS

CAROLINE WEBER

ALFRED A. KNOPF
NEW YORK · 2018

THIS IS A BORZOI BOOK PUBLISHED BY ALFRED A. KNOPF

Copyright © 2018 by Caroline Weber

www.aaknopf.com

Knopf, Borzoi Books, and the colophon are registered trademarks of
Penguin Random House LLC.

Library of Congress Cataloging-in-Publication Data
Names: Weber, Caroline, 1969– author.
Title: Proust's duchess : how three celebrated women captured the
imagination of fin-de-siècle Paris / Caroline Weber.
Description: First edition. | New York : Alfred A. Knopf, 2018. | Includes bibliographical references.
Identifiers: LCCN 2017038855 | ISBN 9780307961785 (hardcover) |
ISBN 9780307961792 (ebook)
Subjects: LCSH: Proust, Marcel, 1871–1922—Sources. | Proust, Marcel, 1871–1922—Contemporaries. |
Proust, Marcel, 1871–1922. À la recherche du temps perdu. | Women—France—Paris—Biography. |
Aristocracy (Social class)—France—Paris—Biography. | Straus, Geneviève, 1849–1926. |
Chevignâe, Laure de, 1859–1936. | Greffulhe, Elisabeth, comtesse, 1860–1952. | Paris (France)—
Social life and customs—19th century. | Paris (France)—Intellectual life—19th century.
Classification: LCC PQ2631.R63 z9818 2018 | DDC 843/.912 [B]—dc23 LC record
available at https://lccn.loc.gov/2017038855

Front-of-jacket image: Lagel-Meier, shoe, circa 1905 © Galliera / Roger-Viollet
Back-of-jacket image: Élisabeth de Riquet de Caraman-Chimay, the Comtesse Greffulhe
by Giuseppe Primoli, Fondazione Primoli, Rome
Jacket design by Jennifer Carrow
Manufactured in the United States of America
First Edition

For Gloria Vanderbilt Cooper,
with admiration and with love

Let my blood flow into your thoughts.
Let my veins pour into your dreams,
Filling them with opals.
Your love will be made of my dreams.

—ÉLISABETH GREFFULHE, *Tua Res Agitur* (c. 1887)

And so it is that the most beautiful flowers of our dreams have
our blood for sap, and our minds for roots.

—MARCEL PROUST, " 'The Little Shoes,' by M. Louis Ganderax" (1892)

CONTENTS

PROUST'S DUCHESS

LIKE A SWAN

Marcel Proust was never a morning person. But for a short while in the spring of 1892, he got out of bed early.

The routine was always the same. After quickly dressing he set out from his family's apartment near the place de la Madeleine—in one of the luxury residential buildings that had sprouted up along the Parisian boulevards a few decades prior—and headed west into the Faubourg Saint-Honoré, the most prestigious neighborhood on the Right Bank.

In the second half of the nineteenth century, this was the province of the *flâneur*, but Proust, then a twenty-year-old law student, was no dandy out for an idle stroll around town. He strode with purpose, in search of elegance, and while he didn't know her yet (for elegance was a woman), he did know where she lived. It was there that he hurried each morning, at some risk to his delicate health. As he would confess to her a quarter of a century later, "I used to have a heart attack every time I saw you."

To make this perilous trip, he took a path he had christened "my route of hope." It began with a sharp right out of the Prousts' apartment building, a seven-story limestone wedge that cleaved the surging traffic of the boulevard Malesherbes like a ship's prow slicing through choppy waters. This turn brought him straightaway into the funereal hush of the rue de la Ville-l'Évêque, a short side street that led past a row of single-family mansions, or *hôtels particuliers*, as big as ocean liners and still as tombs. Approaching the Ministry of the Interior, Proust veered left down the block-long rue des Saussaies and into the place Beauvau, where he paused just long enough to take in the titles on display in the windows of the Émile Paul bookstore. Then he made another right turn into quiet. Five more minutes of brisk walking led him to his destination: a narrow, four-story residential building at 34, rue de Miromesnil.

With its cheap stucco façade and its sooty dormered roof, this structure had nothing visibly special about it. Built a century earlier, it lacked the modern amenities Proust and his family enjoyed at home: an elevator, efficient ventilation, bathrooms with running water. But to him, the shabby sliver of a building was the Promised Land, holy because inhabited by the goddess whose exit he now, stationed on the sidewalk across from the front door, anxiously awaited.

Most mornings, he didn't have to linger for long before she stepped outside. A petite blond countess in her early thirties, she would give no indication that

Every morning in the spring of 1892, Proust passed the Émile Paul bookstore *(far left)*, place Beauvau, on his way to Mme de Chevigné's.

she had spotted the dark-eyed, dark-haired youth gawking at her from across the street, though the rue de Miromesnil being neither busy nor wide, he would have been hard to miss. As she made her habitual left turn toward the place Beauvau, Proust afforded her a brief head start before taking off at a trot behind her. Luckily for him, she tended on these jaunts to eschew the company of a liveried footman—an indispensable chaperone for most women of her class and a deterrent to precisely the sort of behavior in which Proust was engaging.

Dogging his lady's brisk, athletic steps around the quarter (she had a trim figure and liked to keep it that way), he loitered outside the imposing *hôtels* where she stopped to leave her calling cards, outside the boutiques where she did her shopping, and outside a ducal palace off the place de la Concorde where she paid two visits a day, the first and last stops on her busy social round. He jogged up and down her favorite promenade, the Champs-Élysées, in her wake, dodging carriages and pedestrians so as not to lose the trail. From a discreet distance, he strained for glimpses of her aquiline profile and her "bright, blue eyes, the color of the sky of France"—also the color of the cornflowers on her hat. Committing every last detail of her face and dress to memory, he marveled at the alchemy whereby she "turned a simple morning walk . . . into a whole poem of elegance, the finest adornment, the rarest flower under the sun."

Quite obviously, a creature this transfixing couldn't be just anyone, and indeed she was not. The object of Proust's obsession was a celebrity *mondaine* (society woman):* a friend to royals, a muse to artists, a cynosure of the nobility, the darling of the social columns, a fantasy to strangers, and the quintessence, he wrote, of the singular "elevating glory" otherwise found solely in "white peacocks, black swans, . . . queens in captivity." But these qualities also made her maddeningly inaccessible to her young admirer, for while he and his *mondaine* lived in the same part of town, their social milieux—hers the haute noblesse, his the haute bourgeoisie—lay worlds apart.

Still, Proust nurtured the hope that one day she would take him under her wing and bear him aloft to a realm of pure, ineffable glamour. And so he trailed along behind her each morning, a stray puppy imprinting on a swan.

As the biographer George Painter points out, this was "an absurd form [of] wooing"—a conclusion Proust himself would reach only in middle age, when he waxed rueful about his boyish efforts "to catch a bird of paradise beneath the trees of the avenue Gabriel." But at the time, the futility of the hunt was a lesson he would have to learn the hard way. One spring morning, several weeks into his stalking campaign, the countess stunned him by whirling about to face him and issuing a sharp rebuke: *"Feetjahm is waiting for me!"*

The first words she had ever addressed to Proust, they demoralized him for two reasons. Comte Robert de Fitz-James was everything Proust was not: a dashing former naval officer and Bourbon courtier whose family and friends filled the pages of the *Almanach de Gotha,* a social register for royalty and the high nobility. (The head of the comte's family, the Duke of Alba, Berwick, and Fitz-James, was said to be the most titled man in Europe, more heraldically laden than even the queen of England.) An accomplished horseman and shot, Fitz-James, whose surname only bluebloods knew to pronounce "Feetjahm," was a pillar of Paris's sportiest, most selective men's club, the Jockey, famously closed to commoners and Jews. As rivals for his damsel's favor went, the young man could not have conceived of a more daunting opponent than Comte Robert de Feetjahm.†

Even more discouragingly, the voice of Proust's divinity did not fit with the sublime image he had formed of her. When she finally spoke to him, he should have heard the music of the spheres. Instead, he heard the squawk of a hoarse, cantankerous parrot. So much for his rara avis. "Perhaps the most real thing about her beauty lay in my desire," he reflected in an essay he wrote the following year. "She has lived her life, but I alone, perhaps, have dreamed her."

---

* A synonym for this term, which the reader will also encounter in the pages that follow, is *grande mondaine* (woman of the great world); the male and gender-neutral version of this word, as both a noun and an adjective, is *mondain.* For brevity's sake, when using these terms as nouns, I favor them over the slightly more elegant and (in the milieu I am describing) widely used *femme du monde* (woman of society), *homme du monde* (man of society), and *gens du monde* (people of society). The closest approximation to any of these words in English, "socialite," carries grasping, mildly pejorative, or dismissive connotations that do not suit in the fin-de-siècle Parisian context, where *mondains* at least officially commanded respect.

† Readers wishing to know more about the rules that govern modes of nobiliary address, and about the treatment of royal and aristocratic titles in this book, should consult the "Author's Note" in appendix A.

This conclusion was only partially correct. Yes, Proust had dreamed his rare bird into being. But by the time he came along, countless others had dreamed her too, reimagining her as a poem and a queen, an exquisite flower and a mythic swan. More than he knew, perhaps, their dreams suffused and shaped his own.

So did the dreams of the lady herself. She had lived her life, but in two registers, fact and fiction, and like those countless others who had dreamed her too, she strongly favored fiction. Not just in their dreams but in her own, she had seen herself reborn as a poem and a queen, an exquisite flower and a mythic swan. Not just in their eyes but in her own, she had become, in fact, a fiction. And she had undergone this change long before she ever crossed paths with a nobody named Marcel Proust.

THIS IS A BOOK ABOUT REAL PEOPLE turning into fictions, in the context of a class—the French aristocracy—which at the end of the nineteenth century was dying as a political force while resurrecting itself as a myth. Central to that symbolic revival were three doyennes of Parisian high society who transformed themselves, and were transformed by those around them, into living legends: paragons of nobility, elegance, and style. Their names were Geneviève Halévy Bizet Straus (1849–1926); Laure de Sade, Comtesse Adhéaume de Chevigné (1859–1936); and Élisabeth de Riquet de Caraman-Chimay, Vicomtesse (later Comtesse) Greffulhe (1860–1952).

Proust's Duchess is a triple biography of these women. It traces the interweaving paths they took in their rise to social stardom and studies the inventive strategies they used to get there. It relates their conquest of a world where projecting an image was the precondition, and the price, of belonging. It considers what was lost and what won, what was hidden and what laid bare, when selves became characters and lives became stories. It recounts their most dazzling triumphs; it unveils their darkest secrets. It follows them into the heady glare of mass adulation and finds them again in the dim precincts of loneliness. It presents them as they wanted the world to see them and as they were when they thought no one was looking.

Hemmed in by unhappy marriages and restrictive gender norms, the three protagonists of this book sought a measure of freedom and fulfillment by recasting themselves as icons. They reinvented themselves as archetypes of a storied Parisian fiefdom made up of visiting crowned heads and local aristocrats and known variously as the "monde" (short for *le grand monde*, "the great world"), the "gratin" (or "crust") and the Faubourg (short for *le noble Faubourg*).*

---

* Strictly speaking, *le noble Faubourg* referred to the Faubourg Saint-Germain, the stately Left Bank neighborhood where the aristocracy had maintained its stronghold in the French capital during the final century of the ancien régime. But in the nineteenth century, the scope of this term expanded to include the Faubourg Saint-Honoré, a

This society was an anachronism, founded on traditions of hereditary privilege and courtly elegance left over from the defunct ancien régime. These traditions ran counter to the egalitarian principles in the name of which the leaders of the French Revolution (1789–1799) had toppled the monarchy and eradicated the nobility a century earlier, and which the government of the Third Republic (1870–1940) continued to promulgate at those institutions' expense.*

Paradoxically, however, the social and cultural authority of the Faubourg remained absolute throughout the fin de siècle; democratic though France had become, noble rank endured as the ultimate status symbol. None other than the Third Republic's first president, bourgeois statesman Adolphe Thiers, made a candid admission to this effect. In 1871, when the highest-ranked nobleman in France, the Duc d'Uzès, congratulated him on his election to the presidency, Thiers blurted out, "Oh, but Mme Thiers would much rather be a duchess!"

The president's wife was far from alone in her craving for noble glamour. As novelist Jules Renard wrote in 1898,

> Since the Revolution, our republic hasn't made a single step toward [equality] or liberty. It's a republic where all people care about is being invited to [Mme] Greffulhe's.

Described by still another commentator as "the triumph of the duchesses," this contradictory state of affairs persisted for as long as *mondain* society did, only to collapse along with it in the chaos of the First World War.

AS THE GODDESSES OF THIS VALHALLA, Mmes de Chevigné, Greffulhe, and Straus held inexhaustible fascination for their compatriots both inside and outside their privileged sphere. However, none of the three was a duchess, and one, Mme Straus, was not titled at all. This fact highlighted the singularity and the novelty of their achievement. In the monde, the intrinsic superiority of duchesses to countesses (let alone commoners) had traditionally been beyond question. If these three women come to eclipse the duchesses in their milieu, it was not by refuting the time-tested values of hierarchy and rank but by reworking those values in forward-thinking ways. At a moment in history when, with the rise of mass media, popular opinion was emerging in France as a force of unprecedented and unreckoned power, these women infused the snob appeal of class-based privilege with a thoroughly modern knack for publicity and self-promotion.

Bridging history and modernity, Mmes Greffulhe, Straus, and de Chevigné

---

less sedate, more showily opulent district across the Seine. "The Faubourg Saint-Germain is *noblesse*," ran a popular saying. "The Faubourg Saint-Honoré is *richesse*."
* Under the Third Republic as under the First and Second, the precept that all men are created equal applied exclusively to men. French women did not gain the right to vote until 1945.

played to two different audiences at once: the gratin on the one hand, and the general public on the other. To establish and maintain their stature within the noblesse, they adopted its time-honored creed of elegance and exclusivity, perfected its flair for luxurious patrician style, and surrounded themselves with friends to the grandest manner born. At the same time, to appeal to a broader public, they cultivated influential reporters, editors, painters, sculptors, composers, novelists, playwrights, poets, fashion designers, and photographers. Harbingers of a world where celebrity alone suffices to confer social importance and ordain cultural worth, they offered themselves up as "fodder for sonnets and flesh for novels," in the words of one of the many writers who used them in this way.

By the same token, Mmes Straus, de Chevigné, and Greffulhe did not rely solely on others to craft their public images. With the poses they struck and the tales they spun, they played an active, even capital role in shaping their unforgettable personae. In so doing, they engaged in a complex negotiation between creativity and social cachet. Over and above its aesthetic value, the work of the imagination functioned for all three women variously as an escape hatch and a self-marketing gambit, a coping mechanism and a seduction technique, a revision of history and an affirmation of self. It lured them all by turns as a flight from reality, an antidote to loss, a substitute for love. Artistic endeavor, narrowly and broadly defined, allowed them to enact a fantasy of noble distinction, even as the political order that had historically upheld that distinction crumbled around them.

Charting this trio's ascent to the pinnacle of a soon-to-be-extinct society, this book tells the true prehistory of a semi-true story that Proust would go on to recount in his seven-volume, loosely autobiographical novel, *In Search of Lost Time* (1913–1927): the decline and fall of an aristocratic ideal.

Before a swan dies, it sings.

MARCEL PROUST KNEW A THING OR TWO about people turning into fictions. In the opening paragraph of the *Search,* the first-person narrator, later identified as Marcel, remembers reading in bed as a child. As he drifted off to sleep, the adult Marcel recalls of his younger self, "It seemed to me that I myself had become the subject of the book I was reading." This immersion in fantasy saturates the novel, which chronicles the narrator's gradual development into a writer.

The hero of the *Search* grows up in a family that views the world in terms of literature and art. In one of his defining childhood memories, his mother reads to him aloud from George Sand's *The Country Waif* (*François le champi,* 1848). Although she skips over the more suggestive passages in Sand's novel—a love story between the titular waif and the older woman who raised him—the quasi-incestuous passion at its core echoes the intensely close bond between her and Marcel.

Between the narrator's mother and maternal grandmother, the written word is just as important; the two women share a tender private language rooted in the mother-daughter correspondence of Mme de Sévigné (1626–1696), a chronicler of Louis XIV's rule. Sardonic lines from another memoirist of that king's long reign, the Duc de Saint-Simon (1675–1755), pepper the badinage between Marcel's grandfather and a character called Charles Swann, an old family friend. When the former suspects that a schoolmate of his grandson's might be Jewish, he quotes slyly from Fromental Halévy's *La Juive* (*The Jewess,* 1835). The narrator himself recollects an aria from this same opera, "Rachel, when of the Lord," years later, when the madam of a brothel offers him an "exotic" Jewish moll by that name.

For Marcel, the tragedies of playwright Jean Racine (1639–1699) serve as a constant point of reference, whether he is bewailing the fussy outfit his parents make him wear to have his picture taken or noting the prurient interest two closeted gay noblemen take in a bevy of young foreign diplomats at a party. Paintings furnish another rich trove of analogies. Stunned to learn that a venerable marquise has heard of his father—a bourgeois civil servant with no apparent connection to her social set—Marcel likens her to the supersized king of the gods in Gustave Moreau's *Jupiter and Semele* (1895) and envisions his father as one of the antlike figures clustered at the base of Jupiter's throne. A baron in white tie suggests "a 'Harmony in Black and White' by Whistler." At a beach resort in Normandy, seagulls dotting a pastel sky resemble "the water lilies in a . . . canvas by Monet."

Conditioned to see life through the lens of art, the protagonist of the *Search* conceives of love, too, as above all an exercise of the imagination. The earliest object of his affection is his family's neighbor, Oriane de Guermantes, Duchesse de Guermantes, a grande dame who is closer in age to his mother than to him and whom he has never met. The narrator's infatuation originates with his rapturous study of images of Mme de Guermantes's ancestors, scions of France's oldest and greatest noble dynasty.* As a child, he moons over magic-lantern slides depicting the legend of Geneviève de Brabant, a medieval chatelaine from whom the duchesse claims descent, and he admires the likenesses of other feudal-age Guermantes in the stained-glass windows and tapestries of his family's local church.

Based on these representations, Marcel comes to think of the duchesse as an

---

* The real Guermantes were not one of the foremost clans of the *noblesse d'épée,* belonging instead to the less ancient, less prestigious *noblesse de robe,* a class of aristocrats who gained their titles by serving in important judiciary and administrative positions in the king's government. But when Proust wrote the *Search,* he wanted to create a noble dynasty using a family name that had gone extinct, and once he determined that "Guermantes," the sound of which had captured his fancy, had no living bearers, he decided to use it in his novel.

emblem of France's romantic, chivalric, quintessentially noble past. "When I thought of Mme de Guermantes," he explains, "I was picturing her to myself in the colors of a tapestry or a stained-glass window, as a being from another century, made of different stuff from ordinary people." Even the "name of Guermantes" conjures up "fairy-tales, Geneviève de Brabant, . . . a tapestry depicting King Charles VIII," or as scholar Dominique Jullien has noted, "the mythic bird Garamantes," a creature in medieval bestiaries.

As he enters adulthood, the narrator's interest in the duchesse shifts from the Middle Ages to modern times but preserves its basis in fantasy. Having learned from her friend Swann that Mme de Guermantes is "one of the noblest creatures in Paris, the cream of the choicest, most refined society," Marcel now regards her as the gatekeeper and queen of an enchanted kingdom from which his own low birth, he fears, will forever bar him: a realm where history and myth live on, overlain with a gloss of contemporary chic. From the society pages he gleans details of her sensational appearance at a costume ball hosted by the Princesse de Léon (a real-life maven of the fin-de-siècle gratin). At the Opéra, gazing from afar at the duchesse and one of her cousins, the Princesse de Guermantes, the narrator compares "these two poetic creatures" to goddesses from classical myth: "beautiful and ethereal Diana" and "Minerva [with] her glittering fringed shield." The duchesse's understated yet stylish garb looks to him like "a bird's plumage: not just a beautiful ornament, but an actual extension of her body."

For a few months, he even stalks Mme de Guermantes on her daily promenades around the Right Bank. On these outings, Marcel fuels his own excitement by imagining he is on the trail of "a mythological god that has been turned into a laurel or a swan." One day, however, he spots the duchesse anxiously tugging at her veil and coat, fussing over her appearance "as if she were a woman like any other." Unnerved by the ordinariness of this vignette, he ironically reworks his mythological conceit, likening her to "a divine swan that evinces the behavior of its animal species . . . by suddenly pecking at a button or an umbrella as a swan would, not remembering that it was a god."

The narrator's alarm at Mme de Guermantes's lapse in divinity betrays his reflexive habit of overwriting fact with fiction. To him, the unvarnished truth never looks as good as the embellished alternative; reality always lets him down. In the case of the duchesse, all it takes is one dinner party at her house for Marcel to determine that his dream girl is actually a nightmare. Egotistical, cold, pretentious, and shallow, she cares only for trivialities that enhance her fabulous image: paintings and books acquired not for their own sake but as tokens of her self-proclaimed intellectualism; similarly decorative "friendships" with famous artists, about whose work she proves alternately dismissive and ignorant, despite her pompous avowals that "for her, talent is all that matters"; family ties proudly invoked yet devoid of genuine affection; "benevolence" toward her servants, whom she covertly mistreats. Even her wit, which her fellow *mondains* uniformly

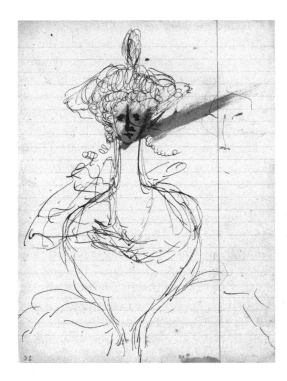

Proust conceived of his ideal noblewoman as a cross between a divinity and a swan, sketched here in one of his unpublished manuscript notes.

praise, "turn[s] out to consist mostly of fat jokes, put-downs, and flat-footed, sophomoric puns." Her titled friends prove disappointing as well—superficial like their hostess but lacking even her thin veneer of culture and charm.

Studying the duchesse and her peers up close, the narrator realizes that in their milieu, "through a topsy-turvy inversion left over from the etiquette of the royal court, . . . it is the surface that [has] become essential and profound." Although he continues to frequent the Guermantes crowd for years to come—having been miraculously (and improbably) welcomed into their midst, he is not about to forfeit the privilege—Marcel ceases to venerate them as "an assembly of gods" on earth.

This disenchantment is of a piece with the many other disillusionments that attend his four-thousand-page search for meaning. While "the Guermantes way" falls far short of his expectations, so does everything else in which the narrator serially seeks his purpose: family, friendship, love, sex, cathedrals, recitals, sleuthing, sloth, tourism, journalism, Impressionism, voyeurism, young girls in flower, young men in uniform, and on and on. Only in the *Search*'s final volume, *Time Regained* (*Le Temps retrouvé*, 1927), does Marcel resolve his conundrum in a eureka moment that, tellingly, echoes his boyhood dream of merging into his bedtime stories.

The scene unfolds at a party at the Paris mansion of the Prince and Princesse de Guermantes, shortly after the end of World War I. Now middle-aged and ailing, the narrator has just returned from a sanatorium outside the city, where he spent the final years of the war. Arriving at the fête, he discovers that during his absence, the grandees of his youth have aged almost beyond recognition. So drastically have they deteriorated that for a moment he wonders if he has overlooked a morbid dress code for the event: Come as your own death mask. This *bal de têtes* (death-masks' ball), as he wryly dubs it, again gives the lie to his former reverence for the gratin's "beautiful people," beautiful no longer. Even Mme de Guermantes has lost her looks, and then some, as she has mutated from a swan goddess into "an old sacred fish," submerged in the primordial goop of lost and wasted time. (*Temps perdu* carries both meanings in French.) Old age has wrought havoc on her appearance, even as war has swept away her world of frivolity and privilege, rendering her obsolete.

After a brief, banal exchange with the duchesse, Marcel withdraws into his hosts' library, where, her peculiarly gruff, raspy voice still ringing in his ears "like the trumpets of the Last Judgment," he has his epiphany at last: "The only life worth living" is one that is "illuminated and . . . realized in a book." Spotting *The Country Waif* on a bookshelf, he suddenly realizes that all the time he feared he had lost or wasted in the past can be redeemed if he transposes it—fleeting pleasures, false hopes, and everything in between—into literature. By mining his experiences for artistic truth, he can infuse them with the significance they seemed to lack the first time around. This resolution knits art and life together in a tight Gordian knot, positioning the book the reader of the *Search* holds in her hands as the book the narrator of the *Search* is just gearing up to write as he concludes his tale. The end. And the beginning.

Proust further blurred the boundaries between writing and reality by peopling his narrative, set among the pampered classes of turn-of-the-century Paris, with characters markedly similar to well-known individuals from that time and place (which happened to be his own time and place). While the resemblances between Proust's characters and his acquaintances were often glaringly obvious, he insisted his magnum opus was not a roman à clef—a novel that cloaks recognizable contemporary personalities in nominally fictive disguises. To Céleste Albaret, the housekeeper who ministered to him while he was working on the *Search*, he groused about a friend who "asked me for the 'keys' to my book. . . . It is impossible for me to give them to him. Not that I am afraid and want to hide them. But there are too many keys for each character."

At the same time, Proust courted speculation that he was writing from life by endowing his narrator, Marcel, with many of his own identifying traits: his haut-bourgeois family; his functionary father (Dr. Adrien Proust was a respected epidemiologist and public health official); his overweening attachment to his mother, an ardent reader of Racine, Sévigné, and Sand; his own dreamy, bookish disposition; his chronic health problems; his disinclination to work for a living; his unluckiness in love; and his keen interest in high society. (Proust did exempt his narrator from two of his own supposed flaws: his Jewishness on his mother's side and his sexual attraction to men. He also made his alter ego an only child, thereby doing away with the existence of his younger brother, Robert.) Proust claimed these points of convergence between his hero and himself were merely effects of his own laziness: "I have spared myself the trouble of inventing my hero [by] giv[ing] him traits that really are mine." Laziness being yet another trait he shared with the fictional Marcel.

To portray the titans of tout-Paris, Proust borrowed liberally from beings of flesh and blood. The character of Charles Swann, an urbane swell embraced by the monde despite his middle-class, German-Jewish heritage, Proust modeled on a well-liked gadabout called Charles Haas (1833–1902). Comte Robert de Montesquiou-Fezensac (1855–1921) unwittingly imparted his high birth, his homosexuality, his erudition, his mean streak, his Whistler-worthy evening dress, and his spectacularly belligerent haughtiness to Marcel's would-be mentor, the Baron de Charlus. Henry, Comte Greffulhe (1848–1932), a cousin of Montesquiou's by marriage, furnished the template for Charlus's rich, smug, and callous brother, Basin, Duc de Guermantes, whose compulsive philandering makes his wife, Oriane, "the most cheated-on, if the most beautiful, woman in Paris," and whose blustering rages earn him a nickname that also belonged to the tantrum-prone Greffulhe: "Thundering Jove" (Jupiter Tonnant).

With the Duchesse de Guermantes, finally, Proust created a composite based on the three grandes dames who together constituted his dream of patrician elegance and grace. He confirmed this triple connection in letters to and about all three women and in many other well-documented exchanges. His friend Fernand Gregh put it the most succinctly: "The Duchesse de Guermantes was Mme Straus combined with Mme de Chevigné, . . . and with a bit of Mme Greffulhe as well."

So famous were these women in their time that even strangers readily pegged them as the models for Mme de Guermantes. Idolized both by their fellow patricians and by the general public, they inspired much the same blend of awe, fascination, and inchoate longing that twenty-first-century American society accords to media personalities, sports stars, and billionaires. Élisabeth Greffulhe received so much fan mail throughout her life that her archives contain a large file marked "Homages and Appreciations from People I Don't Know." (Folders within this file bear such tantalizing labels as "Verses from a Lovelorn Stranger" and "Anonymous Adorations—1888.") Neither Geneviève Straus nor Laure de Chevigné was this scrupulous about preserving personal records, but both women elicited their share of adorations, anonymous and otherwise. They, too, captured the imagination of an era.

IT IS ONE OF THE PARADOXES OF HISTORY that three individuals who enjoyed such outsized celebrity in their lifetimes should today be remembered only for having inadvertently loaned their features to a fictional character, albeit a character in one of the greatest books of all time. And yet, the few biographies that have been written about these women have for the most part been complicit in reducing them to raw materials of the novelist's art. The earliest of these studies, the Princesse Bibesco's *La Duchesse de Guermantes: Laure de Sade, Comtesse de Chevigné* (1950), directly equates the fictive duchesse with the real comtesse, while the most recent work, Laure Hillerin's *La Comtesse Greffulhe: l'ombre des Guermantes* (*The Shadow of the Guermantes*, 2015), offers a point-by-point analysis of its subject's incidental contributions to the character of Mme de Guermantes, from her august genealogy to her Aubusson fauteuils.

Such equations distort the historical picture by tacitly reversing the power dynamic that existed between the novelist and his muses for a full quarter century before he published the first installment of the *Search, Swann's Way* (*Du côté de chez Swann*), in 1913. For the past hundred years, posterity has cared about Mmes de Chevigné, Straus, and Greffulhe because Proust did. But he cared about them because an entire society did, and how an entire society came to care about them is a tale that has not yet been told, not by biographers, not by historians, and not by the author of the *Search*.

As it happens, Proust knew relatively little about the women who "posed" (his term) for his literary portrait of the Duchesse de Guermantes. When in the early 1890s he first embarked upon his long, arduous climb up the peaks of Parisian society, his three protoduchesses already stood firmly at the summit. Between eleven and twenty-two years his senior, they had all ascended to *mondain* glory over the course of the previous decade, while he was still a schoolboy. By the time Proust first began to read about them in the press, all three ladies presided over salons that drew, like Mme de Guermantes's, "the cream of the choicest, most refined society": crowned heads, other grandees, and a select assortment of noted artists. As one of Mme Greffulhe's guests told her, "You invite the dukes and peers to teach the geniuses good manners, and you invite the geniuses to prevent the dukes and peers from getting bored." Or as Proust himself would later say of his invented duchess's philosophy of entertaining, "The quality of a 'salon,' Mme de Guermantes correctly thought, is founded on sacrifice"—on a principle of strict exclusion.

In this setting, the social prospects of an obscure youth of bourgeois, half-Jewish parentage looked anything but bright, though he made much of his lone *mondain* credential: his high-school friendship with Mme Straus's son, Jacques Bizet. On the strength of this connection, Proust began attending Mme Straus's salon in 1889, when he was eighteen, and quickly established himself as a regular there. Even so, it took him a good ten years to form a real friendship with the hostess, and even after that, their bond always bore a trace of its original formality. In the 1910s, Céleste Albaret noticed with some surprise that whenever Mme Straus called on Proust at home (usually after a visit to her dentist, whose office was in the same building), "she would ring at the bell and ask me how Monsieur Proust was. But she never came farther than the hall, and Monsieur Proust never invited her in—she never asked to come in, either."

For his first decade as an habitué of Mme Straus's drawing room, Proust had to resign himself to being treated as a second-class citizen. On the rare occasions when she invited him to lunch or dinner (smaller, more selective affairs than her weekly at-homes), she always placed "little Marcel" at the worst seat at the table. She also once shamed him in front of her other, more valued guests—a carefully curated mix of aristocrats, plutocrats, and artists—by indicating that she only kept Proust around because she wanted his father to help Jacques get into medical school. (Dr. Proust obliged.)

By means of an equally prolonged and obdurate charm offensive, Proust managed in the mid-1890s to develop a cordial relationship with Mme de Chevigné, the birdlike blonde he had shadowed around the Right Bank in 1892. But she put him in his place as well. Like Mme Straus, she held an exclusive salon in Paris, although hers was open only to highborn clubmen like (and including) "Feetjahm." The habitués of Mme de Chevigné's at-homes were the very sort of people Proust was most curious to meet—he himself stood no chance of ever getting into the Jockey (in fact, he would even be rejected from the relatively "bohemian" Cercle de l'Union Artistique), and he knew from the *presse mondaine* (society press) that their cachet was without equal. But Mme de Chevigné stubbornly refused to present Proust to them. In 1909, he pointed out that in the twenty-five years he and the comtesse had known each other, she had never once proposed that he come to her salon—which she had hosted pretty much every day since the early 1880s. She invited Proust only when she socialized with others of his putative ilk: artists of bourgeois and/or Jewish extraction. "Mme de Chevigné is forever trying to put me together with Porto-Riche," he once complained, referencing an eminent Jewish writer twenty-two years his senior. "What she doesn't understand is: *I am Porto-Riche!*" Proust may not have realized quite how true this was. Porto-Riche and Mme de Chevigné were close friends for almost half a century, corresponding far more frequently and candidly than Laure, at least, did with anyone else in her life. Nonetheless, Porto-Riche, too, went to his grave without ever being invited to one of her at-homes.

With Mme Greffulhe, Proust's relations were more tenuous still. It took him the longest time to finagle an introduction to her, without a doubt the most aloof of his three future models. As her cousin and confidant Robert de Montesquiou, whom in 1893 Proust enlisted to act as a go-between, was fond of asking, "Do you not see that your presence in her salon would rid it of the very grandeur you hope to find there?" In 1894, Proust finally prevailed upon Montesquiou for an introduction. But Mme Greffulhe continued to ignore Proust for many years afterward, relenting only when her daughter married his friend Armand, Duc de Guiche, in 1904. From then on, she occasionally deigned to let him fill an empty

Marcel Proust strikes a worldly
pose, circa 1900, photographed
by Otto Wegener.

seat in her box at the opera or function at her dinner parties as a "toothpick": a person brought in after the meal for the amusement of the more important invitees. She never really warmed to him, though; in old age, she remembered Proust to her grandchildren as "a displeasing little man who was forever skulking about in doorways." When asked about him by an American author, Mme Greffulhe said, "I didn't like him. . . . He was tiresome."

Unsurprisingly, given this history, Proust's perspective on these women retained throughout his lifetime the quality of fan-boy worship that had defined it from the start. The air of unreality that envelops the duchesse in his novel also characterized the three *mondaines* who obsessed him in real life. For decades before he set to work on the *Search,* celestial and avian metaphors foreshadowing the narrator's praise for Mme de Guermantes abounded in Proust's (mostly nonfictional) writing about this society troika. Mme Straus is an "angel [who] drives mortals to distraction." Mme de Chevigné "belongs to a special breed, a cross between a goddess and a bird. She is . . . a peacock with wings of snow, a sparrow with jewels for eyes." Mme Greffulhe is "a 'great golden bird'* about to take flight"; her radiance is "like a blessing from on high, like the mysterious and

---

* The allusion here is to José-Maria de Heredia's sonnet "Le Cydnus" (1893), which imagines Cleopatra as a "great golden bird stalking her prey from on high." Proust applied this description to Mme Greffulhe in at least two different essays.

transparent sweetness of the stars." (These last lines are drawn from an unpublished essay Proust wrote about Mme Greffulhe's salon in 1902; long believed to be lost, it is reproduced in translation at the end of this volume.)* Like their variants in the *Search,* these figures of speech describe otherworldly creatures, enshrined in a paradise the earthbound Proust can never hope to enter.

Further presaging the narrator's attitude toward Mme de Guermantes, Proust's idealizing vision of his ladies changed over time into something darker, if no less fantastical and no more human. In the manuscript of *Jean Santeuil,* a disjointed autobiographical novel Proust began writing in 1896 and jettisoned a few years later, he wrote scathingly, "Mme S. has never been to the Louvre, because she doesn't like painting. But because she is rich, she collects drawings by Watteau and the early work of Gustave Moreau." Unabashedly shallow, she values these works only insofar as they advertise her elegant taste. Elsewhere in *Jean Santeuil,* Proust lampoons Mme Straus as "Mme Marmet," a phony middle-class striver whose very name—French for "marmot"—marks her as a nasty critter scrabbling her way up the social food chain.

While he refrained from comparing Mme Greffulhe to a rodent, Proust turned on her with just as much vitriol. In 1907, he scoffed that her much-touted "passion for interesting things" (namely literature and art) was "disagreeable for those interesting things" because it was an act, "enhancing not the woman herself, only her reputation." "Like rouge," he noted, her cultural pretensions allowed her to "look good from across the room," but they would never qualify her to be "a real friend to a man of genius."

By and by, Comtesse Adhéaume de Chevigné, too, lost her luster in Proust's imagination. Although this process began when she first snapped at him about Fitz-James, she continued to disappoint him in the years that followed, as Proust got to know her better and her limitations came more sharply into focus. One of the most vicious letters he ever wrote he addressed to her toward the end of his life; it began: "When what one used to love turns out to be *very, very stupid . . .* " At around the same time, he griped to Céleste Albaret that whereas the comtesse "used to be so beautiful, . . . now she is just an old woman with a hooked nose and a cracked voice." To another confidant, he disparaged her as "a tough old bird I mistook, long ago, for a bird of paradise." Admitting that he had used Mme de Chevigné as a template for Mme de Guermantes, he added, "By making her into a fearsome vulture, at least I have kept others from mistaking her for a mean old hen."

In relation to Proust's "divine swan" encomia, these epithets conform to a pattern the French critic Roland Barthes has identified as the key structuring principle of the *Search* as a whole: "the inversion of essences." Marcel is forever

---

* See appendix C, where I have also translated an 1893 article from *Le Gaulois* that classes Mmes Straus and Greffulhe among the city's leading hostesses. Signed by "Tout-Paris," this essay has not previously been attributed to Proust, but I have provided extensive detail to support my determination that he is its author.

learning to his surprise that people are not as they appear: time after time, he finds that a known self (x) conceals an unknown, opposite self (not x). "Inversion" also being Proust's preferred term for homosexuality, his narrator's discoveries more often than not expose the sexual double lives of gay characters who have been passing as straight. Schoolgirl or widower, diplomat or demimondaine, decorated war hero or ultra-Catholic prince—no matter how seemingly incompatible with "inversion," heterosexual identity (x) invariably turns out to mask homosexual identity (not x).

But the dynamic of inversion operates outside the bedroom as well—in particular when it comes to Mme de Guermantes, one of the few major characters in the *Search* who does not harbor hidden gay proclivities (or any other sexual secrets, for that matter).* With the duchesse what gets inverted is an abstract, aesthetic ideal, bound up with a fantasy about aristocratic glamour, exclusivity, and "class." By the end of the book, the woman whom Marcel once glorified as a bird goddess, a being doubly born for the empyrean, degenerates into a hideous creature from the deep. Her fellow grandees meet with an analogous fate, devolving from an assembly of the gods into the night of the living dead.

For all Proust's objections that he and his narrator were not the same person, one point where the two Marcels absolutely coincide is in the belief that the society belle, the personification of a noble élite, can only be a goddess or a monster. She is either too sacred or too debased to occupy the dull middle ground where regular folks spend their lives, muddling through with the usual messy assortment of good and not so good attributes. In both her idealized and her devalued forms, Mme de Guermantes's dearth of humanity makes her a convenient screen for Marcel's own projections—about the romance of France's feudal history and hereditary gentry; about modern Parisian society and his place in it; about a hazy wonderland where dreams really do come true.

In Marcel's last conversation with the duchesse in *Time Regained,* she remarks in passing, "People think they know me, but they don't." I like to read this comment as a subtle acknowledgment by Proust of both his and his narrator's incapacity to view their exemplary *mondaines* in three dimensions. For better or worse, these women are always ciphers, never people.

It is my hope that *Proust's Duchess* will amend this characterization, a reductive fiction that has for too long been taken as fact. Without question, Mmes de Chevigné, Straus, and Greffulhe did, like their fictional counterpart, embrace a worldview that held the surface to be essential and profound. Yet as I discovered

* In contrast to her perpetually cheating husband, Mme de Guermantes is described throughout the *Search* as a model of wifely fidelity—no secret love life for her. In *Time Regained*, the narrator briefly has a memory that contradicts this perception. He remembers her cousin Charlus once telling him "that the legend of the duchesse's purity was in fact made up of an incalculable number of cleverly dissimulated affairs." Charlus's allegation does not, however, prompt the narrator to investigate further. "I had never heard anything about that," he reflects. "The idea that she had always been above reproach governed everyone's perception." The incalculable number of affairs I describe in the following pages would have given Proust ample material, had he heard (or cared) about it, to complicate considerably the image of his irreproachable duchesse.

from six years' worth of exhaustive archival research, their commitment to surface elegance belied tremendous human complexity. So rich and engaging did I find their stories to be, in fact, that I have not been able to recount them in their totality here. Though all three women lived well into the twentieth century, enjoying colorful, high-profile careers to the last, I have chosen to focus in this book on a relatively short span of time between the late 1870s and the early 1890s. For all the noteworthy directions their lives went on to take, starting with the eruption of the Dreyfus affair as a national political scandal in the fall of 1897, it was during this earlier period that their biographical chronology turned out to be the densest, as it was then that they became the brightest stars in the Parisian social firmament.

From the age of Louis XIV onward, the French aristocracy upheld a tradition that favored appearance and form (*x*) over authenticity and substance (not *x*). This cult of appearances remained a shibboleth in the fin-de-siècle Faubourg, and while Mmes Straus, Greffulhe, and de Chevigné hewed to it in a broad sense, they modified its particulars in unorthodox and far-reaching ways. By taking an age-old, court-based model of elegant surfaces and fusing it with a burgeoning media culture, they presented themselves as new and improved avatars of nobility. They pioneered the by-now-familiar phenomenon of the individual as an image or a "brand" and of public adulation as the ultimate prize.

Crucial to this development was the remarkable creative output the three women fomented among their generation's major and minor talents. Only a few of these artists—Georges Bizet, Guy de Maupassant, Edgar Degas, Gustave Moreau—are still well-known today. But almost all of them were celebrities in their time, their stardom enhancing that of their muses (and vice versa). Like the women who inspired them, these artists were for the most part a good ten to twenty years older than Proust, and many enjoyed a reputation for genius that he himself would begin to attain only a few years before his death at fifty-one in 1922. These men's portrayals of his idols saturated the cultural climate in which Proust came of age, enriching the soil where his hothouse *mondaine,* "the rarest flower under the sun," would eventually take root.

ALL THREE OF THIS BOOK'S HEROINES faced real-world challenges that no amount of glamour, fame, or fantasy could dispel. Their loved ones died prematurely, often without warning. They had difficult relatives and false friends. They ignored their children. Their husbands betrayed their trust. They worried about status and money and growing old. They battled insecurity and scandal; they grappled with mental illness and drug addiction. They had unrequited crushes and unhappy love affairs. They confronted issues of "inversion." Their hearts got broken; one of their noses did, too.

These women bet on the wrong horses not only in love but in other domains, from art to politics to actual horse racing (a pastime dear to Mmes Straus and de Chevigné, both avid gamblers). As an art collector, Mme Straus preferred Jules-Élie Delaunay to Edgar Degas and Alexandre Falguière to Auguste Rodin. Similarly, Mmes de Chevigné and Greffulhe patronized fashionable society portraitists like Federico de Madrazo and Paul César Helleu, overlooking such superior talents as John Singer Sargent and Henri de Toulouse-Lautrec. Mme de Chevigné aligned herself with an exiled royal claimant who never took the throne and backed a royalist military coup that never took place. Mme Greffulhe harbored grandiose ambitions for her husband's political career, which fizzled after sorry, scandal-ridden beginnings. Mme Straus's salon drew visitors of every ideological stripe, including several virulent anti-Semites. But their bigotry only became a problem for her during the Dreyfus affair, when, seeing her take the side of the unjustly persecuted Jewish army captain Alfred Dreyfus, they abandoned and shunned her as a trouble-making Jew.

Alone of the trio, Mme Greffulhe dreamed of becoming a writer, a goal she pursued tirelessly, if secretly, throughout her life, composing hundreds of literary texts, most of them autobiographical. But she published only a handful of these works and none under her own name. As a result, Proust had no way of knowing that the woman he construed as a literary character habitually construed herself as a literary character. He never found out that among the numerous writings in which she gave herself a starring role, several were attempts at a roman à clef set in the contemporary gratin. The inversion would have delighted him, though: aristocrat (*x*) disguises artist (not *x*).

Had he really known them, Proust would have seen that like everyone, his three muses wore many different masks. He would have seen that like everyone, they were fathomless tangles of secrets and longings, sorrows and fears. Above all, he would have seen that if not like everyone, then at least very much like himself, they wanted reality to be other than it was and countered it with a dream of their own transcendence. And however hollow or misguided or doomed, it was that dream that drove them to soar and to sing, and to keep on soaring and singing even as their wings and their voices faltered, even as the darkness gathered, even as extinction loomed. For those with ears to hear, their melody said: I die as a swan would, but remember that I was a god.

PART ONE

CHAPTER ONE

RARA AVIS

JUNE 2, 1885

After the fact, society pages reporting on the Princesse de Sagan's annual costume ball would liken it to Noah's Ark, the *Arabian Nights,* and an opium dream, although for sheer extravagant strangeness, it may well have surpassed all three. Taking the animal kingdom as her theme this year, the hostess had directed her seventeen-hundred-odd guests to model their outfits on the illustrated works of the Comte de Buffon, an Enlightenment naturalist who had studied the "denaturing" effects of environmental change on the fauna.

In the great ceremonial courtyard that separated Mme de Sagan's *hôtel particulier* in the Faubourg Saint-Germain from the street, fifty footmen in powdered wigs and red-and-gold livery danced attendance on arriving guests, handing them down from carriages emblazoned with coats of arms and ushering them inside to an immense reception hall bathed in violet-tinged electric light. (The lady of the house judged "Swan Edison lamps"—lightbulbs, still a relative rarity in Paris—more festive than candles or gaslight.) After a Swiss guard announced them by name and by title, invitees swept up a white marble staircase lined with fifty more liveried footmen and an equal number of porphyry vases. Antique Aubusson carpets cushioned the ascent.

From the top of the stairs, guests entered an enfilade of magnificent formal reception rooms successively decorated à la Louis XVI, Louis XV, and Louis XIV, a sequence that gave visitors the impression of traveling back in time. In one salon hung antique Gobelins tapestries so precious that Mme de Sagan displayed them only once a decade. In a second reception room, the hand-carved boiseries had been gilded with fifty pounds of pure gold, while in a third, floor-to-ceiling mirrors lined the walls, in emulation of the Hall of Mirrors at Versailles. Although the *hôtel* had previously belonged to Henry Thomas Hope, profligate owner of the Hope Diamond, its décor had grown even more opulent since its new proprietress had moved in. Tall and blond with patrician cheekbones and creamy white skin, the Princesse de Sagan, forty-six, liked to think she bore a striking resemblance to Marie Antoinette.

Dazzling though they were, the splendors of the Sagan residence paled beside

The façade and courtyard of the hôtel de Sagan, where the nobility gathered for a lavish costume ball in June 1885.

the menagerie assembled there this evening: a hodgepodge of zoological curiosities defying the dictates of nature—and culture. As denizens of the monde, the revelers were Paris's ordained exemplars of breeding and good taste. Tonight, however, they played against type, making a game of their fabled civility by masquerading as savage beasts.

At this so-called *bal des bêtes* (ball of the beasts) as at all *mondain* functions, the guests were attired with consummate chic, only on this occasion their elegance assumed weird, unsettling forms. Beneath their customary silk top hats, impeccably tailored clubmen—members of such exclusive all-male Parisian social clubs as the Jockey and the Cercle de l'Union—sported oversized papier-mâché heads denoting insects and vermin, crustaceans and big game. To their own uniform of evening dresses and jewels, the women had added furs, masks, and exotic plumage. Statuesque Mme de Sagan, whose "queen of the birds" regalia included a gigantic feather-and-gem-covered mechanical tail that she could unfurl and retract at will, had gone so far as to perch a taxidermied peacock's head atop her own. Its diamond-studded eyes glittered eerily in the electric light.

With similarly macabre wit, slim, haughty-looking Comtesse Adhéaume de Chevigné, twenty-six, had tucked a dead snowy owl's head into her coif. The comtesse, a mythology buff, had dubbed herself "the Friend of Minerva, Goddess of Wisdom [*Sagesse*]," although her take on Minerva's avian mascot contradicted the other meaning of *sagesse:* "decorousness" or "good behavior." On its own, Mme de Chevigné's dress of snow-white tulle and feathers might have exuded decorum, but the giant blood-red rubies sparkling in the eye-sockets of her owl's head told a different story. They were the eyes of a fiend, a devil, a good owl gone bad.

By design, this study in contrasts stressed the contradictory traits for which the comtesse, née Laure de Sade, was famed. She looked like a princess, with the same heavy-lidded blue eyes, silky blond tresses, and chiseled bone structure that the Italian poet Petrarch had cherished in her fourteenth-century ancestress and namesake, Laure de Noves, Comtesse Hugues de Sade. Yet she spoke like a peasant, in an antiquated backwoods drawl, and cursed like a stevedore, in the filthy patois of her other noted literary forebear, the Marquis de Sade. Added to her fondness for shooting, riding, and man-tailored clothing, her tough talk moved one of her friends to brand her "Corporal Petrarch." This sobriquet underlined the antitheses Mme de Chevigné somehow managed to embrace: womanly and virile, sacred and profane.

Her bawdy posturing and provocative "mannish air," as another of her friends termed it, intrigued any number of *mondain* gallants, several of whom were suspected of enjoying Mme de Chevigné's favors in bed. The Sagan ball found her coquetting with one such admirer, Comte Joseph de Gontaut, despite the presence of both their spouses (and despite Gontaut's goofy attire: he was costumed as the hindquarters of a giraffe; two of his kinsmen represented the torso and head). As a rule, such brazen impropriety did not go over well in the gratin, where extramarital affairs were tolerated on the condition that they be conducted in secret. Strangely enough, however, Mme de Chevigné's insubordinate antics endeared her to many of society's grandest figures: crowned heads weary of the joyless formality that necessarily attended their station. To these exalted persons, the young noblewoman's affronts to *bon ton* came as thrilling novelties, like séances or telephones.

The patronage of her high-placed friends allowed Mme de Chevigné to laugh off what she herself saw as her most shameful feature—her relatively modest means—by avowing that she was "poor in income, but rich in highnesses." When society wags speculated that the rubies in her owl's head were presents from a Romanov grand duchess, she neither confirmed nor denied the provenance. But in another virtuoso display of cheek, she disparaged her presumed benefactor's good taste. After relating an anecdote about a different Romanov gift—a sturgeon stuffed with turquoises—she shrugged her shoulders at the tackiness and concluded, "Anyhow, I have *been* to Tsarskoe Selo, and it is *not as chic as all that!*" Lines like these were Mme de Chevigné's masterstrokes. To receive special tokens of a highness's esteem was impressive enough; to scoff at them was downright awe inspiring.

The comtesse flirted with the giraffe's behind until a hummingbird with diamond-speckled wings broke up the colloquy, pulling her aside for a whispered exchange. This interruption restored Gontaut to his fellow giraffe components, who were enjoying their collective stature as the biggest brute at the party.

LE BAL DES BÊTES chez la princesse de SAGAN

A newspaper sketch of the *bal des bêtes* where the aristocrats dressed as bugs, birds, and beasts. Laure de Chevigné, top row, fourth from *right*, dressed as a snowy owl.

Having heard rumors of another guest's intention to show up in an elephant suit, they were relieved to discover that their hostess had vetoed the plan at the last minute, citing the risk of damage to the Old Master frescoes on the ceilings of her *hôtel.*

The princesse had also declared a ban on fish costumes, reasoning that guests thus attired would inevitably want to swim, and she couldn't guarantee them a suitably warm water temperature in her (presumably capacious) aquarium. This caveat hadn't deterred one vixen from decking herself out as a salmon, in a curve-hugging hot-pink mermaid ensemble patently designed to draw stares. Unfortunately, this woman's dress attracted further notice because another femme fatale, known to her peers as "the Blonde Cleopatra," happened to be wearing a skin-tight ibis outfit of a nearly identical hue. The two fuchsia sirens eyed each other charily in the park-sized gardens behind the mansion, where Swan Edison lamps sparkled by the thousands in the old-growth chestnut trees.

Indoors, tension simmered between a portly duchess and a slender vicomtesse, both of whom had elected to appear *en panthère.* Despite her rival's superior rank, the Vicomtesse Greffulhe, twenty-four, held the undisputed advantage. With her regal carriage, willowy frame, swanlike neck, and huge dark eyes the color of crushed pansies, Élisabeth Greffulhe, née Riquet de Caraman-Chimay, was one of Parisian society's most celebrated beauties. Her contemporaries routinely compared her to Venus, the goddess of love, and to Diana, the chaste, ethereal goddess of the moon and the hunt. The matronly Duchesse de Bisaccia

Élisabeth Greffulhe was known for
basing her costumes on famous artworks,
such as Leonardo da Vinci's *John the
Baptist* (1513–1515).

recalled no such deities. Onlookers joked that the only thing funnier than the
contrast between the thin and fat panthers was the discrepancy between Mme
de Bisaccia's disgruntled mien and her family's heraldic motto: "The pleasure is
mine" (*C'est mon plaisir*).

The pleasure should have been Mme Greffulhe's. Yet she gave no sign of
savoring her victory, beyond the chilly Mona Lisa smile that so often played
upon her lips. As one of her relatives noted, "She was beautiful always and
everywhere. But her life was by no means a picnic—it was no laughing matter to
be the most beautiful woman in Paris." By her own admission, the vicomtesse's
prime objective in every circumstance was to project "an image of prestige like
none other." To achieve this effect, she was partial to fashions that provoked
shock and awe, and tonight was no exception. More often than not, she went
in for variations on an ice-queen aesthetic, consistent with her reputation for
spotless virtue. (*Her* family motto was "Piety stands with me"—*Juvat pietas*—to
the despair of many an enamored clubman.) But for the *bal des bêtes,* she had
morphed into something elemental and wild. Eschewing the evening dress that
underlay the other beasts' costumes, she had swathed herself in only a whispery
white chemise, overlain with a genuine panther skin. Her lustrous chestnut-
brown curls, sprinkled with pieces of jet, spilled loose over her shoulders.

Mme Greffulhe's outfit was all the more arresting in that she had based it not,
as the other guests had done, on imagery from Buffon but on one of the treasures of the Louvre's permanent collection: Leonardo da Vinci's *John the Baptist.*
Along with her beauty, the trait on which she most prided herself was her pas-

sion for the arts, and she was infamous for lording it over her peers. Her *John the Baptist* garb typified her high-cultural pretensions, which she believed set her apart from the rest of the gratin. The details of her costume indicated a careful study of Leonardo's painting, from the artful drape of the panther's hide to the curtain of tumbling dark hair, to say nothing of the chilly Mona Lisa smile.

At the same time, her costume raised questions about her rationale for choosing that particular work as her prototype; for Leonardo's John is a comely androgyne, endowed with the features of a young man thought to have been the artist's lover. On a tomboy like Laure de Chevigné, such gender-bending attire would have been equally audacious—cross-dressing had another few decades to go before it would become a mainstay of society costume balls—but at least it would have been consistent with her "mannish air." On Élisabeth Greffulhe, the guise made less sense. Whatever speculation it drew from her peers, the logic behind it remained her own tantalizing little secret.

Meanwhile, the visual clash between the two panthers had caught the eye of a little frog looking on from the sidelines, a dark-eyed, olive-skinned newcomer to the monde. Always quick with a joke, the frog took the dueling panther get-ups as a pretext to crack jokes to her companions: a trio of Rothschild heiresses arrayed as a leopard, a bat, and a bright orange tropical bird. It was then that the frog, mocking the duchesse-panther's heft, first made what would become one of her best-known witticisms, though years of subsequent requoting and revision would transform the fearsome jungle predator into a bland farmyard herbivore. "She isn't a cow," ran the final version of the sally, still circulating in the Faubourg a full generation later. "She's an entire herd!"

If such put-downs passed in Parisian society for the height of cleverness, they also disclosed the undercurrent of malice that subtended the nobility's polish, making that class itself a peculiar hybrid species: part gleaming tooth, part gory claw. At the *bal des bêtes,* this duality surfaced with arresting clarity when the blast of a hunting horn abruptly turned a pack of human staghounds loose in the mansion. Outfitted in dog masks and hunting pinks, the baying creatures raced on all fours across gleaming marble and parquet floors, in hot pursuit of a fleet-footed human stag.

While the outcome of the chase has been lost to history, the scene revealed something essential about its participants. Like the sport it mimicked, this faux stag hunt was a form of ritualized violence, a stylized rechanneling of the latent hostility the French courtier class had once felt toward the king. It was no accident that before he turned a modest royal hunting lodge into the seat of the most magnificent court in Europe, Louis XIV (1638–1715) had come of age at a time when noblemen resentful of the monarchy's absolutist pretensions waged civil war against the throne, nearly toppling it. To forestall any further such sedition, the young sovereign ingeniously transposed his vassals' bloodlust into an arena that he alone could define and control: court ceremony.

Some of the activities that fell under this rubric, such as the royal hunt and the *ballet de cour,* were strenuous enough to provide a physical outlet for the courtiers' aggression. But the Sun King (a persona Louis cultivated by playing the role of the sun in some early court pageants) also addressed this threat more abstractly, by subjecting his retinue at Versailles to an intricate system of etiquette in which nearly every gesture and word bespoke their place in the court hierarchy. When the members of the court gathered each day to watch the king dine, which of them had the right to sit in his presence, and within that tiny élite, who was accorded a stool and who a proper chair? Did a French duke walk into a room ahead of a legitimized royal bastard (Louis XIV had plenty of those) or behind him? To whom did the prerogative of initiating or ending a conversation belong? Who had the privilege of carrying the monarch's candlestick when escorting him to bed, or of removing the royal riding boot from the royal foot after a long, sweaty day in the royal stirrup? The Sun King's genius lay in convincing the members of his court to treat these seeming trivial questions as matters of (symbolic) life and death. By this means, he trained his nobles to envy one another, rather than him, so deflecting from the crown whatever hostile energies might not be exorcised by shooting and dancing alone.

As at the fin de siècle, a century's worth of roiling political upheaval* having finally dethroned Louis's royal heirs, the Bourbons (along with their archrival cousins, the d'Orléans, and the self-made imperial Bonapartes), the French nobility retained an atavistic taste for pomp and circumstance. But the target of its rancor had changed. Instead of an all-powerful king, its most formidable rival now was the bourgeoisie—well educated, high achieving, and, in this industrializing age, increasingly rich. Over the past half century, this demographic had asserted its might in virtually every area that counted: politics, finance, industry, technology, the sciences, the media, the arts. By the time of the Sagan ball, the strides made by the middle classes in all these fields had precipitated a golden age in French history: a period of unprecedented economic, industrial, scientific, and cultural vibrancy that would end only with the outbreak of world war in 1914, and that historians would retroactively label the Belle Époque.

However much good it may have done for the nation as a whole, the bourgeoisie's conspicuous and unstoppable success wounded the pride of the hereditary élite, whose members had been conditioned from birth to view commoners as a congenitally lesser race. As patrician author and aesthete Edmond de Goncourt said with characteristic hauteur, "A bourgeois is an ocean of nothingness." Only somewhat less insultingly, French aristocrats spoke of their presumed inferiors as being "not born," as if to be born without a noble lineage was not to exist at all.

Seen from this perspective, the accomplishments of the lower orders came

---

* For a chronology of the many régime changes—Bourbon monarchy, Bonapartist empire, Orléanist monarchy, and republican government—that occurred between the founding of the First Republic in 1792 and the founding of the Third Republic in 1870, see appendix B.

Louis XIV, aka the Sun King, dressed as Apollo in a *ballet de cour*, a form of pageantry he instituted at Versailles.

as affronts to noble Parisians' sense of innate superiority, to which Victor Hugo (1802–1885) had quite recently dealt a notable, if posthumous, blow. Acclaimed as the greatest French writer of the century, Hugo, eighty-three, died less than two weeks before the *bal des bêtes,* triggering such mass hysteria that Mme de Sagan actually considered canceling her party for fear that his funeral would upstage it.

Her concern was well founded. For decades, the people of France had idolized Hugo for his tremendous gifts as a poet, novelist, and playwright, as well as for his dauntless commitment to freedom, equality, and social justice. Between his meteoric career trajectory and his outspoken liberal politics, Hugo stood in the French national imagination as the heroic embodiment of republican ideals and, by extension, as the antithesis of hereditary entitlement. But for these very reasons, many of his upper-class compatriots abhorred him. The government's decision to honor him with a massive state funeral only exacerbated their ill will.

In the end, the princesse's friends had prevailed upon her not to let the populist fuss over Hugo interfere with their good time. Still, the fuss proved impossible to ignore. On June 1, the day before the Sagan ball, two million mourners had poured into the streets of Paris to watch the great man's catafalque wend its way from the Arc de Triomphe (draped in black in his honor) down the

Champs-Élysées and across the Seine to the Panthéon, where he was laid to rest alongside fellow literary giants Voltaire and Rousseau. As *The New York Times* reported, Hugo's funeral would go down in history as "one of the greatest pageants ever seen in France." Viewing the procession from the terraces of their mansions and clubs, the gentlemen of the monde had shown their scorn for the deceased by refusing to doff their hats to his coffin. It was a petty, ineffectual protest of a situation that rankled these patricians to their core. The author's effective canonization presented them with yet another unwanted reminder of their failure to keep pace with the go-getters of the lower classes.

The relative ineffectuality of the "born" was sustained by a long-standing tradition of inherited, land-based wealth, which nurtured their distaste for the bourgeois touchstones Hugo had embodied: self-improvement and hard work. The aristocrats of the fin de siècle had yet to accept that only by embracing these values could they hope in any material way to approximate, let alone surpass, the achievements of their rivals. Instead, in the words of historian David Higgs, "they found their last redoubt of social power in the control of the criteria of elegant behavior." Like their ancestors at Versailles, they conceived of competition in these primarily symbolic terms, sublimating their thwarted ambition and simmering resentment into a never-ending battle for social prestige.

Deprived of a court, however, the men and women of the nobility had no formally delineated playing field on which to compete for this prize, just as, deprived of a king, they had no single, definitive authority from whom to seek

Victor Hugo's funeral on June 1, 1885: two million people mobbed the streets of Paris to pay their respects to France's most beloved author.

it. These difficulties stemmed from France's reconstitution as a republic in September 1870, the third time since the French Revolution (1789–1799) that the nation had tried to redefine itself along the lines of *liberté, égalité,* and *fraternité.* Invoking that same trifecta, the Third Republic had also eradicated the noblesse as a legal entity, though it did allow the scions of this class to continue using their hereditary titles.

To counter such encroachments, the worthies of the Faubourg drew upon the wisdom of their forebears, adapting the codified posturing of Versailles to a more modern environment. The new backdrop for their splendor was Paris itself, the city to which Napoléon III's visionary urban planner, Georges-Eugène Haussmann, had given a spectacular makeover during the Second Empire (1852–1870). In the vast public spaces of Haussmann's Paris—magnificent boulevards, parks, and performance halls—upper-class Parisians enjoyed far greater visibility than their predecessors had when cooped up in a royal court twelve miles from the city center.

Against this backdrop, the gratin's unremitting and grandiose diversions heightened public awareness not only of its still-abundant privilege but of its resolve to maintain that privilege by keeping commoners at bay. As the Franco-Romanian novelist and society maven Marthe, Princesse Bibesco, recollected in *Equality* (*Égalité,* 1935), the noblesse

> exulted in the grandeur of its pageantry, which carried over into everything it did. It wasn't ostentatious, but prodigal, unselfconscious in its solemnity. It was a citadel with fortresses and bastions that [outsiders] could never enter, that they shouldn't even try to enter. . . . Despite all the revolutions, despite the Revolution itself, this seductive, captivating milieu continued to exist; in the middle of Paris, it formed a world as distant from ordinary people on the streets as the moon is from the earth, an extraterrestrial world where time had no dominion.

The existence of a rarefied parallel universe, inaccessible to the rest of society, represented a maddening enigma to the people it excluded. In defiance of the history that had supposedly destroyed it, the hereditary gentry asserted the abiding power of entitlements conferred by birth.

Carrying on as it did "in the middle of Paris," though, the monde did admit a handful of strategically selected outsiders, a group one clubman termed "a homeopathic dose of bourgeois." The political upheavals of the past century had reduced many aristocratic families to financial circumstances that squared ill with their historic grandeur, turning the vestiges of their glory—great *hôtels particuliers* in town and châteaux in the country—into unsustainable burdens. To avoid the humiliation of dirtying their hands "in trade," cash-strapped patricians resorted to marrying for money. Colloquially referred to as "regilding one's coat of arms" (*redorer son blason*) or "fertilizing one's lands" (*fumer ses terres*), this strategy fell largely to the men of the nobility, who under the tradition of primogeniture most often inherited the monetary stresses of their birthright along with the perquisites. And it was a strategy to which several of the *bal des bêtes'* grandest seigneurs had resorted—including the hostess's own husband, Boson de Talleyrand-Périgord, Prince de Sagan (1832–1910).

The Sagan marriage epitomized the regilding phenomenon and revealed its pitfalls. With his faultlessly elegant clothes, his distinctive shock of white hair, and his classic white carnation boutonnière, the Prince de Sagan, fifty-three, had for the past thirty years reigned as Paris's uncontested "King of Chic." Proud of this distinction, Sagan liked to proclaim: *"Le monde, c'est moi"*—a play on Louis XIV's absolutist dictum *"L'état, c'est moi"*—and no self-respecting aristocrat would have dreamed of challenging him on this point. "The Prince de Sagan's monocle is the sun that illuminates the monde," one of his contemporaries observed. Like the Sun King's political authority, Sagan's social authority was absolute.

But as another of his confrères noted, the prince "was born with two passions, elegance and women, . . . both very expensive," and unlike Louis XIV, he couldn't afford to indulge in either passion without significant financial aid. According to the same observer, Sagan harbored a childlike conviction "that he should have a magician at his disposal, a creature from a fairy tale who could turn rocks into rubies and pearls on demand."

In the absence of such an arrangement, the prince had settled in 1858 for a marriage of convenience to Jeanne Seillière (1839–1905), the daughter of an extremely rich financier and munitions dealer. Disdainful of her low birth, Sagan neither loved nor respected his bride. Having condescended, however, to give her his name, he expected pecuniary carte blanche in return. (As he told her father, "Those who buy a coronet should be willing to pay for it.") Instead, to the prince's astonishment, his wife had balked at his astronomical tailors' bills and gambling debts and placed him on an allowance he found grievously inadequate to his needs. The fact that she showered her best friend, Georgina, Marquise de Galliffet, with cash and expensive gifts only hardened Sagan's heart against his wife. He retaliated by disparaging her to his friends as "Rabble Girl" (Canaillette).

Sagan held his late father-in-law, Achille Seillière, in similarly low regard. Seillière had committed suicide in 1873 after it came to light that he had reaped massive profits during the Franco-Prussian War (1870–1871) by outfitting the nation's soldiers with boots soled with papier-mâché. Once this scandal broke, the prince had indignantly abandoned the hôtel de Sagan, "acquired with money thus ill-gotten," decamping to a modest two-room suite above his club in the rue Royale (and parking his best antiques at a friend's house so that neither his wife nor his creditors could seize them). So complete was Sagan's estrangement from his consort that he refused even to stand beside her in the receiving line at her parties, leaving her notoriously unhinged brother, Raymond Seillière, to do the honors in his stead. (Defensive about his and his sister's origins, Seillière was prone to making wild-eyed pronouncements about his "direct descent from Jupiter and Juno, from Confucius, from King Solomon, from Mohammed!") The prince usually declined to appear at all when his wife entertained, although tonight he had lifted his boycott in the hope of stealing a few moments with Mme Greffulhe.

As for the princesse, she put a brave face on the arrangement, shoring up the position her dearly bought title was meant to have given her by entertaining more lavishly than just about anyone else in town. While a small minority of aristocrats, her husband chief among them, might sneer at her nouveau riche vulgarity, the rest of the monde seemed to appreciate her willingness to devote incalculable sums to its amusement. To the extent that they bankrolled the nobility's penchant for diversion on a princely scale, moneyed arrivistes like Mme de Sagan had an important, if grudgingly tolerated, place in the Faubourg.

In other cases, the gratin opened its doors to outsiders blessed with exceptional personal charm or intellect, since such individuals noticeably augmented what one author would later term the "intelligence coefficient" of a party. It went without saying that an august nobleman like the Prince de Sagan belonged at any *mondain* gathering worthy of the name. But as even his admirers conceded, he was a man "of mediocre intelligence, very superficial and very ignorant," so much so that unless the talk centered on hunting, horses, clothing, or clubs, he was utterly out of his depth. Making a bad situation worse, he would try to mask his discomfort by blurting out non sequiturs he thought poetic, once comparing a starry night sky to "a Negro suffering from smallpox." These clunkers left his interlocutors speechless and forced hostesses to write him off as an unreliable source of sparkling conversation.

The doyennes of the monde made a related, and similarly well-founded, assumption about the majesties and highnesses who formed the apex of the Parisian social hierarchy. Apart from Switzerland, France was the only non-monarchical régime in fin-de-siècle Europe, and since the Third Republic's founding in 1870, the royal European superpowers had been slow to embrace it diplomatically. This reluctance, however, had not lessened the enthusiasm of foreign crowned heads for the pleasures of Paris (commonly held to be more intoxicating than those of all the other world capitals combined). When these illustrious men and women came to Paris, the gratin welcomed them with near-religious reverence, holding its most sumptuous fêtes in their honor. But its adoration stemmed more from its royal guests' stature than from their personalities, which were often stunted by the unique pressures of a princely upbringing. Groomed from birth to project grandeur before an awestruck populace, the scions of Europe's ruling dynasties were often better at feigning charm than at actually deploying it. Exemplary in this regard was the stunning but vapid Princess Alexandra (Alix), who with her husband, Albert Edward (Bertie), Prince of Wales, topped the list of the monde's most prestigious party guests. A French diplomat posted to the court of Princess Alix's father, King Christian IX of Denmark, described her and her siblings' special technique for appearing clever:

> In order to give the public the impression they were holding lively conversations, the princes and princesses had acquired the habit of counting up to a hundred and then starting all over again:
> "1, 2, 3, 4, 5, 6," said the Prince Royal.
> "7, 8, 9, 10, 11," replied the Princess Royal.
> "12, 13, 14," Princess Ingeborg would interpolate with determination.
> "15, 16, 17, 18, 19, 20, 21, 22," replied Princess Thyra, who was a chatterbox.
> "How gay our princes and princesses are this evening!" the public would think with delight.

Tactics like these revealed the dire inadequacy of royal chitchat, which had an unfortunate dampening effect on society banter generally.

Hostesses who wanted their parties to be fun as well as elegant looked outside the monde for live-wires to offset the dullards. As Princesse Mathilde Bonaparte (1820–1904), a prominent *salonnière* during the reign of her cousin Napoléon III, had once declared, when explaining her overtures to celebrity novelist Alexandre Dumas *père,*

> I couldn't invite him because of his high birth, given that he was a half-black bastard; and I couldn't invite him on the basis of his high public office, given that he was nothing. So it was his wit, and his wit alone, that made me seek him out. I wanted his . . . inexhaustible verve to enliven my at-homes.

Despite her frank condescension toward one of their own, artists flocked to Princesse Mathilde's salon throughout the Second Empire, earning her the nickname "Our Lady of the Arts" (Notre-Dame des Arts).

Nevertheless, the princesse's "artistic" coterie remained something of an anomaly in the Faubourg, which tended to regard creative types as a disreputable, if fascinating, breed apart. A more frequent and putatively safer choice was Charles Haas, fifty-two, an affable, amusing clubman whom the Princes of Wales and de Sagan both counted among their closest friends. Over the past quarter century, Haas had risen above his bourgeois Jewish background— his German-born father had worked as stockbroker for the Rothschilds—to become a ubiquitous and beloved member of the gratin. His calling card was his zippy badinage, such as the retort he made when the famously chatty Mélanie, Comtesse de Pourtalès, invited him to accompany her to the opera: "I would be delighted—I've never heard you in *Faust!*"

Haas's gift for genially mordant raillery was a talent he exercised not just at others' expense but at his own. He often joked that the sole reason his royal and noble companions liked him was that he was the only poor Israelite (society speak for "Jew") they had ever met. As applied to Haas, "poor" was a relative term. While not outrageously rich, he had inherited enough money from his father to maintain the leisured lifestyle of his adopted class. But his self-deprecation reassured the "born" that despite their honorary adoption of him, Haas had not lost the humility that a man of his antecedents ought by rights to feel in their midst.

Early in his social career, Haas had shown much the same cheerful self-abnegation by applying to the Jockey-Club for four years in a row: the record for the most rejections in the club's history. On his fifth try, rewarding his docility, the chieftains of the Jockey finally admitted him to their tribe. Even with all the embarrassment that had preceded it, their decision registered as a social miracle of the first order, given the explicit preference the club accorded to bloodline and rank. According to a popular *mondain* anecdote, while serving as club president the irascible Duc de Doudeauville had vetoed "not born" novelist Paul Bourget's bid for membership, exclaiming, "I'd like to think there's still one place in Paris where individual merit doesn't count for anything!" Individual merit was all Haas had going for him, and yet somehow he had made the cut.

Haas's election to the Jockey was all the more remarkable in view of the club's strict policy against accepting Jews. This was a rule that had otherwise been suspended only in the case of three French Rothschild barons whose colossal financial and industrial empire made them among the richest men in the world. Like Mme de Sagan, Barons Alphonse, Gustave, and Edmond de Rothschild owed their provisional *mondain* status to the munificence with which they entertained. With the hôtel de Sagan, their mansions figured on a very short list of private Parisian residences considered grand enough to accommodate royal party guests. Many aristocrats grumbled among themselves about the Rothschilds' obscene wealth, and a few, including the Prince de Sagan, openly disdained them. (In one well-known instance, when organizing a *mondain* fundraiser at the Paris Opéra, Sagan relegated all the Rothschilds to seats behind pillars so that they could neither see nor be seen.) The profound resentment toward the Rothschild family explains why, pointedly "forgetting" their Jockey-Club membership, noble Paris referred to Haas as "the Jockey's only Israelite" and "the Jockey-Club Jew."

Haas wore his taste and artistic expertise as lightly as he did his social ken. Under the Second Empire, he had served as Napoléon III's inspector first of monuments and then of the fine arts. Combined with his naturally discerning

James Tissot, *Cercle de la rue Royale* (1868): A portrait of France's elegant clubmen. Charles Haas, a future model for Proust's Charles Swann, stands at the far *right*.

eye, the relationships and expertise Haas acquired in these functions made him into one of the leading connoisseurs in Paris. Unemployed since the fall of the Second Empire, Haas had to content himself with merely advising his *mondain* friends on their collections. This pastime may not have made optimal use of his abilities, but in the gratin, it turned out to be an invaluable service. For all their proficiency in the minor arts of elegance, aristocratic Parisians were not always so knowledgeable about the fine arts. Yet because works of art were necessary appanages of their station, they liked to know what they were buying, inheriting, or selling. And when, as often happened, they were loath to admit their ignorance, Haas's unthreatening, deferential advisory style put them at ease. Tactfully convincing them that his suggestions had really been their own ideas all along, Haas flattered even the monde's most self-confident aesthetes. As Mme Greffulhe wrote, "I love going to the Salon de Paris"—the annual exhibition of French academic art—"with Haas. He helps me figure out what my opinion is."

Never one to miss a good party, Haas was in attendance at the *bal des bêtes*, where as usual his biggest problem was finding time enough to say a charming word or two to everyone who clamored to chat with him. His choice of costume is unknown, although he may have belonged to the group of cotton-tailed clubmen one reporter mentioned without identifying any of the bunnies by name. (On Haas, such a guise would have made for a characteristically clever sight gag, "Haas" being close to *Hase*, or "hare" in German.) Dispensing jokes, compliments, and gossip, the Jockey-Club Jew was singing for his supper as he always did. In the process, he was setting an example for another, younger Israelite who was also present that night: his friend Geneviève (Bébé) Halévy Bizet, thirty-six, the sassy frog with the gaggle of Rothschild dames, wives of the aforementioned banking barons. Mme Bizet was like Haas in that she had her own engaging personal qualities to thank for her invitation to the ball. But the chipper self-effacement that worked so well for him wasn't really her style. In her own world, she was already a star, and she carried that self-assurance with her into the Faubourg. Nobody put Bébé in a corner.

In a curious way, Mme Bizet's confidence mirrored that of her new *mondain* acquaintances in that it, too, was predicated on birth. In the Jewish community, she qualified as an aristocrat of sorts because she descended on her late mother's side from the Gradis, an ancient and very rich Sephardic clan. Originally from Palestine, the Gradis had in the second century immigrated to Portugal, where one of them had gone on to marry into the ducal house of Braganza. Following the expulsion of the Jews from Iberia in the late fifteenth century, the Gradis relocated to Bordeaux, where they established themselves as moguls of the shipping industry. By the end of the eighteenth century, they so dominated the lucrative trade routes between France and her Caribbean colonies that Louis XVI offered to ennoble them. But their crowning glory—the supreme testament to their grandeur—lay in their rejection of the king's proposal, as acceptance would have required them to swear an oath on the New Testament. In this, the Gradis stood in stark contrast to the Rothschilds, who had readily accepted the noble titles bestowed upon them a generation later by the Austrian emperor Franz I—in exchange for having funded his and his allies' campaigns against the French in the Napoleonic Wars (1803–1815).

The satisfaction Mme Bizet took in her ancestors' uninterest in gaining *titres de noblesse* reflected no animosity toward the Rothschilds, whom she vaunted as her dearest friends, nor did it bespeak her commitment to Judaism, which was minimal. (Once asked if she would ever consider converting to Catholicism, she parried, "I have too little religion to wish to change it.") The Gradis' refusal of ennoblement merely conformed to a conviction Mme Bizet had inherited from her father's side of the family: namely, that true greatness is not a gift bestowed by royalty but a trophy won by genius.

Her own late father had exemplified this principle. The son of an Ashkenazi German immigrant, Fromental Halévy (1799–1862) was a musical prodigy and composer whose masterpiece, *La Juive* (1835), became for a time the single-most-performed opera in Europe. As his international reputation skyrocketed, Halévy's compatriots lavished him with honors and adulation. When he died, tens of thousands of mourners turned out to pay their respects as his coffin traveled from the Institut de France on the Left Bank to the Montmartre Cemetery at the northernmost reaches of the Right Bank, while theaters and concert halls across the city remained dark in tribute to his memory. Though dwarfed by the throngs that more recently had mobbed Hugo's funeral procession, the outpouring of public grief over Halévy's death consecrated him, just as surely, as a national treasure.

In the current generation, Mme Bizet's cousin Ludovic Halévy (1834–1908), the son of Fromental's younger brother, Léon Halévy, had won comparable renown as a novelist, a librettist of light operas, and a playwright of the antic, irreverent "boulevard" school. With his longtime collaborator Henri Meilhac, Ludovic had pioneered an arch, frothy brand of comedy widely acclaimed as the essence of the modern Parisian esprit and popularly known as "Meilhac and Halévy." In December 1884, Ludovic had received the highest accolade available to French men of letters: election to the Académie Française, the 250-year-old, forty-member learned body charged with preserving and promoting the treasures of the French language. (To this day, the Académie Française forms the uppermost rung of the official cultural hierarchy in France; its members are known without irony as "the Immortals.") While the election of a new Immortal always rated as a major event in Paris, Ludovic's had been particularly momentous: he was the first Jew to earn this distinction.

With Meilhac, Ludovic had also co-authored the libretto for *Carmen* (1875), by Mme Bizet's late husband, Georges. Bizet had died prematurely just months after that opera's premiere, but the worldwide acclaim it went on to garner had launched him posthumously into the same stratospheric league as his late father-in-law. By the time of the *bal des bêtes,* the surnames Bizet and Halévy were both synonyms for French musical genius.

As one journalist remarked, those two "glorious names . . . formed a halo of unparalleled brightness" around Mme Bizet. She lived up to her mystique by surrounding herself with Paris's leading artistic talents, who flocked to her weekly salon in Montmartre. Her devotees ranged from Edgar Degas, who brought his peerless eye and exquisite technique to bear on the seedy world of dancers, absinthe drinkers, and prostitutes, to Guy de Maupassant, whose outsized appetite for sex, drugs, and trouble was exceeded only by his towering literary genius. That Mme Bizet attracted such a colorful and accomplished following fueled curiosity about her in the monde, especially after the collapse of the Second Empire, when Princesse Mathilde's star began to fade. While other patrician hostesses might open their doors to one or two arty guests—typically noblemen who dabbled in the belles lettres—Mme Bizet dealt in the genuine article, and unlike Our Lady of the Arts, she was one of them, both by birth and by marriage.

Better yet, the men of genius who frequented Mme Bizet's salon hailed her as the very personification of "Meilhac and Halévy wit." As this claim to fame suggested, her saucy, ironic drollery recalled the beloved comedies of her cousin Ludovic, though to *mondain* ears, it also contained notes of Charles Haas's snappy repartee. As a result, her sense of humor found a doubly appreciative audience in the gratin, landing her on many an exclusive guest list.

But the magnanimity of the noblesse had its limits. In exchange for their inclusion among their betters, commoners like Mme Bizet and Charles Haas were expected not only to be entertaining but to submit graciously to the calculated humiliations *mondain* etiquette prescribed. At formal events like the Sagan ball, for example, bourgeois guests had to contemplate their lowliness whenever they walked from one reception room to the next. Arriving at the pairs of high double doors (*portes à deux battants*) that marked each of these transitions in a noble *hôtel*, protocol demanded that the "not born" had to pause to let the titled pass in front of them on their right-hand side. Perfected at the court of Louis XIV, where it enforced gradations of status between and among royals and aristocrats, this practice was called "giving the hand" (*donner la main*), as in "upper hand." Although its mechanics were subtle, its meaning was anything but, as it subjected the "not born" to a dumb-show of subordination. And while it was *de bon ton* for gentlemen to cede the proverbial hand to all women, even bourgeoises, their female counterparts would have done no such thing. In this symbolic sense, they could and did put Bébé in a corner.

The same type of bias informed the placements at seated dinners, like the one to which Mme de Sagan had convoked Haas, among just forty favored guests, as a prelude to the evening's festivities. Two hours before all the rest of her invitees were slated to arrive, the princesse had plied her inner circle with *truite à la Condé, mousse au foie gras,* and *liqueurs Congrès de Vienne.* Even in animal garb, the gratin observed strict rules of class-based protocol: the higher a person's rank, the more closely he was placed to the head of the table; the lower his standing, the farther he sat toward the foot of the table or *bout de table* ("below the salt" in English parlance). When middle-class subalterns were of the party, this dishonor invariably fell to them, no matter how great their stature in the world at large. A social neophyte once asked Comte Boniface (Boni) de Castellane, widely regarded as the logical heir to his uncle Sagan's "kingdom of chic," to which of two hypothetical dinner guests he would give the better seat, the octogenarian Victor Hugo or an adolescent duke. Castellane's answer was categorical: "The duke, without hesitation. It wouldn't even be a question."

Even when all the guests were aristocrats, seating charts reflected complex calculations based on title and lineage, with the resulting placements sometimes giving offense. Another guest at Mme de Sagan's pre-ball banquet was the supercilious Comte Aimery de La Rochefoucauld, who had once grown so cross at finding himself below the salt (courtesy of a middle-class mother to whom, he would shrug when reluctantly acknowledging her existence, he was "very distantly related") that he demanded of the hostess in a booming voice, "Pray tell, Princesse, will those of us *DOWN HERE* be served all the same dishes you're having *UP THERE*?" The comte's outburst violated a subtler imperative of *mondanité,* which was the preservation of one's composure in the face of any and every travail. Gleeful at his slip, his tablemates tagged him with a moniker he would never be able to shake: "Place à Table" de La Rochefoucauld.

With such intensely fraught assertions of status shaping every interaction, the monde was nothing if not a jungle, a Darwinian universe whose inhabitants were locked in an all-consuming battle for social survival. At the *bal des bêtes,* this much was evident not only in the animal disguises, or the formalities surrounding doorways and dinner placements, or the imitation stag hunt (in which, fittingly enough, a commoner played the stag and noblemen the hounds) but also, and perhaps above all, in the special performance Mme de Sagan had arranged as the soirée's highlight. When the clocks throughout the *hôtel* struck midnight, she herded her guests into the ballroom, a space so cavernous that she had engaged two separate orchestras to play in it simultaneously, one at each end of the dance floor.

Heralded by a drumroll, the princesse tucked up her peacock tail, ascended a platform in the middle of the ballroom, and drew back a curtain to reveal a large golden beehive. As the twin orchestras struck up a tune, eleven pairs of "bee" men and "wasp" women came pouring out of the structure, launching into a stylized mating dance. This piece, devised for the occasion by the Franco-Russian choreographer Joseph Lucien Petipa (brother of Marius Petipa, of *Sleeping Beauty* fame), reworked a celebrated dance number from one of Mme Bizet's late father's operas, *The Wandering Jew* (*Le Juif-Errant,* 1852). Shortly after this opera's sensational premiere, the *ballet des abeilles* had been famously restaged as a *ballet de cour* at the court of Napoléon III, who sought to legitimate his power

Episode du bal costumé donné par S. M. l'Empereur (Ballet des abeilles, l'arrivée des ruches).

The *ballet des abeilles,* as performed here in 1863 at the court of Napoléon III, was revived at the Sagan ball twenty-two years later.

(seized in a coup d'état) by reviving the pageantry of ancien régime Versailles. And now the same spectacle was being reprised once again, under the aegis of Marie Antoinette's would-be double, and in a setting worthy of the Sun King himself.

In the version commissioned by Mme de Sagan, the dancing bees were selected from the highest echelons of the nobility, with names like de Castries, Galliffet, La Rochefoucauld, their identities readily discernible beneath their gold-striped damask tunics and little gold helmets sprigged with filigreed antennae. As the partners gavotted around the golden hive, the swarm assembled, disbanded, and reconstituted itself encircling Comtesse François de Gontaut-Biron (a kinswoman of Mme de Chevigné's giraffe-bottom beau). In an elaborate display of deference, the other wasp ballerinas crowned Mme de Gontaut-Biron their queen bee, whereupon she dubbed the Comte de Beaumont her king. This pair then executed a triumphal *pas de deux* while the others slipped two by two back into the hive. By the time the music ended, only the "royal" couple remained on stage, having conquered the field with their superior rank. The message of the dance was clear: Even in Third Republic France, some animals were more equal than others.

Or were they? According to another "not born" party guest, left-leaning author Juliette Adam, the *ballet des abeilles* marked a turning point in the festivities, and not for the better. In an account she published under the pen name "Count Paul Vassili," Adam wrote that as soon as the applause for the bees died down, a palpable malaise "overtook the whole assembly, spreading doubt through [our midst] like a trail of gunpowder." Whereas before the performance, partygoers had greeted one another "with all the joyfulness in the world," they now looked at one another with distaste. No longer praising their friends' costumes, they began criticizing them. Conversation degenerated into grunts, growls, and lowbrow animal puns ("Hey, you're an odd duck!" "So are you, you old goat!").

Although the evening's program—a mock broadsheet entitled *Le Canard* (the French word "duck" also being slang for "rag," as applied to a newspaper)—promised a cold supper at four thirty in the morning, few guests stayed long enough to partake. "Midnight had barely passed," Adam wrote, "and already most of us were ready to leave early which we did, taking away with us a vague dissatisfaction with each other and with ourselves." The Marquise de Breteuil, a young *mondaine* who had decided against attending the ball on the grounds that the requisite animal gear would "prove inconvenient and probably look stupid," congratulated herself on her decision afterward, her friends having reported that "the ball [had] turned out not to be very gay. . . . It was solemn and not at all lively."

The *bal des bêtes*, then, ended not with a bang but a whimper. What had caused the revelers' discontent? Why hadn't Petipa's proto-royal ballet left them in a sunnier mood? None of the event's commentators ventured a theory. But over and above the catchall hypothesis of party burnout (as the grand finale of the *mondain* season, the Sagan ball represented the last leg of a grueling social marathon that had begun right after Easter), several explanations were possible. First, the *ballet des abeilles* might have struck some attendees as not sufficiently rigorous in its hierarchy: for as everyone present was well aware, Comtesse François de Gontaut-Biron by no means held the highest rank of all the dancing "wasps"—the Duchesse de Gramont did. Mme de Gontaut-Biron's investiture as queen therefore constituted a breach, not an affirmation, of noble precedence.

Conversely, while the Duchesse de Gramont's husband came from a "pure-raced" (*pure souche*) French-Catholic dynasty dating back to the Middle Ages, she herself was Jewish by birth—a Rothschild, granted, and thus a most efficient regilder of the Gramont blazon, but Jewish all the same. And to certain aristocrats these days, Jewishness had unpalatable connotations, evoking the urban, cosmopolitan, capitalistic economy in which parvenus of every faith were routing the landed gentry in the race for monetary gain. Furthermore, French anti-Semites associated the Jews with a specifically Germanic breed of foreignness, a concept the recent depredations of the Franco-Prussian War had turned into a rallying cry for xenophobes both within the Faubourg and beyond it. From this vantage point, some of the guests might have viewed the *corps de ballet*'s coronation of Mme de Gramont—who, coming from the Frankfurt branch of the Rothschild family, spoke French with a hint of a German accent—less as a just honor than as a misplaced one.

Another possibility is that the performance unsettled the company because its confused treatment of rank and hierarchy betrayed the instability of *mondain* classifications as a whole. No matter how fast they held to their traditions of symbolic grandeur, the men and women of the gratin did live in a republic, and in one of the chief centers of modern capitalism at that. Radically different from the agrarian, devoutly Catholic provincial fiefdoms where the nobility's ancestral properties lay, the French capital was rapidly tilting the balance of the nation's economy away from gentleman farming and toward international commerce, industry, and finance. Those aristocrats who lived in Paris even part-time thus found themselves compelled, like specimens in a case study by Buffon, to adapt to the pressures of their alien milieu. And so, brooking the inexorable tide of the bourgeois "ocean of nothingness," they made concessions their ancestors would have deplored: from the Prince de Sagan's and the Duc de Gramont's money-based mésalliances to the presence at the ball of such bourgeois gate-crashers as Haas and Mme Bizet.

Expedient as it was, the incursion of these outsiders into the monde had one especially unwelcome side effect: they sometimes obtained privileges that eluded even their alleged superiors. Haas's election to the Jockey-Club, from which even "born" candidates were routinely blackballed, stood as a prime example of this phenomenon, as did his invitation to Mme de Sagan's pre-ball dinner for forty. Coups like these attested not just to Haas's incredible popularity but to the intrinsic permeability of the borders demarcating the *grand monde* from the wider world around it.

Understood in this way, the bee ballet did not simply present an isolated case of a botched social hierarchy. Rather, it illustrated a far more pervasive and pernicious social phenomenon: *le déclassement du gratin*. And as media commentary about the Sagan ball would demonstrate in the weeks and months that followed, the nobles of Paris were not the only people in France who disapproved of this trend.

No hint of the ball-goers' disgruntlement surfaced in the *presse mondaine*, the large, thriving aggregate of Parisian dailies, weeklies, and monthlies that brought the news of the Faubourg to a much more general public. These publications' coverage of the *bal des bêtes* was as effusive as it was overtly biased. Again exhibiting social instincts that not a few old-guard nobles found inclusive to a fault, the princesse had invited several society reporters to attend her party, and they had returned the favor by praising it at length in their columns.* A reporter for *Le Gaulois* allotted half a dozen paragraphs to the "marvels" of the *ballet des abeilles* alone, going into equally verbose raptures about the costumes, catering, music, and décor. Not to be outdone, the gossip columnist for *Le Figaro,* Étincelle ("Sparkle," the nom de plume of one enterprising Vicomtesse de Peyronny), placed Mme de Sagan's genius for entertaining on par with that of her putative twin, Marie Antoinette. Étincelle further claimed that even the feeble animal puns the guests began trading after midnight were really an "oh-so picturesque form of bestial communication."

The princesse may have gotten her money's worth from these endorsements, insofar as they extolled her as a paragon of *mondanité*. But when they reached the French provinces, where animosity toward decadent, spendthrift, and potentially "foreign" urbanites ran deep, they triggered a violent backlash. Newspapers on both ends of the political spectrum, the secular republican left and the Catholic monarchist right, condemned the Faubourg's willful decline into frivolity and self-abasement. "Go ahead," wrote a journalist for the liberal *Républicain de la Loire et de la Haute Loire,* apostrophizing the Sagan menagerie. "Go ahead and cavort, whistle, and meow, indulge in your own version of Darwinism—but you will regret it, and then it will be too late!" Behind these words lurked the threat of another cataclysmic uprising against the nobility. The implication was that just as the members of that caste hadn't seen it coming in 1789, they obviously didn't see it coming now.

A columnist for the Catholic broadsheet *Le Pèlerin* (*The Pilgrim*) voiced

---

* More typically, the scribes of the *presse mondaine* gleaned details of these events by one of two undignified means: (1) they sneaked into parties in disguise; or (2) they paid bribes to domestics, service providers (coachmen, couturiers, florists), and/or noble guests with gambling debts. A decade later, Proust himself would resort to strategy 2, bribing Mme Greffulhe's servants for information about the goings-on inside her mansion in Paris.

similar disgust. Presuming his readership's familiarity with the Book of Daniel, he likened the monde to the Babylonian king Nebuchadnezzar, whose pride God punishes by forcing him to live for seven years as an animal (with his hair "grown like eagles' feathers, and his nails like birds' claws"):

> In such profane times as the ones we are living in today, this *animalized* (one cannot simply call it *masked*) ball undermines the credibility of those who are meant to serve as examples to the rest of society. Will it teach them a lesson, as it did to Nebuchadnezzar—after *his* "ball," which lasted for seven years—and remind them to stop defying God and bringing shame to Christendom everywhere they go, including in their own salons?

A reporter for another conservative publication, *L'Univers,* didn't necessarily think so, sounding an apocalyptic note:

> The tales of the bizarre divertissement a noble lady offered her friends the other day are not only scandalous—they inspire real terror, terror mixed with righteous indignation. How could it be otherwise when we note the delight these sad festivities seem to inspire in those who have written about them, a delight in seeing all that's left of *la vieille France* [old France] collapse into folly and disappear?

For these commentators, the *bal des bêtes* implied a fundamental crisis in the French class system. Insofar as the nobility still meant anything in a deeper political sense, it meant—all showy posturing aside—the scepter and the cross. It meant the forces of order (a Catholic monarchy) routing the forces of chaos (a godless republic). It meant honor and tradition and "whatever is, is right." For this same demographic to undercut its own God-given authority by attending such an asinine free-for-all as the *bal des bêtes* was not, from this standpoint, merely self-destructive; it was destructive to France—to that glorious kingdom which, though it had perished on the guillotine nearly a hundred years earlier, many conservatives still dreamed of reviving.

Many, but not all. At least one pundit regarded the cause as already lost, its doom sealed by Mme de Sagan's ersatz animal kingdom. In the immediate aftermath of the ball, the name Édouard Drumont did not feature prominently in the vitriol spewed by the Fourth Estate. But a year later, this hitherto obscure critic from Lille detonated a bomb in the French political landscape: *Jewish France* (*La France juive,* 1886), a twelve-hundred-page, savagely anti-Semitic tract denouncing a widespread Jewish conspiracy to destroy the country from within. Drumont posited the "Jew-ified" social chaos at the *bal des bêtes* as proof of the conspiracy's existence and of its triumph. He even mentioned Charles Haas and Laure de Chevigné, among other *mondains,* by name, granting them both a foretaste of the notoriety another writer would bestow upon them a generation later (albeit with significantly different motivations and results).

A bestseller that went into 140 editions within the first ten years of its publication, *Jewish France* unleashed xenophobic racist paranoia as a powerful current in French politics. Instead of voicing nostalgia for a valiant feudal noblesse, the book conjured up a nightmarish contemporary inferno where "everything is controlled by the Jew" and where "the real, established nobility of France" figured among the Jew's many casualties. Three years later, just in time for the centennial of the French Revolution, Drumont rehashed this vituperative argument—again invoking the *bal des bêtes* as proof of "how today's nobility prostitutes itself" to the evil Jewish cabal—in a sequel whose title said it all: *The End of a World* (*La Fin d'un monde,* 1889).

And yet, there must have been another moment, and another imagined outcome. Before Drumont became, with disastrous repercussions for the nation, a household name; before the social columnists filed their unintentionally scandalous articles on the *bal des bêtes*; before the gunpowder trail of fear and (self-) loathing spread through the hôtel de Sagan, inciting the guests to an early exit; there must have been a moment when an alternative, and far more appealing, outcome beckoned. A moment when the dancers' consecration of the "wrong" queen, their unexpected departure from the customary social script, sent up a tiny flare in the blazing electrified ballroom. A moment when three young female guests—a wisecracking frog, a cross-dressing panther, and a good owl gone bad—glimpsed in Mme de Gontaut-Biron's coronation a possibility of their own advancement, elevation, and glory. Charles Haas, an avuncular friend to all three exquisite creatures, had already known such a moment and such an outcome. But as the bees' ballet made clear, *mondain* prestige-seeking was also a women's game. For the time being, the trio saw no reason not to play it, and play it to win.

Much later, they would see the reasons. Much later, they would question and rethink and even rue their choices. Much later, too, they would see the world to which they had pledged themselves—the great world—fall to pieces under the deft, merciless touch of a (half-)Jew, though he served no conspiracy Drumont could have envisioned as he performed his own one-man version of the *ballet des abeilles,* gathering pollen from the gardens of the noblesse and transmuting it into the "black honey" of his novel. But for now, in this moment, these three young women were not endangered species—they were rare birds. For now, in this moment, the world wasn't ending. It had only just begun.

LEITMOTIF

PRETTY BIRDS

Song, I was never the cloud of gold
That once descended in a precious rain
So that it partly quenched the fire of Jove;
But I have certainly been a flame lit by a lovely glance,
And I have been the bird that flies the highest in the air,
Raising her whom in my words I honor.

—PETRARCH, *Rime Sparse* (c. 1327–1374)

It is not always easy for us to understand how certain birds flying over a landscape, a swan rising from the river toward the sky, . . . unceasingly occupy the thoughts of a great genius, . . . and win the admiration of posterity.

—MARCEL PROUST, "Notes on the Mysterious World of Gustave Moreau" (1898)

CHAPTER TWO

MY DON GIOVANNI, MY FAUST

Prince Joseph and Princesse Marie (Mimi) de Caraman-Chimay liked to devise short composition assignments for their six children. In 1874, as they began to consider matrimonial prospects for their eldest daughter, Élisabeth, fourteen, they directed her and her older brother, Joseph, sixteen, to write a dialogue between two birds in a cage. One of the birds, the parents specified, had been born in captivity, the other born free.

Élisabeth's essay focused on the torments of the latter canary, pining for the freedom of his younger days:

> How sad he was when he remembered his childhood, when he thought about the nest he would never see again—the nest where he had grown up and that saw him take his first flight! How sad he was when he recalled how joyously he used to sing with his fellows, in the hawthorns and in the depths of the woods! Now he is a captive in a house made of iron, where all he has is a perch or two on which he is dying of sorrow.

When questioned by his companion, who does not understand his despair, this bird cries out,

> Don't you know that everything on earth and in the sky, the whole, beautiful immensity of nature—all of it used to be mine? Don't you know that I was raised in the hawthorns in a nest lined with feathers? . . . How do you expect me to rejoice, after losing such happiness? I can no longer sing as you do, you who are used to living in this prison . . . I, who have known freedom [and] tasted its charms, . . . I am a prisoner now, and have lost all hope. All that remains is for me to die.

Looking back on these lines after she was married, Élisabeth would weep bitterly to think that without realizing it, she had foretold her own future as the Vicomtesse Greffulhe.

IN THE SUMMER OF 1878, the Franco-Belgian Comtesse Élisabeth de Caraman-Chimay, eighteen, became engaged to Henry, Vicomte Greffulhe, twenty-nine, one of the most eligible bachelors in France. As was typical of aristocratic marriages at that time, the couple's betrothal was conceived by

The engagement photograph of
Comtesse Élisabeth de Caraman-Chimay
and Henry, Vicomte Greffulhe, 1878;
Henry always had Élisabeth sit in
photographs to make himself look taller.

their families as a mutually beneficial business transaction, a matter of practicality rather than passion. As a child of the Belgian Prince Joseph de Riquet
de Caraman-Chimay, soon to be the eighteenth Prince de Chimay, and Mimi
de Montesquiou-Fezensac, who came from one of the French nobility's oldest
clans, Élisabeth boasted a superb pedigree. Like all female Caraman-Chimays,
she was born a countess;* her coat of arms bore a *couronne fermée* (closed crown)
that denoted her family's princely blood. Her ancestors included the Merovingian king Clotaire II, who ruled France in the seventh century; Mme Tallien,
a leading *salonnière* of Directoire Paris; a seventeenth-century knight named
d'Artagnan, purportedly the model for the character of the same name in Alexandre Dumas *père*'s *Three Musketeers* (1844); and the French emperor Napoléon
I, of whom Élisabeth's paternal grandmother, Émilie de Pellapra, claimed to be
the illegitimate daughter. Such roots counted for a lot in fin-de-siècle society,
conferring a level of prestige and authority that money couldn't buy.

Even princes needed money to live, though, and in that regard, Élisabeth's
family had seen better days. Two centuries earlier, her father's forebears the

---

* Many years later, when Élisabeth and her sisters were grown up, the Belgian crown authorized all future daughters
born in the Riquet de Caraman-Chimay line to style themselves princesse (as opposed to comtesse) from birth.
This honor was bestowed upon the family in recognition of the loyal service of Ghislaine (Guigui) de Caraman-
Chimay to Marie-Henriette, queen consort of the Belgians.

Riquets had amassed a fortune by spearheading one of the most ambitious public-works projects of their era, the Canal du Midi, which connected the Garonne River to the Mediterranean Sea. But since then, the family's wealth had dwindled, consumed in no small part by the maintenance costs of their princely real estate holdings. The château de Chimay, the family seat in the Belgian province of Hainaut, was a fortified and turreted pile with architectural elements dating back a thousand years and a private theater modeled on that of the French royal palace at Fontainebleau. The family's house in Paris, a palatial residence known as the hôtel de Chimay, was equally grand, if not even more so. Described by *The New York Times* in 1884 as "one of the most celebrated houses in France," it occupied 54,000 square feet of prime real estate in the Faubourg Saint-Germain, on the quai Malaquais overlooking the River Seine. Everything about the place evoked the glories of the ancien régime, and more specifically of Louis XIV. With architecture by François Mansart, interior murals by Charles Le Brun, and gardens by André Le Nôtre, the hôtel de Chimay was the work of the same design team the Sun King had engaged to beautify Versailles.

As if this were not enough, Prince Joseph had drained much of his fortune while on diplomatic missions for Leopold II, King of the Belgians, in various capitals around Europe—Saint Petersburg, Bern, Paris, Rome—where protocol obliged him to entertain sumptuously at his own expense. (Because it compelled its practitioners to spend, rather than to earn, their money, diplomacy was one of the few professions thought suitable for men of high birth; Élisabeth's paternal grandfather, too, had served honorably in this role.) As a young girl, Élisabeth reveled in her father's foreign postings, eagerly absorbing the languages of each new environment. But these assignments had so eroded Prince Joseph's savings that when Leopold II offered him the governorship of Hainaut in 1870, he accepted without hesitation. Since then, he and Mimi had raised their six children between there and Paris.

The change in living arrangements helped to reduce the couple's expenses somewhat, as did their decision to educate all of their children at home. As the two eldest of the brood, Élisabeth and Joseph took their lessons together. Their tutors came to the house every Tuesday, Thursday, and Saturday, starting when Élisabeth was four and Joseph six. On the other days of the week, the children's governess and parents oversaw their studies, which, by the time Élisabeth reached her teens, focused almost exclusively on literature. Her notebooks from these years are filled with detailed observations on works by Greek, Latin, Spanish, Italian, German, English, and French authors from an impressive variety of genres and historical periods. So absorbing did Élisabeth find this material that when she was sixteen, she persuaded her parents to let her take the qualifying exams to become a teacher. Neither she nor they had any serious expectations that she would follow that career path, but she relished her schoolwork for its own sake. Her training also came in handy when her younger siblings needed help with their lessons.

Keeping the whole family together at home had the added benefit of fostering an appreciable closeness between the parents and their children. Known by the baby-talk nicknames of which patrician Europeans were (and remain) so fond, Élisabeth went by Bebeth, Joseph by Jo, and the two younger daughters, Ghislaine and Geneviève, by Guigui and Minet, respectively. The two younger boys, Pierre and Alexandre, were called Toto and Mousse. The siblings squabbled among themselves, as siblings do, and played wicked pranks on one another. (Bebeth's nastiest one involved making Guigui eat a slug.) Still, they were a close-knit bunch and thrived under their parents' warm, attentive care.

Their father's economizing measures did not restore enough of the family's wealth for him to be able to provide Bebeth, his pet, with the sort of dowry typically required by suitors in her milieu. He and Mimi had long hoped to pair her off with her cousin Louis, Prince de Ligne. Louis had grown up with Élisabeth in Hainaut and over the past several years had given every indication that he was infatuated with her. But he had money troubles of his own. Upon his grandfather's death in 1880, Louis had inherited his family's moated fourteenth-century castle, and he had been struggling to maintain it ever since. Pine as he might for Élisabeth, young Louis de Ligne could not afford to marry for love.

While she liked her cousin well enough, Élisabeth wasn't altogether sorry to be out of the running for Louis's bride. She had always known that sooner or later, she would wind up as somebody's wife. Short of becoming a nun (a path aristocratic girls hadn't routinely taken since before the French Revolution) or a lady-in-waiting at a royal court (the career to which her sister Guigui would devote herself in adulthood), a young woman from her background had few other options; pursuing teaching professionally, though she was qualified to do it, would not have been considered appropriate for a prince's daughter. When privately mulling over her prospects, Élisabeth had entertained vague daydreams of a future with her mother's first cousin, Comte Robert de Montesquiou-Fezensac. In French, first cousins once removed are called uncles and aunts "in the Breton way"; in keeping with that expression, Élisabeth considered and called Robert de Montesquiou her uncle, even though he was just five years older. As children, they had always enjoyed their time together while visiting his and Mimi's grandparents at their castle in France. In particular, Uncle Robert had liked to play dress-up with Élisabeth, combing her tangled curls into elegant hairstyles such as the *coiffure marquise* and inventing new outfits for her dolls. On this basis, she felt her uncle Robert would make "the most charming husband."

Unlike so many gay noblemen of his generation, however, Robert de Montesquiou had no interest in hiding his sexual preferences behind the façade of a sham marriage; he never took a wife. Since he was unavailable for a union, Élisabeth came to suspect that she, too, might be better off remaining single. In an ideal world, she confided in her diary, she would live happily ever after with the two other people she loved best: her father and mother. Even the indignity of having to work for wages as a teacher would be a small price to pay for a lifetime in "heaven," as she called her childhood home.

Both parents had special claims on their eldest daughter's affections. Prince Joseph had always made Élisabeth feel as if she mattered—as if, despite her gender, she might achieve something of substance. In recent years, he had enlisted her help in writing and rehearsing the many speeches he had to deliver as governor, and he took her input seriously enough that Élisabeth thought of the finished products as her own work as much as his. Prince Joseph also liked to bring her abroad with him on the diplomatic junkets he still sometimes undertook at the Belgian king's behest. On these trips Élisabeth acted as her father's unofficial secretary, continuing her work as his speechwriter and public speaking coach. She also served as his official companion, joining him at embassy functions where she chattered away happily, in multiple languages, with attachés and heads of state.

In practical terms, by having Élisabeth accompany him on his travels, Joseph enabled Mimi, who would otherwise have served as his diplomatic helpmeet, to stay at home with their other children. But to Élisabeth, these journeys offered glimpses of a larger world into which girls from backgrounds like hers rarely had a chance to venture. As the novelist Émile Zola wrote in an 1878 newspaper article about "women today,"

> The demoiselle of gentle birth is placed under the strictest supervision—
> she never leaves the house without a chaperone. . . . Her whole education
> can be summed up as follows: constant surveillance and total seclusion
> until she gets married.

By this measure, Élisabeth's trips with her father were exceedingly uncommon. Acutely conscious of this fact, she treasured him all the more for it.

Mimi was just as dear to her, possibly even more so. Élisabeth adored her mother's sweet temperament, her wise counsel, and her pretty, careworn face, crowned by a thick circular braid. She admired Mimi's gentle but firm insistence that Élisabeth and her siblings "be modest, amiable, truthful, unaffected" while also "cultivating a sensitivity to fine ideas and an appreciation for beautiful things," first and foremost the arts. Exceptionally for a noblewoman of her generation, Mimi had trained as a concert pianist in her youth, studying under Clara Schumann and once even performing for Franz Liszt. With the support of her husband, himself an able violinist, Mimi took care to provide her sons and daughters with a similarly rigorous musical education. As part of their training, she created a miniature family orchestra in which each child played a different instrument. Élisabeth, assigned the piano, was never happier than when Mimi joined her at the keyboard, the two of them playing *à quatre mains* while the other children chimed in on brass, woodwinds, and strings—with Prince Joseph accompanying them on his treasured Stradivarius.

Other times, when Élisabeth was struggling with her embroidery or her knitting—conventionally "feminine" arts the family governess insisted on teaching all three sisters—Mimi would encourage her to set the needlework aside and try a more fulfilling activity: read a poem, draw a picture, write a story.

Mimi also encouraged Élisabeth and her sisters to spend time with the four daughters of Prince Joseph's younger brother, Prince Eugène de Riquet de Caraman-Chimay, who with his family lived in Belgium for half of the year and at his country estate in France for other half. Élisabeth, Guigui, and Minet referred to themselves and these cousins collectively as "the seven sisters," and they adored one another. When visiting their paternal grandfather at the château de Chimay, the seven of them staged impromptu plays together in the private theater, costumed in outlandish ancestral outfits they had scavenged from the attic. Élisabeth's favorite of the cousins was dreamy, introverted Marie-Alys, who was eight years Élisabeth's junior and worshipped her.

These were the simple pleasures that made Élisabeth welcome with gratitude any delay in her expulsion from the nest. But expulsion came soon enough. While she savored her dwindling time at home, her parents continued their search for a suitable husband for her, and early in the summer in 1878, they found him in Henry, Vicomte Greffulhe. The vicomte's nickname in Parisian society, drawn from a popular aria in Charles Gounod's *Faust* (1859), was "the Golden Calf," because of the gargantuan fortune he stood to inherit from both his father, Charles, Comte Greffulhe, and his childless paternal uncle, Henri Greffulhe. Originating with their banker ancestors' shrewd financial dealings during the French Revolution, the Greffulhes' wealth now comprised an enormous portfolio of real estate, railroads, canals, and other industrial interests in France and England. In Paris's Faubourg Saint-Honoré, Henry and his family occupied a palatial complex of adjacent *hôtels particuliers* with extensive private gardens and on-site stables (home to thirty horses, an unheard-of number to keep in the center of town). In addition, the Greffulhes owned several estates in the Seine-et-Marne region, an especially desirable destination for upper-class *villégiatures* (stays in the country) because of its proximity to Paris. The family's favorite hunting property, the domaine de Bois-Boudran, lay less than fifty miles southeast of the city.

Suitors with blazons this richly gilded didn't come along every day. As far as Mimi and Joseph could tell, the vicomte's only potential flaw lay in the fact that his Greffulhe forebears had worked "in trade," their *titres de noblesse* dating back a mere seventy years. (For his generous funding of the Bourbon Restoration

Robert de Montesquiou, a kinsman of
Élisabeth, called Henry Greffulhe "the
Big Blockhead" because of the seemingly
rectangular shape of his skull.

that followed Napoléon I's demise, Henry's paternal grandfather had received a
hereditary peerage in 1818.) Nonetheless, the family enjoyed tremendous prestige in the monde—arguably even more than the Caraman-Chimays, by this
point, because of the princely splendor in which the Greffulhes' riches permitted
them to live.

With his father and his uncle Henri, Henry Greffulhe belonged to the two
most élite men's clubs in Paris: the Cercle de l'Union and the Jockey, havens
for French noblemen and crowned heads from all over Europe. Through his
mother, Félicité, Henry belonged to the d'Estissac branch of the La Rochefoucaulds, one of France's great ducal houses; and his two sisters, Jeanne and Louise,
had married into similarly illustrious clans, becoming, respectively, Princesse
Auguste d'Arenberg and the Comtesse (later Marquise) de L'Aigle. The fact that
these dynasties had not balked at contracting alliances with the Greffulhes reassured Joseph and Mimi that if they were to do the same, their peers would not
construe the match as dishonorable. Besides, the prince and princesse knew better than to dismiss this Golden Calf (and his thirty-horse urban stable). Unlike
Louis de Ligne, Henry Greffulhe had far too much money to have to concern
himself with the size of his bride's dowry. On these grounds alone, their Bebeth
would be lucky to have him.

On Henry's side, too, the match had involved a hard-nosed calculus of pros
and cons. In July, after a few brief, strictly chaperoned rendezvous with Élisabeth

and her parents—first in Paris and then in Deauville, where both families rented villas by the sea that summer—the vicomte asked for her hand. Or rather, adhering to noble etiquette for marriage proposals, his father asked Prince Joseph for her hand. When presenting the prince with Henry's offer, the Comte Greffulhe confirmed that his son was prepared to overlook Élisabeth's meager dowry, a mere 5,000 francs in annual income, which was a pittance in comparison to Henry's own yearly allowance of 400,000 francs, let alone the 8 million francs to which he would be entitled upon marrying. (He stood to inherit 60 million francs more when his father and Uncle Henri died.)* But the Greffulhes' offer was no act of charity. As one of Henry's closest confidants, Henri Le Tonnelier, Marquis de Breteuil, theorized, "Greffulhe decided to marry [Élisabeth] for one reason and one reason only: because she was the pretty daughter of a prince, and came from an illustrious family."

Breteuil saw the situation clearly enough. An alliance with the Caraman-Chimays, Henry well knew, would only enhance his already enviable social position; it would also provide a tremendous boost to his future political career. After he married, Henry planned to run for the French national legislature, the National Assembly (Assemblée Nationale), a body in which his uncle Henri and his late paternal grandfather had both served in their time. The young man thought it meet to uphold the family tradition and, ideally, to play a role in bringing the French monarchy back to power.

In the late 1870s, the future of the Third Republic was still far from secure. Not only did petty internecine bickering and periodic scandals plague its leadership, but the heads of the two rival branches of the dispossessed French royal family—the Comte de Chambord, the *chef de famille* of the senior Bourbon branch, and the Comte de Paris, the head of the cadet d'Orléans line—were both waiting in the wings for an opportune moment to return to power. The Greffulhes had cast their lot with the d'Orléans, who looked more kindly on fortunes of recent vintage than did the ultraconservative Bourbons. (France's sole d'Orléans king to date, Louis-Philippe, who ascended the throne in 1830 after the forced abdication of his Bourbon cousin Charles X and ruled until his own overthrow in 1848, had espoused a two-word political platform: "Get rich!") Through his late paternal grandfather, father, and uncle, all longtime stalwarts of the Orléanist cause, Greffulhe had developed amicable relations with the Comte de Paris, whom he hoped to see restored to the throne.

As this was an effort that would require international support, Breteuil—whom Queen Victoria had personally charged with looking after her eldest son and heir, Bertie, Prince of Wales, on his frequent pleasure-trips to Paris—was working to persuade the future king of England to put his support behind a sec-

* The exercise of converting historical currencies into the present-day monetary terms presents methodological difficulties that exceed the scope of this book. However, Greffulhe's friend Comte Albert de Mun qualified in their peer group as a rich man with an annual income of 70,000 francs.

ond d'Orléans reign. The vicomte steered clear of the more substantive political discussions, but he struck up an amicable relationship with the Prince of Wales, predicated on their shared love of hunting. (He and Bertie once earned a scolding from Queen Victoria herself when she caught them shooting game in a bird sanctuary on one of her estates; this episode may have soured the queen on the Vicomte Greffulhe, but it became a favorite memory between Bertie and him.) In Greffulhe's mind, such relationships more than sufficed to qualify him for high political office; he anticipated a brilliant future for himself as a kingmaker and a leader of men. With his limitless resources and the right woman by his side, every vista would surely lie open to him.

Taking this pragmatic view of matrimony, the vicomte assigned little if any importance to the question of attraction between himself and his intended. Breteuil believed his friend "never loved Élisabeth" as he had "loved" the scores of other women the bedding of whom he had made "his only vocation to date." But in marrying Élisabeth, Greffulhe was not looking for love. He was looking for credentials, and hers were beyond reproach. She had a princely surname and a *couronne fermée* to go with it. (The Greffulhe coat of arms featured a lesser *couronne ouverte,* or open crown.) She had three brothers whom her parents were grooming to enter the upper echelons of European diplomacy. She had a father held in the highest esteem by King Leopold II, who was said to be eyeing him as

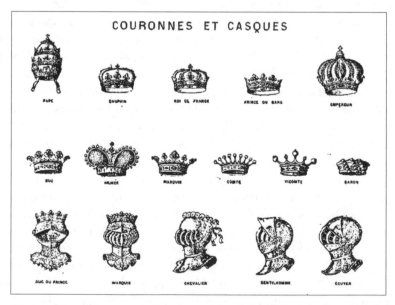

These are the different types of crowns associated with different ranks and titles. As a prince, Élisabeth's father could wear a closed crown *(center row, second from left),* whereas her fiancé, a vicomte, was entitled only to an open crown *(center row, second from right).*

Belgium's next minister for foreign affairs. Once the vicomte entered public life, family ties like these would unquestionably redound to his benefit.

It further enticed him to learn that Élisabeth had her own connections to various European royals, whom she had encountered on her travels with Prince Joseph. While accompanying her father on his diplomatic missions to Russia, for instance, she had won the hearts of Grand-Duc Wladimir of Russia—a son of the current tsar, Alexander II, and a brother of the next one, Alexander III— and his charismatic wife, Maria Pawlowna. (The grande-duchesse was related to the d'Orléans through her father's family, making her and the grand-duc particularly valuable contacts for an Orléanist like Greffulhe.) Élisabeth herself had already told the vicomte that she could easily imagine him as France's ambassador to Russia. Because it would take him to the court of one of the most powerful rulers in the world, this was a posting that suited Greffulhe's inflated sense of self-importance. And if it pleased him that his future wife could envision him in such a prestigious role, it pleased him all the more that she might be able to help him get it.

These factors compensated for what Greffulhe regarded as his fiancée's more regrettable characteristics, from her tearful sentimentality when she talked about how much she would miss home to her professed antipathy to hunting, his favorite sport. What irritated him most about her was her artistic side, notwithstanding the immense pride he took in his own superficial refinement. (As his and Élisabeth's daughter would write to flatter him many years later: "Papa . . . detest[s] everything that isn't poetry, music, and literature.") Like many traditionalists in his milieu, the vicomte believed that a lady who cultivated her mind, a "bluestocking," did so at the expense of her femininity. As another nobleman phrased it: "A bluestocking . . . draws attention to herself without fascinating minds or captivating hearts. She is a poor excuse for decoration." This was how Greffulhe saw things, and he planned to reform his wife accordingly.

Élisabeth's dark hair and dark eyes he was powerless to change, although he had a well-established preference for blue-eyed blondes. But at least her looks promised to hold some redeeming value, for while they did nothing for the vicomte personally, everyone else seemed to find them exquisite. When he groused to Breteuil, who was engaged to Greffulhe's lissome blond cousin Constance de Castelbajac, that Élisabeth was "not at all his type" (*pas du tout son genre*), his friend riposted that the future Mme Greffulhe was stunning in her own dramatic way, "like a siren from the Orient or a princess from a fairy tale." Breteuil praised

> her gorgeous tiny waist, her elegant bearing, and her silhouette, to which no other woman's can compare; when people see her pass by, they turn their heads, astonished, and think she is walking on air.

Breteuil was not the only one struck by Élisabeth's appearance at this early stage. Novelist and *académicien* Octave Feuillet, placed next to her at a dinner at the hôtel de Chimay a few months before her marriage, found her enchanting as well:

> I went to the quai Malaquais on foot, in white tie. At dinner, I was seated next to the young [comtesse], who gazes at the world through wide, black eyes that are almost impossibly large, and whose ripe, merry blossom of a mouth is as pure as a morning flower. Add to that such a mass of dark hair that her head almost bows under the weight of it. Fine like amber, and even more intelligent than fine, with the deep, dazzling eyes of a fairy or a genie, and laughing like a little shepherdess, the girl is . . . a novel unto herself.

The vicomte had no use for feminine intelligence—indeed, his distaste for Élisabeth's "bluestocking" tendencies may have arisen at least in part from a not unjustified suspicion that she was smarter than he. (Although records pertaining to his schooling are sparse, he failed his baccalaureate eight times and apparently gave up on his education after that.) But fineness was another matter entirely. Along with womanizing, horses, and hunting, his favorite pastime was buying art and rare books, expanding upon the collections his father and uncle had built. Greffulhe pursued this hobby with the same competitive, entitled spirit he brought to the other three, chasing only the most coveted objects available. Even though—Breteuil again—"he only responded to beauty in a different guise" (those blue-eyed blondes), the vicomte seems to have concluded that so long as other men found Élisabeth attractive, she would make a suitable addition to his trophy collection.

During their four-month courtship, Élisabeth had no idea that this was how he saw her. When her parents first talked to her about the vicomte, she had blanched at the idea of even meeting him, resentful that a perfect stranger should presume to take her away from the people she loved. During their first encounter, overseen by both their mothers, she had glared at the vicomte with her large black eyes and let Mimi do all the talking. Like most unmarried young women of her class, however, Élisabeth had never had any prolonged contact with men to whom she wasn't related. This left her ill prepared for the charm offensive that Greffulhe, a veteran seducer, launched with minimal effort. He won her over in no time, sounding off about art, books, and politics with a blustering arrogance that she mistook for strength—his booming voice accounted for his other *mondain* nickname, Thundering Jove—and flattering her with canned praise that she mistook for passion.

Breteuil noted that despite his friend's tendency "to say a lot of idiotic things, and tell jokes that only he [found] funny," Greffulhe's self-love—bolstered by

Élisabeth at twenty, two years after her wedding, began to come into her own as a beauty.

his "big sacks of cash" and his La Rochefoucauld parentage—was infectious. Élisabeth's reaction bore out this theory. Instead of noticing the vicomte's limitations, she adopted his unshakable faith in his superior discernment and charm. Within weeks of their first encounter, she informed her parents with a mixture of sheepishness and excitement that if anyone could conquer her reluctance to marry, without question, it was the irresistible Vicomte Greffulhe.

She also admired his "Nordic" handsomeness, waxing rhapsodic about his "superbly regular features, lovely blue eyes, and lush golden beard." Here again she took her cue from the man himself, who, as Breteuil drolly observed, "thought himself one of the handsomest men who ever lived." (Élisabeth would later conclude that Breteuil, attractive of face but hunchbacked of form, envied her husband's hale physique.) Nor would everyone have agreed upon the vicomte's good looks; his beard and head both had an oddly rectangular shape that gave him a more than passing resemblance to a king in a deck of playing cards. But as Élisabeth saw it, this merely underscored the gratifying fact of the royal blood that ran in his veins: Greffulhe's great-grandfather Charles de Vintimille du Luc had been a love child of Louis XV, tagged "Demi-Louis" for his uncanny likeness to that king.

To a more critical bride, Greffulhe's height might have been a deterrent. Élisabeth was tall by the standards of the day—1.68 meters (five feet six) according to her identity card—whereas the vicomte was short, at least a few inches shorter than she. He was, moreover, sensitive enough to this discrepancy that he refused to pose for their engagement photograph unless she sat and he remained standing. But as a man of wealth and taste, he knew how to make the most of his appearance. The tailoring of his Savile Row suits played up his broad shoulders and barrel chest and disguised the degree to which his squat build ran to fatness.

Greffulhe was well-practiced, too, in gallant gestures, which proved irresistible to a girl of Élisabeth's naïve, romantic disposition. One moonlit evening, he serenaded her beneath her bedroom window in the hôtel de Chimay. Dressed in a fitted scarlet riding coat and a black velvet cap, and brandishing a single red rose, he reminded Élisabeth of a hero in an opera, an impression his strong, clear tenor reinforced. Whenever he called on her in the weeks that followed, she talked him into performing duets with her for her parents. Her favorite selections, drawn from Gounod's *Faust* and Mozart's *Don Giovanni,* inspired her to think of him tenderly as "my Don Giovanni" and "my Faust." It didn't yet occur to her that her beloved might incline toward the heartlessness of the one or the soullessness of the other.

Élisabeth did notice that the vicomte's opinions differed from hers on a few important subjects and that he did not take kindly to dissent. Their first tiff occurred in May, when he accompanied her and Mimi to France's first-ever World's Fair, organized by the government in Paris to signal that the nation had definitively recovered from its defeat by the Prussians seven years earlier. Touring the fair's exhibition of contemporary French art, Élisabeth went into raptures over *Salome in the Garden* (1878), an enigmatic watercolor by one of her mother's favorite artists, the Symbolist painter Gustave Moreau. Mimi seconded her daughter's praise and wondered aloud if there might be a way for her and Prince Joseph to buy the piece for the young couple as a wedding gift. To both women's surprise, Greffulhe interrupted their exchange and began to shout, fulminating that Moreau's canvas wasn't beautiful, it was bizarre, and that no one with any taste or sense could possibly think otherwise. Now Charles Chaplin, *there* was an artist! The vicomte was proud to say that he owned several works by Chaplin (a specialist of sugary academic nudes and staid society portraits), but Moreau—what a joke!

Flabbergasted, mother and daughter quickly steered him away from the offending work, and although he soon regained his calm, his outburst troubled Élisabeth for some time afterward. Her Faust had a devil of a temper, it seemed, and she had been frightened to see how ready he had been to take it out on her—not to mention on a painter she liked and on a person she loved. Mimi, less easily intimidated, bought the *Salome* anyway, but as a present just for Élisabeth, rather than for her and the vicomte both.

A few weeks later, he threw another fit, this time concerning the kind of life they were to have together after the wedding. Élisabeth was looking forward to all the parties and balls they would get to attend in Paris. When marooned in dull, provincial Hainaut, she told him, she had devoured press accounts of the dazzling social life enjoyed by her peers in the Faubourg, and she was eager to experience the fun for herself. Hearing this, Greffulhe erupted. The gratin's high-profile festivities, he boomed in his Thundering Jove voice, were symptoms of the crass publicity worship that was ruining their class. No wife of his should expect, or even wish, to participate in such repugnant orgies of *déclassement.*

This time around, Élisabeth's astonishment must have been visible on her face, because in midtirade, he changed course. "Come now, you're not going to like the monde overly much, are you, Bebeth?" he asked in a soft, cajoling tone.

> Surely you're too intelligent to care about the great world—going to a ball is stupid [*bête*]! Waltzing, what an idiotic amusement! No, the only life worth living is a private life, a hidden life.

Lacing her childhood nickname with a hint of condescension (stressing the homophony between "Bebeth" and *bébête,* "stupid" or "infantile"), the vicomte settled the argument as he always did, by declaring the case closed.

Inwardly Élisabeth did not come around to his opinion, continuing to daydream about the gaiety of the monde. Still, she resolved not to challenge him on the subject any further. On August 30, a few weeks before her wedding day, she began a new diary marked "Marriage Journal" ("Journal de mariage"). On the first page, she consoled herself with the thought that her pliability would ensure her happiness with the man to and about whom she now, as his soon-to-be-wife, spoke using his Christian name:

> I love Henry so much that I am utterly absorbed by him. Of course, he has his own habits and his own convictions, but as for me, . . . I must only care about things that will bring me closer to him.

This passage shows that Élisabeth did not suffer the fate of so many girls from her milieu, married off by impecunious families to men they could never hope to love. All the same, her starry-eyed devotion did not exclude a nagging ambivalence about binding herself to Henry for life. In the first entry of her Marriage Journal, she revisited her fantasy about living at home with her parents forever. Reminding herself that she had only given up on this dream because she had unexpectedly fallen for Henry, she realized with some anxiety that she didn't know for certain whether he felt the same way about her. "Will he love *me* more than anyone else in the world?" she wondered. The answer had to be yes—as Mimi, if not Henry himself, had assured her. But if that was the case, Élisabeth wondered, then "why, in the midst of my joy, do I feel so sad?"

She ascribed her pangs of melancholy to the fact that marriage, even to Henry, would put an end to "the reign of the young girl I once was":

Adieu, everything I ever loved—adieu, dreams and poetry of my girl-hood—oh, how I loved you! Soon I will be dead to you—I am *getting married*—I, who always swore I would never get married because I felt I wasn't made for the conjugal state, having nothing but distaste for its consequences. But then love came to me in such an enchanting form that, my heart stricken with a pain it had never known, I let myself be brought round to that terrible word, *marriage*. I'm putting my very life in chains, forever—forever!—and my fate is no longer my own; in marrying, I must accept the consequences . . . and bid my present life farewell bravely, without looking back, lest I burst into tears. Adieu, adieu again, everything I adore.

As a voracious reader of poetry, Élisabeth had come across the Petrarchan trope of "the bittersweet pain of loving" often enough to find some lyricism in her yearning for her beloved. In fact, her maternal grandfather, Comte Anatole de Montesquiou-Fezensac, was a noted translator of Petrarch's verse. Even so, she dreaded certain "consequences" of the commitment she was about to make.

By "consequences," she likely meant at least one of two things. First, by nurturing her intellectual and artistic gifts, Élisabeth's parents had raised her to consider herself as something other—something more—than mere subservient chattel. Nonetheless, in fin-de-siècle society, that was exactly what wives were expected to be. One of the best memoirists of the era, Élisabeth (Lily) de Gramont, Duchesse de Clermont-Tonnerre, whose half-brother, Armand, would go on to marry Élisabeth's and Henry's daughter, Élaine, commented on this imbalanced state of affairs:

In those days, wives had to submit to their husbands to a degree that is almost impossible to believe; they had no right to their own opinions, no right to spend their time or their money as they chose. I once knew a grande dame who respectfully asked her husband for some stamps, to which he replied: "I gave you some yesterday." And when my parents invited my Gramont d'Aster cousin to the Opéra, even though she was so old that all her hair had gone totally white, she turned to her husband and asked: "Will you permit it, Antoine?"

If wedlock as an institution militated against women's independence, then marriage to Henry, so hostile to even the slightest hint of opposition, promised to be particularly stifling. From the two flare-ups she had witnessed thus far, Élisabeth may have intuited that he would not allow her anything like the freedom of thought and self-expression her parents had afforded her. Like the captive bird in the dialogue she and her brother once wrote as a composition assignment, she would look back on that freedom and with her whole being mourn its loss.

Offering a different, though by no means incompatible, explanation for her wariness, Greffulhe family lore holds that Élisabeth had an overpowering aversion to sex and pregnancy. In a caste whose survival depended on the assiduous production of heirs and spares, this was a nonnegotiable consequence of marriage. Her descendants see proof of her phobia in the fact that she "gave" Henry only one child, Élaine, born in March 1882, who as a girl could neither inherit her father's title nor carry on his name (a name that therefore died when he did). For Élisabeth and Henry not, as it would seem, to have tried again, and not to have kept trying until they conceived the all-important son, flew in the face of the aristocratic bias toward populous families—like the one Élisabeth herself came from, and the one her own daughter would eventually create by bearing four sons and one daughter. By this measure, Élisabeth's reproductive performance raised eyebrows among her contemporaries, appearing strange enough to imply that her avowed "distaste" for marriage had a specifically erotic cast. According to one of her great-grandchildren, who uses euphemistic terms straight out of the fin de siècle, "In the family we have always said of her: 'She had a horror of "those things." '"

Élisabeth's horror may have been related to her complete dearth of sexual awareness. Progressive as her upbringing had been in many ways, her parents had instilled in her the profound ignorance of "those things" expected of any girl of breeding. This aspect of a young woman's conditioning can be hard to ascertain because so much of it consists in what she is *not* told, but several documents in Élisabeth's archives offer noteworthy clues. In the diary she kept before her engagement, she wrote that she had trouble distinguishing any one man she met from another: with the exception of her beloved uncle Robert de Montesquiou, all men looked to her "like variations on the same repulsive, yellowish model." And in an unpublished interview she gave toward the end of her life, she divulged that when she was a teenager, her parents expressly forbade her to engage in any form of dancing "in which a man would have had to hold me in his arms." (Even the waltz was verboten.) At one ball in Hainaut, she told the interviewer, a young French officer tried to kiss her when nobody was looking, "which absolutely terrified me, because I thought that that was all it would take for me to conceive a child!"

While typical enough among the nobility's virgin brides, such reflexive dread of even the slightest intimate contact with a man seems to have stayed with Élisabeth long after she learned where babies actually came from. Perhaps not incidentally, her sisters appear to have felt the same way. Her youngest sister, Minet, would remain single until the advanced (in *mondain* terms) age of twenty-four, when she married Charles (Charley) Pochet Le Barbier de Tinan, a career military officer not known for his interest in women. This match produced no children. As for Guigui, the sister to whom Élisabeth would remain closest throughout her life, she elected never to marry at all, instead becoming a lady-in-waiting to Queen Marie-Henriette of the Belgians. "'That sort of thing' frightens me so much," Guigui said when explaining her aversion to the conjugal state. "The very idea of 'that' [cela] terrifies me."

In and of itself, Élisabeth's sexual reticence would have been enough to make her a poor match for Henry. Even in the Faubourg, where men philandered as casually as they breathed, his erotic appetites were thought excessive. According to the *mondain* rumor mill, he kept a "veritable harem" of mistresses all over Paris and bedded them all daily, one after another in rapid succession, when he was in town. So punctiliously, in fact, did Henry adhere to this schedule that the horses drawing his sporty little two-wheeled coupé painted with the Greffulhe coat of arms (blue globe, black griffon, gold crown, and gold stars on a striped silver field) stopped automatically at each address on his daily route, without any prompting from the driver.

If Élisabeth knew nothing of Henry's harem during their engagement, she unknowingly received a hint of its existence on their wedding day, on the short drive from the Église Saint-Germain-des-Prés—the sixth-century church where France's ancient Merovingian kings, her ancestors, lay interred, and where she and her groom wed in great pomp in front of fifteen hundred guests, including a flotilla of d'Orléans princes—to the reception around the corner at the hôtel de Chimay. Henry looked resplendent in his midnight-blue morning suit, and Élisabeth dazzled in an ivory satin dress with a sixteen-foot train. Eliseo Lucat, a composer protégé of her parents, had written a mazurka just for the occasion, "Be Happy" ("Soyez heureuse"), and dedicated it to Élisabeth. Its festive strains merged with the celebratory pealing of the carillons when she and Henry made their exit at the end of the ceremony, only to be drowned out by yet another joyful noise: the cheering of the four thousand strangers who had gathered outside the church to ogle the glamorous newlyweds.

This, Élisabeth wrote in her Marriage Journal, was when her happiness reached its apex, not just because she now belonged to her beloved and he to her, but because the well-wishers straining to get a glimpse of her seemed so bowled over by what they saw:

> When we appeared on the threshold of the church door after the nuptial benediction, we heard all these people exclaiming, "How gorgeous they are," and I must admit that the very church, that dear old church I used to go to every Sunday when we were in Paris, seemed to have been transformed, just as I had been, and I was so very happy. And when they cried, "She is so beautiful!" "What a ravishing young woman!" "He's one lucky man!"—it sounds stupid, but I was elated and proud.

Here Élisabeth revealed a characteristic that would come to define her adult identity: an unalloyed delight in her own beauty, and in the admiration it drew from those around her.

In this case, Élisabeth's elation dimmed as soon as she and Henry settled into his coupé, which had been waiting for them across the church's cobblestone plaza in the rue Bonaparte. For as they drove to the hôtel de Chimay, she noted afterward,

> Henry seemed completely preoccupied with the horses; it actually made me angry, because I was expecting a great show of tenderness from him once we were alone in the coupé, and instead he just kept his eyes riveted on his horses—people were tossing bouquets to us right and left, all the way down the rue Bonaparte, and Henry just kept staring outside and saying, "You must act properly now, darling, people are looking at us." But Papa had joked with me that we would be allowed to pull the little curtains [on the coupé's windows] for privacy! I finally realized that Henry was even watching his horses' movements reflected in the shop windows as we drove past. I was furious, but then all of a sudden we were at the quai Malaquais, where no one had arrived yet except little old Aunt Charlotte, who said to Henry, shaking her head back and forth like a little sorceress (which she is): "*Pretty wife, pretty horses, we'll see what happens, we'll see what happens*"—a rather frightening prognostication, . . . especially from one's own aunt.

Only later would Élisabeth realize that Henry had been watching the horses so fixedly because he worried that they would stop in front of one of his mistresses' houses and so betray the secret of his harem.

The secret came to light during the couple's extended honeymoon in the Seine-et-Marne, but not right away. First, they stopped for two weeks at the château de La Rivière, Henry's parents' estate outside the historic town of Fontainebleau. One glorious fall afternoon, she and Henry went riding in Fontainebleau's sun-dappled forest. Élisabeth found the setting so romantic that she vowed then and there she would never know a happier day in her life. To commemorate the moment, she leaped off her horse and scooped up a small bunch of heather. "I want to be buried with it!" she cried, waving it under her husband's nose, with her little shepherdess's laugh, as Feuillet had called it. When she and Henry got back to La Rivière, she pressed the heather stems between the pages of a book, and once they had dried out, she slipped them into her Marriage Journal for safekeeping. They remain there to this day.

At La Rivière, Élisabeth began to adjust to the trappings of her new position. For the first time in her life, she had her very own maid, Assunta, who addressed her in a thick Spanish accent as "Madam-a la Vicomtess-a" and took over responsibility for dressing her person and her hair. (While Assunta wrestled with corset stays and hairpins, "Madam-a la Vicomtess-a" wrote compulsively: diary entries, to-do lists, creative writing pieces, and endless letters home.) Élisabeth delighted in her elegant, grown-up wardrobe—Mimi had bought her a few new outfits before the wedding—and in the breathtakingly delicate items from her trousseau. Despite their financial worries, her parents had packed her off with a queenly haul: forty-eight chemises, twenty-four embroidered slips, two camisoles, one cashmere bathrobe, thirty-four petticoats, ten peignoirs, ninety-six pairs of stockings, ninety-six towels, and ninety-six handkerchiefs, all lavishly trimmed (except for the towels and the bathrobe) in every variety of handmade lace. "I feel very much the grande dame," she wrote to Mimi.

To look at them, Élisabeth and Henry formed a storybook couple. "You two look just like two monarchs," said her new sister-in-law Louise de L'Aigle. Élisabeth's first impulse was to take the remark as a compliment. Soon gathering, however, that Louise meant it sarcastically, she concluded that Henry's sister was merely jealous. "Ugly women," Élisabeth reflected in her diary, "are personally offended by beauty." In a separate notation, she mused, "There is nothing a woman dislikes more than to see a photograph of another, pretty woman." Élisabeth placed a framed copy of her and Henry's engagement photograph on the mantel in the drawing room at La Rivière.

Beneath the surface, though, trouble was already brewing between her and her handsome groom. Of their wedding night, the usually prolix Élisabeth said nothing in her Marriage Journal, except that her heart had "beat faster" when Henry came into her bedroom for the first time. But a letter Mimi wrote to her at La Rivière implies that Élisabeth didn't exactly warm to her conjugal offices. While cognizant of her daughter's inexperience, Mimi tried to boost her courage:

> I see that you're agitated and upset, but please calm down right away. You love Henry, so trust in him—give yourself to him without fear. You said you were planning to sleep on your chaise longue [rather than in bed], keeping your bathrobe on. Don't do that. . . . If I were there, and could take your chambermaid's place at night, I would tuck you into bed with a kiss, and you would stay there, calmly, like a good girl. That's what you have to do. Go to bed. Give your heart to God, and to [Henry]. Don't make scenes, don't bolt your door. . . . Don't begin your life together by making him suffer—it could do more harm than you think.

The closing line of this letter may have indicated some awareness on Mimi's part of Henry's predisposition to stray and lent urgency to her plea that Élisabeth stop "making him suffer." Nonetheless, Élisabeth balked, demurring with almost comic understatement: "But Maman, there are so many things you didn't tell me!" After this exchange, she and her mother never discussed her sex life again.

But Élisabeth did compose a thinly veiled account of her wedding night, recast as an entry in the diary of one "Marie-Alice, Duchesse de Monteillant." Named after Élisabeth's sweet young cousin, Marie-Alys de Caraman-Chimay, this character is an eighteen-year-old newlywed of uncommon breeding, beauty, and sensitivity. Her loving but impoverished family has married her off to a phenomenally rich French duke,* and Marie-Alice is happy with the arrangement . . . until her wedding night. Decorously, she avoids writing about the encounter in any detail, simply describing it the next morning as the most traumatic experience of her life. All her girlhood dreams "of Princes Charming in green satin, of Knights made of moonbeams," Marie-Alice laments, had left her grotesquely unprepared for the "husband who profaned [her] beauty" in the marriage bed:

> When people first started bringing up the word *marriage* to me, I heard it as a synonym for *commitment* and *constraint*. . . . I understood that it was a social act, one that my family ardently wished me to perform. I did not understand—oh I did *not* understand!—*everything* that the act of marriage entails. . . . *Commitment* and *constraint,* yes. But the unknown brutalities, the *sullying* cloaked in pretty words! Oh, dread! Oh, devastation! Is it really fair to enter into such a contract, when *only one of the two parties knows what it means*? . . . To whom can I protest? Whom can I blame? Customs? Laws? Him, the Duc? He was only "doing his duty as a husband" . . . or at least that's what he says.

Typeset in an unbound page proof in Élisabeth's archive, this passage forms part of an autobiographical novel she worked on sporadically for the next twenty years. Henry never knew of its existence. Whether she found another way to impress upon him her horror of "that sort of thing" is anyone's guess.

After their fortnight at La Rivière, the newlyweds took a brief journey by carriage through the forest of Fontainebleau, heading northeast toward the fortified medieval town of Melun. Along the way, they stopped at La Grande Commune, the first of several hunting properties the Greffulhes owned in the area, where Élisabeth and Henry stayed just long enough for him to deliver a speech to the locals and receive their congratulations on his marriage—a tradition left over from feudal days.

From La Grande Commune, the couple continued on to Bois-Boudran, a 7,500-acre estate where the extended Greffulhe clan convened every fall and winter from the opening of hunting season through New Year's, and where the

---

* NB: Élisabeth's fictional alter ego boasts a much grander title than the real Élisabeth does. Proust effects a similar promotion when making Mme de Guermantes a duchess, whereas two of his three models for this character were countesses and one was bourgeoise. In Proust's earliest notes for the *Search*, Mme de Guermantes is "just" a comtesse.

bride and groom would spend the remainder of their honeymoon. An ungainly L-shaped structure scarcely older than the Greffulhes' *titres de noblesse,* the castle lacked the patina and history of the Montesquiou and Chimay family piles. It reminded Élisabeth of an army barracks. Apart from the allées of stately hemlocks that formed the approach to the château, and a little pond ringed with hawthorn bushes on the grounds behind the rear façade, the landscaping, too, left much to be desired, with a clump of large industrial-looking greenhouses standing in for gardens, with an overall effect Élisabeth found "indescribably sad."

These aesthetic shortcomings did not appear to trouble her husband or in-laws, who went to Bois-Boudran not for atmosphere, but for sport. Henry's paternal grandfather had bought the property in 1814, choosing it because its forests and meadows boasted some of the best shooting in France. Ever since then, the Greffulhes had steadily acquired more and more land contiguous to their own, buying out many tenants and forcing out many more to create what was by now a huge private hunting preserve. In an exposé about "the plague Big Capital has unleashed in our region," the publisher of a local newspaper, *Le Briard,* reported that in gobbling up acreage for their own enjoyment, the Gref-fulhes had displaced entire communities of peasants and small farmers, families that had lived and worked in the area for centuries. Not only had these humble folk been relegated to the outermost fringes of the Greffulhes' estate; they had been banned from the roads, bridle paths, and footpaths that had served as public access routes for generations. Writing under a pseudonym, the publisher of *Le Briard* speculated that "Greffulhe's personal dream would surely be to turn the whole of the Seine-et-Marne into one immense hunting property belong-ing only to him and a few other big landowners like him. . . . At heart, he cares infinitely less about the small farmers [of the region] than about a single covey of partridges."

To protect those partridges, and all the rest of the game on the estate, the Greffulhes engaged a standing army of groundskeepers and guards, led by a professional bruiser named "Big Moustache." These heavily armed men were charged with protecting the family's "sacrosanct quarry" at all costs, meting out brutal punishments to trespassers and poachers. Big Moustache saw a would-be offender in every local—male or female, young or old. "We are the metal instrument, you are the clay pot," he told one group of suspects. "We will break you." As a result, *Le Briard* reported, " 'Big Moustache' is even more hated and feared than the . . . Greffulhes" themselves. But ultimately, "Big Moustache" was indeed an instrument—of his bosses' frank disregard for the common man. The bullying tactics their lieutenants adopted in their name starkly illustrated the divide that still, under the Third Republic, separated the haves from the have-nots.

But for the haves—at least for those who knew their way around a shotgun—Bois-Boudran was heaven on earth, rivaling such legendary hunting estates as

Bois-Boudran was the Greffulhes' favorite hunting estate in the Seine-et-Marne, where they spent most of the fall and winter each year.

the domaine de Chantilly, where the French royals had chased their game for centuries. Chantilly now belonged to the Duc d'Aumale, the youngest surviving son of the late King Louis-Philippe and one of the few Frenchmen alive (besides the Rothschilds) whose wealth exceeded that of the Greffulhes. Even d'Aumale welcomed invitations to Bois-Boudran and with his d'Orléans kinsmen figured from time to time among the Greffulhes' distinguished guests. The men who shot there with Henry on a regular basis were known as "the founders." Along with Henry's brothers-in-law, father, and uncle Henri, this core group included Henri de Breteuil, the Duc de La Force, the Marquis du Lau d'Allemans, the Marquis Costa de Beauregard, Arthur O'Connor, and the Hottinguer brothers, Rodolphe and François, scions of a Protestant banking family like the Greffulhes. As habitués of the Bois-Boudran hunt, the founders all received special buttons emblazoned with the name of the property and the head of a boar.

This creature was the specialty prey at Bois-Boudran, where the Greffulhes kept a dedicated pack (*un vautrait*) of forty dogs specially trained to hunt boar, along with a standard pack of several dozen hounds (*une meute*) for chasing other beasts, which ranged from foxes to wolves to stags. But while the cast of animals varied, the rituals of the hunt remained more or less the same. Turned out in the blue-and-gold livery of Bois-Boudran, the guns pursued their prey on horseback, attended by all the fanfare of the centuries-old *chasse à courre:* master of hounds, huntsmen, hunting horns, and pack. The company galloped for hours through forest and field while their quarry ran for its life, until finally, half dead from fatigue and paralyzed with fear, the cornered animal met its gruesome end in a hailstorm of fangs and weapons (shotguns, rifles, revolvers, even dag-

A postcard of a day's shoot at Bois-Boudran.

The Greffulhes and their extended family were avid hunters, including Bob de L'Aigle, who painted this watercolor.

gers). As the dogs and their masters did their worst, the bugle call of victory, the *hallali,* resounded, only partially muffling their victim's desperate cries.

Though beloved of all the founders, the *chasse à courre* was not the only form of venery on offer at Bois-Boudran. The Greffulhes and their guests also enjoyed the most luxurious form of the *chasse à tir* (shooting): the driven shoot *(battue)*, wherein a team of beaters flushes game birds or boar out of their hiding places, driving them toward the guns en masse. At estates like Bois-Boudran, wrote one veteran of the driven shoot, this sport led to a "veritable holocaust" of animal carnage. Each season the Greffulhes stocked their estate with jaw-dropping quantities of game-birds—thirty thousand pheasants, seven thousand partridges, and so on—to supplement the many thousands of birds nature had already provided. According to the Duc de La Force, on a single day's driven shoot at Bois-Boudran, a good marksman might bag up to fifteen hundred "pieces" without undue effort. One year the Comte de Paris's dashing younger brother, Robert d'Orléans, Duc de Chartres, exceeded this average, felling thirty-four hundred quail in just two days.

For its enthusiasts, the traditions (and the excesses) of the hunt amply justified its historic designation as "the sport of kings." Henry gloried in the association, conceiving of Bois-Boudran—much like his marriage to Élisabeth—as a means of impressing royals and other heads of state. (Officially the château belonged to his uncle Henri, but as the last of the male Greffulhes, Henry was already slated to inherit it.) While taking Bebeth on her first tour of the property, he told her with evident pride that the current president of the Republic, the aristocratic Maréchal de MacMahon, would be joining the founders for a few days' shooting in early December.

This news took Élisabeth by surprise. She was related to MacMahon on the Chimay side of the family—in the parlance of the gratin, she and the maréchal were "a little bit cousins"—and his wife, née Élisabeth de La Croix de Castries, was her godmother and Mimi's best friend. Yet Élisabeth hadn't imagined Mac-Mahon to be someone her husband, who hated republicans and claimed that they all "smelled bad," would wish to cultivate. But Henry insisted that politically as well as socially, the maréchal was "one of ours" and thus worth cultivating. "Besides," he added, "while it is possible to keep one's honor in politics, one must sometimes do curious things." Élisabeth couldn't have realized it at the time, but this comment encapsulated the whole of Henry's political philosophy, in which principle was as nothing compared to personal advancement.

When it came to hunting, Henry demonstrated considerably less flexibility. As he explained it to Bebeth, the routine at Bois-Boudran brooked no exception: house rules dictated that she follow the hunt each day with the rest of the ladies—her mother-in-law, Félicité, Comtesse Greffulhe; her sisters-in-law, Louise, Comtesse de L'Aigle, and Princesse Jeanne d'Arenberg; and the wives of any and all male guests—no matter how inclement the weather and no matter

Although Élisabeth rode well, she did not share her husband's enthusiasm for the sport of kings.

what she might rather be doing instead. Élisabeth's heart sank. She had already tried to impress upon Henry that she thoroughly disliked hunting: disliked the cold and the damp; disliked the endless waiting while the hounds chased their prey and the men set up their shots; disliked the long hours in the saddle or the open calèche; disliked the droves of local peasants and villagers who came rushing from all over the countryside at the sound of the *hallali,* eager to witness the kill; disliked the baying and shrieking and gore in which the whole exercise resulted. Disliked all of it. That she happened to ride well and look elegant on horseback was some consolation, but not enough of one to reconcile her to such a miserable pursuit.

That being said, she already feared her husband's temper too much to oppose him outright. So instead, she urged him to consider the delicate health of his cousin Constance, whose wedding with Henri de Breteuil had preceded Henry's and Élisabeth's by only a week. In the quaint locution of the era, the young Marquise de Breteuil was *poitrinaire* (afflicted with weakness in the lungs and chest). As a result, Élisabeth reasoned, Constance would be much better off staying indoors by the fire and, as the Greffulhes' guest, she should hardly be left there alone.

It was a clever argument, playing to Henry's reflexive, quintessentially "noble" preoccupation with matters of form. (According to one social satirist, the monde rated "thou shalt be polite" more highly than all the Ten Commandments put together.) Detecting the trap, however, Henry told Élisabeth to take up the matter with his father and Uncle Henri, who confounded him by seconding her plan. Henry's father, Charles, was desperate for grandchildren who would carry on his name. So he thought it not only reasonable but politic that the woman responsible for bearing the next generation of Greffulhes should be spared the rigors of the hunt. (In fact, Élisabeth noted with some bemusement, if her father-in-law had his way, he would keep her from locomotion of any sort: "For the sake of my health, I think he would like to see me confined to a wheelchair! He is always bringing me things to eat and drink, and pulling up chairs for me to sit in.") As for Uncle Henri, he was already in the throes of an illness that would claim his life the following spring. He knew all too well how physically punishing the founders' shooting regimen could be. He agreed with Charles: the two young ladies should be allowed to stay at home while the others were in the field.

But if Henry's father and uncle were inclined to exempt the two brides from the sport of kings, his mother was not. Félicité argued that neither Constance's lungs nor Élisabeth's unborn children had any bearing on the matter; at Bois-Boudran, everyone participated in the hunt, end of story. This time it was Élisabeth's turn to be confounded—Charles and Henri Greffulhe capitulated instantly and pleaded with her to do as Félicité wished.

This exchange introduced Élisabeth to another Greffulhe family tradition: absolute, terrified deference to her mother-in-law. While she had never been a beauty, Félicité had the sharp blue eyes and beaked nose of all the La Rochefoucauld d'Estissacs, and in her younger years, these traits had at least given her an air of distinction. Since then, however, she had lost most of her hair and her teeth and now wore obviously false approximations of both. (Her wig, a shoe-polish shade of black, looked especially fake.) These accessories lent her a fearsome air and contributed to her overall resemblance to a drill sergeant or a grenadier, an effect further compounded by her brusque, imperious manner. Her husband, congenial and self-assured in his dealings with others, cringed like a frightened schoolboy in her presence; so did Uncle Henri. As Élisabeth groused in her journal, it was Félicité who "held the reins of government" chez Greffulhe, seconded by Louise de L'Aigle, another "grenadier in petticoats" who visibly enjoyed helping her mother refute Bebeth's challenge to her supremacy.

Élisabeth had no choice but to join the shooting party each day, accompanied by Constance de Breteuil (who would die of pneumonia a few years later). But her surrender did not bring about a truce between her and her female in-laws. Tall, dour-faced Louise, who looked and acted disconcertingly like her mother, remained frosty, silently disapproving, while Félicité ranted openly about Élisabeth's failings as a sportswoman. Of all the Greffulhe women, only Jeanne d'Arenberg, a frail, diminutive blonde, showed her occasional hints of kindness. But like Charles and Uncle Henri, Jeanne was too meek to defy Félicité outright. Élisabeth had landed in enemy territory, with no ally in sight.

Her Marriage Journal now became the repository of her endless frustrations and woes. Describing a typical day in the field, Élisabeth wrote,

> Today I spent five hours following the hunt in my mother-in-law's calèche, I was practically crying, how *freezing* it was!, She kept up a running commentary the entire time: "The hunters are going up there, no, they are going down there, we're going to see something jump out over there . . . ," and all of a sudden, sixteen boar leaped into view. But I only saw six of them, and my mother-in-law was indignant because I couldn't tell her whether or not the last of them was a sow. Apparently I have "a lot to learn."

Her mother-in-law's carping was unpleasant enough, but Élisabeth found it all the more vexing once she figured out its root cause, which was Félicité's belief that no woman could ever be good enough for her only son. As Jeanne and even Louise admitted in private, their mother had raised Henry himself to share this view, making him insufferable to everyone else in the family. In her diary and her letters home, Élisabeth came up with a code name for Félicité: "Cerberus," after the vicious three-headed guard dog of classical myth. "Cerberus watches me constantly, never missing a single detail, and is *so very cold,*" she wrote. "Her personality is the complete antithesis of mine."

That coldness belied a vicious streak that Félicité revealed one day when the hounds attacked an old peasant woman instead of their slated prey. Astonished, Élisabeth watched her mother-in-law "become electrified" as the canine pack "tore off a big chunk" of its elderly victim's lip. All the while, instead of showing concern for the woman her hounds were mauling, Félicité kept screaming at the top of her lungs: "They are biting that horrid creature! Good dogs!" Had Élisabeth ever doubted the aptness of her "Cerberus" moniker, this incident put those doubts to rest. Indeed, she was now seeing firsthand just why her new family was so unpopular with the locals and why the regional press denounced with such vigor "the oppression [the Greffulhes have] visited upon this wretched part of the world, where the master's will is above the law."

It was easy for Élisabeth to cast her mother-in-law as the villain. It was much more difficult for her to accept that Henry could be awful as well—and, more to the point, awful to her. Following his mother's lead, he seized on Bebeth's dislike of the hunt and used it as a pretext for dressing her down at will. On October 19, he flew into a rage at Élisabeth in front of the whole shooting party because, according to him, she was "acting like Ophelia while he was shooting duck." This analogy probably said less about Élisabeth's supposed misconduct than it did about Henry's relative ignorance, given that her offense—huddling beneath a fur blanket with her teeth chattering—had nothing in common with mad Ophelia's death by drowning. But Henry seemed determined to find fault with Élisabeth no matter what. A few days later, he exploded when she giggled at a silly remark Constance made while he was setting up a shot. Once again, he blew up at Bebeth in front of the entire group. She wrote in her journal that the tirade only ended when he had exhausted the full store of his vitriol, leaving him to conclude somewhat flatly, " 'Well, it's obvious *you've* never been hunting in your life!' And with that mortal insult, he turned tail and galloped away."

Neither did Élisabeth's problems at Bois-Boudran cease when the hunt was over and the dinner gong rang. In the country as in the city, everyone dressed formally for dinner. Yet despite this veneer of elegance, mealtime conversation had a guns-and-game focus Élisabeth found unbearably dull. As she complained in a letter to her family, table talk at Bois-Boudran "mainly just rehash[ed] all the details of the day's hunt"—as if those details were exciting enough to warrant repetition and further analysis. She would learn later that this practice was not specific to Bois-Boudran. The de L'Aigles had an immense hunting property of their own, the domaine du Francport—thirteen thousand acres of woodland abutting on the forest of Compiègne—where the founders also liked to convene. There, the dinnertime custom was to read the day's hunting tally aloud at the start of the meal and then enjoy a blow-by-blow retelling of every shot fired and every "piece" missed or slain. After sitting through some of these sessions, Élisabeth would count herself lucky that she hadn't spent her honeymoon at Francport. But she would have counted herself just as lucky had she not had to spend it at Bois-Boudran.

The founders did enjoy conversing about another subject at dinner, but that subject was farming. Like a majority of their peers among the landed gentry, the Greffulhes and their friends regarded agriculture and animal husbandry as the sacred tasks of the country squire. Between her more cerebral, artistic penchants and cosmopolitan upbringing, Élisabeth had never developed this sensibility and was floored by her in-laws' boundless fascination "with chickens, turkeys, even pigs." She could only take part in such discussions, she admitted to Mimi, by "feigning the kind of deep emotion Sarah Bernhardt shows when she asks in [Victor Hugo's] *Hernani* if her lover is still alive." One evening, Élisabeth forced herself to participate in a rousing table-wide argument about the optimal source of nutrition for pheasants. Arguing in her best Sarah Bernhardt mode for worms over ants' eggs, she earned a rare smile of approval from Henry.

Inwardly, though, Élisabeth bridled at "the absolute tedium of evenings here." In her journal, she tried to remind herself that deferring to Henry's tastes and wishes was her duty as his wife:

I must remember that I am leading this kind of life now in order to please my husband. Maybe my feelings about it will change with time, though it is difficult to force oneself to care about things in which one has absolutely no interest.

This rationalization was even harder to accept when she considered the vehemence with which Henry denigrated her own interests: reading, for example. Even though he collected books, he did not particularly care to read them; like the artworks he also spent much of his time acquiring, the rare editions he bought were to him status symbols more than anything else. This, Élisabeth groused to her parents, was why "the library here is always locked. Henry cannot imagine anyone actually wanting to go in and find something to read." Even worse, she was coming to understand that he viewed her love of books as a character flaw it was up to him to correct. He once shouted as he grabbed a volume of poetry from her hands, "Loving me is better than any novel!"

When Élisabeth tried to make him understand that she couldn't live without novels (or poetry), Henry offered a bogus concession. He would get her a subscription to the *Gazette de France,* a royalist newspaper his mother sometimes perused. But it was literature that fed Élisabeth's soul, and she refused to give it up. Catching her curled up with a book by Victor Hugo, Henry threw a fit, shrieking about her "blasted bad taste." His tantrum set Élisabeth off in turn. "When someone attacks the things I admire," she wrote afterward, "I become incensed, and hardly recognize myself."

BECAUSE SHE WAS SO UNHAPPY AT BOIS-BOUDRAN, Élisabeth initially welcomed her and Henry's other principal pastime that fall: paying their obligatory first visits as husband and wife to friends and relatives in the region. She was thankful for these chances to get out of the house and away from her in-laws. Yet it was on one such outing that she gained her first glimpse into her husband's secret love life, a discovery she then chronicled on three tearstained pages in her Marriage Journal. "The blindfold has been ripped from my eyes," reads the first of these pages, dated October 23, 1878. "The entire universe has been illuminated for me in a blinding flash of infinite, inexpressible pain." The second page is blank but for a single name, "Mademoiselle d'Harcourt (Pauline), la Vtesse d'Haussonville," and the third page contains her account of what happened. While at a dinner party earlier that evening, given for her and her husband by the Vicomte and Vicomtesse (later Comte and Comtesse) d'Haussonville at their nearby castle, Gurcy, Élisabeth caught the lady of the house trading sultry glances with Henry and "showering him with a thousand little solicitous shows of affection" that betrayed an unmistakable degree of intimacy between them.

All at once, Henry's frequent absences from Bois-Boudran—including a jaunt into Paris for a wedding to which Élisabeth, too, had been invited, but which he forbade her from attending—assumed a terrible new meaning. (According to *mondain* gossips, Henry spent the better part of his honeymoon trysting with Pauline d'Haussonville not only in Paris but at Les Bouleaux, a manor house on the grounds of Bois-Boudran conveniently proximate to Gurcy.)

Henry's affair with Pauline also explained the tantrums to which he had lately been subjecting Élisabeth almost at random, even when her shortcomings as a huntress were not at issue. She realized during their evening at Gurcy that if Henry was treating her "with neither tenderness nor chivalry nowadays," it was not just because he was short-tempered and callous, although he was both of those things. No, her husband was lashing out at her because she was not Pauline, and because, in her naïveté, Élisabeth wanted him to love her anyway.

It was a futile wish. Pauline, Vicomtesse d'Haussonville, née d'Harcourt, in many respects represented a far better match for Henry than Élisabeth could ever have hoped to be. A consummate grande dame with deep-seated pride in an ancestry she could trace back nearly a millennium, Pauline could and did spend hours in contemplation of her own genealogical greatness and that of her husband, Othenin, who to her infinite satisfaction had a d'Harcourt grandmother of his own. (High-ranking courtiers under Louis XVI, the couple's paternal grandfathers had been friends as well as in-laws—a double bond the two men's sons had reinforced by arranging for their own children to marry.) Pauline's veneration of her forebears made her a kindred spirit for Henry, who liked to point out that his mother's family livery had been purple, the color of royal mourning, ever since the twelfth century, when a La Rochefoucauld king of Jerusalem donned it "to mourn the death of Christ." This anecdote would serve as Pauline's cue to revisit the d'Harcourts' own feats in the Holy Land, where they fought a crusade under the standard of Richard the Lionheart.

After genealogy, Pauline's chief article of faith was the *mondain* virtue of "simplicity." In its ideal patrician usage, this term denotes a laudable blend of understatement and humility, a down-to-earth graciousness intimating that one does not mistake one's station, however lofty, for actual superiority to one's fellow man. But in the fin-de-siècle Faubourg, this quality was scarce, perhaps because the nobility had lost too many of its prerogatives to feel secure in downplaying one of the few it had left: its ostensibly inborn grandeur. As was typical in her peer group, Pauline's "simplicity" was a ruse. By affecting indifference to the values she in fact prized above all others—birth and rank—she conveyed in a roundabout way just how grand she really was. As critic Henri Raczymow has put it, "To praise a person for her 'simplicity' is to point out that she has every reason in the world not to be simple."

No one in the gratin was less "simple," in this sense, than Henry's pompous cousin, Aimery "Place à Table" de La Rochefoucauld. So Pauline exercised her "simplicity" at his expense, deemphasizing her own ancestral vanity by teasing

Aimery for his. According to one of the *hommes du monde* (society gentlemen) who attended her at-homes in Paris,

> Mme d'Haussonville, who was simplicity itself, used to say of "her dear Comte Aimery de La Rochefoucauld" . . . : "Aimery would be charming if he stopped carrying his family tree around with him." She would recount with wry humor how [he] once went boating on Lake Geneva with a number of his [La Rochefoucauld] relatives. When a violent storm suddenly blew up and it looked as if the ship might sink, the comte cried to the rescuers who had rushed out to help them: "Save the senior branch of the family first!"

Aside from promoting the fiction that she herself was above such laughable tribal hubris, Pauline's story had the advantage of shoring up her lover's fragile ego. Smug as he was about his La Rochefoucauld pedigree, Henry was painfully aware that the surname "Greffulhe"—with its middle-class Protestant overtones, its lack of a nobiliary particle ("de"),* and its *titres de noblesse* not even a century old—did not impress genealogical purists like Aimery, who compensated for his own mother's bourgeois origins by "point[ing] up the weak sides of much-vaunted pedigrees, and scoff[ing] even at mésalliances contracted more than a hundred years earlier." This habit of his cousin's brought out the worst in Henry, who thought too highly of himself to tolerate any aspersions cast on his bloodline. Pauline soothed him by putting Aimery on the defensive instead.

Her playfulness on this score did not, however, translate into an approachable demeanor overall. As her friend Gabriel-Louis Pringué remarked, Pauline held herself as if she were "very much above the rest of humanity, . . . and wearing an invisible crown on her head: one felt as if one had to bow to her." In a like vein, Lily de Gramont described her as

> affable but almost willfully banal, as though she were a queen who was only deigning to make small talk with her inferiors. Though she called people by their nicknames and inquired after their health, her big, cold eyes did not appear to participate in the warmth of her words and gestures. . . . She had a very grand air.

Constance de Breteuil offered a harsher assessment: "Mme d'Haussonville has a bad character." But Pauline's hauteur endeared her to Henry, whose mother had trained him to see arrogance as "a mark of distinction and race." He also valued Pauline's close friendship with the Comte and Comtesse de Paris,

---

* While neither necessary nor sufficient to confirm patrician lineage, the particle "de" figures in a majority of noble French surnames. Henry Greffulhe was defensive about lacking this attribute. According to André de Fouquières, he insisted that the Greffulhe name "was greater than any particle."

the d'Orléans pretenders to the French throne. For should those sovereigns ever be restored to power, as Henry hoped and intended, they would undoubtedly conscript Pauline and her husband into their *service d'honneur,* affording the d'Haussonvilles a proximity to the crown that even the Caraman-Chimays, with their ties to the Belgian royal family, could not rival.

But if Pauline's stellar social and political qualities alone might have been enough to arouse Henry's interest, her beauty entranced him as well—not for nothing did the gratin call her "la belle Pauline." Although Pauline was fourteen years her senior, Élisabeth conceded in her journal that Henry's mistress was still

> a beautiful woman, tall and blond and statuesque. Her complexion may be a bit too pink from rosacea, but still, she has a pretty nose, and heavy-lidded eyes in the manner of Louis XV.

This last attribute may point to a narcissistic dimension in Henry's attraction to Pauline: she resembled his own supposed royal ancestor and, perhaps even more important, himself. As Breteuil noted, "Greffulhe's mistresses aren't just all blond—they are all the exact same shade of strawberry blonde which makes for a kind of family resemblance among them." It made for a family resemblance, too, between them and their strawberry-blond-haired lover.

As for Othenin d'Haussonville, if he had any inkling of his wife's involvement with Henry, it did not appear to bother him—perhaps because of his own alleged attachment to someone other than his spouse. While d'Haussonville's contemporaries took note of the "impeccable, almost intimidating courtesy" with which he treated Pauline, he was known in the monde as a loyal devotee of Mme Georges Bizet, the daughter of one great composer and the widow of another. When in Paris, he never missed Mme Bizet's Sunday at-homes, visits on which his wife never joined him. As a bohemian, bourgeoise Israelite, Mme Bizet was just the type of person haughty Pauline preferred to avoid. Truth be told, however, she needn't have worried about rubbing elbows with such a creature; Mme Bizet discouraged her male friends from calling on her with their wives in tow.

It made perfect sense to Élisabeth that the grave, bespectacled Othenin d'Haussonville should gravitate toward Mme Bizet, whose salon in Montmartre drew a famously accomplished crowd. After all, he was himself a serious intellectual, from a family as brainy as it was "born." His mother wrote biographies on subjects ranging from the Renaissance author Marguerite de Navarre to the *modern* literary critic Charles Augustin Sainte-Beuve, while her grandmother Germaine de Staël was one of the most acclaimed female novelists in French literary history. His father, the current Comte d'Haussonville, was a renowned historian and a member of the Académie Française. A respected author in his own right, Othenin aspired to succeed his father in that pantheon, an effort in which Mme Bizet, well-connected with the Immortals, was reportedly working to help him.

Not long before the Greffulhes' visit to Gurcy, Othenin had finished writing a monograph on the negative effects of illiteracy and homelessness on the children of the urban poor. Now he was hard at work on a biography of his great-great-grandmother, Suzanne Necker. In addition to being the mother of Mme de Staël, Mme Necker had been the wife of Louis XVI's finance minister Jacques Necker, whose dismissal by the king on July 11, 1789, had precipitated the storming of the Bastille three days later. In the decade prior to the Revolution, her salon in Paris had drawn the leading minds of the French Enlightenment, including the *philosophes* Denis Diderot and Jean Le Rond d'Alembert and the naturalist Georges, Comte de Buffon.

Othenin's study of Mme Necker intrigued Élisabeth, whose own great-grandmother, Mme Tallien, had held a salon of comparable importance in the decade after the Revolution. (In fact, Mme Tallien had first met her future husband, Élisabeth's great-grandfather the Prince de Chimay, through Mme de Staël.) Élisabeth was also touched by the obvious pride he took in his great-great-grandmother's achievements; apart from her Chimay and Montesquiou kinfolk, she had encountered very few nobles who esteemed their forebears on intellectual or artistic grounds rather than on the antiquity of their *titres de noblesse*. (Abel Hermant, a writer protégé of Mimi's, parodied this attitude to good effect in his 1899 comedy of manners *Le Faubourg*, where a fusty spinster looks down her nose at a noble family who "were still *nobodies* in the middle of the twelfth century!") With her royal Merovingian roots, Élisabeth was eminently qualified to play that game. Yet she always insisted that Mme Tallien was her favorite ancestor, and she liked Othenin for feeling similar pride about Mme Necker.

Pauline did not share in this enthusiasm. Like Henry, she looked askance at artiness as a derogation of *bon ton*. Her own interests lay in philanthropy, the standard avocation for ladies in her milieu. She was an active member of the Faubourg's most prestigious charitable organization, the Société Philanthropique, founded in the late eighteenth century to feed and care for the poor. This was the same charity to which Henry's mother and sisters devoted much of their time when in Paris. In fact, the Greffulhe women were already pressuring Élisabeth to join the Société. Thus far she had demurred, dismissing the group in secret as a gaggle of mean, competitive biddies who cared more about outperforming one another at their annual charity bazaars than about actually doing good works. In this respect as well, Élisabeth's outlook and behavior aligned much less with Henry's than Pauline's did. The discrepancies between the two women fueled his mounting distaste for his wife's alien, bluestocking ways.

On her side, Élisabeth was devastated to learn of Henry's infidelity: agonizing proof that he did not, in fact, love her "more than anyone else in the world." As if to confirm this terrible insight, one of the Bois-Boudran founders, the ebullient Franco-Irish diplomat Arthur O'Connor, presented her with a gag gift not long after the eye-opening dinner at Gurcy: a rare edition of *The Loves of Henri IV* (*Les Amours d'Henri IV*), an historical account of that king's myriad affairs. Henry blew up at O'Connor for spending 450 francs—"a pretty penny!"—on such an asinine joke (the average price of a book at the time being three francs). While Thundering Jove raged at his friend, Élisabeth dashed upstairs to her bedroom in tears.

Though not as steely as Félicité or Pauline, Élisabeth did not make a habit of such overt displays of emotion; placing a premium on her dignity as a woman of high birth, she was determined not to wear her misery on her sleeve. As she would admit to Henry some decades later: "Through all my trials and tribulations, I have done everything possible to keep people from seeing how difficult it is for me to *smile* while my heart is breaking." In the weeks that followed the visit to the d'Haussonvilles, she put that policy into effect, making a concerted effort to present a serene, happy face at Bois-Boudran. Instead of torturing herself with *The Loves of Henri IV,* Élisabeth picked up an anthology of *mondain* adages Uncle Henri had given her and scoured it for helpful hints. From this little book—which Henry only suffered her to read because it had come from his uncle—she deduced that "being beautiful and being ugly make women into two completely different sexes" and that she herself might have an easier time of things if she staked out her place in the beautiful camp. This strategy was obviously working for "la belle Pauline."

For Élisabeth to reinvent herself as an enchantress would require a major commitment of energy and time. But she rose to the challenge, grateful to have a new sense of purpose. She began to spend hours each day in conference with Assunta, experimenting with new ways to wear her hair and jewels. One of her favorite innovations featured a very long pearl sautoir wrapped once around a bun at the nape of her neck, with the remaining "rivers of pearls" spilling down her back between her shoulder blades; for more casual wear, she replaced the pearls with a trailing chiffon scarf. She sent for seamstresses from Paris to whip up dramatic ensembles of her own design, inspired by works in her new family's art and book collections.

Élisabeth's first experiment along these lines was a copy of a demure white court dress that had caught her eye in an antique engraving of a royal princess whose name she shared. Mme Élisabeth, as the pious younger sister of Louis XVI had been called, had been incarcerated with him and Marie Antoinette during the French Revolution and was guillotined not long after they were. Having met her fate with unflinching courage and beatific resignation, Mme Élisabeth was revered in monarchist circles as something close to a saint. The fact that she never married added to her angelic reputation, which royalist iconography tended to underscore by depicting her in white. This was a figure with whom Élisabeth Greffulhe could identify.

The outfit inspired by her royal namesake was made of lustrous white satin: not a fabric in heavy rotation in the other Greffulhe women's wardrobes. (As Élisabeth noted in her diary, Félicité encouraged Louise and Jeanne "to choose all their dresses from one of two shades: *felt* and *dust*," and Jeanne eschewed color altogether, dressing only in black.) With its inflated hoopskirts and dramatic long train, Élisabeth Greffulhe's copy of the dress clearly evoked the ancien régime; it had nothing in common with the wasp-waisted, mutton-sleeved confections currently in vogue in Paris. Putting this dress on, Élisabeth could almost, she wrote, hear a voice "whispering in [her] ear that [she was] not like everyone else."

As would so often be the case for her in the future, Élisabeth's fashion statement was an actual statement, going beyond mere style to make an assertion about who she was, or who she wanted to be. In this instance, her outfit drew an explicit analogy between herself and the virginal Mme Élisabeth. Let her husband keep a mistress, in the tradition of Henri IV; Élisabeth would claim a much loftier role model, the chaste, martyred princess unbowed by persecution. She might have to tolerate Henry's betrayals, Élisabeth seemed to be saying, but she was not about to let him outclass her. When it came to royal posturing, he could learn a thing or two from his "little queen" of a wife.

DESPITE ITS ROYAL OVERTONES, Élisabeth's new ensemble did not lend itself readily to the sport of kings; it was made for the ballroom, not the duck blind. What was more, so long as hunting and farming dominated the dinner conversation each night, her elegant, unusual clothes were not likely to have the desired effect. To create an environment more hospitable to stylish self-display, Élisabeth worked up her courage and resolved to "set the house rules on their ear."

An opportunity to do so presented itself rather unexpectedly in early December, when Uncle Henri came down with the flu. The rapid deterioration of his health, which had been poor to begin with, prompted him and Henry's parents to leave Bois-Boudran for the more salutary climes of the sun-baked Riviera. It was in their absence that Élisabeth stepped up and asserted herself as the new lady of the manor. While she was powerless to prevent the founders from hunting by day, by night she shifted the focus to more sophisticated amusements. These ranged from the sublime (such as the fancy-dress ball she held when the Maréchal de MacMahon came to stay) to the ridiculous (such as a parlor game that ended in general hilarity when a stuffy visiting diplomat consented to "escort the finest goose from the barnyard" around the salon on a leash). By Christmas, such diversions had become the new norm at Bois-Boudran. "Now we are very elegant and very social here," Élisabeth exulted in a letter to Mimi. "We laugh and we sing . . . and we talk about something other than hunting! Bois-Boudran is transformed! To me, it feels like a miracle."

She had a related epiphany at around the same time when she appeared at dinner on Christmas Day—also Henry's thirtieth birthday—in one of her show-stopping new gowns. From the "profound, amazed silence" that fell among the other guests when she made her entrance, Élisabeth realized with elation that "people find me beautiful! Even my mother-in-law looked at me as if she had never seen me before." (By this time, Félicité and Charles were back at Bois-Boudran, while Uncle Henri stayed on in Nice, dying.) As when the crowds had cheered at her on her wedding day, Élisabeth was filled with an intoxicating sense of her own power.

This power had its limits, of course, especially with regard to Henry, who would continue to philander without remission, compunction or, as the years wore on, discretion, until his death in 1932. Long before then, Élisabeth would have to face the fact that no dress in the world was going to make him faithful to her. Still, from the very start of their honeymoon, she had noticed how he was "always checking to see what impression I am making on everyone else," and how he was constantly urging her to "keep up [her] grand air"—shades of Pauline d'Haussonville—so that "people [might] see you and say: 'What a lucky chap, that Henry! He married the most beautiful woman in France!'" Keeping these interactions in mind, Élisabeth came to relish, and actively orchestrate, occasions for "Henry's friends [to] find me *magnificent*—that excites him." It excited his vanity, at least, if not his libido.

More to the point, it excited her own vanity, if not her libido—the latter an incidental concern to her at best. Repelled by the sexual "consequences" of marriage, Élisabeth manifestly preferred the abstract pleasures of the ego to the earthier thrills of the id—a preference that her later dealings with other men would confirm. Confronted with her first glimpse of Henry's infidelity, and with his increasingly hard-hearted treatment of her, Élisabeth chose to look outside her marriage for validation. As she confided to Mimi,

> Having a husband who abandons me, I try to make the best of it and take my little successes wherever I can, rather than wallowing in self-pity because . . . the more care, devotion, and love I show him, the more he enjoys being away from me, and the more . . . he [seems] wrapped around another woman's finger. All I can do is act as though everything is fine, and pursue my own life and my own pleasures [*agréments*] . . . This is all the more convenient because [Henry] himself wants me to shine; otherwise, people will say he married a goose.

By "my own life and pleasures," though, Élisabeth certainly did not (yet) mean parallel romances. She focused her energies and pinned her hopes on *agréments* drawn not from the passion of one man, but from the admiration of many:

I believe there is no ecstasy in the world that can compare to the ecstasy of a woman who feels she is the object of every gaze, and draws nourishment and joy from the crowd. It is a feeling of overwhelming delight, pride, intoxication, generosity, domination, [a feeling] of a crown offered and disdained. Only great poets, great captains, and great orators can understand what such sensations [are] like, at moments when their bravura and talent meet with delirious bursts of public acclaim.

For all the indignities she had suffered, and would continue to suffer, in her marriage, Élisabeth developed an unwavering confidence in her capacity to beguile. She would become the poet, the captain, the orator of her own, wondrous beauty.

Yet just as poetry calls for readers, skippering for a boat, and oratory for listeners, Élisabeth's artful magnetism would amount to little if she only got to exercise it among family members and friends. The revels she had instituted at Bois-Boudran, as chances to savor her male guests' murmurs and stares—and even to elicit the occasional, lingering *baisemain* (hand kiss) or furtively delivered billet-doux—were steps in the right direction. She was particularly gratified to receive a sonnet from none other than Othenin d'Haussonville, comparing her to Diana, the virgin goddess of the hunt and the moon. He concluded the homage with the assertion that Élisabeth's "grand air and enchanting grace [had] conquered all the gods on Olympus."

This sonnet appears to have triggered Élisabeth's lifelong identification with Diana, which would go on to figure centrally in her public image. This identification would also lead her to acquire a magnificent bust of Diana by Jean-Antoine Houdon, which became her most treasured possession. (Describing the bust to her sister Guigui, she wrote, "You will never forget her expression. Her beauty is my legend.") In fact, there was a certain poetic justice in her first interactions with the d'Haussonvilles. Pauline may have forced Élisabeth to confront the fact of Henry's cheating, but Othenin helped her find her way toward a fantasy self: ethereal, untouchable, divine.

But a persona this spectacular required a larger audience than Henry's family and friends, and luckily, Élisabeth knew just where to find it. On New Year's Day 1879, she and Henry left Bois-Boudran for Paris. Recounting the trip in her diary, she confessed that while she did not want to let him see how excited she was to be returning to the capital, she couldn't stop herself from smiling inwardly, a little smile of anticipatory triumph. "You are not going to like the monde overly much, are you, Bebeth?" Henry had wheedled. As a matter of fact, she was going to like it very much indeed.

CHAPTER THREE

THE KINGDOM OF SHADOWS

Amonth after the Greffulhes returned to Paris, another mismatched patrician couple made its way to the altar: Laure de Sade, nineteen, and Comte Adhéaume de Chevigné, thirty-one. Like Élisabeth Greffulhe, who was one year her junior, Laure de Chevigné found little joy in wedlock. Before long, she, too, would seek her solace and purpose in the monde. But also like Élisabeth Greffulhe, Laure de Chevigné transformed from an adolescent bride into a *grande mondaine* only after a discrete period of transition. While Élisabeth's conquest of the Faubourg came after a season at Bois-Boudran, Laure's triumph followed an extended detour in a place she called "the kingdom of shadows."

THE YOUNGER OF COMTE AND COMTESSE Auguste de Sade's two children, Laure de Sade was born in 1859 in Passy, a sleepy riverside township on the westerly outskirts of Paris. In keeping with a five-hundred-year-old family tradition, she was named for her ancestor Laure de Noves, Comtesse Hugues de Sade (1310–1348). Before dying in the Black Plague, Laure de Noves had secured eternal life as "la belle Laure" ("Laura" in Italian): the unattainable damsel with whom Petrarch became infatuated after spying her at church in Avignon on Good Friday of 1327. Following this *coup de foudre,* Petrarch had dedicated himself to writing verse that voiced his forbidden longing for the married comtesse.

His sonnet cycles, in particular the *Rime Sparse,* laid the foundations of lyric poetry throughout the Western world, an achievement that assigned the woman who had inspired his work a uniquely important place in literary history. Half a millennium later, the descendants of "la belle Laure" still prided themselves on her unwitting celebrity and honored her by giving her name to at least one female child per generation. When the Auguste de Sades christened their daughter Laure, they could not have foreseen that she, too, would one day gain lasting renown as an accidental muse to genius.

Laure's father had grown up in her namesake's shadow, his family seat, the château de Condé, being ornamented with portrait medallions of Petrarch and Laure de Noves. This turreted pile represented the bulk of the de Sade family fortune when Auguste was born in 1819, thirty years after the Revolution had decimated the wealth and privilege of noble clans such as his. The tradition of primogeniture, however, had persisted, disqualifying Auguste, as the youngest of his parents' five children, from inheriting the family castle. When or why he chose to relocate to Passy is unclear. He may have had medical reasons for the move, as the village's hot springs attracted people with health problems that taking the waters was thought to cure.

Not unusually for an aristocrat of his era, Comte Auguste de Sade had no formal occupation. Born into the *noblesse d'épée* (nobility of the sword), the ancient hereditary caste that had filled the ranks of the French military since the feudal age, Laure's father would have served as a military officer under the ancien régime.* The de Sades traced their origins to the Provençal city of Avignon, where they had started out as merchants, receiving their *titres de noblesse* after the first of the clan's many Hugues de Sades followed Louis IX (later Saint Louis) in 1249 on a holy crusade into Egypt. While this expedition ended in defeat for the French army and captivity for the French king, the de Sades' participation won a place for their coat of arms—an eight-pointed yellow star on a red field, centered on a two-headed black eagle—both in the Hall of the Crusades at Versailles (a five-room shrine to France's ancient warrior class) and on Avignon's famous bridge.

For every generation since then, the de Sade family had upheld its custom of military service to the crown, turning its sons into officers as proudly as it turned its daughters into Laures. Yet Auguste's chance to follow this path was dashed in 1830 by the so-called July Revolution, when the archconservative Bourbon monarch Charles X was overthrown and replaced by his more liberal d'Orléans cousin, the self-proclaimed "bourgeois king," Louis-Philippe. While some noble families rallied around the new sovereign, many others, including the de Sades, did not.

Generally a more traditionalist bunch than the d'Orléans partisans, the supporters of the fallen Bourbon monarchy styled themselves "legitimists." Haughtily declining to serve a ruler whose authority they did not recognize, they extended the same disapproval to the governments of the Second Republic (1848–1852) and the Second Empire (1852–1870). This series of "illegitimate" régimes spanned Auguste de Sade's adult lifetime; for him, abstention from the French armed forces would have been a matter of political principle.

His politics did not, however, prevent him from marrying Germaine de Maussion in 1844, despite the fact that her father had received his baronetcy from Napoléon I only a quarter century earlier. (Scions of the older, more established *noblesse d'épée* often looked down on the *noblesse d'Empire*, a class created by Napoléon I. This prejudice diminished as the nineteenth century wore on.) The couple welcomed their first child, Valentine, in 1847, three years after their

---

* Younger sons of the *noblesse d'épée* customarily entered the clergy. But this avenue was closed to married noblemen, given the requirement of celibacy for Catholic priests.

The château de Condé, the de Sade family seat, would later become Laure's part-time home when she was orphaned.

wedding. Because Laure did not come along until twelve years later, when her parents were in their forties, her arrival may not have been planned.

When she was growing up, her family lived modestly in Passy, in an unprepossessing red-brick apartment building at 9, rue des Marronniers, today the site of a dental school. As an adult, Laure would remember the street as "the sort of place where one felt one might get one's throat cut after four in the afternoon in the wintertime." But on this point as on so many others, she took license with the facts: the rue des Marronniers was a peaceful suburban lane. Still, compared to the lively streets of Paris, it did have a somewhat desolate feel, especially in the winter, when the sun set early and the eponymous chestnut trees (*marronniers*) stood bare.

Even as a child, Laure hankered for the City of Light. Her parents took her there for the first time when she was four, to attend the wedding of her sister, Valentine, seventeen, to Baron Pierre Laurens de Waru, a young naval lieutenant. The ceremony was held in the Right Bank's ninth arrondissement, a middle-class neighborhood where the newlyweds had decided to settle. After staid Passy, the diversity and bustle of the ninth came to Laure as revelations—from the modern plate-glass-fronted department stores along the boulevard Haussmann to the produce stands on the cobblestoned rue des Martyrs, and from the glitzy Folies-Bergère in the rue Richer to the seedy dance halls and brothels of the place Pigalle.

Although not grand like the Faubourgs Saint-Germain and Saint-Honoré, Valentine's new neighborhood would leave her little sister with an enduring fascination for parts of town disregarded by other *mondains*. (Laure loved the noble districts, too.) She entreated her parents to let her visit the Warus in the city as often as possible and fantasized about living there. According to her friend Lily

2. SADE

Laure liked to remind her contemporaries that her family blazon adorned the famous bridge in Avignon, in the de Sades' ancestral Provence.

de Gramont, Laure "was too taken with her beloved Paris even to consider ever straying any farther afield."

Yet when family tragedy struck, she was forced to do just that. In May 1868, three weeks before Laure's ninth birthday, her father died. Her mother passed away eight years later. At the time of Germaine's death, Laure was still too young to stay on in the rue des Marronniers by herself but too grown-up to move in with Valentine and Pierre in Paris, where the couple were raising several small children of their own.

Responsibility for Laure's welfare fell to a loose network of aunts, uncles, and adult cousins, who cared for her on a rotating basis at their provincial estates: on the de Sade side, the châteaux de Condé, in Brie, and de Mazan, in Provence; and on the Maussion side, the château de Jambville, approximately sixty miles west of Paris. (The relative to whom Laure was closest, her mother's older sister Camille, Baronne Marochetti, lived with her Italian-born husband in London, too far away to be among her caregivers.) Whatever educational program Laure had followed previously (either lessons with tutors at home or schooling at a local convent), her instruction fell by the wayside as her relatives shunted her from one castle to the next.

Laure's nomadic living arrangements were not meant to be permanent; her guardians' intention was to marry her off as soon as they could find a suitable candidate for her hand. (Because women under French civil law were considered lifelong minors, they were expected to pass directly from their fathers' control to their husbands', so essentially, Laure's relations were looking to turn her over to a new guardian.) But brokering a match proved difficult, for though she was charming, vivacious, and well-born, she did not represent a conventionally appealing marriage prospect to men of her caste.

One of the problems was Laure's dowry. While not as meager as Élisabeth de Caraman-Chimay's, it was illiquid enough to give pause, consisting chiefly of a farm near Arles, the domaine de Cabannes, where the main residence was a crude, dilapidated, and, according to Laure, appallingly drafty stone farmhouse. The property had once been a vineyard, but as its vines had stood neglected for generations, it produced little income. As the centerpiece of Laure's dowry, the domaine de Cabannes was hardly a great inducement.

Valentine had likewise gone onto the marriage market with few notable assets to her name, but Pierre de Waru was rich enough for the both of them. His father, Adolphe Laurens, Baron de Waru, was a top banker at the Banque de France and had used his connections there to secure lucrative board positions for Pierre at the Paris–Orléans railway line and the Nationale insurance company. Consequently, Pierre did not have to choose a wife on monetary grounds. Given the aristocratic bias against working "in trade," a bachelor like him was an anomaly in French society. Due to that same prejudice, most of the men with whom Laure's relatives might have hoped to arrange a match would probably have needed rich spouses of their own. As the noblesse grew poorer, so did Laure's chances of finding a husband.

Her surname presented additional complications. Family connections were everything to French aristocrats, as the custom of the *faire-part,* among many others, made plain. Every time a member of the family married or died, an engraved announcement (*faire-part*) was sent out on behalf of any and all parents, grandparents, siblings, children, grandchildren, great-grandchildren, nephews, nieces, great-nephews, great-nieces, aunts, great-aunts, uncles, great-uncles, and cousins to whom the betrothed or deceased was related, by blood or by marriage. Such practices guaranteed that neither Mademoiselle de Sade nor her husband would ever be able to escape her maiden name. Despite the luster lent to it by Petrarch's muse, the name also carried horrific connotations, owing to Laure's other most famous forebear: her paternal great-grandfather, Donatien-Alphonse-François, Marquis de Sade (1740–1814).

As a class, the "born" did not tend to be paragons of rectitude; Henry Greffulhe's affair with Mme d'Haussonville was typical of the rampant adultery in their milieu. Nonetheless, noble Frenchmen and -women were and had ever been scrupulous about keeping up appearances—and this was a principle Donatien de Sade had dedicated his life to flouting. Miring his family in one scandal after another, he had perpetrated a host of offenses he proudly called "crimes of love." These included kidnapping and torturing a beggar; flogging and poisoning several prostitutes; abducting his wife's sister, a cloistered nun, then deflowering her and running off with her to Italy; holding orgies in his castle in Provence; using crucifixes, communion wafers, and other religious paraphernalia as sex toys; and composing reams of explicit, gruesomely violent, and savagely anticlerical pornographic fiction.

An illustration from one of the Marquis de Sade's many pornographic novels, *Justine, or The Misfortunes of Virtue* (1791). The author was Laure's great-grandfather.

As Donatien saw them, his acts of defiance were consistent with his family's heraldic slogan: *Opinione de Sado* (In Sade's opinion). While the spirit of entitlement this motto conveyed was hardly alien to Donatien's fellow aristocrats, he offended them with his refusal to cloak his transgressions in even the flimsiest guise of propriety. No matter how insistently his relatives and peers reproached him for dishonoring his family and his class, he maintained that he would rather "wrap [his] vices in all the colors of hell" than conform to their hollow, hypocritical notions of decency and *bon ton*. "Yes, I am a libertine," he wrote,

> haughty, ferocious, prone to extreme imaginings, because of a disordered moral faculty which has never had its equal . . . : in a word, there you have me; and one more thing, either kill me or take me as I am, because I will not change.

This attitude, to his family's consternation, repeatedly placed Donatien on the wrong side of the law, leading him to rack up a total of twenty-eight years behind bars. To this day, he holds the record for serving time under a greater number of successive political régimes than any other writer in French history, from the reigns of Louis XV and XVI to the First Republic, the Directoire, and the Consulate, and finally to the Empire of Napoléon I. He died in 1814 at Charenton, an asylum for the criminally insane.

Since then, the legend of the lawless marquis had permeated French culture, owing in large part to his idolization by subsequent generations of literary renegades; among nineteenth-century Parisian authors, his most prominent champions were Charles Baudelaire and Guy de Maupassant. At the turn of the twentieth century, de Sade's emphasis on erotic cruelty would make him an important touchstone for Marcel Proust as well as for the poet Guillaume Apollinaire, who would ironically brand him "the divine marquis." Meanwhile, the emergent fin-de-siècle disciplines of psychiatry and psychoanalysis invented the term "sadism," enshrining Donatien's proclivities in language, science, and philosophy. All these factors combined to make his great-granddaughter's surname a watchword for perversion and, as such, a major deterrent to prospective grooms.

In the end, Laure spent two years waiting for her relatives to find someone to take her off their hands. During that limbo period, she shuttled among Condé, Mazan, and Jambville, more or less ignored in all three places and understanding that without a husband, she would be doomed to spend the rest of her days as a family charity case: no longer a provisionally needy *jeune fille à marier* but a permanently dependent *vieille fille* (old maid). Yet all the while, one of her friends recorded, Laure remained "the incarnation of the warrior's soul," with far too much "pluck, good sense, and energy" to wallow in self-pity.

To combat her relative isolation, Laure learned from her athletic Maussion cousins how to ride and shoot as well as any man, forming a deep affection for the gamekeepers, huntsmen, trainers, and stable boys whose labors made her sporting activities possible. From these salt-of-the-earth provincials, she amassed a trove of colorful peasant sayings and pronunciations that infused her speech with incongruous, rusticated charm. She also picked up the lower-class habits of indiscriminate *tutoiement*—using the informal "you" (*tu*) with people of every age and station—and contracting even the shortest words, notably *ça* instead of *cela* for "that." One of her favorite conversational gambits was to invoke an obscure fact or make an outlandish assertion and then shrug: "Everybody knows that" (*Tout le monde connaît ça; tout le monde sait ça*). The last word in this tagline, which to the fin-de-siècle French ear had the slangy sound of "ain't" for "isn't," heightened the surprise or shock value of whatever preceded it. As a corollary to her linguistic transgressions, Laure took up smoking, puffing cigarettes with her roughneck pals in secret behind the barns.

Laure was cerebral as well as athletic, though she was careful not to talk overmuch about her bookish interests; she recognized that in her milieu, bluestockings were not considered attractive. In the libraries of her family's châteaux, she sped through several books a week, a habit she would keep up all her life. Browsing the collections at Condé, she learned that her great-uncle Louis-Marie de Sade had written prolifically—if without the notoriety of his father, "the divine marquis"—on history and myth. His work captivated her because it treated the two subjects as one. In his *History of the French Nation: The First Race* (1805), Louis-Marie asserted as fact that before its occupation by the Romans, who called it Gaul, the territory now known as France had been ruled by Pluto, the god of the underworld and the dead, and had produced a superior human race. This fantastical notion would exert a defining influence on Laure's conception of the French monarchy and later, during the Dreyfus affair, of the French "race" as a whole.

The political treatises of another kinsman, Chevalier Louis de Sade, also shaped her perspective. During the French Revolution, the chevalier had immigrated to England, where he published a slew of pamphlets about the dangers of revolutionary ideology and republican government. He returned to France in 1815, when the Bourbons were restored to the throne, and his support for their rule survived their overthrow fifteen years later. In his *Political Lexicon* (1831), the chevalier issued a rousing appeal to France's "*true ROYALISTS,* those who cherish and respect the legitimate head of the monarchy, [and are deeply] attached to the rights of *royalty* and the stability of *monarchical institutions.*" While this call to arms did nothing to aid the deposed Bourbons, it provides as good a summary as any of Laure's own political views.

Further immersing herself in family lore, she taught herself Provençal, the dialect of the de Sades' native region, and devoured works by and about Petrarch. The Christian name she had inherited from "la belle Laure," she learned, had inspired several Petrarchan riffs on its homophonies with the words "gold" (*l'oro*) and "laurel" (*l'alloro*). This discovery inspired her to form another lifelong habit: signing her letters with a laurel leaf.

Curious to know more about her namesake, she read a dual biography of Petrarch and his muse, written in 1764 by her great-great-uncle, the Abbé de Sade. Despite his clerical position, the abbé had been almost as dissolute as his favorite nephew, Donatien. His study of Petrarch and Laure is rife with scabrous morsels that give the lie to the supposedly platonic nature of the poet's love. For example: "Petrarch *enjoyed* [Laure] in much the same way that a rat in an apothecary *enjoys* the drugs he finds there, *licking the outsides of the bottles that contain them.*" Had Laure's guardians realized that this was the sort of thing she was reading, they would almost surely have intervened, for in their set, such risqué material would have been beyond the pale even for a married woman. But they left Laure to her own devices, thereby fostering her interest in a forbidden subject that she, coached by her stable-boy companions, even dared to call by its forbidden name: "f**king."

This was a topic on which her great-grandfather Donatien had much to tell her. Reading his fiction, Laure reveled in its bawdiness and savage black humor.

De Sade's writings, which run to several thousand pages, extol the joys of torture, rape, sodomy, pedophilia, incest, bestiality, coprophagia, cannibalism, and
murder. It deems prostitution a woman's highest calling and feminine virtue a
crime against nature. It dismisses God as "an inconsequential barbarian," the
Virgin Mary as a "Jewish whore," and Jesus Christ as an "ignorant, weak, and
stupid charlatan" who "deserved to be treated like the king of the lowest scoundrels." In this made-up universe, the villainous are always rewarded and the
virtuous always beaten (to a pulp, and to death). Monasteries are hotbeds of
frantic buggery and palaces, moated human abattoirs where nobody can hear
you scream.

Presumably this reading set a high bar for Laure's definition of bad behavior
and emboldened her to air outrageous views. Throughout her long career in
society, whenever Laure encountered a prig who cast aspersions on her great-
grandfather, she would answer with a smirk that his writings were not immoral
or pornographic but merely "boring." "Besides," she would add, cool as marble, "he really was *quite a good husband.*" As Laure well knew, nothing about
Donatien's treatment of his pious and long-suffering wife supported this assertion. He had squandered her dowry on orgies and prostitutes, run off with her
sister (the cloistered nun), and thrown her life into turmoil with his constant
prison terms. He had even tormented her from prison, forcing her routinely
to replenish his huge collection of custom-built dildoes. It was a testament to
her misery in the marriage that as soon as divorce was legalized in revolutionary France, she took advantage of the new law despite her religious scruples.
It suited Laure's own sense of perversity to confound received wisdom on this
subject. After all, *Opinione de Sado* was her family motto, too, and in Laure's
opinion, she was free to redefine morality or rewrite history as she saw fit.

For Laure as for her great-grandfather, part of that redefinition turned on an
affinity for X-rated language. Donatien had displayed this affinity on virtually
every page of his literary output, and joining theory to practice, he had formu-
lated this axiom to explain why he so enjoyed

> saying obscene or dirty words, [and being] unstinting in [my] use of such
> expressions; the aim is to cause the greatest scandal possible, for it is very
> sweet to be scandalous.

Again given Laure's class, age, and gender, such a justification of scandal was
unthinkable. She belonged to a society where, as one critic noted, "there were
certain words a decent woman went to her grave without pronouncing." This
lexicon ran the gamut from the raunchiest epithets to the blandest terms for
human anatomy and biology. But Laure liked them all. She found that interjecting an obscenity or two into the dinner conversation could enliven even the
dullest provincial evening.

Laure used her time in the countryside to perfect several of the distinctive qualities—the effortless athleticism, the faux-bumpkin patois, the rebellious esprit—that would later make her the toast of Paris. One might even say she was rehearsing for that role. According to her friend Marthe, Princesse Bibesco, Laure never lost sight of her guiding principle: "Paris is amusing—everywhere else is boring. But one must know how to be bored, because paradise is inconceivable without purgatory . . . unless one is a saint." Far from winning any points for sainthood while living with her relatives, Laure was running wild. They couldn't wait to be rid of her.

THEY FINALLY SUCCEEDED IN 1878, when her cousin Laure, Baronne de Raincourt (also née de Sade), mentioned her to Comte Adhéaume de Chevigné, a thirty-year-old bachelor serving with the Raincourts in the retinue of the last pretender from the senior branch of the French royal family, Henri d'Artois, Comte de Chambord. Since the 1830 coup that had ended the Bourbons' rule, Chambord and his cadre of staunch legitimists had been headquartered in the Austrian castle of Frohsdorf. This miniature court was made up of Chambord, called Monseigneur, and hailed by his followers as King Henri V; his queen, Marie-Thérèse de Modène, styled Madame, a querulous, deaf old Habsburg princess; and some two dozen minions whose daily functions included tying Monseigneur's shoelaces and his necktie (two tasks he never learned to perform for himself) and taking dictation for his correspondence. The latter duty fell to Adhéaume de Chevigné, who worked as one of the king's two private secretaries.

Frohsdorf was a solemn, archconservative place, a temple to such *vieille France* values as the divine right of kings and the sanctity of the Catholic faith. The royal couple's devout adherence to the latter—which qualified matrimony, after abstinence, as the holiest human state—put their unmarried attendants under considerable pressure to wed. As a member of the Chambords' inner circle, Chevigné needed a bride from a noble family with legitimist sympathies and established royalist credentials. The de Sades' five-hundred-year-long record of loyalty to the throne counted in Laure's favor, outweighing the peccadilloes of "the divine marquis."

Typified by the *noblesse d'épée,* the tradition of royal service so prized by the legitimists took two principal forms: service in the royal armed forces and service at court and in the king's diplomatic corps. Chevigné, who before coming to Frohsdorf had fought in the Franco-Prussian War, embodied this twofold imperative. On both his father's and his mother's sides, his forebears had distinguished themselves in the military and at court, from the regency of Blanche de Castille, the mother of Louis IX, in the 1220s to the reign of Louis XVIII six centuries later. Chevigné's older brother Olivier had preceded him for a time in Monseigneur's retinue at Frohsdorf and now presided over a group of legitimist

stalwarts in Paris, organizing annual banquets in honor of Henri V's birthday
and the anniversary of Louis XVI's execution.

The de Sades, for their part, had been typically feudal warlords, hunker-
ing down in their fortified castles in the provinces when not off fighting for
the crown. But in the mid-eighteenth century, Donatien de Sade's father, Jean-
Baptiste (c. 1701–1767), had left his native Provence for Versailles, hoping to
parlay his good looks, wicked wit, and penchant for intrigue into an influential
position in the court of Louis XV (1710–1774). Between these attributes and his
taste for debauchery with partners of both sexes, Jean-Baptiste quickly became a
favorite with the king, a jaded voluptuary. Jean-Baptiste reportedly served as His
Majesty's pimp, and possibly as one of his lovers. Louis XV showed his appreciation by naming Jean-Baptiste to a series of plum ambassadorial posts.

In 1733 Louis XV approved Jean-Baptiste's marriage to a lady-in-waiting to the
Princesse de Condé, the wife of a Bourbon prince of the blood. (Jean-Baptiste
and the princesse herself were engaged in a torrid affair, for which his marriage
provided convenient cover.) This union would confer upon the de Sades the ne
plus ultra of prestige: a tie of kinship to the monarch himself.

Jean-Baptiste and his family were given living quarters in the palatial hôtel de
Condé in Paris, where their firstborn child, Donatien, grew up with the Condés'
eldest son, whom he liked to beat up when nobody was looking. When the
Seven Years' War broke out in 1756, Donatien channeled his bellicose streak into
his military service, but seeing combat did not slake his thirst for violence. Soon
after the war, he was arrested for kidnapping and torturing a beggar woman,
who told the authorities that he had blindfolded her, mutilated her with a knife,
poured hot candle wax into the incisions, and forced her to desecrate a cross.
As a personal favor to Jean-Baptiste, Louis XV secured the young man's release
from jail. But Donatien continued to defy the law so brazenly that he soon
landed back in prison on that same king's orders.

The French Revolution opened a new chapter for Donatien. With his fondness for rebellion, he purported to identify with the common man's struggle
for freedom. By chance, he had happened to be a prisoner in the Bastille only
a few days before a mob stormed it on July 14, 1789. He later claimed that he
had incited the crowds to violence by calling to them through a chink in the
wall of his cell. At first this story earned him the goodwill of his fellow citizens.
But with the overthrow of the monarchy in the fall of 1792 and the execution
of Louis XVI the following January, the political climate became dangerous for
aristocrats. The new republic stripped them of their titles and privileges and
rounded them up en masse during the Terror, Maximilien de Robespierre's state-
wide purge of suspected enemies of the state.

Donatien was arrested as a counterrevolutionary in March 1794 and found
himself incarcerated once again while awaiting his trial by the Revolutionary
Tribunal. Such trials were mockeries of justice that almost always ended at the

guillotine. But Robespierre and his henchmen were arresting so many people that the Tribunal couldn't keep up. Donatien would later say that Picpus, the prison where he awaited his day in court, was the most hellish place he had ever seen; it overlooked the mass graves for the victims of the guillotine, and according to him, he and his fellow prisoners were forced to "bury 1,800 [headless cadavers] in thirty-five days, one third of whom came from our own ill-starred institution." He himself escaped decapitation only because Robespierre was overthrown a few weeks before Donatien was scheduled to be tried.

It was his ordeal at Picpus that redeemed the Marquis de Sade in the eyes of men like Chevigné. To many fin-de-siècle nobles, the persecution of their ancestors during the Terror had become a badge of honor, further evidence of the chasm that separated them from the "not born." This conviction gave rise to a parlor game: comparing tallies of ancestors who had died on the guillotine. In her novel *Equality*, the Princesse Bibesco satirized this cult of revolutionary victimhood, noting that of all the headless bodies buried at Picpus, fewer than half came from the nobility.

In royalist circles such as Chevigné's, invoking one's "martyred" forefathers underscored an implicit political commitment to the monarchy, loyalty of a degree that might be needed again if a coup d'état were set in motion to place Henri V on the throne. In assessing Laure as a potential wife, Chevigné would have taken her great-grandfather's travails during the Terror as a satisfactory mark of family honor. In fact, one of Chevigné's own ancestors had been an inmate at Picpus, likewise escaping the scaffold thanks only to Robespierre's fall.

The de Sades' fealty to the crown must also have induced Chevigné to overlook the mésalliances—mixed marriages between the nobility and the lower orders—elsewhere on Laure's family tree. Although she avoided mentioning it, Laure descended on her mother's side from Protestant merchants, the Thellussons, who had fled France in the late seventeenth century to avoid religious persecution and founded a bank in Geneva. During Louis XVI's reign, Laure's maternal great-great-grandfather Georges-Tobie Thellusson had moved his branch of the family back to France, where he purchased a property with a baronetcy attached to it. Through a generous contribution to the royal coffers, he had secured the king's permission to use the nobiliary particle "de" and had celebrated his social elevation by building a monumental *hôtel particulier* in the Marais district of Paris, complete with a thirty-foot-high triumphal arch.

The Thellussons thus adopted the same strategy as the Greffulhes, their fellow Protestant bankers turned aristocrats, intermarrying with better established *nobles d'épée* whose blazons needed regilding. After the Revolution, however, the Thellussons' fortunes waned as the Greffulhes' waxed, and their marriages reflected this divergence. Whereas Henry Greffulhe's father had married into the ducal La Rochefoucauld clan, Laure's mother had had to settle for a penniless younger son from the provincial gentry, saddled with a controversial surname,

Originally Protestant merchants, the Thellussons purchased a baronetcy in the late eighteenth century and built this imposing Parisian *hôtel* before their fortunes dwindled.

while Laure's maternal aunt Camille had been reduced to marrying an Italian sculptor, the Baron Marochetti, whose title was of regrettably recent vintage.

HAVING WEIGHED ALL THESE FACTORS, Chevigné asked for Laure's hand sometime in the winter of 1878–1879. He may have made the proposal by proxy, since he does not appear to have traveled from Austria to France before their wedding. Chevigné's offer presented both advantages and drawbacks. As one of Brittany's old-line patrician surnames, Chevigné would be an honorable one for her to assume upon her marriage, as would the title that came with it: comtesse. In contrast to girls born into foreign princely families such as the Caraman-Chimays, who held titles from birth, the daughters of the French nobility did not generally receive such honorifics until they married. And Laure, a firm believer in Otto von Bismarck's dictum "Life begins at baron," definitely wanted a rank at least as grand as the one her mother, and so many of her female ancestors, had held. One of her grandchildren would later say that Laure's single biggest regret in life had been marrying a count instead of a duke.

As for the peculiar name Adhéaume, unique to Chevigné men, it had a pleasingly feudal resonance: it derived from the word *heaume,* the visor on a knight's helmet. Given the pride Laure took in belonging to the *noblesse d'épée,* Chevigné's patrician social profile came as welcome news. So did his employment at Frohsdorf, where, according to Laure's Raincourt cousins, he was one of Henri V's most trusted advisers. If and when a legitimist coup took place, Chevigné would become one of the most powerful men in the kingdom. (In actuality, the likelihood of another Bourbon Restoration had faded markedly in recent years, for reasons Laure would soon discover.)

Chevigné's position did have its downside: he and the king's other attendants earned no compensation for their service. Several of his colleagues supported themselves by selling off parcels of their hereditary landholdings back home. One of them, a very distant kinsman of Henry Greffulhe, would eventually have to forfeit the château de Guermantes, an estate in the Seine-et-Marne.

Chevigné himself had no property to liquidate. In the early nineteenth century, his great-uncle Arthur, Marquis de Chevigné, then the head of Adhéaume's branch of the family, had nearly gone bankrupt in an ill-advised real estate deal. Against difficult odds, Arthur's younger brother Louis—Adhéaume's paternal grandfather—had held on to the family seat, the château de Saint-Thomas, in the Loire-Atlantique on the western coast of France. At his death, the castle passed to his eldest son, another Louis, Comte de Chevigné—Adhéaume's father. But agriculture on the estate did not throw off enough income to provide well for this Louis's populous brood: when Louis died in 1854, he left behind four sons, of whom Adhéaume was the youngest, and the three older sons were all married, with nine children among them. Moreover, Saint-Thomas belonged to Louis's oldest grandson, Augustin, who had inherited it upon the death of his father, Arthur, Adhéaume's eldest brother, in 1869. As a consequence, Adhéaume had only a meager share of an already modest family fortune with which to underwrite his royal service.

With this economic disadvantage came a social one. In Paris, the Chevignés were known to be very rich and very grand—but these were not Adhéaume's closest relations. Some sixty years earlier, a Louis de Chevigné from a different branch of the family had married the ("not born") heiress to the Veuve Clicquot Champagne fortune. Owing to the resulting cash infusion, the couple's offspring had been able to marry into two of the French nobility's most ancient and illustrious clans: the Mortemarts and the d'Uzès. As a distant cousin to these Chevignés, Adhéaume could legitimately claim them as his kin. But they viewed him as a negligible poor relation. By extension, his wife could expect to hold the same diminished standing in their eyes—unless she found a way to change it.

Considering all this, most aristocratic families with marriageable daughters would not have jumped at a proposal from Comte Adhéaume de Chevigné. But Laure's guardians were in no position to cavil about his weak points. Anxious to conclude the match, they impressed upon Laure that his offer of marriage was probably the best, and perhaps even the only, one she was ever going to receive. The factor that clinched the deal for her was the news that Chevigné had rented a tiny place in the Faubourg Saint-Honoré, at 1, rue du Colisée, for their use when on furlough from Chambord's court.

Laure was not conventionally beautiful, but her fair hair, heavy-lidded blue eyes, and Roman nose gave her an elegant air.

ON FEBRUARY 6, 1879, Mademoiselle Laure de Sade, and Comte Adhéaume de Chevigné, pledged their eternal troth to each other in a traditional Catholic wedding mass in Paris. According to their friends' recollections, the young woman kneeling at the altar that day was a petite strawberry blonde, "narrow of hip, broad of shoulder, and swanlike of neck." Her large, hooded blue eyes sparkled with mischief when they weren't glaring with frosty hauteur. The man who knelt beside her was tall and gangly, with close-set brown eyes, a bushy brown moustache and twin tufts of dark brown hair fringing his balding pate. Chevigné's angular "hatchet face," as one acquaintance called it, was suffused with a deep crimson flush—as if he were forever apologizing for his ungainly height or ashamed of some secret known only to himself. Whatever their initial impressions of each other, the bride and groom would have had to entertain those opinions in the knowledge that the contract they were entering into was for life. Divorce was still illegal in France in 1879.

The Adhéaume de Chevignés did not yet have enough standing in the Faubourg for their nuptials to rate more than one line in *Le Gaulois,* the preeminent daily of the *presse mondaine,* which often devoted several paragraphs or even pages to the marriages among more famous clans. (The paper had run three front-page articles about the Greffulhe/Caraman-Chimay wedding.) But a newer and lesser-known society rag, *Le Triboulet,* ran a lengthier announcement that predictably highlighted the groom's position at Frohsdorf and further stressed the legitimist angle by listing the other Chambord devotees who had attended the ceremony. Other details offered more generic indications of the newlyweds' pedigree, such as Chevigné's service in the Franco-Prussian War and the venue, the Église Saint-Philippe du Roule, one of the most *mondain* churches on the Right Bank.

The article in *Le Triboulet* contained one oddity, however; it gave the bride's surname as "Bade" (French for Baden, the region that gave its name to the German spa town of Baden-Baden) rather than Sade. This mistake allied her with the grand dukes of Baden, a line of fabulously rich Teutonic highnesses, and may have been prompted by the groom's Austrian posting. Or it may have reflected a prejudice against the bride's inglorious surname. "In the world [Mme de Chevigné] inhabited," wrote banking heir André Germain, whom she would later befriend, "one could not exactly revel in being born de Sade."

Flattering as the accidental promotion in rank might have been, Laure did not allow it to stand. The following week, *Le Triboulet* published a detailed correction:

> A misprint in our last issue indicated that M. Adhéaume de Chevigné had married Mademoiselle de Bade, but that name should have been written: "de Sade." Mademoiselle de Sade descends from "la belle Laure" de Noves, immortalized by Petrarch. M. Adhéaume de Chevigné belongs to one of the oldest families in France, and is honored with the very special esteem of Monseigneur [*sic*] le Comte de Chambord.

This addendum could only plausibly have come from Laure herself. As most of her wedding guests lived in the provinces or abroad, they would have been unlikely to come across an obscure Parisian paper like *Le Triboulet*. And no one outside her immediate circle would have been prone to catch the mistake, given her and her husband's as-yet-unnoted standing in the monde. While Chevigné could perhaps have asked for the correction, he disliked publicity too much to call attention to his own wedding announcement. Furthermore, he would never have referred to his master, as the revised notice in *Le Triboulet* did, as "Monseigneur le Comte de Chambord." Etiquette styled the Bourbon pretender either "Monsieur le Comte de Chambord" or "Monseigneur" (My Lord), plain and simple* (a nuance the writer for *Le Triboulet* had gotten right the first time around). The faulty nomenclature pointed to someone unschooled in the finer points of princely address—someone like Laure.

Even more interesting than her protocol gaffe were the three biographical points she brought to the editor's attention: her descent from Petrarch's muse, "la belle Laure"; her husband's ancient bloodline; and the "very special esteem" in which Chambord held him. These were all details she would go on to repeat in Parisian society for the next fifty years, so emphatically and often that even

---

* At that time, "Monseigneur le Comte" was a mode of address reserved for the Comte de Paris, designating his position after the Comte de Chambord in line for the French royal succession.

people who didn't know her personally knew to describe her in these terms. As the Princesse Bibesco noted, Laure had a special ability "to impose a poetic vision of herself on those around her, to reimagine herself as a new and fabulous character, and to project that character—her double, so to speak—into the mirror of the public imagination." The correction in *Le Triboulet* reveals that Laure exercised this talent from the very start of her married life. Not even two weeks after her wedding, she was already presenting an idealized new version of herself to the world.

Laure never spoke or wrote about this effort to reinvent herself, much less about her motives for undertaking it. But it is not difficult to imagine why the nineteen-year-old orphan would have been eager to put the loneliness, dislocation, and precariousness of her recent past behind her. For more than two years after her mother's death, her parentless, homeless, penniless state had left her on the outside looking in—residing in castles, admittedly, but treated like a girl to be pitied, a problem to be solved. And yet, this dismal characterization had never quite meshed with any of the personae she had concocted for herself while in her relatives' care: Laure the literary scion, Laure the intrepid huntress, Laure the tough-talking miscreant, Laure the worldly Parisienne. With her marriage, she gained the opportunity to meld these alter egos into an even more fantastic one—a celebrity grande dame, beloved of poets, clubmen, and kings—while ridding herself of the orphan forever. Whatever shame and sorrow she had endured in the latter capacity would be redeemed, or at least obscured, by the beguiling double she projected into the mirror of the public imagination.

While technically her lord and master, Laure's husband would not exert much influence in shaping her new identity. Those who came to know her well concurred that once he had supplied her with a name, a title, a position at court, and an address in Paris, "her poor Adhéaume wasn't of much use to her" anymore. It wasn't that Chevigné was without his endearing traits. According to one of his army comrades, his "nervous nature and sickly appearance" belied many fine qualities that fostered a certain fondness between him and his new wife. Chevigné was as avid a reader as Laure, although his favorite subjects (geography, opera, and agriculture) left her cold. He was a gifted musician, though extant sources do not reveal which instrument(s) he played. He had flawless manners. Even in a peer group whose highest moral imperative was "Thou shalt be polite," Chevigné was a model of courtesy, once coming to the rescue of three strangers, two women and a child, whose carriage crashed in the Bois de Boulogne. After personally tending to their cuts and bruises, he sent the victims home in his own barouche. Above all, he had a "subtle intelligence" that Laure, so bright herself, could not help but admire. As she liked to say, with the understatement proper to *mondain* boasting, "Adhéaume is *not an idiot*."

For all his good points, however, Chevigné came as a disappointment in one crucial respect: he lacked the ambition and flair necessary to become a person of consequence in the monde. By the time of his and Laure's wedding, he had only taken steps toward joining one club: the Société de Géographie. This was a perfectly respectable institution, the oldest of its kind anywhere in the world, but it was not exactly a hub for Paris's social élite. With Laure's vigorous encouragement, Chevigné soon managed to get himself elected to the Jockey—a feat all the more impressive because he was the first Chevigné ever to be admitted to that club. And yet, to Laure's frustration, he had no interest in parlaying his membership into a conspicuous presence in the Faubourg.

In part, Chevigné stayed aloof from the *mondain* social scene because he didn't yet consider Paris home, nor could he, with his duties at Frohsdorf keeping him abroad eight months a year. In part, too, he steered clear of the gratin because its unending slew of fancy dress parties, horse races, and charity galas cost a good deal of money, and he had to count his pennies—another fact that displeased his young bride. More than anything else, though, Chevigné kept a low profile in the monde because he liked his privacy, and he craved peace and quiet. By contrast, Laure felt that her years in Passy and the provinces had given her enough peace and quiet to last a lifetime. She was bent on discovering Paris and on letting Paris discover her—with or without "her poor Adhéaume" by her side.

Laure's readiness to forge a path for herself independent of her husband may also have had something to do with their sex life, or at least with his. At the time of their wedding, it was common knowledge among Chevigné's relatives and friends that on his periodic visits from Frohsdorf to Paris, he had been keeping company with a middle-aged English courtesan, Émilie Williams, popularly known as "the Seal." Furthermore, he had conveyed to the people who were in on the secret that he had no intention of breaking things off with Williams after he wed. Ordinarily, such a romance would not have raised eyebrows in Parisian society, where liaisons between demimondaines and noblemen, married or otherwise, abounded. But Chevigné's devotion to the Seal puzzled his cohorts because she was homely, a most uncommon defect for a woman in her métier. With the mild, vacant brown eyes and pudgy white belly of the creature that inspired her nickname, "the Seal was never beautiful, nor even nice to look at," according to one gossip columnist.

Even in her prime, which preceded the Chevignés' wedding by a good fifteen years, Williams had been renowned above all as a foil to other, prettier courtesans. On one well-known occasion, a clubman with a spiteful sense of humor ordered an onyx chalice molded on the breast of Cora Pearl, one of the era's most sought-after cocottes, and then gave it to the Seal as evidence of Pearl's superior charms. In another notorious episode, Williams started a savage public brawl with a colleague to whom she had just lost a lover, pulling out her adversary's hair in clumps. The media dubbed this incident "the War of the Chignons."

But if Williams's plainness was axiomatic, she compensated for it with her reputation as "an extremely serviceable and accommodating woman, more open-minded than anyone else around." That open-mindedness extended to a peculiar sex act to which her nom de guerre also referred, and which she had engraved on her writing paper: "The Seal says *mama,* the Seal says *papa.*" As prudishly elliptical in their speech as their contemporaries in Victorian England, fin-de-siècle Parisians left no explicit indications as to what this erotic specialty involved. Did Williams include other women in her frolics with her patrons? Or did she cater to men who, preferring *papa* to *mama,* enlisted her to "play the sodomite," as Laure's own great-grandpapa de Sade would have phrased it? The source record does not say.

But two bits of French cultural lore would appear to confirm that Williams's nickname had something to do with unconventional gender or sexual norms. The first was the Comte de Buffon's categorization of the seal as neither fish nor fowl, "a being so strange" that it seemingly belongs among neither "the inhabitants of the earth" nor the creatures of the sea. The "strangeness" of its amphibian nature made the seal a privileged figure for ambiguous sexuality, as when the author Jean Lorrain caricatured his fellow homosexual and sworn foe, Robert de Montesquiou, as a swishy aesthete, Monsieur de Phocas (Mister Seal), in a 1901 novel by that name. The second, more prosaic clue was the slang expression "gay as a seal," the French equivalent of the English "gay as a goose."

Bandied about as lurid jokes in Parisian boulevard theaters and men's clubs, the Seal and her "*mama/papa*" tagline raised questions about Chevigné's erotic preferences, so much so that for more than a decade after he and Laure married, one of the annually updated directories for the nobility continued to identify him as single and childless: *mondain* doublespeak for "gay" (as a seal). This detail

Before his marriage to Laure, Adhéaume had a longtime mistress known as the Seal. Her cryptic, apparently sexual motto was: "The Seal says *mama,* the Seal says *papa.*"

may provide some explanatory context for one of Laure's most infamous, proto-Sadean pronouncements: "A husband teaches one *nothing about f**king.*"

After the wedding, Laure and Chevigné spent an abbreviated honeymoon in Paris, then set out for Frohsdorf, where protocol obliged him to present his new bride to the king and queen as soon as possible. The train trip to Austria took thirty hours, giving Laure ample time to daydream about her royal destination. She had learned that "Frohsdorf" meant "happy village" in German, and while it obviously wasn't Paris, she hoped it would represent an improvement over the dull abodes of her youth.

When she disembarked in the tiny train station at Frohsdorf, however, she saw that the cheery place-name concealed a depressing reality. According to one of her contemporaries, the town was best described as

> monotonous and mediocre. The locals exist in a haze of indifference and resignation that one never finds in French cities and towns. The whole area is suffused with an atmosphere of profound ennui that even the picturesque Alpine setting cannot dispel. One feels utterly lost, and wonders how the Comte de Chambord can . . . bear having to live there.

As for the Schloss itself, a drab, mustard-colored manor house, it presented far too dreary an aspect to allay anyone's despondency at having to live there. The Duchesse d'Uzès, Laure's new distant cousin by marriage, voiced the typical *mondain* tourist's opinion when she called it "lugubrious." Another of Chevigné's relations, fellow courtier René de Monti de Rezé, tried to cast this defect in a positive light by maintaining that the "admittedly rather severe look of the château befitted the melancholy ambience of princely exile." The manicured *jardins à la française* may have been meant to recall Versailles, but the bone-dry moat encircling the building undercut their splendor, accentuating just how far the Bourbons had fallen. (While one would be hard-pressed to imagine the palace of Versailles repurposed as an office building for the national postal service, Frohsdorf has lent itself altogether credibly to that function since 1955.)

The best thing that could be said about the Schloss was that its grounds boasted first-rate hunting and shooting: a deer park, a shooting range (*tir aux pigeons*), and acres of densely populated forest and field. The large complex of kennels and stables near the castle's northern façade attested to the primacy the sport of kings had assumed at a court whose sovereign, for want of a kingdom, had little else to keep him busy. Although he claimed he was willing to forfeit most luxuries, Monseigneur refused to stint on horses. He owned a hundred pairs of perfectly matched Thoroughbreds, all of them spotlessly white like his family's heraldic emblem: the lily (*fleur de lys*).

Inside, Frohsdorf suggested a cross between a hunting lodge and a mausoleum. In lieu of the lavish gilding, marble, frescoes, mirrors, and boiseries that

Visitors were underwhelmed by the austere architecture and dreary décor of the Schloss at Frohsdorf, the site of the Comte de Chambord's miniature court in exile.

had adorned other seats of Bourbon power, the building's plain whitewashed interior walls were covered with antlers, hoofs, and animal heads; one room was filled with vitrines displaying taxidermied birds. Other rooms featured mementoes of the Bourbons' tragic past: from the diamond-buckled shoes Louis XIV wore for his coronation in 1654 to a Vigée-Lebrun portrait of Monseigneur's great-aunt Marie Antoinette, which still bore the bayonet puncture it had sustained in October 1789, when a revolutionary mob stormed Versailles, clamoring for the queen's head. The bedchamber that had seen the death of Monseigneur's late aunt the Duchesse d'Angoulême—firstborn child of Marie Antoinette and Louis XVI and the sole member of their immediate family to have survived the Revolution—was preserved as a shrine to her memory.

Of all the relics in the Schloss, the most ghastly by far was a crystal reliquary topped with a golden *fleur de lys* and engraved with the letters "L. XVII." It contained the tiny heart of Marie Antoinette's and Louis XVI's son, whom monarchists had recognized as Louis XVII upon his father's execution in 1793 but whose jailers had slain him before he could contest the republic's authority and assert his own. (They killed him before he turned ten.) For Henri V, wrote one of his followers, the little boy's heart "had an almost religious significance," as did the two objects displayed beside it: the tattered white bonnet and blood-stained white fichu Marie Antoinette had worn to the guillotine. Like religious relics, these items were meant to glorify the martyrs to whom they had once belonged, while also standing as reminders of the monarchy's brutal travails.

These macabre tokens aside, Frohsdorf's interior was remarkable above all for its blandness. The private quarters were dark, sparsely appointed rabbit warrens, and nothing about the austerely appointed reception rooms, apart from the family portraits lining the walls and the carpets patterned with *fleurs de lys,* suggested royal majesty. Even the "throne," the centerpiece of the Red Salon (Salon Rouge) where Monseigneur and Madame held court, was just a regular armchair with a bit of gilding on the frame, some armorial woodwork crowning the seat back, and the arms of France (an escutcheon with a closed crown and three *fleurs de lys*) stitched into the upholstery. But the décor may have been underwhelming by design. Having endured the longest exile of any sovereign in European history—forty-nine years and counting—the Comte de Chambord did not want to give the impression that he had accepted Austria as his homeland. "One only settles in when one is in one's fatherland," he proclaimed. "When abroad, one camps out and waits."

All the same, Frohsdorf did preserve one precious feature of its owner's birthright: the elaborate court etiquette his five-times great-grandfather, Louis XIV, had enshrined at Versailles two hundred years before. As exactingly upheld under Henri V as under the Sun King, this protocol obliged courtiers to bow or curtsey (sex depending) before the throne each time they passed it, even when it stood empty; to exit the room backwards when excused from the royal presence; to address Monseigneur and Madame only when spoken to, and only in the third person ("Since Monseigneur has deigned to ask me, I have the honor of telling Him . . ."); to join the sovereigns for Mass every morning at six thirty, lunch at eleven, dinner at six, and for all shooting expeditions, buggy rides, fireside chats, and card games in between; and on and on, empty formalities to fill the empty hours.

Of more immediate relevance to the Chevignés was the stipulation that all newcomers to the Schloss be formally presented to the royal couple without delay. To honor this rule, Laure could not rest or settle in after she and her husband reached their spartan quarters. Instead, she changed straightaway into the prescribed *robe de cour*: a fusty black getup with a clunky hoop skirt and a long train, exactly the sort of outfit tomboyish Laure despised. Then she and Adhéaume proceeded without delay to the Red Salon, where Monseigneur and Madame sat enthroned, flanked by a dozen or so members of their tiny court.

Following the ritual Adhéaume had outlined to her ahead of time, Laure stopped on the threshold of the presence chamber and swept into a very low curtsey—the first of the three the ritual required. Then she advanced slowly toward the royals, taking in the footmen (dressed in the powdered wigs and blue livery of ancien régime Versailles), Élisabeth Vigée-Lebrun's painting of Marie Antoinette in the corner (bayonet puncture very much in evidence), the blood-red walls (painted to match Marie Antoinette's dress in the Vigée portrait), the walnut-sized pearls around Madame's neck (the same ones, in fact, Marie Antoinette was wearing in the Vigée portrait). Laure curtseyed twice more in front of the queen and king, so deeply that her forehead skimmed the parquet floor.

The Comte de Chambord,
photographed eighteen years before
Laure first met him in 1879.

Then, remaining procumbent, she removed her glove from her right hand, took hold of the hem of the Comtesse de Chambord's dress, and kissed it.

Symbolically, these gestures not only affirmed Laure's obedience to the monarchs, but evoked the long history of fealty binding her ancestors to theirs. For her, encountering royalty for the first time in her life, it was an emotional rite of passage. Little did she know the man for whose benefit she was prostrating herself bridled at such practices even as he demanded their observance. When he was in a good mood, Henri V treated the ceremony as little more than an occasion for private mirth: joking with his male attendants, he liked to refer to female courtiers' "presentation gymnastics" as "open-c*nt curtseys."

Chambord's penchant for ribaldry was one of his more engaging qualities. Otherwise, he did not evince much in the way of glorious Bourbon manhood. Mildly cross-eyed, grossly fat, and lame from a long-ago riding accident, the fifty-nine-year-old Monseigneur no more resembled his ancestor the Sun King than his Red Salon did the Hall of Mirrors. In place of a bejeweled court costume, he sported a grubby alpaca-wool cardigan and black bedroom slippers with white socks: "the outfit," wrote one observer, "of a petit-bourgeois Parisian going for a morning walk in the park." His shoulders, moustache, and prodigious rubbery jowls all drooped in an attitude of permanent defeat—an expression they had worn since his aborted return to power five and a half years earlier.

Laure had been too young to follow press reports of Monseigneur's attempted coup. But Chevigné, who had participated in the endeavor, filled her in. In the fall of 1873, encouraged by a royalist majority in the Third Republic's fledgling government, Chambord, then fifty-three, had traveled from Frohsdorf to France incognito, defying the law of exile that had kept him abroad for more than forty years. First stopping in Versailles, he expected the Republic's president, the Maréchal de MacMahon, to welcome him back and usher him into Paris in triumph, securing the people's approval for his restoration to the throne. Chambord even brought along a magnificent white steed named Popular Demand (Vœu Populaire) to ride on that glorious occasion.

But his intractable position on the French flag proved his undoing. Monseigneur ardently favored the reinstatement of the Bourbon standard: white in honor of the Bourbon *fleur de lys*. However, the blue, white, and red *tricolore* first introduced by the revolutionaries of 1789 had become too cherished a political symbol for the French people to consider giving it up. Although clearer heads urged him to yield, precisely, to "popular demand," Chambord dug in. Persisting in his avowal that "Henri V must not abandon the flag of Henri IV," he found that MacMahon, though a royalist at heart, refused so much as to meet with him. This rebuff forced Monseigneur to withdraw from his homeland in disgrace. According to Chevigné, he wept all the way back to Austria.

Monseigneur's failure to regain the crown aggravated the pent-up misery and impotent rage with which he had been struggling for decades. He lived every day with an excruciating consciousness of the trials his family had been forced to endure: the incarceration, overthrow, and execution of his great-uncle, Louis XVI, by the founders of the First Republic (with the deciding vote for the regicide cast by the king's own cousin, the Duc d'Orléans); the imprisonment and murder of Marie Antoinette, Mme Élisabeth, and Louis XVII by the same; the assassination in 1820 of his father, the Duc de Berry, before Monseigneur was even born; the forced abdication in 1830 of his grandfather Charles X, and the subsequent usurpation of the throne by another d'Orléans cousin, Louis-Philippe; the failure of a coup d'état staged against said cousin by his mother, the Duchesse de Berry, in 1832; the Bourbons' banishment from their homeland; and most recently, his and his wife's failure to produce an heir. To have suffered all these indignities only to have scotched his long-awaited chance at redemption was almost more than Chambord could bear.

His followers were crestfallen as well, but they did what they could to rebuild his shattered morale. At the Schloss, they kept the trappings of a Bourbon coronation ever at the ready: ermine-lined purple mantles for Monseigneur and Madame; special uniforms for themselves; an ornate coronation carriage; the horse named Popular Demand. At compulsory Mass each morning, they continued to pray for their leader's reinstatement as king, and with their legitimist cronies back in France, some of them were still plotting to bring it about.

But doom now enveloped their hero like a shroud. In brighter days, Chambord had quoted Saint Paul's line *Spes contra spem* (Hope against hope) as his mantra. Now he preferred such baleful apothegms as "Without my principle"—the principle according to which he, as the sole legitimate Bourbon claimant left, should rule France—"I am nothing but a fat man with a limp" and "The only law that can destroy a prince is the law of exile." By the time she got to Frohsdorf, Laure would later tell her confessor in Paris, Henri V's cumulative sorrows had eradicated any last vestiges of his will to rule. However valiantly his courtiers might try to convince him (and themselves) otherwise, it was perfectly clear to the young lady meeting Chambord for the first time that the Bourbon reign would not revive on his watch. In February 1879, it already lay dying at Frohsdorf, leading Laure to dub it "the kingdom of shadows."

The moribund atmosphere of the Schloss might easily have discouraged Laure about her own circumstances, her marriage having released her from one grim, isolated limbo only to land her in another—one even farther from the exciting metropolis she craved. But she could console herself with the knowledge that the City of Light awaited her, and soon: Adhéaume had already assured her that on this first trip to Frohsdorf, they would only have to stay for a few months before returning to France. He had some political business to attend to in the capital, during which time Laure could begin setting up their household in the Faubourg Saint-Honoré, and then they would go to the château de Saint-Thomas for a brief visit with his widowed mother. After that, she could stay in Paris for as long as she liked on her own, while her husband resumed his premarital work routine in Austria. (As a rule, the Comte de Chambord encouraged his newly wedded attendants to cut their eight-month annual service term in half, the better to start families of their own away from court, but Chevigné had respectfully declined this offer.)

All he asked was that in the future, Laure spend a minimum of two months a year in Austria, to forestall speculation that theirs was a *mariage blanc*, an unconsummated union. To Laure, this condition sounded not only reasonable but permissive beyond her wildest dreams. Most women of her class seldom even left home, much less crossed international borders, by themselves. Custom dictated that they go everywhere with at least one liveried footman in tow and generally with a family member (or several) providing added symbolic protection. An unprecedented departure from the imperatives of feminine *bon ton,* the arrangement Chevigné had proposed would grant Laure unprecedented freedom in the city of her dreams. The prospect of such liberty would make anything bearable—even part-time confinement in the kingdom of shadows.

Laure's first day at Frohsdorf passed in a blur. After three days of train travel in a tight-laced corset, followed by a command performance of curtseys in the Red Salon, she must have been exhausted and eager to turn in. But at that début audience, one thing happened that stuck firmly in her mind. Reverences and hem-kissing completed, she held her semisupine position at the monarchs' feet, Adhéaume having cautioned her that she was only to stand up once Monseigneur uttered a few, usually banal, words of welcome. But the king didn't speak—not right away. He took his time, taking in the slim, crouching figure at his feet. Laure kept her gaze downcast, perhaps wondering if she had botched one of her curtseys, perhaps silently cursing the unflattering cut of her dress. Her husband must have been blushing, as was his wont. The stout, sixty-one-year-old Comtesse de Chambord must have looked puzzled as was *her* wont; being completely deaf, she labored under the constant conviction that she had missed hearing something important. The courtiers stood immobile. The liveried footmen, two of whom were named Charlemagne, held their breath. Seconds ticked by on a grandfather clock in the corner until finally, without warning, Monseigneur broke the silence. "You'd better watch out, Adhéaume!" he barked. "If you're not careful, someone else will run off with her!"

A conventional greeting this was not—something on the order of "You are welcome, my child" would have been more like it—but in its way, it was classic Henri V. In most interactions, one of his courtiers wrote, Monseigneur assumed "a mask of priestly melancholia." But sometimes his blues got the better of him, whereupon he would either throw a blistering tantrum or crack an inappropriate joke. Typical of the latter approach, the sally about Chevigné's bride elicited the usual, cringing smiles from his attendants; they knew their master well enough not to take it at face value. However clumsily, he was trying to be gallant, paying a compliment to the new arrival by pretending to invoke his royal *droit du seigneur.*

Coming from one of the lustier French monarchs, the quip might have betokened a genuine sexual threat: neither Louis XIV nor Louis XV, for instance, would have hesitated to poach an underling's wife, nor would Monseigneur's sixteenth-century namesake, Henri IV, another notorious ladies' man and the founder of the Bourbon royal line. Indeed, since the reign of that earlier Henri, who proudly made it known that both his giant nose and the giant feather (*panache*) he always wore in his hat were but advertisements for his genital endowment, the king's subjects had viewed his sexual potency as a correlate and confirmation of his political might.* But this association had begun to fall apart with the accession of Monseigneur's great-uncle, Louis XVI, who refused to consummate his marriage to Marie Antoinette for almost seven years and whose death by guillotine provided an all-too-fitting end to what some detractors had dubbed his "castrated" rule.

Ever since then, as the Comte de Chambord's followers knew all too well, the crippling mutation of the Bourbons' sexual DNA had persisted, with dire consequences for the crown. One of Louis XVI's two brothers, Louis XVIII, had died without issue, allegedly without ever having slept with his wife, and so had

* This *panache* figured in the exhibition of royal memorabilia at Frohsdorf, standing as a daily reproach to Henri V for failing to perpetuate the dynasty his namesake had begun.

his other brother's son, the Duc d'Angoulême, Monseigneur's late uncle. (In fact, the Duchesse d'Angoulême had left instructions in her will forbidding an autopsy to be performed on her corpse; members of her retinue whispered that she didn't want it known she had died a virgin.)

Much the same end awaited Monseigneur himself, who had never brought any discernible passion to his union with Madame, nor had he given any known proofs of erotic vigor outside the marriage bed. So worrisome did his vassals find this behavior that many years into his marriage, they arranged for a notoriously "fast" patrician beauty to await the prince one night in his bedchamber at Frohsdorf. The plan was for her to relieve him of his virginity, in case the Comtesse de Chambord had failed to do so, and thereby to stir his interest in renewing the experience with his wife. But to the lady's horror and their own, when Monseigneur found her in his bed he bolted from the room, his face as white as his cherished Bourbon flag. The men who had arranged the tryst prevailed upon the would-be royal seductress to swear an oath of secrecy about what had transpired. Within his inner circle, though, the king's reaction confirmed his followers' worst fears about his sexual apathy, fears that even the color of his two hundred horses subsequently appeared to confirm. As one insider said archly of Chambord's all-white equine fleet, "Without a doubt, he had a special fondness for that virginal hue."

To be sure, Henri V's feeble sex drive may have had nothing whatsoever to do with the sterility of his marriage. But the two were linked in the minds of courtiers, for whom his reproductive failure entailed the end of everything they held dear, for "legitimism" meant a royal succession that passed from one legitimate (male, Bourbon) heir to the next. If he died without a successor, as it now seemed certain he would, the legitimist cause would die, too.

When it came to his meals, however, the prince had lustier appetites, as Laure found out almost immediately after her presentation. No sooner had she risen from her curtsey and executed three more at Madame's feet than the clock in the corner struck six, at which signal the royal pair bolted from their thrones and out of the Red Salon, their courtiers hurrying behind them. It was dinnertime at Frohsdorf, and Monseigneur, Adhéaume informed her as they hustled toward the dining room with the rest of the group, liked to dine not only promptly but rapidly, with a minimum of fuss. On her first evening at court, Laure would be given a place of honor to the left of the king. (His wife, being the highest-ranked woman present, always sat to his right.) But she should not expect Monseigneur to speak to her while he ate. And etiquette would again, as always with crowned heads, prohibit her from addressing him first.

Not that Laure would have had much time even to ponder such a breach in protocol, as mealtime with Monseigneur passed with lightning speed. Despite her husband's warning, the unceremonious haste with which dinner was both served and consumed took her by surprise, as indeed it did most newcomers to

Frohsdorf. The Duchesse d'Uzès had grumbled about the "frightening rapidity" of the service. Another visitor, the Marchioness of Waterford, reported a similar experience, noting that she and her friends "were warned that we must not allow anything to pass, or we should not get any dinner," as the small army of liveried footmen who served the meal never offered any dish more than once. Indeed, the Marchioness noted, "when the soup came," her dinner partner "was talking the whole time, and while I was listening, the soup was carried away, and so it was with nearly everything else." She went to bed hungry that night: a standard complaint at the Schloss.

Because Laure tended never to eat much anyway—she was very strict about her diet and chain-smoked to keep her appetite in check—this aspect of the Frohsdorf routine did not strike her as an undue hardship. But the ritual that followed dinner proved more challenging. Every evening after dessert and coffee had been served, the king retired to the *fumoir* to smoke cigars with the rest of the men, while the ladies joined Madame in the parlor for embroidery, cards, and "conversation." This custom became Laure's nightly cross to bear, for while she prided herself on her lively repartee, she had trouble exercising it in connection with any of the royal consort's preferred topics, which were Jesus Christ, the weather, and the treachery of the d'Orléans clan. (The third term in this trinity even featured in the Comtesse de Chambord's version of the Lord's Prayer, in which she asked for deliverance not only from evil but "from the entire d'Orléans family.") Blessed with a dour personality and what one of her more kindly predisposed followers termed "a mediocre intelligence," Madame refused to deviate from these three subjects, which she liked to rehash at amplified volume as her companions feigned interest in her monologue.

Madame's reluctance to broach other matters may well have had to do with her rudimentary command of French (which, after more than thirty years of marriage to the presumptive Bourbon king, she still spoke with a thick Italian accent), and with her hardness of hearing. Unfortunately, Monseigneur's habit of mocking her for both of these limitations—he was especially cruel about her inability to pronounce his Gallic first name, hooting with derision whenever she ventured a querulous "ENRICO?"—only made her more self-conscious.

When first adjusting to Frohsdorf, Laure was unaware of these reasons for sticking to the queen's habitual script and decided to shake things up by steering the talk around to her own idée fixe, Paris. The attempt failed, thanks to an idiosyncrasy of Madame's that Laure, as a newcomer to Frohsdorf, would not have known to take into account. Her face having been misshapen since birth, the Comtesse de Chambord was, in the words of the Duchesse d'Uzès (no beauty queen herself), "so ugly that it was as if the word 'ugly' had been invented just for her." Hypersensitive to her deformity and, sexless though their marriage was, poignantly possessive of her husband, Madame dreaded the French capital, which she pictured as a licentious bedlam teeming with hussies just waiting to lead him astray. "I DO NOT MUCH CARE TO REIGN," she hollered. "PARIS IS TOO FULL OF BEAUTIFUL WOMEN." While the other ladies were impressed that Laure's Paris gambit had managed even to penetrate the thick fog of their mistress's incomprehension, the new courtier learned her lesson: stick to the devils the queen knew (those d'Orléans traitors) and forget the rest.

Early on, Madame's hearing impairment gave Laure a false sense of security about what she might get away with saying in the older woman's company. Shortly after her début in the Red Salon, Laure received a summons to join the queen for a carriage ride around the castle grounds. According to Comte Robert de Fitz-James, a gallant Frohsdorf old-timer who took it upon himself to instruct Laure in the unwritten ways and means of the court, this overture boded well for her future at the Schloss, as it proved she had made a good impression on the royals. Although heartened by Fitz-James's judgment, Laure dreaded the tedium the outing seemed sure to entail. So when she reported for duty and climbed into the carriage beside the queen, Laure did what she had so often done as a girl—she sought solidarity with the help. "God *help* me, Joseph," she called out to the coachman in her gravelly smoker's voice. "I have *never been more bored in my life.*"

To Laure's mortification, it was not the footman but the queen who answered, saying in an uncharacteristically quiet voice, "My poor child, I am so sorry." Madame then explained that sometimes the jostling of the buggy over uneven paving stones momentarily restored her hearing. Laure stammered an apology, and Madame, whose Christian forgiveness extended to everyone except the d'Orléans branch of the family, not only pardoned her but liked her all the more for her momentary show of dismay. From that day forward, the Comtesses de Chambord and de Chevigné took a carriage ride together every afternoon.

Laure had an even easier time ingratiating herself with Henri V, for starters because they both loved to ride, hunt, and shoot. These sports showed Laure to her best advantage, highlighting what another hunting enthusiast described as "her woodsy, chivalric grace and her Amazonian je ne sais quoi." She accentuated her "mannish air" by wearing jodhpurs instead of long skirts and by riding astride instead of sidesaddle. As luck would have it, the hunt had a similarly transformative effect on Monseigneur. Though he limped when he walked, he rode beautifully and was an excellent shot. Leading the *chasse à courre* in the fields and woods around Frohsdorf helped the old pretender forget about his cares, transporting him "beyond space and time" and fostering the blissful, if temporary, illusion that he was "living the life that the king of France, by definition the king of the hunt, had led since Childebert."

Until Laure came to Frohsdorf, women hadn't been regular participants in the royal hunt. Madame herself didn't ride, and her ladies-in-waiting dutifully stayed with her at the castle while the men galloped around the countryside with their weapons, horns, and hounds. For this reason, Monseigneur was both surprised and delighted by Laure's passion for the sport. He particularly savored her zest for the kill: at the smell of gunpowder, her nostrils would flare like a scent hound's as she strained for a whiff of fresh blood. This improbable sight prompted Chambord, guffawing heartily, to pronounce her "a *fine gun*." Coming from the latter-day Childebert, there was no higher compliment.

Equally dissonant, and amusing to the king, was Laure's foul mouth. Monseigneur had a penchant for salty language himself, but he had never encountered such a proclivity in a woman of Laure's breeding and rank. The same went for her affected peasant twang, as when she sneered of his old nemesis, the Maréchal de MacMahon, "MacMahon? Everyone knows he was *uhh* [*sic*] *goose*, he made *that* clear!" Or when, to play down her obviously formidable intelligence, she drawled, "I'm just *uhh* little idiot, *uhh* little peasant."

The kinship Chambord felt for this gutsy young noblewoman grew into such a warm affinity that he came to expect, even demand, her presence on every shoot. Though not prone to nicknaming his attendants, he tagged Laure with a sobriquet—*la vieille* (old girl), an ironic play on her relative youth—that affirmed the chumminess of their bond. With her masculine riding gear, intrepid sportiness, and raunchy sense of humor she became, for all intents and purposes, one of the king's men.

Laure soon found that the sovereign's affection for her enabled her to challenge him in ways that few others in his service would have dared to attempt. For instance, she noticed that he compensated for his lack of real political authority by "reigning like a despot over [every] conversation," no matter who his interlocutors were or what they were trying to tell him. As another of his followers noted, "He never listened to anything, he never wanted to understand anything" except opinions that supported his own. To Laure, with her inborn (if not hereditary) flair for transgression, Monseigneur's "grandiose stubbornness" practically demanded that she rebel. So she got into the habit of deliberately provoking his rages. While the rest of his attendants cowered, she greeted Monseigneur's ravings with a blandly unruffled mien, having determined that it never took long for him to tire himself out with his own shouting, whereupon he would sheepishly ask her forgiveness for his loss of control. When this happened, Laure did not hasten to reassure him, as a typical lackey would have done. Instead, she pressed her advantage, fixing him with an icy blue stare and rasping, "What does Monseigneur want me to say, when He tells me He is sorry? Why does He not just refrain from getting Himself *that worked up in the first place?*"

To a man raised to believe—"mysterious difficulties" notwithstanding—that God had placed him on earth to rule over his compatriots, Laure's insolence came as a shock, but a perversely exciting one. When she scolded him like a naughty child, Laure displayed not only what another grandee described as her "complete absence of fear" but her tantalizing impulse to make her so-called betters squirm. In deference to the Chambords' piety, she avoided mentioning her Sadean roots in their company. All the same, her descent from the miscreant marquis may have heightened the king's titillation at her boldness.

Yet even for Laure, there were limits to Chambord's bonhomie. As much as he enjoyed the occasional mock-challenge to his authority, he only suffered such derogations to take place on his terms, in keeping with his moods, and his moods were ever changing. What amused him one moment might irk him soon afterward: old-timers at the Schloss still trembled to recall an acutely unpleasant episode when one poor wretch, misled by Monseigneur's jolliness, reached out and patted the royal belly. To avoid such disasters, the members of his retinue had to know when to stop joking and start groveling. They also had to follow an established protocol for groveling, seamlessly enacting the rituals of formalized self-abasement that crowned heads expect of those around them, even crowned heads who claimed, as Henri V did, to find such rituals tiresome in the extreme.

As a result, it wasn't advisable for Laure to stake her success at court on her sauciness alone. It was just as important that she master the intricacies of royal etiquette, and with the guidance of Comte Robert de Fitz-James—who spent noticeably more time with her than her husband did—she learned what was expected of her. Fitz-James trained her to use the third rather than the second person when addressing her sovereigns; to cede her turn to the king, or any other royal hunting companion, if a particularly exciting (or easy) shot opened up on the hunt; to lose, but not too obviously, when playing cards with majesties and highnesses; to remain standing until the highest-ranked prince in the room sat down. (Said prince often didn't sit down at all, though royal scions were notorious for deliberately keeping everyone around them standing for long stretches of time, just because they could. Despite his disabled leg, Monseigneur was an expert at this trick.) To crowned heads, these formalities provided daily reassurance about their God-given superiority to the rest of humankind.

Laure's study of protocol instilled in her as well a keen awareness of her other companions' relative social importance. She exhibited this sensitivity when engaged in "marking the distances," a practice that called for minute calibrations of politesse. When greeting someone, the depth of Laure's curtsey was in direct proportion to the grandness of that person's title. When she went in to dinner, she fell into line in front of certain grandees but "gave the hand" to others, those who outranked her. She learned not to be taken aback by a ceremony central to daily life at court, wherein the footmen flanking the double-doored entryways throughout the castle held both doors open for royals but only one for everybody else. Laure would later credit Fitz-James with helping her to master the complex rituals of her new environment. In this way, he groomed her for a long and successful career as a courtier—not only to Henri V and his queen but also, less officially, to the many other crowned heads she would befriend in society in Paris.

Laure's special rapport with Monseigneur did not necessarily endear her to the rest of his suite. After years of strategic toadying and kowtowing, tying his shoes and bearing up under his furies, it galled many of his courtiers to see themselves eclipsed, practically overnight, by a foul-mouthed nineteen-year-old upstart from Passy. But their rancor didn't faze Laure, for as Fitz-James explained, it only confirmed her primacy in the unspoken competition for Chambord's favor. By the same token, Fitz-James did caution her that their envious, idle colleagues would surely look for ways to discredit her in the king's eyes. Thus put on notice, she managed to thwart their schemes to disgrace her.

Whereas Laure's rivals might see the monarch's approval as the ultimate honor, she was playing for a different, if related, prize: stature in the monde. Counting the days until she and her husband went back to Paris, she was determined to become one of the leaders of society, and in this effort, her camaraderie with Chambord would serve her exceedingly well. Laure decided that in her future visits to the capital, she would depict herself—not "poor Adhéaume"—as the prime recipient of Henri V's favor. Like a saint in a medieval painting, shown wielding the instrument of her martyrdom, Laure would appear in the gratin brandishing the "very special esteem" with which the sovereign honored her. And just as Saint Sebastian's arrows and Saint Catherine's wheel occasioned their ascent into heaven, her royal patron's affection would propel her to the summit of the noble Faubourg.

At the same time, Laure foresaw that if her relations with Monseigneur were to perform this miracle, they needed to capture the imagination—and thus would have to appear to be founded on a sentiment more titillating than just-us-guys bonhomie. Casting about for the detail that would bring her Frohsdorf narrative to life, she recalled Chambord's quip at her début in the Red Salon: "If you're not careful, someone else will run off with her!"

This line would become one of the keys to Laure's conquest of the monde. Combined with her "kingdom of shadows" conceit and her freedom to travel abroad without her husband, it provided her with just what she needed to cast herself in a mythical light, updating a classical romance she knew well from Petrarch's "Triumph of Love": "Consider Pluto, there with Proserpine: / Love pursued this deity into the very depths of hell." When speaking in the monde about her life at Frohsdorf, Laure would present herself as Proserpina, the luminous maiden whom Pluto, the god and king of the Roman underworld, abducts and imprisons—but only for part of each year—in his eponymous realm on the banks of the Lethe River. (Conveniently for Laure, the river that flowed through the town of Frohsdorf was called the Leitha.) In this dramatic story, Cham-

Laure called Frohsdorf "the kingdom of shadows," casting herself as Proserpina, the alluring captive of Pluto, the god of the dead. Bernini's representation of the subject *(left)* is in the Borghese Gallery in Rome.

bord would costar as her Pluto: not her back-slapping hunting comrade but her brooding and besotted royal captor.

Laure had the good sense to recognize that she would have to save this richly embroidered version of the facts for people with no firsthand knowledge of Frohsdorf or its king. It went without saying that Henri V hadn't imprisoned her in his Schloss: she had gone there willingly, with a husband who also lived there of his own accord. Just as obviously, the morose, petulant "fat man with a limp" was no ravening lord of hell, holding fast to his nubile blond hostage.

Laure did not need her tale of royal romance to be true, she just needed to make it sound plausible to the scions of the gratin. She also anticipated that in most *mondain* company, no one would question the veracity of her tale, for while all noble Parisians knew of the Comte de Chambord, very few knew him personally. Almost fifty years had passed since the Revolution of 1830 had driven him and the rest of the French Bourbons into exile, and Frohsdorf was both too remote and too grim a location to draw many pilgrims from the Faubourg.

Modeling her own narrative on the myth of Proserpina presented three advantages. First, it relegated "her poor Adhéaume" to the margins of her life's story, which was precisely where Laure intended to keep him. Second, it made that story memorable. Whether by nature (her literary ancestry) or nurture (her robust reading habits), Laure was a gifted raconteur. As such, she recognized that the drama of Proserpina and her kidnapper held considerably more narrative potential than a bored, provincial bride and a sad-sack king without a throne. Third, by painting herself as the apple of Monseigneur's (crossed) eye, Laure placed herself in terrifically privileged company. Throughout history, French kings' infatuations had imbued their ladyloves with unrivaled prestige: Agnès Sorel, Diane de Poitiers, Gabrielle d'Estrées, Mmes de Montespan and de Maintenon, Mmes de Pompadour and du Barry, mistresses who even in death basked in the eternal sunshine of royal favor, an afterglow so dazzling that it encompassed their descendants as well.

This was why, despite the shame otherwise associated with illegitimate birth, Henry Greffulhe boasted about descending from a love child of Louis XV. It was why Robert de Fitz-James was so proud to claim among his ancestors a legitimated bastard of King James II. ("Fitz" was a medieval Norman word for "son.") It was why the Mortemarts, quintessential bluebloods with as old and fine a lineage as any in the noblesse, still dined out on their kinship with Athénaïs de Montespan, whose effervescent wit had enchanted the great Louis XIV. It was why the dukes of Gramont had a tradition of naming their daughters Corisande, after their ancestress Corisande de Guiche, beloved of Henri IV and his virile *panache*.

Laure foresaw that in a world these families ruled, she would never succeed unless she could find a way to beat them at their own status-mongering game. Whereas the Greffulhes, Mortemarts, Fitz-Jameses, and Gramonts stressed their genealogical ties to the royal mistresses past, she invented a fiction that assigned her this enviable role in the present.

Laure's talent for self-aggrandizement had much in common with the flair her future neighbor and friend, Élisabeth Greffulhe, had recently shown by dressing as Louis XVI's virginal, martyred sister. And Laure's mythical posturing, like Élisabeth's, required a bigger and better audience than the one she faced in the earliest days of her marriage. Frohsdorf was Laure's Bois-Boudran: a trial ground for the theatrics she would hone to perfection in Paris.

Less than four months after her wedding day, Laure found herself back in the Faubourg Saint-Honoré, going out, making friends, and telling anyone who would listen that she had returned from Frohsdorf as one would return from the dead: a bit dazed, but terribly glad to feel her heart beating once again.

HABANERA

OISEAUX REBELLES

L'amour est un oiseau rebelle que nul ne peut apprivoiser.
(Love is a rebel bird no man can tame.)

—Habanera, from Georges Bizet, *Carmen* (1875); lyrics by
Henri Meilhac and Ludovic Halévy

I follow the breeze, I follow the girl,
I follow the poets whose hearts beat with hope. . . .
Don't be true to me—just let me kiss your dark eyes,
With their lashes that flutter like hummingbirds' wings.

—GEORGES DE PORTO-RICHE, "Letter," *Eve's Apples*
(*Pommes d'Ève,* 1874)

CHAPTER FOUR

BOHEMIA'S CHILD

"Is Georges cheating on me with my seductive friend Laure? Let me know!"
So wrote Geneviève (Bébé) Bizet, thirty-one, to Liselote (Lizote) de
Porto-Riche from a spa in Switzerland in July 1880. The Georges in question was Liselote's husband, the poet and dramatist Georges de Porto-Riche,
twenty-five. Flirtatious Porto-Riche had been trying for ages to talk his cousin
and close friend Bébé into bed, and his advances had only grown more brazen
since her husband's death five years before. Recently he had sent Bébé such an
erotically charged poem that she had appealed to Lizote to rein in his "impertinence." But the truth was, Bébé reveled in her cousin's infatuation. More than
that, she counted on it. Which was why it so unsettled her to contemplate losing
him to a rival.

In fact, Porto-Riche only knew Laure because Bébé herself had introduced
them at the salon she and Ludovic (Ludo) Halévy, another of her devoted cousins, cohosted on Thursdays at 22, rue de Douai in Montmartre. (Unofficially the
salon was Bébé's, but as unmarried women were not meant to receive male guests
at home, she held her gatherings at Ludovic's place, which was a floor below hers
in the same apartment building.)* At the time, Bébé had caught a palpable
spark between Laure and Porto-Riche, but only now that she had left home for
the summer did it strike her as cause for alarm. Just because Bébé didn't want
to have an affair with Porto-Riche herself didn't mean that she wanted him to
take up with one of her friends, least of all the seductive Comtesse de Chevigné.

As Bébé replayed it now, the encounter between her cousin and Laure had
gone rather too well for her liking. With her airy disregard for the norms of polite
conversation, Laure had treated Porto-Riche from the first as an old friend, nicknaming him "Porto" (whereas good manners called for "Monsieur") and gaily
rattling off a string of obscenities worthy of her great-grandfather de Sade. In
the drawing rooms and ballrooms of the Faubourg, such profanity would have
been unthinkable, yet it was scarcely less shocking in Bébé's salon. Although she
played hostess to artists, Bébé came from a privileged background and spoke

---

* The four-story building at 22, rue de Douai was occupied almost exclusively by the Halévys and their extended
family. Geneviève occupied the third-floor apartment (throughout her marriage to Bizet and the eleven-year widowhood that followed it), and her cousin Ludovic Halévy and his family—his wife, Louise, and his sons, Élie and
Daniel—lived on the second floor. Ludovic's parents, Bébé's uncle Léon and aunt Nanine Halévy, lived with their
unmarried daughter Valentine on the first floor. Between 1873 and 1875, Georges Bizet's father, Adolphe, inhabited
a ground-floor flat in the building as well. (NB: in French, "ground floor" and "first floor" are not synonyms as they
are in English; "first floor" in French translates to "second floor" in English, and so on.)

Georges de Porto-Riche, Geneviève Halévy
Bizet's handsome cousin, pursued her and
many other women. He invented a dramatic
genre called "the theater of love."

as decorously as any cosseted grande dame. Even the rabble-rousers in her set
watched their language around Bébé. But Laure showed no such constraint.

Porto-Riche had clearly been titillated by her daring, all the more so because
she was a comtesse, a title Bébé knew had impressed him. Porto-Riche had fierce
leftist politics; in 1871, he had risked death by firing squad for fighting on the
radical insurgents' side in the Paris Commune. Yet he was hardly inured to the
aristocracy's prestige. Like Bébé, he came from an affluent family in the Jewish
haute bourgeoisie and had been raised with enough refinement to feel a natural
affinity for Paris's social élite. Having alienated his parents by pursuing literature
as a career, Porto-Riche was perpetually moaning about his lack of funds and
selling off precious heirlooms to support his art. But he refused even to consider
divesting himself of his most valuable possession, a rare antique sword that his
friends surmised he kept out of a wishful "identification . . . with the *noblesse
d'épée*." As an as-yet-unknown author—and a Jewish one, at that—Porto-Riche
found few opportunities to socialize with the members of that caste, least of
all its comely hostesses. As an incorrigible roué, he was as tantalized as he was
miffed by the ostensible unattainability of a whole class of Parisiennes. An introduction to a flirty, frisky *mondaine* had thus come to him as an unexpected
stroke of good fortune. He was bound to make the most of it.

Laure had appeared just as enthusiastic about meeting "Porto," treating him
to an animated lecture about her literary ancestry and her innate affinity for
writers. In a society woman, these traits were uncommon to say the least—
indeed, her very presence in Bébé's salon bespoke adventurous leanings that

set Laure apart from the typical society maven. Just as unusually, she made no secret of the fact that she loved men. This was good news for Porto-Riche, as his peers unanimously described him as "one of the most seductive men around." Based on his "tousled black hair [and] shadowy romantic pallor," he reminded portraitist Jacques Blanche of "a poet from Baghdad" and theater impresario André Antoine of "a Renaissance Italian." The *mondain* chronicler André de Fouquières, who would later meet Porto-Riche through Laure, painted him in similarly romantic terms:

> With his fine, chiseled face, his thick shock of hair, which always looked ruffled by the winds of some romantic storm, and his dark, caressing, melancholy gaze, Porto-Riche was a born seducer.

Such overt sex appeal was as rare in Laure's world as noblewomen were in Porto's. It was an unfair comparison, but his smoldering good looks and suave demeanor put the sexually awkward Comtes de Chambord and de Chevigné to shame. In no time at all, Laure was batting her eyes at the poet and inviting him to evaluate the similarities between herself and Petrarch's muse. From this auspicious first meeting, she and Porto became lifelong friends.

Bébé did not welcome a friendship between the two any more than she would have welcomed an affair. Porto-Riche was one of the habitués of Bébé's salon, a group of men whom she called her *fidèles* (faithful ones), and with whom she had a tacit agreement: in exchange for the privilege of her company, they had to place her above any and all other women in their lives. This did not mean she expected them to forgo wives or mistresses—many of the faithful, like Porto-Riche, tended to have both. Nor did Bébé impose this condition because she wanted her acolytes as her own lovers; she was adamant that she would never go to bed with any of them. The kind of love she sought from her *fidèles* was the very kind that Petrarch, in fact, had felt for Laure's namesake: absolute reverence, with no hope of consummation. When Bébé asked whether Porto-Riche was "cheating" on her, then, she understood this infraction above all as a crime of thought—far graver than a physical transgression.

So firmly did Bébé hold this view that she did not hesitate to pepper Lizote, a timid, tender-hearted woman made wretched by her husband's philandering, with questions about Laure's progress as a rival. Nor did she have any compunction about banning Lizote and most other wives from her salon. (Mistresses were categorically excluded.)

In the rare instances where Bébé did admit a female guest into her circle, it was a carefully considered decision on her part, calculated to burnish her own luster in her devotees' eyes. Laure served that purpose to perfection. As a popular and alluring *mondaine*—and a rumored favorite of the exiled Henri V—she was a trophy guest, brought in to impress the faithful with Bébé's high-flown social connections. As Ludovic Halévy's son Daniel later recalled, the sight of Mme de Chevigné gamely loping up the stairs of his family's apartment building signaled to the regulars in Bébé's salon that their hostess, amazing as ever, had done the impossible: lured the "born" to Bohemia.

IN LATE JUNE OR EARLY JULY 1880, Bébé had left her aerie in Montmartre for Gurnigel, Switzerland, in the company of her eight-year-old son, Jacques, and another mother-child duo: Mme Benjamin (Eulalie) Ulmann, the wife of an academic history painter of middling talent, and her daughter, Marcelle, who was six months younger than Jacques. For Bébé, the trip was meant to serve as both vacation and spa cure, a two-for-one palliative to the nervous illness from which she had suffered for most of her life.

Psychological problems ran on both sides of Bébé's family, and in her they took the form of neurasthenia, a disorder that Paris's leading neurologist and alienist, Dr. Jean-Martin Charcot, identified most frequently in women and Jews. In Bébé's case, the disease manifested itself in alternating fits of panicked anxiety and paralyzing despair. Her other symptoms were exhaustion, loss of appetite, vomiting, back spasms, and an aggravation of the facial tics that had first surfaced after a traumatic run-in with her mother, Léonie Halévy, nine years earlier.* Since then, Bébé had avoided Léonie as much as possible. But she had braved a short meeting with her at the beginning of the summer and paid the price with a renewed outbreak of symptoms. The setback had forced Bébé to acknowledge the tenuousness of her mental health. So if her doctors prescribed a few weeks' rest in the Swiss-German Alps—"six hours away from the nearest sign of civilization," she groused in a letter to Ludovic's mother, Alexandrine (Nanine) Halévy—then Bébé knew she should heed their advice, whether she liked it or not.

At the moment, she didn't like it one bit. The fresh mountain air and idyllic setting were supposed to settle her mind, but she found herself more out of sorts than ever, cut off from the comforting distractions of home. Had she been back in Paris, she would have been holding court in Ludovic's drawing room in the rue de Douai, reclining on a chaise longue in one of the racy peignoirs she liked to wear for her guests, gossiping and flirting and feeding bits of croissant to her little black poodle, Vivette (named for a character in her late husband's opera *The Girl from Arles*). She would have been letting Meilhac win at cards—he sulked like a toddler when she didn't. She would have been talking Degas into escorting her to the milliner's. This was an errand he often agreed to run with her on the grounds that he liked to examine the shopgirls' calloused red fingers,

---

* Bébé's tics included a sudden, involuntary widening and then blinking of her eyes, accompanied by the abrupt protrusion of her lower lip and a swooping, sideways dip of her head toward her left shoulder. These spastic movements often startled people meeting her for the first time. But according to Fernand Gregh, once one got to know her, "one grew accustomed to the tics that wracked her beautiful, gypsy face."

but he may have taken at least one of these outings as an opportunity to sketch Bébé herself. She would have been applauding at the opening of her friend Alexandre Dumas *fils*'s newest play or sitting front and center at a revival of an opera by her late husband or her late father. She would have been posing for one of the painter friends whose work she preferred to Degas's: Élie Delaunay, who borrowed her face for his allegorical figures and who had painted her favorite portrait of herself; or Auguste Toulmouche, who used her as a model for his acclaimed (and unidentified) "modern beauties." She would have been riding her horse, Neptune, in the Bois de Boulogne and reveling in the rapt stares she drew from passersby—not least of all the top-hatted, frock-coated clubmen whose names she knew from the social columns and who perhaps recognized hers as well.

As a neurasthenic, Bébé had had to become a seasoned traveler; trips to take the waters were a regular part of her mental-health regimen. Nonetheless, she hated leaving Paris—she always had. Even today, with nearly two decades' distance, she could still recall her indignation when her parents took her and her older sister, Esther, to Nice—on a doctor-ordered spa cure for their father, in fact—in the winter of 1861–1862, when Bébé was just eleven. Esther, who was six years older than she, filled in as her tutor when the family traveled. During the sojourn in Nice, Esther told Bébé to write an essay on the topic of her own choosing. A Parisienne born and bred, Bébé already considered herself too sophisticated for the slow-paced, provincial Riviera and chose to write about the superiority of her hometown. She opened with this thesis statement: "I say and I repeat, there is only one city in the world where one can possibly live, and that city is Paris."

To leave the capital for even a short while, Bébé continued, is for any self-respecting urbanite "to perish of mortal ennui," as "beautiful nature, fresh cream,

Edgar Degas, *At the Milliner* (1882–1885): Degas was an old friend of Geneviève's family. He sometimes joined her when she went shopping for clothes and hats; he also liked to watch her brush her hair.

wild strawberries, and cottages with green shutters" can never adequately replace "the whirlwind of parties and pleasures" on offer back home. To conclude the essay, Bébé restated her opening argument, yoking it to a whimsical vision of a world under her sovereign control:

> If ever I become Emperor, or at least Empress, here is the little trick I would play on everyone who complains about the crowds and the noise of the city: I would force them to live outside of the capital until they too were persuaded that one can only live in Paris, and that everywhere else, one merely vegetates!

Almost twenty years had elapsed since Bébé wrote these lines—and ten years since France had lost its emperor—but her position on Paris was unchanged. She was exceedingly proud of being a "frog," as the courtiers of Versailles had dubbed native Parisians during the ancien régime. Let her aristocratic friends, like Laure de Chevigné, tout their history as *pure souche* landed gentry. As a "frog" and an Israelite, Bébé was cosmopolitan through and through; she liked to say that with these two attributes, she was "Parisian twice over."

Gurnigel was as un-Parisian a place as she had ever been, far duller than Nice; already Bébé had decided she would never return. While submitting to the rituals of her Alpine cure—springwater soaks, gargling sessions, soothing massages, invigorating nature walks—she ruminated anxiously about the effects her absence might be having on her acolytes back home. This far from Paris, she no longer held their loyalty to be self-evident. It was time to take action.

After completing her note to Lizote, Bébé dashed off a separate letter to Porto-Riche, a puckish salvo designed to spark his memory of her, if by any chance he had forgotten:

> My dear friend, here I am at the end of the world, and it's depressing, *so* depressing! Nevertheless, I am selfish enough to wish that you were here with me. . . . Please give me news of you—I need to hear more about all our friends, because the country where I am is as godforsaken as it is Germanic. . . . I am not having any fun here at all, and I'm afraid I'll keep having less and less fun as an effect of my advancing age [thirty-one]. In a moment I am going to try to regain my will to live by going for a ride. If that doesn't work, I won't have any choices left except for interior decorating—or having an affair! Come and see me here, and give me your bad advice!

She might as well have been talking to Porto-Riche directly, so well did these lines convey the bantering, coquettish tone she took with the faithful in person. Though Bébé flirted outrageously with all her male companions, she upheld a strict just-friends policy that pushed many of them to the brink of despair. When it looked as if she might be driving one of them away for good, she would pull him back into her clutches by allowing him to think that maybe, just maybe, she could be persuaded to make an exception in his favor. It was not for nothing that she had inspired the teasing, titular man slayer in her late husband's *Carmen* (1875); according to her cousin Louis Ganderax, also a *fidèle,* Bizet himself identified her as the model for that character. Bébé knew from experience that a hint of sexual promise could go a long way. If she gave Porto-Riche to understand that she was finally open to a love affair, then ideally he would stop thinking about Laure de Chevigné and start thinking about her again instead.

While Bébé's need for reassurance of Porto-Riche's affections may not have rated formally among her neurasthenic symptoms, one did not have to be a mental-health professional to pick up on the "morbid dread of solitude," as one of her friends characterized it, that fueled her relationships. Indeed, Bébé had organized her entire life with a view to keeping loneliness at bay. A more secure woman would have taken her loyal cadre of friends as reliable proof that she was loved. But Bébé could never quite believe that if she didn't manage those friendships with care, she might not wind up bereft and alone.

When broaching this concern with her faithful, she generally used a light touch, as in the playful solicitation of Porto-Riche's "bad advice." She took a similar approach in a card she once sent him when they were both in Paris and he failed to make his usual appearance in the rue de Douai: "I waited impatiently for five minutes and then I started looking for you under the furniture—but no Porto-Riche! Come back to me soon, you frightful defector." On another occasion, she sent him a framed reproduction of one of her portraits "so that you can visit with me, as it were, in effigy" and thereby "not fall out of the habit of loving me!"

Sometimes her fear showed through more nakedly. In yet another missive to Porto-Riche, this one undated, she wrote,

> I hope to see you soon, because once you've tired of letting yourself be *loved a lot* by people who in fact only love you *a little,* . . . surely you will find five minutes for your oldest friend.

As this passage indicates, Bébé was not above a bit of garden-variety manipulation to keep her vassals enthralled. By suggesting that Porto-Riche's new companions didn't care for him like she did, she sent a not-so-subtle message: he should drop them in favor of her, his "oldest friend." But her guile betrayed her gnawing anxiety that within the breast of every *fidèle* lurked a potential *lâcheur* (deserter or defector). This term recurs often in Bébé's correspondence not only with Porto-Riche but with many of her salon's habitués including, eventually, Marcel Proust. Writing to him in 1922, a few months before his death and a few years before hers, she asked whether she had " 'crumbled to dust' in [his] heart," then preemptively thanked him for "not deserting me and leaving me for dead."

While she was particularly nervous about being deserted by the men in her life, Bébé fretted as well about losing her hold on the handful of women with whom she was close. Chief among these was her paternal aunt Nanine Halévy, who shared her whimsical, irreverent sense of humor. (On her deathbed the last words Nanine spoke were, "O, my children, how I have loved . . . *grammar!*") Bébé regarded Nanine as a kindred spirit and engaged her in an active correspondence, hectoring her from time to time about her potentially waning affection. "Don't get too used to doing without me, my dear little aunt," Bébé wrote to her in 1878, "for I have every intention of coming home and reclaiming my place among your *loved ones.*"

Bébé would have been loath to admit it, but to a certain degree, she had inherited her compulsive, possessive social instincts from her mother, Léonie, née Rodrigues-Henriques, who had entertained constantly throughout Bébé's childhood and adolescence. As the wife of world-famous composer Fromental Halévy, and as an ambitious sculptor in her own right, Léonie liked to surround herself with artists and kept an open house seven days a week in the family's apartment in Paris's ninth arrondissement. A scion of the moneyed Jewish community in Bordeaux, Léonie was a Gradis on her mother's side and thus an heiress to a share of that dynasty's legendary shipping fortune. This wealth exempted Léonie from the domestic drudgery that fell to other Parisian artists' wives and left her free to focus all her energies on her friends. Twenty-one years younger than Fromental, she reigned over a large and lively salon.

According to one of the Halévys' regular visitors, painter Eugène Delacroix, at its best the couple's drawing room resembled "a real house of Socrates," brimming with "men of genius" and the products of their toil. (From her Bordelais family, Léonie had inherited a number of valuable artworks and spent prodigiously to expand her collection.) But often, the overcrowding bordered on chaos, even with a battery of footmen and maids to wait on her and her friends. Fromental did his composing at a massive piano desk with a full-sized keyboard in the center drawer. This piece of furniture, which Fromental had invented himself, was too big to fit in any other room than the salon where his wife held her at-homes. This constraint forced him to develop what Édouard Monnais, the director of the Paris Opéra, described as "an imperturbable faculty of attention." Without that faculty, Monnais suspected, Fromental would never have managed "to write his music . . . given all the chatter that surrounded him all the time."

Delacroix joined Monnais in worrying about the negative effect this lifestyle was having on their friend's productivity. "How can he get any serious work done in the midst of all that hubbub?" Delacroix wondered in his diary. One summer when Bébé was small, he convinced the Halévys to take a break from the city in Corbeil, a riverside hamlet where he kept a summer house. Fromental liked the idea so much that he didn't just rent a property in Corbeil—he bought one. After only a few days there, however, Léonie panicked, calling the peace and quiet "stifling" and demanding that they rush back to Paris straightaway. "I've seen the F. Halévys only twice and already they are leaving," Delacroix grumbled. "They are *mondains* who must have their friends over to play cards every night of the week." This cavil about the "F. Halévys" anticipated the complaint Degas would make years later about their younger daughter, when he noted with disapproval that Bébé was "devoured by her social life."

Bébé's feverish absorption in her social life might have been less a willed emulation of Léonie than a delayed response to having grown up in a household where her parents too seldom trained their "imperturbable faculty of attention" on her. When she was born on February 26, 1849, Bébé's father, forty-nine, was in the throes of a creative renaissance. Three months earlier his newest opera, *The Valley of Andorra* (*Le Val d'Andorre*, 1848), had opened to sensational reviews. This was his greatest critical and popular triumph since *La Juive* (1835), a grand opera about the doomed love of a Jewish woman, Rachel, and a Christian prince, Leopold. Hailed by Richard Wagner as "one of the greatest operas ever created" and celebrated the world over, *La Juive* had drawn such spectacular acclaim that Fromental had in the years after its début worried he would never be able to surpass it. The success of *The Valley of Andorra* had revived his artistic self-confidence, sparking a period of frenzied creation. Bébé, the second of his and Léonie's two children, arrived when he was totally absorbed by his next comic opera, *The Rose Fairy* (*La Fée aux roses*, 1849). He was also busy teaching young composers at the Conservatoire de Paris, his alma mater and the finest music school in France. Between his professional commitments and Léonie's social ones, the Halévys had little time for their new baby—or for their precocious elder daughter, Esther, six.

While Bébé was still in diapers, the whole family moved temporarily to London so that Fromental could oversee rehearsals for his musical adaptation—cocreated with Eugène Scribe, the librettist of *La Juive*—of Shakespeare's *The Tempest*, as well as for British productions of *La Juive* and *The Valley of Andorra*. Shortly after the Halévys' arrival, they received an invitation to a personal audience with the French king Louis-Philippe, in exile in England since his overthrow in 1848. This royal summons affirmed Fromental's status as one of France's greatest living artists; it also launched the Halévys' tony social life in London.

A year later, the family returned to Paris, where Fromental continued to work at a manic clip, tossing off two more comic operas, *The Queen of Spades* (*La Dame de pique*, 1850) and *The Wandering Jew* (*Le Juif-Errant*, 1852), and teaching more classes at the Conservatoire. He voluntarily enlisted in the National Guard—a civic duty dear to middle-aged French artists like himself, who had been exempted from military service in their youth upon winning the illustri-

Édouard Dubufé, *Mme Bizet Straus as a Child*
(c. 1850s): Geneviève grew up in material
luxury but without much parental attention.

ous Prix de Rome. All these commitments had already stretched him impossibly
thin when, in 1854, he took on yet another: the perpetual secretaryship of the
Académie des Beaux-Arts. This prestigious sinecure, conferred on him by the
government of Napoléon III, carried with it honorary lodgings in the Left Bank
palace of the Institut de France, home to all five of the nation's learned academies, including the Académie Française. The Halévys' apartment in the gold-
domed palace on the quai de Conti became the new headquarters for Léonie's
around-the-clock open house.

Even in her splendid new apartment, with its panoramic views of the Seine,
Bébé's mother was restless. She supplemented her daily salons with reams of correspondence. Designed to keep tabs on her friends, these letters sound remarkably like those Bébé would write throughout her adult life—in a style at once
nagging and flirtatious. "Tell me all your news," Léonie demanded of one occasional visitor to the quai de Conti:

> Once people are my friends, I want to know what they are doing, what
> they are thinking. . . . Maybe I shouldn't ask what you are doing! Even
> from here I can see your lips pursing and your forehead creasing. Ouf! I
> take it back—I don't want to know anything! I shall confine myself to tell-
> ing you how greatly I like and admire you.

As she later explained to Bébé, "Affection is the only thing that helps me."

Léonie did need help in the clinical sense of the term. Both she and Fromental suffered from hereditary mental illness that would today have qualified as clinical depression. Léonie's, which was probably of the manic variety,

manifested itself in bursts of frantic high energy and loopy grandiosity, followed by plunges into melancholia. When she was manic, her hyperactive attentions flitted between her salon and her sculpture, spanning the two when she pontificated about how her artistic genius would have made her an international celebrity "if only I were a *man*."

In these overexcited states, Léonie also went on epic shopping binges, snapping up decorative items by the cartload and cramming them into the apartment in the quai de Conti. Despite her sophistication, the "objets d'art" she amassed on her sprees were junk: broken space heaters, chipped porcelain, cracked pots and pans. Léonie spent so much money on these ugly, useless items that Delacroix feared she would land the whole family "in the poorhouse." Writer and aesthete Edmond de Goncourt likened the Halévys' increasingly cluttered abode to "a little Charenton" (the madhouse where the Marquis de Sade died in 1814).

As a child in this environment, Bébé had been subjected to tumult and isolation in equal and overwhelming degrees. If these conditions weighed on her more heavily than they did on her older sister, it may have been because Esther, who was engaged to their beloved cousin Ludovic Halévy, could look forward to marriage as an imminent escape. By all accounts a bright and caring young woman, Esther did what she could to be a mother to her little sister. But she couldn't make up for their parents' radical inattentiveness to Bébé's needs. That neglect comes through with wrenching clarity in a letter Bébé wrote to her father and mother when she was eight and they had left her with her paternal grandmother for an open-ended stay:

> My dear parents, it vexes me a lot that you didn't come today, I beg of you please come tomorrow. I shall tell you about my day yesterday. I woke up and had a bath and went for a walk after and then I went upstairs and studied. Then I descendeth [*sic*] and read quietly next to Grandmother. Then we went upstairs and worked until 4. Sometime we had to sort threads until 5, which annoyed me a lot. Then I wenteth [*sic*] downstairs to the front door to see if you were coming because we were not allowed to go looking for you. . . . At the door was a man you sent to tell us on your behalf that you weren't coming, which upset us a lot. . . . That was my day, my beloved father and mother, and I kiss you with all my heart. Bébé.

Like Laure de Sade, Bébé Halévy would react to the stresses of her upbringing by cultivating a winning personality. As an adult, she came up with a memorable stock phrase to describe her girlhood: "When I was a child, my parents abandoned me, like Tom Thumb—except that *I* was left to fend for myself on the rooftops of the Institut!" In one respect, this line foregrounded her cachet as the daughter (and later the wife) of a celebrated artist. Given the French people's unequaled veneration for cultural and intellectual achievement, the palace of the

As perpetual secretary of the Académie des Beaux-Arts, Geneviève's father received an apartment in the Institut de France overlooking the Seine.

Institut was one of the most storied buildings in the country. Tales of playing on the rooftops around its great gleaming cupola, which dominated the skyline of the Left Bank as seen from the Seine, would have sounded as glamorous to French ears as childhood stories set on the roof of Buckingham Palace or the White House might to Anglophones.

On another level, though, her abandonment by her parents had nothing mythical about it, assuming literal form whenever Léonie's manic upswings landed her in a mental clinic. In 1854, when Bébé was five, Léonie spent the better part of the year in Passy at the treatment facility of Dr. Émile Blanche, alienist to Paris's richest and most famous mental patients, including many well-known artists. (Recounting one of her first visits there as a girl, Bébé wrote to her cousin Valentine, "I was very afraid of all the crazy people. But Mme Blanche reassured me by saying that I knew them all already!") Not far from the street where Laure de Sade grew up, Blanche's asylum occupied an eighteenth-century mansion once owned by a French princess of the blood, the Princesse de Lamballe. Its twelve acres of manicured grounds were sprinkled with pavilions where patients underwent a range of treatments, most of which made use of Passy's fabled spring waters: colonics, gargling, cold showers, and baths lasting for hours or even days on end.

The cognoscenti swore by Dr. Blanche, but he was unable to cure Léonie. In the spring of 1864, shortly after Bébé's fifteenth birthday, her mother checked

Many of Geneviève's relatives sought treatment at Dr. Blanche's prestigious mental clinic in Passy. Her sister died there under mysterious circumstances in 1864.

in to his clinic again and stayed for four years. This time, she was joined by Fromental's two elderly unmarried sisters, Flore and Mélanie Halévy, who until then had shared with Esther (and an English governess) in the responsibilities of caring for Bébé. They both, to their younger niece's distress, wound up remaining at the sanatorium for the rest of their lives, Dr. Blanche having diagnosed them with "complete and utter dementia."

By the time her mother and aunts began their extended sojourn in Passy, Bébé had also lost her father, who died in March 1862 after a week of raving delirium. His younger brother, Léon Halévy (also an alumnus of Blanche's clinic), wrote that on the last morning of his life, Fromental had asked Esther and Bébé to lay him out on the sofa "in a scale: *do, re, mi, fa, so, la, ti, do,* until his head rested on the cushions." He died as soon as his daughters lowered him into position.

When it came time for Fromental to be laid to rest in the Montmartre Cemetery, the burial site for many acclaimed French artists, Bébé and Esther had to accompany the funeral procession without their mother by their side; between Léonie's reinternment and their father's death, they had effectively been orphaned. Riding through Paris from the quai de Conti to the butte of Montmartre, with fans mobbing them all along the way, must have been a terrifying experience for the two girls, and it took a noticeable toll on Bébé's mental state. As one of Fromental's pallbearers remarked afterward, "The mother is stark, raving mad, and the younger daughter is becoming more and more like her every day."

Bébé sustained another shattering blow two years later, when Esther—"the only one who made it possible for me to withstand my suffering"—died under mysterious circumstances at Dr. Blanche's clinic. In early April 1864, Esther, twenty-two, had checked in to the facility to keep Léonie company, and perhaps to receive some sort of treatment herself (although her mother later maintained that Esther had been the picture of health upon arrival). Bébé remained in Paris with the governess. Two weeks into her stay, Esther fell ill with a supposed chest cold. Three days later, on April 19, Bébé's nanny rushed her to Passy just in time for her older sister to die in her arms.

Many decades later, Ludovic's son Daniel Halévy wrote that one of Bébé's cousins—Louis Ganderax's brother, Étienne—divulged to him the real circumstances of Esther's death. One evening, Léonie had tried to drown herself in a pond on the asylum grounds. Her older daughter had jumped in and saved her but contracted a deadly fever afterward. Plausible as it sounds, this story doesn't square with the assertion by Dr. Blanche's son, the painter Jacques-Émile (Jacques) Blanche, that there was no pond on the premises of the clinic, a landscaping decision Blanche the elder had deliberately taken "so as not to tempt the suicidal."

Dr. Blanche kept Léonie in the dark about Esther's death for several months after it happened. When he finally did break the news, Léonie erupted in a paranoid, hysterical rage, ranting that Bébé had murdered Esther. Unwilling to be swayed from this belief, Léonie banned Bébé from her presence and had her legally declared a ward of one of their relatives, Émile Pereire, a banking, railroad, and real-estate tycoon in Paris. Kicked out of her parents' flat in the quai de Conti, Bébé moved in to Pereire's mansion in the Monceau plain (*la plaine Monceau*), an opulent residential quarter on the Right Bank that he and his brother Isaac had helped to develop.

Now bereft of her whole immediate family and accused by her mother of an unspeakable crime, Bébé sank into a depression that lasted for several years. Her guardian was in no position to give her a newfound sense of security; in fact he inadvertently added to her stress. In 1852, Émile and Isaac Pereire had founded a bank, the Crédit Mobilier, which had since become one of the most powerful financial institutions in the world. But shortly after Bébé became Émile's ward, the bank had gone into a free fall, undone by speculative investment decisions, dodgy business practices, and a looming international financial crisis, and the Pereires' rivals, the Rothschilds, were showing no mercy. By 1866, the Crédit Mobilier was posting losses of nearly 95 million French francs. A year later, it had collapsed. In 1869, the Rothschilds bought the Pereires' *hôtel* in the Monceau plain for 40 percent less than the brothers had paid for it a decade earlier.

Her guardian's precipitous fall from grace amplified Bébé's misery, as her cousin Ludovic noted with a pang. "How many catastrophes have beset her these many years, the poor dear child!" he wrote. "So much pain! So much loss!" Ludovic, too, was grappling with inordinate sorrow and loss, having been very much in love with Esther. His mother, Nanine Halévy, worried that in his grief, Ludovic might transfer his affections to the manifestly troubled Bébé. So in 1868, Nanine pushed him into a match with Louise Breguet, a Protestant heiress to a Swiss watch-making fortune. After the wedding, Ludovic suffered a nervous breakdown over a period of several weeks, at one point becoming so "aggressive" toward Louise that both her parents and his feared for her safety, and Dr. Blanche intervened to keep him away from her. After a few months, Ludovic regained his wits and was reunited with Louise, allaying her secret fears that "perhaps Ludovic's lack of enthusiasm" for their union arose from his belief that she was "perhaps a monster" of some kind. However, biographers have suggested that Ludovic never really got over Esther's death, carrying a lifelong torch for her and, by extension, for Bébé.

At the time of Ludovic's marriage, Bébé was still struggling mightily with her own bereavement. In her journal, she pleaded with God to alleviate her pain:

> The years pile up in vain, powerless to erase the dreadful memory of the cruel moments that separated me from everything I ever loved. They [the years] can neither erase nor heal my pain. O, Esther, my beloved sister, I could have borne anything with you by my side, God separated us on this earth, may He give me the strength to deserve a place beside you one day. O Lord, You have taken from me what was the most precious to me in the whole world, You took from me a beloved sister who filled my heart and my life with joy, I lost my adored father even before I could understand all the happiness he brought me, and You didn't even leave me with the love of my mother to console me—nor am I allowed to try to ease her suffering and unhappiness with my care! You have made me alone upon this earth, O Lord. . . . Is it really all over for me already, forever, and won't You deign to have pity on me? If I am not as good as I should be, please consider that at least I am very unhappy, and that I am asking for Your forgiveness as well as for Your help. . . . Please do not turn away from me. . . . Have mercy on me in my pain, and help me to become worthy of You and of the people I mourn.

According to biographer Chantal Bischoff, this diary entry is a case study in survivor's guilt:

> Geneviève feels irredeemably guilty—guilty for having outlived her father and her sister, guilty for not having loved her father enough, guilty for not having appreciated her happiness when she had it, guilty for not being able to comfort her mother. . . . If God has deprived her of everyone she loved, it's because she wasn't worthy of them!

Bischoff further points out that while Bébé's prayer may, with its rhetoric of sin and forgiveness, sound "more Christian than Jewish," it in fact echoes the determination of Rachel, the eponymous heroine of *La Juive*, to "be worthy of her father and of her people." Bébé's entreaty to God also belies her subsequent claims about having "too little religion to wish to change it" and suggests that if she had no religious faith as an adult, perhaps it was not because she had never had it but because she had lost it during her dark and tumultuous youth.

Self-recrimination and despair took up permanent residence in Bébé's psyche, resurfacing with a vengeance—accompanied by vivid fantasies of drowning and fears of going insane—whenever more loss threatened. "Tender hearts never forget," she wrote in her diary at nineteen. "For them," she added, anticipating William Faulkner's oft-cited dictum, "the past is not dead—it is merely absent."

The clouds momentarily lifted in the spring of 1869, when Bébé, twenty, became engaged to Georges Bizet, thirty, a strapping, bearded bear of a man who had studied music composition under Bébé's father at the Conservatoire. Bizet had an ebullient manner that contrasted sharply with Bébé's melancholic reserve. A child of the provinces, he was partial to striped sailors' tunics, knitted mufflers, and straw hats: articles seldom if ever worn by her top-hatted Parisian relatives. But beneath his down-home, country-boy demeanor lay a formidable talent, which her late father had recognized. After graduating from the Conservatoire, Bizet had followed Fromental's example by winning the prestigious Prix de Rome.

Bizet's ties to Fromental may have been more than incidental in Bébé's decision to marry him. Before she accepted his proposal, she had been secretly engaged to an academic artist named Henri Regnault, yet another Prix de Rome laureate. Her father's death, however, seems to have predisposed Bébé in his star protégé's favor, a development that appears logical enough when one recalls that for the last many years of his life, Fromental had seen far more of his students than he had of his children. Symbolically, then, the relationship with Bizet would have represented a chance for Bébé to reconnect with her father, whose work had taken him away from her long before his death did.

Much later in life, Bébé would even invent a story in which Fromental had "walked into her room one day and said, 'My student Bizet would like to marry you. I don't know if you would like that, but there, I've told you.' And she had answered, 'I would like that.'" But this scenario, which she recounted to the novelist Julien Benda, would have had her father conveying Bizet's marriage proposal to her when she was twelve at the oldest, for Bébé had only just turned thirteen when Fromental died. Moreover, although she and Bizet had probably crossed paths at various performances throughout her youth, he made no mention of Bébé in his correspondence until she was seventeen, when he confided to one of his own music students, Edmond Galabert, "I have met an adorable girl whom I adore! And in two years, she will be my wife!" Bizet's statement about having to wait until Bébé was nineteen to marry her flatly contradicts the version of events she related to Benda. Yet the fact that she portrayed Fromental as an intermediary in her engagement reveals how present his memory was to her when she decided to accept Bizet's hand.

Perhaps Bébé had imagined her father's blessing as an antidote to her mother's vehement opposition to the match. As a scion of the illustrious Jewish Gradis clan, Léonie considered the penniless, petit-bourgeois, gentile Bizet—the son of a provincial hairdresser turned piano teacher—an unacceptable candidate for her sole surviving daughter's hand. By this time, Léonie was in a different in-patient sanatorium just outside Paris, to which Dr. Blanche had sent her after her four-year stay with him in Passy. So she raged against Bébé's betrothal only by letter but her displeasure wounded Bizet all the same. He groused to Ludovic, "Mme Halévy only respects people who have social status [and] money!!!!!"

Bizet's family members were no less unsupportive. While his widowed father, Adolphe Bizet, came around to the idea of an Israelite daughter-in-law from Paris, his other relatives—rabidly conservative, lower-middle-class, Catholic country folk—echoed Léonie's disapproval. (Where they came from, "marrying a Jewess represented the worst of calamities.") But the couple held firm. On June 3, 1869, they married in a civil ceremony in the ninth arrondissement, attended by just a few family members, including the groom's father and the bride's kindly uncle, Hippolyte (Hippo) Rodrigues, Léonie's brother. A successful financier from Bordeaux, Hippo had stepped forward to offer the newlyweds his moral and financial support.

In the early years of their marriage, Bizet told friends that he and his "Baby," as he nicknamed her, were "immensely happy together," "absolutely happy." Although Bébé abandoned her diary after the wedding, her husband's writings from this period depict their relationship as a loving, harmonious one. Like every marriage, it had its challenges, notably where money was concerned. To make ends meet, Bizet had to teach piano lessons, and Bébé, raised in luxury, was taken aback to learn that they could only afford to hire one maid. At her husband's request, she engaged a young woman named Marie Reiter, who had worked for his parents in the provinces. At the time, Bébé believed what her husband's other family members believed: that Marie Reiter's young son, Jean, was Adolphe Bizet's illegitimate child, and thus Georges's half-brother.

With the Reiters in tow, the newlyweds moved to Montmartre, a rustic township on the northern outskirts of Paris. It perched on a 425-foot-high butte crowned with three windmills, unlikely adornments to a skyline thick with smog. The quaintly bucolic silhouette, visible from all over Paris, stood in contrast to the neighborhood's reputation as a hotbed of insurgency and dereliction. That Montmartre had seen the worst of the civil massacres of 1871 accounted partly for its sinister renown and wholly for the scaffolded, bulbous white outline on its peak: the Sacré-Cœur Basilica, which the government was building

Georges Bizet was Geneviève's
father's student and disciple at the
Paris Conservatoire. She broke off an
engagement with painter Henri Regnault
to marry him.

in dual atonement for the bloodshed of the Paris Commune and the shame of the Franco-Prussian War. But the countercultural mystique of Montmartre also stemmed from the artists who had made it their home, as memorialized in Henri Murger's romantic collection of stories, *Scenes of Bohemian Life* (*Scènes de la vie de Bohème,* 1851). The "bohemians" flocked to the area not only for the lively, free-spirited atmosphere but for the rents, which were among the cheapest in the city. Real estate grew pricier as one descended the butte and proximity to central Paris increased. But at this low elevation, too, Montmartre had the feel of an artists' colony, favored by the more affluent members of the Parisian creative class.

It was in this relatively deluxe sliver of the neighborhood that Bébé and her husband settled, in an elegant, four-story limestone building at 22, rue de Douai. They had found the place through Ludovic Halévy, who lived in a full-floor apartment on the second floor with his wife and two young sons. The Bizets took the flat upstairs. Its best feature was the wraparound outdoor terrace, which afforded picturesque views straight out of Murger: puffing chimney tops; roofs made of slate, tile, even straw; the windmill triptych; and the ruins of an old customshouse, a remnant of the days when fortifications and guarded checkpoints ringed the city. Partway up the butte, livestock grazed on jagged swaths of grass.

Between the Halévy and Bizet households, the building in the rue de Douai became a favorite gathering spot for artists in the area, its cobalt-blue front door a local landmark. Edgar Degas, an old friend of Ludovic's, lived and worked in a studio next door, and despite his professed misanthropy, he stopped by on an almost daily basis—sometimes alone; sometimes with his charming mistress, Hortense Howland, the French-born wife of a rich American expatriate; and sometimes with another Halévy family friend, Albert Boulanger-Cavé, a convivial gadabout and arts connoisseur. (Degas painted the two men together at the Opéra and gave Ludovic the portrait, which occupied a place of honor on the Halévys' drawing-room wall.) Other neighbors, who called with varying degrees of regularity, were novelist Ivan Turgenev; composers Hector Berlioz, Jules Massenet, and Charles Gounod; and painters Gustave Doré, Édouard Detaille, and Gustave Moreau. Pierre Puvis de Chavannes also had a studio nearby but visited less frequently, perhaps put off by the pet name his colleagues coined for him: "Horse's Pubis" (Pubis de Cheval).

At this stage in their marriage, the Bizets struck those around them as a well-matched couple, compatible in their differences. Bébé's deadpan wit found a perfect foil in her husband's jolly farm-boy persona, while his expansive personality counteracted her all-too-understandable tendency to brood. That tendency came as more than a little bit of a shock to Bizet. He hadn't gotten to know Bébé well enough during their courtship to gain a sense of her psychological problems, nor had anyone in her family filled him in about her troubled history with Léonie. Still, he happily assumed responsibility for his bride's well-being. A few months after the wedding, Bizet wrote to Uncle Hippo:

> I am becoming fully experienced in taking precautions for my dear Bébé's health (ha! Geneviève came with an instruction manual!). Her overall condition is very satisfactory: sleep, appetite, everything as it should be— good news from this end!

The couple's happy days came to an abrupt end on July 19, 1870, when France declared war on Prussia. For Bébé, this news brought still more tragedy on the home front, as it drove Ludovic's forty-year-old half brother, Lucien-Anatole (Anatole) Prévost-Paradol, to suicide. The offspring of a liaison between Léon Halévy and the opera singer Lucinde Paradol, Anatole, an illustrious author and diplomat, had been raised alongside his father's legitimate children. They therefore regarded him as one of their own, and so did Bébé. As she and Ludovic reeled from the loss, the Franco-Prussian War shook the nation. In September, the Prussians routed the French at the Battle of Sedan, taking Napoléon III prisoner when he surrendered. Back in Paris, his government collapsed, giving way to the Third Republic; and the fallen emperor's consort, Eugénie, fled town in the carriage of her American dentist. Two weeks later, the kaiser's army marched on Paris and launched a siege that lasted throughout the fall and winter.

During the siege, Bizet tried to keep Bébé's spirits up, though in his correspondence, he lamented the end of the world as they had known it. "It's heartbreaking," he wrote to a friend. "Instead of [peace and brotherhood], we have tears, blood, piles of bodies, and crimes without number and without end!" Perhaps hoping to marshal more support for his sensitive, depressive bride, he encouraged her to write to her mother, who despite the family's legitimate concerns about her ability to function outside a mental hospital had checked herself out of her suburban clinic and returned to her native Bordeaux. To evade the Prussian onslaught, scores of Parisian women and children had relocated there as well, along with the government of the newfound Third Republic.

However, Bébé chose to remain in Montmartre while Bizet served in the National Guard: another Prix de Rome laureate making up for the missed military service of his youth. The couple's decision to stay put furnished Léonie with a pretext for much histrionic fretting, especially once reports began to circulate of widespread famine and fuel shortages in Paris. In late November, Bébé sent Léonie a cheerful letter insisting that amidst all the hardship, she and Georges were doing just fine:

> We are still in perfect health here, Mother, we are not yet dying of hunger and I must say, thus far I have eaten neither cat, nor dog, nor rat, nor mouse, as I hear people are doing in the *best* society. Today I will be tasting donkey for the first time. . . . We've even been eating rather more since this frightful siege began, however much it should have dampened our appetite!

Beneath Bébé's jocular tone, one discerns the unusual privilege she and Georges were still enjoying at that point in the war. Three months of the Prussian stranglehold had indeed reduced many Parisians to eating cats and rats; many more starved. But through Bébé's Pereire kinsmen, she and Bizet had access to more copious and wholesome provisions. At a time when produce had vanished from the city, Émile and Isaac Pereire had fresh fruit and vegetables brought in from their estate in the Seine-et-Marne. At home in Paris, the Pereires also still owned a thousand-bottle wine cellar and continued to drink the same fine vintages that they had in peacetime, until a mob broke in and looted the place.

As the siege wore on, even the Pereires' living standards declined, replaced by the severe austerity the rest of Paris already knew too well. By Christmastime, Bizet was writing to his friend Ernest Guiraud, "We aren't eating anymore. Soon we will be sharing a few horse bones for dinner; every night Geneviève dreams of chickens and lobsters."

Bébé's morale began to degenerate and the sparkling humor to fade from her letters. In a note to her cousin Valentine Halévy, Ludovic's sister, she complained of Bizet's absences from home, which his military service required: "Imagine, I spent twenty-six *hours* all alone, yes, all alone, while Georges was posted to guard the fortifications. . . . Georges took it all well enough, but I found the wait very long." When he did return to their apartment between tours of duty, it was usually late at night, while Bébé was sleeping. Before sneaking out again, he would leave billets-doux on her bedside table for her to find when she awoke. But these tender missives couldn't allay her dread of losing yet another person she loved. ("If I didn't receive little notes from him every day," she told Valentine, "I wouldn't still be alive.")

Before long, Bébé stopped eating, stopped smiling, refused to leave her bedroom or even her bed. So greatly did her deterioration alarm Bizet that a few weeks into the New Year, 1871, he finally determined to get her out of Paris. "Geneviève will be safe and sound! Geneviève is my whole life!" he assured Uncle Hippo, who pleaded with them to come and stay with him and Léonie in Bordeaux. On January 28, Paris fell to the Prussians. A few days later, the Bizets fled the city and went to join Bébé's uncle and mother. And that is when her real troubles began.

Much like the death of her older sister, the nervous collapse Bébé suffered in Bordeaux is still shrouded in mystery, its details discernible only between the lines of the frantic letters Bizet, Ludovic, and Uncle Hippo exchanged in its wake. According to Bizet, the moment she was reunited with her mother, Bébé broke down in hysterical sobs—sobs not of relief but of sheer, uncontrollable panic. Spasms "of unprecedented violence" contorted Bébé's face and racked her body, growing so violent that she lost the ability to speak or walk. In terror, Bizet bundled her off to their hotel room, promising both her and Léonie that after a good night's sleep, Bébé would be herself again. But the next morning, Bizet reported,

> Bébé heard voices in the corridor of the hotel—you should have seen how pale she got! You should have seen how she flung herself into my arms, crying: "That's her! If I see her again, I will die!" How terrifying you would have found her face!

Bébé pleaded with Bizet to take her away from her mother immediately, and he, desperate to placate her, agreed. They boarded the next train for Paris, and Bizet cabled ahead to Ludovic to tell him what had happened:

> Geneviève had been wasting away for the past few months; from the very second Mme Halévy came back into her life, Geneviève was overcome with terror, . . . a real morbid terror. . . . I was in a terrible bind—what was I to do? . . . Suffice it to say that less than twenty-two hours after we arrived, Geneviève, absolutely beside herself, out of her mind, she kept saying to me: "Take me away from here, quickly! Quickly! Or else I shall be killed like Esther!"

Once they got back to Paris, Bébé regained some semblance of equanimity, though her face continued to shudder and twitch with "exterior manifestations of nervous overexcitement that are worse than anything you can imagine. As for Mme Halévy," Bizet concluded, "she mustn't ever know that her very presence could kill her daughter."

Neither then nor afterward did Bébé ever explain why she suddenly became so convinced that her mother, who had accused her of murdering Esther, was the one guilty of that crime, nor did she say why she thought Léonie had plans to kill her as well. Following the return from Bordeaux, Bébé was plagued by horrific nightmares she said she was too ashamed to discuss even with her husband. Her nervous tics persisted, abating only in rare moments of relative calm.

Léonie's self-absorption was such that she barely even noticed her daughter's hasty departure back to Paris. But she continued to manipulate Bébé by mail, writing to her and Bizet, "Thanks be to God, you have no cause to be cold or indifferent to me, *I demand that you love me to excess.*" Then, counting on Bébé's continued guilt over Esther's death, Léonie played her ace: "*The two of you now have to love me enough for four.*" To pay lip service to this demand, Bizet took over corresponding with Léonie so that Bébé would not have to. And the more he got to know his mother-in-law, the less he liked her, characterizing her to Ludovic as "an utterly superficial woman . . . who claims to love everyone, when really she loves no one but herself. . . . Her egotism is incredible!"

This insight confirmed Bizet in the conviction that "it's either her or Geneviève (yet they are both ill)," and his wife's doctors agreed: "All the experts I consulted said it was necessary that [Bébé] never see her mother again." These experts may also have given Bébé sedatives to help her recover from the trauma in Bordeaux, although she didn't refer in her letters to any specific medication until seven years later, when she bemoaned the unpleasant taste of a pill prescribed in the treatment of nervous tics. In time, drugs would become her preferred safeguard against a past that was not really dead. But for the moment, she was depending on her husband to exorcise the ghosts that haunted her.

Outside circumstances again interfered with Bizet's ability to tend to her as she would have liked. Returning to an occupied city, he had rejoined the National Guard, a decision Bébé decried. On March 1, the Prussians staged a triumphal parade on the Champs-Élysées, less than two miles from the Bizets' apartment. For the people of Paris, it was galling to see the invaders marching proudly from the Arc de Triomphe down to the place de la Concorde, brandishing their bayonets and flaunting their victory. Bébé's anxiety, though, was all for Bizet. Writing to Valentine on the day of the parade, she made no mention of the Prussians, instead complaining, "We poor, unhappy wives have to stay inside all by ourselves while our husbands are off, who knows where!" A few weeks later, again to Valentine, she reported, "Georges hasn't been back . . . for three days—you can imagine how little I enjoy this kind of life! I keep blacking out, going into trances."

The blackouts further insulated Bébé from the turmoil besetting her city and her homeland. But that turmoil was about to arrive on her doorstep. On May 10, the Prussian Empire and the Third Republic signed a peace treaty that imposed draconian terms on the latter. France agreed to surrender a significant piece of territory to Prussia (Alsace and the better part of Lorraine, provinces that formed the border between the two countries) and to pay 5 billion francs in reparations. These humiliating concessions to the enemy sparked mass unrest in the French capital, where radical dissidents rallied under the red banner of the Paris Commune. Cited by Karl Marx as an example of the "dictatorship of the proletariat," this insurrectionary socialist body rejected the terms of the armistice and the authority of the Third Republic. Its birthplace was Montmartre.

The Bizets' neighborhood became a flashpoint in the ensuing civil conflict. Their apartment building stood just a few blocks from the place de Clichy, a principal battle site in the so-called Bloody Week (*Semaine Sanglante*) of May 21–28, when government troops marched on Paris and annihilated the Commune. The clash claimed some twenty thousand Parisian lives and resolved in a grisly coda. The aristocratic Marquis-Général de Galliffet ordered the summary execution of several hundred Communard prisoners of war, making good on his infamous pronouncement: "You people of Montmartre may think me cruel, but I am even crueler than you can imagine."

As a child of privilege (and the wife of a National Guardsman), Bébé had not supported the Communard insurgency. But many of her artist friends had, including Porto-Riche, who narrowly escaped with his life after his capture by Galliffet's troops. Mercifully, the building in the rue de Douai survived as well. Nonetheless, the horrors of Bloody Week left Bébé's nerves in tatters. In June she had another breakdown when she learned that Léonie would soon be returning from Bordeaux to Paris, and because Bizet had taken over communications with her mother, Bébé contracted a "strange terror" of him, too. It was a sad paradox of their marriage that Bizet's well-meaning efforts to run interference between her and Léonie made Bébé paranoid that he preferred her mother to her and that the two of them were somehow conspiring against her.

In October, Bébé took up her neglected diary just long enough to scrawl a reprise of her earlier appeal to a higher power:

> My God, I am suffering, I am crying, I am begging You. . . . Even if You don't find me worthy of the joys that I once dreamed of having, can't You at least see to it that everything stops appearing to me in such a somber light? Give me a tiny ray of hope to guide me. Don't let despair alone guide all my actions.

A ray of hope did flicker on the horizon the following summer, in the form of the Bizets' first (and only) child. Jacques-Fromental Bizet, named for his late maternal grandfather, was born in Paris on July 10, 1872. However, Jacques's arrival only increased the pressure on his father to earn a living, leaving Bizet with even less time for Bébé. From Léon Carvalho, one of the most prominent directors in Paris, Bizet accepted a commission to write the score for *The Girl from Arles* (*L'Arlésienne*, 1872), a melodramatic "rural tragedy" slated to open at the Théâtre du Vaudeville in the fall.

Given the stellar reputations of both Carvalho and Alphonse Daudet—the revered author and soon-to-be *académicien* who had adapted the play from one of his own novellas (itself a reworking of a tale by the Provençal poet Frédéric Mistral)—*The Girl from Arles* was to be Georges's highest-profile work to date, and he gave the project his all. In just a few months' time, he churned out more than two dozen mostly brilliant musical numbers for the unconventional twenty-six-piece orchestra Carvalho had specified for the production. The peculiar instrumentation included two flutes, two horns, seven violins, five cellos, two double basses, two bassoons, one oboe, a tambourine, a piano, kettledrums, and an off-stage harmonium.

The Girl from Arles débuted on October 1, earlier than planned; at the last minute, Carvalho had had to substitute it for a different work that wasn't ready to open as scheduled. The audience, angered by the bait and switch, took out their vexation on *The Girl from Arles*. Despite the beauty of Bizet's score, the show met with a stony reaction on opening night and closed after just twenty-one performances.

Bizet responded to this setback by taking four of the numbers from the original score and rearranging them for a full orchestra. The resulting suite premiered a month later to fervid acclaim, marking Bizet's first major professional success. Soon afterward, the directors of the prestigious Opéra-Comique, second only to the Opéra in the hierarchy of Parisian musical venues, commissioned him to write an opera on the subject of his choosing. While working on *The Girl from Arles*, Bizet had grown interested in the folklore of the Mediterranean, so he proposed an adaptation of *Carmen* (1845), a popular novella by Prosper Mérimée. Given the green light by the Opéra-Comique, he engaged Ludovic Halévy and Henri Meilhac—whose hugely successful opera and theater collaborations had long since anointed them as the most famous writing partners in the history of French theater—to author the libretto and began straightaway to compose the score.

If these developments augured a bright future for Bizet, they didn't sit well with Bébé, who felt increasingly abandoned as he lost himself in his music. The exigencies of caring for baby Jacques only worsened her sense of isolation. While motherhood may have been one of the "joys" Bébé had feared God would deny her, she found that the infant's insatiable needs made it all but impossible for her to satisfy her own, and not simply because caring for a newborn was an intrinsically depleting task. Even worse, Bébé had the impression that when her husband did look up from his work, he showed more interest in the child he called his "great, beautiful *baby*" (Jacques had even stolen her nickname) than he did in her.

Chagrined at her perceived demotion in Bizet's affections, Bébé treated their son much as her parents had treated her when she was small—neglectfully. Ludovic's younger son, Daniel, would later criticize his aunt (in the Breton way) for her complete indifference to Jacques's welfare:

> As egotistical as a monster and as unthinking as a doll, she convinced her-
> self that she had done everything for her child when all she did was have
> him brought into her bedroom when she awoke, and let him sit for a few
> moments beside her dog on her cushy, outrageously perfumed bed.

At most, wrote Daniel, "Aunt Geneviève . . . loved and doted on Jacques for one hour a day. I never once saw her cross the threshold into his bedroom, a big dirty room" where she "abandoned him, from morning to night." If correct, this characterization of Bébé's parenting style shows a troubling similarity to that of her self-absorbed mother.

Many years later, Bébé and Ludovic burned all of her letters from this phase of her marriage, and most of Bizet's as well. For this reason, the most detailed account of the couple's relationship comes from Daniel Halévy, probably based on information he gleaned from his parents and other adult relatives. (Like Jacques, Daniel was still in diapers when Bizet and Ludovic were working on *Carmen*.) According to Daniel, while Bizet "labored from morning to night, creating beautiful music and starting to become known for it," Bébé "lacked the seriousness of mind" she would have needed to find this lifestyle fulfilling. Instead, "she wanted to socialize, and her husband loved her so much that he didn't object."

AGAIN REENACTING A PATTERN set by her mother, Bébé became hostess to a sprawling cast of bohemians whom she encouraged to drop by her apartment as often as they pleased. Like Léonie, she had an unquenchable thirst for gossip, cards, and, above all, company, and she found that she seldom if ever had to deprive herself of these amusements. Home to the rowdy nightlife of cabarets like the Moulin Rouge, the Moulin de la Galette, and the Chat-Noir, Montmartre kept late hours, and so did Bébé. From the outset, her drawing room in the rue de Douai attracted the very same creative types with whom she had grown up, along with those she met through Bizet.

The best description of Bébé's salon during this period comes from the painter Jacques Blanche. With so many of Bébé's relatives having sought treatment from his father over the years, Blanche and his parents considered the Halévys part of their own family—"closer to us than our own uncles and cousins." Eleven years older than Jacques Bizet, young Blanche retained lifelong memories of the apartment in the rue de Douai, and of the woman who held court there:

> I can still see the room, hung with flowered wallpaper, and disorderly in a fashion that strikes me as "artistic," rather "bohemian." Pretty Geneviève, in a peignoir, is stretched out on a sofa; I can picture her with her feverish, heavy-lidded black eyes, a sort of benevolent Judith, pale as a camellia beneath her helmet of dark hair, her thick lips trembling ever so slightly.

This portrayal of Bébé foregrounds several characteristics that her subsequent admirers would also single out: her languid pose; her scanty dress, better suited to a boudoir than to a drawing room; her nervous tremors and "feverish" air. And above all, her dark, full-lipped beauty, its Judaic cast highlighted by the Judith reference. Élie Delaunay praised her exotic looks as well, calling her his "velvet-eyed Odalisque" and writing: "How Oriental you are, at least in your eyes!"

Along with the Blanches, Delaunay, and Degas, Bébé's earliest regular callers included her childhood piano teacher Charles Gounod and his fellow composers Jules Massenet, Ernest Guiraud, and Gabriel Fauré; celebrity playwrights Alexandre Dumas *fils*, Henri Meilhac and Victorien Sardou; Symbolist poets José-Maria de Heredia and Henri de Régnier; and a crop of up-and-coming authors hailed as "the princes of young criticism": dramatist cum theater critic Jules Lemaître, novelist cum literary critic Paul Bourget, and novelist cum dramatist Paul Hervieu. And then there were her many artistic cousins: Willie Busnach, who wrote antic boulevard farces such as *The White-Bellied Seal* (*Le Phoque à ventre blanc,* 1883, complete with Émilie Williams's cryptic tagline); Louis and Étienne Ganderax, influential editors and critics; and, of course, Porto-Riche and Ludovic. Porto-Riche determined early on that with such impressive ties as these, Bébé was uniquely well-placed to advance his literary fortunes. "You will make me famous," he told her, positing hope as fact. "You will conduct the rites."

At this stage in her social career, Bébé enjoyed promoting her friends' work. This was Montmartre, after all, and art was the glue that held the community together. With tactfulness and good cheer, she brokered connections between authors and editors, painters and collectors, actors and directors, playwrights and critics. She offered feedback on novels, poems, newspaper columns. She hosted dress rehearsals of new plays and performances of new music. As one of her writer friends would later recall,

> In her salon, she welcomed all that was best . . . in the worlds of art and
> letters, . . . naturally creating an atmosphere of wit, taste, camaraderie,
> and delectable well-being.

Because of Bébé's languorous air and filmy bedroom attire, Paul Bourget teasingly called her "the most indolent of Muses." But in these early years as a
salonnière, Bébé was quite industrious on her friends' behalf.

Her attachment to her *fidèles* may have been a panacea for Bébé, but it troubled Bizet, who was not too busy to notice that he had been displaced. Again
according to Daniel Halévy, "It made Bizet wretched to discover that Aunt
Geneviève belonged less and less to him! Her love for him was still there, but
another love had overtaken it: the passion for society." A hint of Bizet's alarm
comes through in a letter he wrote to Guiraud in 1873, relating a recent dream:

> We were all in Naples, installed in a charming villa; we were living under
> a purely artistic government. The Senate consisted of Beethoven, Michel-
> angelo, Shakespeare, Giorgione, and people like that. The National Guard
> was replaced by an immense orchestra. . . . Bébé got a little too friendly
> with Goethe, but despite this inconvenience, waking up was a bitterly
> cruel business.

Interestingly, in Bizet's dream, Bébé gets "a little too friendly" not with just anyone but with her (and her mother's) favorite type of man: a man of genius. And
while there were no renowned German authors among the faithful—ever since
the war, Bébé had professed a vehement hatred of the Prussians—her husband,
a veteran of that same conflict, would not have been wrong in suspecting that
she was harboring enemy forces: fellow artists ready and willing to lay siege to
his bride.

Battered by their unspoken grievances and incompatible needs, the Bizets'
marriage soon reached a breaking point. Early in 1874, for reasons presumably
outlined in the letters she and Ludovic later destroyed, Bébé moved out of the
rue de Douai and went to live at the Ludovic Halévys' country house in Saint-
Germain-en-Laye, just west of Paris. She left Jacques in the joint care of her
husband, who had stayed behind in Montmartre, and her mother, whom she
had previously tried to keep away from the boy. In one of the few letters to have
survived Bébé's and Ludovic's auto-da-fé, Bizet inquired tenderly about the state
of her "little head," requested her input on the arrangements he and Léonie were
making for Jacques, and assured her of his love. That was in February. By June,
he and Bébé had reconciled.

In what must have felt like a major concession to her spouse—who now
worked at the piano desk once owned by her father but who did not share
Fromental Halévy's "imperturbable faculty of attention"—Bébé agreed not to

resume her social life straightaway. To facilitate Bizet's work on the twelve-hundred-page score he had to complete by the fall, when *Carmen* would go into rehearsals at the Opéra-Comique, she agreed to move with him for the summer into a yellow-painted brick villa he had rented for them in Bougival, a little village on the Seine ten miles west of Paris and close to Saint-Germain-en-Laye.

At first, she griped about the dullness of the boondocks, just as Léonie had done when Bébé was small and Fromental tried to move the family out to Corbeil. Bébé resented her exile in Bougival all the more when Bizet began traveling back to Paris on a regular basis to meet with critics and performers. During his absences, he left her alone in the villa with Jacques and the Reiters: hardly a pleasurable arrangement for Bébé. Whereas Jacques could play happily with little Jean Reiter, Bébé had no wish to keep company with the boy's mother. As close as Marie Reiter had been to Bizet's family while in their service, Bébé did not consider her a suitable friend for herself.

Instead Bébé found herself an arguably even more questionable companion. Rather like Delacroix's Corbeil, Bougival had become a haven for artists looking for fresh air, sunshine, and a respite from the mad rush of the capital. Bébé's friends Dumas *fils* and Ivan Turgenev were the hamlet's best-known literary figures. Its resident painters included Pierre-Auguste Renoir, Alfred Sisley, Claude Monet, and Berthe Morisot, and the music world was represented by Ernest Guiraud and Eraïm (Élie) Delaborde. Being close with the latter two men, Bizet asked them to look in on his wife and son when he wasn't around, and they soon became good friends of Bébé's as well. Bizet scholars have speculated that her relations with Delaborde, however, turned into something more than just friendship, a theory that subsequent events would appear to confirm, although no information exists as to exactly when the two began an affair.

In many respects, Delaborde was similar to Georges Bizet. Like the composer, he was a bit older than Bébé—thirty-five to her twenty-five in the summer of 1874. Also like Bizet, Delaborde had a brawny physique and an outsized personality to match; his contemporaries described him as a force of nature with talent to spare. Supposedly the love child of the composer Charles-Valentin Alkan and one of his aristocratic music pupils, Delaborde had revealed himself as a piano virtuoso at the age of five. Twenty years of study and performance had followed, landing him a prestigious faculty position at the Conservatoire at the age of thirty-four, a sinecure even his brilliant father had never managed to obtain. While Bizet had been Fromental Halévy's student at the Conservatoire, Delaborde had been Halévy's colleague.

In the words of another faculty member there, Antoine Marmontel, as a pianist Delaborde not only executed the most challenging pieces with "the authority and perfection of a consummate musician, . . . with great power of expression and incomparable charm"—but played them from memory. He parlayed this skill into a lucrative sideline as a concert pianist, drawing massive crowds in con-

Pianist Élie Delaborde kept Geneviève company while his friend Bizet "neglected" her to work on *Carmen*. After Bizet's death, she and Delaborde secretly got engaged.

cert halls throughout Europe. Delaborde was so popular in his native Paris that in the winter of 1870–1871, his fans turned out for his performances throughout (and despite) the Prussian siege.

Again like Bébé's husband, Delaborde sought out the company of other artists and impressed them with his multifaceted talent. One of his closest friends was Édouard Manet, who lauded his "real vocation for painting," and whose praise may well have been sincere. Some of Delaborde's canvases, which he signed with his middle name, Miriam, were accepted for exhibition in the annual Salon de Paris—no small achievement for an untrained, part-time painter.

Delaborde also shared Bizet's penchant for colorful accessories, though his ran more to the animal than to the sartorial type. In the spring of 1871, he traveled to London with no less than 121 cockatoos and parrots in tow. (On other journeys, his moveable menagerie included his two pet monkeys as well.) In addition, Delaborde was a superb athlete, fencing daily when in Paris. In Bougival, he took long swims in the bracing waters of the Seine, sometimes joined by Bizet.

But for all they had in common, the two men presented several differences that may have inclined Bébé in Delaborde's favor. To begin with, he was Jewish. Bébé came from a family that prized its Jewishness as a cultural birthright, if not always as a religious faith. On the Halévy side, this tradition went back to her grandfather's founding of the first newspaper ever created for the Jewish community in France. Her father, too, had focused on Jewish themes in his work (from *La Juive* to *The Wandering Jew* to the unfinished *Noah* [*Noé*, 1862]), as had her uncle Léon Halévy, who while moonlighting from his day job as a playwright had authored a magisterial two-part history of the Jews. In Bébé's generation, her cousin Joseph Halévy was an archaeologist of Semitic cultures who, in 1880, joined some members of the Rothschild family in founding an organization to promote Jewish scholarship in France. Coincidentally, another of this group's founding members was Bébé's future second husband, Émile Straus.

On Bébé's mother's side, the intellectual commitment to Judaism was equally strong. Though a stockbroker by trade, Léonie's brother, Hippo Rodrigues, founded the Israelite Scientific and Literary Society (Société scientifique-littéraire israélite) and wrote learned tomes on Jewish history. Also notable was Bébé's late maternal aunt, Eugénie Foa, the first Jewish Frenchwoman to live by her pen; in her novels, Foa was likewise drawn to Jewish subject matter.

Delaborde's Jewish identity derived from his father Alkan, an Ashkenazi with a deep interest in Judaica. In fact, Bébé's father had once tried to recruit Alkan for an organist position at Paris's leading synagogue. Like Bébé's uncles Léon and Hippo, Delaborde's father was a scholar on the side, translating the entire Old Testament from Hebrew into French just for fun. He also referenced his heritage in much of his work as a composer, which musicologist David Conway has identified as "the first published art-music specifically to deploy Jewish themes and ideas." Along with including Hebrew quotations from Genesis and the Song of Solomon, Alkan based many of his compositions on patterns from Jewish liturgical music. Delaborde himself became well versed in this material by compiling an edition of his father's works and incorporating them into his own performance repertoire.

Delaborde further played up his Jewishness by styling himself "Élie" (Elijah), a prevalent name in Israelite families like Bébé's: both her Halévy grandfather and Ludovic's eldest son were called Élie. With Delaborde, she would thus have had the comfort of a shared, inherited frame of reference. For all his talent, her husband's petit-bourgeois, Catholic antecedents had given him no such conditioning, nor could they have.

At least as compelling to Bébé was the fact that Delaborde, too, had a challenging relationship with a parent suffering from severe mental illness. Although raised by an adoptive mother (whose surname he bore), Delaborde grew up knowing of his biological relationship to Alkan and spent decades trying to win his approval, if not his love. This effort was complicated by the fact that Alkan was a notorious eccentric, all but crippled by his terror of his fellow man. He once declined an invitation to perform in a prestigious salon by telling the hostess that an hour and a half of human contact would land him "in the infirmary." So acute was his social phobia that he gave his last concert in 1838, when he was twenty-four, and went into isolation for the next thirty-five years. In 1862, Alkan described his self-imposed solitude in a letter to one of his few remaining friends:

As usual, I've been doing nothing. . . . If it weren't for a bit of reading, I'd be living more or less like a cabbage or a mushroom, a fungus, albeit a fungus with a taste for music.

As he aged, Alkan grew secretive to the point of paranoia, convinced of an elaborate plot to steal his life savings. Musicologist Stephanie McCallum has suggested that these traits may have been symptoms of schizophrenia.

Alkan's quirks made intimacy with his son, or anyone else, impossible. Delaborde tried to bridge the divide by studying with him and by editing and performing his compositions. How Alkan received these expressions of filial devotion is not known. In terms of Delaborde's closeness with Bébé, however, the history of negotiating the trip wires of parental insanity would have provided the pair with a substantial fund of shared experience.

Lastly, due to his success on the concert-tour circuit, Delaborde was relatively affluent, and Bébé, very much her mother's daughter in this regard, had a fondness for luxury that the reduced financial circumstances of her marriage hadn't fully suppressed. (She spent liberally on stylish clothing and stockpiled expensive chocolates and gloves in greater quantities than she would ever consume or wear.) Because she stopped writing in her journal after she married Bizet, and later destroyed any letters that would have compromised her idealized accounts of their love, it is impossible to determine how Bébé felt about the downward economic mobility her union with him had brought. But the change would have been pronounced; for in marrying Bizet, Bébé had gone from being the daughter of an internationally acclaimed artist and a pampered heiress to being the wife of an unknown composer who taught piano lessons to get by.

Because she chose to marry Bizet before he was at all well-known, it would be wrong to assume that like her mother, Bébé "only respect[ed] people who have social status [and] money!!!!!" Even so, those things mattered as much to her as they had to Léonie. As one of Fromental Halévy's loftiest patrons, Princesse Mathilde Bonaparte, would later note with a sneer, "It's incredible, every time there is a Rothschild anywhere in sight, Geneviève just has to latch on to him!" In fairness to Bébé, her attraction to the Rothschilds may have had to do with something more than just their riches and social cachet. As a teenager, she had witnessed firsthand the demise of her mother's Pereire cousins, who in wealth and influence had once rivaled the Rothschilds and who in fact had originally started their railroad company in partnership with Baron James. In Bébé's mind, the Rothschilds may have represented a fantasy alternative to her troubled family of origin. When the Pereires fell, the Rothschilds kept on rising, buying up not only their disgraced rivals' mansion in Paris but, in 1880, their country estate as well. And of course, whereas Bébé's forebears had declined the offer of ennoblement, the Rothschilds had become barons. To the extent that Bébé was attuned to these differences, she may have looked at the Rothschilds as the better articulation of the type of Jewish plutocrats from whom she came.

Apart from his supposedly aristocratic birth mother, Delaborde had no ties to the gratin, and he was certainly not, as was so often said of the Rothschilds, "richer than God." But when Bébé first met him, he was substantially richer than Bizet. Moreover, Delaborde dressed like a man of means. His bespoke suits from London stood in glaring contrast to her husband's coarse, countrified garb—especially after the relocation to Bougival, when Bizet topped off his look with a corncob pipe. As a Parisienne, Bébé took pride in her sophisticated fashion sense, embracing the newest trends with greater religious fervor than she ever brought to the observance of Jewish rites or holidays. There is no question, then, but that she was sensitive to the disparities in the two men's personal styles.

Last but definitely not least, Delaborde was attractive to Bébé because, unlike Bizet, he actually had time for her. When in Bougival, Delaborde was on hiatus from both teaching and touring, with no pressing reasons to leave Bébé alone there as her husband so frequently had to do. With Bizet's attention consumed by *Carmen* (and perhaps also, it was rumored, by his leading lady, Galli-Marié), Delaborde stepped in. Even had he lacked any other redeeming qualities, Delaborde's attentiveness would have meant everything to Bébé, whose morbid dread of loneliness, like the past that had produced it, never entirely left her.

Delaborde's assiduousness in squiring Bizet's wife around Bougival did not go unnoticed by their friends and neighbors. According to some biographers, Bizet himself was conscious of the pair's deepening friendship. Mina Curtiss, who unearthed a cache of his private papers a century after his death, has gone so far as to argue that the composer not only knew but approved of Bébé's romance with Delaborde, as it "relieve[d] him of the burden of his wife's perpetual need for attention" and thus enabled him to focus on *Carmen*. Another biographer has taken the opposite view, arguing that Bébé's liaison with Delaborde made Bizet savagely jealous and tormented him to the last.

In either case, Bébé's infidelity may have been of some artistic value to Bizet if he indeed, as he told Louis Ganderax, was looking to her as a model for his heroine—that exotic, Iberian gypsy untamable by any man. (Whatever its genesis, *Si tu m'aimes, prends garde à toi* was indisputably a fitting slogan for a woman who took up with her husband's friend.) If Bizet did suspect any mischief between his Bébé and Delaborde, he not only made no effort to stop it, but continued to rely on Delaborde to keep her company. Until the day he died, Bizet would depend on his friend for this service.

That day came much sooner than any of them foresaw. On March 3, 1875, *Carmen* premiered at the Opéra-Comique. Although the Bizets had moved back to Paris by then, Bébé did not attend the premiere, having apparently contracted a stye that kept her at home in Montmartre. But Bizet's other friends turned out

Bizet told Geneviève's cousin that he modeled
the fiercely independent, exotic heroine of
Carmen on his (Iberian Sephardic) bride.
But he was suspected of having an affair with
Galli-Marié *(left),* the singer who created the
title role in 1875.

en masse to support him, and when the curtain first rose on the opera, the whole
audience seemed predisposed in his favor. Before long, however, the novelty of
the music and the indecorousness of the heroine alienated the crowd. The next
day, Ludovic Halévy recapped the disaster:

> Act I well received. [Carmen's] first song applauded, also the duet for
> Micaela and José. End of the act good—applause, curtain calls. . . . Every-
> one swarming around Bizet and congratulating him. Act II less fortunate.
> The opening very brilliant. The Toreador Song produced a great effect,
> followed by coldness. From then on, . . . the audience was stunned, dis-
> concerted, perplexed. Fewer people around Bizet at the intermezzo. Con-
> gratulations less sincere—[his friends] embarrassed, constrained. Coldness
> even more pronounced in Act III. . . . After Act IV, which was glacial from
> first to last, no one [was left] except for three or four of Bizet's true friends.
> They had reassuring phrases on their lips but sorrow in their eyes. *Carmen*
> had failed.

By the time the final curtain fell, Bizet was a man in shambles. To Guiraud,
who had stuck around to the end, he confessed that he could not face returning
home to Bébé in defeat—not right away. So the two friends went for a late-night
walk in Paris, meandering for hours through the deserted city streets while Bizet
"poured out the bitterness of his soul."

No sooner did he reach the rue de Douai, though, than he collapsed, beset by a sudden attack of tonsillitis. Over the next several weeks, many more attacks followed, accompanied by crippling rheumatic swelling in Bizet's joints and by the eruption of a large abscess in his left ear. Echoing Bébé's late father, who had lain down to die in a *do-re-mi* sequence, Bizet construed his suffering in musical terms: "Imagine a double pedal A-flat/E-flat pounding in your head from the left ear to the right," he wrote to Guiraud. "I'm quite done in."

In late May, on the grounds that the city air was poisoning him, Bizet talked Bébé into decamping with him to Bougival again until he regained his strength. But the move only seemed to weaken him further. Sometime between May 27 and May 29—historians disagree as to the date—Bizet went for a swim with Delaborde, a decision that in hindsight would appear to support his friend Gounod's theory: that the failure of *Carmen* had made the composer suicidal. Intentionally or otherwise, the dip in the Seine left Bizet with a chill that swiftly gave way to fever and more rheumatic inflammation. On June 1, he had a heart attack. The next day, he had another.

The end came rapidly after that. From his sickbed, Bizet called for Bébé, Jacques, and the Reiters. Jean Reiter, he now revealed, was not his father's illegitimate child but his own. Bizet made Bébé promise to assume responsibility for Jean's future well-being and to keep Marie Reiter on in her service. Distraught and in tears, Bébé promised, and she stayed true to her word. Thereafter she raised her own son to believe that he and Jean Reiter were milk brothers—boys who had suckled at the same breast as infants—and she retained Marie Reiter as a housekeeper for the rest of her life. How she felt about preserving these relationships is unknown; she never spoke of either of the Reiters in her correspondence.

While keeping vigil by her husband's bedside, Bébé at one point thought she heard him gasp, "Delaborde! Go and fetch Delaborde at once!" By the time Delaborde got to the house, Bizet had slipped out of consciousness, and either Bébé or Ludovic, who had also rushed over to offer his help, called for a doctor. When the doctor arrived, he pronounced Bizet dead on sight. It was three o'clock in the morning on June 3, 1875: three months to the day after *Carmen* premiered at the Opéra-Comique and six years to the day after the Bizets' wedding.

Like her mother before her, Bébé, twenty-six, was too distraught to attend her husband's funeral, although four thousand other mourners trooped into the Montmartre Cemetery to pay their respects. At the graveside, Gounod broke down in tears when reading aloud a statement from Bébé, saying "there was not a minute of her married life that she would not gladly have again."

IN THE MONTHS AND YEARS THAT FOLLOWED, Bébé gave a committed performance as Bizet's grieving widow. As custom required, she

Geneviève became famous as the Widow Bizet by wearing full mourning for her husband for five years after his death.

adopted full mourning, dressing wholly in black for a year after her husband's death. But after that date came and went, she decided to keep wearing her widow's weeds, and she was still wearing them two years later when she sat for a portrait by her friend Élie Delaunay. With her permission, Delaunay showed the painting at the 1878 Salon de Paris: a haunting study in black veils, black clothes, and sorrowful black eyes.

The timing of Delaunay's submission turned out to be fortuitous. In the years since *Carmen*'s inauspicious début, the public had changed its mind about that opera and its composer, deeming the former a triumph and the latter a genius. From all over Europe, requests to stage Bizet's work had come pouring in, fielded by Bébé with Ludovic's help. These revivals brought not only royalties—Bébé was suddenly awash in those—but the notice of Europe's loftiest crowned heads. Queen Victoria requested a special performance of *Carmen*. So did Tsar Alexander II, whose letter on the subject Bébé proudly leaked to the press.

Artists and writers joined in the chorus of posthumous praise. Russian composer Peter Ilyich Tchaikovsky called *Carmen* "a masterpiece in the truest sense of the word, . . . one of those rare works destined to reflect most strongly the musical aspirations of an entire epoch," while Friedrich Nietzsche declared that, when listening to that opera, "one becomes a 'masterpiece' oneself." (The German philosopher was particularly impressed by *Carmen*'s "cruel, cynical" portrayal of love as "a tragic joke.")

These ovations combined with Delaunay's arresting *Portrait of Mme Georges Bizet* (1878) to ignite public interest in the composer's exotic-looking young widow. Being a child of show business, Bébé had a sixth sense for reading her audience, and she gave the people what they wanted. In the words of biographer Anne Borrel:

> Delaunay's somber *Portrait of Mme GB* . . . brought a new character into the world: in this composition, the beautiful sitter was reborn as the living, breathing heroine of her very own novel—anticipating all the other novels she would go on to inspire.

To preserve the haunting public image that Delaunay's painting had given her, Bébé continued to wear full mourning for another two years after the 1878 Salon.

Only in 1880 did she finally put her widow's weeds away and switch to half mourning (*demi-deuil*), a wardrobe of soft lilacs, greys, and whites that typically served to ease the transition from black to an unrestricted color palette. For Bébé, however, the change did not represent an end to her "Widow Bizet" persona so much as a refinement of it. She adopted half mourning on a permanent basis, forever reminding all who saw her of the genius she had loved and lost. (She also ordered reams of custom writing paper, in shades of pale grey, violet, and pink: "mauve thoughts edged in black," as one of her correspondents wrote.) Among her nearest and dearest, this fashion statement earned her the nickname "the Mauve Muse."

To the broader Parisian public, Bébé's widow costume signified her readiness to indulge their curiosity about Bizet. Fans made pilgrimages to her apartment in the rue de Douai, where instead of turning the strangers away, she invited them in and gave informal tours. One visitor remembered her leading a group through the composer's office and bedroom, pointing to the desk piano and the Breton sailor shirts and saying, misty-eyed, "This is where he worked, those were his clothes." People came away from the tour touched by Mme Bizet's obvious devotion to her late husband's memory.

But her mournful public image hid a less seemly reality. Bizet was not even ten months dead when Bébé quietly notified the people closest to her that she was engaged to marry Élie Delaborde. Four months after that, in August 1876, she and Delaborde signed a marriage contract in the presence of her mother's notary. Daniel Halévy, always caustic on the subject of his aunt, remarked that while Bébé had lost her husband, "she wasn't a lonely widow for a single day."

EXCEPT THAT SHE WAS ALONE, essentially, here in her Alpine retreat, saddled with Eulalie Ulmann—never mentioned in Bébé's letters as anything more than a convenient sidekick: a placeholder for all the more interesting people she'd had to leave behind. Not even her son, Jacques, whom Bébé could

Geneviève's son, Jacques Bizet, painted at age six by her friend Élie Delaunay, was intensely attached to his indifferent mother.

always count on to go into ecstasies at the sight of her, was around. Shortly after their arrival with the Ulmanns in Gurnigel, little Marcelle had presented symptoms of whooping cough, so the doctor had ordered her and Jacques into separate quarantines. So now Jacques was back in France with his grandpa Bizet, bombarding his mother with badly spelled missives that were long on reproaches ("Why don't you ever write to me? *I* write to *you*! I sleep with your letter on my heart!") but short on news. And it was news that Bébé was longing for, news of Paris and her faithful.

To Aunt Nanine, usually a reliable source of gossip "because the two of us have the same frivolous spirit," she deemed Gurnigel "indescribably sad," less because of its far-flung location per se, though that didn't help matters, than because

> there are no Frenchmen to be found here, only Swiss people who speak German, and Germans who don't speak at all! . . . More than the isolation or the cold, . . . the most frightful thing is never to hear a single word of French. . . . Even the dogs bark in German—*when* they bark, which is rare. There's one big dog I tried to make friends with, but he didn't understand me, and turned his back on me with disdain. Then he trotted off with an old man from Frankfurt.

The line about the dogs only barking in German was typical of the offbeat, improbable formulations with which Bébé liked to amuse her *fidèles*. Yet it spoke as well to her isolation in Switzerland and her eagerness to return home.

Apart from her marriage contract, Bébé left no documentary trace of her romance with Delaborde. But her interaction with Gurnigel's local fauna might have reminded her to be glad she had called it off. While Bébé adored dogs, she did not care for parrots, cockatoos, or monkeys, and the earthy inconveniences of traveling—not to mention cohabiting—with more than a hundred such creatures could easily have negated the allure of Savile Row tailoring and a crazy Jewish father. After a two-year engagement to Delaborde, she had implored Ludovic to break things off with him on her behalf. She was unable to explain her reasoning except to say that "her friends, her freedom—she couldn't think about anything else."

From that standpoint, Bébé's confinement among quiet Germans and their unresponsive pets was frustrating indeed. In a letter to Guiraud, with whom she had remained close since Bizet's death, she groused that while she and Mme Ulmann had identified two potentially appealing prospects among all the Teutons—an American and an Italian—both men seemed inexplicably immune to her charms. (Bébé said nothing of Mme Ulmann's charms, presumably negligible compared to her own.) On July 11, Guiraud replied in a frisky vein:

> Paris has been intolerable since you left. . . . I would tell you that I love you with my whole heart, that I adore you, but you know that as well as I do, and if I were to continue in this vein, I would only bore you to death. So let's talk a bit, if you like, about these two men you've met— your American and your Italian. . . . By now I bet you've already inscribed them both on your famous list of victims—the one that's threatening to grow just as long as Don Giovanni's [*mil e tre*]! All I ask is that you don't let them take my turn.

This note presents one of the more candid expressions of sexual interest Bébé fielded in her correspondence with her admirers; regrettably, her answer hasn't survived. Still, Guiraud's letter indicates that the two of them shared a remarkably comfortable rapport—a playful flirtation in which they both appeared, in other contexts, to delight. Bébé loved amusing her faithful with tales of Guiraud's cavalierly wayward morals, as when she asked him if his illegitimate daughter resembled the mother, and Guiraud smirked, "I don't know. I've never seen her without her hat." This exchange redounded to Bébé's glory as a raconteur, even as it betrayed a distinct breach of decorum between the sexes.

As for Guiraud's assertion that Bébé had been accumulating conquests in numbers comparable to Don Giovanni's, it implied that in her bereavement, the Widow Bizet had been merry indeed. Bébé herself intimated as much when she described to her aunt Nanine the grand plans she had for the latest gentleman to have caught her eye in Gurnigel. She had noticed him in the hotel dining room, reading *Le Figaro* and "speaking French *without an accent*. . . . He has turned out to be a Parisian! The only one here! He looks very rich and distinguished; I am already cultivating him for Ludovic's." By the same token, she mock lamented, "I fear I'll find out that he's just a traveling salesman." Until she could rule out that possibility, Bébé added, she would have to ask her aunt to refrain from telling anyone else in the family about "my new fiancé. I still don't know what his net worth is, and I don't want to get [everyone's] hopes up for nothing!"

By the end of the summer, the "new fiancé," whose name turned out to be Gustave Marx, was forgotten, as, for that matter, were Mme Ulmann and her ailing spawn. Once back in Paris, none of these bit players qualified for admittance to "Ludovic's," where the hostess and star had higher standards for her supporting cast and better players to choose from. Both Porto-Riche and Laure de Chevigné, for example, remained welcome in Bébé's salon, despite her powerlessness to quash their burgeoning friendship. (Bébé may have been pleased to learn that Laure had resettled in Adhéaume's family's château for the fall, awaiting the birth of the couple's first child in October.)

Her attempts at meddling did, however, yield one unexpected benefit. When badgering the Porto-Riches about her seductive friend Laure, she had gleaned a useful bit of intelligence. An extremely eligible Jewish lawyer whom Bébé had met shortly before her departure for Gurnigel—the formidable Maître Émile Straus, thought to be the illegitimate son of the late Baron James de Rothschild—had been asking Porto-Riche about her while she was away. Having heard that "poor Mme Bizet" was marooned in the Alps, and that her little boy was in quarantine, Straus had begged Porto-Riche for updates on their wellbeing. Straus, in other words, was interested in Bébé. And unlike Gustave Marx, Straus was unquestionably somebody: worldly, well-connected, and very rich. Straus would do nicely on Bébé's famous list of victims.

WITHIN MONTHS OF HER RETURN from Switzerland, Bébé and Straus were a couple; or rather, Geneviève and Straus were a couple. Disliking her childhood nickname, he persuaded her to drop it—a seemingly minor change that heralded a major shift in her trajectory. The merry widow was now headed for a second marriage, and for the monde.

She and Straus made their first recorded outing together in March 1881. With Ludovic and another friend as their chaperones, they paid a visit to Ferrières, the Rothschilds' storied castle in the Seine-et-Marne. Built in the 1850s by Baron James de Rothschild, it was the largest château in France, a massive square neo-Renaissance pile with showy domed towers at each of its four corners. The great hall alone was renowned as a "miniature museum": its walls were covered with precious artworks and inlaid with lapis lazuli, marble, and bronze; a crystal roof crowned its sixty-foot ceiling. The castle library housed more than eight thousand volumes, and each of the eighty guest suites—"the Bouquet Bedroom," "the Pheasant Bedroom," and so on, named for the motifs of the antique tapestries lining their walls—offered the ultimate, unheard-of luxury: a private bathroom. (The walls of each suite's bathroom were hung with more tapestries in the same motif.) Another noteworthy feature was the in-house synagogue, a mark of the proprietors' steadfast Judaism (which their gentile *titres de noblesse* did not, in their view, contradict). Back in 1836, German-Jewish poet Heinrich Heine had called Baron James's mansion in Paris "a Versailles for the absolute plutocracy" the Rothschilds had founded. Heine's description applied just as well to Ferrières. For upper-class Parisian Jews, it was the equivalent of a royal court: the summum of Israelite power and prestige.

Such ostentatious splendor met with a good deal of eye rolling among the "born." The Prussian chancellor Otto von Bismarck likened Ferrières to an "overturned chest of drawers," while Edmond de Goncourt, that self-appointed guardian of French taste, dismissed it as "a stupid, ridiculous extravagance, a pudding of every conceivable style." Nevertheless, the princely scale of the interiors (designed by Eugène Lami) and the hunting grounds (eighteen square miles of prime forest, stream, and field) made a slew of converts among Europe's ruling élite, including the future kings of Sweden and England. In 1862, Napoléon III "went into ecstasies" at the splendors of Ferrières. Eight years later, Kaiser Wilhelm I requisitioned it and used it as his personal base of operations during

During the Franco-Prussian War (1870–1871), Kaiser Wilhelm I requisitioned as his personal base of operations Ferrières, the Rothschilds' famous château.

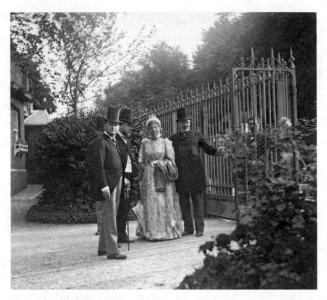

This is the earliest extant photograph of Geneviève with her future husband, Émile Straus *(far left)*. She was drawn to his wealth and Rothschild connections.

the Franco-Prussian War. Refuting his chancellor's negative opinion, the kaiser proclaimed, "What an extraordinary palace! A king could never get away with something like this—only a Rothschild." After the war ended, he returned the castle to its owners, its priceless art and wine collections intact.

For Geneviève, an invitation to Ferrières was a dream come true, a chance not just to spend a few days in an atmosphere of legendary opulence but unofficially to conclude a peace between the Rothschilds and her own kin. It would have to be a posthumous truce, as Geneviève's relative and former guardian, Émile Pereire, had died in 1875, followed by his brother, Isaac, five years later. It was upon Isaac's death that the Rothschilds had purchased the Pereires' property in the country, which, because it conveniently abutted the domaine de Ferrières, the Rothschilds had since absorbed into their own estate. All the same, the rapprochement held deep meaning for Geneviève. She was eager to put her family woes behind her and make a fresh start, allying herself with the winners this time around. She was ready for bigger and better things, things like visits to Ferrières and the considerable social upgrade they implied. With Straus on her arm and the Rothschilds in her sights, Geneviève was on her way.

CHAPTER FIVE

THE FALL AND THE RISE

On August 24, 1883, after a two-month bout of crippling abdominal pain, the Comte de Chambord died at Frohsdorf. Having survived almost until his sixty-third birthday, he had exceeded by more than a decade the median life expectancy for the men in his family. All the same, his death spelled catastrophe for those loyalists who had staked everything on the hope of seeing him restored to the throne. As one chronicler wrote of the tension in the Schloss that summer, the members of Monseigneur's inner circle

> couldn't bring themselves to believe that the King of France might actually die in a foreign land. "Why did he live in the first place," they wondered, "if he wasn't meant to reign?" For them, he stood as the very incarnation of the French monarchy. If he were to disappear, it would mean the end of everything.

An epic geological event intensified the pall over the anxious court. Between late May and late August, a series of volcanic eruptions shook the Indonesian island of Krakatoa, triggering a hundred-foot-high tsunami that claimed 36,000 lives. Another 60,000 victims perished as fire, ash, debris, and atmospheric disturbances from the blast encompassed the globe, blackening skies and roiling seas from Scandinavia to the Cape of Good Hope. It was the deadliest natural disaster since the Lisbon earthquake of 1755, which had exacted a comparable death toll and happened to have coincided with the birth of the Comte de Chambord's great-aunt, Marie Antoinette, the patron saint of Bourbon martyrdom. For courtiers of a superstitious bent, this coincidence betokened ruination on a cosmic scale.

Laure de Chevigné wasn't around for her sovereign's final days, having decamped to Paris a few weeks before his agony began. (Although his team of doctors never reached a consensus about what killed him—stomach cancer, ulcers, heart disease, poison—their initial diagnosis was gastritis, caused by some overripe strawberries he had eaten in June.) But on the morning of August 4, Chambord had tried to summon Laure to his bedside. When Chevigné reminded him that she had gone abroad for the summer, the king suddenly recalled that he had sketched her on the eve of her departure. The little portrait depicted Laure surrounded by steamer trunks, porters, and a multitude of parrots.

Monseigneur had the drawing brought to him and gave it to Chevigné as a

The Comte de Chambord died on August 24, 1883, ending
his followers' hopes for a legitimist restoration.

token of his esteem. He then explained that after his death, Madame would dissolve the court at Frohsdorf and move to Göritz, a town on the Adriatic where the royal couple kept a winter residence and where he would be buried alongside a number of other Bourbons who had died in exile, including his grandfather Charles X, who had succumbed to cholera there in 1836. Before quitting the castle for good, the dying man advised, Chevigné should help himself to a few souvenirs. "Take whatever you like," he rasped with a grin. "If *la vieille* were here, she would fill up two suitcases!" According to Laure's secondhand account, these were the last words Henri V ever spoke. (Other witnesses averred that with his dying breath, he said simply: "France.")

Ten days later, crowned heads from all over Europe descended on balmy Göritz to pay their respects to the last of the French Bourbon pretenders. Having no children, the deceased had named as his successor his forty-five-year-old cousin, Philippe d'Orléans, Comte de Paris, despite the antipathy that had festered between their respective branches of the royal family for a century. Though intended to heal the rifts in the French monarchist party, this act of reconciliation galled such orthodox legitimists as Chevigné, who had spent a lifetime dismissing the d'Orléans as usurpers. Publicly, Chevigné and his colleagues proclaimed their support for their master's anointed heir. But privately, many of them blanched at the prospect of a monarchy headed by Philippe VII.

For these loyalists, Chambord's funeral was a glum occasion, made even glummer by the cost-cutting measures that had impelled Chevigné, charged with organizing the ceremony, to decorate the Göritz cathedral with cardboard facsimiles of the royal arms of France. The cheapness of the crudely painted decorations only exacerbated the legitimists' sorrow at the French Bourbons' inglorious demise. According to Comte Albert de Mun, a royalist statesman who had traveled from Paris for the occasion, these true believers were "in mourning not only for the king but also for the monarchy itself, for the cause [they] had loved and served with such generosity and devotion." To another onlooker, they were visibly struggling with "the awareness that they had wasted their lives; that they had sacrificed their youth, all their talent, and all their energy to . . . a hope that was never to be realized." Some of the Frohsdorf crew wept openly over Monseigneur's corpse, swaddled in the white flag of his ancestors and laid out in a white marble casket carved with *fleurs de lys*.

Other courtiers tittered behind their fans at Madame's decision to place at the head of the funeral cortège her husband's Spanish Borbón relatives and his nephews by his only sibling, the late Duchesse de Parme—a gesture that symbolically denied the Comte de Paris's newfound status as France's presumptive king.* (As such, he should have processed ahead of all the other mourners.) Duly stung, Philippe d'Orléans saw no choice but to boycott the service, despite his lackeys' entreaties that he simply reassert his precedence by moving his prie-dieu ten meters in front of everyone else's in the cathedral. In deference to the slighted prince, the scions of many European royal and noble houses skipped the funeral as well. But as the widow of the deceased might have bellowed in self-justification, quoting a favorite psalm: her hatred of the d'Orléans was STRONG AS DEATH.

With this last, futile assertion of Bourbon supremacy, the Dowager Comtesse de Chambord bade farewell not only to her beloved "Enrico" but to the political life, such as it was, that she had shared with him for the past thirty-seven years. After the funeral, she shuttered the castle at Frohsdorf and dismissed its courtiers and staff. Then she resettled in her sixteenth-century villa in Göritz, where she commissioned the construction in the garden of a special shrine to the Holy Mother—a replica of the Virgin's Grotto at Lourdes. Once it was completed, the quite possibly still-virgin Madame prayed there several times a day for the rest of

* Under the Treaty of Utrecht (1713), Felipe V, Louis XIV's grandson, had as a condition of his accession to the Spanish throne renounced his and his descendants' claims on the French crown. After Henri V's death, a tiny legitimist splinter group favored a French monarchy headed by the Spanish Borbóns' *chef de famille*. This faction, however, played no notable role in the politics of the Third Republic.

The Comtesse de Chambord had a replica of the famous shrine to the Virgin at Lourdes built in the garden of the house she retired to after her husband's death.

her life. She never returned to Frohsdorf, nor did any of its habitués. The court of Henri V had vanished along with its master.

Bereft of his king, his position, and his whole raison d'être, Chevigné was either too distracted, too polite, or just too sad to load up on royal memorabilia before leaving Frohsdorf for the last time. Apart from the legitimist mourning brooches he and Laure would wear for the next six months (along with their black mourning garb), the only mementoes he brought back to France were the uniform he had had made for the aborted legitimist coup ten years earlier and an unspecified keepsake bequeathed to him in the sovereign's will. And the sketch of Laure that Monseigneur had presented to him on his deathbed.

The uniform was relegated to a cupboard in the Chevignés' new apartment in the Faubourg Saint-Honoré. (The couple were now renting a flat at 1, avenue Percier, not far from their former pied-à-terre in the rue du Colisée and just a few doors down from an *hôtel* the Greffulhe family had rented out as an Orléanist headquarters.) But Laure placed the second Frohsdorf keepsake on conspicuous display in the drawing room, hanging it alongside an eighteenth-century watercolor portrait of the Marquis de Sade. Thus enshrined, the royal caricature stood as a constant reminder of Laure's personal legend: the cause célèbre she had served as tirelessly as "poor Adhéaume" had served his monarch's restoration and that, unlike her husband's mission, continued to flourish long after Monseigneur was dead and gone.

Five years had passed since Laure, now twenty-four, had first traveled to

Frohsdorf as a new bride. Since then, in keeping with her husband's request, she had spent at least two months a year with him at the Schloss. She had further obliged him by conceiving two children in short order: Marie-Thérèse, born in October 1880 (and named for her royal godmother, the Comtesse de Chambord), and François, the requisite male heir, who arrived two years later. Once she had fulfilled these wifely obligations, Laure took full advantage of the inducement Chevigné had offered her in exchange, returning to Paris without him for increasingly frequent and extended stays.

Etiquette had obliged Laure to ask the sovereigns' permission whenever she wished to leave their court. As a sop to their Catholic piety, she likely invoked the obligations of new motherhood when petitioning for this boon. Because protocol banned courtiers' children from the king's residence, Marie-Thérèse and François de Chevigné couldn't live in Frohsdorf with their parents, and although Laure sent them to stay with her mother-in-law at the château de Saint-Thomas for a few months a year, the Dowager Comtesse de Chevigné insisted she couldn't afford to feed and lodge the children for any longer than that. (From her own sojourns at the Chevigné family seat, Laure had personal experience of her mother-in-law's parsimony: to cut down on the costs of fuel, Adhéaume's mother decreed a castle-wide nightly curfew of ten o'clock and enforced it by patrolling the darkened hallways late into the night, peering beneath bedroom doors for telltale slivers of fire- or lamplight.) So for the rest of the year, Marie-Thérèse and François had to live in Paris—ostensibly with their mother.

In truth, however, Laure saw little of her children when she was in town. Instead she entrusted them to the supervision of a live-in governess, a corpulent, perennially disgruntled Irishwoman named Frances, and focused on building her social life. On her initial trips back to Paris, Laure relied on local relatives (the Warus, her Chevigné brothers-in-law, and assorted cousins from both sides of the family) and legitimists (kinsmen of the Frohsdorf crew) to introduce her into the monde. But it did not take her long to develop her own friendships in that milieu and to establish herself at the center of the action.

To a large extent, and as she had anticipated, Laure owed her *mondain* success to her self-proclaimed status as Henri V's favorite. When socializing in the Faubourg, she made a point to regale her new acquaintances with anecdotes about "the kingdom of shadows." Her noble peers never seemed to tire of hearing how, at her very first appearance in the Salon Rouge, the Comte de Chambord had joked about running away with her. How only she, of all the women at court, rode to hounds with him each day—"because hunting was my consolation, too." How only she dared to scold Monseigneur for his fits of royal pique. How only she bantered with him in terms so profane they made even the huntsmen blush. How only she had a drawing of herself—right at home here in Paris—by the last of the French Bourbon pretenders. In the telling and retelling of these stories,

Laure's children, Marie-Thérèse and François de Chevigné, circa 1888–1889.

Laure made a virtuoso display of her "simplicity," stressing that the king's august position did not faze her. At the same time, and just as crucially, she encouraged her listeners to dwell on the stunning intimacy these vignettes implied.

Laure sometimes went so far as to hint that Monseigneur had illicitly fathered her children. She raised this possibility by cleverly instructing her audience not to consider it. "*Both* of my children are Adhéaume's—I swear!" she would cry, refuting her own insinuation. "*No bastards*—that is the rule!" Because of the prestige royal bastards had ever enjoyed among the "born," Laure had evidently determined that her red-herring disclaimers about her offspring's paternity would only benefit them when they entered society in turn.

In the meantime, she had calculated that as the presumed lover of a presumptive king, she herself would find few, if any, of the nobility's doors closed to her, and the gamble paid off. Within five years, she had transformed herself from an obscure provincial bride into one of the most sought-after young women in Parisian society.

This change brought with it a barrage of *mondain* engagements, described by one observer as

> a never-ending carnival of grand banquets and intimate dinners, public concerts and private theatricals, garden parties and tea parties, white balls [*bals blancs:* for debutantes], rose balls [*bals roses:* for young married couples], cotillions, assemblies, charity bazaars, and soirées, interspersed with gala performances, art openings, cold suppers, engagement parties, costume parties, embassy parties, and countless other brilliant occasions.

These events topped Laure's list of priorities while she was in Paris, and they would continue to do so even after Monseigneur's death, when she and her husband resettled permanently in the Faubourg Saint-Honoré. Upon returning there from Frohsdorf for good in the fall of 1883, "poor Adhéaume" found that Laure had in his absence developed a busy and altogether self-sufficient routine and that she was disinclined to include him in it now that he was back. Of the pastimes Chevigné pursued in the capital independently of Laure, more will be said later. But from her perspective, Adhéaume's permanent relocation to Paris did not require her to change her social habits in any material way.

Her children, too, remained largely incidental to her existence there, to the nanny's voluble dismay. A visitor to the Chevignés' apartment once overheard Frances berating Laure—in an obstreperous mix of pidgin French and Tipperary brogue—for having "gone out to a fancy-dress ball, disguised as a MEW-GETT" (*muguet*, lily of the valley), even though five-year-old Marie-Thérèse "had measles, and hundred-and-two-degrees of fever she had!" Laure was not one to be bullied, though, not even by an angry Irishwoman twice her size. Having grown up without much parental supervision herself, she saw nothing wrong with depriving her children of her company.

Nor was she by any means alone in putting *mondanité* ahead of motherhood; any number of noble Parisiennes made the same choice. For many such women, Laure included, the "never-ending carnival" of society events represented as much a vocation as a diversion, an opportunity to uphold the grandeur of their family and their caste and thereby to play a role, however limited, in public life. Otherwise, such opportunities were scarce under the Third Republic. Like all Frenchwomen under that régime, female aristocrats had the legal status of minors. They were not eligible to vote or hold political office. They were not allowed to attend the nation's élite universities, military schools, or professional schools. They were barred from the armed services and the diplomatic corps; they could not be named to corporate boards or to learned academies such as the Académie Française. The men of the nobility, by contrast, took all these prerogatives for granted, along with the right to congregate in their clannish social clubs, which also excluded women.

In 1917, Laure would address this last injustice by helping to found the first coed social club in Paris: the Union Interalliée. But in her younger years, she took the monde more or less as she found it, valuing it as her best chance at participating in a bigger, potentially more stimulating, and unquestionably more prestigious sphere than that of hearth and home.

In this respect again, Laure was very much a creature of her milieu. Sparked by the iniquities just cited, the first stirrings of a feminist movement began to make themselves felt in France in about 1890. But noblewomen were conspicuously slow to align with the cause, which even among the lower orders remained a minority enterprise at best. (While Élisabeth Greffulhe bucked convention by writing about the inequalities between the sexes, she took care to keep her thoughts on the matter to herself.) Pondering the apathy of the era's grandes dames, feminist leader Caroline Kaufmann wrote,

> They are and want to remain the phoenix, the rare bird, the priceless object. They don't care at all about women's emancipation, and for good reason—they wouldn't stand to gain anything from it.

Of course, positioning oneself as "the rare bird, the priceless object" was itself a political act of sorts, just not an act that served the sisterhood. For Laure to embrace the fundamentally decorative and symbolic functions of the *grande mondaine* was to pledge allegiance not to her gender but to her class. Her political interests, such as they were, lay more with the ancien régime than with the "second sex."

The carnival of engagements for which Laure signed on was not for the faint of heart; it followed a punishing schedule, dictated by the time of the year, month, week, or day. In the broadest terms, the *mondain* calendar was divided into three parts: a social season in Paris (January to June); a summer trip to the seaside, the mountains, or abroad (July and August); and a fall/winter hunting season in the country (September to December). The summer, autumn, and winter sojourns away from Paris, known as *villégiatures,* were to be spent at villas, country manors, or châteaux belonging to oneself or one's family or friends.

These festivities and holidays accounted for only some of the *grande mondaine*'s social obligations. Women in Laure's set spent endless hours paying and receiving calls (*visites*). According to historian Anne Martin-Fugier, this ritual began each year with

> New Year's visits: the first week of the year was reserved for close family members; the second week for friends; the last two weeks [of January] for relatives. Then came "digestive" calls; these one had to pay within a week following a dinner or a ball to which one had been invited, whether or not one had attended. Then there were visits to offer congratulations (on an engagement, a marriage, an award) or condolences; visits "of convenience," paid three to four times a year to people with whom one wishes to remain on pleasant terms without going any farther; and visits to say hello or good-bye, before or after a trip.

Not all these visits involved face-to-face encounters. If one called at a person's house and found her absent, it sufficed to leave one's *carte de visite,* or calling card, folded on the upper-right-hand corner or along the right-hand edge to indicate that one had stopped by in person. In this case, the recipient of the card had to return the visit. Another option was to send one's footman out to "place cards" (*poser les cartes*) with friends or acquaintances on one's behalf; when a card was delivered in this way, its right side was not folded, and no reciprocal call was required. A card folded in the lower-left-hand corner or along the left-hand side indicated that one was back in town after a trip; here again, no return visit was necessary. In the entrance to their houses, hostesses kept silver trays where cards were to be left; one of Élisabeth Greffulhe's relatives estimated that women in their milieu went through one thousand to fifteen hundred *cartes de visite* per year.

When Laure was in Paris, she typically dispatched with her visits in two rounds, one in the morning after breakfast and one toward the end of the day before dinner. In between, weather permitting, she joined her fellow aristocrats for a midafternoon stroll, ride, or drive in the Bois de Boulogne, a former royal hunting preserve Georges-Eugène Haussmann had in the 1850s turned into a vibrant city park. During the Second Empire (1852–1870), a daily promenade around the lake at the center of the Bois had been a command performance for titled Parisiennes, giving them a chance to show off their élite friendships and elegant fashions, to one another and to the public at large. After the Empire's fall, the monde revived this practice but transferred it from the lake to the allée des Acacias, one of the main thoroughfares through the Bois. Popularly known as "the Bichonne," the broad, leafy allée filled each day at around four o'clock with society worthies looking to see and be seen. For someone like Laure who was still new to the gratin, an appearance in the Bichonne afforded a prime opportunity to draw the notice—and, ideally, the admiration—of more established *mondains*.

Popularly known as "the Bichonne," the allée des Acacias was a thoroughfare in the Bois de Boulogne where Élisabeth, Laure, and Geneviève, among other Parisiennes, went to see and be seen.

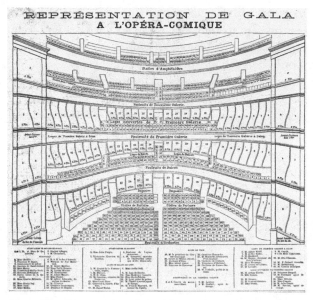

Charts like this one identified who sat where at Paris's leading
performance venues, underscoring the importance of the audience itself as a spectacle.

After sundown, other rituals beckoned, such as the Faubourg's "subscription"
evenings at the city's three top performance halls. For reasons unknown but fixed
by tradition, the gratin went to the Opéra on Mondays, the Théâtre-Français on
Tuesdays, and the Opéra-Comique on Saturdays. On these nights, noble Paris
took over the best seats in the house: loges and *baignoires* ("bathtubs": oversized,
usually first-tier loges) rented for the season by subscription. Decked out in
their evening finery—white tie for the gentlemen; formal dresses, furs, and family jewels for the ladies—the subscribers formed a spectacle unto themselves.
Who was wearing what and who was sitting with whom: More than the events
onstage, these were the dramas that absorbed the theater-going monde. They
also transfixed the gawkers in "Paradise," as the cheap seats up by the rafters
were called.

So rampant was audience voyeurism in the trifecta of Paris's top performance
spaces that newspapers printed diagrams of the venues at the start of every season, pinpointing the location of notable subscribers' boxes. In a further concession to their viewers' curiosity, the managers of Parisian opera halls and theaters
observed a custom of leaving the house lights on for the duration of every show.
This was a practice Élisabeth Greffulhe would attempt to eliminate when spon-
soring a revival of Richard Wagner's *Tristan und Isolde* in 1899, on the grounds
that the composer's work demanded total audience attention. But her peers vig-

orously protested the ban; rarely, if ever, did the action onstage interest them more than the display of their own elegance.

Laure relished subscription evenings for the same reason she enjoyed her rides in the Bichonne: they boosted her profile in the Faubourg, as well as among the reporters covering them for the *presse mondaine*. Season tickets to the best boxes cost more than she and Adhéaume were in a position to spend, but because a royal favorite was a credit to any loge or *baignoire,* Laure seldom lacked for invitations. If she carped every now and again about how the Théâtre-Français or the Opéra "*reek[ed]* of subscribers," it was only to avoid seeming overly grateful for her hosts' charity. "Poor in income" though she was, Laure had her pride.

Thursdays and Sundays found her with the rest of the gratin at the horse races in Longchamp in the Bois de Boulogne and Auteuil, adjacent to her native Passy. For these outings, Laure did not have to worry about ticket prices, as membership fees to the Jockey entitled clubmen and their guests to seats with superior views of the racing. The wives gathered in their own single-sex bandstand, the Ladies' Tribune (*Tribune des Dames*), while their husbands entertained women of easy virtue in a coed bandstand nearby. To avenge themselves on the demimondaines, the *grandes mondaines* went all-out when dressing for the races. According to one habitué of the track, it was among these

> grandes dames that . . . high style reaches its apogee! Fabrics rustle, flowers cascade, and family jewels sparkle, taken out of their cases just for today. The Ladies' Tribune looks like a French garden . . . : toques and hats sprout with blossoms, and on little caps perch hummingbirds and birds of paradise bound to make some onlookers sick with jealousy!

Although Laure would soon come to care about fashion, her chief preoccupation at the races was betting. Confident that her riding expertise gave her an edge in choosing a winning horse, she was in her element as she bustled around the stables and paddocks, examining the Thoroughbreds and interrogating their jockeys and trainers. That she so clearly "loved [the sport] to distraction," as one of her peers noted, endeared her to many prominent racehorse owners, notably Comte and Comtesse Edmond de Pourtalès and Prince and Princesse Joachim Murat, all of whom became her friends for life. But when post time came, Laure was all business, hurrying back to the Ladies' Tribune to watch through her lorgnette as her horse hurtled around the track: starting gate to first turn, five to twenty furlongs, top of the stretch, home stretch, finish line.

The sums Laure wagered were small—fifty francs at most—but her more perceptive companions noticed that the blood drained from her face whenever she lost. Even when her luck was bad, however, the ride from the hippodrome back to Paris restored her spirits. This trip was its own exercise in *mondain* pag-

Jockey-Club members' wives sat in a special Ladies' Tribune at the races at Longchamp. This photograph was taken by Comte Gégé Primoli, an Italian nobleman well-liked in the Faubourg.

eantry. Ensconced in their carriages and mounted on their steeds, the ladies and lords of the noblesse again took stock of their own, and one another's, splendor. Also taking stock were the throngs of hoi polloi who lined the route, goggling at the stately equipages and elegant fashions of the class they called "*la haute*."* The gratin had a reciprocal nickname for these idlers, "the Losers' Club," a designation that stressed their exclusion from all the proper Parisian clubs. To Laure and her companions, the cheers and whistles emanating from this lowly nonclub came as so much agreeable white noise, background expressions of the acclaim they accepted as their due.

As one of her society friends, André de Fouquières, pointed out, the Losers performed another function as well. After taking in "the grand parade" back to Paris from Longchamp or Auteuil, they blended back into the nameless, faceless mass of the capital, where they disseminated their own observations about "this little baroness's outfit or that marquise's trotters." Like the gossipy reports coming out of Paradise after subscription evenings, this chatter filled the pages of the *presse mondaine* and reinforced a widespread fascination with how the elegant half lived. Laure's participation in the postrace parade signaled her élite status not only to her peers but to those numberless Losers who, by talking and reading about her world, "nurtured the illusion that they were not excluded from it."

Another event fostering this illusion was the charity bazaar, where genteel Parisiennes raised money for various philanthropic causes by peddling over-

* Among fin-de-siècle commoners, "*la haute*" ("the high [class]") frequently stood in for the terms noble society used to refer to itself. This designation rankled patrician sensibilities in much the same way the unfortunate word "classy" (*classieux* in French) does today.

priced samples of their (and their servants') handiwork. These items ranged from needlepointed cushions and little lace bonnets to hand-painted fans and gaily ornamented hymnal covers. Some daring souls contributed hand-rolled cigars, while others talked voguish painters like Eugène Lami and Charles Chaplin into donating small works of art. Temporarily overcoming their class prejudice against toiling "in trade," the ladies staffed the sales booths themselves and vied with one another to move the most merchandise. The competition grew particularly fierce when crowned heads browsed their wares; a sales booth, like a party, saw its cachet surge when a majesty or highness deigned to make a cameo appearance. Charity bazaars did not, however, cater exclusively to the élite. For a small admission fee, ordinary Parisians could spend a few tantalizing hours rubbing elbows with *la haute.* If they made a purchase, they might even transact directly with such exalted vendors as the Duchesse d'Uzès and her vivacious young cousin, Comtesse Adhéaume de Chevigné.

WHILE LAURE'S SOCIAL COMMITMENTS were those of a typical *mondaine,* she carried them out with an unorthodox flair that furthered her notoriety and prestige. In particular, as the Princesse Bibesco observed, Laure flouted the gratin's strict prohibition against "young wives accepting any invitations into the great world when their husbands couldn't accompany them," shocking her peers by socializing without "poor Adhéaume" anywhere in sight.

When Laure first started going out in the monde by herself, she was acutely aware of the disapproving glances and huffy whispers that greeted her there. To disarm the naysayers, Laure played up her "rustic" side, drawling with wide-eyed innocence about how she was "dumb as *uhh* goose," "just *uhh* little idiot"—the same stock phrases that had worked so well for her in Austria. Then she would address an earnest little speech to the most obvious skeptic present—usually some old biddy so judgmental and grievance-prone that her company, in one wag's amusing phrase, was "infinitely more unpleasant than a *bag of needles.*" It was frightfully difficult, Laure would say, fixing her probable detractor with the sweetest of smiles, to have to be out in the world without her dear Adhéaume to guide her. And yet—dramatic pause—he couldn't very well accompany her to "'our cousin d'Uzès's' charity bazaar *and wait on Monseigneur at Frohsdorf at the same time.*"

By invoking these magic words, Laure defanged the dragon guards of *bon ton* and forced them to ratify her self-proclaimed exemption from the rules everyone else had to follow. Decades later, Marcel Proust would speak of how the Duchesse de Guermantes, alone in her set, defied the laws of protocol as she saw fit, miraculously turning the phrase "I don't have to" into a point of honor and "the exercise of her '*mondain* free will,' however arbitrary," into an art form. This was Laure's position exactly and uniquely. Even at the very end of her life, when she qualified as something of a "bag of needles" herself, people in society were still referring to her as "one of the very few women in Paris ever to have gone out without her husband."

The Princesse Bibesco framed her friend's unchaperoned sorties in suggestively historic terms: "When in Paris, Mme de Chevigné led the life of an eighteenth-century courtier, escaping from Versailles and traveling into town incognito on an escapade." No one knew better than Laure how poorly Frohsdorf compared to Versailles. Nevertheless, she welcomed comparisons between herself and the denizens of the earlier, grander court. Under the ancien régime, a surfeit of pomp and ceremony at Versailles had famously driven the king's attendants to the occasional, unshackled spree in Paris. By aligning herself with this precedent, Laure did not merely justify her breach of etiquette—she emphasized, yet again, her special affiliation with the Bourbon crown.

She promoted this affiliation as well by violating a second cardinal rule of *bon ton:* she cozied up to the press. By the time Laure entered the monde, the habitués of that world had had a decade to come to terms with the fact that socializing (semi-)publicly at charity sales, horse races, and subscription evenings meant they risked being mentioned in the *presse mondaine,* which inevitably chronicled all such events. Since the founding of the Third Republic in 1870, this sub-industry of the Parisian news media had boomed, the abolition of the class system having counterintuitively pushed popular fascination with the nobility to unprecedented new heights. As a result, the ladies and gentlemen of the gratin had gotten used to seeing their names in the social columns, often followed by breathless praise for their clothing, carriages, horses, hats. Some *mondains* may even have savored these affirmations of their grandeur. But they kept their enjoyment to themselves, for the official line in their set was that the press was vulgar, the mouthpiece of a grubby populace whose opinions did not and could not matter to their illustrious like.

From this belief, it logically followed that courting media attention represented a gross breach of gentility. Such a breach, moreover, was considered particularly grievous when perpetrated by a member of the fairer sex. In the generation ahead of Laure's, the Princesse de Sagan was one of the few women who dared to ignore this precept, and her reputation suffered as a result. The standard line among *mondain* traditionalists was that by fraternizing with the minions of the Fourth Estate, "Rabble Girl" displayed her true, degraded origins.

When Laure undertook the same transgression, she had two things going for her that Mme de Sagan lacked: her *"mondain* free will" and the august lineage to which it supposedly attested. Of necessity, a woman whose coat of arms hung in the Crusaders' Gallery at Versailles could never be dismissed as rabble: "everyone knows that [ça]." Savvy self-promoter that she was, Laure ingratiated herself with the moguls of an industry that was growing more powerful by the day. Among the "born," she was ahead of her time in grasping the potential usefulness of a force that, precisely because its reach extended so far beyond the

As the director of *Le Gaulois*, the leading society daily in Paris, Arthur Meyer eagerly cultivated the "born" and promoted them as celebrities.

small, inward-looking world of the noblesse, exercised immeasurable influence in shaping opinion and bestowing cachet. It was not for nothing that her most powerful media ally, Arthur Meyer, the director of *Le Gaulois,* referred to his business as "Her Majesty the Press."

In the century since the Revolution, the French press had in an essential sense taken over the role previously played by His Majesty the King: that of making and breaking reputations, conferring and withholding prestige. Under the ancien régime, the Bourbon court had constituted the nerve center and the summit of the French social élite, and its members had understood that all blessings flowed from the monarch alone. At the same time, strict royal censorship laws had curbed freedom of expression at Versailles and throughout the realm, further shoring up the sovereign's irrefutable might.

With the fall of the monarchy, everything changed. An explosion of daily and weekly publications fostered the rise of public opinion as a replacement for the king's judgment and favor. Old-line aristocrats grumbled that in the absence of a well-regulated pecking order, France had turned into "an enormous, deformed body without a head." In fact, the body did have a head; they just didn't like the look of it: it was modernity and mass rule, publicity and populism. If anyone wore the crown in fin-de-siècle France, it was Her Majesty the Press.

Laure found a singularly helpful supporter in Meyer, who honored her self-styled grandness without reservation—either despite or because of his own humble origins. The son of Jewish Alsatian ragpickers, Meyer had begun his career as a private secretary to one of the Second Empire's most famous demi-mondaines, Blanche d'Antigny, reputedly the model for the title character of Émile Zola's novel *Nana* (1880). Contact with d'Antigny's high-placed lovers left Meyer with a yen for high society that became his life's obsession. "He knew every nuance of the social hierarchy by heart," one noblewoman observed with surprise. "He knew that there are dukes who outrank serene highnesses, and that there are courtesy titles that sound like nothing, yet take precedence over names that sound a hundred times more impressive." To put this arcane knowledge to use, Meyer went to work as a society reporter, covering *mondanités* first for *La Nouvelle Revue de Paris* and then for *Le Gaulois*.

Since becoming the director of the latter publication in 1879, Meyer had worked hard to cozy up to his aristocratic subscribers, only to be mocked for his lowly Jewish roots. (His enemies joked that his heraldic motto was "Old clothes and used ribbons for sale"; others claimed he "blushed like a little girl in the presence of royalty.") Between her storied ancestry and her position at Frohsdorf, Laure de Chevigné was a dream ally for Meyer, and she went out of her way to cultivate him, seeking him out at social events and offering him her insider's perspective on life at court with Monseigneur.

Her overtures appealed to Meyer's vanity and his politics, which were closely intertwined. Although he had started out as a Bonapartist, a not-uncommon allegiance among self-made Frenchmen, Meyer reinvented himself as a fervid legitimist, and he used *Le Gaulois* as a bully pulpit to call for the restoration of the ultra-Catholic, ultraconservative Henri V, even converting to Catholicism to prove his sincerity. His religious conversion registered in the gratin as the act of a shameless bounder and—a new insult in Parisian patois, imported from England and derived from the Latin *sine nobilitate* (without nobility)—a "snob."

Flattered to be able to claim "the belle of Frohsdorf" as a friend, Meyer rewarded Laure with adulatory mentions in *Le Gaulois,* hailing both her and Adhéaume as paragons of ancient pedigree and legitimist ardor. Over time, he came to focus on Laure alone (almost certainly to her press-shy husband's relief), also taking care to highlight her descent from Petrarch's Laura and/or from the Marquis de Sade.

For all the derision he met with in the Faubourg, Meyer's newspaper was its unofficial bible. As a consequence, Meyer's praise for Laure was extremely effective in elevating her profile in the monde, as well as in the Losers' Club. Taken up by other media outlets, her trademark brand of distinction became the daily bread of social aspiration in Paris. Wrote Meyer's friend Juliette Adam,

> With her classical profile, lovely blue eyes, and supple grace, the Comtesse de Chevigné is one of the most beautiful women in Parisian society today. The descendant of Petrarch's chaste mistress, she too inspires poetry with her limpid gaze. Her irresistible charm wins every vote.

Adam's last sentence captures the paradox upon which Laure's media presence was founded. As a royalist and an aristocrat, she vehemently opposed a social order where everyone had a "vote." But as someone seeking publicity *as* a royalist and an aristocrat, she catered to popular opinion. In this way, she colluded with a system in which the "not born" masses had an important, even an all-important, voice.

FROM HER EARLIEST DAYS IN PARIS, Laure also availed herself of a more elitist means of boosting her stature: she founded a salon. This upper-class institution dated back to the ancien régime, when noblewomen turned their drawing rooms in Paris into havens for lively conversation, unhampered by the rigid formalities of the court. With its patrician origins and overtones, the salon had died out during the Revolution and the Terror, only to reemerge in the nineteenth century as a lynchpin of noble sociability, flourishing during periods of royal and imperial rule. With the collapse of the Second Empire in 1870, the salon had again fallen by the wayside, only to return with a vengeance in the 1880s, its cachet revived by a spate of nostalgic new books about the *salonnières* of the prerevolutionary age. One of the first and most influential of these works was Othenin d'Haussonville's *Mme Necker's Salon* (1882).

As during the ancien régime, a salon was held in the drawing room of a lady's house, usually once a week on her chosen "day." The habitués were known in society—and by hearsay, in the press—as the hostess's inner circle. When that circle was very small and very exclusive, it was reputed to be a "closed" salon: the gold-standard of *mondain* prestige.

Being a newcomer to Paris, Laure charged her old Frohsdorf mentor, Comte Robert de Fitz-James, with helping her assemble an enviably exclusive closed salon. Like Laure, Fitz-James had traveled frequently from Austria to Paris, often timing his jaunts to coincide with hers, and he too moved back to the French capital full-time after Monseigneur's death. In Paris as at court, Fitz-James took an active interest in his young protégée's social trajectory, and as a longtime pillar of the monde, he recruited men of similarly high standing to join him in calling on her at home. They were members of the Jockey or the Cercle de l'Union or both; in contrast to Laure's husband (who wasn't especially friendly with any of them), they were the A-listers of the clubman set, acknowledged leaders of Parisian society.

These men had plenty of other *salonnières* vying for their company. But because they respected Fitz-James, they indulged him when he told them they had to meet Laure, and she won them over straightaway with her irreverent, live-wire personality. With a captive audience of debonair strangers—most of them Fitz-James's contemporaries, so some twenty years older than she—Laure came alive. A columnist for *Le Gaulois*'s biggest competitor, the *Gil Blas,* explained:

Saucy, quick, and a little bit wild, always ready to poke fun at people who take themselves too seriously, the charming Comtesse de Chevigné has conquered the staid old monde. She has brought a noisy, boisterous charm into this most conservative society[;] her conversation leaps and ricochets,

Comte Robert de Fitz-James was Laure's mentor at Frohsdorf and in Paris. He was also her lover for many years.

gallops and flies, never tiring, never stumbling, never landing with a thud. Her wit rises to the very heavens, then flirts with the devil himself. She astonishes with her outrageous jokes, images, analogies, and a laugh like no one else's.

In the best *salonnière* tradition, she injected a sense of levity, unpredictability, and fun into a milieu that tended to be hamstrung by ceremony, convention, and an utter lack of imagination. Laure's callers were entranced, so thoroughly that they insisted on visiting her again and again, no longer as a favor to Fitz-James but as a treat for themselves. Poking fun at their relatively advanced age, Laure christened them "my *vieux*" (old men); they constituted her ultra-prestigious closed salon.

Before long, the *vieux* came to feel that seeing their bubbly young friend just one day a week wasn't enough for them. Abandoning all other salons (and stirring up no end of rancor among the hostesses they left behind), they got into the habit of dropping in to see Laure every day after lunch at the Jockey and refused to leave until they had spent at least two hours chatting with her in her drawing room. None of them, it must be said, went there for the material comforts. Laure's salon was small and cramped, its curtains permanently drawn against the daylight in a superfluous effort to protect the faded and tattered carpets and upholstery from further damage from the sun. The furniture, one visitor noted, "looked as if it must have grown inside the house; it could scarcely have been chosen, bought, and brought into it, it was so entirely without character." The chairs were notoriously uncomfortable, too rickety to have been easy on her callers' middle-aged joints and spines. The *vieux* must have been parched as well, for the air in the room was thick with smoke; Laure burned through one Caporal-brand cigarette after another in her long, amber cigarette holder. Her devotees themselves, according to one of them, "did not smoke much, but [they] would occasionally gather strength . . . by helping [them]selves to a dusty lozenge out of a *bonbonnière* on the comtesse's table." Otherwise, the most refreshment her visitors could hope for was a glass or two of orangeade, probably tepid.

The drab décor at 1, avenue Percier did, however, contain a few zesty clues to Laure's charisma. The drawing of her by Monseigneur was one, but that picture didn't appear in her salon until 1883, by which time the *vieux* were already confirmed fixtures thereof. Another marker of her royal friendships was the collection of Fabergé boxes and pietra-dura knickknacks arrayed on the table beside her: "presents from [her] grand-ducs." These little *objets* confirmed the truth of Laure's self-description: however "poor in income," she was "rich in highnesses."

Another intriguing *objet* was a large bust of General Pierre Cambronne, an officer in the Napoleonic army infamous for having surrendered at Waterloo with an obscenity: *"Merde!"* Ever since, "the word of Cambronne" had been a jokey French synonym for that expletive, and while Laure never resorted to a euphemism when she could use a bawdier term instead, the general's bust stood on her mantel as a campy reminder of her own proclivity to curse. It also referred, more specifically, to one of her more scandalous claims to fame: she was the first *mondaine* ever heard to utter Cambronne's oath in public. The audacity of such an utterance is hard to recapture today, but it was extreme. And beguiling—her boldness kept her acolytes coming back for more, day after day, month after month, and, eventually, decade after decade.

The portrait of Laure's great-grandfather de Sade hinted at the atavistic nature of her rebelliousness and cast it in an even more titillating light. Her kinship with such an infamous degenerate may have scared away some suitors when she was in the market for a husband, but now that she was married—and miraculously free from spousal supervision—it was an incitement to male fantasy. Despite the age difference between them and her, the feeling that bound the *vieux* to Laure was in most cases not avuncular, at least not entirely so. When explaining why she so seldom allowed new guests into her daily conclaves, she joked, "My *vieux* growl when they smell fresh meat." One of the few outsiders to whom she did extend this privilege, an English noblewoman new to Paris, confirmed the predatory dimension of the clubmen's ardor, comparing them to tom-cats slavering at a bird.

Lily de Gramont, who was independently acquainted with most of the *vieux,* was also struck by their palpable attraction to Laure:

The Comtesse de Chevigné sat in a cloud of cigarette smoke, presiding over her group of clubmen. Hunched in their armchairs, they paid court to her, as if to thank her for being so pretty to look at and so droll to listen to, . . . chatting and joking in the slightly husky voice of a woman who smokes too much and stays out too late.

Laure's prettiness was in the eye of her beholders. Her petite figure was all bones, and her facial features all angles: sharp, high cheekbones, a jutting chin, and a curved beak of a nose that invited comparisons to various avian species (eagle, swan, falcon, buzzard, and "bird of the islands"). She wore her strawberry-blond hair pulled back in a tight, severe upsweep; a spray of frizzy curls around her forehead tried, and failed, to soften the effect. On a bad day, she looked like Pulcinella (Polichinelle), the hook-nosed Everyman from the commedia dell'arte and the Grand Guignol. On a good day, she resembled an angel, her eyes too blue and her hair too fair for earthly climes. And just about every day, she lived up to her nickname Corporal Petrarch, her "mannish air" a product not only of her protuberant nose and jaw but also of her trenchant, gravelly voice (which sounded to her contemporaries as if it had been "roughened by centuries of giving orders").

To her friend André Germain, the son of a prominent Parisian banker, Laure had "the uncanny air of a beautiful skeleton that had escaped from the prisons where her great-grandfather [de Sade] languished a hundred years before." To the Princesse Bibesco, she stood as the "very image of the Frenchwoman, the condensation of a thousand years of history, perfect like French roses and decanted like French wines." Germain's and Bibesco's metaphors touched on another vital component of the clubmen's affinity for Laure, and of hers for them. Consistent with her "bony and heraldic" looks, she shared their deep-seated nostalgia for the good old days when the aristocracy, just beneath the sovereign, reigned supreme. Not incidentally, this was the class to which virtually all of Laure's *vieux* belonged. To a man, they decried the forces of liberty

Laure made fun of herself for resembling Pulcinella, the hook-nosed clown from the commedia dell'arte, and she sometimes played up this resemblance at costume balls. This sketch is by Ferdinand Bac, a great-nephew of Napoléon I.

and equality that had toppled the ancien régime and had reached grievous new levels under the Third Republic. The social and political profile of Laure's salon regulars aligned perfectly with her own "belle of Frohsdorf" image.

For two of the *vieux,* Comte Albert de Mun and Henri Le Tonnelier, Marquis de Breteuil, this reactionary stance meant mounting an active opposition effort within the republican government. De Mun was a legitimist by birth (once upon a time, his maternal grandfather too had belonged to Henri V's *service d'honneur* in exile) and by conviction (a fervent Catholic, de Mun denounced the secularism of the republican left), and he had established himself as the voice of the extreme-right faction in the National Assembly. Famous for his rousing, fiery orations, he delivered such *cris de cœur* as "The Revolution is the enemy" and "Disorder and anarchy, social gangrene and moral rot: that is the meaning of the republic."

In addition to his eloquence, de Mun drew his authority from his unique ties to the Vatican. More than anyone else in France, he had the ear of Pope Leo XIII, so much so that his compatriots viewed him as a kind of homegrown papal nuncio, the pontiff's unofficial representative in their midst. When de Mun inveighed against the republic, it was therefore understood that he was voicing not just his party's opinion but the pope's. And for the time being, this was true, the anticlericalism of republican ideology having earned it few friends at St. Peter's.

Laure was proud to count de Mun among her loyalists in spite of his piety, which she found ungallant. When she flirted with him, as she did with all her *vieux,* he protested: "I am terribly sorry, Madame, but you see, I never cheat on my wife." De Mun's refusal to play along irritated Laure, but he more than made up for it with the vicarious papal mystique he brought to her salon. The pope himself, after all, was a crowned head, so de Mun's presence at Laure's at-homes increased her own cherished store of transitive royal cachet.

Henri de Breteuil was another monarchist leader in the Assembly working to combat the encroachments of democracy in France. Through his father, Breteuil descended from a long line of eminent courtiers and statesmen, as well as from one of the eighteenth century's most brilliant *salonnières,* Émilie du Châtelet, the first French translator of Newton and a longtime mistress of Voltaire. Like Laure with her middle-class merchant ancestors, Breteuil was rather less vocal about his "not born" relations on his mother's side. These were the Foulds, a very rich Jewish banking family. Their wealth allowed Breteuil to live in the manner of the *grands seigneurs* whose name he so proudly bore.

Like his good friend Henry Greffulhe, he favored a d'Orléans rather than a Bourbon restoration. He served for more than a decade as the Comte de Paris's official spokesperson in the lower chamber of the National Assembly, the Chamber of Deputies, where he voiced antirepublican sentiments of a piece with de Mun's. In the summer of 1889, as the government prepared to celebrate the hun-

Royalist statesman Albert de Mun *(left)* and monarchist historian Costa de Beauregard *(right)* were members of Laure's exclusive closed salon.

dredth anniversary of the fall of the Bastille on July 14, 1789, Breteuil declared on the floor of the Chamber that the Revolution had been an unmitigated disaster for the nation.

Other members of Laure's clique signaled their disenfranchisement by retreating from public life and devoting themselves conspicuously to patrician leisure. This was Fitz-James's approach. Once his time at Frohsdorf was through, he gave himself over to the pampered indolence to which he felt his birth entitled him and for which his loveless marriage to a Jewish heiress from Vienna, née Rosalie von Gutmann, provided the necessary funds. (While Fitz-James and Breteuil were both casually, reflexively anti-Semitic, they were perfectly willing to regild their blazons with Jewish gold.)

Comte Joseph de Gontaut, who being just eight years Laure's senior was the youngest of the *vieux,* was cut from equally patrician cloth. He came from old-line legitimist stock; several of his forebears had accompanied Charles X, the last of the Bourbons to occupy the French throne, into exile in 1830. In 1871, however, his father, Élie de Gontaut-Biron, had accepted a post as the Third Republic's ambassador to Prussia, only to be recalled six years later after a failed power grab by his royalist cronies at home. This incident led to Gontaut-Biron's forced resignation. Not long afterward, his son Joseph—an alumnus of France's top military academy, Saint-Cyr, and a decorated veteran of the Franco-Prussian War—resigned his own position as an army officer, breaking with a three-hundred-year family tradition of distinguished military service. (During the ancien régime, no fewer than four of Joseph de Gontaut's paternal ancestors had held the highest military post in the land, maréchal de France.) As one of twenty-one siblings, Joseph was "poor in income" himself. But he married a princess, Emma de Polignac, whose dowry helped to sustain his elegant lifestyle. Reputedly the finest horseman in Paris, Gontaut was a national steeplechase champion, and worked to popularize that traditionally English sport in France. He was also master of hounds in the Pyrenean resort town of Pau, home to an élite foxhunt.

Alfred, Marquis du Lau d'Allemans, whose father had served as a gentleman of the bedchamber to Charles X, was another paragon of elective sloth. Though du Lau had had a brief career as an Orléanist deputy in the Chamber, he gave up politics on the grounds that "the traditions of his family and the uprisings of the past hundred years made it [his] duty to wash [his] hands of any and all 'revolutionary' government." With typical *mondain* drollery, du Lau liked to say that he had retired from public life in order to train full-time for the annual clay-pigeon shoot in the Bois de Boulogne, a competition in which he routinely took top honors. He was also an enthusiastic amateur photographer. But his close friends knew that trading politics for clay pigeons and cameras was hard on du Lau. "His mannered idleness," one of them wrote, "was the mask behind which he gracefully hid the waste of his life [*son activité perdue*]"; accepting that there was no place for him in the government of his country "was one of his greatest acts of courage."

Charles-Albert, Marquis Costa de Beauregard—"Costa" to Laure—also acted for a time as a monarchist deputy, likewise stepping down when it became clear that his views would never align with those of the republicans in power. After he left office, he set to work on a four-volume opus, begun by his great-grandfather in 1816, about the Royal House of Savoy, which the Costa de Beauregards had served as valued advisers, courtiers, and officers since the seventeenth century.* Like Othenin d'Haussonville, his future colleague in the Académie Française, Costa comforted himself by resurrecting in writing the lost world where he and his kind had once held sway. As he wrote in an address to his late great-grandfather: "You attach us to the valiant generations of yesteryear," for the sake of whom

> I have endeavored to relive those olden days and to rediscover their memo-
> ries, veritable dried flowers taken from my heart like pages from a book.
> For the sake of those generations, too, and to make their descendants love

* The French royal family had a custom of intermarriage with the House of Savoy that dated back to the fifteenth-century unions of Louis XI with Charlotte de Savoie and of Charles d'Orléans with Louise de Savoie; the latter couple were the parents of François I. This custom survived up to the end of the ancien régime, culminating in the marriages of Louis XVI's two younger brothers, the future Louis XVIII and Charles X, with two daughters of Savoy. Henri V's paternal grandmother was thus a Savoyard. In 1861, Vittorio Emanuele II, Duke of Savoy, became the first king of the unified Kingdom of Italy; his sons were Umberto I of Italy and the Duke d'Aosta, who ruled Spain from 1870 to 1873 as Amadeo I.

the princes they themselves loved so much, [I have] taken up and completed these memoirs of the Royal House of Savoy.

The nostalgia in Costa's writings echoed a sentiment d'Haussonville voiced
in his book about Mme Necker: "Bringing the ashes of the past back to life [in
these] pages . . . may create something of a mirage, but as long as the mirage
lasts, the illusion it imparts is singularly intoxicating and sweet."

Much the same illusion predominated in Laure's salon. In the outside world,
de Mun wrote, he and his peers were beset on all sides by "men of the future."
But among themselves, they remained "men of the past," and they were never
happier than when they could counter the realities of modern democratic society with the mirage of ancien régime entitlement. Between her patrician identity and her legitimist bona fides, Laure was the perfect figurehead for such an
enterprise. As her visiting English friend observed, the *vieux* treated her dim,
musty drawing room as a "Presence Chamber" and the lady of the house as their
queen: a sacred authority in a profane world and a privileged witness to shattered power.

Had Laure lived in a later century, she would almost surely have conceived of
herself as a brand. She anticipated something that has since become the linchpin
of many a celebrity's public-relations strategy—namely, that one's image should
be consistent enough for one's fans to recognize it but variable enough to retain
their interest. At its core, her "bride of Pluto" routine struck a powerful chord
with her contemporaries because it connected to a larger narrative about hereditary privilege and its tragic fall.

Understanding this, Laure expanded her repertoire to include another variation on the theme: the tribulations of the indomitable, intrepid Donatien,
Marquis de Sade. On her salon wall, her placement of her great-grandfather's
portrait right next to Monseigneur's sketch of her and her parrots acted as a
handy conversational prompt. If she sensed her friends growing restive at her
standard conversational fare—that old "kingdom of shadows" routine—she
could flick her cigarette holder in Donatien's direction and switch seamlessly to
another chapter in her extended family history. From playmate of the Prince de
Condé to prisoner in the Bastille, and from grave digger at Picpus to in-patient
at Charenton, de Sade had known a downward trajectory every bit as dramatic
as Henri V's, with a hefty dose of debauchery to make it even more exciting.
Toggling between the dullness of Frohsdorf and the dungeons of "the divine
marquis," Laure fulfilled her companions' yearning for the dark, sexy glamour
of a civilization their ancestors had ruled—and lost.

LAURE'S MYSTIQUE AS A FEUDAL PROSERPINA was so central
to her *mondain* stature that one might have expected her cachet to dwindle
after Monseigneur's death in August 1883. But in fact her celebrity only grew.

Laure went into mourning for the Austro-Hungarian archduke Rudolf, as pictured here, following his suicide in January 1889, even though she had never met him. She took every opportunity to showcase her royalist allegiances.

Besides her media contacts and her closed salon, there were two main reasons for her continued rise. First, in case any of Laure's peers had ever suspected her of overstating Monseigneur's affection for her, his alleged deathbed quip about "*la vieille*" (which she obligingly leaked to Meyer) seemed irrefutably to support her claims, and the *vieux* could confirm the existence of that caricature drawn by his hand. Second, she benefited from the special reverence with which the nobility viewed its royal martyrs. Being the Revolution's best-known princely casualties, Louis XVI, Marie Antoinette, and their young son, Louis XVII, had epitomized royal martyrdom for pretty much the entire nineteenth century. But as the last in a lifelong series of misfortunes, the death on foreign soil of their kinsman, Henri V, had elevated him into their storied ranks.*

Throughout the noble Faubourg, even those who had not rallied around Chambord during his lifetime lionized him in death as the embodiment of a gracious and endangered *temps perdu*. Typical of this response was Princesse Mathilde Bonaparte's decision to adopt "le bouquet du Comte de Chambord" as her new signature fragrance. Politically, Princesse Mathilde was a Bonapartist, as befitted her family name and origins. But because her Bonaparte relatives

---

* To recap the woes of Henri V and his family: Louis XVI and Marie Antoinette dethroned, jailed, beheaded. Their son, Louis XVII, jailed, abused, murdered by his guards. Their daughter, the Duchesse d'Angoulême, traumatized by the Revolution, childless, dead in exile. Monseigneur's grandfather, Charles X, dethroned, banished, dead in exile. His father, the Duc de Berry, assassinated before he (Henri) was even born. His mother, the Duchesse de Berry, jailed for plotting to place him on Louis-Philippe's throne, banished, dead in exile. His marriage, childless. His heirs, the hateful d'Orléans. His flag, abandoned. His kingdom: lost. His horse, Popular Demand. And the rest, so to speak, was history, including his own aborted coup d'état and—the coup de grâce—his own death in exile.

had lost their throne as well, she was sensitive to Chambord's plight and generically nostalgic for a time when crowned heads ruled the land. The same feeling inspired the Princesse de Sagan, a staunch Orléanist, to serve "carp à la Chambord" as a first course at a dinner she hosted for a d'Orléans highness shortly after the Bourbon pretender's death.

Such gestures honored the deceased less for his specific political views (which, centering on the rejection of the tricolor French flag, had been misguided to say the least) or achievements (which had been nil) than for his value as, in one Orléanist pundit's words, "a glorious symbol . . . of the majesty and glory of the past, . . . of the prestige of the monarchy, born of fourteen centuries of honor, faith, and unwavering fortitude." In this climate, Laure's Frohsdorf narrative became more potent than ever. It reassured the gratin that Monseigneur and the royal ideal he represented remained very much alive in spirit if not in fact, embodied by his winning and indomitable favorite.

Fueled by monarchist nostalgia, Laure's popularity translated into a new abundance of invitations to the Faubourg's choicest revels. For her first four years in Paris, she had failed to make the guest list for the Princesse de Sagan's annual costume ball. Nine months after Monseigneur's funeral, however, Mme de Sagan tapped Laure to attend not only the ball but the select dinner for a hundred that preceded it. And there was more: with more than a thousand invitees to choose from, the princesse bestowed upon Laure one of the twenty coveted roles in the professionally choreographed dance number that served as the ball's traditional highlight.

Playing up her affinity for Marie Antoinette, Mme de Sagan had instructed her guests that year to dress in peasant garb, as she would be entertaining them in a quaint half-timbered country village modeled on the Queen's Hamlet at Versailles (a setting the princesse had reconstructed at incalculable expense in the gardens behind her *hôtel*). The Hamlet, as the "born" all knew, had been Marie Antoinette's escape from the rigors of etiquette at Versailles; it was the place where she and her friends had decked themselves out as humble country folk, drinking fresh cream in the queen's picturesque marble dairy and cavorting among flocks of specially perfumed sheep. In light of this history, a formal *ballet de cour* would have been grossly out of place, so Mme de Sagan assigned her dancers a suitably rustic alternative: a raucous foot-stomping bourrée.

This was a daring choice on the hostess's part, and it was not necessarily to the taste of nobles who no longer had the luxury of complaining about the tedium of court ceremony. Even the reliably fawning *Le Gaulois* demurred, calling the bourrée "the cabbage soup of choreography." But Laure must have been delighted with the selection, for which her country-girl persona and natural athleticism were so well suited. The wooden clogs the princesse had asked the dancers to wear tripped up some of the troupe's less agile members. But Laure executed the bourrée with crowd-pleasing élan.

She received another boost from the performance that followed the bourrée: a professional diva's rendition of an aria from Jacques Offenbach's *Geneviève de Brabant* (1859). Thanks to this selection, Laure was able to drop the name of an alleged ancestor whom she invoked less often than she did Laure de Noves or the Marquis de Sade but of whom she was also quite proud. That ancestor was Marie de Brabant, a medieval noblewoman falsely accused of having cheated on her husband while he was off fighting in the Crusades. During her husband's absence, the story went, another man came on to Marie, and when she rebuffed him, he avenged himself by charging her with adultery. She was put to death for her supposed crime, only to have her name cleared afterward, leading to the genesis of a popular folk legend that rechristened her Geneviève in honor of Paris's patron saint. During the Second Empire, Jacques Offenbach had caused a sensation with his opera-buffa adaptation of the tale. But Laure had been an infant at the time, and since then, the popularity of *Geneviève de Brabant* had fizzled along with that of the opera buffa genre generally. As a result, she hadn't found many pretexts for casually mentioning this branch of her family tree. That such an occasion should present itself at her first Sagan ball was a happy coincidence, allowing her to impress her Brabant connection upon her lineage-conscious cohorts.

Laure won further points that evening for her fetchingly simple costume: a little lace mobcap and frilly apron paired with a striped homespun dress. To reporters, she identified herself as "a baker woman à la Louis XVI." This designation was less benign than it may sound, as it alluded to an early chapter

Laure in her cheeky "baker-woman" garb with her friend Costa at the Princesse de Sagan's 1884 peasant ball.

in the story of Louis XVI's and his family's "martyrdom." On the evening of October 5, 1789, a mob of hungry Parisians had marched on Versailles, where they (wrongly) suspected that the king and queen were stockpiling large caches of flour. The marauders stormed the gates and killed the guards. Then they ran amok through the palace, screaming that they wanted to slaughter "the baker-woman"—Marie Antoinette—and drink her blood. In the end, the invaders had settled for capturing the royal family and bringing them back to Paris by force. But the episode had marked the beginning of the end for the French monarchy, as Laure, like all *nobles d'épée,* was well aware. By styling herself "a baker woman à la Louis XVI," Laure thus affiliated herself with Marie Antoinette, and more specifically with the Marie Antoinette victimized by the Revolution. In this way, Laure again cast herself as an archetype of France's martyred ruling class.

Beyond the attention of the other ballgoers, Laure's ensemble earned her one last, special distinction: an illustration in *L'Art et la mode,* a short-lived fashion magazine cofounded by her friend Geneviève Bizet's cousin Ludovic Halévy. The political overtones of her dress were not lost on this publication's pseudonymous reporter, who observed with laconic "Meilhac and Halévy wit": "Looking at pretty Mme de C*******, one is almost tempted to forgive the masses for always pillaging bakeries and starting revolutions!"

Despite her own affinity for Marie Antoinette, the Princesse de Sagan did not appear to resent Laure's baker-woman ploy. As an experienced hostess, she knew a stellar party guest when she saw one, and Laure had decidedly made the grade. From then on, the princesse never failed to include her in the annual Sagan ball and preparty dinner.

She invited Laure as well to smaller, even more selective gatherings with her own personal version of the *vieux:* the d'Orléans princes, who as the new heirs to the French throne became invaluable connections for Laure. In her milieu, what ultimately mattered most was not who wore the crown but who stood the closest to the throne and shone the brightest in its reflected glory. Laure grasped this notion intuitively and embraced it without apology. She hadn't survived Passy, the provinces, and the kingdom of shadows merely to see herself plunged back into obscurity once again. Pluto was dead. Long live Proserpina.

CHAPTER SIX

GOOD FOR THE GOOSE

"Proserpina's husband," as the gratin dubbed Adhéaume de Chevigné, attended the 1884 Sagan ball with Laure, but that was a rarity for him. He tended to feel miserable at such large, frivolous functions, and as well mannered as he was, it showed. One aristocrat noted that when Laure's husband did happen to make an appearance at a big society do, he looked like a bird who had been buffeted about in a tempest and was roosting on the mast of a ship just long enough to gather his strength before he made himself fly back out into the storm. Certainly Chevigné hadn't had to endure such intensive socializing at Frohsdorf. Once he moved back to Paris, it was harder to avoid, but he managed. Although less dismissive than his wife of the imperatives of *bon ton,* Chevigné drew a distinction between public appearances that demonstrated his allegiance to his family or his (late) king—such as weddings, funerals, and commemorations of various Bourbon births and deaths—and those of a more strictly *mondain* nature. The latter he eschewed whenever possible, leaving Laure to pursue her freewheeling social life without him.

Chevigné kept busy in his own way. His years at Frohsdorf having accustomed him to a considerable degree of structure in his schedule, he established a comfortably predictable routine in Paris. After breakfast each morning, he would stroll over to the Jockey-Club in the rue Scribe, a short, easy walk from his and Laure's place in the avenue Percier. Settling into an armchair in the trophy room, named for the taxidermied animal heads that lined its walls, he would read the morning papers until one o'clock. Then he would break for lunch, which at the Jockey was always a tasty affair thanks to the club's cook, vaunted in gourmet circles as the sole living rival to the German kaiser's personal chef de cuisine. While the clubhouse emptied out between lunch and dinner as the members went off to their lady friends' salons (including his wife's) and later to the Bichonne, Chevigné stayed put, resuming his reading in the trophy room until dinner. After taking the latter meal, too, in the members' dining room, he would either indulge in a cigar and a card game in the *fumoir* or head out for an evening on his own. As Parisian clubmen went, Chevigné had an atypical fondness for solitude.

Depending on the night of the week, his preferred destinations were the Opéra, the Opéra-Comique, and the Théâtre-Français. While he seldom missed a new performance at any of these venues—the Jockey had members' loges at all three—he steered clear of them on the subscription evenings that drew Laure

The Jockey-Club was Chevigné's home away from home in Paris. He would spend time here while his fellow club members trooped over to call on his wife each day after lunch.

and her *mondain* pals. To Albert Flament, a sweet-faced homosexual author who became friendly with both him and Laure, Chevigné looked more "like a stern old soldier or hermit" than a sophisticated culture buff. Nevertheless, the comte took the performing arts seriously and preferred to enjoy them undisturbed. The posing and gossip that absorbed Laure and her friends at the theater did not appeal to him in the least. For Chevigné, the play really was the thing.

Some afternoons and evenings his routine varied slightly, if there was an event he was eager to attend at his other favorite haunt in Paris: the Société de Géographie. Whereas the Jockey catered primarily to aristocratic sportsmen (it had been founded in 1833 to promote horse breeding and horse racing in France), the Société de Géographie drew a more studious, intellectual member-ship. At its headquarters in the boulevard Saint-Germain, it offered lectures by noted explorers and scholars, and every few years, its programming committee organized a conference around an international theme.

Chevigné had attended one such colloquium during his and Laure's first trip back from Frohsdorf to Paris in May 1879. The keynote speaker at this event, Ferdinand, Vicomte de Lesseps, had impressed him no end. World famous for having developed the Suez Canal in Africa (completed in 1869), Lesseps unveiled a new plan to the members of the Société de Géographie: the construction of a similar canal in Panama, Central America. His presentation electrified the audience, as his speaking engagements often did. ("Lesseps has total faith in the success of his enterprise . . . ," one of his admirers said. "He could convince God Himself that A equals B.") Chevigné found Lesseps so inspiring that he decided to stake some of his and Laure's savings in the venture, which was formally founded that day as the Panama Canal Company. It was an investment decision the Chevignés would come to regret.

Once retired from Frohsdorf, Chevigné did not rekindle his past relationship with Émilie "the Seal" Williams, who had gone into retirement herself. For a time, rumors circulated in Paris that Williams had abandoned her métier in order to write a tell-all autobiography. But her real motive for leaving the business was less salacious: like many courtesans approaching their twilight years, she had found Christ and abjured her sinful ways. A grizzled clubman who had known Williams before her return to Jesus spotted her at Mass at the Église Saint-Augustin. He wrote in his memoirs,

> If you have been to eleven o'clock services at Saint-Augustin of late, you may have noticed a woman of a certain age, well preserved, dressed with the utmost modesty and plainness, holding a prayer book in her hands, her eyes downcast, kneeling in a humble attitude in a pew on the far-right side of the nave, at a noticeable remove from the rest of the congregation. This respectable-looking *bourgeoise,* who is visibly anxious to avoid prying eyes and familiar faces, is, or used to be, Émilie Williams, latterly an éminence grise of the demimonde. Now she is retired, and wants only privacy in her old age.

Apart from this mention by an old acquaintance, Williams seems to have found the privacy she was looking for. Her name disappeared from the chronicles of the demimonde, and her motto, "the Seal says *mama,* the Seal says *papa,*" fell out of circulation, too. (Avant-garde author Guillaume Apollinaire revived it a generation later, though, in the aptly entitled poem "The Seal.") Nothing in the source record indicates that Chevigné even tried to reconnect with Williams once he moved home from Frohsdorf, nor, for that matter, does he appear to have replaced her with another cocotte.

But he may have replaced her with somebody even more controversial: a bright, bespectacled nobleman fourteen years his junior, Bruno Marie Terrasson, Baron de Senevas. When Chevigné first met him in 1886, probably at the Société de Géographie, Senevas, twenty-four, was still a bachelor, and despite his widowed mother's constant entreaties that he settle down, he was doing his best to remain single. His real passion was traveling. In the summer of 1882, after graduating from law school, he had rewarded himself with a brief jaunt to Belgium and Holland. A year and a half later, he took a longer and more ambitious trip, touring Scandinavia, Russia, the Middle East, and North Africa with a group of friends from university. Senevas's plan had been to remain abroad indefinitely, but in 1885 his paternal grandmother, who had been funding his adventures, died. He returned to France for her funeral and had been living with his mother in Paris ever since.

To avoid her hectoring on the subject of marriage, Senevas took refuge in the library at the Société de Géographie, where he was availing himself of the club's collection of travel materials to chart the itinerary for his next voyage: to America and Southeast Asia. Chevigné, possibly suffering from wanderlust now that he was no longer making regular trips back to Austria, joined him in his research. Together the two men whiled away many a happy afternoon in the hush of the Société's wood-paneled library, plotting exciting journeys to far-flung lands.

In the spring of 1887, they implemented their plans, taking off together on a voyage around the world. On March 19, they boarded the paquebot *Bretagne* at Le Havre and disembarked in Manhattan nine days later. The Personal Intelligence section of the *New York Herald* noted that Chevigné and Senevas had taken rooms at the Hoffman House, a luxury hotel on Madison Square. By June, they were in San Francisco, where their arrival again drew the notice of the local press:

> Count A. de Chevigné and Baron de Senevas, both of Paris, are quartered at the Palace [Hotel in San Francisco]. They are circling the sphere merely on pleasure intent, and will sail for Japan by the next steamer.

Apart from the passenger manifest from the *Bretagne* and the announcement in the *Herald*, this mention in the *Daily Alta California* is the only documented mention of the duo's voyage. If Chevigné or Senevas wrote about it to their loved ones back home, those letters have not survived, although according to Senevas's mother's autobiography, he did notify her that he and his friend were going to make a detour to Siam. He also sent word to her that he was so "exhausted" he was considering staying permanently in Asia. However, both he and Chevigné came back to Paris in the spring of 1888.

Neither their world tour nor their return home wound up in the papers in Paris—an oversight that seems puzzling at first blush given the interest their

Chevigné and the young Baron de Senevas sailed from Le Havre to New York City on this ship in March 1887, beginning a trip around the world that would last for over a year.

This magic-lantern slide depicts the lobby of Hoffman House, the hotel where Chevigné and Senevas stayed while in New York.

adventures would undoubtedly have held for the *presse mondaine*. *Le Gaulois* featured a weekly column about the gratin's travels to parts far (foreign nations and foreign courts) and near (villas in Normandy, castles in the Seine-et-Marne). In excluding the Senevas/Chevigné trip from this column, Arthur Meyer may have been doing a favor for Laure, since the mere announcement that the two men had taken off together for a year would have caused a scandal, even had the report made no insinuations about the nature of their friendship. However she felt about the potential damage to her husband's reputation, Laure would almost surely have wanted to keep the story out of the news to protect her own image. Appealing to Meyer for help would have been a natural move on her part, and given the kindness she had always shown him, granting it would have been a natural move on his. The episode did, however, appear to justify Meyer's private conviction that "in [the] monde, three out of every five men are pederasts."

Senevas's mother, the Dowager Baronne de Senevas, was just as determined to preempt a scandal and independently took action. Before her son's departure for New York, she had been hell-bent on seeing him paired off with a young lady of noble birth. But when he came home, the dowager baronne evidently decided that it would be better for her Bruno to marry a middle-class bride than to remain a bachelor of questionable erotic leanings. So she lowered her sights and arranged a match for him with Marie-Élise Carmier, twenty-two, the daughter of a bourgeois merchant. In her memoirs, the dowager baronne could (and did) go on for pages about seeing the Duchesse de Bisaccia at a charity bazaar or the Comtesse de Paris at a party. Yet so great was her ambivalence about the union her son's misconduct had forced her to make that she dispatched with his engagement and wedding in one short line, identifying neither the Carmiers nor her new daughter-in-law by name. In his own multivolume memoirs, Senevas makes a perhaps related omission. While he writes at length about his prior travels abroad, he avoids all mention of his year-long voyage with Chevigné. The two friends appear to have fallen out of contact after Senevas married in December.

Laure never talked about her husband's trip either, though to the extent that anyone in her milieu caught wind of it, it must have caused her some embarrassment. By the same token, she herself was no model spouse—quite the opposite. Impelled, as she told Coco Chanel some decades later, by "a real taste for '*that*' [*ça*]—for *f**king*," and having concluded that her husband had nothing to teach her on the subject, Laure took it upon herself to "learn about '*that*' from a lover" instead. Furthermore, her infidelity seems to have predated Chevigné's by at least a few years, meaning that it was not just a spiteful reaction to her husband's involvement with Senevas. If anything, her adultery would have justified Chevigné's, not the other way around.

Laure may have rationalized her dalliances using the same logic she brought to bear on all her other acts of rebellion: the standard rules of propriety didn't apply to her. But she did respect the *mondain* convention that called for the utmost discretion when conducting extramarital affairs. She kept her secrets by minimizing written records of her private life, reasoning with a grin that as all letters were either incriminating or boring, the best policy was to avoid writing them at all.

The men from whom Laure sought her sexual education shared her sense of tact, romancing her in their *garçonnières*: bachelor pads in remote parts of town where no one from their world would be likely to spot them. To go to these assignations, Laure would put on a hat with a dainty little veil—the fewer people who saw her face on these excursions, the better—and would toddle off to a museum, a department store, or some other innocuous public place. From there her lover would collect her in a *fiacre*, the horse-drawn equivalent of a taxicab, and whisk her off to his hideaway for an afternoon of love.

THE FIRST OF LAURE'S PARAMOURS was apparently Fitz-James himself. For all the precautions an adulterous couple might take, in a world as small, gossipy, and idle as the Faubourg, secret passions seldom remained secret. And so it was that when, in an undated diary entry from 1886, Constance de Breteuil referred in passing to Laure's involvement with Fitz-James, she treated it as a well-known fact. (As the wife, however, of one of Laure's other *vieux*, Constance may have had inside information about the couple's liaison.) Constance was the same age as Laure, twenty-four years younger than Fitz-James, and described him as an over-the-hill roué whose glory days lay far behind him:

A faded hero with one foot in the grave, Robert de Fitz-James probably made more conquests in his day than any other man of his generation! In his prime he was terribly handsome, debonair, full of breeding [*plein de race*], good at everything, with a mocking, devilish charm that drove women wild and made them fall at his feet like trampled grass.

Casually dismissive of the faded hero's attractions, Constance didn't realize that it was she who had one foot in the grave. She died of tuberculosis in the summer of 1886, within months of writing this journal entry; she was only twenty-seven. Fitz-James lived to be sixty-five, not dying until 1900.

In the meantime, he still had enough of the devil in him to inspire a passionate attachment in Laure. In Austria, he had won her trust with his infallible guidance about court protocol. In Paris, along with helping start her salon, he advised her as to which invitations she should accept or decline, which acquaintances she should cultivate or snub. As at Frohsdorf, these seemingly trivial matters were not trivial at all; how Laure handled them could do much to bolster her social standing or undercut it.

From Fitz-James, Laure learned that the gratin conceived of its social hierarchy somewhat differently from that of a royal court, by taking into consideration factors other than birth and service to the crown. For example, the ravishing Louise, Marquise d'Hervey de Saint-Denys, known as "the Blond Cleopatra," had been born the daughter of a stable boy to the Duc de Parme, the Comte de Chambord's nephew; her older sister was a circus performer, and their mother was a Viennese Jew. Yet by dint of her beauty and title—the latter acquired through her marriage to a distinguished Sinologist twice her age—Louise had reinvented herself as a *grande mondaine*. Similarly, Charles Haas's elegance, charm, and unerring taste made him not only an acceptable but a desirable companion, his Jewishness notwithstanding.

On Fitz-James's advice, Laure befriended both of these society figures, though she would later have an acrimonious falling-out with the Blond Cleopatra when, following the Marquis d'Hervey's death, Louise had the audacity to marry Jacques de Waru, the eldest of Laure's sister's three sons. (Socializing with a stable boy's daughter was one thing; welcoming her into the family was quite another.) Despite this unfortunate incident, Laure would maintain throughout her life that Fitz-James had taught her everything she needed to know about the monde.

Their romance foundered briefly in 1886, when he failed to let Laure know that he had decided to marry Rosalie von Gutmann. Perpetually broke, he regarded the union as a straightforward business deal: Rosalie, a Jewish heiress from Vienna (and presumably no relation to the Blond Cleopatra's mother), would get his title, and Fitz-James would get her cash. But Laure took a different view. In her diary, Constance de Breteuil wrote that Fitz-James's sudden betrothal "has caused rivers of tears to flow all over Paris. It has come as such a violent shock to little Mme de Chevigné, his mistress, that she took to her bed three days ago, pretending to have the flu." Laure herself conceded long afterward that Fitz-James's betrayal had cut her to the quick. She added, however, that her consciousness of her origins had helped her to take it in stride:

> F[itz-James] was in love with me; at least, I thought he was. One day, after I had been away on a trip, I went out to a big dinner party in town. In the foyer, I happened to glance at the guest book and saw: "the Comte and Comtesse R[obert] de F[itz-James]." The scoundrel had gone and gotten hitched without telling me! I thought I was going to fall apart, but I pulled myself up and said to myself: *You are Laure de Chevigné, née de Sade.*

Laure's sangfroid evidently served her well. The proverbial ink on Fitz-James's marriage contract had scarcely dried before reports began to circulate that he had "already revived his previous relationship" with Mme de Chevigné. Punning on the name of the painter Rosa Bonheur (literally: Rosa Happiness), society wags dubbed his bride Rosa Malheur (Unhappiness). The new Comtesse de Fitz-James embraced her position by coining a wittily self-deprecating mantra: "I am ugly, I am dumb, and *that is my chic*." She also started keeping a list of all the French aristocratic houses that had contracted marriages with Israelites. Well aware of the monde's anti-Semitism, Rosa said that the list was for her own protection.

For *her* own protection, Laure diversified her portfolio of lovers. Sometime in the early to mid-1880s, she started up a parallel affair with another of her *vieux,* Joseph de Gontaut. He and Fitz-James were "a little bit cousins" and in fact had much in common. Like Fitz-James, Gontaut came from august stock: his ancestors included Charlemagne, William the Conqueror, and Hugues Capet, the first of the Frankish kings. Thanks, more recently, to his father's stint as ambassador to Prussia, Gontaut was "rich in highnesses"; rather like Élisabeth Greffulhe, he had used his father's time abroad as an opportunity to cultivate his own relationships with Europe's crowned heads.

Gontaut was gregarious and urbane, blessed with a je ne sais quoi known in the Faubourg as "the charm of the Gontauts." Described as "one of the most popular men in all of Paris," he was especially popular with the fairer sex and had cut a swath through the monde and the demimonde alike. Because of his relative penury, he had had to contract a marriage of convenience to the rich, docile, and adoring Princesse Emma de Polignac, whose love for him bordered, Constance de Breteuil felt, on "insane hero worship." While Gontaut did not reciprocate Emma's devotion, he did spend liberally from her dowry.

By all accounts, Laure was crazy for Gontaut as well. But his affections turned out to be as unreliable as Fitz-James's. One day, a few years into his and Laure's

Laure de Chevigné strolls in Paris with Joseph de Gontaut, her good friend and on-again, off-again lover. Photograph by Gégé Primoli.

affair, Gontaut ran off with an American woman named Mrs. Winthrop, who had been living in Pau with her husband, an expatriate Boston Brahmin and foxhunting enthusiast. Unbeknownst to both his wife and Laure, Gontaut had been carrying on a torrid liaison with Mrs. Winthrop in Pau for almost three years. After breaking the news to Emma by letter—again channeling Fitz-James, he didn't bother to send word to Laure—Gontaut announced to all the world that Mrs. Winthrop was the love of his life.

While Laure was galled by this turn of events, once more she kept her cool. Meeting Mrs. Winthrop at a ball in Paris a few years after Gontaut's betrayal, she said to her with a frosty smile, "Thank you so much for sparing me Joseph's old age." In the end, though, Laure wasn't spared Joseph's old age. He and his American sweetheart had to part ways when they realized they couldn't survive without their spouses' wealth. And although Mrs. Winthrop's husband didn't take her back—he had moved on to her sister, whom he said he had always secretly preferred—both Emma and Laure welcomed Gontaut with open arms. He and Laure remained an item off and on for the next twenty-five years.

For all his fickleness, Gontaut possessed something that, to Laure, was arguably even more essential than romantic constancy: a circle of exceptionally high-born, high-placed friends. It was he who first introduced Laure to several of the *mondain* personalities with whom she would become famously linked. The most important introduction Gontaut made for her was to Grand-Duc and Grande-Duchesse Wladimir of Russia, the GDWs to their intimates. In the Faubourg, there were few figures more prestigious than they, for as the eldest of the four (legitimate) younger brothers of Alexander III (Sasha), the grand-duc Wladimir enjoyed a level of power and prestige in his homeland that was second only to that of the tsar himself, the dread Autocrat of All the Russias. For his official functions, he acted as the commander of the Imperial Guard and the governor of Saint Petersburg, where he and his wife, Maria Pawlowna, née Herzogin Marie (Miechen) von Mecklenburg-Schwerin, inhabited a magnificent palace on the Neva. Built to resemble a fifteenth-century Florentine palazzo, the Wladimir Palace became the gathering place for the couple's own glittering royal court, also rivaled only by that of the tsar. Not without some justification, the GDWs were suspected of eyeing the imperial throne for themselves—and later for their son. (In October 1888, the tsar and his family nearly perished in a train wreck that killed twenty-three people, prompting Sasha to joke afterward, "Imagine Wladimir's disappointment when he hears we've survived!")

In the Faubourg, however, the grand-duc cultivated a reputation as the tsar's favorite brother, and this sobriquet stuck. Ardent Francophiles, the GDWs stopped off in Paris at least twice a year on their way to and from Cannes, where their haut-luxe, around-the-clock revelry established the paradigm for jet-setting three or four generations before jets came into existence. In Paris, the press chronicled the culinary excesses of "le Grand-Duc Bon Vivant" (an insatiable gourmand, Wladimir kept annotated menus of all his meals) and the extravagant shopping habits of the grande-duchesse, reputed to be Cartier's single best customer. (She had one of the finest jewelry collections in the world.)

Gontaut had known Miechen since the early years of his father's ambassadorship to her native Germany, when he was in his twenties and she in her late teens. They had stayed in touch after her marriage, and the grand-duc, an impassioned sportsman, had grown immensely fond of Gontaut as well. Both of the GDWs took an immediate liking to their friend's pretty young paramour. Laure's love of hunting and riding met with the grand-duc's immediate approval, as did her predilection for coarse language, which he shared. Not unlike the late Henri V, with whom his wife had been "a little bit cousins," the grand-duc was a stickler for etiquette who nonetheless enjoyed disrupting ceremonial occasions with lewd jokes and puerile clowning. While outwardly more proper than her husband, the grande-duchesse was no shrinking violet. Rumored in Saint Petersburg to "dominate her husband completely," she was tough, intelligent, and fiercely independent. She was the first Romanov bride in history who had refused to convert to Russian Orthodoxy upon her marriage. The self-possession

Grand-Duc and Grande-Duchesse Wladimir of Russia, aka the GDWs, made frequent pleasure trips to Paris, where Laure served as their favorite companion and guide.

and courage that went into that decision were qualities Miechen was delighted to discover in Laure.

Another important introduction Gontaut made for Laure was to a French grande dame nearly twenty years older than she, the Duchesse de La Trémoïlle. Like most of Laure's *vieux,* Henri de Breteuil was a good friend of the duchesse. He described her candidly in his journal:

> Despite the great fondness I have for her, I must say that she is ugly, very ugly, with a huge head, excessively thick hair, coarse features, a mouth that seems to contain only one tooth, and . . . small, if kind and intelligent, eyes. . . . Her waist . . . is too thick, and her complexion too florid. But beneath this crude exterior, one finds the best, noblest, most generous heart, . . . and the sharpest, wittiest mind.

Laure and the duchesse became fast friends and fell into a habit of getting together daily for a late-morning tête-à-tête in the La Trémoïlles' mansion on the place de la Concorde, an easy walk from the Chevignés. Afterward, they would head off on their respective daily social calls, and Laure would go home for her salon. At five o'clock, she would return to the hôtel de La Trémoïlle, where she and the duchesse would debrief each other over a game of whist.

This routine enabled Laure to drop her august friend's name in conversation often yet without appearing to brag. The association with the duchesse was indeed something to brag about, though, and not just because of her rank. The daughter of an influential minister to Louis-Philippe, Marguerite-Jeanne de La Trémoïlle was a longtime intimate of the d'Orléans family, so her *mondain* prestige increased immeasurably once the Comte de Paris became the pretender to the French throne. And just as the d'Orléans' heightened glory reflected well on the duchesse, so did her heightened glory reflect well on Laure.

Mme de La Trémoïlle also happened to be a fanatical sportswoman. The shooting parties she and her husband hosted every fall at Serrant, their majestic castle in the Loire, were high points of the *mondain* hunting season, and Laure never missed a one. Whereas other guests might only be invited for a few days' shooting, she usually stayed for at least a month, another mark of the special esteem in which the hostess held her. During these visits Laure grew fond of the duc as well, even though he preferred poring over his ancestral records (he was an avid genealogist and family historian) to hunting on his ancestral lands.

With his studious, retiring personality and his absorption in noble glories past, the duc had quite a bit in common with Laure's husband. But Chevigné seldom joined his wife at Serrant, preferring to spend his *villégiatures* at the domaine de Cabannes, his and Laure's property in the Midi, where he experimented with irrigation methods for the vineyard. This arrangement made it possible for Gontaut to act as Laure's cavalier at Serrant (leaving his wife Emma at home). Their hostess raised no objection to her young friends' romance, provided that they keep up the requisite façade of decency in front of her other invitees. Nonetheless, rumors swirled in the monde about Laure's wanton antics at Serrant; Élisabeth Greffulhe recorded that while a guest at a certain château, Mme de Chevigné was seen sneaking in and out of "a bedroom other than hers" at odd hours of the night.

The Duc and Duchesse de La Trémoïlle hosted Laure at Serrant, their château in the Loire, every year for a month during hunting season.

If Laure was aware of this chatter, she certainly did not take it as a cue to change her ways. In Paris, too, she spent much of her time with Gontaut, whose sporting habits dovetailed so nicely with her own. They often took afternoon rides together in the see-and-be-seen Bichonne, where, keeping pace with Gontaut, Laure got noticed early and often. Between her own equestrian ability and her presence beside a legend of the horse-and-hound set, she soon became one of the breakout stars of the Bichonne, as an article in the *Gil Blas* confirmed. In June 1884, the paper ran a front-page list of proposed floral nicknames for the city's leading *mondaines*. The idea was that botanical epithets would help to distinguish these ladies from the stylish demimondaines who also paraded up and down the Bichonne and were typically tagged with animal aliases (such as "the Seal"). The floral epithets didn't stick, but Laure's was "Acacia," a reference to the thoroughfare's official name, the allée des Acacias.

As a gathering spot for the city's élite, the Bichonne also served as an unofficial runway for new fashion trends. In this respect, too, Laure benefited from her association with Gontaut, whose rugged athleticism belied an unerring sense of style. His friend Boni de Castellane liked to tell a story about how the republican politician Paul Deschanel sent him, Boni, an urgent plea for clothing advice right after being elected to high office (a request that betrayed the chronic insecurity of the "not born" when it came to matters of taste). As the nephew of the Prince de Sagan and an acclaimed clotheshorse in his own right, Boni could easily have offered a few pointers. But instead, he told Deschanel, "There is one man who can offer you better advice about this than I can, and that is Comte Joseph de Gontaut." Whether Gontaut consented to advise Deschanel is unknown, though the statesman wound up making an unimpeachable choice with Charvet, a renowned tailor on the place Vendôme.

But Gontaut's real fashion specialty was making over the wardrobes of attractive *mondaines*. One of his biggest success stories was Boni's sister-in-law, Comtesse Jean (Dolly) de Castellane, who owed her status as a society belle in large part to Gontaut's good offices. Also the half-sister of the Prince de Sagan, Comtesse Dolly, née Dorothée de Talleyrand-Périgord, had grown up in Germany, where on the arm of her Prussian first husband, Prince Charles Egon von und zu Fürstenberg, she had been lauded as "a principal ornament of the kaiser's court." But when Fürstenberg's death and Dolly's remarriage to one of her French cousins landed her in Paris, her new compatriots smirked at her costumey "Germanic" ensembles. This is where Gontaut stepped in. Encouraging Dolly to accentuate rather than to downplay her Teutonic fashion instincts, while also teaching her the finer points of tailoring and cut, he turned her "Walkyrie allure" into the essence of chic. According to André Germain, the Parisiennes who had poked fun at Dolly soon found themselves imitating her "Wagnerian (as opposed to Worth-ian) audacity" and bemoaning their inability (usually a function of their relatively puny height) to pull it off. When Germain said that

"Dolly de Castellane always looks like she's coming from Wotan's," he meant it as a compliment.

Gontaut seems to have taken a similar approach with Laure, encouraging her to make the most of her sartorial quirks. In her tomboyish youth, she had developed a utilitarian, markedly unfeminine style of dress. Under her lover's tutelage, this idiosyncrasy became the key to her glamour. Several of Laure's contemporaries credited her with being "the first woman in society to get suits made at Creed": slim-fitting, functional, beautifully cut wool suits, like those her well-turned-out lover wore, but with plain floor-length skirts in lieu of trousers. (She also had pants made for riding astride.) In June 1885, *Le Gaulois* identified her by name in an article about the "new vogue for *masculinized* ensembles" that was sweeping the gratin. This mention, too, bespoke her growing reputation for elegance.

Apart from its advantages in field and stream, Laure's man-tailored garb offered an appealing alternative to the overwrought flounces and bulky underthings of mainstream women's dress. In a tirade against the "monstrosity" of the bustle, which was ubiquitous in fin-de-siècle fashion, Constance de Breteuil wrote,

> Parisiennes have a good deal of taste, that much is true. But the craze to be in fashion has destroyed their sense of the female form. . . . What I really don't understand is why we have to wear bustles. It's not natural to drag around behind oneself a second person without a torso or head. And as if this weren't torture enough, in order to keep the whole scaffolding in place, one has to wear other articles that could have been invented by the Spanish Inquisition. First, one has to put on a horsehair pad that attaches around one's corset. . . . Then there is the little stuffed cotton cushion that upholds the pouf, with more laces around the waist, and then two or three enormous iron rings that dig into one's thighs and make it terribly painful to sit down.

In addition to being uncomfortable, these undergarments posed major difficulties for the woman who happened to remove them in the company of a lover rather than a husband. Putting them on required the help of a ladies' maid, and most straying wives were reluctant to bring such assistance with them on their extramarital junkets. Indeed, those ladies who frolicked with their lovers in carriages rather than in *garçonnières* were routinely compelled to toss their corsets out the window during their assignations. This practice left the Bois de Boulogne littered with female undergarments each night when the *cinq à sept* (five to seven o'clock) adultery window closed and married women hurried home to their husbands in a nerve-rackingly disheveled state.

Laure's "masculinized" look did away with these ungainly accoutrements and the problems that went with them. Providing greater comfort and practicality, not to mention a sleeker, more natural line, it gained a keen following among fashion-forward Parisiennes. However, the style looked best on a lean and athletic build, and until then, plump little creampuff bodies had reigned as models of womanly appeal. Sporty by nature and skinny by choice, Laure led the way to a new feminine ideal, anticipating by more than a decade the trim, uncorseted modernity of designers such as Madeleine Vionnet, Paul Poiret, and her future friend Coco Chanel.

Newly confident in her sartorial judgments, Laure took to pronouncing on questions of dress. Reporting on the latest couture confection of her English friend Lady de Grey—a stunning six-foot-tall peeress always gorgeously attired in Worth or Jacques Doucet—Laure would exclaim, "Oh, that Gladys! That Gladys! What chic! What other woman could pull *that* [*ça*] off, here in France?" Similarly, when inspecting the creations of luxury milliner Caroline Reboux, Laure would say in an authoritative voice: "First-rate, my dear! . . . Now *that* is elegant! [*Ça, c'est élégant!*]."

In these instances, Laure's go-to slang contraction, "*ça*," accentuated her approval. But in at least one notorious case, she used it to convey withering scorn. The episode was notorious because the target of Laure's fashion criticism was none other than Grande-Duchesse Wladimir. This imperial princess's top-flight taste in jewels somehow did not extend to her clothing choices, which tended toward the same dowdy conservatism as that of so many royal female wardrobes (past and present). Laure took it upon herself to prescribe a top-to-toe change, seizing the opportunity one day when she went to pick up the grande-duchesse at the Hôtel Continental, the GDWs' favorite hotel in Paris, to escort her to a Rothschild garden party around the corner. Finding the grande-duchesse as frumpily dressed as ever, Laure pulled a face. "*'That*' *[Ça]?!*" she shouted, audibly scare-quoting her buzzword to underscore her disgust. "Possible in Saint Petersburg! Possible in the Hague, or in Copenhagen! *Impossible in Paris!* Wherever did Madame have '*that*' made?" Then, reverting to a pose of courtly obeisance, Laure added smoothly, "If Madame would permit me, I could bring Her to see Worth straightaway. Yes, right now! Gustave?"—Gustave was the Chevignés' footman, authorized to accompany Laure on special occasions—"Have Her Imperial Highness's carriage brought round immediately!"

This incident entered into *mondain* legend, as Laure's moments of glory invariably did, broadcasting both her alleged intimacy with crowned heads and the unheard-of liberties she took with them. The story also showcased the newest feather in her proverbial cap. By presuming to challenge a Romanov grandee on matters of elegance, Laure laid claim to an authority which, in Paris more than anywhere else, rivaled even royalty in its power to enthrall—an authority to which Her Majesty the Press always paid signal attention. In Germain's admiring phrase, the scepter of fashion had passed into Laure's hands.

IMPROVISATION

TRILLS AND FEATHERS

The bird confined to an aviary or a cage is kept for either its feathers or its chirping, either the richness of its plumage or the delicacy of its song. When seen, as it were, from a bird's-eye view, woman trills and preens in much the same way. She employs all the artifices of fashion, transforming herself like a hummingbird, a sparrow, a bird of paradise. . . .

Woman charms, delights or enchants with the unique but inimitable [*sic*] accents of her song. She is a skylark twittering on high, a warbler cheeping in a thicket, a nightingale singing pearly melodies to the dawn. It is no exaggeration to say that when her plumage is as beautiful as her song is sweet, she is a veritable phoenix. . . .

When confined to an aviary or a cage, woman cultivates her plumage and her song for reasons of pleasure, power, . . . elegance, taste; . . . she trills and preens willingly when she hops from branch to branch, . . . or when she looks out at the world through the bars of her cage.

—ÉLISABETH GREFFULHE, "The Woman of Letters"
("La Femme de lettres," c. 1884–1887)

CHAPTER SEVEN

THE ART OF BEING SEEN

Laure de Chevigné did not wield the scepter of fashion alone. At the other end of the spectrum from her man-tailored minimalism, Élisabeth Greffulhe pioneered ornate, fantastical styles that made her, too, a cynosure of the gratin. Although the dress codes in that milieu tended toward the same strict conformity that characterized the rest of its mores, Élisabeth liked outfits that broke all the rules. Her flamboyant nonconformity made her a bit of a conundrum among her peers, as *Le Gaulois* reported in 1882. In a front-page profile of "the beautiful Vicomtesse Greffulhe," the newspaper hailed her on the one hand as "a sweet dream of blueblooded patrician womanhood," and on the other as a sartorial rebel:

> What [Mme] Greffulhe hates more than anything is banality. Original in all things, she can be a bit eccentric in her appearance. . . . Her clothing is designed by her and for her. Everything she wears has to be one of a kind—she would rather look bizarre than look like anyone else. . . . Yet no matter how unusual her caprices, no matter how whimsical her attire, she always retains an air of supreme distinction. One notices it straightaway, and recognizes her for the *grande mondaine* she is.

This characterization rests on a paradox: instead of undermining her "air of supreme distinction," Élisabeth's clothing "caprices" enhanced it. Like Laure, she became a paragon of aristocratic grandeur by blazing her own path and developing a conscious strategy of self-promotion. Determined to recapture in Paris the success she had had on her honeymoon with her "Mme Élisabeth" dress, she set herself one overarching goal: "Always say to myself when meeting someone else: *I want this person to carry away from our encounter an image of prestige like none other.*" With the help of a trusted mentor, Élisabeth perfected this image, and it made her a star. Her "prestige like none other" came to define her for friends and strangers, princes and plebeians alike.

Like most celebrities then and now, Élisabeth owed her fame to a providential confluence of ambition, charisma, talent, and timing. She created and projected her aura of peerless distinction at the very moment when the French monarchy conclusively lost its ability to play that role. While the Comte de Chambord's pathetic career had done irreparable damage to the prospect of a royal restoration in France, his successor, Philippe d'Orléans, Comte de Paris, leveled the deathblow. A retiring, diffident man, the Comte de Paris had a strong sense of duty but no real urge or aptitude to lead and no wish to convey "an image of prestige like none other." To quote the sniffy assessment of the Prince of Wales, who preferred a bit more showmanship from his fellow royals, Philippe d'Orléans was "too bourgeois to be king."

Consistent with this judgment, the Comte de Paris rigorously avoided public displays of royal pomp except on one notable, and fateful, occasion. In May 1886, he and his wife threw an extravagant fête at their residence in Paris, the Galliera Palace, to celebrate the engagement of their eldest daughter, Amélie d'Orléans, to the future king of Portugal. The influx of European crowned heads into the capital, and the fervor the occasion generated in the royalist press, ignited republican fears of a monarchist coup. A month later, the government voted to exile the Comte de Paris and all other princes in line for the French throne.

Philippe went quietly and never returned, yet his departure did not noticeably lessen the glamour quotient in the monde. During his three-year tenure as Paris's resident presumptive king, the Comte de Paris and his wife, a cigar-puffing, hatchet-faced hulk of a matron, had been quite content to leave the spotlight to those who actually enjoyed it, like Élisabeth Greffulhe, who seized the opportunity and didn't let go. Emboldened by the Marquis de Massa's observation that "next to [her], the Comtesse de Paris look[ed] like a chambermaid," Élisabeth came up with an unabashedly vainglorious label to describe herself: "The Woman Who Would Be Queen" ("*La Femme-reine*").

Élisabeth made her first major bid for public attention in May 1880, at a costume ball hosted by the Princesse de Sagan in the Faubourg Saint-Germain. It was a night of many firsts: the first *bal costumé* Mme de Sagan had ever held,

Élisabeth was delighted when a friend told her that next to her, the Comtesse de Paris, the wife of the Orléanist pretender to the French throne, looked like a chambermaid.

For the first Sagan costume ball in 1880, Élisabeth, standing far *right*, dressed as Diana, holding a bow and arrow. Salem, an African page, carried her quiver. An unnamed artist reimagined the scene for *Le Monde Illustré*.

the first grand-scale revel the gratin had enjoyed since the Franco-Prussian War, and the first time since the Greffulhes' wedding that Élisabeth had appeared in Paris before an audience of thousands.

Because the princesse didn't issue any costuming guidelines for the party that year, her guests took free rein in planning their ensembles, and Élisabeth designed hers with infinite care. In a nod to her husband's enthusiasm for the sport of kings (and perhaps in a nod to her own sexual reticence), she dressed as the virginal hunt goddess Diana, with a diamond crescent-moon headpiece and a tutu-like frock made of shimmering diamond-encrusted brocade. Although short enough to reveal her slender ankles—a daring feature in and of itself— the skirt of the dress was inflated by hoops so wide that no one else could fit on the hôtel de Sagan's great ceremonial staircase while Élisabeth was on it. No one, that is, except Salem, the six-year-old African page whom Élisabeth's uncle Robert de Montesquiou had brought back from a recent jaunt to Tangiers. While in standard classical iconography Diana carries her own quiver of arrows, Élisa- beth delegated the task to Salem, who she claimed was madly in love with her.

This was patently not the ensemble of a woman looking to fade into the background. But for all its showiness, it did not eclipse the wearer's beauty—far from it. "This Diana," wrote Gabriel-Louis Pringué, "could have been sculpted by Praxiteles or Houdon; her ravishing little head sat perfectly on her swanlike neck, which was attached to magnificent shoulders." Pringué marveled at how Élisabeth's "long train prolonged the cadenced rhythms and graceful lines of her supple form in motion. . . . She captivated the monde, stupefied it, conquered it, made it worship at her feet." A columnist for Le Monde illustré agreed, exclaiming of her "Louis XIV–style Diana," "What huge dark eyes! What a complexion! What a profusion of dark tresses! What a goddess's way of seeming to walk on the clouds!"

Étincelle, Le Figaro's ubiquitous social scribe, echoed her colleague's verdict. Not only, she wrote, did Mme de Sagan's ball revive the brilliant pageantry of the Faubourg after a decade of postwar austerity; it also revealed

> a dazzling new star on the mondain horizon, the Vicomtesse Greffulhe, née Chimay [sic], a twenty-year-old beauty with black sparkling eyes a thousand times more dazzling than the diamond crescent that beam[ed] its astral light from the abundant darkness of her hair. . . . She [was] the goddess Diana, but Diana from a Versailles ballet de cour. The Sun King himself would have bowed down before this regal Night.

This description of the vicomtesse as a "regal" figure, capable of subjugating Louis XIV himself, represented no small symbolic victory, for it positioned her as royalty.

The queen metaphor, and the outfit that inspired it, remained firmly lodged in the Parisian imagination. In April 1881, one of Étincelle's colleagues at Le Figaro asserted that Mme Greffulhe had "won first prize for beauty at Mme de Sagan's ball last year," even though no such prize had been awarded. In April 1882, the pseudonymous reporter Violetta praised her in Le Gaulois as "the very personification of the aristocracy, 'noble, pale beauty, daughter of wealth, queen of heaven, and mother of love.'" The quotation came from the Romantic poet Alfred de Musset, but according to Violetta, if one really wanted to understand Mme Greffulhe's "absolute superiority," one had only to remember

> the costume she wore to the Princesse de Sagan's ball, where she was the living image of the goddess Diana, with all the majesty of the age of Louis XIV and all the majesty of ancient Olympus, like a figure from the court of the Sun King, her reflection multiplied ad infinitum in the mirrors adorning the galerie des fêtes. . . .

Here again, the vicomtesse appears as a time traveler from Louis XIV's court, a "living image" of royal, even celestial, majesty. "The admiration she inspires, and that she sees in every gaze, is dominated by a feeling of utter respect," Violetta continued. "That is the feeling that all queens command."

That was the feeling Élisabeth set out to re-create with her subsequent party costume. For the next Sagan ball, held in honor of the hostess's close friend and reputed former lover Bertie, Prince of Wales, Élisabeth dressed in a blood-red

At one Sagan ball, Élisabeth beguiled Bertie, Prince of Wales, by dressing as his forebear Queen Elizabeth I.

velvet court dress, a chinchilla cloak, and a ruby crown, an ensemble possibly inspired by a portrait of the young Queen Elizabeth I at Hampton Court. (Fascinated by her virginal royal namesake, Élisabeth kept a postcard reproduction of this portrait in her files.) Élisabeth had been presented to the Prince of Wales once before, at a grouse shoot in Scotland the summer after her marriage. But the setting hadn't given her much of a chance to make an impression—it had been rainy and cold, and everyone had worn tweed the whole time. So she was eager for him to see her in a more glamorous guise, one that paid homage to his royal ancestry while showcasing her own regal aura.

To ensure that she attracted his notice at the ball, Élisabeth timed her arrival at the hôtel de Sagan to coincide with his. Royal highnesses always arrived last, so she made sure she and Henry reached the party very late, and the plan worked like a charm. No sooner had the Greffulhes stepped into the foyer of the mansion than Mme de Sagan's Swiss guards announced the Prince of Wales. Protocol dictated that the princesse greet her royal guest first, but Élisabeth beat her to it, sweeping into such a magnificent curtsey at the prince's feet that he barely glanced at Mme de Sagan when she followed suit. (As Laure de Chevigné would later recall: "Élisabeth Greffulhe—now *there* was a woman who knew how to curtsey!")

As a connoisseur of attractive Parisiennes, the Prince of Wales was visibly delighted with the "Queen Elizabeth" at his feet. But for a few puzzled moments, he couldn't figure out where or how he could have seen her before (as her unsolicited curtsey implied he had). Only when he noticed his old friend Greffulhe standing next to her did he recognize in the bewitching Tudor belle the shy young bride from the grouse shoot. Once he made this connection, the prince launched into such a voluble torrent of praise for Élisabeth that all the guests in the foyer could hear him. They also heard him accept an invitation that Henry had been extending to him for years, without success: he agreed to come shooting that autumn at Bois-Boudran.

From that day forward, the denizens of the monde would say that Élisabeth Greffulhe "made the clouds rain and the sun shine for the Prince of Wales." At the previous year's ball, onlookers had merely speculated about her power to awe a royal highness; this year, they had actually seen her do it. Armed, Pringué wrote, with "the scepter of her beauty, . . . of her opulence, of her grandeur that could never be equaled," Élisabeth emerged once again as the queen of the night.

For the next Sagan revel, she decided to go *as* the Queen of the Night, from Mozart's *Magic Flute* (1791), in a frilly black *robe à la polonaise* with giant tulle bat wings affixed to the back. Henry squired her to the party in a red and white jacquard tunic, red stockings, and a white neck ruff—a King of Diamonds guise supremely well suited to the rectangular shape of his head. He must have gotten a lot of compliments on the ensemble, because afterward, he commissioned the society watercolorist Eugène Lami to paint him and Bebeth in a crowd scene at the ball. The resulting work commemorated one of the few instances when Henry showed as much enthusiasm as his wife for the transformative powers of dress.

For the 1884 Sagan ball, Élisabeth concocted another variation on queenship, in flagrant defiance of the prescribed "peasant" theme. While the princesse and her other guests donned homespun costumes, accessorized with kerchiefs and clogs, Élisabeth dressed as the Duchesse de Bourgogne, Louis XIV's beautiful young granddaughter-in-law, with whom the king had in his old age become scandalously infatuated. (Her death at twenty-six was said to have broken the old king's heart.) The charms of the young duchesse were legendary, inspiring even the persnickety Duc de Saint-Simon to write one of the few unreservedly flattering passages in his multivolume memoir of Louis XIV's court:

> She carried her head valiantly, majestically, gracefully; her mien [was] noble, her smile most expressive, her figure slender, perfectly shaped, her walk that of a goddess upon the clouds: with such qualities she pleased supremely. Grace accompanied her every step. . . . She was the ornament of all diversions.

Élisabeth's peers would have been familiar with the Saint-Simon reference, as his unvarnished gossip about their forebears made his chronicles required reading in their set. Even the least literary-minded of her fellow aristocrats enjoyed the duc's juicy tidbits about their ancestors' machinations at Versailles.

When it came to the Duchesse de Bourgogne, one of Saint-Simon's juiciest tidbits turned on her bitter enmity with the Princesse d'Harcourt, an older, formerly beautiful grande dame known to her fellow courtiers as "the Blond Fury." By means of constant lying, cheating, and backstabbing, Saint-Simon wrote, Mme d'Harcourt had become one of the most "feared, hated, and despised" women in the Sun King's entourage. The Duchesse de Bourgogne hated her more than most and made her feelings known by subjecting the princesse to a range of humiliating practical jokes, from setting off firecrackers beneath her chair to pelting her with rock-hard frozen snowballs to sending twenty Swiss Guards with drums to her bedroom in the middle of the night to "wake her with their racket."

For Élisabeth, these anecdotes would have been enjoyable to recall because Henry's mistress, "la belle Pauline," descended from the Princesse d'Harcourt. At least in the seventeenth century, the lying, cheating d'Harcourt blonde had gotten what she deserved, and with the king's sanction, no less. As Saint-Simon pointed out, "Everything the duchesse did was good" in Louis XIV's eyes, so she was able to torment the princesse with impunity. Élisabeth could expect no such support from Henry, who never took her side against the other women in his life. For that very reason, though, Élisabeth must have savored the fantasy of omnipotence that came with dressing as the Duchesse de Bourgogne.

To clinch the allusion, she donned a replica of the outfit the duchesse wore in her best-known portrait at Versailles, painted by Jean-Baptiste Santerre in 1709. The dress was an ultraformal blue-grey satin *robe de cour,* with multicolored gemstones and gold braid ornamenting the stomacher and a train so long that it required another guest appearance by Salem, Montesquiou's trusty African page. This time around, Salem also toted a parasol as big as a palm tree.

But the real showstopper, both in the Santerre portrait and in Élisabeth's facsimile, was a sumptuous cloak of royal-purple velvet. Lined with ermine and stitched with Bourbon *fleurs de lys* to denote the wearer's royal status, this garment was absurdly ill suited to a down-home "peasant" frolic. Which was exactly why Élisabeth chose it.

Once again, her queenly guise resonated powerfully with her contemporaries. A full five years later, in the summer of 1889, the scribes of the *presse mondaine* were still enjoining their readers to "remember [Mme Greffulhe's] Duchesse de Bourgogne outfit from the Princesse de Sagan's costume ball. She looked like an apparition from the Sun King's court."

The timing of this last plaudit bears noting, as it coincided with the centennial of the French Revolution and with the gargantuan new World's Fair the government held in Paris to mark the occasion. The sensational prelude to the fair was the inauguration on March 31, 1889, of engineer Gustave Eiffel's thousand-foot iron tower, the tallest structure on earth. As a monument to progress, technology, and the indomitable republican spirit, the Eiffel Tower was

For the 1884 Sagan costume ball, Élisabeth copied the Duchesse de Bourgogne's royal ensemble from this 1709 portrait by Jean-Baptiste Santerre. Everyone else dressed in peasant garb.

without equal. Yet it could not and did not eclipse Élisabeth's competing inno-vation: a fashion queen from the Sun King's court, reborn in the pages of the modern-day Parisian press.

TEN YEARS BEFORE THE 1889 WORLD'S FAIR, when Élisa-beth first moved to Paris with Henry, nothing about her life there betokened her future as a style icon. After their honeymoon at Bois-Boudran, the newly-weds had settled into the Greffulhe family compound in the Faubourg Saint-Honoré. Made up of a cluster of adjacent *hôtels particuliers* and residential and commercial buildings—all linked by a network of breezeways, courtyards, and gardens—it occupied the better part of a city block in the peaceful, intersecting side streets of the rue d'Astorg and the rue de la Ville-l'Évêque. With its thirty- to forty-foot-high stone walls and its high ironwork gates, the complex was so vast and imposing that the neighbors referred to it as "the Vatican." Along with the stable for thirty horses, it had thirty-five servants' bedrooms: more a neces-sity than a luxury, given the staggering amount of manpower required to run the place.

When Uncle Henri died that April, Élisabeth and Henry took over his *hôtel particulier* at 8, rue d'Astorg, a grand eighteenth-century house that would be razed with most of the rest of the compound in 1956. The unpublished memoir of Jean-Louis Poirey, who grew up there as the son of the Greffulhes' live-in security guard, contains detailed descriptions of the property. Poirey recalls the garden as "an immense private park second [in size] only to that of the Élysée Palace" (where the president of the Republic lived). With its shady sycamore and chestnut trees, manicured hedges, and formal parterres, it was an oasis of green and quiet in the heart of the capital. Just two blocks away, the carriage wheels and horses' hooves that clattered up and down the boulevard Malesherbes sent up a ceaseless racket audible even behind closed windows and doors. But in the Greffulhes' gardens, singing birds and babbling fountains provided most of the ambient noise, punctuated by occasional peals of laughter coming from the puppet theater the d'Arenbergs had set up behind their house for their children.

In the street beyond the compound's walls, carriage and foot traffic were infrequent. Much of the commercial property the Greffulhes had acquired there served as an added buffer between themselves and the outside world, although Henry's father did rent the ground-floor retail space of a building he owned at 30, rue d'Astorg to Félix Potin, a popular chocolatier. The brand owed its loyal customer following less to the quality of its sweets than to the clever marketing ploy that distinguished it from the competition. Every box and bar of Potin chocolate contained a celebrity trading card: a photograph of a popular contemporary author, artist, statesman, or crowned head, printed on cheap cardboard and collected by many fans.* Apart from the comings and goings at Félix Potin, the hubbub in the rue d'Astorg was restricted mainly to the incongruously rustic sounds of a goatherd's flute or a shepherd's bell as the herdsman went from door to door peddling fresh milk from his animals. Also occasionally wafting in from the street were the cries of a novelty merchant who wandered by every now and then, hawking his wares to the jangling notes of his Barbary organ: "Magic lanterns, magic lanterns, curious things for sale!"

Indoors, the mansion at 8, rue d'Astorg boasted eight cavernous reception rooms on the first floor, covering approximately 17,250 square feet. As the lady of the house, Élisabeth was entitled to claim one of these salons as her own. The one she chose was on the smaller side—still too big to be cozy, but sunny thanks to windows that looked out onto both the gardens behind the house and the entrance courtyard in front. (This double view confirmed the *hôtel*'s conformity to the foremost requirement of aristocratic residential architecture: a location "between courtyard and garden" [*entre cour et jardin*]). The coffered ceilings of her salon were painted sky blue, stippled with fleecy white clouds. The walls were paneled with hand-carved Louis XV boiseries, their swirling tendril and shell motifs offset by the clean neoclassical lines of a white marble Louis XVI mantelpiece. The room was furnished with a rare set of sofas and chairs, also hand-carved and Louis XV, and upholstered with Beauvais tapestry depicting Jean-Baptiste Oudry's illustrations of the *Fables* of Jean de La Fontaine. Apart

---

* Another Parisian chocolate purveyor, Guérin-Boutron, modified Potin's innovation by offering trading cards with color-tinted photographs of the stars. Examples of both brands' cards are reproduced in these pages.

from an ornate bronze clock that had once belonged to Marie Antoinette, a prize from the Greffulhes' collection, the decorative objects reflected Élisabeth's more contemporary tastes. It was here that she hung Moreau's *Salome in the Garden* and displayed photographs of her parents and siblings. These additions created a warm, unfussy atmosphere distinct from that of the other salons in the house, which exuded privilege, grandeur, and silence in equal and imposing measure.

For Élisabeth, the other most welcoming spots in her new residence were a glassed-in conservatory (*jardin d'hiver*) on the ground floor and her dressing room upstairs. The dressing room adjoined her bedroom, which had a large outdoor terrace overlooking the gardens. Henry did not share her sleeping quarters, having his own bedroom and office across the hall.

When he was at home, Henry often communicated with her through notes hand-delivered by the servants. If he tracked Élisabeth down in person, it was generally because he was in a foul mood and spoiling for a fight. ("With H.'s insatiate need to fly off the handle," she recorded, "he could just as well direct his fury at his coachman or the cook, but I am his favorite target.") In these instances, he would yell at her so loudly that the whole building seemed to shake. Otherwise, the hush in the mansion was absolute except in the basement, which housed a sprawling network of kitchens, pantries, wine cellars, laundry rooms, and furnaces. But these spaces, animated by a busy staff, were not Élisabeth's domain. While it was her responsibility to plan her and Henry's menus each day, the cook and the majordomo reported to her upstairs to take her orders.

Élisabeth's most frequent companions in this quiet, insular realm were her in-laws. Henry's parents, Charles and Félicité, lived next door at 10, rue d'Astorg, and his sister Louise and her husband, Robert (Bob) des Acres, Comte de L'Aigle, at number 12. His other sister, Jeanne, and her husband, Prince Auguste d'Arenberg, resided at 20, rue de la Ville-l'Évêque, in an *hôtel* that faced out in back onto the same gardens as the houses in the rue d'Astorg. The d'Arenbergs' house was the only one in the compound not connected to the others by covered walkways, calling for special measures in snow or rain. Their daughter Louise (Riquette) d'Arenberg, who was six years old when Élisabeth first arrived in the rue d'Astorg, remembered fondly how, on inclement days, she and her family would travel around the corner to her grandparents' house in a two-wheeled cart pulled by one of the servants.

These arrangements fostered nearly constant contact among the four households. So did Félicité's daily habit of calling on each of her children and their families after morning Mass. In addition, Félicité required that the whole clan dine together at least four nights a week, preferably at number 10, in a cavernous dining room hung floor-to-ceiling with dark Flemish tapestries. She also expected the whole clan to convene on Sunday afternoons in her salon, where she received perfunctory calls from a restricted group of relatives and family friends.

Félicité's at-homes were dreary affairs. The décor of her somber dark-green drawing room featured a grim unifying aesthetic on the theme "dead family members," achieved with an abundance of framed deathbed portraits and dusty locks of hair under glass. Even the room's one ostensible bit of life and color, a huge "pyramid of flowers" imported daily from the greenhouses at Bois-Boudran and displayed on a central circular table, took on a doleful, oppressive quality, like a funereal wreath on a freshly dug grave. The conversation was equally cheerless, as Félicité dictated not only the choice of guests (most of whom were as fusty as she) but the content of the small talk (more fustiness). In her diary, Élisabeth described the exchanges at number 10 as textbook illustrations of "the banal, ready-made language one is *obligated* to speak in the monde: cold, formulaic words one utters for the sake of *bon ton,* and that disguise one's true emotions." Another guest at these Sunday gatherings commented on their "dearth of charm [and] lively animation," noting that "no member of that household is thoroughly sociable. . . . When the Greffulhes open their salon and light their tapers, they act like they are performing a duty rather than enjoying themselves."

But as Henry was quick to remind Élisabeth, good manners meant nothing so much as performing one's duty and disguising one's true emotions. Take his relationship with Prince Auguste d'Arenberg. The two men despised each other so thoroughly that in their private conversations, d'Arenberg had more than once threatened to build a wall down the middle of the park between his house and Henry's so that they would never have to even look at each other again.* If d'Arenberg didn't act on this threat, it was because, like Henry, he understood that it was their inalienable duty to maintain the appearance of a unified family front. Under the current republican régime, the threat of *déclassement* loomed large for the nobility, and in the rue d'Astorg, common wisdom held that the surest protection against this danger lay in sticking with one's own kind and at least pretending to like it. As a Greffulhe, Élisabeth was expected to follow the same course. Henry had meant it when he told her that "a private life, a hidden life [was] the only life worth living."

Henry's own private life, however, unfolded for the most part outside the home and kept him hidden chiefly from the woman he had married. Though he demanded that Élisabeth attend all the weekly family dinners and all his mother's at-homes, he seldom joined her for these functions. Between his clubs, his horses, his art-buying sprees, his vague political ambitions, and above all, his extramarital affairs, Henry had too many outside interests to want to tend the hearth fires with Bebeth.

---

* The perfunctory nature of aristocratic family feeling was perhaps nowhere more aptly expressed than in a notorious remark made by Henry's cousin Aimery de La Rochefoucauld, on the evening of the *bal des bêtes.* While dressing for the ball, La Rochefoucauld received word that one of his relatives was expected to die within the hour. "You're exaggerating!" La Rochefoucauld shouted to the messenger and waved him away. Had La Rochefoucauld acknowledged the gravity of his kinsman's ordeal, etiquette would have obliged him to skip the ball—one didn't attend parties when in mourning—and he was determined to keep his envied spot in the *ballet des abeilles.* In fact, when the news came of his relation's demise, he was already all suited up and ready for action in his little gold antennae and snappy striped bee tunic.

For her, this bad situation became even worse once she realized that "la belle Pauline" did not represent her only competition for Henry's love. Not long after moving into the rue d'Astorg, Élisabeth learned that one of the footmen had as his sole daily function the delivery of several dozen bouquets of orchids, culled from the hothouses at Bois-Boudran, to women all over the city: Henry's infamous harem. These women, a motley array of *mondaines,* actresses, demimondaines, dancers, domestics, circus performers, and schoolmarms, all had to sign a formal "oath of eternal love," which read: "I, _____, swear to love Henry Greffulhe until I die." (After Greffulhe himself died, Élisabeth found that more than three hundred women in Paris had signed identical copies of this document.) Henry liked to tryst regularly with all his lovers, just as he had done as a bachelor. But now that he was married, he altered his routine somewhat, convening with them in various *garçonnières* instead of in their homes. Eventually, he would take out a lease on the Bagatelle, a diminutive neoclassical château on an island in the middle of the Bois de Boulogne. The property's previous owners included two kings, one Bourbon pretender, and one of Élisabeth's Chimay forebears. Henry would turn it into his own private love nest, holing up there with his paramours, often for days on end.

Henry's extended absences from the rue d'Astorg did not mean that Élisabeth was free to do as she wished while he was away. Invoking the dictates of *bon ton,* he forbade her ever to go out in Paris unattended—not for *his* wife the cheap, freewheeling capers of a Laure de Chevigné. Henry further reminded her that if she crossed him, he would hear about it from his mother or sisters or the servants (whose loyalties ultimately lay with him, the man who paid them), and

After marrying Élisabeth, Henry rented the Bagatelle, a small château on an island in the Bois de Boulogne, for use as a personal love nest, a luxurious version of the clubman's *garçonnière.*

he would make her regret her defiance. This double standard galled Élisabeth almost as much as his cheating and sparked what would become her lifelong interest in women's rights. Meditating on her predicament, Élisabeth wrote, "Women are meant to be trophies, pretty possessions. . . . Smiling, placid, charming. Not leaving the nest, staying in the aviary." Only men, she added, "have the freedom to fly."

In the first years of her marriage, Élisabeth enjoyed what little freedom she could inside her gilded cage. At least in Paris, there was no hunt for her to follow, so she could pursue her indoor hobbies in peace. She clocked in endless hours at the grand piano in her salon and tried to inject some variety into her musical repertoire by teaching herself to play the guitar. Nostalgic for Mimi's home orchestra, she instituted a new family tradition in the rue d'Astorg: private recitals she held in her salon on Sunday evenings, right after Félicité's at-homes. Though she hired professional musicians to provide most of the entertainment, Élisabeth also encouraged her guests to participate as their abilities allowed. To her surprise, even her most straitlaced, least artistic visitors, like Louise de L'Aigle, had jumped at the chance to perform. (Although Henry was no longer willing to sing duets with Élisabeth, he sometimes took a solo if he was around.)

To make the hours pass more quickly in between these little concerts, Élisabeth delved into the rare editions in Henry's book collection: Mme de Sévigné's letters, George Sand's *The Country Waif,* and Prosper Mérimée's *Carmen* were just a few of the titles she devoured as a young bride. Burying herself in literature and music helped Élisabeth to reconnect with the "appreciation for beautiful things" her mother had instilled in her as a girl and with the happiness she had known under her parents' roof.

But even away from Bois-Boudran, her highbrow interests met with stern disapproval from Félicité, who reiterated that Élisabeth's immoderate love of the arts did not befit her station as the Vicomtesse Greffulhe. Not only, charged her mother-in-law, was Bebeth's absorption in books unseemly—it was pretentious. With her aggressively undeveloped intellect and her preoccupation with matters of form, Félicité simply could not imagine reading for pleasure: it had to be an act. "So I'm reading this-and-such a book?" Élisabeth wrote in frustration. "'Friendly' Cerberus re-accuses me of *posing.*"

Cerberus's son proved no friendlier. Catching Élisabeth in an animated discussion about music with Auguste d'Arenberg—whom she had come to appreciate, along with his wife, Jeanne, as the most cultivated of her in-laws—Henry sniped, "Looks like I married the Venus de Mélo!" With this play on words, he took a two-for-one swipe at Élisabeth's beauty and her *mélomanie* (love of music). So pleased was Henry with this pun that he trotted it out often thereafter, ignoring his wife's tearful protests about how "mockery corrodes love."

Given their stated commitment to family unity, Henry and Félicité had no choice but to tolerate at least one of Élisabeth's pastimes: corresponding with her parents, siblings, and cousins back in Belgium. As on her honeymoon, she wrote to her mother and sisters almost daily, and while she tried to sound upbeat, her missives from Paris alarmed them. "At her age," Guigui fretted, "having no distractions, never getting to leave the house, being told only upsetting things—it is all just so sad." Marie-Alys de Caraman-Chimay was rather easier to fool, at least for the first year or two of Élisabeth's marriage. Not yet in her teens at the time, Marie-Alys still stood too much in awe of her beautiful, grown-up cousin to read between the lines of her letters, especially when they accompanied thoughtful presents from Paris: an opal ring, a bottle of violet scent. These gifts heightened Marie-Alys's veneration, drawing her attention even farther away from the strain in Élisabeth's tone. It would never have occurred to the younger girl that her idol (Marie-Alys actually compared Élisabeth to the Eucharist) was so unhappy.

Élisabeth vented her anguish more freely in a prolific body of writings that she worked on in the strictest privacy of her bedroom and dressing room. (She knew that if Henry, Félicité, or Louise saw her thus absorbed, they would only reiterate their jabs about her "posing.") She continued to write regularly in her diary, and she also scribbled in notebooks and on stray scraps of paper while Assunta and a team of other ladies' maids dressed, coiffed, and undressed her each day. For upper-class Parisiennes at that time, seven or eight daily costume changes were the norm, dictated by the time of day (morning, afternoon, evening), the activity (walking, riding, dancing), and the occasion (a night at the theater, a day at the races). All such changes involved the intricate manipulation, by nimble-fingered domestics, of stays, bustles, petticoats, overskirts, stockings, sashes, pins, and endless rows of minuscule buttons—it was all but impossible for ladies to dress themselves. Even for clothes lovers such as Élisabeth, these sessions could be tedious. While her servants fussed with her apparel, she distracted herself by covering page after page with her sloping, unruly hand, processing the sadness and bewilderment her married life had brought.

"What good does it do you to be sad and to cry?" she asked herself rhetorically in one of these notes to self:

> Will that change anything about the human heart? Don't you know that it is your lot in life to suffer? Listen to the voices of the centuries—do you hear the sighs of betrayed lovers, do you hear how the moans and plaints of disillusioned hearts continue to echo long after their sufferings ended? That is how life is—the sincere heart is bound to get broken.

Élisabeth returned to the creative-writing piece she had started on her honeymoon, with her putatively fictional diary entry about the traumatic wedding night of eighteen-year-old Marie-Alice, Duchesse de Monteillant. She also composed essays, including a series of "socio-physiological studies" of different female types. Invented by the novelist Léonce de Larmandie, the popular pseudoscience of socio-physiology examined the customs of the noble Faubourg as if they belonged to an alien tribe. Élisabeth adopted this method primarily so that she could write flattering character sketches about herself ("The Woman Who Would Be Queen"; "The Woman Who Sets the Fashions") and unflattering essays about her female in-laws ("The Ugly Woman," "Vitriolic Women")—without naming names.

Élisabeth did some of her writing in a secret code derived from Duployé shorthand, which she had learned while working as her father's secretary as a girl. In her married life, she often resorted to the cryptic loops and dashes of her pidgin Duployé when she wanted to keep particular observations or feelings a secret from Henry, whose disinclination to spend time with her somehow did not exclude an almost paranoid preoccupation with what she might be getting up to in his absence. On those infrequent evenings when he did come home from his harem, he wasn't above rifling through Bebeth's papers and yelling at her when he objected to what he found. So Guigui and Minet, too, learned to write to her in shorthand and to use code names for the people they gossiped about. Their alias for Henry was "la Jal," short for "the Jealous Woman": the abbreviation and the gender change were meant to guard against his prying eyes.

Nevertheless, Élisabeth wrote most of her letters, journal entries, and literary pieces in undisguised French, so that if Henry had wanted to, he could easily have deciphered this characteristically doleful passage:

> The one I love glanced at me briefly, distracted, then went off to his amours. And here I stay, alone, refusing that which is offered to me, calling out for the one who has fled me. . . . On my knees to observe the disappearance [*Constater la disparition à genoux*]. Fall, my tears, drop by drop on this invisible heart.

This lament frames the crisis in Élisabeth's marriage as a crisis of visibility, ascribing her misery to Henry's literal and figurative refusal to see her. "The disappearance" that brought Élisabeth to her knees consisted both in her husband's physical absence as he "went off to his amours" and in her own sense of existential disintegration as she struggled, and failed, to hold his distracted gaze.

And yet, to hear her mother-in-law tell it, invisibility was precisely the condition to which a well-bred wife should aspire. For Félicité as for the children she had raised to share her views, the prescribed get-togethers in the rue d'Astorg furnished the women in the family with more than sufficient opportunities to socialize. Apart from these modest gatherings, the Greffulhe ladies followed such an inconspicuous, retiring schedule that after the Vatican analogy, the neighbors' favorite quip about their house was "Everyone is sleeping in the rue d'Astorg."

When Félicité and her daughters did go out in public, they kept an exceedingly low profile—Jeanne d'Arenberg was said to be "almost impalpable" in her self-effacement. As a rule, they limited their outings in Paris to the weddings, funerals, and ultraprivate closed salons held by their stuffiest relatives. (These salons were as exclusive as Laure de Chevigné's but lacked all the merriment and spice.) The Greffulhe women also attended meetings of the Société Philanthropique, as well as assorted fund-raising galas and charity bazaars for the other causes they supported. Horsey Louise de L'Aigle allowed herself occasional outings to the Bichonne and the Ladies' Tribune at Longchamp. With Henry's permission, Élisabeth sometimes tagged along on these expeditions; little as she enjoyed her sister-in-law's company, she was grateful to get out of the house.

A few times a year, the entire Greffulhe clan deigned to appear at the Faubourg's larger, more "promiscuous" fêtes, but only when it was expedient for them to do so. For example, although the Greffulhes looked down on the Princesse de Sagan as a vulgar middle-class arriviste, they considered her worth knowing because both the Prince of Wales and Robert, Duc de Chartres, the dashing, blue-eyed younger brother of the Comte de Paris, figured among her good friends (and alleged ex-lovers). Eager to curry favor with these royal scions, Henry and his family made a point of attending the annual *bal Sagan,* despite the publicity it always received in the press.

These calculated sorties aside, Henry's mother seconded his opinion that for noblewomen in particular, "the hidden life" was the most *comme il faut.* As Félicité never tired of remarking, those *mondaines* who showed their faces all over town risked "getting themselves talked about": her phrase for the worst of all social sins.

She deemed it equally inappropriate for a woman of breeding to betray even a hint of vexation if her husband should appear to stray. Everyone knew, for example, that Auguste d'Arenberg often skipped Félicité's closed salon in order to call on the celebrity widow Geneviève Bizet, whose Sunday at-homes, contrary to Félicité's, were reputed to be great fun. But while certain members of the family, Riquette d'Arenberg later remembered, "reproached [Auguste] for his Jewish friendships," Jeanne d'Arenberg never complained about his defections. Instead, citing another of Félicité's (and Henry's) favorite expressions, she "bore up under the conjugal yoke." Jeanne's marriage had made her a serene highness. It behooved her to act like one.

As Félicité saw it, it further behooved the ladies of the rue d'Astorg to dress modestly, even dowdily, on the grounds that only adventuresses like the Princesse de Sagan "got themselves talked about" for their fashion choices. A real grande dame, Félicité declared, had no need of such base gambits; to a well-trained eye, the very restraint of her attire should convey her illustrious birth.

Of all her mother-in-law's ideas about *bon ton,* this one irritated Élisabeth the most. On her wedding day and again in her "Mme Élisabeth" appearance at Bois-Boudran, she had discovered "the joy of feeling myself beautiful" to an admiring crowd. Now, in the city where she had hoped to rekindle that sense of excitement, mean old Félicité, with her yellow dentures and her hideous wig, was demanding that she renounce it. Disclosing her frustration to Guigui, Élisabeth wrote that she felt "obliged to make [my]self ugly in order to find forgiveness in this house." To her growing pile of socio-physiological studies, she added a scathing essay called "Friendly Cerberus, or The Unpaid, Volunteer Duenna":

> Everything invites her commentary; it is difficult to placate Cerberus. To shut her up, one must follow all her precepts: wear the least becoming hats, the most ordinary dresses—an original cut is absolutely forbidden. One must display no individuality whatsoever. *Under no circumstances must one differentiate oneself.*

At the outset of her marriage, Élisabeth did her best to placate Cerberus. Her relations with Henry having been strained since their honeymoon, she knew she would only make things worse if she picked a fight with his mother. And yet, it was in obeying Félicité's rule about socializing with family that Élisabeth hit upon an unexpected way to break free. Even with all the letters she exchanged with her family in Belgium, still she ached for their company. But between her mother's fragile health (like Constance de Breteuil, Mimi was *poitrinaire,* and faring poorly) and her father's financial troubles, they were not able to travel to Paris very often to see her. In fact, Prince Joseph was even considering selling the family house on the quai Malaquais, and while he searched for a buyer, he staved off his creditors by renting out the upper floors to a variety of tenants, including the alienist Dr. Jean-Martin Charcot and a Jewish banking heiress named Flore Ratisbonne Singer.*

Without her loved ones from Belgium nearby, Élisabeth turned to her favorite local relative for companionship. This was Robert de Montesquiou-Fezensac, the uncle in the Breton way with whom she had played dress up and dolls as a girl. Now twenty-three and living in his widowed father's *hôtel particulier* across the river in Saint-Germain, Uncle Robert, as she continued to call him, proved quite happy to renew their childhood bond. His welcoming attitude was by no means a foregone conclusion, for he was a prickly, bellicose man who provoked blood feuds for sport—Ferdinand Bac compared him to "a hurricane of daggers"—and who took as his mantra a line from one of his heroes, Charles Baudelaire, about "the aristocratic pleasure of *displeasing.*" And as it turned out, it pleased Montesquiou greatly to displease Élisabeth's new family, whom he considered uncouth philistines. He called her husband "the Big Blockhead" to his face, deriding Henry's King of Spades noggin and his towering stupidity (as

---

* Élisabeth always said that Henry gave her no money of her own to spend and only authorized her to make large expenditures on entertaining and clothes. Her inability to help her parents hold on to the hôtel de Chimay must have underlined her lack of access to her husband's fortune. The Greffulhes were one of the few Parisian families rich enough to have presented themselves as buyers for the *hôtel.* But they did not intervene, and in 1884, Prince Joseph sold it at a loss to the French government, which annexed it to the École des Beaux-Arts next door.

Montesquiou viewed it) in one fell swoop. The antipathy was mutual; Henry hated him with a passion.

As Élisabeth's relative, though, Montesquiou had every right to call on her at home, and he became the first of her devoted visitors in the rue d'Astorg. He also, in the process, became her guide and accomplice in *mondain* rebellion, encouraging her to equate nobility not with conformity and self-effacement but with artistic refinement and flamboyant self-display. Directly opposed to Félicité's precepts of noble dignity, Montesquiou's teachings found an eager student in the girl with the invisible heart. As she adjusted to her life in Paris, he schooled his lonely niece in the fine art of being seen.

Although he disparaged his native milieu as "the *moribund* Faubourg Saint-Germain," Montesquiou took as much pride in his antecedents as Félicité Greffulhe or Pauline d'Haussonville or Aimery "Place à Table" de La Rochefoucauld, who happened to be first cousins with Montesquiou as well as Henry. (Despite their ducal surnames, Aimery and Montesquiou were sons of two sisters from a "not born" family both men preferred to ignore, whence the former's quip about "the mother to whom I am very distantly related.") Montesquiou reveled in enumerating his exalted (paternal) forebears: the Merovingian kings, the dukes of Aquitaine and Fezensac, and especially the musketeer d'Artagnan, the swashbuckling, seventeenth-century hero romanticized in the 1840s by the histori-

Élisabeth plays coy for photographer Otto Wegener.

cal novelist Alexandre Dumas *père*. When proclaiming his descent from this colorful figure, Montesquiou elected not to dwell on the real-life musketeer's déclassé side as the son of a newly ennobled merchant. Instead he emphasized the purity of d'Artagnan's maternal (Montesquiou) lineage and the romantic derring-do of his exploits performed in the service of Louis XIV. Montesquiou poured limitless sums into the restoration of the crumbling château d'Artagnan in Gascony, where he held sumptuous parties for a select few (the Italian author Gabriele d'Annunzio was one such honored guest) and treated his visitors to florid musings on his ancestral grandeur.

Montesquiou also took pleasure in invoking the rebus-like coats of arms and bygone patrician names that adorned the other branches of his family tree: "I dream of my ancestresses!" he declared in his shrill, exclamatory diction. "Pictavine, Claude, Auriane, Alpais! Blanchefleur, Gelgart, Miraumonde, Aude! . . . A long, divine crown of beauties!" He believed that this lineage made him divine as well. Once asked why he had ignored an acquaintance's greeting, Montesquiou screeched, "People bow when the cross goes by! The cross does not respond!"

When he did acknowledge a being of lesser standing, he enacted a peculiar ritual. Instead of nodding, bowing, or extending his hand—the three components of a typical *mondain* greeting—Montesquiou would bend backward away from the other person. This move exaggerated the already acute convexity of his lumbar spine, which resembled a very long closed parenthesis when seen in profile, and the accentuation of his swaybacked posture pushed his chest out and his face up. Only then, with his eyes trained heavenward, did he flick his chin ever so slightly toward the minion below. Even at rest, he held his proud Roman nose in an uptilted sneer. Author Jules Renard characterized him as "a bird of prey nourished on self-regard."

Yet unlike his cousin Aimery, Montesquiou did not derive his self-regard from his aristocratic birth alone. His vanity also hinged on his self-image as an artist and arts patron, "a high priest," as he phrased it, "in the Church of Beauty." He affirmed his faith by commissioning scores of works from contemporary artists and craftsmen, from Antonio de La Gandara to Émile Gallé, and also by writing volume after volume of poetry, the art form he deemed the greatest love of his life. "I have adorned the ducal coronet of the Fezensacs!" he cried. "With the crown of the poet!"

This, however, was a debatable claim. A hectic jumble of tortured syntax, excessive alliteration, precious neologisms, and grandiose proper nouns, Montesquiou's verse reminded one critic of "a dictionary blowing around in a hurricane." Another dubbed it "a Petri dish for the germs of frivolity." A sample quatrain: "I am Priest-Petronius and Maecenas-Messiah, / volatile volatilizer [*sic*] of words / which, gemmed judge, amidst enamel, / represent this aesthetic of which I am warden." His poems were an acquired taste . . . which few readers acquired. Behind his back, his detractors christened him "Fetch Your Lute" de Montesquiou, after a line from a poem by Alfred de Musset.

But the incomprehension of the people around him had little effect on Montesquiou. He maintained that services rendered to Beauty were the noblest of all human endeavors and that because these activities called for creativity and daring, artists and patrons were entitled to behave however they liked. "It seems to me perfectly natural!" he yelled. "That one's merit should exempt one from the common laws!"

He applied this ethos to all aspects of his life. Like many fin-de-siècle writers, Montesquiou regarded himself and his surroundings as canvases for the elabora-

These caricatures capture Robert de Montesquiou's swaybacked posture, dandyish dress style, and slim, attenuated silhouette.

tion of a bold, original style. His byword was "Love that which will never be seen a second time," and thanks to the fortune he inherited from his middle-class mother, he could afford to make his most outlandish dreams come true. He held a lavish christening ceremony for his cat. He built roaring fires in every room of his house on the hottest day of summer, "to prove to the fire that one loves it *for itself,* for its beauty, not because one is stupidly seeking to warm oneself, like everybody else." He sent his pet tortoise to Fabergé to have its shell gilded and set with precious stones, a project that killed the tortoise but resurfaced in Joris-Karl Huysmans's *Against the Grain* (*A Rebours,* 1884) as the quintessentially decadent *beau geste* of the novel's aesthete antihero, the Duc Des Esseintes, a ringer for Montesquiou.

In describing his protagonist's bizarre home-decorating tastes, Huysmans borrowed many of the touches Montesquiou used in his own residence in Paris: a church bell instead of a doorbell, a Russian sleigh perched on a polar bear skin, a domed ceiling lined in royal blue silk and sprinkled with seraphim in flight. Cherished possessions of Montesquiou's that did not make it into Huysmans's novel included the bullet that had killed the Russian poet Alexander Pushkin, a bust of Empress Eugénie mutilated by the rebels of the Paris Commune, a birdcage once inhabited by the historian Jules Michelet's canary, and the bedpan Napoléon I used after Waterloo. "Style has to be seen to be believed," Montesquiou told Élisabeth in one of his umpteen letters on the subject, all composed in purple ink in his distinctive, flowery hand. "Even when one sees it, one cannot believe it. . . . *Can one believe the* Mona Lisa*?!*"

For his niece, the more pertinent question may have been, could one believe Montesquiou's clothing choices? The man who helped Élisabeth to hone her fashion sense kept his own wardrobe stocked with surprises. Kimonos and sombreros, priests' chasubles and falconers' gloves, cloth-of-gold tunics and Liberty-print foulards—nothing outré was alien to him. Lily de Gramont recalled what a startling figure Montesquiou cut

> in his suit of pale sky blue; in his famous, pistachio-green ensemble with a white velvet waistcoat; and in other, even more bewildering outfits, wildly colorful and flawlessly tailored. . . . He selected his clothes to go with his moods, and his moods were as varied as the rainbow tones of his silk jacket linings. . . . He once attended an all-[Carl Maria von] Weber concert dressed in a mauve jacket, mauve trousers, and a mauve shirt, with a cluster of pinkish pale violets at his throat instead of a tie "because," he explained, "one should always listen to Weber in mauve!" When he wore ties, his tiepins were exotic examples of the jeweler's art, and ranged from an emerald butterfly to an onyx death's head. On a smooth, tapering forefinger he wore a large signet ring set with a crystal that had been hollowed out to contain a single human tear—whose, he never disclosed.

These getups signaled Montesquiou's contempt for "the common laws" of gentlemanly dress, which prescribed a sober palette of grey, black, and white. (The sole exceptions to this rule were riding pinks, formal red suits [*habits rouges*], hunting livery, costume-ball disguises, and, if one were Charles Haas, the vivid green lining of one's grey silk top hat.) However, the paradoxical effect of Montesquiou's effrontery—as in the case of his friend Laure de Chevigné, whom he soon presented to Élisabeth—was to impress his peers with his lordly distinction. Snicker though they might, his contemporaries admired his brio. As one of them conceded, "Were [Montesquiou] to dress head to toe in cabbage leaves, . . . he would still be consummately chic." As it happened, he did venture at least one semivegetal look: a skintight Kelly-green suit that even his friends had to admit made him look like an haricot vert.

Montesquiou's sartorial élan also implied a frank rejection of heterosexual male identity. Raised by an archconservative widowed father and schooled by Jesuit priests, he at once dreaded and craved the "vice" of same-sex attraction. He internalized enough of his elders' fierce homophobia to view the physical act of love with ambivalence bordering on disgust (one of his many commonalities with Élisabeth). For this reason, several of his biographers have speculated that Montesquiou's homosexuality may have been largely theoretical, at least until he met his longtime secretary and companion, Gabriel de Yturri, in the mid-1880s. But well before then, he flouted the sexual norms of his class by cultivating "effeminacy" as an aesthetic and even an ethical position. As he wrote in an uncharacteristically cogent stanza, "The effeminate fights, the effeminate avenges itself; / the effeminate conquers . . . the dull, heavy male. . . . / In itself it contains more than one species, more than one sex, / and is indefatigable."

True to this credo, he assumed a gender-bending persona; as one author noted, "Montesquiou seems to make a show of his difference, flaunting it like a peacock's tail." In fact, peacock feathers were linchpins of his look, along with high heels, face paint, and brightly colored jewels, the latter often set in fantastical shapes. In his clothing proper, Montesquiou went in for sumptuous "feminine" materials such as velvet, *peau de soie,* cloth of gold, and fur. He was one of the first Parisians to trade *mondain* white tie for the Anglo-American tuxedo, having his versions of this garment made in jade green, in purple velvet, and in gold Japanese silk embroidered with black hydrangeas. When he did deign to wear ordinary white tie, he jazzed it up with a chinchilla cape he borrowed from Élisabeth. "This almost ethereal fur," he mused, reminded him of "a bird's plumage, . . . so delicate, so easily ruffled by the first snowflake or raindrop that one cannot call it a *serious* fur."

It was with his niece's chinchilla slung over his arm that Montesquiou posed for a full-length portrait by James Abbott McNeill Whistler, *Arrangement in Black and Gold* (1891–1892), a work that Élisabeth commissioned after meeting the artist through him and that took more than a hundred sittings to complete. (According to Montesquiou, these sessions were so taxing that he only survived them with the aid of a special cocktail: cocaine dissolved in wine.) A leading proponent of "art for art's sake," a phrase he coined, Whistler sought to re-create in painting the abstract shadings and relational harmonies of music. This perspective endeared him to the *mélomane* uncle and niece, who lionized him as their brilliant "Grand Ami."

Montesquiou was taken as well with Whistler's combative persona, epitomized by his score-settling tome, *The Gentle Art of Making Enemies* (1890), and with his lush decorative mural work, exemplified by his famous Peacock Room (1876–1877). This room was the origin of Montesquiou's peacock-feather fixation; he was wont to boast that "the Grand Ami Whistler" had taught him to appreciate "these iridescent plumes, . . . with their hundred eyes representing Knowledge!"

In a reciprocal show of esteem, Whistler nicknamed Montesquiou "the Bat," a pendant to his own nom de guerre, "the Butterfly." Superficially, "the Bat" alluded to the comte's dark-haired, dark-eyed looks and perhaps to the waxen, vampiric air his makeup imparted to them. (The Grand Ami highlighted this ghoulish quality in his portrait of Montesquiou—not altogether amicably.) Yet in its eerie mixture of bird and beast, the bat also evoked the poet's symbolic affiliation with "more than one species, more than one sex." (As mentioned in chapter 3, in its hybridity the seal had comparable associations, and stood in for the bat in Jean Lorrain's 1901 parody of Montesquiou.) The comte made the creature a totem of his unabashed "effeminacy." He paid homage to it in a collection of poems, *The Bats: Chiaroscuro* (*Les Chauves-Souris,* 1892), which he published in a luxury limited edition illustrated by Whistler and Madeleine

Here Montesquiou is shown at Charvet, ordering pants printed with his totem creature, the bat.

Lemaire and bound in grey-green silk embroidered with the titular beasts. So notorious did Montesquiou's alter ego become that the caricaturist Sem sketched him at Charvet, ordering trousers in a zany bat motif.

Another artist who stoked Montesquiou's creative fancy was Sarah Bernhardt, the ruling diva of the French stage and one of the biggest celebrities in the world.* He liked to allege that Bernhardt was the only woman with whom he had ever gone to bed and that after their fling, he had vomited continuously for a week. Despite this claim, the tragedian professed to love Montesquiou "with sweet and infinite tenderness," possibly because he was one of the few Parisians whose outlandishness rivaled her own. "The divine Sarah," as her fans called her, wore men's clothing, took lovers of both sexes (from Charles Haas to the Impressionist painter Louise Abbéma), made love in a hot-air balloon, and slept in a coffin. She wore a Chinese lizard on her breast, tethered to her bodice on a tiny golden chain, and at home kept a menagerie that included a parrot, a puma, a wolfhound, two collies, a boa constrictor, a monkey called Darwin, a hawk named Alexis (after the Russian prince who had given it to her), an Andean wildcat, and an alligator that drank champagne.

Montesquiou took special interest in Bernhardt's cross-dressing, which she showed off in a slew of famous trouser roles. The first was her breakout performance as Zanetto, the wandering minstrel hero of François Coppée's *The Passerby* (*Le Passant*, 1869); after that she went on to play Hamlet, Judas Iscariot, the harlequin Pierrot, Lorenzo de Medici, Romeo, and Napoléon I's ill-fated only son, l'Aiglon (the Eaglet). At a time when the figure of the Doppelgänger haunted Western literature—as in Robert Louis Stevenson's *Strange Case of Dr. Jekyll and Mr. Hyde* (1886) and Wilde's *Picture of Dorian Gray* (1891)—Montesquiou saw in Sarah's androgyny an uncanny reflection of his own. In 1874, when he

---

* The playwright Alexandre Dumas *fils*, in whose *Dame aux camélias* (1852) Bernhardt gave one of her most celebrated performances, told the actress that when a friend of his was dying, he said with his last breath, "I am quite content to die, as I shall have to hear no more of Sarah Bernhardt." Sarah got her revenge on Dumas when her pet puma ate his straw boater.

Sarah Bernhardt in *Le Passant:* the first in a long series of trouser roles, and the inspiration for the matching outfits she and Robert de Montesquiou wore in a photo shoot with Nadar.

was nineteen, he hired the photographer Nadar to take pictures of himself and Bernhardt dressed in matching Zanetto costumes. In the resulting images, the two friends' frilly blouses, velvet capes, billowing trunk hose, and jaunty fezzes blur their gender differences. A decade later, after Mimi and Élisabeth took him to visit the atelier of Gustave Moreau, Montesquiou engaged a team of luxury purveyors to bedeck Sarah like a figure in one of the painter's canvases, "a creature crushed under the weight of innumerable jewels." This makeover coincided with Bernhardt's star turn as the titular Byzantine empress in Victorien Sardou's *Théodora* (1884). Her hyperornamented costumes in that role owed much to Moreau's—and Montesquiou's—febrile imagination.

IN ÉLISABETH, MONTESQUIOU FOUND another kindred spirit, equally game for sartorial follies and mostly exempt (unlike Bernhardt) from competing demands on her time. From the first, his passion for the arts resonated with his niece, who found it a welcome antidote to her in-laws' disparagement of her "posing." She confided in him about her clandestine literary efforts and eagerly accepted his editorial advice. His conflation of aristocracy and aesthetics supported her perception of herself as extraordinary on both counts. Like her uncle Robert, Élisabeth felt that her illustrious origins bestowed on her an implicit but undeniable superiority to people of lesser birth. Her writings contain numerous allusions to her "pride in race."

She did not go out of her way to downplay this pride in her interactions with others. By way of a compliment, she once told the fashion designer Paul Poiret, "I knew you were capable of dressing little Parisian nobodies. But I didn't know you were capable of dressing a grande dame!" (Poiret responded by directing his sales team to cite Mme Greffulhe such extortionate prices for all future purchases that "even she would never be able to afford them.") She was just as high-handed with her peers, particularly on the subject of artistic talent. "My dear T.," she told a clubman who dabbled in music, literature, and drawing. "You are the king of the *also-rans* in every category!" Yet she was endlessly pleased with her own amateurish efforts in those same categories. Ordering her secretary to recopy her "Friendly Cerberus" essay, she wrote, "I find this character *remarkably well described by me*, Élisabeth C-C Greffulhe. Make nine copies."

Like Montesquiou, Élisabeth spoke pompously of her dedication to art and beauty. "The only true great love of my life has been *Harmony*," she announced at a family dinner, perhaps trying to offset the dearth of true great love (and Harmony) between herself and Henry. On another occasion, she declared, "In order to live I must have transcendence. . . . I need to be transported beyond the density of walls and . . . into the realm of the infinite, if only in my thoughts." She was prone to remarking that according to Plato, "the *Beautiful* is the splendor of the *Good*."

By design or not, these statements drew further charges of pretentiousness from Henry, Félicité, and Louise. (Gentle Jeanne, a closet watercolor enthusiast, discreetly sided with Bebeth.) Heartened by her uncle's example, Élisabeth vowed to take their mockery in stride: "I like persecution, which makes me *noble* in my disdain. It lets me take the measure of the distance between myself and those who *infuriate me*." And that distance, she theorized in "Vitriolic Women," was born of her opponents' mediocrity: "Light, beauty, and talent personally offend them, suffocate them. . . . They cannot bear to see others embellished by gifts they [lack]."

But living with people who neither loved nor understood her took its toll. When her husband or in-laws got her down, Élisabeth poured out her sorrows to Montesquiou:

> I find myself overcome by a state of depression more than I ever thought possible. . . . I suffer in silence but rage inwardly against certain, inflexible characters. . . . But what is to be done, the answer is: nothing. Alas! We belong to that race of great, soaring birds who can only live in the plenitude of their aspiration! Sometimes I envy the quietude of those who are not tormented by a need for *fulfillment*.

Her uncle empathized. Beneath his arrogant and bombastic façade, Montesquiou suffered from the same crushing loneliness as Élisabeth. His alienation stemmed not from one blockheaded family but from a whole blockheaded society that reviled "effeminate" men like him and for which he feigned preemptive scorn. By confiding her unhappiness to him, and by echoing his own feelings of rejection and misunderstood genius, Élisabeth enabled him to form one of the only close and enduring friendships he would ever know. Throughout their lives, Montesquiou would joke that his niece was the only person in the monde with whom he had "never managed to have a falling-out."

Gratified to be included in her metaphorical "race of great, soaring birds," he did his best to lift her spirits. "Only barn owls fear the light, whereas the transports of the noble soul are the domain of eagles," he counseled. "So allow yours to soar, eagle-like, above troubling cogitations, . . . and let me be the screen from which you draw your desired dose of brilliance, a reassuring lantern and a guiding beacon."

Mixed metaphors notwithstanding, Élisabeth appreciated her uncle's offer to act as her beacon. She appreciated his eagle analogy even more, for that "great, soaring bird" had been the emblem of her presumed forebear, Napoléon I, one of the many sources of her consoling "pride in race." Montesquiou's letters to her were rife with flattery of this kind, and she had her secretary copy them all for her archives. If she did not do the same for the correspondence she received from her other family members, it may have been because only her uncle's missives portrayed her as she wanted to see herself: a creature ennobled by her princely origins and her cultural refinement alike. To thank Montesquiou for this service, she told him, "Only you and the sun have ever understood me." It was a measure of his love for her that he went on to quote this line often in the years and decades to follow, often adding proudly, "I am delighted that between me and the sun, she put *me* first."

Montesquiou encouraged Élisabeth to develop her own extravagant fashion sense. He brought the city's leading couturiers to see her in the rue d'Astorg and helped her assemble a sumptuous wardrobe on the Big Blockhead's tab. Like unfaithful husbands throughout history, Henry proved willing to fund his wife's retail binges in tacit exchange for his license to stray. Though he refused her even the smallest sums for pocket money, he gave her an annual clothing allowance of 300,000 French francs. The attempt to establish contemporary values for historical currencies yields dubious results at best, but the magnitude of this figure comes into clearer focus when one considers that in 1880, a bespoke three-piece men's suit from a top tailor in Paris cost approximately 160 francs, or that, in the same year, a ladies' maid in Élisabeth's service earned about 140 francs a month.

With essentially no constraints on her clothes spending, Élisabeth gave free rein to her imagination. When engaged in what her uncle called "*le shopping poétique*," she made it her mission to shun the latest vogue. Instead, she opted for pieces that expressed, as she phrased it, her overriding "desire [and] determination not 'to be like everyone else,' to create something new." In her meetings with designers, Élisabeth would review the full gamut of their current offerings; then, with an imperious wave of her hand, she would command them to "make me *anything but that*!" Even Charles Frederick Worth, founder of the Paris couture and style Svengali to empresses and queens the world over, had to submit to this treatment. Élisabeth had taken Montesquiou's watchword to heart—she wanted "only that which [would] never be seen a second time."

She articulated her own version of this philosophy in another of her socio-physiological studies, "The Woman Who Sets the Fashions." Cited here in full, the essay outlines the role Élisabeth saw herself playing as a maker of tastes and a setter of trends:

> She concerns herself with fashion not by following it, but by dictating its course; it is she who decrees new forms and who twists surprised fabrics [*tord les étoffes étonnées*] into new functions. She commissions new styles at will and unveils them to the world, offering up her beauty in the whim of her caprice [*dans la fantaisie de son caprice*]. She is surprising, astonishing, like a rare flower—Eyes and hearts, love and hate fly to her, the unique woman, the woman *nonpareil*—No one dares to emulate her and it is only when she has tired of a particular, transformative look that the vision she has impressed upon others will be nullified by their imitative movements; then "everyone else" will copy her, mechanically picking up that which she has let fall carelessly from her hands—that which she had previously loved.

In a published tribute to Élisabeth's glamour, Montesquiou describes her fashion sensibility in similar terms, highlighting

> the ingenuity, sometimes the magnificence, of her whimsy and her taste. I have seen her in a gown covered entirely in pearls, surpassing in opulence even Caligula's wife, and even her great patroness and name-sake, . . . Queen Elizabeth of England. . . . I have seen her in a velvet dress the color of dawn [and] in a cloak decorated with a hundred thousand swan's plumes, [in which] she resembled an otherworldly cactus with a woman's face. I have seen her in a downy, turquoise muff made entirely from blue-jay feathers [and in] a watered-silk confection, emerald green shot through with violet, that gave her the incontestable air of a Lorelei.

Along with the looks just mentioned, Élisabeth's early exploits in "*le shopping poétique*" yielded: a mauve *robe princesse* with white-gold palm fronds woven into the brocade, which she paired with a mauve tulle toque and a black fox-fur stole so long it skimmed the floor behind her; a frothy white taffeta party dress, anchored to her shoulders with multiple looping strands of pearls that matched her miniature pearl crown; an Empire-waisted tunic of iridescent "stem-green" silk, its ruched hem trimmed with silk anemones; a white satin frock with a pale blue satin sash and a plastron abloom with muslin roses, a real pearl nestling in the petals of each bud; and a bell-shaped party dress of pink and blue brocade, embroidered with sunny yellow acacia blossoms. (Like her uncle's friend Laure de Chevigné, she enjoyed turning heads in the allée des Acacias, though the floral nickname the press gave Élisabeth was "Narcissus," for reasons that should soon become apparent.)

In her accessories as in her outfits, Élisabeth indulged every conceivable "whim of her caprice." Some of her early favorites included a fascinator sprigged with real butterflies; a manila picture hat covered in hundreds of silk violets; a stuffed bird of paradise whose downy tail feathers were molded to trace the curve of her cheek; a pair of black taffeta bat wings (incorporated into her Queen of the Night costume in her uncle's honor); and an elaborate aviary headdress. Neither photographs nor detailed descriptions of this last piece of millinery have survived. But in light of her meditation on women's imprisonment "in the aviary," it suggests that Élisabeth's clothing, like her creative writing, functioned for her as a means of deeply personal self-expression: a commentary, in this case, on her confinement in the rue d'Astorg.

Conversely, the swansdown cloak to which Montesquiou alluded, and that Élisabeth paired with white satin mules covered in more swan's feathers, may have signaled her identification with that elegant, ethereal bird. This was an affinity her uncle strongly encouraged and perhaps even inspired. Admitting her into his winged confraternity with Whistler—and apparently forgetting his eagles versus barn owls trope—he baptized her "the Swan." To praise the graceful lines of her neck and shoulders, he coined an overblown term, "cygniform," and he advised her that if she ever published any of her literary efforts, she should use "the Swan" as her alias. (It was under this name that Montesquiou himself would later excerpt some selections of Élisabeth's prose, in his essay collection *The Thinking Reeds* [*Les Roseaux pensants*, 1897]). Meaningful to both uncle and niece was the iconic significance the swan held in the work of Richard Wagner. Like Europe's most notorious Wagnerian, the flamboyant self-styled "Swan King" Ludwig II of Bavaria, Élisabeth and Montesquiou passionately admired the opera *Lohengrin* (1850), where the swan figures as the mystical bearer of love.

Montesquiou also described Élisabeth as a "pristine specimen of Leda's bird," drawing on the classical myth where Jupiter assumes the form of a swan to ravish a beauty named Leda. For Montesquiou to associate his niece with the male god rather than the mortal woman pointed to an interesting gender reversal, casting the swan (and Élisabeth) as an emblem of indeterminate sexuality—like the bat (and himself). Montesquiou conveyed something similar with these lines:

Virginal ephebe, swan of the heavens,
Celestial damsel . . . ,
Volatile princess, pale and upright bird,
Divine hermaphrodite!

Given her own sexual ambivalence, Élisabeth may have appreciated this dimension of her Swan persona. Certainly it fit well with her Diana alter ego.

Like the virgin hunt goddess, the swan became ubiquitous in Élisabeth's contemporaries' praise for her beauty. André Germain wrote that she "glided like a swan," while Gabriel-Louis Pringué saw the resemblance in the elegant carriage of her neck and head. The painter Jacques Blanche, with whom Montesquiou had a short-lived friendship, noted that whether one saw Élisabeth "at the Opéra or in the country, she was always, indeed, her uncle's *Leda and the Swan.*" Such comparisons shored up Élisabeth's self-image as a rara avis, stranded among coarse, lesser beings with whom she would never see eye to eye. Beings like her in-laws, whose very souls, she wrote in one of her socio-physiological essays, "would have calloused hands if they were to assume human form."

Emboldened by her uncle to flaunt her beauty, she got into the habit of sitting for what would turn out to be an extraordinary number of paintings and photographs. Montesquiou was on a parallel mission to break the eccentric Comtesse de Castiglione's record of having posed for the camera "no less than 189 times." Gleefully undaunted by Henry's and Félicité's ire, he brought one artist after another to the rue d'Astorg to be presented to Élisabeth and encouraged her to commission portraits from each one.

Élisabeth, whose parents had sponsored many artists as well, was happy to meet her uncle's protégés. She was happier still to let them paint, draw, photograph, and sculpt her likeness, although she didn't always like the results. On more than one occasion, she complained, "There are days when one isn't *up to one's beauty,* and those are always the days when one is sitting for one's portrait." She was so disappointed by the bust she commissioned from Alexandre Falguière that she had the head lopped off and saved only the shoulders. Montesquiou kept the chin.

Élisabeth was seldom displeased, however, with the works that played up her likeness to a swan. Paul César Helleu—a young painter whom her uncle Robert discovered through Whistler in 1886—posed her next to a "cygniform" *guéridon,* using the juxtaposition to stress the matched sinuosity of sitter and prop. Another of Helleu's works, a towering full-length portrait still in her descendants' possession, achieves a similar effect, depicting Élisabeth in a fitted floor-length dress of pearlescent white satin, with one hand nestled in the folds of a gigantic swansdown fan. This was a portrayal after the sitter's own heart. Montesquiou was exultant too, complimenting Helleu on his genius in placing "the adorable model . . . under the sign of the White Swan."

Élisabeth placed herself under the same sign in an 1887 photo shoot with Paul Nadar, who had succeeded his father, Nadar (né Gaspard-Félix Tournachon), as the most prestigious portrait photographer in France. Again dressed in a long white gown, this one a poufy strapless Worth confection, Élisabeth brandished another oversized swansdown fan; when she held it behind her head, its plumes appeared to sprout from her shoulders like wings. A few years later, she struck a different avian pose for one of Nadar's rivals, Otto Wegener, vamping for his lens with her downy white cloak aloft on outstretched arms, as if she were about to take flight.

Another session with Wegener yielded a haunting composite image of two Élisabeths, one garbed in white chiffon and lace, the other in black taffeta, a riff on the Odette/Odile *dédoublement* in Tchaikovsky's *Swan Lake* (1877).

In another of her favorite photographs, shot by Nadar in 1883, Élisabeth posed as her great-grandmother Mme Tallien (1773–1835), whose slinky crushed-velvet sheath dress and white neoclassical turban she had unearthed while visiting her family at the château de Chimay. In the Directoire era that followed the Revolution, Thérésa Cabarrus de Fontenay Tallien (later Princesse de Chimay) had held one of the most brilliant salons in Paris. Resurrecting an arts scene that the republicans' Reign of Terror had all but decimated, Mme Tallien had exerted

These photographs of Élisabeth by Nadar *(left)* and Otto Wegener *(right)* present variations on her "swan" persona.

Élisabeth loved this double portrait of her-self, evoking Odette and Odile from *Swan Lake*, by Otto Wegener.

In this 1883 photograph by Nadar, Élisabeth wears a dress belonging to her favorite ances-tor, Mme Tallien, a noted *salonnière* and fash-ion plate.

tremendous influence as a patroness of high culture. As the Nadar photograph made clear, Élisabeth was eager to emulate her on this point.

And on an additional point as well. For all her artistic proclivities, Mme Tallien was also a leader of fashion in the Paris of the Directoire, single-handedly reviving the sartorial excesses of the prerevolutionary age. In one famous instance, Mme Tallien strolled through the Tuileries with sapphire rings on every finger, bejeweled rings on her toes, gold cuffs around both ankles, nine bracelets on each arm, a ruby tiara on her head, and—the past was prologue—a liveried Afri-can page carrying her train. The provenance of Élisabeth's "T.T. ensemble," as she called it, symbolically positioned her as the heir to her great-grandmother's legacy of style.

In fact, Élisabeth promoted the perception that she was the reincarnation of her ancestress by having her milliners make hats that looked like they dated from the Directoire, and by having her hair styled *à la Tallien* in a loose, Directoire-esque chignon threaded with gold ribbon. When complimented, as she so often was, on her large, dark eyes, Élisabeth would answer, "In the family, we call them *Tallien* eyes."

She invoked her "T.T." lineage so frequently that it even made a lasting impression on Grand-Duc Wladimir, who sent her a biography of Mme Tallien as a gift. This seemingly banal gesture was anything but, for the tsar's brother, typically for a crowned head, took little to no interest in nonroyal genealogies. (As another princely scion once quipped, "Seen from such heights as mine, all [ranks] are low.") The fact that he retained the identity of his young friend's great-grandmother long enough to offer her a book on the subject attested to the uniqueness of Élisabeth's pedigree and to her success in impressing it upon those around her. However great their ancestors' contributions as courtiers or soldiers, very few *nobles d'épée* could claim descent from anyone as glamorous—or as famous—as Mme Tallien. Like Montesquiou with the musketeer d'Artagnan, and like Laure de Chevigné with Petrarch's Laura (and the Marquis de Sade), Élisabeth set herself apart by stressing her kinship with an icon of European culture.

As her various Sagan ball outfits indicate, Élisabeth shared Mme Tallien's penchant for theatrical attire, drawing her inspiration from painting (Leonardo), literature (Saint-Simon), and music (Mozart). These sources were not just for party costumes. For everyday dress as well, Élisabeth looked to the patterns, colors, and textures of the fine arts. Henry's collection of treasures was a constant source of new fashion ideas, whether a rare suite of tapestries by François Boucher, an antique vermeil parasol handle set with a lemon-sized citrine, or a minutely detailed rainbow-hued painting, *The Concert of the Birds* (1670), by the Dutch Golden Age painter Melchior d'Hondecoeter.

Keen to affirm the relationship between art and fashion, Élisabeth hired Eugène Lami, the octogenarian watercolorist whom Henry had commissioned to paint them at the 1883 Sagan ball, to tutor her in drawing and painting. (Jeanne d'Arenberg had helpfully set the precedent for this bold initiative by taking private art lessons with the painter Madeleine Lemaire, whose floral still-lifes attracted an avid aristocratic following.) Élisabeth's training with Lami enhanced her ability to sketch her own clothing designs.

Élisabeth also studied photography, serving for a time as an apprentice to Nadar in his studio on the boulevard des Capucines, about a quarter of a mile east of the Madeleine. No information survives about the actual duties she performed there, though one does not imagine her readily pitching in with menial chores. Better documentation remains of her home photography lessons from the Comte de Saint-Priest, an old family friend and an ardent photography buff. He taught Élisabeth how to stage her own photo shoots in her *jardin d'hiver* in the rue d'Astorg. Her models in this setting included Uncle Robert, Henry, and Guigui.

Élisabeth engaged an artist called Deloge to do watercolors of all the pieces in her wardrobe: morning dresses, day dresses, tea gowns, ball gowns, hunting costumes, bathing costumes, and her regal finery for costume balls. As only she, Deloge, and Montesquiou knew about the project, it had to have been one of

Élisabeth frequently sketched her own designs for dresses and hats.

them who mentioned it to someone at the *Gil Blas*. The newspaper duly reported that the completed album would be a precious artifact for posterity, a catalogue raisonné of exquisite garments "all further embellished by the beauty of the woman who wore them so well." The same story appeared in an 1885 monograph by the Baron de Vaux about the most elegant women in Paris; in fact, de Vaux devoted a whole chapter of his book to Élisabeth's fashions as "considered from an artistic point of view." These accounts show how effective she was in presenting both her person and her apparel as works of art, worthy of commemoration and display.

Montesquiou echoed this notion, celebrating her as an "historic beauty" on the order of the Loire Valley's châteaux or the City of Light's museums:

> In twenty years, tourists who come to Paris will have her name in their guidebooks; they will ask to see her—maybe they will come here only for that purpose—and after they do see her . . . , they will die content.

As an alternative to "see Venice and die," Montesquiou proposed "see Élisabeth and die" as the true aesthete's motto. He further stipulated that for the sake of those poor souls who would never have the opportunity to gaze upon her charms in person, it was her sacred "obligation as a Beauty to perpetuate her powers . . . in myriad, faithful portraits that will enchant her contemporaries and generations to come, forever, in Museums."

Showing off her comeliness did pose certain practical challenges, most of them caused by Henry. To guard against her "getting herself talked about," he forbade the public exhibition of any of Élisabeth's portraits. In her diary, she complained bitterly about not being allowed "to *display* Helleu's 'swan,'" and Montesquiou told Goncourt that the Big Blockhead destroyed many of Helleu's sketches of her to prevent anyone from ever seeing them. Élisabeth's portrait by Gustave Moreau may have met with a similar fate. Begun in 1887 and completed over a period of several years, this canvas had somehow gone missing by the time Élisabeth organized a Moreau exhibition at the Galerie Georges-Petit in 1906.

Although she lent her entire collection of Moreau's works to the show, his painting of her did not figure among them, and it has not resurfaced since.

To delimit her public exposure even more, Henry imposed a hard and fast eleven thirty curfew on Élisabeth and reportedly beat her if she came home any later. Evidence in support of this rumor can be found in a "Disagreeable Letters from Henry" file in her archives: letters where he apologizes for having, say, struck her with his cane or spat in her face in front of their dinner guests. These same missives abound in abusive-husband clichés: how he wouldn't have lashed out if she hadn't provoked him; how the blows he struck were "purely involuntary"; how he would never, ever do it again. But he did do it again—over and over again, if Élisabeth's letters to him are any gauge. In 1909, when she was almost fifty and he over sixty, she was still pleading with Henry to spare her "those violent scenes" she felt sure would kill her in the end. "I am not afraid of a swift death," she explained,

> but I am afraid of *being destroyed* . . . That fear has become so morbid [that the mere sound] of a door flying open [can set it off] . . . I hate trembling in terror and spending my [life] in nightmares . . . One might find that one's victim has had a brain aneurysm, then it will be too late.

Some of her other writings also hint at domestic violence, albeit in a more elliptical way. Her journal entries from the late 1880s and early 1890s contain several allusions to a marital homicide case that had scandalized Parisian society a generation earlier. In 1847, at home in the Faubourg Saint-Honoré, the Duc de Praslin had repeatedly stabbed his wife of twenty-three years and then finished the job by smashing in her skull with a blunt object. Before this happened, the monde had long suspected Praslin of beating his wife. Some years earlier he had notoriously tried to instate the governess of his and his wife's nine children as the "real mother" of the brood, becoming abusively violent whenever his wife begged him to let her see them. He poisoned himself in prison while awaiting trial for her murder.

Élisabeth's musings on this episode indicate that she sympathized with the Duchesse de Praslin, whose letters to her husband, published in a newspaper after her death, revealed a woman who had been deeply in love with her spouse and devastated by his cruelty. In her diary, Élisabeth quotes unintentionally ironic tidbits from the duchesse's letters (example: "Life is so short, my darling Théobald"). Her notes about the murder also reveal that Élisabeth asked an unnamed doctor for detailed information about how to kill someone with poison:

> Poisoning—nothing is easier with modern science, and [it can be done] without anybody finding out. Just put a few germs in someone's handker-

chief and give him cholera, typhus, etc., at will. That's what the Ducs de Praslin of the future can look forward to. —The Doctor, '92

The last line of this passage is hard to interpret. Élisabeth could have been imagining herself and Henry in a repeat of the Praslin debacle, with him, a "Duc de Praslin of the future," killing her and then himself. Alternatively, she could have been fantasizing about poisoning Henry before he got the chance to do her in.

It is impossible to say for certain whether Élisabeth drew any such connections between her husband and the adulterous, rage-prone, homicidal duc, but the latter's murder of his wife was the only scandal of its kind Élisabeth mentioned anywhere in her personal writings. What was more, the Praslin murder took place in her own neighborhood, not to mention in her own social set. Indeed, she and the Praslins were even "a little bit cousins" on the Chimay side.

Whether she was fearing murder or plotting it, Élisabeth did take Henry's curfew seriously. At nighttime events in the monde, she often stood out as the first guest to leave or the only guest to depart before midnight. (Laure de Chevigné, by contrast, was the one who could always be counted on to stay at a party to the very end—and then take a group out carousing until dawn.) In a milieu as unrelentingly social as the gratin, these early exits could easily have undermined a lesser woman's stature. But Élisabeth found a way to make the constraint work for her, perfecting a battery of techniques to maximize her limited time in the public eye.

The most daring of these tactics involved her showing up at an event so much later than everyone else that her entrance could not fail to draw every eye, as she did at the Sagan ball with the Prince of Wales. This ploy became known in the Faubourg as Mme Greffulhe's "picturesque lateness," and she gave a much-bruited-about demonstration of it at a concert Montesquiou organized for the GDWs on one of their pleasure trips to Paris. As *mondain* Parisians were universally aware, etiquette required that when a crowned head was expected at a function, all other guests arrive before him or her. Élisabeth, though, sailed into her uncle's concert a full hour late, pausing for a split second in the doorway as all eyes turned from the stage to her. Then she glided through the hall and slipped gracefully into her place of honor beside Grand-Duc Wladimir. The dazzling smile she flashed at him as she sat down betrayed not a hint of embarrassment or remorse.

Fond as he was of Élisabeth, the grand-duc was astounded by her flagrant violation of good manners. Afterward he was overheard wondering aloud, "Could she have done it on purpose? Or maybe she doesn't own a clock?" Some years later, at a revival in Paris of Hector Berlioz's *The Damnation of Faust* (*La Damnation de Faust*, 1846), she pulled the exact same stunt on Queen Amelia of Portugal.

As a pendant to her "spectacular lateness," Élisabeth disciplined herself to leave functions not only ahead of everyone else but often just moments after she arrived. This trick, too, made for excellent theater, presenting her fellow revelers with an image of fugitive, mysterious grace that left them clamoring for more. Other habits that served the same end were her categorical refusal ever to go out (a) two nights in a row and (b) to any dinner parties except those held at the British Embassy. (Like Frenchness in the Anglophone world, Englishness connoted gilt-edged foreign glamour in Paris—whence the gratin's signal reverence for the Prince and Princess of Wales, and whence also the English spelling of Élisabeth's husband's first name.)

Élisabeth developed two more showstopping maneuvers, specific to *mondain* subscription evenings. The first, which she could only execute at the Opéra, found her stationing herself between acts at the top of the double-height staircase that led from the foyer of the building to the loges and *baignoires*. The foyer was where the clubmen congregated during intermission. Leaving their wives behind in their boxes to gossip among themselves, the men spent the break smoking and assessing the sexual availability of the female performers, whom many of them kept as mistresses. By standing alone at the top of the stairs, Élisabeth ensured that when the intermezzo ended and all the gentlemen trooped back upstairs to their seats, every last one of them would lay eyes on her. She liked to believe that the mere sight of her—"a lady of whom it is instantly

Élisabeth treated her public appearances as performances, staging dramatic cameos atop the grand staircase of the Paris Opéra.

said: *She is not like everyone else!"*—would erase from their minds the thought of whatever tawdry little singers or dancers they had been ogling just a few minutes before then.

The second of Élisabeth's subscription evening gambits worked at all three of Paris's main performance venues, as the only backdrop required was her own *baignoire*. In this canny bit of choreography, she would hide in the shadowy recesses of her *baignoire* throughout the performance, knowing that the lorgnettes and monocles of the other audience members would keep turning in her direction to see if she was there. Then, at a carefully chosen moment, she would thrust herself into the blaze of the house lights like a mechanical bird popping out of a cuckoo clock. After holding the pose a few seconds, basking in the crowd's awestruck murmurs and stares, she would dissolve into the darkness once again. From *mondains* like Charles Haas to social columnists like the Baron de Vaux to men of letters like Georges de Porto-Riche, the verdict on these mini-performances was the same: Élisabeth Greffulhe was an "apparition," haunting to all who saw her.

Élisabeth achieved a comparable effect with her daytime appearances at Longchamp, where she covered her face in layers of diaphanous white tulle, "like a precious fruit" (she wrote) "wrapped in gauze." Ostensibly, she did this to protect her face from the sun—since a tan meant hardship and outdoor toil, the gentlewomen of the fin de siècle kept their skin lily-white. But the real purpose of the tulle as deployed by Élisabeth was to cloak her in mystery, promoting intense curiosity about the face it concealed.

ALTHOUGH HENRY AND HIS MOTHER would have balked at the suggestion, with these contrivances, Élisabeth was adapting the Greffulhe creed about the superiority of "the hidden life" to her own model of social distinction. Rather than sequester herself in the closed salons of the old guard, she enhanced her noble prestige by offering the world fleeting glimpses of her splendor—and then withdrawing from view. Stage-managed in this way, her beauty was no less elusive than an invitation to Félicité's at-homes. Its inaccessibility was what gave it cachet. As André Germain observed, it guaranteed that when Élisabeth did make an appearance in society,

> it was as if she were descending from a throne on Mount Olympus to shine her radiance and light on those sumptuous but somewhat dreary parties that her mysterious aura illuminated and filled with excitement.

By the same token, Élisabeth also recognized that if she hid out on Mount Olympus for too long, her radiance and light might fade from people's minds. Taking a page from Laure de Chevigné's playbook, she cultivated the press, developing an amicable (if relatively distant) rapport with Arthur Meyer of

Le Gaulois and a cordial relationship with Gaston Calmette, Meyer's counterpart at *Le Figaro*. Through these men and their underlings, Élisabeth disseminated details about her extravagant fashions. Before her first Sagan ball, she leaked to Meyer that "twenty seamstresses were toiling night and day on the marvelous, classical 'Diana' costume" she would wear for the party, "including a crescent-moon, diamond-encrusted headpiece bound to be the talk of the evening" and a quiver carried by Salem, "a darling little Negro page." Another time, she débuted her pink and blue dress with the acacia-flower embroidery in her mother-in-law's drawing room, where newspapermen were decidedly unwelcome. Yet somehow, the frock still received a glowing mention in *Le Gaulois* the next day.

To guard against imitations, Élisabeth placed her clothing purveyors under strict orders not to replicate her ensembles for anyone else. Their compliance led to a widespread assumption that she did not patronize the Paris couture houses at all. Instead of "letting our couturiers fight over the honor of dressing her," a reporter for *L'Art et la mode* speculated, "this grande dame has all her dresses made from her very own designs, in a private atelier attached to her very own house." This rumor was tantalizing but unfounded. While the complex in the rue d'Astorg was big enough to have accommodated an atelier, no such place existed. Moreover, Élisabeth worked with virtually all the top couturiers—Worth remained a favorite—though for the sake of discretion, they did her fittings at home.

She was more forthcoming in divulging other secrets of her personal style: her descent from Mme Tallien, her rarefied cultural interests, her aversion to "the latest thing." From these bits of information, judiciously shared with the media, a picture took shape in the public imagination: a picture of exquisite, sui generis chic. *Le Figaro* applauded her for "updating Empire dress" (a misnomer for her Directoire "T.T." ensemble) and for "starting a mania for high, upswept hairdos, called 'little Greffulhes' in the monde." (On the woman who launched it, the "little Greffulhe" showed her swanlike neck to its best advantage.) The *Gil Blas* credited her with bringing the flouncy eighteenth-century "rascal dress" (*robe à la polisson*) back into vogue but cautioned that she was one of the only women who could pull it off:

> When a lady wears this dress well, which is a rare feat indeed, it produces a delightful effect; but to do so she must have a narrow, slim, symmetrical, elegant waist—if she has more exuberant proportions, it will make her look like a circus clown. . . . The majority of women today would therefore show great intelligence and common sense if they refrained from adopting such a style, and confined themselves instead to admiring the handful of beauties who do it justice, like the Vicomtesse de [*sic*] Greffulhe, who was the very first to wear it.

Press coverage like this helped Élisabeth embody her two favorite socio-physiological types at once: "The Woman Who Would Be Queen" and "The Woman Who Sets the Fashions." Confirming her success on this score was a front-page feature that *Le Figaro* ran in 1884, comparing her to the ancien régime's best-known "Leaders of Fashion": Mme de Pompadour, the Princesse de Lamballe, and Marie Antoinette. It was no coincidence that all three of these women had imbued their clothing with specifically royal prestige. So the analogy stressed the queenly dimension of Élisabeth's stylishness.

But even as she channeled these historic examples, Élisabeth transcended them, updating them for a brave new world where fame was the ultimate form of power. Unlike a Pompadour, a Lamballe, or a Marie Antoinette, Élisabeth did not derive her authority as a "Leader of Fashion" from a relationship with a crowned head (even if she used the occasional royal as a prop). Her glamour emanated from qualities that were hers and hers alone: her imagination, her creativity, her absolute commitment to self-reinvention and self-display. One of the countless fervid odes she received from her admirers described her as a woman "of a thousand beauties." This sounded about right to Élisabeth. Her beauties were legion, although they sprang from a single source: her matchless ability to exude "prestige like none other."

With every costume change, every public appearance, every media leak, Élisabeth was remaking noble elegance in her own fabulous image. Not just on the Faubourg, but on that "great, anonymous" Parisian public, she cast an irresistible spell. As *Le Figaro* reported in 1891, chronicling a small party she hosted at home in Paris,

> The tastes of the Vicomtesse Greffulhe are thoroughly original, the antithesis of the "common thing." So she gave her guests the joy of applauding a magic lantern, the likes of which had never been seen before.

Considered in connection with Proust's *Search,* these lines are striking because they reference the same medium through which Marcel first discovers the mythic radiance of the Duchesse de Guermantes. But in the context of Élisabeth's evolving media profile, they are interesting because they omit, for once, to mention what she is wearing. Nine years after her first dramatic costume at her first Sagan ball, she is described enacting a different, if related, kind of spectacle: a sequence of luminous, ephemeral images, curated according to her "thoroughly original" tastes and projected by her on a screen of her own choosing—to rapturous applause. The reporter gives no further details about the magic lantern she used in this performance. Maybe the novelty merchant in the rue d'Astorg had finally made a sale. But the prop was beside the point.

Élisabeth was the lantern. Élisabeth was the magic.

BIRDSONG

Poet, fetch your lute! 'Tis I, your immortal
Muse, who, seeing you sad and quiet tonight,
Have come down from the heavens to weep with you,
As a bird to the calls of its covey replies.

—ALFRED DE MUSSET, "The Night in May" ("La Nuit de mai," 1835)

CHAPTER EIGHT

PRINCE CHARMING

The adoration of the public soothed Élisabeth, she said, like a "great, anonymous caress." In another diary entry for Marie-Alice de Monteillant, the unhappy young bride she had invented on her honeymoon, she wrote,

> What a delicious thing to be young, beautiful, and alluring, to feel one's *power* over others . . . ! One almost feels like thanking some unseen person for this gift. And what a pleasurable gift it is—for oneself! . . . If I have any worries or sorrows, my mirror consoles me for everything. I look at my reflection, at my eyes—which I know so well how to make *irresistible*—and I keep looking until I feel good about myself again. The only time I stay in a bad mood, really, is when I don't feel up to being ravishing.

Whereas her uncle Robert had found his idealized double in Sarah Bernhardt, Élisabeth's Doppelgänger of choice was her own "ravishing" image, reflected back to her by the public, the media, her portraitists, her mirror.

As Élisabeth might have anticipated, Félicité deplored her newfound celebrity, which the older woman viewed as a heinous affront to *bon ton*. She reminded Élisabeth that after her wedding announcement, a noblewoman's name ought not to reappear in the newspapers until her obituary.

To discourage Élisabeth's fashion "exaggerations," Félicité seized on any negative comments they drew from her peers. One of the best ones, for Félicité's purposes, came from Hélène Standish, née des Cars, a cousin of Élisabeth's thirteen years her elder. Long regarded as one of the Faubourg's most elegant women, Hélène called in the rue d'Astorg one Sunday when Élisabeth was unveiling a new outfit in Félicité's salon. Élisabeth was miffed to see her—Hélène had an irritating knack for stealing her spotlight—so to keep everyone's focus on herself, she launched into an account of all the admiring gazes that had followed her on her way to and from church that morning. Élisabeth concluded her story with a stagy, wistful sigh: "I suppose I shall know I have lost my beauty when the day comes that the little people no longer stop and stare at me in the street." "Darling," Hélène parried, "they will always stop and stare at you if you keep dressing as you do now."

Félicité didn't have much of a sense of humor, but she thought Hélène's barb was one of the funniest things she had ever heard. Disregarding her own rule about upholding an image of family unity, Félicité made it her business to ensure that the put-down entered the *mondain* lexicon—and she succeeded. More than a quarter century later, Marcel Proust would cite it in a draft version of the *Search*.

Henry had a more complicated reaction to his wife's fame. In some of his letters, he railed against her attention-grabbing fashions, construing them as blights on his honor:

> I will forever wonder, and yet never be able to understand, why a person of more than middling intelligence and appearance should stoop so low as to make herself ridiculous by wearing such willy-nilly, topsy-turvy styles. . . . It is hard for me to see my good name tricked out in such grotesque togs and clownish glad rags.

On other occasions, he blamed Montesquiou for luring her away from "the quiet life, the hidden life" she was supposed to be leading as the Vicomtesse Greffulhe: "You would rather go parading around with your [uncle], who wants only to exploit you for his vanity and his inextinguishable thirst for publicity—*at all costs, come what may.*"

But Henry wasn't consistent in his reproaches. Sometimes he alloyed them with compliments: "Your hat is not *in season,* nor is your coat—I want to see your eyes shining like two stars in a blue [illegible] sky—you don't need to show off your waist." And sometimes he offered unequivocal praise. "My thoughts [yearn] to fly in your air, they are drawn to it," he told her in one undated note. "[I am] like a captive lovebird, cooing his tenderness to his dove, who flies around at liberty without him!"

Henry's volatility stumped Élisabeth at first. Over time, however, she learned to identify his triggers: a stern look from Félicité, a snide word from a paramour,[*] a paranoid belief that his peers were snickering at him for "letting" her make a spectacle of herself. Conversely, what others said about her could also, on occasion, ignite Henry's passion. From the first, he had told her that he wanted his friends to look at her and say, "What a lucky chap, that Henry! He married the most beautiful woman in France!" Thanks to her artful public appearances, they were now saying exactly that.

Élisabeth's most vocal early admirers included Breteuil, who continued to chide Henry for undervaluing her unique allure; Comte Robert de Fitz-James, who all but propositioned her at her first Opéra ball (she sent him packing); the Marquis de Massa, an aging dandy and *mondain* master of ceremonies who organized a fireworks extravaganza in honor of "Diana-Élisabeth" Greffulhe and

---

[*] Élisabeth annotated many "Disagreeable Letters from Henry"—which she kept in a file by that name—with comments such as "His mistress is just jealous because she has gained weight."

composed a sonnet on the same theme, comparing her to her patron goddess. Another clubman who pledged his devotion to her was Gaston, Marquis-Général de Galliffet, a decorated war hero with a silver plate in his stomach—the result of injuries incurred in battle and a source of boundless fascination to the fairer sex. Although his ruthless suppression of the Paris Commune had made him notorious as "the Butcher of Clichy," Galliffet had an impish sense of humor that belied his fearsome reputation. Also a jovially shameless lecher, he enjoyed provoking Henry by flirting outrageously with Élisabeth. (Henry struck back by calling Galliffet "the Drunk Old Assassin of Clichy.") More understated in his approach was François Hottinguer, a slim, sandy-haired clubman and the only bachelor among the Bois-Boudran founders. A senior partner in his family's bank, he shared Élisabeth's literary proclivities and engaged her in a romantic correspondence which Henry seems never to have discovered. But because Hottinguer mooned over Élisabeth whenever he saw her, his passion for her was an open secret in their set. The most improbable of her *mondain* swains, finally, was Prince Edmond de Polignac—an eccentric composer and aesthete, and a self-proclaimed black sheep of his class. His enthrallment with Élisabeth, rooted in their shared *mélomanie*, was the most ardent emotion the gratin had ever seen him display; it was well known that his erotic tastes did not run to women.

Polignac excepted, these men were famously discerning judges of feminine charm, and notwithstanding his vexation with Galliffet, Henry valued their opinion. Like the rare books and artworks he collected, his wife's allure pleased him because of its manifestly high market value. He liked to be reminded that he had the best of everything.

In very rare cases, another man's praise for Élisabeth would fill Henry not only with pride but with lust (or with lust as a consequence of his pride). For the first two and a half years of the Greffulhes' marriage, *mondain* gossips claimed that Henry hadn't darkened Élisabeth's bedroom door—or that she hadn't opened it to him—since their wedding night. This hypothesis seemed consistent with the couple's failure to conceive a child, despite the tremendous pressure they were under to produce an heir to the Greffulhe title and fortune. Just as notable, though, as their presumed embargo on their conjugal duties was the timing of its suspension. Élisabeth and Henry finally welcomed their first and only child, Élaine, into the world on March 19, 1882, just over nine months after the ball where Élisabeth had publicly enchanted the Prince of Wales. This suggested that Henry had looked at her with new eyes after she stopped Bertie, arguably the era's highest-profile (and highest-ranked) seducer, in his tracks. As Laure de Chevigné could have told them, nothing set noble hearts aflutter like the supposition of a princely crush.

But Henry's heart did not flutter for long. After finding out that Bebeth was expecting, he had absented himself indefinitely from the rue d'Astorg; she complained that it was as if "he [were] fleeing a person with an infectious disease."

So prolonged was his disappearance that Élisabeth began to worry that he had married someone else while he was away. (Several decades later, she would find out she was right to entertain this particular fear.) In his nastiest moments, Henry was prone to saying that Élisabeth was not "the *real* Mme Greffulhe"— one (or more) of his mistresses was.

For the time being, he had a different kind of humiliation in store for her. Early in her second trimester, Élisabeth told Mimi about "a very strange letter" she had just gotten—an anonymous letter, the first of many dozen such notes she would receive from Henry's paramours (and sometimes from Henry himself, when he really wanted to goad her) over the next fifty years. Riddled with misspellings, threats, and ugly slang, the unsigned note stated that Henry didn't love her, that he despised her family, that he thought her thinness disgusting ("your [*sic*] a real bag of bones aren't you Missus"), and that she didn't satisfy him in bed.

After almost three years of marriage, this new proof of Henry's adultery did not surprise Élisabeth. What did surprise her was the discovery that in addition to cheating on her, he was denigrating her to her rivals. Yammer on though he might about keeping up appearances, he did not hesitate to run Élisabeth down behind her back. Once again, she was disconsolate. "The love I used to feel has predeceased me," she wrote in an uncoded journal entry, splashed with tears. "There it lies in the grave, *assassinated.*"

Their love was dead, but Élisabeth was trapped; for while divorce had been legalized in France in 1884, it still carried an indelible stigma in her milieu. If she were ever to leave Henry, she would bring lasting shame not only to herself but to her child. Besides, without him, Élisabeth would be penniless, as he never ceased to remind her. "IT IS MY GOOD NAME THAT FEEDS YOU," he would rage, and he meant "feeds" literally. One day Élisabeth and Guigui arrived in the rue d'Astorg a few minutes late for lunch, only to find that Henry had told the kitchen staff, "Don't serve anything to those bitches! Let them starve to death!" Such "unremitting scenes," Élisabeth recorded, "make me blush with shame. If I didn't have to worry about the scandal, would I have the courage to leave?" The answer was always no.

It was a difficult pregnancy; Élisabeth felt as though "an arsenal of rats and mice" were gnawing away at her insides. Her sole consolation lay in her firm if irrational belief that she was having a baby boy. Her fantasy was that once she "gave" her husband and in-laws a male heir, they would have to credit her with saving their GOOD NAME from extinction—Henry was the last of male Greffulhes—and then they would have to treat her more kindly. "If it's a girl, I shan't even see her, you can take her away," she told Mimi, who had promised to come to Paris for the birth. "My honor is at stake now—it has to be a boy."

A girl arrived instead. As if this weren't bad enough, little Élaine bore an unmistakable resemblance to Henry, and even more to Félicité, with her bulg-

Élisabeth's only child, Élaine, took after Henry's side of the family.

ing blue eyes and overlarge nose. Despite Mimi's warm assurances that the baby would grow prettier in time, Élisabeth feared the worst. After six months passed with no sign of improvement, she wrote tersely, "I do not find that Élaine is blossoming."

Élisabeth herself was in full bloom, by all accounts more ravishing than ever when she came out of her confinement. Mimi's extended stay had done wonders for Élisabeth's "state of depression," giving her a newfound radiance that she decided to put to good use. From now on, she was going to go where she was appreciated—into the monde. "I admit it," she wrote to Mimi,

> I have thrown my hat into the ring. Having earned a reputation as a beauty and a wit, I am letting men pay court to me, just a tad. Instead of forever carping about how [Henry fails to] repay my devotion, my effort, even my love, about how he prefers to avoid me, consorting instead with frightful women who aren't worth the dirt beneath my feet, . . . [I have decided] to live my own life, [and] to shine.

Following Élaine's birth, Élisabeth developed what would become a lifelong habit of inciting other men to fall in love with her. As her biographer Laure Hillerin points out, Henry had "revealed himself to be the polar opposite of everything [Élisabeth] longed for, everything to which her soul, with its thirst for love and its passion for beauty, aspired." To make up for this, she set out to win the hearts of men—even beyond her earliest crop of devotees—who shared her high rank and spirit.

She pursued this goal in a manner that often betrayed her own shortcomings: her prudishness, her overweening self-absorption, and her almost infantile naïveté. Élisabeth expected to inspire only the purest and loftiest of feelings in her beaux, who she assumed would ask for nothing in return. She wanted them to be the chivalrous figures that filled her dreams: knights made of moonbeams and Princes Charming in green satin. Consecrated by their worship, her life itself, she imagined, would become a work of art, the fairy-tale romance in which her husband ("my Don Giovanni," "my Faust") had flatly refused to participate.

One of the first candidates Élisabeth auditioned for this role was Henri d'Orléans, Duc d'Aumale, sixty, the fifth son of King Louis-Philippe and an uncle of the Comte de Paris. Of all the d'Orléans princes, d'Aumale was the one the French public found the most appealing—possibly because of his suspected republican sympathies—and as a result, he was something of a national hero. Élisabeth had first met him four years earlier at her wedding, where his attendance had signaled the high esteem in which his branch of the French royal family held the Greffulhes. She had been intrigued to learn that the duc was also a member of the Académie Française, which had admitted him on the strength of his invaluable art collection and thirty-thousand-book library.

Since then, Élisabeth and d'Aumale had crossed paths at many a *mondain* function. But she seems to have first set her sights on him as a swain in the fall of 1884, when he invited her and Henry to a shooting party at Chantilly, his storied, royal estate. On paper, d'Aumale looked like just the right man to assuage Élisabeth's desperate "need for fulfillment." He combined the luster of royal pedigree with the heroism of a warrior (he had fought valiantly in Algeria and later served as the country's governor-general) and the romance of personal tragedy (his wife and all seven of their children had predeceased him) with the cultural authority of an Immortal.

But in close quarters, the duc exhibited no such éclat. When Élisabeth and Henry arrived for the hunt at Chantilly, their host looked even older than his sixty years. Sparse strands of white hair poked out from under his black velvet riding cap, and his wispy white tuft of a goatee looked better suited to an actual goat than to a prince of the blood royal. D'Aumale's gaunt face, scorched to a leathery finish by the Algerian sun, was crisscrossed with furrows, and he reeked of pipe tobacco, which he smoked incessantly. His voice crackled and rasped, "roughened," his contemporaries said, "by years of giving orders." And like his cousin the Comte de Chambord, he walked with a limp. The duc's naughty joke about his handicap would have amused Henri V (and Laure de Chevigné), but it made Élisabeth cringe: "In my youth, I had four supple limbs and a stiff member. Now I have four stiff limbs and a supple member!" She had expected better from her *beau idéal.*

The puerile jest betrayed the limitations of d'Aumale's intellect. His collection of paintings and drawings was the second largest in France, exceeded by only the Louvre's; it included such priceless works as Raphael's *Three Graces,*

COLLECTION FÉLIX POTIN

DUC D'AUMALE

The Duc d'Aumale, a son of the d'Orléans king Louis-Philippe, attracted Élisabeth's interest as a potential suitor.

Giotto's *Dormition of the Virgin,* and a nude preparatory sketch for Leonardo's *Mona Lisa.* His doltishness showed through again, however, when he led his guests on a tour of the picture galleries, for his running commentary always fell one artwork behind. Hobbling up to a painting of a verdant oak tree in a sunny landscape, for instance, he intoned, "Just look at the pallor of death, the paleness of the snow." The canvas he thought he was talking about, a snowy duel scene by Gérôme, hung next to the painting of the oak, but the duc took no notice. He had learned his script by rote.

Unbeknownst to Élisabeth, her disaffection turned out to be mutual. On her first night at Chantilly, she dressed for dinner with her usual flair, in a form-fitting white evening dress and a single, oversized white lily—a tribute to her host's heraldic emblem, the *fleur de lys*—at the nape of her neck. Despite his joke about his impotence, d'Aumale had a well-earned reputation as a ladies' man; he also had a longtime mistress with whom he was quite happy. He thus had no designs on Élisabeth, but she concluded otherwise from his reflexively gallant praise for her in her white ensemble: "Madame, you look like a sylph in this light." This was just the kind of response she had been hoping for. But before she could encourage the duc to expand upon the compliment, Henry came barreling over and grabbed her by the elbow, squeezing it hard. "Why Bebeth, what in the devil are you *doing*?"

Henry's interference left Élisabeth determined to pursue her royal flirtation after all—if only to spite him for his hypocritical possessiveness. During the remainder of their stay at Chantilly, she used every weapon in her arsenal to

The domaine de Chantilly, owned by the Duc d'Aumale, was one of the premier shooting estates in France.

make a conquest of the duc. She did not, however, succeed. D'Aumale must have regretted calling her a "sylph," as he spent the next three days ignoring her coy poses and dodging her meaningful stares. At the end of the visit, d'Aumale was relieved to see her go. "Mme Greffulhe is a lily that could easily turn into a clinging vine," he confided to his friend Edmond Joubert, a prominent Parisian banker. The *mondain* rumor mill being what it was, this line soon got back to Élisabeth—oddly enough by way of Laure de Chevigné, who was related to Joubert by marriage. But if Laure had hoped the quotation would sting, she would have been disappointed. Élisabeth took it as a compliment, proudly ordering her secretary to transcribe it and tuck it away in an "Homages and Appreciations" file.

AFTER CHANTILLY, Élisabeth began a more successful flirtation with another famous French prince. The catalyst for this intrigue was a telegram she received out of the blue in the spring of 1883, while Élaine was still a newborn:

> Yesterday morning, in the rue Royale, a marvelous apparition with the look of a queen, wearing some kind of incredible Directoire cloak, stopped a man dead, seized with admiration. On everyone's lips, a single word: Superb. Synonymous with beauty, with greatness, with the reverence of the masses, this is what the man told his friends afterward. They replied: "Imbecile! You only made this discovery yesterday?" Please help me find the name of this royal beauty. —SAGAN

Boson de Talleyrand-Périgord, Prince de Sagan, had by then reigned for more than a quarter-century as the Faubourg's King of Chic. Élisabeth was overjoyed to have caught his eye, all the more so because she knew Henry couldn't abide him. A note in her archives details the origins of the one-sided feud. A few years before his betrothal to Élisabeth, Henry had had a liaison with a voluptuous blond actress, Blanche Pierson, whom he supported in high style. Because he presumed that his largesse had bought Blanche's fidelity, he was thunderstruck to arrive one day in her apartment (which he paid for) as she was tenderly giving Sagan a footbath. Henry burst into tears on the spot and never forgave the prince for his part in the betrayal. Almost a decade later, tears still sprang to Henry's eyes whenever he recalled this episode: "It is too awful!" he would sob. "A man whom one has had to dinner!"

Knowing that Sagan was friendly with her brother-in-law Auguste d'Arenberg—in fact, the two princes were cousins—Élisabeth contrived to have the d'Arenbergs introduce him to her in their salon, which Henry, in his antipathy to his brother-in-law, assiduously avoided. (In his reciprocal dislike for *his* brother-in-law, Auguste d'Arenberg was only too pleased to orchestrate the encounter.) From their first meeting in the rue de la Ville-l'Évêque, the twenty-three-year-old vicomtesse and the fifty-one-year-old prince hit it off like old friends. Straightaway Sagan treated Élisabeth to some of his famous fashion

Le Prince de Sagan

The Prince de Sagan, known as the King of Chic, became Élisabeth's style mentor and devoted admirer.

advice, sending her to Creed for an overhaul of her equestrian wardrobe. The *Gil Blas* took fulsome note of the makeover:

> The Vicomtesse Greffulhe's new hunting costume is sure to become the model for everyone else's: A narrow pleated skirt, made of forest-green duffel, that doesn't quite skim the ankles; white silk bloomers underneath; supple calfskin boots. On top, a myrtle-colored peacoat trimmed with silver lace and covered with pockets; a suede gilet; a batiste collar; and a wide-brimmed felt hat with a bouquet of real heather adorning the brim.

Delighted, Élisabeth welcomed Sagan into her small circle of confidants, eliciting vehement opposition from that circle's other principal member: Uncle Robert. Quoting Victor Hugo's fustian threat to Napoléon III after the latter's 1851 coup d'état, Montesquiou wrote to her of his new rival, *"If only one of us is left standing, that one will be I."** It never came to that, but he did refuse forever afterward even to be in the same room as Sagan. Many years after Élisabeth and the prince first became friends, Montesquiou stormed out of a luncheon that had been thrown in his honor when he spotted Sagan among the other guests.

Montesquiou's jealousy arose from a misconception, which was that Sagan wanted to unseat him as Élisabeth's most trusted friend and mentor. What the prince wanted was to be her lover. Revealed in a barrage of fiery letters, telegrams, *petits bleus,* and phone calls (the first telephones were installed in the rue d'Astorg in 1883), Sagan's ardor presented her with a conundrum, for while Élisabeth did not reciprocate his feelings, she adored spending time with him. To Henry's aggravation, she had started going out in society with the prince (who as her brother-in-law's cousin notionally qualified as her kin and thus as a suitable chaperone), and she relished the prestige that came with appearing on his arm. It thrilled her to stand beside him and the Prince of Wales in the royal bandstand for the opening of the Thursday races at Auteuil, which Sagan had single-handedly established as a mandatory *mondain* complement to Sundays at Longchamp. It thrilled her to take the place of honor beside him at the Opéra-Comique, where he had (again single-handedly) made Tuesday subscription evenings de rigueur for the gratin. It thrilled her to see her name listed alongside his in the social columns, broadcasting to all the world her friendship with the King of Chic.

Although Sagan knew nothing about art, his good friend Charles Haas, whom he introduced to Élisabeth, did, and together the three of them took in all the latest gallery openings and museum shows. Kind and encouraging where

---

* *"Et s'il n'en reste qu'un, je serai celui-là":* In one of the funniest passages in the *Search*, Proust uses this same quotation to convey the rancorous envy that the sight of "the charming Comtesse G***" inspires in a stodgy, unpopular noblewoman from the provinces.

Élisabeth studied drawing, painting, and photography, and used friends and family as her models, including *(left)* Charles Haas.

Henry was dismissive and cruel, the two men spoke admiringly of her artistic bent, even acting as models for her own creative endeavors. Sagan posed for one of her photo shoots in the *jardin d'hiver* of the rue d'Astorg, and Haas sat for a pen-and-ink portrait she did for one of her drawing lessons. But Haas, for all his charm, was a will o' the wisp—he kept such a busy social calendar that Élisabeth never quite knew when she was going to see him next, whereas Sagan was steadfast in his devotion. Wherever Élisabeth wanted to go, she could always count on him to escort her there and to treat her like the queen he said she was.

Best of all, Sagan was happy to discuss fashion with her for hours on end, offering detailed insights about how the shape of a hat framed her face or how the cut of a dress set off her figure. Talking about her "experiments in beauty" never seemed to bore him. (Perhaps he was relieved not to have to rack his brain for insights on topics not related to clothing.) From time to time, the prince would overstep his boundaries ever so slightly, exclaiming that her gorgeousness "drove him wild." But even these mild transgressions Élisabeth found charming. Sagan never took them too far, and she always welcomed the reminder of her appeal.

In all these respects, the prince was Élisabeth's ideal suitor. "What impassioned understanding between us, whenever we meet!" she wrote in an essay called "False Encounters." "The words you speak to me are like gusts of loving recognition. We are conjoined because you embrace my dream, which is your dream." Yet unfortunately, the dream they had in common was their shared obsession with her beauty—not a mutual attraction. Unlike the Duc d'Aumale, Sagan in his early fifties was still brimming with vitality and ready for love. And while Élisabeth thought him marvelously distinguished, with his lean, exquisitely tailored frame, his echt-patrician features, and his shock of thick white hair, she felt no physical desire for him. In "False Encounters," she decried the unfairness of her dilemma, asking rhetorically, "Why, oh, why must you be enclosed in a body that does not entice me, and that I cannot love?"

Drawn to Sagan only in spirit, Élisabeth came up with a solution she hoped would work for them both. She decided, she told Guigui, to "keep the Prince breathless with anticipation" by flirting with him in writing. And not just in letters, but in a formal tribute that she would compose over the next several months, sending it to him in installments. The text would be her cerebral, asexual way of returning her new friend's love.

The completed pamphlet, which Élisabeth had published on luxurious cardstock by a printer in a town not far from Bois-Boudran, is a hymn to her subject's legendary chic:

> *Making an impression* [*impressionner*] is the distinctive sign of those stamped with that je ne sais quoi that sets them apart from the rest, and makes ordinary people say: "He" or "She" is "not like everyone else."

> Almost always dressed in black, with [his monocle attached to] a black moiré ribbon around his neck, at once sophisticated and simple, he is the most elegant man in Paris. . . .

> The monocle of the Prince de X is a barometer that marks by its position the degree of beauty of the woman he is examining. If he keeps it held up to his fine connoisseur's eye, this expresses the deep satisfaction he derives from [her] brilliant physiognomy. If he lets it fall, with a sharp, dry gesture, then one gleans the *lack* of enthusiasm he feels for the dull physiognomy before him. His monocle is a law-giver, terrible in the finality of its judgments.

On its face, this panegyric merely repeats the stock assertions one finds in all contemporary descriptions of Sagan: that he was the picture of elegance and that his authority as a tastemaker was supreme. What differentiates Élisabeth's version is the praise she showers on herself. From the second page of the pamphlet, she lauds not only a "He" but a "She" who is "not like everyone else"—the same formula she applies to herself in "The Woman Who Sets the Fashions." When she speaks of the prince's trademark monocle—the men's accessory he had brought into fashion after deeming eyeglasses bourgeois—she connects it to his connoisseurship of female "physiognomies." For her, Sagan's greatest mark of distinction is neither his famous monocle nor his equally famous white hair but his expert eye for womanly allure.

In the second half of the pamphlet, Élisabeth shifts focus. Evoking her maternal grandfather's translations of Petrarch, she depicts Sagan as a courtly lover in thrall to an untouchable feminine ideal:

> He obeys, never commands, always following Her lead, attentive to Her heart. He would even go so far as to protect Her from himself if he worried about going *beyond love* [*outre-amour*]! Because he is, first and foremost and above all, a chivalrous, gallant gentleman. . . . Grateful to the beautiful woman for her beauty, he delights in Her as he would in Art, without selfishness, as only true lovers know how to do. He admires grandeur and respects rarity.

The self-congratulation in these lines is unmistakable. If the prince is admirable, it is because he admires "Her" beauty, venerates "Her" as "Art," even "protect[s] Her" from his own baser instincts, renouncing physical pleasure out of sheer gratefulness for "Her" pulchritude, which he construes as its own reward—"as only true lovers know how to do."

As a "lover," then, the prince stands in direct opposition to the fictional Duc de Monteillant—and the all too real Vicomte Greffulhe. Whereas ogres like Élisabeth's fictional and real husbands desecrate their wives' virtue in the marriage bed, Sagan puts his lady on a pedestal, where she belongs. As described in Élisabeth's pamphlet, he is her chivalric ideal, Prince Charming dressed not in green satin but in a white piqué waistcoat and a black Savile Row suit.

Regrettably, Élisabeth's archives shed no light on how Sagan reacted to this essay, though he did remain loyally and, it seems, platonically devoted to her for many years afterward. As she told an interviewer toward the end of her life, "The Prince de Sagan worshipped me until he died." This was not strictly true: Sagan had a stroke in 1897 and lived out the remainder of his days paralyzed and incapable of speech. But before this tragedy struck, he indeed seems to have accepted the conditions Élisabeth's pamphlet laid out for their friendship. He consented to love her with "impassioned understanding": a feeling long on style and short on sex. Anything more, or anything else, would have repelled her as "sullying." As she wrote in a different context, "*bourgeois physical appetites*" were quite beneath her.

Or so she thought, until yet another prince came along and completely rewrote her script for sexless, literary love.

WHEN ÉLISABETH FIRST MET HIM in the summer of 1884, Don Giovanni Battista Borghese, known in France as Prince Jean Borghèse, was twenty-eight, only four years older than she. Consistent with his moniker, "the Prince Charming of Roman society," he was dark and handsome, if not tall, and he had a lithe, feline grace that may have accounted for the code name Élisabeth and Guigui gave him in their letters: "the Panther." Giovanni had a strong jawline, a lanky, aristocratic build, a neatly trimmed black beard, and piercing blue La Rochefoucauld eyes, which Élisabeth may have disliked on her mother-in-law and child but on him found utterly hypnotic. As a son of Félicité's sister, née Thérèse de La Rochefoucauld, he was Henry's first cousin.

Through not only his mother but his father, Marcantonio V, Prince Borghese, ninth Prince of Sulmona, Giovanni belonged to the highest echelons of the Italian and French nobility. Marcantonio V, too, had had a La Rochefoucauld mother, Adélaïde; in Rome it was said that she had poisoned his beloved first wife in order to clear the way for a second marriage between him and her La Rochefoucauld niece, Thérèse. ("Place à Table" de La Rochefoucauld did not have a monopoly on the clan's militant *esprit de famille*.) If this really had been Adélaïde's plan, it worked: Marcantonio had duly married Thérèse and sired nine children by her. Giovanni was the second youngest of the couple's seven sons and was extremely close to his mother. According to one of his confidants, "He adored her above all other family members and friends."

The Borgheses were a bicultural and bilingual family, but despite their deep roots in France, they were based in Rome, dividing their time between the Palazzo Borghese on the River Tiber and the Villa Borghese, home to their storied art collection, in a 148-acre park north of the Spanish Steps. Although they were reputed to be fabulously rich, most of the Borgheses' wealth was tied up in illiquid assets such as land and art. To stay solvent, Marcantonio and his eldest son and heir, Paolo, had begun to dabble in speculative real-estate developments in Rome. Within less than a decade, these schemes would end in scandal, pushing the family to the brink of financial ruin.

Soon to become Prince-Regnant (and later Tsar) of Bulgaria, Prince Ferdinand was a flamboyant eccentric and a good friend of Giovanni Borghese.

Don Giovanni Borghese was an avid explorer, funding and participating in an 1880 expedition across Central Africa.

As a young man, Giovanni was in no hurry to start a family of his own, nor did he have to be, having many older brothers to provide their parents with heirs. But because he was handsome, charming, and from an excellent family, he was a natural target for matchmakers in Rome, and to a lesser extent (because he was there less often) in Paris. To fend off their meddling, he decided to travel the world, starting with a trip in 1883 to attend the coronation of Tsar Alexander III in Moscow as part of a delegation from the Holy See. In theory, only prelates qualified for this honor. But ever since the papacy of their ancestor, Paolo V, the Borgheses had enjoyed considerable influence in the Vatican, as Giovanni's inclusion in the delegation confirmed. On the pontiff's orders, Giovanni received an honorary knighthood in the Order of Malta, a sovereign religious order colloquially dubbed "the Pope's Militia."* Equipped with this title, Giovanni joined the papal expedition to Moscow.

Given the unequaled power then exercised by the "Tsar and Autocrat of All the Russias," Giovanni's attendance at the imperial coronation imbued him with vicarious importance back home; few nobles in either Rome or Paris had been invited to the ceremony. His Russian interlude also boosted his social status because of the royal friend he had made while in Moscow: Prince Ferdinand (Foxy) de Saxe-Cobourg. Born in Vienna in 1861, Ferdinand belonged to the cadet branch of the Saxe-Cobourg and Gothas, who were related by blood or marriage to most of the royal families in Europe—and even to a few Latin American crowned heads. Practically since his infancy, his mother, Princesse Clémentine d'Orléans, the toughest, most ambitious, and reportedly most intelligent of all Louis-Philippe's children, had reportedly been scheming to place Ferdinand on the throne (any throne).

The young prince's d'Orléans blood and vast network of crowned-head cousins made him a subject of boundless fascination in Parisian society. Because he lived in Vienna, though, most information about him in the gratin consisted in rumors, which Giovanni's friends there looked to him to verify—or better yet, to embellish. Giovanni was too discreet to gossip, much less to invent stories

---

* The order's most infamous alumnus was the Marquis de Sade, who had joined up not because he wanted to serve the Holy Father but because it was said to foster sodomy among its members.

for his companions' amusement. But he did refute some of the more scurrilous allegations about his friend, such as Ferdinand's reputed Satanism and his eye for the young sailor boys on Capri.

Marginally less damning claims, which Giovanni acknowledged to be true, included Ferdinand's irrational terror of horses (despite his high-ranking position in the Austro-Hungarian cavalry) and his "womanish" sartorial flair. Dubbed "Ferdinand the Feminine" by his compatriots in Vienna, he wore makeup, women's corsets, and precious jewels and once appeared at a British royal funeral coiffed in a fuchsia satin turban of his own design. In addition, he went everywhere with a wheezing, flatulent pug named Bubi, whom he smugly identified as a gift from his cousin, Queen Victoria. Ferdinand was oblivious to the fact that the queen couldn't stand him and that her intent in giving him Bubi had been anything but benign.

One of the best stories about Ferdinand turned on his obsession with royal insignia, which he collected along with gemstones, butterflies, and exotic birds. During his coronation in Moscow, Tsar Alexander III had bestowed courtesy decorations on his foreign guests. Receiving the Order of Saint Alexander Nevsky, Ferdinand had turned up his (famously prominent) nose and demanded the Order of Saint Andrew, a more prestigious order, instead. Galled by his insolence, the Autocrat of All the Russias shouted in reply: "Even the Saint Alexander is too good for that princeling!" Ferdinand slunk away with his lesser medal, but the tsar never forgave him for his cheek.

For all his idiosyncrasies, Ferdinand impressed those who were fond of him with his intelligence, curiosity, and tremendous cultivation. He was a fearless explorer, having traveled extensively throughout Europe, Africa, and the Americas. In 1879, he had circumnavigated the globe with his older brother Ludwig August, with whom he had made some noted botanical discoveries along the coast of Brazil. Giovanni shared Ferdinand's passion for foreign travel. Three years before the tsar's coronation, he had joined the first group of European explorers to cross Africa from east to west, funding the journey with his own savings (whence its designation in geographic literature as "the Borghese Expedition"). As Giovanni would later explain to Élisabeth, even seasoned explorers had cautioned that the west-to-east crossing could not be done.

Determined to prove them wrong, Giovanni and his two Italian travel companions, Dr. Pellegrino Matteucci and Commandante Alfonso M. Massari, had set out from Suakin, on the Red Sea, in February 1880; their final destination was the Gulf of Guinea on the Atlantic coast. For the next thirteen months, they made their way southwest across the Sudan, traveling on foot and by camel. When they reached Darfur, only about a fifth of the way into their journey, Giovanni received a telegram from his mother. Having, she claimed, fallen gravely ill, she beseeched him to return to Rome at once. (Gossips there later the-

Élisabeth and Giovanni first met during the burial of a mutual relative at the château de Guermantes in 1884.

orized that Principessa Thérèse, who was in perfect health when she ordered her son to come home, had wanted to save him from "the extraordinary dangers that fanatical Islam posed" to a Catholic prince.) His two companions completed the expedition without him. Matteucci died of yellow fever soon afterward.

Before Giovanni left Africa, the Sultan of Nupe had presented him with a special trophy: a big-game animal skin, identified in third-party accounts variously as a leopard or a panther hide. This impressive souvenir, as much as Giovanni's sleek, somewhat feline appearance, may have inspired Élisabeth's and Guigui's code name for him—particularly if he made a gift of the pelt to her, as her ensemble for the *bal des bêtes* may have indicated. That his was the leopard skin she wore on that occasion seems probable when one recalls that she based her costume on Leonardo's portrait of John the Baptist: Giovanni Battista in Italian. A notable departure from her previous, queenly guises, the leopard garb may have been a private homage to her latest Prince Charming.

That fascination began in July 1884, when she and Giovanni were introduced at the funeral of a distant maternal relation of his and Henry's, the twice-widowed octogenarian Comtesse Picot de Dampierre, née Émilie-Ernestine Prondre de Guermantes. Following a memorial service in Paris, the burial took place in the family crypt at the château de Guermantes, a Louis XIII castle in the Seine-et-Marne with a brick-and-stone façade and peaked mansard roofs.

The late Ernestine had been notorious throughout the region for her uninhibited and caustic manner. If the village priest's sermon went on too long for her liking, she would shriek from the Guermantes family pew, "That's enough, Father! *Shut up,* Father!" On a visit to Ferrières, the opulent castle built by the Rothschilds in the 1850s, Ernestine blurted out to her hosts, "*This* place is a boutique. *My* place is a château!" While touring another nearby estate, owned by a prosperous cocoa merchant, she addressed the proprietor as "Baron Cocoa" and bleated "Cocoa! Cocoa!" at random intervals.

To her La Rochefoucauld kin, these bursts of rudeness were righteous expressions of Ernestine's stature; as a very old, very grande dame, she had the right, they felt, to treat her inferiors with disdain. After her interment in the Guermantes crypt—she had been the last person alive to bear that surname—the clan recalled Ernestine fondly and lamented her passing. But as neither Élisabeth nor Giovanni had ever gotten to know her, they did not have much to contribute to the family's reminiscences. Their relegation to the margins of the conversation would have given the two of them a natural reason to gravitate toward each other.

Another commonality may have been their bemusement at the grubbiness of the castle the late Ernestine had compared so favorably to Ferrières. As the scion of a family with one of the greatest private art collections in the world, Giovanni shared Élisabeth's appreciation for beautiful things ("beauty is a veritable Religion for him," she noted approvingly), and the dearth of beauty at Guermantes was so glaring as to be almost comical. Generations of rats had nibbled away at the paintings that hung in the reception rooms, and the frescoes on the ceiling of the thirty-one-meter-long gallery, although they had only been painted twenty years earlier, were thick with grime. Pegs for the servants' brooms had been nailed directly into the seventeenth-century boiseries, and thrifty Ernestine had covered the dining-room walls with cheap wallpaper meant to mimic Córdoba leather.

Giovanni would also have been attractive to Élisabeth because of his intellectual interests. Though an able sportsman, he preferred reading to hunting, contrary to most of the men she knew. He devoured works of fiction, poetry, history, religion, and philosophy and discoursed brilliantly on all these topics. (Marcel Proust, whom Giovanni befriended in the mid-1890s, described him as a superb conversationalist.) Giovanni's favorite subject was literature, and he dreamed of becoming a writer himself. At the least, he told Élisabeth, he hoped someday to move to Paris and join the Cercle de l'Union Artistique, which, as its name suggested, was the most artistic of the men's clubs.

In these respects as well, Giovanni's sensibility meshed with Élisabeth's, and before long, she felt certain that the two of them were soulmates, bound by an invisible but undeniable current. Throughout their stay at Guermantes, the anticipation she felt at the mere prospect of seeing him each day was so intense as to border on physical pain. With Henry, Félicité, and the rest of the family present, Élisabeth took care to mask her excitement. When talking with Giovanni, she affected the cool, formal neutrality good manners required. "The monde," she reflected, "has created a ready-made language one *owes it to oneself* to adopt when one comes from that background; . . . it dissimulates all feelings equally, whether the most complete indifference or the most sincere tenderness." But when talking with Giovanni, she found that this very constraint produced its own form of excitement:

> When the cold, proper words cover up a strong emotion, they ring false by contrast, and lead to an adorable, flustered stammering that causes more joy than the most impassioned phrases.

Élisabeth trusted him to decode the flustered stammering that tripped her up in his presence; she counted on him to understand that between the two of them, small talk was anything but small.

Their time together came to an end far too soon. ("While we chatted at random about banal things and about things we loved," she wrote, "the hours flew maliciously by.") When the family reunion at Guermantes was over, Giovanni returned to Italy with his mother, while Élisabeth took a holiday with Henry and Élaine in Dieppe, a seaside resort in Normandy. The Greffulhes checked in to the sumptuous Hôtel Royal, which advertised itself as the most expensive hotel in the world, and stayed there for the whole month of August.

Neither the Prince de Sagan nor Prince Edmond de Polignac could easily afford the rates at the Royal, but both men soon took rooms there as well, anxious to reenter Élisabeth's orbit. While Henry, as always, found other sources of amusement, she spent her stay in Dieppe strolling with the two princes along the boardwalk (the gratin's summertime stand-in for the allée des Acacias) and taking Élaine out onto the hotel beach to watch the seagulls.

All the while, she kept thinking about Giovanni. Throughout the summer, and then into the fall and winter, she sent him intimate, confessional letters about her unhappy marriage and the "heaviness of her personal burden." She told him how much she longed for an escape. She told him how desperately she envied Marie de Mailly-Nesle, an ethereal young *mondaine* who had left her feckless Jockey-Club husband for a debonair Polish opera singer—and who had looked "radiant," Élisabeth noted, ever since.

Giovanni blew hot and cold in return. In some of his letters, he sounded as smitten as Élisabeth, growing lyrical when he wrote about how much their correspondence meant to him. He once told her of a lonely winter's night when his "thoughts had grown as sad and cold as the sky," only to dissipate in "a burst of radiance" when an envelope from Bois-Boudran arrived, exuding a "fragrance too harmonious for me *ever to forget it!*" But other times, he gave her the impression that she was frightening him by coming on too strong. When she enthused about the Marie de Mailly-Nesle scandal, Giovanni seemed to worry that Élisabeth had brought it up as an example the two of them might follow. In reply, he urged her to put him out of her mind:

My dear friend, do not torture yourself on my account—I feel that I am weighing on your thoughts and it distresses me to add to the already heavy burden you bear. . . . I beg you, do not think any more about me—it is pointless to complain about life, and although mine has had its hardships, I have had opportunities that other men would have known how to turn to their advantage, and from which I have not been able to profit. . . . The "radiant" M—— [Marie de Mailly-Nesle] has more determination and bravery [than I], and she has figured out how to make the most of them in the face of every sacrifice. . . . Life owes her joy in exchange for her courage. Stop worrying about me, I don't deserve it; I have never known how to benefit from "the actions occasioned by my words."

Giovanni's plea for distance did not have the desired result. Accustomed to being pursued, Élisabeth told herself that his withdrawal was merely an expression of his overwhelming ardor. As in her failed flirtation with the Duc d'Aumale, the lily became even more of a clinging vine. She barraged Giovanni with more confessions of her marital discontent and amorous longing. She sent him several pictures of herself (including Nadar's portrait of her in her "T.T." finery), and she extracted at least one photograph of him in return.

As Giovanni continued to send mixed messages, Élisabeth's feelings for him intensified, assuming an erotic charge that caught her unawares. In Henry's library, she came across an 1864 edition of Charles Perrault's *Tales of Mother Goose* (1697), bound in red morocco leather and illustrated with eerie, dreamlike engravings by the artist Gustave Doré. One plate instantly caught her eye: an

Marie de Mailly-Nesle scandalized the gratin when she ran off with the opera singer Jean de Reszké.

image of a girl in a ball gown, gliding down a staircase outside a castle at night. This illustration inspired Élisabeth's only documented sexual fantasy, which she transposed into a fragmentary story about a new fictional alter ego, Éléonore, a spirited young beauty in love with a dashing prince:

> Upon reaching the bottom of the steps, Éléonore would see the Prince, who would escort her into the ball, which could be seen through the blazing windows of the enchanted palace.

> With her arrival at the ball, the music would stop and all heads would turn to watch her glide past in her dress laden with gemstones, and the crowd would whisper its admiration for the beautiful mystery woman.

> The Prince would look at her! A delicious thrill would overtake her; she would feel his presence at her side, as if they were suspended together over a void.

> Then, they would walk out together into the magical garden. With a faraway look in her eyes, she would listen to his sweet, whispered words, blending with the strains of music in the distance, and . . .

The tableau breaks off here, but only, according to a note in the manuscript, after Éléonore's "imagination produces the physical sensation for which [her] body has feverishly, if blindly, been hungering."

Élisabeth's own feverish, blind hunger made her bold. She mailed a copy of her Éléonore text to Giovanni, as if daring him to acknowledge how risqué such a communication was and how strong the desire that fueled it. But all he did was restate his caveat about his inability to follow through on "the actions occasioned by my words," remarking curtly: "Between us, dangerous ground."

Nevertheless, Élisabeth found cause for hope in the fact that Giovanni didn't cut off communication with her as he so easily could have done. More than that, he seized upon her Éléonore sketch as the basis for a proposal that would not only allow but require the two of them to stay in close regular contact. In an uncanny act of poetic justice, Giovanni did to Élisabeth what she had done to the Prince de Sagan: he tried to shift their friendship from "dangerous ground" to the presumably safe, asexual realm of writing.

IN A LONG LETTER DATED DECEMBER 1, 1884, Giovanni outlined his plan: he wanted Élisabeth to write a novel with him. While he didn't yet have any well-developed ideas for the plot, the form would be the exciting part. The book would be an epistolary novel, made up of letters that he and Élisabeth would write either (a) as the novel's protagonists, star-crossed lovers named Éléonore and Gérard; or (b) as themselves, but pretending that Éléonore and Gérard were real people they knew—people about whom two cousins by marriage could reasonably gossip without any derogation of *bon ton.* It is not clear whether Élisabeth warned Giovanni about Henry's propensity to go through her private papers at will. If she did, then writing about their alter egos in the third person would work as an important security measure for her and Giovanni both.

Yet as he was quick to point out, the "double ruse" of writing as and about Éléonore and Gérard would serve the interests not only of privacy but of literary art. By "slip[ping] a bit of divine, lived reality" into their manuscript, he and Élisabeth could reshape the boundaries between truth and fiction—and their efforts could have potentially important implications for the novel as a genre. With her Éléonore fragment, Élisabeth had made an inspired first step in this direction. Now Giovanni was urging her to go farther and to let him make the journey with her.

> What do you say to this idea? How agreeable it would be to write something together like the brothers G[oncourt], who used to work on the same page side by side, sitting at the same table! . . . Their model of collaboration remains unique to this day. . . . Even if our finished product turned out to be flawed, how interesting the process of writing it would have been! Also, wouldn't it be a means of transforming the minute details of our lives, separated as we are by such a distance, into amusing descriptions for each other? . . . Is it not a miracle, a way that fate . . . has given to us to hide in plain sight? . . . How charming it would be to see [our book] in bookstore windows—a mysterious book that everyone would be talking about! . . . Perhaps such a book would take a long time to compose; however, the nests that birds build, scrap by scrap, are quickly finished in the season of love!

This proposition appealed to Élisabeth on a number of levels. First, she loved the idea of their forming a creative partnership. As diligently as she continued to pursue her secret literary efforts, she was beginning to feel stymied with Uncle Robert as her only reader. For all the encouragement he had offered her in the beginning, his enthusiasm for her writing had lessened of late. Not long ago she had finally worked up the courage to show him her Marie-Alice manuscript, only to have him dismiss it in one, biting sentence: "The vague narration of an overgrown little girl." Adding insult to injury, Montesquiou had counseled her to give up on fiction altogether and try her hand at something less ambitious, like a translation of one of their friend Whistler's essays. And when she balked at her uncle's advice, he had countered that a writer had to master basic skills before progressing to real artistry, "just as one must practice one's scales before one can play a fugue!" These words had shaken Élisabeth's faith in her talent; now Giovanni's proposal had the opposite effect, reviving her confidence and her eagerness to create.

She was particularly flattered by the idea that she and Giovanni might become their generation's answer to Edmond and Jules de Goncourt. Before Jules's death in 1870, the Goncourt brothers had cowritten numerous works of fiction, history, and art criticism, toiling "side by side at the same table" and allegedly never spending more than a single day apart. (Neither Edmond, a suspected "invert," nor Jules, afflicted with syphilis, ever married.) To this day, Edmond de Goncourt remained an éminence grise of the literary world; in fact, he was one of the few living authors for whom Montesquiou voiced unqualified esteem. For Élisabeth to model herself on the Goncourts, of all authors, would force her uncle to acknowledge her gifts. Even if she and Giovanni never told anyone else about their joint novel, she would be sure to divulge it to Uncle Robert when the time was right. Then he would have to concede that he had underestimated her as an artist.

Just as thrilling to her, if not even more so, was the opportunity Giovanni seemed to be offering her to deepen their emotional connection. His idea about putting their lives into their letters reminded her of a literary team every bit as prestigious as the Goncourts but bound by romantic rather than fraternal love: George Sand and Alfred de Musset. In their correspondence, these two authors had left an exhilarating chronicle of their passion: an illicit affair that fascinated Élisabeth as much as their fiction and poetry did. That Giovanni was familiar with this aspect of the duo's legend seemed a safe assumption; after all, he knew both writers' works by heart. A few months earlier, Élisabeth had sent him some of her musings on the transcendent power of "Harmony." To her delight, he had replied by quoting a couplet from Musset: "Harmony! Harmony! Daughter of woe, / language invented by genius for love."

This citation had proven to Élisabeth once again how closely Giovanni's sensibility aligned with hers. But it had assumed even greater meaning for her because it was one of the first references, if not the first reference, she had ever seen him make to love. This deviation, however small, from the cool propriety of *mondain* language seemed to confirm what she so dearly wanted to believe: that their common infatuation with the arts was just an extension of a much deeper mutual attraction. By the same logic, the literary project Giovanni had in mind stood to ratify and strengthen this twofold bond.

Élisabeth found additional support for this theory in his metaphor of two birds building a nest "in the season of love." What did this analogy mean if not that he regarded their collaboration as a courtship of sorts? And wasn't there obvious romantic potential, too, in his suggestion that they fold "a bit of divine, lived reality" into the story of Éléonore and Gérard? As far as Élisabeth could tell, this model would permit, and possibly even encourage, the passion between the fictional characters to spill over into the lives of their creators. In this way as well, the project would be conducive to love.

With such compelling reasons to agree to the plan, Élisabeth eagerly gave her assent. Answering his letter that very day, she wrote, "I cannot tell you how much delight I would take in joining our two flames together as one, hidden from other people's eyes but perhaps destined, someday, to touch other people's hearts."

IN THE END, the process of writing their novel would not be nearly as simple as the merging of two flames, or as quick as the building of a birds' nest. The endeavor would take more than a decade, bringing with it many unwelcome twists, including the eventual collapse of their partnership and of the hopes Élisabeth had held out for it. Before their final parting of ways, moreover, the attempt to transpose their "divine, lived reality" into fiction would plunge her and Giovanni into a maze of fun-house mirrors, where the contours between fantasy and truth became increasingly difficult to tease apart.

But to a woman in love with her own reflection, even fun-house mirrors had a certain dizzy appeal. For the time being, Élisabeth welcomed this latest chance to refract, rework, and multiply her captivating image. With Don Giovanni Borghese, she would pioneer a new art of being seen—by hiding in plain sight.

CHAPTER NINE

PARIS HIGH AND LOW

O n paper, Laure de Chevigné and Geneviève Straus looked like opposites. Laure of the provincial gentry and the noble Crusader lineage;
Geneviève of the bohemian bourgeoisie, "Parisian twice over." Laure,
the bony, heraldic "belle of Frohsdorf"; Geneviève, the neurasthenic queen of
Montmartre. Horsey Laure in her little tweed suits, "the incarnation of the warrior spirit"; languid Geneviève in her silky, mauve peignors, "the most indolent
of Muses." Laure, the fair-haired Catholic; Geneviève, the dark-haired Israelite.
In a fairy tale, they would be foils: Snow White, Rose Red. Or rivals: White
Swan, Black Swan. But in reality, they were close friends. They changed each
other's lives in significant ways, while also changing the face of Parisian society.

Beneath their surface differences, Laure and Geneviève had a lot in common.
They were both witty, engaging, sharp as tacks (and mean as hornets when provoked). They both much preferred men to women—themselves and each other
excluded.* Both were tireless social butterflies and shameless coquettes; both
were narcissists and self-promoters and fabulists extraordinaire. Both, finally,
shared a love of Paris, high and low, aristocratic and artistic. Laure, the *mondaine,* was lured by Montmartre; Geneviève, the bohemian, was drawn to the
Faubourg. Neither of them was looking to quit her native element entirely. On
the contrary, each woman was aware of the allure "her" Paris held for outsiders
and counted it a mainstay of her image. More unusual was the fact that each
woman also recognized the glamour of the other's milieu and sought a bit of its
stardust for herself.

LAURE BROUGHT INTO THE GRATIN a spirit of irrepressible playfulness. She was always the first person to volunteer to help paint a live donkey
to look like a zebra (the top prize in a fund-raising raffle for the Opéra) or to
rattle the castanets in a "burlesque symphony" (where party guests banged away
on fanciful noisemakers while a real orchestra played behind a scrim); she was
always the last person to take cover when a rainstorm broke over the racetrack
and the last to leave a skating party when temperatures plunged well below
freezing. In a special nighttime foxhunt in the Bois de Boulogne, conducted by

---

* In the manuscript of Geneviève's will, written in her own hand in 1926, Laure was one of very few women to
receive a bequest. Almost all the other female beneficiaries were either relatives or servants.

torchlight and cohosted by her "cousin d'Uzès" and Henry Greffulhe, Laure galloped at the head of the pack.

Subscription evenings could be crashingly dull affairs, there being only so much excitement one could glean from checking on one's peers through a lorgnette and ignoring the spectacle onstage. To salvage these occasions, Laure would drag a group of her friends out afterward to the latest trendy restaurant (not a standard venue for ladies of gentle birth) or out-of-the-way dance hall (ditto). Most society women turned in early, whereas Laure, wrote Lily de Gramont, "would stay out until two in the morning, only to reappear twelve hours later, bright-eyed, laughing, and as lovely as ever."

Staying out until two in the morning meant venturing outside the noble Faubourg, and in this sense, too, Laure was an original. When the Princesse Bibesco compared her to an eighteenth-century courtier from Versailles, running loose in the capital "on an escapade," she was referring not just to Laure's husbandless hijinks in the monde but to her even more outrageous forays into the gritty, offbeat Parisian neighborhoods that had fascinated her since childhood. These included the vibrant, mostly middle-class ninth arrondissement—where her sister Valentine no longer lived, but where Laure discovered some lively places to eat and drink—and Montmartre, the picturesque butte north of the city, where outlaws and artists roamed free.

On her outings to Montmartre, Laure struck up friendships few other *mondaines*—even those who were interested in the arts—would have deigned, or dared, to pursue. "Being very bright and very curious," wrote Marthe Bibesco,

> Mme de Chevigné made no apologies for going outside her own milieu to explore the margins of society. She socialized with artists, bohemians, musicians, journalists, anyone who pleased or amused her . . . , anyone who had talent or wit—or better yet, anyone who had both.

In truth, Laure valued lineage and rank as highly as anyone else in her set. But by socializing in the counterculture, she invented a new variation on the theme of noble "simplicity," affecting to believe that "nothing mattered but talent" and that her artist chums, whom other noblewomen contented themselves with admiring from afar, were innately superior to "the most illustrious grandees, . . . even [to] certain crowned heads." In this way, Laure sustained the defining, paradoxical fiction of every "simple" grande dame: that she was too "born" to give a hoot about birth.

Improbably enough, Laure owed her entrée into the margins of society to one of the first friends she made in the gratin: the Comtesse de Mailly-Nesle, née Marie de Goulaine. Physically, she and Laure looked uncannily alike; strangers often mistook them for sisters. Marie also shared Laure's respect for artistic talent—she herself was an aspiring singer—and her impatience with the stric-

CHOCOLAT GUÉRIN-BOUTRON

270 Jean de Keské, dans le Cid.

Jean de Reszké, an acclaimed Polish tenor, was one of Laure's first bohemian friends.

tures of *bon ton*. Indeed, Marie went so far as to break with society completely when she left her brutish aristocratic husband for Jean de Reszké, a tall, charismatic Polish tenor who was soon to become one of the greatest opera stars of his generation. (Before she ran off with Reszké, Marie had reportedly been a mistress of her husband's cousin Henry Greffulhe; perhaps this was why her elopement so intrigued Élisabeth.) Unlike most of Marie's fellow bluebloods, who shunned her after her defection, Laure was unwaveringly loyal, calling on her and Reszké often at their studio in Montmartre. It was there that Laure first became friendly with the couple's glamorous friend Geneviève Bizet (still known at the time as Bébé) and began attending her salon in the nearby rue de Douai.

Through Marie and Geneviève, who as doyennes of Montmartre played hostess to their colorful, creative neighbors, Laure absorbed into her social circle a number of writers and artists. After Georges de Porto-Riche, Laure's favorites in this world were three renowned female performers. The first was Yvette Guilbert, a popular chanteuse; Henri de Toulouse-Lautrec, another patrician émigré to Montmartre, immortalized her in all her skeletal, black-gloved glory. The second was Hortense Schneider, a world-famous soprano best known for her triumph in the title role in Jacques Offenbach's *La Grande-Duchesse de Gérolstein* (1867), a popular opera buffa with a Meilhac and Halévy libretto. The third, also a veteran of Meilhac and Halévy theater, was Réjane (née Gabrielle Réjane), acclaimed as the most gifted French actress since "the divine Sarah" Bernhardt.

Laure loved to boast about these friendships to her peers in the Faubourg, who tended not to regard such associations as *comme il faut*. Even a professed arts lover like Élisabeth Greffulhe held this prejudice, treating her protégés like the hired help. (Later in life, she would engage Isadora Duncan to give a private performance in the rue d'Astorg, only to refuse to let the dancer mingle with the guests afterward.) Laure, on the other hand, dropped her celebrity friends' names with breezy familiarity, peppering her conversation with phrases like "*Porto* told me that *Réjane* . . ." If a fellow *mondain* happened to mention some promising new artist she had yet to meet, Laure would become incredulous, exclaiming, "*What?* There is a new talent out there, and *we* haven't heard of her?" Her use of the royal "we" underscored her self-styled authority on *la vie de Bohème*.

With her local friends to guide her, Laure became an aficionado of the nightlife in Montmartre. The haunt she loved most was the Chat-Noir, a notorious gin joint around the corner from Geneviève's apartment. Founded in 1881 in a three-story abandoned post office with a dilapidated half-timbered exterior, the Chat-Noir was the world's first cabaret, a place where patrons could drink until late into the night while enjoying raucous live entertainment. The flamboyant red-haired proprietor, Rodolphe Salis, catered primarily to creative types, who published their writings and artwork in the Chat-Noir's in-house newspaper, gave musical and spoken-word performances on its stage, and covered its walls with their paintings, drawings, and posters. (Toulouse-Lautrec and Théophile Steinlen were regulars there.)

Cabaret singer Yvette Guilbert, drawn here by Toulouse-Lautrec, helped introduce Laure to the nightlife in Montmartre.

The Chat-Noir promoted an aesthetic of "antic madness." Thumbing his nose at high culture, Salis had his waiters dress in the elaborate green-and-gold-silk costumes and bicorn hats of the Académie Française's Immortals. On the third floor of the building, he let artist Caran d'Ache install a shadow theater, where silhouettes of cut-out puppets (*ombres chinoises*, or "Chinese shadows") cavorted against an illuminated scrim, enacting rambunctious parodies of historic events and biblical tales.

As the emcee, Salis was an outrageous showman, singling out new customers, especially the well-heeled ones, for torrents of theatrically obscene abuse. Raunchy language featured as well in the songs of Aristide Bruant, a self-appointed hero of the urban underclass and an avatar of musical provocateurs from Johnny Cash to the Sex Pistols to The Notorious B.I.G. Striding across the stage in musketeer boots and a fiery red muffler, Bruant sang of lowlifes and scoundrels, outcasts defiantly unbowed by the forces of order and law. His rabble-rousing anthems carried a special resonance in Montmartre because of the neighborhood's infamous role in the Paris Commune in 1871. As historian Jerrold Seigel has shown, Bruant cultivated his outlaw image offstage as well, instructing his servants to address him as "Singer for the People" rather than the formal "Monsieur." ("Singer for the People, come along to dinner now, the roast will be over-

The Chat-Noir became one of the most notorious and celebrated nightspots in Montmartre.

done.") As a royalist, Laure had no sympathy for the singer's left-wing politics, but his foul mouth and artful defiance amused her no end.

To those bohemians whose knowledge of the monde was limited to what they read in the gossip columns, Laure confounded their expectations with her peasant patois, her jaw-dropping bursts of profanity, and her *épater la noblesse* cheek. They also stood in awe of her descent from Petrarch's muse. Writers such as Porto-Riche who knew the *Rime Sparse* by heart even saw in Laure's beakish blonde looks traces of the woman Petrarch had hailed as "this phoenix of golden plumage." So captivating was this association to Laure's artist friends that some of them actually referred to her as "Laure de Noves, Comtesse de Chevigné." Others assumed that with such a remarkable literary heritage, she must also be related to the seventeenth-century author Mme de Sévigné, and mistakenly called her by that name.

Even her maiden name—which her "born" confrères primly avoided mentioning—had only positive connotations in this crowd. The young Polish-born pianist Misia Natanson (later the wife of artist José-María Sert), whose salon drew the likes of Mallarmé, Debussy, Toulouse-Lautrec, Monet, and Renoir, noted that because "of her Marquis de Sade ancestry, [Mme de Chevigné] could allow herself to say things that would not have been forgiven anyone else." Misia endeared herself to Laure by sighing, "De Sade! What a beautiful name. What wouldn't I give to have been born de Sade!"

Guy de Maupassant (1850–1893), whom Laure first met through Porto-Riche sometime in the early 1880s, was equally impressed. Renowned in literary circles as the favored protégé of one of the century's most exacting prose stylists, the late Gustave Flaubert (1821–1880), Maupassant was a writer of exceptional talent. (Goncourt put it about that Maupassant was Flaubert's illegitimate son, but this assertion was never proven.) An acclaimed master of the short story, he was wildly prolific in the genre. But Maupassant—a brawny, thrill-seeking boxer, fencer, sailor, hunter, and all-around manly man whose swagger put even Bruant's to shame—seemed to care far less about the life of the mind than about the pleasures of the flesh. He was rumored to have bedded as many women as he had written short stories, which was to say about three hundred, with conquests ranging from streetwalkers to *grandes bourgeoises*. Although he had contracted syphilis in his twenties, Maupassant declared openly that he was "proud to have the disease of François I" and insisted that it had in no way curtailed his prodigious libido. Novelist Joris-Karl Huysmans confirmed the factual basis for this claim after a night on the town with him and Flaubert:

> Maupassant boasted that he could tire a woman out making love. [We] adjourned to a bordello, where Maupassant, put to the test, stripped in front of everyone and came five times with his chosen partner. Flaubert, ecstatic, cried, "How refreshing!"

That Maupassant should identify himself as a rabid fan of "the divine marquis" was wholly consistent with his persona. He claimed that when he wanted to corrupt a new mistress, he gave her one of de Sade's books as a primer. He also belonged for a time to an all-male secret society devoted, like its many counterparts in de Sade's novels, to licentiousness, fornication, and "ferocious obscenity." With Maupassant writing its demented bylaws, the organization expanded its activities into pimping and savage violence, only to dissolve after an aspiring member died from the injuries the rest of the group had inflicted upon him during his initiation. It had been known as the Sadistic Crepitians' Society (Société Sadique des Crépitiens), "Crepitians" being an obscure coinage by Flaubert, and "sadistic" requiring no explanation.

None of Laure's letters to Maupassant has survived—not that she was likely to have written him many, given her chariness about leaving a paper trail. But a handful of his letters to her, recently sold at auction in Paris, suggest that their friendship was warm and long-lasting. One of these documents, an undated missive he wrote to her from Normandy, even implies that Maupassant had an affair with Laure, or at least tried to talk her into having one. Inviting her to come visit him at his beach house there, he offered her the use of his guest room, even as he conceded that by staying with him, she would open herself up to "rumors that could pursue you till the end of your days." Should she wish to avoid a scandal, he suggested, she might instead lodge somewhere nearby and thwart the would-be gossips by coming "over to my place, quite simply dressed as a man!!!" Posterity will never know whether this license to indulge her taste for androgynous clothing persuaded Laure to make the trip.

Maupassant wasn't afraid to put his lady friends into his fiction, and he may have given Laure a cameo in *Bel-Ami* (1885), the novel that made him a household name. The vignette stars a daring grande dame named Mme de Marelle who, left to her own devices by an absentee politician husband, takes advantage of her freedom to troll the nightclubs of Montmartre. Dressed incognito as a working girl, she brings the novel's titular handsome friend (*bel ami*), a lusty, lady-killing writer, on one of her jaunts. At a rowdy cabaret on the boulevard de Clichy (the location of the Chat-Noir), she confides to him above the racket,

> You can't imagine how I love these escapades to all the places where ladies aren't supposed to go. I didn't dare tell you that [*ça*] until now. . . . I love that [*Moi, j'adore ça*]! I have *riffraff* tastes!

In both style and substance, this confession is pure Laure, vaunting the taboo delights of her "escapades" and clinched by her trademark slang word, *ça*. Given his admiration for her great-grandfather de Sade, it was fitting that Maupassant should pay tribute to her as a model of transgressive exploits and "riffraff tastes."

BACK IN THE FAUBOURG, Laure's bohemian exploits set tongues wagging. Some of the stuffier clubmen, polar opposites of the *vieux*, worried that she was setting a bad example for their wives and daughters. Henry Greffulhe, categorically opposed to all misconduct but his own, was a leading voice in this faction. At home, he commanded Bebeth to "watch out for Mme de Chevigné—she is a lost woman!" Translation: do not talk to her in society, do not invite her to our house, and do not even think about emulating her.* (The hypocrisy of this injunction did not escape Élisabeth, who grumbled in her journal, "*He* can get into all the trouble he wants!") But Laure shrugged off the censure. Instead of apologizing for straying from her prescribed milieu, she proclaimed her "delight in the contrasts" between the ballrooms of the monde and the barrooms of Montmartre. *Opinione de Sado:* Laure regretted nothing.

Her insouciance did not prevent her from seeking to get the better of her critics. As a counterweight to the scolding of men like Greffulhe, Laure turned the august GDWs into Montmartre enthusiasts. On one of their trips to Paris, she marched them straight into the Chat-Noir, belly-laughing along with the rest of the crowd when Rodolphe Salis lambasted the princely couple in the vilest scatological and sexual terms. In Russia, to insult a Romanov was to risk Siberia or worse, but for that very reason, the GDWs were exhilarated. In the middle of Salis's tirade, the grand-duc gleefully shouted out a line that, probably thanks to Laure herself, found its way into the gratin's lexicon of royal sayings: "Bravo, *la vieille!*" This compliment was a particular source of pride for Laure because it resuscitated Henri V's pet name for her, simultaneously recalling her old royal friendship and underscoring her new one. Afterward, whenever the GDWs returned to Paris, they insisted that Laure bring them back to Montmartre for more "dangerous thrills."

In another audacious experiment, Laure decided to hold a small luncheon for the GDWs at her apartment in the Faubourg Saint-Honoré. Along with the usual grandees—the Duchesse de La Trémoïlle, Joseph de Gontaut, Henri de Breteuil, and a few of the Romanovs' other specially favored *mondains*—Laure included a surprise guest whom nobody but she would have been so gutsy as to invite with royalty: her celebrity singer friend Hortense Schneider. Laure must have been aware that back in 1867 Grand-Duc Wladimir had traveled to Paris just to see Hortense's star turn in Offenbach's *Grande-Duchesse de Gérolstein*, and that he had been dying to meet her ever since. (Hortense had a reputation for attracting royal lovers; her contemporaries jokingly named her "the Passage of Princes.") Singers and actresses might bed down with royals on the sly, but they

---

* It is possible that in warning his wife away from Laure, Henry Greffulhe was protesting too much, as the blue-eyed, strawberry-blond Laure was his exact physical type. Furthermore, her professed penchant for "f**king" would not have failed to interest a man as sexually insatiable as Henry. But if the two of them did have a liaison of some sort, no evidence of it survives.

Opera diva Hortense Schneider
bedded many of the foreign royals
who visited Paris, whence her
nickname, "The Passage of Princes."

were never, ever permitted to socialize with royalty in the presence of "decent" women, much less "decent" royal wives. While the commingling of heads of state and show-business people may be run-of-the-mill today, it was unthinkable in fin-de-siècle society—until Laure thought of it.

The high point of the luncheon came after a brief performance by Hortense, when Laure demanded of the rest of the group, "Now I ask you, *which* one is the *real* grande-duchesse?" Here again, she astounded her companions by affecting a total indifference to rank and a countervailing regard for talent. As her friend Abel Hermant noted, Laure's daring constituted its own type of sovereignty, so novel that it eclipsed the cachet of the star soprano and the imperial highness combined. To all who heard about the gathering (and Laure made sure everyone did), it affirmed that she "had pulled off a feat no one else in Paris would even have dared to try."

WHILE GENEVIÈVE BIZET'S STRATEGIES for bridging the aristocrat/artist divide were less flamboyant than Laure's, she brought the two worlds together in her own memorable way. Unhappy as her childhood had been, she had grown accustomed at a young age to the luxuries of the very rich: large household staffs; valuable artworks and antiques (interspersed, however, with Léonie's broken crockery); elegant clothes; the finest table settings, food, and wine. So the opulence of the nobility did not faze Geneviève, and she carried herself with the same ease as the denizens of that class. Her comfort with the trappings of privilege made her exceptionally well suited to act as an intermediary between the noble Faubourg and the *vie de Bohème*.

Another factor enabling her to play this role was her triply impressive status as the daughter of Fromental Halévy, cousin of Ludovic Halévy, and widow of Georges Bizet. As Laure's grande-duchesse luncheon made clear, even crowned heads were susceptible to the glamour of famous artists, and that glamour had surrounded Geneviève all her life. Before she even learned to walk, her parents were socializing with the deposed king Louis-Philippe in London. Growing up in Paris under the Second Empire, she saw her father and cousin courted by the most eminent figures of that régime, from the emperor's half brother, the Duc de Morny, a political operative of unbounded influence who yearned only to write for the stage (and with whom Ludovic obligingly coauthored an operetta), to Princesse Mathilde Bonaparte, who recruited both Ludovic and Fromental to her salon. The favor of Our Lady of the Arts launched many an artistic and social career, and Bizet attracted her interest in turn, though he proved too focused on his work to exploit her patronage for his own professional or *mondain* gain. But after his posthumous anointment as a genius, his widow fielded her own invitations from his highborn admirers. In the words of Ludovic's son Daniel—Geneviève's nephew in the Breton way—"She wore the dazzling glory of Bizet's name" with as much éclat as her half-mourning attire of grey, white, and mauve.

Reborn as the Widow Bizet, Geneviève came into her own as a society hostess. Transferring her weekly at-homes from her own apartment in the rue de Douai to Ludovic's place downstairs, she gained a whole new set of acolytes who changed the tenor and composition of her salon. More than anyone else in her family, Ludovic had taken advantage of his celebrity to cultivate the city's social élite. Through his Bonaparte patrons, he made some powerful friends, among them Princesse Mathilde's Franco-Italian nephew, the garrulous Comte Giuseppe (Gégé) Primoli, and the Marquis-Général de Galliffet, years before the Paris Commune turned him into the Butcher of Clichy. Ludovic also joined the ultra-exclusive Bixio Dinner, a weekly invitation-only affair that included Galliffet, Prince Auguste d'Arenberg, and the Duc d'Aumale. First as a candidate for the Académie Française, and then as a member, Ludovic cozied up to its titled Immortals, especially Joseph Othenin de Cléron, Comte d'Haussonville, an historian, and Vicomte Eugène-Melchior (Melchior) de Vogüé, who after a stint as a diplomatic attaché to the Russian court had become France's leading scholar of Tolstoy and Dostoyevsky. Except for the Duc d'Aumale, all these men became regulars at Geneviève's Thursdays, joined by d'Haussonville's son, Othenin (husband of "la belle Pauline"), and the ubiquitous Charles Haas.

According to Ludovic, these gentlemen trooped up to Montmartre each week to pay court to his cousin with the same heady feeling of transgression

DE HÉRÉDIA

BUSNACH
HOMME DE LETTRES

JULES LEMAITRE

GÉNÉRAL DE GALLIFET

These celebrity chocolate cards show (clockwise from *upper left*) poet José-Maria de Heredia, playwright Willie Busnach, Marquis-Général Gaston de Galliffet, and playwright and drama critic Jules Lemaître, all famed habitués of Geneviève's salon.

that brought Laure de Chevigné and the GDWs to the cabaret around the corner: "The Faubourg Saint-Germain [went] to Geneviève's salon as if it were the Chat-Noir." He added that the bohemians in her set were no less excited to mingle with the "born": "The Chat-Noir [went] to Geneviève's salon as if it were the Faubourg Saint-Germain." The meeting of the two contingents was not without explosive potential: Porto-Riche, for instance, had not only fought on the opposite side of the barricades from Galliffet in 1871 but had seen many friends gunned down by the general and his troops (and had narrowly avoided such an end himself). Yet the young poet and the old soldier interacted cordially at Geneviève's, modeling harmony between their respective camps. Both the artists and the noblemen made a concerted effort to be civil with one another, all of them being anxious to retain their visiting privileges in such a uniquely diverse salon. While several other bourgeois hostesses tried to achieve a similarly hybrid mix of guests, few could boast the same success. (All the same, Geneviève did keep tabs on a few of these rivals by occasionally attending their salons and inviting them to hers.)

Geneviève's romance with Émile Straus further expanded her coterie, as he conscripted several high-profile Parisians from his own milieux, separate from but complementary to hers. A leading expert in corporate law, Straus was house counsel to the Rothschilds. In this capacity he had formed relationships with members of all the city's top Jewish banking clans, as well as with the wizard of the Suez Canal, Ferdinand de Lesseps, and Gustave Schlumberger, scion of a Protestant industrialist family. Straus also formed ties with republican leaders like Joseph Reinach (1856–1921), a statesman begrudgingly described by Edmond de Goncourt (who loathed him) as "one of the uncontested masters of France for over twenty years." Because of their "not born" origins and/or their liberal politics, these men would not have been welcome in most aristocratic salons, while because of their power and wealth, they were not natural companions for the bohemians (though many of the bankers collected contemporary French art). At Geneviève's, the tycoons and political leaders added another dash of novelty to the mix, providing yet another inducement unavailable in rival salons.

Of the guests Straus brought into the fold, far and away the most prestigious were Barons Alphonse, Gustave, and Edmond de Rothschild, the grown sons of the late Baron James (né Jakob Mayer) de Rothschild, who had immigrated to France from Frankfurt's Jewish ghetto as a teenager, founded Rothschild Frères, the Parisian branch of his family's multinational financial empire, and wielded power that had rivaled that of Europe's mightiest rulers. Endowed with "the royalty of wealth, which is the scepter of society," poet Alfred de Vigny wrote of him in 1837, "the Jewish banker . . . reigns over the Pope and Christianity. He pays monarchs and buys nations."

Two photos from an Halévy album. From *left*, Degas, Geneviève, Albert Boulanger-Cavé, Louis Ganderax. On the right, from *left:* seated, Melchior de Vogüé, Ludovic Halévy, the Comtesse de Broissia, Louise Halévy, and standing, *left* to *right*, Daniel Halévy, Charles Haas. All the photographs in this album are by the Marquis de Lau, a clubman friend of both Laure and Geneviève, and by Hortense Howland, Degas's longtime mistress.

 Upon Baron James's death in 1868, his sons had inherited his fortune and political clout. The eldest son, Alphonse, took over as the new head of Rothschild Frères, where he and his brothers brought Émile Straus on board as their legal consigliere. This decision lent credence to the widespread rumor that Straus was their father's love child. The three barons further fueled this gossip by treating Straus as a brother, albeit a pesky one. Their presence in the rue de Douai had begun with Straus badgering them for months: "You must see Geneviève!" Only to placate him did they finally make the trek to Montmartre. But when they did, they saw Geneviève's appeal at once and happily joined the growing ranks of her faithful.

 For Geneviève, the Rothschilds' arrival in her salon was a tremendous coup. Still idolizing them as "better" versions of her disgraced Pereire kin, she was drawn to their warmly clannish *esprit de famille.* She also recognized that among Parisian Israelites, no one could match their cachet. Even anti-Semitic *mondains* sought invitations to the parties the Rothschilds held whenever royalty came to town. And even anti-Semitic artists cultivated them for their generous patronage. While given to muttering beneath his moustache about the "dirty Jews," Paul Hervieu confided to Henri de Régnier, "I will never have a falling-out with [Geneviève] and Straus, because they introduced me to the Rothschilds."

IF SHE WERE BEING HONEST, Geneviève might have described her own relationship with Straus in similar terms. Ever since her first trip with him to Ferrières in 1881, she had taken every opportunity to "latch on to" the Rothschilds, as Princesse Mathilde had phrased it. This led Geneviève's loved ones to suspect that Straus's Rothschild affiliation played a major, even conclusive, part in her acceptance of him as a suitor. The consensus among them was that while Straus "love[d] our divine Geneviève madly," she did not love him in return. Daniel Halévy, again echoing his parents' judgments, recorded that his aunt "tolerated" Straus as the man in her life "because he was there, and because he adored her. . . . But he was not loved."

Four years older than Geneviève, Straus was a short, slight man with slumping posture, thinning, frizzy reddish hair, and a large horseshoe-shaped furrow in his brow. His best feature was his strong, sharp chin, notched with a forceful cleft. But in a culture that equated facial hair with manliness, his inability to grow more than a sparse patch of whiskers along his jawline qualified him as somewhat defective. When he was a twenty-six-year-old volunteer fighting in the siege of Paris, a shell had exploded near his face. Ever since then, his blue eyes had been creased in a permanent half-squint, and when he smiled, only one corner of his mouth managed to curl upward. To be sure, Geneviève need not have been put off by her suitor's partial facial paralysis. Given her own struggle with nervous tics, his impairment might have stirred her empathy. It might even, as a lover's quirks sometimes do, have triggered her lust. Still, her nearest and dearest all agreed that she "did not [take Straus] for an Adonis"—a classic *mondain* litotes meant to stress how little she desired him.

Certainly their Geneviève was not, they maintained, with Straus for his winning personality. Though nominally his friend, Schlumberger spoke for many of the faithful when he denigrated Straus as "rather common, quite ill-bred, and willfully impudent, with a lawyer's way of talking too much." ("Schlum," a scholar of the Crusades and Byzantium, had a scholar's way of doing the same thing.) Goncourt, too, objected to Straus's "lawyerly verboseness," and Jean Forain caricatured it by portraying Geneviève's beau in a courtroom in midtirade, his mouth stretched grotesquely wide. Élie Delaunay, who usually had a kind word for everyone, disparaged Straus as "a little twit." One of Geneviève's rare female confidantes, Mme Henri (Laure) Baignères, deemed him arrogant and insecure, "vain about the things he had and envious of the things he didn't."

Hervieu, Bourget, and Porto-Riche were united in their distaste for Straus's "frightful temper," which manifested itself in roaring rages, leading the writers to nickname him "Straus the Tiger," "Straus-Such-a-Tiger" (*Straussitigre*), and "Straus the Terrible." When in a mood, wrote Daniel Halévy, Straus would wreak havoc in Geneviève's salon, "spinning like a top, being a brute, trampling on this lady's dress or that man's feet" and never stopping to apologize for his "carelessness and aggression."

To Ludovic and Louise Halévy, Geneviève's involvement with Straus both stemmed from and amplified her two most regrettable instincts: "black-hearted vanity and social calculation." She had set those impulses aside in marrying Bizet, but they returned with a vengeance in her new relationship. Living up to Bizet's characterization of her mother, Geneviève aligned herself with Straus, and through him, the Rothschilds, for reasons of "social status [and] money!!!!!"

IN HER KEENNESS TO KEEP the Rothschild men happy, Geneviève issued a blanket invitation to their wives and female relatives and friends. This tack enabled her to cultivate Baronnes Alphonse, Gustave, and Edmond, their sister-in-law Mme Maurice Ephrussi (née Béatrice de Rothschild), and two of their kinswomen who had married into the Catholic nobility: the Duchesse (Marguerite) de Gramont and the Princesse (Berthe) de Wagram, sisters from the Frankfurt Rothschild clan. Geneviève also opened her salon to two alluring, well-connected sisters—Lulia Cahen d'Anvers and Marie Kann, wives of prominent Jewish bankers—with whom the Rothschilds fraternized. Jacques Blanche dubbed this new subset of the faithful "the countesses of Judea." Through their offices, wrote Daniel Halévy, his aunt Geneviève was "invited into the very best company," and met with "incredible success."

But her appeal went beyond the unique potpourri of her guest list. Geneviève's perceived influence in the Académie Française remained a significant draw for those of her guests with high-flown literary aspirations. Between Ludovic, his writing partner, Henri Meilhac (elected in 1888), Melchior de Vogüé, and Alexandre Dumas *fils* (a longtime friend of the Halévys), Geneviève had the ear of four out of the forty Immortals, and she was not shy about mobilizing them on her friends' behalf. Over the course of her life, at least nine more habitués of her salon would be named to the Académie: historian Othenin d'Haussonville; novelists Paul Bourget, Paul Hervieu, and Maurice Barrès; poets José-Maria de Heredia, Henri de Régnier, and Fernand Gregh; drama critic (and sometime playwright) Jules Lemaître; and her beloved cousin Porto-Riche.

In d'Haussonville's election, Geneviève was rumored to have played a pivotal role. The fact that his late father had held a seat in the Académie wound up working against him, as the elder d'Haussonville had made an enemy of Dumas *fils* by treating him "with a nobleman's disdain for the lowborn." But Geneviève worked with Ludovic to ensure that the younger d'Haussonville won the necessary votes. (Whether the cousins brokered a truce between him and Dumas *fils* is unknown.) Geneviève declined to involve herself in the candidacy of two other *fidèles:* Schlumberger and Reinach. To the latter, she wrote candidly about his nonexistent chances of election and her inability to help him (effects of the controversial position they both took, in support of Captain Alfred Dreyfus, during the Dreyfus affair). Reinach deferred to Geneviève's judgment with good grace, his compliance itself a testament to her presumed sway with the Immortals.

The more time Geneviève spent with members of the gratin, the more her approach to entertaining changed, becoming less bohemian and more conventionally *mondain.* In the early days of her salon, she treated her guests to special private recitals and performances of her artist friends' new works. She encouraged the writers among them to bring their manuscripts so that she and the rest of the group might offer feedback. She sometimes even recited a few poems or sang a song or two herself, with Gounod or Massenet accompanying her on the piano. These diversions made her at-homes altogether different from those of the Faubourg, where going to a salon usually meant making idle chitchat for a few hours over orangeade, petits fours, and (for the gentlemen and Laure de Chevigné) tobacco. But over time, Geneviève reduced the cultural heft of her salon, having gleaned from her patrician friends that speaking earnestly about highbrow topics violated the monde's basic requirements for elegant conversation (that it remain lighthearted) and womanhood (that it exclude bookishness). As bright and sophisticated as she was, Geneviève held herself scrupulously to

Aesthete, author, and diarist Edmond de Goncourt was an habitué of Geneviève's salon, despite his hatred of Jews; usually he appeared there on the arm of Princesse Mathilde Bonaparte. His unfiltered, persnickety diaries remain an invaluable trove of gossip about the circles in which he and Geneviève moved.

these standards, and according to Lily de Gramont, at least, "her friends were thankful to her for her lack of pedantry."

Edmond de Goncourt frequented Geneviève's salon as a walker for Princesse Mathilde. While he scoffed at the preponderance of Jewish guests, he appreciated the conversational tone Geneviève fostered: "amusing and frivolous, as in an eighteenth-century salon—full of finely malicious double entendres, and barbs like scornful smiles." As Goncourt's analogy indicates, banter of this kind dated back to the salons of ancien régime Paris, where aristocrats on hiatus from Versailles continued the symbolic jockeying for supremacy that consumed them at court. In these drawing-room skirmishes, words were the weapons, and the winners were those who trounced their fellows with the greatest wit and finesse. As Proust would write in his first-ever article for *Le Gaulois,* an overview of the great French salons, "They fought one another with pinpricks."

Of this minor art of war, Charles Haas was the acknowledged master, dusting off such vintage sallies as his decades-old comeback to loudmouthed Mélanie de Pourtalès ("I've never heard you in *Faust!*") and trying out new material. As was typical in his adopted class, he particularly enjoyed cutting down his own friends, such as Robert de Montesquiou, with whom he had been close since before the Franco-Prussian War. Combining two subspecialties of *mondain* humor, impersonation and puns, Haas aped Montesquiou's yelping declamatory style while deliberately butchering his grandiose claim: "I have adorned the ducal coronet of the Fezensacs with the crown [*couronne*] of the poet!" By changing a few letters of the word *couronne,* Haas converted the poet's crown into a heart attack.

Prince Auguste d'Arenberg also excelled in this frothy but deadly genre, although he preferred quoting other people's repartee to coming up with his own. He repeated a snide epigram about Boni de Castellane's fiancée, Anna Gould, an American railroad heiress as homely as she was rich: "She's pretty enough, seen from the back!" (Playing on the homology between the French words for back [*dos*] and dowry [*dot*], this mot suggested that Anna Gould was attractive when considered in light of her wealth.) These were the sorts of arch, cutting insults that qualified as witticisms in the Faubourg—and in Geneviève's increasingly *mondain* salon.

Once she had formed her own salon, Laure de Chevigné had less time to visit Geneviève's. But when she did, she showed the faithful why "her biting wit was the joy and the terror of Parisian society." Once arriving with her little Pomeranian dog, Kiss, tucked under her arm, Laure recoiled when Jean Lorrain, a novelist who wore more makeup than a showgirl at the Folies-Bergère, planted a smooch on the pup's head: "Careful! You'll get face powder all over him!" (Like Haas, Laure was given to recycling her quips: decades later, she would use this same line on Jean Cocteau.)

On another occasion, Laure slammed Geneviève's eccentric friend Emmanu-ela, Comtesse Potocka, whose macabre self-presentation—lacquered black hair, kohl-ringed eyes, and a body as emaciated as that of the greyhounds she kept by the dozens—belied a reputation for sexual wildness. While Laure herself, of course, was no model of feminine virtue, she pretended to take umbrage at Mme Potocka's loose morals. So when the latter woman got up to leave Gene-viève's one day in the company of a suspected lover, Laure took aim. "She's like the sun," she commented, loudly enough for the departing couple to hear. "She rises [*se lève*] in one place and sets [*se couche*] in another."*

Several of the artists in Geneviève's clique were equally adept at such spar-ring. A bohemian by choice but a nobleman by birth, Degas had a natural gift for "assassinating his targets in three lines or less." His preferred victims were the other painters in Geneviève's salon. Of Gustave Moreau, Degas sneered, "He would have us believe the gods wear watch chains!" (This, Daniel Halévy explained in his diary, was meant as a swipe at Moreau's bedazzled mythical figures.) He mocked Édouard Detaille, an academic painter renowned for his battle scenes, as "an arms dealer" and Élie Delaunay as "a watercolorist of cats and dogs." These put-downs didn't win Degas any friends among his fellow art-ists, but they kept the rest of the company amused.

Degas was also known for his fat jokes—expressions of his morbid antipathy to plus-sized women. Daniel Halévy remembered his regaling the group with this anecdote:

> One day at the Opéra, two ladies were resting their big, hefty arms on the velvet ledge at the front of their box. All of a sudden, from up in the gal-lery came a cry: "Down with that ham!" General bafflement. Again the plaintive voice from the gallery: "Down with that ham!" The people in the audience began to whisper, trying to understand. Finally they caught sight of the fat arms and started hooting. The ladies were forced to withdraw.

Geneviève, who like Laure was fanatical about keeping slim, shared Degas's prej-udice, echoed in one of her own often-repeated zingers: "She's not a cow" (or a panther), "she's an entire herd." Jests like these did not sit well with the zaftig Princesse Mathilde, but she was in the minority.

Degas indulged in anti-Semitic mockery as well, apparently unconcerned about offending his Jewish hostess and companions. One of his favorite "funny" stories involved two pet monkeys who got loose during a party at Ferrières. The premise was that it was impossible to distinguish the monkeys, who had been dressed in white tie for the event, from the putatively simian Rothschilds.

---

* This wisecrack was another example of *mondain* wordplay. Because in French the verbs "rise" and "set" also mean "wake up" and "go to bed," Laure's joke referenced Mme Potocka's alleged bed hopping.

To root out the wayward beasts, one guest decided to gather all the celebrants together and ask who among them could spare a two-louis coin. The monkeys blew their own cover when they volunteered the paltry sum—as the inventor of the ruse had anticipated, they were the only ones who did.

Degas did not spare Haas his anti-Semitic ribbing, again demonstrating that when it came to *mondain* persiflage, the taste for cruelty trumped the bonds of friendship. Having turned his back on the idle frivolity of his native caste, the painter disapproved of Haas's dedication to it and saw in his untiring social activity a parvenu's overeagerness to belong. To tease his friend for his habit of ceaselessly hurrying from one party to the next, Degas branded him "the poor Wandering Jew."

Laure de Chevigné shared Degas's penchant for Jewish slurs, which she likewise deployed at her supposed friends' expense. After one of Arthur Meyer's rare cameos in the rue de Douai (he and Geneviève never really got along, each one put off by the other's *mondain* ambition), Laure told the rest of the company, "My yid doesn't have his hair anymore, but he's all right." About Haas, she was even more vicious, reporting behind his back that he owed his membership in the Jockey to a bit of sneaky Hebraic guile. According to Laure, when Haas was preparing to present himself as a candidate there for the fifth (and final) time, he waited until all the club members who might have blackballed him were otherwise occupied . . . fighting against the Prussians in the siege of Paris.

While it won chuckles from the *mondains,* this tall tale played on a deadly serious opposition between the valor of the *noblesse d'épée* and the alleged cunning, cowardice, and traitorous "German" loyalties of the Jew. When the Dreyfus affair erupted in the 1890s, self-proclaimed French patriots would invoke this same stereotype to justify the persecution of an innocent Jewish army officer as a Prussian spy.

How Geneviève's Jewish guests felt about this sort of humor is difficult to determine. Some of them played along, as when Ludovic Halévy made light of his own, stereotypically "Jewish" greed. He recounted how, after turning down an offer of twenty thousand francs to write a serial novel for *Le Gaulois,* "I had to pinch myself. Was it really *I* talking?" Of objections to the anti-Semitic raillery in Geneviève's clique, there appears to be only one recorded instance. An unidentified Jewish friend of hers once moved to cut off a racist tirade by Jean Forain—a caricaturist who had studied under Degas and whose lacerating sense of humor made him a great favorite of Geneviève's—by interjecting, "But your Jesus Christ was Jewish!" Forain, as quick-witted as his master, shot back, "Yes, out of humility." Retorts like these may have deterred the Jewish *fidèles* from protesting more often. As Proust would later surmise in an unpublished manuscript fragment, "Perhaps the humiliations a Jew [has] almost inevitably experienced at some point" in his life make him "fearful of being despised."

As for Geneviève, her line about having "too little religion to wish to change it" may have represented her attempt to put some distance between herself and the racist slurs her "born" friends found so funny. At the same time, she developed a more compelling means of deflecting their bigotry by putting herself forward as the star wit of her salon.

While Geneviève could be as acerbic as any of her callers, she was rarely as mean-spirited. Fernand Gregh described her sense of humor as a fizzy cocktail of

> common sense and surprised merriment, which made her say the most outlandish things with a wholly disingenuous air. Not unlike her cousin Ludovic Halévy, she had a whimsical mind; there was something natural and gentle in its derisiveness and unpredictable in its logic.

Geneviève specialized in tart, playful one-liners that indeed recalled the good-natured irony of Ludovic's and Meilhac's collaborations for the stage. Praised by one theater critic as "biting but restrained, inflicting a blow without ever pouring salt in the wound, . . . impertinent yet sweet at the same time, . . . less annoyed by human folly than amused by it," the "Meilhac and Halévy" esprit enjoyed terrific cultural cachet. To spot a family resemblance between their humor and Geneviève's was to place her in the very best comedic company.

What differentiated Geneviève from the famous duo, and evidently made her company so much more entertaining than theirs, was the look of sweet-faced innocence she assumed when cracking wise. (Goncourt labeled this her "Jewish nonchalance.") Thanks to Geneviève's deadpan delivery, lines that hardly sound like knee-slappers struck her listeners as riotously funny. One of her most celebrated quips came from an exchange with Gounod at the premiere of Massenet's opera Herodias (Hérodiade, 1881). During the intermezzo, Gounod turned to her and declared in sententious tones, "I find the music octagonal." "I was just going to say that!" Geneviève exclaimed, her wide-eyed mien betraying not the slightest glimmer of bemusement. Another of her oft-cited mots was her rejoinder when someone unfamiliar with her background asked her if she liked music: "We made a lot of it in my first family." This line captured Geneviève's own take on upper-class "simplicity," downplaying her ties to two of the greatest composers of the century.

The habitués of her salon professed awe at her cleverness and kept track of her barbs in a continually expanding oral treasury of "Geneviève's latest." Marking time between Sundays, they repeated her sallies among themselves in a ritual of collective self-soothing. They also quoted her epigrams to the uninitiated in their respective peer groups—nobles, plutocrats, artists—introducing each pearl with the question, "Have you heard Geneviève's latest?" Like a stone cast into a lake on a windless day, this refrain sent ripples of excitement through Parisian society, in concentric circles that grew ever wider until they covered the entire surface, leaving no quarter undisturbed. As Boni de Castellane—he of the ugly "dollar princess" bride—remarked with a twinge of regret, "The duchesses of yesteryear are being replaced by witty women."

As time went on, Geneviève would find other methods for honing her mystique. But the legend of her "Meilhac and Halévy" wit, disseminated throughout the city by three distinct, prestigious groups of friends, proved an excellent starting point. Like the reports of Laure's wild nights at the Chat-Noir, this legend not only enhanced the glory of its heroine; it spoke to a new symbolic convergence between Montmartre and the monde. As any collector of Félix Potin trading cards could attest, the old barriers were crumbling in fin-de-siècle Paris, and amidst the wreckage a new social order was taking shape. Between the fortresses of privilege and the ghettos of genius arose a great, bustling marketplace where pedigree and talent, high and low came together to trade in a common coin: celebrity. As catalysts of this rapprochement, Geneviève and Laure emerged as two of its best-known paragons. Although the luster of their names originated with other men's achievements (those of Petrarch, de Sade, Bizet, and the Halévys), the two women made it their own with their unorthodox approach to sociability and self-promotion. Anticipating a world most of their contemporaries had yet to foresee, Geneviève and Laure became famous for being famous.

CHAPTER TEN

A MODERN-DAY ARAMIS

Laure and Geneviève were not the only ones in their respective households to brave controversy and flout convention. Their husbands also bucked the unwritten rules of their milieu. Adhéaume de Chevigné rebelled by taking up, and taking off, with the young Baron de Senevas. Émile Straus rebelled by refusing to stay in his caste of origin: Paris's immigrant working class. Of Adhéaume's transgression, little more remains to be said as no further information seems to survive. Of Straus's anomalous social profile, enough scraps of evidence remain to form a somewhat clearer picture. It reveals a man as bright, ambitious, and complicated as the woman he married; a gumptious, "not born" striver playing his own supporting role in the larger societal drama in which Geneviève, Laure, and Élisabeth costarred: the *déclassement du gratin*.

Straus took many of his contemporaries aback with his naked desire for social advancement. Though merely a bourgeois Jew, he pursued noble and even royal connections with the same mulish tenacity and strategic astuteness that got him so far as a lawyer. According to those who knew him well, Straus's urge to break into the gratin stemmed directly from his insecurity about his family background. As Daniel Halévy phrased it, "Like many self-made men, Straus came from nothing but was extremely snobbish." Also like many self-made men, he avoided talking about the depths from which he had risen. While Straus's name appears hundreds of times in fin-de-siècle newspapers and memoirs, none of these sources ever refers either to the circumstances of his birth or to the years that predated his social and professional climb. Straus himself, although he lived into his eighties, never spoke or wrote about his roots. His effective erasure of them from his public persona is all the more striking given the overweening importance of family in the circles in which he and Geneviève socialized.

To what extent Straus kept even her in the dark about his origins is hard to determine. However, the fact that Geneviève's correspondence contains no letters to or from any of her second husband's relatives suggests either that he chose not to tell her about the other Strauses or that she, too, preferred to ignore their existence. This had by no means been her policy with her first set of in-laws, socially obscure though they had also been. Even after Bizet died, Geneviève had remained close with his widowed father, Adolphe, a retired hairdresser and piano teacher, relying on him often as a babysitter for Jacques. With her encouragement (and likely with her financial help), Adolphe Bizet had even moved in to a small apartment downstairs from hers at 22, rue de Douai, residing there until his death in 1886.

When Geneviève and Straus wed on October 7 of that year, they may both have been seeking a fresh start. The marriage took place at the Grand Synagogue of Paris, a majestic modern basilica with an ornate neo-Romanesque façade and seating for eighteen hundred. Located in the ninth arrondissement, the temple stood in the same neighborhood where the bride had had her first wedding, but the resemblance between the two ceremonies ended there. Geneviève and Bizet had married at the local town hall, the modest civil service attended by only a handful of loved ones (and boycotted by the bride's mother). She and Straus married in great pomp in a religious service officiated by the grand rabbi of Paris, exchanging vows beneath a traditional Jewish chuppah at the foot of a towering marble altar. A phalanx of Rothschilds—the synagogue's leading patrons—witnessed the union, their presence fraught with symbolic meaning for the newlyweds. By this time, Geneviève and Émile had no living parents between them. The Rothschilds, the couple appeared to be saying, would be their family now.

As if to extend this plummy pedigree to his late mother and father, Philippine and Abraham Straus, the bridegroom listed them on the marriage certificate as *rentiers:* people of independent means.* This was the only documented mention he ever made of his legal parents. It was also an untruth that revealed much about his plans for his life with Geneviève. A worthy match for that virtuoso of self-reinvention, Straus would rewrite his history, storm the citadel of privilege, and define himself anew.

ABRAHAM SELIGMANN (1803–1881) was born in Obermoschel in the Rhineland-Palatinate, a Prussian territory in the Rhine valley adjacent to the French province of Alsace. His family belonged to the large Ashkenazi Jewish population that lived in the region; Abraham was one of four siblings, the younger of two sons. His father, Samuel (1774–?), is listed in civil records as a ragpicker from the Frankfurter Judengasse, one of the oldest Jewish ghettos in Europe. There is some chance that he moved to Alsace to join a homegrown forgery ring, for in 1806, two of Samuel's Seligmann relations in the area were arrested for counterfeiting Austrian, French, and Prussian currencies. Once these Seligmanns were tried and convicted, Samuel dissociated himself and his immediate family from the scandal by changing their last name to Strauss. But soon thereafter, in a move his son Abraham would later replicate, Samuel left the country, moving back to the Frankfurt ghetto and leaving his wife and children in Alsace.

---

* *Rentier* was the term people of independent wealth used on civil documents where an occupation had to be specified. Marcel Proust, for instance, was correctly identified as a *rentier* on his death certificate in 1922.

Émile Straus's parents were married in this predominantly Jewish town in the Lower Rhine valley.

Abraham Strauss married Philippine Frank (c. 1812–1884), also an Alsatian
Ashkenazi Jew, in the late 1820s in Obermoschel, where the couple had their
first child, Léopold, in 1830. They immigrated to Paris shortly afterward. In
the move, Abraham's surname changed for a second time, losing its final "s."
Henceforth it would be pronounced in the French manner, as "Strôss,"* rather
than as the Teutonic "Schtrauss." This difference in pronunciation would be
important to the couple's youngest son, Émile, as it would mark an audible
distance between him and his ignoble Rhinish heritage. In Jewish immigrant
communities in the United States in the nineteenth and early twentieth centuries, German Jews formed the pinnacle of the social hierarchy, which happened
to include eminent families named Seligman and Straus (of no known relation
to Abraham, Samuel, et al.). In France, by contrast, the German-speaking Ashkenazi were more commonly regarded as crude, ghettoish stock, inferior to such
old-money, Iberian Sephardic clans as the Gradis, Rodrigues, and Pereires, who
had arrived generations before. The stereotype of the German-Jewish "ghetto
pariah" would grow even more pejorative after the Franco-Prussian War. By
then, as a young attorney starting his career in Paris, Émile would insist upon
the French pronunciation of his name in order to convey his learning, refine-

* Rhyming with the English "dose" or "gross"

ment, and patriotism. During the Dreyfus affair, those wishing to insult him could do so simply by calling him "Schtrauss."

Once in Paris, the Abraham Strauses settled in a blue-collar neighborhood in the second arrondissement, where Philippine gave birth to four more children, two girls and two boys. Émile was the baby, arriving in 1844, eleven years after Daniel, the Strauses' middle son. The children grew up speaking a combination of German and Yiddish at home, a fact that may have attested to their parents' limited grasp of French. Like children of immigrants in so many eras and cultures, the Straus siblings probably picked up the local language from native speakers outside the home: playmates, neighbors, teachers (if the children went to school). Some decades later, Émile would draw upon his boyhood German when translating some poems by Heinrich Heine into French for Baronne Willy de Rothschild.

The second arrondissement was, and still is, home to Les Halles, the sprawling central marketplace aptly known as "the belly of Paris." Abraham found work there as an itinerant flour peddler, eventually rising to become a flour merchant with his own stall in the Grain Exchange on the market's western perimeter. In his gritty novel *The Belly of Paris* (*Le Ventre de Paris,* 1873), Émile Zola describes the Grain Exchange as "a massive and heavy stone cage" piled high with dusty sacks of flour and topped with a vaulted rotunda. In 1885, it would become the new home to the Paris Stock Exchange, previously based in a

This picture shows a typical nineteenth-century worker lugging grain in Les Halles. Straus's father and two older brothers also did this job.

In the "Belly of Paris," women represented a notable part of the workforce.

colonnaded neoclassical building next door. The whole area around Les Halles bustled with activity from before sunrise, when farmers, fishermen, and hunters from the provinces rode into town to offload their bounty from horse-drawn carts, to sundown, when poor people and rats made their meals from scraps in the overflowing trash-bins and gutters.

While Léopold and Daniel Straus were in their early teens, before their youngest brother was born, they joined their father's flour business in the Grain Exchange. (Presumably they never went to high school.) Philippine may have labored alongside them, as many women worked in Les Halles at the time. Apart from the heaviest lifting, the female workers in the marketplace performed all the same tasks as the men, from managing inventories to transacting with buyers. If Philippine did help out in this way, then she would probably have left her infant daughters in the care of a neighbor during the day. Either way, she would still have borne primary responsibility for domestic chores at home, including hauling water for bathing, cleaning, and cooking, up and down narrow flights of stairs; shopping for groceries, which spoiled quickly in the warmer months; cleaning fish, poultry, and meat of its scales, feathers, and hide and preparing it over a smoky coal- or gas-heated stove; and dragging bundles of dirty sheets, clothes, and diapers to the riverbanks to launder them. The cosseted leisure of upper-class Parisiennes, who delegated all such drudgery to their domestic staffs, was not a luxury families like the Strauses could afford.

Another luxury of that sort was the presence of a chaperone, whether a footman or an adult relative, to stand guard over Philippine's virtue whenever she went out in public. For better or worse, this lack of protection would have paved the way for a relationship that a woman in her circumstances could, nevertheless, scarcely have expected to have. And so it was that sometime in the mid-1840s, Philippine entered into an affair with Baron James de Rothschild (1792–1868), one of the richest men in history.

How their romance started is unknown, though the close proximity of the Grain Exchange to the Bourse, a daily destination for Baron James, may have facilitated their initial and/or subsequent encounters. There is also some chance they met through the flour trade. In the mid-1840s, wheat shortages throughout France sent commodity prices soaring. As mass starvation loomed, Baron James took action to forestall the crisis. Convening the grain vendors of Paris, he told them that if they agreed to stop raising their prices, he would fund the shortfall himself (an arrangement he financed by entering into a proto-derivative credit swap with the Russian tsar). If Philippine did work in the business with Abraham and her sons, and if the Strauses were among the merchants the baron summoned to this meeting, she could have caught his attention then.

What drew her and the baron together is another mystery. Philippine left no personal writings—she may not even have known how to write, as schooling in Alsatian Jewish communities tended to be reserved for boys—and Baron James's archives do not seem to contain any hints about the affair. But his public profile, as one of the most powerful men in Europe, was in direct, inverse proportion to Philippine's obscurity, so any theories about the basis of their attraction are bound to skew more toward what was and remains known about him. The most pedestrian, if perhaps also the most plausible, explanation for Philippine's interest in the baron would be that he offered her some material comfort beyond what she was used to in her life with Abraham. Baron James had a legendary

Baron James de Rothschild, presumed to be Émile Straus's real father, was a colossally rich financier, philanthropist, and adviser to Louis-Phillipe.

appetite for the finer things and spent liberally to acquire and enjoy them. As one of his great-great-granddaughters, Anka Muhlstein, writes in her biography of him,

> This Rothschild embraced ostentation with an abandon and an excess that were prodigious, suggesting a fierce . . . resolve to outstrip everyone so as to forge a place for himself apart, and a determination to beat the aristocracy at their own game, that of luxury, taste, and refinement.

In addition, the baron was famously generous toward the poor. If he displayed either or both of these proclivities in his dealings with Philippine, then maybe he won her over with his largesse.

Baron James was not known for his good looks—with his rotund belly, fleshy jowls, and bulbous, thick-lidded blue eyes, he resembled a bullfrog in banker's clothing. The similarity only increased as he grew older, his spherical midsection broadening until he appeared nearly as wide as he was tall. Society wags joked that he had tried to compensate for his ugliness by marrying beauty in the form of his nineteen-year-old niece, née Betty von Rothschild (1805–1886). Described by the German poet Heinrich Heine as a "wingless angel," Betty was a voluptuous, sloe-eyed brunette. A magnificent portrait of her by Jean-Auguste-Dominique Ingres, painted between 1842 and 1848, captures the sheen of her lustrous dark hair, the perfect oval of her face, and the creamy, graceful curves of her shoulders, offset by a sumptuous rose-taffeta dress. While having a gorgeous wife did not deter him from cheating, Baron James did conduct his affairs with an eye to his *mondain* reputation, about which he cared immensely. (According to the Austrian ambassador, "The grand lords all [made] fun of him, but [were] no less charmed" to attend the parties he threw to impress them.) To guard against scandal, the baron preferred to cull his mistresses from the lower orders. So in social terms, a peddler's wife would have been just the kind of woman to catch his roving eye.

No images of Philippine survive; like servants, photographs and portraits lay far beyond the Strauses' means. Assuming she had the same thin frame, light eyes, and fair, reddish hair as her youngest son, then at the very least, she would have represented a different physical type to the baron's wife of twenty years. A more intriguing possibility is that Philippine's hardscrabble background enticed the baron, not just because it kept her out of his social circles but because in an unexpected sense, and again in sharp contrast to Betty, it recalled his own.

Baron James de Rothschild came from an Ashkenazi family in the Frankfurter Judengasse, Philippine's father-in-law's birthplace. The youngest of five sons, James had immigrated to Paris at nineteen, dispatched by his father, German moneychanger turned banker Mayer Amschel, to found a French branch of the family's banking business. (James's older brothers were sent on similar

Baron James's wife, Betty, was also his niece. Painted here by Ingres, she was considered a great beauty.

missions to other cities around Europe, thereby establishing the clan as a multi-national concern.) The Napoleonic Wars (1803–1815) made the Rothschilds' fortunes, earning them their Austrian *titres de noblesse;* in Paris, James grew rich by betting in the stock market that Napoléon I would fall. But he really came into his own as a tycoon during the July Monarchy (1830–1848). Among his many feats of financial wizardry, James branched out, originally in partnership with the Pereires, into a business that became one of the most important and biggest growth industries of the century: railroads. His acumen won him the trust of King Louis-Philippe, whose personal investments he managed and whose favor launched him and Betty in the monde.

But the couple's elevation threw into relief a profound difference between them. As a next-generation Rothschild, Betty had grown up with every advantage, as evidenced, wrote one of her contemporaries, by "that noble indifference that gives the most sumptuous luxury an air of everyday habit." Baron James did not have his wife's innate ease; he came from a world wholly alien to hers—that of the Judengasse—and no matter how much money and power he accrued, he never succeeded in fully leaving it behind. If this discrepancy aggravated the baron's social insecurities, or produced other tensions between him and Betty at home, this, too, may have kindled his attraction to women from humbler walks of life. Women like Philippine Straus.

Apart from their physical appearance, one of the most readily discernible differences between Baron James and his wife was that while she "spoke very pure French," he had a thick German-Jewish accent—"*Ponch*our, Ma*t*ame"—that betrayed his ghetto origins every time he opened his mouth. Novelist Honoré

This postcard of the Jewish ghetto in Frankfurt is marked with an arrow to show where James de Rothschild grew up.

de Balzac endowed the Baron de Nucingen, the omnipotent German-Jewish financier of *The Human Comedy* (*La Comédie humaine*, 1829–1847), with Baron James's uncouth inflections, rendering them phonetically on the page.* It is still thought that Rothschild was the model for Nucingen, even though Balzac is careful not to describe him in any detail, one mention of him as "that fat Jew" aside. In the absence of any other distinguishing traits, the fictional banker's Judengasse patois becomes a central component of his character.

Philippine would have spoken French with a similarly coarse accent. Whereas Betty's "very pure" language attested to a vast, experiential divide between herself and her uncle and spouse, Philippine's immigrant French might perhaps have sounded welcomingly familiar. It might have promised some understanding of the struggles the baron had endured while working tirelessly to make his way in a foreign and not always hospitable land. In their own modest fashion, Philippine and her family still faced those struggles every day.

WHEN ÉMILE WAS BORN IN 1844, Philippine had herself and Abraham Straus listed on the birth certificate as the parents. Within months of the baby's arrival, however, Abraham moved to England and never returned—not

---

* It is not easy to translate for the Anglophone reader how this "Jewish" French sounded and looked (in print) to native French speakers. In his history of the Rothschild family, Niall Ferguson offers this sample, where Baron James is talking about the Pereire brothers: "Vat do you mean? . . . I haf the greatest confidence in the chenius of Messrs. Pereire, . . . such clefer men." In *The Great Gatsby* (1925), Scott Fitzgerald achieves a comparable effect when the grotesquely stereotyped Jewish character Meyer Wolfsheim vaunts his "business goneggtions."

exactly the behavior of a doting new father. Abraham's abrupt and permanent departure signaled the effective end of his marriage to Philippine. The timing of Émile's parents' split would seem to corroborate the claim, to which the society he later entered lent full credence, that he was not Abraham's son but Baron James's.

The unique educational advantages he received further fueled this belief. Of all the Straus siblings, only Émile was sent to private school, boarding as a teen-ager at Bousquet-Basse, an exclusive Right Bank *pension* where the students did their coursework at a prestigious nearby day school, the Lycée Condorcet. The alumni rosters for Bousquet-Basse and Condorcet were a who's who of the city's haut-bourgeois and Jewish élite. Straus's matriculation there could only plausi-bly have been arranged and bankrolled by Baron James, who had already sent two of his sons and one of his grandsons, James Nathaniel de Rothschild, to the same institution. The fact that James Nathaniel and Émile Straus overlapped at Bousquet-Basse (the former being two years Émile's senior, was two classes ahead of him at school) implies that the great financier was not overly concerned with keeping his love child away from his acknowledged offspring. Indeed, after high school, Straus continued to follow in James Nathaniel's footsteps, enrolling in law school two years after him in Paris. When Straus graduated in 1867, he became the first known member of Abraham's and Philippine's family ever to earn a university degree.

Straus's graduation brought with it another family first. He became an author, publishing his thesis on property law with Jouaust, a boutique Parisian publish-ing house with only one other legal monograph on its book list: the law-school thesis of James Nathaniel de Rothschild. Jouaust was better known for its series of pamphlets praising Baron James and other members of the Rothschild clan. One of the house's senior editors was historian Eugène Halphen, whose (as-yet-unborn) granddaughter Noémie Halphen would go on to marry another of Baron James's grandsons, Maurice de Rothschild. (Noémie's maternal grand-father, coincidentally, was Geneviève's former guardian, Eugène Pereire.) In light of its cozy relationship with the Rothschilds, Jouaust's decision to publish the law-school thesis of an unknown student named Émile Straus would again appear to confirm his presumed Rothschild paternity.

During these years, Straus intermittently kept a diary. On its opening page he announced, "I will say only things that are true, and write only for myself." As a repository of his private thoughts, the diary contains several potential bio-graphical clues, although most of them are elliptical at best. The first and most straightforward is the abundance of drawings and short stories he produced in his journal's pages. These doodles illustrate what Straus calls his "bohemian love of all the arts: painting, music, poetry," a love that would remain central to his identity even as he discarded so many other parts of his past. For a young man with no known artistic training (and studying to become a lawyer), his pen-

and-ink drawings display extraordinary promise. One of the finest portrays a dark-haired woman in partial déshabille, standing with her back to the viewer and burning a bundle of letters over an open candle flame. By happenstance, this image evokes his future wife's roughly contemporaneous destruction of her correspondence with Georges Bizet.

A second and related clue is his cryptic account of a meeting he had, apparently while still in law school, with a benefactor identified only as "the Unknown Man" (l'Inconnu). Having heard about Straus's artistic leanings, and being himself a world-class art connoisseur and collector, the Unknown Man asked to see his drawings. Straus handed over his diary and waited nervously while the Unknown Man flipped through it in silence. Finally the latter man spoke, offering gruff, backhanded praise: Had Straus really drawn these pictures? The draftsmanship looked too fine to be his. While this reaction may sound like an insult, Straus does not appear to have taken it that way. He expresses "relief" that the Unknown Man approved of his drawings. He never mentions the stranger again. If Baron James ever had a cameo in the young man's diary, this would have been it—the august aging plutocrat stopping in just long enough to take an ambivalent paternal interest in Straus's artwork and then dissolving back into the Unknown.

As a young man Straus wrote about his "bohemian love of all the arts" and filled the pages of his diary with sketches.

If this clue in Straus's diary points to a fleeting presence, the next one comes through as a glaring absence. Nowhere in the journal's pages does he make even a passing allusion to Abraham, Philippine, or any of his four siblings. As an outsider among affluent boys who regarded boarding school and university as banal rites of passage, not unprecedented opportunities to advance in life, Straus may have been embarrassed by his unsophisticated family. If this was so, then he may have kept quiet about them around his schoolmates to avoid ridicule, either by unexamined habit or conscious intention bringing this silence to bear on his diary entries as well. Whatever its motivation, his suppression of the Strauses from his journal set a pattern he would follow for the rest of his life, distancing himself from them so completely that it was as though he had never known them. So completely that even when he wrote, as he said, "only the truth," they didn't exist.

While Straus was still at Bousquet-Basse, he had some reason to worry about falling prey to bullying. Another alumnus of the school recalled with a shudder "the brutality of the [students'] mores—among themselves they [were] like savages to one another," subjecting the more sensitive boys to a level of "terror and martyrdom" that made them wish they had never been born. For Straus, the risk of persecution would have been bad enough just because he came from a lower social stratum than his peers and in all likelihood, in the beginning at least, had different manners and reference points than theirs. But when Straus was fourteen, his two older brothers were embroiled in a mortifying financial scandal. The notoriety they gained in the press would have provided Émile with another compelling reason to pretend to his peers (and maybe to himself) that those derelict Straus peddlers had nothing to do with him.

After their father's move to England, Léopold and Daniel had gone on working in the Grain Exchange. Sometime in their late teens, they reconfigured the family business as Straus Brothers Flour Merchants, taking aggressive measures to increase their sales. In the early 1850s, Léopold moved across the Channel to open an office in the City of London, while Daniel stayed behind to oversee the domestic operations in Les Halles. But the expansion into foreign markets proved more than the two brothers could handle. In 1858, Straus Brothers Flour Merchants declared bankruptcy. The press in both Paris and London publicized the news of the company's collapse and of the legal actions its coproprietors faced in both countries.

To avoid debtors' prison, Léopold and Daniel fled from their respective cities. Daniel wound up in Alsace, his ancestral homeland, and became a merchant of unspecified wares. Léopold bounced from Bordeaux, where he did a stint as an importer of South American wine and spirits, to Alabama, where he was sued for fraud in state supreme court by a pair of dry-goods entrepreneurs called the Marx Brothers. He eventually landed in San Francisco, where, despite restoring the extra "s" to his last name, he could claim no ties to the Levi Strauss denim juggernaut. If either Léopold or Daniel ever saw each other, their other siblings, or their mother again, the historical record has retained no evident traces of the reunion. With their escape and self-imposed exile, the two brothers not only dishonored the Straus family—they destroyed what was left of it.

Though unstated in Straus's diary, the humiliation and implosion of his family provides a helpful context for decoding the short stories that together form another elliptical biographical clue. While most of these untitled, undated, and unfinished vignettes are mini-comedies of contemporary Parisian manners, they exhibit none of the native flair of Straus's drawings, containing little in the way of sociological insight or psychological depth. Still, they are noteworthy for one striking reason: virtually all of their protagonists belong to the *noblesse d'épée*. As a social type, the swashbuckling scion of France's Catholic warrior class stands as the inverse mirror image of the money-grubbing Jewish immigrant, the craven wretch who fleeces his creditors and changes countries when his swindles come to light. The courtly noble officers in Straus's fiction can be read as palimpsests for the shameful, fractured family he never once brings himself to name.

STRAUS'S NAÏVE IDEALIZATION of the *noblesse d'épée* may have shaped his postgraduate professional path along with his creative writing. Although he earned his law degree in 1867, there is no record of him practicing law in Paris until after the Franco-Prussian War four years later. Sometime during that interval, Straus joined the army. He may not have enlisted until the siege of Paris, when all able-bodied Frenchmen were called up for duty. But it seems likely that he joined up earlier, as no records show him involved in any other professional activity during those years, and a life of gentlemanly leisure would not have been an option for him then. He may thus have done his compulsory military service right after law school and then prolonged his tour of duty with a view to staying on in the army full-time. Baron James died a year after Straus earned his law degree, so even if the baron had been inclined to intervene in Straus's career trajectory, he would not have been around to stage another visit as "the Unknown Man," chastising the youth for the waste of a perfectly good legal education.

Into this interlude, Straus's diary offers some more encrypted insight. In the longest of his short stories, he assigns himself an alter ego, Aramis, named for one of the three musketeers in Dumas *père*'s 1844 historical novel. Though the most ambitious and intelligent, even conniving, of the trio, Dumas's Aramis is as "courtly and distinguished" as his companions, and those are the qualities Straus bestows upon his version of the character. He also endows his "modern-day Aramis" with traits markedly like his own, from his intense "love of all the arts" to his "slight frame, fair hair, hooked nose, [and] pointy chin." Evincing a candid social yearning his contemporaries in the monde, once he got there, would construe as snobbery, Straus reimagined himself as a *noble d'épée*, valiantly longing to do battle for France:

> Ah! I know of nothing more beautiful than to fight for one's country, serve the principles of liberty, bring the enemies of justice to heel! Is there anything more beautiful, anything worthier of a noble heart?

In Straus's diary and in his life, the chivalric fantasy soon ended. In the last installment of the Aramis tale, war breaks out, shocking our hero with its senseless "panic and devastation." Aramis fades to black, his story giving way to a disjointed account of Straus's own experiences in the Franco-Prussian War.

Sometime in January 1871, when the ceasefire was declared, Straus had his run-in with an exploding shell.

AFTER THE ARMISTICE IN MARCH 1871, Straus settled into civilian life in Paris. He took an apartment in the ninth arrondissement, not far from his future wife's building in the rue de Douai. This nearness to Montmartre may have been his way of reasserting his "bohemian love of all the arts" even as he set about founding his law practice and establishing himself in a none-too-bohemian profession.

Some of Straus's early cases were almost comically unglamorous. In one, he represented a woman suing a pharmacist for having incorrectly prepared her dog's bronchitis medicine, causing a fatal overdose. Another was a lawsuit brought by a rich old woman who discovered only after her marriage that her dashing young husband, who styled himself the Marquis de Segarra, had lied to her about his title (which he had fabricated; in fact he was the son of a Spanish gendarme), his blazon (also made up), and his age (thirty-five, but he had told her he was thirty-three). Straus represented the defendant, whom he compared in his closing argument to "Fritz from *The Grande-Duchesse de Gérolstein*," a handsome young soldier upon whom the older duchesse confers a series of unearned promotions, simply because she fancies him. Such apt but unexpected allusions were to become one of Straus's signatures in the courtroom; he always seemed to have just the right literary reference or quotation to clinch his point. His cleverness didn't carry the day for the fake marquis, but that was a rare setback for Straus. The Segarra case and the canine-bronchitis suit were reportedly two of the only cases he ever lost.

Over the next decade, Maître Émile Straus—it pleased him that his job came with an honorific—threw himself wholeheartedly into his work. He approached each case with an obsessive attention to detail, taking a craftsman's pride in the perfection of his briefs. The fastidiousness and concentration he had once brought to his drawing now benefited his legal career, which grew apace. By the time he turned thirty-five, in 1879, he was widely recognized as one of the most formidable attorneys of his generation, "the leading light of the Paris bar."

It was at around this time that the Rothschilds came calling, turning Straus from an impressive lawyer into an indomitable one. The impetus to bring him on board as counsel at Rothschild Frères (which position still left him free to take on other cases, assuming no conflicts of interest) seems to have come from Baron James's eldest son, Baron Alphonse (1827–1905), a soft-spoken, sad-eyed man with pendulous muttonchop sideburns that skimmed the tops of his shirt collars. His late father having anointed him to lead the family and the company into the next generation, Alphonse may have been privy to the secret of Straus's birth and sought him out on that basis. There was a seventeen-year age gap between them, but Alphonse and Straus developed a fond rapport, predicated on their mutual devotion to public service (Alphonse, too, had fought bravely in the siege of Paris; in addition, he had loaned the French government the millions of francs it needed to pay Prussian war reparations in peacetime); to the arts (like Baron James, Alphonse was a discerning, deeply knowledgeable art collector); and to their work. It was this last value that brought the putative half brothers closest together. Alphonse, often identified as the smartest and most industrious of his father's (legitimate) children, admired Straus's keen intelligence and indefatigable work ethic. Straus, for his part, appreciated Alphonse's unentitled manner and unflagging dedication to the family business.

The association with the Rothschilds was life changing for Straus, in at least two ways. The first was financial. Presumably he was well compensated at Rothschild Frères, although as these records did not make their way into the extended clan's archive in London, no information on his salary survives. But Straus also, in the work he did for the company, gained expertise in an area that would today be known as corporate law. (In 1889, *Le Gaulois* described him as Paris's leading "expert in financial affairs.") As France continued to industrialize, with its economy growing ever more modern and complex, this specialty made Straus a rich man.

His new wealth enabled him to adopt the tastes and spending habits of his Rothschild cohort, albeit on a less extravagant scale. Perhaps abetted by Alphonse or Edmond—the Rothschild brother closest to Straus in age, with a fine art collection of his own—he began to buy art. His focus was eclectic, centering on Old Masters, eighteenth-century French works, and modern art. Like Alphonse and Edmond, Straus took his collecting seriously. (None of them would need to turn to Haas for his simplified pointers to the clubmen set.) Perhaps related to his talent as a draftsman, Straus had a sophisticated eye, and in his contemporary collecting especially, this gave him the confidence to select pieces from lesser-known artists. His best early discovery was Claude Monet, from whom he acquired several luminous works.

Straus's riches also afforded him the leisure to expand his practice into less profitable areas, simply because they interested him. He provided legal services pro bono to a cultural-advocacy group, the Society for Dramatic Authors and Composers, that protected the intellectual property rights of artists writing and composing for the stage. Thanks to his involvement with this organization, Straus was able to add intellectual property law to his range of client offerings, and before long, he found himself representing such diverse and prominent artists as Réjane, Guy de Maupassant, Georges de Porto-Riche, and Gustave Moreau (whose work Straus also collected). Unusually for a corporate-law kingpin, Straus made his "bohemian love of all the arts" into a centerpiece of his legal practice.

At the same time, his affiliation with the Rothschilds dramatically altered his social position and outlook. The rumors about his relationship to Baron

Succeeding his father, Baron James, as the
chef de famille of the Parisian Rothschilds,
Baron Alphonse hired Straus as a legal
consigliere.

James accompanied Straus everywhere he went, earning him a degree of consideration not typically granted to a bourgeois (much less a working-class) Jewish lawyer. The pervasiveness of the chatter about his paternity stemmed at least in part from the Rothschilds' notorious insularity. Their tradition of endogamy, of which the Baron James/Betty union was just one of multiple examples, was meant to keep the family and fortune safe from outsiders—an odd but precise parallel with the French nobility's clannish marriage practices under the ancien régime. While the "born" of the fin de siècle still aspired to this dynastic model, their blazons' regilding needs had driven them to compromises to which the Rothschilds were under no such pressure to resort. In 1859, Baron James's and Betty's second eldest son, Baron Gustave (1829–1911), had thrown the family into an uproar by marrying a nonrelative. A quarter century later, Betty had still not reconciled herself to the match. Nor had she forgiven Berthe and Marguerite von Rothschild, two of her nieces from Frankfurt, for marrying Catholic noblemen. In this context, Émile Straus's absorption into the Rothschild family was astounding to say the least. That he was Baron James's natural son seemed the only logical explanation for such an unprecedented development.

Like his enthusiasm for the arts, Straus's worship for the nobility survived his transition from youth to adulthood, although he proved markedly less adroit as a *mondain* than as an art lawyer and collector. When the Rothschilds went out in society, he tagged along with them, hobnobbing with real noblemen for the first time in his life. But his overt eagerness to impress coexisted uncomfortably, for him and those around him, with the combative, arrogant demeanor he had honed in his day job, and perhaps also with a lingering defensiveness about his background. The criticisms Straus would soon draw from Geneviève's friends—that he was obnoxious, aggressive, with a chip on his shoulder—merely rephrased the gratin's complaints about his inelegance and lack of breeding. That the Rothschilds should voluntarily associate with such a boor only lent that much more weight to the conjecture that he was their kin. Why on earth would they tolerate him otherwise?

Straus seemed not to know how to read the cues his *mondain* acquaintances used to try to dodge and snub him. He was dogged in his pursuit of society contacts, having the best luck when the grandees he wanted to befriend happened to need a lawyer. This is how he attached himself to Pauline von Metternich, a monkey-faced Austro-Hungarian princess whose stature in the gratin had peaked during the Second Empire, when her husband was Austria's ambassador to the court of Napoléon III. The fall of the empire had sent the Metternichs back to their homeland, but as a fervid *mélomane* and fashion plate, she returned to Paris from time to time for concerts and couture. By a fluke, Straus chanced to meet her right after the husband of one of her ladies-in-waiting was arrested for murder (caught with bloody knife in hand) in Austria. Straus immediately volunteered to help, despite knowing nothing about Austrian law, and he took advantage of the murderer's long, drawn-out trial to keep up a correspondence with Pauline. She did not save his letters to her. The ones she wrote to him, however, reveal a woman politely enduring the attentions of a man to whom she knows she is beholden but whom she wishes would leave her alone. Straus filed all her letters away in a special folder (a rare move on his part, as he held on to little of his other correspondence) and kept them until he died.

Straus's *mondain* career could easily have stalled here, progressing no further than a sheaf of perfunctory letters from a princess, trifles mistaken for wonders. Yet he gained a second chance to breach the fortress of the monde because somewhere along the way, he encountered Geneviève Bizet, and he knew that she would be the one to help him. Just as her artist friends relied on her to make them famous, and just as her noble friends counted on her to make them interesting, Straus would depend on her to make him clubbable. He did not anticipate that for Geneviève, this endeavor would be the equivalent of the canine-homicide and bogus-heraldry cases: a very rare instance of her special powers failing.

THE ROAD THAT LED STRAUS to his future bride could have originated in any number of places, whether at the Society of Dramatic Authors, to which a number of her friends and relatives belonged, or at a society function where she, as the amusing Widow Bizet, was as eagerly sought after as Straus was artfully avoided. He could have noticed her in the neighborhood, or at the theater, or in the Bichonne. Their lives intersected in so many places, through so many common acquaintances, that by the time they did get together—

sometime between August 1880 and March 1881—their relationship must have felt predestined.

At least it felt that way to Straus. Joseph Reinach, whom he made an early confidant of his infatuation, would later tease him mercilessly in front of Geneviève, telling her that after Straus first met her, he lost all ability to talk about anything or anyone else. Before he used it to rope the Rothschild brothers, and Reinach, and Schlumberger into accompanying him to her salon, the refrain "You must see Geneviève" was an incantation for Straus himself, the operative word in which was "must." Geneviève would be a requirement for him, a principle as absolute and uncompromising as liberty, justice, or chivalric honor. Falling for her would resurrect his inner Aramis. Loving her would make him noble.

The operative word *here,* "noble," is freighted with ambivalence, evoking both the benefits and the drawbacks of Straus's Aramis revival. On the one hand, his by all accounts sincere and unwavering love for Geneviève did, according to her intimates, make him a somewhat better person. Even Ludovic's wife, Louise, who abhorred Straus, acknowledged the improvement. "Straus has absolutely no nobility about him," she complained to her son Daniel. But then she added, "The only noble thing about him is his love for your aunt." In this statement, Louise attached to nobility the same meaning it held for Straus in his Aramis tale: uprightness of character, moral elevation. Straus's love for Geneviève ennobled him in the sense that it brought out his most admirable qualities.

The problem is that "nobility" also denotes the class to which Straus was desperate to belong. As such, it activated all the snobbish impulses that attended and informed his desire. It brought out his least admirable qualities.

This was the human cost of the *déclassement du gratin,* and both Geneviève and Straus paid it when they formed a partnership geared toward *mondain* advancement. The people close to her observed with not a little dismay that once she and Straus became a couple, she evinced more "black-hearted vanity" and social "calculation" than she had ever shown before, and that all the joy went out of her salon.

While regrettable, this evaporation of joy proceeded logically from the choice she had made. For Geneviève, assuming the mandate to make Straus clubbable meant accepting the premise that the arbitrary, exclusionary construct of "class" (or "club") is a worthy end in itself. It meant embracing in a profound and damaging way the logic of this axiom:

> By "Jockey-Club," I mean any association of people from which I would above all be happy to know that others are excluded.

To uphold this precept, as Geneviève came to do, was to decide that associating with people has nothing to do with who they are and everything to do with who they are not.

By this logic, it stands to reason that the faithful felt "Straus was not loved" by Geneviève. In fact, she indicated as much herself when she told them of her decision to marry him in the fall of 1886. "Straus, your husband?! That is going to be dreadful!" they protested. "What else was I to do?" she sighed. "It was the only way I could get rid of him."

As expected, the joke landed in the treasury of "Geneviève's latest," reaffirming her brio as a wit. Still, the world-weariness of the quip pointed to a certain sadness around Geneviève's decision. To marry Straus was to reconcile herself to a life without love, and although she had calculated that the sacrifice would bring bigger gains (her late mother's obsessions, "social status [and] money!!!") than losses, she was neither so hard nor so naïve as to think it would be easy.

For Straus, the difficulty would perhaps be even greater. Even before he and Geneviève married, he struggled with his warring desires for *mondanité* (Geneviève as trophy and social helpmeet) and passion (Geneviève as the love of his life). As Robert Dreyfus said of him, using a metaphor that would have delighted the lawyer formerly known (to himself) as Aramis,

> Straus reminded me of a knight from an old chivalric legend who, as a condition of conquering his miraculous princess, has renounced the temptation to lock her up jealously in a tower to which he alone would hold the key—because he was eager, or at least felt compelled, to open the castle gates to [other] worthy admirers.

In his relationship with Geneviève, Straus faced a classic devil's bargain, weighing his need for exclusive possession (a need so transparent that Galliffet jokingly referred to him as Geneviève's "proprietor") against his collector's urge to show off his prize.

In the end, the collector defeated the spouse. Eager to ingratiate himself with aristocrats who would never otherwise have talked to him, Straus actively encouraged Geneviève to devote herself to her social life and her salon. But by spurring her in this direction, he renounced his proprietary claim on his "miraculous princess." It is telling that virtually all extant photographs of Geneviève and Straus show them in the company of one or more of her *fidèles:* fitting illustrations of a marriage vitiated by *mondanité.*

Although Straus, like Geneviève, elected to make this trade, its attendant emotional burdens weighed on him increasingly as her popularity continued to grow. While Straus "was as proud of his wife's salon as if it were his own," observed Daniel Halévy, "his love of the monde did constant battle with his horror" of having always to compete for Geneviève's attention. Over time, this inner conflict made Straus's rough edges even rougher, his irascibility and combativeness more pronounced.

To the faithful, he gave constant evidence of his "ferocious" and "terrible"

More Halévy family photos: *(left)* Straus and Geneviève, seated, with Boulanger-Cavé, standing; *(right)* Haas, Geneviève, Boulanger-Cavé, and Straus.

character. Once Proust joined the coterie, he noticed that even a gesture as innocent on his part as staying in the salon after the other guests had left, and sitting with Mme Straus for a few moments by the fire, would send Straus into a jealous tailspin. "You should have seen him," Proust recalled to Céleste Albaret:

> He couldn't bear his wife to call me her "dear little Marcel." . . . He would fidget in his chair, get up, walk about, sit down again, pick up the tongs and poke at the fire, then throw them down with a clatter. Mme Straus would say, "Émile, please!" and he would grumble: "My dear Geneviève, you will tire yourself talking. . . ." But she would say, "Please, my dear little Marcel, don't take any notice. Émile, leave us alone!" And all Monsieur Straus could do was bang about with the tongs again.

Another *fidèle* remembered this dynamic in more general terms: "Straus's possessiveness toward [Geneviève] caused him no end of suffering. He was always nursing a grievance, and would have welcomed the chance to tyrannize her."

If Edmond de Goncourt was to be believed, Straus really did tyrannize her. When studying him and Geneviève as a couple, Goncourt concluded that in their relationship, "the woman acted like a man, not wanting to be tied down"—

shades of Carmen, Geneviève's operatic double—"while the man acted like the woman, wanting his beloved to be all his, forever." Furthermore, so intolerable did Geneviève's elusiveness become to Straus that "one day, he threw her to the ground" in a rage, leaving her "in constant terror of more violence from him" from then on. In the end, according to Goncourt, Geneviève only accepted Straus's marriage proposal "because she feared that her pursuer would either assassinate her or kill himself" if she persisted in turning him down.

On Christmas Day 1886, less than three months after the Strauses' wedding, Goncourt remarked in his journal that Geneviève had "married her suitor with regret." Her suitor, now her husband, would have his own regrets, of crushing disappointment to his secret inner Aramis.

CHORALE

LOVEBIRDS

For me, the sky has become but a halo,
Encircling you, shielding you, with azure and light.
Perched on a flower, the bird only flutters
And the flower only smells sweet, and the bird only sighs,
The better to enchant the air you breathe.

—ALFRED DE VIGNY, "The Shepherd's House"
("La Maison du berger," 1844)

Without a doubt, Theseus's wife has fallen victim to one of those ineluctable passions that unsettle the mind and defy the will. . . . But Phaedra is also an infinitely tender and delicate soul, a tormented creature. . . . Pale, languishing, unable to sleep, like a nun consumed in her very cloister by some enigmatic and incurable desire, she is really, despite her criminal flame, as chaste as Hippolytus.

—JULES LEMAÎTRE, review of Racine's *Phaedra* at the
Odéon National Theater (1886)

CHAPTER ELEVEN

THE LUNATIC, THE LOVER,
AND THE POET

Marcel Proust drew the inspiration for his earliest literary works from two of his high-school classmates: Jacques Bizet and Daniel Halévy. As Geneviève's son and nephew (in the Breton way), they introduced him into her salon, catalyzing Proust's involvement in *mondain* society. But first, the two boys did something that established a template for Proust's entire creative output: They transfixed him, and then disappointed him, and thereby drove him to write.

IN OCTOBER 1887, Jacques and Daniel, both fifteen, enrolled in Paris's Lycée Condorcet, where Proust, sixteen, was in the class above theirs. The two cousins had been best friends since infancy, growing up in the same apartment building in the rue de Douai. Their families' cozy cohabitation had come to an end in October 1886, when Geneviève had married Émile Straus after eleven years of widowhood. Following the wedding, the bride and groom had moved with Jacques into a new apartment in the elegant eighth arrondissement, geographically not far from Montmartre, but socially and spiritually a half a world away. For Jacques, a difficult period of adjustment had followed the move, as it had uprooted him from the apartment that had been his home since birth and from the cousin he loved like a brother. The following autumn, however, he and Daniel were reunited at Condorcet.

Founded under Napoléon I—whence its original name, the Lycée Bonaparte—Condorcet was one of the oldest and most prestigious schools in Paris. Despite its location in a former Capuchin monastery, it was the high school of choice for the sons of the Right Bank's Jewish haute bourgeoisie (a category in which the cousins' Halévy heritage placed them both, despite the fact that Jacques's father had been Catholic, Daniel's mother was Protestant, and both boys were baptized). Jacques's new stepfather was a Condorcet alumnus, as were Daniel's older brother, Élie; Ludovic Halévy's late half brother, Anatole Prévost-Paradol; and Jacques's great-uncle Hippo Rodrigues. A number of the boys' parents' influential friends had been educated there as well, from republican politician Joseph Reinach to alienist Dr. Émile Blanche, and from authors Alexandre Dumas *fils* and Edmond de Goncourt to several Rothschild barons. Such connections were typical among Condorcet families, although because of their fathers' celebrity,

Daniel Halévy, here sixteen, was a handsome and popular student at Condorcet, where Proust befriended him.

Jacques and Daniel were likely the two most conspicuous members of their entering class.

Not long after the cousins arrived at the lycée, they struck up a volatile but far-reaching friendship with Proust, who like them came from a respected, afflu-ent half-Jewish family (and was a baptized Christian). He lived with his parents, Dr. and Mme Adrien Proust, and his younger brother, Robert, in a luxurious apartment building in the eighth arrondissement, right off the place de la Made-leine. From modest beginnings as the son of a petit-bourgeois grocer in the provinicial village of Illiers, Adrien had risen through the ranks of the medical profession to become first a brilliant pathologist and then a leading authority in the burgeoning field of epidemiology. By the time his eldest son entered high school, he was one of the Third Republic's leading public-health experts, shaping government policy in response to outbreaks of cholera and malaria and lecturing around the world on the etiology and treatment of infectious disease.

Mme Adrien Proust, née Jeanne Weil, was a bright, cultivated Parisienne whose family, Ashkenazi from Alsace, had made a fortune in manufacturing and finance. She was a great-niece of the late Adolphe Crémieux, a republican states-man and activist who through the Crémieux Decree of 1870 had extended the rights of citizenship to Jews in the French colony of Algeria. This achievement had earned him the rancor of the nascent anti-Semitic movement; according to its ringleader, Édouard Drumont, Crémieux's advocacy for the Jews had "made him the enemy" of Catholics everywhere. But in liberal circles, Crémieux had commanded immense respect. When her parents took her to call on him as a girl, Jeanne had met such luminaries as Alfred de Musset, George Sand, and Fro-mental Halévy. Adolphe Crémieux, too, was a graduate of Condorcet. So was the philosopher Henri Bergson, the future husband of another of Jeanne's relatives.

Beneath the veneer of upper-middle-class privilege, the disparities between the backgrounds of Jeanne Weil and Adrien Proust uncannily resembled those

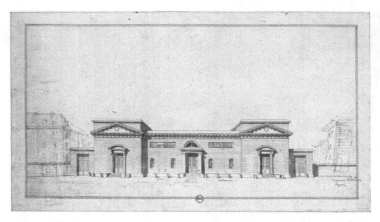

The Lycée Condorcet was housed in a former Capuchin monastery on the Right Bank.

Jacques Bizet's parents had faced while his father was still alive. As biographer Evelyne Bloch-Dano points out, Adrien Proust's uncultured, staunchly Catholic mother had likely never "set eyes on a Jewish person in her entire life" before her son took up with Mademoiselle Weil. But the latter's refinement, charm, and robust dowry, combined with Adrien's formidable ambition and success, melded to advance both spouses' social fortunes. The marriage "opened wide to them the doors of [Paris's] grande bourgeoisie, which otherwise would have remained closed to both the self-made man and the Jewish heiress." As the product of this union, Marcel was typical Condorcet material, although until Jacques and Daniel came along, he had always been something of a loner there.

Jacques and Daniel weren't complete strangers to Proust when he first spotted them in the Condorcet schoolyard, a colonnaded cloister left over from the building's days as a monastery. As little boys, all three youths had matriculated at Pape-Carpentier, a primary-school feeder for Condorcet; Proust nurtured fond if hazy memories of Jacques's striking mother picking up her son and nephew after school. Since then, he had lost sight of the cousins, who in the intervening years had grown into tall and handsome young men. Athletic and outgoing, they both had the easy swagger of the popular students they would swiftly become. Proust cut a diminutive figure by contrast; even when he reached his full adult height, he would stand at only five feet six.

Proust was physically fragile as well. Already beset by the allergies, asthma, digestive troubles, and insomnia that would plague him throughout his life, he had spent long stretches of his childhood in a sickbed, and he had a slight build and invalid's pallor to show for it. Daniel Halévy recalled that "with his big Oriental eyes" and his almost otherworldly frailty, the adolescent Proust looked like "a disturbed and disturbing archangel"—surely not the impression the older boy would have hoped to make on his new schoolmates.

As a *lycéen*, Proust was intellectually very precocious but socially awkward.

Madame Adrien Proust, née Jeanne Weil, was the most important person in her elder son's life.

Proust's somewhat odd demeanor stemmed as much from his upbringing as from his appearance, as his prolonged illnesses had fostered an unusual closeness with his mother. When his sickness kept him from class for extended periods, Jeanne had engaged tutors to help him keep up with his homework, but she herself had assumed primary responsibility for his homeschooling. She had received an uncommonly rigorous education for a woman of her era, mastering an impressive range of academic disciplines and foreign languages, and by all accounts, her intelligence was as great as her erudition. Given the intellectual precocity Marcel demonstrated from a very young age, Jeanne was ideally suited to be his teacher and zealously instilled in him her profound love of literature, music, history, and art history. The extraordinary acuity, unstinting warmth, and wit she brought to their tutorials found echoes in "her little wolf," as she called him, and formed the basis of their intense, symbiotic relationship.

Proust's boyhood playmate Maurice Duplay was struck by the sheer delight Jeanne and Marcel took in each other's company. He observed that they loved to make each other laugh, for instance, by drawing "baroque, improbable" comparisons between episodes from literature and history and "the most banal occurrences" of everyday life. This game had evolved out of Jeanne's strategy for managing her sensitive child's terror of such "unpleasant things as enemas or visits to the dentist." As Duplay remembered:

When Mme Proust had to prepare Marcel for these traumas, she would preface her announcements with lines such as: "Leonidas knew how to remain serene in the most challenging of circumstances," or, "Regulus amazed the world with his calmness in the face of catastrophe."

Such playful juxtapositions would become a trademark of Proust's own literary style, as would his and Jeanne's related habit of working classic quotations into their letters and conversation. (The seventeenth-century dramatist Jean Racine was their favorite source.)

Proust's "exquisite little Maman," as he called her, taught him to equate the joys of mutual affection and understanding with the joys of literature and art. Though he would go on to seek the same combination of pleasures in his other relationships, with no other love object would he ever be able to re-create the perfect meeting of the minds he had found with his mother. She remained the most important person in his life until her death in 1905. Already in 1886, when he first took the questionnaire that today bears his name, Proust defined his worst imaginable misery as "separation from Maman." Six years later, he answered the same question: "Never to have known my mother."

For all the glee Proust took in his and Jeanne's zany, recondite exchanges, this type of banter marked him as a misfit among his fellow students. Robert Dreyfus, a classmate of Jacques's and Daniel's, noted that while Proust's casually encyclopedic range of cultural references may have endeared him to adults, it only incited "us immature boys [to] tease him" without mercy. Even worse, according to Dreyfus, was Proust's unabashed eagerness to please. Accustomed to Jeanne's unqualified love, he did not readily pick up on signs of his peers' dislike. As he also wrote in the "Proust questionnaire," his greatest wish was "to be loved." His failure to conceal that wish further biased his schoolmates against him.

Daniel Halévy took the lead in bullying Proust. Abetted by Jacques Bizet and Robert Dreyfus, Daniel would chase Proust around the cloistered schoolyard during recess, hurling taunts. The boys figured out that removing the letter "s" from their victim's surname yielded the word "fart" (*prout*). Upsetting though it was, this puerile insult may have had one positive consequence, by sparking Proust's lifelong interest in the power of names to mold character and shape destiny.

By his own admission, Daniel was a tyrant at that age. In his memoirs, he described his high-school self in the third person as "forceful and brutal: his comrades looked up to him and obeyed him more than they actually liked him—they didn't dare to cross him." Recalling his and his comrades' mistreatment of Proust, he wrote,

> There was something about him that rubbed us the wrong way, and we responded to it by being harsh with him; we even toyed with the idea of beating him up. We never went that far—it was impossible to hit Proust— but we did let him know that we wanted to, and that was enough to upset

him. He was quite obviously not enough of a *boy* for us. We found his kindness, his thoughtful gestures, his tender solicitousness overly mannered; we thought he was a poseur, a phony, and we told him so to his face—whereupon his big Oriental eyes would get extremely sad, though nothing could stop him from continuing to be nice to us.

Proust had his own reason for putting up with their jeers, and it had to do, it so happened, with the power of names. The fact that the two cousins bore the surnames of their legendary fathers endowed them with unmatched glamour in his eyes. With his broad, winning smile and his precociously woolly beard, Jacques Bizet was the spitting image of his late father, and the resemblance only added to his prestige as the composer's fame continued to grow. By the end of Jacques's first year of high school, his father's final opera, *Carmen* (1875), had already been staged 330 times at Paris's Opéra-Comique alone and had received standing ovations all around the world. As for Daniel's father, Ludovic Halévy, his status as the first Jewish Immortal was more than enough to impress Proust, whose own father liked to joke that one day Marcel would be elected to the Académie Française.

In school, the cousins' fathers' celebrity became a protective cloak for no end of schoolboy mischief. "With your last names, you know full well that you'll never get kicked out!" an exasperated study-hall monitor was heard to cry. For Proust, those last names held a special, almost magical allure that his own could never possess. Although his father's achievements in medicine and public health had brought honor to the family name, these held no interest for Proust. His mother's son through and through, he worshipped the arts. Nicknaming Jacques "Carmen's son" and praising Ludovic Halévy's books to Daniel every chance he got, Proust strove doggedly to win their affection.

The cousins soon found a reason to tolerate (if not exactly welcome) his overtures. For all their rebellious antics, both boys thought of themselves as intellectuals, gravitating toward schoolmates who shared what Robert Dreyfus called their "very lively passion for Literature." With Dreyfus and two other students in their class, Fernand Gregh and Robert de Flers, they formed a clique they called "the little literary gang" and plotted with the unself-conscious grandiosity of youth to take the world of Parisian letters by storm. In November, they founded a "literary and artistic review" called *Mondays* (*Le Lundi*), so named for the *Monday Chats* (*Causeries du lundi,* 1851–1862) of the late critic Charles Augustin Sainte-Beuve, another Condorcet alumnus. The journal's stated mission was to publish "everything that's worth reading, without biases as to content or genre" and to champion "the triumphant eclecticism of the Beautiful"—a quotation cadged from Symbolist poet Paul Verlaine. Halévy appointed himself editor in chief, prompting Ludovic to boast, "Daniel cannot escape literature. It is his destiny."

It was likely as a recruiting effort for *Mondays* that Daniel sought a rapprochement with Proust, who at the end of the previous academic year had garnered a degree of notoriety by winning Condorcet's coveted prize for best French composition. Assigned a standard high-school essay topic—the role of the passions in the neoclassical tragedies of Pierre Corneille and Jean Racine—Proust had written a meditation on the "ferocious realism" and "sublime horror" of Racine's work. His argument diverged markedly from the conventional *lycéen* interpretation, which opposes Racine's portrayal of selfish, all-consuming lust to Corneille's apologia of heroic, community-minded self-sacrifice. Impressed by the older boy's daring, Daniel invited him to contribute a piece to the little literary gang's new magazine. "Proust is more gifted than anyone," he reasoned in his journal, adding presciently, "Perhaps as life goes on, he will display untold flashes of genius."

Jumping at the chance to prove himself to Daniel, Proust dashed off a satirical theater review for *Mondays'* December issue: a pitch-perfect send-up of theater critic Jules Lemaître. The present generation's answer to Sainte-Beuve, whose anecdotal, frankly biased reviewing style had made a virtue of the critic's subjectivity, Lemaître liked not only to give his personal "impressions" of a work, but then to undercut them by anticipating all the ways in which they might be refuted. Proust parodied this approach in a review of Pierre Corneille's tragedy *Horace* (1640), a staple of the Condorcet curriculum. Venturing a series of ridiculously self-evident insights (e.g., *Horace,* which is set in Rome, has Roman characters), Proust qualifies each one with variations on the phrase "Or maybe I am wrong." The wickedness of the lampoon is hard to convey to readers unfamiliar with Lemaître's extravagantly waffling prose, but Daniel, who knew the critic from his aunt Geneviève's salon, recognized him in every sentence. Whatever his foibles, Proust would be an asset to *Mondays.*

Daniel was even more taken with his new contributor's next submission the following spring. This piece was an untitled poem written in the dark, edgy mode of Charles Baudelaire, a favorite poet of both Daniel's and Proust's. Daniel was enrolled that year in an English class taught by Stéphane Mallarmé, one of the most important French poets of the century, and with his guidance, Daniel had fallen under the spell of Baudelaire's *The Flowers of Evil* (*Les Fleurs du mal,* 1857), a work Mallarmé rated as a masterpiece of poetic form. Proust, who had not taken Mallarmé's class, admired Baudelaire as well but viewed him through a different, rather more idiosyncratic lens: as the nineteenth-century heir to Racine.

What intrigued Proust in Baudelaire's poetry, as in Racine's drama, was its focus on the perverse, violent, and self-destructive aspects of desire. In *The Flowers of Evil,* that focus includes an examination of homosexual and sadomasochistic themes of particular interest to Proust, who would maintain throughout his life that "for Baudelaire, these [themes] were so much the main thing that he originally wanted to call the whole volume not *The Flowers of Evil* but *The Lesbians.*" These themes were very much the main thing for Proust himself, whose adoration of his mother went hand in glove with a deep sense of shame about his attraction to men. (His father's attempt to "cure" this defect by sending him to a prostitute—an incident that devolved into farce when, before so much as unbuttoning his overcoat, Proust broke a piece of crockery and fled the scene—only heightened his self-loathing.) Whereas love, for Proust, meant tenderness and intellectual rapport, sex meant debasement and pain, and the latter equation was central to *The Flowers of Evil*. Having pastiched Lemaître for comedic purposes, Proust now channeled Baudelaire in portraying, in dead earnest, the wilder shores of love.

His untitled poem for *Mondays* relates a "macabre dream" about a group of "charming" young men who have been "pierced [by] the evil sting" of a "cruel King, young Killer." Addressing this persecutor in scathing terms (much as Baudelaire apostrophizes his "hypocrite Reader!—my double!—my brother!" in the bellicose preamble to *The Flowers of Evil*), Proust's poetic speaker declares his solidarity with the other victims of the king's abuse:

> *O King! . . . I am transfixed by this Nightmare, riveted*
> *To your palace* [ton palais; also "your palate"],
> *And I want every day to bleed your blood, . . .*
> *I curse you in the name of the pale sleepwalkers who,*
> *Deceived by their troubling heroic dreams,*
> *Curse you too, o cruel, ferocious, white King.*

Here, as in *The Flowers of Evil*, the disturbing imagery and menacing tone stand in bracing contrast to the sonority of the classical alexandrine favored by Baudelaire (as well as by Racine). However, Proust's poem goes beyond mere imitative homage. Rife with torturers and insomniacs, inhuman torments and unreachable ideals, it bears many of the hallmarks of his mature work.

Regarding Proust's relationship with Daniel, this poem had a more tactical function: it scored a palpable hit against the "cruel, ferocious . . . King" of the Condorcet playground. Between his insomnia and his delicate health, Proust himself could fairly be described as a "pale sleepwalker," and he was all too familiar with the "evil sting" of Daniel's schoolyard teasing. Yet with his poem, Proust showed that he was quite capable of striking back: if not physically, then in writing.

One feature of this work bears particular note. Simultaneously resentful of and enthralled by the king's cruelty, the poetic speaker twice treats his foe to a shattering malediction—a rhetorical device borrowed from Racine's tragedy *Phaedra* (*Phèdre*, 1677), which Proust and his mother knew by heart and which contains the best-known curse scene in all of French literature. When the play's eponymous heroine confesses her forbidden love for her stepson, Hippolytus, he recoils in horror. She retaliates by letting her husband, King Theseus, believe that Hippolytus tried to seduce *her*. Theseus, enraged, curses his son, calling on the sea god Neptune to do away with him. Hippolytus bravely combats the ensuing sea monster until his terrified horses bolt, dragging him to his death and bringing about the play's tragic conclusion.

Hinging as it does on Theseus's damning injunction, *Phaedra* highlights something important about curses in general. They are speech-acts, taking place wholly in words. Using this rhetorical device in his poem was Proust's way of asserting, once again, that the pen was a creditable match for the sword. He demonstrated that his own strength lay in his mastery of the literary language of Baudelaire and Racine: the very language to which Daniel, the poem's first reader, wished to lay claim. (While he would go on to become the first French translator and biographer of Friedrich Nietzsche, at this stage Daniel wanted to be a poet when he grew up.) And lest Proust's targeted attack escape the "cruel King" whom, in real life, he both idolized and abhorred, he inscribed the poem "For Daniel Halévy, written while gazing at him during the first fifteen minutes of detention."

Peeved but impressed, Daniel copied these lines into his journal, along with the poem itself, thereby instituting a habit of transcribing for posterity all of Proust's letters to him and to Jacques. In the margins, Daniel wrote, "Proust (Marcel), detention, May 13, 1888—his first verses ever, or so he says—what an intolerable fellow!" This comment betrayed his envy of the older boy's obvious talent. Supposedly destined for literature himself, Daniel would continue to marvel at Proust's brilliance, as when he remarked of a long letter Jacques received from Proust some months later,

> Proust . . . has written the entire thing without scratching out or changing a single word. The crazy fellow has enormous talent, and I don't know of ANYTHING that is . . . more marvelously written than this.

As for Proust's Baudelairean poem, it unsettled Daniel not only with its literary acumen but with its hints about the author's sexual proclivities. From the sadomasochistic bond between the "cruel King" and his victims (who, "pierced" by the monarch's "sting," are riveted both to his palace and, courtesy of a French wordplay, to his palate), to the naked yearning of the dedication ("For Daniel Halévy, written while gazing at him . . ."), its homoeroticism was unmistakable.

At least, this was how Daniel read the poem. In a subsequent diary entry, he noted that while Proust was "more gifted than anyone," he was also "young and weak, [and] he coitus-es [*sic*], he masturbates, maybe he even *pederasts* [*sic*]!" Having regarded Proust from the first as "not enough of a *boy* for us," the rest of the little literary gang agreed. According to Dreyfus,

> We admired Proust, and sensed that he was an exceptional being, but we were appalled, the way one can be at sixteen, by his sexual tenden-

cies. . . . That even became our principal reason for mocking and mistreating him, and [for trying to] distance him from our group of friends.

Needless to say, Proust's sexuality had also played a role in drawing him to Daniel and Jacques, and he wrote the two cousins a series of letters expressing his attraction to them both. The erotic allure they held for Proust accounted for the tenacity with which he tried to win them over. His pursuit of the cousins would introduce him to the humiliation and pain of unrequited longing. But by the time Proust graduated from Condorcet, these feelings would give way to a more creative, and constructive, stance: as a portrayer of the boys' forbidden appeal, and of his struggle to renounce them as love objects.

Initially, Proust focused on Bizet, whom he found more approachable and sympathetic than Daniel. This perception may have had something to do with Jacques's devotion to his own mother, who was born in the same year as Proust's "exquisite little Maman." Both mothers had a dry, offhand sense of humor that belied their fierce intelligence, and they were both unconventionally attractive. With their dark hair, dark eyes, and "beautiful Jewish features" (Proust's description of Jeanne), they reminded their sons' friends of heroines from the Old Testament.

In other respects, however, the two women were nothing alike. Geneviève was a consummate *mondaine,* known throughout Paris for her high-stepping social life and her famous friends. Jeanne was a homebody—when her husband had to mingle with the power brokers of his profession, she preferred that he do it without her. Geneviève was vain; like her friend Laure de Chevigné, she embraced the modern female body type of extreme slimness and starved herself to achieve it. Zaftig Jeanne was utterly uninterested in losing weight or following fashion. Perhaps their biggest difference, though, lay in their parenting styles. Whereas Jeanne tended to hover and dote, Geneviève treated her son as an afterthought, when not ignoring him outright.

Jacques ached for his mother with a fervor that Proust, incapable of bearing any "separation from Maman," knew only too well. Throughout his childhood, when Geneviève's spa cures and social obligations kept her away from home for extended periods, Jacques bombarded her with letters imploring her to return, or at least to write him back. Even when she was at home, she never ventured into her son's bedroom. According to Daniel, her negligence left Jacques free to play with a secret stash of knives—an early presage of the self-destructive impulses that would plunge him as an adult into alcoholism, drug addiction, and, finally, suicide.

Proust made his first move on "Carmen's son" sometime in the winter of 1887–1888, when Jacques, who had entered a rebellious phase following his mother's remarriage the previous fall, was behaving with a recklessness that landed him in detention on a regular basis. Jacques kept getting into trouble at home as well.

Early one morning, Straus apprehended him sneaking back into the apartment through a window after an unauthorized night on the town. While Geneviève laughed off the caper, Straus insisted that they consider disciplining the boy with stricter measures, such as boarding school, where they would end up sending him a few years later. (Ludovic hinted that Geneviève's habit of "dashing around from one château to the next" had necessitated the move.)

Jacques's run-ins with authority presented Proust with an opening. He wrote to Jacques to say that he, too, faced difficulties at home. He suggested that they lean on each other for support:

> My dear little Jacques, My family treats me very badly. They want to send me to boarding school in the provinces. My only consolation when I am really sad is to love and to be loved. And truly, it is you who respond to that need, the *you* who have had so many problems of your own this winter, the *you* who wrote me 1 exquisite letter the other day. I kiss you and love you with all my heart.

Because Daniel did not copy the letters he and Jacques wrote to Proust, only the ones Proust wrote to them, the contents of Jacques's "exquisite letter" have been lost. However, the adjective Proust used to describe it is suggestive, insofar as it was also his stock qualifier for his beloved Maman.

The reference to boarding school was similarly pointed. It was also patently made-up—there is no evidence to suggest that Proust ever faced banishment to a school "in the provinces." Nowhere in his voluminous correspondence with his mother and other family members is such a possibility even mentioned, nor would it have been, as the prospect of being kept apart from her "little wolf" was as unthinkable for Jeanne as it was for him. It would thus appear that Proust fabricated the boarding-school threat—and the broader claim about how poorly his parents treated him—in the hope of winning Jacques's trust. That his lie was motivated by something more than empathy comes through in his lines about "lov[ing] and be[ing] loved," and loving Bizet "with all [his] heart." Even "I kiss you," while a common enough valediction in French, had potentially amorous overtones. Its closest approximation in English is "love and kisses"—not a typical good-bye among heterosexual teenage boys.

Later that spring, Proust propositioned Jacques more directly. The letter in which he did so has not survived, but the one he wrote as a follow-up makes it plain that Jacques had turned him down:

> My darling Jacques, I respect your uprightness even as I deplore it. Your reasons [for saying no] are excellent, and I do admire the soundness of your thinking on the matter. And yet . . . the heart—or the body [*le cœur—ou le corps*]—has reasons of which reason knows nothing. So I accept with

great admiration for you . . . , but also with great sadness, the cruel yoke that you have imposed on me. Maybe you're right. Still, it saddens me not to get to pluck that delicious flower while we still can, because if we were to pluck it later [as adults], by then it would have ripened into—forbidden fruit. True, it's a fruit you find poisonous, so let's neither think nor speak of it further.

As noteworthy as Jacques's implied rebuff is Proust's refusal to take no for an answer. Even as he pledges to respect Jacques's wish that they keep their friendship platonic, Proust reasserts his lust by way of a witty pun on the seventeenth-century philosopher Blaise Pascal's truism, "The heart [*le cœur*] has reasons of which reason knows nothing," amending the homonymous *corps* to *cœur*. In this way, Proust appeals to the "very lively passion for Literature" that had first drawn him into Jacques's and Daniel's orbit. To stress that passion even more strongly, he praises Jacques's astuteness and moral probity. Chafe though he might under the "cruel yoke" of rejection, Proust suggests that his love springs as much from the spirit as from the flesh.

This dextrous reasoning did not change Jacques's mind about plucking the proverbial flower. But he did not take umbrage at the come-on. According to both Daniel and Robert Dreyfus, he was so secure in his heterosexuality that he "just shrugged his shoulders and laughed off Proust's effusions, knowing that he himself was above all suspicions of that kind."

Proust admitted defeat, but only to a degree. Jacques's indifference became the pretext for his first overture to Daniel, to whom he wrote in May expressing his yearning "to stare at Jacques forever, to kiss [him], to sit in [his] lap, to love [him] carnally, in the flesh, . . . to call [him] 'my little darling' and 'my angel' in all sincerity, without ever, for all the world, thinking of these actions as 'pederasty.'" He ended this letter on a defensive note, as if anticipating Daniel's scorn: "I don't know why such impulses should be thought any dirtier than the usual sort of love."

Although presented as a confidence about his passion for Jacques, this argument was actually directed at Daniel. Appealing to the latter's rational, analytical sensibility, Proust reminded him in a second letter that two of the greatest thinkers in the Western canon had loved men:

In their lifetime, [at least] two Masters of wisdom plucked the flower: Socrates and Montaigne. . . . They thought that, for young men, friendships that were at once sensual and intellectual were far preferable to entanglements with stupid, corrupt women.

A relationship "at once sensual and intellectual" is clearly what Proust was after here—and it was Daniel, he now revealed, who aroused him in these ways:

I'm going to explain my line of reasoning to you, an exquisite boy, on a subject that warrants our interest, even if we aren't generally comfortable discussing it together. . . . You think I am jaded and effete, you are wrong. If you are delectable, if you have pretty, clear eyes in which the refined grace of your mind is reflected so limpidly that I feel I can't completely love your mind without also kissing your eyes, if your body and your eyes are as graceful and subtle as your thoughts, so much so that I feel I would be able to enter into your thoughts much better if I were sitting on your lap, if, finally, it appears that your *you,* your *you* in which your lively brain is, for me, inseparable from your lithe body, would both refine and augment for me "the sweet joy of loving," none of that means that I deserve your scornful words. . . . I know plenty of extremely intelligent and upstanding men who fooled around with other boys when they were young. Later on, they returned to women. . . . So don't treat me like a pederast—that only hurts me.

In this appeal to Daniel, Proust uses many of the same tactics that feature in his letters to Jacques: the praise for his friend's intelligence; the fantasy about sitting in his lap; the premise that same-sex experimentation is acceptable teenage behavior; and the insistence that such experimentation would not count as actual "pederasty." (This was the term the young Proust tended to use for homosexuality; he switched to "inversion" much later.) The only material difference between this letter and its predecessors lies in Proust's plea for tolerance. Protesting that he is neither "jaded" nor "effete," he begs Daniel not to spurn him as a thrill-seeking deviant when all he, Proust, wants is "the sweet joy of loving" another boy.

Once again, Proust's entreaty got him nowhere. It may even have undermined his cause, as it seemed to precipitate a rupture between him and both cousins. Not long after receiving this letter, Daniel stopped writing and speaking to Proust altogether, and Jacques followed suit. Through the end of classes in the spring, and throughout the summer vacation, the two boys acted as if Proust didn't exist. The more obstinately they ignored him, the more desperate he grew. In one melodramatic note, he claimed that his mother, having picked up on the "excessive, *sensual* affection" between him and Jacques, had forbidden them ever to see each other again. This was probably another fabricated claim, improvised to create a sense of urgency—as if it were Jeanne's prohibition, not the cousins' silent treatment, that was tearing him and Jacques apart. At all events, Proust proclaimed, he stood ready to "love you *extra muros*" if necessary. "My little darling, we can turn a café into our little home for two."

Melodramatically, Proust labeled this missive "the hardest letter I have ever had to write in my life." Nevertheless, it left Jacques, and Daniel, unmoved.

Transcribing it in his diary on June 14, Daniel wrote, "That poor Proust is absolutely insane. Witness this letter."

As the new academic year approached, the cousins' embargo showed no signs of thawing, driving Proust into a frenzy of despair. In August, he turned to Robert Dreyfus (who had made the mistake of contacting him with some questions about the curriculum for the coming semester) to help him make sense of the situation. He begged Dreyfus to tell him why Jacques, "who used to be so nice to me, has dropped me" and why "his cousin has dropped me even more completely." Dreyfus's answers have not survived. September found Proust still quizzing him about the cousins' mindset ("Do they want to make fun of me, or get rid of me, or what?") and pining for a reconciliation.

In his letters to Dreyfus, Proust went so far as to compare himself to Racine's Phaedra, a paragon of ill-fated sexual transgression. Adulterous, incestuous, and criminal (because traitorous to her husband the king), Phaedra's infatuation with her stepson, Hippolytus, is triply taboo. As such, it is agonizing in a way that must have resonated with the seventeen-year-old Proust, as he made clear when telling Dreyfus about a recent sighting of Daniel and Jacques. "I could have said, like Phaedra: *My eyes are once more dazzled by the light of day, / And my trembling knees beneath me give way.*"

This letter dates from around the time Proust first took his later-to-be-famous questionnaire, which included a question about one's favorite literary character. Proust answered "Phaedra" (though he later crossed her off and substituted another of Racine's heroines, Bérénice, who succeeds in overcoming her problematic desire). As he explained to Dreyfus, he could relate to Phaedra's mooning over Hippolytus, "*charming, young, dragging all hearts behind him.*"

By the time Condorcet opened its doors again in October, marking Proust's final year at the lycée, his despondency had reached its nadir. Yet he soon had an epiphany, finding that the antidote to his distress lay in the one realm where Daniel and Jacques had reliably and willingly met him before. The one realm in which hypothetical desires and speculative utterances were not only tolerated but encouraged: literature.

In early October, Proust wrote two poems, one for each cousin. The very title of his new poem for Daniel, "Pederasty," indicated that his idée fixe hadn't changed. But it had assumed a different and, to a reader with Daniel's particular literary tastes, more palatable form—one that, beginning with Petrarch half a millennium earlier, had ever been the province of the thwarted lover. More recently, Baudelaire and Mallarmé had given this form dazzling new expression, and now Proust had adapted it to his own ends. "Pederasty" was a sonnet.

True to the French conventions of the genre, Proust's sonnet opens with two quatrains (four-line stanzas), rendered in the limpid alexandrine meter of Baudelaire, Mallarmé, and Racine:

If I had a great sack filled with silver, gold, and bronze,
And if I had a bit of boldness in my loins, my lips, my hands,
I would leave city life—with its books, its horses, and its politics—
And run away there immediately, today, tomorrow,
To a raspberry-strewn lawn—emerald or carmine!—
Where without the rustic hassles of wasps, dew, and frost,
I would want [je voudrais] forever to sleep with, to live with, and to love
A warm-bodied boy named Jacques, Pierre or Firmin.

By using only conditional verbs to describe his homosexual utopia, Proust stresses its divergence from the actual circumstances of the poetic speaker's life. With the litany of "if"s and "I would"s delineating a safe divide between what is (reality) and what could be (literature), "pederasty" ceases to be a threatening or off-putting possibility that the "real" Proust is trying to explore with his friends. It becomes instead a poetic trope like any other—like the quasi-incestuous love in *Phaedra*, say, or the "hypocrite reader" in *The Flowers of Evil.* Similarly, once "Jacques" takes his place alongside the fictitious "Pierre" and "Firmin," he loses his obvious affiliation with Jacques Bizet. He emerges instead as simply one invented character among many, inhabiting a world that, whatever its resemblance to the author's reality, remains separate from it.

After repositioning his verboten sexual partner and impulses as rhetorical devices, Proust abandons the conditional tense in which he first described them. In the sonnet's last two tercets (three-line stanzas), he restates his taboo urges in the present tense:

Away with prudish men's timid scorn!
Rain down, pigeons! Young elms, sing! Apples, ripen!
I want [je veux] to inhale his perfume until I die
Beneath the gold of ruddy sunsets, beneath the nacre of the moon,
I want [je veux]—to swoon and think I've died
Far from the death-knell of bothersome Virtue!

Twice proclaiming "I want," the speaker underlines the immediacy, rather than the conditionality, of his wants—a shift in emphasis known as a *volta* (turn), which the two closing tercets of a sonnet typically effect. In "Pederasty," the *volta* pairs sex with death, as the sensual pleasures the speaker craves—inhaling his lover's scent and swooning in his arms—are implicitly orgasmic *"petites morts"* (little deaths).

The tercets in this poem also attempt something on the order of a Racinian speech-act, in that the hortatory line "away with prudish men's timid scorn!" prescribes the banishment of homophobes from the speaker's sexual oasis. By means of this line, Proust follows Racine in summoning forth a new reality in language—a reality which, yet again, is both derived and distinct from the one he himself inhabits. While the reference to uptight, scornful men could be read as a pointed allusion to Proust's recent difficulties with Daniel and Jacques, the speaker's call for the expulsion of "prudish" homophobes from his idyll marks a sharp divide between literature and life. (So does the elimination of "wasps, dew, and frost," all elements unavoidable in nature.) By giving voice to an impermissible yearning, and dismissing those who would condemn it, Proust conjures up an enchanted realm where other, better norms apply. His sonnet *is* the paradise it evokes—a world "far from the death-knell of bothersome Virtue," where a young man might "pederast," in Daniel's parlance, to his heart's content.

Even outside this poetic never-never land, "Pederasty" seems to have improved Proust's situation with the cousins, as Daniel finally broke his silence upon receiving it, marking it up with suggested edits. Rigorous, sober minded, and focused on the work's formal properties, Daniel's feedback indicated that he had come around to viewing Proust again as a writer to be courted, rather than as a pervert to be shunned. Restored by the poem's literary merit, Daniel's confidence in the older boy's talent again moved to the foreground of their relationship.

In a second response to "Pederasty," Daniel sent Proust an example of his own verse, a rambling, fourteen-stanza poem called "Love" ("Amour"). This text also draws its inspiration from Baudelaire, but it reads like a hackneyed imitation or an unintentional parody. Its opening stanza alone includes three of Baudelaire's most sensationalistic tropes—a vampire, a rotting corpse, and a tangle of feasting worms—and things only get worse in the stanzas that follow. If Proust's high-school poetry contained "flashes of [the] genius" that would illuminate his mature oeuvre, Daniel's efforts in that vein confirmed the wisdom of his eventual decision to pursue philosophy and history instead of belles lettres.

The awfulness of "Love" came as a bonanza for Proust, who took the opportunity to trounce Daniel with his superior literary acumen. "The whole thing is v. bad," he wrote. "It shows no talent, to my despair, and is wholly unworthy of you." He peppered the margins with comments such as, "childish, horrible verse," "incomprehensible periphrasis, disheartening cliché," and "idiotic at the level of thought, language, and versification." In an attempt to offer constructive criticism, Proust urged Daniel to reread the classics—"Homer, Plato, . . . Shakespeare, La Fontaine, Racine, . . . La Bruyère, Flaubert, Sainte-Beuve, . . . and above all, Ludovic Halévy"—as correctives to his graceless style.

For both Proust and Daniel, this exchange was important in that it reestablished their relations as fellow aspiring authors. When the little literary gang decided that fall to relaunch its magazine as *The Lilac Review* (*La Revue lilas,* named for the lilac paper on which it was printed), Daniel not only solicited Proust's writings, as he had for the journal's previous incarnation, but also approved his election to the board as secretary general. Paradoxically, it had taken a sonnet on pederasty to convince Daniel that Proust's talent mattered more than his sexuality—or at least that the two were inextricably connected. Comparing his friend's "pederasty" to Baudelaire's notorious hashish addiction, Daniel hypothesized that "if [Proust] lost his vile side, he would lose the source of his greatness."

Proust sent as his first contribution to the new magazine an untitled prose poem—a genre upon which, though pioneered by Baudelaire, Proust again placed his own distinctive stamp. Dedicated "to my dear friend Jacques Bizet" and suffused with homosexual longing, it describes a sleepless night in a Paris apartment. The first of its two stanzas reads:

> *Fifteen years old. 7 o'clock at night. October.*
> The sky is a dark violet, stippled with light. Everything is black. Oh, my little friend [*mon petit ami*], why oh why am I not sitting in your lap with my face in your neck? Why oh why don't you love me? Here comes the lamp, the horror of usual things. They oppress me. . . . Here is the horror of usual things, and the insomnia of the first hours of the evening, while upstairs someone is playing waltzes and I can hear the jarring noise of dishes being washed in another room. Oh, my little friend [*mon petit ami*] . . . !

Like "Pederasty," this passage deftly reclaims for literature readily identifiable features of the author's existence, from the anguish of Proust's nocturnal solitude to his fantasy about curling up in the lap of a male friend.

Proust then introduces a *volta,* underlining a notable shift. This change is brought to bear not only on the speaker's erotic flights of fancy but on the whole panoply of concrete "usual things" for which the speaker used to feel only "horror," enumerated in the second and final stanza:

> *Seventeen years old. 11 o'clock at night. October.*
> The lamp weakly illuminates the dark corners of my room, and casts a great bright circle of light upon my hand, suddenly amber-colored, my book, my desk. . . . Everyone is asleep in the big, silent apartment. . . . I open the window to take one last look at the sweet, round face of the friendly moon. . . . I have closed the window. I am in bed. My lamp, beside me on the bedside table, amidst a jumble of glasses, flasks of cool liquids, small books with precious bindings, letters from friends, love letters, casts a dim light into the depths of my library. The holy hour! Usual things, like nature—being unable to vanquish them, I have made them sacred. I have cloaked them in my soul and in intimate or splendid images. I live in a sanctuary, in the middle of a spectacle. . . . Splendid visions dance before my eyes. This bed is soft. I fall asleep.

Contrasted with Proust's other writings to and for the cousins, and even with the stanza that directly precedes it, this passage is devoid of homoeroticism. Despite the muted sensuality of lines like "I am in bed" and "This bed is soft," the speaker no longer dwells on the anguish of his impossible love but instead highlights the compensatory joys of his own creativity. "Usual things, like nature— being unable to vanquish them, I have made them sacred." The erstwhile horror of nature—of an implacable status quo unwilling or unable to accommodate the speaker's taboo desires—dissipates when confronted with the splendid images he summons forth. The poet's art is the sanctuary; the rest is spectacle.

Aside from improving his relations with Jacques, this work led the younger boy to go out of his way to treat him kindly. Familiar with Proust's mania for collecting photographs of people he admired (a habit that took many of these people aback, since at that time one gave one's photograph only to family members and close friends), Jacques gave him a picture of himself, signed with congenial flattery: "For Marcel Proust, my dearest friend (with Halévy), February 1889."

Jacques also began inviting Proust on after-school visits to his family's apartment. Living up to his reputation as a favorite with adults, Proust flattered Jacques's parents with his deference and impressed them with his erudition. So favorable an impression did he make on them, in fact, that the Strauses temporarily tabled their plan to send Jacques to boarding school. "Just ask M. Straus what a good influence I have had on Jacques," Proust gloated to Daniel in November 1888. "One's morality is best gauged by one's influence [on others]." As for his "pederasty," Proust continued, it need no longer trouble either Jacques or Daniel, because "I am trying to remain pure, if only for the sake of elegance."

Proust may have found an impetus for his purity in a poem he discovered at right around this time, Alfred de Vigny's "The Shepherd's House" ("La Maison du berger," 1844). This work, an ode to poetry, "pure Spirit," and "peaceful, loving Reverie," emphasizes that literature, unlike sex, is impervious to "the tumults of the heart" and that the "pure, diamond-bright mirror" of great art is the sole "imperishable love" there is. At the same time, Vigny's poem acknowledges that the pursuit of such love can be an isolating business, insofar as most "base souls," when confronted with true genius, can bear "neither its ardor nor its weight." This message may have carried special, consolatory meaning for Proust in the spring of 1889, when Daniel and Jacques voted to reject his latest submission to *The Lilac Review*—a short story about a young hero in ancient Greece who learns to value platonic male friendship over homosexual lust. As much as the cousins had hurt Proust when spurning his sexual advances, their dismissal of his writing stung even more, and may explain why he gravitated toward Vigny's lonely but lofty worldview. By telling himself that his talent lay beyond the ken of mere mortals like the cousins, he could shrug off their disregard and remind himself of the superior fulfillment that awaited him in art.

This shift in Proust's way of thinking tempered his feelings for Daniel and Jacques, leading him to see that they were not the brilliant creative spirits their surnames had once led him to expect. In a letter he sent to Daniel that May, Proust indicated that both cousins, lacking the superior intellect he had originally ascribed to them, had fallen sharply in his estimation:

> Yesterday evening . . . I think I may not have made myself clear when I said that I love Jacques less than I used to. I didn't at all mean to say I find him stupid—just that the ideal image I used to have of him has faded a bit, as when one falls out of love. . . . However, I still think he has a certain number of [fine] traits—traits you yourself might not admire, given that they have to do with feelings, and that feelings aren't strictly literary; subtleties of character and nuances of emotion that he understands infinitely better than you do. But if you think about it, those things are the very stuff of art; they are what give great books their staying power. . . . So you see that I still have a lot of admiration for Bizet, since I admire him more than I admire you.

In offering such a backhanded statement of his esteem, Proust makes it known that his days of blindly worshipping the duo are over. He further indicates that if the cousins still have any claim on his admiration, it is only insofar as they stand to teach him about the "very stuff of art." The criterion by which Proust judged the pair was no longer romantic or erotic; it was aesthetic. They now mattered to him only as springboards for his own creative activity, as glass to be molten into the diamond-bright mirror of his art.

But when Proust said he had stopped pining for Jacques, it wasn't quite the case that he was through with love. Rather, he had turned his idealizing gaze on a muse of a finer, more promising alloy: a woman who had already inspired innumerable Parisian artists and who held one of the city's leading salons; a woman who, like her friend Charles Haas, had transcended her Jewishness to become an honorary member of the "born." A woman who was related to Jacques and Daniel but whose gender and age—along with her dazzling social position and her notoriously possessive husband—conveniently exempted her from Proust's "impure," same-sex longings, freeing him to concentrate on her aesthetic and social allure. A woman whom Daniel called "aunt" and Jacques called "Maman," and whom the society columns—a staple of Proust's reading regimen as the Condorcet chapter of his life wound down—designated by any number of her boldfaced names: Geneviève Halévy Bizet Straus.

LAME DUCKS

On November 11, 1889, Henry, Comte Greffulhe, forty, made an announcement that took the people closest to him aback. On September 22, he had been elected to a seat in the Chamber of Deputies. When campaigning in Melun, the electoral district for Bois-Boudran, Henry had described himself as "conservative, independent, liberal" and "not exclusively royalist," yet sympathetic to the cause of the d'Orléans princes, with whom the Greffulhes had been linked for generations. He had also sold himself as an outspoken critic of the republican left, which he denounced as a "band of brigands and thieves, exploitative and corrupt." Anyone who knew Henry knew that unlike his avowed "liberal" sentiments, his antirepublican vitriol was genuine. He had led his entire life as one long, haughty refutation of the credo *Liberté, égalité, fraternité* and was given to making statements like, "Republicans are dreadful and smell bad!" Which was why his family and friends were stunned when after six weeks in office, he claimed to have had a change of heart. He was a republican now.

To Élisabeth, twenty-nine, the news of Henry's political conversion came as a shock of a particularly unpleasant sort. For the past two years, for reasons she had no intention of sharing with him, she had inwardly withdrawn into feelings of wrenching despair, and Henry had for the most part let her be. But when the two of them did talk, they had talked about politics, which ever since the d'Orléans' exile had been a major topic of conversation at dinners in the rue d'Astorg. In these exchanges, Élisabeth and Henry had found to their surprise that for all the dysfunction in other areas of their marriage, they got along unusually well when pondering the future of the French monarchy and the role Henry should play in it. Élisabeth had even flat-

Henri Greffulhe, photographed by Nadar, became Comte Greffulhe in 1888.

tered herself that between his wealth and Orléanist ties and her media savvy and mystique, theirs would be an unbeatable political partnership. His defection to the republican camp, a move he failed to discuss with her ahead of time, disabused Élisabeth of this hope. It smarted all the more because without her, Henry would never have won the election in the first place. Or so she initially believed. The truth, when it came to light, would make her feel even worse.

AS ÉLISABETH SAW IT, Henry's political career had only really gotten under way in the summer of 1886, when she decided to take matters into her own hands. Before then she had waited anxiously, year in and year out, to see if he was going to follow through on his stated ambition to enter public life. But year after year he stalled, frustrating the ambitions Élisabeth had formed during their courtship, when she envisioned him as an ambassador to Russia or the Court of Saint James. Fearful of Henry's temper, she had been reluctant to press him about his inertia. But that changed on June 22, 1886, when the government passed the law of exile, banishing all pretenders to the French throne. This development gave Élisabeth an impetus and an opening to nudge her husband to fulfill his political destiny.

It was a counterintuitive moment for her to bring up such a matter, given that the princes Henry had supported all his life were being expelled from the country. But before their departure for England on June 24, the d'Orléans held a two-day farewell ceremony at their family seat in Normandy, the château d'Eu, built in the time and style of their kingly forebear Louis-Philippe. Along with royal relatives from all over Europe, the d'Orléans family had summoned their inner

The d'Orléans princes, exiled in the summer of 1886, had a farewell gathering at the château d'Eu, their family seat in Normandy. Élisabeth and Laure were guests at the party.

circle of loyalists from the Faubourg: the Greffulhes, La Trémoïlles, d'Haussonvilles, de Muns, Breteuils, Standishes, Sagans, and Galliffets (the wives in the last two couples attending together, separately from the husbands). It was among these, the d'Orléans' core loyalists, that Élisabeth had her epiphany about her husband's political future and resolved to see him more actively and centrally involved in the cause of Orléanist rule.

Élisabeth's revelation arose less from political ideology than from personal instinct, dawning on her when she found herself in the presence of more royals than she had ever before seen gathered in one place. Of the crowned heads who had traveled to Eu to see off the d'Orléans princes, some she had already met before, such as the members of the Belgian royal family, while others—such as Princesse Clémentine de Saxe-Cobourg and her favorite son,

Since the death of his cousin the Comte de Chambord in 1883, the Comte de Paris had been the presumptive heir to the French throne.

Giovanni Borghese's friend Prince Ferdinand—Élisabeth was encountering for the first time. At night in the castle's Gothic Revival banquet hall, where boiseries by Eugène Viollet-le-Duc framed antique Flemish tapestries depicting the sport of kings, Élisabeth had been awed by the spectacle of several dozen majesties and highnesses dining together by candlelight. Taken individually, few of these dignitaries would have met Élisabeth's high standards for attractiveness. To her eye, the Comtesse de Paris still looked rather like a washerwoman and the Duc d'Aumale rather like a goat, and nothing had prepared Élisabeth for the mountainous heft of old Princesse Clémentine. But as an ensemble, with the men in the gleaming medals and satin sashes of their poetic-sounding orders (the Holy Spirit, the Starry Cross, the Golden Fleece, the Golden Spur, the Garter, the Holy Sepulchre, the Elephant) and the women in their royal diadems and priceless crown jewels, they took her breath away. In this setting, Élisabeth suddenly realized what she and her peers had been missing for so long without a monarch on the throne: the unsurpassable glamour of a royal court. It was for this, above all else, that she decided Henry should assume his rightful place in the Orléanist high command. For if he were instrumental in helping to restore the princes to power, then he and Élisabeth would assume their rightful place in the new court: a place befitting their own matchless beauty, fortune, and favor.

Like Henry, Élisabeth had been raised in a monarchist household, although on the matter of the French succession, her parents' allegiance had lain more with the Bourbons than with the d'Orléans. Also like Henry, Élisabeth had no truck with the egalitarian ideals of the republican left. As she reflected in a one-page essay, "Equality," written in 1887,

> The word *equality* is dangerous, harmful to the public good. . . . Consider the hive. There are workers and queen bees. If everyone were a queen, nothing would function. *Inequality is a social good.*

The visit to Eu brought home to Élisabeth as never before the power and the glory of the royal scions as a separate, and decidedly not equal, species. While other biographers and scholars have tried to cast her as a political progressive, in this fundamental sense she was an élitist through and through. Élisabeth sincerely believed that birth and station endowed some men and women with a natural and necessary right to rule over others. (Her progressivism was limited to her inclusion of women in this category.) Despite her openness to such democratic modes of influence as the press, Élisabeth did not consider her celebrity with the general public a substitute for a more exclusive kind of social authority, born of proximity to monarchical power. It was time for her to turn "The Woman Who Would Be Queen" into something more than a party costume.

As she embarked on that effort at Eu, Élisabeth found an unexpected ally in Laure de Chevigné, who had come alone for the d'Orléans' send-off and seemed happy to find the Greffulhes there. Given Laure's well-known affiliation with Henri V, her presence at the château had puzzled Élisabeth until she noticed two things. First, Laure was exceedingly chummy with such Orléanist diehards as the Duchesse de La Trémoïlle, the Princesse de Sagan, Albert de Mun, and Henri de Breteuil. Clearly it was through these friends that Laure had insinuated herself into the princes' inner circle, despite her much-touted legitimist connections. Second, Laure was winningly at ease in the rigidly formal court environment at Eu, which closely resembled that of Frohsdorf. For aristocrats who had come of age under the Third Republic, the subtleties of such stringent court protocol could be rather daunting, all the more so as the Duc d'Aumale did not enforce it at Chantilly, which of all the d'Orléans residences was the closest to Paris and the most often visited by denizens of the monde. (At one recent dinner there, d'Aumale had scandalized his royal family when he gave the seat of honor to Baronne Alphonse de Rothschild, demoting his royal kinswoman Grande-Duchesse Wladimir to the second-best seat.) In such a setting, Laure stood out for her breezy facility with her hosts' customs. To see her so seamlessly revive her Frohsdorf training was to understand why the d'Orléans liked having her around. Quite apart from all her other engaging traits, she understood their way of life as few other Frenchwomen of her generation did or could.

During their stay at Eu, Laure provided indispensable guidance to Élisabeth, who for all her queenly posturing did not have nearly as much experience of court customs. When traveling with her father to foreign courts as a girl, Élisabeth had not, being unmarried, qualified for formal presentation there. As newlyweds, she and Henry had been presented to the Belgian monarchs in Brussels. Since then, however, her contact with royalty had been restricted chiefly to social events in Paris and shooting parties at Bois-Boudran and other hunting estates where *mondain* as opposed to royal etiquette held sway. Élisabeth did not like having to admit her ignorance in such matters, and part of her may have resented Laure for outshining her at Eu. But the company at the d'Orléans' château that weekend presented her with no viable alternative mentors. Constance de Breteuil was very sick (and would die less than a week later), and her husband visibly torn between caring for her and tending to his royal masters. Mmes de Sagan and de Galliffet only had eyes for each other; the same went for the Général de Galliffet and Mme Standish, whose love affair had become an open secret in their milieu. Mme de La Trémoïlle was too ugly, and Mme de Mun too priggish, to inspire Élisabeth's confidence, and for obvious reasons, "la belle Pauline" d'Haussonville was the last person whose help she would have wished to seek out. In any other context, Élisabeth would have turned to Sagan for counsel. But with Henry around, Élisabeth didn't want to act too friendly with his nemesis. She settled on Laure as her guide by process of elimination.

Élisabeth wound up being happy with the choice, not only because Laure's courtly savoir-faire proved so helpful but because her company was so amusing. To Élisabeth, getting to spend time laughing and gossiping with a woman her own age (twenty-seven to her twenty-six that summer) was a fairly new experience. Élisabeth didn't tend to confide in any women other than her mother, sisters, and cousin Marie-Alys, as she believed that female competitiveness made friendship between women difficult and between attractive women impossible. However, Laure's looks, fashion sense, and personality were all so different from her own that Élisabeth did not anticipate a rivalry. More than that: she liked Laure's wicked sense of humor and the feeling of playful complicity it inspired; it was as if Laure were silently daring her at every moment to spot the absurdity beneath all the solemnity and the pomp. At one point, the two young women caught each other's eye when Prince Ferdinand, spilling beer on himself at dinner, pulled his jacket off to reveal an arm covered wrist-to-shoulder in sparkling bracelets. Laure and Élisabeth had goggled at each other in mute hilarity, delighted not to be alone in seeing what they had seen.

WHILE AT EU, ÉLISABETH also set out to build alliances for Henry among the probable leaders of any Orléanist coup. Because these men, if they succeeded in crowning the Comte de Paris king, would influence the allocation of plum positions in the new régime, Élisabeth wanted them in Henry's corner, and luckily, three of them—Breteuil, de Mun, and d'Haussonville—already were. To make a new convert, Élisabeth focused her energies on fifty-one-year-old Émmanuel Bocher, whom she had not known well beforehand. With his father, the Comte de Paris's personal banker, Bocher was among that prince's most trusted advisers and as such was one of the chieftains of the Orléanist party. When they encountered each other at Eu, Élisabeth could tell from Bocher's attentiveness that he found her captivating, and she made a conscious decision to lead him on in the interests of Henry's career.

As usual, Élisabeth wasn't really attracted to her new swain. But Bocher made flirting easy with his gallantry and lively erudition. Despite his weighty political role, he considered himself a scholar rather than a statesman. Along with rare books, Bocher's real passions were archaeology and eighteenth-century French etchings. The latter he had collected for decades, documenting his holdings in a two-volume catalogue raisonné. When telling Élisabeth about his collection, he divulged that he kept his favorite etchings in a studio in Montmartre that even his wife of twenty-three years didn't know he had; he dearly hoped Élisabeth would visit him there someday. This disclosure put her on notice that Bocher's intentions toward her were anything but pure. But Élisabeth felt confident that by stringing him along, she could secure his support for Henry. "The Woman Who Would Be Queen," she wrote in her essay by that name, "perjures and prostitutes herself, a sacrificial virgin." Bocher would be her great conquest from Eu, although her "prostitution" was and would remain a matter of words, not deeds.

On the morning of June 24, the d'Orléans gathering came to an end. After exchanging emotional farewells with their loved ones, the princes exited the château to find the lawn teeming with well-wishers from all over Normandy and beyond. Breteuil, temporarily distracted from his wife's steady deterioration, took in the scene:

> Peasants in their smocks and sailors from the coast stood cheek by jowl with former [Orléanist] ministers, dukes, banking tycoons, and all kinds of other notables. The greatest ladies of France rubbed elbows with peasant women from the fields and sailors' wives from Le Tréport. Very few eyes were dry, and never will this great, imposing, and silent demonstration of fealty fade from the memory of those who witnessed it. An estimated 12,000 people came [to Eu] to pay their respects to the princes on that day.

With the d'Orléans bound by private train car to the coast and from there by steamship to England, their royal and noble houseguests dispersed. A handful, including Breteuil, rode with the princes all the way to Le Tréport, where the docks swarmed with another 25,000 of their devotees. Breteuil recorded that as the ship set sail, the Comte de Paris stayed on deck and addressed to the crowd one final "sad and noble salute. A single cry escaped from his lips: *'Vive la France!'* Thousands of other mouths took up the cry. Shouts of *'Vive le roi!'*

were rarer because the prince had made it known that he wished to avoid any demonstration" of overt royalist feeling. To the last, the would-be Philippe VII wanted to preserve law and order in the homeland that was forcing him to go.

ÉLISABETH AND HENRY RETURNED to Paris from Eu in a flush of revived royalist ardor. This was when their political partnership, as she thought of it then, really came into its own. In the past, when Élisabeth had reproached Henry for his extended absences from home, he would counter that he stayed away in order to avoid her jealous outbursts about the other women in his life. From Henry's vantage point, Élisabeth's newfound interest in his career represented a most agreeable change from those tantrums, while for her, his willingness to talk with her about his political trajectory gave her some comfort that as his confidante, at least, she meant more to him than his mistresses did. The détente did not lead Henry to curb his infidelities, nor did it blunt the pain they continued to cause Élisabeth. But while it lasted, the couple's shared sense of political purpose did afford them a modicum of the domestic harmony their marriage had lacked almost from the start.

To Émmanuel Bocher, with whom Élisabeth began secretly corresponding after they left Eu, she downplayed her marital rapprochement, stressing instead her feelings of sadness and isolation. These may have been authentic, but her intimation that Bocher was the man to alleviate them was not. At a party in Paris in the spring of 1887, she confided in him that she had "never allowed a certain word"—love—"to pass [her] lips." This admission ignited in Bocher a fiery resolve to make her say that word to him, and Élisabeth played coy, letting him live in hope. That autumn, Bocher and his father helped engineer Henry's election to the town council of Melun, a modest but necessary first step on the path to political glory.

Bocher may have been under the impression that by doing this service for Élisabeth's husband, he would win her love in return. If that was the case, then he was cruelly deceived, as the letters he sent her after Henry's election reveal. On May 31, 1888, Bocher wrote,

> Your lips never parted to tell me *yes* or *no* in good faith. Your hand refused to write the words you didn't wish to say. Don't you see? When it comes to certain feelings, one needs courage, which you don't have, and an ability to rise above trivial *mondain* concerns. I feel sorry for you, that's all.

But that wasn't all. In closing, Bocher declared that "despite all my suffering . . . , the deep, unwavering love I feel for you will never leave my heart." Élisabeth was unmoved, even annoyed. On the back of another of his letters, she scrawled: "DUPE! Not a word of it is true. I'll never love him; I just need him. Let him crawl like all the others. It's not my fault." If Bocher persisted in loving

After his wife's death in 1886, Henri de Breteuil formed a close friendship with Élisabeth and began an affair with Laure.

her, then that was his problem—she would show him no mercy. She would continue to manipulate him, and he would continue to crawl.

By this time, Élisabeth may have felt she could afford to be reckless with Bocher's heart, as the next phase of Henry's political ascent looked like it would depend on a different Orléanist leader, one whose loyalty was already assured. Since the death of his wife after the d'Orléans' departure, Henri de Breteuil had formed a close attachment to Élisabeth, turning to her as a confidante in his grief and dining regularly with her and Henry to avoid going home to a house without Constance. Breteuil had also tried to forget his heartache by throwing himself with renewed fervor into the cause of the d'Orléans, racking his brain for a way to bring the Comte de Paris back to France and to power.

Breteuil soon found a way, or so he hoped, in the person of General Georges Boulanger (1837–1891), a charismatic ex–minister of war who in the wake of the d'Orléans' expulsion was swiftly emerging as a national populist hero. Boulanger's own political sympathies were all over the map. He had gone from helping to crush the Paris Commune—gunning down the radicals alongside his arch-rival, Galliffet—to becoming the Duc d'Aumale's protégé to joining a far-left faction led by Georges Clemenceau, one of the most forceful proponents of the law of exile. The general had even cozied up to the d'Orléans' rival claimants, the Bonapartes, spinning himself as a military dictator in the Napoleonic mold. Most recently, Boulanger had tapped into a deep spring of class hatred and nationalist anxiety among disenfranchised citizens across the sociopolitical spectrum, from workers resentful of corrupt government officials and greedy capitalist bosses to conservative noblemen equally hostile to those guardians of the bourgeois republican status quo.

The general's growing popular base encompassed the same malcontents to whose xenophobia Édouard Drumont had recently appealed in *Jewish France* (1886), by scapegoating the Jews as foreign menaces who were wrecking the country from within. In a related move, Boulanger blamed the Prussians, ascribing France's economic and social ills to her humiliating defeat in the Franco-Prussian War and calling for a full-scale military rematch. With his saber-rattling jingoism and his dashing appearance on his trademark black horse, Boulanger stirred the masses into a frenzy of rage against the establishment and of worship for him as their savior.

At the suggestion of the Duchesse d'Uzès, a rabid monarchist like himself, Breteuil decided to try to harness Boulanger's popularity for the Orléanist agenda. The spectacle that clinched the idea for Breteuil occurred on April 19, 1888, when more than 100,000 citizens poured into the streets of Paris to cheer the general on as he rode past in a gaudy red-and-green open calèche, pulled by glossy black horses with red carnations, Boulanger's emblems, on their halters and red-and-green pompons in their manes. In his journal, Breteuil noted that it was "the equipage of a real charlatan," but a charlatan who had made it clear that even though the people "were shouting '*Vive la République!*,'" what they really loved was a man, and what they really wanted was a master." Based on the public fervor the Comte de Paris had elicited on his final day in France, Breteuil believed that prince could be just such a master, if only the army and the people would rally behind him.

On the strength of this insight, Breteuil and the Duchesse d'Uzès approached Boulanger with a proposition. They offered to back him politically and financially in a military coup that would topple the Third Republic and instate the Comte de Paris as Philippe VII. The general eagerly assented, flattered by their confidence in his greatness, as well as by a gracious letter of thanks from the would-be king himself. With the Comte de Paris's blessing, Breteuil and the duchesse canvassed their friends in the Faubourg to join their seditious undertaking. The resulting coalition was a hodgepodge of Orléanists, Bonapartists, and former legitimists such as Laure and Adhéaume de Chevigné, Valentine and Pierre de Waru, and Arthur Meyer. Whatever factional antipathies had divided them in the past, these *mondains* were united in their wish to see the hated Republic fall.

Solicited by Breteuil, Henry Greffulhe agreed to add his name to the roster of the new "Boulangist committee." But on Élisabeth's advice, he held off on participating any further until the success of the plan seemed assured. Despite her eagerness to see Henry make himself invaluable to the prince, she had misgivings about Boulanger's fitness to lead the d'Orléans to victory. As a *mélomane,* she abhorred the general's xenophobic attempts to ban performances of one of her favorite operas, Wagner's *Lohengrin* (1850), on French soil. (Twenty years earlier, the Prince de Sagan had tried to instigate a similar ban, also on patriotic grounds. But he had since come around to Élisabeth's way of thinking.) And as a "Woman Who Sets the Fashions," she viewed the pompons on Boulanger's horses as the height of bad taste—a judgment that would stay with her daughter well into adulthood. But even setting these cavils aside, Élisabeth worried that the general was simply not to be trusted. Her high-placed friends in the army, such as Galliffet, described him as a self-seeking, amoral con artist. Even Breteuil jokingly disparaged him as "General Bel-Ami," after the seductive but unscrupulous hero in Maupassant's novel. To Élisabeth, Breteuil's jest belied the risks he was taking by placing his hopes in such a dubious character. She wasn't at all certain that Henry should follow suit.

For once, Élisabeth found herself on the same side of an argument as Félicité, who groused to her by letter,

> I always thought the Duchesse d'Uzès was crazy, but not to quite such an extent, I have always said one must be prudent when it comes to politics, and it is probable that sooner or later Henry, too, will wind up making himself look ridiculous, if not worse, whereas if he would only follow our advice he would have nothing to worry about.

Félicité was fit to be tied when Henry finally admitted that he had nominally signed on to the d'Uzès/Breteuil committee. "Only an ambitious idiot would go over to Boulanger's side," she scowled. Élisabeth concurred, but she encouraged Henry to proceed carefully when managing the Boulangist group's expectations about his commitment to their cause. Perhaps thinking about her dealings with Bocher, she recommended tactical deception:

> It is simply a matter of being cleverer than everyone else, of playing a part, and expressing yourself in such a way that you mislead others as to your meaning, without compromising what you actually believe.

By holding himself somewhat aloof from the Boulangists, Élisabeth reasoned, Henry would keep his options open. If the putsch succeeded, he could make himself out as having backed it all along. If it failed, he could distance himself from Breteuil and the other conspirators and emphasize that his own brand of royalism was more measured, less divisive, than theirs. Either way, Élisabeth wrote to him, "I would like to see you more than anything else as an independent, getting along with everyone yet holding yourself *above* everyone."

In fact, there was an argument to be made that given the fierce partisanship of the current political environment, Henry might be even more useful to his prince as an independent than as another card-carrying Orléanist. At the moment, the republican and royalist factions in government were locked in a state of intractable mutual opposition. If Henry cast himself as an independent and advocated for the Comte de Paris's interests under a seemingly neutral guise, then perhaps the republicans in the Chamber would give his ideas a fighting chance, whereas they would reject the same ideas if proposed by a known Orléanist. Élisabeth believed that the prince would value Henry all the more for serving the cause in such a clever way and would be sure to promote him accordingly once the new monarchy was established.

ABOVE: Élisabeth de Riquet de Caraman-Chimay, Vicomtesse (later Comtesse) Greffulhe (c. 1887) at twenty-seven, around the time when Porto-Riche started leaving anonymous love poems for her on her pew at the Église de la Madeleine. By Nadar.

ABOVE RIGHT: Laure de Sade, Comtesse Adhéaume de Chevigné (1885) at twenty-six. Proust admired her hooded blue eyes, reddish gold hair, and delicately beaked nose. By Nadar.

RIGHT: Madame Émile Straus (1887), Geneviève, at thirty-eight, just when Proust, sixteen, first struck up a friendship in high school with her son, Jacques Bizet. By Nadar.

LEFT: The Italian Renaissance poet Petrarch wrote much of his lyric poetry for Laure's ancestress Laure de Noves, with whom he fell in love from afar in Avignon in 1327. Laure's descent from this famous muse became an integral feature of her persona.

BELOW: In the *Search,* Marcel's fascination with Oriane, Duchesse de Guermantes, begins in his childhood, when he views magic lantern slides relating the legend of one of her medieval ancestors, Geneviève de Brabant. Laure claimed to descend from her.

HISTOIRE DE GENEVIÈVE DE BRABANT.

Bienfaisance de Geneviève de Brabant.

Mariage de Geneviève avec le comte Sifroy, seigneur palatin.

Départ de Sifroy pour la guerre.

Geneviève de Brabant reçoit un message de son mari.

Golo déclare son amour à Geneviève de Brabant.

Geneviève, enfermée dans sa prison par ordre du traître Golo, met au monde un fils.

Apparition de Drogan à Sifroy.

Les serviteurs, chargés de mettre à mort Geneviève de Brabant, lui laissent la vie.

Geneviève de Brabant dans la forêt.

Reconnaissance de Geneviève et de son fils par le comte Sifroy son époux.

Innocence de Geneviève proclamée par Sifroy, et son retour au château de son époux.

Mort de Geneviève de Brabant.

Fabrique de PELLERIN, Imprimeur-Libraire, à ÉPINAL.

ABOVE: The Champs-Élysées, one of the most fashionable avenues in Paris, figures in many events in this book, from Victor Hugo's funeral in June 1885 to Élisabeth Greffulhe's appearance in *les drags* (society drag races) in May 1887 to Marcel Proust's stalking of Laure de Chevigné in the spring of 1892.

BELOW: The Right Bank at the fin de siècle.

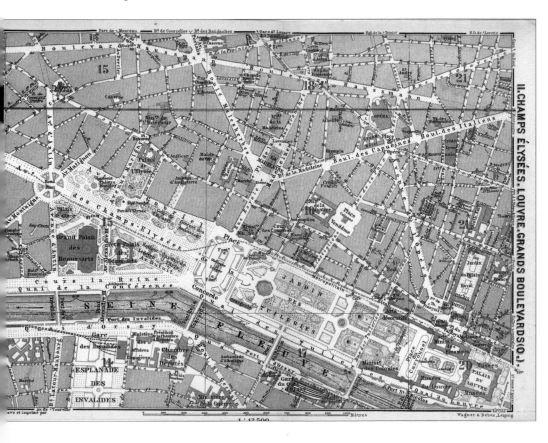

LEFT: The *ballet des abeilles* (bees' ballet) at the 1885 Sagan ball was based on a dance number from Fromental Halévy's *The Wandering Jew*. The Princesse de Sagan's version starred twenty-four "bees" drawn from the highest echelons of the French nobility.

BELOW: The ancient moated château de Chimay, in Hainaut, Belgium, was Élisabeth's father's family seat. As children, she and her siblings and cousins staged plays in the castle's private theater, modeled on the theater in the French royal palace of Fontainebleau.

LEFT: Gustave Moreau, *Salome in the Garden* (1878). Élisabeth's mother, Mimi, bought this watercolor as a present for her after they saw it together at the World's Fair in Paris in 1878. Élisabeth felt a special kinship with the fatally alluring biblical princess.

BELOW: This caricature of the exiled Comte de Chambord, the last of the French Bourbon royal claimants, depicts him on his horse, Popular Demand. His failed bid to reclaim the throne in 1873 gave the lie to his belief that the French people popularly demanded his return.

LES PRETENDANTS, PAR GILL

Edgar Degas, *Ludovic Halévy and Albert Boulanger-Cavé Backstage at the Opéra* (1878–1879). Geneviève's cousin Ludovic, left, was an acclaimed librettist, playwright, and novelist. A number of his artist friends, including Degas, became habitués of her salon.

Fromental Halévy was one of the most celebrated composers of the nineteenth century. As his daughter, Geneviève grew up surrounded by musicians, writers, and artists. Her first husband, Georges Bizet, studied under Fromental at the Paris Conservatoire.

Jean Béraud, *A Soirée* (1877). This mondain party scene captures the elegant, formal atmosphere of fin-de-siècle Parisian society, where evening dress meant tightly corseted, floor-length dresses for women, white tie for men, and gloves for both sexes.

RIGHT: Eugène Lami, study for *A Costume Ball Given by the Princesse de Sagan* (1883). Henry Greffulhe, who commissioned this work, dressed for the 1883 Sagan ball as a playing-card king, center. Élisabeth, left, dressed as the Queen of the Night. The red-haired, mustachioed man in the white ruff behind her is the ubiquitous Charles Haas.

BELOW: The museum-quality French antiques in both Élisabeth's and Geneviève's salons included eighteenth-century settees upholstered with Beauvais tapestries re-creating the painter Jean-Baptiste Oudry's illustrations for *The Fables of La Fontaine* (1694).

The Bat-Hunter by Robert de Montesquiou (1885). Élisabeth's "uncle in the Breton way," thirty in this self-portrait, was a flamboyant homosexual aesthete and poet who encouraged her to develop an extravagant personal style. The bat was his totem.

The Comtesse Greffulhe by Paul César Helleu (c. 1891). Of her many portraitists, Élisabeth liked Helleu for his emphasis on her swanlike silhouette. In 1891, she invited him to spend a weekend alone with her in the country. The visit yielded more than a hundred watercolors and sketches, but Henry, deeming them too intimate, destroyed most of them.

Jules-Élie Delaunay, *Portrait of Mme Georges Bizet* (1878). This portrait of a twenty-nine-year-old Geneviève in mourning caused a sensation at the 1878 Salon de Paris, cementing her public image as the Widow Bizet. It inspired the "painting of sunshine and mourning" in Maupassant's *Strong as Death*.

James A. M. Whistler, *Arrangement in Black and Gold: Comte Robert de Montesquiou-Fezensac* (1891–1892). Élisabeth and Montesquiou both fervently admired the painter they called their "Grand Ami" Whistler. In this portrait, commissioned by Élisabeth, Montesquiou poses with her chinchilla cloak slung over his arm.

RIGHT: The eccentric Prince Ferdinand de Saxe-Cobourg was one of Giovanni's closest friends. In the summer of 1887, Giovanni canceled his plans to visit Élisabeth in Dieppe so that he could travel to Sofia for Ferdinand's accession as Prince-Regnant of Bulgaria.

BELOW: Élisabeth engaged in a longtime secret correspondence with Henry's Franco-Italian cousin Don Giovanni Battista Borghese. She and Giovanni collaborated for nearly a decade on an epistolary novel about their star-crossed alter egos, Éléonore and Gérard.

ABOVE: Guy de Maupassant (1888) at thirty-eight, one of the most gifted writers of his generation. His last two novels, *Strong as Death* (1889) and *Our Heart* (1890), were widely thought to be based on his covert love affair with Geneviève. By Nadar.

Élisabeth cultivated friendships with numerous crowned heads, including members of the Russian imperial family. When the tsar gave her a Russian liturgical garment as a gift in 1896, she had Worth refashion it into a dramatic evening cape.

In his poetry, Petrarch imagined his love for the unattainable Laure de Noves as a phoenix, which burns, dies, and is rekindled. He also represented Laure herself as that mythical bird, recasting her blond hair as "golden plumage." Lord Lytton borrowed the phoenix trope in *Marah* (1892), the sonnet cycle he wrote for Élisabeth.

RIGHT: Aristide Bruant was a popular singer in Montmartre, where he performed at the legendary Chat-Noir cabaret (and later at his own establishment). He was famed for his outlaw swagger and his slang-laden ditties about the poor and criminal classes.

BELOW LEFT: Proust was fascinated by the regalia of the noblesse, including the elaborate livery uniforms of its footmen. One of the preeminent livery makers in Paris, Sutton, had his shop in the ground floor of the Strauses' building at 134, boulevard Haussmann.

ABOVE: Élisabeth studied photography with society shutterbug Nadar and staged her own photo shoots in her *jardin d'hiver* in the rue d'Astorg, with family and friends acting as her models. This is a photograph she took of the Prince de Sagan, aka the "King of Chic."

Ludovic Halévy   Le Comte d'Haussonville

Melchior de Vogüé   Paul Bourget

Geneviève's salon drew a unique mix of artists and aristocrats. Fame was the common denominator among her devotees, many of whom figured on the celebrity trading cards produced by fin-de-siecle chocolate companies.

LEFT: General Georges Boulanger, pictured as the King of Hearts due to his good looks and broad popular appeal, emerged as a national populist hero by advocating for military reengagement with Prussia. Laure joined a group of royalists conspiring to back him in a military coup d'état, but the plot collapsed when he fled the country on April 1, 1889.

LORD LYTTON.
Governor-General of India, 1876-80.

RIGHT: Before coming to Paris as British ambassador, Lord Lytton was viceroy of India, where his decadent entertaining style earned him the sobriquet "The Great Ornamental."

LEFT: Fromental Halévy's opera *The Wandering Jew* (1852) was a point of reference for many mondains, from Edgar Degas, who teasingly called Haas "the Wandering Jew," to Lord Lytton and Élisabeth, who adapted the story separately in their creative writings.

Robert de Montesquiou
likely drew his sobriquet
for Élisabeth, "the Swan,"
from Richard Wagner's
Lohengrin (1850).
Georges de Porto-Riche
envisioned himself and
Élisabeth as the two lovers
in the opera, the Swan-
Knight Lohengrin and
the Belgian noblewoman
Elsa of Brabant.

LEFT: Jacques-Émile Blanche, *Portrait of Marcel Proust* (1892). This painting depicts Proust, twenty-one, at the start of his so-called "camellia period," his phase of youthful mondanité. According to Blanche, the gardenia boutonnière was a gift from Lord Lytton.

BELOW: Snapped at the Strauses' estate in Trouville (c.1893), this photograph shows, left to right (standing): Fernand Gregh, Georges de Porto-Riche, Louis de La Salle; and (seated): Proust, Louis Ganderax, and Geneviève.

BEFORE LONG, Élisabeth and Henry got a promotion of a different sort. On September 27, 1888, Charles Greffulhe died at seventy-four after a long illness, making Henry and Élisabeth the new Comte and Comtesse Greffulhe and demoting Félicité to dowager comtesse. In addition to leaving them an incalculable fortune, the old man's passing plunged his family into six months (and his widow into two years) of obligatory mourning, a ritual suspension of sociability and enjoyment. The reception rooms in the rue d'Astorg and Bois-Boudran were hung with black, as were the windows of the family's many carriages and coupés, drawn by all-black horses with black rosettes on their bridles and black ribbons woven into their manes. The coachmen and servants traded their blue-and-gold Greffulhe livery for black mourning clothes, coarser versions of their masters' solemn garb. The family canceled all shooting and hunting for the rest of the year and recused themselves in advance from the Paris social season the following spring.

This enforced withdrawal from society came at a fortuitous time for Élisabeth and Henry both. Of Élisabeth's reasons for welcoming it, more will be said later. As for Henry, the loss of his father provided him with a handily convincing pretext for his noninvolvement in the Boulangist committee, whose activities accelerated over the autumn and winter as popular support for the general continued to grow at a stupefying rate.

While the Greffulhes hid behind the trappings and the suits of mourning, Breteuil and his cohort were having a gay old time preparing to bring down the government. The fact that they were plotting treason lent a cloak-and-dagger frisson to their meetings, which involved decoy carriages, secret doorways, and silly disguises, complete with fake beards for the men. They incorporated the red carnation into their daily dress, a jaunty splash of dissidence on their bosoms and lapels. Carried away by the dizzy optimism and furtive thrill of the whole business, Breteuil and Laure de Chevigné fell into a love affair. Arthur Meyer, drunk with excitement about his prestigious new "friends," praised them gratuitously in the pages of *Le Gaulois.* He even talked the Duchesse d'Uzès into standing as his godmother when he converted to Catholicism. (When persuading her to play this role, Meyer expressed the paradoxical hope that being baptized at the hands of the country's highest-ranked peeress would "cleanse [him of] the urge for social advancement," which according to him afflicted all Jews from birth.)

Breteuil and his accomplices made some effort to stay focused on the weighty issues at hand. In the faded splendor of the British Embassy, they had discussions with the ambassador, Lord Lytton, and the Prince of Wales about the sunny future of Franco-British relations under Philippe VII's rule. In the not-at-all-faded splendor of the Duchesse d'Uzès's mansion—refurbished with the riches of her "not born" ancestors, the founders of the Veuve Clicquot Champagne company—the conspirators politely questioned Boulanger himself about his plan of attack. That he avoided going into tedious detail struck most of them as a sign of good manners, which they were pleased if rather surprised to discover in a man they took to be descended from bakers. (In fact, the general's father was a lawyer, but to the "born" that distinction meant next to nothing; that his surname meant "baker" told them all they cared to know about his origins.) Rather than enter into questions of strategy or policy, Boulanger spoke to the group in vague but stirring terms about his unique ability to make the people of France do his bidding. "I will stop at nothing to stir up public opinion," he told them. "I still have more than one trick up my sleeve."

His supply of tricks was soon to run out. By the end of 1888, Boulanger had "won the voices of over a million Frenchmen," in Breteuil's accounting, as self-described Boulangists throughout the country ran for office, albeit without legal party status, and won in many districts. In January 1889, the general himself ran for a seat representing Paris in the Chamber of Deputies and carried the vote by a landslide. The government voided his win on the grounds of his military affiliation, a policy aimed at blocking the very sort of junta Breteuil's crew was hoping to pull off. This setback drew wrathful indignation from Boulanger's followers in Paris and beyond. Civil unrest mushroomed. The Republic teetered. The conditions seemed ripe for a coup.

The general did not, however, rise to the challenge with the swashbuckling valor and resoluteness of purpose his adherents had expected of him. Quite the opposite: he became unhinged, overwhelmed by his sudden fame and paranoid about the mounting risk he faced of imprisonment or assassination. He sought comfort and guidance from his mistress, who supposedly gave him bad drugs as well as bad advice. On April 1, just hours after the government inaugurated the new Eiffel Tower with much patriotic fanfare, Boulanger fled to Belgium to avoid arrest on conspiracy and treason charges. He took his mistress and his *mondain* backers' money with him (including three million francs from the Duchesse d'Uzès alone), never to return. According to historian Frederick Brown, "The Eiffel Tower seemed to plant a gigantic exclamation mark after the announcement of his flight," broadcasting for all to see that the republic was here to stay.

OF HER PROTÉGÉ'S IGNOMINIOUS ESCAPE, the Duchesse d'Uzès wrote tersely, "With that, the general's star didn't fade; it was extinguished." His disappearance left scores of disgruntled Frenchmen without a spokesman for their inchoate anger, prejudice, and fear. Wasting no time, Drumont churned out a battery of new anti-Semitic tracts (*The End of a World*, 1889; *The Last Battle*, 1890; *An Anti-Semite's Testament*, 1891) and founded an anti-Semitic newspaper, *Free Speech* (*La Libre parole*, 1892–1924). In these publications, he reiterated his arguments about the rapacity and perniciousness of "the Jew," to whose list of alleged crimes against France Drumont now added the desecration of the Parisian skyline by the Eiffel Tower (even though Eiffel was Christian).

His call for all French patriots to join forces against the Jewish "foreigner" was soon taken up by other nationalist ideologues, including Maurice Barrès (1862–1923), a young, formerly Boulangist author and politician who had recently begun frequenting Geneviève Straus's salon. At the other end of the political spectrum, socialist and anarchist agitators gained ground among the working classes, prescribing radical solutions to the iniquities of capitalism. With extremism on the rise on both the left and the right, the Third Republic was headed toward an explosive fin de siècle. In hindsight, the Boulangist crisis would look like the beginning, not the end, of the régime's seismic troubles.

Another, nearer-term effect of Boulanger's flight was to annihilate not just Breteuil's and his friends' plans for a coup but any last meager shred of legitimacy that French royalists might still, three years after the princes' exile, have tried to claim for their political doctrine. With a new round of general elections coming up in the fall, Orléanist politicians scrambled to persuade the electorate that theirs remained a viable platform. When their compatriots voted on September 22, Breteuil, de Mun, and d'Haussonville all managed to hold on to their seats in the Chamber. But throughout the country, their party sustained crushing losses. After hearing the grim election returns at Meyer's office at *Le Gaulois,* Breteuil reflected on his colleagues' defeat:

> There was no choice—we had to win or die, become the majority or remain an impotent minority! There was no middle ground between the two situations, nothing else to hope for. There's no point in hiding it—we are beaten, and no matter what comes next, nothing will change that now.

The collapse of the Boulangist plot changed everything for Henry Greffulhe, though, and seemingly for the better. In the chaos around the general's rise and fall, Henry launched his first bid for national office, running for the Chamber as a representative of the district of Melun. Untainted by association with Breteuil's aborted coup, he presented himself as a salutary alternative to royalists and republicans alike. While unstinting in his censure of the current régime, he pledged to be all things to all people, a champion for "conservative, independent, *and* liberal" interests (emphasis added). This impossible claim inspired the opposition to dub Henry "the bat candidate" (*le candidat chauve-souris*), presumably as a swipe at his grotesque ideological hybridity. Given his loathing for Robert "the Bat" de Montesquiou, Henry was unlikely to have savored the comparison.

But the name-calling did not stop him from continuing to push his catchall political agenda. Sounding not unlike the departed Boulanger, Henry spouted hollow phrases about his unique ability to lead his compatriots to a brighter future. He vowed to reconcile "the France of yesterday [with] the France of tomorrow" and riffed to the press about founding his own political party,

Henry was caricatured as "the bat candidate" because of his hybrid political position.

"one that would place itself between warring factions to protect them against each other's blows, like the Sabine women" in a famous history painting by Jacques-Louis David. When pressed for specifics about his platform, he replied that "being brand-new to politics, [he did] not yet belong to any party, and [did] not wish to be labeled or classified" in partisan terms.

Thus far, it appeared that Henry was following Élisabeth's counsel to the letter, positioning himself as an independent in a category of one. As was perhaps to be expected, the fatuousness of his campaign promises rankled Breteuil, who predicted that Henry would "stop at nothing to get himself elected deputy from Melun, come what may and at all costs." (This last clause was one of Henry's own stock qualifiers, typically used when he was scolding Bebeth for an infringement of *bon ton*.) But the Orléanists needed all the deputies they could get, and given Henry's historic allegiance to their party, they decided to back him as their candidate in Melun. Despite Boulanger's demise, the Orléanist machine retained some of its influence in that traditionally conservative district, so its backing proved valuable to Henry. On September 22, he was swept into office with 60.5 percent of the vote.

Even allowing for the efficacy of the local Orléanist bosses, the decisiveness of Henry's victory was stunning. Not only had he appeared to stand for nothing while campaigning; he had never been well-liked in or around Melun. Since inheriting Bois-Boudran from his uncle ten years earlier, Henry had kept "Big Moustache" on as his enforcer in the area, terrorizing suspected poachers and trespassers and sparking criticism in the regional press. Brutalizing his neighbors by proxy gave Henry a reputation for cowardice, whence the local saying that even his elegant wife was "more of a man than the Comte Greffulhe."

Henry preferred to think of himself as the Sabine woman keeping two enemy armies from killing each other in David's *The Sabine Women (above).*

(Not only that, he complained to Élisabeth, "my adversaries went so far as to say that I beat my wife!") Knowing how unpopular he was with the electorate, Henry had avoided making public appearances during the campaign, relying instead on a staff of four to five hundred paid supporters—in a district where fewer than eight thousand people would vote—to proselytize on his behalf. His opponent, by contrast, had given speech after rousing speech and held a series of well-received town hall meetings. At only one of these had Henry deigned to show his face, and when his suite of armed guards started roughing up the people in the crowd, the event had devolved into an outright brawl. Yet somehow, in spite of all this, he had carried the district in an irrefutable win.

To Élisabeth, her husband's triumph seemed to validate her own strategic acuity. By maintaining his neutrality as she had recommended, Henry had won a seat in a now predominantly republican Chamber—a feat that impressed even the Comte de Paris, who sent his personal congratulations: "The large majority you secured has come to me as the most agreeable surprise." This mark of royal approval buoyed Élisabeth's optimism about Henry's future as the man behind the prince and her own future as the woman behind the man.

But then came Henry's apostasy. Less than two months after his election, he recanted his independence and threw in his lot with the republicans in the Chamber. Élisabeth, who had not been privy to his decision ahead of time, was scandalized. Henry's abrupt change in course threatened to negate everything she had thought the two of them were working to achieve. Rebuking him for the shift, she did not mince her words:

> Regrettable, regrettable, M. le Comte Greffulhe a "republican of tomorrow"—not elegant! I can see that in spite of your best intentions you are going to compromise yourself. And the more concessions you make, the more prestige you will lose. You'll wind up being lumped in with *them* [the republicans], dropped by your friends and despised by all. A man like you does not sell his name. Believe me. I am not saying this out of chagrin at finding myself married to a republican. I am saying this to get you to think twice about the slippery slope you are on. *I* would have preferred to see you as an independent, getting along with everyone and especially holding yourself *above* everyone. . . . The role of the disennobled [*désanobli*] republican does not suit you.

Quite aside from the anger it was bound to cause in the Orléanist camp, Henry's defection to the republican side appalled Élisabeth because in her view, it amounted to a forfeiture of his birthright. As a grand seigneur, her husband was supposed to stand "*above* everyone" else, not just in politics, but in general. This was the ethos by which the members of their caste had always lived. At present as in the past, their elegance and prestige were what defined them, relative to their noble peers and to humanity at large, as Henry himself reminded her every time he upbraided her for compromising the family name. Yet he was guilty of this very compromise, this very crime. To "sell his name" to the republicans was to cater to the lowest common denominator, abetting the *déclassement du gratin.*

Aghast at his shameful conduct, Élisabeth was hypersensitive to the ill will it generated among their peers, not to mention in the Comte de Paris. In a second note from England, the prince wrote to Henry with acid understatement, "Know that you may count on me, my dear Greffulhe, as I have been able to count on you"—in other words, not at all.

The worst was still to come. Within days of Henry's change of allegiance, the news broke that he had led a dirty campaign, bribing some voters and preventing others from casting their ballots. Henry issued a categorical denial: if any of the alleged wrongdoing had taken place, his election agents had carried it out without his knowledge. But the scandal cast suspicion on his 60.5 percent electoral majority and exposed his newfound republicanism for what it almost surely was: a craven bid to preempt prosecution by the Chamber's majority party. In this endeavor, at least, Henry failed. At the behest of radical deputy Camille Pelletan, the legislators opened a formal investigation into his election in Melun.

The investigation lasted for the remainder of the year. The deputies pored over a massive dossier, evaluating charges that the Greffulhe campaign (1) paid citizens for their votes, usually in five- to ten-franc sums; (2) kept other citizens from voting; (3) plied still others with free alcohol in exchange for their support; and (4) contracted implicit quid-pro-quo bargains with various municipal groups and leaders ("Does the commune of Guignes need a pump? M. Greffulhe buys them a pump. Do the firemen of Champeaux want a banquet? M. Greffulhe pays for their banquet"). Camille Pelletan repeatedly complained that many key documents in the dossier had gone missing and that other materials looked as if they had been falsified. If this was true, then the fact that Henry and his team were the ones responsible for compiling the dossier may have accounted for the irregularities.

With the information available, the deputies determined that Henry had gotten only 52 percent of the vote in Melun—still a winning margin but obviously less than the original tally. In addition, they discovered that Henry, having real estate holdings in the Nangis district, had also considered running there. But he had changed his mind about Nangis when, even after endowing a hospital and a school there, he came in dead last in the preliminary polls. This bit of evidence seemed consistent with the picture Pelletan was trying to paint of Henry as a rich swindler looking to buy his way into office. While the deputies discussed their findings on the floor of the Chamber, Henri de Breteuil, sitting with his Orléanist colleagues, refrained from making a comment. But he had been saying it all along: his old friend Henry Greffulhe "would stop at nothing to get himself elected deputy from Melun, come what may and at all costs."

On December 23, 1889, two days before Henry's forty-first birthday, the deputies wound down the investigation and put the matter to a vote. In his closing address to his colleagues, Pelletan urged them to invalidate the election of the Comte Greffulhe. He reminded his leftist confrères that before defecting to their ranks the comte had repeatedly accused them of thievishness and corruption—the two defining features, it now turned out, of his own campaign. According to Pelletan, the moral rot at the heart of Greffulhe's candidacy was evident not only in his financial skullduggery but in the "infinite, ahem, plasticity" with which "he offered . . . to mediate between the passions of the right and the left, likening himself to the Sabine women of David's painting!" Playing this grandiose analogy for laughs, Pelletan went in for the kill:

> But he is too modest! The Sabine women were abducted, but nobody abducted [Greffulhe]—he abducted himself, by spontaneously joining our great republican family with no encouragement from us!

At these words, the deputies erupted in hoots, whistles, and uproarious laughter. Pelletan paused for long enough to let his audience's gaiety run its course, then he resumed a more sober enumeration of Greffulhe's misdeeds. But the line that stayed with everyone afterward, and that was reprinted the next day in the national press coverage of the session, was Pelletan's coup de grâce: "He abducted himself."

The flippant yet deadly irony of this line was very much in the spirit of Meilhac, Halévy, and Geneviève Bizet Straus. But whereas such wit had made those individuals' reputations, it destroyed Henry's. In the end, he was not forced out of office: while 192 deputies voted for the annulment of his election, 261 voted against. Nonetheless, his standing in the Chamber was permanently undermined by Pelletan's ridicule.

Before long, he stopped going to the Chamber even for important votes. "I can't take it anymore," he told Élisabeth. "I don't go anymore because I never know how to vote without turning the left and the right against me." Their daughter, Élaine, now seven years old, tried to cheer him up with an original work entitled "Elections: A Moral Poem." After listing the many challenges that attend "the battle to crush one's opponent," the poem concludes:

> *And why all the running around?*
> *Just to win a position*
> *Where giving one's opinion*
> *Makes one a thousand enemies.*
> *Moral:*
> *The happy life is the hidden life;*
> *We should pity those poor deputies.*

Henry pitied himself so much that he took off for Bois-Boudran for the remainder of hunting season. Perhaps he took some small comfort in the fact that his only child agreed with him about the superiority of the hidden life. On that subject, he and his wife remained as far apart as ever.

FOR HER PART, Élisabeth did not lord it over Henry that, once again, she had been right. She was too downcast to gloat, her triumph too Pyrrhic to mitigate her blues. For a short, soothing while, her dream of a brilliant future at court, of a life spent basking in a husband's (and a king's) reflected glory, had carried her through, shining a light in the darkness at just the moment when another, infinitely more precious dream of hers was dying. But now, with Henry's political career in ruins, that consoling fantasy was dead as well.

The lesson she learned from the whole debacle was, Elegance and prestige really are everything.

The lesson she did not learn from it was, Reflected glory really is nothing at all.

PART TWO

PART TWO

VARIATIONS

CAGED BIRDS

Every loving feeling in my heart is struggling to break free, like
thousands of birds beating their wings against the bars of a cage.

—ÉLISABETH GREFFULHE, *Tua Res Agitur* (c. 1887)

Salome: Let me kiss your mouth.
Iokanaan: Never, daughter of Babylon! Daughter of Sodom, never!
Salome: I will kiss your mouth, Iokanaan. I will kiss your mouth.
Young Syrian: Princess, Princess, you who are like a bouquet of myrtle,
you who are the dove of doves, do not look at that man! Do not look at
him! Do not say such things to him. I cannot bear it.

—OSCAR WILDE, *Salome* (1893)

My poem will be a sad bird in a cage,
Carried outside beneath treetops in bloom,
And puzzling to the free, wild bird
Who is drawn to its echoing laments.

—ÉLAINE GREFFULHE, *The Sad Roses* (*Les Roses tristes*, 1906)

CHAPTER THIRTEEN

KISSES NEVER GIVEN

I n the spring of 1887, *les drags* were only in their fourth year, but already they had become a highlight of the Paris social season. Sponsored by the National Steeplechase Society and presided over by the Prince de Sagan, the event was a drag race in the fashionable English style. Seven clubmen, handpicked by Sagan, drove four-in-hand stagecoaches at breakneck speed from the place de la Concorde to the hippodrome in Auteuil, where a Champagne picnic awaited.

The custom-built lacquered coaches, the fin-de-siècle equivalents of professional race cars, were brightly painted in the drivers' family colors, with enough seating on top and inside to accommodate a dozen or so relatives and friends. In a nod to medieval and Renaissance tournaments, when noblemen jousted with their ladyloves' insignia on chivalrous display, the custom in *les drags* was for the wife of each of the seven competitors to sit beside him in the driver's seat. This practice upheld an essential fiction of *bon ton,* namely that the wife of the grand seigneur was the most important woman in his life. It was a pretense that even the most incorrigible philanderers sought to maintain in public, with one glaring exception: Henry Greffulhe.

After nearly ten years of marriage, Élisabeth had learned that at any given moment, Henry's harem always had a reigning queen, a woman he called "La Principale" ("The Main One"). Pauline d'Haussonville had occupied this position for a decade or more, but recently, a chubby, vindictive minx named the Baronne de Noirmont had unseated her. Élisabeth suspected that the plain little baronne was romancing Henry above all out of a petty wish to upstage her, his famously alluring wife. But Élisabeth had had no concrete support for her theory until an evening in April 1887, when Henry had barged into her bedroom in the rue d'Astorg with a horrifying announcement: Mme de Noirmont wanted to sit between him and Bebeth in the place of honor when he raced in this year's *drags.* Élisabeth had objected strenuously, appealing to her husband's own oft-proclaimed concern for appearances. But Henry had shouted her down, reminding her with his usual brutality that obeying him was her only choice.

Élisabeth had spent the next several weeks trying to forget about the impending *drags.* She busied herself with cultural activities, going to concerts and art exhibitions, and with her secret literary projects and correspondence. But on May 10, race day dawned bright and clear over Paris, and the whole Faubourg gathered on the place de la Concorde, the gentlemen dapper in their tailcoats,

In the first leg of *les drags,* clubmen raced their stagecoaches from the place de la Concorde up the Champs-Élysées.

cabbage-sized carnations in their buttonholes, and the ladies festive in their summer-print dresses and flower-garden hats. Élisabeth wrapped her features in an opaque white veil and carried a frilly white parasol. Most of the time, she used such accessories as props in her ongoing flirtation with the Parisian public, to preserve her air of mystery. But today, she was using them for self-protection. She didn't want anyone to see her blushing in desperate humiliation when, handed up into Henry's blue-and-gold stagecoach by a footman in blue-and-gold Greffulhe livery, she found herself face-to-face with a beaming Mme de Noirmont. As Élisabeth settled into her seat, pulling her ruffled white skirts in close so as not to touch those of her rival, Henry glowered at her through her veil, as if daring her to contest his perverse idea of chivalry.

When all the drivers and passengers were in place, a volley of trumpet blares sounded. The Prince de Sagan appeared atop a bandstand, his white mane gleaming beneath a black silk top hat, and surveyed the crowd through his monocle. Raising his right arm and pointing it upward, as stiff and straight as the three-thousand-year-old obelisk behind him, he fired the starting gun. On this signal, seven long whips cracked in unison over the backs of twenty-eight horses, and twenty-eight stagecoach wheels rolled into motion, rapidly picking up speed. The 5.5-kilometer race course ran up the Champs-Élysées, around the Arc de Triomphe, and through the Bois de Boulogne to Auteuil. From start to finish spectators lined the route, cheering at the *mondain* pageantry. For Élisabeth, every second of the jolting, clamorous ride was misery, as thousands of Parisians watched her go by in her disgrace, forced to share her seat of honor with her husband's "Principale."

The next day, Élisabeth fled to London. The pretext she gave for her trip was the unveiling of her newest portrait, by Carolus-Duran, at the Royal Academy on May 14. But the truth was, she just couldn't stay in Paris. Nothing any of her admirers might say to her about her unequaled beauty could console her for her public embarrassment. Or rather, she had one prospective beau whose reassurance would have meant everything to her, but he hadn't been in town for *les drags,* nor had he mentioned them by letter. Maybe it was just as well—Élisabeth didn't want his pity. She wanted his love.

Her shaming at *les drags* did turn out to have one positive consequence. Élisabeth's father-in-law, Charles, was so aghast at his son's mistreatment of her that when she returned home from England, he presented her with the most extravagant gift she had ever received: an estate of her own in Dieppe, her favorite resort town on the Norman coast. When handing her the keys to the property, known as the Villa La Case, Charles stressed that it was to be hers and hers alone.

Henry was none too pleased about this gift, and not only because it implicitly reproached him for his shoddy behavior. He preferred quiet spa towns such as Royat-les-Bains to the Norman seaside, which he disliked for its showy *mondain* social circuit, ruled by the unsavory likes of the Princesse de Sagan. But Élisabeth was overjoyed. She knew immediately what she wanted to do with the place: turn it into her own haut-luxe artists' colony, a retreat where she and her uncle Robert and their like-minded friends could write and paint and play music to their hearts' content. While Henry carried on with his "Principale," in Royat or Paris or parts unknown, Élisabeth would make a refuge of La Case, pursuing her creative projects in the company of people who understood and adored her.

Uncle Robert found this an excellent plan and agreed to help inaugurate the villa by cohosting a house party there with Élisabeth in August. Together they drew up a small but perfect guest list: two composers, Prince Edmond de Polignac and Gabriel Fauré, the latter a new protégé of Élisabeth's (he had recently begun work on a haunting *pavane* in her honor); one painter, Paul César Helleu; and one aspiring writer, Don Giovanni Borghese. Unbeknownst to Uncle Robert, it was really with Giovanni in mind that Élisabeth had come up with the idea for a party. It was Giovanni whom she wanted to console her in her dejection. It was from Giovanni that she wanted not pity, but love.

THREE YEARS HAD PASSED since Élisabeth's first meeting with Henry's handsome half-Italian cousin at the Dampierre funeral at Guermantes, and still the prince haunted her daydreams and bedeviled her slumber. "The minutes die painfully unless my thoughts are attached to him," she wrote. The minutes died painfully when her thoughts were attached to him, too, although those moments brought a different, more delectable sort of pain. On his sporadic trips to Paris with his mother and on his own, Giovanni had become a popular figure in the gratin, appreciated for his courtly charm and engaging conversation.

Not to mention for his striking and exotic looks, his La Rochefoucauld eyes as bright as sapphires against his dusky Borghese complexion. Lily de Gramont's description of him as "an Italian from the Renaissance" put Élisabeth in mind of Petrarch, who had opened her eyes as a girl to the bittersweet pain of romantic longing. Thanks to Giovanni, Élisabeth had since become something of an expert on the subject.

Over the years, her friendship with him had proceeded by fits and starts, interrupted by family tragedy (the deaths of her mother and his father, in 1884 and 1886) and conducted primarily by mail. Though he still lived with his mother in Rome, Giovanni continued to talk about moving to Paris someday, and whenever he came to town, he stayed with his aunt Félicité in the rue d'Astorg. During these visits, the Greffulhe model of family-based socializing allowed Élisabeth to see him on a daily basis. The more she saw of him, the more deeply she became convinced that he was the soulmate she had been yearning for all these years.

Élisabeth had hoped that her literary collaboration with Giovanni would help bridge the distance between them when he was in Rome, and to some degree it had. Writing as "Éléonore" and "Gérard" (also identified in Giovanni's manuscript pages as "G.B." and "the Prince"), the two of them had exchanged dozens of letters and journal entries. The premise that they were working on a novel had given Élisabeth the courage to reveal more of herself to Giovanni than she would ever have thought possible. "How sweet it is," she wrote as Éléonore, "to know

Élisabeth kept this photograph of Giovanni in her private archives.

that you will see through this transparent veil and grasp my real meaning." She confided in Gérard that she never felt more alive than when a man—or better yet, a crowd—was looking at her. ("I find that anonymous stares give me the same sort of frisson as Harmony does; the gaze is the music of Beauty!") She admitted that despite her reputation for spotless virtue, in reality it didn't "take any merit on my part to turn my suitors down" because nearly all of them—all but one of them, in fact—repulsed her. She even confessed that the very thought of that one uniquely appealing male friend "envelops me and caresses me as if I were lying in his arms, with my head on his shoulder."

Such disclosures deviated sharply from the regimented conversation Élisabeth found so limiting in the gratin: "the banal, ready-made language one is *obligated* to speak in the monde: cold, formulaic words one utters for the sake of *bon ton,* and which disguise one's true emotions." Through the transparent veil of fiction, she had been showing Giovanni her true emotions.

A transparent veil, or a magic mirror that dissolved the sorrows of her real existence, transforming them into everything she craved and lacked: romance, connection, freedom, joy. Not long ago, Élisabeth had reread "The Shepherd's House" by Alfred de Vigny, and its description of poetry as a "diamond-bright mirror" had reminded her of what she and Giovanni were trying to do with their novel. As she saw it, at least, the two of them were building a sanctuary for "imperishable love" (Vigny again), an alternative to the restrictive, soulless milieu that conspired to keep them apart. She had quoted this couplet from the poem in one early letter to Giovanni: "What do I care for the day? What do I care for the world [*Que m'importe le monde*]? / I will say they are beautiful when your eyes say they are!"

Élisabeth knew that Vigny meant *le monde* as the world in the broadest sense, but she wanted to insist on the narrower, social meaning of the term, having come to regard *mondain* society as the real enemy. Where she had once been drawn to its elegance and excitement, she now found herself bristling at its suffocating propriety, its flagrant hypocrisy, its rigid intolerance for sincere emotion. This was the world she dreamed of defying for Giovanni's sake, as she had been trying to let him know in letter upon letter to him in Rome.

But Giovanni had yet to meet her even halfway. Although he and Élisabeth were supposedly writing a love story, his contributions to their manuscript skirted the issue of love. Thus far, his pieces had consisted chiefly of fictional diary entries, relating a trip through Africa that seemed to be based on the Borghese Expedition. In these sections, which Élisabeth had a secretary transcribe in a notebook bound in blood-red leather covers, passages like this one predominated:

1 October 18__, 7 o'clock in the morning. Recalled to Europe by urgent letters, I left Dar Gueri, the residence of the Sultan of Tama, on the border of

Waddai. . . . My two companions were to continue the expedition without me, heading toward Chad.

Such dry, factual entries also made Élisabeth want to scream or cry whenever she
tore into his latest packet from Rome. The logistics of Giovanni's African travels
hardly seemed a fitting response to her heartfelt confessions.

She granted that from a literary standpoint, Giovanni had valid reasons for
developing this subplot. His thought was that the African journal would function as a frame narrative for their novel, which would open with Gérard's trun-
cated journey across the Sahara, undertaken after the demise of his love affair
with Éléonore. (How or why the couple's affair fell apart, Giovanni had yet
to explain—Élisabeth couldn't bring herself to think about it.) On the eve of
his departure, Gérard would give a packet of his and Éléonore's old love letters to one of his fellow travelers for safekeeping. This minor character, "P.M."
(probably named after Pellegrino Matteucci, a companion of Giovanni's on the
Borghese Expedition), would act as the book's fictional "editor," publishing
the correspondence "under the veil of anonymity, after both lovers' untimely
deaths." The novel would open with a preface by P.M., explaining how the letters came into his possession; the letters themselves would follow, taking the
reader back in time to the story of the couple's doomed romance.

Presented with this proposed structure, Élisabeth conceded the African diary's value as a literary device. But as a clue to Giovanni's feelings for her, it was
of maddeningly little use. Writing to him under her own name, she ventured a
flirty taunt: "I'm starting to get jealous of these foreign lands that absorb you so
completely!" Giovanni did not take the bait.

Nor did he offer much ground for encouragement in the few places in his
writings where his characters did refer to women and romance. P.M., for example, comments at one point that although his relationship with "G.B. [is] much
more intimate than an ordinary friendship," he has never heard Gérard "utter
any woman's name except with the utmost indifference." True to this characterization, Gérard steers rigorously clear of sentimental territory in all but one of
his extant letters. At the end of a long digression about Wagner (for whose music
Giovanni, like Élisabeth, was mad), Gérard makes his only remark about love:

Reality is always more beautiful when seen from afar; very little can
withstand closer scrutiny. I once looked through a magnifying lens at
the "admirable" complexion of a woman I used to love, and I must confess: . . . her pores terrified me.

Élisabeth did not believe for a second that her own pores were terrifying—if
anyone's complexion could withstand closer scrutiny, hers could. Still, Giovanni's attitude puzzled her. Except for Henry, not a single man Élisabeth knew

regarded her with indifference. Even her hairdresser claimed to be in love with her—she had a sheaf of impassioned letters to prove it.

Élisabeth was not alone in being stumped by Giovanni's evasiveness, or in trying to make sense of it in fiction. That very spring, an author named Francis Marion Crawford, born in Italy to American parents, published a roman à clef called *Saracinesca* (1887), setting Roman society abuzz about the striking similarities between its hero, Don Giovanni Saracinesca, and Don Giovanni Borghese. Along with his princely rank, his "non-Roman" bloodline (which owes its "distinct character [to] the influence of a foreign mother"), his family ties to the papacy, and his appearance ("His features stood out in stark relief from the setting of his short black hair and pointed beard"), the trait the fictitious Giovanni most obviously shares with the real one is a "restless energy" that drives him to seek adventure and avoid romantic entanglements. As one of the most eligible noblemen in Rome, he confounds the ladies of his set with his obdurate bachelorhood:

> Don Giovanni was not married, but there were few marriageable women in Rome who would not have been overjoyed to become his wife. But hitherto he had hesitated—or, to speak more accurately, he had not hesitated at all in his celibacy. His conduct in refusing to marry had elicited much criticism. . . . His reputation for wildness rested rather upon his taste for dangerous amusements than upon such scandalous exploits as made up the lives of many of his contemporaries. But to all matrimonial proposals he answered that he . . . had plenty of time before him, that he had not yet seen the woman whom he would be willing to marry, and that he intended to please himself.

In Crawford's narrative, Giovanni's lack of interest in the opposite sex hides his unspoken passion for Corona del Carmine, a "very beautiful" duchess with "splendid black eyes" that she "wielded [like] magnificent weapons." Corona's noble but impoverished family has made her marry the duke for his prodigious wealth. It has turned out to be an unhappy match because her husband, a "wretched remnant of dissipated humanity," cheats on her with countless women. Yet Corona is too virtuous to resort to adultery herself ("There was never a breath of scandal breathed about the Duchessa"), and Giovanni Saracinesca is too virtuous to try to tempt her.

Élisabeth, who had read *Saracinesca* at Giovanni's prompting, wanted to believe that her prince had kept his distance for similar reasons. In fact, he himself had admitted to her that he was the model for the book's protagonist, and though he warned her that "the portrait [was] immoderately flattering," Élisabeth thought it captured him quite accurately. Not just in the surface details, either, but in his admirable moral fiber. Like Giovanni Saracinesca, Giovanni

Borghese was a staunch Catholic, proud of his ancestral links to the Vatican. While in Africa, he had bought a seventeen-year-old, arrestingly handsome slave boy, Mahraghian, at the bazaar in Khartoum. In addition to having Mahraghian baptized, Giovanni had brought him back to Rome to live and arranged for him to receive a first-rate Catholic education there. Such nobility of character was one of the many traits Élisabeth cherished in her Giovanni, even if, as seemed likely, it was stopping him from declaring himself to her. After all, in the eyes of the Church, a liaison between them would qualify as not only adultery, but incest.

But for all Giovanni's reticence, she felt so much closer to him than he seemed to realize, close enough that she always thought of him as "*tu*" and "*toi*," although neither in person nor in her (or even Éléonore's) letters would she ever have dared to address him in such an intimate way. With everyone other than her daughter, siblings, and younger female cousins, Élisabeth used the more distant and formal "*vous*," as good manners required. Given that this was even the pronoun she used with Henry and Uncle Robert, it was unquestionably the proper mode of address for an adult male cousin by marriage. In her diary, Élisabeth imagined coming clean to Giovanni about the linguistic liberties she took with him in her mind:

> When I am with you [*toi*] I will coldly say *monsieur* and you will never know you are my lover, with all the delicacy of platonic love and all the frenzies of the flesh.

And yet, she wanted him to know. And when he accepted her invitation for the housewarming in Dieppe in August, she made a promise to herself: she would bare her soul to him then.

HER FIRST AUGUST AT LA CASE. Élisabeth was making the final preparations to welcome Giovanni, Uncle Robert, and her two other guests. While a silent army of domestics swept through the villa, plumping cushions and polishing floors, she surveyed the gardens outside. The estate stood atop a high, craggy peak, a lone promontory jutting out into the English Channel, but the lawn was a miracle of lushness. A hundred thousand geraniums overflowed from the parterres, forming a fragrant red tide around the whitewashed half-timbered façade of the house. The Greffulhe standard flew from a faux-medieval donjon. Leaded glass, freshly cleaned and smelling faintly of lemon, sparkled in the open windows. Apart from the calls of the seagulls swooping and dipping overhead, Élisabeth could hear only the crashing of the surf at the base of the cliff below. And the swift, steady pounding of her own heart.

Her most cherished hope, which had consumed her all summer, was that Giovanni would be as taken with La Case as she was. She had even allowed herself to daydream about the romantic life the two of them could lead there,

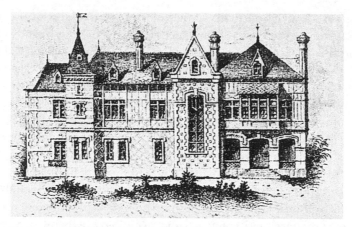

La Case, a villa in Dieppe overlooking the English Channel, was a gift to
Élisabeth from her father-in-law.

free from their families and the monde. With Uncle Robert's help, she had had
a folly built in the garden, meant to charm her handsome prince: a diminutive Japanese pagoda. Like Uncle Robert and Edmond de Polignac, Giovanni
had become a keen partisan of *japonisme,* a craze for Japanese decorative arts
launched by Edmond de Goncourt and Charles Ephrussi (a Jewish art connoisseur more erudite, if less *mondain,** than Charles Haas). According to
Henry, belligerent as always, *japonisme* was merely a byword for effeminacy, as
evidenced not just by the sexual proclivities of Montesquiou and Polignac but
by the confirmed-bachelor status of Goncourt, Ephrussi, *and* Giovanni. But
to Élisabeth, Giovanni's *japonisme* attested to his refinement, and thus to his
spiritual kinship with her. Besides, his zeal for Japanese art (as well as for Wagner) fostered unexpectedly amicable relations among him, Uncle Robert, and
Edmond. Despite their homosexuality, the latter two men were fiercely possessive of Élisabeth and openly hostile to most of her male devotees. The fact that
they both liked Giovanni also boded well, she thought, for her future with him.

The pagoda was not the only surprise Élisabeth had in store for Giovanni
during his stay. Over the past many months, she had written a cycle of verse and
prose poems she hoped would enlighten him once and for all as to her passion.
On the dedication page, she transcribed the "you will never know that you are
my lover" passage from her diary, addressing it "to You [*Toi*], the Unreal One"
and adding, "Your heart is the cool oasis where I have been hiding without you
knowing it." In a nod to Giovanni's Roman heritage, she entitled the collection
Tua Res Agitur (*It Concerns You*), referencing a line from the Roman poet Hor-

---

* Ephrussi spoke with a heavy Yiddish accent, which, as in the case of Baron James de Rothschild, curtailed his
mondain assimilation. Indeed, Ephrussi's nickname in the monde was "Matame"—the "ghetto" pronunciation of
"Madame."

ace: "If your neighbor's wall is on fire, it concerns you." If Giovanni caught this allusion, as he surely would, he would have to acknowledge the searing intensity of her desire. No more evasions; no more feints between them.

The publisher in Nangis who had printed Élisabeth's homage to the Prince de Sagan produced a copy of *Tua Res Agitur* in the same format, a booklet with thick, beautifully engraved pages the size of calling cards. The last significant thing she had to do before Giovanni's arrival was to work out her strategy for gauging his reaction to her text, which she planned to leave in his room for him to discover on the first night of his visit. A few days earlier, she had thought she would simply wait for him to bring it up, sometime when the other guests had left the two of them alone. It now occurred to her, though, that she could have Éléonore write a note to Gérard, asking for his opinion of *Tua Res Agitur;* given how often their two characters talked about art, this would be a natural question in their correspondence. Élisabeth liked the idea of her own poetry for Giovanni becoming "a bit of [the] divine, lived reality" from which they were creating their novel. Yes, this would be her strategy for engaging him about her poems. She took one last, long look around the garden and went inside for the evening. Before bed, she played Wagner on the piano: *Siegfried Idyll.* It was the most transporting music she had ever heard.

ÉLISABETH WOKE UP THE NEXT MORNING feeling more hopeful and excited than she had in years. Her house party would be perfect. *Tua Res Agitur* would be perfect. Giovanni would be perfect. Uncle Robert was to arrive the following day, and the others a few days after that. She could hardly wait.

While having her breakfast in bed, Élisabeth went through the mail stacked neatly on a separate silver tray. A telegram from Rome sat on the top of the pile; she grabbed it, tore it open, and read it. Then she read it again to make sure she hadn't misunderstood. Giovanni regretted that he would be unable to come to La Case after all; another matter demanding his immediate attention was going to take him abroad indefinitely.

Élisabeth's heart imploded.

Her wall burned down.

Her neighbor, who was supposed to be concerned, was nowhere to be found.

Giovanni followed his telegram with a massive arrangement of Japanese lilies, a second apology. The scent of the flowers made Élisabeth nauseous, but she kept them by her bedside anyway, tokens of her runaway prince.

Without thinking, she reached for *Le Gaulois.* On the front page, she read: "Prince Jean Borghèse has just left Rome to go and stay in Bulgaria with Prince Ferdinand de Saxe-Cobourg, to whom he is bound by ties of the greatest intimacy."

Fuzzily, Élisabeth remembered. Last month, Giovanni's old friend Prince Ferdinand de Saxe-Cobourg had been named prince regnant of Bulgaria; the press

Prince Ferdinand de Saxe-Cobourg (*far right*) ascended the Bulgarian throne in 1887. The short, top-hatted (bearded figure, rear third from *left*) is Giovanni; he traveled from Sofia for the occasion.

had reported that he would assume power in Sofia by summer's end. She remembered laughing with Henri de Breteuil when the Prince of Wales told them of his mother's indignant reaction to the news: "Prince Ferdinand of Cobourg [*sic*] is totally unfit—delicate, eccentric, and effeminate . . . and should be stopped at once!" (Like Tsar Alexander III, Queen Victoria loathed him.) Her friend Henri had issued a similar verdict:

> If [the Bulgarians] really have been reduced to offering their empty throne to Prince Ferdinand de Saxe-Cobourg-Gotha [*sic*], then at least the matter has its comical side. I can't think of anything more grotesque than that young prince with the big nose and the nasal voice—the only two traits he inherited from the d'Orléans—who covers himself in jewels [and] drenches himself in perfume. . . . His French relatives ridicule him mercilessly, [but] his mother, that excellent Princesse Clémentine, spoils him rotten.

Reading the notice in *Le Gaulois*, Élisabeth could not recall why Bulgaria mattered geopolitically—something to do with the balance of power between Russia, the Ottoman Empire, and the West. To her only one fact pertained: Giovanni was off to Sofia to share in the triumph of his friend. His eccentric, effeminate, intimate friend. Of course.

She should have guessed it, should have seen the signs, if not in Giovanni himself—she still viewed him as nothing if not virile—then in Prince Ferdinand. All those bracelets on his arm when he took off his jacket at Eu last summer: that alone should have tipped her off.

Élisabeth ought to have noticed these things. She ought to have realized. As Dr. Pasteur had told her on a recent tour of his laboratory in Paris, "The greatest disorder of the mind consists in seeing things as one wishes they were." Another thing she should have registered but didn't: the greatest scientist alive dismissing the retreat into the imagination as sheer folly. By Pasteur's standards, how would one qualify the Éléonore/Gérard manuscript? Or *Tua Res Agitur*? As diamond-bright mirrors? No—as disorders of the mind.

TIME PASSED. Taking up *Tua Res Agitur* again, Élisabeth rewrote its first and last pages. In the revised dedication, she struck an elegiac note: "To You, the Unreal One [*Toi, l'Irréel*], are dedicated these fugitive pages, furtive and brief like moments of happiness."

The same mood pervaded the new ending, which evoked Giovanni's apology bouquet:

> *Murderous odor of great Japanese lilies!*
> *Intensity of love cutting into my soul; . . .*
> *We exchanged the supreme vows of the happiness*
> *That we dreamed, and hid, beneath inflexible masks.*
> *Our imaginary lips met in kisses never given.*

La Case, the house in which she had placed so much hope, was unbearable to her now. Everywhere she looked, she saw her lover's absent form and ached for his kisses never given. Sending telegrams to Uncle Robert and her other invitees, she postponed the house party until early September. Etiquette prevented her from canceling it altogether; in a heartless society, heartbreak was not a valid excuse for reneging on one's commitments. Élisabeth would come back in a few weeks and dutifully play hostess to her friends. But in the meantime, she had to get away. "Like an animal that goes into hiding to die," she wrote, "I go into hiding to suffer."

As if to punish herself for her failing to see the truth about the man she loved the most, she went to stay with the woman she loved the least, her mother-in-law. Félicité was spending the end of the summer at the château de La Rivière, where Élisabeth and Henry had passed the first few weeks of their honeymoon nine years before. Henry and his father were at Bois-Boudran, getting organized for the upcoming hunting season, so Félicité was on her own. Her sour, dull personality could not have been further removed from Giovanni's irresistible intellect and charm. But for that very reason, Élisabeth figured her mother-in-law's company would force her to readjust to the grim, loveless reality she had so foolishly dreamed she might escape.

Élisabeth also needed privacy in order to lick her wounds—"My brain," she wrote on August 22, "is like a workshop of malice, where the wheels and cogs exist only to cause pain." Mercifully, Félicité seemed content to leave her in peace. She didn't bully Élisabeth into staying in the château proper, granting her request to hole up instead in one of the outbuildings, the Penthièvre Pavilion. The Duc de Penthièvre, who had owned the property before the Revolution, was not an ancestor of the Greffulhes—they had inherited it from a forebear who acquired it after the Revolution. Nonetheless, Félicité took inordinate pride in the fact that her estate had once belonged to a grandson of Louis XIV and a cousin of Louis XVI. Élisabeth suspected that her mother-in-law's very willingness to let her stay in the Penthièvre Pavilion had to do with nothing so much as the immense satisfaction it gave Félicité merely to pronounce that ducal name.

The pavilion was an enchanting little folly in the Louis XVI style, but Félicité did not often have volunteers to stay there, for legend held that it was haunted by its original proprietor. Penthièvre, one of the richest men of his era, had used the place as a workshop where he tinkered with the watches and clocks that he collected by the hundreds. Since his death in 1793, these objects had remained untouched, scattered on tabletops and filling vitrines throughout the pavilion, and to this day, they struck the hours correctly, unwound by human hands. Local superstition ascribed their exactitude to midnight visitations by the old duc, whose soul was said to take on the form of an eerie, amorphous light when returning to tend to his timepieces. The constant ambient chimes and tolls gave Élisabeth the sense that she had been frozen in time, her hopes and future arrested by that telegram from Rome. "Everybody *else* is moving forward," she wrote wistfully. "I am like a stopped clock." She was almost sorry that Penthièvre did not appear to her while she was living among his treasures. Having lost his beloved wife in childbirth, buried five of his seven children in infancy, seen his surviving son and heir engage in the most dissolute behavior only to have him, too, die prematurely, and, finally, in his dotage, lost his beautiful and blameless daughter-in-law, Marie-Thérèse de Carignan, Princesse de Lamballe (1749–1792), to the murderous rage of a revolutionary horde, the duc was a man who understood loss.

In fact, if anyone's spirit haunted Élisabeth during her stay in the pavilion, it was that of the ill-fated princesse, whose life story suddenly seemed eerily akin to her own. The Princesse de Lamballe had been an exquisite, highborn virgin packed off to France from her happy home abroad to marry, at seventeen, one of the nobility's most eligible scions. Her husband, Penthièvre's aforementioned heir, had proceeded to treat her with brazen contempt, philandering with scores of mistresses, squandering his fortune, and leaving his mortified father to try to console her with the gift of real estate (the hôtel de Lamballe in Passy, now home to Dr. Blanche's mental clinic). As an antidote to her miserable marriage, the princesse had cultivated a close, passionate friendship with Marie Antoinette, remaining unconditionally loyal to her to the end—and paying dearly for her devotion. In a series of riots in Paris in September of 1792, a mob had dragged the princesse into the street and demanded that she publicly disavow the queen, whom they accused of being her lover. When the princesse demurred, the crowd had hacked her to pieces, impaled her head, her breasts, and (according to some reports) her genitals on pikes, and marched the gruesome trophies past the windows of Marie Antoinette's jail cell, screaming for the royal prisoner to "kiss the lips of her beloved."

Along with Marie Antoinette, Madame Élisabeth, and the rest of the royal family, the Princesse de Lamballe was remembered to this day in noble circles as a martyr to the monarchist cause. (Élisabeth's uncle Robert even wrote some poetry on the subject.) As Élisabeth now thought of it, however, the princesse had been a martyr not to politics, but to love. Ultimately she had died because nothing could induce her to give up on her most cherished friend. "A sincere heart is bound to get broken," Élisabeth mused. Her suffering may not have found the same lurid physical expression as the Princesse de Lamballe's, but it was killing her nonetheless.

During her first few days at La Rivière, it occurred to her that she might dress as the Princesse de Lamballe for some future ball; like all her best costumes, this one would connote both royalty and purity. But at some point during her stay, Élisabeth remembered that because of the Princesse de Sagan's well-known identification with Marie Antoinette, the gratin referred to her best friend, Georgina, Marquise de Galliffet, as the Princesse de Lamballe. Élisabeth further recalled that this epithet carried more than a whiff of scandal; for like their eighteenth-century namesakes, the two women were presumed to be lovers. Estranged from her husband (the chronically unfaithful Général de Galliffet), Mme de Galliffet lived in a pretty house Mme de Sagan had had built for her in the gardens behind her hôtel in the Faubourg Saint-Germain. The two women went everywhere in society together, sometimes dressed in matching outfits, and took their summer *villégiatures* in neighboring villas in Deauville, a few towns southwest of Dieppe along the Norman coast. They had even arranged for one of Mme de Sagan's brothers to marry Mme de Galliffet's daughter, Antoinette. Allegedly the mothers had brokered this union as a cover for their own undue closeness, which according to *mondain* rumormongers combined "all the devotion of friends" with "all the tenderness of sisters."

From Uncle Robert, Élisabeth had learned that such expressions were seldom as innocent as they sounded. Like the other phrases that recurred in connection with Mmes de Sagan and Galliffet—"intimate and inseparable friendship," "the very closest ties," "the sweetest intimacy"—they were euphemisms for same-sex love. Uncle Robert seethed when people used language like this to describe his bosom friendship with Edmond de Polignac, say, or his relationship with his live-in personal secretary, Gabriel de Yturri. But he relished applying such terms to others.

So, as it happened, did Giovanni. While in Paris a few years back, he had sent

Élisabeth a (for him) startlingly risqué account of an evening at the Opéra with friends. Gossiping with one of the ladies in his group, "Mme de C.," Giovanni noticed that another of their companions, "Mme H.," had grown agitated at the sight of a couple canoodling in a *baignoire* across the way. Together he and Mme de C. came to the conclusion that Mme H. was jealous not of the woman in the couple but of the man. Mme H.'s dismay, Giovanni reported to Élisabeth in his letter, confirmed "suspicions [he had] already had about her for six months now."*

At the time, Élisabeth had not dwelled on this story, except to wonder what, technically speaking, intimacy between female lovers might involve. In one of their coded exchanges, she and Guigui had envisioned a scenario in which two women bit and tore at each other's clothing, pinched one another's nipples, and tumbled into a bath together. But in hindsight, she realized that Giovanni's anecdote had been yet another crucial bit of information about his own leanings. Yet another clue Élisabeth had ignored to her own detriment.

Although she could no longer stand to look at the Éléonore/Gérard manuscript, writing remained a release for Élisabeth, and she needed it more than ever. Returning to her story about Marie-Alice de Monteillant, she added two new characters to create a love triangle. Blanche de Vauguyon, a naïve young bride madly in love with her new husband, a dashing world traveler named Aymard de Verteuil, has a nervous collapse when she finds out that he has been carrying on a secret romance with her kinswoman Marie-Alice. When Blanche learns of the affair, she bewails Aymard's infidelity in a series of diary entries and letters addressed to him on his travels in Africa and Asia. Here is a standard Blanche lament:

> Why did you let me believe you when you were bound to deceive me, I know that you are a liar but still I long to believe you. . . . I submit to your strange power to the point where I make myself blind of my own volition. In a rage I fling oil on the mirror so as not to see the truth reflected in its surface. Oh not to see it. Not to see.

To Élisabeth, the introduction of this subplot enabled her to give voice to her despair while also exploring conflicting facets of her own personality: the woman who breaks hearts (she now described Marie-Alice as "an executioner" whose "supreme allure vanquishes all who see her: men, animals, . . . even women") and the woman whose heart gets broken.

As for Aymard de Verteuil, his globe-trotting habits linked him rather point-

---

* "Mme de C." probably designates Mme de Chevigné, who was friendly with Giovanni Borghese via her cousin Charles Marochetti, the Italian ambassador to Russia and thus another satellite in the GDWs' orbit. "Mme H." would seem to be the "not born" *salonnière* Mme Hochon, who ran a hospital for underprivileged girls afflicted with tuberculosis.

edly to Giovanni. So did the name Élisabeth chose for him: Verteuil was a fortified château the La Rochefoucaulds had owned for eight hundred years; in the twelfth century one of its proprietors was called Aymar II de La Rochefoucauld. In more recent family history, the same Christian name had been borne by the Marquis de Dampierre, a noted legitimist statesman. The fictional Verteuil's first name, modernized as "Aymard," was thus a veiled allusion to Ernestine Picot de Dampierre, whose funeral had first brought Élisabeth and Giovanni together.

With these characters and these clues, Élisabeth's Marie-Alice manuscript itself became something like a mirror doused in oil, at once revealing and disguising the secrets of her broken heart. She drafted a new entry in Blanche's journal:

> Now I understand, oh how I understand, the legend of the bird that used to make me laugh—the bird that hides its head in the sand in order not to see that it is in peril, its body exposed. One wishes one could hide one's head and one's heart in a similar manner, deceiving oneself by siding with one's deceivers, in order not to see, not to see.

For Élisabeth as for Blanche, the grave beckoned, kinder than love: "I have entered the austerity of death, from which those of us who suffer this much should never be released."

JUST OVER A YEAR LATER, on September 27, 1888, death came in earnest to the rue d'Astorg. It claimed Élisabeth's father-in-law, turning her and Henry into the Comtesse and Comte Greffulhe. The promotion in rank and fortune did not raise Élisabeth's spirits, which were still as low as they had been at La Rivière. She found herself too downcast even to appreciate the "*incredible sparkle*" (as she put it) that her all-black mourning clothes had brought out in her eyes. She noted this enhancement as a phenomenon exterior and irrelevant to herself, so that when Uncle Robert commented on it with an improvised line of verse—"Beautiful lily, with black pistils for eyes!"—Élisabeth turned to her sister, who had come to town for the funeral, and said matter-of-factly, "Quite right, don't you think so, Ghislaine?" In the hush of the hôtel Greffulhe, where the windows and mirrors were all hung with black, Guigui had laughed aloud at Bebeth's conceitedness.

What Guigui didn't understand—what nobody understood—was that Élisabeth had lost all pleasure in her own beauty. Try as she might, she simply could not connect her inner wretchedness with the outward appearance that fascinated everybody else—everybody, that is, except the one person she would have given anything to attract. "Why must *others* be the ones to marvel at my sparkling eyes?" she wondered. Since "that 'somebody' whom I do not wish to name" was unmoved by it, her dazzling gaze was of no use to her.

At least Henry hadn't yet gotten angry with her for her melancholy. As a rule, the slightest hint of sadness in Élisabeth enraged him, sparking fierce vituperations. ("One does not cry *like a servant!*") Insofar, though, as his father's death called for a formal display of grief, Henry was prepared to tolerate her despondency.

Élisabeth was thankful to have this camouflage for her desolate mood, all the more so as she couldn't discuss its real cause with anyone. As one of her newer admirers, the British ambassador Lord Lytton, perceptively wrote to her, "The worst sorrows are not always those for which we wear mourning, and receive condolences."

For the past several months, Lord Lytton had been trying to confide in Élisabeth about his own secret sorrows, hinting that she herself was their cause. All the same, he had described her state of mind exactly. She was suffering not because her father-in-law was dead—as fond as she had been of Charles, he had been old and sick, and she was reconciled to his loss—but because she herself was still alive. In an unsent letter addressed to a male correspondent identified only as "G.," she stated that her life had become "a chaos of untold, inexplicable pain," a "sea of knives" slicing her heart to ribbons. As ever, she longed for death as a deliverance: "From now on, my mind in its blackness will crave only the silence that extinguishes thought."

Suicide both tempted and scared her. Writing as Blanche, she mused,

> If I were given the chance to end it all, without a thought or a feeling for what *is*, wouldn't I raise my hand? What frightens me is everything that still attaches me to life; without that I would fling myself joyfully into the arms of anything that should say to me: "I am nothingness," "the mystery . . . death."

Writing as herself, Élisabeth drew up her will, bequeathing Moreau's *Salome in the Garden* to Uncle Robert, her private papers to Guigui, and the antique clock from her salon—the one once owned by Marie Antoinette—to Giovanni. To Henry, she left instructions for the clothes she wanted to wear in her coffin: a white dress and a white veil, "like a bride on her wedding day." In place of her wedding band, however, she wanted to wear two special rings, gifts from someone other than her husband. One was engraved with an arrow, the other with a swan. She did not say who had given them to her.

As her adviser on all things aesthetic, Uncle Robert was the only person she told about her burial ensemble. He responded by writing a poem for her, "The Dead Woman's Final Rest" ("Le Coucher de la morte"), in which a beautiful young woman decides that, her legions of would-be suitors notwithstanding, she will never find true love. Unable to bear the pain of living with this knowledge, she lies down to die in a picturesque tableau. For her deathbed, she chooses an ebony bier piled high with cushions, the latter stuffed not with down, but with letters from the innumerable men who desired her and whom she turned away. When Élisabeth read this poem, she broke down in tears; it was her uncle's best work yet. Like Lord Lytton's maxim, it captured her misery perfectly.

AT ODDS WITH HER AS USUAL, Henry had been uncommonly upbeat. Élisabeth found his jollity incongruous in a man still mourning his father, although she blamed herself for some part of his good mood. After all, it was she who had pushed Henry to involve himself more actively in the Orléanist cause, and with a Boulangist coup on the horizon, he had reason to feel optimistic about his political future. She could only hope that he would recommit to the monarchists once the coup came off, and that the Comte de Paris would reward him accordingly. In the meantime, she wished Henry would temper his buoyancy. It only made her feel sadder by comparison.

Henry's rosy political prospects weren't the only source of his good cheer. He had also been talking excitedly about how he would spend his inheritance, thanks to which he had become one of the richest men in France. He was planning major additions at Bois-Boudran, including a ballroom, several elegant new bedroom suites, and a private theater to rival the one at the château de Chimay. The pièce de résistance was to be a double-height formal banquet hall with a dining table for a hundred that would rise at the flick of a switch from a vast hidden crawlspace beneath the parquet floors.

In addition, Henry's architectural overhaul would equip Bois-Boudran with luxurious modern amenities such as telephones, electric light, and an underground train running between the dining room and the kitchen. (This last innovation, introduced by the Rothschilds at Ferrières, was designed to prevent dishes from growing cold in transit from the kitchen while keeping guests at a civilized remove from the sounds and smells of cooking.) While etiquette forbade him from socializing for six months after his father's death, it did not stop Henry from fantasizing about the parties he would throw once the mourning period was over—parties fit "to dazzle not only the gratin, but the whole of Europe's Gotha." He even, fleetingly uxorious, granted Élisabeth a place in his Xanadu. "Guests, theater, music," he rhapsodized to her by letter, "I can already see you flitting about like a fairy in the middle of it all."

Élisabeth blinked back her tears and kept her own counsel.

THERE HAD BEEN A TIME not too long ago when she would have welcomed her husband's vision of a more festive Bois-Boudran. Over the years, she had gradually established her own salon in the rue d'Astorg, a Sunday-evening postlude to her mother-in-law's weekly gathering of the clan. Élisabeth's at-homes had grown out of the little recitals she organized for friends and family, the success of which had emboldened her to attempt more ambitious programs. With Uncle Robert's help, she had scoured Paris for promising artists and intellectuals and offered them her patronage. Her protégés ranged from Gabriel Fauré, whom she had indeed welcomed to La Case in September of the previous year (with all her original invitees except Giovanni), to Louis Pasteur, a brilliant microbiologist whose new research institute she helped to fund. To repay her generosity, these men agreed to make special appearances from time to time in her salon, where they shared their new compositions and discoveries with her and her guests. The novelty, if not always the substance, of these programs delighted Élisabeth's friends, especially those who came to her house straight from her mother-in-law's mausoleum of a drawing room. Félicité, of course, was not amused.

Neither was Henry at first. He had been willing to fund Élisabeth's support for "men of genius" because it grew out of a long-standing, honorable tradition of aristocratic patronage. But he drew the line at fraternizing with such lowly characters. "Never must a lady expose her husband's house to pillage and shameless publicity [by] opening its doors to barbarians," he inveighed in one angry dispatch. In another, he explained that Bebeth's habit of inviting these men into her salon offended his sense of hierarchy:

> I am a logical man—I see that no good can come of opening one's doors to nobodies, strangers, and parasites, . . . all these vile, self-interested peons who only . . . accentuate how much better off one is with one's own kind and how justified I am in my savage misanthropy.

What saved Élisabeth in the end was the fact that so many of Henry's own closest friends—from Breteuil to du Lau to both Hottinguer brothers to de Mun—raved about her cultural programs, which were unlike anything the gratin's other hostesses provided in their salons. Like their admiration for her beauty, the praise Henry's peers voiced for her original, somewhat bohemian salon changed his opinion in her favor. He reserved the right to continue fulminating about any nobody, stranger, or parasite who happened to rub him the wrong way. (Henry bore a particular animus toward Jews, complaining of one of Élisabeth's parties: "You can smell the *yid* from miles away!") But he became more supportive of her artistic gatherings. Indeed, the private theater he intended to build at Bois-Boudran would allow her to replicate them on a grand scale in the country, as she herself, nostalgic for her and her cousins' productions in the private theater at Chimay, had often wished she could do.

As Élisabeth could have predicted, Henry's mother vehemently opposed his plan for a private theater, which according to her would subject the family to irreversible *déclassement*. Félicité warned him that if he and Élisabeth wound up "inviting half the city" to stay with them in the country, then she herself would "renounce Bois-Boudran forever." Once so complaisant about her son's profligate lifestyle, Félicité had finally started to see it as a problem. "Unquestionably," she sniped, "having too much money makes one stupid, until it makes one downright contemptible."

Little did Félicité know that her daughter-in-law had been voicing this very complaint about Henry—in private, in her diary—for ages, and that Élisabeth held her responsible for Henry's moral turpitude. In her journal, Élisabeth pictured her mother-in-law telling him, "Here is 50 million francs. Go help yourself to all the most beautiful mistresses in Paris!"

If Mimi were still alive, Élisabeth knew what she would advise: devote yourself to motherhood, to raising Élaine. But Mimi had died at age fifty on Christmas Day 1884, leaving Élisabeth too grief-stricken to care for herself, much less for Élaine, who had been only a toddler at the time. For more than a year afterward, Élisabeth had delegated Élaine's upbringing to Félicité. Aided by an English governess called Annie and an armada of nursemaids and domestics, the old woman had lost no time inculcating her granddaughter with respect for the Greffulhe family trinity: pedigree, hunting, and *bon ton*.

Between this stern conditioning and Élaine's homely appearance (she had inherited the broad, round face of the Greffulhes and the protuberant La Rochefoucauld nose), she now, at age six, struck Élisabeth as being "too much like *them*": the barn owls of the rue d'Astorg. Élisabeth couldn't help thinking that if only the child had looked more like her, she might have felt a greater maternal attachment.

As it was, a drawing Élaine did of herself, Élisabeth, and Henry during a vacation in Royat captured their family dynamic with poignant accuracy. The picture shows a baleful little girl slumped behind her mother, separated from her by the long train of her dress. With her gaze fixed straight ahead, Élisabeth looks as if she is about to exit the drawing on the left side of the page, leaving

Élisabeth and Henry's daughter, Élaine, drew this revealing picture of herself with them, reflecting the tension in their marriage.

Élisabeth poses for Nadar with Élaine, age four. Élisabeth considered her daughter disappointingly plain.

her daughter behind. Henry occupies the far right side of the page, at as great a remove from his wife as the horizontally positioned sheet of paper will allow. Staring out at the viewer, he too ignores his child. Although framed by her parents, Élaine stands alone.

Precocious beyond her years, the girl had clearly intuited that her looks came as a disappointment to her mother, whom she idolized and longed to resemble. "I never forget my origin," she told Élisabeth solemnly. "I don't want something [*sic*] that is supposed to be like you make you fall from heaven to earth!" Another time Élaine whooped for joy when noticing a heartening change in her features: "I don't look like Papa anymore! My eyes have turned almost black!" Unfortunately for both mother and daughter, the transformation of Élaine's eye color from La Rochefoucauld blue to Tallien brown did not alter Élisabeth's perception of her as a fundamentally alien being. Nor did Élaine's cheery reports, a few years later, that the iron corset Élisabeth compelled her to wear was really making her spine "*much* straighter." The contraption may have allayed somewhat Élisabeth's fears that her child would grow up to be deformed, but it gave her no confidence that Élaine would develop into a swanlike beauty like herself.

The one similarity to herself Élisabeth did recognize in her daughter was her artistic bent. Élaine loved to draw, read, and write and wanted to grow up to be a poet like her godfather, Uncle Robert. Her mother encouraged her to develop her literary skills by writing prose poems on a subject dear to both of their hearts: Élisabeth's beauty. Élaine obligingly called her first creative effort "All About Maman":

December 1887. Maman is lovely, she has lovely little ears that are short not long like a donkey's, let me tell you. She has pretty little eyes that are very big. She has a pretty tiny waist and teeth that are white as snow; she has a chin as pretty as two roses. When she comes down for dinner she is graceful and, wow! She gives a pretty little bow. Everyone stares at her beauty. She has diamonds in her hair: she has a pretty little waistcoat like a man's. If you see her, you will fall down for joy. I find her ravishing.

In Uncle Robert's estimation, "All About Maman" showed genuine promise, proving that some Montesquiou and Chimay blood ran in his goddaughter's veins, however little one might guess it to look at her. (He could not resist adding that in spite of her talent, Élaine would "undoubtedly grow up to be a strapping, sturdy huntress"—a chip off the old Blockhead. Her Greffulhe looks displeased him as well.)

While Montesquiou's verdict about Élaine's literary gifts mollified Élisabeth somewhat, it did not allay the darkness all around her. For her, only one source of light would do. "You who made the sun shine [*toi qui fis le soleil*]!" she wrote, sobbing.

It used to be that when Élisabeth's morale flagged, the admiration of a crowd could revive it. But how flat and stale such elixir tasted to her now. In "Call Without an Echo," she analyzed her disquiet:

A woman who is young and beautiful feels that Paris is her kingdom; she adorns herself, shows herself off, sacrifices herself to the monde by offering up her beauty at random, to anyone who happens to see her.
   Maybe I will hear a divine song!
   Anxiously she listens, and always she hears only the worn-out refrains that sicken her! They are empty clichés, the words people say to a pretty young woman, and she laments: *O! To be nothing more than a pretty young woman!*
   A futile result for the resounding lyre that calls out in a poignant voice to hearts that know how to love.

The point of departure for this essay was the myth of Narcissus, the youth who gave his name to the flower that became Élisabeth's floral nom de guerre in the

Gégé Primoli photographed Élisabeth in a Narcissus pose in
the garden at Bois-Boudran.

press, and who was too transfixed by his own reflection to heed Echo begging
in borrowed words for his love. Like this ill-fated pair, Élisabeth had come to
an impasse. From her fellow *mondains,* her beauty elicited only pointless, rote
compliments that condemned her to be "nothing more than a pretty young
woman," isolated in and by her surface allure.

The only deliverance Élisabeth could imagine from this fate (other than suicide) would take the form of divine song, addressed to her beautiful soul rather
than to her pretty face. Such a song would herald the arrival of her kindred
spirit—someone with the same rare inner gifts as she. It would dispel her loneliness and usher in the storybook ending she had dreamed she would have with
Giovanni: perfect bliss for two hearts that know how to love.

Yet Élisabeth did not see how she would ever find another kindred spirit,
not in her current milieu. The Faubourg was the kingdom of pretty faces. No
country for beautiful souls.

Like the death in her family, Élisabeth's disenchantment with the monde
served as a convenient pretext for her woe. She raised her frustration again and
again in her conversations with her closest friends, but they had trouble relating. As the King of Chic, Sagan loved the kingdom of pretty faces and could not

fathom why Élisabeth, the prettiest of them all, should find it wanting. Breteuil, too, was *mondain* to his fingertips, even though he often claimed he wished he could spend less time at parties and more time in museums. (Élisabeth knew this was a ruse: whenever Breteuil crowed to her about having toured some cultural attraction, like the Sacré-Cœur or the Louvre, he had really been trysting with his paramour, Laure de Chevigné.)

As for Uncle Robert, when Élisabeth complained to him about the intellectual and emotional limitations of their peers, he huffed that these were defects she should have recognized long ago. The "born," he reminded her, were ignorant, unfeeling, and baselessly arrogant. As such, they warranted only derision, "for nothing is as comical as the illusion that one is *great*, when in fact one is *small*, [or] that one can soar like an eagle, when at best one has the wings of a chicken."

Edmond de Polignac shrugged off her laments as well. As a composer and an "invert," he claimed to abhor the womanizing dimwits of the Jockey-Club, but still he lunched there every day—like Breteuil's, his reservations about the monde were an act, a perverse form of *mondain* "simplicity." Consistent with this stance, Edmond told Élisabeth that she had only herself to blame for her angst. "All the lunches, all the dinners, this never-ending social round, this constant public exhibition of your person, it all just wears me out," he grumbled. Edmond's implication was clear: if Élisabeth's social life wore him out, then it could only take an even greater toll on her.

Although she would have liked Uncle Robert and Edmond to be more supportive, Élisabeth disregarded their testy comments about her social life. She felt it was fairly obvious that in their possessiveness of her, the two men disapproved less of her *mondanité* in general than of her affection for one *mondain* in particular: Lord Lytton, who had arrived in town the previous December as Great Britain's new ambassador to France. Already well-known in Paris from an earlier stint as a diplomatic attaché, the fifty-seven-year-old Englishman had met with a hero's welcome from his old friends in the gratin. Urbane, distinguished, and perfectly bilingual, he was society's newest darling, and had quickly singled out Élisabeth as his favorite doyenne.

For her as for the rest of noble Paris, association with Lord Lytton carried prestige because of his semi-royal stature. He claimed a remote kinship with Owen Tudor, whose grandson Henry VI founded the Tudor dynasty and whose wife, Catherine de Valois, had been the daughter of France's own Charles VI. Lord Lytton himself, moreover, qualified as a crowned head because he had governed India as viceroy from 1876 to 1880. These credentials had made him a coveted addition to all the most select parties and salons, Élisabeth's included.

In his private conversations with Élisabeth, Lord Lytton professed astonishment at her compatriots' enthusiasm for his viceroyalty, which his subjects in India and his compatriots back home had almost universally deemed a failure.

The whole experience had begun under a black cloud as his accession as viceroy had coincided with the outbreak of a famine that claimed more than six million lives. Instead of providing relief to the poor, who were hardest hit by the famine, Lord Lytton had decided that letting them starve would act as a much-needed check on overpopulation. The public furor provoked by this policy had been aggravated by his profligate spending on other measures. As viceroy, Lord Lytton had plowed immeasurable sums into an inconclusive war with Afghanistan. He had also racked up a £500,000 deficit trying to expand opium production in India. (He himself partook liberally of the drug.) Most damningly of all, from his critics' perspective, he had thrown parties of unprecedented extravagance, such as a week-long banquet rumored to have been the most expensive dinner party in history. On this occasion, Lord Lytton and 68,000 dignitaries glutted themselves on rare delicacies and drank from "deep golden cauldrons seething with champagne," while 100,000 people starved to death in Mysore and Madras alone. These many sources of controversy had accounted for the assassination attempt he ducked in 1879, as well as for the derogatory nicknames with which Indians and Britons had tagged him: "India's Nero" and "the Great Ornamental."

In the monde, however, Lord Lytton's disastrous record in India paled in importance beside the fact that he had occupied its throne. Furthermore, noble Parisians regarded his fondness for pageantry as a virtue instead of a vice. Royal

Edward Robert Bulwer-Lytton, in his viceregal finery, was a fervent admirer of Élisabeth's, and former viceroy of India.

memorabilia buffs traded tobacco cards—cheaply produced celebrity portraits like those that came with Félix Potin's chocolates but enclosed in packs of cigarettes—that showed the earl looking dashing in a pith helmet. Society mavens swooned over photographs of him in his coronation regalia, complete with skintight white breeches that left little to the imagination.

The Faubourg further esteemed Lord Lytton because of his cordial relations with many European sovereigns (courtesy of his previous postings to the British embassies in Spain, Portugal, and Austria) and his signal friendship with his sovereign back home. Although known to be dour and unloving toward her own offspring, particularly Bertie, Queen Victoria treated Lord Lytton like a favorite son. She showered him with honors, elevating him from a baronet—his father's title—to an earl, naming his wife, née Edith Villiers, one of her ladies of the bedchamber, and appointing him to her own Privy Council. She had even insisted upon standing as godmother to one of his and Edith's children, named Victor in the queen's honor, and had authorized Lord Lytton to address her in the second rather than the third person—a privilege otherwise reserved exclusively for members of the royal family. Along with his flair for entertaining on a lavish scale, the special place Lord Lytton held in Queen Victoria's affections made invitations to his fêtes at the British Embassy among the most coveted in Paris.

The suave, ornamental earl was a particular favorite with the gratin's hostesses, whom he charmed with his colorful tales of India and his florid gallantry. The word among expatriate Parisians was that the British diplomatic corps had never produced a better dancer or a livelier party guest than Lord Lytton: two more reasons the ladies adored him.

To Élisabeth, he had been a most diverting companion, taking her on adventures in a city he seemed to know better than she. He brought her to watch a surgeon dissect a human cadaver; to hear clairvoyants communicate with the spirit world; to see Shakespeare's *The Tempest* performed by an all-puppet cast. He took her and Henri de Breteuil (an old friend of Lord Lytton's through the Prince of Wales) on a tour of the neurology clinic of Dr. Jean-Martin Charcot, the alienist who had once rented a wing of the hôtel de Chimay. Now based in the Salpêtrière Hospital, Charcot was an expert on hysteria, a variant of neurasthenia that was supposedly rampant among women. To show Élisabeth and her companions how he treated the disease, Charcot hypnotized a patient in front of them—a pretty but disheveled girl in a shapeless white nightgown—and then invited them to "suggest" a fantastical idea to her. After shooting a meaningful look at Élisabeth, Lord Lytton told the patient she was "present at a conflagration." These words sent the girl into a panic, choking, shrieking, and frantically trying to put out a fire visible only to her.

Élisabeth so enjoyed Lord Lytton's company that while she declined virtually all dinner-party invitations ("picturesque lateness" was much trickier to pull off when issues of seating and food service came into play), she dined regularly with him at the British Embassy. Because of his *mondain* cachet, Élisabeth's mystique benefited from the exception she made on his behalf—the line "she only dines out at the British Embassy" became as central to her image as "poor in income, but rich in highnesses" was to Laure de Chevigné's. But Élisabeth's dinners with Lord Lytton also held a secret sentimental appeal for her. Located in the rue du Faubourg Saint-Honoré, around the corner from the rue d'Astorg, the British Embassy occupied a beautiful eighteenth-century mansion called the hôtel Borghèse. It was named for its most famous former owner, Princess Pauline Borghese, Napoléon I's sister—and Giovanni Borghese's great-aunt by marriage. As dismayed as Élisabeth still was by Giovanni's trip to Sofia, some small, stubborn part of her persisted in hoping that sooner or later he would realize she was his one true love. Seeing his family crest dotted around the embassy struck her as a good omen. It reminded her to keep the faith.

Some of the dinners Élisabeth attended in the hôtel Borghèse were state occasions attended by hundreds or even thousands of guests. More often, however, they were cozy, informal suppers with just her host and Breteuil. To these more intimate gatherings, Lord Lytton invited neither Élisabeth's husband nor his own wife of twenty-five years. Henry tolerated the snub only because he was convinced that Bebeth's rapport with Lord Lytton would strengthen his own clout with the Prince of Wales. (He also trusted Breteuil as a chaperone.) As for Edith, Countess Lytton, she made a point of laughing off the slight. According to her confidants, she was privately vexed by her husband's fascination with Mme Greffulhe but "wisely pretend[ed] to treat it as a joke." A handsome, statuesque blonde who stood a full head taller than Lord Lytton, Edith found solace in her own busy *mondain* schedule and also in the Paris couture. While the costs of running the embassy weighed heavily on her and her husband's family, she was one of Worth's biggest clients. A Francophile like her spouse, Edith followed the "born" Parisienne's golden rule: always look perfect, no matter how shaky one's finances or one's marriage.

For all his success in the monde, Lord Lytton had shown Élisabeth considerably more empathy than her other society friends when she vented to him about their shallow, convention-bound milieu. In her able if stilted English, Élisabeth complained to him about "how usual" it was for their *mondain* brethren "to follow the beaten tracks that we call '*la Routine*,'" never thinking for themselves or yearning for something more. Lord Lytton heartily agreed, telling her in one of their exchanges on the subject,

> It is as if there were no place in social life for all that is elevated, genuine, and profound; by contrast the monde embraces all that is base, artificial, and trivial. Flirtation is allowed, but love, real love, is dismissed as troubling, improper, tiresome.

This comment reminded Élisabeth of Uncle Robert's distinction between barn owls and eagles. "All I know," she reflected, "is that I am no longer at home with anyone who is not ardent of spirit." In Lord Lytton, Élisabeth had found a fellow ardent spirit.

THE GRATIN BEING WHAT IT WAS, the earl did have his detractors, prickly, "bag of needles" types who impugned his "originality"—*mondain* jargon for "weirdness." These people tittered about how both Lord Lytton and his mother, the Irish beauty Rosina Wheeler Bulwer-Lytton, had spent time in mental hospitals, and about how his late father had been subject to "frequent fits of melancholy and dejection, . . . followed by impatient cravings for excitement." Lord Lytton was notorious for similarly volatile moods, which by his own admission oscillated between uncontrollable excitement and a state he described alternately as "the blue devils" and "an almost intolerable hysterical depression." Joseph Reinach, envious of Lord Lytton's growing favor with Geneviève Straus (whose salon the Englishman also frequented), disparaged him in the press as "three-quarters insane."

Insane or not, Lord Lytton's mental state could not have been helped by his heavy opium use, which had persisted since his years in the East. Nellie Melba, an Australian diva who occasionally appeared in the monde on the arm of a princely lover, liked to tell a funny story about the earl's "very frequent" consumption of the substance he tried to pass off as snuff:

[Lord Lytton] would take from his pocket a little gold snuff box with an enameled miniature on its lid, carefully dip his finger into it, lift his eyes up to the ceiling, and then, very slowly and very delicately, sniff it up his nose, with an air of infinite relish. But that was not all. When the snuff had procured for him its utmost sensation, he would flick his fingers and take from his breast pocket a large red handkerchief, which with infinite precision he would apply to his nose. Then he would say "Ahhh," clasp his hands behind his back, and walk with a happy smile toward the window. It made me feel that there must be something *very attractive* about his *particular brand* of snuff.

Auguste d'Arenberg, who met Lord Lytton often at Mme Straus's at-homes, reported that the "snuff" pretense fooled none of the regulars there—not Jean Lorrain, "who always smell[ed] of ether," not Guy de Maupassant, a great aficionado of psychotropic drugs, and not Geneviève herself, with her undisguised dependence on morphine. In this knowing crowd, Lord Lytton's blissed-out snorting confirmed him as a fellow user. Jacques Blanche, whom Élisabeth commended to the earl one summer while both men were vacationing in Normandy, described him as "a voluptuous pasha in his harem, an old libertine glutted with opium."

Mondain gossips spoke in captious tones as well of Lord Lytton's parents' scandalous marriage, which had ended amidst explosive allegations by his mother about his father's moral degeneracy. In a sensational roman à clef, Rosina Bulwer-Lytton had parodied her husband, the celebrity author Edward Bulwer-Lytton, as a decadent, ruthless egomaniac whose smile reveals "a mouthful of man-traps," and whose sinister mien, with its "hook nose, sensual mouth, [and] hard, seared, worldly lines [denoting] bad passions," could only appeal to "an artist gleaning illustrations for *Faust,* and wanting a model Mephistopheles."

According to Rosina, homosexuality had been the worst of her husband's "bad passions," and she publicly accused him of having had an affair with Jewish statesman Benjamin Disraeli. Both now deceased, the two men had lent apparent truth to these charges by aping the effeminate dress of their shared idol, the poet Lord Byron, an infamous debauchee and "pederast." Like their hero, Disraeli and Bulwer-Lytton had gone in for long, flowing hairdos, sparkly jewelry, and rainbow-colored costumes swagged with lace. When the lore about Bulwer-Lytton's "pederasty" surfaced in the monde, Robert de Montesquiou chimed in with damning evidence of his own. He reported that traveling as a youth on a yacht in the Mediterranean, he had fallen overboard and nearly drowned in an effort to dodge the predatory old Englishman's advances. In a letter to Élisabeth, he recalled the encounter with rather less certainty but just as much scorn.

To Uncle Robert's undisguised regret, this story did not bias Élisabeth against Lord Lytton, whom she had every reason to assume liked women. She did have to admit, though, that his fashion sense conveyed a different impression, giving his enemies yet another reason to talk behind his back. Eschewing (not unlike her uncle) the sober color palette and understated tailoring of his peers, the ambassador favored chocolate-brown velvet suits with tight pants and oversized lapels, accessorized with brightly patterned Liberty scarves, and wore rings set with multicolored gemstones on several fingers of each hand—including a large turquoise nearly identical to one Élisabeth had inherited from Mimi. He also went around in a thick cloud of cologne, and had a smooth, soft manner that some described as feminine. Along with his opium habit and his viceregal past, Lord Lytton's ambiguous masculinity had earned him another derogatory nickname among his compatriots back in London: "the Vice Empress."

Given Uncle Robert's strident praise for "the effeminate," Élisabeth would have expected him and the colorful earl to feel a certain mutual sympathy. But in fact the two men despised each other. Of all the writings she had submitted to her uncle for editing over the years, the one he liked best was a short essay about how "nothing vexes a beautiful woman more than seeing a photograph of another beautiful woman." Maybe he detested Lord Lytton for similar reasons;

they were too alike not to view each other as rivals. She had once made the mistake of telling Uncle Robert that her English friend had described him as "*très* ladylike," a characterization her uncle had taken (again despite his hymn to effeminacy) as nothing less than a declaration of war. Since then, Élisabeth had had to accept that the two Roberts in her life would never be friends.

She regretted that this was so, because the quality that appealed to her the most in Lord Lytton was the very one that bound her so closely to Uncle Robert: literary talent. Yet this commonality may also have fueled her uncle's competitive rancor, because Lord Lytton was the author of more than half a dozen books of poetry. Edward Bulwer-Lytton had been a hugely successful novelist and playwright, responsible for such enduring bromides as "The pen is mightier than the sword," "the great unwashed," and "It was a dark and stormy night," and Lord Lytton had grown up idolizing his father's genius as fervently as Élaine revered Élisabeth's beauty. From the age of fourteen, he had known that he, too, wanted to be a writer, only to be told by his father that the literary world was not big enough for "two famous Bulwer-Lyttons." As a compromise, Bulwer-Lytton the younger had agreed to enter the foreign service and pursue the belles lettres as a sideline rather than a profession. He had also promised to publish all his work using a nom de plume, "Owen Meredith," taking the first name from his alleged Tudor forebear, and proceeding to churn out reams of florid verse under that alias. Meredith's poetry had not always found favor with the critics, but Queen Victoria was said to prefer it to that of any other British poet, living or dead.

Over the summer, Lord Lytton had presented Élisabeth with a translation of his *Glenaveril* (1885), a six-canto epic newly published in French. While she had yet to cut the volume's pages—she preferred to read the English original—she loved talking with its author about his creative endeavors. At the moment, Lord Lytton was working on his magnum opus, *King Poppy* (1892), a satirical verse fantasia about the power of the imagination (and the pleasures of opium consumption). Perhaps as a tribute to his friend Laure de Chevigné, he identified the work's titular poppy as the lone blossom smuggled by Proserpina into the underworld.

Perhaps as a tribute to his friend Geneviève Straus, Lord Lytton was also taking notes for a long comedic poem about the Wandering Jew, the subject of an opera by Fromental Halévy. Lord Lytton did extensive research on this folkloric figure, condemned to wander the earth forever in penance for his coreligionists' betrayal of Christ. When the earl shared his findings with Élisabeth, she borrowed them for her own literary purposes, opening one of her prose pieces with this epigraph: " 'One must keep marching ahead,' said the Wandering Jew."

It gratified Lord Lytton to think that he was influencing such "an accomplished, pretty little lady of *la haute*," as he described her in a letter home, wryly using the lower-class term for the society to which they both ambivalently belonged. Élisabeth, for her part, refrained from telling him that her conception

of the Wandering Jew was nothing at all like his. Lord Lytton conceived of the
character as a mythic version of Disraeli, Britain's first Jewish prime minister,
undermined by political foes and reviled by "the great unwashed." Élisabeth had
a different perspective. In her art as in her life, she was trying to understand why
men stray, to other countries and other loves. To this point, she flagged a quotation from Alexandre Dumas *père:*

> Nothing overcomes us more quickly than wanderlust; once the fever to
> travel consumes us, it pushes us to move ahead, and to keep moving ahead
> forever: the Wandering Jew is just a symbol.

In Élisabeth's literary imagination, the Wandering Jew was Aymard de Verteuil,
roving the world entire yet unable to shake off the burden of his sin, which is his
betrayal not of Christ but of his adoring wife, Blanche. The millstone he carries
with him in punishment is his consciousness of Blanche's love for him, which
even his treachery cannot destroy:

> Alas irony irony [*sic*], the more he distances himself, the heavier the chain
> grows, the links uncoiling and stretching out and multiplying [until] he
> cries out in his harassment: *My God take this burden away from me!* But
> everywhere he goes, he drags the dead weight with him, reproaching him,
> proclaiming its humiliation, its captivity; it is a heart that is dead and that
> will never be given to another for as long as he is alive.

Although Élisabeth shared some of her other writings with Lord Lytton, she
kept this one to herself, knowing it would only give him an opening to talk
about his own, insuperable passion—for her. More and more frequently at their
embassy dinners of late, she had caught him fixing her with a leer that had gone
from smoldering to almost deranged, his bulging, bright green eyes aglow with
an unsettling new fire. Toward the end of the summer, he had shown up without warning on her doorstep in Dieppe. When Élisabeth asked him why he had
come without his wife and children, he had grabbed her hand, given her that
maniacal, bright green stare, and whispered hoarsely: *"I think you know why."*

If only she felt the same way in return. But with his foppish scarves, rings,
and fitted velvet pants, Lord Lytton was not Élisabeth's type of man. Besides,
at nearly twice her age, he was just too old to attract her. Even so, unlike his
contemporary the Prince de Sagan, Lord Lytton had not resigned himself to the
asexual role Élisabeth preferred for her adorers to play. She outlined this role in
an essay called "The True Friend":

> The true friend loves you with the unselfish affection of a mother. . . .
> Such an attachment is based on respect, on trust, on love—but love puri-

fied of all that is incompatible with respect. . . . The true friend wins your trust little by little, he only enters your life as much as you let him; he never tries to steal anything that isn't given to him. . . . True friends act as each other's guardian angels. . . . When they are together, they feel as if they are enveloped in white wings, rather than being in a forest full of roaring wolves.

Lord Lytton was not convinced by this argument, protesting to Élisabeth that there was nothing avuncular, and still less maternal, about his feelings for her. He further let her know that her "just friends" cajolery was not going to keep those feelings in check forever. Along with the unnerving, wolfish gleam in his eyes, she had recently noticed a palpable undercurrent of aggression in the way he spoke to her, as if he were already preparing himself to hate her for the rejection they both knew was imminent. If the earl were ever to try to kiss her, she imagined, he would probably bite her instead.

Odi et amo, wrote Catullus, one of the Latin poets she had studied as a girl: "I hate and I love." Over the years, other men purporting to love her had evinced the same duality, switching from adoration to outrage when she rebuffed them.

IN HER MORE PHILOSOPHICAL MOMENTS, she tried to look at these interactions as opportunities to gain insight into the male psyche. She pictured her character Marie-Alice de Monteillant, "a divinity for innumerable worshippers," engaged in a similar analysis:

> She was always hoping to learn what was meant by that word ["love"], examining the faces of her suitors before she showed them the door. They would go on and on about *happiness, heaven, dreams,* and while they talked their eyes would goggle ridiculously and their faces would turn crimson; and then, when she gave them to understand that "she didn't feel the same way," they would pass without transition to words like *hell, agony, torture,* at which point her study would come to an end.

But despite Élisabeth's extensive experience with outbursts of this kind, she couldn't face such a scene with Lord Lytton. She had no wish to be reminded that he could not live without her, whereas Giovanni so obviously could. The contrast between the two men's attitudes was dispiriting, if not downright insulting. "What an indignity," she recorded, "to be an object of rapturous veneration for one man, and an object of revulsion for another."

DURING THE SIX MONTHS OF MOURNING for Henry's father, the Greffulhes stayed in seclusion in the rue d'Astorg. (To Henry's great irritation, etiquette prevented him from hunting that season at Bois-Boudran.) The isolation suited Élisabeth's bleak frame of mind, but as winter turned to spring, she could tell that Henry was losing patience with her. He reminded her that more than a year earlier, he had paid Gustave Moreau a hefty commission to paint her portrait, and he chided her for failing to schedule the necessary sittings.

Élisabeth had deliberately avoided following up with Moreau; she didn't want him to paint her looking as morose as she continued to feel. But to placate her husband, she contacted the artist and set a date in April to pose for him in his studio. Having always enjoyed her trips to Moreau's atelier in the past, Élisabeth tried to tell herself that the visit would do her good. She always found him easy to talk to—maybe because he said so little himself.

Tucked behind the stone-and-brick façade of a small *hôtel* in the ninth arrondissement, Moreau's studio was reasonably close to the rue d'Astorg, only a few minutes away by carriage. But to Élisabeth, it felt like another world, equal parts magic lantern and curiosity cabinet. The walls were lined with wonders, conjured by the master's brush. Phantom gems glinted on talons, diadems, daggers; hair and haloes shone with the warmth of burnished gold. Uncanny beasts abounded: chimeras and hydras, sirens and simurghs, unicorns and sphinxes. A peacock pestered Juno. Leda loved a swan. Orpheus strummed a lyre, glanced behind him, doomed Eurydice; maenads tore him limb from limb. Dido and Sappho teetered on ledges; when they jumped, they would take their heartache with them. John the Baptist's head floated in midair while Salome vamped for King Herod. Unfurling her veils one by one, she unwrapped herself like a present.

This last painting, *The Apparition* (1876), differed dramatically from the watercolor of Salome that Mimi had bought for Élisabeth after Henry's blowup at the 1878 World's Fair. In Élisabeth's version, *Salome in the Garden,* Herod's stepdaughter did not perform her notorious striptease. Instead, she stood motionless, clad in a billowing cloak of lapis-blue velvet. Holding her victim's head at arm's length, she contemplated it like a memento mori, a reminder that all things come to dust. Her face wore a pensive expression, and her blue robe hid every curve of the body that drove Herod to murder. In this portrayal, the Jewish temptress could almost have been a nun or a saint, Mary Magdalene renouncing the vanities of the world.

On the eve of her marriage, Élisabeth had been drawn to the grave, virginal heroine of *Salome in the Garden,* whereas what riveted her now, in *The Apparition,* was the young woman's brazen eroticism. Élisabeth had already read about the latter painting in Huysmans's novel *Against the Grain,* where it figured in the art collection of Des Esseintes, her uncle Robert's fictional double. For Des Esseintes, this Salome represented

the symbolic deity of inextinguishable Lust, the goddess of immortal Hysteria, of cursèd Beauty, . . . indifferent, irresponsible, unfeeling, like antiq-

While posing for her portrait at Moreau's atelier, Élisabeth admired his *Apparition.*

uity's Helen [of Troy], poisoning all who come near her, all who behold her, all those whom she touches.

Moreau himself had once characterized the Salome of *The Apparition* as "the Eternal Feminine, free as a bird, but deadly, but terrible, going through life with a flower in her hand, in search of her vague ideal, trampling everything beneath her feet." Élisabeth recognized herself in both of these archetypes. She had lost count of all the men who had described her in such terms.

At the start of the sitting, she and Moreau, a slight old man with an unkempt white beard, alert dark eyes, and a thatch of tousled silver hair, traded pleasantries. He asked after Uncle Robert, whom he said he admired, and listened with a polite but guarded air as Élisabeth talked about the full-length portrait she had recently engaged the American painter James A. M. Whistler to paint of him. She rhapsodized about the genius of her and her uncle's Grand Ami and confided that in order to give Whistler his due, she was working with some of her politician friends to secure him the Légion d'honneur. While the British ambassador, whom she had asked to advocate for Whistler with the French government, had not come through, Élisabeth was confident that she could succeed where a career diplomat had failed. She had already decided she would embroider Whistler's red rosette—the insignia of the award—with her own hands.

Moreau greeted this news impassively. As quiet and unassuming as Whistler was self-promoting and brash, he had no interest in the other painter's quest for fame and fortune—nor, Élisabeth suddenly worried, in her own self-important chatter. It was an awful habit of hers; her siblings always used to tease her for it: bragging about herself whenever she felt anxious, or angry, or sad. Nowadays, she felt all three of those emotions pretty much all the time.

Which may have been why she caught herself already at it again, boasting to Moreau about more of her impressive achievements. At the moment, the city of Paris was preparing for the opening in May of the 1889 World's Fair, a mammoth exhibition of art, technology, and culture expected to draw hundreds of thousands of visitors from all over the world. Because the Third Republic was holding it to celebrate the centennial of the Revolution, Élisabeth's peers in the Faubourg were for the most part planning to boycott the event; their standard line about the rabble-rousers of 1789 was, "They cut my grandmother's head off. I don't want to hear about it." However, she heard herself telling Moreau, the unprecedented publicity the fair would attract was an opportunity not to be wasted. She had decided to harness it for a good cause by organizing a special fund-raising performance of George Handel's *Messiah* (1742) at the Trocadéro, with all proceeds going to the Société Philanthropique.

Scheduled for June 10, this occasion would mark two firsts: the first time French audiences heard Handel's masterwork played in its entirety and the first time a Parisian charity gala featured a grand-scale orchestral production. Through the respective efforts of Philippe de Massa and Charles Ephrussi, sketch comedies and art openings had become mainstays of society benefits in Paris, but a major musical event would be something new. Over the objections of her mother-in-law, averse to novelty in all its forms, Élisabeth had sold the Société Philanthropique on the proposal. Her contacts in the media were already predicting a triumph.

Again, Moreau looked unimpressed, answering after a brief pause that he had decided not to show any of his paintings in this year's World's Fair. Having participated in the last one eleven years ago, he had no desire to repeat the experience; the media fanfare and intense public attention had come as unwelcome distractions from his work. "Violent impressions," he explained, "detract from the purity of the Dream." Whereupon, his store of small talk visibly depleted, he picked up his brush and palette and set to work.

Quiet filled the studio, interrupted only by an occasional lapidary comment coming from behind Moreau's easel. In these moments he appeared to have fallen into a trance. His gaze glassy, he talked to Élisabeth in koans, such as "Pain is necessary. It is a purification." And "One must withdraw from the world in order to see with new eyes."

Élisabeth transcribed his sayings afterward in her journal and pondered their relevance to herself. Her own suffering felt nothing like a purification. It felt like a curse. And her attempts to withdraw from the world had not given her a salutary new perspective on her pain. To the contrary, they had let her wallow in it, lose herself in it. Feel herself disappear.

Élisabeth knew that the men who thought her heartless might see her as a Salome figure, felling them with her "cursèd Beauty." Little did they know that she identified just as closely with Salome's victim, John the Baptist, consumed by "inextinguishable Lust." "Oh, I can feel stirring deep within me the seeds of eternal desire, bitter, frightful pangs," she wrote. "I feel like a ball of flame, rising and falling. . . . My pain assumes every possible guise to hunt me down."

It tracked her like a beast, at all times and in all places—even in Moreau's atelier, where when arriving for her sitting she noticed for the first time a small reproduction of Leonardo's painting of John the Baptist hanging in the vestibule: *Giovanni Battista,* the panther-clad androgyne. Once a treasured memory, Élisabeth's costume for the *bal des bêtes* now struck her as a cruel joke she had unwittingly played on herself, a mockery of the tender hopes that had inspired it.

Back home in the rue d'Astorg, she mulled desperate acts. "One roars, one's blood boils, one hates, and wants to die. One feels capable of crime, of madness, oh madness!" She felt reckless, destructive. Unable to answer for what she would do next.

While not particularly devout, she prayed for deliverance. "Give me strength, my God, to keep hiding my pain. I beseech Thee to remove me from this cruel, unhappy life if I no longer have the strength to resist." She watched for signs that the Lord had heard her cry. Taking a solitary ramble along the banks of the Seine, she noticed that Eiffel's tower had finally been completed, just in time for the World's Fair. In its spindly, metal silhouette she thought she discerned "two long lace arms, joined at the top like two hands praying to heaven."

On Sunday, April 21, Élisabeth went by herself to Easter services at the Église de la Madeleine, the Right Bank's answer to a classical temple. At the end of the Mass she remained kneeling on her prie-dieu, her head bowed, while the central doors of the church flew open behind her and sunshine flooded the nave. The rest of the congregation rose as one to the pealing of the carillons, hailing the resurrection of Christ and the rebirth of the world. Élisabeth did not share in the jubilation.

But in that instant, a tiny, private miracle occurred, reminding her that she was not, after all, irremediably alone. On April 22, she wrote, "When I was at the Madeleine yesterday I was crying, not praying, and I felt a pair of fretful eyes upon me, anxiously trying to guess at the meaning of my tears."

CHAPTER FOURTEEN

FODDER FOR SONNETS

P*aris. Winter 1887–1888.* Georges de Porto-Riche had a new muse. She was beautiful, married, rich, and "born"—in other words, totally out of his league. Still, he predicted that the Vicomtesse Greffulhe would be the great love of his life. "She makes a man dissatisfied with all the women he has had," he wrote. And Porto-Riche had had a lot of women.

He first laid eyes on her a few months earlier, a white sylph in a black dress, and the sight of her unspooled something knotted up deep within him, dissolving the writer's block that had stalled him for more than a decade. As a young man he had withstood intense pressure from his father, an affluent arms dealer from Bordeaux, to go into banking or law, becoming a writer instead. While still in his early twenties he had published several well-received poems and one-act plays; the positive reviews they garnered seemed to justify his choice of vocation. His literary future looked bright; Porto-Riche was proud to have stood up to his father and met life on his own terms. Then everything fell apart.

At twenty-six, his confidence in his gifts at its peak, Porto-Riche had attempted his most ambitious work to date, *Drama Under Philip II (Drame sous Philippe II,* 1875). Departing from the romantic and lyrical themes of his earlier work, this play centered on an obscure historical event: a sixteenth-century uprising in the Belgian duchy of Brabant. With the help of his cousin Geneviève (still Bébé back then), Porto-Riche had even prevailed upon Jules Massenet to compose an original score. But the play had been a flop, dismissed by the critics as the vanity project of a spoiled dilettante. His biggest fault in their eyes had apparently been that he came from money—a fact unfortunately highlighted by the word "*riche*" in his surname, and although he tried to make it known that he had forfeited his inheritance to pursue his art, the naysayers gave him no credit for the sacrifice. One reviewer had even accused him not only of paying the theater to stage his work "but offer[ing] money to certain critics in exchange for their praise."

The savage response to *Philip II* rattled Porto-Riche so thoroughly that after the play closed, he had resolved never to write again. And with a few piddling exceptions, he had stayed true to his vow. Until he saw Mme Greffulhe. Before that, his only serious temptation to break it had come in the summer of 1886, when rereading Petrarch had reminded him of just how forceful and exalted literary expression could be. But at the time, Porto-Riche had lacked a muse. Now he had found her, and without knowing it, she had rekindled his creative spark.

Georges de Porto-Riche fell in love with Élisabeth from afar, writing her a series of poems later published as *Happiness Manqué.*

As he explained to a theater impresario who had recently expressed interest in working with him, "After my initial successes I was childish enough to give up on my career, and spent ten years basically doing nothing. But now, I am filled once more with a burning need to write." At thirty-seven Porto-Riche felt young again, inspired, capable of great things: poems he would strew at her feet like flowers. Plays that would make her proud to know him.

Except she had no idea he existed—a situation Porto-Riche was doing his best to change. As luck would have it, Mme Greffulhe lived around the corner from the apartment he shared with his wife, Lizote, their seven-year-old son, Marcel, and their fittingly named dog, Misère (Penury), across from the Élysée Palace in the rue du Faubourg-Saint-Honoré. Benefiting from the proximity, he spent the fall and winter learning as much as he could about the beautiful vicomtesse. Stationed outside her walled fortress in the rue d'Astorg, he tracked her comings and goings. He followed her all over the neighborhood, trailing her sleek horse-drawn coupé on foot for as long as possible until it left him in the dust. He strolled behind her when she went out walking with her daughter and her dogs. Mme Greffulhe had a small spaniel and a large greyhound, and on his walks with Misère, Porto-Riche took to carrying bread crusts in his pockets, like an urchin in a fairy tale, lest he get close enough to his beloved to offer her pets a treat. (The towering liveried footman who accompanied her everywhere had yet to give him an opening, but Porto-Riche lived in hope.)

He staked out her favorite nearby bookstore, the Librairie Achille, and her favorite local art gallery, the Galerie Georges-Petit. He watched for her among the lovelies showing off their new dresses in the Bichonne. He scoured the announcements in the *presse mondaine* to find out which concerts, plays, and operas she planned to attend and bought a ticket to every one. Training his opera glass on her from his nosebleed seat in Paradise, he could examine the vicomtesse at length. Or at least for as long as she chose to stay at a given performance, which typically wasn't very long at all.

He peppered one of his few society friends, Laure de Chevigné, with questions about Mme Greffulhe's private life. What books did she read? What friends did she see? When she left Paris *en villégiature*, where did she go? When she put on one of her opulent, old-fashioned gowns, whom was she looking to impress? Was it true that her husband was brutal to her, and unfaithful? Was she faithful to him? Might she welcome a chance to stray? Did her affection for her cousin Montesquiou extend to other men of letters?

As Laure had told Porto-Riche many times already, she herself had a soft spot for writers—as a descendant of Petrarch's Laura, how could she not? So she did what she could to satisfy his curiosity, albeit by pretending to know more than she did. Laure gushed about how fine Henry and "Bebeth" had looked on their wedding day, neglecting to mention that she herself had not been a guest at the ceremony. She described the incredible luxury of their compound in Paris, even though she had been inside it only once, for a recital the vicomtesse had organized there last spring. (While Henry Greffulhe still considered her a potentially bad influence on his wife, her ducal and grand-ducal friendships had raised Laure in his estimation somewhat.)

In her throaty voice, she conjured up a world where all the men were princes and all the houses castles. She talked about how she and the Greffulhes were among the "très *select*" coterie of loyalists invited to the château d'Eu, the d'Orléans family seat in Normandy—"everyone knows that [*ça*]"—to see off the Comte de Paris when he went into exile two summers ago. She said that the second most powerful man in Russia, Grand-Duc Wladimir, never turned down an invitation to hunt at the Greffulhes' property in the Seine-et-Marne, despite a protocol glitch that had surprised him on one recent shoot. In a *battue,* a card marked with a crowned head's full name and title identifies his assigned shooting position, or butt. (Nonroyal butts, by contrast, are merely numbered: according to Laure, everyone knew that, too.) When preparing this special marker for the grand-duc, a huntsman at Bois-Boudran had bungled the job, dropping "His Imperial Highness" and shortening the rest of the prince's name to "the Big Wlad."

Porto-Riche didn't chuckle along with Laure when she delivered this punchline: he didn't care about *battues,* butts, or the Big Wlad. He cared about Mme Greffulhe, perhaps to a degree that his trusted friend found tiresome. Still, Laure had been patient with him. Beneath all her tough talk, she had a soft heart. Porto's quandary touched her. She was trying to help.

He had yet to tell the other *mondaine* in his life, his cousin Geneviève, about his infatuation, though he suspected that she could glean some useful information from her friend Auguste d'Arenberg, Mme Greffulhe's brother-in-law, if she wanted to. The problem was, Geneviève most definitely wouldn't want to. Every now and again she confided in Porto-Riche about her flirtations, but it annoyed her when he tried to talk to her about his. The Mauve Muse abhorred a rival.

Porto-Riche had a better idea. When the vicomtesse was in Paris, she went to church most Sundays at the Madeleine, usually joined by her husband's two sisters (one big and loud, the other small and quiet) and her mother-in-law (bad wig, mean mouth). Because she always perched at the far end of the family pew, at a bit of a remove from the other women, Porto-Riche had calculated that he could leave a letter for her there without anyone else noticing. Like Petrarch, come to think of it, gazing at Laure de Sade during Good Friday services in Avignon, he would treat the church as a place of strictly amorous worship. Under Napoléon I—from whom "Bebeth," reportedly, descended—the Madeleine was known as the Temple of Glory: a monument to France's soldiers. When Porto-Riche was finished with it, it would be known as the Temple of Love.

Being Jewish, he didn't worry about sacrilege. "Your blond-bearded Jesus . . . died for the world," he wrote, already making his case to his muse, "but . . . I will die for you." You (*toi*): Élisabeth. Unable to talk to her in person, he would talk to her on paper, as intimately as if she were already his. Every Sunday from now on, she would find an unsigned love poem from him waiting on her prie-dieu at the Madeleine.

Porto-Riche intended to keep his identity a secret from her, at least at first.

Porto-Riche began his attempt to woo Élisabeth by leaving unsigned love poems on her prie-dieu at the Église de la Madeleine.

To disguise his identity from Élisabeth, Porto-Riche gave his billets-doux to his friend Paul Hervieu, *left,* who copied them out in his own hand.

He didn't want her to ask around about him before he had a chance to woo her with his poetry. He didn't want the first thing she heard about him to be, "People *used* to read him." Let her read his new work, the work she had inspired, before she drew any conclusions. If she liked what he had written, then she would consent to meet him. And once she met him, Porto-Riche felt confident that she would fall for him. Women always did.

In the meantime, to protect his anonymity, he charged his fellow author Paul Hervieu, thirty, with copying out the love poems on his behalf. As Hervieu's compact right-slanting penmanship bore no resemblance to Porto-Riche's vertical calligraphic whorls, it formed the perfect disguise. Hervieu's character, too, promised discretion; in Geneviève's gossipy salon, he stood out for his tight-lipped reserve. Granted, some of the *fidèles* considered him a snake in the grass. For instance, the young writer Léon Daudet, upon whose father Alphonse's novella Georges Bizet had based *The Girl from Arles,* thought of Hervieu as

> an uptight, ambitious sort who coldly calculates his every move. He is clever, underhanded, flattering, discreet, the ideal lackey.

Henri de Régnier took a similar view, opining, "Hervieu seems to base his politeness toward others on a careful calculation of their worth," and "I'm afraid even his much-vaunted probity is just an artifice of his ambition. . . . He's a cashier, a calculator; his entire life is a calculation." But among Geneviève's friends, at least, Daudet and Régnier were in the minority. Taking their cue from their hostess, who adored Hervieu, most of the faithful maintained that no one was more "elegantly discreet" than he; little Marcel Proust, laudatory to a fault, went so far as to describe him as the ideal model for "a statue of Friendship"—just to look at Hervieu was to know he would never betray a confidence. Porto-Riche was staking a lot on the supposition that Proust was right.

Where his ladylove was concerned, Porto-Riche's hope was that the mystery of his identity would intrigue her. The previous May, he had ogled her from afar at a Parisian revival of Richard Wagner's *Lohengrin* (1850), in which the titular hero pledges his troth to Elsa, Duchess of Brabant, on one condition: she must never know his name. Perhaps, given Élisabeth's reputation for *mélomanie,* it would titillate her to think of herself and him as characters in a Wagner opera.

(On this point he had made a lucky guess. Right around this time, Élisabeth had begun using "Elsa" as an alias in some of her diary entries, written in her special coded shorthand. She was keeping secrets as well, though they had nothing to do with Porto-Riche.)

Porto-Riche left her his first offering shortly before Christmas. Here is the poem in its entirety:

> *I have been writing verses ever since I first saw her,*
> *But she is true to her husband.*
> *When I am walking home, she passes by my street;*
> *She is ensconced in a coupé.*
> *Her face is not aglow from recent caresses;*
> *She wears dresses from yesteryear.*
> *All you queens, held prisoner by jealous kings,*
> *I think of you when I see her.*

If he stuck around in the church to see what happened when she found his message, he didn't write about it in his diary. She did, however, take the poem home with her, squirreling it away in her files under "Homages and Appreciations from People I Don't Know."

Porto-Riche decided to continue with the experiment. For the next six months, it consumed him. He wrote her a new poem every week or two, always untitled, always just a few lines long. He wrote about her eyes and how they haunted him. Her "black eyes"; "big Moorish eyes"; "soft, sweet eyes"; "eyes so full of impertinences"; "eyes too beautiful to do without"; "the Promised Land of [her] eyes."

He wrote about her marriage, which Laure had told him was troubled: "She rarely goes out; she is an honest wife. / They say she isn't happy. / They say she reads poetry / While she waits for her harsh master to come home."

He wrote about "all the efforts, all the stratagems" he had devised to pursue her: "I have stood watch outside your house since December"; "I look for you everywhere, / at the theater [and] in the Bois / . . . I scan the papers for your name"; "I have knelt in your frescoed church." Apropos of church, he hinted at his Jewishness ("I have desecrated the sacristy, not for Mass, but for you, my pretty Christian") and boasted that the Son of God had nothing on him: "I have more heart than Jesus does"; "more than your Christian fetish, / I will bring you eternal love." He described her clothes with, indeed, a fetishist's ardor, as stand-ins for the body he ached to hold. "In a crowd at the theater, I grazed your medieval bodice." "Kneeling behind you, I am touching the hem of your dress; / that outfit suits your body perfectly. / You absolutely dress as if I were your lover." In these verses as in all the ones he wrote for her, she was *toi,* the soul of his soul and the flesh of his flesh. His passion for her transcended all formality.

One day, Élisabeth left her fan behind in church. Porto-Riche absconded with it and scribbled his next poem on its silken folds: "Someday, when this fan flutters against her mouth, / men will see her blush, and they will wonder why. / It will be because she feels on her faithless lips / this invisible kiss from me."

Read in sequence, his poems trace a volatile emotional arc. In the initial ones, he grovels. "I am a commoner, in love with the queen, / but the queen does not love me back." "A poor devil is in your life . . . / If only you knew, beautiful stranger, how earnestly he loves you!" "My loyal heart belongs to you; / humiliate it if you must." The position of the supplicant did not come naturally to Porto-Riche, who had always thought of himself as a Lovelace, the cold-blooded roué of Samuel Richardson's *Clarissa* (1747). Porto-Riche was used to claiming women's hearts as his due and breaking them without a second thought.

In late January, the close encounter with Élisabeth's bodice gave him back a bit of his Lovelace swagger: "You *will* meet the lover who dogs your steps . . . / Do you have any idea what kisses await you?" But his optimism soon dwindled, eroded by the pain of unrequited love: "People are asking if I have fallen ill; / Heartache has given me white hairs and wrinkles, / I feel the weight of my thirty-seven years." In another note, he threatened to vanish from her life forever: "I thought that I could brighten my dark days / by writing you these sorrowful verses. / But I can bear it no longer. . . . / I have suffered too deeply / to keep singing of my anguish."

Leaving poems for her was growing old as well. Yearning to talk with her face-to-face, Porto-Riche pleaded with her by letter to let him call on her at home. But nothing swayed her. "I cannot take a step into the world where you live," he complained. He knew that she invited other artists to her salon. Why not him?

February brought another blow. Following Élisabeth and a group of her friends into the Librairie Achille, Porto-Riche ducked behind a bookshelf to eavesdrop. What he overheard erased his confidence. Marked *"February 188_. Librairie Achille,"* his terse account of the incident reads: "I heard everything. Your friends described me to you / as a poet without glory and a man without breeding. / It's true, I am nothing; but despite my humble birth, / I have felt, I have suffered like the greatest of men."

Once again he hinted at his Judaism, echoing Shylock's plaint from *The Merchant of Venice* (presently in rehearsals at the Odéon—he and Élisabeth would both attend opening night, each of them alone): "I am a Jew. . . . Hath not a Jew . . . eyes [and] passions? . . . If you prick us, do we not bleed? If you tickle us, do we not laugh? . . . And if you wrong us, shall we not revenge?"

We should indeed, Porto-Riche decided. For the first time, a trace of vengefulness stole into his verse. Bitterly he imagined his future literary greatness trouncing the snobs for all eternity:

> *Who will remember your friends tomorrow?*
> *In death, they will be unknown skulls, vulgar ashes,*
> *Whereas I, who may not count for much today,*
> *Will count for a lot to posterity.*
> *Once the days of shame and rancor are behind me,*
> *My name just might live on in the annals of Love.*

This outburst was cathartic, but the relief was short-lived. After revealing himself to Élisabeth as the "poet without glory" her companions had vilified in the bookshop, Porto-Riche could no longer reassure himself that her unresponsiveness to his suit was nothing personal. She now knew exactly who he was, yet still she ignored him.

Worried that Hervieu had double-crossed him somehow, Porto-Riche stopped using him as an intermediary. He now wrote his poems to her in his own hand and mailed them to her at home in Paris. Throughout the spring, he begged her repeatedly for a tête-à-tête. He informed her that he had better social credentials than she may have thought: "I have friends who are invited to your house . . . / Please, open your doors to me, too . . . / Though I come from Bohemia, / I know how to behave in a salon!" To affect *mondain* elegance, he grew his hair long like the Prince de Sagan and wore it in the same artfully untamed style, erupting from the crown of his head like a volcano. Porto-Riche's thick locks were still predominantly black; once they turned white, they would be all but indistinguishable from those of the King of Chic.

Élisabeth did not react to Porto-Riche's new hairstyle (if she even saw it—her opera glasses never seemed to swivel up toward Paradise on her evenings at the theater). Changing tacks, he invoked his sexual prowess: "I have dreamed of giving you the five best minutes of your life." Only five minutes? He adjusted his pitch:

> *Once I have held you in my arms for a long time,*
> *You will stop caring about my lowly birth.*

Porto-Riche adopted a bushy, mane-like hairstyle in emulation of the Prince de Sagan. This new look was captured here by the Franco-Italian poster designer Leonetto Cappiello.

You will count the minutes between raptures past and future,
I will wake your sleeping lips with untold kisses. . . .
My talent for loving makes other men jealous.

Again receiving no answer, he appealed to her love of the arts, well-known to the readers of the *presse mondaine:*

Ah! You are an artist as much as a grande dame . . . ,
With your inspiring eyes and your hidden penchants.
In the name of all the romances that have ever touched you,
In the name of all the geniuses who would have cherished you,
Be kind to the obscure wretch who asks only to admire you.

She was not kind. She relented not a bit, prompting him to revert to the fantasy in which he became famous and those who shunned him were sorry. "You will buy my novels and applaud my plays. . . . / One day, when I am a celebrity, / maybe then, you'll wish you knew me, / and you'll regret all this wasted time [*temps perdu*]."

But it was Porto-Riche who was wasting his time, "spending my days in rancor and shame." By June, he had reached his wits' end. Lashing out, he warned Élisabeth that once she lost her looks, she would regret having spurned him:

The future is just, and will see to my revenge.
In ten years, I will laugh at your derision . . . ,
And will be much happier than you. . . .
No one will follow you anymore; and I, a poet becalmed,

Will send you my stanzas no longer.
Then you will regret your past coldness:
You will be ugly and old and you will never have loved.

Predictions about her future ugliness were apparently not the way to his beauty's heart. So Porto-Riche played his trump card. In July, he embarked on an affair with a different woman and gloated about it to Élisabeth by poem: "My lover looks like you; / she is fragile like you. . . . / When our debauches are over, / we'll take a walk past your house." Then he stopped writing to her, for the time being. Let her wonder. Let her stew.

PARIS. WINTER 1888–1889. Porto-Riche hated himself for it, but he had had to declare defeat. For nearly six months, he had refrained from contacting Élisabeth—the Comtesse Greffulhe, since her father-in-law's death in September—yet he owed this feat more to her disappearance from the social scene than to his own restraint. (The newspapers had kept him abreast of her travels outside the city, as well as of her father-in-law's death and ensuing period of mourning.) As soon as he spotted her in town again in December, "dressed all in black as when [she] first enchained my heart," all his willpower left him. Nearly a year to the day after he left his first billet-doux for her in the Madeleine, he broke down and wrote her a new poem. From now on he would number his odes in the manner of Petrarch, Ronsard, and Shakespeare: "all the geniuses who would have cherished you." He resumed his courtship with these lines:

So here she is, she is back again, as haughty as she was last season. . . .
For six long months, her little heart, so sure of its power, never
Thought to ask how I survived in her absence, it never asked
What I did, or even whether loving her was still my great affair. . . .
She rode past, her horses at a trot; her soul, a doll's soul,
Seemed preoccupied with other avowals, other kisses.
I should have liked to follow her, the cruel woman—
But her little heart asked nothing at all.

As before, Élisabeth ignored him, unmoved by his taunts about her "doll's soul," which he had hoped would goad her out of her silence. He rationalized that perhaps she was still smarting from the news of his infidelity. So he followed up with a poem notifying her that his competing fling was over: "Coldly I have dismissed / my interim lover. / She wept, not unattractively, / in her mediocre lace dress." He was all Élisabeth's now, if she would have him.

Her unflagging silence forced him to think more seriously about what he had once called her "hidden penchants." What if Élisabeth's mind really was on other avowals, other kisses? A year ago, Porto-Riche had described her as "an honest wife," "true to her husband," but what if her virtue was just a front? What if she was willing to break her marriage vows—just not with him?

Looking for clues, Porto-Riche examined her through his opera glass at a concert in February. Her face was as white as stone against her black mourning dress, her gaze as lifeless as unlit coal. But then the music changed and so did she. When a surging harmony in the strings section "evoke[d] the *tristesse* of love," a dazzling flame leapt back into her eyes. The metamorphosis confirmed his deepest fear: "Someone will take her away from me."

Before long, his anxiety turned to anger. After all Porto-Riche had done to win her, it enraged him to think that she pined for another man—a man of high birth, no doubt. In his diary, he ranted, "So she cares only for princely lovers—I spit upon them all!" He let Élisabeth know he was onto her, writing of (and to) her caustically in the third person, "No doubt she would have agreed to a *titled* indiscretion." Porto-Riche was a commoner, in love with the queen, but the queen did not love him back. "After a year-long, epic struggle, I cannot so much as touch her hand."

He could do something else, though: ferret out her secret. He put her on notice: "I know her better than she knows herself, / for a year, I have followed her, / body and soul, step by step; / I see everything, I know everything. . . . / I will be the first one to guess whom she loves."

When he asked Laure de Chevigné whether Élisabeth might be having an affair, Laure laughed in his face. "You are mad, you are *mad,* you are *MAD!*" she exclaimed, her standard protest whenever her mind boggled. Then she told him why. First, Henry Greffulhe would never have stood for such a betrayal; supposedly he hit his wife for even trivial infractions, so adultery would have been out of the question. Besides, everyone knew that Élisabeth had no taste for "*that*"—as she was forever reminding everyone with her virgin-queen and virgin-goddess costumes. In addition, Henri de Breteuil had told Laure that on a recent visit to Dieppe, he had found Élisabeth "thin and nervous, feverish and unable to eat"—symptoms of an unspecified malady that had been afflicting her for at least a year. In Laure's expert opinion, this did not sound like a woman in love.

As a man whose friends had misconstrued his own infatuation as an illness, Porto-Riche begged to differ. "If Bebeth is unwell," he sighed, "then Bebeth is in love." Laure smirked at the pun, but Porto wasn't laughing.*

He forced himself to concentrate on work. In January, he published a one-act comedy called *Françoise's Luck* (*La Chance de Françoise,* 1889) in *La Revue illustrée,* the same literary review that had just begun to serialize his friend Maupas-

* Porto-Riche's lament, "*Si Bebeth a du mal, Bebeth est amoureuse,*" was a play on a well-known line from Jean Racine's tragedy *Bérénice* (1670): "*Si Titus est jaloux, Titus est amoureux*" (if Titus is jealous, then Titus is in love). After founding the so-called *théâtre d'amour,* Porto-Riche would become known as "the Jewish Racine."

sant's latest novel, *Strong as Death* (*Fort comme la mort*), also inspired by an unhappy love affair. In *Françoise's Luck,* the title character is abjectly devoted to her husband, Marcel, a self-styled Lovelace who tolerates her worship but regrets having married her. Over the course of the play, Françoise confronts mounting evidence of Marcel's connubial misgivings and his propensity to cheat. Yet she clings all the same to the baseless conviction that one day, her luck will change—"*la chance de Françoise!*"—and her husband will recognize that he loves her and her alone. This delusion accounts both for the play's bracing irony and for its unexpected pathos.

To Porto-Riche's astonishment, *Françoise's Luck* was a hit, acclaimed for its acerbic, unsentimental take on the relations between the sexes. The critics hailed him as a genius, the inventor of his very own, quintessentially modern dramatic genre: the theater of love (*le théâtre d'amour*). Practically overnight, he went from a washed-up dilettante to the toast of the Parisian stage.

To people who knew him well, Porto-Riche's breakthrough play depicted a marriage suspiciously like his own. (As his friend Jules Lemaître raved in a front-page review, "Now *here* is a husband drawn from life! Drawn from life!") Originally his family and Lizote's—she was Porto-Riche's first cousin on his mother's side—had tried to stop them from marrying, and these obstacles had excited his passion. But he had lost interest in Lizote as soon as she became his wife, falling into one affair after another, and rationalizing that he was gathering material for his work: "It's not infidelity—it's research!" While Lizote, stuck at home with their son, was excruciatingly conscious of Porto-Riche's dalliances, she continued to adore him and to hold out faith in his eventual reform. When Françoise deprecated herself as "just a little idiot [*une petite bête*] who will always love only one man her whole life long," Laure de Chevigné might have discerned a jokey homage to herself, but Porto-Riche's other friends heard the voice of poor, mistreated Lizote.

Not being privy to his secret heartbreak, these friends couldn't have known that Porto-Riche had painted himself in Françoise. Beneath his caddish persona, he was a hopeless romantic like her, persisting in his adoration without the least bit of encouragement from his beloved, and even despite a probable betrayal. "It would be so much easier if I had the right to be sad," sighs Françoise when Marcel rebukes her for getting upset at his philandering. Porto-Riche had no right to be sad either. He had no claim on Élisabeth's heart.

WHAT HE HADN'T COUNTED ON was his newfound celebrity, which apparently changed everything in her eyes. Shortly after the opening of *Françoise's Luck,* Élisabeth broke her silence and issued the long-awaited invitation to Porto-Riche to visit her at home. Thunderstruck, he committed her instructions to verse:

I will leave my card at her house while her husband is out of town;
In keeping with the new policy, her door will then open to me.
Later on, if her husband asks, she will say to him with a smile
That the poet was introduced to her in her loge at the Opéra one night.
The friends we have in common, who have seen my suffering,
Will lend us their assistance.

For the first time in as long as he could remember, he exulted in *"la chance de Georges."*

SEELISBERG. JULY 1889. Porto-Riche was in the Swiss Alps on vacation with his wife and son. To (and of) Élisabeth, he wrote, "I have escaped her disquieting eyes. . . . / I am not as good as she thinks / and did well to go away." He did well to go away because in the end, an affair with her would not have made him happy. Upon reflection, all the pleasure Porto-Riche took in their relationship had lain in the fantasy, in the chase: "I was craving and pursuing / the truest desire, the purest dream; / I found the stranger beautiful / for the *future* bliss she promised." It was her unattainability that had stoked his desire. Once it looked as if he might actually have her, he had stopped wanting her, as simple as that.

Maybe not quite as simple as that.

Admittedly, Porto-Riche's ardor hadn't cooled overnight. For the first month and a half after Élisabeth broke her silence, he had wanted her more than ever, piqued by her unexpected talent for seduction. After telling him to leave his card with the concierge in the rue d'Astorg, she had cleverly omitted to propose a date for their tête-à-tête. Instead, she had presented him with a series of more challenging directives: look for a letter tucked in the petals of a carnation that I will drop from my corsage at the horse races; leave your answer inside a volume of Heinrich Heine's poetry at the Librairie Achille; slip me a note at intermission in the lobby of the Opéra-Comique. Though a touch sophomoric, these ploys heightened Porto-Riche's anticipation, fostering the illusion that he and Élisabeth had stepped into the pages of a Tolstoy novel or a Shakespeare tragedy, where passion was dangerous but irresistible, worth the deadliest of risks. So long as she adhered to this strategy, Élisabeth owned him.

In April, however, she had begun to sound overeager, almost desperate, pressing Porto-Riche for an assignation, *soon*. He tried to warn her that she was ruining the fun:

Ah! Don't be so quick to cherish me! Be scornful, be mercurial;
You don't know, dear indulgent one, how much more suffering I can take. . . .
Let's wait for my feelings to grow even stronger from your resistance; . . .

And tell your too-audacious dress not to show so much cleavage.
You will yield to me in August—by that time, I will have earned you.

Yet rather than take the hint, Élisabeth had kept pushing for a rendezvous, insistently enough to arouse his suspicions. Why had she changed her mind about him, anyway? To a woman like her, was the success of a one-act play really an incentive to romance? And even if it was, why was she so eager to end the merry chase that she had led him on, and that he was so obviously enjoying?

Pondering these questions, Porto-Riche had wondered again whether she might have another love interest. If she did, then her sudden keenness to meet him could well be an act, intended to pique his rival's jealousy.

Porto-Riche had again looked for answers by studying Élisabeth from afar. On Easter Sunday, he followed her to church at the Madeleine and spied on her during the Mass. Although a mauve veil hid her features, her hand kept darting beneath it, clutching a soggy handkerchief. This told Porto-Riche all he needed to know. He himself had given her no reason to weep (as yet); ergo she was crying for someone else. One of those "princely lovers," he mused bitterly. "Mine is a heart without importance."

Shylock would have his vengeance yet: Porto-Riche knew just how he would make her pay. He would agree to an assignation and would try to bed her when they met. Whether she yielded to him or not, he would tell the world afterward that she had. "I would ruin her reputation / to compensate for my defeat. / With my rancorous claims, / I would blacken her precious honor, / and not a soul would doubt me, / as I've succeeded so many times before." If Élisabeth was going to scorn him as a vulgarian, then he might as well act like one.

But when it came right down to it, Porto-Riche couldn't bring himself to sink that low. After fixing a date for their tryst, he canceled on her with this callous send-off:

I don't know why I am recoiling at the love she is offering me;
Maybe I am still calculating the time wasted [temps perdu], *and the pain endured.*
The thrill of hoping and pleading has vanished from my breast;
I am rediscovering the vile Lovelace I used to be; . . .
I will betray her, that's for certain; and once my pleasure has died,
I will have the unexpected joy of feeling no remorse.

Porto-Riche delivered the coup de grâce, too, with a stroke of the pen. In *La Revue illustrée,* he published the complete series of poems he had written for her, under the title *Happiness Manqué: The Diary of a Man in Love* (*Bonheur manqué: carnet d'un amoureux,* 1889). By going public with his verse, he wanted to make Élisabeth think that all along, he had been using her and not the other way around, that artistic ambition, not love, had driven his pursuit. He coined a little axiom about why women like her should not underestimate men like him: "Even in bed, writers are thinking / not about their mistresses, but about fame. / You are nothing more, beloved beauties, / than fodder for sonnets and flesh for novels." To leave her feeling exploited and exposed—that was revenge of a kind. That was justice.

Yet Porto-Riche softened this blow as well, by declining to name her as the woman to whom *Happiness Manqué* was addressed. Given her legendary aloofness and stature, the revelation about their secret literary entanglement would have brought Porto-Riche more publicity than a lifetime's worth of successful plays. Nonetheless, before submitting his poems to *La Revue illustrée,* he had changed the woman in them from a brunette to a blonde and scrambled all the places and dates that could have connected her to Élisabeth.

The only remaining clue to her identity lay in the epigraph he chose for the cycle. In one of the last letters he received from her, she had told Porto-Riche about her fascination for the intense bond between Alfred de Musset and George Sand. At the time, Porto-Riche had taken the reference as an encouraging sign. As paradigms for his and Élisabeth's romance, the model of Musset and Sand was just as appealing as the one he had originally had in mind: Lohengrin and Elsa de Brabant. So in a last, sentimental gesture, he prefaced *Happiness Manqué* with a quotation from Musset that sounded like it could have come from *Lohengrin.* It was a vow to protect a sacred passion by keeping a lover's name forever secret: "If you think I shall tell you / whom I dare to love / I wouldn't name her to you / if you offered me a kingdom." Only Élisabeth would know that these lines were meant for her—the reverent farewell of a vassal to his queen.

Then, his opus completed, he had packed up Lizote, Marcel, and Misère and headed off to Switzerland for the summer. Porto-Riche had claimed that he wanted to get out of Paris during the mayhem of the World's Fair, but he was fibbing. Only to Élisabeth did he admit the truth: "I am going to a land far away from France, a land where the birds don't all sing with your voice."

DIEPPE. AUGUST 1889. In the end, Porto-Riche was unable to stay away. Ditching Lizote and Marcel in Switzerland, he rushed back to Paris on his own, and from there on to Dieppe, where Élisabeth was spending her summer *villégiature.* He ignored a series of nosy letters from Geneviève, who knew him well enough to sense that he was up to no good. Sounding like Laure de Chevigné, she demanded to know whether Porto-Riche was mad.

He was not. His senseless infatuation had brought him to Normandy, but his art had kept him there. This is how it happened: No sooner had he reached Seelisberg than a letter from Élisabeth had reached him there, forwarded from Paris. In it she urged him to "brave the 'zone of terror' that you believe encircles"

In the summer of 1889, Porto-Riche cut short his family vacation in the Alps to answer a summons from Élisabeth, who invited him to call on her at the Villa La Case.

her place of residence, and to come and call on her at the beach. A few hectic days later he was in Dieppe, checked in to a hotel in the rue Aguado. From his room, which faced out over the boardwalk to the ocean, he could just make out the Greffulhes' estate on the horizon, a distinct if distant speck on the coastline west of town. Perched atop an isolated, windswept cliff, the house stood apart from and above the rest of the world. When Porto-Riche trekked up the promontory to visit her there, he was overcome by the old familiar feeling of his own inadequacy, encapsulated in a line from Victor Hugo he quoted in his diary: "I am an earthworm in love with a star."

Steeling himself for Élisabeth's disdain, Porto-Riche had been taken aback when he arrived at the house and she greeted him like an old friend, or at least like a human being. She had opened the door to him herself, although servants flitted busily in the background, one of them bringing orangeade in crystal glasses, another a tiny lace handkerchief—"for Madame la Comtesse"—on a gleaming silver tray. Apart from her staff, Élisabeth appeared to be alone in her high baronial keep, striking him for the first time as human herself, maybe even a little bit lonely.

Afterward, Porto-Riche recorded the details of their interview only as a series of fragmentary notations. But these notes indicate that Élisabeth had wanted to speak that day of her own feelings rather than of his:

So there she is, all geared up to tell me what it is like, what a joy it is, to be pretty, to be beautiful, and surrounded by admirers. She knows no sweeter feeling. She knows only the sweetness of men's homages.

Élisabeth had also made it clear that the homages she found the sweetest came from much loftier suitors than Porto-Riche, prompting him to rage anew against those "princely lovers" who outranked him in her esteem. He repeated in his journal: "I spit upon them all!"

The saving grace: Élisabeth's confession had given him an idea for a new project, his first-ever work of fiction. Porto-Riche jotted down the central concept:

"Novella"

A married lady, still elegant and beautiful to other men, is left alone, neglected, abandoned by her husband, whom she does not love.

She sets out to cheat on him with a very grand, very elusive [crossed out] baron. They will [illegible] about art. Their love affair will unfold in the letters they exchange.

In a separate scribbling, he wrote: "Gérard jealous?"

These lines, Porto-Riche told himself, pointed the way to his deliverance; they would help him redeem his folly. Yes, he had been a fool to interrupt his vacation and hurry all the way from the Swiss Alps to the English Channel only to have Élisabeth confirm, yet again, that he was not the one she loved. But this time, in return for his fealty, she had given him something infinitely more precious than her heart. Whether intentionally or not, she had given him her story.

CHAPTER FIFTEEN

BIRDS OF PARADISE

As a young man, Proust dreamed of a voyage of discovery to remote enchanted lands. Geographically, this terra incognita did not lie at all far from his own native habitat in the boulevard Malesherbes. In social terms, however, the distance he would have to cover to reach it appeared measureless and fraught with peril. As his friend Fernand Gregh recalled,

> Back in 1890 or so, Proust's birth barred him, or at least he believed that it barred him, from the Faubourg. . . . When he was first starting out in society, Proust saw the Faubourg as a forbidden realm; and that is why he dreamed of it with such passion, the way a child who collects postcards or stamps dreams of Tahiti or Ceylon. And like the early cartographers of Africa, Proust filled this terra incognita with roaring lions and birds of paradise. The lions, for him, were the men, all those noblemen with their celebrated names . . . ; the birds were the women.

Proust was never a sporting type. But beginning in the early 1890s, he turned himself into an explorer, forging fearlessly into the province of roaring lions and rare birds.

Unfortunately for Proust, his family background did not facilitate his entry into this world. As he would later tell Céleste Albaret,

> The people my parents knew were one thing. With my father in the position he was [in], theirs was the social circle of an eminent doctor and his eminent colleagues, along with some prominent patients. But I wanted to get to know society people, the cream of what was called "the Faubourg Saint-Germain." . . . Mother could not have introduced me to those people.

Mother could not have, but his friend Jacques Bizet's mother could, and did. When Proust first started going over to Jacques's apartment in the late 1880s, Geneviève Straus's social cachet was nearing its apogee. Along with her old friend Haas, whom Proust would encounter for the first time in her drawing room, Mme Straus stood as living proof that bourgeois Jewish origins did not preclude a brilliant career in the monde. So Proust quite naturally looked to her to facilitate his investigation of that world and duly established himself as an habitué of her salon.

At the time, Proust's school friends worried that his "deadly *mondain* obsession," as Robert Dreyfus called it, would stymie his artistic potential. Many of them would later acknowledge in their memoirs that they mistook his curiosity about society for social climbing, plain and simple. "In those days," Dreyfus remembered, "Proust seemed much more determined to get invited to certain aristocratic houses than to devote himself to literature, and this preference made no sense to us." Fernand Gregh cautioned that by spending so much time in the monde, Proust risked becoming an "incomparable dilettante." Jacques Blanche piled on, urging his friend not to turn into "one of those frightful intellectual 'apprentices' to the gratin."

But Proust evidently knew what he was doing. From the first, he divined the richness of the terrain into which Mme Straus could and did lead him. The alien creatures and customs of her élite milieu would provide him with a lifetime's supply of literary material, assuming its final contours in the fictional "Guermantes way."

Of necessity, spending time with Mme Straus and her friends was not all Proust did as a young man. Following his graduation from Condorcet in the summer of 1889, a host of other duties, rites of passage, and distractions made competing claims on his time. In November 1889, when he was eighteen, he reported to an infantry regiment stationed in Orléans, a city on the Loire seventy miles southwest of Paris, for a year of military service. To his great surprise, he enjoyed his experience in the army, his ineptitude as a soldier notwithstanding. (Of the sixty-four recruits in his battalion, Proust was ranked sixty-third; when he offered to extend his tour of duty by another year, his superiors turned him down flatly.) Recognizing Proust's physical limitations—his obstreperous asthma cough was impossible to ignore—his commanding officers treated him with leniency. He sat out the most punishing training exercises, spent his Sundays back home in Paris, and hired an orderly to look after his uniform and equipment. He also ditched the barracks for a comfortable apartment in Orléans; his fellow recruits suspected that in his cushy special quarters, Proust took his breakfast in bed.

Despite the laxity of his training, Proust did learn how to fire a gun and handle a sword, necessary skills not only in the military, but in the monde, where the aristocratic custom of dueling remained the preferred method for settling disputes of honor. (In February 1897, Proust himself would fight a duel, meeting the challenge with an unruffled courage that impressed his friends.) He gave up his attempt to master a third, equally essential gentleman's sport—riding—after a traumatic fall from his horse.

The army brought Proust into contact with his first acquaintances from the Jockey-Club: two of his commanding officers, Charles, Comte Walewski and

Armand-Pierre, Comte de Cholet, were members. Scholars have established that the two counts later furnished the rough outlines of two highborn military characters in both the *Search* and *Jean Santeuil.* But in addition, Walewski and Cholet represented Proust's earliest documented connections to two of his models for Mme de Guermantes. Charles Walewski was the son of a love child borne by a Polish noblewoman to Napoléon I, Élisabeth Greffulhe's supposed ancestor; Walewski impressed Proust with his kindness, once complimenting him on his elegant pink writing paper. As for the Comte de Cholet, he was "a little bit cousins" with Laure de Chevigné. (One of her aunts on the de Sade side, the mother of her cousin Laure de Raincourt, had been born a Cholet.) Like Walewski, Cholet was kind to Proust, even giving him a signed photograph of himself at the younger man's request. Cholet autographed the picture with a Sadean flourish: "To the provisional recruit Marcel Proust, from one of his torturers."

When his military service ended in November 1890, Proust moved back to his family's apartment in Paris. At his parents' behest, he enrolled in the Sorbonne and the École Libre des Sciences Politiques to read law and diplomacy, the two fields from which they hoped he would choose a respectable bourgeois profession. (His younger brother, Robert, was already planning to be a doctor like their father and would become a noted gynecologist.) But as Proust warned his father, he regarded his legal and diplomatic studies as so much *temps perdu* (wasted time); the only vocation that appealed to him was literature.

Neglecting his classes, Proust followed a busy educational program of his own devising. He went to the theater and the opera. He took in museum exhibitions and cabaret shows. He read voraciously and catholically, his choices ranging from old favorites (Racine, Saint-Simon, Vigny, Baudelaire) to contemporary writers (Guy de Maupassant, Paul Bourget, Paul Hervieu, Anatole France) to Anglophone masters (Emerson, Shakespeare, Shelley, George Eliot), whom he read in translation, while his mother read them in English. Upon graduating from Condorcet, he had won one last prize for French composition; the award, an edition of Jean de La Bruyère's *Characters* (1688), lapidary comments on life at the court of Louis XIV, became another of Proust's touchstone texts. The *Characters* would come in especially handy once he began his investigation of high society.

Proust's independent studies proved of negligible value when it came time for him to take his exams; he failed more than one. But within a few years he completed both of his university programs. Upon receiving his law degree in the fall of 1893, he accepted an internship at a law office as a sop to his parents, who continued to press him to embark upon a proper career. Proust toiled as an intern for two weeks and then proceeded to shirk formal employment for the rest of his adult life.

Proust's parents were disappointed with their elder son's apparent lack of direction, equating as they did success with gainful professional endeavor. However, as biographer William Carter points out, Jeanne and Adrien Proust did not realize that "what seemed like Marcel's wastefulness and insouciance constituted [the] highly particularized apprenticeship" of an author in search of his subject and his voice. At the same time, Proust's mother and father did not punish him by withholding their financial support. Their wealth would sustain him for the rest of his life, affording him the leisure to discover and practice his true vocation.

In his copious free time, Proust kept up with the little literary gang, which gained several new members in the early 1890s: Georges de Lauris, Louis de La Salle, Robert de Billy, and Jacques Baignères (the son of Mme Straus's friend Mme Henri Baignères). The group also welcomed Jacques Blanche—a slightly older Condorcet alumnus, and an old family friend of the Prousts as well as the Bizet/Halévys—who became the group's token painter. They were a focused, hard-driving lot, many of them already making names for themselves in their chosen fields: Daniel in philosophy, Gregh in poetry, Blanche in portraiture. Jacques Bizet had decided to study medicine, but he continued to identify nominally with the group's intellectual and artistic leanings.

Alternately humbled and inspired by his peers' ambitions, Proust fitfully honed his craft. While still in the army, he began publishing short works of fiction, poetry, and criticism in a variety of newspapers and magazines, including *The White Review* (*La Revue blanche*), an avant-garde periodical favored by Symbolist poets such as Paul Verlaine and Stéphane Mallarmé, the English teacher from Condorcet. In another publication, Proust wrote a glowing review of a book about Turkey by the Comte de Cholet; Cholet's signed photograph may have been a thank-you for this service.

In January 1892, Proust helped Daniel, Gregh, and the others cofound the last of their literary magazines, *The Banquet* (*Le Banquet*), which appeared on a more or less monthly basis until March 1893, when it merged with *The White Review*. *The Banquet* was a family affair, professionally printed by Jacques Bizet's half brother, Jean Reiter, on the presses of the newspaper where Reiter worked as a typesetter. The young men sold subscriptions of their journal to the devotees of Mme Straus's salon.

For aspiring young writers, the readership base Proust and his cohorts developed in this milieu was heady to say the least, from Mme Straus's resident Immortals (d'Haussonville, Vogüé, Dumas *fils*, Meilhac, and Halévy) to her influential critic friends (Jules Lemaître, the Ganderax brothers), to poets José-Maria de Heredia and Henri de Régnier and novelists Guy de Maupassant and Jean Lorrain. Even those authors in the group who had not been famous when Geneviève first befriended them were becoming so now. Paul Hervieu had had a big success with his first novel about the gratin, *Flirt* (1890), and an even bigger one with the sequel, *In Their Own Words* (*Peints par eux-mêmes*, 1893). Paul Bourget had also made a stir with his fiction about the monde; in 1893, the *New York Herald* named him "one of the literary lions of Paris." Porto-Riche was on a roll as well. Although *Happiness Manqué* (1889) had not drawn much acclaim, *Françoise's Luck* (1889) had sparked considerable excitement for his "theater of love," and Porto-Riche's follow-up effort in that genre, *The Unfaithful One* (*L'Infidèle*, 1891), with Réjane in the leading female role, had cemented his stardom. The ultimate proof of his success? Laure de Chevigné's exultant claims that the GDWs found him "charming."

With luminaries like these subscribing to *The Banquet,* Proust took advantage of the chance to make a good impression, offering his own sharp-eyed take on the phenomenon that drew them, too, to Mme Straus's salon: *mondanité.* Proust's first contribution to the magazine was a review of a short story by Louis Ganderax, "The Little Shoes: A Christmas Story" (1892), a saccharine tale about a Parisian nobleman who wants to leave his wife and child for a courtesan but decides against it in the end, swayed by the heartrending sight of his child's little shoes. The bathos of Ganderax's story has rightfully consigned it to oblivion, but in Proust's review, it becomes a springboard for two noteworthy ideas. First, Proust argues that because marital infidelity is rampant in the Faubourg, Ganderax must have written "The Little Shoes" to bring solace to a real-life society maven whose husband has been untrue. Here Proust articulates a supposition made about so many literary portrayals of the fin-de-siècle gratin, including his own future masterwork: that they are based on lived experience.

Proust would later deny this thesis in connection with the *Search;* he would also postulate more generally that a writer's life and his work unfold in two radically separate spheres. Throughout the 1890s, however, Proust repeatedly and explicitly spoke of his creative output as the product of a symbiosis between his imagination and the world around him, and by the latter term, more often than not, he meant the great world. Indeed, when Proust anthologized his writings from these years in *Pleasures and Days* (*Les Plaisirs et les jours,* 1896), Geneviève's friend Jean Lorrain published a review dismissing the book's contents as "little nothings about elegance." Without question, Lorrain meant the phrase pejoratively; his review was malicious and included a barb about Proust's sexuality that led to the aforementioned duel. Yet in terms of both their abbreviated format and their thematic focus, "little nothings about elegance" is as apt a characterization as any of Proust's publications from his twenties, beginning with the essay on "The Little Shoes." This piece set the tone for his subsequent contributions to *The Banquet,* almost all of which took the form of novelized reportage, or short fiction *à clef,* about contemporary Parisian society.

In his review of "The Little Shoes," Proust also returns to the insight he had had during his final year at Condorcet: that where reality disappoints, art consoles and redeems. At the end of the article, Proust speculates that the flesh-and-blood counterpart of the tale's unhappily married noblewoman "will probably wait in vain for the miracle M. Ganderax seemed to promise her by recounting it." Nevertheless, Proust continues,

It doesn't matter—she won't be too cruelly let down, for by transposing, as it were, her suffering, M. Ganderax has rid it of its selfish aspect and offered ingenious comfort. His lies are the only realities; even if we genuinely love them, the existence of the "real" things that surround us and have a hold on us starts, little by little, to fade. The power those things have to make us happy or unhappy diminishes, allowing them instead to take root in our souls, where we convert their color into beauty. That is what real happiness is; that is true freedom.

It is a testament to Proust's perceptiveness that a work as trite as "The Little Shoes" could have inspired such a thoughtful meditation on the transformative powers of literary art. But he was only just getting started. He was not yet ready to renounce those "things that had a hold" on him—things such as the monde's exotic fauna. Before he could renounce them, he had to meet them, take their measure. And to do that, he had first to make the journey to his friend's mother's salon.

GENEVIÈVE STRAUS ENTERTAINED her faithful on Sunday afternoons in her entresol apartment at 134, boulevard Haussmann, overlooking a recently erected statue of William Shakespeare. Her street bore the name of the city planner who during the Second Empire carved out the broad, leafy thoroughfares that made that swath of the eighth arrondissement, tucked between the Faubourg Saint-Honoré and the Monceau plain, a newly desirable home address. Daniel Halévy griped that in razing the cluttered buildings and twisting side streets of old Paris, Haussmann had reduced that whole swath of the Right Bank to "a land without a history, an insipid Australia." Even so, the convenience and modern comforts of the neighborhood attracted pampered, discerning residents. To Geneviève's gratification, several Rothschilds lived nearby.

To Proust's gratification, so did he, at approximately half a mile's distance from chez Straus. Like the "route of hope" he would soon be taking to Mme de Chevigné's building in the rue de Miromesnil, his Sunday walk from 9, boulevard Malesherbes to 134, boulevard Haussmann followed a short and not very scenic path. But it did feature two landmarks that primed his imagination, preparing him for the world he would discover at the entresol, and conditioning his portrayals of it in print.

The first of the two landmarks on Proust's Sunday pilgrimage stood at 46, boulevard Malesherbes, marking the approximate halfway point between his family's building and the Strauses'. This milestone, the Église de Saint-Augustin, was another product of the Haussmann era: one of the first churches in Paris to be built primarily out of iron. Even its 260-foot-high dome was sheathed in iron, and could be seen all the way from the Arc de Triomphe. Between the dome's disproportionate hugeness and the hodgepodge of Gothic, Byzantine,

The boulevard Malesherbes was one of the broad new thoroughfares Napoléon III's urban planner, Georges-Eugène Haussmann, created on the Right Bank between 1853 and 1870. Proust's family moved there in 1873.

and Romanesque styles that characterized the church as a whole, Saint-Augustin was often criticized as an eyesore. Proust, though, liked to think of it as a little piece of Rome in his own backyard. Its vaulting, metallic silhouette, topped with a belfry that took on the shifting colors of the fickle Parisian sky, looked to him like something out of Piranesi's sketches of the Eternal City.

This aura of ancient grandeur melded in Proust's daydreams with the glamour of Saint-Augustin's present-day congregation. Like the Madeleine, its pendant place of worship at the southern terminus of the boulevard Malesherbes, the church drew an illustrious Catholic flock. During the Second Empire, Napoléon III and his stylish consort, Empress Eugénie, had worshipped there, and the church's cachet had not lessened since the imperial couple's fall. Under the Third Republic, the *presse mondaine* reported that Saint-Augustin remained "the most elegant parish in Paris": a favorite perch for Proust's birds of paradise.

If he timed his trip to the entresol correctly, he could pause to admire these colorful specimens as they exited the church after Mass. Tilting their parasols and fluttering their fans, they twittered among themselves for a few bright moments as they waited for their carriages to pull up to the parvis. While they harbored in their midst at least one reformed courtesan, Émilie "the Seal" Williams, Proust only had eyes for the noblewomen, whose titles and surnames he could deduce from the colors of their footmen's livery and the coats of arms lacquered and gilded onto their carriage doors.

He loved to contemplate the dizzying heights at which these rare birds roosted. This mental exercise yielded, among other works, a paragraph-long essay called "To a [Female] Snob" ("À une snob," 1893). The piece opens with a mock-heroic

The Église de Saint-Augustin marked
the midpoint on the short walk from
Proust's apartment to the Strauses'.
He liked to linger on the parvis
to catch a glimpse of the elegant
parishioners after Sunday Mass.

description of the Faubourg's spiritual aeries: "family trees with roots plunging
deep into the most ancient French earth." It then suggests (and concludes) that
at the heart of this "dazzling, symbolic conception of the monde"—aristocratic
society as "a forest of family trees"—lies

> [a] dream [that] brings together the present and the past. The soul of
> the Crusades animates the banal faces of contemporary [nobles]. In each
> of their names, can you not feel the quickening, the almost melodious
> reawakening of sumptuous old France, like a dead woman rising up from
> beneath her blazoned tombstone?

The simile of a noblewoman rising from the dead recalls Laure de Chevigné's
Proserpina pose and conveys essentially the same message: "sumptuous old
France," with her ancient arms-bearing Crusader caste, is neither gone nor for-
gotten. Or in the words of the woman whom Proust was on his way to visit,
"The past is not dead."

Elsewhere in his writings from these years, Proust attributes the rebirth of
the past specifically to the resonant magic of noble names. Bourgeois names
lack this power, he theorizes, because of the "impenetrable night [that] covers
their origins in the distant past." By contrast, the names of France's great patrician families can be traced back for centuries, if not longer. Thus anchored in

"the distant past," they connect their modern-day bearers to figures of history and legend. "Through the naïve colors of the magic-lantern slides that such names offer us," he suggests in another essay, it is possible to "see [a] mighty lord with [a] blue beard or [a damsel imprisoned] in a tower . . . or men-at-arms riding along thirteenth-century roads." Such romantic associations spring not only from the landed gentry's surnames, made famous by heroes of the Crusades and courtiers of the king, but from its antiquated, often clan-specific Christian names, which its contemporary scions also carry into the present:

> Odon, Ghislain, Nivelon, . . . Tucdual, Adhéaume or Raynulphe: fine baptismal names coming from a past so profound that in their unwonted luster they seem to sparkle mysteriously, like those names of prophets and saints inscribed in the stained glass of our cathedrals.

Readers of the *Search* will recognize in this passage an early articulation of the "poetic pleasure" Marcel extracts from such grand seigneurial names as "Guermantes," investing them with the spectral luminosity of stained glass, magic lantern slides, and the ghost of Geneviève de Brabant.

The second of the two key attractions on Proust's walk to the Strauses' marked the endpoint of his journey: Sutton's, the tailor's shop that occupied the ground-floor retail space directly beneath the entresol. Commercial setups of this kind were not uncommon in the modernized sections of Paris; two tailors' boutiques, Eppler's and Sandt & Laborde, were housed in the ground floor of Proust's own building, which likewise dated to the Haussmann era. But these establishments did not beguile him like Sutton's did. Whereas Eppler's and Sandt & Laborde were all-purpose tailors, Sutton specialized in livery for noble households: another picturesque relic of "sumptuous old France" that took hold of the young Proust's imagination.

The livery made by Sutton fell into two categories: livery for the hunt and livery for domestic staff. Having never been invited on a shooting party, Proust was unfamiliar with the rituals and pageantry of the hunt and does not seem to have been interested in their sartorial dimensions. But he was fascinated by the eye-catching clothing he saw daily on the footmen who squired the ladies of the monde around Paris. The uniform of French livery (*livrée à la française*) these domestics wore harked back to the ancien régime, when the footmen in royal and aristocratic households wore powdered wigs, knee breeches (*culottes*), silk stockings, and formal jackets in the colors of the family they served, with buttons bearing the family's coat of arms. A hundred years after the Revolution, this archaic dress remained de rigueur for footmen in the Faubourg. When not acting as chaperones for the womenfolk, these footmen played a dual function at their masters' houses on the days or nights when guests came to call. Verbally, the footmen notified their masters of every guest's arrival. Visually,

This postcard shows the Strauses' building after the erection in 1888 of a bronze statue of Shakespeare. Their entresol apartment nestled below the *piano nobile* and above the storefront of Sutton the livery-maker.

they impressed upon each visitor the high standing of their employer—a duty Riquette d'Arenberg fancifully described as "intellectual labor." Whole battalions of such sentinels staffed Paris's greatest houses, posted at the entrance to all reception rooms and at the foot of all staircases.

With its expensive fabric and trimmings, its formal, restrictive cut, and its white silk stockings, easily stained and torn, the *livrée à la française* was clearly ill suited to menial chores—though the footmen's third function, serving at dinner parties, did impel them to lift the occasional plate or tray. Their evident exemption from more strenuous tasks highlighted their importance as status symbols. As Proust would have read in La Bruyère, "the liveried valets . . . of the great" existed above all to make one "feel inferior to . . . their masters; for one must always suffer from the great and from everything that belongs to them."

To Proust, whose family did not have heraldic colors in which to outfit their staff, the regalia the nobility prescribed to its valets quite obviously contradicted that caste's "simplicity"—its affectation of unaffectedness. He elaborated on this idea in an unpublished fragment of a manuscript that would eventually turn into *Swann's Way*. This fragment, which he cut from the final version of the novel, is a meditation on the pretenses of *mondanité*, as exemplified by two fictive ladies on a social call:

When the Princesse de Beauvais called at the house of her sister-in-law, the Vicomtesse de Hainaut, an invisible force in the antechamber kept a footman standing there motionless and expressionless, and although neither of the two sisters-in-law attached the slightest importance to rank, this force had dictated that the footman be liveried in the colors of the Hainaut family. . . . It was a law of the Monde that ran the vicomtesse's household, selected her dresses, [and] ordained her every gesture, entrance, and exit, [actions] she performed like the steps of a ballet. . . . The vicomtesse had no concern whatsoever for nobility or for luxury . . . , it was a law of the Monde that had outfitted her footmen in liveries in the Hainaut colors and kept them as immobile as statues.

These lines target the hypocrisy of those aristocrats who gainsay the "importance of rank" even as they actively strive to uphold it. If people like Proust's hypothetical Mmes de Beauvais and Hainaut were honest, they would admit that they chose to assert their standing by means of such showy markers as *livrée à la française*. Instead, they attribute their choices to a "law of the Monde" that absolves them of all agency, an "invisible force" as inexorable and impersonal as gravity.

Just as intriguing to Proust as this invisible force was its grubby underside, debt, for while the past had conditioned noble Parisians to regard a staff *en livrée* as an entitlement, the present had in many cases failed to provide them with the means to pay for it. "Half the Faubourg," Proust learned, owed Sutton amounts in the six figures. As a result, a fortuitous peek into the livery-maker's shop could reveal a grand seigneur or grande dame in improbably awkward straits: a vivid demonstration of history and modernity colliding.

The voyeuristic thrill this tableau afforded also made its way into Proust's writings, though he transferred it into scenes exposing perversion, rather than penury, as the *mondain*'s dirtiest secret. In his short novella *The Indifferent Man* (*L'Indifférent*, 1893, published in 1896), a clubman called Lepré, with "a delicate and noble Louis XIII face," unknowingly wins the heart of one Madeleine de Gouvres. Madeleine is a high-spirited, black-haired widow to whom many illustrious gentlemen pay court but who spurns them all. Lepré attracts Madeleine because he alone seems indifferent to her allure. Consistent with "the maxim of flirtation contained in the famous line *Si tu ne m'aimes pas, je t'aime*" (Proust couldn't resist this wink at the spirited, black-haired Widow Bizet), Madeleine becomes "consumed with a crazy need" to make Lepré fall in love with her. But her every attempt to charm him fails. She finally learns to her horror that Lepré prowls by night through the slums of Paris, trolling for "ignoble women one picks up out of the gutter." His princely mien masks a sordid vice: "He loves only women covered in mud, and he loves them to the point of madness."

Not only does this penchant disqualify Madeleine as a candidate for Lepré's affections; it disqualifies him, as his late father's only son, from perpetuating the family line. Unwilling to bed a woman of his own class, one of his friends explains to Madeleine, "Lepré is too honorable even to consider marriage. . . . And his sons won't be like him, because he won't have any." By condemning him to couplings that can never produce a legitimate heir, Lepré's erotic preference inverts in a striking way Proust's model of onomastic rebirth. Whereas a name like "Adhéaume" revives an ancient ancestral history, a perversion like Lepré's dooms a name and lineage to extinction.

A scene in *Sodom and Gomorrah* (*Sodome et Gomorrhe,* 1921–1922) presents a more direct transposition of the tawdry reveal in Sutton's shop. The narrator spies a cousin of the Duchesse de Guermantes, the imperious Baron de Charlus, entering the livery-maker's workshop in the ground-floor of the Guermantes' Right Bank abode. Sensing something off about Charlus's errand, Marcel sneaks into an empty boutique adjacent to the tailor's, where the sounds he makes out through the flimsy wall "revolutionize" his perspective "as instantly and thoroughly as if a magic wand" had given him second sight: "Until then, I hadn't understood, I hadn't seen." What Marcel sees, or more accurately hears, is a noisy sexual encounter between the tailor and Charlus, a widower and reputed ladies' man. Afterward, peering out into the courtyard from his hiding place, Marcel watches the baron offer to pay his partner for the tryst. In Charlus's case as in Lepré's, the taint of sexual deviancy replaces the shame of financial distress—and appears to betoken, as mere poverty could not, the end of a noble family line.

In addition, these scenarios enable Proust to explore a complicated interplay between surface and depth, semblance and truth. Like the name that "brings together the present and the past," the nobleman with the secret sin straddles two putatively antithetical worlds: elegance and abjection. His high birth and lordly privilege coexist, however tenuously, with the very debasement they are supposed to exclude.

Glimpsed on Proust's Sunday travels to 134, boulevard Haussmann, the juxtaposition of surface elegance and hidden corruption would become a defining feature of his portrayal of the monde. He would get a much closer look at these seeming opposites, and a much deeper sense of them, when he reached his destination. Bearing right at the statue of Shakespeare (a monument which, despite his admiration for the Bard, left no trace in Proust's writings) and arriving at the Strauses' address, he would push open the building's heavy wooden front door, just to the right of Sutton's storefront. Once in the lobby, he would climb a single short flight of steps, his gloved hand skimming the sinuous iron curve of the art nouveau banister. If his asthma was acting up, he would skip the stairs and ride up in a funny little elevator made to resemble a Louis XV bergère. As his friend Georges de Lauris would later note, Proust's sense of excitement reached its peak during this last and shortest leg of his journey, and for good reason. For when he crossed the threshold into Mme Straus's salon, his real voyage of discovery would begin.

CHAPTER SIXTEEN

THE PICTURE OF MME BIZET

For all their complaints about the "deadly *mondain* obsession" that brought Proust to Mme Straus's salon week after week, several of his peers from the little literary gang—Jacques Blanche, Fernand Gregh, Robert Dreyfus, Robert de Billy, and Georges de Lauris—were regulars there as well. They insisted they did not share their friend's enthusiasm for high society; whether or not this was true, Blanche recalled afterward, they continued to "deplore Proust's interest in the monde." Only in hindsight would they realize what Proust had known all along: that his artistic imagination demanded a rigorous study of that rarefied sphere. If he was going to write anything worthwhile about the gratin, then he had to educate himself about its denizens in the only environment, as yet, where he could examine them up close. As Gregh commented in his memoirs, "Everything Proust knew about the monde, he learned at Mme Straus's."

True to his purpose, Proust approached her entresol with the assumption that there was information to be gleaned from its habitués' every turn of phrase, gesture, and pretense. Blanche was struck by Proust's formidable powers of observation, likening them to "the bee's antennae and thousand-faceted insect eyes." This analogy was consistent with Proust's later remarks that he went into society to gather pollen for the "black honey" of his art. Like another of his literary heroes, novelist Honoré de Balzac, Proust would draw on his encyclopedic observations to create characters and settings with astonishing precision. The habits and quirks of the gratin would inform both his youthful and his mature writings.

What Proust learned in Mme Straus's salon shaped his work in a deeper and broader way as well. His early years there coincided with the publication, by several of her older *fidèles*, of writings born of real-life passions for unattainable society doyennes. Notable among these is Maupassant's *Strong as Death* (*Fort comme la mort*, 1889)—a novel published serially, and concurrently, with his friend Porto-Riche's *Happiness Manqué* (1889). Both *Strong as Death* and Maupassant's subsequent novel, *Our Heart* (*Notre cœur*, 1890), were widely thought to have been inspired by a romance between him and Mme Straus. This would mean that Maupassant, like Porto-Riche, found his muse in one of the future models for Proust's Duchesse de Guermantes—just as the younger man was beginning his own career as a bard of Parisian elegance.

The author of *Strong as Death* represented a particularly important role model for Proust because, unlike Porto-Riche—who went to his grave without naming

Élisabeth Greffulhe as the dedicatee of *Happiness Manqué*—Maupassant kissed and told. Or rather, by larding his fiction with details that conspicuously evoked Mme Straus's circumstances and his own, he gave a persuasive impression of having kissed, and then he told. In the process, he set a precedent of twofold relevance to Proust. First, he underlined a putative convergence between his life and his work, reshuffling elements of reality into configurations that bore the stamp of artistic truth. While Proust had already toyed with this aesthetic in his high-school writings, Maupassant, an accomplished novelist twenty years his senior, gave it a more mature articulation.

Second, Maupassant deployed his art-meets-life method to criticize the culture of elegance to which Mme Straus and her friends were beholden. In his personal life, as will soon be seen, Maupassant was determined to join the *mondains*. But in his literary life, he was just as determined to beat them. His creative integrity would not permit him to idealize in his writings a class that, no matter how eagerly he pursued it as a man, he knew as an artist to be hollow and corrupt. "Society people ought to realize," Maupassant remarked elsewhere, "that it is as dangerous for them to open their doors to novelists as it is for a grain merchant to raise rats in his store." This analogy may not have been innocent; if he and Geneviève were on terms as intimate as their friends suspected, then there is some chance that she confided in Maupassant about her husband's ignoble family background. (If she did, it would have been a signal admission on her part, for none of the other *fidèles*, who between them generated several thousands of pages' worth of public and private writings, ever alluded to Straus's grain-merchant kin.)

But for Proust, the more salient point was this: Maupassant showed that it was possible, even imperative, to write about the monde without idealizing it. In *Strong as Death,* he suggests that the literary value of the gratin lies not in its elegance per se, but in the misplaced ambition, frustrated longing, and wholesale duplicity that such elegance at once occasions and conceals. Although Proust would not fully absorb this lesson as a young man, in time it would come to inform his most astute depictions of the gratin.

Thirty years later, in *The Guermantes Way* (*Le Côté de Guermantes,* 1920–1921), Proust would write that the Duchesse de Guermantes never sounded as "literary, to my mind, as when she spoke about the Faubourg Saint-Germain, and never seemed to me more stupidly 'Faubourg Saint-Germain' than when she spoke about literature." Taken in context, these lines refer to a slightly different phenomenon from the one explored in *Strong as Death.* When Proust's narrator extols Mme de Guermantes's "literary" qualities, he is talking about the evocative symbols of her lineage: Crusader forebears, coats of arms, and ancient, poetic family names. According to the narrator, these emblems of nobility constitute richer artistic fodder than whatever vapid small talk the duchess might have made when she was trying to sound cultured.

In *Strong as Death* (1889), Guy de
Maupassant lambasted the culture
of *mondanité* he encountered in
Geneviève's salon.

However, the statement about the Faubourg's literariness applies in a broader
way to the dynamics both Proust and Maupassant witnessed in Geneviève
Straus's salon. The interactions that unfolded there were shadow plays—as incidental to the real dramas unfolding beneath the surface as the onstage action
was to a *mondaine* on a subscription evening at the Opéra. Going into society
meant wearing a mask, presenting a polished façade that hid any and all vestiges
of private, "inelegant" truth. In this crucial regard, noble society may well have
been the most literary of all fin-de-siècle Parisian settings, because it obliged its
members to exist as fictions. "In the monde," says a character in *Strong as Death,*
"everything is a simulacrum." That is its deepest truth.

IN MARRYING STRAUS and relocating to the eighth arrondissement,
Geneviève had left arty, rough-and-tumble Montmartre behind her. But in
order to retain a bit of the bohemian flair that had made her salon in the rue
de Douai such a success, she exacted a compromise from her husband. The
patrician families in their new neighborhood typically lived either in elegant
old *hôtels particuliers* or in grand apartments on the *piano nobile* of one of the
area's many luxurious, Second Empire–era residential buildings. The building
the Strauses moved in to at 134, boulevard Haussmann was duly luxurious, and
was possessed of *piano nobile* apartment, complete with the double-height ceilings, ceremonial *portes à deux battants,* and large wrought-iron balconies common to such residences. But at Geneviève's prompting, the Strauses forwent this
option and chose instead to move in to the building's entresol: a low-ceilinged

space that nestled beneath the *piano nobile* and above the high arched windows of Sutton's tailor shop on the ground floor. In other such buildings, tradesmen like Sutton used the entresol either for storage or as their own living quarters "above the store." For a couple as moneyed and *mondain* as the Strauses, it was a peculiar real-estate choice to say the least. But for Geneviève and her faithful, the entresol represented, like her Montmartre flat before it, a tantalizing and unique alternative to the staid grandeur of the monde. Indeed, Lily de Gramont, who called there as a girl with her stepmother the Duchesse de Gramont (née Rothschild), recalled it as a charming, almost magical place. Because its windows faced out onto the treetops of the boulevard Haussmann, the apartment gave visitors the delightful sense of having climbed into a treehouse, and because its ceilings were low, it fostered a feeling of coziness. In Gramont's recollection, the "indescribably seductive, intimate charm" of the entresol extended to its lone female inhabitant: "Mme Émile Straus never looked more alluring than she did in those low salons, where the sunlight filtered in through the leaves of the chestnut trees outside."

Geneviève's salon occupied the graceful, oval-shaped room in the building's rotunda, and it was here that the affluence she now enjoyed as Straus's wife appeared—entresol or no—in all its glory. As one of her *fidèles* noted, Straus regarded her as "his masterpiece," and he installed her in a setting of exquisite beauty, furnished with an array of superb Louis XV and Louis XVI antiques. Visitors took their seats in hand-carved chairs and settees signed by Georges Jacob, cabinetmaker to Marie Antoinette. The Aubusson upholstery on the furniture showed peasant gambols, flower garlands, and—like the Beauvais tapestry on Élisabeth Greffulhe's drawing-room suite—vignettes from La Fontaine's *Fables*. Aubusson tapestries hung from the rococo boiseries, their pastoral tableaux vying for wall space with pieces from Straus's art collection: an eclectic but first-rate mix of eighteenth-century French masters (Watteau, Nattier, Greuze, Fragonard, Boucher) and contemporary painters (Monet, Pissarro, Renoir, Vuillard, Seurat, and family friends such as Forain, Delaunay, Moreau, and Detaille). Of all the nineteenth-century French artists, the one Straus collected most avidly was Eugène Boudin, an obsessive portrayer of beaches, ports, jetties, boats, low tides, and high seas. "I am *encumbered* by Boudins," Geneviève would sometimes sigh. She wasn't a fan of his watery scenes, perhaps because of her sister's death by drowning.

Some juxtapositions in the art installation were thematic. A Fortuny watercolor of a peasant girl adjoined a Millet pastel of the same subject; semi-naked damsels by Greuze and Forain formed another toothsome pair. Other combinations evinced the whimsical humor for which the lady of the house was famed. Jupiter violated two different women in two different disguises in two different canvases. A Millet pencil sketch of Venus and Cupid was sandwiched between

Lami's *Othello and Iago* and Bayre's *Two Bengal Tigers Fighting*. The message of this triptych? Love hurts, particularly if you're married to "Straus the Tiger." A nearby Daumier caricature of a balding lawyer pontificating in a courtroom drove the message home.

On an étagère by the fireplace stood a clutch of academic animal sculptures: a lion and a greyhound in plaster; a basset hound and a dromedary camel in bronze. These unlikely pairings, too, suggested the hand of Geneviève, who in her darker moods spoke of the conjugal state as a tragic mismatch, a yoking of two beasts doomed never to walk in synchrony. Other arrangements were more cheering, such as a phalanx of eighteenth-century terra-cotta figurines, fragile and perfect, that lined the mantelpiece.

A vitrine in a corner displayed a collection of costly, kitschy little animal statuettes by Royal Copenhagen. When no Rothschilds were present, Geneviève would roll her eyes at "the frightful Copenhagens" and explain that she couldn't throw them away because Adèle de Rothschild had been giving them to Jacques as birthday presents for years. With this ritual complaint, Geneviève affected her own version of the daring irreverence Laure de Chevigné displayed when mocking her Romanov friends for their questionable taste. ("I have *been* to Tsarskoe Selo, and it is *not as chic as all that.*") It was an audacious gambit insofar as even those *mondains* who begrudged the Rothschilds their wealth and social station tended to recognize their unparalleled discernment as art collectors. Geneviève's disparagement of the "frightful Copenhagens" conveyed her indifference to received wisdom and her nonchalance toward the very worthies upon whose cachet she based part of her own. Indeed, Geneviève claimed that Jacques had received the figurines as birthday gifts because Adèle and her late husband, Baron Salomon de Rothschild, were his godparents. In fact, Baron Salomon had died eight years before Jacques's birth in 1872, and neither his name nor his wife's figures among the godparents listed on the boy's certificate of baptism.

Less contentious was the garden of white porcelain flowers abloom in another display case. In a third clustered several portrait busts by Geneviève's mother, who had died in 1884. The little sculptures represented virtually every member of their family except Geneviève herself, Léonie having pointedly refused to portray her. Above this vitrine hung a famous portrait of Voltaire by Quentin de La Tour. With his stringy wig and his demoniac grin, the philosopher looked to Jacques Blanche like "an exact effigy" of Geneviève's batty old aunt Mélanie.

After her remarriage and relocation to the entresol, Geneviève had divested herself of the piano-desk contraption upon which her father and first husband had composed. In its stead, a new grand piano nestled between two oversized jardinières stuffed with fresh roses. The flowers were another of Straus's obsessions: he was said to love his wife, his art collection, and his roses, in that order.

Stacked on scattered *guéridons,* piles of books and journals bore fulsome inscriptions to Geneviève. She didn't always read, or admit to reading, the works in question, but she liked to show them off. The minutes ticked by on antique clocks, reflected in antique mirrors.

Dead center, on the wall across from the fireplace, hung the pièce de résistance: the portrait of Mme Bizet in mourning, with her eyes like smoke and her face like glass.

DISPLAYED RIGHT ABOVE the Louis XV divan where Geneviève reclined when she entertained, Delaunay's portrait was the beating heart of her salon. The party line among the faithful was that it made "all the Pissarros, La Tours, Seurats, and Monets in the world look downright boring" by comparison. Proust went even further, asking more than one first-time visitor to the salon, "Say, monsieur, isn't it more beautiful than the *Mona Lisa*?" Ever since its début at the 1878 Salon de Paris, the canvas had drawn accolades like this one:

> On Mme Bizet's lips floats a wan smile, and an unsettling fire glows in her burning gaze. Hers is a problematic, disquieting beauty that must have been very difficult to paint. M. Delaunay has rendered it to perfection: he has made a masterpiece.

Another typical review highlighted the sitter's "disconcerting charm" and dubbed the overall composition "a rare symphony in black and gold," anticipating the title of Whistler's painting of Robert de Montesquiou, *Arrangement in Black and Gold* (1890–1891). In fact, Montesquiou was a client of Straus's and became a friend of Geneviève's. He wrote an ode to her fabled likeness: "Delaunay did a portrait of your soul, / where your eyes burn with a flame / that defies the passage of time."

Among Geneviève's friends, only Degas refused to hail the Delaunay portrait as a work of genius. He argued that its theatrical emphasis on her black mourning garb was a gimmicky shortcut to conveying sorrow. Degas may have had a point, given that Geneviève had been secretly engaged to Delaborde for several years by the time she sat for Delaunay. But Degas's grousing did not diminish the others' appreciation for the painting. According to Maupassant, they treated it like a religious relic, praising it upon their arrival "much as one makes the sign of the cross when entering a church."

Geneviève enjoyed these homages, even though they violated her embargo on artistic discussion. Georges de Lauris speculated that she made this exception because "in her salon, everything was dedicated to *her*." Otherwise, she continued to discourage highbrow talk among the faithful. In Lauris's paraphrase, she justified her policy by pointing out that "naturally any books or [paintings] by *her* friends could only be very good. Why belabor the obvious?"

Considering the exceptional concentration of talent in her salon, Geneviève's ban on highbrow conversation topics took Proust by surprise. Accustomed to talking about books and art with his "exquisite little Maman" and his high-school friends, he found it frustrating not to be able to broach the subject of literature with so many well-known writers. He was unable to pepper Jules Lemaître, the drama critic whom he had parodied in his first submission to *Mondays,* with questions about Corneille and Racine; unable to discuss *In Their Own Words,* a *mondain* epistolary novel that Proust would briefly try to emulate in the summer of 1893, with Paul Hervieu; unable to ask Porto-Riche about *Happiness Manqué* (which in private Proust deemed "a book of very bad poems" but which, according to *Le Gaulois,* had found its way into "the hands of all the women" in Paris). Jacques Blanche recorded that Proust was particularly frustrated not to get to talk about English literature with Lord Lytton.

In middle age, Proust would transpose this predicament into *The Guermantes Way* (1920–1921). During his first dinner party at the Duchesse de Guermantes's house, the narrator is exasperated to discover that "when she was with a poet or a musician, she found it [more] elegant to converse with them about the weather" than about their work. "To the uninformed visitor," the narrator remarks, "there was something disturbing, even mysterious, about this abstention," above all when the Duchesse brought it to bear on "a celebrated poet he had been dying to meet." But for Geneviève, the refusal to talk about her famous friends' accomplishments constituted her own studied version of noble "simplicity." Like an aristocrat's feigned indifference to lineage, her disregard for genius accentuated her inborn right to take it for granted.

Even at this early stage, Geneviève's antibluestocking manner did not sit altogether well with Proust. "How could it be," he wondered to Lauris, "that we should prefer the company of Mme Straus, who at bottom has so little interest in anything we care about, to that of Mme X, who knows so much about literature and art?" Lauris surmised that her appeal as a hostess "had something to do with the seduction of her natural gifts," and initially, Proust concurred. It would not take him long to see, however, that her seductive gifts were anything but natural.

SINCE HER MARRIAGE TO STRAUS, Geneviève had fine-tuned her winning persona. Along with her wit (which had evolved), she entranced her devotees with three principal traits. The first was her singular brand of beauty, which had become even more "problematic" in person than in the Delaunay portrait, owing to the depredations of age, neurasthenia, and drug use. The vials and syringes on the table beside her chaise longue bespoke her weakness for Veronal and morphine. Paul Bourget, who as a self-styled "psychologist of the human heart" took note of her growing dependency on opiates, repeatedly begged her to cut back, but she ignored him.

Although Geneviève claimed to take drugs for medical purposes, they did little to allay the tics that still periodically jolted across her face "like flashes of lightning in a summer sky." Yet as this simile suggests, her fragile constitution was part of her charm, and she knew it. Reprising the ideal of peaked, ailing femininity launched a generation earlier by her friend Dumas *fils*'s wildly popular novel-turned-melodrama, *The Lady of the Camellias* (*La Dame aux camélias*, 1848), Geneviève played the sensual invalid. As in her Montmartre days, she received callers in risqué bedroom attire: slinky housedresses and lacy peignoirs in her signature palette of grey, mauve, and white. She sprayed herself so liberally with her favorite eau de parfum, Peau d'Espagne, that Élie Delaunay pleaded with her "not to wear *quite that much* Peau d'Espagne—you do not smell bad naturally!" But like Bourget's drug lectures, Delaunay's entreaty fell on deaf ears. According to her nephew Daniel, Geneviève persisted in keeping herself "outrageously perfumed" at all times.

Lolling on her plush satin-upholstered divan, Geneviève would complain about the chill despite the roaring fire that blazed in her drawing room year-round. She would shiver fetchingly as she clutched an expensive fur stole or cashmere shawl around her neck and chest, while at the same time allowing the lower half of her peignoir to gape open to expose her ankles and feet, parts of the anatomy "decent" women of the era were never supposed to reveal. Stepping up the provocation, she wore stockings of flesh-colored silk that made her look bare legged. This illusion scandalized Goncourt, who grumbled in his journal that Mme Straus was "not a lady of the monde, but a pseudo-cocotte!" Princesse Mathilde felt the same way, ruing the decline of social standards since her own heyday as a hostess (and a would-be femme fatale). But Geneviève's other callers—at least the straight men in the group—were transfixed. "Those sorts of wiles should be forbidden by law," teased Joseph Reinach.

As Reinach and Geneviève were both aware, however, those wiles were essential to her charm, enticing the faithful with a subtle but distinct promise of sexual availability. For the majority of her followers, that promise turned out to be illusory. Geneviève knew her flirtiness kept them interested, but she also knew she could only take it so far without compromising her reputation. The gender double standards of the monde were such that if she showed much more than a hint of erotic complaisance, she could be found in violation of the decorum society ladies were meant to project. While Laure de Chevigné might thumb her nose at this stricture, Geneviève's bourgeois Jewish roots did not entitle her to take such liberties. As an honorary member of the gratin, she was under special pressure to conform to its doctrines of feminine decency. And conform she did, so adroitly that strangers sometimes assumed she had been educated by nuns.*

In the interests of propriety, then, Geneviève tempered her sultriness with

---

* Geneviève may have picked up some tips from the two members of her family who *were* educated by nuns: the daughters of Ludovic's late half brother, Anatole Prévost-Paradol. One of the daughters, Thérèse, even took holy orders and has a brief cameo later in this story.

an air of prudish reserve that constituted her second signature attraction. Cool when her devotees burned hot, she hinted that her aloofness arose from her unwavering fidelity to her husband—her first husband. Straus's "frightful temper" notwithstanding, Geneviève intuited that for the men who chased her, he represented a much less formidable rival than his predecessor. So she gave her *fidèles* to understand that she was immured in eternal mourning for the late, great Georges Bizet. She encouraged this perception by positioning her favorite divan right beneath the Delaunay portrait of her in her widow's weeds and, again, by dressing exclusively in the muted colors of half mourning.

These contrivances made a lasting impression on Geneviève's acolytes, from Paul Hervieu, who referred to her as "the lovely perfumed lady in a mauve dressing gown," to Paul Bourget, who borrowed some of her features for the enticing widowed heroine of his *mondain* novel *A Woman's Heart* (*Un cœur de femme*, 1890). Robert de Montesquiou, fascinated by her adroit manipulation of his heterosexual confrères, wrote a poem comparing her to Penelope, the wife who stays true to Odysseus during his long years of wandering, despite an army of suitors vying for her hand: "She is a famous composer's widow . . . / Still bewitched by the echo of the dead man's motifs . . . / She is Penelope, forever keeping her suitors at bay / and accepting none of them— / even though this Penelope has dared to remarry." It was one of Montesquiou's most insightful poems. From one poseur to another, he appreciated the cleverness of Geneviève's gambit. By definition, a remarried Penelope was an oxymoron, but that was precisely what made her so intriguing.

Although he stood in awe of Montesquiou's pedigree, Straus could not have welcomed his portrayal of Geneviève as another man's Penelope. But even Straus had to recognize that to a certain extent, Geneviève remained, or pretended to remain, in thrall to Bizet's memory. Proust observed that Straus "became agitated whenever his wife brought up Georges Bizet, with whom she had been very much in love," and Goncourt noticed a similar reaction, remarking that nothing drove Straus crazier than the faraway look that stole into Geneviève's eyes whenever she caught herself "accidentally" humming a tune from *The Girl from Arles* or *Carmen*.

And yet, nothing about her Widow Bizet posture was accidental: not the recitals of Bizet's music she sometimes organized at home (in another calculated exception to her anti-artistic policy); not her habit of naming her miniature poodles after characters in his operas; not her attendance at every new revival of his work; not her efforts to have a monument to him installed at the Opéra-Comique, where a bust to her late father was already enshrined. Geneviève's involvement in the Bizet monument campaign threw Straus into such a jealous frenzy that Goncourt wondered if maybe one of the lawyer's enemies hadn't approached her with the plan.

As much as it agitated Straus, Geneviève held fast to her image as the Widow

Bizet, understanding its importance in helping her negotiate the fine line between leading her faithful on and pushing them away. Like the wild temptress whom Bizet had modeled on her in his *Carmen,* Geneviève refused to let any man claim her. Or at least, that was what she wanted everybody to believe.

The third of Geneviève's most engaging attributes, Lily de Gramont recorded, lay in her

> rare and delicious knack for intuiting, with her fine feminine antennae, your innermost thoughts and deepest desires. She knew what you wanted, what you were hoping for, what you were worried about; she flattered and caressed.

Gramont particularly admired Geneviève's finesse in coddling the Baronne de Rothschild, whose husband, Alphonse, Straus's putative half brother, was the current *chef de famille* and thus the richest and most powerful member of the Parisian branch of the clan. Known in the monde as Baronne Laurie, Alphonse's wife was his niece from the English branch of the family. Having been a Rothschild since birth, she had spent her whole life insulated by staggering wealth and found the world outside baffling in the extreme. (Touring a friend's estate in England, she once asked in genuine wonder, "Whatever do you do to get so many dead leaves?") Baronne Laurie had only grown more out of touch since the death of her father-in-law, Baron James, in 1868, when she and Alphonse inherited 300 million francs, a sum equal to fifteen thousand times the annual salary of a midlevel executive in the Rothschild Frères bank.

Baronne Laurie's unease outside the family cocoon may have been compounded by anxiety about her closeted lesbian leanings. Under the Second Empire, the Parisian secret police had kept tabs on a discreet romance between her and Georgina de Galliffet, the Princesse de Sagan's best friend. That police force having disbanded with the empire's fall, Baronne Laurie's sexual proclivities had since stayed a closely guarded secret. But that secret was potentially unsafe in Geneviève's salon, where novelist and reporter Jean Lorrain, one of the few openly gay *fidèles,* reveled in gossiping about clandestine homosexuality among *mondain* Parisians. Cognizant, however, of the special importance the Rothschilds held for his hostess, Lorrain kept mum about Baronne Laurie's Sapphic tendencies, and Geneviève made an extra effort to put her at ease:

> If Baronne Laurie walked in, looking tentative and anxious, Mme Straus would immediately bring her a comforting cup of tea with cream, along with some chocolates, reminding her repeatedly that these excellent chocolates came from Marquis. Then she would murmur: "Ferrières . . . Your beautiful Worth dress . . . How are the birds in the big aviary doing?"

Geneviève, thirty-nine, poses with one of her most treasured guests, "Baronne Laurie" de Rothschild, fifty.

This smooth, reassuring patter worked like a tranquilizer on Baronne Laurie. The peace that came over the Rothschild matriarch within minutes demonstrated the remarkable efficacy of Geneviève's solicitous charm.

To the noninitiated, Geneviève's attentiveness might have looked like kindness; Proust, for example, admired (or professed to admire) her "goodness," "benevolence," and "refined moral charm." But those who knew her better, like Lily de Gramont, believed that Geneviève's "art of taking a passionate interest" in her friends was first and foremost "an art of making herself indispensable to them." If Lauris regarded her as "a *woman* to the core," it was because "she knew just how to flatter you so that you would flatter her in return." Maupassant traced her "unimaginably thoughtful gestures, delicious attentions, [and] infinite sweetness" to her all-consuming need "to keep her captives close and subjugated."

Though Geneviève's wit remained an official draw for the faithful, like her physical appearance, it was beginning to show its age. Some of her best-loved one-liners were now more than a decade old, such as "I was *just* going to say that!" (the rejoinder to Gounod's line about Massenet's "octagonal" music) and "It was the only way I could get rid of him" (her mock explanation of her marriage to Straus). But she continued to trot them out often, with an ever less sensational impact on her audience. Even younger visitors like Lauris, for whom her riffs were relatively fresh, commented on their "reheated" (tepid) quality, while Arthur Meyer, not being one of her core loyalists, went so far as to say that

> It was her misfortune to have a surfeit of wit but without the good grace to downplay it. . . . A real hostess should know how to start a conversation and keep it going without ever dominating it. . . . She should hand her guests a tennis racket but refrain from hitting the ball herself.

By these criteria, Geneviève was a less than exemplary *salonnière*. But her true believers refused to admit such heresy. They pretended to find her as side-splittingly funny as ever, rewarding her quips with a show of false hilarity that Maupassant, for one, found quintessentially *mondain:*

> In the *grand monde,* laughter is never genuine. When good manners require it, people put on an amused air and pretend to laugh. They present a reasonable facsimile of laughing, but they never actually do it.

Perhaps the faithful amplified the magic of Geneviève's wit to bolster their self-satisfaction in her company—to reassure themselves that, socially speaking, they had thrown in their lot with the best hostess in Paris. ("Your conversation," Proust gushed to her, sincerely or otherwise, "is a work of art!") And perhaps their fake laughter blunted its sting when the humor in her salon came at their own expense, as when Haas endured Degas's anti-Semitic mockery. Or when Proust suffered Lorrain—who had somehow found out about his humiliating high-school nickname—to greet him as Marcel Fart.

Such a defense against ridicule would have been particularly helpful to the man Geneviève most enjoyed ribbing in the longer tales she told to supplement her one-liners. That man was Henri Meilhac, Ludovic's writing partner, who had known Geneviève all her life and prided himself on being her biggest fan. Without question, he was the biggest in a literal sense: a balding, red-faced bachelor with a bushy grey walrus moustache, Meilhac was so obese that he couldn't tie his shoes, hence his habit of going about with his laces trailing. Geneviève and her friends nicknamed him "the Blob"—a moniker Hervieu changed to "the Blob of the Académie Française," almost surely out of envy, when Meilhac was elected to that august body in 1888.

Given his success in the opera and theater worlds, Meilhac had his pick of singers and actresses to share his bed, and outside the entresol, this was the company he kept. But in Geneviève's presence, he fervidly maintained that she was the only woman for him and went to great lengths to try to prove his devotion. Whenever she left town on one of her many spa cures, he insisted on tagging

COLLECTION FÉLIX POTIN

HENRI MEILHAC

Henri Meilhac was Ludovic Halévy's longtime writing partner, and Geneviève's most slavishly devoted *fidèle*. She and Paul Hervieu nicknamed him "the Blob of the Académie Française."

along on her travels. In so doing, though, he turned himself into the butt of the "funny" stories she recounted when she came home. Being a creature of the Parisian boulevards, Meilhac was woefully ill-equipped to function outside the city, and his haplessness proved a comedic goldmine for Geneviève. She regaled the faithful with stories about how in an effort to impress her at a lakeside spa in Switzerland, he had reinvented himself as a yachtsman—"Meilhac rented a little motorboat and started talking about having anchors embroidered on all his flannels"—and how, on a trip to the Pyrenees, he had tried to "become a hiker and an excursionist, parading around in a beret and brandishing a [shepherd's crook]. It was a beautiful sight to see."

These anecdotes turned into mainstays of Geneviève's humor, to such an extent that when habitués of her salon spoke of her "Meilhac and Halévy" wit, as Proust would later do in the *Search,* they may have been referring not just to the ironic sensibility she shared with Halévy, but to the ridicule she heaped on Meilhac. They may also have been underlining the Carmenesque nature of her hold on her cousin's co-author ("*Si tu m'aimes, prends garde à toi*"), who only loved her more abjectly the more she abused him. In a letter she showed off to her friends, Meilhac slavishly assured her that "everything Lemaître calls my 'talent' begins with you, is because of you. . . . Everything good that I have ever written comes from you." Not a bad tribute from one of the nation's forty Immortals.

Not all of Geneviève's stories featured the bumbling Blob. Most of them did, however, center on her trips away from Paris—maybe the prospect of gaining some new conversational material made these absences frustrate her slightly less. One of her tales grew out of a ferry ride she took across Lake Maggiore, Meilhac-free, in a rainstorm:

> There I was, beneath the beautiful Italian skies—which were the most inclement skies I have ever seen. . . . And the rain! Everyone tried to take refuge in the hold and if I tell you that an Italian marching band got there first, that will give you some idea of how crowded it was. . . . It's totally dark, no one can move, the boat is being pitched about. Umbrellas open, luggage drenched or lost, thunder, lightning, and then, because the Italians are a festive people, the bandleader gives the signal and *boom, boom*—the fanfare begins! I was wedged between a steamer trunk and a trombone.

Another vignette culminated in her discovery, at a spa in Royat, of a "curious object" that combined a prie-dieu with a bidet: "I never saw such a thing—it must have been invented by someone *very busy!*"

Meilhac resurfaced in Geneviève's account of the "four unforgettable and almost *unrecountable* hours" she spent with him and Straus touring the shrine to the Virgin Mary at Lourdes (the same shrine the widowed Comtesse de Chambord had reproduced in miniature in her garden at Göritz). But in this story, for once, someone other than Meilhac figured in the punch line:

> Imagine a whole city in delirium, crazy people kneeling in the middle of the streets, women walking around with candles, priests filing past and singing, scrofulous paralytic epileptics and madwomen being pulled to the Grotto in little carts, and crowds of people hurling themselves into the mud and screaming supplications to the Virgin so loudly that their prayers sound like insults. . . . There were maybe 10,000 pilgrims at Lourdes that day. . . . It was curious to see what a minor role God plays in that city . . . Everything is dedicated to the Virgin: statues, prayers, banners, etc. People talk only about her, and God struck me as being treated like "the husband who counts for very little," and whom people greet only out of politeness.

To the perceptive listener, "the husband who counts for very little" also described Straus's position in Geneviève's salon. In the years since his marriage to their friend, the grandees whose noble stature so impressed him had made it clear to him that their sole business in the entresol was with his wife. More gallingly still, she herself now treated Straus with contempt, as Goncourt noticed in this exchange: " 'Last night I had the stupidest, stupidest dream,' the husband blurted out. Mme S. answered: 'Are you quite sure, darling, that you weren't already awake?' " To avoid these blows, Straus absented himself from her salon more and more often, and according to Daniel Halévy, nobody missed him.

Least of all Geneviève and Maupassant, who had been involved in a covert flirtation dating back to late 1885 or early 1886. The two of them were likely first introduced by Porto-Riche, Laure de Chevigné, or Princesse Mathilde, who claimed Maupassant as her protégé via her friendship with his late mentor, Gustave Flaubert. Back then, Geneviève had been trying to decide whether she should "finally say *yes*" to Straus, while Maupassant, a year and a half her junior, was riding high on the reception of his second novel, *Bel-Ami* (1885), which went into its thirty-seventh printing four months after its release. The story of a loutish womanizing reporter who sleeps his way to the top of Parisian society, *Bel-Ami* had made its author not only famous but rich enough to buy a beach house, a yacht, and the legal services of Émile Straus. Fellow novelist Paul Morand estimated that Maupassant's blockbuster brought in ninety thousand francs a year, an unprecedented sum for literary fiction.

The success of *Bel-Ami* trained a spotlight on Maupassant's own scandalous reputation. Encouraging gossip about the autobiographical basis for the book, he signed his letters "Bel-Ami" and bragged, "Bel-Ami, c'est moi" (echoing Flaubert's dictum, "Mme Bovary, c'est moi"). Like his fictional hero, Maupassant was a sometime journalist known for his swaggering, uncouth manner, his muscular boxer's build, his luxuriant moustache (a key symbol of virility in his oeuvre), and, with a rumored three hundred conquests to his name, his irresistible way with women. For as long as he had been in the public eye, Maupassant's sexual prowess had been one of his defining features. The presumed resemblance between him and his protagonist only solidified that aspect of his legend.

Like most legends, this one had its dark side: syphilis. By 1889, Maupassant's disease had led to severe eye problems and, more disturbing to those around him, bouts of demented behavior. One of his friends reported that while taking a walk with him in the country, Maupassant grabbed a fallen branch, jammed it into the ground, and bellowed that in a year's time, it would yield "hundreds of little Maupassants."

In 1887, Maupassant had joined some three hundred other French artists in signing a protest against the Eiffel Tower, which was being built for the World's Fair of 1889. Later, he took to dining frequently at the restaurant *in* the tower, "because it was the only place in Paris where [he didn't] have to look at" the structure. Less wittily, he alleged that "God has proclaimed from the top of the Eiffel Tower: 'M. de Maupassant is the son of God and Jesus Christ.'" Taken in isolation, such megalomaniacal pronouncements may have appeared as mere symptoms of celebrity narcissism: the inflated self-regard that an overabundance of wealth and adulation seldom fail to produce. One had to know him much better to see that he was teetering on the brink of full-blown madness.

To Geneviève, on the verge of marrying a straitlaced lawyer, the bad-boy novelist presented a dangerous temptation. After all, she was no stranger to mental imbalance, and although she herself was becoming ever more *mondaine,* her attraction to bohemians remained as strong as ever. (As Gregh remarked, even after marrying Straus, she "never lost her taste for *outlaw* artists.") With his fame and fortune as two further enticements, Maupassant was very much Geneviève's masculine ideal. Playing up his naughty repute, he inscribed her copy of his best seller, "With the compliments of Bel-Ami himself."

Bel-Ami himself, for his part, wasn't immediately drawn to the Widow Bizet, with her dark hair and strong "Semitic" features—he liked blondes and disliked Jews. (In another novel, Maupassant surmises that the Jews of the era were "avenging their oppression as a race by oppressing others with the power of their money.") But Geneviève's celebrity piqued his interest and so—even more so—did her social network. Despite the nobiliary particle in his surname, Maupassant was not an aristocrat; his father had added the "de" in 1846, and his mother came from respectable bourgeois Norman stock. However, Maupassant was anxious to conquer the Faubourg, and he recognized the degree to which Geneviève might help in that endeavor. To Goncourt, Maupassant's *mondain* ambition was a symptom of his deteriorating mental health; the older man remarked with disdain that "the only book [Maupassant] kept at home was the *[Almanach de] Gotha.*"

Léon Daudet saw other evidence of Maupassant's craving for social advancement:

> One fine day, we learned he had bought himself three dozen pairs of rose-colored underwear, two dozen pairs of patent leather shoes, suits in every color, and that he had been having solemn colloquies with all the most fashionable shirtmakers, whom he deemed remarkably intelligent. He also began eagerly seeking out people with titles, club memberships, salons, . . . and solicited their guidance in helping him change his (previously crude) manner of eating, dressing, walking, and riding. When his pals teased him about his sudden snobbery, he retorted: "I'm sick of being a pariah—I'm going to make my way up in the world—if I ever have a child, I want him to be an *homme du monde*—I'll take a well-bred layabout over a lowborn genius any day!"

Daudet further noted that while he and his friends could not resist teasing Maupassant about his snobbishness, "we also felt sad for him." It struck them as perverse that a man of such great talent should have "fallen into the *mondain* trap," distracting himself with trivialities and toadying to unworthy, unappreciative dolts.

In light of his social ambitions, Maupassant's initial advances toward Geneviève could have been motivated as much by arrivisme as by lust. What is certain is that before she married Straus in October 1886, Maupassant approached her with at least two risqué propositions. In May, he invited her to dinner at his place with the Porto-Riches—Porto was a good friend of his, too—"and possibly with Straus." "I realize it isn't 'done' for a lady to dine with a bachelor at his house," the novelist owned, "but I don't see how it could really be that shocking if the lady were to be joined by other women of her acquaintance." (By "other women," he really meant just Lizote de Porto-Riche.) None of Geneviève's letters to Maupassant survive—it would appear that at some point, he destroyed them—and nothing else in the source record indicates whether the dinner at his place ever occurred. Soon afterward, though, he wrote to her again, apparently replying to an invitation to her salon:

> I am going to be indiscreet. Might it not be possible to meet you sometime outside the normal hours of *mondain* interchange? If you find me impertinent, say so. I don't offend easily. [But] isn't it natural to want to see more of women who interest one, and to see them *alone,* the better to savor their charm and grace—the better to be seduced by them?
>
> At-homes are unbearable. . . . I prefer to visit when I am the only one expected, the only one seen, the only one heard, the only one who gets to find you beautiful and charming—and I won't stay for too long, I promise.

Although Maupassant allowed here for the possibility that Geneviève might rebuff him outright, that was not what she did. His second letter, written in the summer of 1886, reveals that she answered his request for special favors with an admission that she had recently started to lose her hair, an almost unthinkably personal disclosure for a society woman of that time (or any time) to make to a new acquaintance. To circumvent Straus, with whom Geneviève had taken off for a long vacation in Switzerland, Maupassant mailed his response in care of one of the couple's traveling companions, the Dowager Duchesse de Richelieu, née Alice Heine (1858–1925). A statuesque blonde with soulful brown eyes and dainty buck teeth, Alice had been born in New Orleans, the daughter of a rich Jewish banker from Bordeaux. Moving back to France during the American Civil War, she had gotten to know Bébé through their mutual ties to the Bordelais Jewish élite. In 1875, Alice had married an impoverished French duke—yet another case of modern blazon regilding—only to be widowed five years later. Since then, she and Geneviève had become inseparable companions, united in their widowhood, their music-world connections (Alice was a fanatical opera buff and patron), and their *mondanité*. Throughout their lives, they would keep each other's secrets, upholding a pact that may have begun with Alice receiving Maupassant's letter for Geneviève.

The trip the two girlfriends were taking with Straus that summer was the very one that would culminate in his and Geneviève's engagement. Nonetheless, Geneviève was still interested enough in Maupassant to go to some trouble to stay in touch with him on her travels by having Alice act as a go-between. The

COLLECTION FÉLIX POTIN

ALICE
PRINCESSE DE MONACO

The scion of a rich Jewish banking family, Alice
Heine converted to Catholicism to marry the
Duc de Richelieu in 1879. Prematurely widowed
like Geneviève, she went on to marry Prince
Albert I of Monaco in October 1889. The union
would be an unhappy one, ending in a legal
separation in 1902.

ruse was necessary insofar as Straus would undoubtedly have been angered by
Maupassant's letter: not just the fact of it, but the intimate subject matter and
tone. Because hair loss was one of the symptoms of his syphilis, Maupassant
was able to supply Geneviève with detailed instructions for a home remedy:
hot water mixed with ammonia, glycerine, and a "foaming coal-tar compound
available in any good pharmacy." That she expected him to know how to advise
her suggests that he had already told her about his disease, unless she had merely
deduced from the hero's phallic moustache in *Bel-Ami* that Maupassant had a
hair fixation. (If so, she was right: in the French literary canon, only Baudelaire
rivals Maupassant in his eroticized treatment of hair.) In any case, to conclude
his letter, he petitioned her for a small fetish object in exchange: "If my methods
succeed as I hope, then I ask you (and I promise I won't tell anyone) to give me
a few of the hairs that I will have saved, as the price of my services."

After Geneviève and Straus married that autumn, she and Maupassant continued to correspond, presumably still without the lawyer's knowledge. Because
Maupassant was an inveterate wanderer and seducer, his epistolary flirtation with
Geneviève tended to wane whenever his travels or sexual conquests demanded
his attention. (In fact, seemingly unbeknownst to Geneviève, he romanced
at least two of her female *fidèles*, Marie Kann and the Comtesse Potocka, and
he may have had an affair with Marie's sister Lulia as well.) But 1888 brought
with it a pivotal change in their friendship, demonstrated by a noticeable new
intensity in Maupassant's letters to Geneviève. While on a month-long trip to

Algeria to work on his next novel, he sent her long, lyrical missives about his surroundings: "ravines filled with virgin forests"; rooftop hammocks "beneath a sky filled with huge, fiery, miraculous African stars"; flea-infested mosques "that I frequent like a good Muslim, tranquil asylums of stone." Sounding more like a lovelorn knight-errant than a randy Bel-Ami, he impressed upon Geneviève that he was alone, and that in his solitude, his heart was full of "the people" he had left behind:

> At night I drink in the desert air and I devour the isolation. It is good, and it is sad. There are evenings when I arrive in a humble African inn and in my whitewashed single room I feel the full weight of the distance separating me from those I love, because I do love them.

Following up on this last loaded statement, he sent her a suggestive gift: a pair of "slave-girl" earrings from the souk in Algiers. Though he spoke of "those," not "the one," he loved, Maupassant brought no such presents, and wrote no such letters, to any of the other women in his life. Geneviève was starting to eclipse them all.

When she and Maupassant were both in Paris, they arranged to see each other often, typically with mutual friends acting as chaperones or pretexts for their meetings. One summer afternoon, Geneviève turned out with José-Maria de Heredia and Madeleine Lemaire in the Champ-de-Mars to watch Maupassant fly over Paris in a hot-air balloon, *Le Horla,* named for his best-known short story. Another time, she went with Gégé Primoli, Meilhac, and Dumas *fils*'s daughter Colette Dumas Lippmann to visit Maupassant in Triel-sur-Seine,

In the summer of 1889, Gégé Primoli photographed Geneviève *(left)*, Colette Dumas Lippmann, and Guy de Maupassant boating on the Seine.

Maupassant, thirty-nine, flirts with Geneviève, forty, in the garden at
Triel-sur-Seine. Photo by Gégé Primoli.

a riverside hamlet where he had rented a villa as a quiet place to work. Primoli
snapped photographs of Maupassant paddling the two women about in a row-
boat marked "MADAME" and gallantly offering Geneviève a flower.

Geneviève and Maupassant may also have found ways to spend time with
each other alone. In June 1888, he wrote to her to confirm a rendezvous outside Paris: "I will be in Poissy first thing tomorrow morning. If I don't see
you there on the 2 o'clock train, I'll go into the woods ahead of you, on the
road from Saint-Germain[-en-Laye]." Given that Ludovic had a house nearby,
Geneviève could have arranged to stay with him and Louise as cover for a tryst
with Maupassant. She later griped to Reinach about Louise's refusal to "turn a
blind eye"—she didn't specify to what—when she, Geneviève, was the Halévys'
houseguest in the country.

In July, Maupassant visited Geneviève at the villa she and Straus had rented
in Trouville-sur-Mer, a fashionable resort town in Normandy where the couple
would later buy a grand estate of their own. (Maupassant, a native of the region,
had a house in Étretat, thirty-five miles northeast of Trouville.) Photographs in
an Halévy family album show Geneviève and Maupassant posing on the terrace
alongside several noted *mondains,* including Melchior de Vogüé, his Russian
father-in-law, General Annenkoff, and a charming (but, for Geneviève's pur-

poses, unthreateningly plain) society doyenne, the Comtesse de Broissia. That fall, Geneviève arranged for Maupassant to join a shooting party at Ferrières. He accepted the invitation, only to scoff at the travesty of sportsmanship he found there, complaining to Goncourt that instead of allowing their guests to track a live beast, the Rothschilds had their huntsmen carry a dead deer out into the woods and release the hounds in that direction. But because many crowned heads and other grandees hunted at Ferrières, the experience gave Maupassant invaluable bragging rights afterward, confirming the value of Geneviève's patronage.

Along with opening doors for Maupassant socially, Geneviève seems to have been providing him with material. In February 1889, just in time for her fortieth birthday, *La Revue illustrée* published the first installment of the novel Maupassant had been working on while in Algeria: *Strong as Death*. The work came out in book form in May, surprising critics and fans because it was about the monde, an environment barely mentioned in the author's previous writings. (In *Bel-Ami,* the hero only ascends to that pinnacle at the very end of the

Geneviève *(center)* introduced Maupassant *(far left)* to her many patrician friends, including (from *left* to *right*), the Comtesse de Broissia, Vicomte Eugène-Melchior de Vogüé, and Vogüé's Russian father-in-law, General Annenkoff.

book.) And to readers in the know, *Strong as Death* reflected a significant shift in Maupassant's priorities not only as a writer but as a man. More specifically, it prompted speculation that it was based on a romance between him and Geneviève Straus. According to *Le Gaulois,* this perception in turn fueled the "sensational public response" to the novel.

The heroine of *Strong as Death,* Anne (Any) de Guilleroy, is a flirty, forty-year-old society hostess whom the gratin has adopted despite her bourgeois origins. She wears slinky outfits, nude stockings, and is married to a charmless, socially aggressive plutocrat whom she has never loved and who sees her as the "masterpiece" of his art collection. Though the Guilleroys could easily afford to live in an *hôtel particulier,* they choose to make their home in a quirky, cozy flat on the boulevard Malesherbes. (In an early draft of the novel, the Guilleroys live on the boulevard Haussmann.) Their only child has been living with a family in the provinces since she was small, to facilitate her mother's busy *mondain* schedule. That schedule serves as Any's consolation for her loveless marriage, and as her cover for a longtime, passionate affair with a fellow adoptive *mondain.*

Any has won over the gratin with her lively wit, "troubling" beauty, and deft social instincts: "She knew just how to . . . read people and figure out what they needed to hear to put them at ease." Her salon, "a mysterious fusion of artists and *mondains,*" has a loyal following. Her *fidèles,* as she calls her regular guests, include a hefty, imperious old dowager who prides herself on her arts patronage but understands nothing of her protégés' work; a clever retired arts inspector who squanders his erudition on obtuse society swells; and Any's secret lover, Olivier Bertin, a ruggedly good-looking celebrity painter turned clubman, whom the Faubourg has likewise accepted as one of its own. Bertin is the creator of the painting to which her faithful pay ritual homage every time they visit: a portrait of "a pretty woman [in] gold and black, made of sunshine and mourning," depicting her in mourning dress for a long-dead relative.

That these elements recalled Geneviève was glaringly evident, and appeared to her friends to confirm their suspicions about a clandestine attachment between her and the novelist. Gossiping with Goncourt, Mme Baignères claimed to have it on Geneviève's own authority that "at a certain point, if Maupassant had asked her to, [she] would have left everything to be with him." According to Porto-Riche, who passed the news on to Gégé Primoli, Maupassant confessed to him directly about a love affair with Geneviève but later specified that they slept together only once, sometime after *Strong as Death* came out. As Geneviève herself left no documented reaction to the novel, it is impossible to know how she felt about it. But the portrayal was not exactly a flattering one.

OF ALL THE BIOGRAPHICAL DETAILS in *Strong as Death,* the most arresting is the portrait made of sunshine and mourning painted by Olivier Bertin at the start of his romance with Any de Guilleroy. When the action begins in the spring of 1887, the two of them have been a couple for twelve years. Both of them are honorary, not "born" *mondains*, who have carried on their affair discreetly but happily beneath the noses of their socially prominent friends. But as they approach middle age, Bertin's painting of his mistress, because it portrays her as a much younger woman, comes to remind both of them that they will soon lose the only thing they have ever truly cared about, in each other or themselves: their surface allure. It is to this supreme noble value that the two lovers have dedicated their lives, and over the course of the few months recounted in the novel, they discover to their horror that their passion is as flimsy and two-dimensional as the painting that brought them together in the first place.

Their demise is inadvertently triggered by Any's teenage daughter, Annette, who at the beginning of the story returns to Paris after a childhood spent in the provinces. Her parents having sent her away in order to focus on their social lives, they have now brought her back in order to marry her off to a debonair young marquis. When Annette makes her début in the monde, her parents' friends are struck by the uncanny similarity between her and the Bertin portrait of Any. While their praise for the girl's radiant beauty bodes well for Annette's future in a society fixated on appearances, Any takes it to mean that her own days as a queen of that milieu are numbered. Terrified that her physical charms, which bewitched her *fidèles* for so long, are on the wane, she develops a neurotic compulsion: looking in the mirror every few minutes to check for new wrinkles. Her self-consciousness grows so morbid and acute that she eventually stops going out in public. Withdrawing into morphine abuse, she isolates herself in the elegant drawing room where she once ruled as a goddess, and where her portrait, formerly the focal point and the glory of her salon, constantly reminds her of her lapse into mortality.

Like Any, Bertin is a bourgeois who owes his provisional place in the gratin to his youthful good looks and the charisma they once sustained. Also like Any, he undergoes a midlife crisis when he realizes that his appeal is fading—an epiphany yet again catalyzed by Annette and the portrait. While Bertin falls hopelessly in love with the girl because of her resemblance to his painting of her mother, Annette does not even register his crush. She regards him as an inconsequential old man, less handsome and less eminent than her highborn future husband. She also reads in a magazine that Bertin's artwork has fallen out of fashion. For this last shortcoming, at least, Bertin knows he is responsible; for after painting Any, he gave up on his great artistic ambitions in order to devote himself to her and to *mondanité*. But the ferocity of his attraction to Annette upends his longtime rationale that he sacrificed his talent for the sake of a once-in-a-lifetime passion. According to the psalm referenced in the book's title, love is as strong as death, yet Bertin is forced to see that his feelings for Any were skin-deep all along; it is the image not the woman that enthralls him. Although he desperately wants to think otherwise, whenever he contemplates

Any's portrait, "it was Annette who now emerged from the canvas. The mother had disappeared."

Bertin's insight into his own shallowness pains him even more insofar as he has always believed that his middle-class origins and artistic pursuits exempt him from the superficiality of the "born." He even, sick with jealousy of Annette's titled fiancé, treats Annette to a self-righteous lecture on the vapidity of the noblesse, informing her that

> the intelligence of the [men and women] of the monde is without value, substance or consequence; [that] their convictions are unfounded [and] their tastes fickle and dubious; . . . that there is nothing profound, genu-inely feeling, or sincere about them; that their cultivation is nil and their sophistication a façade; that, in short, they are mannequins who create the illusion and go through the motions of élite beings, which they are not.

In the novel's climactic scene, set at a gala performance of *Faust,* Bertin inwardly rages as he watches Annette stare with adoration at the "overly made-up mannequin" in the starring role. In her attraction to the handsome but musically mediocre tenor, she exhibits the very frivolity against which Bertin had warned her. Aghast, the painter realizes he has fallen prey to the same warped perspec-tive; like the hero of Gounod's opera, he has traded his soul for insubstantial, ultimately ruinous pleasures: "It seemed to him that he himself was becoming a Faust." Later that evening, crazed with self-recrimination, Bertin throws himself under the wheels of an omnibus.

Though he is mortally wounded, his mania for appearances stays with him to the end. When Any rushes to his deathbed, Bertin expresses two wishes. First: he wants her daughter's face to be the last one he gazes upon as he expires. Second: he begs Any to destroy their correspondence, as in the wrong hands it could shatter her virtuous façade. Throwing her and Bertin's love letters into the fire and watching them burn, she has the feeling that "their love itself was turning to ash" and that the liquefying sealing wax on the envelopes is blood gushing from a wound. The metaphor of wax turning to blood then inverts in the novel's closing passage. Bertin dies, leaving Any to look on in dread as his body takes on the pallid chill of a waxworks figure. In death, he becomes the perfect *mondain:* an "impassive, unfeeling" mannequin.

A WARNING TO THE LOVERS' real-life counterparts? Maybe. Little good would it do them.

CADENZA

PAINTERS, WRITERS, PARROTS, PROPHETS

The writer is envious of the painter; he wishes he could make sketches, take notes, but if he does so, he is lost. Yet when he writes, there is not a single gesture of one of his characters, not a single tic or accent, that his inspiration hasn't taken from his memory; there is not one invented character under whose name he could not put the names of sixty people he has seen, borrowing from one a grimace, from another a monocle, from still another a flash of anger or an attractive arm gesture, etc. And then the writer sees that even if his dream of being a painter couldn't be realized in a conscious and voluntary sense, he, too, has been filling his notebook with sketches all along, without even being aware of it. For all the while the writer, long before he knew that that was what he would become someday, was . . . instructing his eyes and ears to retain forever things that seemed to others like childish little nothings, the accent with which a phrase was uttered, or the facial expression and movement of the shoulders made at a certain moment by someone about whom he knew nothing else, long ago, and all because [the writer] felt that he would someday be able to hear that accent again, that it was something that could be renewed, that could endure; it is the feeling for general principles that, in the future writer, selects of its own accord that which is general and which can be put into a work of art. For never was there a moment when, listening to people talk, however stupid or foolish they may have sounded, repeating like parrots the things that all people of their type always say, he did not see and hear them transformed by their very chatter into birds of prophecy, mouthpieces of a psychological law. He remembers only what is general.

—MARCEL PROUST, *Time Regained* (*Le Temps retrouvé*, 1927)

CHAPTER SEVENTEEN

ELEGANCE FOR BEGINNERS

With *Strong as Death,* Maupassant had set forth a devastating critique of a society where appearance conquered substance and form vanquished feeling. Over the years, Proust would grow savagely critical of this phenomenon as well, inveighing in the *Search* against the "topsy-turvy inversion left over from the etiquette of the royal court" whereby "the surface [had] become essential and profound." But while still a neophyte in the monde, he adapted eagerly to its codes of studied shallowness, again taking Mme Straus and her friends as his exemplars.

As Proust applied it to himself at this early stage, the doctrine of *mondain* superficiality governed two main areas of his behavior. The first had to do with his sexual mores. Already in his high-school dealings with Jacques Bizet and Daniel Halévy, Proust had come to the conclusion that he should try to stifle his homosexual leanings, "if only for the sake of elegance." This same assumption informed his conduct for his first five years as a regular visitor to the entresol. In his effort to project "straightness," Proust benefited from finding himself in a salon where all the (male) guests were expected to be infatuated with the hostess yet were emphatically discouraged from acting on their desire. While this dual prescription was hard on some of the faithful—as Maupassant's next roman à clef would demonstrate—for Proust it was the perfect arrangement. Following the lead of Mme Straus's other acolytes, he placed her on a pedestal and treated her as an untouchable Belle Dame sans Merci. He barraged her with compliments and bouquets; he sent her impassioned letters, sprinkled with statements like "You are unique, as in all else, in possessing the art of making hearts vibrate until they break." When she would let him (which wasn't often), Proust literally sat at her feet, on a stool or ottoman at the foot of her favorite divan. In this posture, he reminded his friend Jacques Blanche of Cherubino, the tender ephebe hopelessly besotted with his godmother in Mozart's opera *The Marriage of Figaro* (*Le nozze di Figaro,* 1786).

Blanche's comparison was fitting, not only because Cherubino is a trouser role, his effeteness underscored by the singer's femininity (and soprano register) but also because Proust's ardor was itself a performance, corresponding to no underlying carnal urges. Proust himself intimated as much in one of his earliest letters to Mme Straus:

You are not sufficiently persuaded of the truth (I think you aren't persuaded of any truth!) that *one must accord a great deal* to platonic love. . . .
As I want to follow your pretty precepts against bad form I will say no
more. But please, I beg you, deign to look kindly on the keen platonic love
that attaches [me] to you.

The hint of defensiveness in these lines suggests that Proust's passion may have
been a bit too chaste for Geneviève's liking, for while she claimed not to reciprocate her devotees' lust, she made no secret of the pleasure she took in inspiring
it. For Proust, however, the role of the platonic lover was a comfortable and
even, according to his friends, agreeable default position. The consensus in the
little literary gang was that "no one enjoyed that sort of make-believe more than
Proust."

Consistent with his courtly pose, Proust attached special significance to the
fact that the first time Mme Straus ever wrote him a letter was on Good Friday
in 1890. (He had been writing to her for well over a year before she finally graced
him with a reply.) This coincidence established a symbolic link in his imagination between his asexual attachment to Mme Straus and Petrarch's unconsummated passion for Laure de Sade, upon whom the Italian poet had first laid
eyes on Good Friday more than half a millennium before. This parallel in turn
reflected the cerebral and literary nature of Proust's devotion, captured in this
line from another of his earliest letters to Mme Straus: "Having not wanted to
give you a headache by doing so in reality, here, in fiction, I kiss you tenderly."

In addition to disguising his homosexuality, the fiction of Proust's infatuation
with Mme Straus served as an alibi for his assiduous presence at her at-homes. In
this way as well, he was acting "for the sake of elegance," for nothing qualified as
less elegant than a parvenu's keenness to break into the monde, and while it was
that very keenness that made Proust so diligent about attending her salon each
week, he understood that admitting as much would amount to social suicide. As
he would joke a few years later in *Jean Santeuil,* "the words by which Lohengrin
reveals his name and origins to Elsa are every bit as dangerous and destructive"
to the aspiring *mondain* as the words "How charmed I am to see you; might
we have dinner together?" Such phrases, he reasoned, "irrevocably destroy" the
speaker's standing because they betray his overeagerness to please; "one is only
nice to people who are situated above oneself." This could well have been one
of the "pretty precepts against bad form" Proust inferred from Mme Straus, to
whom he protested in the summer of 1892, "You are very wrong to think that
I . . . desire to become *mondain.*"

Of all Mme Straus's faithful, it was perhaps Maupassant who most dramatically illustrated the perils of arrivisme. As his foppish fashion makeover and his
dog-eared copy of the *Almanach de Gotha* implied, Maupassant was unabashed

in his hankering for the monde, and for this cardinal sin, two of Geneviève's "countesses of Judea" punished him cruelly. According to Léon Daudet, Marie Kann and her sister, Lulia Cahen d'Anvers, subjected the novelist to a series of practical jokes:

> They once told Maupassant to dress for a dinner party in a red suit [*habit rouge*], then exulted in his mortification when he came to dinner thus attired, and stood out like a parakeet among all the gentlemen in white tie. Another time, [either Marie or Lulia] gave him an assignation, and when he got to her house, he found her friends hiding under every piece of furniture, crying with laughter. Another time, they sent him fiery love letters signed by a maid.

These pranks had the effect of exposing Maupassant as a pathetic clod. Recounted to general hilarity in the entresol, they highlighted the contempt in which the gratin held overzealous strivers.

Another of Geneviève's acolytes to fall victim to this sentiment was Fernand Vandérem (né Vanderheym), a clever novelist whom Maupassant introduced into her salon. Paul Hervieu, whose cool disposition and suave manners aligned him with the group's clubmen despite his haut-bourgeois provenance, looked down on Vandérem as a wretched Jewish upstart, vituperating to Goncourt that "such people defile everything, debase everything." It was true that Vandérem nurtured grand social ambitions—as one of his contemporaries said, he didn't "just want a place at the table; he want[ed] the place of honor"—but he also worried about his Jewishness hindering his advancement. Hervieu, knowing this, started a malicious rumor that one of Geneviève's highest-ranking guests, Prince Auguste d'Arenberg, secretly hated Vandérem. Tipped off by Hervieu, Vandérem fell for the ploy, turning into a bundle of nerves whenever the prince was around. When d'Arenberg wasn't around, Vandérem entreated the rest of the faithful to explain how he, a lowly professional scribbler, had managed to offend His Serene Highness. Vandérem's torment became a running joke in the entresol, confirming for Proust, who was fond of him, the importance of concealing his own *mondain* aspirations, and further motivating him to assert his "make-believe passion" for Mme Straus.

THE LONGING TO SEE the monde from within shaped not only Proust's sexual persona but his manners more generally. When studying Mme Straus's upper-class friends, he did not content himself with remarking upon their overweening investment in matters of form. He observed the myriad, subtle shadings of speech and deportment that characterized their interactions. As an outsider, Proust quickly grasped the extent to which his ignorance of such nuances could discredit him in that world. If Mme Straus and her coterie dismissed him as a vulgarian, then even his precarious foothold among them would be jeopardized. This unwelcome possibility may have fueled Proust's determination to initiate himself into the rites and mysteries of *mondain* elegance.

To begin with, he noticed that in the gratin, the word "elegance" was itself the subject of an essential, unstated law. This word was (and remains) the shibboleth of Parisian *mondanité,* denoting not merely politeness and *bon ton,* but an effortless grasp of their dictates, an unforced yet infallible ease in the ways of gracious living. Lacking an equivalent of the Italian *sprezzatura,* French society had (and still has) to make do with *élégance.* For the social novice, Proust saw, the danger lay in the abundance of apparent synonyms for this all-important term—variants which, perversely enough, betrayed a fundamental lack of elegance. "Swankiness" was for yokels, "classiness" for boors, and "chic," perhaps worst of all, for people who cared too much and tried too hard—for "snobs."

Proust had fun pointing up this prejudice in "Snobs," an article that appeared in the May 1892 issue of *The Banquet.* Along with mimicking the dry, knowing tone of La Bruyère, the essay adopts that author's caustic perspective on the petty, prestige-obsessed courtiers of Louis XIV's Versailles. "Snobs" opens with a description of a generic contemporary grande dame who deceives herself and others about how much she actually cares and how hard she actually tries:

> A woman does not attempt to hide the fact that she loves balls, horse races, even gambling. She makes no bones about it, acknowledging it simply or even proclaiming it openly. But try to get her to admit that she loves "chic," and she'll object and become genuinely angry. . . . Women of the world are so afraid of being accused of caring about chic that they never call it by its name; when pressed, they resort to a euphemism in order to avoid naming the lover who would compromise them. They cling to the word Elegance, which . . . at least conveys the impression that their lives are ruled by artistic considerations rather by vanity.

Very much in the spirit of La Bruyère, Proust advances a trenchant sociological conclusion: "elegance" is a code word for the *mondain* love or self-love—snobbery, vanity—that dares not speak its name.

Proust was further struck by the insipidness of "elegant" badinage chez Straus. By proscribing highbrow subjects and promoting frivolity, he observed, it forced people to assume "superficial selves," divorced from their most cherished "tastes, beliefs, [and] opinions." Restricted to such trivialities as the latest sensational news story or the "pretty things in [a lady's] apartment," he wrote, social banter was at best "an agreeable folly [that] in our heart of hearts we know to be no more reasonable than the delusion of a man who talks to the furniture because he knows it is alive."

As anxious as he was to curry favor with Mme Straus and her friends, when chatting with them Proust found he could only tamp down his intellectual firepower for so long. His lapse into "pedantry" came at a cost, though, as he would recall some twenty years later:

> A youth stands a better chance of succeeding in [the monde] if he is dull rather than intelligent. . . . I was very young in that milieu. At first I only said the silliest things. One day, I spoke intelligently. I was banned from [smaller gatherings] for six months, and only invited to the [bigger] crushes.

The neutral tone of this reminiscence belies the mortification Proust felt at the time. A more revealing, and contemporary, account is a fragment in *Jean Santeuil* where Mme Marmet, an ambitious, "not born" society hostess modeled on Mme Straus, humiliates the young protagonist in front of her friends. Jean admires Mme Marmet's "facility with words [and] concise, lucid wit," but for his brainy enthusiasms, she has nothing but contempt. When he brings them up in her salon, she "greet[s] his opinions with sarcasm," exclaiming to her other guests, "How pretentious and stupid he sounds whenever he opens his mouth!" Jean, sensing "confusedly that somehow he had been naïve, at fault, lacking in good judgment, [is] overcome with shame." The rebuff pains Jean all the more because it brings back his worst memories of high school, when a group of boys whose seeming "intelligence had inspired a certain affection in Jean . . . made fun of him when he talked, pushed him around in the schoolyard," and ignored his "most sincere and eloquent letter[s]." The analogy between Jean's former classmates and Mme Marmet hints at a comparable relationship between the little literary gang and Mme Straus, unified in their scorn for a youth too bookish and earnest to be suave.

Proust was also critical of what Élisabeth Greffulhe dubbed the "banal, ready-made" character of *mondain* niceties. In Mme Straus's salon, the aristocrats set the tone with their reliance on stock formulas that projected courtesy while neither containing nor inviting any genuine fellow feeling. One example came from Prince Albert I of Monaco, an honorary *fidèle* through his 1889 marriage to Alice de Richelieu. To every new artist he met at Mme Straus's, Prince Albert said with a winning smile: "You are very well known in Monaco." More often than not, he himself had never heard of the individual to whom he paid this compliment. But he delivered it with such congenial grace that the unworldly addressee was duped into thinking him sincere. More seasoned *mondains* knew better. They understood that a line like Prince Albert's was a mere formula, graciously bestowed "as if he were conferring a diploma or offering a box of petits fours." "Discerning the fictive character of such amiability was what they called being well brought up," Proust noted, whereas "believing that the friendliness was real" was a telltale sign of bad manners.

Proust decried the *mondain* fondness for worn-out aphorisms. Mme Straus's noble guests, good Catholics in principle if not necessarily in practice, favored trite biblical palaver. When pondering the immeasurable economic disparities between France's upper and lower classes, Othenin d'Haussonville cited the Gospels: "For ye have the poor always with you." In light of d'Haussonville's renown as an expert on urban poverty, one might fairly have expected him to proffer a more edifying view. His fellow Immortal Melchior de Vogüé displayed marginally more pep by quoting his saws in Latin: *Misereor super turbam* (I have pity on the multitude). To Proust, such platitudes were interesting only in their unself-conscious smugness. Born to immense wealth and privilege, d'Haussonville and Vogüé invoked timeless Christian truths to affirm the rightness of a world order where people other than themselves were poor and needed pity.

These gentlemen's pat, uninspired language aggravated Proust even more because they were highly regarded writers, and as he pointed out to Mme Straus, the best writers "create their own language." Compounding Proust's annoyance, the epidemic of hackneyed self-expression infected the "not born" authors as well, though their buzzwords tended to be secular. Vandérem, for example, spoke obsessively about social class. But whether out of anxiety, neurotic self-sabotage or just plain cluelessness, he framed his ideas in an unrefined idiom that made the *mondains* cringe. Vandérem said "swanky." He said "classy." Instead of "the gratin," he said "the *cream* of the gratin" or, even worse, "*la haute.*" He referred to noblemen as "quality folks." So jarring did this vocabulary sound to upper-class ears that it may well have made Auguste d'Arenberg recoil, thus appearing to ratify his rumored vendetta against Vandérem. It is even possible that Hervieu started the rumor when he noticed the revulsion with which d'Arenberg endured Vandérem's uncouth patter.

Although he edited one of the most prestigious literary journals in France, *La Revue de Paris,* Mme Straus's cousin Louis Ganderax was partial to a different kind of cliché: the kind employed by third-rate literary hacks. In reviewing Ganderax's "The Little Shoes" for *The Banquet,* Proust had taken a laudatory tone—eager to be published in *La Revue de Paris* someday, he likely praised the editor with that end in mind. But in private, he railed against Ganderax's weakness for "fine phrases," the fineness of which had long since dulled from overuse. It took Proust almost two decades to admit to Mme Straus how much he detested her cousin's shopworn prose, finally venting to her in 1908:

> Why does [M. Ganderax] write that way? Why, when he says "1871,"*
> does he have to add: "that most abominable of years"? Why does he auto-
> matically qualify Paris as "the big city," [and] Delaunay as "the master

---

* It was in 1871 that the Third Republic ceded Alsace and much of Lorraine to Prussia and that twenty thousand people were killed in the Paris Commune. That it was also the year of Proust's birth would perforce have made it less "abominable" to him than to Ganderax.

2ᵉ COLLECTION FÉLIX POTIN

GANDERAX
HOMME DE LETTRES

Louis Ganderax and his brother, Étienne, were lifelong friends of their cousin Geneviève. Louis, the editor of a prestigious literary magazine, was the more accomplished of the two.

painter"? Why must . . . bonhomie inevitably be "smiling" and bereavement "cruel"?

Proust scholars often cite these lines as a kind of negative *ars poetica,* a denunciation of lazy, threadbare writing by an artist to whom those two adjectives seldom (at least in his mature work) apply. But Alain de Botton's gloss on this harangue goes deeper, suggesting an important link between Proust's literary philosophy and his *mondain* experience:

> The problem with clichés is not that they contain false ideas, but rather that they are superficial articulations of very good ones. . . . Clichés are detrimental insofar as they inspire us to believe they adequately describe a situation while merely grazing its surface.

Jewish jokes formed a third subset of the platitudes that flourished at Mme Straus's. Anti-Semitism traffics in mindless stereotypes, and so did the banter of her *fidèles,* even and often at her and her husband's expense. Seconding Degas's gibes about Moreau's ornate aesthetic, Jean Lorrain quipped that the latter's paintings, several of which hung in the Strauses' salon, appealed to Jewish collectors "because of all the jewelry." Goncourt declared that Straus "admirably incarnated the very physical type of the satanic lorgnette merchant." This recycled an old anti-Semitic chestnut, lampooned by Gustave Flaubert in his *Dictionary of Received Wisdom* (*Dictionnaire des idées reçues*): "Jews: Sons of Israel. Jews are all lorgnette merchants." Flaubert's point in restating such bromides was to show how trite and imbecilic they were. Proust agreed, and was stunned that authors as accomplished as Goncourt and Lorrain apparently did not.

NOT ALL THE LANGUAGE LESSONS in the entresol were this dispiriting. From Mme Straus's patrician friends, Proust became attuned to the oddities of pronunciation governing a set of words particularly dear to his heart: family names. It fascinated him to discover that many old aristocratic names were not pronounced as they were spelled. The unwritten rules of noble speech styled Bisaccia "Bisac"; Broglie, "Broy"; Castellane, "Cast'lane"; Castries, "Castr"; Greffulhe, "Greffoy"; Rohan, "Rouen"; Talleyrand, "Tahl'rahn"; d'Uzès, "d'Uzay"; and so forth. Certain élite place-names invited this secret-handshake treatment as well. The realm of the late Comte de Chambord, for instance, was pronounced "Frozhdorf," the first syllable rhyming not (as both French and German phonetics would dictate) with "rose" but with "loge" or "doge."

These minute distinctions sensitized Proust to unsuspected layers of complexity and richness. Aesthetically, such improbable pronunciations as "Broy" and "d'Uzay" contained an element of the poetry Proust found in so many noble names, rooted in the sediment of *la vieille France* and suffused with the crepuscular glamour of crumbling turrets and Merovingian kings. Developing this idea in the *Search*, he wrote,

> This manner of pronouncing words was a veritable museum of French history. [To hear someone speak of] "my great-uncle Feetjahm" was no surprise, for it is common knowledge that the Fitz-James are very proud of being French noblemen, and do not like hearing their name pronounced in the English way. Incidentally, one has to admire the touching pliability of people who used to think they were supposed to pronounce certain names phonetically, and all of a sudden, after hearing them pronounced [by an aristocrat] in a different manner, affect a pronunciation they could never have arrived at on their own. Thus the Duchesse [de Guermantes], whose great-grandfather served in the retinue of the Comte de Chambord, liked to make fun of her husband's Orléanism by proclaiming: "*We* old Frozhdorf types . . ." A new visitor [to her salon], who had previously always thought he was speaking correctly when he said "Frohsdorf," changed his tune immediately, and forever afterward could be heard to say "Frozhdorf."

Proust contemplated the social function of these minutiae in an unpublished manuscript fragment about an awkward Jewish social climber who, à la Vandérem, "says things nobody in the *monde* would ever say." With arch, La Bruyère–like worldliness, the narrator of this text asks rhetorically, "Does not the mere fact of pronouncing the 'i' in 'Castries' signify that one is a stranger to the monde?" But the irony of this observation extends to the observer himself—to Proust. After all, no more than Vandérem or any other bourgeois, had he grown up knowing to drop the "i" in "Castries." In consciously making this adjustment as an adult, Proust displayed the same "touching pliability" as the ignoramus who switches to "Frozhdorf" as soon as he realizes that is how duchesses say it.

Proust also learned to notice the sartorial details that further distinguished the cognoscenti from the rubes. Mme Straus's risqué hostess attire presented a calculated and daring exception to the rule of dressy formality that prevailed in other salons, not to mention among her own guests. Female visitors wore hats, gloves, and stylish floor-length day dresses, inflated around the hips by petticoats and a bustle and nipped in at the waist by a daytime corset (an article somewhat more forgiving than its rigid evening counterpart, although Laure de Chevigné preferred to forgo both garments). Male callers dressed in dark frock coats, matching or subtly contrasting vests and trousers, silk cravats, bouton-nières, gloves, and top hats. These last they doffed when entering the drawing room, placing them crown first on the floor by the doorway or beside their chairs. When performed by Charles Haas, this ritual disclosed a jaunty disc of green silk lining. But innovations like Haas's were not for the beginner, in whom any variation from the norm conveyed ignorance as opposed to flair.

Because ignorance meant inelegance, it drew harsh reprobation from the "born." Comte Léonce de Larmandie, whose socio-physiologies of the Faubourg inspired Élisabeth Greffulhe's, told of a petit-bourgeois Parisian who, having saved the life of a grand seigneur, earned an invitation to dine at the latter's house—and proceeded to alienate him forever by showing up dressed in black rather than white tie. Larmandie published this story in 1889, but it so haunted Proust that a full fifteen years later, he still felt compelled to err in the opposite direction, arriving in white tie for a luncheon at the country estate of his friend Armand, Duc de Guiche, only to find the rest of the company outfitted in shooting and riding apparel. A month or so afterward, as if to overwrite this gaffe, Proust swung to the other end of the fashion spectrum, sporting a casual bowler hat to Guiche's wedding in Paris. But this choice, too, was a flub: top hats were obligatory at *mondain* weddings. In a recently discovered film clip, a thin-faced, moustachioed figure historians have identified as Proust can be spot-ted hurrying out of the Madeleine behind the wedding party (Élaine Greffulhe was the bride), his unsuitable felt bowler bobbing alone on a tide of black silk top hats.

Style slipups dogged Proust from the very start of his *mondain* career. When first attending Mme Straus's at-homes on his Sunday furloughs from his army regiment in Orléans, he became painfully self-conscious about his standard-issue infantryman's uniform, which looked distinctly shabby in that setting. He once wrote to her to apologize for his "frightful" uniform jacket and to assure her that he would not reappear in her salon until he had something nicer to wear. In his own recollections of the entresol, Jacques Blanche remembered Proust in his ungainly army attire:

> I can still see Marcel in his soldier's uniform, his unbuttoned cloak and shako cap. What a strange contrast between his military uniform, which he was not wearing for the fun of it, and the dark hair and pure oval of his face, which made him look like a young Assyrian. . . . I can see Marcel now, perched on an ottoman, unconcerned about his two-day beard, knocking over a china cup as he helps pour the tea.

The painter also noted that Proust's hat always looked "like a Skye terrier or a hedgehog," covered in lint and brushed the wrong way.

Yet Blanche went on to say that once Proust's military service ended, he emerged from his uniform and two-day beard like a butterfly from its chrysalis. Gone was the scruffy cadet, to say nothing of the tortured misfit from the lycée Condorcet. In their place stood (or perched on an ottoman) a debonair "apprentice dandy," "dressed in a carelessly knotted green cravat, corkscrew trousers," with a camellia sprouting from the lapel of his frock coat. This was the Proust whose portrait Blanche painted in 1892, changing only the color of the sitter's tie (to white) and the type of flower (to an orchid). Despite the latter modification, Proust would always refer back to this phase of his life—his *mondain* twenties—as his "camellia period." According to Fernand Gregh, Proust took special pride in his exotic boutonnière, a stylish alternative to the failsafe white carnation, because it had been a gift from Lord Lytton.

Proust, twenty-one, called regularly at Geneviève's while on his weekly furlough from his military service.

Along with honing his fashion sense, Proust developed an eye for the subtle power plays that underpinned even the most banal-seeming social encounters. Princesse Mathilde Bonaparte, aka Our Lady of the Arts, furnished him with much material along these lines. By the time he first met her in the entresol, the sexagenarian princesse had long since lost the trim waistline of her youth—once her best apology for her piggy eyes and broad, doughy face. In its place she had acquired the sturdy rotundity of a peasant matriarch in the Bonapartes' native Corsica. While she dressed like a princess—in stiff satin confections typically involving a train and accessorized with a strand of egg-sized Tahitian pearls—her hearty physique suggested a woman who knew her way around a laundry mangle. At first blush, so did her manner. Proud of her fame as a patron to men of genius, the princesse liked to assure them that she didn't stand on ceremony. To the artists who frequented Geneviève's salon, as to those who still came to Princesse Mathilde's own Tuesday at-homes, the older woman thus made a great show of her "simplicity," sweetly reminding the bohemians that as a Bonaparte, she, too, came from parvenu stock: "Without the French Revolution, I'd be selling oranges on the streets of Ajaccio!"

But to watch the princesse closely was to see that her humility was a put-on, belied not only by her infamous statement about Dumas *père* ("I couldn't invite him because of his high birth, given that he was a half-black bastard"), but by her imperious attachment to the prerogatives of her rank. "Princesse Mathilde encourages a particular kind of groveling from [the rest of us]," wrote Henri de Régnier. "As a sign of respect, voices must be lowered and verbs conjugated in the third person, and [we must] happily oblige." Furthermore, when Régnier and his artist brethren went to greet her with the requisite *baisemain* (kiss on the hand), the princesse held her hand so low to the ground that as they bowed, their foreheads practically scraped the floor. By enforcing these rites of deference, she pulled rank among the very artists she purported to esteem.

The internal contradictions of Princesse Mathilde's "simplicity" exposed the disingenuousness of that classic *mondain* charade. The hypocrisy of the down-to-earth grande dame would become one of Proust's favorite themes when he wrote about the Faubourg, as in a scene in *The Guermantes Way* where the narrator remarks caustically upon "the curious happenstance whereby Mme de Guermantes's majordomo would always address her as 'Mme la Duchesse.'" This comment is ironic because the situation Marcel is describing has nothing to do with happenstance. It is the duchesse herself who insists that her domestic use her title, notwithstanding her oft-made assertion that she "believes only in intelligence" (and not at all in hereditary titles). And yet it would never cross her mind to question the "invisible force"—as Proust called it in his earlier sketch about the fictional Vicomtesse de Hainaut and her liveried staff—that compels the duchesse to wield the markers of her standing: "It would never have crossed her mind to urge the majordomo to call her 'Madame,' plain and simple. And whenever she gave him an errand to run for her husband, she would say: 'You will remind Monsieur le Duc that . . .'." Like her "elegance," Mme de Guer-

Geneviève, in black (fourth from *far left*) attended the 1889 World's Fair in Paris with a group that included Straus (to Geneviève's *immediate right*), Princesse Mathilde Bonaparte *(far left)*, Ludovic (third top-hatted figure from *right*), and Meilhac *(far right)*. Photograph by Gégé Primoli.

mantes's "simplicity" is a fiction, camouflage for the supreme importance she attaches to her ducal rank.

In time, Proust would come to identify this form of bad faith as one of Mme Straus's (and later, one of Mme de Chevigné's) most off-putting traits. But in Princesse Mathilde, the same characteristic didn't irritate him as much. This may have been because she was the first crowned head he ever met, and like any *mondain,* Proust was susceptible to the putative glamour of crowned heads. While his tenure in the gratin would eventually bring him into contact with many more royals, to the end of his days, he would speak of Princesse Mathilde with misty nostalgia as "my first highness."

In fact, he not only included this epithet in the *Search* (in a sardonic passage about how "Princesse Mathilde Bonaparte . . . didn't put on all the airs of a highness"); he also worked it into his first and last conversation with James Joyce in 1922, in a manner repellent to the Irishman. Afterward, Joyce grumbled that his fellow genius "would only talk about duchesses," although as Proust would have hastened to point out, Princesse Mathilde was not a duchess but an imperial highness. This was a distinction he had learned to make when he first met her in the entresol. He took pride in his acquaintance with a princely scion, even as he took note of the arrogance her "simplicity" did little to hide.

The third-person locutions the princesse extracted from Mme Straus's callers attuned Proust in a more general way to the intricacies of royal and noble address.* In "*Mondanité* of Bouvard and Pécuchet" (1893), he mined these byzantine subtleties for absurdist comic effect. Resurrecting his gift for pastiche, he imagined the eponymous duo of Gustave Flaubert's *Bouvard and Pécuchet* (1881), a dim-witted pair of petit-bourgeois polymaths, deciding they want to enter the monde. In Flaubert's satirical novel, the two men try to educate themselves on a crazy-quilt assortment of subjects, from medicine to child rearing and landscape architecture to occultism. But their "knowledge" is a mishmash of dubious information, half-baked opinion, and commonplace, and their every attempt to apply it comes ludicrously to failure. In Proust's parody, Bouvard and Pécuchet contemplate the ways and means of the noblesse and are likewise undone by their own irremediable haplessness.

The two friends begin their would-be social conversion by trying to work out how they ought to bow to the grandees of the monde: "With the whole body, or just the head? Quickly or slowly, stepping forward or staying in place? . . . Should the hands stay beside the body, hold the hat, be gloved?" They then rehearse other "debonair" attitudes with unintentionally silly results: "Bouvard leaned on the mantel, toying carefully, so as not to dirty them, with a pair of light-colored gloves he had brought just for that purpose, and addressing Pécuchet as 'Madame' or 'Général' to complete the effect." The pair's befuddlement mounts when they confront the problem of making introductions: "Whose name should be said first? Should one indicate the person one is naming with one's hand, or with a nod, or should one remain immobile, with an air of indifference?"

Their confusion reaches its farcical climax when Bouvard and Pécuchet broach the matter of "giving everyone his correct title," a topic so daunting that it soon forces them to admit defeat:

> One says "Monsieur" to a baron, to a vicomte, to a comte; but "Bonjour, Monsieur le Marquis," sounded flat to them, and "Bonjour, Marquis," too cavalier. They resigned themselves to saying "Prince" and "Monsieur le Duc," even though they found the latter usage revolting. When they came to Highnesses, they had trouble; Bouvard, flattered at the thought of all his royal acquaintances, imagined a thousand sentences featuring this appellation in all its forms; he uttered it with a small, blushing smile, bowing his head a little, and hopping about on his legs. But Pécuchet declared

---

* For more detail on the French conventions governing royal and noble address, see the Author's Note, appendix A at the end of this book.

that he would lose track, or get all muddled, or burst out laughing in the prince's face. In short, to spare themselves the hassle, they would avoid going into the Faubourg Saint-Germain.

While ridiculous on its face, Bouvard's and Pécuchet's decision to "avoid going into the Faubourg Saint-Germain" altogether highlights the exclusionary function that world's codes of elegance were expressly designed to play. Those codes were intended to intimidate and shame outsiders; they were meant to show up an unbridgeable divide between the d'Arenbergs and the Vandérems, the Jockey-Club and the Losers' Club.

In the final paragraph of Proust's pastiche, Bouvard and Pécuchet veer off on a contemptuous digression about the one social group that even they, as cloddish as they are, feel wholly entitled to scorn:

> As for the Jews, Bouvard and Pécuchet admitted that they hated being around them. They [the Jews] had all been lorgnette merchants in Germany in their youth. They all had hook noses, exceptional minds, and vile souls consumed only with turning a profit. Plus they formed some kind of vast secret society, placing their inexhaustible riches at the disposal of unnamed enemies, to a frightening and mysterious end.

As the conclusion to a send-up of *mondain* elegance, this litany of anti-Semitic clichés is not as much of a non sequitur as it may at first appear. For while Proust, like Flaubert before him, had no patience for such hokum, Mme Straus's other friends repeated it in earnest. In the entresol, one laughed at anti-Semitic slurs no matter what one's religion, for the simple reason that anti-Semitism was "elegant"; Jewishness was not.

If one were Proust, one's amusement was more equivocal. One laughed out of embarrassment, or self-loathing, or bogus nonchalance ("simplicity"). One laughed to seem like a good sport, or goy (as Proust was anyway by baptism, if not altogether by blood); or one laughed to keep from crying. But one also laughed, perhaps, out of an outrageous secret hope that someday, by the force of one's own implacable talent, one would consign the haughty to a losers' club all their own. One laughed to imagine just how little their elegance would help them then.

CHAPTER EIGHTEEN

OUR HEART

Paris in February was no place to get over the flu, so Lord Lytton was in Nice for a few weeks on doctor's orders, staying at the Hôtel des Étrangers in the Cimiez district in the hills above town. The sea air and sunshine were meant to restore his physical well-being; the previous May, he had had a tumor removed from his nose, and his health had been precarious ever since. (The Englishman's "snuff" habit was catching up with him.) But whatever their effects on his body, the tonics of the Riviera had yet to calm Lord Lytton's mind. And it was his mind that had been giving him the most trouble of late.

On February 16, 1890, in a letter to his wife's sister, Theresa Earle, he described his restive condition:

> I think I am as variable as a wind, and I certainly am conscious that I don't know myself. Indeed, I am a great puzzle to myself. All I know is that I have at least half-a-dozen different persons in me, each utterly unlike the other—all pulling different ways, and continually getting in each other's way—and I don't think anybody else knows all of them a bit better than I do myself.

As he didn't elaborate on the identities of these conflicting selves, Theresa Earle might have assumed her brother-in-law was referring to his two professional personae: His Excellency the Ambassador on the one hand, and Owen Meredith on the other. It was true that juggling his diplomatic and literary duties presented challenges, albeit necessary ones: Lord Lytton depended on the (modest) revenues from his book sales to help defray the (exorbitant) costs of running an embassy. Just in the last week, he told his sister-in-law, he had "recast and rewritten the greater part of *King Poppy*" with a view to publishing it as soon as possible. He confessed that in revising his magnum opus, he was trying not to fret too much about "the commercial fate of its publication, even if it should seem to fall stillborn."

But in fact, the commercial fate of his poem mattered a good deal to him. As a boy at Harrow, his schoolmates had branded him "Poor Lytton," and the nickname still applied. Although he tried to make light of his financial stresses—he had even named a favorite dog Budget, recently deceased—he was tired of being the poorest person he knew.

Theresa Earle might also have suspected a recurrence of her brother-in-law's infamous blue devils. For some time now, he had complained of feeling "tortured by the unbridgeable distance between [himself] and [his] ideals" and had ascribed his woes to the constraints of his diplomatic and *mondain* position. To his other closest confidante, his married daughter Lady Betty Balfour, he wrote,

> I feel like a wild bird in a poultry yard, and if now and then the cramped wings flutter under the coop, they are subdued at once by a perception of the unseemliness in such flutterings of a diseased personality.

Opium helped to still those flutterings, but its effects never lasted.

What Lord Lytton did not tell either Betty or Theresa Earle was that he had been discreetly paying court to two different married women in Paris, and the situation was growing untenable. While the two women, Geneviève Straus and Élisabeth Greffulhe, were not friends, their social circles overlapped enough that his duplicity seemed bound to come to the surface sooner or later. This prospect only aggravated Lord Lytton's malaise, but he knew better than to raise it with his daughter or his sister-in-law—they would have both taken umbrage on his wife's behalf.

Lord Lytton's trip to Nice may have complicated his love life further. He checked in to the Hôtel des Étrangers on February 7. Two days later, Geneviève showed up alone and took rooms there as well. Officially, she was spending a couple of months at the Prince's Palace in Monte Carlo with her old friend Alice de Richelieu, now Princess Alice of Monaco. Alice was preparing for her first ball as royal consort and had asked Geneviève to stay with her in Monte Carlo long enough "to help her with that dreary chore," as well as to attend a touring production of *Carmen,* starring Jean de Reszké as Don José. (To face the public at both events, Alice was going to need all the moral support Geneviève could give her, as Prince Albert had opted to take an extended honeymoon on his new yacht, the *Princess Alice*—all by himself.) But unofficially, Geneviève's trip to Monaco gave her the chance to tour the region unsupervised by her husband. While Straus had accompanied her on the journey to Monte Carlo, he was called back to Paris on a case just days after he and Geneviève reached the palace. His absence left Geneviève free to travel to Nice on her own, and also to make a twenty-four-hour stopover in Cannes.

Whether by coincidence or design, Guy de Maupassant, who had been sailing his own yacht, the *Bel-Ami,* around the Mediterranean since mid-January, also surfaced in Cannes and Nice during Geneviève's visits to both cities. While she was in Cimiez, Maupassant, too, put up at the Hôtel des Étrangers—despite the fact that when in Nice he usually stayed with his mother, who had a house nearby.

A conspicuous gap in Geneviève's correspondence while she was on the Riviera makes it hard to determine just what she did, when, and with whom. In February, she wrote to her aunt Nanine Halévy from Monte Carlo, relating her adventures as a houseguest in the Prince's Palace and pretend-complaining about its drawbacks: from its "very own Hall of Mirrors, aptly named because it is *freezing*,"* to a "terrifying bedroom where some or other Duke of York passed away" to the "marble- and porphyry-covered floors, where one is forever slipping and sliding about." Later that month, she sent Porto-Riche a cryptic note from Nice: "With any luck, things will all turn out fine." What those things were, and why they would need luck to "turn out," she did not explain.

Then her correspondence falls silent for six months.

However, a letter Élie Delaunay sent to welcome Geneviève back to Paris in March suggests that she had confided in him about having seen the earl on her travels. She may have made this admission when passing along Lord Lytton's praise for Delaunay's portrait of her, as the painter wrote, "My unhappy, velvet-eyed odalisque, . . . I am flattered that Lord Lytton should love my portrait [of you], but I think he is *damn* right to love the original even more!" Her cause for unhappiness remains another mystery, although her husband may have had something to do with it, as Paul Bourget wrote to her on March 18 to ask, "Has Straus managed to rein in his frightful temper?" Whether or not he knew anything about her assignation in the South of France, Bourget was clearly worried about the trouble Geneviève now faced at home.

Lord Lytton's correspondence offers even fewer clues as to what transpired between him and her in Nice. A few months beforehand, in one of his few extant letters to refer to Geneviève by name, Lord Lytton had described her as "a most intelligent and charming woman, daughter of Halévy the composer, and widow of Bizet the composer, whose opera of *Carmen* is all the rage." This correspondence, too, presents an approximately six-month gap after the trip to the Riviera, perhaps also due to strategic censorship after the fact. (In editing his letters for posthumous publication, Lady Betty Balfour suppressed any documents her father would not have wanted to be made public; this service, which Lord Lytton had likewise performed for his own late father, drew a veil over the earl's many indiscretions.)

But Geneviève's presence is discernible between the lines of Lord Lytton's other writings from this period. For instance, although he did not live to finish his satirical reworking of *The Wandering Jew,* he did complete an English-language adaptation of another of her late father's operas, *La Juive.* (Lord Lytton's version, entitled simply *The Play,* was never performed.) He also wrote fulsomely of the literary titans he encountered in her salon, voicing his preference for the "exceedingly witty, if shy, rather silent, clumsy-looking" Meilhac, whom he likened to "an awkward elephant with a wonderfully intelligent sensitive trunk."

Lord Lytton prized such connections and knew that in Paris, no one was better poised than Geneviève to help him make them. In England, his author friends

* In French, Hall of Mirrors is *Galerie des Glaces; glace* means "ice" as well as "mirror."

ranged from Charles Dickens to Robert Browning to Oscar Wilde; these associations gave Lord Lytton some reassurance that despite his aristocratic background and diplomatic career, his fellow authors took him seriously as an artist. (He had good reason to be defensive, as outspoken denigrators of his talent included his father, who had gone to his grave dismissing Owen Meredith as a plagiarist and a hack; of his son's friendship with Dickens, Edward Bulwer-Lytton had famously shrugged, "A cat may look on a king.") While serving as ambassador to France, Lord Lytton was hoping to win the respect of the nation's preeminent writers. He gravitated to the entresol as the ideal place to meet them.

Geneviève may also have inspired him creatively. Under his pseudonym, Owen Meredith, he composed a bittersweet love poem, "A l'entresol" ("At the Entresol"), addressed to a beguiling Parisienne with a "sorrowful look" in her "dark, deep, humid orbs" and a nervous "tremble in [her] cheek." The poem is written in English, but its French title alludes to its setting: the elegant drawing room of an entresol on the Right Bank, where the poetic speaker and his hostess spend a cozy evening alone. The contents of the salon recall those of Geneviève's own, whether "the brow of the great Voltaire" reflected in a "large and limpid mirror," the "little French beauty by Greuze," the "Leda, weighed over her white swan's back / by the weight of her passionate kiss," or the profusion of fresh-cut roses, "with their bells shut tight" against the winter chill outside.

In companionable silence with the lady of the house, the speaker stands at the windows of the salon, contemplating "the heaving Boulevard [that] flares and roars" below. Meanwhile, on the mantel behind him, "the flitting hand of the Time-piece" registers the minutes slipping by. This reminder that time flies stirs up mixed emotions in the speaker. At first, it makes him keen to seize the day with his sad-eyed hostess: "Ah well, / when time is flown, how it fled / is better not to ask or tell / . . . Let us kiss and break the spell!" Just as he is about to embrace her, though, he recoils, as the glint of her dark eyes in the firelight abruptly reminds him of a different salon, and a different *salonnière*. In the closing lines of "A l'entresol," he stops addressing his companion and instead makes a plea to his own heart, where another woman lives and reigns: "O my heart, how fearfully like *her* she seemed! / Hide me up from my own despair, / And the ghost of a dream I dreamed!"

These verses may show where the Mauve Muse's influence ended and a rival muse's began, for the ghost in Lord Lytton's dreams was not Geneviève, but Élisabeth. Six months before his trip to Nice, he had grown fed up with Élisabeth's mixed signals and summarily put an end to their relationship. His effort to break free of her had not, however, quashed what he had once described to her as the "incredible feeling that has enveloped me from the very first moment I saw you." Élisabeth continued to dominate Lord Lytton's emotional life long after he told her he wanted to be friends with her no more.

From his published correspondence, his daughter Betty posthumously excised all but one allusion to Mme Greffulhe (that "accomplished, pretty little lady of *la haute*"). But letters preserved in Élisabeth's archive reveal that Lord Lytton cut ties with her in late August or early September 1889, just after they had both vacationed in Dieppe without their spouses or children. She had not invited him to stay with her at La Case, leaving him to bunk in town at the Hôtel Royal (an extravagance he could ill afford). However, Lord Lytton had declared himself to her anyway, and it was her demurral that provoked their rupture. He took his leave of her with this curt dispatch:

> Given that you have both said and demonstrated to me that your feelings for me were of a purely intellectual nature, I must tell you that I overestimated my ability to pursue our relationship under those conditions.

Lord Lytton had then decamped to Trouville-sur-Mer, Geneviève's preferred haunt on the Norman coast, where columnists spotted him at the races and the casino with her and Meilhac.

Élisabeth had anticipated that sooner or later her English friend would force such a confrontation. But his decision to end their relationship outright shook her all the same. In October 1889, she rewrote their unconsummated love story as a pithy morality tale: "He loved her. She remained virtuous. He stopped loving her. The moral of the story: Love one another [*Aimez-vous les uns les autres*]." Here again, she reflected on the resentment that had simmered beneath Lord Lytton's gallantry, remembering how at the lowest point of her despair over Giovanni, the earl had been "the first to notice when my complexion started to look dull; he would have *liked* to see me old, ugly, atrocious. A peculiarity that set his love apart from everyone else's."

Since their fateful last meeting in Dieppe, Lord Lytton had stayed firm in his resolve never to see Élisabeth again, except at big *mondain* crushes where they could avoid each other without attracting undue notice. Even so, he had been unable to stop writing to her, confessing to her in one letter that winter that all it took was "a single line, a single word, a single thought to reawaken my all-consuming passion for you." "Reawaken" was a misnomer—his longing for her never really went dormant. At best, it merely ebbed for short stretches of time. Whenever it came over him again, he found that the only way he could appease it was by giving vent to it on paper.

One such text is a fanciful character sketch of Élisabeth that she didn't receive until after Lord Lytton's death. Cited here in condensed form, and originally written in French, it begins and ends with the assertion that she haunts him:

> I write to speak to you of a vision that has been haunting me so obstinately that its smallest minutiae seem closer and more real to me than do the dirty streets of London, where everything looks so sad this evening.

The vision is of a young woman. . . . She is a lady and even a queen to the tips of her fingers, although she is also very much a woman. But she bears no more resemblance to other women than a princess in a fairy tale does to the princesses whom one sees every day.

Her outfit tonight is an exquisite sort of pink *déshabille;* . . . its floating, diaphanous folds envelop the beautiful contours of her svelte and graceful figure in such an *atmospheric* glow that she looks like a cloud suspended on the rosy beams of a fading sunset. . . .

From time to time an adorable little foot, shod in a pink silk slipper and encased in a pink silk stocking, flits out from beneath the undulating cloud, . . . disappearing and reappearing, like a dove attached to the person of an unseen goddess!

The proprietor of this little foot seems lost in thought . . . ; her big brown eyes—deep, wild, enigmatic eyes—wear the far-off expression of a doe that stops in the forest and listens, affrighted, to a distant echo audible to her alone. A doe that would never be at home except in a forest, and transformed by a magic wand into a princess who would never be at home except in the world of princesses. . . . This woman is made of pure poetry; she is a poem unto herself. . . . She turns prose into poetry and poetry into music.

Now let the mocking little demon that sometimes nestles in the corners of her beautiful mouth entreat her not to make fun of this hasty, unfinished sketch of the vision which haunts the dreams of

—R. Earl of Lytton, London, Sunday evening, August 4, 1890

The date of this document is telling: by the time Lord Lytton wrote it, almost a year had passed since their ostensible parting of ways. But still he pined for Élisabeth, the ghost who gave him no peace.

Some part of Lord Lytton must have been hoping that, sooner or later, his strategy of avoiding her in person but continuing to pay court to her in writing would induce her to seek him out again, perhaps even, someday, surrendering to his love. All hope of such an outcome would have evaporated, though, had she learned of his parallel flirtation with Geneviève. On more than one occasion, Lord Lytton had assured Élisabeth that his feelings for her "made it utterly impossible for him to have anything whatsoever to do with any other woman, or even to desire any other woman." Based on what he had gleaned from her and Breteuil about Henry Greffulhe's harem, Lord Lytton knew that Élisabeth was hypersensitive about infidelity. She would never forgive Lord Lytton if she found out that while purporting to love only her, he had also been chasing the Widow Bizet.

And yet, chase Geneviève he did. Reports in the society press indicate that in the months after their return from Nice, the bond between her and Lord Lytton grew stronger. Whereas previously Geneviève had received invitations only to the largest of the British Embassy's parties (which up to two thousand people might attend), she now enjoyed frequent, intimate lunches there with just the ambassador and a few other guests. Lord Lytton chose the other invitees to these gatherings—the daytime equivalents of his erstwhile dinners with Élisabeth and Breteuil—from among Geneviève's faithful, singling out his personal favorites in the group: Meilhac, Halévy, Dumas *fils,* Hervieu, Bourget. But Geneviève's own preferred escort was Maupassant, whom the Englishman did not like at all. (A romantic to his core, Lord Lytton decried Maupassant's ruthlessly cynical portrayal of the relations between the sexes.) By conscripting Maupassant into her lunches at the hôtel Borghèse, Geneviève enmeshed Lord Lytton in a second, unsustainable love triangle—one that had him vying with the novelist for her fickle attentions.

Maupassant's activities at the time confirm this development. He started work on his second novel about the gratin, *Our Heart* (*Notre cœur,* 1890), after he got back to Paris from the South of France in March 1890; Ollendorff published the book on June 20. The three months Maupassant spent writing *Our Heart* coincided with his forays to the British Embassy on Geneviève's arm. He lunched there with her and Lord Lytton for the first time on March 12 and for the last time three months later. That April, Maupassant made a short, secret journey to Rouen, where he wrote to his friend Robert Pinchon that he was "not alone, but don't breathe a word to anyone about my trip. It must stay shrouded in mystery because the woman who has come here with me has a jealous husband." He identified this woman neither in his letter to Pinchon nor anywhere else in his correspondence. Writing to Geneviève later that spring, however, Maupassant alluded to "the Rouen voyage" as if it were a secret the two of them shared.

Based, moreover, on his confidences to Porto-Riche, it would appear that Maupassant and Geneviève had their first and only sexual encounter shortly before he completed his last round of revisions to the manuscript of *Our Heart.* According to Gégé Primoli, summarizing Porto-Riche's account, Geneviève had been so "disgusted by Maupassant's brutality" in bed that afterward she told him she "never wanted to submit to a second experience." This incident, Porto-Riche told Primoli, had become the basis for Maupassant's new novel:* "Having left

---

* The fact that Geneviève's first sexual experience with Maupassant also turned out to be her last may have saved her from catching syphilis, although not long after their supposed assignation, she did develop two symptoms that Maupassant suffered from as a result of his disease: migraines and debilitating eye pain. Geneviève's mental illness also worsened markedly in the years that followed; this development, accompanied by a newfound terror of being locked away at Dr. Blanche's clinic, culminated in a suicide attempt during World War One. Because of her long history of neurasthenia, however, it is impossible to ascribe her psychological decline conclusively to syphilis.

him famished after she had aroused his appetite," Geneviève gave him the inspiration for *Our Heart*. Once Maupassant completed that novel, his contact with her dropped off precipitously.

LIKE *STRONG AS DEATH*, *OUR HEART* relates the sub rosa amours of a vain and vapid *mondaine* with a conspicuous resemblance to Mme Straus. This second portrayal is even more damning than the first. While Any de Guilleroy is an adulteress, and while her shallowness severely impairs her capacity for real love, she at least has the integrity to care for only one man: Olivier Bertin. By contrast, the heroine of *Our Heart*, Michèle de Burne, toys with multiple suitors while feeling nothing for any of them. A widow in the "final flowering of her mature beauty," she was married at a young age to "a demanding, jealous, even violent master, . . . one of those domestic tyrants before whom everything and everyone must yield, and with whom she was most unhappy." In addition to bullying his wife, à la Straus, the late M. de Burne "trained her to be a polished, elegant hostess, almost a slave" to his own *mondain* ambitions. When he died of an aneurysm five years into their marriage, Michèle de Burne vowed never to let another man control her.

In her widowhood, Michèle has developed a loyal following of artists, clubmen, and financiers. Her flirty disposition and "unpredictable, vivacious wit" have made her "the idol, . . . the fetish, . . . the human goddess" of this "cult of adoring men"; their worship provides the "incense [that] exalts and deifies her."

Our Heart opens with the first visit by the protagonist, André Mariolle, to Michèle's entresol, escorted by his friend Massival, a famous composer who is a regular there. Mariolle is a handsome, athletic, rich, and artistic thirty-seven-year-old bachelor for whom the opposite sex holds few surprises. It excites him to meet a woman so hell-bent on preserving her independence. Having been warned by Massival that her *fidèles* have all tried and failed to seduce her, he sees her as an irresistible sexual challenge. Over the next several months, he pays court to her by letter, and eventually, she yields to him.

But she turns out to be an ice-cold lover, balking at any further physical contact with Mariolle after their first sexual encounter. When visiting him in his *garçonnière*, she acts as if she were paying a routine social call. Rebuffing his advances, she prefers to talk about banalities: her newest fashionable outfit, her latest social triumph, the foibles of her *fidèles*. These unsatisfying rendezvous impress upon Mariolle that what his mistress offers him is a mere "simulacrum of tenderness," and that Michèle herself is a mere simulacrum of a woman.

Yet perversely, the more she eludes his touch, the more Mariolle's "ferocious, insatiable appetite" for her grows. His torment reaches new heights when she starts up a flirtation with Comte Rodolphe de Bernhaus, a "charming, well-spoken, excellently distinguished" Austrian diplomat. Though relatively new to Paris, Bernhaus is already the toast of the Faubourg, where he enjoys "celebrity akin to Sarah Bernhardt's." Michèle, who like her late husband is obsessed with her *mondain* status, eagerly pursues the comte as the "crown jewel" of her salon, and Mariolle learns from her other *fidèles* that she and Bernhaus may be carrying on an affair in secret. This information sends Mariolle into a tailspin, driving him to flee to the countryside, where in the book's closing pages he seeks comfort in the arms of an adoring peasant girl. But even then, he cannot escape the thought of his coy mistress. The end of the novel finds Mariolle making love with his peasant girl but pretending to himself that she is Michèle de Burne, the woman without a heart.

To readers who knew Geneviève personally or by reputation, Maupassant's fictional siren seemed like a barely disguised depiction of her. As Goncourt, who like many Parisian literati rushed to read *Our Heart* as soon as it came out, wrote on July 5,

In Mme de Burne of *Our Heart* Maupassant has painted the portrait of the modern-day Parisian *mondaine:* he took Mme Strauss [*sic*] as his model. . . . Yes, Geneviève is indeed the heartless, pitiless, thoughtless man-eater that is Mme de Burne; in her little group of friends, that has ever been her role. Consider how she treats Meilhac!

In fact, Maupassant *had* considered how she treated Meilhac—and had skewered the relationship in the book. The most abject of all Michèle's vassals is the shambolic "fat Fresnel," a "tubby, wheezing, boring, beardless old windbag whose only merit, disagreeable to everyone else but essential in her eyes, was to love her blindly, better, and more than anyone else." In *Our Heart,* this Meilhac clone dogs Michèle's every step, hopelessly pining for her all the while. His groveling ubiquity so annoys her other admirers that they brand him "the Seal" (presumably a reference to his body type rather than to the obscure erotic specialty of Adhéaume de Chevigné's ex-mistress). When the *fidèles* reproach her for "her condemnable, selfish, and vulgar taste" in flunkeys, "Mme de Burne smile[s]: 'I love him like a devoted old uncle.'" This was Geneviève's standard self-justification when her friends groused to her about Meilhac.

No evidence survives to suggest that Meilhac read *Our Heart,* or that if he read it, he saw himself in "the Seal" and Geneviève in Michèle de Burne. However, several of her other intimates reached the same conclusion as Goncourt. In a family album, Daniel Halévy wrote as a caption to a photograph of his aunt: "Mme Straus—here she is—the heroine of *Our Heart,* by Guy de Maupassant." Atypically, Daniel did not take this opportunity to reiterate his harsh opinion of his kinswoman's character: "as egotistical as a monster and as unthinking as a doll." Maybe he thought that simply identifying her with Michèle de Burne made Geneviève's flaws clear enough. Daniel's mother, Louise, was more outspoken in her distaste. Again according to Goncourt, she went around town

Geneviève playfully adjusts Meilhac's boutonnière.

proclaiming high and low that "in Geneviève's place, I would be revolted, I would be *indignant* with Maupassant!" Another friend chided Geneviève for her alter ego's unfeeling treatment of Mariolle. "It's exactly what men deserve!" countered Geneviève, her reaction lending further credence to the view that Mme de Burne was her Doppelgänger.

Lord Lytton weighed in on *Our Heart* as well but voiced a dissenting view. "Mme Straus is said to be the heroine of a novel by Maupassant, which I think horrid, called *Notre cœur*," he wrote to an English friend. While omitting to mention the numerous similarities between Bernhaus and himself—a "charming, well-spoken, excellently distinguished" diplomat of Sarah Bernhardt–level renown*—Lord Lytton declared that Geneviève was "not at all" like Mme de Burne.

As for Straus, he may not have been as ready as Lord Lytton to give Geneviève the benefit of the doubt, although here again, there is some uncertainty as to what transpired. What is known is that a week after the release of *Our Heart*, Maupassant, Geneviève, and Lord Lytton had their final lunch together at the British Embassy. After that, all three of them left town for the summer, while Straus stayed behind to work on a lawsuit Maupassant had asked him to bring against a publisher for reproducing a portrait of him without his permission. (As he ranted to Straus in June, Maupassant could not stand the sight of his own face in bookstore windows; he found all photographs of himself "detestable.") Geneviève spent the month of July in Normandy, where she joined Laure de

---

* Educated at the University of Bonn, Lytton spoke fluent German and had been posted to the British Embassy in Austria earlier in his career. Also, because "earl" is the British equivalent of the French title "comte," the *presse mondaine* sometimes referred to him as "le Comte de Lytton."

Chevigné at the races in Deauville and scouted properties for sale in nearby Trouville-sur-Mer. Then, accompanied by Meilhac and Delaunay, she went on a spa cure at Bagnères-de-Luchon, a picturesque watering hole in the Pyrenees. She stayed for the whole month of August and the first three weeks of September, residing at Luchon's top hotel, the Sacaron. Supposedly Geneviève was there to receive treatment for her migraines, a new addition to her panoply of ailments.

This time around, Maupassant seemed to go out of his way to avoid Geneviève on his travels. When she headed north to Trouville, he journeyed south to Nice and Aix (where he met Dr. Adrien Proust, in town on a business trip, through a mutual friend—news that greatly excited Marcel). When Geneviève went south to Luchon, Maupassant moved north to his beach house in Étretat. Lord Lytton, meanwhile, returned home to England for a few months, his wife and younger children having settled for the summer in a cottage on the grounds of Knebworth, the Bulwer-Lyttons' ancestral estate in Hertfordshire. (To offset the carrying costs of the property, Lord Lytton had found tenants to rent the main house.)

But by August 4, he was in London by himself—this was when he wrote the sketch of Élisabeth Greffulhe cited earlier—and by the end of the following week, after a three-day stopover in Dieppe, he had relocated to the Hôtel de Sacaron in Bagnères-de-Luchon, also without his family. Like Geneviève, he stayed in Luchon until late September.

With Meilhac, Delaunay, and Lord Lytton to keep her company, it is unclear

In the summer of 1890, Geneviève and Lord Lytton were both ostensibly in Bagnères-de-Luchon to take the waters at its well-known thermal spa.

whether Geneviève was expecting her husband to join her in Luchon. Anticipated or not, though, Straus turned up at the Sacaron sometime after August 5 and before August 27. And at some point between those two dates, Geneviève wound up with a broken nose.

Geneviève's gap-ridden correspondence resumes briefly during her sojourn in Luchon, in the form of four letters to her aunt Nanine Halévy. In the longest of these, dated August 27, Geneviève explained that while attempting to drive a horse-drawn buggy herself, she had tumbled from the driver's seat and landed face-first on the ground. Afterward, true to form, she played the accident for comic effect, joking that perhaps it would qualify her to join the circus "as a female 'human cannon.'"

Less typical was the defensive note on which Geneviève concluded her letter: "Émile isn't hiding anything from you, I swear! You will see my nose in its entirety!" This statement implies that Nanine had voiced some doubt as to the veracity of Straus's account of his wife's injury. Given his reputedly savage temper, it is possible that Nanine suspected him of having harmed Geneviève and then inventing the accident as a cover story.

If Straus was responsible for Geneviève's broken nose, then the question remains as to what specifically prompted the assault. *Our Heart* itself would not likely have been the immediate cause for provocation; for as Maupassant's attorney, Straus would have been thoroughly familiar with the novel—and with the resemblance between its heroine and his wife—well before he arrived in Luchon in late August. (Straus's correspondence with Maupassant suggests that

While in Luchon, Geneviève and Lord Lytton stayed in this hotel, both leaving their spouses at home.

he made a point of reading his client's books.) However, it may be that finding Lord Lytton staying in the same hotel as Geneviève opened Straus's eyes to the possibility of a real-life basis for the romance between Michèle de Burne and the Comte de Bernhaus. If that were the case, then Straus's suspicions could have erupted in a rage, and if his rage turned violent, then afterward he may have tried to misrepresent to Nanine the real cause of Geneviève's fracture.

Whatever occurred between the Strauses in Luchon, domestic violence was one of those unseemly matters that elegant society preferred not to acknowledge; even with a broken nose, a *mondaine* was expected to put a pretty face on any such unpleasantness. So it is possible that Geneviève was playacting when she returned to Paris and declared to all and sundry her "immense satisfaction at having been painted in Maupassant's book." According to Goncourt, "Mme Strauss [*sic*] has gone around repeating until she is blue in the face that Maupassant has never written anything better" than *Our Heart*. "Mme S.'s entourage feels she has no cause to be proud of [Maupassant's] portrait of her," Goncourt commented drily, yet for Geneviève, the mere fact that Maupassant had made her the heroine of his novel seemed amply to justify her delight.

"Mme S.'s entourage" was indeed appalled. Again finding fault with Geneviève's morals, one *fidèle* griped that "the women in society who have a taste for *common* men . . . like Maupassant . . . are Jewesses who only want to whore themselves out to men of celebrity, in order to raise their own profile by association." Porto-Riche, who had a falling-out with Geneviève at around this time, expressed his disapproval as well, sniping, "Little does she care about the character's morality, or lack thereof; little does she care about the heroine's virtues or vices; all that matters is that the heroine be famous, and conflated with *her*!" Without naming her outright, Porto-Riche took his cousin to task for her vanity.

While such criticisms were by no means unfounded, Geneviève's friends may have misread her reasons for claiming to admire *Our Heart*. Precisely because she cared so much about how she was perceived, she may have felt as though she had to go into raptures over the book. Even if the characterization of Michèle de Burne had upset her, letting her distress show would only have done her further harm. She had a reputation to uphold, not just as a virtuous wife (and widow) but as a model of elegance, a breaker of hearts, and a muse nonpareil. For her to voice any misgivings about *Our Heart* would have been to admit her embarrassment and pain. Such an acknowledgment would have undermined the image she worked so hard to project.

Critics and scholars tend to consider *Our Heart* one of the weakest texts in Maupassant's oeuvre. The plot is slight, the dénouement unsatisfying, and the characters two-dimensional and trite: the jealous lover, the unfeeling tease, the country girl with the heart of gold. Several commentators have attributed these flaws to the fact that the symptoms of Maupassant's syphilis grew significantly worse while he was working on *Our Heart*. In March 1890, he complained to his father that reading or writing even a few lines "awakens intolerable pain in my eyes." He also suffered from debilitating migraines. Both of these conditions now also plagued Geneviève.

During this period, Maupassant's mental health deteriorated as well. To Paul Bourget he confessed,

> One out of every two times I walk into my house, I come face-to-face with my double. When I open the door, I see myself already sitting in my armchair.

Perhaps this hallucination may have explained Maupassant's inordinate hostility toward his own likeness, as in the unauthorized portrait he had directed Straus to block. But he had other delusions, too. He claimed the pills one of his doctors had prescribed "spoke to him with their little voices, offering advice, dictating sentences better than anything he had ever written." He excoriated François Tassart, his loyal valet of almost ten years, for having "written to God to accuse me of sodomizing a chicken, a goat, etc." He accused another domestic of stealing "first 70,000, then 4 million, then 6 million francs" from his personal savings, and he ranted about needing to dig holes in which to hide his "millions and billions and trillions." In a pitiful resurgence of his *mondain* pretensions, he ordered all servants in his employ to address him as "Monsieur le Comte."

But the most heartrending testament to Maupassant's psychological decline is a fragmentary letter he drafted in June 1890, addressed to an unnamed woman who may or may not have been Geneviève:

> My senses are swelling up inside me and poisoning me as bile poisons the bilious. But if I could spit them out, then maybe they would evaporate and I would be left with a light and joyful heart, who knows? Thinking is an abominable torment when one's brain is nothing but an open wound. I have so many gashes inside my head that my ideas can't move around without making me want to scream. Why? Why? Dumas would say it's because I have a bad stomach. But I think it's because I have a poor, proud, shameful heart, a human heart, that old heart that everyone laughs at, but that feels things and hurts, and in my head too it hurts, I have a worn-out, Latin soul. And then there are some days when I don't think like this but I suffer all the same, because I belong to the family of the flayed. But I don't say this, I don't show it, I even cover it up rather well, I think. No doubt I come across as the most indifferent of men. I am a skeptic, but that's not the same thing, I am a skeptic because my eyes are open. And my eyes say to my heart: "Hide, you grotesque old thing," and it hides.

Writing *Our Heart* under these conditions, Maupassant was perhaps bound to fall short of the high standard he had set with his previous work. Only Geneviève tried to claim that he had triumphed once again.

After the release of his novel, Maupassant's physical symptoms grew even more severe, forcing him to stop working altogether; *Our Heart* would be the last book he ever published. For the rest of the year and throughout the following one, Maupassant pursued a haphazard regimen of medical cures and pleasure cruises, but his disintegration proceeded apace. On December 31, 1891, he wrote to one of his doctors to announce that a self-prescribed course of nasal lavages had flooded his head with so much saltwater that he could

> feel my brains dripping from my nose and mouth in a gluey paste. Death is nigh and I'm insane! My mind is beating a hasty retreat. Good-bye, friend, you will never see me again.

The next night, January 1, 1892, Maupassant tried to shoot himself in the head. Upon pulling the trigger he realized that François Tassart, to guard against just such a scenario, had removed the bullets from his gun. So Maupassant then grabbed a letter opener and raked it beneath his chin, crying out as blood gushed from the wound: "Look what I've done, François, I've slit my throat: *it is a clear case of madness!*"

Tassart called for a doctor, who arrived in time to stitch up the gash before Maupassant bled to death. The doctor sedated the novelist and then, assisted by a burly sailor from the crew of the *Bel-Ami,* forced him into a straitjacket. Before Maupassant could harm himself any further, he was carted off to Dr. Blanche's clinic in Passy.

Gégé Primoli later told a sad story about his friend's breakdown:

> When they came in to fetch Maupassant to take him away to Dr. Blanche's, the poor man, who was all strapped down, with tears in his eyes, begged his minders to bring him to the seashore to take a last look at "the boat so dear to his heart" [the *Bel-Ami*]. Don't . . . these touching farewells to the confidant of his dreams recall those that Lohengrin addressed to his swan when he was about to quit the land of the ideal to grapple with the rock of reality?

But Maupassant would never grapple with reality again. For the next year and a half, as an inpatient at Blanche's sanatorium in the hôtel de Lamballe, he did battle only with the figments of his own deluded imagination: insects that stung him with morphine "from a distance"; "a ball of cholera" rotting in his gut; an angry mob determined to kill him "because I burned down my own house!" It did not help that his quarters in the *hôtel*—room number 15, "decorated in the

Florentine style"—looked out across the Seine. Every day until the day he died, Maupassant had to stare down his nemesis on the opposite riverbank: the Eiffel Tower.

During Maupassant's internment, Geneviève traveled to Passy repeatedly to check on him, but the staffers at Dr. Blanche's clinic turned her away every time at the patient's mother's behest. Upon learning of her son's collapse, Laure de Maupassant's first reaction had been to try to strangle herself with her own hair—an act that raises interesting questions about the etiology of Guy's erotic hair fixation. Like mother, like son: Laure de Maupassant survived her suicide attempt—a medic saved her by cutting the thick braid she had tugged into a choke hold around her neck. Once she had regained her wits (or at least her voice), she notified Dr. Blanche that under no circumstances should any female visitors be allowed to see her boy. In her estimation, women lay at the root of all his problems. It is possible she put herself in that category as well. In the eighteen months Maupassant spent at the hôtel de Lamballe, his mother never once went there to see him.

Unbeknownst to Laure de Maupassant, Gégé Primoli and Georges de Porto-Riche entertained a similar hypothesis about her son's breakdown, though they pointed the finger at just one woman. They speculated that with her enervating wiles, "the delicate heroine of *Our Heart* . . . may have hastened the fatal crisis" that had laid the novelist low. Had Porto-Riche and Primoli brought their theory to François Tassart, they might have found validation in the evidence he had been independently gathering about his master's demise. He blamed the tragedy on an unfeeling vamp he identified only as "the lady in grey."

Maupassant hated the Eiffel Tower, describing it as a "gigantic, disgraceful skeleton" and a "tarted-up boiler."

Since the publication of Tassart's memoirs, generations of scholars have debated this woman's identity, focusing chiefly on (and ruling out) the possibility that it was either Lulia Cahen d'Anvers or Marie Kann, the two "countesses of Judea" who had so often made a game of humiliating Maupassant. But these commentators have all managed to overlook what a careful study of Tassart's recollections strongly suggests, which is that Geneviève was the lady in grey.

In his memoirs, Tassart describes the mystery woman as a "bourgeoise of the greatest chic," always dressed in hues of dove or pearl grey and always "perfumed to excess, yet she is *not* a cocotte." (This observation recalls Delaunay's gripe about Geneviève's overuse of Peau d'Espagne, Daniel Halévy's reference to her "outrageously perfumed" self-presentation, and Goncourt's description of her as a "pseudo-cocotte.") In Tassart's account, this woman's other distinguishing traits are her "very good manners" ("as if she had been educated in [a] convent"), her "surprising intelligence," and a peculiar glaze in her eyes, potentially an effect of morphine use.

Tassart reports that the lady in grey turned up for the first time at Maupassant's flat in the rue Boccador on May 18, 1890, the approximate chronological midpoint between the author's assignation in Rouen in April and the publication of *Our Heart* in June. From the outset, Tassart found it odd that the grey lady should call at his employer's "'official' residence" rather than at the *garçonnière* where Maupassant typically conducted his love affairs. On many more occasions in May and June, the woman again eschewed Maupassant's love nest for the apartment in the rue Boccador, and the sexual reticence this maneuver implied may, the valet surmised, have accounted for "the great pain" she was causing his employer. On the eve of Maupassant's departure for Aix in June, the novelist confessed to Tassart that he wanted to "get away from 'the lady in grey' at all costs."

A hiatus ensued, consistent with Maupassant's and Geneviève's nonoverlapping travel itineraries in the summer and early fall. But the lady in grey resumed her visits to the rue Boccador in February 1891, just when Maupassant and Geneviève renewed contact with each other. The novelist dined with her alone at the entresol on February 15 and made plans to go with her and Laure de Chevigné to the Chat-Noir later that month. Then the documentary trail goes cold again until August, when Maupassant and Geneviève both went to Lake Geneva to take the waters. She rented a villa at Évian-les-Bains, while he checked in to a spa at Divonne-les-Bains, which boasted a special hydrotherapy treatment for patients with acute eye problems.

Writing to Aunt Nanine from Évian in early September, Geneviève mentioned that Maupassant had recently "given [her] a two-day tour of Divonne." This detail conforms to Tassart's notation that the lady in grey visited his master there. According to Maupassant's own correspondence, he went to see Geneviève at least once in Évian, on September 4. A few days later, he returned to Évian to escort her to a party at the Villa Bassaraba, the Princesse Brancovan's lake-side palazzo, where Geneviève flirted up a storm. Remarking on her "coquettish dress . . . strewn with lilac flowers," a society reporter compared "the daughter of the great Halévy" to "a flirty heroine straight out of [Eugène] Scribe" (her late father's collaborator on *La Juive, The Tempest,* and *The Wandering Jew*).

Shortly before they were to leave Switzerland, Tassart wrote, Maupassant negated the curative benefits of his treatment by "riding for hours in the blazing sun all the way from Divonne to the gates of Geneva, to call on the Baronne de R. at Pregny." (The château de Pregny, owned by the Rothschilds, was Gene-viève's home away from home on Lake Geneva.) When Maupassant reached the castle, the baronne and her friends had gone out, leaving no word as to where he might find them. Tassart believed that this futile expedition harmed his employer irreparably, in body and in mind. Once again, the manservant sus-pected foul play by the grey-clad siren and concluded that she had to be "made of marble" to toy with Maupassant so cruelly.

With foreboding, Tassart predicted that this woman's games would be the end of his employer—a forecast Maupassant came close to realizing with his suicide attempt four months later. According to the valet, it was a telegram from the lady in grey, sent "from the Orient," that triggered Maupassant's frenzied burst of self-harm. Indeed, when the fateful telegram arrived in Cannes, Lulia Cahen d'Anvers and Marie Kann were in France, not the Orient. But Geneviève was in Alexandria with Ludovic, visiting Thérèse Prévost-Paradol, the daughter of his late half-brother, Anatole. Thérèse had entered a Catholic convent there after her father's suicide in 1870 and had recently been promoted to mother superior.

MAUPASSANT DIED at Dr. Blanche's facility on July 6, 1893, a month shy of his forty-third birthday. The doctor told Goncourt that by the end, Maupas-sant had "become *animalized* [*sic*]," and was "hopelessly insane." His last words were: "The shadows! The shadows!"

In the flippant spirit of Geneviève's salon, Léon Daudet punned that Mau-passant had "passed badly" [*maupassa*].

He was buried in Paris two days later. Geneviève attended the funeral; Straus did not. At Émile Zola's initiative, and with funds contributed by the Roths-childs, a monument to Maupassant's memory was erected in the parc Monceau, not far from the entresol. Sculpted by Raoul Vernet, it depicts the novelist in the company of a fin-de-siècle temptress markedly reminiscent of Geneviève. Dr. Max Nordau, a pundit whose best-known work, *Degeneration* (1892), explored the relationship between moral depravity and genius, left a telling description of this double portrait in stone:

> On a chaise longue . . . a woman reclines languorously, amidst a fetching disorder of cushions. Her every trait bears the stamp of authentic Parisian

The monument to Maupassant features an unnamed woman
with a notable resemblance to Geneviève.

elegance. . . . Her feet, which poke out coyly from beneath her dress, are
clad in embroidered silk stockings and high-heeled mules. The dress, a
housedress, is richly trimmed in lace. . . . M. Vernet has taken great care
to render these "underthings" because they furnish, as it were, the SYM-
BOLIC MEANING [sic] with which he wants to imbue both the figure
of the woman and the monument as a whole. The Parisienne with the
tantalizing "underthings" and the witty [sic!] shoes holds in her hands,
rather nonchalantly, a book . . . sprung from Maupassant's imagination.
Behind her stands a bust of [the man] himself, frighteningly lifelike with
its low forehead, . . . its short, thick nose, its bushy moustache, its vulgar,
brutally sensual mouth. . . . Maupassant stares fixedly at the woman—not
at his novel in her hands, not at her hands either, but lower down, at her
expressive feet, and especially at those underthings that seem to promise so
much. M. Vernet's work . . . tells a tale of erotic hypnotism, of the power
of feminine seduction.

While aptly conveying the strangeness of the statue, Nordau commits a subtle error. He writes that Vernet's Maupassant gazes raptly "not at his novel" but
at the silk-stockinged vixen who holds it. This phrase rests on a tacit distinction
between the book and the woman. But for the author of *Our Heart,* in the
throes of his fatal folly, they just might have been one and the same.

PAVANE

PAIR-BONDING

We will silence their clucking! We will soon be their slaves!
It is always the same! It is always like this!
We love one another! We hate one another!
We curse those we love!

—GABRIEL FAURÉ, Pavane, op. 50 (1887), dedicated to Élisabeth Greffulhe;
lyrics by Robert de Montesquiou

The phoenix, a wonderful but solitary bird, . . . fed on perfumes, lived
in the purest regions of the air, and terminated his brilliant existence on
a funeral pyre of fragrant wood, whose flames were kindled by the sun.
But doubtless, he had more than one occasion to envy the fate of the
white dove, because she had a companion like herself! I would not make
you better than you are; you are all too conscious of the impression you
produce; you intoxicate yourself with the perfumes and incense that are
burnt at your feet. You are an angel in many respects, but a woman in
others.

—PIERRE-SIMON BALLANCHE to Juliette Récamier (c. 1805)

CHAPTER NINETEEN

IN WHICH PROUST IS
DISAPPOINTED

By the time Maupassant died, Mme Straus had fallen substantially in Proust's estimation. How much he knew about her entanglement with the novelist is a mystery, for by a maddening fluke, the single biggest gap in Proust's twenty-two-volume correspondence coincides with the sad dénouement of the Geneviève/Maupassant affair. From the entire year of 1890, only two of Proust's letters seem to have survived, one of them a brief note to his father, where he indulges in a little shy bragging about how the famous Guy de Maupassant "must know more or less who I am" and the other an even briefer note to Mme Straus, accompanying a bouquet of chrysanthemums. A letter Jeanne wrote to him in 1891 indicates that Proust and his mother were trading opinions about *Our Heart,* but his opinions cannot be extrapolated from her text. From 1891 and 1892, a total of four of his letters appear to be extant, and while three of the four, perhaps tellingly, are addressed to Mme Straus, none of them makes any allusion to Maupassant, Lord Lytton, or even Émile Straus. They do, however, make it possible to trace a distinct evolution, or diminution, of Proust's feelings for the Mauve Muse.

In the first letter, dating from around Easter 1891, Proust subtly compared himself to Petrarch and Mme Straus to Laure de Noves by pointing out that he considered Good Friday a kind of anniversary in their relationship, because that was when Mme Straus had written to him for the first time (yet another missing document), captivating him with her "strangely moving" handwriting. By indirectly drawing an analogy between himself and Petrarch and Mme Straus and "la belle Laure," Proust suggested that he had high hopes for the inspiration his friend's mother would provide him.

A year later, those hopes had waned. Sometime in the spring of 1892, Proust wrote Mme Straus a letter that began as a courtly homage but quickly turned into a personal attack:

Madame,
I love mysterious women, because that's what you are, and I have often said so in *The Banquet,* where I often wished you might recognize yourself. But I can no longer completely love you, and I am going to tell you why. . . . One generally sees you with twenty other people, or rather one

sees you *through* twenty other people, because it is always the young man who is kept at the greatest distance [from you]. But even supposing that one should manage, after many attempts, to see you alone for a change, then you have only five minutes to talk, and even during those five minutes, you're thinking about something else. Even worse, if one speaks to you about books, you find one pedantic; if one speaks to you about people, you find one indiscreet or nosy; and if one speaks to you about you, you find one ridiculous.

That Mme Straus had hurt his pride is clear, whether by placing him at "the greatest distance" from herself in company or by appearing distracted when he managed to get her alone. But Proust was also growing weary of her "pretty precepts against bad form," which led to such dull and pointless conversations. He was too sharp and curious by far to be content with idle chitchat, especially when talking with someone he felt certain could do better.

In his third letter from this sequence, Proust sketched a sly, double-edged portrait of his addressee:

"The Truth about Mme Straus"

At first, I thought you loved only beautiful things, and that you understood them very well—then I realized you don't give a toss about them. Then I thought you loved only People, [until] I figured out that you don't care a whit about them either. Now I think you love only a certain lifestyle, one that shows off not so much your intelligence as your wit, not so much your wit as your social graces, and not so much your social graces as your clothes. [You are] a person who loves this sort of lifestyle above everything and everyone else—and [yet you] are charming all the same. And it is because you are charming that you must not gloat and conclude that I love you any less. To prove to you that the opposite is the case (because you know that actions are more effective proofs than words—you who are all words and no actions), I would send you the most beautiful flowers—which would annoy you, because you do not deign to look favorably on the sentiments with which I have the painful ecstasy of being, of Your Sovereign Indifference, the most respectful servant,

Marcel Proust

Had Geneviève had access to Daniel Halévy's journal, she might have been struck by the similarity between this faint-praise panegyric and the kiss-off letter Proust had sent her nephew and son in high school, insisting that he still liked the cousins even though they weren't as smart as he had once hoped. In "The Truth about Mme Straus," only the content of Proust's critique has changed, as he tags her not with stupidity but with the same character flaws Maupassant ascribes to the heroines of *Strong as Death* and *Our Heart:* frivolous values, flimsy charms, and empty promises ("all words and no actions"). For Proust, his passions always on the knife edge between rapture and abasement, there is a "painful ecstasy" to the discovery that he has been prostrating himself before a false idol. In this case, it is not that the empress has no clothes; it is that her clothes are all she has.

That Geneviève's calamitous involvement with Maupassant sparked this epiphany seems a fair possibility, if only because of how much time Proust spent in her salon while the whole messy drama was unfolding. After all, the debacle surrounding *Our Heart* led at least one other *fidèle,* Georges de Porto-Riche, to decide that Geneviève was irredeemably shallow—and as Proust would later realize, "*I am Porto-Riche!*" But even if Proust knew nothing of Geneviève's love affairs, the increased familiarity he gained just by hanging around the entresol may have been enough to foster his contempt. As Maupassant had stressed in his last two novels, but as Proust could also see for himself, all those lessons in elegance showed the teacher in a most unflattering light. Petrarch had never gotten near enough to Laure to be let down by her defects, whatever they were. Seen for who she was, Proust's goddess lost her heavenly aura.

FORTUNATELY, PROUST HAD ALREADY LEARNED from Geneviève's son and nephew that the collapse of a dream could be a fruitful alternative source of creative inspiration. Sometime in 1892, he investigated this notion by writing a fairy tale about disenchantment. What follows is a synopsis of the story (all quoted language is Proust's): "Once upon a time, there was an "obscure youth" called Percy. He lived alone in a humble dwelling, commensurate with his humble origins. In fairy-tale society—which is to say princely society—Percy was no one special, despite the moniker he shared with the Romantic poet Percy Bysshe Shelley, one of his creator's new favorite authors."

But in Proust's writings, names are always destiny. Accordingly, Percy's poetic name called for a poetic fate. One day two fairies, Beauty and Fame, decided that they wanted to do something special for him. So they waved their magic wands and filled Percy's mind "with the most splendid visions of fame and of beauty"—visions in which he soared high above the circumstances of his ignoble birth. As they had hoped, their protégé reveled in his imaginary powers. Eager to conquer a beautiful highness (the ultimate prize in fairyland), he summoned Cleopatra herself to share his modest table, and she consented to join him. More than that: she made a habit of doing so. "Drawn to her conjuror's splendid mind, the queen regularly accepted his invitations." In the world into which the fairies had spirited him, everything else about Percy's life became similarly grand. His simple abode turned into "a palace, and two-bit trinkets, into priceless treasures."

That his reveries squared ill with the actual conditions of his existence never bothered Percy until one day, when he was in his early twenties,

> his vanity asked to have a brief sit-down with him. In this conversation, [Percy's vanity] told him: "The fairies have duped you, my friend. They have given you a taste for Fame and for Beauty—they have given you dreams of fame and beauty—but they have not given you Beauty and Fame as such."

By way of an example, his vanity pointed out that Percy had invested his ideal woman with "graces she probably never had to begin with" and that the youth's absorption in fantasy had blinded him to the disdain with which not only queens but perfectly ordinary women treated him in real life: "Even Madame X, who is none too difficult to possess, and who has lovers much less worthy than you are, would turn her back on you should you dare to speak to her of love."

Stung by these observations, Percy called upon Fame and Beauty. With honeyed words that "fell like large pearls on their luminous flesh," he implored them to make his splendid dreams come true. He specified that he would like to have a queen for a mistress—a flesh-and-blood replacement for Cleopatra—to avenge himself on the snobbish Madame X. With sorrow in their eyes, the fairies explained that they could grant his wish, but at a cost: once they did so, they would vanish from his life forever. When Percy, determined to show up Madame X, agreed to these terms, Beauty and Fame bade him a sad farewell: "Good-bye, dear boy, the spell is broken, but we must oblige you."

And so they did. The next day, Percy inherited a princely fortune, and a château to go with it. He also met a gorgeous queen who fell instantly in love with him—"defying all logic, she entreated him to go to bed with her." As Percy had hoped, Madame X was sick with jealousy.

As the fairies had cautioned, however, the realization of our hero's wishes broke the very spell that had made those wishes enticing in the first place. Rather than live happily ever after in his castle with his queen,

> Percy was surprised to find that he no longer desired the beautiful princesses [*sic*] whose charm had once seduced him so, when they only existed in his dreams. Now he found them mediocre; the more he got to know them, the more their allure faded. Their power was no longer something rarefied, intoxicating, and mysterious.

After this, Proust's narrative breaks down, devolving into such jumbled fragments as "the flower despoiled by his hand, which clutched with too much effort when he plucked it" and notations like "STraus/STandish," suggestive if unexplained.

Proust never completed Percy's tale, and he never published it. Yet its basic premise never left him. He would spend the next three decades writing and rewriting variations on this theme: the unreachable muse whose charm evaporates upon contact. The flower plucked, then despoiled. The swan that comes crashing to earth.

In the nearer term, Proust would have to go hunting for a new rare bird.

LAMENT

OISEAUX TRISTES

Once upon a time,
There was a princess, who was captive bound
In an enchanted tower beside the sea:
And when that princess from her tower looked round,
Nothing beneath her, nor above, saw she,
But waves, and clouds, and birds. . . .
She thought that she was, too,
A bird herself. And to the birds one day,
"O sisters, take me with you far," she sighed,
"Away from here!" "Put forth thy wings," said they.
She spread her arms, and drooped them, and replied,
"I cannot! Oh, for wings to fly away!
Wherefore to me alone are wings denied?
And wherefore was I made the only one
Of mine own kind, to live and die alone?"
"Princess," said a bird to her, "thou art not
Of all thy kind the only one. Far, far
Away from here, there is a distant spot
Beyond the sea, where other birds there are,
Like thee. No visible wings those birds have got,
Yet I have heard them many a time declare
That by a single word to them is given
A power that can lift them into Heaven."
"What is that word? O tell it me!" said she.
"Tell it I can," replied the little bird,
"But if I do, 'twill be no use to thee . . ."
"Tell me the word!" "It is I-love-thee." Then
The princess became pensive. But she muttered

That word I-love-thee o'er and o'er again,
And every time that to herself she uttered
The sound of it, she sighed: and strangely, when
She sighed, her little bosom heaved and fluttered.
"To none can I that sweet word breathe," sighed she,
"And none will ever breathe it back to me!"

—OWEN MEREDITH (pseud. Edward Robert Bulwer-Lytton,
Earl of Lytton), *Glenaveril, or The Metamorphoses* (1885)

The birds of the sea are sad,
They are crying, they say:
We shall no longer drink
The water of the sea,
Because it is made of our tears.

—ÉLAINE GREFFULHE, *The Book of Amber* (*Le Livre d'ambre*, 1887–1889)

CHAPTER TWENTY

DEAD LOVE, STILL UNDYING

Concerning her romance with Lord Lytton, the truth about Mme Straus is difficult to pin down; once again, the paucity of extant sources shrinks the field of the knowable. After their time in the Pyrenees, another sizable hole opens up in the correspondence of both friends, almost as if they were in league with each other (as well, impossibly, as with the young Marcel Proust). The gap in Geneviève's letters stretches from September 1890 to August 1891; in Lord Lytton's, from December 1890 to May 1891. Only one clue survives, but it is a good one: an undated, unpublished note to Geneviève that scholars have previously failed to attribute because it is signed merely "L.," even though it is unmistakably written in Lord Lytton's hand, on writing paper engraved with his family crest. In this short missive, he says that the unspecified, "unhappy news" of "the lady from Luchon . . . pains me greatly," and he proposes that they discuss it "at the house of my Serene Neighbor—at whatever time you wish." (The neighbor mentioned here was in all probability His Serene Highness Prince Auguste d'Arenberg, whose mansion in the rue de la Ville-l'Évêque stood at five minutes' walking distance from the hôtel Borghèse.) Lord Lytton closes by asserting that no matter what happens in the aftermath of the Luchon lady's ordeal, he remains her "very, very, *very* devoted" admirer.

That devotion took on a different quality, however, after the duo returned from their summer vacation. Various contemporary memoirs and press accounts indicate that beginning in the fall of 1890, Lord Lytton and Geneviève discontinued their private lunches at the British Embassy and stopped appearing together at social functions. (Before the trip to the Pyrenees, they had frequently been spotted together in the monde.) That these changes occurred right after the interlude at the Hôtel de Sacaron may support the conjecture that Straus broke Geneviève's nose in response to finding Lord Lytton there. Such a catastrophe could quite plausibly have induced the (illicit) couple to part ways, and the historical record, such as it is, suggests that this is what happened.

But their relationship did not end altogether. Once back in Paris, Lord Lytton still made occasional visits to the entresol. On its face, this might seem to contradict the premise that he and Geneviève had had to part ways to pacify Straus. But as old hands at the game of *mondain* appearances, the two friends would have known that a formal rupture, signaled by Lord Lytton's abrupt disappearance from her salon, would only stir up gossip about what had caused it. Those readers of *Our Heart* who had recognized Robert, Earl of Lytton in Rodolphe,

Comte de Bernhaus would be especially quick to put two and two together. Had they done so, then scandal would have ensued, exposing Geneviève to the risk of further reprisals from "Straus the Tiger." It was thus a safer course by far for Lord Lytton to keep up some semblance of normalcy among the faithful.

This shadow play preserved for Lord Lytton, Geneviève, *and* Straus the superficial benefits each of them drew from the association. As a jealous husband, Straus would hardly have relished seeing his rival in Geneviève's drawing room, but as a social climber, he would have hated to strike such a prestigious name from her guest list. For her part, Geneviève, ever insecure as to her acolytes' loyalty, had the satisfaction of knowing that the earl hadn't abandoned her entirely, while Lord Lytton, symmetrically insecure about his reputation as an author, got to keep his honorary place among her esteemed literary *fidèles*.

At least on the surface, then, the love triangle had resolved itself fairly pleasantly—more bedroom farce than *Othello*. Not unlike Michèle de Burne's "simulacrum of tenderness" for Mariolle, the Strauses and Lord Lytton upheld a facsimile of friendship, even having an off-site reunion in April 1891, when they all found themselves in Monte Carlo as guests at the Prince's Palace. Princess Alice must have warned Geneviève ahead of time—the two of them were too close for her not to have known something of the Lord Lytton drama—and perhaps the two men were prepared for the encounter as well. If any tensions flared during the visit, no direct evidence of it survives. The only indirect evidence is a group photograph of the Monacos and Strauses in which Lord Lytton declined to appear. But this recusal may have had more to do with his own marriage than with Geneviève's; when he wrote to his wife from the palace, he gave her to understand that he was the Monacos' only houseguest. Perhaps Edith, too, needed reassurance that her spouse's extramarital flirtation was over.

LORD LYTTON PAID HIS LAST CALL at 134, boulevard Haussmann in the autumn of 1891, when his friend Oscar Wilde, in Paris for a few months to work on his French-language play, *Salomé* (1893), requested an introduction to the fabled Mauve Muse. The visit did not go well, albeit through no fault of Lord Lytton's. Wilde miffed his hostess from the first by greeting her as "Madame Straus," the form of address for a social inferior. In the effusive welcome he received from a pretty little fop named Marcel Proust ("Say, monsieur, isn't it more beautiful than the *Mona Lisa*?"), Wilde incorrectly discerned a sexual advance; he would later realize his mistake in an incident embarrassing to them both. He paid a patronizing compliment to Degas: "You know how well-known you are in London," only to have the painter strike back: "Fortunately less so than you." Both Degas and Joseph Reinach were openly disgusted by what Lord Lytton himself might have termed Wilde's "*très* ladylike" mannerisms.

Afterward, Reinach teased Geneviève that her tolerance for homosexuals would be the ruin of her salon. "They don't hunt the same prey as we do," she parried, "so where's the harm?" Although this particular "invert" hadn't charmed Geneviève, his growing fame inclined her to act as if he had. As Wilde's notoriety increased over the next several years, culminating in his sensational trials, conviction, and imprisonment for public indecency in 1895, his cameo at the entresol became ever more central to the myth of Mme Straus. In this context, her "friendship" with Britain's most controversial living writer became yet another sign of her far-reaching influence. Geneviève even liked to hint that Delaunay's portrait of her had inspired *The Picture of Dorian Gray* (1891)—which was impossible, as the book had appeared six months before Wilde's first visit to her salon.

Had she read *Dorian Gray*, Geneviève might have thought twice about proclaiming a kinship between its antihero's portrait and her own. In Wilde's novel, the eponymous picture manifests the inner ugliness of its superficially beautiful subject, presenting an image of Dorian Gray's corrupt, degenerate soul. More incidentally, but just as pertinently to Geneviève, a friend of Dorian's cautions him against "women who wear sentimental colors" in tribute to the men they love, specifying, "Never trust a woman who wears mauve." Given Geneviève's mauve-based, explicitly sentimental mode of dress, this adage was not one that was likely to have pleased her.

Then again, maybe these aspects of Wilde's novel wouldn't have discouraged Geneviève from claiming a role in its genesis. It is quite possible that she took the same attitude toward *Dorian Gray* as she had toward *Our Heart,* prompting Porto-Riche to scoff, "Little does she care about the character's morality. [A]ll that matters is that the [protagonist] be famous, and conflated with *her*!"

It was certainly the case that after returning to Paris from Luchon, Geneviève chased the limelight more assiduously than ever. In the autumn and winter of 1890, she was a ubiquitous presence on the *mondain* circuit. (If Degas had been inclined to tease her in the same terms he used with Charles Haas, he might have called her a "Wandering Jew" as well.) In addition, Geneviève redoubled her efforts to present herself as the public face of her father's and her late husband's legacies. In October, she sat front and center at the opening of a new production of *La Juive*—an event that may have marked the beginning of the young Proust's lifelong fascination with that opera. Shortly thereafter, the campaign to erect a Bizet monument in the lobby of the Opéra-Comique went into high gear, culminating in gala performances of *The Girl from Arles* in November and *Carmen* in December. Geneviève did not involve herself in the planning of these events, but her name featured prominently in the advance publicity for them both. With her symbolic blessing, both productions drew standing-room-only crowds.

These events constituted new high points in Geneviève's career as a public figure. At the premieres, she attracted as much attention as any of the other celebrities present, on or off the stage. This was a particularly impressive feat at

Carmen, where the two internationally famous leads, Jean de Reszké and Australian diva Nellie Melba, stood as the equivalents of music-world royalty; while in
the audience, loyal Princess Alice of Monaco represented the real thing. (Proust
was thrilled to be included in this star-studded gala, albeit relegated to a low-
status "man's spot," standing up at the very back of Mme Straus's loge.) Other
grandees in the box seats included the Duc d'Aumale, the Duchesse d'Uzès, the
Prince de Sagan, Comte Robert de Fitz-James, Comte Albert de Mun, Comte
Adhéaume de Chevigné (without Laure but with his new American friend James
Gordon Bennett, the flamboyant, Paris-based owner of the *New York Herald*),
and the expected battery of Rothschilds. But the uncontested queen of the evening was Geneviève—or rather, the Widow Bizet. For the opening nights of
both *Carmen* and *The Girl from Arles,* she traded her customary grey, white, and
mauve half mourning for all-black ensembles, evoking her widow's weeds in the
Delaunay portrait.

More than a decade had gone by since Geneviève had posed for that painting,
and up close, her face continued to betray both the passage of the years and the
ravaging effects of her opiate dependency. But from a distance, she looked as if
she had stepped right out of Delaunay's canvas, art come to life. Even Édouard
Drumont, who hated Straus, and Geneviève by extension, reluctantly admitted
that her appearance at the *Carmen* premiere was a triumph—"an apotheosis of
the Widow Bizet," he conceded, "in her black lace and black velvet." The Bizet
monument itself further burnished Geneviève's image as the keeper of Bizet's
flame. The statue was the work of Alexandre Falguière, who had approached the
commission rather as Vernet did in the Maupassant monument, choosing to represent his subject not as a solitary artist but as a man in a woman's thrall. Beside a
relatively diminutive bust of the composer, Falguière sculpted a full-sized statue
of Bizet's anointed muse. At first glimpse, this figure appears to be Carmen, clad
in her exotic "gypsy" wear. But her face is unmistakably Geneviève's. Yet again,
the latter's love affair with a genius was enshrined in stone, immortalized in art.

The completion of the Bizet monument postdated the publication of *Our
Heart* by several years. However, Falguière's creation may have helped attentive
readers make sense of an otherwise inexplicable detail in that book. A minor
character called Prédolé—invited to Michèle de Burne's salon because of his
growing renown as one of the greatest sculptors who ever lived—admires an
"altogether modern group sculpture" displayed on her mantel. When Prédolé asks her who made the statue, she says Falguière, and then she bursts out
laughing for no apparent reason. To Maupassant's contemporaries, Prédolé was
a ringer for Auguste Rodin, brilliant but notorious in Parisian society for his
gauche attempts to engage his hostesses in earnest discussions about art. (This
may explain why Rodin never hit it off with Geneviève, and why he hit it off
very well with Élisabeth Greffulhe.) The fact that the Rodin character in *Our
Heart* has an invented name, whereas Falguière is identified by his real name,

Through her involvement in a campaign to have this monument to Bizet installed in the lobby of the Opéra-Comique, Geneviève promoted her image as the Widow Bizet.

throws the reference to the latter artist into high relief. So does Michèle's unexplained laughter when she mentions him. Because there is nothing intrinsically funny about Falguière's name or art, she seems to be chortling at an in-joke between herself and her real-life counterpart—who was also, of course, a collector of that sculptor's work.

DECOUPLED FROM GENEVIÈVE, Lord Lytton maintained a social profile as low as hers was high. "Paris is just now a complete solitude," he wrote on September 20. It was a solitude of his own choosing, interrupted by a bare minimum of public appearances. In October he went to see his friend Sarah Bernhardt in *Cleopatra* (1890), an overwrought commercial drama by Victorien Sardou, and called on her at home the next day to say how much he had enjoyed the play (although he had not). Lord Lytton also hosted an "informal" lunch for the Prince of Wales at the Hotel Bristol—Bertie selected the location, preferring its plush ultramodern comforts to the creaky grandeur of the hôtel Borghèse—and attended a séance with Henri de Breteuil's lady friend, Laure de Chevigné. The soothsayer failed to notify Laure that she was about to lose a lover to a foreign woman for the third time in five years: on March 3, 1891, Henri de Breteuil, forty-three, would wed Marcellita Garner, twenty-three, the orphaned heiress to a multimillion-dollar "bleachery" fortune in Wappingers

Falls, New York. If the séance yielded any other occult messages, for Laure or Lord Lytton, neither of the pair committed them to paper.

These outings aside, Lord Lytton stayed put in the embassy, "passing all of my afternoons and evenings at home, with a minimum of cigarettes," and with Budget's successor, a bear-sized Great Pyrenees dog named Goblin, snoozing at his feet. His daughter Betty commented with alarm on his "condition of almost constant pain, . . . physical suffering, [and] mental depression." November 8, 1890, marked Lord Lytton's fifty-ninth birthday. He would live to see his sixtieth, but only just.

From Lord Lytton's perspective, the one advantage of his infirmity was that it allowed him to turn over most of his day-to-day ambassadorial responsibilities to his wife, Edith, who enjoyed such work, and to focus instead on his writing. He was still tinkering with *King Poppy*, to which the *presse mondaine* irksomely but consistently referred as *King Pappy*. The project that came to consume most of his attention in the final year of his life, however, was a cycle of lyric poems called *Marah* (1892). Rife with arcane literary allusions and untranslated snippets of Latin, the book did not have the makings of a best seller. But as he told Theresa Earle, "No man who writes with an eye to popularity or to please a present taste ever produced a great work in *poetry*. The poet must please himself."

While the subject of *Marah*, "an ill-starred, unhappy passion," was not exactly pleasing, it preoccupied the poet utterly. On Christmas Day 1890, Lord Lytton griped to Theresa Earle "that (apart from Tennyson and Browning . . .) our contemporary English poetry is marked by a singular absence of either passion or sentiment." Yet as he saw it, that dearth made no sense, least of all in lyric poetry. Ever since Petrarch, Lord Lytton told his sister-in-law, that genre had existed to voice the "strong emotions" that were "branded into [the poet's] own inmost consciousness, [and] fetched by himself, at his own cost, out of the dimmest region" of his heart.

Pursuing the same line of argument with his daughter Betty, he wrote, "A certain element of personal emotion seems to me indispensable to the truth of all love poetry." However unhappy and ill-starred the passion he sought to express in *Marah*, it was Lord Lytton's own innermost truth, and it had only intensified since his quasi-separation from Geneviève. He felt it like a pair of hands closing around his throat, squeezing the air from his windpipe and hurling him, in the words of Owen Meredith, "down into the breathless blue cone of the night." Lord Lytton's abiding passion for Élisabeth was the fire that burned his skin and the chill that froze his blood. It was his benediction and his curse, his virtue and his crime, and if he couldn't capture it in writing, then maybe his father had been right: he had no business calling himself a poet.

With *Marah*, Lord Lytton had set himself a daunting task. As he "became more and more absorbed in its composition," Betty Balfour observed, "he felt with an acute pang . . . the irremediable antagonism between himself and his circumstances." Although Lord Lytton frequently bemoaned the "antagonisms" that kept him forever at war with himself, he described this one to Betty not, as he did in other contexts, as a conflict between his public and private identities but as a mismatch between his high ambitions for his art and his limited ability to realize them. He worried that he lacked the genius necessary to convey all the complex shadings of his love. In writing to his daughter, he did not add that that love was itself an irremediable antagonism and that its internal contradictions were what made it so challenging to convey.

In one of the early *Marah* poems, "Idolatry," the speaker declares that "to love is to create, down here below / A god on earth." Yet because "naught perfect is on earth, . . . / The god on earth created / Is but a half-divine, half-devilish one; / A god half loved, half hated." The topos of adoration fraught with hatred recurs in "Twins." Cut from the final version of *Marah,* this text shows the speaker torn between "a woman that I hate, . . . / In all her intimacies pure of taint, / In all her conduct carefully correct— / A social saint" and "a woman that I love . . . , / Neither saint nor sinner, / But a wild creature unashamed of truth." At the end of the poem, he reveals that the two women are one. *Odi et amo* (I hate and I love) indeed: Élisabeth had been right to construe Lord Lytton's attachment to her in those terms, for it was to her that *Marah* was secretly addressed.

Lord Lytton told Betty he had drawn this title from John Bunyan's Christian allegory *The Pilgrim's Progress* (1678), which contrasts Marah, "the waters of bitterness," to Beulah, "the pleasant land," and in which the titular pilgrim travels from the former, associated with the world of mortality and sin, to the latter, "beyond the Valley of the Shadow of Death, and out of the reach of Giant Despair." *Marah,* he explained, would reverse this trajectory. Over the course of the volume's four cantos, the poetic speaker would find himself driven farther and farther away from redemption and into woe—a spiritual journey inspired not, as in Bunyan's text, by God but by the speaker's "pagan idol," the lady he both worships and reviles. Though seeking paradise in his beloved, the speaker would wind up in hell instead.

In keeping with the mutable logic of such antitheses, though, no sooner had Lord Lytton begun his work on *Marah* than his acrimony toward Élisabeth changed into its opposite. At some point before the end of the year, the two friends reconciled. "Oh darling, darling!" he wrote to her. "The days I don't see you, don't hear from you, and don't know where you are nor what you are doing, nor how you are feeling, these are dark days for me." According to biographer Anne de Cossé-Brissac, Élisabeth's great-great-granddaughter, this note dates from the autumn of 1890. Its language suggests that Élisabeth and Lord Lytton had by this time resumed not only communicating but meeting with each other on a regular basis. When this turnabout happened or what precipitated it is unclear, though the earl added to *Marah's* first canto a poem, "Telepathy," relating how the mere locking of eyes with his ex-love across a crowded room instantly restores their passionate bond: "And then your glance met mine midway / Across the chattering crowd; / And all that heart to heart can say / Was in that glance avow'd."

Lord Lytton's only documented encounter with Élisabeth that season took place in December at a skating party in the Bois de Boulogne, where he joined his wife, Edith, and their teenage daughter Constance; Élisabeth was there alone. But it is possible the two of them reconnected as early as the séance Lord Lytton attended with Laure de Chevigné in October; Élisabeth's date book from this time mentions several such gatherings, which were then gaining popularity among the more open-minded (or gullible) members of their set. The occult had appealed to Élisabeth ever since Mimi's death, and Lord Lytton, who maintained that Knebworth, his ancestral house in England, was "haunted by an apparition called the Yellow Boy," shared her interest. If his rapprochement with Élisabeth did occur at a séance, then the title "Telepathy" may have been a private joke, a coded reference to the backdrop for their truce.

The Prince of Wales's luncheon at the Bristol, also in October, presented another occasion when Élisabeth and Lord Lytton might have reestablished their ties. As the woman who "made the clouds rain and the sun shine" for Bertie in Paris, Élisabeth would have been an obvious choice for the guest list (which Lord Lytton withheld from the media at the prince's request). She would moreover have accepted the invitation with alacrity, and not simply because she never refused a royal summons. That fall Giovanni Borghese was back in town, evading rumors in Rome about his family's looming bankruptcy, and Élisabeth had resolved to lure him away from his intimate friend Ferdinand by flaunting her own high-placed admirers. In other words, she would have eagerly attended the luncheon for the Prince of Wales, if for no other reason than because he outranked Bulgaria's prince regnant.

That winter, Élisabeth also trained her sights on a second crowned head: Kaiser Wilhelm II of Germany, the son of Bertie's beloved older sister, Princess Vicky. Although Élisabeth had yet to meet him, the kaiser, thirty-one to her thirty, had fascinated her ever since his accession two years earlier in 1888. In the photographs she had discreetly collected since then, she found the German ruler most distinguished-looking and decided he would make a superb addition to her stable of admirers. (Half a century later, she would reach a similar conclusion about Benito Mussolini, also without knowing him.) In her emotional chess game with Giovanni, the kaiser could become an invaluable pawn. Or more accurately, a king.

"As you know," she wrote to Guigui early in the New Year, "I have long been looking for a way to make myself known to Wilhelm II," and thanks to the Prince of Wales, she had found one. Élisabeth had learned from Bertie and Breteuil that Vicky—the Dowager Empress Friedrich to her subjects in Prussia—planned to visit Paris in February, but incognito, as the government of her son, the kaiser, still hadn't formally recognized the Third Republic. Realizing that even incognito, the Dowager Empress Friedrich would require a certain standard of elegant hospitality on her trip, Élisabeth offered to hold a top-secret tea party for her in the rue d'Astorg.

It was just the opportunity Élisabeth had been looking for. To Guigui, she exulted, "My doing this favor, *which is really a diplomatic mission,* for His Majesty, . . . will ensure that He *never forgets me!*" Better yet, she continued, "I have asked if Giovanni—'my first cousin'!—might receive with me," Henry having refused to host for political reasons. (Now lampooned in the press as "the founder of the Sabine women's party," he couldn't risk the added controversy of being seen to fraternize with a German royal.)

To bring off her tea without a hitch, Élisabeth would have had to coordinate behind the scenes with the embassy of her guest's native England. In this context, the timing of her truce with Lord Lytton may not have been accidental. Whether or not she had other motives for reconciling with him, the ambassador's help would be indispensable in bringing off her plan to welcome the dowager empress—and by extension, to charm the kaiser and make Giovanni jealous.

Lord Lytton knew nothing of Élisabeth's hidden agenda, and for a few giddy months, the rapprochement had him walking on air. He told Betty that he now intended to give *Marah* a happy ending, transforming the "ill-starred, unhappy passion" of the early pages into a "serene and felicitous affection" in the final canto. He even changed the volume's title to *Marah and Beulah* to indicate that the poetic speaker, like Bunyan's Christian pilgrim, would progress from abjection to joy.

In "Absence," toward the end of the first canto, the speaker reiterates his complete dependence on his ladylove: "Unlit by you, no light have I, / A fainting lamp that's fed by none! / The earth seems left without a sky, / The sky without a sun. / Come back! Come back!" And so on. Along with "Her Portrait" and a few other poems and letters (including the earlier, doe-turned-princess essay), Lord Lytton put a copy of "Absence" aside to have sent to Élisabeth after his death. These texts would serve to remind her that he had never stopped loving her and that he had written *Marah and Beulah* to prove it.

Given all the misery he had already suffered at Élisabeth's hands, Lord Lytton may have sensed that he was opening himself up to more of the same. In "Omens and Oracles," the speaker acknowledges the need for caution: "All the phantoms of the future, all the spectres of the past, / In the wakeful night came round me, sighing, crying, 'Fool, beware! / Check the feeling o'er thee stealing!'" Nevertheless, Lord Lytton disregarded his own advice, letting himself believe that this time around, things were going to be different between him and his beloved.

But as he discovered all too soon, Élisabeth had not lost her old habit of cutting him to the quick. Sometime in the months that followed the kaiser's mother's visit to the rue d'Astorg on February 24 (a triumph, Élisabeth reported to

Élisabeth collected postcards of Kaiser Wilhelm II, whom she had yet to meet but whom she hoped to impress with her beauty and *mondain* cachet.

Guigui, thanks to Giovanni: "The Empress chatted at length with the Panther, who was perfect; he tactfully said all the right things"), Lord Lytton and Élisabeth had another row, and this time, he worried the break was final. Crestfallen, he bewailed Élisabeth's "dreadful letter, with its heartless words," suggesting that this time around, she had been the one to instigate the rupture. This letter, too, has since been lost, and with it an explanation of why Élisabeth acted as she did. However, it is possible that after she had made use of Lord Lytton in carrying out her "diplomatic mission" for the kaiser, she had no further need of him. Her callous comment about Emmanuel Bocher—"DUPE! I will never love him, I just need him"—betrayed the utilitarian view she often took of her adorers. Maybe she "duped" Lord Lytton as well.

Certainly that would appear to be the case, judging by a letter she wrote that fall confiding in an addressee whose name is crossed out and replaced by "X":

> Lord Lytton writes me seventy-page letters and I can barely bring myself to answer with one syllable: it's frightful. The people from whom one would *like* to receive so many pages write one very little or not at all, that's how it goes.

These lines reveal that even in the midst of what Lord Lytton construed as the rebirth of their magical romantic bond, Élisabeth thought of him as a nuisance. In that sense, it had only been a matter of time before she discarded him once again.

Equally noteworthy in this passage is the way she uses her complaint about Lord Lytton's assiduousness to impress upon her reader that "the people from whom one would *like* to receive" such marks of devotion invariably (and irksomely) fail to comply with her wishes. Of all the laments in her writings to and about Giovanni Borghese, this is the one that recurs the most often. It can be summarized as: "Everyone else on earth loves me—why don't you?" Indeed, in her archives, this letter to X is filed under "Borghese," suggesting that perhaps she dropped Lord Lytton because, by then, Giovanni filled her thoughts too completely to leave room for the earl and his "frightful" seventy-page missives.

Besides, she had not shared her Éléonore/Gérard novel with Lord Lytton, and in the spring of 1891 that project again came to consume most of her attention, even though on her coauthor's side it continued to advance at a slower pace than she would have liked. Remembering Giovanni's initial idea about modeling their partnership on that of the brothers Goncourt, she made overtures to the surviving brother, Edmond, summoning him to the rue d'Astorg in April. Goncourt recorded afterward that to his astonishment, she had invited him there not to socialize but to talk with him about "doing a novel about a society woman, a woman of the *grand monde,* a character that nobody has accurately captured yet, not Maupassant, not anyone." Goncourt inferred from all this that Mme Greffulhe was trying to persuade him to write a novel about her, but in fact, she was laying the groundwork for the day when she would ask for his opinion of her own (and Giovanni's) manuscript. For the time being, she had contented herself with "accidentally" showing the old man some of Élaine's prose poems.

By reaching out to Goncourt, Élisabeth may have hoped to impress Giovanni with her literary wherewithal. However, she was even more anxious to remind him of her desirability as a woman. The letters she traded with him throughout the spring point to a concerted effort on Élisabeth's (or Éléonore's) part to taunt Giovanni (or Gérard) by bragging about the scores of men who were smitten with her. In response, his "fictional" letters took on an *odi et amo* quality of their own. In some, Gérard rails against Éléonore's "morbid need to offer up [her] body as a feast for every eye and for every ignoble desire" and accuses her of caring less about him than about her "newest triumph with an eminent man" or her latest "successful royal audience." In others, he advances the hope that "the heavenly dream she used to inspire in me" (whatever that was) might still come true.

From the heightened emotion of these letters, Élisabeth could congratulate herself on having prodded her writing partner out of his indifference. She had even persuaded him to travel with her, Guigui, Montesquiou, and Gégé Primoli to Bayreuth, Germany, in July. The summer opera festival there had recently become a fashionable destination for fans of Richard Wagner, and her uncle Robert, who had already made the trip once, had insisted that Élisabeth follow suit. ("I don't even say I prescribe it; I *require* it.") As a fellow Wagnerian, Giovanni was a natural person to include in the adventure. But Élisabeth's reasons for inviting him were of course not purely cultural. Neither, perhaps, were Giovanni's; he agreed to join the excursion but wanted to stop off for a few days in Gotha, one of the two capitals of Prince Ferdinand's family's dukedom.

Writing as himself, Giovanni also sent Élisabeth a maddening note that heartened and demoralized her all at once. In it he apologized for having treated her with "perhaps excessive coldness." He explained that until he met her, he had "never come across a woman whose affinities, tastes, and intellect are more in line with my own." All the same, he beseeched her "once and for all to forget about my old animal"—his old-fashioned term for his body—and love "only the best of me, my mind, which I have never given to anyone else."

Even read selectively for only signs of encouragement, such letters hardly constituted the impassioned declaration Élisabeth had been wanting from Giovanni for so long. Telling herself that their trip to Germany would surely, finally, allow him to speak his heart, she was counting the days till their departure. As far as her relationship with Lord Lytton was concerned, the imminent jaunt to Bayreuth would have given her another compelling reason to have done with him and his high-maintenance courtship. It was time, she wrote in her diary, to "gather [her] forces" and focus on snaring her elusive prince.

In the summer of 1891, Élisabeth (*far left*), thirty-one, traveled to Bayreuth with Montesquiou (to Élisabeth's *right*), Giovanni (*far right*), and Gégé Primoli, who took this photograph.

Another altogether different possibility is that she cut ties with Lord Lytton because she heard about his liaison with Geneviève Straus. To Élisabeth's "dreadful" letter of farewell, he replied with a poem inveighing against the "ill-ominous denunciators" who had made him out to be "Your worst of foes, / The man of whom you should be most afraid, / . . . Your young life's most menacing / And deadliest danger." In Élisabeth's inner circle, two individuals stand out as Lord Lytton's likeliest defamers. The first was her uncle Robert, who in his correspondence from this period repeatedly admonished her for having revived an unworthy friendship with an unsavory man. That man was not necessarily Lord Lytton—Montesquiou was jealous of practically all of his niece's male friends, and he didn't name names in his epistolary harangues—but the Englishman's "*très* ladylike" barb had placed him at the top of Élisabeth's kinsman's long list of enemies. If he had caught wind of any rumored improprieties between Lord Lytton and Geneviève, Montesquiou would have jumped at the chance to tattle to his niece.

The same held true for Lord Lytton's other most probable "denunciator," Auguste d'Arenberg. For the past year, d'Arenberg and Élisabeth had been meeting almost daily to work out the details of her newest cultural venture, the Société des Grandes Auditions Musicales de France. Founded in the spring of

1890, the Société was a philanthropic organization that sponsored performances of music by unknown or underappreciated French composers. It was Élisabeth's brainchild and the first entity of its kind in Europe. But for propriety's sake, she had asked her brother-in-law to serve as its titular head. In working with her so closely, d'Arenberg had gained an uneasy new perspective on Élisabeth's flirtatious friendships with a host of different men.

Years before, d'Arenberg himself had abetted just such a friendship by brokering her initial encounters with the Prince de Sagan. However, he had not expected his sister-in-law to make a habit of such meetings. Ever protective of the family's honor, d'Arenberg recoiled to see Élisabeth playing fast and loose with her reputation. Her villa in Dieppe struck him as a dangerous catalyst to dishonor; he pointed out to Félicité that it was indecent for Élisabeth to entertain male visitors there when Henry wasn't around. And of all the men who swarmed around her at La Case, Lord Lytton—with his jewelry, poems, blue devils and drugs—seemed to d'Arenberg to present a particular cause for concern.

Had d'Arenberg wanted to blow up the friendship between his sister-in-law and the earl, his own closeness with Geneviève Straus could easily have given him the necessary ammunition. As one of her longtime *fidèles,* d'Arenberg would have been as well-placed as, say, Porto-Riche or Delaunay to receive her confidences. He may even, as Lord Lytton's reference to the meeting at "His Serene Highness's" house implies, have facilitated the Englishman's secret romance with Geneviève. If d'Arenberg did help the two of them in this manner, then he would unquestionably have had inside information about their involvement. And having already proven, with his priggish quibbles about La Case, his willingness to meddle in his sister-in-law's affairs, he would not have hesitated to turn her against her questionable English friend.

Whoever or whatever caused it, the falling-out with Élisabeth crushed Lord Lytton. He reverted to his old policy of avoiding any gatherings where they might cross paths, but the monde was a small place, and he couldn't keep away from her indefinitely. One painful encounter took place at a costume ball held on May 26 by the Princesse de Léon. A thirty-eight-year-old blueblood until then known primarily for her dazzling marriage (to the Duc de Rohan's eldest son and heir), extensive doll collection, and fondness for abstruse poetry, the princesse had taken it upon herself to challenge Mme de Sagan's monopoly on the costume-party genre. As a "born" aristocrat, Mme de Léon generated considerable excitement by encroaching onto the territory Rabble Girl had controlled for more than a decade. *Mondain* anticipation mounted when the younger princesse revealed that her guest of honor was to be the queen of Spain. This announcement meant that Lord Lytton, as the queen of England's ambassador, had to go to the party, even if it meant running into Élisabeth. The best he could hope for

Because of his viceregal posting, his effeminacy, and his opium habit, Lord Lytton was caricatured in *Vanity Fair* as "the Vice Empress."

was not to see her in the crowd, and between the length of the Princesse de Léon's guest list (seventeen hundred people) and the brevity of Élisabeth's typical social forays, this seemed a reasonable possibility.

It was not to be. To differentiate her party from the *bal Sagan,* Mme de Léon had issued sartorial guidelines quite unlike her rival's maximalist whimsies: the only dress requirement was that guests wear no color. (Truman Capote may not have known of the precedent, but this was the original Black and White Ball.) A smattering of guests ignored this stricture, among them Laure de Chevigné, who gaily drew stares in a checkered yellow-and-blue harlequin ensemble. But most of the revelers obeyed, from Lord Lytton's wife and daughter, who both turned out in white silk ball gowns from Worth, to Élisabeth Greffulhe, whom the earl cursed himself for spotting right away. Even in a sea of black and white she had appeared to stand alone, luminous in a simple white tunic and a plain gold fillet in her hair. From across the ballroom, her eyes hooked at Lord Lytton's heart. His anguish hovered in the space between them, ignored. He looked away and then looked back—she was gone.

AFTER THE LÉON BALL, THE *PRESSE MONDAINE* reported that once again, Mme Greffulhe had based her party disguise on a masterpiece from the Louvre: David's *Portrait of Mme Récamier* (c. 1800). As a self-marketing strategy, it was a brilliant choice on Élisabeth's part, consistent with Laure de

Chevigné's insight that a celebrity's image should preserve a foundation of consistency while offering enough variety to hold the public's interest. By dressing as Juliette Récamier (1777–1849), one of the two most celebrated hostesses of the Directoire era, Élisabeth did both of these things. On the one hand, she reasserted her descent from Mme Tallien, the Directoire's other best-known *salonnière* and a friend and rival of Mme Récamier's. On the other, Élisabeth associated herself with a new and different legend: that of the virtuous seductress. Mme Récamier had bewitched the greatest men of her time, from French dukes to German highnesses, from Napoléon I's brother Lucien to novelist René de Chateaubriand. (Chateaubriand had also, coincidentally, carried a torch for Henry's great-aunt Cordélia Greffulhe, a scandal-prone renegade seldom mentioned in the rue d'Astorg.) Yet for all the passion she inspired, Mme Récamier's relationships had remained famously platonic, leaving her womanly honor unblemished. It was said that she never even consummated the union with her husband, a rich, brutish banker who didn't love her.

While Mme Récamier's purity had been legendary since her own lifetime, it had recently been the subject of an adulatory essay published by Oscar Wilde in a ladies' magazine he edited in England. According to this essay,

> Mme Récamier invented a new kind of feeling which was neither friendship nor love, but a mixture of both. It was not unlike that which Beatrice and Laura inspired [in Dante and Petrarch], only their lovers worshipped from afar, while Mme Récamier's enjoyed the companionship of their idol without flagging in the zeal . . . of their adoration.

Élisabeth based her costume for the 1891 Léon ball on David's 1800 portrait of Juliette Récamier, a famous beauty of the Directoire.

These lines echo the prescriptions for "True Friendship" with which Élisabeth had once presented Lord Lytton, and which she encouraged all her admirers to follow. This facet of Mme Récamier's mystique must have made her seem a kindred spirit to Élisabeth.

Élisabeth may also have appreciated Mme Récamier's well-known adoption of the phoenix as her totem. Along with its miraculous capacity to rise from a predecessor's ashes, this bird was renowned for its stringent refusal to pair-bond, a bit of trivia that meshed well with Mme Récamier's claims of imperviousness to physical desire. Not unlike the Napoleonic eagle or the Wagnerian swan, the phoenix occupied a transcendent category of one. By dressing as Mme Récamier, Élisabeth thus aligned herself symbolically with yet another rara avis, again using costume to assert her grandeur. At the same time, the association with the phoenix would have served, like the rest of the Récamier legend, to emphasize Élisabeth's blameless sexual morals. Underscored by her immaculate white dress, her air of purity would have stood as an eloquent retort to Giovanni's peevish imputations about her/Éléonore's "morbid need to offer [her] body up as a feast for every eye."

Unfortunately, no mention of Élisabeth's Récamier party guise—or of the party itself—appears in her extant correspondence with Giovanni. Her costume did, however, generate plenty of attention in other quarters, encapsulated by Montesquiou's verdict: "The Comtesse Greffulhe is our modern Mme Récamier." Echoed in the society columns, this judgment ratified her supreme powers of enchantment.

Élisabeth's high-profile appearance at the Léon ball met with predictable hostility from Henry. Despite the undeniable prestige of the Rohan family (not to mention the queen of Spain), he had refused to squire her to the party, probably because he and the rest of the Greffulhe clan were still officially in mourning for Jeanne d'Arenberg, who had died of tuberculosis that March. Élisabeth's decision to attend the ball anyway represented a flagrant breach of etiquette, amplifying Henry's indignation at what he disparaged as her "Mme *Réclamier*" publicity stunt.* "It would have been more *comme il faut* to stay at home, but you didn't," he wrote. "It is high time for you to realize that the only true grande dame, the *grandest* grande dame, is the one nobody talks about!!"

Élisabeth evidently felt no guilt at having violated mourning for her sister-in-law, even though Jeanne had been one of her only allies in the rue d'Astorg. As for Henry's "Réclamier" scolding, she chalked it up to the jealousy of his "Principale": "Mme de Noirmont dislikes it when everybody is talking about me," she scribbled in the margins of his note. For Élisabeth, the escape to Germany could not come soon enough.

---

* Henry attributed this insult to an unidentified "chap in [his] circle," of whom the quickest-witted were du Lau, Fitz-James, and Haas. The barb indeed displays a verbal facility more nimble than Henry's own: "Réclamier" is a portmanteau, fusing "Récamier" with *réclame* (publicity).

FOR LORD LYTTON, the sighting of her at the Léon ball reopened the floodgates to his "intolerable sorrow." He renamed his poem cycle *Marah:* there would be no happy ending after all. Despondency now clouded his poems. And also his letters. To Theresa Earle, he confided,

> I am tired, sick, and weary of all things. The roses are too red for me—the sunbeams too sunny. In every rose I recognize a canker—in every sunbeam a potential ague—and beneath all flesh, however fair, the skeleton that will outlast it.

Never mind that his own flesh was failing him. On top of the respiratory problems he had developed after his nasal surgery the previous spring, Lord Lytton was suffering from an acute inflammation of the bladder. More recently, he had begun experiencing chest pains as well. To spare him the strain of climbing the stairs to his upper-floor bedroom and study in the hôtel Borghèse, Edith had set up a bed and desk for him in the Green Salon on the first floor.

These new arrangements were palliative at best, as the earl's physical and mental health continued to decline. To Betty he reported that he felt himself increasingly detaching from the world of men (and women), as if the whole of human existence were but a hollow spectacle staged for him alone. "All people are to me as *ombres chinoises* [shadow puppets]," he admitted. At the same time, he had the uneasy sense that inanimate objects were taking on lives of their own. According to his youngest daughter, Emily Bulwer-Lytton, Lord Lytton became convinced at this time that the allegorical figure on the French twenty- and one-hundred-franc coins, "the Spirit of the Republic drafting the Constitution," was his "very last friend on earth." He was no more a republican than any of his patrician French friends, so his attachment to the coin did not arise from

Toward the end of his life, Lord Lytton's mental health deteriorated to such an extent that he believed the allegorical figure on the twenty-franc coin was his only friend.

his political preferences. His desperation had pushed him into a realm beyond politics, even beyond logic.

Alarmed by her husband's deterioration, Edith proposed that in July they travel together to Bayreuth, where she had always wanted to attend the annual festival of Wagner's music. Although Lord Lytton wasn't a *mélomane* like his wife, he had loved Germany since his university days at Bonn and readily agreed that a trip there would do him good. His longtime fondness for Paris had abandoned him; he now spoke of it as a "loathsome" place, "with its *esprit,* its *amours,* its well-dressed women and witty men who all do and say the same thing, exceedingly well, but with a fatiguing repetition of ever the same type and note—brilliantly superficial." As Élisabeth had put it, the Faubourg was the kingdom of pretty faces, no country for beautiful souls. Or, Lord Lytton might have added, for broken hearts. Anywhere, even the Wagner capital of the world, would feel more hospitable to him than where he was now.

Reaching Bayreuth, he was pleasantly surprised to learn that despite its popularity with music-loving Parisians, it presented a "most welcome contrast" to the City of Light. "The life here [is] rough and simple," he told Betty in an unusually sanguine letter, "the sensations strong and serious." This was the life best suited to his somber frame of mind. Yet the festival came as another happy surprise. To his younger daughter Constance, he wrote that while he was "not very susceptible to musical effects and wholly ignorant of the art by which they are produced," he found Wagner's music unexpectedly stirring.

Lord Lytton was also impressed by the Bayreuth Festival Theater (Festspielhaus), which had been designed as a dedicated performance space for Wagner's operas. Two of its more innovative features, a hidden orchestra pit and a double proscenium, opened up what the composer had termed a "mystic gulf" (*mystische Abgrund*) between the public and the stage; the result was an otherworldly mise-en-scène unlike anything Lord Lytton had ever seen. Wagner had created his last great work, *Parsifal* (1882), a complex, controversial adaptation of the Arthurian Grail legend, specifically for the stage at Bayreuth, and had left instructions forbidding it to be performed elsewhere. Hearing the composer's music in this setting, Lord Lytton savored the illusion that he had journeyed "safe in[to] the very heart of the world of dreams."

But he wasn't safe, as various omens kept reminding him. During *Parsifal,* it gave him an unpleasant start to discover that one of the aliases used by that opera's shape-shifting temptress, Kundry, was Herodias, Salome's mother, and that in devising that character, Wagner had borrowed heavily from the legend of the Wandering Jew. Given Élisabeth's fascination with both of these figures, as well as with Wagner, Lord Lytton found himself ruminating about her once more. Kundry's wicked wiles reminded him of Élisabeth, too. In this character, as one critic observed, Wagner had sketched a type of woman not uncommon in fin-de-siècle Parisian society: the "demoniacal" vixen, whom "nothing enchants more . . . than [the] trembling adoration her supernatural powers" command from men, and whose slogan was "You are not to love me, but to lie, full of dread and terror, in the dust at my feet." This was exactly what Élisabeth had demanded of Lord Lytton; this was the death sentence to which she had condemned him.

She pushed her way back into his memory yet again on July 20, when he and Edith were invited to tea with Wagner's widow, née Cosima Liszt. Among Wagnerians, there was no more coveted privilege than an audience with the great man's wife; Geneviève's mystique as the Widow Bizet paled in comparison with the cult that had grown up around Frau Wagner, the high priestess of Bayreuth. Lord Lytton enjoyed meeting Cosima. Having been friendly with her late father, Franz Liszt, he had been delighted to recognize in her "a great deal of Liszt's wonderful charm." But he was shaken when she remarked that he and Edith had just missed the Comtesse Greffulhe on her own maiden voyage to Bayreuth. The comtesse and her traveling companions, a group of relatives from Paris, Brussels, and Rome, had also taken tea at Cosima's house.

For Lord Lytton, the mere mention of Élisabeth's name was enough to reignite all the suppressed rage and frustrated longing (a key *Parsifal* trope) he had come to Bayreuth to escape. The incantatory power of his lady's name was a phenomenon he had already described in the first canto of *Marah,* where the speaker exclaims, "Ah, still even strangers' lips renew / The magic of your name! / Last night, when someone spoke of you, / I felt my blood turn flame." In this work, the fire metaphor has positive associations. Optimistic about his chances with her, the poetic speaker welcomes the conflagration as a testament to the force of his passion. But for the poet himself, by the summer of 1891, his beloved's name had become an evil incantation, riling up his demons with a vengeance. Even Bayreuth's world of dreams could give him no quarter from the nightmare brewing back in Paris.

At this point Élisabeth started to figure in Lord Lytton's imagination as someone—or something—more nefarious than just an omnipresent ghost. He replayed a conversation the two of them had had after one of their tours of a medical facility in Paris, where they had witnessed the dissection and cremation of a human cadaver. Lord Lytton had been stunned at the fascination this sight had held for Élisabeth, who enthused to him afterward, "Remember, Professor Dieulafoy said that when a body is cremated, the heart is the last of all the organs to burn!" At the time, Lord Lytton had been rather pleased with his gallant rejoinder: "That must be why it is so flammable while we are alive." In hindsight, though, the exchange struck him as ominous. This was a woman who took the durability of the human heart as a challenge to her own superhuman capacity for destruction. He now feared that she wouldn't rest until she had torn his heart from his chest and burnt it to ash.

After he and Edith returned from Bayreuth to Paris, he wrote a long, not at all lyrical poem to bring *Marah*'s fourth and final canto to a close. This poem, "Somnium Belluinum" ("Bestial Dream"), reworks Lord Lytton's nightmare of a disembodied heart on fire. It opens with a phantasmagoric "monstrous procession" of animals, stampeding past the speaker in his fitful, uneasy dreams. Each animal in the cavalcade "thrill[s]" him "with a different pang": "passionate longing," "indescribable desolation," "a frenzy of burning flame," and "life's cessation." The beasts vary as widely as the feelings they induce. Some belong to known natural species: "the lithe Leopards, and Ounces, and Lynxes: / then the Jaguars, Panthers, and Pumas." Many more do not. There are forty-footed dragons and "golden-crown'd" gryphons; "supernatural Apes with divining rods"; and "two-leggèd Dogs with the airs of gods." There are "sleek Basilisks" that kill with their eyes; "blithe Centaurs" rattling their quivers; and "a ponderous phalanx . . . / Of the man-faced Bulls of Chaldea, / Whose bewildering bulks dread embodiments are / Of the strength of a dread Idea." The whole "grim multitude" reads like a deranged breeding experiment cooked up by the Princesse de Sagan and Gustave Moreau, as if the fauna from the latter's studio had mated with those from the former's *bal des bêtes*.

As for the "dread Idea" the wild things embody, it only dawns upon the speaker once "a tumultuous pageant of strange-color'd birds" swoops in and joins the creatures of the ground. "There were Peacocks, and Parrots, and Loories, / And Flamingoes, and Hoopoes, and Fowls obscene / With the eyeballs and talons of Furies." As the birds circle around him, the poet is filled with dread, and soon he understands why. They are joined by their leader, the cruel, omnipotent phoenix, carrying in its beak "a fiery coal" the speaker recognizes as his "own heart burning."

In terror, the speaker cries out, "What are you going to do / with my heart . . . / For what sacrifice fierce have you kindled it so / with infernal fire?" By way of an answer, the phoenix and its "trooping . . . herds" begin to squawk, flap, and scratch with uncontrolled fury. They drown the sun in a heaving black squall, effecting an eclipse in broad daylight. They turn on the speaker and "pursue him like murderous priests" while "a blood-red pall . . . the shuddering land enshroud[s]." Perversely, the horror of the ordeal only reaches its apex when the speaker jolts out of his slumber: "And the Birds and the Basilisks madden'd the air / With a horrible screeching and hissing: / Till at last I awoke with a clutch of despair / At my heart. But too late! It was missing."

With these lines ends the last canto of *Marah*.

EDWARD ROBERT BULWER-LYTTON, first Earl of Lytton, age sixty, died at home in Paris in the hôtel Borghèse on November 24, 1891. *The New York Times* reported that he had fallen victim to "a sudden attack of heart disease." Other publications mentioned aneurysm and cardiac arrest; a newsletter for a British anti-opium group alleged that the deceased had been done in by his "fondness for the opium pipe." *Le Gaulois,* recalling the flu Lord Lytton had contracted two years earlier following an operation on his nose, noted that he had never seemed quite the same after that. The news outlets all concurred that the public outpouring of grief for him in Paris was extraordinary. Lord Lytton was one of the few foreigners ever to receive a state funeral in France, though he was not buried there. After the obsequies in Paris, his body was dispatched to England and buried among his ancestors at Knebworth.

According to his wife and daughters, when Lord Lytton died he had not left his sickbed for more than a month, having landed there after a brief trip to Knebworth, where he had contracted a deathly chill, followed by "internal inflammation" exacerbating his infection of the bladder. The latter condition grew so excruciating during his return trip across the English Channel that by the time he got back to Paris, he could scarcely stand up for the pain. His doctors again prescribed total bed rest. One of them even advised him to resign his ambassadorship—a measure Lord Lytton did not dismiss out of hand, hating the city as he now did. They all exhorted him to desist from work of any kind, cautioning that the slightest exertion could cost him his life.

Against their counsel, Lord Lytton continued to work on his poetry. In bed in the Green Salon, he obsessively fine-tuned *Marah.* Edith, Betty, and Emily all observed that he was composing an addendum to the volume at the very moment of his death. He had already directed Edith to have his publisher place this final piece at the end of the book, as the last poem in the cycle. Here is Betty's account of his demise:

> His manuscript was always beside him, and he was actually writing a line of a new poem when an arterial clot passed from the heart to the brain. . . . The end came with merciful swiftness, and the rest for which he had yearned was won.

The autopsy confirmed the blood clot. It also disclosed "a doubly abscessed kidney" and "a heart about an inch less thick than normal." Biographer Laure Hillerin ventures a more symbolic diagnosis: "Without a doubt, his heart was too weak and old for his tempestuous nature."

Weak and old, maybe it was, but there is some evidence to suggest that Lord Lytton's heart was not broken when he died. Although Betty Balfour attempted to strike this evidence, too, from the historical record, traces of it persist both in Élisabeth's archives and in the contemporary press. These sources reveal that Lord Lytton's confinement to the hôtel Borghèse was not as absolute as his family would subsequently claim. For a few days in the final week of his life, he defied his doctors' instructions and left his sickbed—to attend a house party at Bois-Boudran for Grand-Duc and Grande-Duchesse Wladimir.

As one of just twenty-six guests included in this "*très* select" occasion, Lord

Lytton would not have been invited, nor would he have endured the physical pain of the journey, unless he and Élisabeth had had yet another rapprochement. In this respect, the phoenix depicted at the end of *Marah* was an apt figure for the poet's infatuation. As Petrarch, the progenitor of the lyric genre in which Owen Meredith worked, wrote of his passion for Laura, "Thus is my desire. . . . It burns, and dies, and regains its strength, vying with the phoenix." In the fall of 1891, Lord Lytton's "dead love, still undying" performed a similar feat.

The GDWs arrived at Bois-Boudran on the afternoon of Thursday, November 19, and returned to Paris on the evening of Saturday, November 21, making both trips in a plush private train car Henry Greffulhe had paid the railroad company to send for them. Nearly all the founders turned out for the royal visit: the d'Arenbergs, the de L'Aigles, the La Forces, the Hottinguers, du Lau, and Costa de Beauregard. The only missing member of the regular gang was Breteuil, who was then on the other side of the Atlantic Ocean, visiting his new wife's family in Wappingers Falls, New York (and unfortunately not documenting his impressions of the trip).

The Greffulhes' other guests that weekend included the Prince de Sagan (to whose presence Henry agreed only because the GDWs adored him), the Général de Galliffet (ditto), the British ambassador, and the Duchesse d'Uzès (in need of cheering up since the suicide a few months earlier of her disgraced former protégé, General Boulanger). Despite his ailing condition, Lord Lytton would have been obliged to stay for the full two and a half days of the party, as etiquette required that all guests be present when the crowned heads arrived and remain until after they left. This was a rule with which, although Élisabeth often broke it, a career diplomat most definitely had to comply.

The program for the GDWs' stay at Bois-Boudran consisted of lavish driven shoots during the daytime—their host imported fourteen thousand pheasants from Hungary to ensure that the grand-duc came away with an abundant haul—and sumptuous dinner parties at night. The evening feasts were held in the new wing of the castle, which the Greffulhes took the GDWs' visit as a pretext to unveil. True to Henry's extravagant vision, the addition featured a monumental double-height banquet hall connected to the kitchen by an underground train. Activated by a switch, the gleaming parquet floorboards would part and a dining table with seating for one hundred guests would rise from below like a deus ex machina at the opera. Indeed, the Greffulhes' architect had designed the space in the overwrought style of Garnier's Opéra in Paris; visiting some years later, Jacques Blanche would describe the banquet hall as "an orgy of balustrades, pilasters, galleries, loggias, girandoles, and festoons, these flourishes all dripping with gold, insolently illuminated by rock-crystal lustres." Similar adornments bedecked Bois-Boudran's new private theater, also equipped with seating for a hundred. On the second evening of the Romanovs' stay, a professional men's choir performed the Russian national anthem on the theater's stage.

The opulent wing Henry had added to Bois-Boudran in 1888 was a "château unto itself." It featured a dining hall that could seat a hundred guests, an underground train between the dining room and the kitchen, and a private theater.

These alterations to Bois-Boudran garnered mixed reviews. Gaston Calmette, the editor-in-chief of *Le Figaro,* described the new wing to his readers as "a veritable château unto itself"—though not having been invited to the inaugural party, he may have been repeating a line fed to him by Élisabeth. The Duc de La Force, brutally honest as only an old friend (and a duke) felt entitled to be, ribbed Henry for having grafted "the Versailles of the Sun King onto the house of a bourgeois." For better or worse, the splendor of the renovations accounts for Élisabeth's underwhelmed reaction, later in life, when visiting the English royal family's country estate in Norfolk: "Sandringham has nothing even close to the luxury with which Henry surrounds me at Bois-Boudran."

For "poor Lytton," the luxury with which his ladylove was surrounded at Bois-Boudran could have been a demoralizing sight, unless perhaps it brought back fond memories of his days as India's Grand Ornamental. He elected not to participate in the driven shoots the Greffulhes had organized—he had never really gone in for hunting and was in no condition to start now. With his recusal, the earl may have cheated death by at least a few days, as Grand-Duc Wladimir, notoriously cavalier about firearms safety, almost blew off the head of one of the other guns by taking a shot out of turn. (To the scandalized Duchesse d'Uzès, a stickler for the protocol of the hunt, the grand-duc shrugged that he had been aware of the danger but sure he would hit his mark.) By abstaining from the sport of kings, Lord Lytton also gained some time alone with his hostess while everyone else was in the field; the Duc de La Force noticed that Élisabeth declined to join the shooting party as well.

Through all the rancor and misery of *Marah,* somehow Lord Lytton's love for Élisabeth had survived, and now, by some miracle, he found her prepared to encourage it once again. A cryptic letter she wrote to him from Dieppe at the end of the summer reads: "You alone eliminate all other considerations. So much turmoil, so much confusion, so much limbo [*sic*]—until one day a little flower blossoms, and fixes the dream in an enameled definition." What dream was she talking about? And why had she decided, as Lord Lytton phrased it in a card he enclosed in a bouquet of flowers he sent her that August, to "let [him] back into [her] good graces a little bit"?

Impossible to say. However, her change of heart may have had something to do with her own journey to Bayreuth that July. Apart from the photographs Gégé Primoli snapped of their group along the way, no documentation of the outing survives. That Élisabeth and Giovanni did not trade letters while travel-ing together is not, of course, surprising. But the fact that they never mentioned the trip in their subsequent correspondence presents a puzzle. An undated letter in Giovanni's hand, rebuking her for "being too demanding with me during the performance the other night," indicates that where he was concerned, Élisabeth's threshold for disappointment was inordinately low. So it may have been that their time together in Germany had fallen short of her expectations. Another hint in this direction surfaces in her only journal entry to refer to the trip. Returning to Dieppe afterward, she recorded that the music at Bayreuth had "transported her" with its promise of "awakened faith and . . . love revealed." Yet that promise, she wrote, had not transformed her real-life relationships into fairy-tale romances; it had left her alone, with only the music to love:

> One begins by loving things for themselves. Then, one needs *someone* to love, and no longer loves things for themselves, only in relation to that someone. Then, later on, one again starts to love things for themselves.

This passage appears in Élisabeth's diary on the same page as her transcription of the note about how the thought of Lord Lytton "alone eliminate[d] all other considerations" in her life. It would therefore appear that on his travels with Élisabeth, Giovanni had somehow managed to eliminate himself as a consider-ation, at least for the time being, and that once she was back in Paris, she went back to Lord Lytton one last time to fill the void.

Neither of Élisabeth's two other biographers make any mention—in this con-nection or in general—of her tortured passion for Giovanni. But one of them, Anne de Cossé-Brissac, confirms that after Bayreuth, Élisabeth's morale sank to a new low, and that by the time Lord Lytton came to Bois-Boudran in Novem-ber, "she had for the first time come to feel her solitude as a physical sensation." Overcome with loneliness, Cossé-Brissac writes, "Élisabeth was filled with a sudden longing to feel [Lord Lytton's] eyes, hands, and lips all over her, giving her the reassuring illusion . . . that she was not all alone."

Whether Élisabeth conveyed these feelings to Lord Lytton is also impossible to say, though the searing pain in his urinary tract could not have been conducive to physical love. Yet he did imagine his literary alter ego finally consummating his desire. Two poems Lord Lytton wrote in the days just before he died evoke a rapturous erotic encounter with a "woman who had long struggled against surrendering herself to him." The first of these writings is undated, untitled, and unsigned, scrawled in Lord Lytton's hand on Bois-Boudran writing paper. Composed in French in alexandrine meter, this eight-line text celebrates "the ineffable delirium of moments of love, [when] one heart responds to another as a lyre to the air." To "help his beloved overcome her prudery," the speaker "explains the desire he has awakened in her" and "more than half-conquer[s]" her with his eloquence. As she tumbles "weak and smitten" into his arms, the poet feels "like a young man in love," "drunk with hope" to find himself "adored," at long last, in return. The pathos here is arresting: a dying man of sixty dreams of being young again.

The second poem is the addendum to *Marah* the earl was working on when he died, and to which either his family or his editor gave the title "Lord Lytton's Last Poem." Like the rest of the poems in *Marah,* this unfinished work does not claim to document lived experience as such. Rather, it presents the final stage of an evolving relationship that may or may not have paralleled the poet's relationship with Élisabeth, to whom he had dedicated the volume. By the same token, the circumstances of the poem's composition—Edith noted that her husband started "writing it, as if in haste" the very day he came back from Bois-Boudran—might reasonably indicate that the weekend with Élisabeth had inspired him. The fact that he kept working on this piece right up to the moment of his death suggests that as the end drew near, nothing mattered more to Lord Lytton than his poem: his poem, and the passion it expressed.

Lord Lytton's stated goal for *Marah* had been to give voice to a sentiment "fetched by [the writer] himself, at his own cost, from the dimmest region" of his soul. Published shortly after his death, the book was hailed as a compelling demonstration of this approach, with "Lord Lytton's Last Poem" receiving special notice for its resounding ring of authenticity. A reporter for London's *National Review* concluded, "To men who are neither critics nor poets, the work of Lord Lytton . . . will speak through the force of [its] unmistakable sincerity. While reading these poems many will murmur, 'How sad!' Some will add, 'How true!'"

As the last installment of the *Marah* cycle, "Lord Lytton's Last Poem" brings the speaker's volatile emotional pilgrimage to a close. The ending is an unexpectedly happy one, when we recall that when we last saw our hero, a sadistic phoenix was making off with his heart clamped in its beak. After all the tribulations he has borne since first he drank from the bitter springs of Marah—after all the hurts and ghosts and angry birds that have plagued him along the way—the speaker finally gets the girl.

The miracle takes place while he and she are out walking together in a green, forested land that she knows well, but to which he is a stranger. After leading him up a "wood-girt hillside" to a scenic overlook, she stops and does her watchful-doe impression:

You looked and listened,
And your woodland eyes deepened. . . .
You shook your brown curls free,
And made an effort vain to smooth them flat,
And laughed.

She wonders aloud where the rest of the company have got off to, then an awkward pause ensues: having until then only "met in the sight of others," she and the speaker are unused to finding themselves alone.

The tension between them mounts until she abruptly turns her "face full on mine, . . . with swimming eyes and half heartbroken smile." As soon as their eyes meet, they lose all control:

And shudderingly,
Like things caught up, and seized, and swept away
By the unconquerable hurricane,
We rushed together in a faint wild cry,
Closed in a mute embrace.

As in the Bois-Boudran poem, the woman's "surrender" has a rejuvenating effect on her companion, although here the renewal encompasses and reshapes the world around them, too: "We / to one another all at once became, / The sole man I, and the sole woman she, / Of a new world where nothing is the same / As in the world that was."

With this transformation, the speaker gains a heartening new insight into his beloved. Examining her "surrender'd beautiful soft face" "pillow'd on my breast," he grasps for the first time that the "proud revolts" and "start[s] / of sudden coldness" with which she once tortured him had been so many signs of her love, not of her scorn. Unbeknownst to him, the severest "agonies, / [and] pangs" had wracked her "highborn heart" as she struggled not to give in to her forbidden passion: "the shamed acknowledgment of love's success." But now, with their embrace, she has set aside the "cruel feminine art / Of self-protection practiced in disdain / Of love's good faith." The poem breaks off here—the writer could write no more.

If this was the version of his and Élisabeth's love story that he was telling himself when he breathed his last, then it seems fair to imagine that Lord Lytton died a happy man.

CHAPTER TWENTY-ONE

THE REPLACEMENTS

Lord Lytton left instructions that a package he had addressed to Élisabeth be delivered to her in Paris after his death. It is a testament to Edith Bulwer-Lytton's integrity and love for her husband that she carried out his wish. Along with the sheaf of letters and poems he had set aside for Élisabeth while writing *Marah*—"verses written for the Comtesse Greffulhe and dedicated to Her"—the parcel contained a large gemstone carved with indecipherable runes. She kept it until a soothsayer told her that it was cursed and killed everyone into whose possession it came, including Lord Lytton. Hearing this, Élisabeth flung it into the Seine. Montesquiou later put it about that the water in Paris had turned undrinkable the moment the jewel landed in the river.

Élisabeth did hold on to Lord Lytton's poems and letters. But nothing in her own writings suggests that she regarded his death as an inordinately troubling loss; it had merely relieved her of one of the pawns on her chessboard. As usual, and in spite of herself, her thoughts lay with Giovanni. A week after Lord Lytton's funeral in Paris, she wrote, "The absoluteness of his love made me understand mine—my love, suffocated but still alive, and distracting itself with a sensuous literary idyll. The lover who truly *has* me, body and soul, keeps his distance, is passive."

On her better days, Élisabeth tried to chalk Giovanni's remoteness up to outside circumstances. While their trip to Bayreuth had not gone as well as she had hoped, she had expected to have a chance to reconnect with him afterward, away from their traveling companions, in either Paris or Dieppe. But no sooner had they returned to France than a dispatch from Giovanni's mother sent him hurrying back to Rome, where the longtime rumors about their family's financial woes had finally erupted in a massive public scandal. In August, the Borgheses began selling off their assets, a difficult, drawn-out process that captured headlines around the world. In Paris, Schadenfreude, celebrity worship's evil twin, ran amok in the pages of the *presse mondaine,* trumpeting every detail of the princes' humiliating fall. (One particularly embarrassing news story involved the Borgheses' sale to Baron Alphonse de Rothschild of a Raphael portrait that turned out to be a forgery.) Reading this coverage, Élisabeth could almost convince herself that Giovanni's worries about money had been the real obstacle between them all along and that once this problem was resolved, he would rush back to Paris to be with her. To Guigui, she wrote optimistically, "Good things will surely happen if G. comes back!"

Élisabeth's good cheer became harder to maintain, however, as rivals for his affection seemed to be multiplying all around her. Uncle Robert, for one thing, had grown fonder than ever of Giovanni on their Bayreuth trip, as evidenced by Gégé Primoli's photographs: the two men appear together in every shot. Moreover, her cousin Marie-Alys de Caraman-Chimay, now twenty-two and styling herself just "Alys," had begun her own correspondence with Giovanni at some point without Élisabeth's knowledge, possibly after meeting him on one of her infrequent visits to the rue d'Astorg. Living with her widowed mother in the provinces and condemned, for want of a dowry, to a spinster's fate, Alys had written cryptically to Élisabeth in recent years about her unfulfillable romantic longings and her struggle "to stop wishing for the thing that has been my greatest wish." Élisabeth had always assumed that Alys was speaking generally of her wish to get married. But the information—passed along by Guigui, who heard it from Minet—that Alys was in touch with Giovanni put her forbidden desire in a different and more troubling light. Élisabeth did not intend to let the situation continue. She would start by impressing upon her cousin that Giovanni did "not have a penny to his name," as this fact alone would indeed make it impossible for him and Alys to have a future together. Still, Élisabeth did not like to have to think of Alys as competition for her prince.

More threatening still, however, was the emergent rumor that the Borgheses were trying to finagle a marriage between their peripatetic bachelor scion and the American heiress Gertrude Vanderbilt. Élisabeth looked down on "dollar princesses," although she now counted just such a specimen in her immediate family, her brother Jo having married Clara Ward, the daughter of a Michigan steel and timber tycoon, a year earlier. Jo's new bride spoke loudly, dressed badly, and wore too much rouge. Yet to Élisabeth's vexation, Clara not only considered herself a great beauty but somehow caught the eye of none other than King Leopold II of the Belgians, and was openly carrying on an affair with him. It galled Élisabeth to imagine Giovanni in the clutches of such a "savage" (as she called Clara behind her back, further noting that as she was "from a different race than ours," she would "not be the Princesse de Caraman-Chimay for long!"). If the king of the Belgians could fall for a common American vamp like her sister-in-law, then anything was possible.

Brooding over this scenario dampened Élisabeth's hope that Giovanni would return to her of his own accord. She ruminated afresh about his long history of apathetic behavior toward her. A few weeks after her cheerful note to Guigui, Élisabeth recorded, "He does not see me. I am an empty space for him," and "If someone loves me, that's all it takes for me to detest him, whereas you [*toi*], whom I love, are repelled by me. A kiss from me would disgust you." The echo of Bizet's *Carmen* (*Si tu ne m'aimes pas, je t'aime*) may or may not have been intentional. While Bizet was not one of Élisabeth's favorites, she sometimes included selections from his operas on the program for her recitals in the rue d'Astorg.

Her claim to be repelled by any man who loved her was not exactly true, however. Lord Lytton having died, and her overtures to the kaiser having stalled since his mother's visit to Paris, Élisabeth was at loose ends without some romantic intrigues to absorb her. Whether to get a rise out of Giovanni or simply to soothe her own bruised ego, she entered a phase of hyperactive flirtation, recruiting new admirers as fast as she could find them. At least one of her targets, the poet Henri de Régnier, deflected her attentions, put off by a rapacious glint in her eye. "Her roving gaze," he wrote, "has something of the bird of prey about it." But Élisabeth found plenty of other willing victims, accruing a collection of vassals as varied and abundant as the clothes in her closets (or the emotions in *Marah*).

One of her new devotees was Paul César Helleu, the portraitist whom she and Montesquiou had invited to their first house party in Dieppe in the summer of 1887. Since then, Élisabeth had continued to cultivate Helleu. She was drawn to his proud, almost haughty reserve (an intriguing quality, she thought, in a petit bourgeois from Brittany) and to his absolute reverence for the female form. As one contemporary critic said of him, "The contour of a girl's cheek and the curve of a woman's shoulder are to Helleu . . . things to be taken quite seriously, studied with assiduous care." To Élisabeth's mind, Helleu was uniquely well suited not just to capturing but to appreciating her "cygniform" grace.

To put the painter's attraction to the test, she invited him to spend a weekend at Bois-Boudran, where she would be staying on her own; she proposed to put him up nearby at Les Bouleaux, the house on the grounds of the estate where Henry had romanced "la belle Pauline" during his and Élisabeth's honeymoon. The ostensible purpose of Helleu's visit would be for him to sketch Élisabeth at his leisure in a variety of attitudes, indoors and out, over the course of several days. But in her diary, she revealed that she was really angling to push the limits of propriety with a handsome and (she presumed) adoring man of genius. That she kept the painter's visit a secret from Henry, who would never have stood for it, also indicated that she knew she was treading on dangerous ground, looking for something more, perhaps, than just another slew of portraits.

Those, Helleu did wind up producing during his stay, in impressively large quantities: some one hundred sketches in total. Writing about the weekend in her journal, however, Élisabeth did not refer to any of these works. Instead, she gushed about how thrilling it had been for "the Beauty" to find herself having dinner with the Artist . . . "all alone!!!! As if we were in the middle of a forest!!!" and how the conversation between them had kept "coming back to that inevitable subject: Love!!!" In recording these encounters in her journal, Élisabeth did not appear to notice that it was she who had repeatedly steered the conversation in that direction. In one late-night posing session, for example, she had pretended to believe that "in the presence of Beauty, . . . the Artist" remained

Paul César Helleu sketched and painted Élisabeth more often than any other portraitist did. Her patronage made him a highly fashionable artist. Years later he would paint the ceiling frescoes of Grand Central Terminal in New York City.

detached, "cold as marble"; this was Helleu's cue to protest that "quite the opposite was the case!!!!" During another sitting, she asked him if he had ever shown any of his portraits of her to his wife of five years, Alice, a luscious redhead who was his favorite model. Helleu replied in the affirmative and gratified the Beauty by quoting his wife as having said, "These look like the sketches you did of me when we were first married." From this Élisabeth deduced that the Artist wished he were married to the Beauty instead.

As ever, what Élisabeth was after in these exchanges seems to have been adoration, not passion, and whether out of professional courtesy or courtly gallantry, Helleu played along, unstinting in his praise. Even when her attempt to pose for him with her newest pet, a white peacock she had acquired on Uncle Robert's advice, ended in a bruising struggle, Helleu reassured her: "You looked beautiful that way." At the same time, he never made the slightest move to take advantage of finding himself alone with her. Élisabeth's diary entries about the weekend do not mention Helleu's reserve as a source of disappointment; on the contrary, they are some of the giddiest pages she ever wrote.

The escapade with Helleu did have one unpleasant consequence. Henry found out about it shortly afterward and went berserk, convinced that she had compromised herself with the painter in some unthinkable way. As incidental as the drawings may have been to Élisabeth's experience of the weekend, Henry treated them as the smoking guns in his case against her and Helleu. The Artist had indeed rendered her swanlike form with sensuous grace; to Henry's eye, the resulting images were so intimate as to be obscene, proof positive that Helleu had had his way with Bebeth. So great was Henry's fury that he even considered challenging the artist to a duel, only to conclude that as the Comte Greffulhe, it would be beneath him to recognize such a serf as a rival. According to Montesquiou, the Big Blockhead got his revenge by destroying the bulk of Helleu's sketches, although some of them have survived.

Henry's conniptions over this episode did not deter Élisabeth from pursuing other admirers, even under his very nose. Within months of Helleu's visit, she was engaged in a heady flirtation with one of her husband's own friends, Comte Albert de Mun, whom she also invited to Bois-Boudran. This was not a secret tête-à-tête like the one she had finagled with Helleu. Henry and the founders were all in attendance, and officially, de Mun had come up to go shooting with them. But after the shoot was over, he wrote to Élisabeth privately to express his "profound gratitude for those three days we had together," adding: "Thank you for what you have been to me, what you have been for *us*."

The intimacy implied in this last pronoun seems to have been purely emotional, just as Élisabeth preferred. De Mun's willingness to behave himself was probably a function of his oft-proclaimed religious fervor—the very creed he invoked when fending off Laure de Chevigné's saltier advances. As a devout, married Catholic, de Mun told Élisabeth, he allowed himself to covet his neighbor's wife "with only the utmost tender respect"; any other sentiment "would be a frightful sacrilege!"

For epistolary fervor, even the eloquent de Mun could not match Colonel Albert de Rochas, a grizzled army veteran pursuing a second career as a paranormal psychologist. Of all Élisabeth's devotees from this period, Rochas was the most prolific correspondent, assailing her with extravagantly amorous letters for more than five years. It seems that Élisabeth first turned to him after her father died in March 1892, hoping Rochas would help her contact both of her parents in the afterlife. He humored her, hoping she would fall in love with him. In the end, they were both sorely disappointed, though not before Élisabeth learned much from him about reincarnation, levitation, telepathy, and telekinesis. Rochas's theories about psychic possession and "exteriorized feelings" inspired her to think of her beauty as a supernatural force unto itself.

Rounding out the ranks of Élisabeth's new suitors were two handsome and brilliant men named Paul. Both were just a few years older than she—a nice change of pace from all her geriatric beaux—and both were fast emerging as leaders in their chosen fields. The first of the two was Paul Deschanel (1855–1922), the republican deputy who had once sought tailoring advice from Boni de Castellane. Since his discovery of Charvet, Deschanel had become one of the nattiest men in the government. He was also one of its most charismatic and

Albert de Rochas, a military officer turned paranormal specialist, intrigued Élisabeth with his research into the occult. This illustration is taken from one of his books on hypnosis.

influential members, with a gift for inspiring oratory that made him the progressive left's answer to Albert de Mun. Élisabeth had first gotten to know Deschanel when he and Henry were colleagues in the Chamber, but while Henry's career there had foundered, Deschanel's star just kept rising. He would go on to win the presidency of the National Assembly (a position rather like the Speaker of the House in the United States Congress) multiple times before he turned forty, and in 1920, he would become the president of the Republic. If Élisabeth was looking for the politician most likely to succeed in her own generation, Deschanel was her man.

In fact, she had been looking for just such an ally in the republican camp, despite of her enduring royalist sympathies and distaste for egalitarian ideology. Since Henry's conversion to republicanism in 1889, the political winds had shifted in a direction that would have favored his career had he not compromised it so thoroughly from the outset. Over the past few years the monarchist faction had continued to lose ground, and as its hopes for a restoration died out, the Comte de Paris, passive in his exile, had made no move to resuscitate them. In February 1892, Pope Leo XIII added his own fatal nail to the Orléanist coffin when he called on all French Catholics to set aside their political differences and "rally" to the Third Republic. (Until then, the Vatican had officially deplored the secularism of the régime in France, enabling right-wingers there to oppose the government on religious grounds.) As a self-styled defender of the faith, Albert de Mun had seen no alternative but to bend to the pontiff's will and encourage his colleagues to follow suit. Some diehards, like Breteuil, preferred to quit politics instead, but their renunciation only solidified their enemies' victory. Élisabeth, recognizing that the republic had prevailed, chose to side with the winners, just as Laure de Chevigné had done when aligning with the d'Orléans after the Comte de Chambord's death. Having proven her mettle as a patroness of the arts and sciences, Élisabeth wanted to extend the scope of her influence into politics, and unlike her discredited husband, Deschanel proved an excellent steward. Aided by him and another leftist young Turk, Gabriel Hanotaux, Élisabeth would successfully reinvent herself as a figure of some influence in the upper echelons of the republican government. Suffice it to say this was not a distinction many other women in her set were able (or willing) to achieve—as usual, Félicité was aghast—and Deschanel was instrumental in helping Élisabeth obtain it.

In and of itself, however, Deschanel's political backing probably wouldn't have moved Élisabeth to make a conquest of him. His good looks, sophisticated dress style, and magnetic personality were the more obvious attractions, making it no hardship for her to field his exuberant professions of love. She also took considerable interest in his accomplishments as an author, in particular his monograph about the *salonnières* of the ancien régime, *Feminine Figures* (*Figures de femmes,* 1889)—part of the fin-de-siècle explosion of books on this subject. Between her Tallien roots and her own prestige as a hostess, Élisabeth was intrigued by Deschanel's research. She was especially drawn to his description of Mme Récamier, as "that beauty universally recognized and saluted by Europe's élite, . . . captivating all men because none could say he had had her." In fact, Deschanel's book may have been one of the sources of inspiration for Élisabeth's Mme Récamier costume at the Léon ball in 1891.

Despite her elitist political convictions, Élisabeth cultivated many republican leaders in the 1890s, among them the charismatic Paul Deschanel, who would later become president of the Republic.

Élisabeth's identification with this decorous femme fatale did not prevent her from giving Deschanel some cause for hope on the romantic front. His letters to her from the early to mid-1890s refer to at least a few private encounters between them. "I want to tell you in all sincerity," he wrote to her one winter at Bois-Boudran, "that those moments I spent alone with you [there recently] were the best moments of my entire life—since those morning walks we took together in Dieppe." Contrary to Laure de Chevigné, Élisabeth was not in the habit of going out without the requisite footman to guard her. As a result, her strolls alone with Deschanel would have been momentous occasions for her, requiring special planning, and serving, one might think, a special purpose. As her chosen companion on these walks, Deschanel would have had some grounds to believe he was not pursuing her in vain.

But despite Élisabeth's evident willingness to bend the rules of propriety for his sake, Deschanel ultimately had to come to terms with the fact that their thrilling tête-à-têtes were never going to lead to anything more. Of Mme Récamier, he wrote,

> One must admit, hers is a particularly cruel kind of "goodness." . . . She accepts love without compassion for the one who loves her; she gives her mind, but not her body, over to the strangest kind of intercourse, in which the most refined coquetry passes itself off as virtue.

While Élisabeth savored her Récamier persona, Deschanel knew enough about that model to recognize that it imposed no end of suffering on her beaux. Once he understood that "giv[ing] her mind, but not her body" was Élisabeth's modus operandi as well, he did not fall out with her—he was nothing if not ambitious and did not underestimate the value of her patronage—but the fervor in his letters to her cooled.

Élisabeth's abstract notions of true love met with a more appreciative response from the other Paul who loomed large in her emotional double life, the celebrated author Paul Hervieu (1857–1915). A former diplomatic attaché from a well-to-do family in Neuilly, Hervieu had the polished manners and aloof bearing of the *mondains* who starred in his novels and plays. So frosty and stiff was his demeanor that according to one of his fellow regulars in Geneviève Straus's salon, he had "tiny icicles in the corners of his moustache"; another *fidèle* speculated that he was made out of cardboard. But Hervieu's reserve disguised his ferocious ambition, which would land him in the Académie Française at the relatively young age of forty-three. When he first came into contact with Élisabeth in the winter of 1887–1888, acting as a scribe for Porto-Riche's unsigned billets-doux, Hervieu was still finding his footing in the literary world, his talent admired by the cognoscenti but not more popularly known. A few years later, he was one of the most famous writers in France, acclaimed for his incisive com-

COLLECTION FÉLIX POTIN

PAUL HERVIEU

While copying Porto-Riche's poems to Élisabeth, Hervieu began writing her impassioned letters of his own.

edies of manners about the contemporary Faubourg. During that same period, Hervieu transformed from the unseen intermediary in Porto-Riche's courtship of Élisabeth to a suitor bound and determined to win her for himself.

Hervieu began writing to Élisabeth on his own account in the spring of 1888, right around the time when Porto-Riche, correctly fearing a double-cross, relieved him of his duties as go-between. Hervieu's initial overtures to Élisabeth were not letters as such but collages of quotations from a miscellany of classic authors—Diderot and Keats, Rousseau and Goethe, Shelley and Musset—about life-changing, all-consuming passion. Like Porto-Riche's poems, these texts played to Élisabeth's literary bent, feeding her craving for fairy-tale romance. But unlike Porto-Riche's poems, which by that spring had turned sulky and importunate, Hervieu's quote collages spoke of his love in only the most exalted terms. As Porto-Riche's communiqués grew testier, Hervieu, profiting from his inside knowledge of his rival, presented himself to Élisabeth as the quintessential courtly lover, worshipful, submissive, asking only to admire and to serve. In a rare attempt at writing poetry of his own, Hervieu pledged to Élisabeth his "patient and submissive heart," a "heart filled only with you" and with "infinite love."

This was the tone Élisabeth wished all her men would take with her; it corresponded perfectly to the ideal of chaste, cerebral love she had been preaching for nearly a decade, with woefully little success. While some of her admirers started out by paying lip service to her platonic creed, sooner or later they all tired of it. And once they did, they gave free rein to their torments, their grievances, their sullying urges and demands; they hassled and hounded Élisabeth until the very sight of them filled her with disgust. But not Hervieu. Those metaphorical icicles on his moustache bespoke a level of self-containment that made him an exceptionally good candidate for her new Prince Charming.

It is quite possible that her virginal, Récamier posturing struck a chord with Hervieu as well. He would remain a bachelor all his life, although he would go on to have a publicly acknowledged, long-lasting relationship with another *mondaine,* Baronne Aimery-Harty (Marguerite) de Pierrebourg. Mme de Pierrebourg would leave her husband for him in the 1890s, but she and Hervieu would never live together. Literature may have been the chief binding agent in their union, for she was a writer, too, publishing well-regarded novels under the gender-neutral alias Claude Ferval. According to Georges de Lauris, who married Mme de Pierrebourg's daughter in 1910, his mother-in-law and Hervieu thought of themselves as latter-day versions of George Sand and Alfred de Musset—the very partners in genius Élisabeth had looked to as models for her relationships with both Giovanni and Porto-Riche.

That same type of model now presented itself to Élisabeth's mind as a prospective template for her friendship with Hervieu, unbeknownst to the two men who had preceded him in that scenario. Neither Giovanni nor Porto-Riche was aware of her clandestine involvement with Hervieu (though Porto-Riche, having smelled a rat in the spring of 1888, had ceased to regard him as a friend). Consequently, neither of them could have realized that with the sensational success of his writings about the monde, and with his genius for epistolary fiction especially, Hervieu had assumed newfound potential for her as an artistic, if not a romantic, partner. Outstripping the cagey Italian prince and the volatile Jewish poet, the famous young novelist—driven yet docile, besotted yet bloodless—was coming into focus as a man singularly well equipped to help tell her story. Perhaps someday, if she decided she really wanted him in the role, he would be the coauthor of Élisabeth's dreams.

CHAPTER TWENTY-TWO

GODDESSES AND MONSTERS

In the spring of 1892, Proust had an encounter with Geneviève that confirmed his worst suspicions about her soulless character. He took almost thirty years to give literary form to his discontent, reworking the fateful experience in the final scene of *The Guermantes Way* (1920–1921), where the hollowness of the *mondain* obsession with appearances appears in stark, shocking relief. Just before this volume of the *Search* came out, Proust warned Mme Straus that he had "incorporated the red shoes" into the storyline, "but without naming you." By withholding Mme Straus's name, he manifestly sought to do her a kindness, as the vignette exposes the Duchesse de Guermantes and her husband, the book's paragons of noble elegance, as ogres of superficiality and self-absorption.

As Proust did not write about the original "red shoes" incident in any other context, the version recounted in *The Guermantes Way* offers the only available information as to what he might have witnessed with Mme Straus half a lifetime before. In the novel, Jewish clubman Charles Swann (whom Geneviève, discerning his likeness to the Jockey-Club Jew, renamed "Swann-Haas") appears at the Guermantes' house in Paris just as the duc and duchesse are on their way out to a fancy-dress ball at a friend's house near the parc Monceau. Atypically for such a stalwart party fixture, Swann has no plans to join them at the fête; he explains that his doctors have recently told him he is terminally ill, with no more than three or four months left to live. As one of his oldest and dearest friends, the duchesse might be expected to be saddened by this news. But her overriding commitment to her social duties leaves no room for sorrow. In their eagerness to get to the ball, she and the duc pretend to take Swann's announcement as a joke, for if he were kidding, they would be under no obligation to keep talking with him. Again acting out of character, Swann proves unwilling to let them off so easily. "That would be a joke in charming taste," he answers in a sarcastic tone. By placing jokes and taste, two staples of *mondain* sociability, in opposition to the pathos of a man's looming death, Proust stresses the shallowness and frivolity of *bon ton*.

In the name of that very code, the Duc de Guermantes hastens to cut the interview short, pointing out that if he and his wife tarry any longer, they will be late for their party—an unpardonable social sin. But then he notices that the duchesse has put on black shoes with her red dress, a pairing he finds so ugly that he barks at her to go back into the house and change into red shoes at once. For an anxious beat she demurs, reminding the duc of what he has just said to

Swann about them running late. "But we have all the time in the world!" the duc counters, unfazed. "It won't even take us ten minutes to get to the parc Monceau!" Defeated, the duchesse obeys her husband's orders, showing that while she has not a minute to spare to comfort her dying friend, she has "all the time in the world" to make adjustments to her outfit. Once again, matters of elegance override the most rudimentary imperatives of human kindness.

According to biographer George Painter, the real encounter that inspired this vignette occurred when Proust was in his early twenties and went to the entresol to pick up the Strauses for a ball they were to attend nearby with a whole group of *fidèles*. Mme Straus came downstairs to Proust's waiting carriage attired in a red gown with black shoes, whereupon Straus, who prided himself on his unimpeachable dress sense, flew into a rage at the inelegant color combination. And so, writes Painter, "Mme Straus, like the duchesse, was compelled by her angry husband to change" into red shoes and sent "Proust himself . . . upstairs to fetch" them for her. Painter identifies neither the function the Strauses were going to nor which, if any, of their companions tried to divulge a terminal illness at that time.

However, Geneviève's red dress makes it possible to pinpoint the event with reasonable certainty, as there is only one documented case of her ever having worn that color, so alien to the tones of her habitual half mourning. That was on March 2, when she and Straus went with Proust, Ganderax, Jacques Blanche, and Édouard Detaille to a costume ball at Madeleine Lemaire's house near the parc Monceau. In observance of the party's theme, "paper," Geneviève dressed as a playing card, the Queen of Hearts; *Le Gaulois* described her costume as a red satin ball gown and a red-and-black "Rubens hat." With two illicit love affairs in her recent past, Geneviève may have opted for this guise in a saucy attempt to defuse any lingering hint of scandal. By appearing as the Queen of Hearts, she acknowledged her reputation as a manslayer head-on, yet made light of it with her famous nonchalant wit.

The press said nothing about either her husband's or Proust's party attire, although it did report that Jacques Blanche went as Lohengrin in a giant papier-mâché swan's head. More regrettably still, no public or private accounts of the Lemaire ball mention a soon-to-be-dying member of the Strauses' entourage, and while Haas, as Swann's Doppelgänger, might come to mind first in this connection, he did not die until 1902. Nonetheless, another of Geneviève's most devoted, longtime friends, composer Ernest Guiraud, did pass away at age fifty-five just two months after the ball. It is thus not out of the question that Guiraud showed up at the entresol on the evening of the Lemaire ball with tidings akin to Swann's. And if one considers Proust's theory that Geneviève didn't "care a whit" about other people—or Daniel Halévy's observation that she was "as egotistical as a monster and as unthinking as a doll"—it is not improbable that if Guiraud did try to tell her about his failing health, she reacted flippantly, in the manner of the future Mme de Guermantes. Whatever happened that night, it made a lasting impression on Proust, compounding his disenchantment with Mme Straus and accelerating his search for a new model of *mondanité*.

THAT PROUST HIMSELF WAS INVITED to the "paper" ball reflected the progress he had been making as a society swell, for the friendship of Madeleine Lemaire was its own badge of *mondain* prestige, and primed him for further social advancement. The mavens of the Faubourg regarded Lemaire's vaporous, decorative aesthetic as the last word in painterly elegance. According to Lily de Gramont, "every [grande] dame owned a fan decorated with a watercolor by M[me] Lemaire," typically in one of her signature floral motifs, and Lemaire's drawings adorned luxury editions of works by such socially prominent authors as Comte Robert de Montesquiou, Paul Hervieu, and the late Lord Lytton. A gregarious, rich, and clever bourgeoise, Mme Lemaire had parlayed her success as an artist into a provisional *mondain* status akin to that of Mme Straus. The at-homes she held on Tuesdays in her glass-roofed studio in the rue de Monceau drew the same mixed demographic, and often the same people, as Geneviève's Sundays in the boulevard Haussmann, from Dumas *fils* to Princesse Mathilde and d'Haussonville to Réjane.

This overlap led to a superficially friendly rivalry between the two hostesses, who poached guests from each other's salons on the sly. This was how Proust found himself pulled into Mme Lemaire's starry orbit. First meeting him in the entresol when he was twenty, and she forty-seven, the painter was charmed by

COLLECTION FÉLIX POTIN

MADELEINE LEMAIRE

As he became disenchanted with Mme Straus, Proust began to rely on other society mavens to facilitate his entrée into the monde, including Madeleine Lemaire, a well-connected painter and *salonnière*.

Madeleine Lemaire, *An Elegant Tea-Party in the Artist's Studio* (1891): Mme Lemaire, *far right,* cultivated many of Geneviève's acolytes, among them Hervieu (shown seated, in profile, at *far left*), Louis Ganderax (center figure in standing trio at *left*), and Maupassant (moustachioed standing figure at *center*).

Proust's sparkling intelligence and wicked sense of humor and adopted him as her "delicious little page." Condescending as this epithet sounded, it belied her sincere affection for him, endearing her to Proust in turn. He appreciated that unlike Mme Straus, who still tended to treat him as an irksome nonentity, Mme Lemaire considered him a delightful addition to her guest list. She welcomed Proust not only to her weekly salon but to the high-profile crushes she sometimes held in the little lilac garden behind her studio. Her soirée on March 2, where the blueblood-meets-bohemian crowd was grander than any Proust had yet encountered in the entresol, may have been the first real "society" function he ever attended. Then and at Lemaire's subsequent gatherings, Proust cultivated several A-list contacts who became new guides for him in his exploration of the gratin.

In fact, the more Proust ventured into the monde, the less impressed he was by Mme Straus's standing there. After all, as Fernand Gregh said of her, "This charming woman was not a born *mondaine,*" and to certain, more conservative aristocrats, even the excitement surrounding "Geneviève's latest" and her tantalizing, hybrid salon did not make up for the double stigma of her plebeian Jewish birth. For Proust, laboring under the same two disadvantages, Mme Straus's background had struck him less as a drawback than a reassuring precedent for himself. But between his growing reservations about her as a person and his decreasing dependence on her for *mondain* entrée, he began to assess her social position with a flintier eye.

He noticed, for example, that Mme Straus had failed to receive an invitation for the most prestigious party of the 1891 social season: the Princesse de Léon's black-and-white ball. This extravaganza had drawn the gratin's most exalted worthies, receiving grandiloquent coverage in the *presse mondaine*. The accounts of this ball so captivated Proust that he would later evoke it repeatedly in the *Search*, without even changing the hostess's name. Mme Straus's exclusion from the Léon party signaled to him, and to anybody else who might have been keeping track, that for all her cachet, some doors would remain closed to her forever.

Proust could not help but observe that for other *grandes mondaines*, by contrast, all doors appeared to be open. Take Comtesse Adhéaume de Chevigné. He saw her for the first time either at Mme Lemaire's costume ball or shortly thereafter and could tell without even speaking to her that she was the epitome of noble breeding. As a loyal reader of *Le Gaulois*, Proust knew that Mme de Chevigné, thirty-two to his twenty in the spring of 1892, went to all the best parties, whether Mme de Sagan's "peasant" frolic, where she wowed the assembly in a bourrée, or Mme de Léon's famous fête, where she acted in a commedia dell'arte skit with a troupe of clubmen twice her age. (Laure had signed on for this performance because it gave her a chance to poke fun at her own resemblance to Pulcinella.) As the wife of a Jockey-Club member, finally, Mme de Chevigné was a fixture in the Ladies' Tribune at Longchamp, a queenly assembly in which Mme Straus could only appear as someone else's guest, as Proust definitively realized when he overheard a *mondain* prince remarking that there was no conceivable scenario in which Émile Straus would ever be admitted to the Jockey-Club.

Mme de Chevigné fascinated Proust for other reasons as well. He was enchanted by her husband's echt-feudal name, "Adhéaume," including it in his litany of "baptismal names that . . . come from a past so profound" they seem to belong "in the stained glass of our cathedrals." He pined to know more about the exclusive redoubts where royals and nobles came under the comtesse's spell, whether Henri V at his court at Frohsdorf or the clubmen in her closed salon in Paris. He goggled at her sleek, minimalist dress style and her preternatural grace on horseback. He obsessed over her "mannish air," which combined square-jawed bone structure and virile swagger on the one hand with angelic blue eyes, "golden hair, and swanlike neck" on the other. (Proust may also have noticed that in covering the Léon ball, at least one reporter mistook Mme de Chevigné, in her yellow-and-blue harlequin outfit, for a man.) Even her countrified twang and salty locutions added to Proust's idea of her as "the incarnation of *landed-gentry* chic." With these attributes, Mme de Chevigné presented a model

Although Mme de Léon directed her guests to wear only black and white to her 1891 ball, Laure *(left, at center)* dressed in a yellow-and-blue harlequin ensemble. This outfit seems to have been her sly way of making fun of her own resemblance to Pulcinella *(right)*, the hook-nosed everyman of the commedia dell'arte.

of patrician elegance that Mme Straus could never have hoped to approximate: a model of noble lineage, with roots reaching deep into the past.

In thrall to his new muse, Proust recast his visions of upper-class glamour in the sepia tones of feudal history and royal myth. In the words of biographer Claude Arnaud, for Proust to fixate on "this heraldic monument [of a woman], whose coat of arms had adorned the bridge at Avignon since 1177, was to hoist himself up into the very highest company," while to daydream about "a lady whose existence at the court of the 'would-be' Henri V had followed the pattern of life at ancien régime Versailles was to harbor the illusion that he [Proust] was re-creating a court, if not a kingdom," in his mind. One of the many friends in whom Proust confided about his new crush, Robert de Billy, confirmed its formative influence on the future novelist's creative vision. According to Billy, it was "the Comtesse [A. de Chevigné], the wife of a descendant of an equerry of Blanche de Castille, [who] first inspired Marcel to effect that curious super-position of memories, images, and ideas that later enriched" his portrayal of the Duchesse de Guermantes, "like sunlight streaming through a stained-glass window, like a heraldic device, like a figure out of Petrarch."

Billy's reference to the Italian poet was particularly fitting, of course, in view of Mme de Chevigné's descent from "la belle Laure"—a relationship that appeared to justify the specifically artistic quality of Proust's infatuation. Although he had learned that society looked down on people who wore their emotions on their sleeve, when it came to the "bony and heraldic" comtesse, Proust had difficulty containing himself. Before long, his acquaintances in the gratin were snicker-ing: "Proust wants to persuade Laure de Chevigné that he's her Petrarch!" This association would outlive his actual fascination with her by several decades. In 1920, Proust told a friend that when writing about the society belles of his youth, he found that in spite of himself, he could "only, like Petrarch, keep repeating *Laure*" to convey womanly perfection.

Or, again, not so womanly, for as it happened, Mme de Chevigné was not the first member of her family to prompt Proust's literary effusions. A little over a year before he laid eyes on her for the first time, some of Proust's university classmates had presented him to Gustave Laurens de Waru, the youngest of Laure's sister Valentine's three sons. Proust and Waru were exact contemporaries—nineteen in the winter of 1890–1891—but Laure's nephew put Proust in mind of a medi-eval Crusader or knight-errant, the product of an ancient and exalted race. That Waru was not only a *noble d'épée* but an alumnus of the storied military academy Saint-Cyr may have encouraged this fantasy on Proust's part, although like him Waru had proven a mediocre soldier, graduating 411th in a class of 451 cadets.

Proust was entranced above all by Waru's patrician looks, which he would soon rediscover in the boy's aunt: blue eyes, blond hair, trim, athletic build, jutting chin, and prominent, delicately hooked nose. Proust found these traits exotically unlike his own, perhaps with the encouraging exception of the last one. Gregh observed that Proust "used to complain about the small bump on the bridge of his nose"—until he noticed the same imperfection on Waru's. With its similarity to a bird's beak, Waru's nose looked to Proust like an exter-nal expression of innate, seigneurial hauteur. Having made this determination, Gregh wrote, Proust became "coquettishly" fixated on his own beakish profile, as if it authorized him, too, to claim some share of inborn grandeur.

To ingratiate himself with Waru, Proust wrote a poem for him—an atypi-cally dull, uninspired ode to a beloved of unspecified gender, in whose "indif-ferent, languorous, mystical eyes" the speaker wishes to drown. Published in *Le Mensuel* (*The Monthly*) in February 1891, it appeared with a dedication as pointed as its title was vague: "Poetry, for Gustave L. de W." This grand gesture did not noticeably affect Waru's feelings for Proust, which remained cordial but noncommittal. Proust may have erred in thinking that poetry would win the young nobleman's heart; for unlike Daniel Halévy, about whom he had once made the same supposition, Waru did not have a literary bent—physics was his strong suit. Yet one aspect of Proust's dynamic with Daniel carried over into his dealings with Waru. Finding his homosexual feelings unrequited, Proust shifted his fixation to the young man's aunt: an older, more gender-appropriate, if no less unavailable version of his original love object. Anxious as ever to downplay his attraction to other men—"if only for the sake of elegance"—Proust revered Mme de Chevigné with the same ostentatious, platonic fervor he had brought to his relationship with Mme Straus.

AT THE ONSET OF HIS PASSION for Mme de Chevigné, Proust begged Mme Straus to play Cupid on his behalf; he wanted the striking grande dame to know she had won his heart. Geneviève let Proust think that she had passed along the message and that her friend Laure had opted to brush it off, but this was a lie. Having just lived through the double loss of Maupassant and Lord Lytton, Geneviève was not prepared to risk losing another of her swains, even one as negligible as "little Marcel." In fact, the previous fall, Geneviève had picked a fight with Proust upon learning that he had taken to calling on Laure Hayman, a cocotte to whom another *fidèle*, Paul Bourget, was also devoted. (Proust was presented to Hayman by his maternal uncle Louis Weil, one of her many satisfied customers; Proust's father may have sampled her favors as well.) Geneviève's fundamentally dismissive attitude toward Proust did not make her any less hypersensitive about his potential to "desert" her. As Porto-Riche had concluded when looking for allies in his quest to seduce Mme Greffulhe, it was useless to ask Geneviève for her help in such matters. The Mauve Muse abhorred a rival.

What Geneviève didn't realize was that making Proust think Mme de Chevigné had rejected him only intensified his attraction. As he had already demonstrated in his relations with Daniel and Jacques, and to a lesser extent with Mme Straus herself, Proust was prepared, even inclined, to withstand a fair amount of agony in the name of love. As when he was in high school, Proust still, following Racine and Baudelaire, conceived of sexual longing as an intrinsically nasty, brutish, and perverse phenomenon, a bonanza of suffering and debasement. Whether passive (like Mme Straus's treatment of him as the least important person in her salon) or active (like her son's and nephew's persecution of him at Condorcet), the humiliations Proust's crushes inflicted on him were and would ever be the bitter food on which his desire fed. In the words of scholar Antoine Compagnon, "Cruelty, by turns Sadean and sadistic," was the bedrock of Proust's sexuality. For this reason, Mme de Chevigné's lack of interest, as reported by Geneviève, would have functioned for him much more as an aphrodisiac than as a deterrent.

Mme de Chevigné's Sadean lineage would have been another significant enticement for Proust, for whom "the divine marquis" held enormous appeal. He classed de Sade's pornographic novels in the same important category as Racine's tragedies and Baudelaire's poems: unflinching portrayals of Eros as violence and degradation. Indeed, it is revealing that the only time Proust ever toyed with writing drama—a genre that during his lifetime was far more prestigious and lucrative than fiction—was when he tried to talk a friend into collaborating with him on a play called *The Sadist*. The project never materialized, but its title indicated clearly enough Proust's attraction to the Sadean legend, which intrigued him all the more because of its homosexual component. A well-known 1878 edition of de Sade's work advanced the claim that the author had extolled

Laure's artist friend Federico de Madrazo captured her indulging in one of her great secret pleasures: reading.

the pleasures of sodomy not only in theory but in practice. For Proust, this information would have heightened the piquancy of Mme de Chevigné's "mannish air"—as if, by falling for her, he were really allowing himself to fall for a fellow male "invert."*

Following his first glimpse of Mme de Chevigné in March, Proust came up with a two-pronged strategy of courtship. One of the two prongs was stalking. Like Porto-Riche before him, Proust found out where his goddess lived and followed her around her neighborhood each day. By the late 1880s the Chevignés were living in a small, unglamorous building at 34, rue de Miromesnil, one of the blander streets in the Faubourg Saint-Honoré. Wags in the monde averred that Laure had chosen the new place because it was conveniently located for her *vieux*, "on the way to their clubs." But it was conveniently located for Proust as well; he could get there from his parents' apartment in a little more than ten minutes, following his "route of hope."

Based on careful observation, Proust determined that the optimal time for intersecting with Mme de Chevigné was in the morning, when she left her apartment and strode down to the La Trémoïlle mansion off the place de la Concorde

* The same dynamic still informed Proust's relationship to *mondain* society twenty years later, when he asked the actress Réjane for a photograph of herself dressed up as the Prince de Sagan. Because Proust had just won a major literary award for *Within a Budding Grove* (*A l'ombre des jeunes filles en fleurs,* 1919), she granted his request. When a reporter tried to interview him about his prize-winning novel, Proust talked instead about the photo of the actress in drag, saying, "I value it greatly. I worship Réjane." What he really valued in this case was the image of a feminized King of Chic.

for the first of her two daily confabs with the duchesse. Waking up and getting himself over to the rue de Miromesnil early enough to catch the comtesse as she was leaving home represented something of a challenge for Proust, who liked to stay up late reading and writing. But it was a sacrifice he gladly made for his love.

And for his art, which constituted the second prong of his courtship strategy. Because he and his friends sold subscriptions to their literary magazine, *The Banquet,* to Mme Straus's *fidèles,* Proust had reason to hope that if he praised Mme de Chevigné in its pages, there was some chance she would notice. In April, he wrote a panegyric to her, publishing it in the May issue of *The Banquet.*

Entitled "A Sketch Based on Mme de ***," Proust's homage to Mme de Chevigné formed part of a larger series of *mondain* set pieces, *Fragments of Italian Comedy* (1892–1893). He may have intended the series title as a reference to Mme de Chevigné's stint as Pulcinella in the commedia dell'arte at the Léon ball the previous year. Otherwise, the "Italian" dimension of the texts was limited primarily to the precious, in fact Greek *and* Italianate names—Cydalise, Myrto, Hippolyta—of the characters portrayed. To his friends, Proust acknowledged that he had based these characters on well-known Parisian *mondaines,* modeling Cydalise after Marie de Mailly-Nesle ("exud[ing] something loving and painful, . . . a dolorous grace"), Myrto after Mme Straus ("witty . . . and alluring, but a slave to chic"), and Hippolyta, the heroine of "A Sketch Based on Mme de ***," after Mme de Chevigné.

In this last case especially, the character's name bears noting, as it is a feminized version of Hippolytus, the love object of the title character in Racine's *Phaedra.* On one level, the name evokes Proust's own taboo desire—for a married comtesse old enough to be his mother (and/or for her heterosexual nephew). On another, it subtly inverts the gender roles between the author and his subject, aligning Mme de Chevigné with Hippolytus, the youth impervious to the illicit passion of his stepmother, Phaedra, and Proust with that tragic queen, whose love for him consumes her all the same. (The reader will recall from chapter eleven that when bemoaning his unrequited longing for Jacques Bizet and Daniel Halévy, Proust explicitly compared himself to Phaedra.) Third, the sobriquet pays tribute to Mme de Chevigné's horsey proclivities—Hippolytus meaning "unleasher of horses" in Greek.

Last but not least, the name recalls the Greco-Roman aliases another seventeenth-century author Proust admired, Jean de La Bruyère, used to veil the identities of the real-life aristocrats depicted in *Characters,* his incisive study of life at Louis XIV's court. La Bruyère's writings often begin *in medias res* and develop their thesis through a "philosophical" dialogue. Both of these techniques figure in Proust's "Sketch," which he frames as a debate between a first-person narrator smitten with Hippolyta and a companion less convinced than he of her beaky attractions. Here is the essay in its entirety:

How can you prefer Hippolyta to the five other women I have just named, and who are the uncontested beauties of Verona? For starters, her nose is too long and too hooked.

You might as well add that her skin is too fragile and her upper lip too thin, so that when she laughs, it pulls her mouth upward into a very acute angle. And yet, her laugh delights me no end; and the purest profiles leave me cold compared to the silhouette of her overly (in your view) hooked nose, which moves me so much and reminds me of a bird. Her head has something of a bird about it as well—tracing a line between her forehead and the blond nape of her neck—and her sweet, piercing eyes even more so. Often, at the theater, she sits with her elbows resting on the balustrade of her loge; her white-gloved arm shoots straight up to her chin, which she cradles in the fingers of her hand. Her perfect figure fills out her customary, gauzy white wrappings like folded wings. One thinks of a bird lost in reverie, perched on a frail and elegant claw. I have never been able to encounter her children or her nephews, all of whom have the same hooked nose, thin lips, piercing eyes, and fragile skin as she, without being moved to recognize a race born, no doubt, of a cross between a goddess and a bird. Beneath the metamorphosis that today fastens some or other winged desire to this woman's body, I recognize the regal little head of a peacock, behind which no longer flows a sea-blue or sea-green torrent, or the foam of her mythic plumage. She is woman and dream, an energetic yet delicate beast, a peacock with wings of snow, a sparrow with precious gems for eyes. She evokes the idea of the fabulous, with the frisson of the beautiful.

Here again, Proust's appropriation of another writer's strategies goes beyond elementary pastiche. These lines show his imagination taking flight, turning a white-clad blonde at the theater into an emblem of highborn, avian grace. From her distinctively beaked nose, a replica of her nephew Waru's, Proust draws out the conceit of the celestial rare bird. Hippolyta may have traded her "mythic plumage" for "customary" *mondain* evening dress, but her looks and bearing lose none of their ornithological charm. Spurring the narrator's "winged desire," they elevate him metaphorically into her own lofty sphere, home to deities and birds, the fabulous and the beautiful.

If Mme Straus molded Proust's understanding of the *mondaine*'s mentality— her biases, habits, and countless pretty hypocrisies—Mme de Chevigné shaped his ideal of the grande dame as a physical specimen. Forever afterward, the blue-eyed, blond-haired, hook-nosed bird goddess would stand as his archetype of patrician elegance, the harbinger of a realm reachable only, to mortals like himself, on the wings of sacred desire.

A PUBLISHED WORK IS LIKE a message in a bottle—one casts it into the "sea-blue or sea-green torrent" and hopes for the best. Long though he might for Mme de Chevigné to recognize herself in his Hippolyta sketch, beyond publishing it in *The Banquet,* there was nothing Proust could do to ensure that she read it. If Laure did read it, no trace of her reaction survives.

Yet there is some evidence to suggest that another noblewoman read Proust's essay. And not just any noblewoman, but the very one who before too long would replace Laure as Proust's *muse mondaine,* just as Laure had replaced Geneviève. At some point after the d'Orléans' farewell at Eu, Élisabeth Greffulhe added a secondary character to her Marie-Alice novel: the Baronne de Thélus, a self-seeking, rule-breaking society maven with a pronounced resemblance to Laure de Chevigné. In Élisabeth's narrative, the baronne has arrived in the Faubourg after spending her youth at the Mitteleuropean court of an exiled king, the moody, sexually dysfunctional owner of a broken-down nag named Popular Demand. To her *mondain* friends, the baronne brags (with faux "simplicity") about her royal connections, but she is a rebel in courtier's clothing. Inspired by the novels of the Marquis de Sade, she enjoys an "existence independent from [that of] the husband [she] does not love." When in the city, she spends "amusing evenings exploring the underbelly of Paris" in places like Montmartre. When in the country, at the château of an older duchess who adores her, she sneaks into her paramour's bedroom in the middle of the night (and plays dastardly practical jokes on the Général de Galliffet). The baronne's character is a study in contradictions, at once refined and coarse, formal and familiar, feminine and virile.

In short, she is a Laure de Chevigné epigone. The connection is even apparent in the baronne's surname, which abbreviates Thellusson, the name of Laure's merchant-turned-baron ancestors. For the baronne's first name, while Élisabeth eventually settled on Maximilienne, this was not her only choice. Her corrections to the page proofs of her manuscript indicate that she considered naming the character Hippolyta—or even, perhaps to highlight the baronne's ambiguous sexuality and "mannish air," Hippolytus (Hippolyte in French).

Given Élisabeth's catholic literary tastes, there is some chance that she borrowed the name Hippolyta from Shakespeare's *Midsummer Night's Dream.* But except for her fondness for horses and hunting, the Bard's docile queen of the Amazons has nothing in common with Élisabeth's mischievous, on-the-make baronne. Admittedly, Proust's Hippolyta bears no resemblance to her Shakespearean counterpart either. That, however, is because the narrator of the "Sketch" only sees his dream woman from a distance—as an image, not a person. And without question, that image is Laure de Chevigné's. As such, Proust's homage seems a more probable source than Shakespeare's play for the name of Élisabeth's Laure-esque baronne.

Which is not to imply that Élisabeth herself was one of the entresol regulars to whom Proust and his friends hawked *The Banquet*. As far as anyone knows, Élisabeth never frequented Geneviève's salon, and the detailed records she kept as a hostess indicate that she never invited her to the rue d'Astorg, much less to Bois-Boudran or Dieppe. Not only were the two women not friends; their one-time rivalry over Lord Lytton may have left a lasting animosity between them. Élisabeth's brother-in-law d'Arenberg, though, remained devoted to Geneviève. More than that, by the time *The Banquet* came out, he owed Geneviève a favor, as through some of her influential republican friends she was working on getting d'Arenberg named to the presidency of the Suez Canal Company, an esteemed and highly profitable appointment. While he was not named to the post until 1894, it was a long process; in the meantime, shelling out ten francs a month for Geneviève's son's and nephew's magazine would have been the least the prince could do to thank her. So if *The Banquet* did find its way into Élisabeth's hands, d'Arenberg would almost surely have been the conduit. It is even plausible that Élisabeth liked what she read, as she went on to take out her own subscription to *The White Review* after it merged with *The Banquet* a year later.

AS FOR PROUST, he discovered all too soon that in Mme de Chevigné, what had enticed him was the image, not the person. He walked his "route of hope" for several weeks, maybe two months at most, and so long as the object of his passion stayed just out of reach, a "great golden bird" fluttering at the outer limits of the visible, her hold on him was absolute. From his respectful stalker's remove, he could go into ecstasies at the perfect match between her heavy-lidded blue eyes and the cheerful blue cornflowers in her hat. When the springtime wind blew in brisk jags across the Champs-Élysées, he could gaze tenderly upon the splotches of rosacea that blossomed beneath the surface of her fair, delicate skin. He could observe her interactions with passing strangers—free from a footman's surveillance, Mme de Chevigné sometimes drew catcalls from workmen in the street, to her undisguised amusement. (To one randy fellow who whistled at her derrière, she yelled without missing a beat: "Hang on there, darlin'! You ain't seen the front yet!") Taking in these exchanges from a distance, Proust couldn't hear her words. But he could and did memorize the "very acute angle" Mme de Chevigné's lips formed when she laughed, outlining neither the shape of a rosebud nor the promise of a kiss but the sharp, proud sliver of a vestigial second beak—a duplicate marker of her mythic, avian race.

Best of all, Proust could lose himself in his dreams of the life Mme de Chevigné led when she disappeared from view: what books she read, what friends she saw, what châteaux she visited when she left town. Proust could make her anyone he wanted her to be, within the regal parameters—physical traits, genealogical particulars, *mondain* credentials—she had unwittingly supplied to his fancy.

He could worship her as a bird goddess come to earth, he wrote, "because he saw her with his imagination, which ennobles everything."

Then came the terrible spring morning when Mme de Chevigné spun around midwalk, glared at him, and screeched, "*Fitz-James is waiting for me!*" Why she lost her temper with Proust just then, after ignoring him for so many weeks running, remains an enigma. Maybe she was late for a tryst with Fitz-James—Proust did notice that she had concealed her features behind a little veil. Maybe she was feeling testy because another of her off-again, on-again lovers, Henri de Breteuil, and his young American wife had recently announced the birth of their first child, a bonny male heir. Maybe she was on edge because of the anarchist bombs that had recently started exploding all over Paris, including at the house of her good friend Jeanne de Sagan. Maybe she was fretting about money, which had been tighter than ever since Adhéaume's investment in the Panama Canal went up in smoke. Maybe she was miffed that her husband had resorted to earning a living of sorts, writing music reviews for his friend Gordon Bennett's newspaper, the *New York Herald;* or that one of his first articles, a piece about Wagner, identified the Comtesse Greffulhe as the leader of fashionable Paris. (While fond enough of Élisabeth, Laure would perhaps have preferred to see herself so named.) Maybe she was irritable because of an ill-placed hairpin poking into her scalp, or mud seeping into her shoes after a rain shower. Maybe she was stewing over a squabble with Frances, her children's judgmental Irish nanny. Maybe she was peeved that her old friend Albert de Mun, who always invoked his piety when faced with her flirty gambits, had overcome his religious scruples and fallen desperately in love with another woman. (Whom, he refused to say.) Maybe Laure had just had enough of the saucer-eyed young stranger tagging along on her errands uninvited. Or maybe she wasn't annoyed, at all, and Proust simply misread her mien and tone.

At all events, he would never uncover the cause of what he took to be Mme de Chevigné's pique. While he would later get to know her fairly well through mutual friends in the gratin, Proust never dared to ask her why she had spoken to him in that manner, on that day. But he never forgot how imperiously she had "marked the distances" between grandees like herself (and "Feetjahm") and peons like him. Even for a young man inclined to equate pain with love, the cruelty of the rebuff was hard to take. According to Céleste Albaret, the wound Mme de Chevigné inflicted on Proust in that moment stayed with him until he died: a lasting reminder that he should perhaps have been more careful what he wished for when he wished for a blueblood née de Sade.

CHAPTER TWENTY-THREE

SO LONG AS THE GESTURE
IS BEAUTIFUL

Proust's fascination with the aristocratic tier of Parisian society began with his pursuit of Mme de Chevigné in the spring of 1892 but did not end with it. After, and despite, her stinging rebuke, he persevered in his attempt to conquer what he now called "the *real* gratin." He relied less and less on Mme Straus, though he remained a regular in her salon, and more and more on several of the other hostesses he met through her: Madeleine Lemaire, Princesse Mathilde Bonaparte, and two Rothschild "countesses of Judea," the Princesse de Wagram and the Duchesse de Gramont. While none of these women belonged by birth to the *noblesse d'épée,* the latter two had married into it, and all four of them presided over exclusive social coteries. Proust charmed his way onto the ladies' guest lists and took every chance to ingratiate himself with their friends.

Not all the *mondains* fell for his Cherubino act—Charles Haas dismissed him out of hand, refusing "to speak to him and not even deign[ing] to look at him" when they crossed paths. Lily de Gramont's theory was that Haas looked down on Proust because when they saw each other at dinners in the gratin, the younger man was always seated at the foot of the table, and the Jockey-Club Jew hadn't gotten where he was by wasting his time on nonentities. (Another possibility is that Haas felt the monde wasn't big enough for two bourgeois Israelites with only their wit to recommend them.) But other society figures took a liking to Proust, from the curmudgeonly "invert" Prince Edmond de Polignac to the haughty and beautiful Pauline, Comtesse d'Haussonville. Reflecting on his rising currency in this elite set, Proust said, "The main thing is to gain entrée. After that it just builds up on its own." The mirror in his bedroom became a shrine to his newfound popularity, festooned with calling cards, thank-you notes (for the flowers he sent "pretty much right and left"), and engraved invitations to dinner parties, charity galas, art openings, balls.

So successfully did Proust navigate this milieu that on May 30, 1894, he earned an introduction to the grandest grande dame of them all, Élisabeth, Comtesse Greffulhe. He was twenty-two and she was thirty-three; they both had birthdays coming up in July, hers just a day after his. Their meeting would not beget a warm friendship, but it provided Proust with another indispensable ingredient for his fiction and marked the apex of his social trajectory to date.

In most scholarly and biographical accounts, as in most of Proust's own writings from these years, his fascination with the *grandes mondaines* tends to overshadow the historical circumstances in which it emerged. His preoccupation with the Comtesses de Chevigné, Greffulhe, and their world coincided with a phase of violent sedition in Paris. On February 29, 1892, right around the time Proust started trailing Mme de Chevigné on her morning tours of the Faubourg Saint-Honoré, an anarchist bomb exploded across the river in the Faubourg Saint-Germain. The blast inaugurated a two-year anarchist "black terror" that saw many more bombings all over the city, and culminated in the assassination of the president of the Third Republic, Marie-François Sadi Carnot, on June 25, 1894, less than a month after Proust first met Mme Greffulhe. Although generally ignored in the existing literature on Proust's "camellia period," this historical backdrop is important, as it throws into relief another profound ambiguity in his pursuit of elegance.

THE LEAP DAY BOMBING in the noble Faubourg didn't happen just anywhere. It happened at one of the gratin's most storied meeting places, the hôtel de Sagan. On the morning of February 29, two sticks of dynamite detonated on the doorstep of the mansion. The blast shattered fifty windowpanes in the building and nearly two hundred more in the surrounding area.

The Princesse de Sagan herself was not at home at the time, having fled the icebound capital a few days prior to spend Carnaval in sunny Cannes with Mme de Galliffet. The only wounded party was the princesse's concierge, who had happened upon the explosives while sweeping up; with its rounded edges and its brown paper wrapping, the dynamite had looked to him like a package of jam. "The escape of the servant from death was almost miraculous," wrote an American reporter. "He was a great deal more frightened than hurt," sustaining only minor cuts and bruises.

The ensuing police investigation revealed that the explosion was the handiwork of anarchists, possibly the same ones who had sent Mme de Sagan an anonymous letter the previous spring, threatening to set off a bomb during her upcoming annual ball. Having just been upstaged by the Léon extravaganza, the princesse had pared down her list that year to a mere five hundred invitees—not even one-third the usual number—and instructed them to wear the same black-and-white outfits they had donned for her rival's party. Presumably to protect her guests from a potential bombing, Mme de Sagan had confined the festivities to "an immense tent, supported by four beribboned pillars and covered in flowers, [that she had] set up in the garden." The *hôtel* remained closed for the night, and so did its ceremonial courtyard, which in normal circumstances would have been filled with idling carriages, horses, and drivers, and arriving and departing revelers. While these precautions had cast a tomblike

When anarchists threatened to bomb her annual costume ball in the spring of 1891, the Princesse de Sagan held the party in the parklike gardens behind her house, closing off the ceremonial courtyard and the *hôtel* proper.

pall over the mansion, the soirée had come off without a hitch. Since then, the princesse hadn't given the anarchist scare a second thought, until the blast at her front door.

Mme de Sagan hurried back to the city to assess the damage. By then the social season in Paris was just getting started, but she didn't plunge into the merriment with her customary élan. In fact, she would never host another costume ball again, and the police would never find the perpetrator of the attack.

The bombing gave dramatic expression to the sociopolitical discontent that had grown even more acute since the flight of General Boulanger two years before. One factor in the rising public outrage was a series of skirmishes between government forces and radical demonstrators (anarchists and striking workers) on May Day of 1891, in both Paris and the provincial town of Fourmies. In Fourmies, the army had opened fire on an unarmed crowd and slaughtered ten civilians, including two children. The massacre sparked a furor, and an anarchist named Ravachol (né François Koenigstein) vowed to avenge the victims. On March 11, 1892, he dynamited a building on the boulevard Saint-Germain. His ostensible target was a judge who lived there and who was presiding over one of the May Day trials. But because the building was owned by Comte Wlodimir de Montesquiou, Robert's uncle and Élisabeth Greffulhe's great-uncle, Ravachol's bombing also struck a symbolic blow at the Parisian noblesse.

Public outrage was further stoked by a huge financial scandal connected to the Panama Canal Company. Between 1882 and 1888, more than 600,000 small investors had poured their life savings into a venture for a new transoceanic canal in Central America. Led by Ferdinand de Lesseps, the legendary builder of the Suez Canal, and engineer Gustave Eiffel of the eponymous tower, the company raised 1.4 billion francs through a series of securities offerings but failed to disclose the multitude of costly problems that, half a world away, were rapidly dooming the project to failure. Though their coffers were empty by 1885, Lesseps, Eiffel, and their colleagues kept investors in the dark by bribing more than 150 government officials.

A civil court in Paris decreed the dissolution of the Panama Canal Company in February 1890, and ordered a forensic inquiry. Over the next two years, the details of the fraud coalesced into a picture of gross corporate malfeasance and staggering political corruption. Even as hundreds of thousands of people (including the Chevignés) had lost everything they had invested in the company, the management team and its government cronies had pocketed millions. A Franco-German financier who played a central role in the swindle, Baron Jacques de Reinach, netted 6.1 million francs from one fraudulent bond issue alone. He killed himself in November 1892; prison sentences for Eiffel, Lesseps, and other conspirators soon followed.

In this toxic atmosphere, anarchist cells sprouted like mushrooms. As reactionary and persnickety as ever, Goncourt complained in May 1892, "The anarchist party is recruiting all the failures, all the losers, all the hunchbacks, all those who are unhappy with their lives." The most hard-bitten malcontents, such as Ravachol, found their voice in dynamite. After the two attacks in Saint-Germain, anarchists bombed more redoubts of Parisian wealth and influ-

Between 1892 and 1894, a series of anarchist bombings shook
Paris, targeting bastions of law, order, and privilege.

ence, including a restaurant and a police station in the fashionable Palais-Royal district of the Right Bank. Ravachol was executed on July 11, 1892. He went to the guillotine singing, "To be happy, goddammit, you've got to kill those who own property. . . ." He was shouting, "*Vive la Révolution!*" just as the blade fell.

Ravachol's death galvanized his comrades. On December 9, 1893, anarchist Auguste Vaillant tossed a homemade bomb into the Chamber of Deputies, sending a forceful message about the discredit into which that body had fallen. (None of Élisabeth's, Geneviève's, or Laure's deputy friends were among the twenty injured; Henry Greffulhe, having aborted his campaign for reelection that fall, escaped the blast entirely.) Vaillant was guillotined two months later, and the government passed a series of "scoundrel laws" (*lois scélérates*) to crack down on other agitators. But still the attacks kept coming. In March, a bomb went off at a café in a Parisian train station, and in April, another one detonated in a restaurant where the Prince of Wales was expected after a night at the theater. While the prince ended up dining elsewhere that evening, the explosion injured and maimed many others and brought some twenty thousand rubberneckers rushing to the scene.

In Montmartre, the countercultural stylings of Rodolphe Salis and Aristide Bruant took on a new edge that was either sinister or electrifying, depending on one's politics. Anarchists sang Bruant's rebel ditties, supplemented by anthems of their own invention, such as:

> *Kings, gods are dead, and we don't care.*
> *Tomorrow we'll live as free as air.*
> *No faith, no laws, no slaves, no past.*
> *We are the iconoclasts.*

And:

> *I got enough daggers, pikes, and guns . . .*
>   *To hit Galliffet and the cops where it hurts. . . .*
> *I got potassium picrate, and nitrogen chloride . . .*
>   *And damn! Enough dynamite . . .*
> *To strike the whole of France.*

The reference to Galliffet posited a link between the new generation of anarchists and the Communard insurgents whose massacre the general had overseen in 1871. For the bomber of the train and police stations, twenty-one-year-old Émile Henry, the link was personal; his father had fought in the Commune against the Butcher of Clichy. For Émile Henry and his fellow travelers, Galliffet exemplified the brutality of the ruling élite.

Extremist pundits were quick to pinpoint another bête noire. In the autumn of 1892, a pseudonymous reporter for Édouard Drumont's new weekly broad-sheet, *Free Speech (La Libre Parole),* incited his readers to "attack the Golden Calf of yesteryear." While generic enough to encompass corrupt politicians, decadent aristocrats, and murderous generals, the metaphor in fact took aim at Drumont's perennial bugbear: the Jews. Before his suicide, Jacques de Reinach had given Drumont a list of all the guilty parties in the Panama scandal and urged him to publish it. The scoop made *Free Speech* famous overnight but earned no thanks from Drumont. He and his fellow anti-Semites took Reinach's Jewishness—and the falsely alleged Jewishness of Eiffel and Lesseps—as more evidence of "the Jewish peril" endangering France. Henri Rochefort, the founder of the socialist daily *The Intransigent (L'Intransigeant)* and the self-proclaimed "king of the gutter press," made this case in an article so rabid Drumont reprinted it wholesale:

> It seems that all of Jewry, high and low, [colluded] in the disaster that cost so many citizens their savings and so many good deputies their reputations. . . . The Jews . . . were the authors of this foul mess.

This perspective earned Rochefort and Drumont the "profound respect and high esteem" of the anarchists, who found in the vilification of the Jews support for their own belief that the power brokers of the republic were "monsters [who must] be exterminated." The anarchists lumped these monsters into a single aggregate foe, "Monsieur Vulture," whom caricaturists often endowed with an oversized "Jewish" beak.

Free Speech flooded Paris with anti-Semitic cartoons. In December 1893, Drumont circulated a free special issue of the weekly with a full-page cover illustration entitled "The Qualities of the Jew." Sketched as compartments in the head of a hook-nosed Semitic grotesque, these qualities bore such labels as "Honesty," "Charity," "Veneration," and "Patriotism." Each compartment showed a tiny stick figure contravening the attribute listed: picking a man's pocket, thumbing his hook nose at charity, worshipping a gold coin, and refusing to serve in the army. This last vignette conjured up the avoidance of military duty with which Laure de Chevigné faulted her good friend Haas, the Jockey-Club Jew.

The "Patriotism" box also foreshadowed Drumont's stance on a national scandal that would soon eclipse the anarchists and the Panama affair: the trumped-up conviction in the winter of 1894 of Captain Alfred Dreyfus, an Alsatian Jewish artillery officer in the French army, as a Prussian spy: *Free Speech* was the first publication to give prominent coverage to Dreyfus's "treason." On the cover of the issue that broke the news of the captain's arrest, Drumont ran a full-page caricature of himself sweeping "Judas Dreyfus" into a sewer with a pair of garbage tongs. The caption read: "People of France, what have I been telling you every day for the past eight years?" Aside from the spiked Prussian helmet

These characters on the front of Édouard Drumont's *Free Speech* fueled anti-Semitic feeling among Proust's contemporaries. "The Qualities of the Jew According to Gall's Method," December 23, 1893 *(left)* and "About Judas Dreyfus," November 16, 1894 *(right)*.

on his head, the word "TRAITOR" on his brow, and the lorgnette on his huge hook nose, the Dreyfus clamped in Drumont's tongs was identical to the wretch from "The Qualities of the Jew."

In the gratin, the intermittent shocks of the anarchist frenzy came as unnerving reminders of the vulnerability of privilege. In their ritualized customs and backward-looking lore, the *mondains* existed in a time warp. It paradoxically took less imagination for them to situate themselves under the monarchy of a Louis XIV or a Louis XVI than under the presidency of a Thiers or a Carnot. Nonetheless, living in constant reference to the ancien régime entailed a hovering awareness of the catastrophe that had ended it. That awareness varied from one individual to the next—finding its most accomplished representative in Laure de Chevigné, who now spoke of herself as "the ghost of Frohsdorf"—but it settled around a median of nagging discomfort.

The news of the world turned on the fragility of royal institutions. In March 1881, Grand-Duc Wladimir's father, Tsar Alexander II, had died a gruesome death in an explosion staged by anarchists in Saint Petersburg. For the rest of his life, Grand-Duc Wladimir tried to preempt assassination by sitting with his back against the wall wherever he went, even during his pleasure trips to France. His richest Parisian friends, like the Greffulhes, always hired extra security when he and the grande-duchesse came shooting in the Seine-et-Marne.

Just a month before the Sagan bombing, police in the Bulgarian capital of

Sofia had foiled a plot to murder the country's ruler, Prince Ferdinand.* Élisabeth Greffulhe may have gloated in private about her rival's ordeal; she saved a clipping about it in one of her international affairs files. (She also redoubled her efforts to educate herself on current events, enlisting her republican friend Gabriel Hanotaux, soon to be named France's minister of foreign affairs, to send her weekly news summaries.) Otherwise, Prince Ferdinand's brush with death heightened anxieties in the gratin, to which he belonged, odd and far away as he was, by dint of his d'Orléans blood. The execution of his would-be killers in August 1892 brought little comfort to his sympathizers in Paris; it even threatened to stir up more trouble for them at home. Reporting on the hanging of the assassins in Sofia, Rochefort invited French "socialists and revolutionaries" to rise up against "slaughterers like . . . Machine-Gun Galliffet," as the Bulgarians would doubtless continue to rebel against "Ferdinand the Hangman."

In response to the vitriol, Galliffet drove around Paris in a bulletproof carriage. But he remained a defiantly assiduous presence in the monde. *Hôtels* positioned "between courtyard and garden" would have afforded a degree of security for him and his companions, as the reception rooms in those houses stood at some remove from the street. Apartment buildings like the Strauses', though, lacked this buffer. The windows of Geneviève's drawing room faced directly out onto, and were perfectly visible from, the boulevard. So lobbing a bomb into the entresol when Galliffet was there would have been relatively easy had any of his enemies thought to do it.

The years of Parisian anarchism coincide with another extended gap in Geneviève's correspondence, so one cannot say whether she worried about the anarchist terror following Galliffet to her door. In his extant letters to her, the general made light of the risk. "The 'Machine-Gunner of 1871'—that's a bit of an exaggeration," he assured her, quoting from his latest bit of bad press. "But seeing as the legend has taken hold, it would be in poor taste for me to try to shirk the responsibilities that come with it." As a military man, a *noble d'épée,* and an *homme du monde,* Galliffet was triply inclined to shrug off any such threat, recasting the prescribed reaction of valiant nonchalance as a matter of simple good taste.

EVEN THOSE SOCIETY STALWARTS who didn't regularly fraternize with Galliffet had cause for concern, as the bombers' targeting of such civilian figures as Jeanne de Sagan, Wlodimir de Montesquiou, and Bertie, Prince of Wales, implied that anyone in the gratin could be next. At parties, the standard

---

* Despite Tsar Alexander III's antipathy to Prince Ferdinand, the latter man inadvertently saved the entire Russian imperial family from another assassination attempt in 1880. An anarchist had planted dynamite in the dining room of the Winter Palace and set it on a timer to explode when the Romanovs went in to dinner. But that evening Prince Ferdinand, who was the family's guest at the time, took so long to dress for dinner that the bomb went off when the dining room was still empty. His rudeness and vanity saved the imperial family's life.

The Strauses' entresol apartment, *right* (in the arched windows just above Sutton's shop), was perilously exposed to potential attacks from the street.

mondain reflex was to dispatch with the latest unpleasantness quickly—"How horrible, all these explosions!"—and then revert to more congenial subject matter. However, some aristocrats dared to evoke the menace head-on. The Duchesse d'Uzès announced that because she was "good to [her] workers" (those employed in her household and at her family's Champagne company, Veuve Clicquot), "they wouldn't dream of dynamiting anyone or anything. If only everyone did as I do!" Because of her unsurpassed rank, she felt entitled to play the schoolmarm now and then—she knew full well that her peers weren't as "good" to their underlings as she—but nobody thanked her for it.

Robert de Montesquiou, with his usual effrontery, voiced admiration for the rebels, sporting a red anarchist cockade in his top hat and crowing about his friendship with Henri Rochefort. In the monde, he would corner stuffy dowagers whom he knew to be easily shocked and lecture them about the grue-some sublimity of bloodshed and "the eternal black poetry" of revolution. If the upheaval killed some members of their set, he argued, then the survivors would be all the grander for it, "like those flowers that, the Far East teaches us, become more beautiful when the buds of the neighboring stems are pruned." He even cited an anarchist poet's quip about the Chamber of Deputies attack: "Who cares about the victim, so long as the gesture is beautiful?" Although intended to provoke his fellow aristocrats, Montesquiou's radical speechifying adhered in a roundabout way to their own ethos of superficiality. By aestheticizing the very real dangers of social chaos, he reclaimed them for the orthodoxy of pure form, thereby blunting their fearsome edge.

Mondain clichés achieved the same end with less panache. By clinging to the surface of things, they too drew a veil of "elegance" over the horrors of dynamite and deadly class struggle. Given the economic motivations for the anarchists' revolt, such biblical truisms as d'Haussonville's "For ye have the poor always with you" took on an unexpected topicality. If one interpreted this line to mean that poverty was an inevitable feature of human existence, then one might logically persuade oneself that the likes of Ravachol and Émile Henry were fighting a losing battle, whether against "Monsieur Vulture" or the very will of God. However specious, an inference of this sort could provide some illusory comfort against the menace of the next terrorist bomb.

Proust dramatizes the *mondain* retreat into platitude in "A Dinner Party in Town" ("Un dîner en ville," 1895), his only published piece from these years to reference the anarchist attacks. The story is set at a dinner party on the Right Bank hosted by one Mme Fremer, an "ambitious, conniving," middle-class hostess "who [is] in the habit of presenting great writers to duchesses" and who prides herself on fostering "harmonious conversation" between the two camps. Her guests include a "relative of M. de Vogüé," a "disciple of M. Maurice Barrès" (two names drawn from Mme Straus's clique), a "very beautiful" young man called Honoré who knows better than to talk to his dinner partners about literature, and some insipid ladies from the Monceau plain. Honoré observes that along with the hostess and her husband (a rich and grasping bourgeois), the guests "all suffer from the same collective folly: snobbery." Thus afflicted, the group spends the dinner chatting about trifles.

Only as the meal draws to an end does the conversation veer toward substance. In the postprandial lull, with the candles on the table burning low and the wine flowing freely, defenses go down. "The gentlemen start touching the knees of the ladies next to them," and before long, Mme Fremer's guests stumble into a "grave discussion about anarchists." But instead of relating the particulars of the group's discussion, Proust gives the floor to their hostess, who with a soothing cliché brings the talk of terrorism (and the story) to a close:

> As if bowing down in resignation to an incontrovertible natural law, Mme Fremer said slowly: "What use is there in talking about it? There will always be rich people and poor people." And with that, all her guests, even the poorest of whom had an income of 100,000 pounds a year, were delivered from their cares, and cheerfully downed one last glass of Champagne.

Commoner though she is, Mme Fremer displays the instincts of a "born" *mondaine.* Redirecting attention away from an unwelcome political reality, she sustains her guests in the pleasing illusion that their cosseted, moneyed existence is immutable and everlasting.

WITH THE BONE-DRY IRONY of its conclusion, "A Dinner Party in Town" reprises the arch social critique of some of the other *mondain* sketches from Proust's "camellia period." Yet just because he mocks the self-seeking smugness of a rich lady's claim that "there will always be . . . poor people" does not mean he concerned himself with the societal ills the rest of the monde preferred to ignore. Quite the opposite: not only do Proust's literary publications from the 1890s avoid (apart from the passage just cited) all mention of the contemporary political disorder, in none of the hundreds of letters he wrote during that decade does he once refer to the anarchist terror, the execution of the bombers, the "scoundrel laws," or the assassination of President Carnot. Nor does he allude even in passing to the May Day clashes, the Panama Canal imbroglio, or the anti-Jewish polemics of Drumont and Rochefort. Although Proust would later side against the anti-Semites in the Dreyfus affair, before then he took no demonstrable interest in the sociopolitical issues of his day.

To some degree, one might blame his inattention on the callowness of youth. After all, Proust was only twenty when the bombings in Paris started and twenty-two when Carnot was killed. However, some of the anarchists were just as young as Proust and came from similarly prosperous backgrounds. At least one of his friends, moreover, began at that time to engage seriously with questions of economic inequality, workers' rights, and social and educational reform. Having graduated from Condorcet in 1890, a year after Proust, Daniel Halévy became a fervid reader of Marxist and socialist thought. To his Orléanist parents' chagrin, Daniel spent much of his time as a university student in Paris touring poor working-class neighborhoods, interviewing the locals, and taking notes for a (never completed) study of modern socialism.

Even setting Daniel and his research aside, Proust's social circle did not exactly insulate him from the political turbulence of the era. Through Dr. Adrien, whose stature as public-health expert continued to earn him important government honors and commissions, Proust and his family were well acquainted with many eminent republican officials, including Félix Faure, a future president of the republic, and his family. (Faure's daughters, Lucie and Antoinette, had been two of Proust's favorite playmates since childhood, and it was Antoinette who first gave him the questionnaire eventually renamed in his honor.) The Prousts were also close to one of the primary villains of the Panama Canal affair: Gustave Eiffel. Eiffel's sister was one of Jeanne Proust's dearest friends.

As an habitué of Mme Straus's salon, Proust had even more ties to compatriots caught up, like Eiffel, in the Panama debacle. Newly minted *fidèle* Maurice Barrès, then a freshman Boulangist deputy, emerged as one of the fiercest government critics of the scam, while Émile Straus mounted the legal defense for one of the culprits. Because both he and his client were Jewish, Straus became a target of the anti-Semites' ire, as did Joseph Reinach, a nephew of the disgraced Baron Jacques. Like all of Geneviève's faithful, moreover, Proust had to contend with the potentially dangerous presence of Galliffet in the entresol. (In his correspondence from these years, however, Proust only speaks of the general in relation to a point of protocol: "The Prince de Polignac calls Galliffet [by the informal] *tu*.")

Finally, *The White Review*—the literary journal that merged with *The Banquet* in 1893, and to which Proust contributed several articles—became at this time a leading literary outlet for anarchist sympathizers. One of the members of its editorial board was even tried as a suspected conspirator in Carnot's assassination.

To the extent that Proust held any political views during this time, they were vague but skewed to the right, perhaps as surprising to his father as Daniel Halévy's socialism was to Ludovic. Dr. Adrien Proust was a stalwart republican, as befitted his trajectory as a self-made man and his stature in the government. Jeanne Proust's politics were less easily categorized. Like many established, well-to-do Jewish French families (including the Halévys), the Weils had historically favored the liberal d'Orléans monarchy. Jeanne retained that bias while also—as an obedient wife and a citizen deprived of a vote—professing her support for her husband's convictions. Proust described her sympathies as an incongruous hybrid: "Orléanist-republican."

As a young man Proust seems to have absorbed the royalist part of his mother's outlook—his friend Antoinette Faure teased him about his "Orléanist preoccupations"—while rejecting the republican component. Still absorbed in the literature of Louis XIV's reign, he seems above all to have been nostalgic for an idealized vision of the ancien régime. In April 1894, he attended the opening of a new gallery exhibition about Marie Antoinette, with relics from her life and death loaned by many illustrious noble clans (La Rochefoucauld, Montesquiou, d'Uzès).* Afterward he commented to a friend,

> What I reproach the Revolution with is having systematically destroyed all that was gracious and beautiful . . . , the dignity of Marie Antoinette . . . , the sumptuary follies of [Louis XV's mistress] Mme du Barry.

To Antoinette Faure, Proust's "poetic" antipathy to the Revolution revealed, "if not [his] snobbishness, then at least [his] inveterate *mondanité.*" He objected that he was "not a mere snob like Straus" and that it "saddened" him to be lumped in with such an unsubtle, unpopular arriviste. Of his ideological convictions he said nothing. With some justification, Antoinette's verdict still resonates in Proust scholarship today. As Jeanne Canavaggia writes, "Proust and politics? In general, to pose this question is to invite the smiling response: 'Duchesses.'"

The essential point here is that if Proust ignored politics during his early twenties, he did so by choice. He made a conscious decision to focus on society and its mavens, to the exclusion of current affairs. Not only his literary work from the 1890s, but also his letters, validate Antoinette Faure's assessment with the sheer profusion of noble names they reference. As often as not, the names

---

* For reasons unstated, the Greffulhes did not lend to the exhibition their clock that had once belonged to Marie Antoinette.

belonged to people Proust either had yet to meet (e.g., the Duc de Doudeau-ville, the cantankerous clubman who wanted the Jockey to remain "one place in Paris where individual merit doesn't count for anything!") or would never meet (e.g., the Comte de Paris's family). Not knowing the objects of his curiosity did not deter Proust from avidly discussing them. He relished passing along sec-ondhand gossip ("I hear the Princesse de Léon [is] deliciously intelligent") and solicited information from friends better connected than he ("Was it Mme de La Trémoïlle who once, when . . . asked her opinion on love, replied brusquely: 'I make it often but I never talk about it!'?").

To the little literary gang, Proust's rapturous reports about the monde con-firmed their fear that he was turning into a horrible snob. Jacques Blanche pleaded with him to regard his *mondain* acquaintances more skeptically: "You have to look at them as if they were beneath you—the way they look down on us." At their most incisive, Proust's early sketches of the gratin show that he was capable of looking at "them" harshly indeed. Yet at this young age, he did not always maintain such an unflinching perspective. Blanche cringed to see his brilliant friend submit "calmly, even cooperatively" to the most "impertinent affronts" from the nobles. "And if I deplored the fact that he was wasting himself on these scions of the aristocracy," Blanche wrote,

> [Proust] would say to defend himself: "I assure you that dear old X" (or some other ducal name) "has a good heart; please forgive me if I tell you I know of no better friend than he; I owe him so much! If only you knew what Loulou has done for me! He showed me Ricard's portrait of his grandmother, the Marquise de X, and the cane that belonged to his uncle, the Maréchal-Prince de X, which in a secret little compartment one opens with a pin contains a love letter from Catherine the Great—isn't it sublime?"

It was not sublime, and to read Proust at his best, even in his early twenties, one would have thought him above such facile self-mystification. But like an astronomer propelled against all odds into a galaxy he had long viewed through a telescope, Proust "let himself be dazzled" by the "stars . . . of the *Almanach de Gotha*."

When his friends groused about his enthusiasm for the Faubourg, Proust insisted that he was looking to it for literary inspiration, not social advance-ment. In *Jean Santeuil* (1896–1899), he speaks with a mixture of earnestness, defensiveness, and self-deprecation about writers "whose fancy is captured by the monde":

> Seldom are the[se] men of letters as naïvely snobbish as the world makes them out to be. When [such a man goes into society] he does not say to

himself: "I want to *arrive,* I want to be sought after in the monde. . . ." No, [he] says to himself: "I want to feel everything, experience everything. . . . In order to be able to depict life someday, I want to live it." (Still, this rationale does not impel him to seek out poverty . . . , which just as much as opulence qualifies as a form of life.)

In the wry parenthetical closing, Proust concedes that a man of letters might just as fruitfully write about the impoverished as about the privileged. He goes on to explain, however, that when authors pursue "opulence," what really motivates them is a longing for the unattainable. They "desire that which—because all they know about the monde is what they have imagined . . . —they have always lacked." The gratin intrigues them as artists because it is not readily accessible to them (whereas poverty presumably is). To reiterate the Princesse Bibesco's formulation: "In the middle of Paris, [the monde] formed a world as distant from ordinary people on the streets as the moon is from the earth." It is this distance, according to Proust, that sparks the writer's imagination and impels him to create. In order to portray it accurately, he may do all he can to launch himself into that realm and examine it up close. But the first, indispensable precondition of his art is a perception of infinite space between himself and the stratosphere that lures him, twinkling brightly and untouchably from on high.

This would always be his view. Already in 1892, Proust was writing his unhappy fairy tale about Percy, whose infatuation with princesses and castles flourishes only for as long as they lie beyond his grasp. Twenty years later, he would rewrite that fairy tale as the *Search,* cycling his narrator through a four-thousand-page sequence of comparable enchantments and deceptions. Against the backdrop of political cataclysm, anti-Semitic hysteria, and anarchist furor of his early adulthood, though, Proust's aesthetic of unreachable elegance takes on a different meaning. His attraction to "all that [is] gracious and beautiful" belies a troubling affinity for the patrician ethos of shallowness he purports, in his more critical moments, to condemn.

Even as a young man, Proust may already have been too exacting a reader and too gifted a writer to have much patience for trite, superficial turns of phrase. But he was not yet mature, self-aware, or ruthlessly disillusioned enough to grasp that his fantasy of a world where illustrious names reliably correspond to splendid personal qualities (the Princesse de Léon: "delicious intelligence"; "some or other ducal name": exemplary friendship) was itself superficial and trite. While disorder, bigotry, and terror raged in his city and his country, Proust pledged a part of himself, a not negligible part of himself, to the *mondain* cult of appearances.

CHAPTER TWENTY-FOUR

SOVEREIGNS OF
TRANSITORY THINGS

MAY 30, 1894

This time around, and provisionally for Proust, elegance was a man.
Montesquiou, thin and hostile, wielded his cane like a duelist's foil.
He never had a hair out of place, his dark curls arrayed in a seascape
tempestuous yet frozen: a triumph of pomade and discipline. He dressed with
dandyish flair, "in a suit of fog or blotting-paper grey, the nuance and cut of a
charming pretension," a bunch of violets in place of a tie and a red anarchist
cockade in his hatband, a pendant to the red cross of the Knights of Malta on his
friend Giovanni Borghese's shirtfront. Montesquiou was inseparable from, yet
implacably cruel to, the Italian prince, mocking his well-known penury in verse:

Of his patron, John the Baptist,
All Giovanni Battista has left
Is his beggar's bowl, a plate to pass around,
For alms for his next meal.

Montesquiou and Jimmy Whistler, comrades in venom, enjoyed a good cackle
over this one.

As many poetic tropes as he devised, Montesquiou inspired even more. His
wiry frame looked like a greyhound in a topcoat or "a gladiola being whipped
about in a ceaseless storm." His temperament was "as unstable as his body,
which, on his high heels, would bend over backwards so far that it threatened
his equilibrium." He fixed his adversaries with a volcanic glare, twin pools of
black lava simmering beneath a chalky face-paint crust. He had an impudent
hawk's nose, a jaunty d'Artagnan moustache, an aloof and princely mien. He
barricaded himself behind a fortress of legends which, "though based on nothing, took on the solidity of prehistoric boulders."

Montesquiou pursed his lips as if tasting something foul—air breathed by
peons soured on his tongue. An offshoot of the Merovingian dynasty—"my uncle

By the time Montesquiou moved to Versailles in 1894, the former royal palace had been turned into a museum, but did not draw many visitors.

Childebert," thirteen hundred years dead, cleaved to him in spirit—he lived "like a king in exile." Now more than ever, in fact, did he dwell in royal style, since his recent move from the Faubourg Saint-Germain to an eighteenth-century pavilion in Versailles, a half a mile up the road from the Bourbon palace. The history of the house pleased him: its prior owners included a sword bearer to Louis XVI, a butler to Marie Antoinette, and a daughter of Louis XV. After spending 458 million francs restoring the place, the comte renamed it after himself: the Montesquiou Pavilion.

With his change of address, he took on a new persona: "the Moon King of the Bats," the spooky shadow cast by the Bourbons' fallen sun. Montesquiou, an elegist, sang hymns to a sunken kingdom, a holocaust of "stones that ask only to crumble *magnificently.*" Behind lowered eyelids he saw "the Sun King expiring on his deathbed, . . . the King-Sun [*sic*] dying nightly beneath the royal purple shroud of yellow-mauve mirrored waters." In his dreams he saw the guillotine, a necklace of blood-splashed pearls.

For Montesquiou, every conversation was a monologue and every monologue a performance. He "cackled and screamed in weird attitudes, giggling in high soprano [and] hiding his little black teeth behind an exquisitely gloved hand" heavy with jeweled rings. When he held forth, his slim, glittering fingers drew arabesques in space. He was a shadow puppeteer, a phantom calligrapher, "a sculptor of clouds!" He wrapped his pronouncements, gifts to the hearer, in ribbons of verse from the century's greatest poets: Hugo, Baudelaire, himself.

When Montesquiou threw a party, as he was doing today to inaugurate his new residence, he didn't just fetch his lute; he hired a whole orchestra. He installed the musicians in a decorative grove in the *jardin à la française* behind the house, planted to resemble the grounds of the castle up the street. Some of the statues in Montesquiou's garden replicated those that still stood in the abandoned copses behind the palace: Diana, the lunar virgin huntress; Proserpina, the queen of

65 — Versailles (S.-et-O.) - Avenue de Paris

Montesquiou's new residence was on one of the three main east-to-west thoroughfares leading through the town of Versailles to the palace.

shadows. Other sculptures recalled the occupants of Louis XIV's menagerie, long dispersed: a leggy bronze heron; an elephant the size of a haystack.

Manicured allées radiated outward from the low white pavilion, leading past the mossy statuary down a sloping lawn to Montesquiou's Japanese greenhouse, a miniature museum of chrysanthemums and potted bonsai. But the focal point of the outdoor mise-en-scène was the small rococo theater he had had erected in the center of the garden, surrounded by lush blue hydrangeas. Built from fragrant planks of young pine, the structure had a tented canvas roof and walls hung with trompe-l'oeil paintings of crumbling colonnades—more simulacra of the landscape of Versailles.

Inside the theater stood a low platform where a teenage piano virtuoso would play compositions by Chopin, Liszt, and Fauré. After that, the stars of the Parisian stage would recite the works of the century's greatest poets (same as before), positioned beneath a frieze that read EPHEMERAL (*ÉPHÉMÈRE*). The adjective, a homonym for the comte's cipher in reverse (FMR: Fezensac Montesquiou Robert), evoked his mantra: "I am the sovereign of transitory things." Things like poems recited and music played, like strands of gossamer, "delicate—, diaphanous—," dissolving even as they are spun. Montesquiou's *"fête littéraire,"* as he called it, would pay homage to these fleeting wonders, and to himself as their king.

For his guest list, Montesquiou chose invitees from the rival tribes to which he claimed allegiance, respectively embodied by his two guests of honor, Élisabeth Greffulhe and Sarah Bernhardt. From the gratin, he convoked his friends (Laure de Chevigné, Rosa de Fitz-James) and his enemies (the Prince de Sagan, Henry Greffulhe), each of their names a bright sacred bead on the rosary of the

Montesquiou had a *japoniste* folly built in gardens otherwise landscaped to resemble those at Versailles. Here he strikes a meditative pose while writing with a swan's feather. Photograph by Gégé Primoli.

"born." Montesquiou rationalized the inclusion of his foes with the knowledge that the highbrow pleasures of his happening would only plunge them further into the depths of their own idiocy. It amused him to picture them panicked and submerged, paddling furiously upward toward an ever-receding surface of murky green sunlight, lungs constricting, eyes bulging, bloated fish mouths forming doomed entreaties to a heedless god. Greffulhe, clearly cowed by this prospect, declined the invitation. But Sagan, stupid Sagan, accepted, and so unknowingly prepared to fulfill the prophecy Montesquiou had foreseen for him long ago, quoting Hugo's defiant dictum: *If one of us is left standing, that one will be I.*

From his adopted family, the race of genius, Montesquiou gathered famous painters (Lemaire, Detaille), poets (Porto-Riche, Régnier), and other "magicians of the Word" (Ganderax, Barrès). He also summoned his niece's three pet Pauls: Helleu, Hervieu, Deschanel. Of this trio, only the novelist had the impertinence to beg off, pleading an attack of gout that swelled his feet so painfully he couldn't wear shoes. The comte avenged the slight in a snippy tercet: "The author Paul Hervieu / is looking ever older [*plus vieux*] / and ever rainier [*pluvieux*]." At thirty-six, Hervieu was three years younger than Montesquiou.

Last and least, the comte invited somebody—nobody, really, undistinguished by birth or genius—to write about the party for the *presse mondaine:* a twenty-two-year-old university student and aspiring author whom he had a year earlier adopted as his disciple. Albeit a disciple of uncertain promise, the youth's talent for flattery and superb taste in literature (*The Bats*) were undercut by his dismal bourgeois manners and confounding mutinous streak. (In the salons of Mmes Lemaire and Straus, he was said to impersonate the comte with uncanny and ruthless accuracy.) Due to these flaws, Montesquiou had already broken with his acolyte once; their relationship would undergo many more such ruptures in the decades ahead. But of the *fête littéraire,* he trusted the boy to work up a suitably reverent account, extolling the refinement of the ladies' dresses and the host's literary selections.

In this mission, the amanuensis would not disappoint, though he himself would be disappointed by the finished product of his toil. Finding his article on the cover of *Le Gaulois* the morning after the party, published under the pseudonym "Tout-Paris," he would see that his extensive fashion descriptions had been abridged. Worse, his list of revelers would be missing the name he had been most excited to add to it: his own. Tout-Paris would try not to take the omission as a slight, a sign of his ineligibility for the exclusive club his alias denoted. It would mollify him somewhat to note that the names of a few of the grander guests, such as Don Giovanni Borghese, had been cut as well.

Montesquiou owned a replica of this statue, François Girardon's *The Abduction of Proserpina* (c. 1675–1695), which stood on the grounds of the palace of Versailles.

Besides, Tout-Paris's assignment would bring with it a different reward, of greater and more lasting import. At Versailles, he would at last be presented to the Comtesse Greffulhe: the newest Laura to his Petrarch and his latest ideal of aristocratic glamour. "Never have I seen a woman so beautiful." To this statement, Tout-Paris would sign his real name: Marcel Proust.

ONE EVENING IN APRIL 1893, at Madeleine Lemaire's glass-roofed studio in the Monceau plain, Proust attended a party celebrating the upcoming release of Comte Robert de Montesquiou's latest book of poems, *The Chieftain of Suave Odors* (*Le Chef des odeurs suaves*, 1894). Montesquiou's reputation preceded him, to a degree. Even before Mme Lemaire introduced them, Proust knew the comte was a grand seigneur who held the key to some of the Faubourg's leading salons, including Mme Greffulhe's. He was also familiar with Montesquiou's image as a nervy, decadent aesthete, collector of Moreaus and gilder of turtles. But he was surprised by the comte's "baroque erudition," a match for Proust's own, as well as by his demented grandiosity, irresistible to a budding satirist. Along with Montesquiou's pedigree and social access, these were the traits that drew Proust in from the first, activating an impulse known in the little literary gang as "Proustifying": the extemporization of rapt, effulgent praise. Such as: "You are the sovereign not merely of transitory but of eternal things." And: "Your verses and your eyes reflect continents the rest of us will never see."

Montesquiou reveled in the compliments, which were eloquent enough to gratify him as an author yet groveling enough to satisfy him as a grandee. Proust's looks were another enticement. Though eight years into a lifelong relationship with his secretary, Gabriel de Yturri, a former tie salesman from Argentina, the comte still had an eye for exotically handsome brunettes, as evidenced by his constant companionship with Giovanni Borghese (newly resettled in Paris after his family's bankruptcy in Rome). According to Fernand Gregh, Proust in his early twenties had a similarly foreign allure: "He was beautiful, in an almost Eastern or Italian way; he would laugh when I said he looked like a Neapolitan prince." Jacques Blanche's portrait of Proust in evening dress, exhibited in the Salon de Paris that May, showed him in this incarnation, scrubbed of the last outward traces of his misfit teenage self. Proust would later describe a version of this portrait in *Jean Santeuil,* where it reveals to the crowds at the Salon

> a dazzling young man . . . gazing out from beautiful, elongated eyes with whites the color of fresh almonds, . . . his rosy white complexion . . . flushed only a bit at the ears, which a few stray curls of his soft, shiny, silky black hair caressed . . . , his face as luminous and fresh as a spring morning, [radiant] with sweetly thoughtful beauty.

Proust's thoughtful beauty got Montesquiou thinking. Suspending his usual contempt for strangers, he suggested that the young man write to him after the party. Proust, recognizing the rarity of this opening, would not hesitate to take it. According to Céleste Albaret, he "never concealed the fact that he, too, was eager to pursue the acquaintance" with the comte.

Yet Proust's eagerness, contrary to Montesquiou's, had no basis in physical attraction. In the monde, Proust had settled comfortably into his role as "a delicious little page," dutifully paying court to women old enough to be his mother. Nonetheless, when socializing within his peer group, he continued to form crushes on men his own age. Most recently, he had fallen for a dapper young Englishman, Willie Heath, whose cherubic androgyny and inscrutable reserve reminded Proust of Leonardo's *John the Baptist*. He and Heath first met in the summer of 1892. By the spring of 1893, they were taking regular walks together in the Bois de Boulogne and mulling over (in Proust's words) a shared "dream, almost a plan, to live more and more in each other's company." The dream ended when Heath died—suddenly, from dysentery—in October 1893. But neither before nor after Heath's death would Montesquiou be the one to dislodge his boyish image from Proust's heart; Proust's erotic preferences ran to ephebes. His interest in the comte was and would ever be a matter of intellectual camaraderie, psychological curiosity, and social expedience.

Proust did not so much discourage Montesquiou's attraction as redirect it. Proustifying to keep his "Professor of Beauty" happy (the nickname itself was a Proustification), he engaged the comte in a lively correspondence. In his letters, Proust unleashed more torrents of praise for Montesquiou's literary opus, calling it "a glorious trophy," "heavenly opium," and "a meadow filled with stars beneath a sky filled with flowers." At the same time, Proust cast himself as an aesthetic naïf who had everything to learn from the comte's artistic expertise. "It would be an artist," he later would write of his alter ego in *Jean Santeuil*, "who, . . . with the prestige of his authoritative and revealing speech, initiated [Jean into] beauty; for his mind, which often found itself alone, needed guidance." For this guidance, Jean Santeuil would look, like his creator, to "M. de Montesquiou, that consummate connoisseur of artistic beauty."

Accustomed to playing this role for Élisabeth, Montesquiou undertook Proust's tutelage with zeal, if without mercy. In his billowy purple script, he critiqued his pupil's letters, issuing stern appraisals of their vocabulary (he had nothing nice to say about the word "nice") and style (he rated Proust's prose "no more than 15 on a 20-point scale"). *Mondain* despite his protestations to the contrary, Montesquiou could not abide infractions of form. A large ink blot on one of Proust's missives earned a crude edit, "CRAP," and an ad hominem verdict: "No breeding." He issued another reprimand of this type when Proust asked him to mail him a signed photograph of himself. A gentleman, the count countered, would know that such an intimate token was best given in person.

Proust took this admonition as his cue to call on Montesquiou at home in Paris, making his first pilgrimage there less than two weeks after their initial meeting chez Lemaire. The comte rewarded his initiative with the longed-for photograph, a moody head shot inscribed, "I AM THE SOVEREIGN OF TRANSITORY THINGS." The same motto hovered above Montesquiou's signature on the title page of the book he also bestowed upon his new follower: a deluxe edition of *The Bats,* "transformed into a bibelot" by its sumptuous silk binding and illustrations by Whistler and Lemaire. In return, Proust flattered the comte by adapting a conceit from Victor Hugo's *Ruy Blas:* "an earthworm in love with a star." "*The Bats,*" he enthused, "are a star that is traveling through space to bring light to all the planets, and which has very much dazzled this earthworm from above."

Proust barraged the comte with inventive gifts: a bluebird in a cage; a bouquet of Liberty ties; a noseless Christ child from an antique Italian crèche. He also sent Montesquiou a copy of one of his own published pieces, with a cover letter claiming that for him to present a sample of his humble prose to a writer of the comte's caliber was as "absurd" as offering "an earthworm in exchange for a firmament of stars." But in private, the earthworm was making a study of those stars.

His findings were mixed. Proust's growing awareness of the gratin's conformist mentality made him admire the comte's unabashed weirdness, particularly in matters of language. Except for the occasional biblical adage (fittingly enough for a "Professor of Beauty," he liked the line from Psalms: "Be wise now therefore . . . ; be instructed"), Montesquiou did not evince the *mondain* penchant for clichés. On the contrary: he favored arcane vocabulary words ("sardonyx" instead of "onyx," "moray" instead of "eel") and coined ungainly neologisms ("Pompadourity" for "rococo"). His manner of speaking was no less outlandish (all those shrieks and yells). "Your diction has for me a properly magical quality," Proust told him.

The younger man would later try to capture this magic in "A Professor of Beauty" ("Un professeur de beauté," 1904), an article naming Montesquiou as a worthy candidate for the Académie Française. Reminding the reader that the Académie is responsible for producing the official dictionary of the French language, Proust describes the comte's special aptitude for that task:

> Anyone who has seen [M. de Montesquiou] pause and rear up as he is about to utter a word, almost bucking like a horse at having seen a gaping abyss suddenly open up between the word's past and its present, made banal to us by day-to-day usage, and in the vertigo of having perceived that word's primordial grace, trembling like a flower on the edge of a cliff, anyone who has seen him seize at a word, show all its beauties, taste it (almost grimacing at the strength and specificity of its flavor), assert it,

repeat it, shout it, chant it, sing it, use it as the basis for a thousand dazzling variations, improvising with a richness that boggles the imagination and thwarts the mind's efforts to make sense of it all, anyone who has seen him do this can just imagine how marvelous he would be at the Académie on dictionary days.

As an account of Montesquiou's crazed verbal theatrics, Proust's crazed verbal theatrics convey more affection than derision; they feel less like a parody than an homage. And this was his attitude after ten years of friendship with the man. In the beginning, Proust so appreciated the comte's linguistic brio that he treated even his most absurd affectations as intentionally rather than accidentally funny. "In the beginning," Proust admitted to Robert Dreyfus in middle age, "I didn't know that Montesquiou didn't know he was ridiculous."

The young Proust was more ambivalent about his mentor's fanaticism for home décor. This preoccupation came into focus as Proust got into the habit of calling on the comte at home, first in Paris and then, from early 1894 onward, at the Montesquiou Pavilion. Interior decorating was one area in which the earthworm-to-a-star analogy may have legitimately described the two men's relative capacities, as Proust came from a family utterly uninterested in owning beautiful things. Despite their wealth and Jeanne's sophistication, his parents collected neither fine art nor fine furniture; their decorative tastes were fusty and middlebrow. Gregh remembered their apartment in the boulevard Malesherbes as a

> plush, . . . dark interior crammed with heavy furnishings, shrouded in curtains, muffled by carpets, the whole lot of it black and red, . . . a run-of-the-mill bourgeois apartment not too far removed from what [we picture when] we think of the somber clutter in a Balzac novel.

During Proust's "camellia period," this dowdy atmosphere drew scornful reactions from such discerning callers as Émile Straus, Oscar Wilde, and Montesquiou himself. Proust registered their distaste but did not share it. While he loved looking at great works of art in the Louvre and in private collections such as the Strauses', he said he didn't wish to acquire such treasures for himself because he already had "an incomparable museum" in his mind. But Montesquiou had an incomparable museum in his house, and although his décor schemes were considerably more recherché than those typically found in the Faubourg, the same commitment to noble grandeur obtained. Even at their most eccentric, the comte's interiors were theatrical displays, shrines to his matchless distinction.

To interact with Montesquiou in these settings was to submit to interminable disquisitions about his "religion of Beauty." By design, many tenets of this religion contradicted the prevailing dogmas of upper-class taste. When it came to furniture, for example, aristocratic Paris tended to favor the quiet elegance of eighteenth-century Louis XV "Pompadourity" and Louis XVI neoclassicism, shunning the florid opulence that had succeeded them under Napoléon I. The comte flouted this bias, commingling the three styles. In the Montesquiou Pavilion, he interspersed graceful Louis XV and Louis XVI pieces, natural complements to the eighteenth-century architecture, with incongruously showy Empire chairs and *guéridons,* their high-gloss cherry frames ablaze with ormolu emblems of Napoleonic rule: sphinxes, eagles, swans. If a guest happened to look askance at the Empire furnishings, Montesquiou would point out that they had come down to him from his great-grandmother "Maman Quiou," whom Napoléon I had personally chosen as the governess for his only son, the king of Rome. (Like "bastard child," the label "governess" went from lowly to lofty whenever crowned heads were involved.) Proust filed this detail away for use in the *Search,* where Mme de Guermantes stuns her friends by declaring, "The Empire [furniture] suite we inherited from Quiou-Quiou is a splendor!"

Splendor was Montesquiou's taskmaster and his god. In its service he reworked his home environment, wherever he happened to be living, as obsessively as his poems. Daily did he tinker, adding a touch of *japonisme* here, a splash of art nouveau there. Buying sustained the tinkering, a decorative-arts variant of his and Élisabeth's sartorial *shopping poétique.* Tireless in his search for the peculiar and the rare, Montesquiou pillaged antique shops and bore down on auction houses. He snapped up literary curiosities: "a cigarette butt from Mme Sand, . . . an absinthe bottle swigged by Musset." With his fellow collector friends—Goncourt, Haas, Charles Ephrussi—he traded notes and compared treasures. He shed old flourishes (peacock feathers) and tried out new ones (Lalique crystal). He scrapped formats while preserving motifs, retiring his polar-bear rug but commissioning from glass artist Émile Gallé a vase etched with polar-bear silhouettes.

Montesquiou arranged his trinkets in elaborate still lifes, of which his friend Abel Hermant described a representative sample:

> On the shelves sleep bats and hydrangeas, sculpted into ceramics and painted on vases, chiseled and engraved on wood and metal, shimmering with mother-of-pearl inlay, ivory and pietra-dura openwork, separated by glass partitions from green or pink or blue saucers and cups of precious china and souvenirs from olden times, . . . painted Japanese scrolls, bookbindings, cane handles, and plaster casts of the beautiful Comtesse Castiglione.

Hermant's tangled cumulative syntax mirrors the disparateness of the objects displayed, and conveys their disorienting collective impact. Yet as Montesquiou declared in equally tortured prose, his aesthetic aim was to stupefy, not to soothe:

The Montesquiou Pavilion: Montesquiou (in boater, at *right*) and his live-in secretary, Gabriel de Yturri (in top hat, *far left*), pose in front of his eighteenth-century residence in Versailles, two weeks after the May 1894 *fête littéraire*.

The grouping of *objets* in as it were an association, an ingenious and at times startling conversation, one that arouses the appetite of the eyes and astonishes the soul, that is what I have instinctively, voluptuously, and brilliantly sought to achieve, with the self-renewing drunkenness of the opium eater.

Such pride did Montesquiou take in his achievements as a decorator that he even deigned to invite reporters on his house tours from time to time, reasoning that press coverage could only help to spread his "religion of Beauty."

According to Léon Daudet, who accompanied Proust on one early trip to the Montesquiou Pavilion, their host's "mania not just for showing, but for extolling and exhaustively explaining his collections" was fatiguing in the extreme. His house tours took eons, yet if his charges grew weary, the comte either didn't see or didn't care. He had more, always more, trivia to impart to them; "he would grow emotional, irritable, excited, then, suddenly calm, he would groan after a long silence: 'How BOOOOOTIFUL it is!'" Recalled another guest,

He led us through gigantic salons, filled with vitrines, sideboards, reliquaries. He opened them up from time to time and pulled out a rare item, balanced between his index finger and his thumb: "Here is a *lacrymatory* that holds [Empress] Agrippina's tears. Here are Cleopatra's mirror and comb.

Nothing more nor less. This is the little silk jacket Marie Antoinette wore on January 13, 1776. This is the scalpel the surgeon Félix used to operate on Louis XIV's fistula."

Again reflecting the prejudices of his class, Montesquiou seemed to equate value with royal ownership: "The names [of their former owners] say enough about them to endow even [the] paltriest items with glory."

While mesmerized by the comte's mannerisms, Proust didn't much care for the arid provenance patter that went with them. Despite his own fascination with names (and royals), he did not embrace the idea that an object was intrinsically interesting just because it had once belonged to a majesty or a highness. Unlike Daudet, Proust did not resent their host for talking too much. He resented Montesquiou for talking too much about things and not enough about the human dramas in which those things might have participated. The scalpel, for instance, had featured in a remarkable demonstration of Louis XIV's iron political will. In 1686, he had to have a fistula removed from his anus, a surgical procedure so excruciating (in the days before anesthesia) that he lost consciousness for some time. Because his body was held to be coterminous with France itself, the king's syncope terrified his attendants. When he came to, his first instinct was to reassure them that his superhuman majesty had in no way been compromised: "The man is suffering, but the king is fine." This was the type of story that would have brought Montesquiou's bric-à-brac to life for Proust. It was also the type of story Montesquiou consistently neglected to tell.

When touring the comte's collections, one suspects that Proust Proustified to try to disguise his boredom. On one visit, however, Montesquiou apparently picked up on his ennui, as he later sent him a blistering letter of ostensible farewell. The letter has been lost, but Proust quoted the comte as having written, "I put you to the test of inordinate amiability, the only one that can separate the wheat from the chaff." The point: Proust was the chaff, too thankless and graceless to give Montesquiou's "BOOOOOTIFUL" possessions their due. The nobleman's fury subsided soon afterward, and he summoned Proust back to his house as if nothing had happened. Montesquiou had taught him a lesson, however, about his exacting standards for friendship, and about the risks one ran by failing to meet them.

Scholars have suggested that Proust later transposed Montesquiou's blowup into *Sodom and Gomorrah,* in a chapter where the Baron de Charlus, who "loved to play at being the king," berates the twenty-something narrator as an ungrateful, ignorant "*bourgeois* (a [word] he voiced with a hiss of impertinence)." There is no proof that this part of the novel replicates a clash between Montesquiou and Proust. However, the scene is full of tidbits that connect the fictional baron to the actual comte. The encounter takes place when the narrator calls on Charlus at home in Paris and inadvertently offends him, prompting the older man to announce,

> As any nobleman must, I made the first steps toward you, I who was everything and you who were nothing. . . . I put you to the test that the only eminent mind in our milieu astutely calls the test of inordinate amiability, the only one that can separate the wheat from the chaff.

Charlus then proceeds to insult the narrator for several pages, remarking in between put-downs that "these are . . . the last words we shall ever exchange on earth." And yet, like Montesquiou, the baron has more, always more, trivia to impart to his companion, even as he rants about their eternal rupture. Holding forth in a salon filled with strange artifacts and historically diverse furnishings, he continues,

> I cannot expect much . . . of someone who would easily mistake a Chippendale piece for a rococo pulpit. . . . Verily my affection for you is dead. Nothing can revive it. I always feel rather like Victor Hugo's Boaz: *I am bereft, I am alone, darkness is falling on me.*

With the furniture lecture and the Hugo citation, Proust again channels Montesquiou, in whose testy and didactic voice the baron unmistakably speaks.

And keeps on speaking as he shepherds the narrator through the reception rooms of his mansion to the front door, prating about his possessions all the while:

> I walked back with him through the large greenish salon, and said in passing how beautiful it was. "It is, isn't it? One must love something. The boiserie . . . come from the old hôtel de Chimay, which they opened up just for me. . . . Look, in this display case, here are all the hats worn by Mme Élisabeth, the Princesse de Lamballe, and the Queen [Marie Antoinette]. That doesn't interest you, one would think you couldn't see. Perhaps you are suffering from an affliction of the optic nerve. . . . You can't wait to get out of here . . . ," he added with a sorrowful expression. . . . Despite his solemn avowals that we would never see each other again, I could have sworn that M. de Charlus would not have minded seeing me again.

Once more, Montesquiou references abound, from the royal fashion flotsam to the insider's connection to the old hôtel de Chimay. More interesting, though, is Proust's condensed yet subtle portrayal of the baron's chameleonic character. In the space of a few lines, Charlus changes from a blasé dilettante ("one must love something"), to an entitled grandee ("they opened [it] up just for me"), to a memorabilia obsessive ("here are all the hats" of Marie Antoinette and company), to a passive-aggressive churl ("perhaps you are suffering from an affliction of the optic nerve"), to a lonesome crank upon whom it dawns too late that once he sends his visitor packing, he will have no one left to talk to. This metamorphosis is a small masterpiece of literary bravura, proceeding from the comedy of the baron's pompous chatter to the pathos of the loneliness and neediness his hauteur cannot wholly conceal.

BUT IN HIS EARLY LITERARY WORKS, Proust was neither this adept at nor this focused on capturing human complexity. As much as Montesquiou's provenance fixation irked him, he indulged in equally vacuous blather when writing about his own favorite fetish: the unreachable *grande mondaine*. Published in *The White Review* in the summer of 1893, "Other Relics" ("Autres reliques") is a two-page first-person narrative by an unnamed young man who has just bought up the belongings of a grande dame recently deceased. He explains in the opening line that he purchased them because the noblewoman had been someone "whom I should have liked to befriend, and who did not deign to speak to me for even a second." After making this disclosure, the narrator provides no further detail about the lady, her death, or his own interactions with her. Instead, he launches into a description of his loot from her estate: a deck of cards, some novels in bindings stamped with her coat of arms, two marmosets, and a dog. The house pets vanish from his narrative after the first mention. But he is mesmerized by the books and cards, which he construes as witnesses to the dead woman's "most unguarded, inviolable, secret hours":

> Her cards, which she played in the evenings with her favorite friends, . . . which were present at the beginning of her love affair, and which she put down to kiss [the man she loved]; her novels, which she opened or closed depending on her mood or her fatigue, . . . and the lives of whose characters and authors filled her dreams . . . while allowing her to dream about her own life in turn.

That the narrator ignores the woman's living companions (her pets) in favor of these inanimate objects highlights the morbid futility of his fascination. So does the question he poses to her books and cards: "Haven't you retained anything of her, and won't you tell me anything about her?" Predictably enough, they make no answer, their muteness appearing to suggest that the effort to reconstruct a life from relics is a dead end.

Reading "Other Relics" up to this point, one might take it as a veiled critique of Montesquiou's reverence for the castoffs of the dead, a refutation of the claim that provenance alone suffices to "endow even [the] paltriest items with glory." But the second half of the story reverses this perspective, as the narrator arrives at the conclusion that his lady's relics may retain something of her essence after all:

> Cards, novels, because she so often held you in her hands, . . . not all the fragrance that infused the air in her bedroom [and] the fabric of her clothes . . . has evaporated from you; it impregnated you. . . . You have conserved the creases made by her joyful or nervous hand; if she cried over a heartbreak, either in her life or in a book, maybe you're still holding her tears captive. . . . I tremble when I touch you, anxious about your revelations, nervous about your silence.

This paragraph is an apologia for "transitory things." It does not guarantee that such things will break their silence about the woman to whose "grace [they] unconsciously [bore] witness." But it does imply that the slightest material trace of that woman, a lingering whiff of perfume or a crease on a playing card, may germinate new life, albeit of a fragile and solipsistic kind. The passage ends with these lines, also the last in the story: "Perhaps the most real thing about her beauty lay in my desire. . . . She has lived her life, but I alone, perhaps, have dreamed her." The woman is dead; long live the man who dreams her.

By this logic, a woman does not have to exist to ignite passion in another's breast. In a deck of cards or a stack of novels, a stranger of a certain inward-looking disposition may find enough material to sustain his fancy. He may content himself with fetishes, disposing them in a vague approximation of a human silhouette. In fact, if distance breeds his longing and nearness kills it, then he may even prefer a silhouette, a shadow puppet flickering against an impassable blank wall, to a being of flesh and blood. He may give his heart to a simulacrum and call the gesture love.

It is either a stunning coincidence, or no coincidence at all, that Proust wrote "Other Relics" within days of his first-ever glimpse of Mme Greffulhe. He spied her from a distance at a ball at the Princesse de Wagram's house in Paris on July 1. The next day, he rhapsodized in a letter to Montesquiou:

> I finally saw the Comtesse Greffülhe [*sic*] (yesterday at Mme de Wagram's). And by the same impulse that moved me to tell you of my emotion upon reading *The Bats,* I must confide in you about the emotion I felt last night. Her hair was styled in a graceful, Polynesian coiffure, with mauve orchids trailing down the nape of her neck, like a "hat made of flowers" . . . It is hard to evaluate her, because evaluation implies comparison, and there is not a single element in her that one has ever seen in any other woman or even *anywhere* else. But the whole mystery of her beauty is in the sparkle, and above all the enigma, of her eyes.

Kindling the third and last of Proust's formative *mondain* obsessions, this sighting may explain why he called the story he wrote so soon afterward "*Other Relics*," a title that made it sound as if he were expanding upon a pre-existing relic collection. In a way, he was, for by the summer of 1893, Proust already had Mmes Straus and de Chevigné neatly tucked away in the museum case of his mind, ready at a moment's notice to be rearranged into a vivid new tableau of splendor or disenchantment. "Nothing more nor less": Montesquiou's line about Cleopatra's comb and mirror could also have been Proust's motto for his prototypical grandes dames. As he saw them, they were nothing more nor less than spurs to his own creativity. Without question, they were more valuable to him as relics than as real women, more pliable to his wishes and his needs. In Mme Greffulhe, his imaginary vitrine would gain an exquisite new specimen.

Her notorious aloofness heightened not only her snob appeal but her artistic utility, as her elusiveness would make it impossible for her to reveal some gross human imperfection, as Mmes Straus and de Chevigné had done. Confident that Mme Greffulhe's glamour, unlike theirs, would not fade on contact, Proust longed to meet her. He longed to bask in the sparkle, and above all the enigma, of her eyes. He longed to amuse her with clever literary allusions (for unlike her fellow specimens, she made no apologies for loving books) and be rewarded with her tinkling peals of laughter, "chiming like the carillons of Bruges." If he had read or heard about her panther costume from the *bal des bêtes,* then perhaps he longed to scan her features for hints of a resemblance to Willie Heath, of whom he would soon eulogistically write, "You reminded me of a da Vinci [painting] with the inscrutable intensity of your inner life. Often, with your eyes impenetrable and smiling in the face of a mystery you declined to reveal, you looked to me like Leonardo's *John the Baptist.*" He longed to study her da Vinci smile and guess at the secrets it withheld. He longed desperately for all these things, and he knew only one man could help him achieve them. Even if he did find Montesquiou ridiculous, Proust would never let him know it. Not before meeting Mme Greffulhe.

Montesquiou was not going to make it easy for him, however. Reading *The Chieftain of Suave Odors* over the summer, Proust noticed that the poet had dedicated the book to Mme Greffulhe and one of the sonnets to the Princesse de Léon. Proust used this observation as a pretext to tell the comte how greatly he wished to meet "some of those lady friends in connection with whom you are most often mentioned (the Comtesse Greffulhe, the Princesse de Léon)." Montesquiou had shrugged off Proust's earlier praise for Élisabeth, but this new mention set his teeth on edge. While it was he who had first trained her in the art of being seen, the comte did not like to think by this point she had surpassed him. He did not enjoy feeling that many *mondains,* and even many artists, now cultivated (or tolerated) him not for his own sake but for that of his niece. Still less did he welcome the prospect of her winning his new acolyte away from him (although arguably Montesquiou had effected a comparable betrayal by growing close to Giovanni on their Bayreuth trip). So when Proust dropped Élisabeth's name to him a second time, the comte struck back with a single question: "Do you not see that your presence in her salon would rid it of the very grandeur you hope to find there?"

Proust swallowed the insult (and plenty more like it, according to his worried friends). He was playing a long game with Montesquiou. He would bide his time.

While he waited, Proust developed a literary outlet for his fantasies about Mme Greffulhe. In late July, he suggested to three of his cofounders of the recently shuttered *Banquet*—Fernand Gregh, Daniel Halévy, and Louis de La Salle—that the four of them collaborate on a new literary venture: a *mondain* epistolary novel in the manner of Hervieu's latest best seller, *In Their Own Words*, with each of them contributing letters in the voice of a different character. The friends agreed and together they devised their alter egos. Proust created Pauline de Dives, a young married noblewoman secretly pining for a ne'er-do-well bachelor named Nulleroy, whom La Salle volunteered to voice. Gregh invented Chalgrain, a dapper bourgeois writer fascinated by the monde. Daniel offered his services as Pauline's confidant, the Abbé de Traismes, a kindly, worldly priest based on the Abbé Mugnier, genial confessor to Mmes Greffulhe, de Chevigné, and many of their peers.

Proust seems to have had Mme Greffulhe in mind as a model for Pauline and to have hit upon a doomed infatuation with Nulleroy as the key to her character and to the book as a whole. As he effused to Daniel on August 3, "Truly, the life of a lovesick young woman of the monde is a mute poem, made all the more touching by her melancholy and suffering." Mme Greffulhe would remain a mutely poetic presence in his imagination for as long as Montesquiou persisted in keeping them apart. As Pauline, Proust would fill his muse's silence; she would speak to him in his own words.

The letters Proust wrote as Pauline indicate that he had been doing his research on Mme Greffulhe. His heroine is an elegant aesthete, proud of her sophisticated (if somewhat affected) tastes. She claims that when she goes walking in the country, she looks for Walkyries behind the trees. She mulls over a plan to acquire some peacocks for her garden, citing as her inspiration "two marvelous poems" about such birds in "Robert de Montesquiou's *Chieftain of Suave Odors;* it is not in bookstores yet, but there are luxury editions." She turns up her nose at "young American women" who think they can buy their way into "our world." She boasts that Chalgrain draws his inspiration from her and would be her lover if only she would let him.

More striking than these letters' evocation of Mme Greffulhe, though, is their failure to touch on the feelings Proust had said he intended to explore: "melancholy and suffering." Only in one letter does Pauline come close to broaching the issue of emotional pain, and even then, she does not identify it as her own. In a playful, lighthearted dispatch to the abbé, Pauline refers in passing to the aristocratic tradition of marriage without love as "an abominable work of destruction," spawning "lives soaked in tears, husbands who go off with their mistresses in front of their distraught wives, etc." Avoiding any mention of her own marriage, she goes on to remark, in similarly generic terms, that it is "tragic . . . for an infatuated woman" to wait anxiously day after day for the arrival of a love letter that never comes. Nowhere in this note to the abbé, nor in any other part of the manuscript, does Pauline indicate that she herself might be the "infatuated woman" in question (that inference only occurs to the reader because she is the sole female character in the novel). Perhaps if Proust had been aware that Mme Greffulhe herself had been waiting anxiously for years for a love letter that never came—an unequivocal declaration from Giovanni—he would have done more to develop this aspect of his character.

But as it was, Proust went no farther in plumbing the mysteries of his "lovesick young woman of the monde." That he deprived Pauline of emotional depth might seem like a defensible, even logical, authorial choice, given the frivolity of the milieu he and his friends aimed to portray. Still, Pauline's shallowness conflicts with his own stated interest in her hidden, suffering side; it also stands in marked contrast to the wrenching despair of Gregh's Chalgrain (whose lamentations about the unattainable Pauline could have been lifted directly from Porto-Riche's *Happiness Manqué*). Although Proust had conceived of Pauline's hopeless passion as the fulcrum of the novel, it is almost as if he became too preoccupied with her elegant exterior to grant her an inner life. For neither the first time nor the last, Proust the *mondain* apologist edged out Proust the *mondain* critic, to say nothing of Proust the writer. It would be no great loss to literature when the project fizzled a few months later.

Proust and his writing partners did most of the work on their manuscript during their holidays in August and early September 1893, corresponding with one another in their characters' voices. After a few weeks in Switzerland, Proust went to Trouville, where he put up at the luxurious Hôtel des Roches-Noires on the boardwalk overlooking the sea. Just that July, the Strauses had moved in to their new villa in Trouville, Le Clos des Mûriers, a half-timbered chalet-style construction surrounded by rose gardens so dense and trees so tall one could easily forget one was at the beach. (This landscaping feature may have been a concession to Geneviève's fear of drowning, while also indulging her husband's passion for roses.) Proust reconvened there for a spell with Daniel, Gregh, and La Salle, all of whom were vacationing in the area. A photograph taken by Degas's longtime mistress, Hortense Howland, shows three of the four coauthors posing on the terrace with Mme Straus, Louis Ganderax, and Porto-Riche. The young men decided to add a seaside subplot to their novel, using a house like Le Clos des Mûriers as a backdrop. Proust may have liked this idea because of Daniel's claim

Postcard of the Strauses' seaside villa, Le Clos des Mûriers, with Geneviève's writing on the front.

that in their inveterate snobbery, the Strauses had had the place built to resemble the Greffulhes' villa in Dieppe.

When the friends returned to Paris in the fall, their enthusiasm for the project dwindled as other obligations crowded to the fore. Proust hunkered down just long enough to pass his final round of law-school exams, receiving his degree in October and seemingly forgetting about it soon afterward. That same month, his friend Willie Heath died. Proust reacted to the loss by busying himself with plans to publish a "little book" of his literary sketches and to dedicate it to the memory of a "being I loved with all my heart." By November 5, he had already persuaded Mme Lemaire to agree to do the illustrations, which would depict not only her trademark floral bouquets but fine-boned patrician beauties with wistful, faraway eyes. Maybe Proust had decided he would rely on Lemaire to convey the melancholy and suffering of his young women of the monde.

Despite having given up on the Pauline de Dives story, Proust continued to write about *mondanité*. In September, he contributed his first article to *Le Gaulois,* "The Great Parisian Salons."* In this piece, credited to "Tout-Paris," he gave a minutely detailed account of the endless gradations, some obvious and some obscure, that formed the hierarchies of "aristocratic and elegant society." It was a measure of his hyperbolic ardor for Mme Greffulhe that while his essay turned on a distinction between two putatively incompatible types of salon, "elegant and open" and "closed," he named her salon under both rubrics.

* A translation of this article appears in appendix C.

Madeleine Lemaire's illustrations for Proust's first book, *Pleasures and Days* (1896), conveyed the sense of melancholic longing he ascribed to his fictional society doyennes.

Mme Straus's he placed in a small subgroup of bourgeois "literary salons." Given her determination not to seem like a bluestocking or a bourgeoise, the Mauve Muse may have taken this categorization as an affront, and Proust may have meant it that way. Mme de Chevigné he excluded altogether, possibly in vengeance for the snub that rankled him still.

After "The Great Parisian Salons" came out, Montesquiou upbraided Proust for yet another protocol error. The article listed the Princesse de Léon as the hostess of a noted "open" salon. As the comte informed Proust, however, there *was* no longer a Princesse de Léon; upon the death of her father-in-law on August 6, she had succeeded to a new title, Duchesse de Rohan, making her unmarried, fourteen-year-old son the new Prince de Léon. This correction must have come as a bitter pill to Proust, implying as it did that for all the progress he felt he had been making in the gratin, he was still on the outside looking in. Even worse, he had publicized his ignorance of noble nomenclature in the pages of the monde's own favorite daily. He had studied the "born" closely enough by then to know that they would catch his mistake and judge him harshly for it, and although Proust had published his article under an alias (standard practice in the *presse mondaine*), he had no reason to trust that the comte would keep quiet about his gaffe. If anything, Montesquiou would gloat about having assessed him correctly: no breeding.

IN THIS CONTEXT, the opportunity to write a second piece for *Le Gaulois* would have presented Proust with a means to recover his dignity vis-à-vis the paper's readership. The chance arose the following May, when the comte made it known he would be holding a *fête littéraire* in Versailles at the end of the month. Eager to publicize the festivities but unwilling to appear involved in their promotion, he authorized Proust to offer to report on them for *Le Gaulois*. Arthur Meyer said yes, on the supposition that Montesquiou's plan to invite only 120 people would make the party the most talked-about event of the *mondain* season. The editor's instinct proved spot-on. In a society where the "best" gatherings routinely drew upwards of a thousand people, the news of the comte's drastically abbreviated guest list stirred up a frenzy of anticipation. And competitive glee—many *mondains'* hearts beat a little faster at the thought of attending a function from which their friends had been turned away in droves. Once the invitations were sent out, this excitement turned (in all but 120 cases) to incredulous rage; Montesquiou's peers were not used to being treated like a losers' club. But their indignation only served the comte's "aristocratic pleasure of displeasing," to say nothing of his notoriety. As for Proust, his assignment to chronicle the fête seemed to come as a saving grace insofar as it would allow him (he thought) to name himself among the happy few chosen to attend. He would put the Faubourg on notice that he, a mere bourgeois, had succeeded where hundreds of grandees had failed. It would be his own modest version of Haas's Jockey-Club admittance.

With a stroke of his pen, Meyer denied Proust this small social victory. But for once in the younger man's life, the disappointment did not undo the rapture that had come before it. Because rapture had indeed come before it. And it seemed liable, for a change, to withstand any letdown.

This bliss befell him at the party proper, where his introduction to Mme Greffulhe could no longer be avoided. Montesquiou was presenting all the guests to her that day—as the uncrowned queen of the occasion, she had to have every last one brought to her, to pay obeisance. Much as the comte might have wished to deprive Proust of this honor, there was no way around it. The earthworm would have to meet the star.

Proust was ready and rose to the occasion. From his intent study of *mondain* customs, he had learned how to doff his top hat just so, swivel his Malacca walking stick into the crook of his arm, and fold his spine in half, a pretty black forelock spilling over his brow. He had learned how to take her right hand in his right hand, two gloves touching, and pantomime a kiss that grazed only air. (It went without saying that any lip-smacking, mouth-to-hand contact would have been unthinkably vulgar.) She looked to him for all the world like a cattleya orchid grown to his exact height (five feet six), "deliciously attired in a dress of rosy lilac silk, strewn with [painted] orchids and covered in matching silk muslin, and a hat all abloom with orchids and swathed in lilac tulle." The cloud of tulle that floated around her face was so opaque that one could scarcely make out beneath it the dark fire of her eyes, the pale crescent of her cheek. Many of the guests grumbled about her veil, even citing it afterward as one of the main failings of the event (which they would admit, bringing some solace to the shunned, had been grossly overhyped). Georges de Porto-Riche went so far as to chide Élisabeth directly, writing to her afterward: "Too thick was your veil!" But Proust had no such complaints.

To him, it did not matter that her outfit clashed with the red carpet Montesquiou had laid out for her in the garden, again in deference to her queenly stature. Nor did it matter that mauve, according to the comte, was "a none-too-flattering shade" on his niece. Neither did it temper Proust's elation that the anarchist Émile Henry had been guillotined nine days earlier.

It fazed him neither that Mme de Chevigné was among the revelers at the party (who was *she* next to the sublime Comtesse Greffulhe?) nor that Mme Straus was not (truth be told, her exclusion from the proceedings may well have intensified Proust's pleasure at being there). It decidedly did not concern him that the festivities, postponed by a week due to heavy rainstorms, unfolded beneath cloudless skies and a white-hot summer sun. It did not worry him that

Émile Henry, twenty-one, was responsible for at least two anarchist bombings in Paris. He was executed in May 1894.

several guests grew faint in the heat, sweltering in their finery and finding only scant relief inside the tented theater where their host, resplendent in a pearl-grey redingote, subjected them to a series of ponderous odes, declaimed by over-dressed actresses and punctuated by his own cries of: "Isn't it BOOOOOtiful?" It did not even trouble Proust to see that "the poor things listened to the pro-gram with resignation, looking for all the world like cats who had been caught in the rain."

In the monde's idiomatic parlance, he had other cats to whip.* Momen-tarily pulled from his reveries of Mme Greffulhe, he found his attention drawn by another compelling creature, as ferocious and catlike as the comtesse was vaporous and floral. Sarah Bernhardt, fresh off a triumphant run in Paris as Phaedre, stalked onto the stage for the finale, her lithe form clad in a slithery white dress. The hard, feline glitter in her eyes may have recalled for some of Montesquiou's guests a media firestorm that had swirled around the actress five years earlier. While entertaining at home in Paris, the story went, she had grown impatient with one of her many pets, a cat she felt was purring too loudly. To silence the beast, she had grabbed it by the scruff of the neck, stuffed it into a hot coal-burning stove, and proceeded to ignore its "heartrending cries as it slowly roasted to death." Reports of this incident had made headlines around the world, and although Bernhardt had vehemently refuted them, the aura of savagery clung to her still. Not that Proust, equating as he did brutality with attraction, minded that, either.

Nor, obviously, did Montesquiou, who had enlisted Bernhardt to perform on the grounds that she alone was worthy to recite his poetry. For those of his guests who might privately have thought his verse unworthy of her, she had a surprise, rendering it in "cruel, languorous inflections" that stripped it of its bombast and infused it with mesmeric power. The magic of her art redeemed the mediocrity of his.

She cast her spell on "Aria": "Shadows of tree glens, / and skeletons of wrens." She brought her sorcery to "Salome": "I love jade, color of the eyes of Herodias, / and amethyst, color of the eyes of John the Baptist." To close out the program, she worked necromancy on "The Dead Woman's Final Rest," summoning forth a bier piled with cushions

> Filled with all the love letters that had left her weary. . . .
> A symphony of avowals, entreaties, tears,
> Adorations and imprecations . . . ,
> Singing her to her eternal rest . . . , whispering . . . :
> "She who has known such love will never die."

---

* The English equivalent of this expression—a favorite of Laure de Chevigné's—is "other fish to fry."

Montesquiou believed his poetry was too great to be recited by anyone but a world-famous talent like Sarah Bernhardt, painted here by
Georges Clairin.

If the Comtesse Greffulhe, who had wept the first time she read this poem, did so upon hearing it again now, her mauve veil covered her tears. As for Proust, he did not know that Montesquiou had written "The Dead Woman's Final Rest" for her, but it impressed him so much that he cited it at length in his article for *Le Gaulois*. Which Élisabeth clipped from the front page the next morning and saved for the next sixty years—yet another of her secrets Proust would never know.

Proust himself had been thinking quite a bit about dead women lately. About the enigmas they took with them to the grave and the clues they left behind. Dead women were mysterious, and as he had once told Mme Straus, he loved mysterious women, although by "mystery," he might have added, he meant "blank canvas." And by "blank canvas," he meant "shadow puppet," or "magic-lantern slide," or "simulacrum." Or "sanctuary," or "specimen," or "relic." Proust's twenty-third birthday was only six weeks away, leaving him with more than half of his life still to live. Yet already he was moving purposefully, joyfully, toward death. Toward his very own kingdom of shadows.

In that mythic kingdom—and herein lay the crux of his happiness, at the fête and forever after—he would need no more than the very little his muse had chanced to give him. No more than she, in her several incarnations, had already given him, without meaning to or even noticing. From the cloud of tulle, the face unseen, he would spin the book and volume of his dream. And that dream would fill endless cushions on endless biers with endless love letters to which the dead, the elegant dead, would be indifferent, but which would carry him with them into eternity.

Because he who had known such love would never die.

Because his love would bear all things, believe all things, hope all things, endure all things. Until it would not.

Because he could do better.

Because he could imagine.

(Because he could not help himself.)

Because he could write.

THE REAL KING OF BIRDS, OR
*VIVE LE ROITELET**

A legend holds that when it came time to establish a hierarchy among themselves, the various species of birds agreed to bestow the crown upon the one who could fly the highest in the air, closest to the sun.

The eagle rose skyward past all visible competitors until at length, growing tired, he rested his mighty wings—whereupon a little wren who, unbeknownst to the eagle, had stowed away on his back suddenly took flight and found his consecration in the solitude of the heavens, far above all the other creatures.

The alleged impropriety of the wren's gambit invalidated his triumph, and so it was the eagle who figured forever afterward as a symbol of royalty on flags and thrones.

For those of us who don't believe that cleverness should disqualify us from ruling the world, the wren remains the real king of birds.

—PAUL HERVIEU, *Parisian Silliness* (*La Bêtise parisienne,* 1897)

---

* *Roitelet* means not only "sparrow" but also, in a more archaic usage, "little king."

CODA

SWAN SONG

A crown, a swan, a kiss never given. And so much wasted time.

We all want to mean something in this world. We all want to matter. Every life a solar system in miniature, a whorl of planets moons comets undetected by outside eyes; every self a star burning fiercely at its center. I am a sun, we say. The galaxies in their vastness cannot dwarf me, the gods in their mystery negate me. You, singular or plural—you will see me, and know my light. You will remember my name.

Strewing our minutes like pennies, we spend with kingly abandon. Our pockets empty, we plead hardship, pining for riches we never knew we had. We gather talismans: a crown, a swan, a kiss never given. We chase fairy favors, line our nests with fools' gold. If we can and as we can, we build sanctuaries in the void, bulwarks against forgetting.

Time wasted, replenish what we have squandered. Time lost, and by each sun mourned, redeem us. Let us live again.

ACKNOWLEDGMENTS

Although writing a book may often seem and feel like a solitary endeavor, it is seldom if ever a one-woman show. Many people helped me in my work on the present volume, and I owe them all a tremendous debt of gratitude. I hope I have not forgotten to acknowledge any of them here.

I must start by thanking a number of my descendants' subjects, contemporary aristocrats without whose assistance I could never have reconstructed their forebears' *temps perdu*. In particular, I am grateful to Laure de Gramont; her brother, Guy, Comte de Gramont; and their late cousin Antoine XIV, Duc de Gramont and Prince de Bidache, for granting me access to Élisabeth Greffulhe's enormous personal archive: thirty-two linear yards' worth of private writings still largely unknown to scholars of the *Search* and historians of the fin de siècle. Not all the discoveries I made in this incredible trove were straightforward or conclusive. For example, I spent more than a year trying to decipher the private language Élisabeth developed on the basis of a nineteenth-century form of stenography, yet in the end I only partially cracked the code. All the same, the contents of her files went a long way toward helping me see her as a woman in full; they also illuminated previously dark corners of my other two heroines' lives. Last but not least, one of the 208 file boxes in Élisabeth's archive yielded the manuscript of Proust's unfinished, previously unpublished, and untranslated essay about her salon. Admittedly, *Proust's Duchess* would have been much shorter had the Gramonts not entrusted me with these materials. Yet it would also have been much the poorer both as a work of scholarship and, I hope, as a piece of storytelling.

For sharing their own family reminiscences, documents, gossip, and contacts, I am indebted to these other descendants of my book's characters: Prince Dimitri of Yugoslavia; Prince Pierre d'Arenberg; Princesse Alexandra de Riquet de Caraman-Chimay; Comte Marc de Gontaut-Biron; Armand-Ghislain, Comte de Maigret; Philippe, Comte d'Ornano; Comte Bertrand de Vogüé; Baron Roland de L'Espée; Achille Murat Guest; and Carlo Perrone. My thanks as well to Jean-Louis Poirey, who grew up in the staff quarters of the Greffulhe compound in the rue d'Astorg, for sending me his unpublished memoir of those years, and to Xavier Guiraud de Saint-Eymard, for taking me through the fascinating history of the Gontaut-Birons.

Élisabeth's great-great-granddaughter and first biographer, Anne de Cossé-Brissac, deserves special mention for her generosity. Not only did she share her own notes and files with me, she and her husband, Comte Patrice de Rambuteau, invited me to do further research at the château de Rambuteau in Burgundy, and they persuaded her brother, Philippe, Comte de Cossé-Brissac, and his in-laws, Bikem and Roger de Montebello, to extend the same gracious hospitality to me at the Palazzo Contarini Polignac in Venice. The kindness shown to me by this branch of the family has made me feel all the more acutely the responsibility that comes with writing about a relative who is not my own.* Because so much of what I reveal about Élisabeth's private life does not appear in Anne de Cossé-Brissac's biography (or anywhere else), it perhaps goes without saying that any errors in my account are mine alone. I do want to stress, though, that exposing Élisabeth's—and Geneviève's and Laure's—secrets reflects not my lack of respect for my subjects but my commitment to portraying them as truthfully as possible. As I have already noted, Proust's failure to see his *mondaines* in three dimensions was one of his rare deficiencies as an artist. Had I been content to idealize or caricature these women in turn, I would have defeated the very purpose of my book, which was to reinvest them with a modicum of the complexity, depth, and nuance they lost when they became Proust's Duchess.

The librarians, archivists, curators, and collections managers who facilitated my research in the United States and Europe include: Valentine Weiss, Section des archives privées, Archives Nationales de France, Paris; Moira Fitzgerald, Beinecke Rare Book & Manuscript Library, Yale University; Dr. Charles-Éloi Vidal, Anaïs Dupuy-Olivier, and Guillaume Fau, all three in Département des manuscrits et des estampes, Bibliothèque Nationale de France, Paris; Pauline Savoyini, Domaine national de Chambord, Chambord; Valeria Petitto, Fondazione Primoli, Rome; Meredith Friedman, the Metropolitan Museum of Art, New York; John Vincler, the Morgan Library & Museum, New York; Pamela Golbin, Musée des Arts Décoratifs, Paris; Valerie Steele, the Museum at the Fashion Institute of Technology, New York; Emma Butterfield, the National Portrait Gallery, London; David Rosado, the New York Public Library, New York; and Justin Cavernelis-Frost, the Rothschild Archive, London. Securing reproduction rights for the images in this book was a pharaonic task unto itself, executed with aplomb by my research assistants, Julia Elsky and Laura Jensen, and expedited in a few dozen cases by Robbi Siegel at Art Resource, New York. For manuscript formatting, I relied on the good offices of Tomara Aldrich and Sondra Phifer.

At Barnard and Columbia, I benefitted from the support of Provost Linda Bell, Anne Boyman, Peter Connor, Pierre Force, Serge Gavronsky, Ross Hamilton, Anne Higonnet, Laurie Postlewate, and my favorite Proust scholar, Elisabeth Ladenson. Colleagues at other institutions—Christie McDonald at Harvard, François Proulx at the University of Illinois–Urbana, Laure Murat at UCLA, and Nathalie Mauriac Dyer at the École Normale Supérieure—were also generous with their Proust expertise, as was Patrick Mimouni, an encyclopedically knowledgeable Proustian who first gave me a sense for Geneviève's

---

* In the interest of full disclosure, I should note that in researching this book, I found out that a medieval ancestor on my mother's side of the family, which is French, married a Chevigné. This was not a connection of which I had previously been aware, and it certainly did not bias me in my portrayal of the Chevigné family.

and Laure's colorful backgrounds. With this book as with its predecessor, Rob McQuilkin, my agent, was my best first reader and my most trusted adviser—a font of faith, hope, charity, and 100 percent market share.

At Knopf, I had the good fortune to work with a terrific team, led by my brilliant and beloved editor, Shelley Wanger. I cannot thank her enough for the indefatigable effort and unerring acuity she brought to bear on this project, not to mention for the multiple extensions she granted me as it ballooned to more than twice its original intended size, and for her wry sense of humor, which made even our most stressful moments fun. Shelley's assistant, Brenna McDuffie, and their colleagues Victoria Pearson, Zakiya Harris, Nicholas Latimer, Kathryn Zuckerman, and Yaima Villarreal all made indispensable contributions to the project known in-house as *Proust's Posse*. Copyeditor Amy Ryan and proofreader Benjamin Hamilton brought unparalleled rigor to their revisions of the book, purging it of hundreds of horrifying mistakes, and jacket designer Jennifer Carrow chose the perfect symbol of "Guermantes" glamour (and moral bankruptcy) for the cover. When I write the sequel to this book, I can only hope to get to collaborate again with this most talented group of people.

Probably the hardest thing for me about writing *Proust's Duchess* was that in order to complete it, I had to isolate myself for years from everyone I cared about. Yet even in my monklike solitude, many of my friends gamely pitched in to help. Robert Couturier and Isaac Mizrahi advised me on aristocratic protocol and livery, respectively. Caroline Rennolds Milbank cast a helpful eye on a key Nadar photo and Amanda Foreman disclosed a handy trick for managing chapter transitions. Anne Bass understood about the red shoes, and Gloria Vanderbilt Cooper understood about everything else. Samantha Boardman, Bernard-Henri Lévy, Catie Marron, Kathy Rayner, and Cécile David-Weill all lured me away from my Proust bunker at various points in my writing process, ensconcing me in extremely luxurious versions of a room of one's own. Other acts of book-related kindness came from: Tanya Blumstein, Jonathan Burnham, Lea Carpenter, Pietro Cicognani, Amy Fine Collins, David Patrick Columbia, Tayyibe Gülek Domaç, Peter Duchin, Susan Fales-Hill, Jennifer Fellowes, Fred Iseman, Barbara Liberman, Francine du Plessix Gray, Alice Kaplan, Suzanne Kennedy, Anne de Marnhac, the late Bernard Minoret, Gretchen Rubin, Sheryl Sandberg, Jeannette Sanger, Sally Spooner, Marie-Monique Steckel, Marcelita Swann, and Jackie Drake. Maurice Samuels offered astute feedback on several sections of the manuscript, while John Habich Solomon, my heroic *miglior fabbro,* read it from start to finish, providing ingenious suggestions on virtually every page, and reminding me repeatedly, with consummate wisdom and unfailing good cheer, that I was not in fact trapped in a crazy word-prison of my own devising. I will never be able to repay him for all that he did for this book and for me.

My mother and father, Carol and Jack Weber, and my brother, Jonathan, have been unwavering in their support, as constant today as in the era of *A Birthday for Cinnamon*. Alexandra and Annabelle Hayes patiently bore with me as Proust made me an absentee godmother; they are The Most Important. Finally, I am grateful to my boyfriend, Paul Romer, who has never once complained that when I moved into his house five years ago, I brought a quartet of demanding, if long-dead, Parisians to live with us (along with four equally demanding, and not at all dead, rescue dogs). It has helped that Paul shares my workaholic tendencies and, economist though he be, my obsessive preoccupation with the *mot juste*. He has not yet read this book in its entirety, having vowed to tackle it only once it is in published form. When he does read it, I hope that he will enjoy it, or at very least, that it will move him to take another crack at *Swann's Way*. That, indeed, is my hope for every reader of this book.

AUTHOR'S NOTE

A few remarks about capitalization and nomenclature in this book. To the extent that these explanations sound hairsplitting and pedantic, I apologize. They relate to subtleties of etiquette and social hierarchy that may appear trivial today but that mattered enormously in the world I have described in these pages.

1. In a concession to English grammatical convention, I have capitalized the first letters of royal and nobiliary titles. These titles begin with lower-case letters in French (e.g., the comte d'Haussonville, the prince de Sagan).

2. In some cases I have deviated from the rule whereby the head of a family (*chef de famille*) is designated only by his honorific and surname, whereas younger sons go by their honorific, first name, and surname. Being a younger son, Adhéaume de Chevigné should technically be identified as "Comte Adhéaume de Chevigné." But for the sake of relative concision, I sometimes refer to him as "the Comte de Chevigné," a title held during his lifetime first by his father and then successively by all three of his elder brothers.

3. A convention related to (2), above, dictates that when (a) one does wish to specify the Christian name of a *chef de famille* or (b) one is referring to a nobleman who is the only one in his family to bear a given title, his first name precede his honorific, as in (a) Henry, Comte Greffulhe and (b) Boson de Talleyrand-Périgord, Prince de Sagan—*not* (a) Comte Henry Greffulhe or (b) Prince Boson de Sagan. Because it requires neither extra verbiage on my part nor special knowledge on the part of the reader, I have respected this convention in my book.

4. I have also observed the French convention of dropping the nobiliary particle "de" when mentioning noble surnames without their honorifics (e.g., "she said to La Force," versus "she said to the Duc de La Force") . . . *except* when those surnames have only one syllable ("she said to de Mun") or begin with a vowel or a silent "h" ("she said to d'Arenberg and d'Haussonville").

5. Duc is the highest of the French nobiliary titles, ranking just below the monarch and typically taking precedence (in descending order) over marquis, comte, vicomte, and baron. When a French prince is not of the blood royal, a duc outranks him too; in fact, "prince" is often the title

held by a duc's eldest son. As a rule, French princes of the blood outrank ducs, even though the former often hold ducal titles of their own: Louis XIV's younger brother, for example, was the Duc d'Orléans. Perhaps more confusingly to the lay reader, certain members of the French royal family choose for various reasons to style themselves comtes, such as the Comte de Chambord (1820–1883) and the Comte de Paris (1838–1894), respectively the Bourbon and Orléanist pretenders to the French throne in the final decades of the nineteenth century. In the *Search* Proust plays on this murky area of princely address by having Odette de Crécy, a socially unschooled courtesan, mistake the Comte de Chambord for a "mere" count.

6. Due to the hereditary nature of royal and nobiliary titles, these do not always remain the same throughout the lifetime of the individuals who hold them. To take another example from the *Search:* the Duc and Duchesse de Guermantes are initially the Prince and Princesse des Laumes, only succeeding to their ducal status when the prince's father dies. Or to take an historical example familiar to an Anglophone audience: the Greffulhes' friend Bertie, Prince of Wales, ascends the throne as Edward VII, King of the United Kingdom, upon the death of his mother, Queen Victoria, in 1901.

TIMELINE OF POLITICAL RÉGIME CHANGES IN FRANCE, 1792–1870

- **September 1792:** French revolutionaries overthrow King Louis XVI and with him the Bourbon monarchy. A new, republican government is declared, known as the **First Republic.**
- **January 21, 1793:** Louis XVI is guillotined on the place de la Concorde in Paris. Ten months later, on October 16, his queen, Marie Antoinette, is executed on the same spot.
- **August 1793–July 1794:** Under the leadership of Jacobin militant Maximilien de Robespierre, the **Committee of Public Safety** (Comité de Salut Public) rules France, purging "counterrevolutionaries" in a bloody **Reign of Terror.** The Terror ends with the fall of Robespierre and his cronies in a coup d'état known as the **Thermidorian Reaction.**
- **1795–1799:** Following the dissolution of the Committee of Public Safety, a five-person committee called the **Directory** (Directoire) governs France.
- **November 8–9, 1799:** In the so-called coup of 18 Brumaire, General Napoléon Bonaparte overthrows the Directory and puts himself at the head of the body that replaces it, the **Consulate** (Consulat). This will be the First Republic's final governing body.
- **December 2, 1804:** Having effectively established a military dictatorship, First Consul Bonaparte crowns himself Napoléon I, Emperor of the French. The **first Napoleonic Empire** is founded.
- **April 1814:** After a protracted war with the Allied forces of Europe, Napoléon I is forced to abdicate. The older of Louis XVI's two surviving brothers ascends the throne as Louis XVIII, marking the first phase of the **Bourbon Restoration.** Napoléon Bonaparte is exiled to Elba.
- **February–March 1815:** Bonaparte returns from exile and stages a comeback. Marching on Paris with an army of supporters, he regains power for a period known as the **Hundred Days.**
- **June 18, 1815:** At the Battle of Waterloo, Bonaparte is again defeated by the Allied forces. Four days later, he abdicates for a second time and goes into exile on St. Helena, where he dies in 1821.
- **July 1815:** Louis XVIII returns to power, ushering in the second and longer phase of the Bourbon Restoration.

- **September 1824:** Louis XVIII dies, succeeded by his younger brother, who ascends the throne as Charles X.
- **July 26–29, 1830:** The increasingly autocratic style of Charles X's rule triggers an uprising, the **July Revolution**, which culminates in the sacking of the Tuileries Palace and the fall of the Bourbon monarchy.
- **August 1830:** Charles X abdicates and goes into exile with his family. He is replaced on the throne by his cousin, Louis-Philippe, Duc d'Orléans, the head of the cadet branch of the Royal House of France. D'Orléans ascends the throne as Louis-Philippe, King of the French. His reign, a relatively liberal, constitutional monarchy, is known as the **July Monarchy**.
- **February 1848:** The July Monarchy falls in the Revolution of 1848; the **Second Republic** is declared.
- **December 10, 1848:** In a landslide victory, Napoléon Bonaparte's nephew and heir, Prince Louis-Napoléon Bonaparte, is elected president of the Second Republic.
- **December 2, 1851:** In a coup d'état, President Bonaparte dissolves France's national legislature, the **National Assembly** (Assemblée Nationale), establishing himself as sole ruler of France.
- **December 2, 1852:** The **Second Empire** is founded, with ex-president Bonaparte reigning as Napoléon III, Emperor of the French.
- **September 2, 1870:** At war with Prussia since July, Napoléon III surrenders to the enemy at the Battle of Sedan. Three days later, republican statesman Léon Gambetta officially declares the end of the Second Empire. The **Third Republic** is founded and endures for the next seventy years. It collapses in the summer of 1940, when France falls to Nazi Germany and the **Vichy** government is created.

APPENDIX C

PROUST AS SOCIAL COLUMNIST*

I. "THE SALON OF THE COMTESSE GREFFULHE" (C. 1902–1903)[†]

Author's note: Élisabeth filed this article away in an unmarked box in her archives and later believed it had been lost, remarking in a note cited by Laure Hillerin: "[Proust] sent me a profile of me that he wrote after seeing me, which had been one of the great desires of his life. He asked me to return it to him if I thought it was good [enough to publish.] But because my husband had made me fearful of publicity, I hid it away at Bois-Boudran. Alas! Has it been lost?"

The article is fragmentary, beginning on page 3 of eight hand-numbered, type-written pages. All breaks, gaps, and incomplete words are preserved as they appear in the original text.

. . . ersons invited. Perhaps the original plan was to invite only ten, but this number soon grew. But this party will be the opposite of the crew Victor Hugo sang about:

> *Leaving Cadix [sic], we were ten.*
> *Reaching Otrante, we were thirty.*[‡]

And I am convinced that soon, we will be two hundred. Soon, because [the party] is in an hour. If one could only peer beneath the roofs of Paris's most beautiful *hôtels*, how amusing and charming it would be to see the graceful agitation of the beautiful women inside who are getting ready. As the weather is fine, their victorias await them by the front door or in the courtyard, and before long, a hundred coachmen in different parts of town will be given the same address, gliding through warm, sunny streets as their charges, arrayed in flowery, multicolored dresses, trade pretty salutations in passing.

The first guests are starting to arrive and Mme Greffulhe places them along the walls in the great reception rooms of the *hôtel*, keeping the middle of the salon free and clear for the arrival and progress of His Majesty. Just a handful

---

* The translations of both of these articles are mine, as are all footnotes. The first article, being unfinished, contains several rough spots, which I have tried to leave intact in translating it into English.
† The gathering Proust chronicles here is a "*matinée littéraire et musicale*" Élisabeth held in the rue d'Astorg in honor of King Oscar II (r. 1872–1905) of Sweden on the afternoon of Wednesday, May 14, 1902. Two hundred people attended, including (among those not mentioned by Proust) Robert de Montesquiou, Laure de Chevigné, Joseph de Gontaut, Melchior de Vogüé, and Georges de Porto-Riche.
‡ These lines come from Victor Hugo's epic poem *The Legend of the Ages* (*La Légende des siècles*, publ. 1859–1883).

of men still linger there, as on the day of a military review when a few stray soldiers pass through the empty courtyard of the barracks before the general's arrival, only to fall in to line at the first clarion call. All the ladies who are to be presented first to His Majesty are placed toward the front. There is Mme de Pourtalès, who is also a Majesty in her way, but who is above all Her Serene Grace Comtesse Edmond de Pourtalès, so thoroughly does the serene grace with which she has ever charmed the world remain intact. When the King, who knew her during the [Second] Empire, sees her, he will not be able to believe his eyes, so little has she changed, and Mme Greffulhe will seem to him like a fairy who has worked a miracle for him by conjuring up such an unchanged apparition of beauty from the past. Next to her, the Duchesse de Luynes, née La Rochefoucauld, exudes a charm that is particular to her and also to her two children, seated beside her: the Duchesse de Noailles, with her ravishing eyes; the Duc de Luynes, so refined, so courtly, the very embodiment of grace. Next to her, Comtesse Paul de Pourtalès, tall and blond with symmetrical features; Mme Ternaux-Compans; the Princesse de Caraman-Chimay, née Werlé;* Mme Casimir-Périer; the Duchesse de Gramont. Now people are arriving in greater numbers. Mme Greffulhe, standing in the entryway, "resembles a great golden bird"[†] preparing to take flight. Her marvelous eyes change from moment to moment. "Do you see that cloud up there that looks like a camel?"[‡] Hamlet asks Polonius, continuing to see new shapes in it from one minute to the next. Mme Greffulhe's eyes are no less ever-changing. At present, they are immobile, with the mineral beauty of precious gems; one knows that if they were put in a vitrine, they would light up a Louvre. Now her pupils look, in her eyes, like stones that have been tossed into limpid waters. But as soon as she smiles at the arrival of a friend, they are dematerialized, taking on a kind of benevolence from on high, akin to the mysterious, transparent sweetness of stars. At every minute they are "other." Here is the Marquis du Lau, an old friend of M. Greffulhe's who once served with General Galliffet, a figure out of Ghirlandaio with his florid face and bright blue eyes. Another old officer talking with him is Comte Louis [sic] de Turenne, the most charming man in this milieu. Decent, upright, and affable no matter what the circumstance, M. de Turenne is also a man of great cultivation, known for his distinguished achievements;[§] his little apartment in the rue de la Bienfaisance is as much a haven for reflection and study as it is a center of elegance. M. de Turenne is one of those men of whom one says that they make the rain fall and the sun shine, which is perhaps to grant them a

---

* Marthe Mathilde Werlé was the first wife of Élisabeth's younger brother Pierre.
[†] As noted in the Overture, this image is taken from "Le Cydnus," a sonnet from José-Maria de Heredia's *The Trophies* (*Les Trophées*, 1893).
[‡] *Hamlet* (III, ii).
[§] In the mid-1870s, Louis, Comte de Turenne d'Aynac, traveled around the United States and Canada, afterward publishing an account of his experiences in *Fourteen Months in North America* (*Quatorze mois dans l'Amérique du Nord,* 1879).

bit gratuitously a prerogative once reserved for the good Lord, and which today belongs in a certain measure to physicists. But it is nevertheless true that in this narrowly restricted universe, which extends from the rue Tronchet (hôtel Pourtalès) to the avenue d'Iéna (hôtel Standish) and from the avenue de Marigny (hôtels de La Trémoïlle and Gustave de Rothschild) to the rue Saint-Dominique (hôtel Sagan), his power is essentially without limits.

He says hello successively to: the Duc de Montmorency, the youthful-looking bearer of an historic name;* M. Charles Ephrussi, a great friend of the Comte and Comtesse Greffulhe; the Marquis de Castellane and the Comte de Rambuteau. Mme Greffulhe now places, beside her friend the Comtesse de Kersaint, née Mailly-Nesle, the tall, young, dark-haired Marquise d'Eyragues, her cousin, née Montesquiou (the sister and sister-in-law of the Comte and Comtesse Henri de Montesquiou, née Noailles), a woman of delicious wit captivating to all who know her. Hers is the genuine and charming wit that consists in seeing everything in such an original and nuanced way that for her there is no such thing as an insignificant event or a boring person; from the dullest stone she extracts a sparkling grain of gold. Thus no sooner does she take her seat than the other guests crowd around her, and you can see how delighted the people sitting closest to her are by her fanciful conversation. The Marquise de Massa, the Comtesse de Gabriac, and the Duchesse de Reggio, having spotted Mme d'Eyragues, leave their places and come over to find seats near hers. Among themselves they point out the illustrious writers and scientists who have come to be presented to His Majesty. Talent always clusters around centers of feminine influence. But today, the day of (to reprise our earlier image) a great military review, where the veterans of French thought will appear in honor of the King, the vanguard and the rearguard, the majors-general and the reserves, have all been called to arms. Such that alongside the young [painters] Helleu, La Gandara, Lobre, [and] La Sizeranne, here is M. Berthelot, the great chemist; the imperturbable, perspicacious M. Albert Sorel, with his astute and profound historian's mind; M. Camille Saint-Saëns; M. Paul Hervieu, still young, but illustrious, too, expressing himself with slow, musical diction, with a harmonious, lagging cadence, that keeps us all hanging on his every, profound and charming word. M. Janssen, the great astronomer, has shown up in evening dress, even though it is 4 o'clock in the afternoon—whether out of an excess concern for officialdom, or out of a scientist's disdain for the contingencies of dress, or out of a touching desire, utterly ignorant of fashion, to do the right thing. On anyone else and anywhere else, it would look ridiculous, but on M. Janssen it takes on a noble and very touching air, and one feels that the other intelligent men in attendance would

---

* This title dated back to the fifteenth century but was re-created twice after that. The Duc de Montmorency to whom Proust refers here, Nicolas de Talleyrand-Périgord, inherited the title from his uncle. Nicolas's son and heir, Napoléon Louis Eugène de Talleyrand-Périgord, was to be the last Duc de Montmorency; the title went extinct upon his death in the 1950s.

gladly change into evening dress to be like him and would say to him as Dumas *fils* once said to George Sand: "I would rather be wrong with you than right with everyone else." The King has still not arrived. It is like being in a classroom and waiting for the examiner to appear. Everyone continues to chat. Through the open window facing out onto the gardens wafts a delicious odor of lilac, mingled with a goldfinch's song. Now and then a witty comment draws a burst of laughter from Mme Greffulhe. Ah! What a lovely thing! For a split second she looks unsure of herself, as if hesitating before the lit fuse of her own laughter, which explodes all at once in a lavish burst of chimes.

AND ONE CANNOT KEEP one's eyes off her. She is "Beautiful from the blaze of the eyes all fixed on her."[*]

She has one rival today for everyone's charmed attention: the Houdon [bust of] Diana on the mantelpiece. For before the curtain rises on this little *mondain* performance, I have introduced to you, like a good dramatic author, all the characters, but I haven't told you about one inanimate spectator, who is however the liveliest spectator of them all, the Houdon Diana, an oversight that is all the more egregious in that it is she who gave me the title for this article.[†] Let me tell you the story quickly before the party begins; for some movement is now afoot, M. Greffulhe just hurried out of the salon, I suspect His Majesty is not far off. So, about ten years ago, Mme Greffulhe wanted to dress as Diana for a costume ball, and to research her costume she wished to see an Houdon Diana owned by some of her neighbors in the country, very humble, rustic folk with whom she was unacquainted. So she called on them, only to find the household in mourning, I'm not sure whether it was for the wife or the daughter of the owner of the Houdon bust, but Mme Greffulhe felt she ought to console the family, and she did so quite naturally, speaking eloquently from the heart. Ten years later, the owner of the bust himself died, and left it to her in his will in memory of her visit. (The full account of this incident appears in the Goncourt brothers' journal, which I don't have to hand.) And that is how this adorable marble "guest" has the privilege—coveted by so many people of flesh and blood—of attending all Mme Greffulhe's parties. No, it wasn't the King, I had enough time to finish my story and he still isn't here.

But isn't punctuality the . . . you know.[‡] Here are a few latecomers: the Comte and Comtesse Edouard de La Rochefoucauld, née Colbert; the Comte and Comtesse Henri de Montesquiou, née Noailles; the Comte and the Comtesse Mathieu de Noailles, née Brancovan; and the Prince and Princesse Alexandre de

---

[*] "Elle est *'Belle du flamboiement des yeux fixés sur elle'*": This is another line, albeit slightly modified, from Hugo's *The Legend of the Ages*, where Cyris, the goddess of love, is "encircled by the blaze of the eyes all fixed on her" (*ceinte du flamboiement des yeux fixés sur elle*).

[†] Because the first page of this article is missing, the title Proust gave it is unknown.

[‡] Here Proust makes as if to venture a platitude but playfully stops himself before completing the adage: Punctuality is the politeness of kings (*l'exactitude est la politesse des rois*).

Caraman-Chimay, also née Brancovan.* But here I must open a parenthesis. I mentioned these last two names with an emotion that is difficult to define. The Comtesse de Noailles and the Princesse de Chimay [*sic*]† are already respectively such a great poet and such a great prose writer—though as of a month ago one has been able to call Mme de Noailles a great prose writer as well—that it seems one ought to be speaking of them in a volume of literary criticism, or in a history of French literature, rather than in the *presse mondaine.* To see them included in a list of "elegant ladies" would produce a feeling of cognitive dissonance similar to the impression one gets when reading in a memoir from the Restoration period: "Today, a beautiful party at the Duchesse de ***'s. The guests included MM. de *** and de ***. One of them, brought by M. de Castrie [*sic*]‡ or M. de Broglie, M. de Lamartine read some verses he called *Poetic Meditations*."§ I know that it's not quite the same thing when one is talking about women [writers]. But no such cases have yet presented themselves in literary history, so there are no precedents. M. Paul Hervieu goes over to congratulate Mme de Noailles on her admirable novel, while everyone looking at them remains as it were transfixed by her infinite eyes, which are filled with light and shadow, and with an afterglow that sings a hymn to her perfect beauty, her absolute divinity and grace.¶

Deliciously molded by the most stirringly subtle and delicate hand, the exquisite face of the Princesse de Chimay casts a no less powerful spell. Her beautiful eyes, although nearsighted, see so deeply into the essence of things; her charming figure, energetic and frail; everything about her conveys a sense of untamable sweetness. Comte Mathieu de Noailles and the Prince de Chimay** [*sic*] are equal to the exquisite and difficult task of being married to two women of genius; at the same time, the [two men] are more than that, they have merits of their own. And their wives find in them the strength and the kindness that serve as a much-needed refuge from the fatigues and the doubts of thought and artistic creation. But I will have to return to this portrait sometime soon, for the King has walked in on the arm of Mme Greffulhe. I will not describe him so as to prevent him from being recognized; that way I can protect his incognito.

* Princesse Hélène de Caraman-Chimay was the wife of Élisabeth's youngest brother, Alexandre, and was a good friend of Proust's. She and her sister, Anna de Noailles, were Franco-Romanian noblewomen by birth; Anna, a poet, was friendly with both Laure de Chevigné and Geneviève Straus.
† Even after twenty years of *mondanité*, Proust was still prone to getting people's titles wrong. "Princesse de Chimay" was the title of the wife of the *chef de famille*, who in 1902 was Élisabeth's oldest brother, Joseph. Joseph divorced his first wife, Clara Ward, in 1897 (after she ran off with a Roma violinist) and would remarry in 1920, making his second wife the new Princesse de Chimay. In marrying Joseph's youngest brother, Hélène de Brancovan would thus "only" have become a Princesse de Caraman-Chimay. This was the same title Élisabeth's and her siblings' mother, Mimi, had held until she and their father Joseph acceded to the title in 1886.
‡ This [*sic*] is Proust's, meant to point out that unlike the memoirist he is citing, he knows that "Castries" is spelled with an "s" (despite the silent pronunciation of the final "ies").
§ Proust's point here is that Alphonse de Lamartine (1790–1869), a highly celebrated poet, is too important a literary figure to appear in a *mondain* chronicle as nothing more than the evening's entertainment. Indeed, Lamartine's *Poetic Meditations* (1820) was and is considered a masterpiece.
¶ Anna de Noailles's *Shadow of the Days* (*L'Ombre des jours,* 1902) appeared earlier that spring. The book was dear to Proust's heart because it featured a quotation from Racine's *Phaedra* on the cover.
** Again: this is in fact Prince Alexandre de Caraman-Chimay, the youngest brother of Élisabeth Greffulhe and Joseph, Prince de Chimay.

You will say that that scarcely matters, for what king hasn't been to the rue d'Astorg or to Bois-Boudran? A visit to Mme Greffulhe's is as inevitable a part of any royal visit to Paris as a trip to the Élysée [Palace], the Louvre or Notre-Dame. Mme Greffulhe, inspiring to poets, regal with kings, kind to everyone, and beautiful for everyone, advances on the arm of the King and presents to him or reintroduces to him the Comtesse Edmond de Pourtalès, the Duchesse de Fezensac, the Dowager Duchesse de Luynes, the Duchesse de La Trémoïlle, Mme Casimir-Perier, the Duchesse de Bisaccia, the Duchesse d'Uzès, née de Chaulnes,* la Duchesse de Rohan, Comtesse Mathieu de Noailles, Princesse Alexandre de Chimay [sic], the Duchesse de Mortemart, the Duchesse des Cars. The King congratulates the Duchesse de Rohan on her latest poem†

Calmette who comes up to

in the prime

Mme Greffulhe ap

the men

[gr]eet the sovereign as if offering them a crown. Slim, immobile, with an unerring finger, she designates [them], she calls out in a clear voice: "M. Berthelot." M. Berthelot steps forward and speaks for a moment with His Majesty; M. Vandal, who has such refinement and delicate charm; "M. Fauré," the great musician with the handsome and inspired face, his blue eyes like Alpine milk-wort flowers blossoming beneath the precocious and almost artificial-seeming snow of his white hair; "M. Jules Roche." His Majesty seems particularly to enjoy talking with the eminent statesman [Roche], with his fiery eyes, his ardent and colorful speech, his inexhaustible intelligence. Then the King sits down and the program begins. It is entirely made up of Beethoven sonatas and preludes and polonaises by Chopin, executed by M. [Francis] Planté. Those who haven't heard M. Planté don't know what a metamorphosis a piano can undergo at the hands of a great artist, alternately roaring like a stormy sea, singing sweetly like a nightingale, echoing like the depths of a forest. Making an exception, as one must always do, for M. Risler, no pianist has ever reached this level. But those who don't know M. Planté are also unaware of this original artist's amusing idiosyncrasies. M. Planté does not play so much as a single measure without offering a reflection, underlining it with a gesture, prefacing it with a warning to the audience, following it with an appreciative commentary. We should add that because this peculiarity comes naturally to him, it is most agreeable, unlike the affectation one finds in certain pianists, such as M. Delafosse, whose genuine talent as a musician and a composer often produces a less than beautiful effect due to his tiresome, mannered style.

---

* This is the daughter-in-law of the Duchesse d'Uzès (by 1902 the Dowager Duchesse d'Uzès) mentioned throughout this book.
† In the 1900s, Herminie, Duchesse de Rohan (1853–1926), formerly the Princesse de Léon, published several volumes of poetry.

Everyone is waiting. M. Planté is about to begin. He places his fingers on the keyboard, sound is about to issue forth, no. M. Planté stops and, turning toward the King, [says:] "Since His Majesty wishes to hear a bit of music, I am first going to play a prelude for him. I call it *The Rocks of Biarritz*." Turning toward M. Bonnat [he adds]: "Yes, old fellow, Biarritz. Ah! What a delightful place!" He starts to play; one hears an exquisite trill. As he plays, [he comments:] "That is a wave, you can hear it, hear its pearly laughter." Looking at Mme Greffulhe: "Ah! I see that the comtesse can hear it; I am so glad." He laughs. (The trills continue, easily, unceasingly, while he talks.) "How crystalline it [the wave] is! Oh, but we have to watch out, or it will get us wet!" He turns toward the orchestra that is accompanying him: "Oh, dear viola, not too loudly, let me sing, since I love to sing" (and without stopping, he makes the piano sing beneath his fingertips in a truly sublime manner), "There!" (still playing without stopping) "Let's sing together . . . *the-e-e-re! The-e-re!* Let's sing, let's sing" (addressing the orchestra once again), "Ah, what you are saying is pretty, let me answer you now" (and, indeed, the piano answers the phrase begun by the orchestra). And then the piece is over, the program is interrupted. M. Planté, who is overheated, has expressed a desire to go take a shower. At that moment an alert, glorious, still youthful old man comes in, the illustrious [painter Ernest] Hébert, who takes an interest in all new artistic developments and all *mondain* pleasures. "Here is the wonderful, the charming M. Hébert, sire," Mme Greffulhe says, in her unusual voice that seems almost to skate over the words, designating M. Hébert to the King. The King, full of respect for M. Hébert's great reputation and advanced age,* rises, hurries over to him, and invites him to sit down beside him; they chat together for a long time. Then M. Planté, freshly showered and ready to get back to it, reappears, dressed in a different, lighter-weight suit, takes his place at the piano and announces a Chopin nocturne that he has decided to call *Hébert's Melancholy.* "Watch out, old friend," he says to the great painter, "I am aiming for the heart." And indeed, he plays in a way that divinely touches the heart. Hébert, clearly moved, embraces him when he is done. But alas! The King got here so late that the matinée was only halfway through and it was already 6 o'clock; I had to leave. Too soon for my taste, but perhaps too late for yours, so long and cumbersome must my account of these minutes have seemed to you, minutes that to me seemed to flit so swiftly by.

—Dominique†

* In May 1902, Oscar II was seventy-three; Hébert eighty-four.
† Proust borrowed this pseudonym from the novelist Stendhal, also using it as his byline for "The Salon of Her Imperial Highness Princesse Mathilde" and "The Salon of Mme Madeleine Lemaire," articles that appeared in *Le Figaro* on February 25, 1903, and May 11, 1903, respectively. Proust apparently intended to publish "The Salon of the Comtesse Greffulhe" in *Le Figaro* as well, as he wrote in pencil on the back: "Calmette article—unfinished." Élisabeth held on to it after he sent it to her, however, leading Proust to complain in April 1903 that Gaston Calmette, the editor-in-chief of *Le Figaro*, had still not agreed to its publication, "for a reason I cannot fathom." As noted above, that reason was Élisabeth's fear that the "publicity" would anger Henry.

2. "THE GREAT PARISIAN SALONS" ("LES GRANDS SALONS PARISIENS") IN *LE GAULOIS* (SEPTEMBER 1, 1893)

In a recent letter, one of our subscribers asked us this question: "Which are the ten or twenty most 'closed' salons in Paris? Which are the ten or twenty most elegant salons? The ten or twenty most aristocratic salons? Do you think the last two questions are the same as the first one?"

Not wishing to offer a personal perspective on such a matter, we have solicited the experts for their views, and apologize for any omissions or errors our findings might contain.

Closed salons: We are no longer living under the [Bourbon] Restoration, the July Monarchy, or the [Napoleonic] Empire. In the absence of a Court [*sic*], nothing can protect society against the invasion of newcomers whose merit, fortune or education earns them a place in the best salons.

To exclude these individuals would be to display an inordinate *esprit de caste;* to admit them all would be to turn aristocratic salons into crowded casinos.

Of these two evils, the lesser one would obviously be preferable, but who is to say which is the lesser? As always in cases like these, different people take different approaches, and those who aim for a compromise resort to coming up with three separate guest lists: a long list, for guests one invites once a year; a "half list," for those one invites two or three times a year; and a short list, for people one invites as often as possible.

"Either a door is open or it's closed," says the proverb; here one proceeds as one used to do at Court [*sic*], opening a door either by one or two *battants*, depending on the circumstances.

The clubs [e.g., the Jockey, the Cercle de l'Union, etc.] have also brought about a change in our salons. Salons used to play the role the clubs play now; they were places where people talked about everything, from literature to politics. It was in salons that reputations were made or new ideas came under fire. Each salon took a clearly defined position, its habitués either promoting or attacking the new idea.

In those days, very few great men succeeded without first passing through a salon, where they had the good sense to befriend an influential woman or two. It was in Barras's drawing room that Bonaparte first met and conquered Mme Tallien's friend Mme [Joséphine de] Beauharnais, who helped to secure him the command of the Egyptian army, which was the first step in his rise to power. He was right to make her his empress in return for this invaluable favor.

Under the Restoration, the salons were more or less exclusively royalist, as the marshals [of Napoléon I's army] rallied to the throne. Mme Récamier commanded respectful adoration, and left [author René de] Chateaubriand in charge of the conversation, together with Duc Mathieu de Montmorency and a handful of other distinguished guests. These privileged gentlemen were given seats in her salon, but they were surrounded by throngs of listeners who had to stand, murmuring their approval and admiration at every word that fell from the oracles' lips.

In Mme de Staël's salon there was less academic posing and more relaxed, wittier conversation, but it was still a closed salon, notably at Coppet [her castle in Switzerland], where exile kept the crowds at bay. Because she died in 1817, Mme de Staël was unable to leave any memoirs of the monde during the Restoration.

The mystical Mme de Komar, who was almost Alexandre's muse, also had a closed salon, which drew a high-minded élite.*

Under the July Monarchy, salons divided into two camps, royalist [legitimist] and liberal [Orléanist]. They stirred up trouble, spread gossip, fought one another with pinpricks.

The Duchesse Pozzo di Borgo, a stalwart of the legitimate [Bourbon] monarchy, played hostess to the entire Faubourg Saint-Germain; the Princesse de Lieven, beautiful and charming in her particular, Russian way, supported the new [Orléanist] régime, but she couldn't decide between M. Guizot and M. Thiers, and even had a smile for M. Berryer.† She would have received everyone in Paris, but then she realized her mistake, so she went with Guizot; as soon as she did, Thiers called her "a moron and a liar." Her open salon had become closed.

The Second Empire brought about a reconciliation of sorts between previously warring salons, and also saw the emergence of new ones supportive of its policies. At that time, Princesse Mathilde [Bonaparte] had the foremost salon in Paris. Her doors were open to all illustrious writers and artists, [among them] Sainte-Beuve, the brothers Goncourt, Flaubert, Théophile Gautier, Mérimée; and to this day, her salon retains its reputation for the warm welcome it extends to French genius.

The Duchesse de Galliera continued to host brilliant parties, but they were now limited to the Orléanist faction: M. Thiers, M. de Rémusat, the Duc [de] Pasquier . . . all gathered there. The Comte d'Haussonville's was a meeting place for the Académie [Française], both its actual and its aspiring members. M. de Hübner, the Austrian ambassador, alternated between holding official receptions and entertaining the Faubourg Saint-Germain.

After the fall of the Empire and the [Franco-Prussian] War, it took some time before the salons reopened their doors. Once again, a Russian lady led the way, Princesse Lise Troubetskoy, whose hospitality was astonishing. M. Thiers

---

* Alexandre, Comte de Komar, and his wife, Pélagie, were Polish aristocrats living in Paris, where she was a noted *salonnière*. One of the couple's grandsons, Clément de Maugny, became a good friend of Proust's, serving as the first model for the character of Robert de Saint-Loup in the *Search*.
† Adolphe Thiers was an historian and political power broker who played a key role in the overthrow of Charles X and the establishment of the July Monarchy. He and fellow Orléanist François Guizot, also an historian cum statesman, were rivals, both serving at different points as prime ministers to King Louis-Philippe. (Thiers later went on to become the first president of the Third Republic.) In a different context, Proust himself evaluated the two men solely in terms of their literary abilities, which he deemed "frightful" in both cases. Thiers and Guizot were sworn enemies of Antoine Berryer, one of the leaders of the legitimist opposition to Louis-Philippe's reign.

was her first guest; she wanted [to found] a political salon, but she didn't succeed. But another Russian, the Comtesse de Rainneville, opened up her drawing rooms [in her house] two steps from the place Beauvau, and that was where the debates in the National Assembly began and ended. A salon open to everyone of importance in the conservative party.

Meanwhile, political and literary exchanges migrated to the clubs, reducing the salons to mere places of amusement. From then on, their authority dwindled, and closed salons had only one goal: to conserve a precious sense of intimacy in a serious, aristocratic milieu.

It is easy to cite up to ten closed salons [in Paris] today; naturally, they are all aristocratic.

If we had to cite the most elegant salons, we would necessarily cite the aristocratic ones, and vice versa.

Thus we can only establish two, rather than three, divisions in categorizing them: closed salons on the one hand, and the most elegant and most aristocratic salons on the other.

An aristocratic salon is one where the hosts are aristocrats, and receive members of noble and elegant society. An elegant salon is one where the hosts, without belonging to the aristocracy at all, nonetheless receive certain of its members, as well as members of elegant society.

Today the most esteemed closed salons in Paris are those of the Duchesse de Noailles; the Dowager Duchesse de Mortemart, whose recent mourning prohibits her from receiving; the Dowager Duchesse de Maillé; the Duchesse de La Trémoïlle; the Duchesse d'Avarny; Comtesse Aimery de La Rochefoucauld; the Comtesse Greffulhe; the Marquise de Lévis; Mme Standish; the Marquise de Montboissier; the Comtesse de Croix; and the Comtesse de Gramont d'Aster.

That's twelve. We don't think we can make any more additions to this exclusive list of names.

Some people will call these salons coteries, others [will call them beacons of] good taste. We believe these salons deserve *neither this excess of honor, nor this indignity.**

The aristocratic and elegant salons that are open to a larger number of guests, and are quite accepting of newcomers, are many in Paris; in enumerating these, we shall have to give an extensive list of names, lest we appear uninformed.

Which salons are more aristocratic than elegant, and which ones more elegant than aristocratic? Where is the dividing line, and how can it be established without giving [certain hostesses] legitimate cause for offense?

We will limit ourselves to noting that among these open salons, several are closed on certain days, depending on whether the guests are drawn from the

---

* This is a famous line from Racine's tragedy *Britannicus* (1669), which Proust studied in his first year at Condorcet, and which the title character reads in his unfinished autobiographical novel, *Jean Santeuil*. See my comments at the end of the article for more on why this quotation bears noting.

short list, the "half list" or the long list. Here we shall simply categorize them as the most aristocratic *and* the most elegant open salons:

The Duchesse de Doudeauville; the Princesse de Léon, currently in mourning; the Comtesse Greffulhe, née Caraman-Chimay; the Comtesse de Pourtalès; the Princesse de Sagan; the Comtesse de La Ferronays; the Duchesse de Gramont; . . . the Comtesse Jean de Montebello; the Comtesse O. de Montesquiou; the Rothschilds; the Princesse de Wagram [née Rothschild]; the Princesse de Brancovan; the Princesse Murat; Mme Heine-Furtado; Mme Porgès; . . . the Comtesse d'Haussonville; . . . Mme Stern; . . . the Marquise de Jaucourt; the Baronne Hottinguer; [etc.]

To this list we must add the more specifically literary and artistic salons, such as those of Mme Hochon, Mme Straus, and Mme Aubernon. . . .

In none of these categories can we place those princely salons where only the most eminent figures from politics, the arts and letters, and society are invited.

The Duc d'Aumale doesn't hold a salon in Paris, but Chantilly isn't far away, and he frequently entertains guests from the Institut, the army, and the literary world. The Duc and Duchesse de Chartres receive on certain days in their salons in the rue Jean-Goujon, but without fanfare, limiting their company to a small number of faithful friends. As for Princesse Mathilde, she still graciously receives anyone who has made a name for himself in literature or the arts, and to the loyalists of the Empire.

Open salons: For the past several years, this term has frightened many a hostess, as the tide of newcomers has continued to rise. Whether driven by curiosity, or by snobbery, or by a natural desire to frequent a *comme il faut* milieu, the number of requests for invitations has grown greater with each passing year. And because these requests come from friends of friends to whom hostesses find it difficult to say no, even the largest salons have started to feel crowded.

That is why, today, the short list finds the greatest favor.

—Tout-Paris

Author's note: As I mention earlier in the book, "The Great Parisian Salons" has never before been attributed to Proust. I have therefore detailed below my reasons for making this attribution, which I unreservedly believe is correct:

1. **The pseudonym:** "Tout-Paris" is the same pseudonym Proust adopted nine months later when publishing "Une Fête littéraire à Versailles," also in *Le Gaulois* (and discussed in detail in chapter 24).

2. **The timing and subject matter of the piece and the forum in which it appears:** In the early to mid-1890s, Proust's literary output was predominantly (a) journalistic, appearing in a range of newspapers and magazines, and (b) focused on the monde. An overview of "the most aristocratic and the most elegant salons" is thus wholly consistent with

Proust's preoccupations at this time, and *Le Gaulois* was the ideal outlet for his writings about *mondanité*—as he himself remarked in a letter in 1893.

3. **The erroneous reference to "the Princesse de Léon":** Again as discussed in chapter 24, the father-in-law of Herminie, Princesse de Léon, died on August 6, 1893. So she was indeed still in mourning a month later, as Tout-Paris correctly reports. But he errs in identifying her as the Princesse de Léon, for since her father-in-law's death, she had been the Duchesse de Rohan. Robert de Montesquiou wrote to Proust in the fall of 1893 to correct him for making this very mistake. It seems highly unlikely that another *mondain* reporter would have gotten this exact detail wrong, at the very same moment as Proust did.

4. **The double mention of Mme Greffulhe:** As noted in chapter 24, the Comtesse Greffulhe is the only woman to appear on both of Tout-Paris's (supposedly) mutually exclusive lists—hostesses of closed salons and hostesses of "aristocratic" and "elegant," yet open, salons. This idiosyncrasy bespeaks a fascination with Mme Greffulhe that was of course not at all unique to Proust but which, in his case, began in the summer of 1893, a few months before Tout-Paris's "Great Salons" article appeared. On July 3, Proust wrote to Montesquiou to announce that he had "finally seen (yesterday at Mme de Wagram's) the Comtesse Greffulhe" for the first time and that he had never seen a more beautiful woman. Less than a week later, he wrote to Montesquiou again, asking, "Did you pass along my message to the Comtesse Greffulhe?" (Proust's exact phrase was *faire ma commission* [run my errand], the same expression he used when asking Mme Straus to tell Mme de Chevigné about his crush on her.) The newness and intensity of Proust's preoccupation with Mme Greffulhe offers a plausible explanation for Tout-Paris's otherwise inexplicable decision to name her in two antithetical categories.

5. **The incongruous quotation from Racine:** As discussed in chapter 11, Proust loved to cite classic literary works—especially the plays of Jean Racine—in improbable contexts. In this article, Tout-Paris quotes from a scene in Racine's tragedy *Britannicus* (1669), where the evil Nero, future emperor of Rome, is trying to woo his adoptive brother's fiancée, Junie, against her will. When Nero proposes marriage, Junie demurs with a withering retort: "I dare say that I have deserved / neither this excess of honor nor this indignity" (*J'ose dire pourtant que je n'ai mérité / ni cet excès d'honneur, ni cette indignité*). To suggest that calling a Parisian salon a "coterie" is like the Roman tyrant Nero trying to seduce his brother-in-law's fiancée is to create just the type of incongruous juxtaposition Proust so enjoyed devising. Except in other articles written by him, such

a juxtaposition appears nowhere in any of the hundreds of fin-de-siècle social columns I read when researching this book.

6. **The inclusion of "not born" Jewish hostesses on the list of leading** *salonnières:* Until the Dreyfus affair, the stature of the Barons and Baronnes de Rothschild was unquestioned (if secretly begrudged by anti-Semites) in the gratin. But while the *mondain* position of other Parisian Jews, even the very rich ones, was much less assured, Tout-Paris matter-of-factly names several women from these families—the Furtado-Heines (financiers), the Porgès (diamond moguls), and the Sterns (bankers related to the Rothschilds by marriage)—on his list of society mavens. These were the families to which the "countesses of Judea" Proust met through Mme Straus belonged.

7. **The Proustian signature in the last paragraph:** When speculating as to why the number of requests for invitations to salons has grown in recent years, Tout-Paris performs one of Proust's hallmark rhetorical gestures, launching into a list of incompatible theories about potential hidden motivations: "Whether driven by curiosity, or by snobbery, or by a natural desire to frequent a *comme il faut* milieu" (*Soit curiosité, soit snobisme, soit désir naturel . . .*). As his first German translator, Walter Benjamin, observed in 1929, one of Proust's most distinctive narrative strategies is "the endless succession of '*soit que . . . ,*' by means of which an action is shown in an exhaustive . . . way in the light of the countless motives upon which it may have been based."

Ubiquitous in the *Search,* this construction is already present in Proust's *Jean Santeuil.* Here is one example from that unfinished novel, a meditation on the complex emotional responses that may arise when a person has just finished reading a delightful book:

> Once one has closed the book, one doesn't dare to proclaim one's complete satisfaction, whether out of shame [*soit honte*], or out of a desire [*soit désir*] always to be an object of pity, or in order not to seem too happy, or because happiness [*soit que le bonheur*], as soon as it is examined or called into question, disappears.

NOTES

The unabridged version of these endnotes runs to more than three hundred pages. To reduce book length and reader fatigue, I have condensed my citations as much as possible and appended a detailed bibliography. Unless otherwise noted, all translations of quotations from non-English-language sources are my own.

ABBREVIATIONS

For primary-source authors frequently cited

For simplicity's sake, I use the same abbreviations to designate the three main female figures in this book, instead of providing different abbreviations to reflect their maiden names or, in Geneviève Straus's case, her married name from her first marriage.

CA: Céleste Albaret
CCB: Constance de Breteuil, née Castelbajac
FB: Ferdinand Bac (pseud. Ferdinand-Sigismond Bach)
GB: Georges Bizet
GBB: Giovanni Battista Borghese
HB: Henri de Breteuil
JB: Jacques Bizet
JEB: Jacques-Émile (Jacques) Blanche
MB: Marthe Bibesco, née Lahovary
RB: Robert de Billy
AC: Adhéaume de Chevigné
GCC: Ghislaine de Caraman-Chimay
LC: Laure de Chevigné, née de Sade
MACC: Marie-Alys de Caraman-Chimay
MCC: Marie (Mimi) de Caraman-Chimay, née Montesquiou-Fezensac
ED: Édouard Drumont
LD: Léon Daudet
RD: Robert Dreyfus
AF: Albert Flament
AdF: André de Fouquières
RF: Robert de Flers
AG: André Germain
AGG: Armand de Gramont, Duc de Guiche (later Duc de Gramont)
EG: Élisabeth Greffulhe, née Riquet de Caraman-Chimay
EdG: Edmond de Goncourt
FG: Fernand Gregh
HG: Henry Greffulhe

LG: Élisabeth (Lily) de Gramont, Duchesse de Clermont-Tonnerre
DH: Daniel Halévy
LH: Ludovic Halévy
NH: Alexandrine (Nanine) Halévy, née Le Bas
BL: Barbara Lister (Lady Wilson)
GL: Georges de Lauris
LL: Robert Bulwer-Lytton, Lord Lytton
AM: the Abbé Mugnier
GM: Guy de Maupassant
OM: Owen Meredith (pseud. LL)
PM: Paul Morand
RM: Robert de Montesquiou-Fezensac
GLP: Gabriel-Louis Pringué
MP: Marcel Proust
GPR: Georges de Porto-Riche
HR: Henri de Régnier
ES: Émile Straus
GS: Geneviève Bizet Straus, née Halévy
PV: Paul Vasili (pseud. Juliette Adam)

For book-length works by Marcel Proust

Unless specified below, all bibliographical details for these texts appear in Works Consulted.

RTP: À la recherche du temps perdu
AD: Albertine disparue, in RTP, volume IV
CCS: Du côté de chez Swann, in RTP, volume I
CG: Le Côté de Guermantes, in RTP, volume II
CSB: Contre Sainte-Beuve
JS: Jean Santeuil
LP: La Prisonnière, in RTP, volume III
OJFF: A l'ombre des jeunes filles en fleurs, in RTP, volumes I and II
MPG: Matinée chez la Princesse de Guermantes
PJ: Les Plaisirs et les Jours
SG: Sodome et Gomorrhe, in RTP, volume III
TR: Le Temps retrouvé, in RTP, volume IV

OVERTURE: LIKE A SWAN

1   Marcel Proust was never a morning person: Maurice Duplay, *Mon ami Marcel Proust: Souvenirs intimes* (Paris: Gallimard, 1972), 23.

1   "I used to have a heart attack every time I saw you": MP to LC, in MP, *Correspondance*, ed. Philip Kolb, vol. 19 (Paris: Plon, 1970–1992) (hereafter Kolb, ed.), 212; also cited in Jeanine

Huas, *Proust et les femmes* (Paris: Hachette, 1971), 163; George D. Painter, *Marcel Proust: A Biography*, vol. 1 (London: Chatto & Windus, 1959), 110; and Henri Raczymow, *Le Paris retrouvé de Proust* (Paris: Parigramme, 2005), 134. MP was notorious for not dating his letters, as RD notes in a humorous passage in RD, *De Monsieur Thiers à Marcel Proust* (Paris: Plon, 1939), 15. In many cases, Kolb's extensive research, supplemented by research in contemporary periodicals and other people's correspondence, makes it possible to determine when, either approximately or exactly, MP wrote particular letters. Wherever such information is available and pertinent, I provide it in the body of the text. To cut down on verbiage, when citing MP's letters, I do not include the name of the addressee if s/he does not figure in the story told in these pages.

1   "my route of hope": MP, in Kolb, ed., ibid., vol. 1, 382. On MP's "route of hope," see also Huas, ibid., 162–63.

2   "bright, blue eyes, the color of the sky of France": Helene Iswolsky, *No Time to Grieve: An Autobiographical Journey* (Philadelphia: Winchell, 1985), 91.

2   "turned a simple morning walk": MP, CG, 358. MP once conscripted RB to join him in "stalking" LC; for a firsthand account of this experience, see RB, *Marcel Proust: Lettres et conversations* (Paris: Portiques, 1930), 79–80. MP describes a similar experience in his essay "La Comtesse" in CSB, 86–93, 90.

3   "elevating glory": MP, "Portrait de Mme ***," in MP, PJ, 225. This essay, discussed at length in chapter 22, was originally published as "A Sketch Based on Mme de ***," in *The Banquet* (*Le Banquet*), a literary journal MP cofounded in 1892 with a group of friends. MP told the cofounders of the magazine that "Mme de ***" was LC; see RD, *Souvenirs sur Marcel Proust* (Paris: Grasset, 1926), 71.

3   "an absurd form [of] wooing": Painter, op. cit., vol. 1, 110.

3   "to catch a bird of paradise": MP to AGG, in Kolb, ed., op. cit., vol. 20, 349. This letter is also cited in Carassus, op. cit., 540 and is reproduced in full in MB, *Le Voyageur voilé* (Geneva: La Palatine, 1947), 106–11.

3   *"Feetjahm is waiting for me!"*: Cited in MP to AGG, in Kolb (ed.), op. cit., vol. 20, 349; and in Painter, op. cit., vol. 1, 112.

3   "Perhaps the most real thing": MP, "Reliques," in PJ, 176. Similarly, MP writes in "La Comtesse," "When I think of the comtesse today, I realize that she . . . was one of those people who have a little magic lamp, but are unaware of their own light. And when one gets to know them, talks with them, one becomes like them, one no longer sees their mysterious light, their charm, their color; they lose all their poetry." MP, CSB, 87–88.

5   "Mme Thiers would much rather be a duchess!": Cited in Anne de Rochechouart de Mortemart, Duchesse d'Uzès, *Souvenirs 1847–1933* (Paris: Lacurne, 2011), 41.

5   "Since the Revolution": Jules Renard, *Journal inédit* (Paris: Bernouard, 1927), entry of January 3, 1898; cited in Richard Langham Smith and Caroline Potter, eds., *French Music Since Berlioz* (London: Ashgate, 2006), 111, n. 1.

5   "the triumph of the duchesses": Cited in Suzanne Fiette, *La noblesse française des Lumières à la Belle Époque* (Paris: Perrin, 2015), 206. On the gratin and its demise see also GLP, "Gratin (Le)," in *Dictionnaire du snobisme*, ed. Philippe Jullian (Paris: Plon, 1958), 87; and Alice Bernard, "Le grand monde parisien à l'épreuve de la guerre," in *Vingtième siècle* 99 (July–September 2008): 13–32.

6   "fodder for sonnets and flesh for novels": GPR, *Théâtre d'amour* (Paris: Paul Ollendorff, 1921), 344.

6   "It seemed to me": MP, CCS, 3.

6   For a brief discussion of the mother/son bond in RTP, see Judith Thurman, "I Never Took My Eyes off My Mother," in *The Proust Project,* ed. André Aciman (New York: FSG/Books & Co./ Helen Marx Books, 2004), 6–7.

7   On the treatment of art-historical sources in RTP, see Eric Karpeles, *Proust and Painting: A Visual Companion to "In Search of Lost Time"* (London: Thames & Hudson, 2008). Karpeles reproduces and illustrates the passage about Moreau's *Jupiter and Semele* on pages 110–111; he cites "a 'Harmony in Black and White' by Whistler" and "like the water-lilies on a . . . canvas by Monet" on pages 198 and 211, respectively.

7   Mme de Guermantes's ancestors: see MP, CCS, op. cit., 9–10 and 59–60; Samuel Beckett, *Proust* (London: Chatto & Windus, 1931), 45; and Howard Moss, *The Magic Lantern of Marcel Proust: A Critical Study of* "The Remembrance of Things Past" (Philadelphia: Paul Dry Books, 2012 [1962]), 62–63.

8   "the mythic bird Garamantes": Dominique Jullien, *Proust et ses modèles* (Paris: José Corti, 1989), 134.

8   "one of the noblest creatures in Paris,": MP, CG, 356.

8   "these two poetic creatures": Ibid.

8   "beautiful and ethereal Diana": Ibid., 357.

8   "Minerva [with] her glittering fringed shield": Ibid., 357.

8   "a bird's plumage": Ibid.

8   "a divine swan": Ibid., 329.

8   On the limitations of the "esprit de Guermantes," see James Litvak, "Strange Gourmet: Taste, Waste, Proust," in *Studies in the Novel*, 28, no. 3 (Fall 1996): 338–56, 348.

9   "through a topsy-turvy inversion": MP, CG, 719.

9   On MP's disillusionment with the monde, see Léon Pierre-Quint, *Marcel Proust: Sa vie, son œuvre* (Paris: Simon Kra, 1925), 176–77; on disenchantment as a constitutive feature of RTP, see Walter Benjamin, *Sur Proust* (Caen: Nous, 2010), 22–23.

10   *bal de têtes:* This pun is a play on the Princesse de Sagan's 1885 *bal des bêtes,* discussed in chapter 1. "*Le bal de têtes*" was MP's original title for the final party scene in RTP, posthumously published as *Une matinée chez la Princesse de Guermantes.* See MP, MPG, 15. For an astute analysis of Proust's *bal de têtes* in relation to the *Memoirs* of the Duc de Saint-Simon, see Marc Hersant and Muriel Ades, "D'un bal de têtes à l'autre," in *"Le Temps retrouvé" 80 ans après: Essais critiques,* ed. Adam Andrew Watt (New York: Peter Lang, 2009), 10–21.

10   "The only life worth living": MP, TR, 337; see also ibid., 899, where MP writes that the work of art is "the only way of regaining lost time."

10   On the circular structure of RTP, see Antoine Compagnon's preface to the French Folio edition of MP, CCS, ed. Antoine Compagnon (Paris: Gallimard/Folio, 1988), xxv.

10   boundaries between writing and reality: Howard Moss, op. cit., 22: "A book in which real people, natural objects, and institutions appear, yet resorting, like a fairy tale, to deception to reach the truth, [the *Search*] is a house of mirrors."

10   "asked me for the 'keys' ": Cited in CA, *Monsieur Proust,* as told to Georges Belmont, trans. Barbara Bray, foreword by André Aciman (New York: New York Review Books, 2003), 241; on the issue of "keys" in MP, see also ibid., 153–57, 243–45, and 248; A. Adam, "Le Roman de Proust et le problème des clefs," *La Revue des sciences humaines,* 65 (1952); RD, *De Monsieur Thiers à Marcel Proust,* op. cit., "Les Clefs de Proust," 37–44; Jacques de Lacretelle, "Les Clefs de l'œuvre de Proust," in *La Nouvelle Revue Française* 112 (January 1923); André Maurois, *Quest for Proust,* trans. Gerald Hopkins (New York: Penguin, 1962 [1950]); Henri Raczymow, *Le Cygne de Proust* (Paris: Gallimard, 1989), 51–63; and Roland Barthes, *The Preparation of the Novel,* trans. Kate Briggs (New York: Columbia University Press, 2011), 313–15.

11   "I have spared myself": MP, in Kolb, ed., op. cit., vol. 19, **.

11   The character of Charles Swann: See above all RB, op. cit., 65; RD, *Souvenirs sur Marcel Proust,* 190–92; DH, *Pays parisiens* (Paris: Grasset, 1932), 81–83; and Raczymow, *Le Cygne de Proust,* 51–64. In her correspondence with MP, GS referred to Haas, whom MP first met in her salon, as "Swann-Haas" (cited in Raczymow, op. cit., 51). (According to RB, MP told him on at least two separate occasions that Haas was the model for Swann.) Edmund de Waal discusses the relationship of another "key," Charles Ephrussi, to Charles Haas in his magnificent family biography *The Hare with Amber Eyes: A Hidden Inheritance* (New York: Picador, 2010), 104–7; Ephrussi eventually became a good friend of both EG and HG, but as that friendship postdates the period I am examining here, and as Ephrussi was close neither to GS nor to LC, he does not feature in the present study.

11   Comte Robert de Montesquiou-Fezensac: See (among many sources): CA, op. cit., 255–65; William C. Carter, *Marcel Proust: A Life* (New Haven and London: Yale University Press, 2013), 126, 147, 176, 243–44, 442–43, and 756–57; Patrick Chaleyssin, *Robert de Montesquiou: Mécène et dandy* (Paris: Somology, 1992), 185–97; FG, *Mon amitié avec Marcel Proust* (Paris: Grasset, 1958), 33–34; LG, *Robert de Montesquiou et Marcel Proust* (Paris: Flammarion, 1925); Philippe Jullian, *Robert de Montesquiou, prince de 1900* (Paris: Perrin, 1965); Ursula Link-Heer, "Mode, Möbel, façons et manières: Robert de Montesquiou und Marcel Proust," in *Marcel Proust und die Belle Époque,* ed. Thomas Hunkeler (Frankfurt: Insel, 2002), 84–120; and Edgar Munhall, ed., *Whistler and Montesquiou: The Butterfly and the Bat* (New York and Paris: The Frick Collection & Flammarion, 1995), 28 and 53.

11   "Thundering Jove": Cited in Painter, op. cit., vol. 1, 148. On HG as a model for the Duc de Guermantes, see also Philippe Michel-Thiriet, *Le Livre de Proust* (London: Chatto & Windus, 1989), 186.

11   Proust created a composite: FG, *Mon amitié,* 45. CA states that according to MP, "the character of the Duchesse de Guermantes was based partly on the Comtesse Greffulhe, and partly

on Mme Straus and the Comtesse de Chevigné." See CA, op. cit., 241, as well as 153–57 and 243–48. While other mentions of LC, EG, and/or GS as the models for Mme de Guerman-tes are too numerous to cite in full, a few notable sources are: Anne-Marie Bernard, ed., *The World of Proust as Seen by Paul Nadar*, trans. Susan Wise (Cambridge and London: The MIT Press, 2002), 69, 72, and 97; MB, *La Duchesse de Guermantes: Laure de Sade, Comtesse de Chevigné* (Paris: Plon, 1950), i–xii, 35, 133–35, and 138–42; MB, *Le Voyageur voilé*, op cit., 49–118; RB, op. cit., 79–80; Carter, *Marcel Proust*, 129–30, 144, and 673; RD, "Madame Straus et Marcel Proust," in *La Revue de Paris* 42 (October 15, 1936): 803–14; RD, *De Monsieur Thiers à Marcel Proust*, 17–25 and 34; AdF, *Mon Paris et ses Parisiens*, vol. 1: *Les Quartiers de l'Étoile* (Paris: Pierre Horay, 1953), 105 and 138–39; AdF, *Mon Paris et ses Parisiens*, vol. 1: *Le Faubourg Saint-Honoré* (Paris: Pierre Horay, 1956), 88; FG, *L'Âge d'or* (Paris: Grasset, 1947), 158; AG, *Les Clés de Proust, suivies de Portraits*, "La Duchesse de Guermantes" (Paris: Sun, 1953), 29–45; Huas, op. cit., "Oriane," 155–98; Maurois, *Quest for Proust*, op. cit., 160–79; Painter, op. cit., vol. 1, 150; and Jean-Yves Tadié, *Marcel Proust*, trans. Euan Cameron (New York: Viking, 2000), 117. That MP modeled Mme de Guermantes on these three women even receives men-tion in such generalist works as William Amos, *The Originals: Who's Really Who in Literature* (London: Cardinal, 1990), 221.

11 "Anonymous Adorations—1888": EG, in AP(II)/101/1. The majority of EG's archival docu-ments are untitled and undated, but I do provide that information whenever it is available.

12 In her biography of LC, MB even refers to her as "Laure-Oriane"; see MB, *La Duchesse de Guermantes*, 56. For a point-by-point comparison of EG to Mme de Guermantes, see Laure Hillerin, *La Comtesse Greffulhe, l'ombre des Guermantes* (Paris: Flammarion, 2014), 16–17, 423–47, and 539–43.

12 "The quality of a 'salon'": MP, CG, 744.

13 Proust had to resign himself: See MP, *Lettres à Madame et Monsieur Émile Straus*, ed. Robert Proust (Paris: Plon, 1936), 11.

13 She had never once proposed: See Jean-Baptiste Proyart, "Marcel Proust et la Comtesse de Chevigné: envoi autographe sur *Le Côté de Guermantes* I et correspondance" (June 2008): 4. MP makes his complaint about never being invited to LC's salon in a letter addressed not to her but to AC, who took pity on MP and invited him over at last. On MP's specific desire, and failure, to meet the clubmen of the gratin, see Émilien Carassus, *Le Snobisme et les lettres françaises de Paul Bourget à Marcel Proust, 1884–1914* (Paris: Armand Colin, 1966), 543, n. 80.

13 "Mme de Chevigné is forever trying": Cited in LG, *Robert de Montesquiou et Marcel Proust* (Paris: Flammarion, 1925), 19; and in Maurois, *Quest for Proust*, 67.

13 "Do you not see that your presence": Cited in Bernard Briais, *Au temps des Frou-Frou: Femmes célèbres de la Belle Époque* (Paris: Imprimerie de Frou-Frou, 1902), 267; and in Chaleyssin, op. cit., 110.

14 "a displeasing little man": Cited in Joseph Confavreux and Nathalie Battus, *Guermantes en héritage*, a documentary aired by France-Culture on February 19, 2007.

14 "I didn't like him": Cited in Mina Curtiss, *Other People's Letters* (New York: Helen Marx Books, 2005), 168.

14 the quality of fan-boy worship: Litvak, op. cit.; and Wayne Koestenbaum, "I Went by a Devi-ous Route," in Aciman, ed., op. cit., 57–58. Litvak describes Mme de Guermantes's hold on MP's narrator's imagination as "the fascination of the forbidden object" and the lady herself as a "simultaneously straight and gay" version of Marcel's ultimate forbidden object: "The Mother." "Without for a moment doubting the intensity of his love for her [the duchesse]," Litvak writes, "we could compare it to a certain gay male 'love' for, say, Marlene Dietrich" (Litvak, op. cit., 347). In MP's (as opposed to Marcel's) life, much the same idealizing "gay male 'love'" informs his attitude toward LC, GS, and EG. When commenting on this phe-nomenon, MP's contemporaries substituted "religious" for "gay," as in: "His respect for soci-ety's grandes dames was almost religious; [RM] and [EG] particularly awed him." See AdF, *Cinquante ans de panache* (Paris: Pierre Horay, 1951), 71. It bears noting that AdF identifies both EG *and* RM as "grandes dames."

14 an "angel [who] drives mortals to distraction": MP to GS, in MP, *Correspondance avec Mme Straus*, preface by Susy Mante-Proust (Paris: Plon, 1936), 15–16.

14 "a 'great golden bird'": Dominique (pseud. MP), "Le Salon de la Comtesse Greffulhe." Trans-lated and published for the first time in English in appendix C.

15 "Mme S. has never been to the Louvre": MP, JS, 435.

15 "passion for interesting things": MP, in Kolb, ed., op. cit., vol. 7, 77. MP further remarks

that EG is not "a Récamier"—a reference to a legendary *salonnière* with whom, as I discuss in chapter 20, EG in fact sought to identify herself.

15 "When what one used to love": Cited in Huas, op. cit., 168.

15 "used to be so beautiful": Cited in CA, op. cit., 243–44.

15 "a tough old bird": MP to AGG, in Kolb, ed., op. cit., vol. 20, 349.

15 "making her into a fearsome vulture": Ibid.

15 "the inversion of essences": Barthes first developed the thesis of inversion as "the basic principle" of RTP at a colloquium at Cerisy in 1977, expanding upon it in Roland Barthes, *The Rustle of Language,* trans. Richard Howard (Berkeley: University of California Press, 1989), 272–80. On the paradigm of "inversion" in RTP, see also Pierre Zoberman, "L'Inversion comme prisme universel," in *Le Magazine Littéraire: Marcel Proust* (2013): 81–86; Laure Murat, "Les Souliers rouges de la duchesse, ou la vulgarité de l'aristocratie française," in Forest and Audeguy, eds., op. cit., 97 ("The *Search* [is] the great book of inversion"); and Peter Brooks's as-yet unpublished lecture, presented at a 2013 colloquium at the Columbia University Maison Française. Discussing the hidden homosexuality of the characters in the *Search,* Brooks notes, "The lives of 'inverts' in Proust invert precisely our optics of and on reality" as such. (Brooks also refers to this matter in his article "Persons and Optics," in *Arcade* [March 16, 2015]: n.p.) Nicolas Grimaldi provides a cogent synopsis of this phenomenon of (*x*) turning into (not *x*) when he writes, "One can never be sure that one really knows anyone else. There is no more continually verified theorem in the whole of the *Search.* . . . There is not one interpersonal relationship that is not founded on [mutual] misperception." See Nicolas Grimaldi, *Proust, les horreurs de l'amour* (Paris: PUF, 2008), 87.

16 major characters in the *Search:* MP, TR, 328.

16 In contrast to her perpetually: RTP, tome IV, 600.

16 On the aesthetic dimension of the young MP's "mystical" reverence for ancient French bloodlines, see Jean Recanti, *Profils juifs de Marcel Proust* (Paris: Buchet/Chastel, 1979), 18; and RB, op. cit., 86.

16 "People think they know me, but they don't": Ibid.

16 When commissioning one of her early portraits, EG considered Sargent, only to decide against him in favor of the now-forgotten society portraitist Carolus-Duran; see James S. Harding, "Art Notes from Paris," *Art Amateur* 17, no. 2 (July 1887): 31. This decision was emblematic of EG's taste in painting. Madrazo's portrait of LC is reproduced later in this book. According to A. Adam, op. cit., Madrazo was a model for the sculptor Ski in RTP.

CHAPTER ONE: RARA AVIS

21 an immense reception hall: Prior to its acquisition by the Seillière/Sagan family, the residence at 57, rue Saint-Dominique was known as the hôtel de Monaco, after its late-eighteenth-century proprietor, the estranged wife of a Monegasque prince. The material for the description of the hôtel de Sagan and the *bal des bêtes* is drawn from a large selection of mostly contemporary sources, including: *L'Art et la mode* (June 16, 1885): 6–7; Jules Claretie, *La Vie à Paris: 1880–1885,* vols. 1–6 (Paris: Victor Havard, 1880–1885), vol. 1, 175; Étincelle (pseud. Vtesse Peyronny), *Carnet d'un mondain* (Paris: Édouard Rouveyre, 1881), 47–60; *Le Figaro* (May 28, 1885): 1; *Le Figaro* (June 3, 1885): 1; *Le Figaro* (June 5, 1885): 1–2; *Le Gaulois* (May 26, 1880): 1; *Le Gaulois* (May 10, 1885): 2; *Le Gaulois* (May 29, 1885): 1; *Le Gaulois* (June 3, 1885): 1–2; *La Lanterne* (June 1885): 2; Parisis (pseud. Émile Blavet), "Le bal Sagan," in *La Vie parisienne: la ville et le théâtre,* preface by Aurélien Scholl (Paris: Paul Ollendorff, 1886), 116–23; Abbé Sadinet, "Le Bal des bêtes," in *La Vie moderne* (June 15, 1885): 392–93; *Truth: A Weekly Journal* 7, no. 174 (June 3, 1880): 713–15; and *Le Voleur illustré* (June 11, 1885): 382–83. For additional descriptions of the Sagan residence and marriage, see An American (pseud.), "To Blow Up a Princess: Dynamite Bombs Explode in the Doorway of the Princesse de Sagan," *Baltimore American* (March 1, 1892): 1; J. Sillery, *Monographie de l'hôtel de Sagan* (Paris: Frazier, 1909); "Historic Residences of Paris Now Occupied by Antiquaries," *New York Herald* (January 2, 1910): 11; A Veteran Diplomat (pseud.), "The Passing of Talleyrand, *le roi du chic: A Chapter in the Fall of Past Grandeur,*" *New York Times* (February 27, 1910): n.p.; AdF, "Une saison de printemps commence," *La Semaine à Paris* (May 8, 1936): 4; and Pierre Guiral, "Les Écrivains français et la notion de la décadence," *Romantisme* 13, no. 32 (1983): 9–22.

21 she bore a striking resemblance to Marie Antoinette: *Truth: A Weekly Journal* 7, no. 176

(May 13, 1880): 682; and de V . . . (pseud.), "Nos Grandes Mondaines: la Princesse de Sagan," *La Revue mondaine illustrée* (February 10, 1893), n.p.

22 With similarly macabre wit: On the appearance of "la belle Laure," see Stéphanie-Félicité du Crest de Saint-Aubin, Comtesse de Genlis, *Pétrarque et Laure* (Paris: E. Ladvocat, 1819), 174.

23 cursed like a stevedore: MB, *La Duchesse de Guermantes,* 89; and Claude Arnaud, *Proust contre Cocteau* (Paris: Grasset, 2013), 75.

23 "Corporal Petrarch": Arnaud, 77.

23 "mannish air": Ibid., 74.

23 On the gratin's tolerance for (discreet) adultery, see GLP, "Gratin (Le)," in *Dictionnaire du snobisme,* ed. Jullian, 89.

23 "poor in income, but rich in highnesses": AG, *Les Clés de Proust,* 30.

23 "Anyhow, I have *been* to Tsarskoe Selo": Cited in AF, *Le Bal du Pré-Catelan* (Paris: Arthème Fayard, 1946), 312–13.

23 a hummingbird with diamond-speckled wings: Sadinet, op. cit., 392.

24 *en panthère:* Good descriptions of EG's panther costume appear in RM, *Têtes couronnées* (Paris: Sansot, 1916), 253–54; and in RM's preface to the *Catalogue des tableaux par Gustave Jacquet* (Paris: Galerie Georges Petit, 1909), 10.

25 "The pleasure is mine": Comte O. de Bessas de la Mégie, ed., *Légendaire de la noblesse française: devises, cris de guerre, dictons, etc.* (Paris: Librairie Centrale, 1865), 119.

25 "She was beautiful always": LG, *Mémoires,* vol. 2, *Les Marronniers en fleurs* (Paris: Grasset, 1929), 22.

25 "an image of prestige like none other": EG, in AP(II)/101/150; also cited in Anne de Cossé-Brissac, *La Comtesse Greffulhe* (Paris: Perrin, 1991), 53.

25 "Piety stands with me": Louis de la Roque, ed., *Bulletin héraldique de France, ou revue historique de la noblesse,* vol. 9 (Paris: Administration du Bulletin Héraldique de France, 1890), 49.

26 thought to have been: See Inti Landauro, "Louvre to Restore da Vinci's *John the Baptist,*" *Wall Street Journal* (January 13 2016); and James M. Saslow, *Ganymede in the Renaissance: Homosexuality in Art and Society* (New Haven and London: Yale University Press, 1986), 89–90.

27 On protocol in the Royal Chapel at Versailles, see Alexandre Maral, *La Chapelle royale de Versailles sous Louis XIV* (Wavre: Mardaga, 2010), 109–22.

27 On etiquette at Louis XIV's court, see Pierre Dominique, "Sous le règne de l'étiquette," *Le Crapouillot: Les Bonnes Manières* 19 (1952): 19–25; Norbert Elias, *La Société de cour* (Paris: Calmann-Lévy, 1974), 79–93; Lucy Norton, ed., *Saint-Simon at Versailles* (London: Hamish Hamilton, 1980), 223–35; and Louis de Rouvroy, Duc de Saint-Simon, *Mémoires,* ed. M. Chéruel, preface by Charles-Augustin Sainte-Beuve, vol. 12 (Paris: Hachette, 1858), ch. 19. Elias points out that prestige was a zero-sum game among Louis XIV's courtiers, as "every improvement in one person's rank necessarily brought about the degradation of another's" (79).

27 "A bourgeois is an ocean of nothingness": EdG, *Journal,* op. cit., entry of September 5, 1867.

27 "not born": On this expression, see Georges Renard, "Les Femmes du monde et leur rôle politique," in *La Revue politique et parlementaire,* tome XXXVII, no. 3 (September 1903), 601–16.

28 the people of France had idolized Hugo: On "the great and universal adulation" of the French people for Victor Hugo, and on the latter's "middle-class liberalism," see Robert Harborough Sherard, *Twenty Years in Paris: Being Some Recollections of a Literary Life* (London: Hutchinson, 1905), 6, 11.

28 two million mourners: CCB, *Journal: 1885–1886,* ed. Éric Mension-Rigau (Paris: Perrin, 2003), 39–41; AM, *Journal (1879–1939),* ed. Marcel Billot (Paris: Mercure de France, 1985), 49–52; and Graham Robb, *Victor Hugo: A Biography* (New York: W. W. Norton, 1999), 525–32. On Mme de Sagan's brief thought of postponing the ball because of Hugo's funeral, see *Le Gaulois* (May 29, 1885): 1.

29 "one of the greatest pageants": Cited in Frederick Brown, *For the Soul of France: Culture Wars in the Age of Dreyfus* (New York: Alfred A. Knopf, 2010), 126.

29 "they found their last redoubt": David Higgs, *Nobles in Nineteenth-Century France: The Practice of Inegalitarianism* (Baltimore and London: The Johns Hopkins University Press, 1987), 229. Suzanne Fiette makes the same point, writing that "at the fin de siècle, the high nobility avenges the eclipse of its political power by occupying the superb summit of elegant life"; see *La Noblesse française,* 206. Other sources on the fin-de-siècle nobility's commitment to social distinction include Jean-Pierre Chaline, "La Sociabilité mondaine au XIXe siècle," in *Élites*

et sociabilité en France: Actes du colloque de Paris, 23 janvier 2003, ed. Marc Fumaroli, Gabriel de Broglie, and Jean-Pierre Chaline (Paris: Perrin, 2003), 25; Christophe Charle, "Noblesses et élites en France au début du XXe siècle," in *Les Noblesses européennes au XIXe siècle: Actes du colloque organisé par l'École Française de Rome et l'Université de Milan, Milan-Rome, 21–23 novembre 1985* (Milan: EFR, 1988), 427; Anne Martin-Fugier, *Les Salons de la IIIe République* (Paris: Perrin, 2003); and Guillaume Pinson, *Fiction du monde: analyse littéraire et médiatique de la mondanité*, Ph.D. dissertation (Montreal: McGill University, 2005), 19–28.

30   The new backdrop for their splendor: Marie-Claire Bancquart, *Paris "Fin-de-Siècle"* (Paris: SNELA, 2009), 372–83.

30   "exulted in the grandeur": MB, *Égalité* (Paris: Grasset, 1935), 167.

30   dirtying their hands "in trade": Fiette, op. cit., 211; and Vicomte André de Royer-Saint-Micaud, "Avons-nous une noblesse française?" *La Revue des revues* (October 1898): 1–20, 12.

31   "King of Chic": Gaston Jollivet, *Souvenirs de la vie de plaisir sous le Second Empire* (Paris: Tallandier, 1927), 97; A Veteran Diplomat (pseud.), op. cit. On the Prince de Sagan's tastes, finances, and marriage, see also AdF, *Cinquante ans de panache*, op. cit., 48–50; and Martin-Fugier, *Les Salons de la IIIe République*, 23–24.

31   *"Le monde, c'est moi"*: Cited in Marcel Fouquier, *Jours heureux d'autrefois: Une société et son époque, 1885–1935* (Paris: Albin Michel, 1941), 53.

31   "that he should have a magician at his disposal": CCB, op. cit., 215.

31   "Those who buy a coronet": Cited in An American (pseud.), op. cit., 1.

31   he had reaped massive profits: Léon Techener, *Bulletin du bibliophile et du bibliothécaire* (Paris: L. Techener, 1873), 193; A Veteran Diplomat (pseud.), op. cit.; and AdF, *Cinquante ans de panache*, 49.

32   "direct descent from Jupiter and Juno": Cited in "Société Medico-Psychologique—le cas du Baron Seillière," *La Petite République française*, June 30, 1887; reproduced in *Papers Relating to the Foreign Relations of the United States in the Year 1887* (Washington, DC: US Government Printing Office, 1888), 336.

32   "intelligence coefficient": MP, CG, 744.

32   "of mediocre intelligence": CCB, op. cit., 214.

32   "a Negro suffering from smallpox": Cited in A Veteran Diplomat (pseud.), op. cit.

32   On France's diplomatic isolation as one of only two republics on a continent ruled by a network of "crowned cousins that formed one single family," see FB, *Intimités de la IIIe République: La Fin des temps "délicieux"* (Paris: Hachette, 1935), 38–39.

33   "I couldn't invite him": Cited in Horace de Viel-Castel, *Mémoires sur le règne de Napoléon III*, vol. 2 (Paris: Guy Le Prat, 1979), 95.

33   "Our Lady of the Arts": Cited in Raczymow, *Le Paris retrouvé de Proust*, 137.

34   "I've never heard you in *Faust*!": Cited in Chaleyssin, op. cit., 77.

34   He often joked: See Raczymow, *Le Cygne de Proust*, 17; on Haas's record for the most rejections in the Jockey-Club's history, see ibid., 16.

34   society speak for "Jew": Luc Sante explains that an "Israelite" was a French Jew of long standing (and typically of Sephardic origin, like GS's mother), whereas a "Jew" was a recent immigrant (stereotypically of Ashkenazi origin, like GS's father). See Luc Sante, *The Other Paris* (New York: Farrar, Straus & Giroux, 2015), 82.

34   "I'd like to think there's still one place": Cited in Guillaume Hanoteau, *Paris: Anecdotes et portraits* (Paris: Fayard, 1974), 90. On the importance of family history and pedigree in Jockey-Club admissions, see also Robert Burnand, *La Vie quotidienne en France de 1870 à 1900* (Paris: Hachette, 1948), 147.

34   When organizing a *mondain*: CCB, op. cit., 135.

34   "the Jockey's only Israelite": Cited in Raczymow, *Le Cygne de Proust*, 17.

34   Under the Second Empire, he had served: X. (pseud.), "Choses et autres," *La Vie parisienne* (February 5, 1870): 113; and Raoul Chéron, "Nécrologie: M. Charles Haas," *Le Gaulois* (July 6, 1902): 2.

35   "I love going to the Salon": EG, undated note in AP(II)/101/149.

36   "I have too little religion": Cited in RD, *De Monsieur Thiers à Marcel Proust*, 31, n. 1.

36   *La Juive*: The standard claim is that this was the most performed opera for about twenty-five to thirty years after its début. Mathias Énard offers a slightly different account, identifying it as "the most frequently performed work at the Paris Opéra until the 1930s." See Mathias Énard, *Boussole* (Paris: Actes Sud, 2015), 262. I am thankful to Julie Elsky for calling my attention to this source.

36   tens of thousands of mourners turned out: Ruth Jordan, *Fromental Halévy: His Life and Music* (New York: Limelight, 1996), 197–99 and 208.

36   For a detailed discussion of LH's "special esprit, his unique brand of irony, his original and inimitable grace," see Claretie, *La Vie à Paris: 1880,* vol. 1, 225–32.

37   "glorious names": AF, *Le Bal du Pré-Catelan,* 158.

37   On the monde's ambivalence toward artists, see Martin-Fugier, *Les Salons de la IIIᵉ République,* 12–15.

38   "giving the hand": On the genesis and import of this ritual, see Daria Galateria, *L'Étiquette à la cour de Versailles,* trans. Françoise Antoine (Paris: Flammarion, 2017), 115–17.

38   "The duke, without hesitation": Cited in Misia Sert, *Misia and the Muses: The Memoirs of Misia Sert* (New York: The John Day Company, 1953), 126–27.

38   "very distantly related": Cited in Jullian, *Robert de Montesquiou,* 30.

38   "Pray tell, Princesse": Cited in GLP, *Trente ans de dîners en ville* (Paris: Revue Adam, 1948), 45. On Comte Aimery de La Rochefoucauld as "a regular Saint-Simon," see PW, *Society in Paris: Letters to a Young French Diplomat,* trans. Raphael Ledos de Beaufort (London: Chatto & Windus, 1890), 134. It is GLP who identifies PV as Juliette Adam (ibid., 29).

39   a celebrated dance number from: On the *ballet des abeilles* in Halévy's opera, see Paul Smith, "Théâtre du Grand Opéra: *Le Juif-Errant,*" *Revue et gazette musicale de Paris,* 17 (April 25, 1852): 137–40, 139. On the popularity of the *ballet des abeilles* under the Second Empire, see Damien Colas, "Halévy and His Contribution to the Evolution of the Orchestra," in Niels Martin Jensen and Franco Piperno, *The Impact of Composers and Works on the Orchestra: Case Studies* (Berlin: Berliner Wissenschafts Verlag, 2007), 143–84 and 177–78.

40   the dancing bees were selected: For a complete list of the dancers in the *ballet des abeilles* at the Sagan ball, see ED, *La France juive: Essai d'histoire contemporaine,* vol. 2, 43rd ed. (Paris: Marpon & Flammarion, 1886), 180–81.

40   "overtook the whole assembly": PV, *Le Grand Monde* (Paris: La Nouvelle Revue, 1887), 306. See also PV, *Society in Paris,* 202.

40   "prove inconvenient": CCB, op. cit., 203.

42   Étincelle: On the real identity of this leading gossip columnist for *Le Figaro* as the Vicomtesse de Peyronny, see "Le mariage d'Étincelle," *La Revue des grands procès contemporains* 14 (1896): 266–348. Her contemporaries ascribed her professional success to the fact that when she wrote, "one could hear a genuine *mondaine* speaking her own native language; one could tell that hers was not the artificial work of some professional"—read "not born"—"journalist" (cited in "Le Mariage d'Étincelle," ibid., 266). On the girlish sobriquets used by pseudonymous writers in the Parisian fashion and society press, see Lisa Tiersten, *Marianne in the Market: Envisioning Consumer Society in Fin-de-Siècle France* (Berkeley: University of California Press, 2001), 137.

42   On the xenophobic dimension of fin-de-siècle French anti-Semitism, see Jérôme Hélie, "L'Arche sainte fracturée," in Général André Bach, *L'Année Dreyfus: Une histoire politique de l'armée française de Charles X à "l'Affaire"* (Paris: Tallandier, 2004). To many fin-de-siècle French conservatives, Hélie writes, "the Jew strongly signals the rise of 'new' men—men not legitimated by blood and by ancestral roots in the land, [men] easy to conflate with 'hateful Germany' " (231).

43   "grown like eagles' feathers": Daniel 4:33.

43   "In such profane times": *Le Pèlerin* (July 1885). For additional right-wing coverage of the *bal des bêtes,* see *Annales catholiques* (June 27, 1885, and July 16, 1885); *La Croix* (June 18, 1885, February 16, 1889, and February 13, 1894); and *La Légitimité* (August 1, 1896): 165–66.

43   "The tales of the bizarre": *L'Univers,* June 7, 1885.

43   Drumont posited the "Jew-ified" social chaos: ED, *La France juive,* vol. 2, 94–97 and 177–82; and *La Fin d'un monde* (Paris: Savine, 1889), 386–89. ED also criticizes the fin-de-siècle Faubourg's ultimate sacred cows, the Comte de Chambord (hereafter "Monseigneur") and his legitimist followers, for their singular inefficacy in mounting a defense against the tides of "Jewish" republicanism in France; see *La France juive,* vol. 1, 436–44; he reiterates this thesis in ED, *Testament d'un antisémite* (Paris: E. Dentu, 1891), 4–10.

44   "everything is controlled by the Jew": ED, *La France juive,* vol. 1, 174. See also ED, *Testament d'un antisémite,* "It is the Jew. It is the Jew who holds everything in his hands" (115).

44   MP's description of his artistic process as that of a bee making honey is cited in Duplay, op. cit., 72; and in CA, op. cit., 145. On MP drawing the pollen for his "black honey" from the ladies of the gratin, see William Fifield, "Interview with Jean Cocteau," *Paris Review* 32 (Summer–Fall 1964).

CHAPTER TWO: MY DON GIOVANNI, MY FAUST

46 On EG's ancestry, see Cossé-Brissac, op. cit., 44–45; AG, *Les Clefs de Proust,* 34–37; and miscellaneous genealogical documents in AP(II)/101/3.

48 the Canal du Midi: On the Riquets' construction of this canal, also known as the Canal de Languedoc, see A. Borel d'Hauterive, ed., *Annuaire de la pairie et de la noblesse de France et des maisons souveraines de l'Europe,* no. 3 (Paris: Bureau de la Revue Pittoresque, 1845), 245.

48 Her notebooks from these years: AP(II)/101/1–2.

49 making Guigui eat a slug: AG, *Les Clés de Proust,* 39.

49 Uncle Robert had liked to play dress-up: Hillerin, op. cit., 41.

50 "The demoiselle of gentle birth": Émile Zola, "Types de femmes en France," *Le Messager de l'Europe,* June 1878, n.p.

50 Élisabeth adored her mother's sweet temperament: Cossé-Brissac, op. cit., 44.

50 "cultivating a sensitivity to fine ideas": EG to MCC, letter dated September 20, 1880, in AP(II)/101/ 40.

51 "the seven sisters": MACC to EG, letter dated December 30, 1900, in AP(II)/101/53.

51 dreamy, introverted Marie-Alys: MACC's letters to EG and her sisters fill a large file in EG's personal archives; see AP(II)/101/53.

51 "the Golden Calf": RM wrote a snide poem about HG in which all the verses rhymed with "Veau d'Or" (Golden Calf), and which is cited in Chaleyssin, op. cit., 84; and in Jullian, *Robert de Montesquiou,* 103.

51 on-site stables: Béatrice de Andia, ed., *Autour de la Madeleine* (Paris: Action Artistique de la Ville de Paris, 2005), 83.

51 in the Seine-et-Marne region: See Tom (pseud.), "La Grande Villégiature," *L'Illustration* 92 (July 21, 1888): 39.

52 On HG's wealth, see Cossé-Brissac, op. cit., 18–21.

52 On HG's paternal ancestry, see Guy Antonetti, *Une maison de banque à Paris au XVIIIe siècle: Greffulhe Montz et Cie* (Paris: Cujas, 1963); Jean-Baptiste de Courcelles, ed., *Histoire généalogique et héraldique des pairs de France, des grands dignitaires de la couronne, des principales familles nobles du royaume,* vol. 7 (Paris: Arthus, 1826), 93; FB, op. cit.; and JEB, *La Pêche aux souvenirs* (Paris: Flammarion, 1949): "The origins of the Greffulhes are not lost in the mists of time" (202).

53 5,000 francs in annual income: Éric Legay, *Le Comte Henry Greffulhe, un grand notable en Seine-et-Marne.* Master's thesis presented at the Université de Paris X Nanterre (1986–1987), 55, note 1.

53 "Greffulhe decided to marry": HB, *La Haute Société: journal secret 1886–1889* (Paris: Atelier Marcel Jullian, 1979), 40.

54 He and Bertie once earned a scolding: appears in LG, *Mémoires,* vol. 2, 20. LG adds that when the two young men saw Queen Victoria coming toward them during their illicit shoot, they "hid in the bushes like schoolboys."

54 "his only vocation to date": HB, op. cit., 39.

55 France's ambassador to Russia: Hillerin, op. cit., 66–67.

55 "Papa . . . detest[s] everything": Élaine Greffulhe, "Papa," in AP(II)/101/33.

55 "A bluestocking": Astolphe-Louis-Léonor, Marquis de Custine, "Bas-bleu," in *Dictionnaire du snobisme,* ed. Jullian, 35.

55 "her gorgeous tiny waist": Ibid., 40.

56 "I went to the quai Malaquais": Octave Feuillet, in "Hommages et appréciations," AP(II)/101/1.

56 he failed his baccalaureate eight times: Legay, op. cit., 49–50. Legay's research in the nineteenth-century baccalaureate registries in the French national archives suggests that after his first eight efforts, HG never passed this exam. Legay's research further indicates that HG managed to avoid military service, which was compulsory for all Frenchmen but which, according to Legay, HG likely paid someone else to fulfill in his stead. Given HG's oft-proclaimed concern for his honor as a *noble d'épée,* one might fairly have expected him to carry out this duty himself. See Legay, op. cit., 50.

56 Like most unmarried young women: See EG's girlhood diary, labeled *Mes premières amours,* in AP(II)/101/1, n.p.

56 "to say a lot of idiotic things": HB, op. cit., 40.

57 "superbly regular features": AdF, *Mon Paris et ses Parisiens,* vol. 4, 90.

57 hunchbacked of form: Painter, op. cit., vol. 1, 151. Painter points out that this deformity later caught the notice of MP, who in the *Search* makes a reference to "Quasimodo de Breteuil," 151.

57   resemblance to a king in a deck of playing cards: JEB, *La Pêche aux souvenirs,* op. cit., 203; on HG's descent from "Demi-Louis," see Pauline de Broglie, Comtesse de Pange, *Comment j'ai vu 1900* (Paris: Grasset, 1962), 49; and AdF, *Mon Paris et ses Parisiens,* vol. 4, 90.

57   according to her identity card: EG's identity card is filed in AP(II)/101/1. On the same card, she makes herself eight years younger, giving 1868 as the year of her birth.

58   *Salome in the Garden:* On EG's acquisition of this painting, see Jean Laran, ed., *L'Art de notre temps: Gustave Moreau* (Paris: Librairie Centrale des Beaux-Arts, 1914), 73; RM, *Les Pas effacés,* vol. 2 (Paris: Émile-Paul, 1923), 233–34; and RM, *Altesses sérénissimes* (Paris: Félix Juven, 1907), 11, 44.

58   On MCC's and EG's admiration for Moreau, see RM's preface to *Exposition Gustave Moreau* (Paris: Galerie Georges Petit, 1906), 11–12; on HG's tirade against Moreau (and in favor of Charles Chaplin), see Cossé-Brissac, op. cit., 15 and 34–35.

59   "Surely you're too intelligent": HG cited by EG in her Journal de Mariage (1878–1879), n.p., in AP(II)/101/1.

59   "I love Henry": Ibid., entry of October 19, 1878.

59   "why, in the midst of my joy": Ibid., entry of September 26, 1878.

60   "the bittersweet pain of loving": The sixteenth-century *pétrarquiste* poet Pernette du Guillet, for instance, invokes the "bitter sweetness" (*doulx amer*) of the "pain of love" (*mal d'aymer*) in Song Three of her *Rymes,* ed. Victor E. Graham (Geneva: Droz, 1968), 41. On EG's fascination with Petrarch's verse, and specifically with Petrarch's Laura, see EG's lesson notebooks in AP(II)/101/1; and Hillerin, op. cit., 25. Hillerin does not note that EG's maternal grandfather translated Petrarch into French.

60   "In those days": LG, *Souvenirs du monde: 1890 à 1940* (Paris: Grasset, 1966), 87–88.

61   aristocratic bias toward populous families: On the *mondain* belief that "was not enough" for the Greffulhes; see HB, op. cit., 44.

61   "In the family we have always said of her": Interview with Armand-Ghislain, Comte de Maigret, Paris, March 14, 2012.

61   "like variations on the same repulsive, yellowish model": EG, *Mes premières amours,* op. cit., entry of February 3, 1877.

61   "in which a man would": EG to an unidentified interviewer in notes for an unpublished, undated interview, in AP(II)/101/1.

62   "The very idea of 'that'": Cited in Hillerin, op. cit., 231.

62   "veritable harem": LG, *Souvenirs du monde,* 131.

62   the cheering of the four thousand strangers: *Le Petit Parisien,* September 27, 1887, 1.

63   "Henry seemed completely preoccupied": EG, Journal de Mariage, entry of September 25, 1878.

63   "I want to be buried with it!": Cited in Cossé-Brissac, op. cit., 25.

64   breathtakingly delicate items: On EG's trousseau, see a full accounting in AP(II)/101/1. See also Jean-Philippe Bouilloud, ed., *Un univers d'artistes* (Paris: L'Harmattan, 2004), 31.

64   "You two look just like two monarchs": Cited in Cossé-Brissac, op. cit., 27.

64   "Ugly women": EG, in AP(II)/101/150.

64   "I see that you're agitated": MCC to EG, in AP(II)/101/41.

64   "But Maman": EG to MCC, in AP(II)/101/40.

65   "of Princes Charming in green satin": Unbound, typeset page in a sheaf of pages forming an untitled "Journal de Marie-Alice." The paragraph cited here comes from a page marked with the header "Au château de Monteillant, le lendemain du mariage," in AP(II)/101/149 (and also in duplicate in AP(II)/101/152). Though EG never gave a title to this text, I refer to it hereafter as her "Marie-Alice" project.

65   "When people first started bringing up the word *marriage*": Ibid. Some decades later, EG seems to have passed along at least this part of her "Marie-Alice" narrative to a novelist with whom she had by then become friendly, Adolphe Aderer, as the latter's *Une Grande Dame aima* (Paris: Calmann-Lévy, 1906) contains an account of a wedding night that is uncannily like the one written by EG and features a heroine strikingly similar to Marie-Alice de Monteillant. Aderer dedicated another novel, *L'Impossible Amour* (Paris: Calmann-Lévy, 1903), to EG a few years before writing *Une Grande Dame aima.* I am currently doing further research into this relationship, and into EG's other secret literary collaborations from the mid-1890s onward.

66   It reminded Élisabeth of an army barracks: EG, Journal de Mariage, entry of October 6, 1878; on the hemlock allées, see Agnes Herrick and George Herrick, *Paris Embassy Diary* (Lanham, Md.: University Press of America, 2007), 20–21.

66   "indescribably sad": JEB, *La Pêche aux souvenirs*, 203.
66   "Greffulhe's personal dream": Le Père Gérôme (pseud. A. Vernant), "Notes sur la Grande
      Propriété: Chez M. le Comte Greffulhe," *Le Briard* (October 22, 1892): 1. I bought a copy of
      this issue of *Le Briard* from a rare-books dealer in France. However, the article cited here is
      the second installment of a three-part exposé by the same title, which ran between October 21
      and October 25, 1892. All three installments are preserved in the Archives Départementales de
      Seine-et-Marne, microfilm PZ 34/44Mi306.
66   "Big Moustache": Ibid.
66   "We are the metal instrument": Cited in ibid.
66   " 'Big Moustache' is even more hated": Ibid.
66   rivaling such legendary hunting estates: On the superb quality of the hunting at Bois-Boudran
      and Chantilly, see Georges de Wailly, "La Vénérie moderne," in *La Nouvelle Revue,* vol. 80
      (January–February 1893): 167–77, 168–69; and Legay, op. cit., 111–112.
69   the driven shoot (*battue*): For more information on the *battue* and on the *chasse à tir* generally,
      see Gaston, Marquis de Castelbajac, "La Chasse à tir," in *Le Protocole mondain,* ed. AdF (Paris:
      Levallois-Perret, n.d.), 359–64; Crafty (pseud.), *La Chasse à tir: Notes et croquis* (Paris: Plon,
      1887); and "Les Battues," in *La Chasse moderne. Encyclopédie du chasseur,* ed. M. H. Adelon, G.
      Benoist, et al. (Paris: Larousse, 1912), 291–314.
69   thirty thousand pheasants, seven thousand partridges: See Le Père Gérôme (pseud. Vernant),
      "Notes sur la Grande Propriété: Chez M. le Comte Greffulhe," *Le Briard* (October 21, 1892):
      1; for the figure of fifteen hundred "pieces," see La Force, op. cit., 77; on the Duc de Char-
      tres shooting 3,400 birds in two days, see Olivier Coutau-Bégarie, ed., *Souvenirs historiques:
      Archives et collections de la princesse Marie d'Orléans* (Paris: Drouot, 2014), 52.
69   "while it is possible to keep one's honor": HG, cited by EG in AP(II)/101/150.
71   "thou shalt be polite": Cited in Quint, op. cit., 180.
71   "For the sake of my health": EG, Journal de Mariage, entry of November 20, 1878.
71   While she had never been a beauty: On Félicité's appearance, see CCB, op. cit., 43; and Hil-
      lerin, op. cit., 29; on Félicité's intimidation of her husband and Uncle Henri, see PW, *Les
      Soirées de Paris* (Paris: La Nouvelle Revue, 1887); and Hillerin, op. cit., 30.
72   "Today I spent five hours": EG, Journal de Mariage, entry of November 20, 1878.
72   On Louise de L'Aigle admitting that Félicité's favoritism toward HG had been a disaster for
      the whole family, see AP(II)/101/54.
72   "Her personality is the complete antithesis of mine": EG, Journal de Mariage, entry of Octo-
      ber 11, 1878.
72   "They are biting that horrid creature!": Ibid., entry of November 10, 1878.
72   "the oppression [the Greffulhes have] visited": Le Père Gérôme (pseud. Vernant), "Notes sur
      la Grande Propriété: Chez M. le Comte Greffulhe," *Le Briard* (October 21, 1892): 1.
72   "acting like Ophelia": EG, Journal de Mariage, entry of October 9, 1878.
73   " 'Well, it's obvious *you've* never been hunting' ": Ibid., entry of November 5, 1878.
73   the domaine du Francport: See "Society," *Lady's Realm* 14 (May–October 1903): 675–78, 676.
73   "feigning the kind of deep emotion": Cited in Cossé-Brissac, op. cit, 49.
74   "I must remember": EG, Journal de Mariage, entry of November 20, 1878.
74   He would get her a subscription: On HG's approval of, and EG's disinterest in, the *Gazette de
      France,* see Hillerin, op. cit., 31.
74   "When someone attacks the things I admire": EG in AP(II)/101/5. In her Journal de Mariage,
      EG wrote, "Henry *blows up* at anything I find beautiful," entry of November 13, 1878.
75   "to mourn the death of Christ": GLP, *Trente ans de dîners en ville,* 45.
75   "To praise a person for her 'simplicity' ": Raczymow, *Le Cygne de Proust,* 90.
75   On Aimery de La Rochefoucauld's genealogical "purism," see AdF, *Mon Paris et ses Parisiens,*
      vol. 4, 87.
76   by "point[ing] up the weak sides": PV, *Les Soirées de Paris,* 135.
76   "affable but almost willfully banal": LG, *Mémoires,* vol. 1, 110.
76   "Mme d'Haussonville has a bad character": CCB, op. cit., 122. MP later wrote a fawning
      article, "Le Salon de Mme la Comtesse d'Haussonville," which appeared under the pseud-
      onym Horatio in *Le Figaro* (January 4, 1904). This essay is reproduced in MP, *Le Salon de
      Mme de . . .* (Paris: L'Herne, 2009), 64–75. In this essay, MP posits Pauline and Othenin as
      two examples of "intellectual, moral [and] physical nobility" (66). But apart from two lines of
      perfunctory praise for Pauline (72), the entire essay is about the achievements and character of
      Othenin, whom MP knew through GS.

76 He also valued Pauline's close friendship: Paul-Gabriel Othenin, Comte d'Haussonville, *Le Comte de Paris: souvenirs personnels* (Paris: Calmann-Lévy, 1895); and MB, *La Duchesse de Guermantes,* 104.

77 "Greffulhe's mistresses aren't just all blond": HB, op. cit., 40.

77 "impeccable, almost intimidating courtesy": GLP, *Trente ans de dîners en ville,* op. cit., 105.

78 "were still *nobodies* in the middle of the twelfth century!": Abel Hermant, *Le Faubourg* (Paris: Paul Ollendorff, 1900 [1899]), 32. According to PM, MP credited Comte Aimery de La Rochefoucauld with a similar mantra: "They had no social standing to speak of in the year 1000." See PM, *Journal d'un attaché d'ambassade* (Paris: Gallimard/NRF, 1963), 194. Painter cites this line somewhat differently, though still ascribing it to "Place à Table": "They were nobodies in the year 1000." See Painter, op. cit., vol. 1, 153.

78 the standard avocation for ladies: Boniface de Castellane, *Vingt ans de Paris* (Paris: Fayard, 1925), 105; and Marie-Thérèse Guichard, *Les Égéries de la IIIᵉ République* (Paris: Payot, 1991), 114–15. In one of the hundreds of unbound, typeset page proofs archived as her literary oeuvre, EG satirizes two noblewomen passive-aggressively, running down each other's contributions to an upcoming charity bazaar; see EG, in AP(II)/101/150.

79 a rare edition: EG to MCC, letter dated January 8, 1881, in AP(II)/101/40; and Cossé-Brissac, op. cit., 52.

79 "Through all my trials": EG to HG, letter dated October 14, 1912, in AP(I)/101/22.

79 "being beautiful and being ugly": EG, Journal de Mariage, entry of November 10, 1878; on the great effort EG put into being beautiful, see LG, *Mémoires,* vol. 2, 22.

80 "to choose all their dresses": EG, in AP(II)/101/150.

80 Jeanne eschewed color altogether: Louise d'Arenberg, marquise de Vogüé, *Logis d'autrefois* (Paris: n.p.), n.p. NB: Some portions of this typewritten manuscript are numbered and others are not, whence the occasional lack of page numbers in my citations from it.

80 "whispering in [her] ear": EG, in AP(II)/101/151.

80 "Now we are very elegant": EG, Journal de Mariage, entry of December 12, 1878.

80 "We laugh and we sing": Ibid., entry of December 15, 1878.

81 "profound, amazed silence": Ibid., entry of November 16, 1878.

81 "always checking to see": Ibid., entry of October 7, 1878.

81 "keep up [her] grand air": Ibid., entry of October 26, 1878.

81 "Henry's friends [to] find me *magnificent*": Ibid.

81 "Having a husband who abandons me": EG to MCC, letter dated November 18, 1882, in AP(II)/101/40.

82 "I believe there is no ecstasy": Cited in RM, *La Divine Comtesse* (Paris: Manzi, Joyant, 1913), 205.

82 She was particularly gratified: D'Haussonville's untitled sonnet, subsequently retyped by one of EG's secretaries, is filed under "Hommages et appréciations" in AP(II)/101/1.

82 "You will never forget": EG to GCC, in AP(II)/101/50. On EG's acquisition of this bust, see EdG, *Journal,* entry of July 7, 1891; and Dominique (pseud. MP), "The Salon of the Comtesse Greffulhe," reproduced in appendix C.

82 Recounting the trip in her diary: On EG's return to Paris, see EG, Journal de Mariage, entry of December 25, 1878.

CHAPTER THREE: THE KINGDOM OF SHADOWS

83 "the kingdom of shadows": Marcel Schneider, *Innocence et vérité,* vol. 2, *L'Éternité fragile* (Paris, Grasset: 1991), 295. According to MB, LC also referred to Frohsdorf as "the empire of the dead"; see MB, *La Duchesse de Guermantes,* 29.

84 a place for their coat of arms: A. Borel d'Hauterive, "Musée de Versailles: notice sur les cinq salles des Croisades," *Annuaire historique pour la Société de l'Histoire de France* 9 (1845): 127–95, 180.

85 "the sort of place": Cited in LG, *Souvenirs du monde,* 153. See also LG, *Mémoires,* vol. 2, 30. LG correctly identifies the street on which LC grew up but wrongly places it in Auteuil rather than in Passy. Under Haussmann's redesign of Paris, both townships, historically conjoined, were absorbed into the capital's sixteenth arrondissement in 1860, a year before LC was born.

85 the wedding of her sister: On Valentine's marriage to Pierre de Waru, see *Le Gaulois* (July 15, 1868): 1; and *L'Indicateur des mariages* (August 21–28, 1864): 3. For additional biographical

information about Waru, see his obituary and the brief report on his funeral in *Le Gaulois* (April 29, 1914): 2 and (May 2, 1914), respectively.

86 "was too taken with her beloved Paris": LG, *Souvenirs du monde*, 153.

86 her mother's older sister: Silvia Silvestri, "Marochetti, Carlo," in *Dizionaio biografico degli Italiani*, vol. 70 (Rome: Treccani, 2008), n.p.

87 the domaine de Cabannes: Very little information survives about (alternately referred to as Les Cabannes, Mas-de-Cabannes, or La Cabanne). The property evidently first passed into the de Sade family when "Jean de Sade, the eleventh to bear that name," became "co-lord of La Cabanne" in the 1590s. See François-Alexandre Aubert de La Chesnaye-Desbois, ed., *Diction-naire de la noblesse*, vol. 18 (Paris: Schlesinger Frères, 1873), 32. The Chevigné family sold it to the French government after World War II.

87 was a top banker: On Adolphe de Waru's employment with the Banque de France, and on the Waru family generally, see Alain Plessis, *Régents et gouverneurs de la Banque de France sous le Second Empire* (Geneva: Droz, 1985), 48–51.

88 *Opinione de Sado:* Comte de Burey, ed., *Annuaire général héraldique* (Paris: Jules Wigniolle, 1902), 986.

88 "wrap [his] vices": Cited in Lawrence W. Lynch, *The Marquis de Sade* (Boston: Twayne, 1984), ii.

88 "haughty, ferocious": Cited in ibid., 13–14.

89 the legend of the lawless marquis: This legend took off with the publication of Jules Janin's influential biography, *Le Marquis de Sade* (Paris: Chez les marchands de nouveautés, 1834).

89 among nineteenth-century Parisian authors: On de Sade's influence on Baudelaire, see Damian Catani, "Notions of Evil in Baudelaire," *Modern Language Review*, vol. 102, no. 4, 996–98.

89 On GM's interest in de Sade, see Bancquart, op. cit., 234. On MP's interest in de Sade (by way of Baudelaire), see especially Simone Kadi, *Proust et Baudelaire* (Paris: La Pensée Universelle, 1975), 93–96.

89 "the divine marquis": Guillaume Apollinaire, "Le Divin Marquis" (1909), in *Œuvres en prose complètes*, ed. Michel Décaudin, vol. 3 (Paris: Gallimard, 1993), 785. The marquis's work was also a major influence on the artists of the Surrealist movement; see Paul Éluard, "L'Intelligence révolutionnaire du Marquis de Sade," *Clarté* (February 1927); and Claude Mauriac, "Sade déi-fié," in *Hommes et idées d'aujourd'hui* (Paris: Albin Michel, 1953), 117–30.

89 Fin-de-siècle commentaries on "sadism" in Baudelaire include Paul Bourget, *Essais de psy-chologie contemporaine*, vol. 1 (Paris: Plon, 1920 [1883]), 5–9; and Max Nordau, *Degeneration* (London: D. Appleton & Co., 1895), 286–87 and 317. Clinical discussions of sadism from the late nineteenth century include Nordau, ibid., 450–51; F. C. Forberg, *Manuel d'érotologie classique* (Paris: Isidore Liseux, 1883); Dr. Jacobus X. (pseud.), *Le Marquis de Sade et son œuvre devant la science médicale et la littérature moderne* (Paris: Charles Carrington, 1901), 19–28; and Dr. Marciat, "Le Marquis de Sade et le sadisme," in *Vacher l'éventreur et les crimes sadiques*, ed. A. Lacassagne (Paris: Masson, 1899), 185–237. In a 1972 television interview, Xavier, Marquis de Sade, launched a campaign to have the word *"sadisme"* and its variants "suppressed from the French language" on the grounds that this terminology had "done harm to an entire family." The interview is available online at http://www.ina.fr/video/CAF97037725.

89 "the incarnation of the warrior's soul": MB, *La Duchesse de Guermantes*, 74.

89 "pluck, good sense, and energy": BL, *The House of Memories* (London: William Heinemann, 1929). MB adds that in the face of every loss, LC "held her head high, and refused to com-plain" (90).

89 On LC's affected rustic speech as ascribed to Mme de Guermantes, see especially MP, CSB, 234: "The comtesse affected a pretty, 'earthy' manner of speaking. She would say: '*C'est une cousine à Astolphe [sic], elle est bête comme eun oie.*'" See also MP, *Carnets*, Florence Callu and Antoine Compagnon, eds. (Paris: Gallimard/NRF, 2002), 397: "*C'est l'ami à Mme de Guer-mantes. Mme de Guermantes capital contiendra l'esprit Straus dans la voix Chevigné eun bête*"; and the footnoted line from RTP: "*Moi, je suis eun bête, je parle comme une paysanne*" (n. 220). NB: I have translated "*eun*" as "uhh."

89 indiscriminate *tutoiement:* MB, *La Duchesse de Guermantes*, 13.

89 "Everybody knows that": Cited in AM, op. cit., 104; on LC's use of "*ça*," see also MB, *La Duchesse de Guermantes*, 104; and AF, "Le Salon de l'Europe," *La Revue de Paris* 7, no. 44 (November 15, 1936): 457–76, 464, and 469.

89 "she was careful not to talk overmuch": see MB, *La Duchesse de Guermantes*, 69.

90 Louis-Marie de Sade had written prolifically: For a condensed overview of Louis-Marie de

Sade's literary career, see Ernest Desplaces and Louis Gabriel Michaud, eds., *Biographie universelle, ancienne et moderne,* vol. 37 (Paris: Chez Mme Desplaces, 1843), 224.

90 In his *History of the French Nation:* Louis-Marie de Sade, *Histoire de la nation française, première race* (Paris: Delaunay, 1805), v–vi.

90 *"true ROYALISTS":* Chevalier Louis de Sade, *Extraits du "Lexicon politique"* (Paris: A. Barbier, 1831), 1.

90 "Petrarch *enjoyed*": Abbé de Sade, *Mémoires pour la vie de François Pétrarque,* vol. 2 (Amsterdam: Arskée & Mercus, 1764), 478.

91 "saying obscene or dirty words": D.A.F., Marquis de Sade, *La Philosophie dans le boudoir, ou les instituteurs immoraux* (Quebec: Bibliothèque Électronique de Québec, n.d. [1795]), 134.

92 "Paris is amusing": Cited in MB, *La Duchesse de Guermantes,* 80.

92 On the courtiers' daily functions at Frohsdorf, see Monti de Rézé, *Souvenirs sur le Comte de Chambord* (Paris: Émile-Paul, 1930), 41. On AC's military service, see Fidus (pseud. Arthur Meyer), "Le Jour de l'An à Goritz," *Le Gaulois* (January 2, 1881): 1; and *Le Vétéran,* 10 (May 20, 1910): 20.

93 Donatien channeled his bellicose streak: Maurice Lever, *Sade: A Biography,* trans. Arthur Goldhammer (New York: Farrar Straus & Giroux, 1993), 77–78, 83.

94 "bury 1,800 [headless cadavers]": Cited in Lynch, op. cit., 18. On the "martyrology" of the nineteenth-century noblesse, see Fiette, op. cit., 125; on the nobility's exaggeration of the headless bodies at Picpus, see MB, *Égalité,* 166; on AC's ancestor who survived Picpus, see René Pocard de Cosquer de Kerviler, Sir Humphrey Davy, and Louis-Marie Chauffier, eds., *Répertoire général de bio-bibliographie bretonne,* book 1, vol. 9 (Rennes: Plihon & Hervé, 1897), 201.

95 As for the peculiar name: On the derivation of the name "Adhéaume," see Kerviler, Davy, and Chauffier, eds., op. cit., 200.

96 position did have its downside: On the financial sacrifices made by Monseigneur's courtiers, see CCB, op. cit., 211.

96 Chevigné had rented: On the apartment in the rue du Colisée, see MB, *La Duchesse de Guermantes,* 60; and Huas, op. cit., 164. By 1884, the couple had moved a few blocks away to 1, avenue Percier. See *Bulletin de la Société d'Acclimatation Nationale de France* 1, no. 4 (May 3, 1884): xxiii.

97 "hatchet face": BL, op. cit., 76; other information on AC's physical appearance appears in MB, *La Duchesse de Guermantes,* 29; Françoise Benaïm, *Marie-Laure de Noailles, vicomtesse du bizarre* (Paris: Grasset, 2002), 37; Bernard Xau, "Derniers échos de Göritz," *Gil Blas* (September 9, 1883): 1–2; and Painter, op. cit., vol. 1, 111. The sole extant photograph of AC to figure in any public sources appears in a memoir written by one of his cousins and fellow courtiers at Frohsdorf; Monti de Rezé, op. cit., 175.

97 rate more than one line in *La Gaulois: Le Gaulois* (February 2, 1879): 4; for the front-page articles on the HG/EG wedding, see *Le Gaulois* (July 27, 1878): 1; *Le Gaulois* (August 23, 1878): 1; and *Le Gaulois* (September 27, 1878): 1. For the longer notice about the AC/LC wedding, see *Le Triboulet* (February 9, 1879): 12.

98 On Monseigneur's retinue and court at Frohsdorf, see *Le Gaulois* (August 23, 1885): 2; *Le Gaulois* (September 8, 1883): 37; and Théodore Anne, *M. le Comte de Chambord: souvenirs d'août 1850* (Paris: E. Dentu, 1850), 199–216.

98 "In the world [Mme de Chevigné] inhabited": AG, *Les Clés de Proust,* 31.

98 "A misprint in our last issue": *Le Triboulet* (February 16, 1879): 12.

98 Characteristic of LC's contemporaries' repetition of her favorite biographical details is PV, *Les Soirées de Paris,* 403.

99 "to impose a poetic vision": MB, *La Duchesse de Guermantes,* 34.

99 "her poor Adhéaume wasn't of much use": AG, *Les Clés de Proust,* 30.

99 "Thou shalt be polite": Cited in Quint, op. cit., 180; AC's chivalry toward the carriage-crash victims was reported in *Gil Blas* (July 13, 1883): 1.

99 "subtle intelligence": L. Massenet de Marancour, *Les Échos du Vatican* (Paris: n.p., 1864), 113–14.

99 "Adhéaume is *not an idiot*": Cited in MB, *La Duchesse de Guermantes,* 105.

100 With Laure's vigorous encouragement: Le Diable Boiteux (pseud. Baron de Vaux), "Nouvelles et échos," *Gil Blas* (January 31, 1880).

100 Chevigné stayed aloof: AF, "Le Salon de l'Europe," *La Revue de Paris* 7, no. 44 (November 15, 1936): 457–76, 467.

100 he had been keeping company: Bénaïm, op. cit., 37; other lore about the Seal appears in Arsène Houssaye, *Les Mille et une nuits parisiennes,* vol. 4 (Paris: E. Dentu, 1878), n.p.; Cora Pearl

(pseud. Emma Crouch), *Mémoires de Cora Pearl* (Paris: J. Lévy, 1886), 245; Richard O'Monroy, *La Soirée parisienne* (Paris: Arnould, 1891), 128–29; Virginia Rounding, *Grandes Horizontales: The Lives and Legends of Four Nineteenth-Century Courtesans* (New York: Bloomsbury USA, 2003); and Zed (pseud. Comte Albert de Maugny), *Le Demi-monde sous le Second Empire: souvenirs d'un sybarite* (Paris: E. Kolb, 1892), 105. Arsène Houssaye also names the Seal as a minor figure among the "princesses of ruin" who reigned over the demimonde in the 1860s.

100   the media dubbed this incident: Gabrielle Houbre, ed., *Le Livre des courtisanes: Archives secrètes de la police des mœurs 1861–1876* (Paris: Tallandier, 2006), 197–98.

101   "an extremely serviceable and accommodating woman": Ibid., 198; and Zed, op. cit., 106.

101   "The Seal says *mama*, the Seal says *papa*": Étincelle (pseud. Vicomtesse de Peyronny), *Carnet d'un mondain*; "La Journée parisienne," *Le Gaulois* (January 21, 1880); Maxime Gaucher, "Causerie littéraire," in *La Revue bleue* (July 4, 1885): 663–67, 666.

101   Many fin-de-siècle discussions of the Marquis de Sade explicitly labeled him an "invert." See for instance D.A.F., Marquis de Sade, *Idée sur les romans,* preface by Octave Uzanne (Paris: Rouveyre, 1878), 7; and Dr. Jacobus X, op. cit., 19–28.

101   "a being so strange": Buffon, *Œuvres complètes,* vol. 6, 384.

101   Monsieur de Phocas: The French word for seal, *phoque,* derives from the Latin *phoca;* the two words are roughly homophonous. For Lorrain's parody of RM, see especially Jean Lorrain (pseud. Paul Duval), *Monsieur de Phocas: Astarté* (Paris: Paul Ollendorff, 1901), 1–12.

101   for more than a decade after he and Laure married: René Pocard de Cosquer de Kerviler, Sir Humphrey Davy, and Louis-Marie Chauffier, eds., *Répertoire général de la biographie bretonne* (Rennes: 1898), 207.

101   In Willie Busnach's comedy *The White-Bellied Seal* (*Le Phoque à ventre blanc,* 1883), one of the characters cites "the Seal says *mama*, the Seal says *papa*" as an example of the scabrous humor favored by clubmen.

102   "A husband teaches one *nothing about f**king*": cited in PM, *L'Allure de Chanel* (Paris: Hermann, 1996), 107–8 and 196; and Arnaud, op. cit., 75. Descriptions of Frohsdorf are taken from (in order cited): Fidus (pseud. Meyer), "Le Château de Frohsdorf," *Le Gaulois* (July 5, 1883): 1; Xau, op. cit., 1–2; d'Uzès, op. cit., 18; Monti de Rezé, op. cit., 10–12; Gyp (pseud. Comtesse de Mirabeau-Martel), *La Joyeuse Enfance de la IIIᵉ République* (Paris: Calmann-Lévy, 1931), 131; and Jules Cornély, *Le Czar et le roi* (Paris: Clairon, 1884), 252–54.

102   had little else to keep him busy: Comte de Pimodan, *Simples Souvenirs, 1859–1907* (Paris: Plon, 1908), 162.

103   Monseigneur's late aunt: Bader, op. cit., 66–67; on the reliquary containing Louis XVII's heart, and on its "almost religious significance," see Jan Bondeson, *The Great Pretenders* (New York: W. W. Norton, 2005), 69–70.

104   centerpiece of the Red Salon: Descriptions of the Salon Rouge and the interiors at Frohsdorf are taken from Cornély, op. cit., 255 and 262; and Homme d'État (pseud.), *Histoire du Comte de Chambord* (Paris: Bray & Retaux, 1880), 249–50.

104   "When abroad, one camps out and waits": Cited in Fidus (pseud. Meyer), "Le Jour de l'An à Göritz," *Le Gaulois* (January 2, 1880): 1.

104   Frohsdorf did preserve one precious feature: MB, *La Duchesse de Guermantes,* 99–100; and Monti de Rezé, op. cit., 21–31; on the livery at Frohsdorf, see MB, *La Duchesse de Guermantes,* 99.

105   "presentation gymnastics": Cited in Monti de Rezé, op. cit., 33.

105   Mildly cross-eyed: Homme d'État (pseud.), op. cit., 250.

105   "the outfit": Cornély, op. cit., 255.

106   But his intractable position: Monseigneur unequivocally expressed his position on the French flag in his "Manifeste de Salzbourg" of October 1873, reprinted in Henri d'Artois, Comte de Chambord, *Lettres d'Henri V depuis 1841 jusqu'à présent,* ed. Adrien Peladan (Nîmes: P. Lafare, 1873), 234–36; see also Comte [Albert] de Maugny, *Cinquante ans de souvenirs, 1859–1909,* ed. René Doumic (Paris: Plon, 1914), 195–96; and La Force, op. cit., 107–10. On the political impact of Monseigneur's stance on the flag, see Alan Grubb, *The Politics of Pessimism: Albert de Broglie and Conservative Politics in the Early Third Republic* (Wilmington: University of Delaware Press, 1996), 50. On AC's account of Monseigneur crying all the way back to Frohsdorf, see AM, op. cit., 304–5.

106   an ornate coronation carriage: Luigi Bader, *Album: le Comte de Chambord et les siens en exil* (Paris: Diffusion Université-Culture, 1983), 88. On the uniforms his attendants, including AC, had made for their master's aborted return to power, see AM, op. cit., 343. According to AM, LC saved the uniform like a relic.

106   *"Spes contra spem":* Romans 4:18.
107   "The only law that can destroy a prince": Cited in AM, op. cit., 344.
107   "the kingdom of shadows": Cited in Schneider, *L'Éternité fragile,* 295; AF, "Le Salon de l'Europe," 457–76; and MB, *La Duchesse de Guermantes,* 81 and 105–6.
107   his premarital work routine in Austria: On AC's term at Frohsdorf, see *Le Figaro* (September 24, 1884): 1; on the unusual freedom AC granted to LC to travel back to Paris alone, see Schneider, *L'Éternité fragile,* 295–96.
108   two of whom were named Charlemagne: The two footmen were a father-son duo. The elder Charlemagne served Monseigneur for more than fifty years and held him as he breathed his dying breath; see Cornély, op. cit., 277 and 362.
108   "You'd better watch out": Cited in LG, *Mémoires,* vol. 2, 29–30.
108   "a mask of priestly melancholia": Monti de Rezé, op. cit., 33. On Monseigneur's "salty bonhomie," see Dubosc de Pesquidoux, *Le Comte de Chambord d'après lui-même* (Paris: Victor Palmé, 1887), 68–70.
109   "Without a doubt, he had a special fondness": LG, *Mémoires,* vol. 2, 28.
109   But the two were linked: René de La Croix, Duc de Castries, *Le Testament de la Monarchie,* vol. 5 (Paris: Fayard, 1970), 33.
110   "frightening rapidity": d'Uzès, op. cit., 19.
110   "were warned that we must not allow": Augustus Hare, *The Story of Two Noble Lives: Memoirs of Louisa, Marchioness of Waterford,* vol. 3 (London: George Allen, 1893), 265.
110   the royal consort's preferred topics: d'Uzès, op. cit., 19; and LG, *Mémoires,* vol. 2, 28.
110   "from the entire d'Orléans family": Cited in Luz, *Henri V,* 130. On Madame's hatred of the d'Orléans, see also Guillelmine Lucie Marie de La Ferronays, *Mémoires de Mme de La Ferronays* (Paris: Ollendorf, 1900), 261–62; and Otto Friedrichs, "Desinit in Piscem," *La Légitimité* 19 (May 16, 1886): 289–93, 290. LC later told AM and MB that Monseigneur, too, hated the d'Orléans and that he would have adopted the Prince Imperial Napoléon IV and made him his heir (instead of the Comte de Paris) had the young prince not been killed in Africa. See MB, *La Duchesse de Guermantes,* 108.
110   "so ugly that it was as if the word 'ugly'": d'Uzès, op. cit., 18.
111   "I DO NOT MUCH CARE TO REIGN": Cited in LG, *Mémoires,* vol. 2, 29. On the link between Madame's reluctance to see her husband ascend the throne and her dread of pretty Parisiennes, see also La Force, op. cit., 110.
111   "I have *never been more bored in my life*": Cited in Huas, *Les Femmes de Proust,* 164–65; and in MB, *La Duchesse de Guermantes,* 101. On LC and Madame riding together every afternoon following this gaffe, see AF, "Le Salon de l'Europe," 461–62.
111   "her woodsy, chivalric grace": MB, *La Duchesse de Guermantes,* 70; on Monseigneur's riding and shooting, see LG, *Mémoires,* vol. 2, 28; and Cornély, op. cit., 263.
111   "beyond space and time": MB, *La Duchesse de Guermantes,* 70.
112   "MacMahon?": Cited in ibid., 10.
112   *la vieille:* Cited in AM, op. cit., 343.
112   "He never listened to anything": PV, *Les Soirées de Paris,* 33.
112   "What does Monseigneur want me to say": Cited in AM, op. cit., 344.
113   patted the royal belly: LH, *Carnets: 1878–1883* (Paris: Calmann-Lévy, 1935), 838. LH heard this story from one of AC's fellow courtiers at Frohsdorf, the Comte de Blacas.
113   "marking the distances": MB, *La Duchesse de Guermantes,* 49. Another renowned virtuoso of "marking the distances" was Pauline d'Haussonville; see MP, "Le Salon de la Comtesse d'Haussonville," 72.
114   "Consider Pluto": Francesco Petrarch, "Le Triomphe de l'Amour," in *Pétrarque: Épîtres, éclogues, triomphes,* trans. (into French) by Comte Anatole de Montesquiou-Fezensac (Paris: Aymont, 1843), 97.
114   Laure would present herself: See especially MB, *La Duchesse de Guermantes,* 29; and MB on LC in NAF 28220, carton 57.
116   Less than four months after her wedding: Schneider, *L'Éternité fragile,* 296; and "Échos du High-Life," *Le Triboulet* (June 29, 1879): 12.

CHAPTER FOUR: BOHEMIA'S CHILD

118   "Is Georges cheating on me": Cited in Bischoff, op. cit., 100; GPR's erotic poem for GS is "A Carmen," in GPR, *Tout n'est pas rose* (Paris: Calmann-Lévy, 1877), 169–70; GS complains

to Lizote about this poem's "impertinence" in NAF 24981, folio 240. Another of GPR's early poems for GS is "A Mme B" (1870), in GPR, *Pommes d'Ève* (Paris: 1874), 84–85. On GS's relationship with GPR, see Bischoff, op. cit., 246–50.

118 she held her gatherings at Ludovic's place: Sébastien Laurent, *Daniel Halévy: Du libéralisme au traditionalisme* (Paris: Grasset, 2001), 60.

119 "identification . . . with the *noblesse d'épée*": Henri Lavedan, "Un raffiné: Georges de Porto-Riche," *Le Journal* (May 16, 1894): 1. On the critics' perceptions of GPR, see Un Monsieur de l'Orchestre (pseud. Émile Blavet), "La Soirée théâtrale: *L'Infidèle*," *Le Figaro* (April 26, 1891): 2; and Hendrik Brugmans, *Georges de Porto-Riche: sa vie, son œuvre* (Geneva: Slatkine, 1976), 121. On GPR's antique sword, see HR, *Nos rencontres* (Paris: Mercure de France, 1931), 124–25.

120 "a poet from Baghdad": JEB, *Mes modèles: souvenirs littéraires* (Paris: Stock, 1984 [1928]), 114.

120 "with his fine, chiseled face": AdF, *Mon Paris et ses Parisiens*, vol. 4, 143. On GPR's seductive qualities, see also FG, "Hommage à Porto-Riche," *Les Nouvelles littéraires* (September 13, 1930): 46–47.

121 Mme de Chevigné gamely loping: DH, "Deux portraits de Mme Straus," reproduced in *Marcel Proust: Correspondance avec Daniel Halévy*, ed. Anne Borrel and Jean-Pierre Halévy (hereafter Borrel & J.-P. Halévy, eds.) (Paris: Fallos, 1992), 173–180, 177.

121 neurasthenia: Georges Guinon, ed., *Clinique des maladies du système nerveux: M. le Professeur Charcot, Hospice de la Salpêtrière*, vol. 2 (Paris: Progrès Médical, 1893), 319. See also George Miller Beard, *A Practical Treatise on Nervous Exhaustion (Neurasthenia)* (New York: Treat, 1880), 53; and Michael R. Finn, *Proust, the Body, and Literary Form* (Cambridge and London: Cambridge University Press, 1999), 10–12 and 38–41. As for GS's specific symptomology, she refers to it throughout her correspondence, as do her family and friends. To give just one example, GPR describes GS's "alternating agitation and despondency"; cited in Françoise Balard, ed., *Geneviève Straus: Biographie et correspondance avec Ludovic Halévy: 1855–1908* (Paris: CNRS Éditions, 2002), 249.

121 aggravation of the facial tics: FG, *L'Âge d'or*, 168; and AF, *Le Bal du Pré-Catelan*, 158; it is AF who cites another friend's line about GS's tics as "flashes of lightning in a summer sky." In a less kindly vein, Comte Giuseppe (Gégé) Primoli said that GS's facial spasms made her "resemble a madwoman, . . . so out of politeness, I avoided looking at her"; see Primoli, *Notes intimes*, n.p., cited in Emily D. Bilsky and Emily Braun, eds., *Jewish Women and Their Salons: The Power of Conversation* (New York: Jewish Museum, 2005), 230, n. 103. GS's tics are also discussed in Bilsky and Braun, eds., 72; and in George Painter, op. cit., vol. 1, 91.

121 "six hours away": GS to Mme Léon (Nanine) Halévy, letter of July 6, 1880, reproduced in Balard, ed., op. cit., 134. When citing from GS's correspondence, I have tried wherever possible to provide published-source information, rather than or along with archival-source information, as the former will be considerably easier for interested readers to track down. More detail on the archives of GB, LH, GPR, ES, and GS appears in the Works Consulted section.

121 On GS's penchant for entertaining in boudoir attire, see GS to GPR, undated letter in NAF 24944, folio 442/443.

121 he sulked like a toddler: HR, *Les Cahiers inédits*, ed. David J. Niederauer and François Broche (Paris: Pygmalion/Gérard Watelet, 2002), 322.

121 talking Degas into escorting her: On GS's activities with Degas and her other artist friends, see Bischoff, op. cit., 131–47; LG, *Souvenirs du monde*, op. cit., 289; Laurent, op. cit., 60.

122 She would have been posing: GS to NH, letter dated September 20, 1881, in Balard, ed., op. cit., 138. In this letter, GS specifies that Delaunay cast her variously as Autumn, Night, and a nurse. GS does not specify which of Toulmouche's paintings she posed for; she simply reports that he asked her to wear fashionable, contemporary dress when she sat for him. The paintings in which Toulmouche appears to have borrowed GS's features include *Awaiting the Visitor* (*Attendant le visiteur*, 1878); *Exotic Beauty* (*Beauté exotique*, c. 1880s); and *The Love Letter* (*Le Billet-doux*, 1883). He also painted her portrait in 1886, a work that has since been lost.

122 "I say and I repeat": GS, *Journal*, entry marked January 1862; reprinted in Bischoff, op. cit., 34.

123 "If ever I become Emperor": Ibid., 34–35.

123 as a "frog": Louis-Sébastien Mercier, *Tableau de Paris*, vol. 1 (Paris: Virchaux, 1781), 44. This may be why GS chose to dress as a frog for Mme de Sagan's *bal des bêtes*.

123 "Parisian twice over": Cited in LG, *Mémoires*, vol. 2, op. cit., 199; LG, "L'entresol," *Le Figaro: supplément littéraire* (March 3, 1926): 3; and FG, *L'Âge d'or*, 164.

123 "My dear friend": Cited in Bischoff, op. cit., 99.

124   "morbid dread of solitude": Lucien Corpechot, *Souvenirs d'un journaliste* (Paris: Plon, 1936), 119; and Bischoff, op. cit., 114 and 132.

124   "I waited impatiently": Cited in Bischoff, op. cit., 248–49. For a sampling of other letters in which GS calls GPR a "defector" (*lâcheur*), see NAF 24971, folio 270/271, folio 290/291, and folio 276/277; and NAF 24944, folio 295, folio 329, and folio 337.

125   "'crumbled to dust'": GS to MP, letter marked "samedi 27 mai," in the Proust archival papers at Yale University, GEN MSS 601, box 49, folder 1022.

125   "O, my children": Cited in JEB, *La Pêche aux souvenirs*, op. cit., 108, n. 1.

125   "for I have every intention": GS to NH, letter of August 6, 1878, in Balard, ed., op. cit., 133.

125   According to one of the Halévys' regular visitors: Bischoff, op. cit., 18–23; and Eugène Delacroix, *Journal* (Paris: Plon, 1932), 422–25 and passim.

125   "to write his music": Édouard Monnais, *Souvenir d'un ami pour joindre à ceux d'un frère* (Paris: Imprimerie Centrale, n.d.), 12. See also Bischoff, op. cit., 23.

126   "devoured by her social life": Cited in Bischoff, op. cit., 141.

126   moved temporarily to London: R. Jordan, op. cit., 139; on Fromental Halévy's busy schedule of commitments in Paris, see Bischoff, op. cit., 105–12.

127   "Once people are my friends": Cited in Bischoff, ibid., 112.

127   "Affection is the only thing that helps me": Cited in Mina Curtiss, *Bizet and His World* (New York: Alfred A. Knopf, 1958), 266.

128   In these overexcited states: Bischoff, op. cit., 19–23; R. Jordan, op. cit., 110 and 168–69, and Laure Murat, *La Maison du docteur Blanche* (Paris: Hachette/Lattès, 2001), 139–43 and 199–202.

128   "My dear parents": This letter is reproduced in full in Bischoff, op. cit., 19.

128   "When I was a child": Cited in ibid., 29; and Balard, ed., op. cit., 111. See also Huas, op. cit., 188.

129   landed her in a mental clinic: Balard, op. cit., 12 and 23; Delacroix, *Journal*, 499; and Murat, *La Maison du docteur Blanche*, 199–201.

129   "I was very afraid": GS to Valentine Halévy, undated letter of 1863, in Balard, ed., op. cit., 52.

130   "complete and utter dementia": Murat, *La Maison du docteur Blanche*, 180–81.

130   "The mother is stark, raving mad": Cited in Andrée Jacob, *Il y a un siècle . . . quand les dames tenaient salon* (Paris: Arnaud Seydoux, 1991), 141.

131   "the only one who made it possible": Cited in Balard, ed., op. cit., 49.

131   "so as not to tempt the suicidal": JEB, *La Pêche aux souvenirs*, 30; also cited in Murat, *La Maison du docteur Blanche*, 200.

131   legally declared a ward: See a notarized document signed by Émile Pereire and dated October 18, 1864, inv. 2000.24.038, digital archives, Musée d'Art et d'Histoire du Judaïsme. Curiously, this document also states that Esther Halévy did not die at Dr. Blanche's clinic in Passy but in the ninth arrondissement of Paris at 19 bis, rue de la Chaussée d'Antin. I have been unable to find any additional supporting evidence for this puzzling assertion, to which no other scholars or biographers of the Halévy family allude. According to a contemporary guidebook issued by Galignani, an English-language bookstore in Paris, 19 bis, rue de la Chaussée d'Antin was the address of a school for young ladies from "the wealthier classes" of the city's Protestants. See *Gaglignani's New Paris Guide* (London: Simpkin, Marshall & Co., 1863), 116.

131   the bank had gone into a free fall: On the Pereires' demise, and the Rothschilds' role therein, see Romaric Godin, "Les Frères Pereire, le salut par le crédit," *La Tribune* (December 26, 2011); and Niall Ferguson, *House of Rothschild*, vol. 2, *The World's Banker, 1849–1999* (New York: Penguin, 2000), 158–59.

131   "How many catastrophes": Cited in Bischoff, op. cit., 61.

132   "aggressive": The source of this story is EdG, who heard it from the Halévys' friend Mme Sichel, who heard it from Dr. Blanche. See J.-P. Halévy, "Ludovic Halévy par lui-même," 143–44.

132   "perhaps a monster": Cited in ibid., 144.

132   "The years pile up": Cited in Bischoff, op. cit., 39.

132   "Geneviève feels": Ibid., 40.

133   "more Christian than Jewish": Ibid., 40.

133   "For them," she added: Cited in ibid., 68.

133   William Faulkner's oft-cited dictum: "The past is never dead. It's not even past." See William Faulkner, *Requiem for a Nun* (New York: Knopf Doubleday, 2011 [1951]), 69.

133   she had been secretly engaged: AG, *Les Clefs de Proust*, 29.

133   "walked into her room": Cited in Bischoff, op. cit., 54.

133 "I have met an adorable girl": Cited in ibid., 53.

134 "Mme Halévy only respects people": Cited in ibid.

134 "marrying a Jewess": Ibid., 54.

134 For the home addresses of these visitors to the Halévy/Bizet households, see Jetta Sophia Wolff, *Historic Paris* (Paris: John Lane, 1923), 227–28; *Tout-Paris: Annuaire de la société parisienne* (Paris: A. La Fare, 1893), 69, 80, 155, 237, and 400. I am grateful to Alain Bertaud for telling me about "Pubis de Cheval," a razz that originated with the irreverent students of the École des Beaux-Arts.

134 "immensely happy together": GB to Hippo Rodrigues, in NAF 14345, folio 267.

134 "absolutely happy": Cited in Bischoff, op. cit., 62.

136 "I am becoming": Cited in ibid., 64.

136 still more tragedy on the home front: Jean-Pierre Halévy, "La Famille Halévy," in *Entre le théâtre et l'histoire: la famille Halévy*, ed. Henri Loyrette (Paris: Fayard, 1996), 18–37.

136 "It's heartbreaking": Cited in Hugh MacDonald, *Bizet* (Oxford: Oxford University Press, 2014), 166.

137 "We are still in perfect health": Cited in Bischoff, op. cit., 67.

137 "We aren't eating anymore": Cited in Borrel, "Geneviève Straus," 106–27, 116.

137 "Imagine, I spent twenty-six *hours*": Cited in Bischoff, op. cit., 67.

139 "exterior manifestations": Cited in Winton Dean, *Georges Bizet: His Life and His Work* (London: J. M. Dent & Sons, 1965), 87; and in Bischoff, op. cit., 71–72.

139 "Thanks be to God": Cited in Rémy Stricker, *Georges Bizet* (Paris: Gallimard, 1999), 153.

139 "an utterly superficial woman": Cited in Borrel, "Geneviève Straus," 117.

139 "it's either her": Cited in Bischoff, op. cit., 72 and 74–75.

139 the Prussians staged a triumphal parade: Peter Brooks, *Flaubert in the Ruins of Paris: The Story of a Friendship, a Novel, and a Terrible Year* (New York: Basic Books, 2017), 37.

140 "dictatorship of the proletariat": Jacques Rougerie, *Paris libre: 1871* (Paris: Seuil, 2004), 265–70.

140 the ensuing civil conflict: On GS and GB during the Paris Commune, see ibid., 76–81. On the Paris Commune more generally, see ibid. Alistair Horne, *The Fall of Paris: The Siege and the Commune 1870–71* (London: Reprint Society, 1965), 245–433; and John Merriman, *Massacre: The Life and Death of the Paris Commune* (New York: Basic Books, 2014).

140 "You people of Montmartre": Cited in Horne, op. cit., 406.

140 "strange terror": Cited in Dean, op. cit., 91.

140 "My God, I am suffering": Cited in Bischoff, op. cit., 103.

141 the show met with a stony reaction: On the critical response to *The Girl from Arles,* see Dean, op. cit., 103; and Bradford Robinson, program notes to a performance of Bizet's *The Girl from Arles* conducted by Konrad von Abel, Jürgen Höflich Musikproduktion (Munich, 2005): n.p.

142 "As egotistical as a monster": Balard, ed., op. cit., 118; and Hervé Lacombe, *Georges Bizet: Naissance d'une identité créatrice* (Paris: Fayard, 2000), 744.

142 Bébé and Ludovic burned all of her letters: Borrel, "Geneviève Straus," 119.

142 "labored from morning to night": Cited in Balard, ed., op. cit., 106.

143 "closer to us": JEB, *La Pêche aux souvenirs,* 107.

143 "I can still see the room": Ibid.; also cited in Jacob, op. cit., 150.

143 "How Oriental you are": Élie Delaunay to GS, letters dated September 1884 and May 18, 1890, in NAF 24384 folio 66/67 and folio 82/83, respectively.

143 "the princes of young criticism": Georges François Renard, *Les Princes de la jeune critique* (Paris: La Nouvelle Revue, 1890).

143 "You will make me famous": Cited in Bischoff, op. cit., 134. When seeking GS's help in his bid for election to the Académie Française, Joseph Reinach made a similar comment: "You have so many friends that through you I will be able to recruit many elegant and influential associates." Reinach to GS, undated letter marked "Porter's Lodge [Pavillon du Concierge], Montjoye, Rambouillet, Friday," in NAF 14383, folio 106/107.

144 "In her salon": RF, "Mort de Mme Émile Straus," *Le Figaro* (December 23, 1926): 2.

144 "the most indolent of Muses": Paul Bourget to GS, letter dated December 28, 1887; cited in Bischoff, op. cit., 261.

144 "We were all in Naples": Cited in Dean, op. cit., 86; and in Curtiss, *Bizet and His World,* 266–67.

144 Bébé moved out of the rue de Douai: Curtiss, *Bizet and His World,* 366. Curtiss quotes a letter from GB to GS dated February 1874, reporting that Léonie "wants to have the child either constantly with her or not at all. We came to the latter arrangement. Do give me the satis-

faction of keeping Jacquot or sending him elsewhere" (366); which option GS took remains unknown. On GS's prior efforts to keep Léonie away from JB, see Dean, op. cit., 101.

144 "little head": Cited in Curtiss, *Bizet and His World,* 366.

145 To facilitate Bizet's work: LH recorded in his diary that *Carmen* was in rehearsal by September 1, 1874. But for reasons that remain obscure, rehearsals were "turbulent" and "stormy," rife with unexplained interruptions and delays. See ibid., 373–74; and Dean, op. cit., 105.

145 "the authority and perfection": Cited in Jean-Yves Bras, "Qui était Éraïm Miriam Delaborde?" *Bulletin de la Société Alkan* 4 (March 1987): 3–6.

146 "real vocation for painting": cited in Curtiss, *Bizet and His World,* 369.

146 121 cockatoos: Balard, ed., op. cit., 116; Curtiss, ibid., 368; and Ruth Harris, *Dreyfus: Politics, Emotion, and the Scandal of the Century* (Macmillan: New York, 2010), 284.

147 an organization to promote Jewish scholarship: This organization, Société des Études Juives, is still in existence today. For a list of its founding members, see the manifesto in the first volume of the journal the Société published as part of its mission: "Appel pour la fondation de la Société des Études Juives," *La Revue des études juives,* vol. 1 (1880): 160–61. On ES's involvement in the Société, see also "Procès-verbaux des Assemblées Générales et du Conseil (1879–1880)," in ibid., 152–59.

147 On the contributions to Franco-Jewish culture by the Halévy and Rodrigues-Henriques/Gradis/Foa families, see Michèle Bo Bramsen, *Portrait d'Élie Halévy* (Amsterdam: John Benjamins Publishing Company, 1968), 1–5; Loyrette, ed., op. cit.; and Maurice Samuels's path-breaking study, *Inventing the Israelite: Jewish Fiction in Nineteenth-Century France* (Palo Alto, Calif.: Stanford University Press, 2008), 39–46.

147 On Alkan's Jewish cultural activities, see Bras, op. cit., 5; and David Conway, *Jewry in Music: Entry to the Profession from the Enlightenment to Richard Wagner* (Cambridge and London: Cambridge University Press, 2011), 231; and R. Jordan, op. cit., 179.

147 "the first published art-music": Conway, ibid., 235; on Alkan's adaptation of patterns from Jewish liturgical music, see ibid., 222–37.

147 Alkan was a notorious eccentric: The principal source for this discussion of Alkan's mental illness is Stephanie McCallum, "Alkan: Enigma or Schizophrenia?" *Alkan Society Bulletin* 75 (April 2007): 2–10.

148 "As usual": Cited in ibid., 8.

148 She spent liberally: RD, *De Monsieur Thiers à Marcel Proust,* 28–29; and Maurice Sachs, *Le Sabbat: souvenirs d'une jeunesse orageuse* (Paris: Gallimard, 1960), 16.

148 "It's incredible": Cited in EdG, *Journal,* entry of December 28, 1887. According to EdG, Princesse Mathilde said this in GS's presence, loudly enough for her to hear.

148 their country estate as well: Ferguson, op. cit., 158.

149 Bizet himself was conscious: Lacombe, op. cit., 744; and Dean, op. cit., 111.

150 "Act I well received": Cited in Dean, op. cit., 114–15.

150 "poured out the bitterness of his soul": Ibid., 116.

151 "Imagine a double pedal": Ibid.

151 his friend Gounod's theory: Lacombe, op. cit., 736.

151 not his father's illegitimate child: The relationship between and among GB, GS, and the Reiters bears further research. A small trove of photographs of Jean and Marie Reiter formerly belonging to GB are archived in the Mina Curtiss Collection in the Music Division of the New York Public Library, JPB 93–95, series 7, box 4, folios 193–99.

151 "Go and fetch Delaborde": Hugues Imbert, *Médaillons contemporains* (Paris: Fischbacher, 1902), 51.

151 Bébé, twenty-six, was too distraught: Borrel, "Geneviève Straus," 120.

151 four thousand other mourners: Bischoff, op. cit., 94. Although GB was buried at the Montmartre Cemetery, his body was later moved to Père-Lachaise Cemetery.

151 Gounod broke down: Jacques-Gabriel Prod'homme and Arthur Dandelot, *Gounod: sa vie et ses œuvres, d'après des documents inédits* (Paris: Charles Delagrave, 1919), 182, n. 4.

151 "there was not a minute": Cited in Dean, op. cit., 128. Dean suggests that Gounod, not GS, wrote this statement.

152 So did Tsar Alexander II: His letter requesting a performance of *Carmen* was excerpted in *Le Gaulois* (July 24, 1877): 2.

152 "a masterpiece": Cited in Susan McClary, *Georges Bizet: Carmen* (Cambridge and London: Cambridge University Press, 1992), 117.

152 "one becomes a 'masterpiece' oneself": Cited in ibid., 118.

152   "a tragic joke": Cited in ibid., 118.
153   "Delaunay's somber *Portrait*": Borrel, "Geneviève Straus," 120.
153   "mauve thoughts edged in black": Cited in Borrell, "Geneviève Straus," 210; see also Reinach to GS, undated letter in NAF 14826, folio 100/101.
153   "This is where he worked": Cited in Balard, ed., op. cit., 116.
153   she was engaged: Leslie A. Wright, *Bizet Before Carmen* (New York: 1985), 14. For press coverage of GS's engagement and planned marriage to Delaborde, see the *Musical Standard* (October 14, 1876): 247.
153   "she wasn't a lonely widow for a single day": Cited in Borrel, "Geneviève Straus," 121.
154   "Why don't you ever write to me?": JB to GS, NAF 14383, folio 9/10. For JB's other unpublished childhood letters to GS, see folios 5–28.
154   "because the two of us": GS to NH, letter dated July 24, 1878, in Balard, ed., op. cit., 132–33.
154   "there are no Frenchmen": GS to NH, letter dated July 6, 1880, in ibid., 134.
155   "her friends": DH, "Deux portraits de Mme Straus," 176.
155   "Paris has been intolerable": Cited in Bischoff, op. cit., 97–98.
155   "I don't know": Cited in Carter, *Marcel Proust,* 207.
155   "speaking French": GS to NH, letter dated July 6, 1880, in Balard, ed., op. cit., 134.
156   "I fear I'll find out": Ibid.
156   thought to be the illegitimate son: On ES's alleged Rothschild paternity, discussed at greater length in chapter 10, see Borrel, "Geneviève Straus," 106; EdG, *Journal,* entries of November 23, 1883, and June 6, 1885; Jacob, op. cit., 165; and Herbert Lottman, *The Return of the Rothschilds: The Great Banking Dynasty Through Two Turbulent Centuries* (London: I. B. Tauris, 1995), 88.
156   Straus had begged: Bischoff, op. cit., 98–99; and GPR to GS, in NAF 24971, folio 240/241.
156   Ferrières: Fredric Bedoire, *The Jewish Contribution to Modern Architecture: 1830–1930,* trans. Roger Tanner (Stockholm: Ktav, 2004), 18 and 85–92; Ferguson, op. cit., 45–48 and 108–10; and Guy de Rothschild, *Contre bonne fortune . . .* (Paris: Pierre Belfond, 1983), 11–42.
157   Such ostentatious splendor met: On anti-Semitic discourse about the Rothschilds' unbounded power, prior to the Dreyfus affair, see for example Anka Muhlstein, *Baron James: The Rise of the French Rothschilds* (New York and Paris: The Vendome Press, 1983), 114; Jacques de Biez, *Rothschild et le péril juif* (Paris: Chez l'Auteur, 1891); and Un Banquier (pseud.), *Que nous veut-on avec ce Rothschild Iᵉʳ, roi des Juifs et dieu de la finance?* (Brussels: Chez les Principaux Libraires de la Belgique, 1846), 7: "The royalty of Rothschild Ist," the pseudonymous "Banker" states, "is an officially recognized fact, as indisputable as that of a Bourbon, a d'Orléans or a Cobourg."
157   "a stupid, ridiculous extravagance": Cited in Bedoire, op. cit., 88.
157   "went into ecstasies": Cited in G. de Rothschild, op. cit., 18. Niall Ferguson cites this last line somewhat differently: "Folks like us can't rise to this; only a Rothschild can achieve it." See Ferguson, op. cit., 199. On the Prussians' occupation of Ferrières, see ibid., 198–201; and G. de Rothschild, op. cit., 19.

CHAPTER FIVE: THE FALL AND THE RISE

159   a two-month bout of crippling abdominal pain: On the illness and death of Monseigneur, see Joseph du Bourg, *Les Entrevues des princes à Frohsdorf: la vérité et la légende* (Paris: Perrin, 1910), and Monti de Rézé, op. cit., 202–30; Pierre de Luz (pseud. Pierre Henry de La Blanchetai), *Henri V* (Paris: n.p., 1931), reprinted as vol. 58 of *Les Amis du Comte de Chambord* (Paris: Plon, 2007), 459–60; Cornély, op. cit., 284–352.
160   "Take whatever you like": Cited in AM, op. cit., 343. AM also provides a description of Monseigneur's drawing of LC and her parrots.
160   "France": Cited in Hyacinthe de Paule de La Motte Ango, Marquis de Flers, *Le Comte de Paris,* trans. Constance Majendie (London: Allen & Co., 1889), 204.
160   named as his successor: Dubosc de Pesquidoux, op. cit., 448–89 and 465–66.
161   Publicly, Chevigné and his colleagues: Un Domino (pseud. Meyer), "Les Fidèles," *Le Gaulois* (August 24, 1883): 2.
161   "in mourning not only": Comte Albert de Mun, "Les Dernières Heures du drapeau blanc," *La Revue hebdomadaire* 46 (November 13, 1909): 141–63, 141.
161   "the awareness": PV, *Society in Paris,* 27.
161   other courtiers tittered: On the kerfuffle over precedence at the funeral, and the suggestion

to move the Comte de Paris's prie-dieu ahead of all the others, see H. de Flers, op. cit., 206; Cornély, op. cit., 365.

161 the Dowager Comtesse de Chambord bade farewell: On Madame's intention to move to, and Monseigneur's plan to be buried in, Göritz, see Cornély, op. cit., 357–58; and Du Bourg, op. cit., 303.

162 now renting a flat: The Société de Géographie membership roster for 1885 places AC and LC at 1, avenue Percier. Sometime in the late 1880s, after 1886 but before 1889, they moved to 34, rue de Miromesnil, the endpoint of the young MP's aforementioned "route of hope." On the Orléanist headquarters in the avenue Percier, paid for by the Greffulhe family, see "Ça manque de pigeons!" *La Lanterne* (August 3, 1878): 1.

163 As a sop to their Catholic piety: On Monseigneur's Catholic family values, see Chambord, op. cit., 227.

163 her mother-in-law's parsimony: MB, *La Duchesse de Guermantes,* 78.

164 *"No bastards":* Cited in PM, *L'Allure de Chanel,* 106.

165 "had measles": Cited in BL, op. cit., 80. It is likely that this incident occurred in the spring of 1885, when LC was seen in a lily-of-the-valley-based ensemble. See Vicomtesse de Renneville, "Chronique de l'élégance," *La Nouvelle Revue* 34 (May–June 1885): 444.

165 such opportunities were scarce: Laurence Klejman and Florence Rochefort, *L'Égalité en marche: Le Féminisme sous la Troisième République* (Paris: PFNSP/des femmes, 1989).

165 "a minority enterprise": Diana Holmes and Carrie Tarr, eds., *A Belle Époque? Women in French Society and Culture, 1890–1914* (New York and Oxford; Berghahn, 2007), 12.

166 "They are and want to remain": Cited in Guichard, op. cit., 17. On the emergence and limitations of fin-de-siècle French feminism, see also Holmes and Tarr, op. cit., 12.

166 "second sex": The reference here of course is to Simone de Beauvoir's foundational feminist treatise, *The Second Sex* (*Le Deuxième Sexe,* 1949). Of all the main characters in this biography, only EG was still alive when Beauvoir's book was published.

166 the *mondain* calendar: On "the golden triangle of upper-class sociability: seaside villa, Paris *hôtel,* and hunting château," see Fiette, op. cit., 217.

166 "New Year's visits": Martin-Fugier, *Les Salons de la IIIe République,* 100. This is also the source for the figure of one thousand to fifteen hundred *cartes de visite* per year.

167 "the Bichonne": CCB, op. cit., 47–48; Jean Lorrain (pseud. Paul Duval), *La Ville empoisonnée: Pall-Mall parisien* (Paris: Jean Crès, 1936), 210; *Gil Blas* (May 29, 1883): 1; and Sally Britton Spottiswood Mackin, *A Society Woman on Two Continents* (New York and London: Transatlantic, 1896), 172–73.

168 the Faubourg's "subscription" evenings: Burnand, op. cit., 226; Carassus, op. cit., 232–33; Aurélien Scholl, "Abomination!" in *Le Fruit défendu* (Paris: Librairie Universelle, 1888), n.p.; and GLP, *Trente ans de dîners en ville,* 82. GLP specifies that Friday was for haut-bourgeois and Saturday for aristocratic Opéra subscribers.

168 the dramas that absorbed the theater-going monde: On the subscribers' lack of interest in the spectacle onstage, see GLP, *Trente ans de dîners en ville,* 82 and 121; and AGG, *Souvenirs* (n.p., n.d.), 29.

169 horse races in Longchamp: LG, *Mémoires,* vol. 2, 168; and AGG, op. cit., 31–33.

169 The wives gathered: Marie-Alice Hennessy, "Courses," in *Dictionnaire du snobisme,* ed. Jullian, 53–54.

169 "grandes dames that . . . high style": Lysiane Sarah-Bernhardt (pseud.), "Les Courses," in *Le Protocole mondain,* ed. AdF, 340–41.

169 her chief preoccupation: BL, op. cit., 81.

170 On the Losers' Club: AdF, *Mon Paris et ses Parisiens,* vol. 1, 231. The Losers' Club makes an appearance in OJFF, where MP describes the "insurmountable barriers" that, "in the eyes and imagination of the 'losers,'" appear to separate them from the elegant ladies driving past. See MP, OJFF, 627.

170 "this little baroness's outfit": AdF, *Mon Paris et ses Parisiens,* vol. 1, 231. On "la haute" as plebeian slang for the upper class, see Aristide Bruant, ed., *Dictionnaire français: argot* (Paris: Flammarion, 1905), 28.

170 the charity bazaar, where genteel Parisiennes: For an account of one charity bazaar in which LC participated at the Duchesse d'Uzès's invitation, see Louis Prudent (pseud.), *"À la rue de Sèze: fête de charité,"* *Le Gaulois,* May 1, 1885, 2.

171 "young wives": MB, *La Duchesse de Guermantes,* 80.

171 "a *bag of needles*": Comte Léonce de Larmandie, *Du Faubourg Saint-Germain en l'an de grâce 1889* (Paris: E. Dentu, 1889), 122.

171 "'our cousin d'Uzès's'": *Le Gaulois* (May 1, 1885): 1. See also AF, "Le Salon de l'Europe": "When Mme de Chevigné said 'Adhéaume,' she was invoking an authority that brooked no appeal" (op. cit., 466), even if (as was usually the case) AC had no idea LC was using his name for that purpose.

172 "one of the very few women in Paris": Arnaud, op. cit., 76.

172 "When in Paris": MB, *La Duchesse de Guermantes,* 80.

173 "Her Majesty the Press": Arthur Meyer, *Ce que mes yeux ont vu* (Paris: Plon-Nourrit, 1912), 359.

173 the French press had in an essential sense: For a brief history of the pre- and postrevolutionary French press, see Henri Avenel, *Histoire de la presse française, depuis 1789 jusqu'à nos jours* (Paris: Flammarion, 1900), 18–20 and 35–63; on the dramatic rise in circulation rates after 1789, see Rolf Reichardt, "The French Revolution as a European Media Event," *EGO: European History Online* (August 27, 2012): 5.

173 An explosion of daily and weekly publications: According to historian Rolf Reichardt, before the storming of the Bastille on July 14, 1789, the number of broadsheet periodicals published in France "could be counted on one hand," whereas eight years later, "the total daily circulation of the Parisian newspapers alone amounted to 150,000" copies. Over the course of the next hundred years, that figure continued to grow exponentially.

173 Meyer had begun his career: Odette Carasso, *Arthur Meyer, directeur du Gaulois: Un patron de presse juif, royaliste et antidreyfusard* (Paris: Imago, 2003), 19–35.

174 "Old clothes and used ribbons": Cited in ED, *La France juive,* vol. 2, 183.

174 "blushed like a little girl": Corpechot, op. cit., 104.

174 a "snob": On the entry of "snobbery" into fin-de-siècle French social discourse, see Carassus, op. cit., 47–60; Meyer, *Ce que mes yeux ont vu,* 409–10; and Zed (pseud. Maugny), *Parisiens et Parisiennes en déshabillé* (Paris: Ernest Kolb, 1889), 3–12.

174 its unofficial bible: On the Faubourg's fascination with *Le Gaulois,* see de Pange, who describes it as "the official newspaper of the *mondain*" set (op. cit., 272).

174 "With her classical profile": PV, *La Vie à Paris,* 103.

175 This upper-class institution: On the French salon tradition, see especially Benedetta Craveri, *The Age of Conversation,* trans. Teresa Waugh (New York: New York Review Books, 2006); and Antoine Lilti, *Le Monde des salons: Sociabilité et mondanité à Paris au XVIIIᵉ siècle* (Paris: Fayard, 2005).

175 "Saucy, quick": Larillière (pseud.), "La Société de Paris: La Comtesse de Chevigné," *Gil Blas* (August 17, 1903): 1.

176 "my *vieux*": Cited in Painter, op. cit., vol. 1, 111–12.

176 "looked as if it must have grown": BL, op. cit., 75. Other details regarding LC's salon appear on pp. 75–79; in AF, "Le Salon de l'Europe," 463–65; and in Huas, op. cit., 165.

177 "the word of Cambronne": One of LC's granddaughters later wrote a little essay about LC's fondness for this word and for the bust of the general who made it famous. See Marie-Laure de Noailles, "Clefs (les mots)," in Jullian (ed.), *Dictionnaire du snobisme,* op. cit., 51–52.

177 "My *vieux* growl": Cited in BL, op. cit., 78.

177 tom-cats: Ibid.; also cited in MB, *La Duchesse de Guermantes,* 32.

177 "The Comtesse de Chevigné sat": LG, *Mémoires,* vol. 2, 30–31.

178 Laure's prettiness: For varying assessments of LC's appearance, see Arnaud, op. cit., 75–76; Pierre Grenaud and Gatien Marcailhou, *Boni de Castellane et le Palais Rose* (Paris: Les Auteurs Associés, 1983), 158; PM, *L'Allure de Chanel,* 168–71; LG, *Mémoires,* vol. 2, 31; MB, *La Duchesse de Guermantes,* 33; and BL, op. cit., 78.

178 "roughened by centuries": Cited in Arnaud, op. cit., 75–76. Because, as discussed in chapter 8, this exact same description was applied by EdG to the Duc d'Aumale's voice, LC's raspy voice may have contributed to what Arnaud calls her "emphatic virility"; see Arnaud, op. cit., 75.

178 "the uncanny air": AG, *Les Clés de Proust,* 31.

178 "very image of the Frenchwoman": MB, *La Duchesse de Guermantes,* 46–47.

178 "bony and heraldic": Gilbert Guilleminault, *Prélude à la Belle Époque* (Paris: Denoël, 1957), 212.

179 "Disorder and anarchy": Jacques Piou, *Le Comte Albert de Mun: sa vie publique* (Paris: Spes, 1925), 8; for a critical assessment of de Mun's efforts to "erect himself as the leader of a Catholic party" in France, see "Count Albert de Mun," *Public Opinion* 48 (November 13, 1885): 615.

179 "I am terribly sorry": Cited in LG, *Souvenirs du monde,* 39.

180 On the domestic political crisis that resulted in Gontaut's father's recall from Berlin to Paris, see Albert, Duc de Broglie, *Ambassador of the Vanquished: The Viscount Élie de Gontaut-Biron's Mission to Berlin* (London: William Heinemann, 1896), 267–98.

181   On Gontaut's family and leisure activities, see Robert R. Locke, *French Legitimists and the Politics of Moral Order in the Early Third Republic* (Princeton, NJ: Princeton University Press, 2015), 56–57; and *La Revue des Basses-Pyrénées et des Landes* 1 (1884): 334.

181   "the traditions of his family": DH, *Pays parisiens,* 84.

181   On du Lau's leisure activities, see de Vaux, *Le Sport en France,* 199–202; *La Revue des Basses-Pyrénées et des Landes,* 334. Also, du Lau is one of the two photographers to whom many of the photographs reproduced in this book are credited; his photography partner was Hortense Howland, the longtime mistress of Edgar Degas, and the pictures they took went into an Halévy family photo album now held by the Metropolitan Museum of Art in New York.

181   "His mannered idleness": DH, *Pays parisiens,* 83–84.

181   "You attach us": Charles-Albert, Marquis Costa de Beauregard, *Un homme d'autrefois: Souvenirs recueillis par son arrière petit-fils* (Paris: Plon, 1878), vi.

181   "I have endeavored to relive": Ibid., 468.

182   "Bringing the ashes of the past": Paul-Gabriel Othenin de Cléron, Vicomte (later Comte) d'Haussonville, *Le Salon de Mme Necker* (Paris: Calmann-Lévy, 1882), 3.

182   "Presence Chamber": BL, op. cit., 78.

182   a privileged witness: MB, *La Duchesse de Guermantes,* 107, and AM, op. cit., 81.

183   lionized him in death: Posthumous appreciations for Monseigneur, from nonlegitimist sources, appear in Georges de Nouvion and Émile Landrodie, *Le Comte de Chambord: 1820–1883* (Paris: Jouvet, 1884), 396; Eugène Veuillot, "La Mort du Comte de Chambord," *L'Univers* (August 25, 1883): 1; and Dubosc de Pesquidoux, op. cit., 492–93.

183   For a more general account of the fin-de-siècle French nobility's "autarkic legitimist dream" of its heroic past, and its concomitant "rejection of the modern world," see Fiette, op. cit., 216.

183   "le bouquet du Comte de Chambord": Burnand, op. cit., 84. As Burnand points out, this was a "paradoxical" name for a fragrance, as "lilies"—the Bourbons' floral emblem—"have no odor."

184   "carp à la Chambord": Un Domino (pseud. Meyer), "Échos de Paris," *Le Gaulois* (April 29, 1888): 1.

184   dress in peasant garb: On Mme de Sagan's peasant ball and LC's appearance there, see "Bloc-notes parisien: au village," *Le Gaulois* (June 11, 1884): 1–2; Diable Boiteux (pseud.), "Nouvelles et échos," *Gil Blas* (June 11, 1884): 1–2, (June 12, 1884): 1, and (June 13, 1884): 1; and Hy de Hem (pseud.), "La Fête villageoise de la Princesse de Sagan, *L'Art et la mode* 30 (June 21, 1884): 8–9. The quotation about LC's costume comes from Hy de Hem's article.

185   an alleged ancestor: On LC's descent from "Geneviève" (Marie) de Brabant and Laure de Noves, see Henri Raczymow, *Le Paris littéraire et intime de Proust* (Paris: Parigramme, 1997), 26; and Henri Raczymow, *Le Paris retrouvé de Proust,* 196. In my own study of Laure's and her husband's family tree, I have been unable to verify the kinship between her and the Brabants.

186   "the baker-woman": Cited in François-René de Chateaubriand, *Mémoires d'outre-tombe,* tome I (Paris: Garnier Frères, 1899), 281.

CHAPTER SIX: GOOD FOR THE GOOSE

187   "Proserpina's husband": MB, *La Duchesse de Guermantes,* 30; the comparison of AC to a bird in a storm appears on that same page as well as in BL, op. cit., 76.

187   always a tasty affair: Scrutator (pseud.), "Dinners *à la Russe,*" *Truth* (July 31, 1879): 138–40, 139.

188   For a detailed description of the interiors of both the Jockey and the Cercle de l'Union, and of the habits of their members, see Charles Yriarte, *Les Cercles de Paris: 1862–1867* (Paris: Dupray de la Mahérie, 1864). Although Yriarte describes these clubs in a period prior to the one discussed here, by the fin de siècle very little had changed in either club's culture.

188   "He could convince God Himself": CCB, op. cit., 49.

189   Émilie "the Seal" Williams: For more on the Seal, see Zed (pseud. Maugny), *Le Demi-monde sous le Second Empire: souvenirs d'un sybarite* (Paris: E. Kolb, 1892), 105–7; and Guillaume Apollinaire, *Selected Writings,* trans. Roger Shattuck (New York: New Directions, 1971), 198: "I've the eyes of a sea-going calf . . . / I'm merely a seal by profession. / A seal-lion proud of its past / Papa Mama / Pipe and spittoon and a café concert / Heigh ho."

189   Baron de Senevas: Details of Senevas's life and travels appear in Bruno-Marie Terrasson, Baron de Senevas, *Une famille française du XIVe au XXe siècles* (Paris: J. Moulin, 1939), vol. 2, 304–10, and vol. 3, 242–44.

190 taking off together: Press mentions of AC's trip with Senevas are "Personal Intelligence," *New York Herald* (March 28, 1887): 3; and "Personals," *Daily Alta California* (June 13, 1887), n.p.

190 "exhausted": Senevas published his mother's autobiography as part of his own multivolume memoir and family history; see Senevas, op. cit., vol. 3.

191 "three out of every five men are pederasts": Cited in HR, *Les Cahiers*, 635.

191 In her memoirs: For the dowager baronne's references to her social encounters with the Duchesse de Bisaccia and the Comtesse de Paris, see Senevas, op. cit., vol. 3, 243–44. For her one-line account of Bruno's wedding, see Senevas, op. cit., vol. 3, 245. The dowager baronne also comments with some anxiety about the refusal of one of Bruno's uncles "in the Breton way," Auguste Grandin de L'Eprevier, to serve as a witness to the wedding, as he had done for her daughter, Marthe, a few years earlier. While L'Eprevier claimed he was too sick to attend the ceremony, the baronne worried that he was really boycotting it for some other reason (ibid.). She did not say what she thought that reason might have been, but based on her own bias, she likely assumed it had to do with the bride's ignoble birth.

192 In his own multivolume memoirs: For Senevas's detailed description of his other travels, and his curious omission of his year-long trip with AC, see ibid., vol. 2, 304–10.

192 she herself was no model spouse: On LC's extramarital affairs and her lovers' *garçonnières,* see PM, *L'Allure de Chanel,* 106; and GLP, *Trente ans de dîners en ville,* 43.

193 "A faded hero": CCB, op. cit., 194.

193 Louise, Marquise d'Hervey de Saint-Denys: Anonymous, "A Leader of French Fashion," *The Searchlight* (January 21, 1905): 27; on LC's falling-out with her, see AdF, *Mon Paris et ses Parisiens,* 104–5; and AG, *Les Clefs de Proust,* 31–32.

194 "has caused rivers of tears": CCB, op. cit., 194.

194 "F[itz-James] was in love with me": Cited in PM, *L'Allure de Chanel,* 107.

194 "already revived his previous relationship": AG, *La Bourgeoisie qui brûle: propos d'un témoin, 1890–1940* (Paris: Sun, 1951), 74.

194 "I am ugly": Cited in AG, *Les Clés de Proust,* 139.

194 She also started keeping a list: AG, *La Bourgeoisie qui brûle,* 185–86.

194 "the charm of the Gontauts": A. de Gramont, op. cit., 256.

194 "one of the most popular men in all of Paris": PV, *France from Behind the Veil,* 349.

194 "insane hero worship": CCB, op. cit., 192–93.

195 "Thank you so much": Cited in MB, *La Duchesse de Guermantes,* 73. Painter misquotes this barb as "Thank you for sparing me the sight of Henri's old age," referencing it in the context of Laure's subsequent affair with HB, who also left her for an American woman. LC may have recycled the insult when encountering HB's new love, whom he married in March 1891, but if she did, Painter does not provide a corroborating source. See Painter, op. cit., vol. 1, 112.

196 exceptionally highborn, high-placed friends: A. de Gramont, op. cit., 454.

196 the GDWs to their intimates: HB, op. cit., 194–95 and 204–5; and Galina Korneva and Tatiana Cheboksarova, *Grand Duchess Maria Pavlovna* (East Richmond Heights, CA: Eurohistory, 2015), 22–52.

196 "Imagine Wladimir's disappointment": Cited in Simon Sebag Montefiore, *The Romanovs: 1613–1918* (New York: Alfred A. Knopf, 2016), 470.

196 She had one of the finest jewelry collections: Korneva and Cheboksarova, op. cit., ch. 6, "Passion for Perfection and Jewels," 169–79.

197 "Despite the great fondness": HB, op. cit., 56.

198 Laure never missed a one: On LC's annual trips to Serrant, see BL, op. cit., 82–83; on AC's viticultural experiments at Cabannes, see *Le Journal de l'agriculture, de la ferme et des maisons de campagne* 3 (1892): 502–3; *Le Progrès agricole et viticole* 22 (1894): 392; *Le Bulletin du Ministère de l'Agriculture* 16 (1897): 821; *La Géologie agricole* 3 (1897): 249–50; *Les Annales de la science agronomique française et étrangère* 1 (1898): 348; and *Le Bulletin de la Société des agriculteurs de France* 59 (January–June 1906): 265. AC and LC did host at least one hunt together at Cabannes in 1894: see Gant de Saxe (pseud.), "Mondanités: réceptions," *Le Gaulois* (January 20, 1894): 2.

199 "There is one man": Cited in Grenaud and Marcailhou, op. cit., 72; on Deschanel choosing Charvet, see PM, *1900* (Paris: Marianne, 1931), 13.

199 One of his biggest success stories: PV, *France from Behind the Veil,* 350. Boni de Castellane wrote that Dolly (his sister-in-law) had the "international" look of a "grande-duchesse" rather than the "essentially French" appearance of a Parisian *femme du monde.* See Castellane, *Vingt ans de Paris,* 107.

199 "a principal ornament of the kaiser's court": AG, *Les Clés de Proust,* 127.

200   "Dolly de Castellane always looks": AG, *La Bourgeoisie qui brûle,* 189.
200   "the first woman in society": MB, op. cit., 12; according to MB, LC thereby "revolutionized women's fashion" (ibid.).
200   "new vogue for *masculinized* ensembles": "Bloc-notes parisien," *Le Gaulois* (June 11, 1885): 2.
200   "monstrosity": CCB, op. cit., 223.
201   a new feminine ideal: On the shift in the ideal female body type, as catalyzed by the fashion for man-tailored women's suits, see Eugen Weber, op. cit., 99–100.
201   Laure took to pronouncing: MB, *La Duchesse de Guermantes,* 169.
201   "Oh, that Gladys!": Cited in AF, "Le Salon de l'Europe," 469.
201   "First-rate, my dear!": Cited in ibid., 464. Reboux's relatively small, understated, and unstructured straw and felt hats were to the gigantic, hyperornamented hats of the fin de siècle what Laure's unfussy suits were to the era's bustled, flouncy confections: avatars of modern fashion. While Reboux's invention of the cloche hat did not come until much later, she was beginning to experiment with a pared-down molded silhouette as early as the 1870s and 1880s. See for instance a delicate little blue hat in the collection of the Costume Institute at the Metropolitan Museum of Art in New York: Caroline Reboux, *Hat* (1870–1880); accession number CI.38.47.5.
201   "'*That*' *[Ça]?!*": Cited in ibid., 49.

CHAPTER SEVEN: THE ART OF BEING SEEN

203   The Art of Being Seen: The title I have given this chapter references that of curator Philippe Thiébaut's exhibition catalogue, *Robert de Montesquiou, ou l'art de paraître* (Paris: Éditions de la RMN, 1999), best translated as *Robert de Montesquiou, or the Art of Appearances.*
203   ornate, fantastical styles: In 2016, Olivier Saillard and Dr. Valerie Steele organized a museum exhibition of EG's clothes, held first at the Palais Galliera in Paris and then at the Fashion Institute of Technology in New York. In the press, this exhibition prompted a handful of articles about EG's pioneering sartorial style and her importance as a "fashion icon." See for example Madison Mainwaring, "Fashion Regained: Looking for Proust's Muse in Paris," *Paris Review* (March 16, 2016); and Isabelle Cerboneschi, "La Comtesse Greffulhe, icône de mode," *Le Temps,* December 23, 2015 (online editions). But the best and most scholarly article on the subject is Valerie Steele, "L'Aristocrate comme œuvre d'art," trans. Delphine Nègre-Bouvet, in Saillard, ed., op. cit., 60–65. Another good article in the same catalogue is Alexandra Bosc, "Elle n'a pas suivi les modes, elle était faite pour les créer" (76–80).
203   "What [Mme] Greffulhe hates": Violetta (pseud. Laincel), "Sous le masque," *Le Gaulois* (April 5, 1882): 1.
203   "Always say to myself": EG, in AP(II)/101/150; also cited in Cossé-Brissac, op. cit., 53. Hillerin speaks aptly of EG's "strategy of prestige" and her "art of putting herself onstage"; see Hillerin, op. cit., 211–14.
204   assessment of the Prince of Wales: HB, op. cit., 355.
204   "next to [her]": EG transcribed Massa's compliment in "Hommages et appréciations," in AP/101/1.
205   she dressed as the virginal hunt goddess: For a good description of EG as Diana, and for general information on this ball, see Vicomte Georges Letorière (pseud.), "Le Bal costumé de la Princesse de Sagan," *Le Monde illustré* (June 19, 1880): 382–83.
205   "could have been sculpted": GLP, "La Souveraine de la Belle Époque," *Crapouillot: Les Bonnes manières* 19 (1949): 26–27, 26.
205   "long train prolonged": *Le Crapouillot: Le Savoir-vivre à travers les âges, l'étiquette des cours* (1952): 25.
206   "What huge dark eyes!": Letorière, "Le Bal costumé . . . ," 393.
206   "a dazzling new star": Étincelle (pseud. Peyronny), *Carnet d'un mondain,* n.p.
206   "the costume she wore": Violetta (pseud. Laincel), "Sous le masque," *Le Gaulois* (April 5, 1882): 1; reprinted in an expanded form in Alice, Comtesse de Laincel, *Les Grandes Dames d'aujourd'hui* (Paris: Société d'Imprimerie, 1885), 267–72. The Musset line quoted by Violetta ("noble, pale beauty," etc.) is taken from "Les Pensées secrètes de Rafaël, gentilhomme français"; see Alfred de Musset, *Poésies complètes* (Paris: Charpentier, 1840), 151.
206   "The admiration she inspires": Violetta (pseud.), op. cit.
206   For the next Sagan ball: The description of EG's red velvet dress at her second Sagan ball, and of her timing her arrival to coincide with that of the Prince of Wales, appears in GLP, "La

Souveraine de la Belle Époque," 27. That EG may have based this costume on a portrait of the young Elizabeth I is suggested by a picture postcard in her archive, featuring such a dress and marked in EG's hand: "Photograph of Queen Elizabeth—Hampton Court." She likely went to Hampton Court on one of her and HG's many trips to Great Britain between 1879 and 1881; these trips mostly revolved around grouse shoots in Scotland, but they also allowed for visits to London and various estates in the country.

208 "made the clouds rain": This is an idiom, not unlike the English expression whereby "the sun rises and sets on" someone who is much admired.

208 he commissioned the society watercolorist Eugène Lami: LG, *Marcel Proust* (Paris: Flammarion, 1948), 60.

208 "She carried her head": Cited in James Eugene Farmer, *Versailles and the Court Under Louis XIV* (Philadelphia: Century, 1905), 290–91.

209 "the Blond Fury": Saint-Simon, op. cit., vol. 4, 53.

209 "feared, hated, and despised": Ibid., 56.

209 "wake her with their racket": Ibid.

209 she donned a replica of the outfit: Two excellent contemporary descriptions of EG's "Duchesse de Bourgogne" costume come from one of her great admirers: see Le Diable Boiteux (pseud. de Vaux), "Nouvelles et échos," *Gil Blas* (September 2, 1884): 1; and the Baron de Vaux, *Les Femmes de sport* (Paris: Marpon & Flammarion, 1885), 148–49.

209 "remember [Mme Greffulhe's] Duchesse de Bourgogne outfit": Le Diable Boiteux (pseud.), "Nouvelles et échos," *Le Gaulois* (June 13, 1889): 1.

209 the tallest structure on earth: Jill Jonnes, *Eiffel's Tower: The Thrilling Story Behind Paris's Beloved Monument and the Extraordinary World's Fair That Introduced It to the World* (New York: Penguin, 2009). Jill Jonnes specifies that "the pinnacle [of the Eiffel Tower] achieved a final height of 300 meters, or 984 feet. With the addition of a flagpole, the tower reached 1,000 feet."

210 Poirey recalls the garden: Jean-Louis Poirey, "Ma comtesse: souvenirs d'un enfant, 8–10 rue d'Astorg, 1944–1956" (Gy: n.p., 2015). I am tremendously grateful to M. Poirey for sharing this unpublished document with me.

211 a goatherd's flute: L. de Vogüé, *Logis d'autrefois,* op. cit., 8.

211 "Magic lanterns, magic lanterns": HG, *Quantum mutatus ab illo* (n.p., 1913–1921), in AP(I)/101/32; also cited in Cossé-Brissac, op. cit., 147.

211 Indoors: On the square footage and the layout of the Greffulhes' house in the rue d'Astorg, see Poirey, op. cit., 5.

211 The coffered ceilings of her salon: On the furnishings and décor of EG's salon, see Gerald Reitlinger, *The Rise and Fall of the Objets d'Art Market Since 1750* (New York: Holt, Reinhart & Winston, 1965), 436; Hillerin, op. cit., 263; and Curtiss, *Other People's Letters,* 165. Curtiss notes that César Ritz later borrowed the device of the ceiling painted to resemble a sky for the dining rooms of his eponymous hotels in Paris and London. In the late 1880s, the boiseries from EG's salon were moved to Bois-Boudran; they now hang in the Colombe d'Or Hotel in Houston, Texas. See John Harris, *Moving Rooms: The Trade in Architectural Salvage* (New Haven and London: Yale University Press, 2007), 208. In 1999, a chair from EG's salon that did not belong to the Beauvais suite—a giltwood chair signed by Jacob and once owned by Marie Antoinette—was sold at auction in Paris for 2.5 million French francs, or approximately $500,000. See Judith Benhamou-Huet, "Pourquoi les meubles flambent," Les Échos.fr, December 5, 2000. On the settees and chairs with the Beauvais tapestry in Oudry's designs from La Fontaine, see Hillerin, op. cit., 135. Hillerin claims that this furniture gave MP the idea for some Guermantes furniture in RTP, but in fact GS also had a suite of eighteenth-century furniture with tapestry illustrating scenes from La Fontaine, and as MP spent immeasurably more time at GS's apartment than at EG's house, GS's furniture is the more likely source of inspiration here. By 1891, the Oudry suite had been moved into the dining room; see EdG, *Journal,* entry of April 25, 1891.

212 a two-wheeled cart: Ibid.

212 These arrangements fostered: On the living arrangements and weekly routine in the rue d'Astorg, see L. de Vogüé, op. cit., n.p.; and Cossé-Brissac, op. cit., 54.

213 The two men despised each other: A. de Gramont, *L'Ami du Prince,* op. cit., 326.

214 Henry's infamous harem: Hillerin, op. cit., 279.

215 This double standard galled Élisabeth: Of EG's interest in women's rights, Hillerin identifies as the prime expression an unpublished essay she wrote in 1904, "Mon étude sur les droits à donner aux femmes" ("My Study on the Rights to Be Granted to Women"). See Hillerin, op.

cit., 473–74; and AP(II)/101/150 for the original essay. But in fact, EG first wrote about issues of gender equality and gender roles several decades before then, in a series of articles entitled *Les Femmes: une physiologie sociale* (*Women: A Social Physiology*), in AP(II)/101/151.

215   "Women are meant to be trophies": EG, *Les Femmes*; also cited in Hillerin, op. cit., 280.

215   Élisabeth delved into the rare editions: On EG's reading habits and selections, see Cossé-Brissac, op. cit., 64; on HG's library, see *Collection des livres anciens et modernes, provenant de la famille Greffulhe* (Monte-Carlo: Sotheby Parke Bernet Monaco, February 1982): 27 and 102.

215   "appreciation for beautiful things": EG to Mimi, letter dated September 20, 1880, in AP(II)/101/40. On November 13, 1887, in her Journal de Mariage, EG had already dolefully concluded, "Decidedly this family has no taste for art [except for] the Prince d'Arenberg, who is almost always of my opinion."

215   "Looks like I married": Cited in Hillerin, op. cit., 286; and in Jean Cocteau, *Le Passé défini* (Paris: NRF/Gallimard, 1983), 301.

215   "mockery corrodes love": EG, in AP(II)/101/150.

216   "At her age": AP(II)/101/45; also cited in Hillerin, op. cit., 279.

216   Marie-Alys actually compared Élisabeth to the Eucharist: See MACC to EG, letter dated April 7, 1893, in AP(II)/101/53.

216   seven or eight daily costume changes: Eugen Weber, *France Fin de Siècle* (Cambridge and London: Harvard University Press, 1986), 97.

216   "What good does it do": EG, untitled note marked "La Rivière '89," in AP(II)/101/150.

217   "almost impalpable": PV, *Society in Paris*, 95. See also L. de Vogüé, op. cit., 12–13.

218   "reproached [Auguste] for his Jewish friendships": L. de Vogüé, ibid., n.p.

218   "bore up under the conjugal yoke": HG to EG, undated letter in AP(II)/101/14.

218   "the joy of feeling myself beautiful": EG, in AP(II)/101/150.

219   "obliged to make [my]self ugly": Cited in Hillerin, op. cit., 48.

219   "Everything invites her commentary": EG, "The Volunteer Duenna," one of twenty-one unpublished essays archived in AP(II)/101/152.

219   Prince Joseph was even considering: On EG's family's inability to keep the hôtel de Chimay, see JEB, *La Pêche aux souvenirs*, 201. On the sale of the house in 1884, see Parisis (pseud. Émile Blavet), "L'Hôtel de Chimay," *Le Figaro* (June 14, 1884): 1; and The Paris Galignani's Messenger (pseud.), "The Fate of the Hôtel de Chimay," *New York Times* (July 4, 1884): n.p. On the "Israelite . . . political and artistic salon" that Mme Ratisbonne Singer held in the hôtel de Chimay, see JEB, ibid., 97.

219   "a hurricane of daggers": FB, op. cit., 180.

219   "the aristocratic pleasure of *displeasing*": Cited in RM, *Notes et réflexions inédites*, in NAF 15108, folio 46; and in RM, *Les Pas effacés*, vol. 2 (Paris: Émile Paul, 1923), 53.

220   "the *moribund* Faubourg Saint-Germain": RM, "Aristos," in NAF 15183, folio 46/47.

220   "the mother to whom I am very distantly related": Cited in Jullian, *Robert de Montesquiou*, 154.

220   d'Annunzio was one such honored guest: "D'Artagnan's Château Sold for £350" in *The Illustrated London News*, vol. 182 (1933): 42.

221   "I dream of my ancestresses!": Cited in ibid., 36.

221   shrill, exclamatory diction: HR, *Les Cahiers inédits*, 368, 432, and 433; and LG, *Robert de Montesquiou et Marcel Proust*, 22–23.

221   "People bow when the cross goes by!": Cited in Chaleyssin, op. cit., 70.

221   "a bird of prey nourished on self-regard": Cited in Jullian, *Robert de Montesquiou*, 175.

221   "I have adorned": Cited in Jullian, *Robert de Montesquiou*, 105.

221   A hectic jumble: For one contemporary critique of RM's "very bad" poetry, see Lorrain (pseud.), *La Ville empoisonnée*, 97 and 103–4. More on RM's "religion of Beauty" appears in chapter 24. RM is described as "the high priest" of his own religion of aesthetics in *La Revue mondiale* (January 1, 1899): 97.

221   "a Petri dish": Cited in Raczymow, *Le Cygne de Proust*, 114.

221   "I am Priest-Petronius": Cited in Chaleyssin, op. cit., 85.

221   "Fetch Your Lute": Thiébaut, ed., op. cit., 8.

222   "Love that which will never be seen": RM, *Les Pas effacés*, vol. 3, 121.

222   "to prove to the fire": Cited in FB, op. cit., 176.

222   a ringer for Montesquiou: On the resemblances between RM and Des Esseintes (including the tortoise's fatal bedazzling), see Carassus, op..cit., 484–86; Chaleyssin, "Des Esseintes," in op. cit., 27–36; and Marc Fumaroli's excellent preface to Joris-Karl Huysmans, *A Rebours* (Paris: Gallimard, 1977 [1884]). AM, a friend and confessor to many fin-de-siècle artists and

mondains, claimed to have been told by Huysmans himself: "Des Esseintes is half Montesquiou and half me." Though RM enjoyed the notoriety that came with the Des Esseintes association, it came to irk him over time; see RM, *Les Roseaux pensants* (Paris: Eugène Fasquelle, 1897); and EdG, *Journal,* entry of May 18, 1892.

222   "Style has to be seen": RM to EG, in AP(II)/101/150.

223   "in his suit of pale sky blue": Cited in Cornelia Otis Skinner, *Elegant Wits and Grand Horizontals: Paris—La Belle Époque* (New York: Houghton Mifflin, 1962), 45–46.

223   These getups: On male evening dress and RM's variants thereon, see Burnand, op. cit., 91; and Thiébaut, ed., op. cit., 9.

223   "the common laws" of gentlemanly dress: On the *mondain* dress code for men, see GLP, "La Haute Société de la Belle Époque," *Le Crapouillot: La Belle Époque* 29 (1949): 2–7, 5. On RM's high heels, see FB, op. cit., 70.

223   On RM's elegance, see Raoul Ponchon, "Gazette rimée: le mot 'chic,'" *Le Journal* (April 16, 1902): 2. Even the ultradiscerning Boni de Castellane, who succeeded his uncle Sagan as the Faubourg's "King of Chic," has high praise for RM's style. See Boni de Castellane, *Comment j'ai découvert l'Amérique* (Paris: G. Crès, 1925), 90–91. RM's skintight Kelly-green suit may have inspired the outfit worn by the title character, a caricature of RM, in Jean Lorrain (pseud. Paul Duval), *Monsieur Phocas* (Paris: Paul Ollendorff, 1901), 1–3.

223   On RM's sexual ambivalence, see Jullian, *Robert de Montesquiou,* 155–58. On his relationship with Gabriel de Yturri, see especially Rubén Gallo, "An Argentinian in Paris," ch. 2 in *Proust's Latin Americans* (Baltimore and London: The Johns Hopkins University Press, 2014), 90–133.

223   "The effeminate fights": Cited in Jullian, *Robert de Montesquiou,* 154.

223   "This almost ethereal fur": Magali (pseud.), "Le Monde et la mode," *La Vie élégante* 2 (July 15, 1882): 261–272, 271. This text specifically mentions EG's fondness for chinchilla. EG later accused Yturri of having stolen her chinchilla, as he and RM did not return it to her after the portrait by Whistler was completed. On the wine/cocaine mixture RM drank to get through all the sittings, see EdG, *Journal,* entry of July 7, 1891.

224   This perspective endeared him: On RM's "friendship" with Whistler, see Chaleyssin, op. cit., 143; Jullian, *Robert de Montesquiou,* 130–36; Munhall, ed., op. cit.; and Whistler's correspondence with RM, digitally searchable at: http://www.whistler.arts.gla.ac.uk/correspondence /people/result/?nameid=Montesquiou_Rde&year1=1829&year2=1903&sr=0&firstname=& surname=Montesquiou.

224   "Grand Ami": On Whistler as EG's and RM's "Grand Ami," see EG to RM, various letters in AP(II)/101/150; EG to Whistler, letter dated March 16, 1891, in AP(II)101/26; and EG to Whistler, various letters in AP(II)/101/116.

224   "the Bat": On the bat as RM's totem, see Munhall, ed., op. cit.; Jullian, *Robert de Montesquiou,* 156; and RM, *Les Chauves-souris: clairs-obscurs* (Paris: Georges Richard, 1892). On the opulence of the limited edition of *The Bats,* see LG, *Robert de Montesquiou et Marcel Proust,* 38.

225   Another artist who stoked: On RM's friendship with Sarah Bernhardt, see Cornelia Otis Skinner, *Madame Sarah* (Boston: Houghton Mifflin, 1967), 101; on Bernhardt's home zoo and other eccentricities, see ibid., 93–94 and 238; Sarah Bernhardt (apocryphal), *My Double Life* (London: William Heinemann, 1907), 316–18; and Robert Gottlieb, *Sarah: The Life of Sarah Bernhardt* (New Haven and London: Yale University Press, 2013). Dumas *fils*'s story about his dying friend appears in Bernhardt, op. cit., 256.

226   "a creature crushed": Cited in Chaleyssin, op. cit., 29. Jullian draws a distinction between Moreau's and Whistler's influence, noting, "Whistler had held up to him the dandy's polished metal mirror. In Moreau he had found the magician's crystal ball." See Jullian, *Robert de Montesquiou,* 165. With respect to RM's transformation of Sarah Bernhardt into a figure out of a Moreau painting, it bears noting that Oscar Wilde, whom RM regarded with a mixture of fascination and repulsion, envisioned a similar makeover for the actress when writing for her the title role of his French drama, *Salomé.* For an excellent discussion of the "decadent" aesthetic of Wilde's *Salomé* (which did not get performed until he was in prison), see Rhonda Garelick, *Rising Star: Dandyism, Gender, and Performance in the Fin de Siècle* (Princeton: Princeton University Press, 1999), 149.

226   another kindred spirit: On EG's admiration of, as she put it to MCC, RM's "extreme taste and distinction," see Hillerin, op. cit., 41–42; and Steele, op. cit., 61.

227   "I knew you were capable": Cited in Paul Poiret, *Vestendo la Belle Époque,* trans. Simona Broglie (Milan: Excelsior, 2009 [1930]), 163.

227   "even she would never be able to afford them": Ibid.

227 "I find this character": AP(II)/101/50; emphasis EG's.

228 "never managed to have a falling-out": Cited in AG, *Les Clés de Proust,* 129. See also RM, *Les Pas effacés,* vol. 2, 53.

228 "Only barn owls": RM to EG, in AP(II)/101/150.

228 "Only you and the sun": Cited in Chaleyssin, op. cit., 22.

228 an annual clothing allowance: Huas, op. cit., 180.

228 a bespoke three-piece men's suit: Senevas, op. cit., vol. 2, 302.

228 about 140 francs a month: "Relevé des recettes et des dépenses faites pour Madame la Vicomtesse Greffulhe (1880)," in AP(I)/101/16.

228 "desire [and] determination": EG, "La Mode," manuscript dated 1887, in AP(II)/101/150.

229 "*anything but that!*": Cited in RM, *La Divine Comtesse,* 203. See also Steele, op. cit., 64; and Bosc, op. cit., 78.

229 "only that which [would] never be seen": EG, in AP(II)/101/151.

229 "She concerns herself": EG, "La Femme qui donne la mode," in ibid.; also cited in Bosc, op. cit., 77.

229 "the ingenuity": RM, *La Divine Comtesse,* 203–4.

229 Along with the looks just mentioned: Descriptions of dresses and accessories not otherwise attributed appear in Étincelle (pseud.), "Carnet d'un mondain," *Le Figaro* (June 25, 1883): 1; *La Grande Revue* (May 1889): 322; *Le Gaulois* (April 29, 1887); Hillerin, op. cit., 220–25; *La Nouvelle Revue* (June 1884): 446; Steele, op. cit., 64; Violetta (pseud. Laincel), "Sous le masque," *Le Gaulois* (May 27, 1882): 1; and Valérie Laforge, *Talons et tentations* (Quebec: Fides, 2001), 68.

230 excerpt some selections: The chapter of *Les Roseaux pensants* in which RM includes excerpts of EG's creative writing, attributed to "The Swan" (*Le Cygne*), is entitled "The Quartet of Masks" ("Le Quatuor des masques"), and reproduces as well work by three other unnamed "amateurs." One of those other amateurs is Élaine Greffulhe, whose prose poetry RM ascribes to "the Hummingbird, . . . daughter of the Swan." See RM, *Les Roseaux pensants,* 292–313.

230 "Swan King" Ludwig II: Unsurprisingly, RM worshipped the swan-and-Wagner-loving King Ludwig II of Bavaria as well and wrote at least two poems about him, "Armenta" and "Passionspiel," in *Les Chauves-souris,* 305–8.

231 "Virginal ephebe": RM, Poem LXXXIV, in *Les Paons* (Paris: Georges Richard, 1908 [1901]), 144.

231 "glided like a swan": AG, *La Bourgeoisie qui brûle,* 190.

231 the elegant carriage of her neck and head: GLP, *Trente ans de dîners en ville,* 109.

231 "at the Opéra": JEB, *La Pêche aux souvenirs,* 204.

231 "no less than 189 times": Cited in Thiébaut, ed., op. cit., 35. A helpful summary of EG's many portraitists appears in Hillerin, op. cit., 506–7, n. 7.

231 "There are days when one": Cited in Huas, op. cit., 181.

231 She was so disappointed: LG, *Mémoires,* vol. 2, op. cit., 25.

231 a gigantic swansdown fan: For close-up photographs of two of EG's extravagant feathered fans, see Saillard, ed., op. cit., 66–67. Neither of these is the one that appears in the Helleu portrait or the Nadar photo—one is too small and the other too brown, and they are both made from ostrich feathers.

231 "the adorable model": Cited by JEB in *Propos de peintre,* ed. Frédéric Mitterrand (Paris: Séguier, 2013), 384–85.

232 she struck a different avian pose: Mary Bergstein convincingly connects Wegener's "double photograph" of EG to a burgeoning taste for "photographic spiritualism" in fashionable circles at the fin de siècle. See Mary Bergstein, *Looking Back One Learns to See: Marcel Proust and Photography* (Amsterdam and New York: Ropoli, 2014), 156.

233 "In the family, we call them *Tallien* eyes": Interview with Armand-Ghislain, Comte de Maigret, Paris, March 14, 2012.

233 she invoked her "T.T." lineage so frequently: MB, *Le Voyageur voilé,* 33.

233 a lasting impression on Grand-Duc Wladimir: EG thanks him for the Tallien biography in an undated letter in AP(II)/101/24; an excerpt of this letter is cited in Hillerin, op. cit., 174.

234 Henry's collection of treasures: For details on the art and furnishings in the rue d'Astorg, see *La Collection Greffulhe: vente le lundi 6 mars 2000* (Paris: Drouot, 2000); *Catalogue on a Selected Portion of the Renowned Collection of Pictures and Drawings Formed by the Comte Greffulhe* (London: Sotheby's, June 22, 1937); and Charles Gueullette, *Les Cabinets d'amateurs à Paris, la collection du comte Henri de* [sic] *Greffulhe* (Paris: Detaille, 1887), 5–6.

234 Élisabeth hired Eugène Lami: EG to MCC, letter dated August 13, 1882, in AP(II)/101/40;

Cossé-Brissac, op. cit., 59; and Hillerin, op. cit., 266–77. On Jeanne d'Arenberg's lessons with Mme Lemaire, see Horatio (pseud. MP), "Le Salon de Mme Madeleine Lemaire," in MP, *Le Salon de Mme de . . .* , 39.

234 Élisabeth also studied photography: Cossé-Brissac, op. cit., 63–64. Some of the photographs EG took in her *jardin d'hiver* in Paris are now viewable digitally on the website of the Musée d'Orsay, categorized under "Fonds autour de la comtesse Greffulhe (1860–1890)." The inventory numbers for these photographs are PHO 2010 5 19 and PHO 2010 5 20 (HG); PHO 2010 5 16 (Guigui); and PHO 2010 5 17 (the Prince de Sagan, incorrectly identified on the d'Orsay website as "the comte de Caraman-Chimay?? [*sic*]").

234 engaged an artist called Deloge: Le Diable Boiteux (pseud. de Vaux), "Nouvelles et échos," *Gil Blas* (November 3, 1883): 1.

235 "all further embellished": Ibid.

235 "considered from an artistic point of view": de Vaux, *Les Femmes de sport,* 148.

235 "In twenty years": RM, *La Divine Comtesse,* 199.

235 "getting herself talked about": HG to EG, undated letter in AP(II)/101/32.

235 "*display* Helleu's 'swan'": RM describes Helleu's "swan" portraiture in detail in *La Divine Comtesse,* 200–201.

236 To delimit her public exposure: Painter, op. cit., vol. 1, 148; and Cossé-Brissac, op. cit., 133.

236 "Disagreeable Letters from Henry": HG to EG, in AP(II)/101/32.

236 abusive-husband clichés: Typical of HG's schizoid "apologies" is a *petit bleu* he sent EG in 1902, in which he alternates between the first and the third persons: "When he leaves her in pain, it tears at his heart and that hurts *him.* I was holding the walking stick and I just happened to get impatient. I regret it. Movements like those [illegible] more pain to him than to anyone else. . . . It breaks his heart. He begs her pardon. He will never do it again. He adores her—Her Henry." HG to EG, in ibid.

236 "I am not afraid of a swift death": EG to HG, letter dated January 4, 1909, in AP(I)/101/22.

237 "picturesque lateness": FB, op. cit., 183–84. EG formulates the theory behind her "picturesque latenesses" in an unpublished essay called "On the Influence of That Which Is Not Unveiled." The thesis of this essay is "The source of prestige is mystery!" See EG, "De l'influence du non-dévoilé," in AP(II)/101/150. She wrote another essay on the same subject, "Aperçu sur le prestige," in ibid., theorizing that "Prestige is 'imagined reality.' " Further citations from both essays are given in Hillerin, op. cit., 213.

237 "Could she have done it on purpose?": FB, op. cit., 184; also cited in Hillerin, ibid., 215. On EG being "picturesquely late" for the Queen of Portugal, see A. de Gramont, op. cit., 275.

238 "a lady of whom": EG, in AP(II)/101/151.

239 In this canny bit of choreography: On EG's trick of hiding in, and briefly emerging from, the shadows of her *baignoire,* see MB, *Le Voyageur voilé,* 49.

239 "apparition": Haas, cited in Cossé-Brissac, op. cit., 129; Le Diable Boiteux (pseud. de Vaux), "Nouvelles et échos," *Le Gaulois* (June 13, 1889): 1; GPR to EG, letter dated January 1925, in AP(II)/101/107; and EdG, *Journal,* April 25, 1891.

239 "like a precious fruit": EG, in AP(II)/101/149.

239 "it was as if she were descending": AG, *Les Clés de Proust,* 33.

240 "twenty seamstresses were toiling": *Le Gaulois* (May 26, 1880): 1.

240 "letting our couturiers fight": Cited in Hillerin, op. cit., 223.

240 her descent from Mme Tallien: In one of his accounts of EG's "goddess"-like presence, AF, too, stresses her descent from Mme Tallien, in *Le Bal du Pré-Catelan,* 258–59.

240 "updating Empire dress": Étincelle (pseud.), "Carnet d'un mondain," *Le Figaro* (June 5, 1891): 1; also cited in Bosc, op. cit., 77.

240 "When a lady wears": Santillane (pseud.), "Courrier de Paris," *Gil Blas* (November 24, 1883): 1.

241 "Leaders of Fashion": Étincelle (pseud.), "Les Maréchales de la mode," *Le Figaro* (September 1, 1884): 1–2.

241 "of a thousand beauties": Cited in Hillerin, op. cit., 203.

241 "The tastes of the Vicomtesse": Étincelle (pseud. Peyronny), "Mondains et mondaines," *Le Monde illustré* (January 10, 1891): 1.

CHAPTER EIGHT: PRINCE CHARMING

243 "great, anonymous caress": AP(II)/101/151; also cited in RM, *Les Roseaux pensants,* 307.

243 "What a delicious thing": EG, in AP(II)/101/152.

243 one of the Faubourg's most elegant women: GLP, *Trente ans de dîners en ville,* 40.
243 "I suppose I shall know": Cited in Huas, op. cit., 180; and in Painter, op. cit., vol. 1, 152. Both Huas and Painter note that MP used this mot in a discarded passage of the second volume of SG. Interestingly, MP believed that EG borrowed her statement about "the little people" from Mme Récamier; see Jeanne Maurice Pouquet, *The Last Salon,* trans. Lewis Galantière (New York: Harcourt, Brace, 1927), 325. On EG's identification with Mme Récamier, see chapter 20.
244 "I will forever wonder": Cited in Hillerin, op. cit., 223.
244 "Your hat is not *in season*": This letter from HG to EG is written on his count's letterhead, so it must date from after September 1888; AP(II)/101/32. The other citations from HG to EG here are also taken from letters filed under this archival code.
244 "What a lucky chap": EG, Journal de Mariage, entry of October 26, 1878.
244 organized a fireworks extravaganza: For its grand finale, Massa's fireworks display for EG spelled out the initials D-E ("Diana-Élisabeth") in the sky; the sonnet he wrote for EG is also entitled "Diana-Élisabeth" and is dated 1886. Nearly a quarter of a century later, in 1909, Judith Gautier would compare EG to both Diana and Venus, in an untitled sonnet that begins *"Diane a convié Vénus, en la forêt."* EG saved both of these poems, along with many more from Massa (and other admirers), in "Hommages et appréciations," AP(II)/101/1.
245 notorious as "the Butcher of Clichy": On Galliffet's role in the Paris Commune, see Horne, op. cit., 406–7.
245 "the Drunk Old Assassin of Clichy": HG to EG, in AP(II)/101/32.
245 engaged her in a romantic correspondence: Hottinguer's letters to EG are filed in AP(II)/101/89. The most passionate of them date from an approximately ten-year period between 1884 and 1894.
245 "he [were] fleeing a person": Cited in Cossé-Brissac, op. cit., 52.
246 "a very strange letter": EG to MCC, letter dated October 13, 1881, in AP(II)/101/32. A number of other anonymous letters to EG—including one annotated in EG's hand, "anonymous letter written by Henry"—are archived in the same file.
246 "Don't serve anything": Cited in Cocteau, *Le Passé défini,* 301.
246 "an arsenal of rats and mice": EG to MCC, letter dated October 2, 1881; AP(II)/101/40.
246 "If it's a girl": EG to MCC, letter dated October 12, 1881, in ibid.
247 "I do not find that Élaine is blossoming": EG to MCC, letter dated December 8, 1882, in ibid.
247 "I admit it": EG to MCC, letter dated November 18, 1882, in ibid.
247 "revealed himself to be": Hillerin, op. cit., 290–91.
248 But in close quarters: On the Duc d'Aumale's appearance and demeanor, see X. (pseud.), "Choses et autres," *La Vie parisienne* (June 7, 1890): 319; Burnand, op. cit., 150; and Raymond de Monbel to EG, undated letter in AP(II)/101/99.
248 "roughened": EdG, *Journal,* entry of December 14, 1874; and EG, in AP(II)/101/59 and AP(II)/101/150.
248 "In my youth": Cited in LG, *Mémoires,* vol. 2, 169.
249 "Just look at the pallor of death": Cited in ibid., 168. For a comprehensive fin-de-siècle catalogue of d'Aumale's collection, see *Chantilly: Visite de l'Institut de France—26 octobre 1895* (Paris: Plon, 1896). The *Dormition of the Virgin,* displayed in a special gallery called the Giotto Room, was later proven to have been painted by a follower of Giotto's.
250 "Mme Greffulhe is a lily": EG, note labeled "cited by Monsieur Joubert," in AP(II)/101/150. On the marriage of LC's niece Yvonne de Chevigné to Jean Joubert, and on the Duc d'Aumale's friendship with the bridegroom's father, see the Marquise de Dangeau (pseud.), "Chronique mondaine," *La Mode de style* (February 11, 1891): 51–54, 52.
250 "Yesterday morning": Prince de Sagan to EG, telegram in AP/101/(II)/112; also cited in Cossé-Brissac, op. cit., 62.
251 Henry had a liaison: On HG's affair with Blanche Pierson, see Houbre, ed., op. cit., 153 and 188; and HB, op. cit., 40.
251 "It is too awful!": Cited in LG, *Mémoires,* vol. 2, 26.
251 Sagan treated Élisabeth: Cossé-Brissac, op. cit., 63.
252 "The Vicomtesse Greffulhe's new hunting costume": Le Diable Boiteux (pseud.), "Nouvelles et échos," *Gil Blas,* August 12, 1885, 1.
252 *"If only one of us is left standing":* Cited in RM to EG, undated letter in AP(II)/101/150. This alexandrine comes from Victor Hugo's "Ultima Verba," in *Punishments* (*Les Châtiments*) (1853). For MP's use of this quote, see CG, 735.

254   "Why, oh, why": EG, "Fausses rencontres," in AP(II)/101/152.

254   "keep the Prince breathless": EG to GCC, in AP(II)/101/151.

254   The completed pamphlet: The title EG eventually gave this pamphlet is *Portrait du Prince de X;* see AP(II)/101/152. The pamphlet was typeset and printed but does not have page numbers. For three characteristic contemporary accounts of Sagan's elegance, see AdF, *Cinquante ans de panache,* 48–50; GLP, *Trente ans de dîners en ville,* 31; and Scrutator (pseud.), "Notes from Paris: Intermarriage and Degeneracy," *Truth* (August 14, 1902), 386.

254   "The monocle": EG, *Portrait du Prince de X.*

255   "He obeys": Ibid.

255   "the Prince Charming of Roman society": LG, *Mémoires,* vol. 2, 37.

256   "the Panther": EG to GCC, letter dated February 24, 1891, in AP(II)/101/45.

256   it was said that she had poisoned: Augustus Hare, *Story of My Life,* vol. 1 (Library of Alexandria: n.d.). Four of Don Marcantonio's children with his first wife, née Lady Gwendoline (Guendalina) Talbot, also died prematurely, but Hare does not suggest that Adélaïde de La Rochefoucauld poisoned them, too. According to his friend Conte Edoardo Soderini, Don Marcantonio only consented to remarry because "in Thérèse [de La Rochefoucauld] he found the perfect copy of his Guendalina." See Conte Edoardo Soderini, *Il Principe Don Marco Antonio Borghese* (Rome: Bafani, 1886), 12.

256   "He adored her above all other": Commandante Alfonso M. Massari, *Don Giovanni Borghese: Cenni necrologici* (Rome: Presse della Reale Società Geografica Italiana, 1918), 6.

256   the brink of financial ruin: On the financial woes of the Borghese family at the fin de siècle, see Frances Elliot, *Roman Gossip* (London: John Murray, 1894); Ian Chilvers, ed., *The Oxford Dictionary of Art* (Oxford: Oxford University Press, n.d.), 90; and René Guimard, "Les Borghèse," *Gil Blas* (August 30, 1891): 1–2; biographical information for GBB and his family is drawn principally from the *Almanach de Gotha,* vol. 144 (1904): 281–83; and from Elliot, op. cit.

257   it was said to foster sodomy: Enea Balmas, *Studi di letteratura francese* 18 (Florence: Olschki, 1990), 170. On homosexuality among the Knights of Malta, see also Carlo Carasi, *L'Ordre de Malte dévoilé, ou voyage de Malte* (Cologne: n.p., 1790), 184–186; and Edward Prime-Stevenson, *Du similisexualisme dans les armées et de la prostitution homosexuelle à la Belle Époque,* trans. Jean-Claude Féray (Paris: Quinte-Feuilles, 2000), 23.

257   Prince Ferdinand: Details on Prince Ferdinand de Saxe-Cobourg are taken from Henry Fischer, ed., *Secret Memoirs of the Court of Royal Saxony (1891–1922): The Story of Louise, Crown Princess* (Bensonhurst, NY: Fischer's Foreign Letters, 1912), 36; Stephen Constant (pseud.), *Foxy Ferdinand, Tsar of Bulgaria* (London: Sidgwick & Jackson, 1979), 37–46; and John MacDonald, *Czar Ferdinand and His People* (New York: F. A. Stokes, 1945), 94.

258   "womanish" sartorial flair: Constant (pseud.), op. cit., 37 and 44; Anonymous (pseud.), "Ferdinand the Feminine," in *Ferdinand of Bulgaria: The Amazing Career of a Shoddy Czar* (London: A. Melrose, 1916), 125–34; Duncan M. Perry, *Stefan Stambolov and the Emergence of Modern Bulgaria* (Durham, NC: Duke University Press, 1993), 216–17; and A. Nekludoff, "Auprès de Ferdinand de Bulgarie," *La Revue des deux mondes* 54 (November–December 1919): 546–76, 551.

258   gemstones, butterflies: Constant (pseud.), op. cit., 44; and the Baron Beyens, "L'Avenir des petits états: la Bulgarie," *La Revue des deux mondes* 44 (April 1818): 874–94, 875. On his aviaries, see Anonymous, *Ferdinand of Bulgaria,* 128.

258   "Even the Saint Alexander": Cited in S. Constant (pseud.), op. cit., 37; and in J. V. Köingslöw, *Ferdinand von Bulgarien* (Munich, 1970), 34.

258   noted botanical discoveries: Heinrich Wawra de Fernsee, *Les Broméliacées découvertes pendant les voyages des princes Auguste et Ferdinand de Saxe-Cobourg* (Liège: C. Anoot-Braeckman, 1880).

258   the first group of European explorers: For firsthand details of the Borghese Expedition, see the testimony of Dr. Pellegrino Matteucci, excerpted in Pietro Amat di San Filippo, *Gli illustri viaggiatori italiani con una antologia dei loro scritti* (Rome: 1885), 498–507; and Massari, op. cit. For secondhand accounts of the expedition, see Sir Harry Hamilton Johnston, *A History of the Colonization of Africa by Alien Races* (Cambridge and London: Cambridge University Press, 1899), 213–14; *Le Tour du monde: nouveau journal des voyages,* vol. 40–41 (Paris: n.p., 1881), 437; and *L'Exploration* 17 (1884): 228–29.

258   beseeched him to return to Rome: Massari, op. cit., 6; and "La Traversée de l'Afrique," in *Bulletin de la Société Royale Belge de Géographie* (1885): 861.

259   "the extraordinary dangers": *Bulletin de la Société Royale Belge de Géographie* (1881): 457; on the fate of GBB's two companions after he left Africa, see *Bulletin de la Société Royale Belge de Géographie* (1883): 861; and *Le Tour du Monde: Nouveau Journal des Voyages* 40–41 (1881): 437.

259   a big-game animal skin: Sonia Bompiani, *Italian Explorers in Africa* (London: Religious Tract Society: 1891), 53; *Bulletin de la Société Royale Belge de Géographie* (1882): 117; and Massari, op. cit., 6.

259   a distant maternal relation: HG's mother's maternal grandmother, Anne Picot de Dampierre, had four brothers, one of whom married Émilie Ernestine Prondre de Guermantes, the daughter of Emmanuel Paulin Prondre, the last Comte de Guermantes. (Several online genealogies incorrectly write "Prondre" as "Pondre," as in "pondre un oeuf": to lay an egg.) Ernestine Picot de Dampierre was thus HG's great-great-aunt by marriage. On the genealogy of the Guermantes family, see A. Borel d'Hauterive and Vicomte Albert Révérend, eds., *Annuaire de la noblesse de France*, vol 54 (Paris: Bureau de la Publication, 1896): 369. On the successive owners of the château de Guermantes after Ernestine's death, see Suzanne Verne, *Guermantes de Louis XIII à nos jours* (Paris: Ferenczi, 1961), 182–86. On Ernestine's funeral services in Paris and at Guermantes, see "Hommes et choses," *Le Matin* (July 10, 1884): 3.

259   "That's enough, Father!": Cited in Verne, op. cit., 175.

259   "*This* place is a boutique": Ibid.

260   "Cocoa! Cocoa!": Cited in A. de Gramont, op. cit., 159.

260   grubbiness of the castle: On the décor of Guermantes in the 1880s, see Verne, op. cit., 177–82.

260   On GBB's conversational charm, see Luca Bartolotti, *Roma fuori le mura* (Rome: La Terza, 1988), 78; and Countess Maria Tarnowska, *The Future Will Tell: A Memoir* (Victoria, BC: Friesen, 2016), 31. On GBB's literary interests, see Massari, op. cit., 5.

260   "The monde": EG, in a text marked "4ᵉ volume: Le Revoir," dated in EG's pidgin shorthand (translation: "dix février 1885"), 1 (the pages are hand numbered just for this section of one of EG's notebooks) in AP(II)/101/151. Judging by the date, and by a reference in the text to how she is seeing him again (*revoir*) for the first time in nearly half a year, EG seems to have written this about her first reunion with GBB since Guermantes. But I cite it here because it usefully condenses much of her writing about what it was like for her to have to communicate with him "in the language of the monde."

261   "While we chatted": Ibid., 3.

261   the sumptuous Hôtel Royal: JEB, *Dieppe* (Paris: Berthout 1992 [1926]), 21.

261   "thoughts had grown as sad": GBB to EG, letter dated December 28, 1887, in AP(II)/101/53.

261   exuding a "fragrance": Ibid.

262   "My dear friend": GBB to EG, letter dated December 1, 1884, in AP(II)/101/151.

263   "Upon reaching the bottom of the steps": EG, unnumbered manuscript page in AP(II)/101/151. The first line on this page begins with "*Ce soir-là, vibrante de plénitude elle chantait. . . .*"

263   star-crossed lovers named Éléonore and Gérard: In naming his alter ego Gérard, GBB may have meant to pay tribute to one of the most famous nineteenth-century French explorers of Africa, Jules Gérard, "killer of lions" (1817–1864); GBB himself, after all, had been credited with killing either a lion or a leopard on his expedition there. In an odd coincidence, in 1887, Stéphane Mallarmé assigned DH and JB a story about "Gérard, killer of lions" as a translation exercise in their English class at the Lycée Condorcet. See DH, *Pays parisiens*, 113.

264   "What do you say": GBB to EG, letter marked "1 décembre 1884," in AP(II)/101/151. EG's response to this letter, GBB's follow-up correspondence, and many of the Éléonore and Gérard texts, are also archived in this file.

265   unqualified esteem: RM to José-Maria de Heredia, letter marked "avril [1883]," in Heredia, *Correspondance*, ms. 5689, vol. 12.

265   "Harmony!": Taken from Musset's poem "Lucie," this line also appears as the epigraph to the chapter on music in GBB's only published book. See GBB [Prince Jean Borghèse], *L'Italie moderne* (Paris: Flammarion, 1913), 257.

CHAPTER NINE: PARIS HIGH AND LOW

267   they were close friends: Bischoff, op. cit., 186; DH, "Deux portraits de Mme Straus," 177; and AM, op. cit., 430.

267   irrepressible playfulness: Sources for this brief sample of LC's *mondain* mischief are Eugène Hubert, "La Fête de l'Opéra," *Gil Blas* (April 8, 1883): 3–4; "La Journée," *Le Gaulois* (April 29, 1885): 2; and "Bloc-notes parisien," *Le Gaulois* (March 17, 1889): 1.

268   "would stay out until two": LG, *Mémoires,* vol. 2, 31.
268   "Being very bright": Ibid., 79–80.
268   "nothing mattered but talent": AdF, *Mon Paris et ses Parisiens,* vol. 4, 118. On this aspect of LC's character, see also AF, *Le Bal du Pré-Catelan,* 156–57.
268   one of the first friends she made: MB, *La Duchesse de Guermantes,* 80; and AF, "Le Salon de l'Europe," 467–70. On the Reszkés' scandalous love story, see Garry O'Connor, *The Pursuit of Perfection* (Philadelphia: Atheneum, 1979), 49. Unable to secure a divorce, Marie de Mailly-Nesle had to wait until her husband died to marry Reszké; by the time that day finally came, she and the tenor had been living together for more than a decade. On HG's rumored liaison with Marie de Mailly-Nesle, see HB, op. cit., 40.
270   "*Porto told me that Réjane*": Cited in AF, "La Salon de l'Europe," 463.
270   "*What?* There is new talent": Cited in ibid., 450.
271   "antic madness": Cited in Harold B. Segal, *Turn-of-the-Century Cabaret: Paris, Barcelona, Berlin, Munich, Vienna* (New York: Columbia University Press, 1987), 20. Unless otherwise noted, details about the Chat-Noir are drawn from Segal's account (19–37); from Theodore Child, "Characteristic Parisian Cafés," *Harper's New Monthly Magazine* 77 (April 1889): 687–703 and 700–703; and from Jerrold Seigel, *Bohemian Paris: Culture, Politics, and the Boundaries of Bourgeois Life, 1830–1930* (Baltimore and London: The Johns Hopkins University Press, 1996), 223–24 and 231–36. On Bruant's popularity with upper-class Parisians, see Seigel, op. cit., 238–39; and Alcanter et Saint-Jean (pseud. Marcel Bernhardt), "Les Vendredis d'Aristide," *Le Nouvel Echo* 3 (February 1892): 78–80.
271   silhouettes of cut-out puppets: The historical and biblical figures parodied in the Chat-Noir's shadow theater included Napoléon I, Saint Anthony, and the Queen of Sheba; see Segal, op. cit., 31. One particularly daring shadow play satirized the life of Christ; see the *Chap-Book* (August 1, 1894): 201–2.
271   Aristide Bruant: On Bruant's rabble-rousing persona and musical repertoire, see Seigel, op. cit., 235–39.
271   "Singer for the People": Cited in ibid., 239. In French, the honorific Bruant had his servants use with him was *Chansonnier populaire,* which translates more literally to "Popular Singer." But in French, "*populaire*" does not simply mean well-liked; it connotes "the people," "the masses," a nuance that was particularly important to Bruant in positioning himself as a spokesperson for the common man.
272   Porto-Riche who knew the *Rime Sparse*: On GPR's interest in Petrarch, also discussed in chapter 14, see NAF 24951, folio 156; and Walter Müller, *Georges de Porto-Riche, 1849–1930: l'homme, le poète, le dramaturge* (Paris: J. Vrin, 1934), 51.
272   "this phoenix of golden plumage": Francesco Petrarca, "CLXII. *Questa fenice dell'aurata piuma,*" in *Il Canzoniere,* vol. 1, ed. Lorenzo Mascetta (Lanciano: Rocco Carabba, 1895). In this line, "*dell'aurata*" (of golden) contains, like so many of Petrarch's wordplays, a reference to his lady's name: Laura.
272   some of them actually referred to her: Gratin (pseud.), "Femmes et fleurs," *Le Gaulois* (August 30, 1885): 1; on people mistakenly calling LC "Mme de Sévigné," see AF, "Le Salon de l'Europe," 460.
272   confrères primly avoided mentioning: AG, *Les Clés de Proust,* 31; and Jean-Pascal Hesse, *Donatien Alphonse François de Sade* (Paris: Assouline, 2014), 418–19. In his interview with Hesse, Xavier de Sade says that after his forebear Donatien's death in 1814, "any mention of the marquis [was] strictly forbidden in my family for more than a century" (418). As a young man in the 1930s, Xavier adds, he was warned by one of his uncles, "If you ever, ever speak about your great-great-grandfather, you will be damned!" (419).
272   "of her Marquis de Sade ancestry": Sert, op. cit., 87.
272   "De Sade! What a beautiful name.": Cited in PM, *L'Allure de Chanel,* 107.
272   He was rumored to have bedded: On GM's alleged three hundred conquests, see Armand Lanoux, *Maupassant le Bel-Ami* (Paris: Fayard, 1967), p. 241; and *La Revue des deux mondes* (October–December 1970): 84.
272   "Maupassant boasted": Louis Auchincloss, *The Man Behind the Book* (New York: Houghton Mifflin, 1996), 99.
273   when he wanted to corrupt a new mistress: LD, *Devant la douleur,* 119.
273   "ferocious obscenity": Cited in René Maizeroy, "Guy de Maupassant à Sartrouville," in *Le Gaulois* (July 3, 1912): 1. Maizeroy identifies himself in this essay as GM's best friend. He provides much of the information I have cited about GM's secret society. For more on the Crepitians, see Bancquart, op. cit., 131; and the editors' notes to GM, *Contes et nouvelles,*

ed. Dominique Frémy, Brigitte Monglon, and Bernard Fremech (Paris: Robert Laffont, 1988), 209.

273   "rumors that could pursue you": GM, undated letter to a female friend sold at auction as lot #272, and transribed in *Autographes et manuscrits* (Paris: Ader, June 23, 2013). This lot is not identified as a letter to LC; however, it was sold along with a sheaf of other letters confirmed to have been written to LC from GM, and from some of LC's other artist friends (Yvette Guibert, Frédéric Mistral, and FB). These letters were described as having all come from the same family estate.

273   "quite simply dressed as a man!!!": Ibid.

273   "You can't imagine": GM, *Bel-Ami* (Paris: L. Conard, 1910 [1885]), 146.

274   "watch out for Mme de Chevigné": Cited in Cossé-Brissac, op. cit., 138.

274   "*He* can get into all the trouble he wants!": EG, in AP(II)/101/8.

274   "Bravo, *la vieille!*": In RTP, MP correctly attributes this line to Grand-Duc Wladimir, who has a cameo appearance at a Guermantes party at the beginning of SG. However, the trigger for the grand-duc's mirth is the humiliation of a *grande mondaine* who accidentally gets drenched by a fountain in her hosts' garden.

274   her celebrity singer friend Hortense Schneider: AF, "Le Salon de l'Europe," 464–66.

274   "the Passage of Princes": Cited in F. W. J. Hemmings, *Culture and Society in France, 1848–1898: Dissidents and Philistines* (London: Batsford, 1971), 136. On the fascination Schneider, known in her prime as "the queen of Paris," held for actual royalty, see Jacques Heugel, "Hortense Schneider," *Le Ménestrel* (May 14, 1920): 208.

275   "Now I ask you": AF provides a slightly different account of this episode in "Le Salon de l'Europe," 464.

275   "had pulled off a feat": Ibid., 465.

276   "She wore the dazzling glory of Bizet's name": DH, "Deux portraits de Mme Straus," 177.

276   Ludovic had taken advantage of his celebrity: On LH's *mondanité*, see Laurent, op. cit., 92; and J.-P. Halévy, "Ludovic Halévy par lui-même," 141. On his involvement in the "Bixio dinner," see Laurent, op. cit., 43.

278   "The Faubourg Saint-Germain [went] to Geneviève's salon": Cited in FG, *Mon amitié*, 42–43; and in Carassus, op. cit., 86; on the uniqueness and cachet of GS's "hybrid" salon, see Balard, ed., op. cit., 162–63; DH, "Deux portraits de Mme Straus," 175; and Jacob, op. cit., 168–70. On her literary friends' continued reliance on her for help in their careers, see Bischoff, op. cit., 134–36.

278   "one of the uncontested masters": EdG, *Journal*, entry from February 17, 1893.

278   "the royalty of wealth": Cited in Muhlstein, *Baron James*, 105.

279   "You must see Geneviève!": Cited in Bischoff, op. cit., 111. On Reinach teasing ES about how all he could talk about was GS, see LG, *Mémoires*, 200.

280   "I will never have a falling-out": Cited in HR, *Les Cahiers*, 447.

280   "because he was there": DH, "Deux portraits de Mme Straus," 177.

280   "for an Adonis": Cited in Jacob, op. cit., 165.

280   "vain about the things he had": Cited in HR, *Les Cahiers*, 278.

280   "frightful temper": Unless otherwise noted, all complaints about and characterological assessments of ES by GS's *fidèles* are cited in Bischoff, op. cit., 113–16. Bischoff rather curiously insists that these individuals' many anxious comments about ES's volcanic temper and violent possessiveness cannot "be taken seriously" (115). Of all the faithful, however, only Paul Hervieu ever seemed to make light of ES's propensity to anger. See PH to GS, undated letter in NAF 13026, folio 37.

281   "carelessness and aggression": DH, "Deux portraits de Mme Straus," 178.

281   "invited into the very best company": Ibid., 175.

283   "her friends were thankful": LG, "L'entresol," 3. Similarly, on GS's "not at all *bluestocking*, not at all *literary* or *intellectual* character," see RD, "Madame Straus et Marcel Proust," 806.

283   "amusing and frivolous": EdG, *Journal*, entry of February 18, 1895. JEB describes the banter in GS's salon in similar terms; see *Mes modèles*, 114.

283   "They fought one another with pinpricks": Tout-Paris (pseud. MP), "Les Grands Salons de Paris," *Le Gaulois* (September 1, 1893): 1–2; reproduced in translation in appendix C.

283   Of this minor art of war: On Haas's and d'Arenberg's wit, see Painter, op. cit., vol. 1, 128; and FG, *Mon amitié*, 43.

283   with whom he had been close: Chaleyssin, op. cit., 223.

283   "She's pretty enough": Cited in Paul Grelière, *Les Talleyrand-Périgord dans l'histoire* (Paris: Éditions Clairvivre, 1962), 181.

283 "her biting wit": AdF, *Cinquante ans de panache,* 52.

283 "Careful!": Cited in Arnaud, op. cit., 76; and in AG, *Les Clefs de Proust,* 15.

284 "She's like the sun": Cited in Huas, op. cit., 166.

284 "assassinating his targets": FG, *Mon amitié,* 43. Here FG is actually referring to the biting sarcasm of Degas's student and friend, caricaturist Jean-Louis Forain. But it applies equally well to Degas, Forain's acknowledged master in both art and wit. On Forain as GS's "favorite" wit, see Bischoff, op. cit., 138, n. 1.

284 "He would have us believe": Cited in DH, *My Friend Degas,* trans. Mina Curtiss (Middletown, CT: Wesleyan University Press, 1964), 47, n. 5.

284 "an arms dealer": Ibid.

284 "a watercolorist of cats and dogs": Cited in EdG, *Journal,* entry of June 6, 1885. While she did not particularly care for paintings of battle scenes, GS had a soft spot for Detaille because he painted the original stage-sets for *Carmen.*

284 "One day at the Opéra": Cited in DH, *My Friend Degas,* 47.

285 "the poor Wandering Jew": Cited in Raczymow, *Le Cygne de Proust,* 92.

285 "My yid doesn't have his hair": Cited in André Magué, *La France bourgeoise actuelle* (Paris: Février, 1891), 229. LC's claim about the secret to Haas's Jockey-Club election is cited in PM, *L'Allure de Chanel,* 106; and in DH, *Pays parisiens,* 82. On the members of the Jockey who did fight in the Franco-Prussian War, see "Le Jockey-Club à l'armée," *Le Figaro* (October 25, 1870): 2.

285 "I had to pinch myself": LH, *Carnets,* 590.

285 "But your Jesus Christ was Jewish!": Cited in AGG, *Souvenirs,* 144.

285 "Perhaps the humiliations": This fragment is reprinted in the scholarly notes to the Pléiade edition of RTP. See MP, RTP, vol. 1, 902.

286 "common sense and surprised merriment": FG, "Sur Marcel Proust" *Le Journal des débats* (February 7, 1937): 3; and FG, *L'Âge d'or,* 168. In a like vein, on her "repartee, where she so skillfully infused her irony with benevolence," see RF, "Mort de Mme Émile Straus," 2. On GS's "Meilhac and Halévy" wit, see also RD, *De Monsieur Thiers à Marcel Proust,* 21 and 29. On Mme de Guermantes's "Meilhac and Halévy" wit, see MP, TR, 785.

286 "biting but restrained": Cited in Jean-Claude Yon, "Le théâtre de Meilhac et Halévy: satire et indulgence," in Loyrette, ed., op. cit., 162–77, 168.

286 her "Jewish nonchalance": EdG, *Journal,* entry of March 28, 1887.

286 "I was *just* going to say that!": Cited in LG, *Mémoires,* vol. 2, 201; and in FG, *L'Âge d'or,* 168. (It is FG who specifies that GS and Gounod were at *Hérodiade* at the time.) Many years later, MP cites this line, ascribing it to GS but altering the context in which she said it, in his pastiche of the memoirs of Saint-Simon. See MP, *Pastiches et mélanges* (Paris: Gallimard, 1947 [1919]), 84.

286 "We made a lot of it in my first family": Cited in LG, *Mémoires,* vol. 2, 201. For a list of GS's other most frequently cited quips, see ibid., 200–201; and MP to GS, in MP, *Correspondance avec Mme Straus,* 99–100.

286 "Have you heard Geneviève's latest?": Cited in RD, *De Monsieur Thiers à Marcel Proust,* 18.

287 "The duchesses of yesteryear": Castellane, *Vingt ans de Paris,* 106. In the same passage, Castellane also notes that "the old houses [of the nobility in Paris] are entertaining less and less, and people are getting used to a new sort of society" (ibid.). That new sort of society included not only "witty women," but nonaristocratic, often foreign-born heiresses like Castellane's own wife, Anna Gould. More on the crumbling of the old social barriers in fin-de-siècle Paris appears in Fiette, op. cit., 205–7; and in an 1886 diary entry by CCB: "It seems as if, wherever one looks, the old world, old society, is coming apart," CCB, op. cit., 196.

287 most of their contemporaries had yet to foresee: An important exception here is Arthur Meyer, who joined (and helped) LC and EG in bringing about their era's cult of celebrity; according to JEB, Meyer's guiding "doctrine" was "Notoriety matters more than talent." See JEB, "Mes modèles" *Les Nouvelles littéraires, artistiques et scientifiques* (July 14, 1928): 2.

CHAPTER TEN: A MODERN-DAY ARAMIS

288 "Like many self-made men": Cited in Balard, ed., op. cit., 399.

289 The marriage took place at the Grand Synagogue: Because French law does not recognize religious marriages as legally binding, ES and GS also had to marry civilly in the town hall of the ninth arrondissement; see "Faits divers," *Le Temps* (October 9, 1886): 3.

289 listed in civil records as a ragpicker: *Staats- und Adress-Handbuch der Freien Stadt Frankfurt,* vol. 114 (Frankfurt: Krugs Verlag, 1852), 308.

289 arrested for counterfeiting: On the Seligmann relations' involvement in a counterfeiting ring, see *Journal politique de Mannheim* 107 (April 18, 1886): 4; and Maurice Mejan, *Recueil des causes célèbres et des arrêts qui les ont décidés,* vol. 1 (Paris: Plisson, 1807), 193–234.

290 "Schtrauss": As MP and FG would both later note, the Strauses' longtime "friend" d'Haussonville, who sided against them in the Dreyfus affair, deliberately began mispronouncing their surname to insult them. See FG, *L'Âge d'or,* 169; and Painter, op. cit., vol. 1, 225. MP depicts a similar dynamic in RTP when Swann becomes a Dreyfusard, offending many of his *mondain* friends; after this, certain people in the monde (including his own daughter, adopted after his death by her mother's aristocratic second husband) take to pronouncing his last name "Svann," "turning this name of English origin into a German surname." For a discussion of this shift, see Raczymow, *Le Cygne de Proust,* 28.

290 In Jewish immigrant communities: On the social cachet of German Jews in the United States, see Stephen Birmingham, *Our Crowd: The Great Jewish Families of New York* (New York: Harper & Row, 1967); on the prestige of Sephardic Jews in France, see Philippe Erlanger, "Israélites français devant le snobisme," in Jullian, ed., 95–96.

290 "ghetto pariah": On the origins and implications of this noxious stereotype, see especially Hannah Arendt, *The Jew as Pariah* (New York: Grove, 1978) and *The Origins of Totalitarianism,* Part I: *Anti-Semitism* (New York: Harcourt Brace Janovich, 1951), 54–88.

291 "a massive and heavy stone cage": Émile Zola, *Le Ventre de Paris,* 3rd ed. (Paris: Charpentier, 1874), 213.

292 Philippine may have labored alongside them: On the mixed-gender labor force of Les Halles, see Sante, op. cit., 104.

293 one of the richest men in history: See for instance Ignotus (pseud.), "Les Rothschild," *Le Figaro* (January 30, 1878): 1; on his daily visits to the Bourse, see Muhlstein, *Baron James,* 86; on his intervention in the grain crisis and his deal with the tsar, see G. de Rothschild, op. cit., 73–74.

294 "This Rothschild embraced ostentation": Muhlstein, *Baron James,* 78.

294 the baron was famously generous: See Ignotus (pseud.), op. cit., 1; Septfontaines (pseud.), *L'Année mondaine 1889* (Paris: Firmin-Didot, 1890), 329; and Ferguson, op. cit., 19–20. On the philanthropic spirit of the Rothschild family generally, see HB, op. cit., 46–48; Ferguson, op. cit., 19–20, 233, and 273–80; and RM, "Saints d'Israël," *Têtes couronnées,* 98–106.

294 he resembled a bullfrog: EdG cited in Ferguson, op. cit., 111.

294 marrying beauty: Muhlstein, *Baron James,* 76–78.

294 "wingless angel": Heinrich Heine, "Die Engel," in *Neue Gedichte* (Hamburg: Hoffmann & Campe, 1852), 219. On Betty as the inspiration for this poem, see Virginia Cowles, *The Rothschilds: A Family of Fortune* (New York: Alfred A. Knopf, 1973), 72. On the Ingres portrait of Betty, see Tinterow and Conisbee, eds., op. cit., 414–25.

294 "The grand lords": Cited in Tinterow and Conisbee, eds., op. cit., 414. On Baron James's *mondain* ambitions, see also Nicault, op. cit., 9; and Muhlstein, *Baron James,* 81. Muhlstein notes that Baron James held four parties a week when in Paris.

294 the baron preferred to cull his mistresses: In the mid-1860s, when he was in his seventies, Baron James struck up a flirtation with the Comtesse Walewska, the beautiful wife of a minister of Napoléon III (and the mother of a future commanding officer of MP). But up until that point, he had been known for avoiding entanglements with well-bred Parisiennes. See Ferguson, op. cit., 109.

295 "that noble indifference": Cited in Muhlstein, *Baron James,* 78.

295 one of the most readily discernible differences: See Nicault, op. cit., 10; and Ferguson, op. cit., 58. On Baron James's pronunciation "à la Nucingen," see Ferguson, op. cit., 91.

297 Straus continued to follow in James Nathaniel's footsteps: ES wrote his law-school thesis on the distinction in the Napoleonic Code between movable and immovable property. See ES, *La Distinction des biens* (Paris: Jouaust, 1867). The work by Baron James Nathaniel de Rothschild, published at the same publishing house as ES's thesis, was *Des conventions qui modifient la composition de la communauté* (Paris: Jouaust, 1865).

297 "I will say only things that are true": ES, *Journal,* 5, in NAF 14386. Unlike most archives held by the Bibliothèque Nationale de France, this manuscript has not been assigned folio numbers for each page, so I have used page numbers instead.

297 "bohemian love of all the arts": Ibid., 19.

298   "the Unknown Man": Ibid. The bullying manner of "the Unknown Man" toward the young ES is consistent with descriptions of Baron James as a "domineering father" figure to his children, relatives, and underlings; see Ferguson, op. cit., 228–29.

299   "the brutality of the [students'] mores": Constant Coquelin, *Un Poète philosophe: Sully Prud-homme* (Paris: Paul Ollendorff, 1882), 9.

299   "terror and martyrdom": Sully Prudomme, "Première solitude," cited in Coquelin, op. cit., 10–11.

299   mortifying financial scandal: Baudouin, "Tribunal de commerce: Faillites," *Gazette des tribu-naux: journal de jurisprudence et de débats judiciaires* (January 24, 1857): 38; "Bankrupts," *Solic-itor's Journal & Reporter* (March 14, 1857): 281; and "Meetings for Proof of Debts," *Solicitor's Journal & Reporter* (December 25, 1858): 139. On Léopold Straus's activities after he fled Paris, see *Revue des vins et liqueurs et des produits alimentaires pour l'exportation* 12, no. 12 (1888): 24.

299   fraud in state supreme court: "Marx et al. v. Strauss [*sic*] et al.," *Southern Reporter* 9 (April 1891): 818–20.

300   "courtly and distinguished": ES, *Journal,* op. cit., 24.

300   "modern-day Aramis": Ibid., 19.

300   "slight frame": Ibid.

300   "Ah! I know of nothing": Ibid., 22.

301   a woman suing a pharmacist: The details appear in *Le Monde illustré* (March 20, 1880): 186; on Straus's remarkable record of wins in court, see "Maître Émile Straus," *Le Gaulois* (June 22, 1889): 3.

301   "Fritz from *The Grande-Duchesse de Gérolstein*": Albert Bataille, "Gazette des tribunaux," *Le Figaro,* March 13, 1884, 3. Another example of this kind of literary flourish came when ES represented an obscure poet, Louis Ratisbonne, in a lawsuit against a literary journal that had published someone else's bad poetry under his, Ratisbonne's, name. In his closing argument, ES quoted a funny line from a poem by Musset about plagiarism: "My glass may not be big, / but I am the one who drinks from it" (*"Mon verre n'est pas grand, / mais je bois dans mon verre"*); the preceding line in this couplet, which ES did not quote on the assumption that his audience would get the reference, is "I hate plagiarism as much as I hate death" (*"Je hais comme la mort l'état de plagiaire"*). This case was covered in an untitled news item in *Le Livre* 4 (1883): 140.

301   "the leading light of the Paris bar": Paul Hervieu cited in Alphonse France, "Courrier des théâtres," *Le Figaro* (May 26, 1905): 5.

302   the smartest and most industrious: On Alphonse de Rothschild's considerable work ethic, see HB, op. cit., 46–47; and Ferguson, op. cit., 228.

302   "expert in financial affairs": "Maître Émile Straus," op. cit., 3.

302   he began to buy art: An excellent source of information on ES's art collection is *Collection Émile Straus: tableaux modernes, aquarelles, pastels, dessins, sculptures, tableaux anciens, terre cuites, meubles et sièges anciens, tapisseries Aubusson* (Paris: Galerie Georges Petit, June 1–2, 1929); on ES's involvement with the Société des Auteurs, see Alphonse France, op. cit., 5; and Malcolm Daniel, *Edgar Degas, Photographer* (New York: Metropolitan Museum of Art, 1998), 62.

303   Nor had she forgiven Berthe and Marguerite: HB, op. cit., 46.

304   a correspondence with Pauline: Pauline von Metternich's letters to ES are archived as NAF 14383, folio 118/119 through folio 134/135.

305   "Straus has absolutely no nobility": Cited in DH, "Deux portraits de Mme Straus," op. cit., 177.

305   "black-hearted vanity" and social "calculation": Cited in ibid. FG noticed a similar change, observing that GS stopped inviting people just because she liked them and started inviting "people who were 'chic,' merely because they were 'chic.'" See FG, *Mon amitié,* 42.

305   "By 'Jockey-Club'": Racyzmow, op. cit., 23. A similar version of this statement appears in Louis de Beauchamp, *Marcel Proust et le Jockey-Club* (Paris: n.p., 1973), 17.

306   "It was the only way I could get rid of him": Cited in DH, "Deux portraits de Mme Straus," 179; and in FG, *L'Âge d'or,* 169. FG adds, "I don't know if perhaps she was exasperated by Straus and his indiscreet admiration [for her]."

306   "Straus reminded me": RD, *De Monsieur Thiers à Marcel Proust,* 117.

306   "proprietor": Cited in Bischoff, op. cit., 116.

306   "was as proud of his wife's salon": DH, "Deux portraits de Mme Straus," 175.

306   "ferocious" and "terrible" character: Cited in Bischoff, op. cit., 115–16.

307 "You should have seen him": Cited in CA, op. cit., 154–55.
307 "Straus's possessiveness": GL, *Souvenirs d'une belle époque* (Paris: Amiot Dumont, 1948), 156.
308 "one day, he threw her to the ground": EdG, *Journal,* entry of December 25, 1886.
308 of crushing disappointment: ES would go on to write a series of fictional sketches that were coded expressions of his disillusionment with GS and her *mondain* friends. Those stories, collectively titled "Tales of Woe" ("Contes chagrins," 1892), are listed under Works Consulted in this book.

CHAPTER ELEVEN: THE LUNATIC, THE LOVER, AND THE POET

310 Founded under Napoléon I: On Condorcet's origins in and as the Lycée Bonaparte (which became the Collège Bourbon during the Restoration and the July Monarchy), see Charles Lefeuve, *Histoire du Lycée Bonaparte (Collège Bourbon)* (Paris: Bureau des Anciennes Maisons de Paris sous Napoléon III, 1862). On the large Jewish contingent at the Lycée Condorcet, see DH, *Pays parisiens,* 102.
310 the high school of choice: Though technically a day school, Condorcet also opened its doors to students boarding at various respected Parisian *pensions.* As discussed in chapter 10, ES matriculated there while boarding at the Pension Bousquet-Basse. For an extensive, if nonetheless incomplete, list of the Lycée Bonaparte/Condorcet's leading alumni as of 1862, see Lefeuve, op. cit., 107–270. See also Taylor, op. cit., 9.
311 "made him the enemy": ED, *Testament d'un antisémite,* 86, n. 1.
311 Jeanne had met such luminaries: Carter, *Marcel Proust,* 6; and Benjamin Taylor, *Proust: The Search* (New Haven and London: Yale University Press, 2015). On the importance (and limitations) of the Crémieux Decree, see Maurice Samuels, *The Right to Difference: French Universalism and the Jews* (Chicago and London: University of Chicago Press, 2016), 74.
311 the disparities between the backgrounds: Évelyne Bloch-Dano, *Madame Proust: A Biography,* trans. Alice Kaplan (Chicago and London: University of Chicago Press, 2007); and Jean-Yves Tadié, *Marcel Proust,* trans. Euan Cameron (New York: Viking, 2000), 13–36; and Duplay, op. cit., 13.
312 As little boys: Tadié, *Marcel Proust,* 55 and 68; Taylor, op. cit., 9; and Racyzmow, *Le Paris retrouvé de Proust,* 50.
312 "with his big Oriental eyes": DH, *Pays parisiens,* 123; also cited, in a slightly different translation, in Edmund White, *Marcel Proust: A Life* (New York: Penguin, 1999), 28.
313 For more detail on Mme Proust's considerable culture and excellent education, see Bloch-Dano, *Madame Proust,* op. cit., 41–42 and 101–3. On the young MP's "sickly years" as "a time of extraordinary ferment," a "period of insatiable reading," see Taylor, op. cit., 11–12.
313 "unpleasant things as enemas": Cited in Duplay, op. cit., 23.
314 Racine was their favorite source: One of the earliest documented examples of the mother-son tic of quoting Racine to each other appears in MP, *Correspondance avec sa mère: 1887–1905,* ed. Philip Kolb (Paris: Plon, 1953), 23, where Jeanne Proust ends a letter to MP with a line from Racine's *Esther:* "How long the time seems to my impatience!" (*Que ce temps est long à mon impatience!*). Evidently MP even "chatted about his beloved Racine" when he was a little boy, playing with a group of neighborhood children in the Champs-Élysées; see Carter, *Marcel Proust,* 817, n. 36. I return to MP's relationship to Racine, and cite a number of important academic sources on the subject, later in this chapter.
314 "separation from Maman": Scholars have not reached a consensus as to when MP filled out this questionnaire for the first time. But Philip Kolb, the scholar who has probably done the most exhaustive work in reconstructing the chronology of MP's life, maintains that it was in 1886. For more on the Proust questionnaire, see Carter, *Marcel Proust,* 55, and (crossing my desk just before this book went to press) Évelyne Bloch-Dano, *Une jeunesse de Marcel Proust: une enquête sur le questionnaire* (Paris: Stock, 2017). MP's answers to his first questionnaire are reproduced in Maurois, *Quest for Proust,* 52–54. A facsimile of MP's subsequent version of the questionnaire, completed in 1892, is reproduced in Mireille Naturel, *Marcel Proust in Pictures and Documents,* ed. Suzy Mante-Proust and trans. Josephine Bacon (Zurich: Edition Olms, 2012), 118. For a witty discussion of MP's questionnaire answers about his mother, see Elisabeth Ladenson, "Someone like Maman," *London Review of Books* 30, no. 9 (May 8, 2008): 19–20.

314   As one of MP's best biographers, William Carter, puts it, "The adolescent Marcel . . . incarnated the wretched, insecure mama's boy." Carter, *Marcel Proust*, 75.

314   "us immature boys [to] tease him": RD, *Souvenirs*, 43. On MP's unpopularity with his fellow lycéens, see also JEB, *Mes modèles*, 103. On his popularity with their parents, see, again, RD: "The ones Marcel really impressed were people of a more respectable age [than his little classmates]: they were unanimous in marveling at the refinements of his politeness, of his graciousness, of his gentleness, of his goodness" (25). Similarly, Lucien Daudet recalls how impressive his adult family members found MP. "My grandmother declared 'that she had never met a young man who was as amiable and well-mannered as that little Monsieur Proust,'" and Lucien's mother described MP as "a charming boy, extremely well-read and exceptionally amiable." See Lucien Daudet, *Autour de soixante lettres de Marcel Proust* (Paris: Gallimard, 1929), 11–13.

314   On the boys taunting MP in the schoolyard, see RD, *Souvenirs*, 31.

314   lifelong interest in the power of names: See Roland Barthes, *Le Degré zéro de l'écriture* (Paris: Seuil, 1972), 133; and Benjamin, *Sur Proust*, 9–11.

314   "forceful and brutal": DH, "Autoportrait inédit," in Cahier 2 (January 1889); reproduced in MP, *Écrits de jeunesse 1887–1895*, ed. Anne Borrel (Paris: Institut Marcel Proust International, 1991), 30.

314   "There was something about him": DH, *Pays parisiens*, 122–23.

315   endowed them with unmatched glamour: MP wasn't alone in being dazzled by the cousins' famous patronymics. Maurice Sachs, who later became related to JB by marriage, describes a similar reaction in Sachs, *Le Sabbat*, 45.

315   "With your last names": Cited in FG, *L'Âge d'or*, 136.

315   "little literary gang": RD, *Souvenirs*, 56.

315   "everything that's worth reading": MP, *Écrits de jeunesse*, 94.

315   "Daniel cannot escape literature": Cited in RD, *Souvenirs*, 54. On the creation and the mission of *Mondays*, see MP, *Écrits de jeunesse*, 91–94. On the prestige of MP's prize for French composition, see RD, *Souvenirs*, 22.

316   Assigned a standard high-school essay topic: MP's essay on Racine versus Corneille appears in André Maurois, *A la recherche de Marcel Proust* (Paris: Hachette, 1949), 33–49. Biographer Jean-Yves Tadié writes that this essay presents "the first trace of [MP's] fondness for Racine, whom he considered a brother and someone very much like himself"; in another essay written while at Condorcet, MP "noted 'the influence of Racine on modern literature,' who [*sic*] affirms the power of love." See Tadié, op. cit., 65. MP also discusses the profound kinship between Baudelaire and Racine in CSB, 329–32 and 432–34. In an important study of the relationship between MP and Racine, Antoine Compagnon points out that MP's appreciation of "the sublime horror" of Racinian passion was not wholly original; at the fin de siècle, a number of prominent critics a generation above MP were advancing a similar interpretation—most notably Ferdinand Brunetière, who praised Racine as the progenitor of an entire "literature on the passions of love." See Antoine Compagnon, *Proust entre deux siècles* (Paris: Seuil, 1989), 95–102; as well as Ferdinand Brunetière, "La tragédie de Racine," *La Revue des deux mondes* 62 (1884): 213–24. Compagnon rightly notes that "the originality of Proust's Racine is a function of its constant association with Baudelaire" (101). I discuss this juxtaposition at some length, with further reference to Compagnon's work on the subject, later in this chapter. On MP's "extraordinary familiarity with Racine's texts," see also Anka Muhlstein, *Monsieur Proust's Library* (New York: Other Press, 2012), 94.

316   "ferocious realism": Antoine Compagnon, "Racine and the Moderns," *Theatrum Mundi: Studies in Honor of Ronald W. Tobin*, ed. Claire Carlin, Ronald W. Tobin, and Kathleen Wine (Charlottesville, VA: Rookwood Press, 2003), 241–49, 242.

316   "Perhaps as life goes on": DH, Carnet 1, 1886–1888, reprinted in MP, *Écrits de jeunesse*, 53.

316   his personal "impressions": See Theodore Child, "Literary Paris," *Harper's New Monthly Magazine* 35 (August 1892): 337–39; for MP's later critique of Lemaître, see MP, "Pendant le Carême," originally printed in *Le Mensuel* 5 (February 1891): 4–5 and reprinted in MP, *Écrits de jeunesse*, 174–75. MP's Lemaître pastiche for *Mondays* is reprinted in MP, *Écrits de jeunesse*, 101–2.

316   On Mallarmé's considerable influence on DH, see DH, *Pays parisiens*, 105–17; and Sébastien, op. cit., 53–56. On Mallarmé as the one who first got DH excited about Baudelaire, see DH, *Pays parisiens*, 117.

316   What intrigued Proust in Baudelaire's poetry: See again Compagnon, *Proust entre les deux*

siècles, 101–7. See also MP, "A propos de Baudelaire," in MP, CSB, 632. On the importance that both Baudelaire and Alfred de Vigny (also the author of the poem that would inspire MP's SG) hold for MP's literary treatment of homoeroticism, see Elisabeth Ladenson, *Proust's Lesbians* (Ithaca, NY: Cornell University Press, 2006), 18–22.

317   His father's attempt to "cure" this defect: William C. Carter, *Proust in Love* (New Haven and London: Yale University Press, 2006), 14; and Carter, *Marcel Proust,* 70.

317   "O King!": MP, untitled poem dated May 13, 1888; reproduced as "Premiers vers de Marcel Proust" in Borrel and J.-P. Halévy, eds., op. cit., 35–36.

318   biographer of Friedrich Nietzsche: On DH's work on Nietzsche, see especially Laurent, op. cit., 75–82, and 201–21. On DH's activity as a diarist, see Laurent, op. cit., 51–52.

318   "For Daniel Halévy": Borrel and J.-P. Halévy, eds., op. cit., 35. I disagree strongly with Carter's assertion that unlike MP's other texts from this period, this poem "contained no homoerotic longings"; see Carter, *Marcel Proust,* 66.

318   "Proust (Marcel), detention": Borrel and J.-P. Halévy, eds., op. cit., 36.

318   "Proust . . . has written the entire thing": MP, *Écrits de jeunesse,* 52.

318   "We admired Proust": Cited in Borrel and J.-P. Halévy, eds., 37–38.

319   Initially, Proust focused on Bizet: See Borrel and J.-P. Halévy, eds., 66.

319   In other respects: Huas, op. cit., 189. For JB's letters to GS, see, again, JB to GS in NAF 14383, folios 20–48. On the longing JB voices in these letters, and on GS's indifference to them (and to him), see Bischoff, op. cit., 103.

320   "My dear little Jacques": MP, *Écrits de jeunesse,* 41.

320   "My darling Jacques": MP to JB, in Kolb, ed., *Correspondance,* vol. 1, 101–2.

321   "just shrugged": Cited in MP, *Écrits de jeunesse,* 120.

321   "to stare at Jacques": Borrel and J.-P. Halévy, eds., op. cit., 40–41.

321   "In their lifetime": Ibid., 51.

322   "I'm going to explain": MP to DH, in Kolb, ed., op. cit., vol. 1, 121–22. For a discussion of how this letter anticipates MP's later literary treatment of homosexuality, see Carter, *Proust in Love,* 15–16.

322   "the hardest letter": Borrel and J.-P. Halévy, eds., op. cit., 43.

323   "that poor Proust": Ibid. On MP perhaps having "invented" the boarding school threat, see Tadié, op. cit., 69; on the "rupture" between MP and the cousins, see ibid., 69–71. On Jeanne Proust's concern about MP's "sensual affection" for JB, see Carter, *Marcel Proust,* 69.

323   "who used to be so nice to me": MP to RD, in Kolb, ed., op. cit., vol. 1, 105–6; also discussed in Tadié, op. cit., 71.

323   "I could have said": Cited in Landes-Ferrali, op. cit., 200. As Landes-Ferrali notes, this couplet had been on MP's mind since at least 1886, when he jokingly readapted its second line in a letter to his maternal grandmother to describe the difficulties he was having with a school paper: "And the words [I need], frightened, beneath me give way" (200). When taking the Proust questionnaire for the second time in 1892, MP still counted Phaedra among his "favorite heroines in fiction." See Naturel, op. cit., 118.

323   another of Racine's heroines, Bérénice: Bloch-Dano, *Une jeunesse de Marcel Proust,* op. cit., 203.

323   *"charming, young":* Racine, *Phaedra* (*Phèdre,* act 2, scene 5); cited by MP, but with the first two adjectives of the line reversed to *"jeune, charmant,"* in MP, *Chroniques* (Paris: Gallimard, 1927), 32. As Antoine Compagnon and Anka Muhlstein, among others, have pointed out, the narrator of RTP compares himself to Phaedra in a famous passage in CCS; see Compagnon, *Proust entre les deux siècles,* 84; and Muhlstein, *Monsieur Proust's Library,* 94–95.

324   "If I had a great sack": MP, "Pederasty," in *The Collected Poems of Marcel Proust,* ed. Harold Augenbraum (New York: Penguin, 2013), 4–5. This collection offers superb, facing-page versions of the original French poems and their translations into English. I have provided my own translation here, however, because the Penguin translation of "Pederasty" inexplicably cuts the name "Jacques" from the list of boys' names MP gives to the speaker's would-be paramours in this poem.

324   Proust follows Racine: Later in life, MP explicitly identified the performative "avowal" (confession of forbidden love) in *Phaedra* as one of that drama's most "inimitably animating" devices. See MP's untitled preface to PM, *Tendres stocks* (Paris: NRF, 1923), 31–32.

325   Daniel sent Proust an example of his own verse: DH's poem is reprinted in MP, *Écrits de jeunesse,* 157; on its Baudelairean influence, see Laurent, op. cit., 56–57. For MP's criticism of this poem, including the comments cited here, see MP, *Écrits de jeunesse,* 160. See also DH, *Pays parisiens,* 118–20.

325   "Homer, Plato": Borrel and J.-P. Halévy, eds., op. cit., 60–61.
325   relaunch its magazine as *The Lilac Review*: RD, who with MP, DH, and JB was a founding
      editor of this magazine and its successors, *The Green Review* (*La Revue verte*) and *The Banquet*
      (*Le Banquet*), states that *The Lilac Review* was founded in November 1888; see RD, *Souvenirs*,
      44.
326   "if [Proust] lost his vile side": Borrel and J.-P. Halévy, eds., op. cit., 44.
326   "The sky is a dark violet": MP, *Écrits de jeunesse*, 123.
326   "Seventeen years old": Ibid., 123–24.
327   "I am trying to remain pure": MP to DH, in Kolb, ed., vol. 1, 122.
327   "pure Spirit": Alfred de Vigny, "La Maison du berger," *Œuvres complètes*, vol. 1 (Paris: A.
      Lemerre, 1883). This poem would remain a touchstone for MP for many years to come; see for
      instance MP, letter dated first week of October 1898, in Kolb, ed., op. cit., vol. 3, 473.
328   "Yesterday evening": Borrel and J.-P. Halévy, eds., op. cit., 65–66.
328   a muse of a finer, more promising alloy: On the transference of MP's affection from JB and
      DH to GS, see Tadié, op. cit., 73–76. Later in this book, I discuss the relationship between
      MP and GS in greater detail. But the best condensed treatment of their relationship, in any
      biography, is the one given in White, op. cit., 30–31.

CHAPTER TWELVE: LAME DUCKS

329   "brigands and thieves, exploitative and corrupt": Cited in the *Journal officiel de la République
      française: débats parlementaires, Chambre des Députés*, session of December 23, 1889, 520.
329   "Republicans are dreadful and smell bad!": Cited in Cossé-Brissac, op. cit., 123.
329   He was a republican now: On HG's soi disant conversion to republicanism, see especially
      Legay, op. cit., 77–81. MP refers to this conversion to republicanism in a passage in JS where
      the Duc de Réveillon, a precursor of the Duc de Guermantes, fulminates about "scumbags"
      like HG who vote "with the republicans" and says, "I would like to have all of them shot!" MP,
      JS, 403.
332   "The word *equality*": EG, "*Égalité*," in AP(II)/101/149. EG signs this essay "Elsa" in her pidgin
      shorthand, an alter ego also referenced in chapter 14.
332   On the strictness of court etiquette, see X. Brahma (pseud. EG), *Âmes sociales* (Paris: G.
      Richard, 1897), 68–69. On LC's rapprochement with EG, see various documents in AP(II)/
      101/77. On the sight of Prince Ferdinand's bracelet-covered arm, see also PM, *Journal d'un
      attaché d'ambassade*, 438.
334   Bocher's real passions: Emmanuel Bocher, *Les Gravures françaises du XIXe siècle: Catalogue
      raisonné des estampes, pièces en couleur, au bistre et au lavis, de 1700 à 1800*, 2 vols. (Paris: D.
      Morgant, 1872–1880). On his secret studio in Montmartre, see Bocher to EG, undated letter
      (c. 1887–1888) in AP(II)/101/1. I should add here that Anne de Cossé-Brissac identifies the
      author of this letter as Édouard Bocher, Emmanuel's seventy-eight-year-old father. But it was
      Emmanuel who had the studio in Montmartre, and collected engravings, and corresponded
      secretly with EG for several years.
334   "The Woman Who Would Be Queen": EG, "La Femme-Reine," in AP(II)/101/151.
334   "Peasants in their smocks": HB, op. cit., 16.
335   "never allowed a certain word": Bocher quotes this claim back to EG in one of his undated
      letters, in AP(II)/101/1.
335   "despite all my suffering": Emmanuel Bocher (unsigned) to EG, letter dated Thursday,
      May 31, 1888, in AP(II)/101/1.
335   "DUPE!": In ibid.; also cited in Cossé-Brissac, op. cit., 121–22.
336   joining a far-left faction: On Boulanger's affiliation with Clemenceau, and the latter's support
      for "that unjust law of exile," see d'Uzès, op. cit., 54. On Boulanger's erratic relationship with
      the Duc d'Aumale, see Frederick Brown, *For the Soul of France: Culture Wars in the Age of
      Dreyfus* (New York: Anchor Books, 2010), 93–94. On the public's admiration for Boulanger on
      his glossy black steed, see Brown, op. cit., 95–103. On the Duchesse d'Uzès's decision to place
      her support behind him, see d'Uzès, op. cit., 55–56.
337   "the equipage of a real charlatan": HB, op. cit., 252. Boulanger's mass appeal inspired a similar
      insight in HB's political adversaries, such as republican deputy Jules Ferry. Writes historian
      Frederick Brown, "During troubled times, the 'popular imagination,' as Ferry put it, wanted
      its passions and fantasies embodied in one man." See Brown, op. cit., 103.
337   For a scholarly account of the improbable convergence between the "populist" Boulanger and

the élitist French nobility, see William D. Irvine, "French Royalists and Boulangism," *French Historical Studies* 15, no. 3 (Spring 1988): 395–406.

338   "General Bel-Ami": HB, op. cit., 281.

338   "I always thought the Duchesse d'Uzès": Félicité Greffulhe to EG, letter sent from La Rivière in September [no date], 1890, in AP(II)/101/7.

338   "Only an ambitious idiot": Félicité Greffulhe to HG, letter dated December 20, 1888, in AP(II)/101/7; also cited in Cossé-Brissac, op. cit., 120. I am indebted to Cossé-Brissac's excellent synopsis of the Boulangist affair as viewed by EG and HG, and of the latter's subsequent course of action.

338   "It is simply a matter": EG to HG, letter dated July 1888, in AP(I)/101/22; cited in Crossé-Brissac, op. cit., 121.

338   "I would like to see you": EG to HG, letter dated November 1889, AP(I)/101/22.

339   a cloak-and-dagger frisson: HB, op. cit., 299.

339   standing as his godmother: Corpechot, op. cit., 97.

339   "cleanse [him of]": Cited in ibid., 98.

340   "I will stop at nothing": Cited in HB, op. cit., 245.

340   Boulanger fled to Belgium: Brown, op. cit., 124 and 146.

340   "With that, the general's star": d'Uzès, op. cit., 60.

341   "There was no choice": HB, op. cit., 386.

341   "the France of yesterday": Cited in Cossé-Brissac, op. cit., 122.

342   "one that would place itself": *Le Nouvelliste de Lyon* (October 16, 1889): 1.

342   "being brand-new": Cited in *Journal officiel de la République française,* op. cit., session of December 23, 1889, 521.

342   "stop at nothing": HB, op. cit., 327–28.

342   60.5 percent of the vote: Legay, op. cit., 61.

342   "more of a man than the Comte Greffulhe": Cited in Le Père Gérôme, *Le Briard* (November 14, 1891): 1.

343   "my adversaries went so far": HG to EG, letter dated August 5, 1888, in AP(II)/101/32.

343   Knowing how unpopular: Legay, op. cit., 70–71.

343   "The large majority": Cited in Cossé-Brissac, op. cit., 120.

344   "Regrettable, regrettable": EG to HG, letter dated November 1889, in AP(I)/101/22; cited in Cossé-Brissac, op. cit., 124.

344   At the behest of radical deputy Camille Pelletan: See "Fin de session" and "Le Parlement: vérification des pouvoirs," *Le Petit Journal* (December 25, 1889): 1 and 3.

345   the deputies determined: On HG winning by a 52 percent versus a 60.5 percent margin, see, respectively, *Le Journal officiel de la République française,* session of December 14, 1889, 403; and Cossé-Brissac, op. cit., 120, n. 3.

345   "But he is too modest!": Cited in the *Annales de la Chambre des Députés: débats parlementaires* 29 (November 12–December 23, 1889): 653.

346   "He abducted himself": Cited in "Bulletin du jour: Chambre des Députés," *Le Journal des débats politiques et littéraires* (December 24, 1889): 1; Pas Perdus (pseud.), "La Chambre," *Le Figaro* (December 24, 1889): 1–2, 2; "Chambre des Députés: La Séance," op. cit.; "L'Election Greffulhe: Discours de M. Camille Pelletan," *La Justice* (December 25, 1889): 1–3, 2; and "Le Parlement: Vérification des pouvoirs," op. cit. *Le Gaulois* stands out for having declined to cover the HG scandal; Arthur Meyer may have done this as a favor to EG, just as he may have done a favor to LC by avoiding any mention of AC's trip around the world.

346   In the end, he was not forced out: The results of the vote on the matter of the invalidation of HG's election to the Chamber are reported in "Chambre des Députés: La Séance," *Le Temps* (December 25, 1889): 3. Despite HG's victory, he continued to draw criticism, for instance as "a new republican who evidently can offer his merchandise to any and all buyers"; see "Opportuno-réactionnaires," *La Lanterne* (December 28, 1889): 1.

346   "I can't take it anymore": Cited in Hillerin, op. cit., 180.

346   "Élections: A Moral Poem": Élaine Greffulhe, "Les Élections: poésie morale," in AP(II)/101/35.

346   Henry pitied himself so much: See HG to EG, letter dated November 15, 1889, in AP(II)/101/32.

CHAPTER THIRTEEN: KISSES NEVER GIVEN

350   *les drags:* The best account of this *journée des drags* appears in *Le Figaro* (May 11, 1887), 1; even this article made note of the fact that the Baronne de Noirmont rode with EG in HG's stage-

coach. On the *drags,* also known as *les mails* (for "mail coaches"), see also Élisabeth Hausser, *Paris au jour le jour: 1900–1919, les évenenements vus par la presse* (Paris: Minuit, 1968), 455; and GLP, *Trente ans de dîners en ville,* 76–77.

352 unveiling of her newest portrait: Carolus-Duran's portrait of EG has since been lost, but reviewers identified it as one of the stand-out works of the exhibition. See for instance William Sharp, "The Royal Academy and the Salon," *The National and English Review* 9 (March–August 1887): 513–24, 514 and 518.

352 Henry was none too pleased: See EG to HG, undated letter on writing paper from the Hotel Sacher in Vienna, in AP(I)/101/22.

352 her own haut-luxe artists' colony: See Sylvia Kahan, *In Search of New Scales: Prince Edmond de Polignac, Octatonic Explorer* (Rochester, NY: University of Rochester Press, 2009), 59; and AGG, op. cit., 139.

352 "The minutes die": EG, in AP(II)/101/150.

353 "an Italian from the Renaissance": LG, *Mémoires,* vol. 2, 37.

353 "How sweet it is": Éléonore [EG] to Gérard [GBB], letter marked "4 janvier 1885, 8 heures," in AP(II)/101/151.

354 "I find that anonymous stares": EG, in AP(II)/101/152.

354 "the banal, ready-made language": EG, "4ᵉ volume: Le Revoir," op. cit.

354 "What do I care for the day?": Vigny, "La Maison du berger," cited by EG in a letter marked "Trois décembre 84," in AP(II)/101/151.

354 she now found herself bristling: On EG's growing distaste for *mondain* society, see a fragment in AP(II)/101/150; the opening line reads: "Je n'aime plus tant le monde . . ."

355 "I'm starting to get jealous": Éléonore [EG] to Gérard [GBB], in AP(II)/101/150. On this typewritten page of the novel, EG has crossed off "Gérard" and written "Gaston" over it. She does not, however, appear to have made this name change anywhere else in the manuscript.

355 "[is] much more intimate": Entry in an unmarked red notebook in GBB's hand, in AP(II)/101/150 (hereafter "Journal de Gérard").

355 "her pores terrified me": Ibid.

356 a sheaf of impassioned letters: EG saved these letters in an "Hommages et appréciations" file in AP(II)/101/1.

356 striking similarities: Jane Hanna Pease, *Romance Novels, Romantic Novelist: Francis Marion Crawford* (Bloomington, IN: AuthorHouse, 2011), 72. A French translation of *Saracinesca* was published serially in *Le Temps* in the spring of 1890 (with the first installment appearing on March 12) and came out in book form a year later; see *La Nouvelle Revue* (June 1891): 893.

356 "non-Roman": F. Marion Crawford, *Saracinesca* (New York: Macmillan, 1893 [1887]), 8.

356 "distinct character": Ibid., 11.

356 "Don Giovanni was not married": Ibid., 17.

356 "very beautiful": Ibid., 18.

356 "the portrait [was] immoderately flattering": GBB to EG, letter dated December 28, 1887, in AP(II)/101/53.

357 seventeen-year-old arrestingly handsome slave boy: *Les Missions catholiques* (November 5, 1880): 529; and EG, in AP(II)/101/53. GBB's commitment to Catholicism seems to have been driven more by familial pride than by faith. A cleric with whom he was friendly recalled that he had a "saying: 'I believe in nothing, but on my deathbed I shall ask for a priest; it runs in my blood.'" See Albert Houtin, *The Life of a Priest: My Own Experience* (London: Watts & Co., 1927), 227.

357 "When I am with you": EG, entry dated November 24, 1887, in AP(II)/101/150.

358 a keen partisan of *japonisme*: On *japonisme* in fin-de-siècle Paris, see Burnand, op. cit., 142; and Junji Suzuki, "Le Jardinier japonais de Robert de Montesquiou," *Cahiers Edmond et Jules de Goncourt* 18 (2011), 103–4. RM himself wrote about his (and Goncourt's) *japonisme* in RM, "Japonais d'Europe," *Le Gaulois* (March 9, 1897): 1.

358 On Polignac's frustration with EG's *mondanité*, see Kahan, op. cit., 55.

358 "Your heart is the cool oasis": EG, *Tua Res Agitur*, in AP(II)/101/150. All subsequent citations from *Tua Res Agitur* come from this same source; edits of this work and paratextual documents relating to its composition are also archived in this source.

359 "If your neighbor's wall is on fire": The original Latin reads "*Nam tua res agitur, paries cum proximus ardet*" and appears in Horace, *Epistles*, I, xiii (l.84).

359 "Prince Jean Borghèse has just left Rome": "Échos de l'étranger," *Le Gaulois* (August 29, 1887): 1. This news also ran in "Petites annonces," *La Croix* (August 30, 1887): 4.

360 "delicate, eccentric, and effeminate": Cited in Constant, op. cit., 36.

360   "If [the Bulgarians]": HB, op. cit., 83. For detailed contemporary commentary on "the Bulgarian question," see Sir Edward Hertslet and Edward Cecil Hertslet, eds., *British and Foreign State Papers: 1886–1887,* vol. 78 (London: William Ridgway, 1894): 908–18; for EG's musings on the subject, see AP(II)/101/197.

361   "The greatest disorder of the mind": EG, in AP(II)/101/149.

361   disorders of the mind: A few years later, EG returns to the idea that her romantic fantasies are a kind of madness, writing to an unidentified male addressee: "These illusions I have [of you] populate my life—oh, let me rock these chimeras in my arms the way a madwoman cradles a doll whom she is convinced is the baby she lost—who would dare to cry out to her that the doll is made out of wood?" EG note on Bois-Boudran letterhead, dated March 6, 1892, in AP(II)/101/150; the opening lines of this letter are: "*Oh je t'en prie révèle moi à moi-même . . .*"

361   "To You, the Unreal One": EG, *Tua Res Agitur.* Many years later, EG sent this modified copy of *Tua Res Agitur* to EdG, asking him whether he thought she should publish it (beyond the "three to five" existing copies she had had privately printed in Nangis), and if so, whether he would write a preface. See EdG, *Journal,* entry of July 5, 1894. On his delicate attempt to discourage her from publishing this work, see EdG, *Journal,* entry of August 8, 1894; he commented in his diary, "I fear my response will not satisfy the comtesse's craving for publicity."

362   haunted by its original proprietor: L. de Vogüé, *Souvenirs,* op. cit., n.p.

362   "Everybody *else* is moving": EG, undated note in AP(II)/101/149.

363   even wrote some poetry: RM, *Les Perles rouges; les paroles diaprées* (Paris: G. Richard, 1910), xx, 82–83.

363   "A sincere heart": EG in AP(II)/101/152.

363   the mothers had brokered this union: Brusquet (pseud.), "Le Régime du sabre," *Le Triboulet* (May 23, 1880): 5; and A. de Gramont, *L'Ami du prince,* 399, n. 2. Alexandre Seillière, incidentally, was not Mme de Sagan's mentally unstable brother; that was Raymond Seillière, whom Mme de Galliffet apparently tried to get the Princesse de Sagan to institutionalize. On this scandal, see "France," *Papers Relating to the Foreign Relations,* op. cit., 303–55.

364   "suspicions [he had] already had": GBB to EG, unsigned note dated April 1884, page 21 of a red notebook (pages numbered by hand) in AP(II)/101/151. On Mme Hochon's hospital for underprivileged girls stricken with tuberculosis, see Maxime Du Camp, *La Charité privée à Paris* (Paris: Hachette, 1892), 257.

364   "Why did you let me believe you": EG, another typeset page marked "Journal de Blanche," in AP(II)/101/152. This entry begins: "*Il y a des choses qu'il vaut mieux ne jamais écrire.*"

364   "supreme allure vanquishes": EG, unnumbered manuscript page in AP(II)/101/152.

365   Verteuil was a fortified château: Marquis de Amodio, "Le Château de Verteuil," an electronic guidebook available at andre.j.balout.free.fr/Charente(16)_pdf/verteuil_chateau003.pdf. On Aymard de La Rochefoucauld (whose name appears in some early historical records as Aymard de La Roche), see *Documents historiques sur l'Angoumois* (Angoulême: n.p., 1864): 255; and *Bulletins et mémoires de la Société Archéologique et Historique de la Charente,* vol. 6 (Angoulême: L. Coquemard, 1897): 123.

365   "Now I understand": EG, "Journal de Blanche," in AP(II)/101/152.

365   "Why must *others* be the ones": EG, AP(II)/101/[152].

366   "One does not cry *like a servant!*": HG to EG, undated letter, in AP(II)/101/32.

366   "The worst sorrows": LL to EG, retyped letter fragment dated January 9, 1884, in AP(II)/101/151.

366   "From now on": EG, in AP(II)/101/152.

366   "If I were given the chance": EG, fragment of a typeset page that has been cut down to an approximately one-inch by three-inch rectangle, in ibid. She outlines her plan to be buried in a white dress and veil in another page in AP(II)/101/152; the note begins: "*Tout préparé pour mourir dans un tiroir une chemise sa plus belle un châle en tissue blanc . . .*" A few years later, in 1892, EG changes this plan and decides she wants to be buried dressed in black. On RM's "Le Coucher de la morte," see EG to EdG, undated letter in AP(II)/101/151.

367   major additions at Bois-Boudran: See Hillerin, op. cit., 253–54; and JEB, *La Pêche aux souvenirs,* 204.

367   "to dazzle": Cited in Hillerin, 253.

368   "Never must a lady": HG to EG, undated postcard in AP(II)/101/32.

368   "I am a logical man": HG to EG, undated letter in ibid.

368   "You can smell the *yid* from miles away!" HG to EG, letter dated July 3, 1897, in AP(II)/101/32.

369   "Unquestionably": Cited in Hillerin, op. cit., 254.

369   "Here is 50 million francs": EG, undated note in AP(II)/101/149.

369   "too much like *them*": Ibid., 296.

370   "I never forget my origin": Élaine Greffulhe to EG, letter sent from Royat-les-Bains, in AP(II)/101/37.
370   "I don't look like Papa anymore!": Élaine Greffulhe to EG, undated letter in AP(II)/101/34.
370   "*much* straighter": Élaine to EG, letter dated July 21, 1896, in AP(II)/101/37. In this same letter, Élaine refers to having also undergone electrical treatments to improve her posture.
371   "All About Maman": This work appears in Élaine Greffulhe, *Le Livre d'ambre par Élaine Greffulhe de 5 à 7 ans,* preface by Robert de Montesquiou (Nangis; L. Ratel, 1892 [1887–1889]), n.p. RM expresses his views on Élaine's literary talent in idem; in his preface to Élaine Greffulhe, Duchesse de Guiche, *Les Roses tristes* (Paris: Presses de l'Imprimerie Nationale, 1923 [1906]), vii–viii; and in a letter to EG, dated November 1890 ("will undoubtedly grow up to be a hefty huntress"), in AP(II)/101/150.
371   "A woman who is young and beautiful": EG, "Un appel sans écho," in a collection of hand-written essays entitled *Essais d'esquisse sur vingt motifs,* p. 12, in AP(II)/101/152. EG develops this somewhat incoherent notion of a "divine song" in her poem cycle *Tua Res Agitur,* discussed later in this chapter: *"Il faudrait douce et tendre la passion d'une main à la hauteur de la mienne—tandis qu'allongée sans voir—Presque sans penser—sans parler—une mélodie divine traduirait cette extase"* and *"J'entendis de si douces choses en écoutant mon cœur que je me taisais."* See EG, *Tua Res Agitur,* in AP(II)/101/150.
371   the myth of Narcissus: On EG as Narcissus, see, again, Larmandie, op. cit., 218.
373   Élisabeth knew this was a ruse: EG, in AP(II)/101/1; and HB, op. cit., 384.
373   "for nothing is as comical": RM, *Les Quarante Bergères: portraits satiriques en vers inédits* (Paris: Librairie de France, 1925), 54. This collection was published posthumously, but RM had circulated many of the satirical ditties it contained several decades earlier.
373   claimed to abhor the womanizing dimwits: Kahan, op. cit., 56.
374   a £500,000 deficit: *The Spectator* (12 August 1876): 2–3.
374   most expensive dinner party in history: Mike Davis, *Late Victorian Holocausts: El Niño Famines and the Making of the Third World* (New York: Verso, 2001), chapter 1, n.p. A digital version of this chapter is excerpted at www.nytimes.com/books/first/d/davis-victorian.html.
374   "India's Nero": "G. Aberigh-Mackay's *21 Days in India,*" in Sujit Bose, ed., *Essays on Anglo-Indian Literature* (New Delhi: Northern Book Center, 2004): 41–49; and Edward Hower, *Shadows and Elephants* (Wellfleet: Leapfrog Press, 2002), 91.
375   a tour of the neurology clinic: On the tour of Charcot's facility and the interaction with the hypnotized patient, complete with quotations from LL ("present at a conflagration"), see "T.P. in His Anecdotage," *T.P.'s Weekly* (December 7, 1906): 723.
376   "she only dines out": Cited in LG, *Souvenirs,* op. cit., 148.
376   the British Embassy occupied: Located at 39, rue du Faubourg-Saint-Honoré, the building that houses the British Embassy was originally known as the hôtel de Charost, after the French duke who had it built in the 1720s. It became the Parisian residence of Pauline Bonaparte in 1803, after she married Don Camillo Borghese (GBB's great-uncle) at her brother Napoléon's behest. Following Napoléon's defeat in 1814, Pauline sold the building to the Duke of Wellington, who donated it to the British crown. For a condensed history of the hôtel Borghèse, see Anne Martin-Fugier, *La Vie élégante, ou la formation de Tout-Paris* (Paris: Fayard, 1993), 149–50. For more detail, see Jean-Dominique Ronfort and Jean-Mérée Ronfort, *À l'ombre de Pauline: La Residence de l'ambassadeur de Grande-Bretagne à Paris* (Paris: Éditions de Centre de Recherches Historiques).
376   "wisely pretend[ed] to treat it as a joke": Mary Lutyens, *The Lyttons in India: An Account of Lord Lytton's Viceroyalty 1876–1880* (London: John Murray, 1979), 10. On Lady Lytton's fondness for Worth couture, see Diana de Marly, *Worth: Father of Haute Couture* (London: Elm Tree Books, 1980), 162–63.
377   "All I know": EG, in AP(II)/101/149.
377   a fellow ardent spirit: On EG's appreciation of LL's "spirit," see JEB to EG, undated letter in AP(II)/101/67.
377   "frequent fits of melancholy": John Ferguson Nisbet, *The Insanity of Genius* (New York: Scribner's, 1912 [1891]), 129. Nisbet also discusses the instances of mental illness in other members of LL's family (128).
377   "the blue devils": LL in Lady Betty Balfour, ed., *Personal and Literary Letters of Robert Lytton, First Earl of Lytton* (hereafter Balfour, ed.), vol. 2 (London: Longmans, Green, & Co., 1906).
377   "an almost intolerable hysterical depression": Cited in Lutyens, op. cit., 5.
377   "three-quarters insane": Cited in HB, op. cit., 330.
377   his heavy opium use: "The Late Lord Lytton an Opium-Smoker," *Friend of China* 16, no. 4

(October 1896): 109; "Owen Meredith," *Illustrated American* (December 12, 1891): 165. Neither of these articles was published under a byline, and, for the passage quoted in this chapter, Nellie Melba (pseud.), *Melodies and Memories* (New York and Cambridge: Cambridge University Press, 2011 [1925]), 90.

377 "who always smell[ed] of ether": Cited in Chaleyssin, op. cit., 31.

377 commended to the earl: JEB to EG, letter dated December 25, 1885, in AP(II)101/67.

378 "a voluptuous pasha": JEB, *Mes modèles*, 114.

378 scandalous marriage: Rosina Bulwer-Lytton, Baroness Lytton, *A Blighted Life* (London: Bloomsbury, 1994), 219–29. For further commentary on the perceived homosexual bond between, and the "Byronic" affectations of, Disraeli and Edward George Bulwer-Lytton, see Andrew Elfenbein, *Byron and the Victorians* (Cambridge: Cambridge University Press, 1995), 206–29; Andrew Elfenbein, "The Shady Side of the Sword: Bulwer-Lytton, Disraeli, and Byron's Homosexuality," in *Byron,* ed. Jane Stabler (London and New York: Routledge, 2014), 110–22. On Disraeli's "ambiguous sexuality," see William Kuhn, *The Politics of Pleasure: A Portait of Benjamin Disraeli* (London: Free Press, 2006), 5, 12, and 125. Adam Gopnik's review of Kuhn's book, "The Life of the Party," *New Yorker* (July 3, 2006), contains a memorable characterization of "Dizzy's" flamboyant image: "He did what would-be Byronic heroes without the means to swim the Hellespont or fight for Greece have always done: he became a dandy, [dressing] like a cross between Cecil Beaton and a member of the Village People; on holiday in Malta, he dressed in full pirate regalia, complete with pistols and daggers. Later, . . . he wore, according to an affectionate observer, 'a scarlet waistcoat, long lace ruffles, . . . white gloves, with several brilliant rings outside them.' His gold chains, worn many at a time, were a wonder, his lacquered curls an event."

378 RM to EG, letter postmarked Dieppe, September (?), 1890, in AP(II)/101/150.

378 "the Vice Empress": Sir Salar Jung, "An Indian Mayor of the Palace," *Today* 1 (July 1883): 342–52, 351; and Jehu Junior (pseud. Thomas Gibson Bowles), "Statesman: Lord Lytton," *Vanity Fair* 219 (March 18, 1876): 223.

378 "nothing vexes a beautiful woman": EG, "La Preuve," in AP(II)/101/150. This essay is marked in RM's hand with a single word: "*GOOD.*"

379 "Owen Meredith": On LL's literary career, see Louise Dalq, "Lord Lytton: philosophe et poète," *Le Figaro: supplément littéraire* (November 12, 1887): 1–2; on his father's attempt to dissuade him from said career, see Leslie George Mitchell, *Bulwer-Lytton: The Rise and Fall of a Victorian Man of Letters* (London: Bloomsbury/A&C Black, 2003), 83–84. On "Owen Tudor" as the basis for "Owen Meredith," see Harlan, op. cit., 67. The surname "Meredith" derives from this same, not altogether sturdy branch of the Bulwer-Lytton family tree: it was a "tradition," Harlan writes, to affirm "that a certain Ann Meredith married into the Bulwer-Lytton family, and was either a sister or a niece of Owen Tudor" (67). On the publication of *Glenaveril* in French, see *Le Monde illustré* (June 2, 1888): 1.

379 about the Wandering Jew: Balfour, ed., op. cit., vol. 2, 364. On LL's English adaptation of Halévy's *La Juive,* entitled simply *The Play* (1887), see E. Neill Raymond, *Victorian Viceroy: The Life of Robert, the First Earl of Lytton* (London and New York: Regency, 1980), 265–66. It may bear noting that LL's great-grandfather, Richard Warburton Lytton, was a scholar of ancient languages and composed a drama in Hebrew. This work was never performed—according to its author, this was because he "could not find Jews sufficiently versed in Hebrew to act in it." See Nisbet, op. cit., 128.

379 "an accomplished, pretty little lady": Balfour, ed., op. cit., vol. 2, 387.

380 "Nothing overcomes us": Alexandre Dumas *père, Quinze jours au Sinaï* (Paris: Charles Gosselin, 1841), 289.

380 "Alas irony irony": EG, "Journal de Blanche," in AP(II)/101/152; this passage appears on a cut-out piece of a page proof that begins "*Quel mépris angoisseux s'empare de celui qui ne voit pas aimé . . .*"; the quote itself begins "*Hélas ironie ironie . . .*"

380 *"I think you know why":* Lord Lytton to EG, in AP(II)/101/95; on EG's supposition that if LL tried to kiss her, he would bite hard enough to draw blood, see her diary entry dated October 27, 1889, in AP(II)/101/150.

380 "The true friend loves you": EG, "L'Ami vrai," in AP(II)/101/150. Hillerin aptly observes that "The True Friend" "is the anti-portrait of Henry" (235).

381 *Odi et amo:* On EG's studies of Greek and Roman literature, including Catullus, see her lesson notebooks in AP(II)/101/1.

381 "She was always hoping to learn": EG, unnumbered page proof marked "Journal de Marie-Alice," in AP(II)/101/152.

381   "What an indignity": EG in AP(II)/101/150; also cited in Cossé-Brissac, op. cit., 93.

382   to Élisabeth, it felt like another world: For EG's notes on her visits to Moreau's studio, see "Visite chez Gustave Moreau," along with several untitled pages of fragmentary notes, in AP/101/151 and 152. On the décor of Moreau's studio and house, see also Geneviève Lacambre, "De la maison au musée" and "Des œuvres pour le musée," in *La Maison-musée de Gustave Moreau* ed. Marie-Cécile Forest (Paris: Somogy, 2014), 25–68.

382   "the symbolic deity": Huysmans, op. cit., 145.

383   "the Eternal Feminine": Gustave Moreau, *L'Assembleur de rêves: Écrits complets de Gustave Moreau,* ed. Pierre-Louis Matthieu (Paris: Fata Morgana, 1984), 78. With Flaubert and Wilde, Moreau and Huysmans were the main instigators of fin-de-siècle culture's fascination with Salome. See Toni Bentley, *Sisters of Salome* (New Haven and London: Yale University Press, 2002), 22–25.

384   "They cut my grandmother's head off": MB, *Égalité,* 48.

384   fund-raising performance of George Handel's *Messiah*: Kahan, op. cit., 67.

384   "Violent impressions": EG, page marked "Visite chez Gustave Moreau," in AP(II)/101/151.

384   "Pain is necessary": EG, untitled note in AP(II)/101/152.

384   "One must withdraw": Ibid.

385   see her as a Salome figure: OM, for example, compares EG to Salome in "Saturnalia": "Now she has it in her hands. It is / a dead man's head. And how her burning eyes / gloat on its horror! How her red lips kiss / those white ones! / Yes, 'tis she. I recognize / Herodias"—Herodias being Salome's mother's name, sometimes used for the daughter as well. "Saturnalia" appears in a volume, *Marah* (1892), which after LL's death EG learned had been written for her; I discuss that volume at greater length in chapter 20. See OM, "Saturnalia," *Marah* (London: Longmans, Green, 1892), 150.

385   "I feel like a ball of flame": EG in AP(II)/101/152. On the reproduction of Leonardo's *John the Baptist* in Moreau's vestibule, see RM's preface to *Exposition Gustave Moreau,* 13.

385   "One roars": EG, "Journal de Blanche," in AP(II)/101/152.

385   "Give me strength": Ibid.

385   "two long lace arms": EG, in AP(II)/101/152.

385   "When I was at the Madeleine": EG, diary entry dated April 22, 1889, in AP(II)/101/150.

CHAPTER FOURTEEN: FODDER FOR SONNETS

386   "She makes a man dissatisfied": GPR, *Bonheur manqué,* first published in *La Revue illustrée* 81 (May 15, 1889): 313–23. Unless otherwise noted, citations refer to the poems in this version of *Happiness Manqué,* as they hew most closely to the handwritten originals EG received from GPR, initially in church and later by post. She saved most of the original poems and letters in her archive, in AP(II)/101/1. The chronology of these poems, corroborated by postmarks in the case of the ones the author sent by mail, is substantially altered in the book version of *Happiness Manqué.*

386   Porto-Riche had had a lot of women: Published sources for biographical information on GPR in this chapter, from his sexual conquests to his early literary success to his ten-year writer's block, include Edmond Sée, *Porto-Riche* (Paris: Firmin-Didot, 1932); AdF, *Mon Paris et ses Parisiens: le Faubourg Saint-Honoré;* A. Antoine, *Mes souvenirs sur le Théâtre-Libre* (Paris: Fayard, 1921); Brugmans, op. cit.; Lavedan, "Un raffiné: Georges de Porto-Riche"; Charles Monselet, "Théâtres," in *Le Monde illustré* (July 5, 1873): 11; HR, *Nos rencontres.*

386   Along with those specified below, archival sources for this chapter include (and please note that inconsistencies in the folio numbering for GPR's archives are original to the files in the Bibliothèque Nationale de France): GPR's and Hervieu's unsigned letters to EG, archived as "Lettres d'un soupirant inconnu," in AP(II)/101/1; GPR's other letters to EG, in AP(II)/101/107; GPR, NAF 24951, folios 16, 30, 76, 80, and 88; GPR, fragments and drafts of *Happiness Manqué* in NAF 24951, folios 40–70; GS to GPR, in NAF 24944, folios 260/261, 262/263, and 494/495; LC to GPR, NAF 24954–24955 and NAF 24980; EG to GPR, in NAF 24971, folios 185–91; and GS to GPR in NAF 24971, folios 262/263 and 358/359.

386   rereading Petrarch: GPR, NAF 24951, folio 156.

387   Plays that would make her proud: On GPR's renewed determination to write works of genius, see GPR, in NAF 24951, folios 5 and 79.

387   the Librairie Achille: This bookstore was something of a celebrity haunt at the fin de siècle. Jules Claretie recorded that visitors chez Achille could expect to run across prominent states-

men and famous writers (like himself). Claretie once overheard an elegant old lady asking the sales staff at Achille to point her toward "the newest titles of a *serious* nature"—she turned out to be the Empress Eugénie, the widow of the deposed emperor Napoléon III. See Jules Claretie, *La Vie à Paris: 1898* (Paris: Charpentier, 1899), 9.

388   questions about Mme Greffulhe's private life: GPR, in NAF 24951, folio 24; and GPR to LC in NAF 24980, folio 17/18. AF confirms LC's fib about attending EG's wedding in AF, "Le Salon de l'Europe," 476.

388   she had a soft heart: LC to GPR, NAF 24955, folio 228; and GPR to LC, NAF 24974, folio 31.

389   Under Napoléon I: *Le Guide pittoresque de l'étranger dans Paris et ses environs* (Paris: Jules Renouard, 1843), 92; *Description du fronton de l'église de la Madeleine* (Paris: Gauthier, 1834), 6; and Lebrun (pseud.), *Manuel complet du voyageur dans Paris* (Paris: Roret, 1843), 294.

390   Porto-Riche felt confident: GPR, in NAF 24951, folio 44.

390   "an uptight, ambitious": LD, *La Melancholia* (Paris: Grasset, 1928), 205.

390   "Hervieu seems to base": HR, *Les Cahiers,* 468.

390   "I'm afraid": Ibid., 492.

391   "elegantly discreet": *Les Hommes du jour: annales politiques, sociales, littéraires et artistiques* (1911): n.p. (See the untitled theater review that begins, "*Des gens, sans doute bien intentionnés, ne cessent de nous proposer, depuis dix ans, pour modèle parfait, le théâtre de M. Paul Hervieu,*").

391   "a statue of Friendship": MP, *Letters to a Friend,* preface by GL, trans. Alexander and Elizabeth Henderson (London: Falcon Press, 1949), 22.

391   revival of Richard Wagner's *Lohengrin*: Albert Gier, "Marcel Proust und Richard Wagner: Zeittypisches und Einmaliges in einer Beziehung zwischen Literatur und Musik," in Hunkeler, ed., op. cit., 142; and Prod'homme and Dandelot, op. cit., 213. Prod'homme and Dandelot note that with this production, *Lohengrin* dethroned *Faust* as *mondain* Paris's favorite opera.

392   "I am a commoner": The original reads: *Je suis comme Ruy-Blas, amoureux de la reine, / Mais la reine ne m'aime pas.* Ruy-Blas is the hero of an 1838 Victor Hugo drama by that name, an indentured commoner besotted with the Queen of Spain, who against all odds falls in love with him in return. Perhaps GPR knew that Hugo was one of EG's favorite poets; perhaps not. Either way, the reference seemed to me too cumbersome to include in my translation of the couplet.

393   presently in rehearsals: A three-act French adaptation of Shakespeare's *Merchant of Venice,* by Edmond Haraucourt, with music by Gabriel Fauré, opened at the Odéon National Theater in December 1889. See Edmond Haraucourt, *Shylock ou le marchand de Venise* (Paris: n.p., 1889); and *Le Monde illustré* (December 28, 1889): 402. In fact, unbeknownst to GPR, Fauré wrote to EG in October 1889 to inform her that a visit to her "beautiful gardens" had inspired him to compose one particularly "subtle musical phrase—a Venetian clair de lune—for *Shylock.*" EG's patronage of Fauré had begun, through RM's offices, a year earlier. The letter about the *Shylock* clair de lune is cited in Jean-Michel Nectoux, *Gabriel Fauré: A Musical Life,* trans. Roger Nichols (Cambridge and London: Cambridge University Press, 2004), 145.

393   "I am a Jew": William Shakespeare, *The Merchant of Venice,* act 3, scene 1.

393   Worried that Hervieu had double-crossed him: See GPR's notes on the "traitorous villainy" of his friend "P" in the matter of "Mme G[reffulhe] and G[eorges] and P[aul]," in NAF 24979, folio 17; see also GPR's comments about "Lost Friendship, Rupture," in NAF 24951, folio 70. GPR also complained to HR about Hervieu's "malevolent machinations"; see HR, *Nos rencontres,* 124. GPR's suspicions were well founded; as discussed in chapter 21, Hervieu began writing to EG on his own account in the spring of 1888; see AP(II)/101/1.

394   "spending my days in rancor and shame": GPR, in NAF 24951, folio 66.

395   "My lover looks like you": This is one of the poems GPR left out of the manuscript of *Bonheur manqué* when he submitted it to *La Revue illustrée.* This poem does, however, appear in the book version; see GPR, *Bonheur manqué* (Paris: Ollendorff, 1908 [1889]), 26.

396   "So she cares only for princely lovers": GPR, in NAF 24951, folio 16.

396   *théâtre d'amour:* RF, "Théâtre d'amour: Georges de Porto-Riche," *La Presse* (July 13, 1898): 4.

397   "Now *here* is a husband": Jules Lemaître, "*La Chance de Françoise* de Georges de Porto-Riche," *La Revue illustrée* (January 1, 1889): 1.

397   "just a little idiot": GPR, *La Chance de Françoise* (1888), in *Théâtre d'amour,* 15.

397   "It would be so much easier": Ibid., 41. On GPR's own "chance," see NAF 24974, folio 88.

398   "Ah! Don't be so quick": GPR, in NAF 24951, folio 56.

399   "I would ruin her reputation": GPR explores this idea as well in an unpublished text called

"Poème," in NAF 24951, folio 91: "He loves her, and wants to behave like an honest man; but when he sees that he is looked down upon, he becomes rabble (*canaille*) once again. And how better to show that he is rabble than by calumny? He will say that this woman became his mistress, and people will believe him . . . because he is a libertine whom women find irresistible."

400 "Even in bed": GPR, *Théâtre de l'amour,* 344.

400 declining to name her: In his unpublished notes for *Happiness Manqué,* GPR discusses his decision not to identify EG as the book's dedicatee; see NAF 24951, folio 60. On the mystery surrounding GPR's muse's identity, see also Marc Gérard, "Bonheur manqué," in *Le Gaulois* (July 14, 1889): 2.

400 "If you think": GPR dropped this epigraph when he had the poems republished as a book.

400 "I am going to a land": GPR, NAF 24951, folio 56.

400 a series of nosy letters: GS to GPR, letter dated July 17, 1889, NAF 24516, folio 47; GS to GPR, letter dated August 18, 1889, NAF 24944, folio 262/263; and GS to GPR, postcard dated August 2 (?), 1889, NAF 24944, folio 494/495.

400 "brave the 'zone of terror' ": EG to GPR, in NAF 24971, folio 185.

401 "I am an earthworm in love with a star": The reference here is to Hugo's tragic verse drama *Ruy Blas,* in which, as noted earlier, a commoner falls in love with a queen. In addition to quoting this play in his manuscript notes, GPR explicitly compares himself to the hero of *Ruy Blas* in one of the poems in *Happiness Manqué.*

401 "So there she is": GPR in NAF 24951, folio 30.

402 "I spit upon them all!": GPR, diary entry marked "Friday August 9, [1889]," in NAF 24951, folio 70.

402 "A married lady": GPR, "Nouvelle" (notes), in NAF 24951, folio 26.

402 "Gérard jealous?": GPR, "Trop honnête" (notes), in NAF 24951, unnumbered folio.

CHAPTER FIFTEEN: BIRDS OF PARADISE

404 "deadly *mondain* obsession": RD, *Souvenirs,* 57.

404 "incomparable dilettante": FG cited in RD, ibid.

404 "one of those frightful intellectual 'apprentices' ": JEB, *Mes modèles,* 108.

404 he reported to an infantry regiment: Sources on MP's military service include Carter, *Marcel Proust,* 103–5; AG, *Les Clés de Proust,* 115; Tadié, op. cit., 58; Taylor, op. cit., 19–23; and Marie Miguet, "Le Séjour à Doncières dans *Le Côté de Guermantes:* Textes et avant-textes," *in Vers une sémiotique différentielle,* ed. Anne Chovin and François Migeot (Besançon: Presses Universitaires Franc-comtoises, 1999), 27–50. I am thankful to Philippe d'Ornano for kindly sharing his knowledge about the connections between the Bonapartes and his ancestors the Walewskis.

405 "To the provisional recruit Marcel Proust": Cited in Chovin and Migeot, op. cit., 30.

405 *temps perdu:* MP to Dr. Adrien Proust, letter dated September 28 (?) 1893, in Kolb, ed., vol. 1, 236.

405 to Anglophone masters: On MP's English literary interests at this time, see Daniel Karlin, *Proust's English* (Oxford: Oxford University Press, 2007), 27.

406 "what seemed like Marcel's wastefulness": Carter, *Marcel Proust,* 160.

406 the last of their literary magazines: RD, *Souvenirs,* 79–133; FG, *L'Âge d'or,* 148–52; Carter, *Marcel Proust,* 131–32; and Painter, op. cit., vol. 1, 114–15. On Jean Reiter producing *The Banquet* on the printing presses of the newspaper where he worked (*Le Temps*), see FG, *Mon amitié,* 59–60; and Raczymow, *Le Paris retrouvé de Proust,* 137. On the little literary gang selling subscriptions of *The Banquet* to GS's salon guests, see RD, "Madame Straus et Marcel Proust," 16.

406 Paul Bourget had also made a stir: "Paul Bourget in New York," *Pittsburgh Press,* August 21, 1893, 2; on GPR's success, see HR, *Nos rencontres,* 122; on Paul Hervieu's success, see Octave Mirbeau, *Combats littéraires* (Paris: L'Âge d'homme, 2006), 82.

407 The GDWs found him "charming": For LC's reports on the GDWs' newfound appreciation for GPR, see NAF 24955, folios 208, 211, 245, and 264.

407 a writer's life and his work: On the young MP's insistence that an author's life is inseparable from (not, as he would claim from CSB onward, radically incommensurable with) his art, see especially JS, which opens with the disclaimer "Can this book be called a novel? It is less and perhaps much more than that: it is the very essence of my life, gathered without any embellishment. . . . I didn't write this book; I harvested it." See MP, JS, 183. MP returns to this

notion throughout JS, as when he writes, "Our life is not absolutely separate from our work. All the scenes I am recounting to you are scenes I have lived" (490), or when, having posited the writer's life "circumstances, happy or terrible" as the "materials" of art, MP concludes, "For whatever kind of life we lead, our life is always the alphabet in which we learn to read" (477)— and to write about—the world around us. The reader may notice the similarity between this conception of the art-life symbiosis and the one GBB sought to explore with EG, transposing "a bit of divine lived reality" into their joint literary project.

407   "little nothings about elegance": Jean Lorrain (pseud. Duval), untitled review reproduced in PJ, 294–296, 295. Touching upon the same problem, FG writes that although PJ contains "some delightful pages," it has "too many princesses, too many melancholy beauties, too much elegance"; see FG, *Mon amitié*, 65. FG detects a similar quality in MP's review of Ganderax's "The Little Shoes," which FG describes as "fairly *mondain* in tone—*mondanité* was his cute little sin at the time and would remain one of his chief inspirations," in ibid., 53.

407   his review of "The Little Shoes": Quotations from this text are taken from MP, "'Les Petits Souliers,' par M. Louis Ganderax," *Le Banquet* 1 (March 1892). Ganderax's story itself, "Les Petits Souliers: conte de Noël," ran in *La Revue des deux mondes* 109 (January 1, 1892).

408   "a land without a history": DH, *Pays parisiens*, 148.

408   the Église de Saint-Augustin: David Jordan, *Transforming Paris: The Life and Labors of the Baron Haussmann* (New York: Simon & Schuster, 1995), 194–95.

409   "the most elegant parish in Paris": X. (pseud.), "Choses et autres," *La Vie parisienne* (November 13, 1875): 642.

410   "family trees with roots plunging deep": MP, "A une snob," in PJ, 89. This text originally appeared in *La Revue blanche* 26 (December 1893): 392–93.

411   "see [a] mighty lord": MP, *Days of Reading*, trans. by John Sturrock (London and New York: Penguin Books/Great Ideas, 2008), 104.

411   "Odon, Ghislain, Nivelon": Ibid., 103.

411   "poetic pleasure": MP, CG, 825. This last line appears in an extended discussion of the resonances of noble names, a discussion in which MP specifies, "My curiosity about history was weak in comparison to my aesthetic pleasure." See also MP, CSB, 248: "The Guermantes, for me, were their name. . . . The name Guermantes amalgamated [such] wonders as Geneviève de Brabant, [a] tapestry depicting Charles VIII, [a] stained-glass window representing Charles the Bad. . . . When I was invited to mingle with these legendary creatures, beings from a magic lantern, a stained-glass window, a tapestry [out of] the ninth century, this proud name Guermantes seem[ed] to come to life, to recognize me, to call out to me."

411   Sutton specialized in livery: "Le Livre d'or du *Figaro*," *Le Figaro* (December 26, 1877): 2.

411   these footmen played a dual function: de Pange, op. cit., 23.

412   "intellectual labor": L. de Vogüé, op. cit., n.p.

412   "the liveried valets": La Bruyère, op. cit., 132.

412   "When the Princesse de Beauvais": MP, *Manuscrits autographes: Soixante-deux cahiers de brouillons, etc.*, NAF 16652, cahier 12, folios 124–29.

413   a "law of the Monde": In RTP, MP refers to this same "law" or "force" as *le génie des Guermantes*. Meaning both the genius and the genie of the Guermantes, this phrase connotes a mystical blend of human invention and supernatural magic. MP discusses a similar version of this phenomenon in JS, in a digression about aristocrats who "graciously devalue their nobility in their speech, manner, and artistic . . . interests," while "ingeniously" asserting their rank by more subtle means, such as "writing paper adorned with little ducal crowns; hosts of footmen constantly calling them, seemingly without their knowing or even noticing it, 'monsieur le duc,' 'madame la duchesse'; portraits of their ancestors; castles bearing their names; and silver engraved with their family crests." See MP, JS, 448.

413   "a delicate and noble Louis XIII face": MP, *L'Indifférent*, PJ, 263. Although he did not publish it until 1896, MP wrote this work in the summer of 1893; see ibid., 348; and Kolb, ed., op. cit., vol. 1, 133.

413   "the maxim of flirtation": MP, *L'Indifférent*, 257. MP's account of Madeleine's widowhood also reads like a reference to GS: "In her four years of widowhood, [society's most] remarkable men had been coming to see her several times a day"; "she knew by the unanimity of their opinions that she was one of the most alluring women in Paris, that her reputation for intelligence [and] wit . . . added prestige to her beauty" (261).

413   "consumed with a crazy need"; Ibid., 264.

413   "He loves only women covered in mud": Ibid., 266.

413   "Lepré is too honorable": Ibid.

414   "revolutionize" his perspective: MP, SG, 11.
414   his real voyage of discovery would begin: GL, op. cit., 145.

CHAPTER SIXTEEN: THE PICTURE OF MME BIZET

415   he had to educate himself: Information and quotations from MP's contemporaries about
       his *mondain* apprenticeship in GS's salon are taken from JEB, *Mes modèles* and *La Pêche aux
       Souvenirs;* RD, *Mon amitié* and "Madame Straus & Marcel Proust"; AGG, op. cit.; FG, *L'Âge
       d'or;* and GL, op. cit.

415   a particularly important role model: For an astute meditation on GM's influence on MP, see
       Patrick Mimouni, "La Vocation talmudique de Marcel Proust: I. Les Lois causales," in *La
       Règle du jeu* 35 (September 2007): 82–114, 83–85. Tadié also speaks briefly of GM's influence
       on MP's earliest writings in op. cit., 57.

416   "Society people ought to realize": Cited in PM, *Vie de Guy de Maupassant,* 144.

416   "literary, to my mind": MP, CG, 786. Interestingly, this quotation comes just a few pages after
       the narrator observes that Mme de Guermantes's "favorite writers [are] Mérimée, Meilhac,
       and Halévy" (ibid., 285)—a remark that evokes GS with its reference not just to Meilhac (and
       through him, indirectly, to his writing partner, LH), but to Mérimée, upon whose novella
       Meilhac and LH based the libretto for GB's *Carmen.* Earlier in the same chapter, the Duchesse
       de Guermantes holds forth about GB's *The Girl from Arles;* see MP, CG, 776.

417   "In the monde": GM, *Fort comme la mort,* in *Romans de Guy de Maupassant,* ed. Louis Fores-
       tier (Paris: Gallimard/Pléiade, 1987), 877.

418   "Mme Émile Straus never looked more alluring": LG, *Mémoires,* vol. 1, 198.

418   "his masterpiece": Bischoff, op. cit., 123.

418   a setting of exquisite beauty: Precise information about the furnishings, artworks, and bibe-
       lots in GS's salon comes from the auction catalogue *Collection Émile Straus.* All the objects
       described in this chapter were sold at that auction, with one exception: the Delaunay portrait
       of Geneviève Halévy Bizet. The Strauses' heirs donated that painting to the Louvre; it is now
       held in the Musée d'Orsay.

418   "I am *encumbered* by Boudins": Cited in Bischoff, op. cit., 118.

419   a tragic mismatch: On GS's description of love as two beasts doomed never to walk in syn-
       chrony, see EdG, *Journal,* entry of March 28, 1887.

419   "the frightful Copenhagens": Bischoff, op. cit., 119; and Racyzmow, *Le Paris retrouvé de
       Proust,* 50.

420   "Say, monsieur": Cited in JEB, *Mes modèles,* 113.

420   the canvas had drawn accolades: Contemporary reviews of Delaunay's portrait of GS cited
       here are A. Surmay, "Exposition de peinture: Salon de 1878," *Musée des familles: lectures du
       soir* 45 (September 1878): 258; and "Le Salon des Beaux-Arts de 1878," *Gazette des beaux-arts*
       (July 1878): 58. RM's poem about the painting is RM, "Dédicace à Mme Émile Straus," in *Les
       Paroles diaprées* (Paris: Sansot, 1910). On Degas's dislike of the Delaunay portrait, see DH, *My
       Friend Degas,* 37. The other *fidèles'* admiring comments about it are cited in Balard, ed., op.
       cit., 116–17.

420   "much as one makes the sign of the cross": GM, *Fort comme la mort,* 878.

420   "naturally any books": GL, op. cit., 154.

421   "a book of very bad poems": MP, in Kolb, ed., op. cit., vol. 3, 44.

421   "the hands of all the women": M. Gérard, "Bonheur manqué," 2.

421   "was with a poet or a musician": MP, CG, 505. In this passage, MP ascribes the duchesse's
       unwillingness to talk with artists "only about the food they were about to eat or the card game
       they were about to play" to the irreverent "Meilhac and Halévy wit, which was hers." See MP,
       CG, 506.

421   "How could it be": Cited by GL in op. cit., 155.

421   "had something to do with the seduction of her natural gifts": Ibid.

421   her weakness for Veronal: EdG, *Journal,* entry of June 18, 1894; Bischoff, op. cit., 132; Florence
       Callu, "Madame Straus," in Tadié, ed., *Le Cercle de Marcel Proust,* 203 and 207; and Sachs,
       Le Sabbat, 16. On GS's tics, "like flashes of lightning," etc., see, again, AF, *Le Bal du Pré-
       Catelan,* 158.

422   "not to wear *quite that much* Peau d'Espagne": Delaunay to GS, letter from 1890 in NAF
       14383, folio 82/83.

422   "outrageously perfumed": DH, Carnet 3, May 30, 1890; cited in Balard, ed., op. cit., n. 118.

422   "not a lady of the monde": EdG, *Journal,* entry of April 15, 1889. On GS's nude lace stockings, see ibid., entries of February 22, 1891 and April 16, 1886.

422   "Those sorts of wiles": Cited in Bischoff, op. cit., 141.

423   "the lovely perfumed lady": Cited in Bischoff, op. cit., 261.

423   "She is a famous composer's widow": RM, "Ginevra," *Les Quarante Bergères,* n.p.

423   "became agitated": Cited in Bischoff, op. cit., 122.

423   nothing drove Straus crazier: EdG, *Journal,* entry of December 25, 1886.

424   "rare and delicious knack": LG, *Mémoires,* vol. 2, 201.

424   she and Alphonse inherited: HB, op. cit., 120; the figure for the midlevel banker's annual salary, given in 1880 French francs, comes from PM, raised in connection with GM's financial success. See PM, *Vie de Guy de Maupassant* (Paris: Pygmalion/Gérard Watelet, 1998 [1942]), 120–21.

424   a sum equal to fifteen thousand times: In Paris in 1880, a ladies' maid earned an average annual salary of approximately 360 francs and a midlevel bank employee at Rothschild Frères earned an average annual salary of 2,000 francs. Carassus, op. cit., 117.

424   "If Baronne Laurie walked in": LG, *Mémoires,* vol. 2, 201.

425   "art of taking a passionate interest": Ibid., 202.

425   "a *woman* to the core": GL, op. cit., 154.

426   "reheated": GL, op. cit.; see also JEB, *Mes modèles,* 114; and HR, *Les Cahiers,* 382.

426   "It was her misfortune": Meyer, *Ce que je peux dire,* op. cit., 89–90.

426   "In the *grand monde*": GM, *Fort comme la mort,* 877.

426   "the Blob": Bischoff, op. cit., 240. In French, GS's nickname for Meilhac was "la Tourte," literally a dense, round loaf of bread; idiomatically a "lug" or a "blob."

426   "the Blob of the Académie Française": Letter from Paul Hervieu to GS dated September 11, 1892, cited in Bischoff, op. cit., 241. On Meilhac being too fat to tie his own shoes, see LG, *Mémoires,* vol. 2, 201.

427   "Meilhac rented a little motorboat": Balard, ed., op. cit., 191.

427   "become a hiker": Ibid., 181. The best account of Meilhac's masochistic devotion to GS appears in Bischoff, op. cit., "Meilhac: La 'Tourte' Amoureuse": 240–45.

427   "everything Lemaître calls my 'talent' ": Meilhac to GS, letter dated June 30, 1890, on letterhead marked "Casino de Vittel" and cited in Bischoff, op. cit., 242.

428   "There I was": Balard, ed., op. cit., 155.

428   a "curious object": Ibid., 175.

428   "four unforgettable and almost *unrecountable* hours": Ibid., 182.

428   " 'Last night' ": EdG, *Journal,* entry of February 18, 1895.

429   his second novel, *Bel-Ami*: Information about the popular, critical, and financial success of *Bel-Ami* is taken from PM, *Vie de Guy de Maupassant,* 120–21.

429   "Bel-Ami, c'est moi": Cited in ibid., 121; and in GPR, *Sous mes yeux* (Abbeville: F. Payart, 1927), 46.

429   "hundreds of little Maupassants": Cited in Dr. Zacharie Lacassagne, *La Folie de Maupassant* (Toulouse: Gimet-Pisseau, 1907), 46. On GM and the Eiffel Tower, see PM, *Vie de Guy de Maupassant,* 139–41; and Jacob T. Harskamp, *The Anatomy of Despondency* (Leiden: Brill, 2011), 282.

429   "God has proclaimed": Cited in Alain-Claude Gicquel, *Maupassant: tel un météore* (Paris: Castor Astral, 1993), 242.

429   the brink of full-blown madness: Sherard, op. cit., 55.

430   "never lost her taste for *outlaw* artists": FG, *L'Âge d'or,* 125.

430   "With the compliments of Bel-Ami himself": Cited in PM, *Vie de Guy de Maupassant,* 121.

430   "avenging their oppression": Cited in ibid., 138.

430   "the only book": EdG, *Journal,* entry of January 1, 1892; also cited in Édouard Maynial, *Guy de Maupassant: la vie et l'œuvre* (Paris: Société du Mercure de France, 1906), 200.

430   "One fine day": LD, *Devant la douleur* (Paris: Nouvelle Librairie Nationale, 1915), 116–17.

430   "we also felt sad for him": Ibid.

430   at least two risqué propositions: EdG claims that GM "tried to have her [GS] before she married Straus, [and] continued to pursue her after that." See EdG, *Journal,* entry of July 5, 1890.

432   she and Maupassant continued to correspond: All citations from GM's letters to GS can be found on the easily searchable digitized edition of his correspondence at www.maupassant .free.fr (hereafter GM, *Correspondance*). The letters are numbered in chronological order; the ones cited and referenced in this chapter are 417, 418, 514–20, 526, 529, 531, 535, 536, 588, 614, and 615. As mentioned in this chapter, none of GS's letters to GM survive. Perhaps not

incidentally, in the final scene of *Strong as Death,* the heroine, supposedly based on GS, burns all her correspondence with the hero, supposedly based on GM, to prevent her husband or anyone else from finding out about their affair. We know that GS and LH destroyed much of her correspondence with GB; who destroyed her correspondence with GM is unknown. It is plausible, though, that GM himself was a willing participant; writing to an unidentified female correspondent in 1890, at the peak of his romance with GS, he wrote that he dreaded the prospect of "posterity being curious about my private life. . . . The idea that people might talk about Her and Me, that men might judge her and women make comments, that journalists might talk about us, that my respectful tenderness might be stripped (forgive the dreadful expression but it fits) of its very underwear . . . makes me violently angry and profoundly sad" (letter 645).

434   "turn a blind eye": Reinach to GS, in NAF 14383, folio 148/149.

435   *Strong as Death:* On the critical reception of *Strong as Death,* see Louis Forestier's "Notice" to GM, *Fort comme la mort,* 1560–61. On the belief that the novel was about a real-life romance between GM and GS, see JEB, *La Pêche aux souvenirs,* 173; EdG, *Journal,* entry of January 28, 1895.

436   And to readers in the know: Sherard, op. cit., 59–63.

436   The heroine of *Strong as Death*: I have significantly condensed my summary and analysis of GM's book in order to reduce the overall length of my own, though I plan to make my unabridged reading of the former available either online or in print. In the meantime, I refer the interested reader to a cogent synopsis of *Strong as Death* in Anka Mulhstein, *The Pen and the Brush: How Passion for Art Shaped Nineteenth-Century French Novels,* trans. Adriana Hunter (New York: Other Press, 2017), 146–51.

436   "a mysterious fusion of artists and *mondains*": GM, *Fort comme la mort,* 869.

436   "a pretty woman": Ibid., 848.

437   "Love is as strong as death": Song of Solomon 8:6.

438   "it was Annette who now emerged from the canvas": Ibid., 987–88.

438   "the intelligence of the [men and women] of the monde": Ibid., 875–76.

438   set at a gala performance: Ibid., 1000. This scene recalls a real fundraiser performance that took place at the Opéra-Comique in the autumn of 1887, to celebrate the five hundredth performance of *Faust* in that venue, with GS's and LC's friend Jean de Reszké in the title role. Several details about the tenor who attracts Annette seem to point to Reszké, notably his scandalous love life.

438   "overly made-up mannequin": Ibid., 1003.

438   "It seemed to him that he himself was becoming a Faust": Ibid., 1001. The reader may notice an echo here of the line from MP I quoted in the Overture: "It seemed to me that I myself had become the subject of the book I was reading." Indeed, much more remains to be said about the influence of *Strong as Death* on RTP. As I intend to show in another context, the connection between the two books resides not only in the critique of *mondanité,* but in the elaboration of a model of "involuntary memory" wherein a sensory experience affectively (and effectively) brings a forgotten moment back to life. In RTP, of course, the narrator is transported back into his childhood by the taste of a madeleine dipped in tea. In *Strong as Death,* Bertin has a similar experience while strolling with Annette in the parc Monceau. In the sound of the girl's voice he suddenly hears that of her mother when Any and Bertin first fell in love years earlier, and "the mystery of that resuscitated voice" (900) brings "his old life bubbling up to the surface" (899), flooding him "with recollections [he thought had] disappeared, plunged into oblivion. . . . It was as if a hand were stirring up the sediment of his memory" (899).

438   "their love itself was turning to ash": Ibid., 1027.

438   "impassive, unfeeling": Ibid., 1028.

CHAPTER SEVENTEEN: ELEGANCE FOR BEGINNERS

440   "You are unique": MP to GS, letter postmarked November 13, 1892, in MP, *Lettres à Madame et Monsieur Émile Straus,* 6.

440   reminded his friend Jacques Blanche of Cherubino: JEB, *Mes modèles,* 113. Gustave Schlumberger had a somewhat different opinion, characterizing the young man on the footstool as "bizarre." See Gustave Schlumberger, *Mes souvenirs: 1844–1928,* vol. 1 (Paris: Plon, 1934), 304.

441   "You are not sufficiently persuaded": MP to GS, letter from "1892", in MP, *Lettres à Madame et Monsieur Émile Straus,* 11; MP refers to his "Good Friday" anniversary with GS on p. 4.

441   "Having not wanted to give you a headache": MP to GS, undated letter in ibid., 5.

441   "The words by which": MP, JS, 667.

441   "one is only *nice*": Ibid.

441   "You are very wrong": MP to GS, letter from the summer of 1892, in R. Proust, ed., op. cit., 7.

442   a series of practical jokes: LD, *Devant la douleur,* 118. LD's narrative does not identify Lulia and Marie as the masterminds of these pranks; that information appears in Bischoff, op. cit., 231.

442   "such people defile everything": Cited in EdG, op. cit., entry of December 11, 1889.

442   "just want a place at the table": Paul Allain, "En passant: La Place à table," *Le Radical* (November 9, 1922): 1.

442   worried about his Jewishness: LD, *Fantômes et vivants* (Paris: Nouvelle Librairie Nationale, 1914), 293.

442   "make-believe passion": Taylor, op. cit., 26. As Taylor so incisively remarks, MP "never in his life wanted women. He only wanted to want them" (27).

442   investment in matters of form: MP did, however, posit this investment as the bedrock of *mondanité,* writing while still in his twenties, "It is a commonplace among people of the monde that the monde judges everything based on appearances." See MP, JS, 628.

443   "Swankiness": Bruant, ed., op. cit., 180–82.

443   "A woman does not attempt": MP, "Études I. Snobs," *Le Banquet* 3 (May 1892); reprinted as "Snobs" in MP, PJ, 86–88;

443   "tastes, beliefs": MP, JS, 677.

443   sensational news story: HR notes, for example, that in the spring of 1891, GS and her faithful spoke obsessively about an adulterous young Frenchwoman in North Africa who had poisoned her husband and then killed herself. See HR, *Les Cahiers,* 256. For news coverage of this scandal, see Amédée Blondeau, "L'Empoisonneuse d'Aïn-Fezza: Mme Weiss," *Le Rappel* (May 30, 1890): 1; Émile Massard, "Jeanne Weiss," *La Presse* (May 30, 1891): 1; Notre Envoyé Spécial (pseud.), "L'Empoisonneuse d'Aïn-Fezza" (May 31, 1891): 1–2; and "Le Suicide de Mme Weiss," *L'Avenir de Bel-Abbès* (June 3, 1891): 1–2.

443   "pretty things in [a lady's] apartment": MP, JS, 678.

443   "an agreeable folly": Cited in Alain de Botton, *How Proust Can Change Your Life* (New York: Pantheon, 1997), 108.

444   "A youth stands a better chance": MP, in Kolb, ed., vol. 3, 247.

444   "facility with words": MP, JS, 677–78.

444   "How pretentious": Ibid., 678.

444   "confusedly": Ibid., 679.

444   "intelligence had inspired": Ibid., 258. See also ibid., 1068, n. 3. This note contains a short passage cut from the manuscript of JS, where MP explicitly compares Mme Marmet to Jean's "little gang" of high school tormentors and writes that they are similar not just in their cruelty, but in the intellect with which he had wrongly credited them.

444   "the banal, ready-made": EG, "Le Revoir," op. cit. A few years later, in JS, MP would make a similar complaint about the restrictions the rote forms of *mondanité* place on emotional, psychological, and creative freedom: "The automatic responses known as 'good manners' destroy all spontaneity, all independent exercise of thought, all possibility of poetry"; see MP, JS, 525.

444   "You are very well known in Monaco": Cited in Bischoff, op. cit., 127. For further discussion of MP's analysis of meaningless *mondain* niceties, see Gilles Deleuze, *Proust et les signes* (Paris: PUF, 1964), 10–11.

444   "formula . . . a box of petits fours": MP, CG, 833.

444   "Discerning the fictive character": MP, SG, 62. This sense of what MP elsewhere calls the "honorific function" (CG, 834) of conversational niceties is not limited to the fin-de-siècle noblesse. Most English speakers today come sooner or later to the realization that "how are you?" is, like Prince Albert's all-purpose compliment to strangers, a pure formula. Seldom does the person asking this question expect an earnest answer, much less wish for one.

445   "For ye have the poor always with you": Matthew 26:11. D'Haussonville also cites this line in at least one of his books. See Paul-Gabriel Othenin de Cléron, Comte d'Haussonville, *Socialisme et charité* (Paris: Calmann-Lévy, 1895), 381.

445   *Misereor super turbam:* This is a line from a twelfth-century antiphonary from the Monastery of Saint-Maur-des-Fossés; in the manuscripts department of the Bibliothèque Nationale, siglum F-Pnm lat.12044. Also cited in Vicomte Eugène-Melchior de Vogüé, *Le Roman russe* (Paris: Nourrit-Plon, 1888), xxiii.

445 affirm the rightness of a world order: In his wittiest take on this phenomenon, MP describes a fictional crowned head who has been raised to believe that "divine Providence wanted you to be superior by birth and also by wealth. . . . In His goodness God willed it that you should own almost all the shares of the Suez Canal and three times as many shares as . . . Rothschild in [the] Royal Dutch Petroleum Company." See MP, CG, 720.

445 Vandérem said "swanky": Lucien Descaves, "Opinions et souvenirs: Fernand Vandérem," *Le Journal* (February 6, 1938): 3; Robert de Traz, "Chroniques," *La Revue hebdomadaire*, 2, no. 7 (February 12, 1938); 229–35.

445 "Why does [M. Ganderax] write that way?": MP to GS, in MP, *Correspondance avec Mme Straus,* 109. Later in the same letter, MP explains that formulaic language does not make for great literature because "only that which bears the mark of our taste, our uncertainty, our desire, our weakness can be beautiful" (112). Indeed, "the problem with clichés" in expressing or describing reality, is that they only "graz[e] its surface": Botton, op. cit., 88.

446 "physical type of the satanic lorgnette merchant": EdG, *Journal,* entry of June 6, 1885.

446 "Jews are all lorgnette merchants": Gustave Flaubert, *Dictionnaire des idées reçues, suivi des "Mémoires d'un fou"* (Paris: Nouvel Office d'Édition, 1964), 84. EdG, I should add, did not always temper his anti-Semitic views by making jokes; he described himself straightforwardly as a "theoretical enemy of the Jewish race"; see EdG, *Journal,* entry of June 24, 1891.

447 aristocratic names were not pronounced: On French noble names that are not pronounced as they are spelled, see also Cécile David-Weill, *The Suitors,* trans. Linda Coverdale (New York: Other Press, 2012), 101. In this hilarious study of twenty-first-century *mondanité,* the excursus on name pronunciations is prompted by the fact that the surname of the heroine, Laure Ettinguer, is pronounced "Ettingre"—just as EG's and HG's friends the Hottinguers pronounced their name "Ottingre."

447 "This manner of pronouncing words": MP, LP, 543.

447 "says things nobody in the monde would ever say": MP, in NAF 18324, folio 83/84.

447 "Does not the mere fact": Ibid., 86. In this same notebook, MP discusses other erroneous "word choices" and "forms of names" that expose the self-styled *mondain* as a fraud; e.g., "calling the Duc . . . de Doudeauville 'the Duc de La Rochefoucauld Doudeauville' " and "not eliding the 'e' and the 'ey' in Cast'llane and Tall'rand, etc.": ibid., 84. In SG, he returns to the pronunciation of d'Uzès when he notes that, for a middle-class woman who marries into a noble family, one of the chief pleasures of the marriage is the fact that it entitles her to speak of "my aunt d'Uzai," pronouncing it in a "way that had stupefied her" at first. MP, SG, 213.

448 black rather than white tie: Larmandie, op. cit., 91.

448 In a recently discovered film clip: Some scholars believe this depicts MP leaving the church right after the bridal party; available online at http://www.france24.com/en/20170215-france-literature-marcel-proust-footage-wedding-clip. The wedding took place in November 1904, and MP's trip to AGG's château a month or so earlier.

449 "I can still see Marcel": JEB, *Mes modèles,* 112–13.

449 "Skye terrier": Ibid., 111.

449 "apprentice dandy": Ibid., 113. On MP's newfound attentiveness to the details of *mondain* style, see also Sisley Huddleston, *Paris Salons, Cafés, Studios* (New York: Blue Ribbon Press, 1928), 277: "It was necessary for him, he said, to know how a Prince [*sic*], the arbiter elegantarium, wore his monocle," and he regarded LC's hat collection as "a museum that lived and moved."

449 "camellia period": Cited in CA, op. cit., 145.

450 the sturdy rotundity: Anonymous, *Biographie de Mme Demidoff: la Princesse Mathilde* (London and Brussels, 1870), 31. The analogy the anonymous author draws here is between the "flabby-shouldered" Princesse Mathilde "and a big fat peasant woman from the Beauce."

450 "Without the French Revolution": Cited in MP, "Un Salon historique: le Salon de S.A.I. Princesse Mathilde," in *Le Salon de Mme de . . .* (Paris: L'Herne, 2009), 15–35, 16.

450 "Princesse Mathilde encourages": HR, *Les Cahiers,* 278. GPR also complains about Princesse Mathilde's hauteur in NAF 24951, folio 44.

450 "the curious happenstance": MP, CG, 732–33.

451 "my first highness": In OJFF, the narrator refers to the fictitious Princesse de Luxembourg, supposedly modeled on the Princesse de Sagan, as "my first Highness," then qualifies the statement: "I say she was my first, because Princesse Mathilde"—whom the narrator had encountered earlier—"didn't act like a Highness in all her ways." The joke here is that both the Princesse de Luxembourg and Princesse Mathilde believe they are being "simple"—

unassuming, down-to-earth—toward lesser mortals, when really they are being incredibly condescending. The scene that showcases the Princesse de Luxembourg's inadvertent obnoxiousness toward the narrator and his grandmother is one of the funniest passages in RTP. See MP, OJFF, 58. MP's first German translator, Walter Benjamin, quotes Joyce quoting MP as having told him: "She was my first Highness." See Walter Benjamin, "Pariser Köpfe," in *Walter Benjamin Passagen: Schriften zur französische Literatur,* ed. Gérard Raulet (Frankfurt: Suhrkamp, 2007), 174–81.

451   "would only talk about duchesses": Cited in Carter, *Marcel Proust,* 778.

452   "Bouvard and Pécuchet": For an overview, see Brooks, *Flaubert in the Ruins of Paris,* 161–63.

452   "With the whole body": MP, "Mondanité et mélomanie de Bouvard et Pécuchet," in *La Revue blanche* 21–22 (July–August 1893); reprinted in MP, JS, 57–65, 59.

452   "Bouvard leaned on the mantel": Ibid., 57.

452   "One says 'Monsieur' ": Ibid., 59–60.

453   "As for the Jews": Ibid., 62. For a brief but astute commentary on this passage, see Carter, *Marcel Proust,* 152. On MP's equivocal amusement in the face of *mondain* anti-Semitism, see JEB, *Mes modèles,* 121.

CHAPTER EIGHTEEN: OUR HEART

454   a tumor removed from his nose: *Archives diplomatiques: mensuel international* (April–June 1889): 352; and Balfour, ed., op. cit., vol. 2, 384–85.

454   "I think I am as variable as a wind": Balfour, ed., ibid., 395.

454   "recast and rewritten": Ibid., 395.

455   "I feel like a wild bird": Ibid., 424.

455   all by himself: AdF, *Mon Paris et ses Parisiens,* vol. 4, 23; Baron de Vaux, ed., *Le Sport en France et à l'étranger* (Paris: J. Rothschild, 1899), 84.

455   Maupassant, too, put up at the Hôtel des Étrangers: In a telegram dated February 16, 1890, GM states, "In Nice Hôtel des Étrangers." GM's last surviving bit of correspondence before then is dated January 26, 1890, and puts him at the Pension Marie-Louise in Cannes. Like his decision not to stay with his mother while in Nice, GM's choice of the Pension Marie-Louise was unusual for him, for he moored the *Bel-Ami* in Cannes and habitually slept on the boat when he was in port there. See GM, letters 596 and 595, respectively. On the proximity of GM's mother's house to Cimiez, see Jacques-Louis Douchin, *Vie érotique de Guy de Maupassant* (Paris: Suger/Pauvert, 1986), 150.

456   "very own Hall of Mirrors": GS to NH, letter marked "Palais de Monaco" and dated February 1890, in Balard, ed., op. cit., 184–85.

456   "With any luck": GS to GPR, letter sent from Nice in February 1890, in NAF 24971, folio 276.

456   "My unhappy, velvet-eyed odalisque": Élie Delaunay to GS, letter dated March 18, 1890, in NAF 14383, folio 82/83.

456   "Has Straus managed to rein in his frightful temper?": Paul Bourget to GS, letter dated March 18, 1890, cited in Bischoff, op. cit., 116.

456   "a most intelligent and charming woman": Balfour, ed., op. cit., vol. 2, 402.

456   Lord Lytton had likewise performed for his own late father: On LL's posthumous censorship of his father's letters, see Louisa Devey, *Life of Rosina, Lady Lytton* (London: S. Sonnenschein, Lowrey, & Co., 1887), vi–x. On the gaps in GS's and LL's extant letters: GS's correspondence resumes on August 27 and LL's correspondence September 8, 1890. On the latter date, LL wrote a letter on letterhead from the Hôtel Sacaron, which GS gave as her return address on the letter she wrote on the former date. See Balard, ed., op. cit., 187.

456   "an awkward elephant": Balfour, ed., op. cit., vol. 2, 402.

457   "A cat may look on a king": Cited in L. G. Mitchell, op. cit., 83.

457   "O my heart": OM (pseud. LL), "A l'entresol," in *The Poetical Works of Owen Meredith* (New York: New York Publishing Company, 1895), 213.

457   "incredible feeling": LL to EG, letter dated July 17, 1889, in AP(II)/101/95.

458   they had both vacationed in Dieppe: LL's correspondence with Lady Dorothy Nevill places him at the Hôtel Royal in Dieppe beginning in August 1889. See Lady Dorothy Nevill, *Under Five Reigns* (London: Methuen, 1910), 245.

458   "Given that you have both": LL to EG in AP(II)/101/95.

458 "He loved her": EG, diary entry from 1890, in AP(II)/101/150.

458 "the first to notice": EG, untitled note dated October 27, 1889, in ibid.

458 "a single line": LL to EG, in AP(II)/101/95.

458 "I write to speak to you of a vision": LL to EG, letter dated August 4, 1890, in AP(II)/101/95; also cited in Hillerin, op. cit., 245–46.

459 "made it utterly impossible": LL to EG, letter dated September 20, 1890, in AP(II)/101/95; also cited in Cossé-Brissac, op. cit., 93.

460 Lord Lytton decried Maupassant's ruthlessly cynical portrayal: Balfour, ed., op. cit., vol. 2, 405.

460 writing to Geneviève: The letters from GM to GS consulted for this chapter, from GM, *Correspondance,* op. cit., are: 669, 672, 673, 700, 706, 707, 771, 772, and 773.

460 "disgusted by Maupassant's brutality": Cited in Joanna Richardson, *Portrait of a Bonaparte: The Life and Times of Joseph-Napoléon Bonaparte* (London: Quartet, 1987), 195.

461 his contact with her dropped off: To some extent, this diminution in GM's involvement with GS can be quantified. In 1888, when GM began *Strong as Death,* 20 percent of the letters he wrote were addressed to GS (twelve out of sixty). In 1890, that figure dropped to 1.4 percent (one out of seventy-two letters written that year).

461 "final flowering": GM, *Notre cœur,* in *Romans de Guy de Maupassant,* ed. Forestier, 1032.

461 "a demanding, jealous": Ibid., 1034.

461 "trained her to be a polished, elegant hostess": Ibid., 1035.

461 "financiers": Ibid., 1042.

461 "unpredictable, vivacious wit": Ibid., 1058.

461 "the idol . . . the fetish": Ibid., 1115.

461 "Michèle's entresol": Ibid., 1033.

461 turns out to be an ice-cold lover: Michèle de Burne's extreme reluctance to sleep with her lover again, a decision that obviously recalls the GPR/GM/Primoli gossip about GS's refusal to "renew the experience" with GM, is more interesting than my short plot summary indicates. Michèle's nearest and dearest consider her "asexual," despite her compulsive flirtiness, while GM hints in a few places that she may be involved in a lesbian relationship with the Princesse de Malten (ibid., 1120 and 1128–29), a character seemingly based on GS's and LC's friend Lady (Gladys) de Grey. One eminent critic and editor was so struck by the lesbian overtones of Michèle's character that in a letter to GM he called her "a Sappho"; see GM, *Correspondance,* letter 617.

461 her newest fashionable outfit: In another suggestive detail, redolent of the ornithological imagery in so much of the literature surrounding GS, EG, and LC, GM describes Mme de Burne modeling a new outfit for her lover, a stunning cloak covered in feathers, that gives her "the bizarre appearance of a wild bird"; see GM, *Notre cœur,* 1128. This cloak sounds uncannily like the one RM describes as belonging to EG in chapter 7; it also evokes Petrarch's description of Laura as a plumed creature. In the context of GM's novel, Michèle's implied lesbian leanings and her avian costume both serve his portrayal of the *grande mondaine* as "perverse" or "unnatural," a perspective discussed in a general way in Bancquart, op. cit., 213–14.

461 "charming, well-spoken": GM, *Notre cœur,* 1100–1 and 1103.

462 a barely disguised depiction: On the perception that "for Maupassant, she [GS] is Mme de Burne," see Borrel, "Geneviève Straus," 124.

462 "In Mme de Burne of *Our Heart*": EdG, *Journal,* entry of July 5, 1890.

462 "Mme Straus—here she is": DH, Carnet 3, 189; this page from DH's scrapbook is reproduced in Loyrette, ed., op. cit., 117.

462 "as egotistical as a monster": Cited in Balard, ed., op. cit., 118; and in Hervé Lacombe, *Georges Bizet: Naissance d'une identité créatrice* (Paris: Fayard, 2000), 744.

463 "in Geneviève's place": Cited in Jacob, ed., op. cit., 175.

463 "is said to be the heroine": Balfour, ed., op. cit., vol. 1, 402; letter of September 8, 1890.

463 "not at all": Ibid.

463 "detestable": GM to ES, letter 628, dated June 20, 1890, in *Correspondance.*

464 a three-day stopover in Dieppe: EG alludes to this visit, and notes that from Dieppe, LL went on to Luchon, in a letter to "X," dated September 3, 1890, in AP(II)/101/26.

464 "Émile isn't hiding anything from you": GS to NH, letter dated August 27, 1890, in Balard, ed., op. cit., 167.

466 "the women in society": Cited in Bischoff, op. cit., 231.

466 "Little does she care": GPR, *Sous mes yeux,* 47–48. In a like vein, EdG complained that with her love of notoriety, GS had brought a "show-business" dimension into the monde; see EdG, *Journal,* entry of May 17, 1892.

466 one of the weakest texts: Negative critical assessments of *Our Heart* include Douchin, *La Vie érotique de Guy de Maupassant;* René Doumic, *Les Écrivains d'aujourd'hui: Bourget—Maupassant—Loti—Lemaître* (Paris: Perrin, 1895), 91; Remy de Gourmont, *Promenades littéraires,* vol. 4 (Paris: Mercure de France, 1927), 145–48. Sherard speculates that the novel must "have been written entirely for commercial purposes." See Sherard, 62.

467 while he was working on *Our Heart:* Louis Forestier's "Notice" to GM, *Notre cœur,* 1621–22.

467 "One out of every two times": Cited in Sven Kellner, *Maupassant, un météore dans le ciel littéraire de l'époque* (Paris: Publibook, 2012), 58.

467 "spoke to him": Cited in EdG, *Journal,* entry of October 1, 1893. According to EdG, GM was ranting about the pills and their "little voices" the night before his suicide attempt in Cannes.

467 "written to God": Cited in Georges Normandy, *La Fin de Maupassant* (Paris: Albin Michel, 754), 194.

467 "first 70,000": Cited in Murat, *La Maison du docteur Blanche,* 336.

467 "millions and billions and trillions": Sherard, op. cit., 65.

467 "My senses are swelling up inside me": GM to an unidentified female correspondent, undated letter 646, in GM, *Correspondance.*

468 "feel my brains dripping from my nose and mouth": GM to Dr. Henri Cazalis, letter 751, dated late December, 1891, in GM, *Correspondance.*

468 "Look what I've done": Cited in PM, *Vie de Guy de Maupassant,* 250.

468 "When they came in to fetch Maupassant": Cited in J. Richardson, op. cit., 132; and Bruno Haliou, "Comment la syphilis emporta Maupassant," *La Revue du practicien* 53 (2003): 1386–89.

469 Laure de Maupassant's first reaction: Bancquart, op. cit., 194; and Murat, *La Maison du docteur Blanche,* 338. Murat also provides an invaluable account of GM's tenure at Blanche's clinic, "Fou? Maupassant et le docteur trois-étoiles," in ibid., 328–48.

469 "the delicate heroine of *Our Heart*": Cited in J. Richardson, op. cit., 195.

470 generations of scholars: A good synopsis of the debate about Marie Kann, Lulia Cahen d'Anvers, and GM's "lady in grey" appears in Douchin, *La Vie érotique de Guy de Maupassant.* All citations from François Tassart are taken from his *Souvenirs sur Guy de Maupassant par François, son valet de chambre, 1883–1893* (Paris: Plon, 1911). The detail about the telegram "from the Orient" that, according to Tassart, precipitated GM's suicide attempt definitively excludes Marie Kann and Lulia Cahen d'Anvers from consideration as "the lady in grey," since they were both in France when GM received it, whereas GS was in Alexandria with LH. On the Convent of Ramlah, see Liévain de Hamme, *Guide-indicateur des sanctuaires et lieux historiques de la Terre Sainte* (Paris: Imprimerie des Pères Franciscains, 1897), 138. On Thérèse Prévost-Paradol's taking of the holy orders there, see *The Nation* 59 (September 24, 1894): 215. On Thérèse Prévost-Paradol and her two siblings, Lucy and Hjalmar, see JEB, *La Pêche aux souvenirs,* 92–103; and Pierre Guiral, "Anatole Prévost-Paradol," in Loyrette, ed., op. cit., 128–35, 133–34.

470 "a two-day tour of Divonne": GS to NH, letter marked "début septembre 1891," in Balard, ed., op. cit., 192.

471 "coquettish dress": Étincelle (pseud.), "Les Parisiennes au Léman," reprinted in *La Grande Dame* 1, no. 1 (1893): 5–7. GS discusses her visits to the Princesse de Brancovan's and to the Rothschilds' places on Lake Geneva in Balard, ed., op. cit., 191–92.

471 "become *animalized*": EdG, *Journal,* entry of January 30, 1893.

471 "passed badly": LD, *Souvenirs littéraires* (Paris: Grasset, 1968), 100.

471 a monument: On the inauguration of the GM monument, see *La Gazette anecdotique* 21 (November 15, 1897): 258–59.

471 "On a chaise longue": Cited in Douchin, *La Vie érotique de Guy de Maupassant,* 10–11.

CHAPTER NINETEEN: IN WHICH PROUST IS DISAPPOINTED

474 "Madame, I love mysterious": MP to GS, in MP, *Correspondance avec Mme Straus,* 21–22.

475 "The Truth about Mme Straus": MP to GS, in Kolb, ed., op. cit., vol. 1, 163–64.

476 by writing a fairy tale: Reprinted in MP, *Écrits de jeunesse,* 207–10.

CHAPTER TWENTY: DEAD LOVE, STILL UNDYING

481   "unhappy news": LL to GS, unsigned letter on LL's writing paper, in NAF 14826, folio 110.

482   greeting her as "Madame Straus": NAF 14383, folio 181/183. On the faux pas this mode of address still constitutes in French society today, see David-Weill, op. cit., 101, in a comical scene where an outsider "manag[es] to cram so many gaffes into one greeting [that it is] in fact a kind of triumph" (100).

482   "Say, monsieur": Cited in JEB, *Mes modèles*, 113.

482   an incident embarrassing to them both: The incident was a dinner at the latter's family's apartment, to which MP invited Wilde after they met again at Mme Baignères's in December 1891. Arriving at 9, boulevard Malesherbes, Wilde was taken aback to discover that MP's parents intended to join them. In his discomfort, Wilde opined rudely on the apartment's "tasteless, . . . old-fashioned, bourgeois" décor and then made to leave, having stayed for all of a few minutes. MP asked him if he was feeling unwell; Wilde answered, "No, I am not ill in the slightest. I was under the impression that I was to have the pleasure of dining [with you] alone, but I was ushered into the drawing room. I looked in and your parents were sitting at the far end, so my courage dissolved. Au revoir, Monsieur Proust." In this encounter as in his introduction to GS, Wilde addressed his host as a social inferior ("Monsieur Proust"). For more on this episode, see Robert Fraser, *Proust and the Victorians: The Lamp of Memory* (New York: St. Martin's, 1994), 212–13; and Emily Eells, "Proust et Wilde," in *Le Cercle de Proust,* ed. Jean-Yves Tadié (Paris: Honoré Champion, 2013): 225–36.

482   "You know how well-known you are in London": Cited in DH, *My Friend Degas,* 84.

482   "They don't hunt the same prey as we do": GS to Joseph Reinach, in NAF 14383, folio 49.

483   "women who wear sentimental colors": Oscar Wilde, *The Picture of Dorian Gray,* ed. Robert Mighal (London: Penguin Classics, 2006 [1891]), 99.

483   "Little does she care": GPR, *Sous mes yeux,* 47–48.

483   For media coverage of the Bizet monument fund-raising campaign, see *Le Temps* (December 3, 1890): 4; *Le Temps* (December 27, 1890): 3; and the interview LH gave to *Le Gaulois* (December 11, 1890): 2, to publicize the revival of *Carmen,* which opened the following night. A vituperative account of the campaign and the *Carmen* benefit performance appears in ED, *Testament d'un antisémite,* 244–47.

484   the ravaging effects of her opiate dependency: The deterioration of GS's appearance comes through with arresting clarity in an untitled painting of her by Jean-Louis Forain. This painting shows Geneviève on her divan in a mauve peignoir, with her little black poodle at her feet, but while the pose is coquettish, her face is a death's mask, her cheeks emaciated, her complexion ghostlike, her eyes two gigantic black sockets ringed with red. Regrettably, the painting belongs to a private collection and was unavailable for reproduction here, but the woman it depicts has an all-too-evident problem with drugs.

484   "an apotheosis": ED, *Testament d'un antisémite,* 244.

484   gauche attempts to engage his hostesses: See FB, op. cit., 104.

485   Sarah Bernhardt in *Cleopatra*: To Betty, LL called *Cleopatra* a "great disappointment." See Balfour, ed., op. cit., vol. 2, 406.

485   attended a séance: On the table-turning with LC, see Cossé-Brissac, op. cit., 141–42; on LL's interest in "spiritism," see C. Nelson Stewart, *Bulwer-Lytton as Occultist* (LaVergne, TN: Kessinger, 2010).

485   on March 3, 1891: HB's remarriage is reported in "Married to a Marquis," *New York Times* (March 3, 1891): 1; and Our Own Reporter (pseud.), "A Visit to Wappingers Falls," *Poughkeepsie Eagle* (June 12, 1891): 1.

486   Lord Lytton stayed put: Unless otherwise noted, all information and quotations from LL regarding his self-imposed confinement at the hôtel Borghèse and his work on *Marah* appear in Balfour, ed., op. cit., vol. 2; and all quotations from *Marah* are taken from that volume.

486   the fire that burned his skin: For the topoi of fire and ice, night and sun, etc., that moved LL to write *Marah,* see especially, in that volume, "Absence," "Death," "Amari Aliquid," "By the Gates of Hell," "Selene," "Travelling Acquaintance," and "Somnium Belluinum." See also OM (pseud. LL), "The Earl's Return," in *The Poetical Works,* 314. On LL's sense that his abilities didn't match his ambitions as a poet, see also Raymond, op. cit., 296.

487   "Oh darling, darling!": LL to EG, undated, in AP(II)/101/92; also cited in Cossé-Brissac, op. cit., 136, n. 1.

488   Élisabeth also trained her sights: On EG's interest in Kaiser Wilhelm II, see various docu-

ments in AP(II)/101/151. The very fact that these documents wound up not in her international relations file but in one of her "literary" files, mixed in with writings for her novel with GBB, suggests that her pursuit of the kaiser was connected in her mind to her involvement with GBB.

488   she would reach a similar conclusion: On her later interest in Mussolini, see EG, a typed and undated note in AP(II)/101/149 that reads, "There is obviously only one man in Europe [today], and that man is Mussolini! So I am pained, I who have always searched in vain for a way to get to know him, to say that I will never meet him!" (EG goes on to note that the Comte Manzoni from the Italian embassy has given her a "very important and original" book entitled *Mussolini Speaks: Speeches Are Facts.*)

489   "My doing this favor": EG to GCC, letter of February 24, 1891, in AP(II)/101/151.

489   "the founder of the Sabine women's party": *Annales de la Chambre des Députés: débats parlementaires—session extraordinaire de 1889* (Paris: Imprimerie des Journaux Officiels, 1890), 653.

489   "All the phantoms of the future": OM, "Omens and Oracles," in *Marah*, 44. I cannot resist including this particular quotation here, for while LL's literary oeuvre has not furnished posterity with as many trite phrases as that of his father, Edward Bulwer-Lytton, "check the feeling o'er thee stealing" might be read as the Victorian precursor to "check yourself before you wreck yourself."

489   the kaiser's mother's visit: For the details on the dowager empress's visit and the Léon ball, see especially, and respectively, EG's above-cited letter of February 24, 1891, to GCC; *Le Gaulois* (May 27, 1891): 1; and *Le Monde illustré* (May 30, 1891): 425.

491   "dreadful letter": Balfour, ed., op. cit., vol. 2, 66.

491   "Lord Lytton writes me seventy-page letters": EG to "X," letter dated September 3, 1890, in AP(II)/101/26. NB: This letter is filed along with a number of other letters to and from GBB.

491   "doing a novel about a society woman": EdG, *Journal,* entry of April 25, 1891.

492   "morbid need to offer up": GBB, "Journal de Gérard," entry dated "9 avril . . . 1h45 du soir," p.7 (marked in blue pencil at the top of the page).

492   "newest triumph with an eminent man": GBB in ibid., entry marked "16 avril . . . midi," p. 14 (marked in blue pencil at the top of the page).

492   "perhaps excessive coldness": GBB to EG, in AP/101(II)/150.

492   "gather [her] forces": EG, note dated November 1890, in ibid.

493   "ill-ominous denunciators": OM, "Lord Lytton's Last Poem," in *Marah,* 202. On the murder of d'Arenberg's twin brother, see PV, "La Société étrangère à Paris," *La Nouvelle Revue* 70 (May–June 1891): 677–701, 680.

493   her newest cultural venture: The manifesto announcing the founding of the Société des Grandes Auditions Musicales de France ran in *Le Figaro* that April; see Gaston Calmette, "Les Compositeurs français joués en France," *Le Figaro* (April 10, 1890): 1–2; and "Musical Notes," *Monthly Musical Review* 20 (May 1, 1890): 116–17. For more information about the Société des Grandes Auditions and its role in French musical culture at the fin de siècle, see Cossé-Brissac, op. cit., 87–91; Kahan, op. cit.; Jann Pasler, "Countess Greffulhe as Entrepreneur: Negotiating Class, Gender, and Nation," in *The Musician as Entrepreneur,* ed. William Weber (Bloomington: Indiana University Press, 2004); and James Ross, "Music in the French Salon," in *French Music Since Berlioz,* ed. Smith and Potter, 91–116.

497   "the Comtesse Greffulhe is our modern Mme Récamier": RM, *La Divine Comtesse,* 198. In fact, because Mme Récamier was more famous than Mme Tallien, the press often described EG's Directoire-style dresses in terms of the former, not the latter, *salonnière.* See, for example, the commentary on "Mme G***'s legendary beauty and *Récamier* hat" in Frivoline (pseud.), "Art et chiffons," *L'Art et la mode* 29 (June 20, 1885): 337–38, 337.

497   "Mme *Réclamier*" publicity stunt: HG to EG, undated letter in AP(II)/101/32.

498   "I am tired, sick, and weary of all things": Balfour, ed., op. cit., vol. 2, 416; also cited in Raymond, op. cit., 295.

498   his own flesh was failing him: Raymond, op. cit., 295; on LL's statement to his daughter that the figure on the twenty-franc coin was his last friend on earth, see ibid., 302; on his trip to Bayreuth, see ibid., 295.

499   "with its *esprit*, its *amours*": Balfour, ed., op. cit., vol. 2, 419.

499   "not very susceptible to musical effects": Ibid., 420.

499   "mystic gulf": On Wagner's notion of the *mystische Abgrund,* see the composer's comments "On the Name 'Music-Drama'" ("Music-Drama," not "opera," was his term for *Parsifal*), in

Richard Wagner, *Actors and Singers*, trans. William Ashton Ellis (London: Kegan Paul, Trench, Trübner, & Co., 1896), 354. See also William James Henderson, *Richard Wagner: His Life and His Dramas* (New York: G. P. Putnam & Sons, 1910), 140; and Daniel H. Foster, *Wagner's Ring Cycle and the Greeks* (Cambridge and London: Cambridge University Press, 2010), 76.

499   unlike anything Lord Lytton had ever seen: On LL's impressions of the mise-en-scène at Bayreuth, see Balfour, ed., op. cit., vol. 2, 419–20.

499   "safe in[to] the very heart of the world of dreams": Ibid., 419. On Wagner's debt to the Wandering Jew in creating Kundry, see Dieter Borchmeyer, *Drama and the World of Richard Wagner* (Princeton, NJ: Princeton University Press, 2003), 90.

500   the mere mention of Élisabeth's name: OM, "Figures of Speech," in *Marah*, 67.

500   "when a body is cremated": Cited in Cossé-Brissac, op. cit., 92.

501   "monstrous procession": OM, "Somnium Belluinum," in ibid., 179–86.

501   "a sudden attack of heart disease": *New York Times* (November 25, 1891): 1. On LL's death and funeral, see also: Balfour, ed., op. cit., vol. 2, 430–33; Raymond, op. cit., 303; Scott (pseud.), "Les Obsèques de Lord Lytton," *Le Monde illustré* (December 5, 1891): 1–2.

502   "His manuscript was always beside him": Balfour, ed., op. cit., vol. 2, 430–31. This detail appears in many of LL's obituaries, for instance in the *Annual Register*, which notes that he "had been writing verses, of which the ink was not dry when he succumbed to a sudden cessation of the action of the heart." See "Obituary of Eminent Persons: The Earl of Lytton," *Annual Register and Review of Public Events at Home and Abroad* (November 1891): 197–98.

502   "Without a doubt": Hillerin, op. cit., 245.

503   "Thus is my desire": Petrarch, "XCV. *Qual più diversa e nova*," in *Il Canzoniere*, 482–83.

503   fourteen thousand pheasants: Du Bled, op. cit., 164; on the performance by the professional men's choir, see "Nouvelles et faits: Seine-et-Marne," *Le Journal du Loiret* (November 24, 1891): 3.

503   "an orgy of balustrades": JEB, *La Pêche aux souvenirs*, 149.

504   "the Versailles of the Sun King": La Force, op. cit., 77.

504   he had never really gone in for hunting: "Lytton: Edward Robert Bulwer-Lytton," in *The New Volumes of the Encyclopaedia Britannica*, vol. 6, ed. Sir Donald Wallace, Arthur Hadley, and Hugh Chisholm (London and Edinburgh: Adam and Charles Black, 1902), 386–88, 386. On the Grand-Duc Wladimir's flippant violation of firearms protocol, see d'Uzès, op. cit., 88.

505   "You alone eliminate all other considerations": EG, diary entry marked "A [Robert]" (with the bracketed name written in her version of shorthand) and dated "Dieppe, 1 septembre, 1891"; the "Robert" in this case was definitely LL and not RM, as her relationship with the latter Robert was singularly—and for RM, uncharacteristically—devoid of turmoil, confusion, and "limbo."

505   "being too demanding": GBB to EG, undated entry in the same small red notebook in AP(II)/101/152.

505   "she had for the first time": Cossé-Brissac, op. cit., 135–36.

506   "woman who had long struggled": Raymond, op. cit., 302.

506   In EG's archives, this text, along with several of the *Marah* poems, is filed not in the carton that contains the rest of her correspondence with LL, but in a carton assembling the "Hommages et Appréciations" to EG received from many of the people she knew (as opposed to the appreciations and homages written by strangers, which are filed separately). The untitled poem LL drafted for her on Bois-Boudran letterhead begins: "*Ô des instants d'amour l'ineffable délire*"; see AP(II)/101/1. "Lord Lytton's Last Poem," posthumously added by Betty or Edith Bulwer-Lytton, appears at the end of *Marah*, 197–202.

506   "To men who are neither critics nor poets": A.B. (pseud.), "Marah," *National Review* 19 (March–August 1892): 200–11, 203.

507   "You looked and listened": OM, "Lord Lytton's Last Poem," in *Marah*, 197–98.

CHAPTER TWENTY-ONE: THE REPLACEMENTS

508   Élisabeth flung it into the Seine: This story is retold in EdG, *Journal*, entry of August 15, 1895.

508   "The absoluteness of his love": EG note to self dated December 6, 1891. The note begins, "*J'ai compris par l'absolu de son amour . . .*" In this text, "the lover" is written in EG's secret-code version of shorthand; the rest is written in French. See AP(II)/101/149.

508   family's financial woes: On the Borgheses' bankruptcy scandal and series of asset sales, see

Elliot, *Roman Gossip*, 117; Chilvers, ed., *The Oxford Dictionary of Art*, 90; and Guimard, "Les Borghèse," 1–2.

508   On the fake Raphael scandal: When the Borgheses sold their portrait of Cesare Borgia to Rothschild in October, the transaction made news around the world because it was billed as "one of Raphael's finest efforts" and had been a "Borghese art heirloom since it was first painted"; see "Rothschild Buys a Raphael," *Chicago Tribune* (October 4, 1891): 2. The hype surrounding the purchase only exacerbated the family's embarrassment when the forgery was uncovered a month later.

508   "Good things will surely happen": EG to GCC, in AP(II)/101/151. Regarding the rumored Borghese/Vanderbilt engagement, I am thankful to my friend Gloria Vanderbilt, Gertrude Vanderbilt Whitney's niece, for fielding my nosy questions on this subject.

509   "to stop wishing for the thing": MACC to EG, letter dated February 26, 1893, in AP(II)/101/53. See also, in the same file, MACC to EG, letters dated July 14, 1889, July 6, 1892, and April 7, 1893.

509   "not have a penny to his name": MACC to GCC, letter dated July 1894, in ibid.

509   "from a different race": EG, note dated September 1890, in AP(II)/101/26.

509   "He does not see me": EG, handwritten note marked at the top of the page "*Mort atroce celle des cœurs*" and at the bottom of the page "[18]92," in AP(II)/101/149.

510   "Her roving gaze": HR, *Les Cahiers*, 378. In HR's sense that EG was looking at him in a predatory, tacitly erotic way, one sees a precursor of MP's narrator briefly thinking, upon seeing Mme de Guermantes for the first time, that her eyes contained a hint of sexual availability or interest. See MP, CCS, 175. See also Beckett, op. cit., on the "gently wanton" allure the duchesse exudes in this scene in MP's novel.

510   "The contour of a girl's cheek": Perriton Maxwell, "Helleu and His Art," *The Cosmopolitan*, 43 (May–October 1907): 119–27, 120.

510   "the Beauty": EG, in AP(II)/101/150.

511   "quite the opposite was the case!!!!": Ibid.

511   "You looked beautiful that way": Cited in HR, *Les Cahiers*, 378.

512   "those three days we had together": Comte Albert de Mun to EG, unsigned letter dated 1892, in AP/101/150.

512   "with only the utmost tender respect": Comte Albert de Mun to EG, unsigned letter dated October 30, 1893 (opening line: "*Je n'ai pu vous dire merci!*"), in ibid.

512   Colonel Albert de Rochas: Rochas's friendship with EG began in 1892, and over the next several years he seems to have repeatedly begged her to become his mistress, without success. On January 13, 1896, he wrote her to say that she had "made my life *unbearable*" by "adopting with respect to me a policy of *inertia* and *silence* worse than anything one would inflict upon one's worst enemies in diplomacy. . . . I am battered, bruised, mortally wounded by your tactics. . . . How can you tell me to 'play nice' when I have placed in you all the vitality of my being, all the aspirations of my heart; now I am discovering, o despair!, that the goddess at whose altar I placed my very life as a burnt offering has been laughing at my naïveté and my old-fashioned sentimentality, and takes my love for madness! Is it really possible to 'play nice' under such circumstances?" EG annotated on the back of this letter: "I am *through* with confidences like these" (though she was not); see AP(II)/101/109.

514   "that beauty universally recognized": Paul Deschanel, *Figures de femmes* (Paris: Calmann-Lévy, 1889), 266 and 268.

515   "I want to tell you": Paul Deschanel to EG, letter dated December 30(?), 1895, in AP/101(II)/79.

515   "One must admit": Deschanel, *Figures de femmes*, 309–10.

515   the other Paul who loomed large: For Hervieu's letters to EG, see AP(II)/101/1 and AP(II)/101/88. On Hervieu's diplomatic background and elegant manners, see LG, *Mémoires*, vol. 1, 205–7; and FG, *Mon amitié*, 40. On Hervieu's stiff and chilly demeanor, see HR, *Les Cahiers*, 200, 478.

515   "tiny icicles": FG, *L'Âge d'or*, 263.

515   made out of cardboard: LD, *Souvenirs littéraires*, 169; and LD, *Au Temps de Judas* (Paris: Nouvelle Librairie Nationale, 1920), 76. On Hervieu's success as a "*mondain* novelist," see Henri Lavedan, "Paul Hervieu," *Le Figaro* (September 26, 1895): 1.

516   "patient and submissive heart": Hervieu to EG, letter dated April 10, 1888, in AP(II)/101/1.

517   Baronne Aimery-Harty (Marguerite) de Pierrebourg: Writing as Claude Ferval, Mme de Pierrebourg won the Académie's Prix Montyon in 1903 and its most prestigious award, the Prix Académie, in 1934. See http://www.academie-francaise.fr/claude-ferval. On her and Her-

vieu's identification with Sand and Musset, see AdF, *Cinquante ans de panache*, 61. On the Pierrebourg/Hervieu liaison, see also Painter, op. cit., vol. 1, 104.

517   driven yet docile: Hervieu may not have been as submissive and neutered as he led EG to believe. At around this same time, a rumor circulated in the literary world that an ill-fated passion for a woman from outside the milieu had turned Hervieu suicidal; see Auchincloss, op. cit., 125.

CHAPTER TWENTY-TWO: GODDESSES AND MONSTERS

518   "incorporated the red shoes": MP to GS in MP, *Correspondance avec Mme Straus*, 268.

518   "Swann-Haas": Cited in Bischoff, op. cit., 281. Similarly, in his reminiscences about GS's salon, FG refers to "Haas-Swann"; see FG, *Mon amitié*, 46.

518   "That would be a joke in charming taste": MP, CG, 883. Not incidentally, this was a quip MP had heard Haas use in the monde, making fun of a friend who had asked him to evaluate a painting in his, the friend's, collection. See Painter, op. cit., vol. 1, 94.

519   "But we have all the time in the world!": MP, CG, 884.

519   "Mme Straus, like the duchesse": Painter, op. cit., vol. 1, 90–91. The best scholarly treatment of the "red shoes" episode is Murat, "Les Souliers rouges de la duchesse," 96–105. On GS's red-and-black costume for the Lemaire ball, see Gant de Saxe (pseud. M. Ferrari), "Mondanités: Tout au papier," *Le Gaulois* (March 2, 1892): 1; see also EdG, *Journal*, entry of March 2, 1892. EdG names Ganderax and Detaille as two other *fidèles* who attended Lemaire's ball.

519   composer Ernest Guiraud: On Guiraud's death, see Imbert, *Médaillons contemporains,* 293.

520   The at-homes she held: On Mme Lemaire's "hybrid" salon emerging as a formidable rival to GS's, see George Painter: "Soon the Faubourg Saint-Germain arrived, because it was so delightful to meet artists, and then still more artists, because it was so delightful to meet the Faubourg." Painter, op. cit., vol. 1, 105. These lines, of course, recall LH's: "The Faubourg Saint-Germain [went] to Geneviève's salon as if it were the Chat-Noir; [and] the Chat-Noir [went there] as if it were the Faubourg Saint-Germain."

521   "delicious little page": Cited in Link-Heer, op. cit., 84.

521   "This charming woman": FG, *Mon amitié*, 41. JEB echoes this judgment when he states that while Marcel "attended the salon of Mme Émile Straus in its heyday," that wasn't the same as "being invited into the 'real gratin,'" where he went very little." See JEB, *Mes modèles,* 112.

522   grandiloquent coverage in the *presse mondaine*: Étincelle, (pseud.), "Les Grandes Réceptions: le bal blanc de la Princesse de Léon," *Le Figaro* (April 11, 1891): 1–2; Comtesse de Vérissey, "Chronique mondaine," *La Mode de style* (June 3, 1891): 179–180; and Gant de Saxe (pseud.), "Mondanités," *Le Gaulois* (June 23, 1891): 3.

522   this ball so captivated Proust: MP, CCS, 26, 97, and 172.

522   he overheard a *mondain* prince: MP explicitly made a note of this fact, recording that he once heard one of the club's members, Prince Edmond de Polignac, say, "'But no, of course he wasn't of the Jockey . . .' (Polignac on Strauss) [*sic*]." See MP, *Carnets,* 152.

522   "golden hair, and swanlike neck": MP, *Days of Reading,* 79.

522   "the incarnation of *landed-gentry* chic": Arnaud, op. cit., 76. Similarly, Painter writes that the "peasant-like roughness" of LC's voice was for MP "part of her supreme distinction" because it "came from her provincial ancestry." See Painter, op. cit., vol. 1, 113.

523   "this heraldic monument": Arnaud, op. cit., 75.

523   "the Comtesse [A. de Chevigné]": Billy, op. cit., 79. On MP's transposition of LC into his writings, from *The Banquet* to the *Search,* see also RD, *De Monsieur Thiers à Marcel Proust,* 17.

524   "Proust wants to persuade Laure de Chevigné": Cited in Benaïm, op. cit., 36.

524   "only, like Petrarch, keep repeating *Laure*": Cited in Christian Gury, *Proust: clés inédites et retrouvées* (Paris: Kimé, 2003), 203.

524   "used to complain": FG, *Mon amitié*, 33.

524   "coquettishly": Ibid. FG adds that MP liked to think that LC had "inherited her aquiline nose from the de Sades" (ibid.).

524   "indifferent, langorous, mystical eyes": MP, "Poésie," in MP, *The Collected Poems of Marcel Proust,* ed. Augenbraum, 19. Very little information about Gustave de Waru seems to survive, apart from the notice of his Saint-Cyr class ranking published in *Le Figaro* (October 23, 1889): 4. But while in school he did receive a prize for physics. As an adult, he undertook a not at all *mondain* professional path—he managed the Marais paper mill in the Seine-et-Marne,

specializing in the production of high-quality paper stock. He was a "confirmed bachelor" until 1912, when at age forty-one he married his thirty-four-year-old cousin Nicole de Waru. The marriage was without issue.

524 Anxious as ever: On MP's continued eagerness to downplay his homosexuality, see Arnaud, op. cit., 74. On GS lying to MP about having told LC about his crush, see AM, op. cit., 504.

525 Geneviève had picked a fight with Proust: MP to GS, in MP, *Correspondance avec Mme Straus,* 14–16 and 23. On Hayman's relationship with MP and his uncle Louis, see Carter, *Marcel Proust,* 84–85. On Hayman's possible involvement with Dr. Adrien Proust, see Taylor, op. cit., 15.

525 "Cruelty, by turns Sadean and sadistic": Compagnon, *Proust entre deux siècles,* 182. Compagnon makes this tacit distinction between "Sadean" and "sadistic" because MP tended to "conflate 'sadism' with perversion more broadly defined, including masochism, fetishism" and other impulses that de Sade appreciated (in art and in life), but which "sadism," in clinical terms, does not encompass (ibid., 171, n. 3).

525 a play called *The Sadist:* René Peter, *Une saison avec Marcel Proust,* ed. Jean-Yves Tadié (Paris: Gallimard/NRF, 2005), 136. Without mentioning its title, William Carter briefly discusses this play in *Proust in Love,* 75. As outlined by MP, the titular sadist would have "liaisons with whores and enjoy . . . soiling his own good sentiments" (cited in ibid., 75), a penchant MP also ascribes to the hero of *L'Indifférent.*

526 The same dynamic: The story in the footnote about Proust and the photo of Réjane dressed as the Prince de Sagan appears in Brassaï (pseud. Gyula Halász), *Proust in the Power of Photography,* trans. Richard Howard (Chicago and London: University of Chicago Press, 2001), 10.

527 *Fragments of Italian Comedy:* In his annotations to *Fragments of Italian Comedy,* editor Thierry Laget remarks upon the potential *commedia dell'arte* reference in the title but does not relate it to LC or the *commedia dell'arte* divertissement at the Léon ball in 1891. See PJ, 309, n. 1.

527 modeling Cydalise: See MP, in Kolb, ed., op. cit., vol. 7, 239–40.

527 "exud[ing] something loving": MP, "Cires perdues," *Fragments de comédie italienne,* in PJ, 85.

527 Myrto after Mme Straus: MP to GS, in Kolb, ed., op. cit., vol. 1, 195; MP, PJ, 310, n. 1.

527 "witty . . . and alluring": MP, "Les Amies de la Comtesse Myrto," *Fragments,* 81. On Hippolyta as LC, see RB, op. cit., 79–80; RD, *De Monsieur Thiers à Marcel Proust,* 17; RD, *Souvenirs,* 71; and Karlin, op. cit., 56, n. 88.

527 In classical myth, Hippolytus gets his name from his mother, Hippolyta, the Amazonian warrior-queen who precedes Phaedra as Theseus's wife. While Hippolyta does not appear in Racine's *Phaedra,* she is a minor character in Shakespeare's *A Midsummer Night's Dream* (1595–1596), marrying Theseus in the fourth act. But the latter play would have been far less likely than Racine's to have served as Proust's inspiration here. From his childhood letters to his mature literary work, his writings abound in allusions to Racine in general and *Phaedra* in particular. By contrast, although Proust did read Shakespeare, the sole reference to *A Midsummer Night's Dream* in the former's work was added by Scott Moncrieff, the first English translator of the *Search,* when rendering a generic mention in that novel of "a Shakespeare fantasia [*féerie*]." (Moncrieff also used Shakespearean, not Proustian, language to translate the title of RTP itself: *Remembrance of Things Past* is taken from Shakespeare's Sonnet 30.)

527 Jean de La Bruyère: On MP's early writings as pastiches of La Bruyère, see Nicola Luckhurst, *Science and Structure in Proust's "A la recherche du temps perdu"* (Oxford: Clarendon, 2000), 18–21. While Luckhurst does not mention "A Sketch Based on Mme de ***," she discusses MP's use of two of La Bruyère's key devices—the dialogic form and the *in medias res* beginning—in other texts MP wrote during this period.

528 "How can you prefer Hippolyta": This essay originally appeared in *Le Banquet* 3 (May 1892) and is reprinted in its entirety in RD, *Souvenirs,* 71–72. A slightly shortened version, missing the penultimate sentence, appears as "Cires perdues, II," in MP, PJ, 85–86.

529 All details about EG's fictional Baronne de Thélus are taken from X. Brahma (pseud. EG), *Âmes sociales,* op. cit. EG's page proofs for this novel contain many fascinating variations and are archived chiefly in AP(II)/101/152.

530 Proust and his friends hawked *The Banquet:* FG, "Hommage à Marcel Proust," *La Nouvelle Revue française* (January 1923): 41.

530 he owed Geneviève a favor: LG, *Mémoires,* vol. 2, 201; and "L'entresol," 3.

530 if *The Banquet* did find its way: Racyzmow, *Le Paris retrouvé de Proust,* 137.

530 in Mme de Chevigné, what had enticed him: On this point see Iswolsky, op. cit.: "Proust fell deeply in love with her image" (91).

530 "Hang on there, darlin'!": Cited in Huas, op. cit., 168.

531 "because he saw her with his imagination": MP, *La Fin de la jalousie et autres nouvelles,* ed. Thierry Laget (Paris: Gallimard, 1993), 82.

531 the wound Mme de Chevigné inflicted: On MP's abiding "rage" over LC's Feetjahm snub, see Huas, op. cit., 171; Painter, op. cit., vol. 1, 110–11; and Albaret, op. cit., 244.

CHAPTER TWENTY-THREE: SO LONG AS THE GESTURE IS BEAUTIFUL

532 "the *real* gratin": Cited in Chaleyssin, op. cit., 65.

532 "to speak to him": LG, *Robert de Montesquiou et Marcel Proust,* 60. MP himself writes in RTP that his alter ego, Marcel, must have seemed "like a little imbecile" to Haas's alter ego, Swann; see Carassus, op. cit., 543.

532 "The main thing is to gain entrée": Cited in CA, op. cit., 149.

533 "black terror": Carassus, op. cit., 372. On this "two-year anarchist frenzy," see also E. Weber, op. cit., 109–17. On the contemporaneous rise of anarchism throughout Europe and in the United States, see E. Weber, ibid.; "Les Attentats anarchistes," in *L'Intransigeant,* December 12, 1893, 2; and Albert Bataille, *Causes criminelles et mondaines de 1894: Les Procès anarchistes* (Paris: E. Dentu, 1895), xi–xvi.

533 The Leap Day bombing: Jean de Paris (pseud.), "La Dynamite chez la Princesse de Sagan," *Le Figaro* (March 1, 1892): 2–3; "La Dynamite à Paris: L'Hôtel de Sagan," *Le Petit Parisien* (March 1, 1892): 1; Le Masque de fer (pseud.), "Hors Paris," *Le Figaro* (March 2, 1892): 1–2; "La Dynamite: Attentat contre l'hôtel de la Princesse de Sagan," *Le Petit Journal* (March 1, 1892): 1–2; and "Faits divers: La Dynamite à l'hôtel de Sagan," *Gil Blas* (March 2, 1892): 2.

533 "The escape of the servant": An American (pseud.), idem.

533 "an immense tent": Marquise de Dangeau (pseud. Comtesse de Vérissey), "Chronique mondaine," *La Mode de style* (July 1, 1891): 208–211, 211; and Diable Boiteux (pseud.), "Nouvelles et échos," *Gil Blas* (June 7, 1891): 1.

534 a symbolic blow at the Parisian noblesse: On the target of the second bombing in the Faubourg, see Sante, op. cit., 248; and Will-Furet (pseud.), "Faits divers: L'Attentat du boulevard Saint-Germain," *Le Gaulois* (March 14, 1892): 2. On the *mondain* anxiety about "anarchist plots and infernal bombs," see de Pange, op. cit., 58.

534 The information given about the Panama Canal is taken from Arendt, *The Origins of Totalitarianism,* 95–99; Maurice Barrès, "The Panama Scandal," *The Cosmopolitan* 17 (May–October 1894): 203–10; HB, op. cit., 316–17; and Augustin Hamon and Georges Bachot, *L'Agonie d'une société: histoire d'aujourd'hui* (Paris: Albert Savine, 1889), 12.

535 "The anarchist party": EdG, *Journal,* entry of May 1, 1892. On anarchists who turned to dynamite as a weapon, see E.C. [*sic*], "Dynamite," *L'Oued-Sahel* (March 20, 1892): 1; and "La Dynamite," *Le XIXᵉ siècle* (October 31, 1892): 1.

536 "To be happy": Cited in John Merriman, *The Dynamite Club: How a Bombing in Fin-de-siècle Paris Ignited the Age of Modern Terror* (Boston and New York: Houghton Mifflin Harcourt, 2009), 82. On Ravachol, see also Philippe Dubois, "L'Affaire Ravachol-Koenigstein," *L'Intransigeant* (April 8, 1892): 1–2; Jean de Paris (pseud.), "Les Anarchistes," *Le Figaro* (April 5, 1892): 2; Saint-Réal (pseud.), "La Détente mondaine," *Le Gaulois* (April 6, 1892): 1; and "Ravachol," *Le Petit Parisien* (April 3, 1892): 1–2.

536 Auguste Vaillant tossed a homemade bomb: See "LA DYNAMITE AU PALAIS-BOURBON," *Le Journal* (December 10, 1893): 1–2; Jules Dietz, "L'Attentat du Palais-Bourbon," *Journal des débats* (December 10, 1893): 1; "L'Attentat du Palais-Bourbon," *Journal des débats* (December 11, 1893): 1–2; "L'Attentat du Palais-Bourbon: Découverte du coupable, ses aveux," *L'Intransigeant* (December 12, 1893): 1–2; Saint-Réal (pseud.), "Chez le défenseur de Vaillant," *Le Gaulois* (December 13, 1893): 1. Interestingly, Vaillant's lawyer was one Maître Albert Crémieux. As discussed in chapter 11, MP was related through his mother to an influential Crémieux family. I have been unable to determine whether Albert Crémieux belonged to that family.

536 having aborted his campaign: "Chronique électorale: conscience et liberté," *La Croix* (August 11, 1893): 2; "Chronique électorale: dans les départements—Melun," *Le Rappel* (August 12, 1893): 1; and Jacques Saint-Cère (pseud.), "Les Nouveaux Elus," *Le Figaro* (September 13, 1893): 2.

536 in April, another one detonated: On the April 26 bombing, see Associated Press Dispatches, "Panic-Stricken Paris: Consternation Reigning at the French Capital," *Los Angeles Herald*

(April 27, 1892): 2; Walter F. Lonergan, *Forty Years of Paris* (London: T. Fisher Unwin, 1907), 177–78; and Alan Sheridan, *Time and Place* (London: Scribner, 2003), 229.

536   In Montmartre: On Montmartre as a hotbed of socialist and anarchist fervor, see Merriman, *The Dynamite Club*, 60–62.

536   "Kings, gods are dead": Cited in E. Weber, op. cit., 110.

536   "I got enough daggers": Cited in Flor O'Squarr (pseud. Charles Flor), *Les Coulisses de l'anarchie* (Paris: Albert Lavine, 1892), 88–89. On Galliffet as a scapegoat for the anarchists, see Charles Malato, *De la Commune à l'anarchie*, 3rd ed. (Paris: Tresse & Stock, 1894).

537   "attack the Golden Calf of yesteryear": Cited in Brown, op. cit., 167.

537   "king of the gutter press": Cited in Merriman, *The Dynamite Club*, 125. Merriman correctly notes that Rochefort, an outspoken Boulangist, went into exile in England after the general's escape. But Merriman errs in identifying Rochefort as a "correspondent" (ibid.) for *The Intransigent;* he was the paper's founder.

537   "It seems that all of Jewry": Cited in Brown, op. cit., 171.

537   "profound respect and high esteem": O'Squarr, op. cit., 84.

537   "monsters [who must] be exterminated": Ibid., 311.

537   "Monsieur Vulture": Jean Conti, *Monsieur Vautour: pièce en un acte* (Paris: Éditions Théâtrales, 1911).

538   "the ghost of Frohsdorf": MB, *La Duchesse de Guermantes,* 67 and 106.

539   foiled a plot: On the assassination attempt against Prince Ferdinand, and on the execution of the would-be regicides, see Félix de Régamey, "La Guerre de demain," *Le Figaro-graphic* (January 25, 1892): 3.

539   "socialists and revolutionaries": Henri Rochefort, "Les Policiers possibilistes," *L'Intransigeant* (August 8, 1892): 1.

539   the general made light of the risk: Galliffet to GS, NAF 14383, folios 93/94–109/110.

539   "The 'Machine-Gunner of 1871' ": Galliffet to GS in ibid., folio 104/105.

540   "good to [her] workers": Cited in O'Squarr, op. cit., 51.

540   voiced admiration for the rebels: LD, *Fantômes et vivants,* 283–84; and Bertrand, op. cit., vol. 1, 33, n. 2.

540   "the eternal black poetry": RM filched this expression from Émile Zola. See Patrick McGuinness, *Poetry and Radical Politics in Fin-de-siècle France: Anarchism to Action Française* (Oxford: Oxford University Press, 2015), 90.

540   "like those flowers": Cited in Thiébaut, op. cit., 17.

540   "Who cares about the victim": Cited in Alvan Francis Sanborn, *Paris and the Social Revolution* (Boston: Small, Maynard & Co., 1905), 367.

541   "who [is] in the habit": MP, "Un dîner en ville," PJ, 159.

541   "relative of M. de Vogüé": Ibid., 153.

541   "very beautiful": Ibid.

541   "the same collective folly": Ibid., 158.

541   "The gentlemen start": Ibid., 159.

541   "As if bowing down": Ibid.

542   the anti-Jewish polemics of Drumont and Rochefort: Even during the Dreyfus affair, MP never named either Rochefort or ED in his letters, a peculiar omission I plan to investigate further in a sequel to the present volume.

542   he took no demonstrable interest: JS does include an extensive section on the Dreyfus affair, a shorter bit on the Panama scandal, and a throwaway line about Ravachol (invoked for comedic effect by a pompous petit-bourgeois who thinks it makes him sound "artistic" to claim an affinity for "Ravachol's *beau geste*"). But JS (a) was not published during MP's lifetime, and (b) was written between 1896 and 1899, after the period under discussion here.

542   Daniel Halévy became a fervid reader: On DH's flirtation with socialism, see Laurent, op. cit., 67–70. For a sample of Barrès's fierce criticism of the Panama swindlers, see Barrès, "The Panama Scandal," 203–10. On the anti-Semitic response to ES representing a defendant in the Panama scandal, see Hamon and Bachot, op. cit., 19.

542   "The Prince de Polignac": MP to his mother, letter dated [September 10, 1899], in Kolb, ed., op. cit., vol. 2, 304. At this point, Galliffet was serving as Minister of War and had become a controversial figure in the Dreyfus affair.

543   *The White Review:* See Claire Paulhan, "*La Revue blanche: tout l'esprit d'une époque*," *Le Monde: Le Monde des livres* (December 6, 2007), n.p.; and Carassus, op. cit., 372–73.

543   "Orléanist-republican": MP to Antoinette Faure, letter dated [July 15, 1887], in Kolb, ed., op. cit., vol. 1, 96.

543 "Orléanist preoccupations": Ibid., 95. In fact if MP did harbor any fondness for the monarchy, it is possible that here, as in all other areas of his life, his literary outlook came into play, for loving seventeenth-century literature as he did, he immersed himself in a world where the king reigned supreme. As MP's and LC's future friend René Boylesve writes in *Feuilles tombées* (Paris; Schiffrin, 1927), 147, "Racine [depicts] humanity qua subject of the king, humanity 'monarchized' to the ultimate degree." This "monarchized" world is also the context for and the subject of Saint-Simon's and Sévigné's writings, likewise key references for MP.

543 he attended the opening: MP had in fact planned to meet RM and Gabriel de Yturri at the Marie Antoinette exhibition but arrived too late; see MP to Yturri, letter dated [April 1894], in Kolb, ed., op. cit., vol. 1, 286–87. The catalogue for the exhibition, with the names of families lending objects from their own collections, is *Catalogue de l'exposition de Marie Antoinette et son temps,* preface by Germain Bapst (Paris: Galerie Sedelmeyer, 1894).

543 "What I reproach the Revolution with": Cited in Duplay, op. cit., 123.

543 "if not [his] snobbishness": MP to Antoinette Faure, letter dated [July 15, 1887], in Kolb, ed., op. cit., vol. 1, 95.

543 "Proust and politics?": J. Canavaggia, *Proust et la politique* (Paris: A.-G. Nizet, 1986), 7. In this book, Canavaggia briefly examines MP's treatment of the Panama scandal in JS (21–25).

544 "one place in Paris where individual merit doesn't count": Cited in Hanoteau, op. cit., 90.

544 "I hear the Princesse de Léon": MP, in Kolb, ed., op. cit., vol. 1, 226.

544 "Was it Mme de La Trémoïlle": MP to RB, letter dated "This Thursday" (January 26?, 1893), in ibid., 199.

544 "You have to look at them": JEB, *Mes modèles,* 109.

544 "let himself be dazzled": Ibid.

544 "Seldom are the[se] men of letters": MP, JS, 427–28.

545 They "desire that which": Ibid., 426–27.

CHAPTER TWENTY-FOUR: SOVEREIGNS OF TRANSITORY THINGS

546 wielded his cane like a duelist's foil: Jacques Saint-Cère (pseud. Armand Rosenthal), "Une heure chez le Comte Robert de Montesquiou," *La Revue illustrée* (June 15, 1894): 117–24, 118. This gesture would come back to haunt RM a few years later.

546 "a suit of fog": RM, in NAF 15038, folio 95/96.

546 "Of his patron": Cited in Valentino Brosio, *Ritratti parigini del Secondo Impero e della Belle Époque* (Paris: Nuovedizioni E. Vallecchi, 1975), 182; and in Jullian, *Robert de Montesquiou,* 205.

546 "a gladiola being whipped": Cited in Chaleyssin, op. cit., 95.

546 "as unstable as his body": FB, op. cit., 173.

546 "though based on nothing": Saint-Cère (pseud.), "Une heure chez le Comte de Montesquiou," 119.

546 "my uncle Childebert": Cited in Brosio, op. cit., 182.

547 "like a king in exile": Lucien Corpechot, "Les Lettres françaises: le Comte Robert de Montesquiou," *La Revue de France* 2, no. 23 (February 15, 1922): 435–44, 435.

547 the Montesquiou Pavilion: The sources for this description of RM and the Montesquiou Pavilion are RM, untitled notes on the Montesquiou Pavilion, in NAF 15040, folio 7/8; Chaleyssin, op. cit., 71; Munhall, op. cit., 94; HR, *Nos rencontres,* 161; and Saint-Cère (pseud.), "Une heure chez le Comte de Montesquiou." The house is still standing today. It is located at 53, avenue de Paris, a broad, tree-lined thoroughfare that begins at the place d'Armes, the vast open courtyard in front of the château de Versailles, and leads northeast to Paris.

547 "the Moon King of the Bats": Cited in HR, *Les Cahiers,* 159. On RM's aesthetic of elegant, regal ruination, see Bertrand, op. cit., vol. 1, 226–28; and RM, "Apollon aux lanternes (Versailles)," in *Autels privilégiés* (Paris: Bibliothèque Charpentier, 1898), 329–44.

547 "stones that ask only to crumble *magnificently*": RM, "Apollon aux lanternes," 332.

547 "the Sun King expiring": Ibid., 334.

547 In his dreams he saw the guillotine: RM, *Les Pas effacés,* vol. 3, 32–33. On RM's vision of blood-splashed pearls, see RM, *Les Perles rouges,* viii. (The poems in this volume were published after an almost twenty-year delay; MP refers to some of them in his correspondence with RM during this period.)

547   "cackled and screamed": William Samson, *The World of Proust* (New York: Scribner, 1973) and André Maurois, *Le Monde de Proust* (Paris: Hachette, 1960), 33.

547   "a sculptor of clouds!": Saint-Cère (pseud.), "Une heure chez le Comte Robert de Montesquiou," 119. On RM's pompous, poetic statements as (in his mind) gifts to the hearer, see Lorrain (pseud.), *La Ville empoisonnée*, 105.

547   Proserpina: A few years after his *"fête littéraire,"* RM sold this statue, a replica of François Girardon's *The Rape of Proserpina,* to American collector George Gould, a brother of Boni de Castellane's (and later Hélie de Talleyrand-Périgord's) "dollar bride," Anna Gould. See Jules Huret, *En Amérique de New York à La Nouvelle-Orléans* (Paris: Fasquelle, 1904), 199.

548   the focal point: On the theater RM had built for his party, see HR, *Nos rencontres,* 161.

548   "I am the sovereign of transitory things": This is the opening line of "Maëstro" [*sic*], a poem in RM, *The Bats,* 13. On this slogan, see also MP, "Robert de Montesquiou," in CSB, 426–35.

548   "delicate—, diaphanous—": Cited in Tout-Paris (pseud. MP), "Une fête littéraire à Versailles," *Le Gaulois* (May 31, 1894): 1.

548   Montesquiou's *"fête littéraire"*: RM, "Programme du jeudi 24 mai, 1894," in NAF 15040, folio 73. The twenty-fourth was the original date of the party, postponed, as mentioned, due to rainy weather. On RM's delight at imagining his foes having a bad time at his party, see RM, *Les Pas effacés,* vol. 3; RM, "Le Pavillon Montesquiou à Versailles"; and RM to EG, in AP(II)/101/150. On Hervieu's last-minute cancelation of his plan to attend RM's party, see Hervieu to RM, letter dated May 30, 1894, in NAF 15247, vol. 236, folio 41.

550   "The author Paul Hervieu": RM to Paul Hervieu, in NAF 15247, unnumbered folio.

550   he was said to impersonate the comte: MP's impersonations precipitated the two men's first temporary rupture. See LG, *Robert de Montesquiou et Marcel Proust,* 34. On the excision of his (and other guests') names and of his fashion descriptions from his article in *Le Gaulois,* see MP to RM, letter dated [Thursday, May 31, 1894], in Kolb, ed., op. cit., vol. 1, 297. See also Jullian, *Robert de Montesquiou,* 222; and Carter, *Marcel Proust,* 170.

551   "Never have I seen": MP to RM, letter marked "Sunday July 2, 1893," in Kolb, ed., op. cit., vol. 1, 217. As MP later told CA, "I believe I was conquered the very first time I set eyes on her. She had such breeding, such class [*sic*], such presence, and such a marvelous way of carrying her head. The way she wore a bird of paradise in her hair. Unique!" Cited in CA, op. cit., 156.

551   Proust attended a party: *Le Gaulois* published an account of Madeleine Lemaire's soirée on Thursday, April 13, 1893. As Mme Lemaire usually entertained on Tuesdays, the party for RM was thus likely held on April 11. See Carter, *Marcel Proust,* 145.

551   the key to some of the Faubourg's leading salons: Ibid., 148.

551   "baroque erudition": HR, *Nos rencontres,* 161.

551   "Proustifying": FG, *Mon amitié,* 47.

551   "You are the sovereign": MP would later rework this line in "Robert de Montesquiou," in CSB, 435, saying "that [RM's] kingdom is not only of this world and that eternal things, just as much as transitory ones, have preoccupied him."

551   "Your verses": MP to RM, undated letter probably from late spring or early summer 1893, in *Lettres à Robert de Montesquiou,* ed. Robert Proust and Paul Brach (Paris: Plon, 1930), 6. Robert Proust and Brach do not attempt to date the letters in this edition.

551   newly resettled in Paris: GBB's move to Paris seems to have happened sometime in the first few months of 1893. Whistler mentions going to the theater with GBB, RM, and EG in late January of that year. Based on reports in the *presse mondaine,* GBB became a weekly presence on the Parisian society circuit beginning that February, showing up at parties more often with RM than with EG, though sometimes with the two of them together. It appears that the group outing to Bayreuth in the summer of 1891 had brought RM and GBB closer together; this would explain not only the shift in their relationship but EG's apparent disappointment with the trip.

551   A few months after GBB moved, he was approved as a temporary member of the Cercle de l'Union Artistique and was granted permanent membership there in June 1894, with EG's brother-in-law Bob de L'Aigle acting as his sponsor. See *Le Gaulois* (June 28, 1894): 4.

551   "He was beautiful": FG, *Mon amitié,* 33.

551   "a dazzling young man": MP, JS, 675. In this novel, MP attributes the painting to *mondain* portraitist Antonio de La Gandara, a rival of JEB and a protégé of RM (675).

552   "never concealed the fact": CA, op. cit., 256.

552   "a delicious little page": Cited in Chaleyssin, op. cit., 64.

552   reminded Proust: MP, "A mon ami Willie Heath" (July 1894), in PJ, 40.

552   "dream, almost a plan": Ibid. On Heath's death, see Painter, op. cit., vol. 2, 138.

552   His interest in the comte: On MP's (nonerotic) motives for befriending RM, see Painter, op. cit., 134; Chaleyssin, op. cit., 76–77; and Maurois, *Quest for Proust,* 66.

552   "Professor of Beauty": MP, "Un professeur de beauté," *Les Arts de la vie* (August 15, 1905), reprinted in Léon Guichard, "Un article inconnu de Marcel Proust: Marcel Proust et Robert de Montesquiou," *La Revue d'histoire littéraire de la France* 2 (1949): 161–75, 163–72. See also RM and MP, *Le Professeur de beauté,* preface by Jean-David Jumeau Lafond (Paris: La Bibliothèque, 1999); and Jullian, *Robert de Montesquiou,* 18.

552   "heavenly opium": MP to RM, letter marked "This Thursday evening" (June 29, 1893), in Kolb, ed., op. cit., vol. 1, 216.

552   "a meadow filled with stars": MP to RM, Proust and Brach, eds., op. cit., 7.

552   "It would be an artist": MP, JS, 332.

552   "no more than 15": Cited in Jullian, *Robert de Montesquiou,* 220.

552   "CRAP": Cited in CA, op. cit., 258. On the issue of RM's photograph, see MP to RM, letter dated [June 28, 1893], in Kolb, ed., op. cit., vol. 1, 214; and Carter, *Marcel Proust,* 160.

553   "transformed into a bibelot": LG, *Robert de Montesquiou et Marcel Proust,* 38.

553   *"The Bats,"* he enthused: MP to RM, in Proust and Brach, eds., op. cit., 15.

553   a bluebird in a cage: MP to RM, letter dated [March 11, 1894], in Kolb, ed., op. cit., vol. 1, 277. Kolb notes that RM wrote in MP's inscribed copy of *The Bats,* "A memento for M. Marcel Proust, who gave me a bluebird" (280, n. 2). On the gift of the Liberty ties, see Jullian, *Robert de Montesquiou,* op. cit., 221. On the gift of the crèche, see MP to RM, letter dated [March 28, 1894], in Kolb, ed., op. cit., 284.

553   "absurd": MP to RM, letter dated [June 25, 1893] in Kolb, ed., op. cit., vol. 1, 213. The same letter appears, without any editorial surmise as to the date, in Proust and Brach, eds., op. cit., 8.

553   "Be wise": Psalms 2:10. Like Melchior de Vogüé, RM was partial to quoting in Latin, so he delivered this command: *Nunc erudimini.* See Chaleyssin, op. cit., 69. FG liked to quote this line when making fun of RM.

553   "sardonyx": Cited in Jullian, *Robert de Montesquiou,* 184, 189, and 190. See also 18.

553   "Your diction": Cited in Chaleyssin, op. cit., 67. For LD's much less flattering account of RM's oratorical style, see LD, *Fantômes et vivants,* 185.

553   "Anyone who has seen": MP, "Un professeur de beauté," 163–64.

554   "In the beginning": Cited in Jullian, *Robert de Montesquiou,* 216. Unbeknownst to MP, EG had come around to a similar perspective about RM, saying of him behind his back, "It's a shame he is ridiculous"; cited in Hillerin, op. cit., 41–42.

554   "plush, . . . dark interior": FG, *Mon amitié,* 32. On the "frightful, cushy" décor of the Proust family's apartment, see also Duplay, op. cit., 24.

554   "an incomparable museum": Cited in ibid.

554   the comte's interiors: RM's interior decorating interests and ventures form a huge subject unto themselves; for one good overview, see Bertrand, op. cit., vol. 1, "Partie I: L'Espace intérieur," 53–258. On RM's interiors as "universes of theatricality," see ibid., vol. 2, 703–4.

555   "a cigarette butt": Cited in LD, *Fantômes et vivants,* 284.

555   "On the shelves": Abel Hermant, "Jours de guerre," *Le Monde illustré* (July 15, 1917): 40.

556   "The grouping of *objets*": RM, *Les Pas perdus,* vol. 2, 94.

556   "he would grow emotional": LD, *Fantômes et vivants,* 284–85.

556   "He led us through": Cited in Bertrand, op. cit., vol. 1, 87–88.

557   "The names [of their former owners]": RM, *Brelan de Dames* (Paris: Fontemoigne, 1912), 15.

557   "The man is suffering": Special thanks to HRH Prince Dimitri of Yugoslavia for bringing my attention to this bit of his family lore. The fistula and operation are also discussed in Stanis Perez, *La Santé de Louis XIV* (Paris: Perrin, 2010), 73–83.

557   "I put you to the test": Cited in Chaleyssin, op. cit., 67; see also MP to RM, in Kolb, ed., op. cit., vol. 1, 410; and MP, RTP, vol. 2, 1813, n. 2.

557   "loved to play at being the king": MP, CG, 842.

557   *"bourgeois":* Ibid., 845.

558   "As any nobleman must": Ibid., 844.

558   "the last words": Ibid.

558   "I cannot expect much": Ibid., 849.

558   "I walked back": Ibid., 849–50.

558   "Despite his solemn avowals": Ibid., 851.

559   The issue of *La Revue blanche* in which "Other Relics" appeared was published on July 15. From his correspondence with the editor, Thadée Natanson, it seems that MP finished and filed his story about a week before the issue went to press; see Kolb, ed., op. cit., vol. 1, 231, n. 3.

559   "whom I should have liked to befriend": MP, "Autres reliques," originally published in *La Revue blanche* 21–22 (July–August 1893): 51–52, 51; and reprinted as "Reliques" in PJ, 175–76.

559   "most unguarded, inviolable": Ibid.

559   "Haven't you retained": MP, "Reliques," PJ, 176.

560   "Cards, novels": Ibid.

560   "I finally saw": MP to RM, letter dated [Sunday, July 2, 1893?], in Kolb, ed., op. cit., 217.

561   they were more valuable to him as relics: Toward the end of his life, reflecting to CA on the society people (including LC, GS, and EG) who had "posed" for his novel, MP explicitly spoke of them as relics on display, dead objects trapped under glass: "'Ah Céleste,' he sighed, 'all that is crumbling to dust. It is like a collection of beautiful antique fans on a wall. You admire them, but there is no hand now to bring them alive. The very fact that they are under glass now proves that the ball is over.'" Cited in CA, op. cit., 159.

561   "chiming like the carillons of Bruges": Cited in Huas, op. cit., 185.

561   "You reminded me": MP, "A Willie Heath," PJ, 40. MP dated this dedication July 1894 but would not publish it until 1896, when he used it as the preface to PJ.

561   Not before meeting Mme Greffulhe: On MP's determination to meet EG through RM, see Huas, op. cit., 181; and Taylor, op. cit., 30. Taylor amusingly writes that "an introduction to [RM's] cousin the Comtesse Greffulhe [was] every snob's highest goal."

561   "some of those lady friends": MP to RM, undated letter from 1893, in Proust and Brach, eds., op. cit., 9.

562   "Do you not see": Cited in Briais, *Au temps des Frou-Frou: Femmes célèbres de la Belle Époque* (Paris: Imprimerie de Frou-Frou, 1902), 267; and in Chaleyssin, op. cit., 110.

562   according to his worried friends: FG was particularly concerned about the degree to which RM humiliated MP; see FG, *Mon amitié,* 33–35. FG adds that according to Helleu, CA went "crazy with joy" when she learned of RM's (rather miserable) death in 1921. Mulling over this news, FG writes, "What did she know? Why so much hatred?" (ibid., 35) In MP's letters to RM, one certainly sees an almost "Blob"-like capacity for abjection. After one apparently vicious tongue-lashing from RM, MP wrote to him, "Dear sir, one doesn't get angry at lightning, even when it strikes one, because it comes from on high"; MP to RM in Proust and Brach, ed., op. cit., 13.

562   a *mondain* epistolary novel: On the genesis of the group epistolary project and on the characters assumed by each of the four writers, see MP, *Écrits de jeunesse,* 218–19. FG would soon change Chalgrain from a novelist into a painter, but he would preserve the character's essential identity as an artist who was not born into the monde yet wants to socialize there, like Olivier Bertin in *Strong as Death,* or like any number of GS's *fidèles.* For a useful overview of *In Their Own Words,* see Auchincloss, op. cit., 125–31. The final line of this commentary on the novel is "One can see why [MP] so admired Hervieu's treatment of the 'old Faubourg.' It is not unlike his own" (131). Apropos, on MP's admiration for the "unforeseen richness" Hervieu's novel brought to the epistolary genre and the *mondain* comedy of manners, see MP to Mme de Pierrebourg, in Kolb, ed., op. cit., vol. 21, 244. All citations given here in connection with MP's group epistolary novel and his characterization of Pauline de Dives appear in MP, *Écrits de jeunesse,* 252–66.

563   their new villa: On Le Clos des Mûriers as an imitation of the Greffulhes' villa in Dieppe, see DH cited in Bischoff, op. cit., 203.

564   "little book": MP to RB, letter dated Sunday [November 5, 1893], in Kolb, ed., op. cit., vol. 1, 245. It is in this letter, too, that MP mentions that Mme Lemaire has already agreed to illustrate his "little book."

564   "aristocratic and elegant society": Tout-Paris (pseud. MP), "Les Grands Salons parisiens," *Le Gaulois* (September 1, 1893): 2.

565   As the comte informed Proust: On RM's correction of MP regarding the Princesse de Léon (versus the Duchesse de Rohan), see Philip Kolb, "La Correspondance de Marcel Proust: Chronologie et commentaire critique," *Illinois Studies in Language and Literature* 33, nos. 1–2 (1949), 5 and 9; and Carassus, op. cit., 538–39.

566   "deliciously attired": Tout-Paris (pseud.), "Une fête littéraire à Versailles."

566   The cloud of tulle: On EG's opaque mauve veil, and on the complaints it engendered from the other party guests (who were presumably hoping for a glimpse of her face), see EdG, *Journal,* entries of May 30, 1894, and May 31, 1894. For another less than glowing account of the party, see HR, *Nos rencontres,* 161–65.

567   "Too thick was your veil!": GPR to EG, undated note in NAF 24974, folio 169.

567   "a none-too-flattering shade": RM, *Les Pas effacés,* vol. 3, 165; cited in Florence Callu and Jacques Lethève, eds., *Marcel Proust—Exposition à la Bibliothèque Nationale, juin–septembre 1965* (Paris: Tournon & Cie., 1965), 34.

568   finding only scant relief: LD, *Souvenirs littéraires,* 145.

568   "the poor things": Ibid.

568   "heartrending cries as it slowly roasted to death": Cited in Sherard, op. cit., 331.

568   "cruel, languorous inflections": HR, *Nos rencontres,* 161. On the mediocrity of RM's art, in the context of his own *"fête littéraire,"* see Jean Ajalbert, "Rimes riches," *Gil Blas* (June 5, 1894): 1–2.

568   "Shadows of tree glens": RM, "Aria," in *Les Chauves-souris,* 22.

568   "I love jade": RM, "Salomé" (per RM's program for the party in NAF 15040), published many years later as "L'Irresponsable," in *Les Paons: édition définitive* (Paris: G. Richard, 1908), 90; also cited in HR, *Nos rencontres,* 165.

568   "Filled with all the love letters": RM, "Le Coucher de la morte," in *Les Chauves-souris,* 393–94.

569   cited it at length in his article: MP quotes three full stanzas of the poem in Tout-Paris (pseud.), "Une fête littéraire à Versailles." Introducing the poem, MP describes it as "a page that will endure."

569   Élisabeth clipped from the front page: "Une fête littéraire" remains in EG's archive to this day, filed under AP(II)/101/136–38.

WORKS CONSULTED

I · ARCHIVAL SOURCES

A · Archives Nationales de France, Paris

Private archive of the Comtesse Greffulhe. AP(II)/101/1–203; and six "noncoded, supplementary" files
Private archive of the Comte Greffulhe. AP(I)/101/1–63
Private papers of the Gramont family. AP/101/A1–J5
Private papers of the Greffulhe family. AQ/61/1–6

B · Bibliothèque Nationale de France, Paris

1. Département des Manuscrits

Letters of Georges Bizet and Geneviève Halévy, later Mme Bizet. NAF 14345
Letters and papers of the Halévy, Bizet, and Straus families. NAF 13205; NAF 13208; NAF 13209–13210; NAF 13212–13222; NAF 14346–14355; and NAF 14383–14386
Letters addressed to Mme Bizet, later Mme Straus. NAF 14826; NAF 24838–24839
Letters of Paul Hervieu, addressed to Mme Bizet, later Mme Straus. NAF 13206–13207
Letters of Georges de Porto-Riche, addressed to Mme Bizet, later Mme Straus. NAF 13211
Letters of Comte and Comtesse Adhéaume de Chevigné, addressed to Georges de Porto-Riche. NAF 24954–24955; NAF 24980
Letters and papers of Georges de Porto-Riche. NAF 24510–25021
Letters and papers of Ludovic Halévy. NAF 19801–19915
Letters and papers of Comte Robert de Montesquiou-Fezensac. NAF 15012–15380
Papers of the Guérin and Straus families. NAF 14826
Selected writings of the Princesse Bibesco. NAF 28220
Selected writings of Marcel Proust. NAF 16612–16616; NAF 16696; NAF 18313–18325; NAF 24884; NAF 27350–27352

2. Département de la Musique

Letters of the Comtesse Greffulhe, addressed to various composers. NLA 305–334; VM BOB-20541

3. Bibliothèque de l'Arsenal

Correspondence of Comtesse Adhéaume de Chevigné with Ferdinand Bac. Ms. 14159
Papers of Paul Hervieu. Ms. 13969

4. Bibliothèque–Musée de l'Opéra

Letters of Eraïm Miriam Delaborde. VM BOB-19470
Dossier pertaining to the composition and premiere of Georges Bizet's *Carmen* (1875). FOL-ICO THE-648
Letters of Mme Straus, addressed to various composers and musicians. NLAS-119(49); LAS BIZET (GENEVIEVE)

C · The Metropolitan Museum of Art, New York

Halévy family album, containing photographs by and of various members of the Halévy, Bizet/Straus, and Chevigné families; Edgar Degas; Mme Meredith (Hortense) Howland; Charles Haas; Alfred, Marquis du Lau d'Allemans; Vicomte Eugène-Melchior de Vogüé; General Mikhail Annenkov; Guy de Maupassant; and Georges de Porto-Riche. Accession Number 2005.1001.587.1-29

D · The Morgan Library and Museum, New York

Letters of Émile Straus. MLT H148.S912; LHMS 193335
Letters of Lord Lytton. MA 1714-120627; MA 3944-120670; MA 4500-186849

Manuscript of Mme Straus's last will and testament. LHMS 193949. NB: Although Émile
Straus is listed as the author of this document, it is written in Mme Straus's hand.

E · *Beinecke Rare Books and Manuscript Library, Yale University*

Frederick R. Koch Collection: GEN MSS 601, box 49
Letters of Mme Straus and Marcel Proust. Folder 1022
Manuscript writings of Marcel Proust. Folder 1034

F · *Digital Archives and Resources*

Archives départementales de Seine-et-Marne. Melun. http://archives.seine-et-marne.fr
/archives-en-ligne
Archives du Musée d'Art et d'Histoire du Judaïsme. Paris. https://www.mahj.org/fr
/ressources-documentaires/archives
Archivio fotografico digitale della Fondazione Primoli. Rome. http://www.archivioprimoli.it
Correspondance de Guy de Maupassant. www.maupassant.free.fr
Correspondence of James A. M. Whistler. University of Glasgow. http://www.whistler.arts
.gla.ac.uk/
Fonds autour de la Comtesse Greffulhe. Musée d'Orsay. Paris. http://www.musee-orsay.fr/fr
/collections/
Journal des Goncourt. https://fr.wikisource.org/wiki/Journal_des_Goncourt/I
The Kolb-Proust Archive for Research. University of Illinois at Urbana-Champaign. http://
www.library.illinois.edu/kolbp/
Mémoire des équipages: Équipage de Bois-Boudran (1836–1912). http://www
.memoiredesequipages.fr/fiche/2691
The Rothschild Archive. London. https://www.Rothschildarchive.org/

G · *Other Archives*

Mina Curtiss Collection. Music Division, New York Public Library. New York. JBP 93–95,
Series 1–7
Correspondence of Comte Albert de Mun. Archives Jésuites de la Province de France. Vanves.
HDu61-70
Greffulhe family films. Centre National de la Cinématographie. Paris. Thirty-six home
movies shot between 1899 and 1913 and filed under "[Film de famille Greffulhe]."
Greffulhe family papers. Centre des Archives Nationales du Monde du Travail. Paris.
2006/064/Mi-6

II · BIOGRAPHIES, CORRESPONDENCE, AND OTHER WRITINGS ABOUT AND BY MMES DE CHEVIGNÉ, GREFFULHE, AND STRAUS

Acker, Paul. "La Comtesse Greffulhe." In *Portraits de femmes*. Paris: Dorbon Aîné, 1912.
Balard, Françoise, ed. *Geneviève Straus: Biographie et correspondance avec Ludovic Halévy: 1855–1908*.
Paris: CNRS Éditions, 2002.
Bibesco, Marthe, Princesse. *La Duchesse de Guermantes: Laure de Sade, Comtesse de Chevigné*. Paris:
Plon, 1950.
Bischoff, Chantal. *Geneviève Straus: Trilogie d'une égérie*. Paris: Balland, 1992.
Bled, Victor du. "Comtesse Greffülhe [*sic*] née Caraman-Chimay." In *Le Salon de la Revue des deux
mondes*. Paris: Bloud & Gay, 1930.
Borrel, Anne. "Geneviève Straus, la 'muse mauve'." In *Entre le théâtre et l'histoire: la famille Halévy
1760–1960*. Edited by Henri Loyrette. Paris: Fayard, 1996.
Bosc, Alexandra. "Elle n'a pas suivi les modes, elle était faite pour les créer." In *La Mode retrouvée: les
robes trésors de la Comtesse Greffulhe*. Edited by Olivier Saillard. Paris: Palais Galliera, 2015.
Brahma, X. (pseud. Comtesse Greffulhe). *Âmes sociales*. Paris: Georges Richard, 1898.
Brisman, Shira. "Biographies: Geneviève Straus." In *Jewish Women and their Salons: The Power of
Conversation*. Edited by Emily D. Bilsky and Emily Braun. New York: The Jewish Museum, 2005.
Buffenoir, Hippolyte. *Grandes dames contemporaines: la Comtesse Greffulhe, née Caraman-Chimay*.
Paris: Librairie du Mirabeau, 1894.

Callu, Florence. "Madame Straus." In *Le Cercle de Marcel Proust.* Edited by Jean-Yves Tadié. Paris: Honoré Champion, 2013.

Cerboneschi, Isabelle. "La Comtesse Greffulhe, icône de mode." *Le Temps* (December 23, 2015).

Clermont-Tonnere, Élisabeth de Gramont, Duchesse de. "L'Entresol." *Le Figaro: supplément littéraire* (March 3, 1928): 3.

Cossé-Brissac, Anne de. *La Comtesse Greffulhe.* Paris: Perrin, 1993.

Dreyfus, Robert. "Madame Straus et Marcel Proust." *La Revue de Paris* 42 (October 15, 1936): 803–14.

Flament, Albert. "Quelques apparitions de la Comtesse Greffulhe." *La Revue des deux mondes* (March 1953).

———. "Le Salon de l'Europe: La Comtesse Adhéaume de Chevigné." *La Revue de Paris* 44 (November 15, 1936).

de Flers, Robert. "Mort de Mme Émile Straus." *Le Figaro* (December 23, 1926).

Halévy, Daniel. "Deux portraits de Mme Straus." In *Marcel Proust: Correspondance avec Daniel Halévy.* Edited by Anne Borrel and Jean-Pierre Halévy. Paris: Fallos, 1992.

Hillerin, Laure. *La Comtesse Greffulhe: l'ombre des Guermantes.* Paris: Flammarion, 2015.

———. "Trajectoire d'une étoile oubliée." In *La Mode retrouvée: les robes-trésors de la comtesse Greffulhe.* Edited by Olivier Saillard and Valerie Steele. Paris: Paris-Musées, 2015.

Jacob, Andrée. *Il y a un siècle . . . quand les dames tenaient salon.* Paris: Arnaud Seydoux, 1991.

Laincel, Comtesse Alice de. *Les Grandes Dames d'aujourd'hui.* Paris: Société d'Imprimerie, 1885.

Largillière (pseud.). "La Société de Paris: la Comtesse de Chevigné." *Gil Blas* (August 17, 1903).

Loyrette, Henri, ed. *Entre le théâtre et l'histoire: la famille Halévy 1760–1960.* Paris: Fayard, 1996.

Mainwaring, Madison. "Fashion Regained: Looking for Proust's Muse in Paris." *Paris Review* (March 16, 2016).

Meyer, Arthur. "Salons d'aujourd'hui et d'hier." In *Ce que je peux dire.* Paris: Plon, 1912.

Pasler, Jann. "Countess Greffulhe as Entrepreneur: Negotiating Class, Gender, and Nation." In *The Musician as Entrepreneur 1700–1914.* Edited by William Weber. Bloomington: Indiana University Press, 2004.

Poirey, Jean-Louis. "Ma Comtesse: Souvenirs d'un enfant, 8-10, rue d'Astorg, 1944–1956." Gy: n.p., 2015.

Pringué, Gabriel-Louis. "La Souveraine de la Belle Époque." *Le Crapouillot: les Bonnes manières* 19 (1952): 26-29.

Proyart, Jean-Baptiste de. "Marcel Proust et la Comtesse de Chevigné: Envoi autographe sur *Le Côté de Guermantes* I et correspondance" (June 2008).

Romani, Bruno. "La Regina degli Snob: la Contessa Greffulhe." *Il Messaggero* (September 9, 1956).

Steele, Valerie. "L'Aristocrate comme œuvre d'art." In *La Mode retrouvée: les robes-trésors de la comtesse Greffulhe.* Edited by Olivier Saillard and Valerie Steele. Paris: Paris-Musées, 2015.

Steta, Annick. "À la recherche de la Comtesse Greffulhe." *La Revue des deux mondes* (February 12, 2016).

Vaux, Baron de. "La Vicomtesse de [*sic*] Greffulhe." In *Les Femmes de sport.* Paris: Marpon & Flammarion, 1885.

III · MARCEL PROUST BIBLIOGRAPHY

A · Selected Correspondence, Journalism, and Literary Works

De Brabant (pseud.). "Exposition Internationale: Galerie Georges-Petit." *Le Mensuel* (December 1890).

Proust, Marcel. *A la recherche du temps perdu.* 4 vols. Edited by Jean-Yves Tadié et al. Paris: Gallimard/ Pléiade, 2005.

———. "A une Snob." *La Revue blanche* 26 (December 1893).

———. "Les Amies de la Comtesse Myrto." *Le Banquet* 2 (April 1892).

———. "Autres reliques." *La Revue blanche* 21–22 (July–August 1893).

———. *Les Cahiers 1 à 75 de la Bibliothèque Nationale de France.* Edited by Nathalie Mauriac Dyer, Bernard Brun, Antoine Compagnon, et al. Tournhout: Brepols, 2008.

———. *Carnet de 1908.* Edited by Philip Kolb. Paris: Gallimard/NRF, 1976.

———. *Carnets.* Edited by Florence Callu and Antoine Compagnon. Paris: Gallimard/NRF, 2002.

———. *Chroniques.* Edited by Robert Proust. Paris: Gallimard/ NRF, 1927.

———. *The Collected Poems.* Edited by Harold Augenbraum. New York: Penguin, 2013.

———. *Contre Sainte-Beuve, suivi de nouveaux mélanges.* Paris: Gallimard/NRF, 1954 [c. 1895–1900].

———. "Contre une Snob." *La Revue blanche* 26 (December 1893).

———. "Conversation avec Maman." In *Contre Sainte-Beuve*. Paris: Gallimard/NRF, 1954.

———. *Correspondance, 1880–1922.* 21 vols. Edited by Philip Kolb. Paris: Plon, 1971–1993.

———. *Correspondance.* Edited by Jérôme Picon. Paris: Flammarion, 2007.

———. *Correspondance avec Daniel Halévy.* Edited by Anne Borrel and J.-P. Halévy, op. cit.

———. *Correspondance avec Madame Straus.* Introduction by Susy Mante-Proust. Paris: Plon, 1936.

———. *Correspondance avec sa mère: 1887–1905.* Edited by Philip Kolb. Paris: Plon, 1953.

———. "Cydalise." *Le Banquet* 2 (April 1892).

———. *Days of Reading.* Translated by John Sturrock. New York: Penguin/Great Ideas, 2008.

———. *Écrits de jeunesse: 1887–1895.* Edited by Anne Borrel. Paris: Institut Marcel Proust International, 1991.

———. *Écrits sur l'art.* Edited by Jérôme Picon. Paris: Flammarion, 1999.

———. "Esquisse d'après Madame de ***." *Le Banquet* 3 (May 1892).

———. "Esquisse de vie mondaine." *Bulletin de la Société de Marcel Proust* 11 (1961).

———. "Étude I [Les Maîtresses de Fabrice]." *Le Banquet* 2 (April 1892).

———. "Étude II [Les Snobs]." *Le Banquet* 3 (May 1892).

———. "Étude IX [Amitié]." *La Revue blanche* 21–22 (July–August 1893).

———. *La Fin de la jalousie et autres nouvelles.* Edited by Thierry Laget. Paris: Gallimard, 1993.

———. *Fragments de comédie italienne.* In *Les Plaisirs et les jours.* Paris: Gallimard, 1993.

———. "Gustave Moreau." In *Contre Sainte-Beuve*. Gallimard/NRF, 1954.

———. "Henri de Régnier." In *Contre Sainte-Beuve*. Paris: Gallimard/NRF, 1954.

———. *Jean Santeuil.* Edited by Pierre Clarac. Paris: Gallimard/Pléiade, 1971.

———. *Letters to a Friend.* Preface by Georges de Lauris. Translated by Alexander and Elizabeth Henderson. London: Falcon Press, 1949.

———. *Letters to His Mother.* Translated and edited by George D. Painter. New York: Citadel, 1957.

———. *Lettres à Madame et Monsieur Émile Straus.* Edited by Robert Proust. Paris: Plon, 1936.

———. *Lettres à M. et Mme Sydney Schiff, Paul Souday, J.-É. Blanche, etc.* Edited by Robert Proust and Paul Brach. Paris: Plon, 1932.

———. *Lettres à Robert de Montesquiou.* Edited by Robert Proust and Paul Brach. Paris: Plon, 1930.

———. "Un livre contre l'élégance: *Sens dessus dessous.*" *Le Banquet* 2 (April 1892).

———. *Matinée chez la Princesse de Guermantes.* Edited by Henri Bonnet. Paris: NRF/Gallimard, 1982.

———. "Mondanité de Bouvard et Pécuchet." *La Revue blanche* 21–22 (July–August 1893).

———. "Noms de personnes." In *Contre Sainte-Beuve*. Paris: Gallimard/NRF, 1954.

———. *Pastiches et mélanges.* Paris: Gallimard, 1947 [1919].

———. "Pendant le Carême." *Le Mensuel* (February 1891).

———. "'*Les Petits Souliers*' par M. Louis Ganderax." *Le Banquet* 1 (March 1892).

———. *Les Plaisirs et les jours, suivis de "L'Indifférent."* Edited by Thierry Laurent. Paris: Gallimard, 1993.

———. Preface to Paul Morand, *Tendres stocks.* Paris: NRF/ Gallimard, 1923.

———. "Un professeur de beauté." *Les Arts de la vie* (August 15, 1905).

———. "Robert de Montesquiou." In *Contre Sainte-Beuve*. Paris: NRF/Gallimard, 1954.

———. "Le Salon de la Comtesse Greffulhe." Unpublished manuscript from AP(II)/101, in one of six "cartons non cotés, supplémentaires." Reproduced in translation in appendix C.

———. *Le Salon de Mme de . . . .* Paris: L'Herne, 2009.

———. "Sixteen Letters of Marcel Proust to Joseph Reinach." Translated and edited by D. R. Watson. *Modern Languages Review* 63, no. 3 (July 1968).

———. *Swann's Way.* Translated by C. K. Scott Moncrieff. Edited and annotated by William C. Carter. New Haven and London: Yale University Press, 2013.

———. *Textes retrouvés.* Edited by Philip Kolb and Larkin B. Price. Urbana and Chicago: University of Illinois Press, 1968.

———. "La Vie mondaine." *Le Mensuel* 3 (January 1891).

Tout-Paris (pseud.). "Une Fête littéraire à Versailles." *Le Gaulois* (May 31, 1894).

———. "Les Grands Salons de Paris." *Le Gaulois* (September 1, 1893). Reproduced in translation in appendix C.

———. "Mondanités." *Le Gaulois* (August 24, 1895, and June 18, 1896).

B · Selected Memoirs, Biographies

Albaret, Céleste. *Monsieur Proust.* Translated by Barbara Bray. New York: New York Review Books, 2003.

Bibesco, Marthe, Princesse. *Au bal avec Marcel Proust.* Paris: Gallimard/L'Imaginaire, 1989 [1928].

———. *Le Voyageur voilé.* Geneva: La Palatine, 1947.

Billy, Robert de. *Marcel Proust: Lettres et conversations.* Paris: Portiques, 1930.

Blanche, Jacques-Émile. "Mes modèles." *Les Nouvelles littéraires, artistiques et scientifiques* (July 14, 1928).

———. *Mes modèles: Souvenirs littéraires.* Paris: Stock, 1984 [1928].

———. *La Pêche aux souvenirs.* Paris: Flammarion, 1949.

———. *Propos de peintre.* Edited by Frédéric Mitterrand. Paris: Séguier, 2013 [1919–1928].

Bloch-Dano, Évelyne. *Madame Proust: A Biography.* Translated by Alice Kaplan. Chicago and London: University of Chicago Press, 2007.

———. *Une jeunesse de Marcel Proust: enquête sur le questionnaire.* Paris: Stock, 2017.

Carter, William C. *Marcel Proust: A Life.* New Haven and London: Yale University Press, 2013.

———. *Proust in Love.* New Haven and London: Yale University Press, 2006.

Colette (pseud. Gabrielle-Sidonie Colette). "Préface: Marcel Proust." In *Marcel Proust.* Paris: Le Capitole, 1926.

Daudet, Lucien. *Autour de soixante lettres de Marcel Proust.* Paris: Gallimard, 1929.

Dreyfus, Robert. *De Monsieur Thiers à Marcel Proust: histoire et souvenirs.* Paris: Plon, 1939.

———. *Souvenirs sur Marcel Proust, accompagnés de lettres inédites.* Paris: Grasset, 1926.

———. "Souvenirs sur Marcel Proust: L'Année du *Banquet,* 1892–1893." *Le Figaro* (April 10, 1926): 1–2.

Duplay, Maurice. *Mon ami Marcel Proust: souvenirs intimes.* Paris: Gallimard, 1972.

Gramont, Armand, Duc de Guiche, later Duc de. *Souvenirs: 1879–1962.* Unpublished manuscript.

Gramont, Élisabeth de (Duchesse de Clermont-Tonnerre). *Marcel Proust.* Paris: Flammarion, 1948.

———. *Robert de Montesquiou et Marcel Proust.* Paris: Flammarion, 1925.

Gregh, Fernand. *L'Age d'or.* Paris: Grasset, 1947.

———. "Hommage à Marcel Proust." *La Nouvelle Revue française* (January 1923).

———. *Mon amitié avec Marcel Proust: Souvenirs et lettres inédites.* Paris: Grasset, 1958.

Hayman, Ronald. *Proust: A Biography.* New York: Carrol & Graf, 1992.

Lhéritier, Gérard, ed. *Proust, du temps perdu au temps retrouvé: Précieuse collection de lettres et manuscrits provenant d'André et Simone Maurois et de Susy Mante-Proust.* Paris: Équateurs, 2010.

Maurois, André. *Le Monde de Marcel Proust.* Paris: Hachette, 1960.

Montesquiou-Fezensac, Comte Robert de, and Marcel Proust. *Le Professeur de beauté.* Preface by Jean-David Jumeau-Lafond. Paris: La Bibliothèque, 1999.

Painter, George D. *Marcel Proust: A Biography.* 2 vols. London: Chatto & Windus, 1959–1965.

Peter, René. *Une saison avec Marcel Proust.* Preface by Jean-Yves Tadié. Paris: Gallimard/NRF, 2005.

Pierre-Quint, Léon. *Marcel Proust: sa vie, son œuvre.* Paris: Simon Kra, 1925.

Sollers, Philippe. *L'Œil de Proust: les dessins de Marcel Proust.* Paris: Stock, 1999.

Souday, Paul. *Marcel Proust.* Paris: Simon Kra, 1927.

Tadié, Jean-Yves. *Marcel Proust.* Translated by Euan Cameron. New York: Viking, 2000.

Tadié, Jean-Yves, ed. *Le Cercle de Marcel Proust.* Paris: Honoré Champion, 2013.

———. *Marcel Proust et ses amis.* Paris: Gallimard/NRF, 2010.

Taylor, Benjamin. *Proust: The Search.* New Haven and London: Yale University Press/Jewish Lives, 2015.

White, Edmund. *Marcel Proust: A Life.* New York: Penguin, 1999.

C · Criticism and Scholarship—Books

Aciman, André, ed. *The Proust Project.* New York: FSG/Books & Co./Helen Marx Books, 2004.

Adorno, Theodor W. *Notes to Literature.* 2 vols. Translated by Shierry W. Nicholsen. New York: Columbia University Press, 1991–1992.

Arnaud, Claude. *Proust contre Cocteau.* Paris: Grasset, 2013.

Bardèche, Maurice. *Marcel Proust romancier.* 2 vols. Paris: Sept Couleurs, 1971.

Barthes, Roland. *The Preparation of the Novel.* Translated by Kate Briggs. New York: Columbia University Press, 2011.

Beckett, Samuel. *Proust.* London: Chatto & Windus, 1931.

Benjamin, Walter. *Sur Proust.* Translated by Robert Kahn. Paris: Nous, 2010.

Bergstein, Mary. *Looking Back One Learns to See: Marcel Proust and Photography.* Amsterdam and New York: Ropoli, 2014.

Bernard, Anne-Marie, ed. *The World of Proust as Seen by Paul Nadar.* Photographs by Paul Nadar. Translated by Susan Wise. Cambridge and London: The MIT Press, 2002.

Bersani, Leo. *Marcel Proust: The Fictions of Life and of Art.* Oxford: Oxford University Press, 1965.

Botton, Alain de. *How Proust Can Change Your Life.* New York: Pantheon, 1997.

Bowie, Malcolm. *Proust Among the Stars.* New York: Columbia University Press, 2000.

Brassaï (pseud. Gyula Halász). *Proust in the Power of Photography.* Translated by Richard Howard. Chicago and London: University of Chicago Press, 2001.
Canavaggia, J. *Proust et la politique.* Paris: A.-G. Nizet, 1986.
Carassus, Émilien. *Le Snobisme dans les lettres françaises de Paul Bourget à Marcel Proust: 1884–1914.* Paris: Armand Colin, 1966.
Clarac, Pierre, and André Ferré, eds. *Album Proust.* Paris: Gallimard/Pléïade, 1965.
Compagnon, Antoine. *Proust entre deux siècles.* Paris: Seuil, 1989.
Deleuze, Gilles. *Proust et les signes.* Paris: PUF, 2007.
Diesbach, Ghislain de. *Proust.* Paris: Perrin, 1991.
Finn, Michael R. *Proust, the Body, and Literary Form.* Cambridge and London: Cambridge University Press, 1999.
Forest, Philippe, and Stéphane Audeguy, eds. *La Nouvelle Revue française: D'après Proust 203–4* (March 2013).
Francis, Claude, and Fernande Gontier. *Marcel Proust et les siens.* Paris: Plon, 1981.
Fraser, Robert. *Proust and the Victorians: The Lamp of Memory.* London: Macmillan/Springer, 1994.
Gallo, Rubén. *Proust's Latin Americans.* Baltimore and London: The Johns Hopkins University Press, 2014.
Germain, André. *Les Clés de Proust, suivies de Portraits.* Paris: Sun, 1953.
Grimaldi, Nicolas. *Proust, les horreurs de l'amour.* Paris: PUF, 2008.
Guichard, Léon. "Un article inconnu de Marcel Proust: Marcel Proust et Robert de Montesquiou." *La Revue d'histoire littéraire de la France* 2 (1949).
Harris, Frederick John. *Friend and Foe: Marcel Proust and André Gide.* Lanham, MD: University Press of America, 2002.
Huas, Jeanine. *Les Femmes chez Proust.* Paris: Hachette, 1971.
———. *L'Homosexualité au temps de Proust.* Paris: Danclau, 1992.
Hunkeler, Thomas, ed. *Marcel Proust und die Belle Époque.* Frankfurt: Insel/Marcel Proust Gesellschaft, 2002.
Jullien, Dominique. *Proust et ses modèles: Les "Mille et une Nuits" et les "Mémoires" de Saint-Simon.* Paris: José Corti, 1989.
Kadi, Simone. *Proust et Baudelaire.* Paris: Pensée Universelle, 1975.
Karlin, Daniel. *Proust's English.* Oxford: Oxford University Press, 2007.
Karpeles, Eric. *Paintings in Proust: A Visual Companion to "In Search of Lost Time."* London: Thames & Hudson, 2008.
Ladenson, Elisabeth. *Proust's Lesbians.* Ithaca, NY: Cornell University Press, 2006.
Landes-Ferrali, Sylvaine. *Proust et le Grand Siècle: formes et significations de la référence.* Preface by Antoine Compagnon. Tübingen: Gunter Narr, 2004.
Luckhurst, Nicola. *Science and Structure in Proust's "A la recherche du temps perdu."* Oxford: Clarendon, 2000.
Mante-Proust, Suzy, and Mireille Naturel, eds. *Marcel Proust in / Pictures and Documents.* Translated by Josephine Bacon. Zurich: Olms, 2012.
Mauriac, François. *Proust's Way.* Translated by Elsie Pell. New York: Philosophical Library, 1950.
Maurois, André. *Quest for Proust.* Translated by Gerard Hopkins. New York: Penguin, 1962 [1950].
McDonald, Christie, and François Proulx, eds. *Proust and the Arts.* Cambridge and London: Cambridge University Press, 2015.
Moss, Howard. *The Magic Lantern of Marcel Proust.* Foreword by Damion Searls. Philadelphia: Paul Dry Books, 2012 [1962].
Muhlstein, Anka. *Monsieur Proust's Library.* New York: Other Press, 2012.
Oriol, Judith. *Femmes Proustiennes.* Paris: EST, 2009.
Raczymow, Henri. *Le Cygne de Proust.* Paris: Gallimard, 1989.
———. *Le Paris littéraire et intime de Proust.* Paris: Parigramme, 1997.
———. *Le Paris retrouvé de Marcel Proust.* Paris: Parigramme, 2005.
Recanti, Jean. *Profils juifs de Marcel Proust.* Paris: Buchet/Chastel, 1979.
Shattuck, Roger. *Proust's Way: A Field Guide to "In Search of Lost Time."* New York: W. W. Norton & Co., 2001.
Vignal, Louis Gautier. *Proust connu et inconnu.* Paris: Laffont, 1976.

D · Criticism and Scholarship—Articles and Chapters

Adam, A. "Le Roman de Proust et le problème des clefs." *Revue des sciences humaines* 65 (1952).
Beauchamp, Louis de. *Marcel Proust et le Jockey-Club* (Paris: n.p., 1973).

Benjamin, Walter. "The Image of Proust." In *Illuminations*. Translated by Harry Zorn. Edited by Hannah Arendt. New York: Schocken Books, 1968.

Borrel, Anne. "'La Petite Société des quatre amis'." In *Marcel Proust et ses amis*. Edited by Jean-Yves Tadié. Paris: Gallimard/NRF, 2010.

Compagnon, Antoine. "Morales de Proust." In *Résumés des cours et travaux du Collège de France* (2009).

———. "Note sur 'La Simplicité de M. de Montesquiou.'" *Romanic Review* 81, no. 1 (1990).

———. Preface to MP, *Sodome et Gomorrhe*. Paris: Gallimard/Folio, 1989.

———. "Proust et le judaïsme." *Critique* 54 (1991).

———. "Proust on Racine." *Yale French Studies* 76 (1989).

———. "Racine and the Moderns." In *Theatrum Mundi: Studies in Honor of Ronald W. Tobin*. Edited by Claire Carlin, Ronald W. Tobin, and Kathleen Wine. Charlottesville, VA: Rookwood Press, 2003.

Enthoven, Jean-Paul. *Saisons de papier*. Paris: Grasset, 2016.

Fernández, Ramón. "La Vie sociale dans l'œuvre de Marcel Proust." *Les Cahiers Marcel Proust* 1 (1927).

Fifield, William. "Interview with Jean Cocteau." *Paris Review* 32 (Summer–Fall 1964).

Gantrel, Martine. "Jeu de pistes autour d'un nom: Guermantes." *Revue d'histoire littéraire de la France* 3 (October–December 2004): 919–34.

Gier, Albert. "Marcel Proust und Richard Wagner: Zeittypisches und Einmaliges in einer Beziehung zwischen Literatur und Musik." In *Marcel Proust und die Belle Époque*. Edited by Thomas Hunkeler. Frankfurt: Insel/Marcel Proust Gesellschaft, 2002.

Goux, Jean-Joseph. "Un inédit. Le *Carnet de syntaxe* de Proust." *La Nouvelle Revue française: D'après Proust*, op. cit.

Gregh, Fernand. "Sur Marcel Proust." *Le Journal des débats* (February 7, 1937): 3.

Gury, Christian. *Proust: Clés inédites et retrouvées*. Paris: Kimé, 2003.

Hersant, Marc, and Muriel Ades. "D'un bal de têtes à l'autre." In *"Le Temps retrouvé" quatre-vingts ans après: essais critiques*. Edited by Adam Andrew Watt. New York: Peter Lang, 2009.

Johnson, Theodore. "Marcel Proust et Gustave Moreau." *Bulletin de la Société des Amis de Marcel Proust* 28 (1978).

Keller, Luzius. "Proust und die Belle Époque." In *Marcel Proust und die Belle Époque*. Edited by Thomas Hunkeler. Frankfurt: Insel/Marcel Proust Gesellschaft, 2002.

Koestenbaum, Wayne. "I Went by a Devious Route." In *The Proust Project*. Edited by André Aciman. New York: FSG/Books & Co./Helen Marx Books, 2004.

Kolb, Philip. "Marcel Proust et les dames Lemaire, avec des lettres de Proust à Suzy Lemaire." *Bulletin de la Société des Amis de Marcel Proust* 14 (1964).

Lacretelle, Jacques de. "Les Clefs de l'œuvre de Proust." *La Nouvelle Revue française* 112 (January 1923).

Ladenson, Elisabeth. "Proust and the Marx Brothers." In *Proust and the Arts*. Edited by Christie McDonald and François Proulx. Cambridge and London: Cambridge University Press, 2015.

———. "Someone like Maman." *London Review of Books* 30, no. 9 (May 8, 2008): 19–20.

Lamont, Rosette C. "Le bonheur chez Proust." *Bulletin de la Société des Amis de Marcel Proust et de Combray* 16 (1966).

Link-Heer, Ursula. "Mode, Möbel, Nippes, *façons et manières*: Robert de Montesquiou und Marcel Proust." In *Marcel Proust und die Belle Époque*. Edited by Thomas Hunkeler. Frankfurt: Insel/Marcel Proust Gesellschaft, 2002.

Litvak, James. "Strange Gourmet: Taste, Waste, Proust." *Studies in the Novel* 28, no. 3 (Fall 1996).

Maurois, André. *A la recherche de Marcel Proust*. Paris: Hachette, 1949.

———. *Le Monde de Marcel Proust*. Paris: Hachette, 1960.

Miguet, Marie. "Le Séjour à Doncières dans *Le Côté de Guermantes*: textes et avant-textes." In *Vers une sémiotique différentielle*. Edited by Anne Chovin and François Migeot. Besançon: Presses Universitaires Franc-comtoises, 1999.

Mimouni, Patrick. "Fumer avec Proust." *La Règle du jeu* 60 (April 2010).

———. "La Vocation talmudique de Proust: I. Les Lois causales." *La Règle du jeu* 35 (September 2007).

Murat, Laure. "Les souliers de la duchesse, ou la vulgarité de l'aristocratie française." *La Nouvelle Revue française: D'après Proust*. Edited by Philippe Forest and Stéphane Audegy (March 2013).

Samuels, Maurice. "Proust, Jews, and the Arts." In *Proust and the Arts*. Edited by Christie McDonald and François Proulx. Cambridge and London: Cambridge University Press, 2015.

Sonnenfeld, Albert. "Marcel Proust: Antisémite?" *The French Review* 62, no. 1 (October 1988).

Thurman, Judith. "I Never Took My Eyes off My Mother." In *The Proust Project*. Edited by André Aciman. New York: FSG/Books & Co./Helen Marx Books, 2004.

Zoberman, Pierre. "L'inversion comme prisme universel." *Magazine littéraire: Marcel Proust* (2013).

IV · GENERAL BIBLIOGRAPHY

A · Primary and Secondary Sources—Books

Adelon, M. H., G. Benoist, et al., eds. *La Chasse moderne. Encyclopédie du chasseur moderne.* Paris: Larousse, 1912.

Aderer, Adolphe. *Une Grande Dame aima.* Paris: Calmann-Lévy, 1906.

Aesop. *Fables.* New York: Cricket House Books, 2010.

d'Albiousse, Lionel. *Les Fiefs nobles du château ducal d'Uzès.* Uzès: Malige, 1906.

Aldobrandini, Giovanni. *Élites dell'Ottocento: Politica e cultura in Gran Bretagna e Italia.* Rome: Gangemi, n.d.

Andia, Béatrice de, ed. *Autour de la Madeleine: art, littérature et société.* Paris: Action Artistique de la Ville de Paris, 2005.

Anne, Théodore. *M. le Comte de Chambord: Souvenirs d'août 1850.* Paris: E. Dentu, 1850.

Anonymous. *Ferdinand of Bulgaria: The Amazing Career of a Shoddy Czar.* London: A. Melrose, 1916.

Anonymous. *Biographie de Mme Demidoff, Princesse Mathilde.* London and Brussels: n.p., 1870.

Antoine, A. *Mes souvenirs sur le Théâtre-Libre.* Paris: Fayard, 1921.

Antonetti, Guy. *Une maison de banque à Paris au XVIIIe siècle: Greffulhe Montz et Cie.* Paris: Cujas, 1963.

Apollinaire, Guillaume. *Œuvres en prose complètes.* Vol. 3. Edited by Michel Décaudin. Paris: Gallimard, 1993.

———. *Selected Writings.* Translated by Roger Shattuck. New York: New Directions, 1971.

Apostolescu, Ginette. *Mon journal: 1879–1880.* Paris: Cercle des Amis de Marie Bashkirtseff, 2004.

d'Arenberg, Princesse Louise-Marie (Marquise de Vogüé). *Logis d'autrefois.* Paris: n.p., n.d.

———. *Souvenirs: 1903–1939.* Paris: n.p. 1941.

Armstrong, Carol. *Odd Man Out: Readings of the Work and Reputation of Edgar Degas.* Chicago and London: University of Chicago Press, 1991.

Astruc, Gabriel. *Le Pavillon des fantômes.* Paris: Belfond, 1987.

Auchincloss, Louis. *The Man Behind the Book.* New York: Houghton Mifflin, 1996.

Austin, J. L. *How to Do Things with Words.* Edited by J. O. Urmson and Marina Sbísa. Cambridge: Harvard University Press, 1962.

Avenel, Henri. *Histoire de la presse française, depuis 1789 jusqu'à nos jours.* Paris: Flammarion, 1900.

Bac, Ferdinand (pseud. Ferdinand Sigismond Bach). *Intimités de la IIIe République: La Fin des temps "délicieux."* Paris: Hachette, 1935.

Bach, Général André. *L'Année Dreyfus: Une histoire politique de l'armée française de Charles X à "l'Affaire."* Paris: Tallandier, 2004.

Bachaumont (pseud. Émile Gérard). *Les Femmes du monde.* Paris: E. Dentu, 1876.

Bader, Luigi. *Album: Le Comte de Chambord et les siens en exil.* Paris: Diffusion Université-Culture, 1983.

Balfour, Betty Bulwer-Lytton, Lady. *The History of Lord Lytton's Indian Administration, 1876 to 1880; Compiled from Letters and Official Papers.* London: Longmans, Green, 1899.

Bancquart, Marie-Claire. *Paris "Fin-de-Siècle."* Paris: SNELA La Différence, 2009.

Un Banquier (pseud.). *Que nous veut-on avec ce Rothschild Ier, roi des Juifs et dieu de la finance?* Brussels: Chez les principaux libraires de la Belgique, 1846.

Barrès, Maurice. *Le Culte du moi.* Paris: Plon, 1922 [1888–1891].

Barthes, Roland. *Le Degré zéro de l'écriture.* Paris: Seuil, 1972.

———. *The Rustle of Language.* Translated by Richard Howard. Berkeley: University of California Press, 1989.

———. *Sur Racine.* Paris: Seuil, 1963.

Bartolotti, Luca. *Roma fuori le mura.* Rome: La Terza, 1988.

Baudelaire, Charles. *Les Fleurs du mal: Édition définitive.* Paris: Calmann-Lévy, 1919.

Beard, George Miller. *A Practical Treatise on Nervous Exhaustion (Neurasthenia).* New York: Treat, 1880.

Bellenger, Marguerite. *Les Courtisanes du Second Empire.* Brussels: Office de Publicité, 1871.

Benaïm, Françoise. *Marie-Laure de Noailles, vicomtesse du bizarre.* Paris: Grasset, 2002.

Bentley, Toni. *Sisters of Salome.* New Haven and London: Yale University Press, 2002.

Bergerat, Émile. *Souvenirs d'un enfant de Paris: 1879–1884.* Paris: Charpentier, 1912.

Bernhardt, Sarah (apocryphal). *My Double Life.* London: William Heinemann, 1907.

Bertrand, Antoine. *Les Curiosités esthétiques de Robert de Montesquiou.* 2 vols. Geneva: Droz, 1996.

Bienvenu, Jacques. *Maupassant inédit.* Aix: Edisud, 1993.

Biez, Jacques de. *Rothschild et le péril juif.* Paris: Chez l'auteur, 1891.

Bizet, Georges. *Lettres; Impressions de Rome; la Commune.* Preface by Louis Ganderax. Paris: Calmann-Lévy, 1907.

Blanche, Jacques-Émile. *Dieppe.* Paris: Berthout, 1992 [1927].

du Bled, Victor. *La Société française depuis cent ans.* Paris: Bloud & Gay, 1923.

Blount, Sir Edward. *Memoirs.* Edited by Stuart J. Reid. London: Longmans, Green, 1902.

Bocher, Émmanuel. *Les Gravures françaises du XVIIIe siècle: Catalogue raisonné des estampes, pièces en couleur, au bistre et au lavis, de 1700 à 1800.* 2 vols. Paris: D. Morgant, 1872–1880.

Bompiani, Sofia. *Italian Explorers in Africa.* London: Religious Tract Society, 1891.

Bondeson, Jan. *The Great Pretenders.* New York: W. W. Norton, 2005.

Borchmeyer, Dieter. *Drama and the World of Richard Wagner.* Princeton, NJ: Princeton University Press, 2003.

Borghèse, Prince Jean (Giovanni Battista). *L'Italie moderne.* Paris: Flammarion, 1913.

Bouilloud, Jean-Philippe, ed. *Un univers d'artistes.* Paris: L'Harmattan, 2004.

du Bourg, Joseph. *Les Entrevues des princes à Frohsdorf: La Vérité et la légende.* Paris: Perrin, 1910.

Bourget, Paul. *Un cœur de femme.* Paris: Alphonse Lemerre, 1890.

———. *Essais de psychologie contemporaine.* Vol. 1. Paris: Plon, 1920 [1883].

Boutet de Monvel, Roger. *Eminent English Men and Women in Paris.* Translated by G. Herring. New York: Scribner's, 1913.

Bouvier, Jean. *Les Rothschild: Histoire d'un capitalisme familial.* Brussels: Complexe, 1992.

Boylesve, René. *Feuilles tombées.* Paris: La Pléiade, 1927.

Bramsen, Michèle Bo. *Portrait d'Élie Halévy.* Amsterdam: John Benjamins Publishing Company, 1978.

Bredin, Jean-Denis. *The Affair: The Case of Alfred Dreyfus.* Translated by Jeffrey Mehlman. New York: George Braziller, 1986.

Breteuil, Henri Le Tonnelier, Marquis de. *La Haute Société: Journal secret 1886–1889.* Paris: Atelier Marcel Jullian, 1979.

Briais, Bernard. *Au temps des Frou-Frou: Femmes célèbres de la Belle Époque.* Paris: France Empire, 1985.

de Broglie, Albert-Jacques-Victor, Duc. *Ambassador of the Vanquished: The Viscount Élie de Gontaut-Biron's Mission to Berlin.* London: Heinemann, 1896.

Brook-Shepard, Gordon. *Uncle of Europe: The Social and Diplomatic Life of Edward VII.* New York: Harcourt Brace Jovanovich, 1976.

Brooks, Peter. *Flaubert in the Ruins of Paris: The Story of a Friendship, a Novel, and a Terrible Year.* New York: Basic Books, 2017.

Brosio, Valentino. *Ritratti parigini del Secondo Imperio e della Belle Époque.* Paris: Nuovedizioni E. Vallecchi, 1975.

Brown, Frederick. *For the Soul of France: Culture Wars in the Age of Dreyfus.* New York: Anchor Books, 2010.

Brugmans, Hendrik. *Georges de Porto-Riche: Sa vie, son œuvre.* Geneva: Slatkine, 1976.

Buffon, Georges Louis Leclerc, Comte de. *Œuvres complètes.* Vols. 1 and 6. Paris: Abel Ledoux, 1844–1846.

Bulwer-Lytton, Edward Robert, Lord Lytton. *Personal and Literary Letters of Robert, First Earl of Lytton.* 2 vols. Edited by Lady Betty Balfour. London: Longmans, Green, 1906.

———. *The Ring of Amasis.* London: Macmillan, 1890.

Bulwer-Lytton, Rosina (Baroness Lytton). *A Blighted Life.* London: Bloomsbury, 1994.

Burnand, Robert. *La Vie quotidienne en France de 1870 à 1900.* Paris: Hachette, 1948.

Busnach, Willie. *Le Phoque à ventre blanc.* Paris: E. Chatot, 1883.

Carassi, Carlo. *L'Ordre de Malte dévoilé ou voyage de Malte.* Cologne: n.p., 1790.

Carasso, Odette. *Arthur Meyer, directeur du Gaulois: un patron de presse juif, royaliste et antidreyfusard.* Paris: Imago, 2003.

Castelbajac, Constance de (Marquise de Breteuil). *Journal: 1885–1886.* Edited by Éric Mension-Rigau. Paris: Perrin, 2003.

Castellane, Boni de. *Comment j'ai découvert l'Amérique.* Paris: G. Crès, 1925.

———. *Vingt ans de Paris.* Paris: Fayard, 1925.

de Castries, René de La Croix, Duc. *Le Testament de la monarchie.* Vol. 5: *Le Grand Refus du Comte de Chambord.* Paris: A. Fayard, 1970.

Chaleyssin, Patrick. *Robert de Montesquiou: Mécène et dandy.* Paris: Somogy, 1992.

Chambord, Henri d'Artois, Comte de. *Lettres d'Henri V depuis 1841 jusqu'à nos jours.* Edited by Adrien Peladan. Nîmes: P. Lafare, 1873.

Charle, Christophe. *Histoire sociale de la France au XIXe siècle.* Paris: Seuil, 1991.

Chateaubriand, François-René. *Mémoires d'outre-tombe.* Vol. I. Paris: Garnier Frères, 1899 [1849–1850].

Claretie, Jules. *La Vie à Paris: 1880–1885.* Vols. 1–6. Paris: Victor Havard, 1880–1885.

————. *La Vie à Paris: 1898.* Paris: Charpentier, 1899.

Cocteau, Jean. *La Fin du Potomak.* Paris: Gallimard/NRF, 1939.

————. *Le Passé défini.* Paris: Gallimard/NRF, 1983.

————. *Portraits-souvenir.* Paris: Grasset, 1935.

Condé, Gérard. *Gounod.* Paris: Fayard, 2009.

Constant, Stephen. *Foxy Ferdinand, Tsar of Bulgaria.* London: Sidgwick & Jackson, 1979.

Conway, David. *Jewry in Music: Entry to the Profession from the Enlightenment to Richard Wagner.* Cambridge and London: Cambridge University Press, 2011.

Coquelin, Constant. *Un poète philosophe: Sully Prudhomme.* Paris: Paul Ollendorff, 1882.

Cornély, Jules. *Le Czar et le roi.* Paris: Clairon, 1884.

Corpechot, Lucien. *Souvenirs d'un journaliste.* Paris: Plon, 1936.

Costa de Beauregard, Charles-Albert, Marquis. *Un homme d'autrefois: souvenirs recueillis par son arrière petit-fils.* Paris: Plon, 1878.

Cotterel, François-Frédéric. *Tableau historique du procès des fabricateurs des faux-billets de la Banque de Vienne, et autres valeurs de la plupart des gouvernements d'Europe.* Strasbourg: F.-G. Levrault, 1807.

Cowles, Virginia. *The Rothschilds: A Family of Fortune.* New York: Alfred A. Knopf, 1973.

Crafty. *La Chasse à tir: Notes et croquis.* Paris: Plon, 1887.

Craveri, Benedetta. *The Age of Conversation.* Translated by Teresa Waugh. New York: New York Review Books, 2006.

Crawford, F. Marion. *Saracinesca.* New York: Macmillan, 1893.

Crémieux, Hector-Jonathan, and Étienne Tréfeu. *Geneviève de Brabant.* Libretto to the opera buffa by Jacques Offenbach. Paris: Michel Lévy Frères, 1868 [1859].

Crouthamel, James L. *Bennett's "New York Herald" and the Rise of the Popular Press.* Syracuse, NY: Syracuse University Press, 1989.

Curtiss, Mina. *Other People's Letters.* New York: Houghton Mifflin, 1978.

————. *Bizet and His World.* New York: Alfred A. Knopf, 1958.

Dahan, Philippe. *Guy de Maupassant et les femmes.* Paris: Bertout, 1996.

Daudet, Ernest. *Ferdinand Ier, tsar de Bulgarie.* Paris: Attinger Frères, 1917.

Daudet, Léon. *Au temps de Judas.* Paris: Nouvelle Librairie Nationale, 1920.

————. *Devant la douleur.* Paris: Nouvelle Librairie Nationale, 1915.

————. *Fantômes et vivants.* Paris: Nouvelle Librairie Nationale, 1914.

————. *La Melancholia.* Paris: Grasset, 1928.

————. *Souvenirs littéraires.* Paris: Grasset, 1968.

David-Weill, Cécile. *The Suitors.* Translated by Linda Coverdale. New York: Other Press, 2012.

Davies, Helen M. *Émile and Isaac Pereire: Bankers, Socialists, and Sephardic Jews in Nineteenth-Century France.* Oxford: Oxford University Press, 2016.

Davis, Mike. *Late Victorian Holocausts: El Niño Famines and the Making of the Third World.* New York: Verso, 2001.

Dean, Winton. *Georges Bizet: His Life and His Work.* London: J. M. Dent & Sons, 1965.

Delacour, Alfred, and Alfred Hennequin. *Le Phoque.* Paris: Allouard, 1878.

Delacroix, Eugène. *Journal.* Paris: Plon, 1932.

Demachy, Édouard. *Les Rothschild: Une famille de financiers juifs au XIXe siècle.* Paris: Chez l'auteur, 1896.

Dermenjian, Geneviève, Jacques Guilhaumou, and Martine Lapied, eds. *Femmes entre ombre et lumière: recherches sur la visibilité sociale, XVIe–XXe siècles.* Paris: Publisud, 2000.

Deschanel, Paul. *Figures de femmes.* Paris: Calmann-Lévy, 1889.

Desplaces, Ernest, and Louis Gabriel Michaud, eds. *Biographie universelle, ancienne et moderne.* Vol. 37. Paris: Chez Mme C. Desplaces, 1843.

Devey, Louisa. *Life of Rosina, Lady Lytton.* London: S. Sonnenschein, Lowrey, & Co., 1887.

Dickens, Charles. *A Tale of Two Cities.* London: James Nisbet & Co., 1902.

Diesbach, Ghislain de. *Secrets of the Gotha.* Translated by Margaret Crosland. New York: Meredith Press, 1968.

Doré, Gustave, and Pierre Dupont. *La Légende du Juif-Errant.* Paris: Garnier-Frères, 1859.

Douchin, Jacques-Louis. *Vie érotique de Guy de Maupassant.* Paris: Suger/Pauvert, 1986.

Doumic, René. *Écrivains d'aujourd'hui: Paul Bourget, Guy de Maupassant, Pierre Loti, Jules Lemaître.* 2nd ed. Paris: Perrin, 1895.

Drumont, Édouard. *La Dernière Bataille: nouvelle étude psychologique et sociale.* Paris: E. Dentu, 1890.

————. *La Fin d'un monde.* Paris: Savine, 1889.

————. *La France juive: Essai d'histoire contemporaine.* 2 vols. 43rd ed. Paris: C. Marpon & E. Flammarion, 1886.

———. *Le Testament d'un antisémite.* Paris: E. Dentu, 1891.

Du Camp, Maxime. *La Charité privée à Paris.* Paris: Hachette, 1892.

Dumas, Alexandre, *fils. La Dame aux camélias.* Paris: Librairie Théâtrale, 1853.

Dumas, Alexandre, *père. Quinze jours au Sinaï.* Paris: Charles Gosselin, 1841.

Dürhen, Dr. Emil (pseud. Iwan Bloch). *Der Marquis de Sade und seine Zeit.* Berlin: H. Barsdorf, 1901 (1899).

Eddie, William A. *Charles-Valentin Alkan: His Life and His Music.* London: Ashgate, 2007.

Elfenbein, Andrew. *Byron and the Victorians.* Cambridge and London: Cambridge University Press, 1995.

Elias, Norbert. *La Société de cour.* Translated by Pierre Kamnitzer. Paris: Calmann-Lévy, 1974.

Elliot, Frances. *Roman Gossip.* London: John Murray, 1894.

Enard, Mathias. *Boussole.* Paris: Actes Sud, 2015.

Étincelle (pseud. Vicomtese de Peyronny). *Carnet d'un mondain.* 2 vols. Paris: Rouveyre, 1881–1882.

Farmer, James Eugene. *Versailles and the Court Under Louis XIV.* Philadelphia: Century, 1905.

Fauré, Gabriel. *Correspondance.* Edited by Jean-Michel Nectoux. Paris: Fayard, 2015.

———. *A Life in Letters.* Translated and edited by J. Barrie Jones. London: B. T. Batsford, 1989.

Fauser, Annegret. *Musical Encounters at the 1889 World's Fair.* Boydell & Brewer: Suffolk, 2005.

Ferguson, Niall. *House of Rothschild.* Vol. 2: *The World's Banker (1849–1999).* New York: Penguin, 2000.

Ferval, Claude (pseud. Baronne Aimery-Harty de Pierrebourg). *Paul Hervieu: deux portraits hors texte.* Paris: Fayard, 1916.

Fiette, Suzanne. *La Noblesse française des Lumières à la Belle Époque.* Paris: Perrin, 2015.

Fischer, Henry, ed. *Secret Memoirs of the Court of Royal Saxony, 1891–1922: The Story of Louise, Crown Princess.* Bensonhurst, NY: Fischer's Foreign Letters, 1912.

Flament, Albert. *Le Bal du Pré-Catelan.* Paris: Arthème Fayard, 1946.

Flaubert, Gustave. *Dictionnaire des idées reçues, suivi des "Mémoires d'un fou."* Paris: Nouvel Office d'Édition, 1964.

de Flers, Hyacinthe de Paule de La Motte Ango, Marquis. *Le Comte de Paris.* Translated by Constance Majendie. London: Allen & Co., 1889.

Forberg, F. C. *Manuel d'érotologie classique.* Paris: Isidore Liseux, 1883.

Fouquier, Marcel. *Jours heureux d'autrefois: une société et son époque, 1885–1935.* Paris: Albin Michel, 1941.

Fouquières, André de. *Cinquante ans de panache.* Paris: Pierre Horay, 1951.

———. *Mon Paris et ses Parisiens.* 4 vols. Paris: Pierre Horay, 1953–1956.

Fournel, Victor. *Ce qu'on voit dans les rues de Paris.* Paris: E. Dentu, 1867.

Fournier, Alfred. *The Treatment and Prophylaxis of Syphilis.* Translated by C. M. Marshall, M.D. New York: Rebman, 1907.

Fumaroli, Marc, Gabriel de Broglie, and Jean-Pierre Chaline, eds. *Élites et sociabilité en France: actes du colloque de Paris, 23 janvier 2003.* Paris: Perrin, 2003.

Galateria, Daria. *L'Étiquette à la cour de Versailles.* Paris: Flammarion, 2017.

Garelick, Rhonda. *Rising Star: Dandyism, Gender, and Performance in the Fin de Siècle.* Princeton, NJ: Princeton University Press, 1999.

Genlis, Stéphanie-Félicité du Crest de Saint-Aubin, Comtesse de. *Pétrarque et Laure.* Paris: E. Ladvocat, 1819.

Germain, André. *La Bourgeoisie qui brûle: propos d'un témoin, 1890–1940.* Paris: Sun, 1951.

Gicquel, Alain-Claude. *Maupassant: tel un météore.* Paris: Castor Astral, 1993.

Giraud, Victor. *Un Grand Français: Albert de Mun.* Paris: Bloud & Gay, 1919.

Goncourt, Edmond de, and Jules de Goncourt. *Journal: Mémoires de la vie littéraires.* Edited by Robert Ricatte. 21 vols. Paris: Fasquelle & Flammarion, 1936–1956.

Gosse, Edmund. *Portraits and Sketches.* London: William Heinemann, 1913.

Gottlieb, Robert. *Sarah: The Life of Sarah Bernhardt.* New Haven and London: Yale University Press, 2010.

Gourmont, Remy de. *Épilogues: réflexions sur la vie 1895–1898.* Paris: Mercure de France, 1903.

———. *Promenades littéraires.* Vol. 4. Paris: Mercure de France, 1927.

Graham, Victor E., ed. *Rymes: Édition critique.* Geneva: Droz, 1968.

Gramont, Alfred, Comte de. *L'Ami du Prince: Journal inédit, 1892–1915.* Edited by Eric Mension-Rigau. Paris: Fayard, 2011.

Gramont, Élisabeth de (Duchesse de Clermont-Tonnerre). *Mémoires.* Vol. 1: *Au temps des équipages.* Paris: Grasset, 1928.

———. *Mémoires.* Vol. 2: *Les Marronniers en fleurs.* Paris: Grasset, 1929.

———. *Mémoires.* Vol. 4: *La Treizième Heure.* Paris: Grasset, 1935.

———. *Souvenirs du monde: 1890 à 1940.* Paris: Grasset, 1966.

Gray, Francine du Plessix. *At Home with the Marquis de Sade: A Life.* New York: Simon & Schuster, 1998.

Greffulhe, Élaine (later Duchesse de Guiche, then Gramont). *Le Livre d'ambre.* Paris, 1887–1889.

———. *Les Roses tristes.* Preface by Robert de Montesquiou. Paris: Presses de l'Imprimerie Nationale, 1923 [1906].

Grelière, Paul. *Les Talleyrand-Périgord dans l'histoire.* Paris: Éditions Clairvivre, 1962.

Grenaud, Pierre and Gatien Marcailhou. *Boni de Castellane et le Palais Rose.* Paris: Les Auteurs Associés, 1983.

Grubb, Alan. *The Politics of Pessimism: Albert de Broglie and Conservative Politics in the Early Third Republic.* Wilmington: University of Delaware Press, 1996.

Gueullette, Charles. *Les Cabinets d'amateurs à Paris, la collection du comte Henri de* [sic] *Greffulhe.* Paris: Detaille, 1887.

Guichard, Marie-Thérèse. *Les Égéries de la République.* Paris: Payot, 1991.

Guilleminault, Gilbert. *Prélude à la Belle Époque.* Paris: Denoël, 1957.

Guinon, Georges, ed. *Clinique des maladies du système nerveux: M. le Professeur Charcot, hospice de la Salpêtrière.* Vol. 2. Paris: Progrès Médical, 1893.

Gyp (pseud. Comtesse de Mirabeau-Martel). *La Joyeuse Enfance de la IIIᵉ République.* Paris: Calmann-Lévy, 1931.

Halévy, Daniel. *My Friend Degas.* Translated by Mina Curtiss. Middletown, CT: Wesleyan University Press, 1964.

———. *Pays parisiens.* Paris: Grasset, 1932.

———. *La République des ducs.* Paris: Grasset, 1937.

Halévy, Léon. *Fromental Halévy, sa vie et ses œuvres.* Paris: Ménestrel, Heugel, 1863.

Halévy, Ludovic. *Carnets: 1878–1883.* Paris: Calmann-Lévy, 1935.

———. *Parisian Points of View.* Translated by Edith Matthews. New York: Harper, 1894.

———. *Princesse.* Paris: Calmann-Lévy, 1889.

Hallman, Diana R. *Opera, Liberalism, and Antisemitism in Nineteenth-Century France.* Cambridge and London: Cambridge University Press, 2007.

de Hamme, Liévan. *Guide-indicateur des sanctuaires et lieux historiques de la Terre Sainte.* Paris: Imprimerie des Pères Franciscains, 1897.

Hamon, Augustin, and Georges Bachot. *L'Agonie d'une société: histoire d'aujourd'hui.* Paris: Albert Savine, 1889.

Hanoteau, Guillaume. *Paris: Anecdotes et portraits.* Paris: Fayard, 1974.

Haraucourt, Edmond. *Shylock ou le marchand de Venise.* Paris, 1889.

Hare, Augustus. *Story of My Life.* 2 vols. Virginia: Library of Alexandria, n.d.

———. *The Story of Two Noble Lives: Memoirs of Louisa, Marchioness of Waterford.* London: George Allen, 1893.

Harlan, Aurelia Brooks. *Owen Meredith: A Critical Biography of Robert, First Earl of Lytton.* New York: Columbia University Press, 1946.

Harris, John. *Moving Rooms: The Trade in Architectural Salvage.* New Haven and London: Yale University Press, 2007.

Harris, Ruth. *Dreyfus: Politics, Emotion, and the Scandal of the Century.* New York: Metropolitan, 2010.

Harris, Trevor A. *Maupassant et "Fort comme la mort."* Paris: Nizet, 1991.

Harskamp, Jacob T. *The Anatomy of Despondency.* Leiden: Brill, 2011.

d'Haussonville, Paul-Gabriel Othenin Cléron, Comte (initially Vicomte). *Le Comte de Paris: souvenirs personnels.* Paris: Calmann-Lévy, 1895.

———. *Femmes d'autrefois, hommes d'aujourd'hui.* Paris: Perrin, 1912.

———. *Le Salon de Mme Necker, d'après des documents tirés des archives de Coppet.* Paris: Calmann-Lévy, 1882.

———. *Socialisme et charité.* Paris: Calmann-Lévy, 1895.

Heine, Heinrich. *Neue Gedichte.* Hamburg: Hoffmann & Campe, 1852.

Hemmings, F. W. F. *Culture and Society in France, 1848–1898: Dissidents and Philistines.* London: Batsford, 1971.

Henderson, William James. *Richard Wagner: His Life and His Dramas.* New York: G. P. Putnam & Sons, 1910.

Heredia, José-Maria de. *Les Trophées.* Paris: Alphonse Lemerre, 1893.

Hermant, Abel. *Le Faubourg: comédie en quatre actes.* 4th ed. Paris: Paul Ollendorff, 1900.

———. *Vie littéraire.* Paris: Flammarion, 1923.

Herrick, Agnes, and George Herrick. *Paris Embassy Diary.* Lanham, MD: University Press of America, 2007.

Hertslet, Sir Edward, and Edward Cecil Hertslet, eds. *British and Foreign State Papers: 1886–1887.* Vol. 78. London: William Ridgway, 1894.

Hervieu, Paul. *L'Armature.* Paris: Alphonse Lemerre, 1895.

———. *La Chasse au réel.* Introduction by Henri Malherbe. Paris: E. Sansot, 1913.

———. *Flirt.* Paris: Alphonse Lemerre, 1890.

———. *Œuvres choisies: romans, nouvelles, théâtre.* Edited by Henri Guyot. Paris: Delagrave, 1919.

———. *Peints par eux-mêmes.* Paris: Fayard, 1907 [1893].

Hesse, Jean-Pascal. *Donatien Alphonse François de Sade.* Paris: Assouline, 2014.

Higgs, David. *Nobles in Nineteenth-Century France: The Practice of Inegalitarianism.* Baltimore and London: The John Hopkins University Press, 1987.

Holmes, Diana, and Carrie Tarr, eds. *A Belle Époque? Women in French Society and Culture, 1890–1914.* New York and Oxford: Berghahn, 2007.

Un Homme d'état (pseud.) *Histoire du Comte de Chambord.* Paris: Bray & Retaux, 1880.

Horne, Alistair. *The Fall of Paris: The Siege and the Commune 1870–1871.* London: Reprint Society, 1965.

Houbre, Gabrielle, ed. *Le Livre des courtisanes: Archives secrètes de la police des mœurs 1861–1876.* Paris: Tallandier, 2006.

Houssaye, Arsène. *Les Mille et une Nuits parisiennes.* Vol. 4. Paris: E. Dentu, 1878.

Houtin, Albert. *The Life of a Priest: My Own Experience.* London: Watts & Co., 1927.

Hower, Edward. *Shadows and Elephants.* Wellfleet: Leapfrog Press, 2002.

Huddleston, Sisley. *Paris Salons, Cafés, Studios.* New York: Blue Ribbon, 1928.

Huret, Jules. *En Amérique de New York à La Nouvelle-Orléans.* Paris: Fasquelle, 1904.

———. *Tout yeux, tout oreilles.* Preface by Octave Mirbeau. Paris: Eugène Fasquelle, 1901.

Huysmans, Joris-Karl. *A Rebours.* Preface by Marc Fumaroli. Paris: Gallimard/Folio, 1977.

Iacometti, Francesco. *Marco Antonio Borghese.* Rome: Tipografia A. Befani, 1886.

Imber, Hugues. *Georges Bizet.* Paris: Paul Ollendorff, 1899.

———. *Médaillons contemporains.* Paris: Fischbacher, 1902.

———. *Portraits et études—Georges Bizet: lettres inédites.* Paris: Paul Ollendorff, 1894.

Iswolsky, Helene. *No Time to Grieve: An Autobiographical Journey.* Philadelphia: Winchell, 1985.

Janin, Jules. *Le Marquis de Sade.* Paris: Chez les marchands de nouveautés, 1834.

Johnston, Sir Harry Hamilton. *A History of the Colonization of Africa by Alien Races.* Cambridge and London: Cambridge University Press, 1899.

Joliet, Charles. *Les Pseudonymes du jour.* Paris: E. Dentu, 1884.

Jollivet, Gaston. *L'Art de vivre.* Paris: Maison Quantin, 1887.

———. *Souvenirs de la vie de plaisir sous le Second Empire.* Preface by Paul Bourget. Paris: Tallandier, 1927.

Jonnes, Jill. *Eiffel's Tower: The Thrilling Story Behind Paris's Beloved Monument and the Extraordinary World's Fair That Introduced It to the World.* New York: Penguin, 2009.

Jordan, David. *Transforming Paris: The Life and Labors of the Baron Haussmann.* New York: Simon & Schuster, 1995.

Jordan, Ruth. *Fromental Halévy: His Life & Music, 1799–1862.* New York: Limelight, 1996.

Julia, Isabelle, ed. *Jules-Élie Delaunay, 1828–1891.* Nantes: Musée Hébert, 1988.

Jullian, Philippe. *Robert de Montesquiou, prince de 1900.* Paris: Perrin, 1965.

Jullian, Philippe, ed. *Dictionnaire du snobisme.* Paris: Plon, 1958.

Jungle, Ernest. *Profils parisiens.* Paris: A. Melet, 1898.

Kahan, Sylvia. *In Search of New Scales: Prince Edmond de Polignac, Octatonic Explorer.* Rochester, NY: University of Rochester Press, 2009.

Kellner, Sven. *Maupassant, un météore dans le ciel littéraire de l'époque.* Saint-Denis: Éditions Publibook, 2012.

Kleinmichel, Marie von Keller, Countess von. *Memories of a Shipwrecked World.* New York: Brentano's, 1923.

Königslöw, J. *Ferdinand von Bulgarien.* Munich: n.p., 1970.

Korneva, Galina, and Tatiana Cheboksarova. *Grand Duchess Maria Pavlovna.* East Richmond Heights, CA: Eurohistory, 2015.

Kuhn, William. *The Politics of Pleasure: A Portrait of Benjamin Disraeli.* London: Free Press, 2006.

La Douasnerie, Dominique Lambert de, ed. *Autour du congrès légitimiste d'Angers du 7 août 1887.* Angers: Congrès légitimiste, 1888.

La Ferronays, Guillemine Lucie Marie de. *Mémoires de Mme de La Ferronays.* Paris: Paul Ollendorff, 1900.

La Force, Auguste de Caumont, duc de. *La Fin de la douceur de vivre: souvenirs, 1878–1914.* Paris: Plon, 1961.

Lacassagne, Dr. Zacharie. *La Folie de Maupassant.* Toulouse: Gimet-Pisseau, 1907.

———. *Vacher l'éventreur et les crimes sadiques.* Paris: Masson & Stock, 1899.

Lacombe, Hervé. *Georges Bizet: Naissance d'une identité créatrice.* Paris: Fayard, 2000.

Laforge, Valérie. *Talons et tentations.* Quebec: Fides, 2001.

Lanoux, Armand. *Maupassant le Bel-Ami.* Paris: Grasset, 1995.

Larmandie, Comte Léonce de. *Le Faubourg Saint-Germain en l'an de grâce 1889.* Paris: E. Dentu, 1889.

Laurent, Sébastien. *Daniel Halévy: du libéralisme au traditionalisme.* Paris: Grasset, 2001.

Lauris, Georges, Marquis de. *Souvenirs d'une belle époque.* Paris: Amiot Dumont, 1948.

Lefeuve, Charles. *Les Anciennes Maisons de Paris sous Napoléon III.* 3 vols. Paris: Achille Faure, 1863–1865.

———. *Histoire du Lycée Bonaparte (Collège Bourbon).* Paris: Bureau des Anciennes Maisons de Paris sous Napoléon III, 1862.

Legay, Éric. *Le Comte Henry Greffulhe: Un grand notable en Seine-et-Marne.* Unpublished master's thesis. Université de Paris X Nanterre, 1986–1987.

Lemaître, Jules. *Les Contemporains: Guy de Maupassant, Stéphane Mallarmé, Général Boulanger, Guillaume II.* Paris: Société Française d'Imprimerie, 1898.

———. *Impressions de théâtre.* Paris: Lecène, Oudin, 1888–1892.

Leprieur, Paul. *Gustave Moreau et son œuvre.* Paris: Bureaux de l'Artiste, 1889.

Lerner, Michel. *Maupassant.* New York: Braziller, 1975.

Leroy, Géraldi, and Julie Sabiani. *La Vie littéraire à la Belle Époque.* Paris: PUF, 1998.

Lever, Maurice. *Sade: A Biography.* Translated by Arthur Goldhammer. New York: Farrar, Straus & Giroux, 1993.

Liégeard, Stéphen. *La Côte d'Azur.* Paris: Libraires-Imprimeries Réunies, 1891.

Lilti, Antoine. *Le Monde des salons. Sociabilité et mondanité à Paris au XVIIIe siècle.* Paris: Fayard, 2005.

Locke, Robert. *French Legitimists and the Politics of Moral Order in the Early Third Republic.* Princeton, NJ: Princeton University Press, 2015.

Loliée, Frédéric. *Women of the Second Empire: Chronicles of the Court of Napoleon III.* Translated by Alice Ivimy. London and New York: John Lane, 1907.

Lonergan, Walter F. *Forty Years of Paris.* London: T. Fisher Unwin, 1907.

Lorrain, Jean (pseud. Paul Duval). *Lettres à Marcel Schwob.* Edited by Eric Walbecq. Tusson: Lérot, 2006.

———. *Monsieur de Phocas: Astarté.* Paris: Paul Ollendorff, 1901.

———. *Le Vice errant.* Paris: Paul Ollendorff, 1902.

———. *La Ville empoisonnée: Pall-Mall Paris.* Preface by Georges Normandy. Paris: Jean Crès, 1936.

Lottman, Herbert. *The Return of the Rothschilds: The Great Banking Dynasty Through Two Turbulent Centuries.* London: I. B. Tauris, 1995.

Lumbroso, Albert. *Souvenirs sur Maupassant: sa maladie, sa mort.* Rome: Bocca Frères, 1905.

Lutyens, Mary. *The Lyttons in India: An Account of Lord Lytton's Viceroyalty, 1876–1880.* London: John Murray, 1979.

de Luz, Pierre (pseud. Pierre Henry de La Blanchetai). *Les Amis du Comte de Chambord.* Vol. 58: *Henri V.* Paris: Plon, 2007 [1913].

Lynch, Lawrence W. *The Marquis de Sade.* Boston: Twayne, 1984.

MacDonald, Hugh. *Bizet.* Oxford: Oxford University Press, 2014.

MacDonald, John. *Czar Ferdinand and His People.* New York: F. A. Stokes, 1945.

Mackin, Sally Britton Spottiswood. *A Society Woman on Two Continents.* New York and London: Transatlantic, 1896.

Magué, André. *La France bourgeoise actuelle.* Paris: Février, 1891.

Malato, Charles. *De la Commune à l'anarchie.* 3rd ed. Paris: Tresse & Stock, 1894.

Maral, Alexandre. *La Chapelle royale de Versailles sous Louis XIV.* Wavre, Belgium: Mardaga, 2010.

Marancour, L. *Massenet de.* *Les Échos du Vatican.* Paris: Hachette, 1864.

Marie-Laure (pseud. Vicomtesse de Noailles). *La Chambre des écureuils.* Paris: Plon, 1955.

Marly, Diana de. *Worth: Father of Haute Couture.* London: Elm Tree Books, 1980.

Martin-Fugier, Anne. *Les Salons de la IIIe République.* Paris: Perrin, 1993.

———. *La Vie élégante, ou la formation de Tout-Paris.* Paris: Fayard, 1993.

Massa, Philippe, Marquis de. *Au mont Ida: comédie en un acte.* Paris: Paul Ollendorff, 1887.

Massari, Commandante Alfonso M. *Don Giovanni Borghese: cenni necrologici.* Rome: Presse della Reale Società Geografica Italiana, 1918.

Maugny, Comte de. *Cinquante ans de souvenirs, 1859–1909.* Edited by René Doumic. Paris: Plon, 1914.

Maupassant, Guy de. *Bel-Ami.* Paris: L. Conard, 1910 [1885].

———. *Correspondance.* Edited by Jacques Suffel. Évreux: Cercle du Bibliophile, 1973.

———. *Romans.* Edited by Louis Forestier. Paris: Gallimard/Pléïade, 1987.

Mauriac, Claude. *Hommes et idées d'aujourd'hui.* Paris: Albin Michel, 1953.

Maussion, Baronne de, née Thellusson. *Contes aux enfants du château de Vaux.* Paris: Aymot, 1846.

Mayeur, Jean-Marie, and Madeleine Rebérioux. *The Third Republic from Its Origins to the Great War, 1871–1914.* Translated by J. R. Foster. Cambridge and London: Cambridge University Press, 1984.

Maynial, Édouard. *Guy de Maupassant: la vie et l'œuvre.* Paris: Mercure de France, 1906.

McClary, Susan. *Georges Bizet: Carmen.* Cambridge and London: Cambridge University Press, 1992.

McGuinness, Patrick. *Poetry and Radical Politics in Fin-de-Siècle France: Anarchism to Action Française.* Oxford: Oxford University Press, 2015.

Meilhac, Henri, and Ludovic Halévy. *Carmen: An Opera in Four Acts.* Libretto to the opera by Georges Bizet, adapted from the novella by Prosper Mérimée. Introduction by Philip Hale. Boston: Oliver Ditson, 1914.

———. *Théâtre.* 8 vols. Paris: Calmann-Lévy, 1899–1902.

Mejan, Maurice. *Recueil des causes célèbres et des arrêts qui les ont décidés.* Vol. 1. Paris: Plisson, 1807.

Melba, Nellie (pseud. Helen Porter Mitchell). *Melodies and Memories.* Cambridge and London: Cambridge University Press, 2011.

Mercier, Louis-Sébastien. *Tableau de Paris.* Vol. 1. Paris: Virchaux, 1781.

Meredith, Owen (pseud. Edward Robert Bulwer-Lytton, Lord Lytton). *Glenaveril, or The Metamorphoses.* 2 vols. London: Longmans, Green, 1885.

———. *King Poppy: A Fantasia.* London: Longmans, Green, 1892.

———. *Marah.* London: Longmans, Green, 1892.

———. *Poetical Works.* New York: New York Publishing Company, 1895.

———. *Selected Poems.* London: Longmans, Green, 1894.

Mergier-Bourdeix, ed. *Jules Janin: 735 lettres à sa femme.* Paris: Klincksieck, 1976.

Merriman, John. *The Dynamite Club: How a Bombing in Fin-de-Siècle Paris Ignited the Age of Modern Terror.* Boston and New York: Houghton Mifflin Harcourt, 2009.

———. *Massacre: The Life and Death of the Paris Commune.* New York: Basic Books, 2014.

Meyer, Arthur. *Ce que je peux dire.* Paris: Plon, 1912.

———. *Ce que mes yeux ont vu.* 50th ed. Preface by Émile Faguet. Paris: Nourrit-Plon, 1912.

Mitchell, Leslie George. *Bulwer-Lytton: The Rise and Fall of a Victorian Man of Letters.* London: Bloomsbury, 2003.

Montefiore, Simon Sebag. *The Romanovs 1613–1918.* New York: Alfred A. Knopf, 2016.

Montesquiou-Fezensac, Comte Robert de. *Autels privilégiés.* Paris: Bibliothèque Charpentier, 1898.

———. *Brelan de Dames.* Paris: Fontemoigne, 1912.

———. *Les Chauves-souris, clairs-obscurs.* Paris: Georges Richard, 1892.

———. *Le Chef des odeurs suaves.* Paris: Georges Richard, 1893.

———. *La Divine Comtesse.* Paris: Manzi, Joyant, 1913.

———. *Les Paons.* Paris: Georges Richard, 1908 [1901].

———. *Les Pas effacés.* 3 vols. Paris: Émile-Paul, 1923.

———. *Paul Helleu: Peintre et graveur.* Paris: Sansot, 1913.

———. *Les Perles rouges; Les Paroles diaprées.* Paris: G. Richard, 1910.

———. *Les Quarante Bergères: portraits satiriques en vers inédits.* Paris: Librairie de France, 1925.

———. *Les Roseaux pensants.* Paris: Fasquelle, 1897.

———. *Les Têtes couronnées.* Paris: Sansot, 1916.

Monti de Rezé, Comte René de. *Souvenirs sur le Comte de Chambord.* Paris: Émile-Paul, 1930.

Montréal, Fernand de. *Les dernières heures d'une monarchie.* Paris: Victorion, 1893.

Moonen, Antonius. *Petit Bréviaire du snobisme.* Paris: L'Inventaire, 2000.

Morand, Paul. *L'Allure de Chanel.* Paris: Hermann, 1996.

———. *Fin de siècle.* Paris: Stock, 1957.

———. *Journal d'un attaché d'ambassade.* Paris: Gallimard/NRF, 1963.

———. *1900.* Paris: Marianne, 1931.

———. *Vie de Guy de Maupassant.* Paris: Pygmalion/Gérard Watelet, 1998.

Moreau, Gustave. *L'Assembleur de rêves: écrits complets.* Edited by Pierre-Louis Matthieu. Paris: Fata Morgana, 1984.

Mugnier, Abbé. *Journal, 1879–1939.* Edited by Marcel Billot. Paris: Mercure de France, 1985.

Muhlfeld, Lucien. *Le Monde où l'on imprime.* Paris: Perrin, 1897.

Muhlstein, Anka. *Baron James: The Rise of the French Rothschilds.* New York and Paris: The Vendome Press, 1983.

————. *The Pen and the Brush: How Passion for Art Shaped Nineteenth-Century French Novels.* Translated by Adriana Hunter. New York: Other Press, 2017.

Müller, Walter. *Georges de Porto-Riche, 1849–1930: l'homme, le poète, le dramaturge.* Paris: J. Vrin, 1934.

de Mun, Comte Albert. *Dieu et le roi.* Paris: Librairie de la Société Bibliographique, 1881.

————. *Pour la Patrie.* Paris: Émile-Paul, 1912.

Murat, Laure. *La Maison du docteur Blanche.* Paris: Hachette/Lattès, 2001.

Musset, Alfred de. *Poésies complètes.* Paris: Charpentier, 1840.

Nectoux, Jean-Michel. *Gabriel Fauré: A Musical Life.* Translated by Roger Nichols. Cambridge and London: Cambridge University Press, 2004.

Nevill, Lady Dorothy. *Reminiscences.* Edited by Ralph Nevill. London: Edward Arnold, 1907.

————. *Under Five Reigns.* Edited by Ralph Nevill. New York: John Lane, 1910.

Nisbet, John Ferguson. *The Insanity of Genius.* New York: Scribner's, 1912.

Nordau, Max. *Degeneration.* London: D. Appleton & Co., 1895 [1892].

Nouvion, Georges de, and Émile Landrodie. *Le Comte de Chambord: 1820–1883.* Paris: Jouvet, 1884.

O'Connor, Garry. *The Pursuit of Perfection.* Philadelphia: Atheneum, 1979.

O'Monroy, Richard. *La Soirée parisienne.* Paris: Arnould, 1891.

O'Squarr, Flor (pseud. Charles Flor). *Les Coulisses de l'anarchie.* Paris: Albert Savine, 1892.

de Pange, Pauline de Broglie, Comtesse. *Comment j'ai vu 1900.* Paris: Grasset, 2013.

Paris, Gaston. *Le Juif-Errant.* Paris: Sandoz & Fischacher, 1880.

Parisis (pseud. Émile Blavet). *La Vie parisienne: la ville et le théâtre.* Preface by Aurélien Scholl. Paris: Paul Ollendorff, 1886.

Pasler, Jann. *Writing Through Music: Essays on Music, Culture, and Politics.* Oxford: Oxford University Press, 2007.

Pearl, Cora (pseud. Emma Crouch). *Mémoires de Cora Pearl.* Paris: J. Lévy, 1886.

Pease, Jane Hanna. *Romance Novels, Romantic Novelist: Francis Marion Crawford.* Bloomington, IN: AuthorHouse, 2011.

Pellapra, Émilie de (Comtesse de Brigode, Princesse de Chimay). *Mémoires publiées.* Paris: La Sirène, 1921.

Perez, Stanis. *La Santé de Louis XIV.* Paris: Perrin, 2010.

Perry, Duncan M. *Stefan Stambolov and the Emergence of Modern Bulgaria.* Durham, NC: Duke University Press, 1993.

Pesquidoux, Dubosc de. *Le Comte de Chambord d'après lui-même.* Paris: Victor Palmé, 1887.

Petrarcah, Francesco. *Il Canzoniere.* Edited by Lorenzo Mascetta. Lanciano: Rocco Carabba, 1895.

————. *Épîtres, éclogues, triomphes.* Translated by Comte Anatole de Montesquiou-Fezensac. Paris: Aymot, 1843.

————. *Petrarch's Lyric Poems.* Translated and edited by Robert M. During. Cambridge: Harvard University Press, 1979.

Pierrefeu, Jean de. "Société d'écrivains?" *Les Nouvelles littéraires* (July 14, 1928): 1.

Pimodan, Comte de. *Simples souvenirs, 1859–1907.* Paris: Plon, 1908.

Pinson, Guillaume. *Fiction du monde: analyse littéraire et médiatique de la mondanité, 1885–1914.* Ph.D. dissertation. Montreal: McGill University, 2005.

Piou, Jacques. *Le Comte Albert de Mun: sa vie publique.* Paris: Spes, 1925.

Plessis, Alain. *Régents et gouverneurs de la Banque de France sous le Second Empire.* Geneva: Droz, 1985.

Poiret, Paul. *Vestendo la Belle Époque.* Translated by Simona Broglie. Milan: Excelsior, 2009.

Porto-Riche, Georges de. "Bonheur manqué: Carnet d'un amoureux." *La Revue illustrée* 81 (May 15, 1889): 313–23.

————. *Bonheur manqué: Carnet d'un amoureux.* Paris: Paul Ollendorff, 1905.

————. *Sous mes yeux.* Paris: F. Payart, 1927.

————. *Théâtre d'amour.* Paris: Paul Ollendorff, 1921.

————. *Tout n'est pas rose.* Paris: Calmann-Lévy, 1877.

Pottier, André. *Histoire de la faïence de Rouen.* Rouen: Le Brument, 1870.

Pougy, Liane de (Princesse Ghika). *Mes cahiers bleus.* Paris: Plon, 1977.

Pouquet, Jeanne Maurice. *The Last Salon: Anatole France and His Muse.* Translated by Lewis Galantière. New York: Harcourt, Brace, 1927.

Pringué, Gabriel-Louis. *Trente ans de dîners en ville.* Paris: Revue Adam, 1948.

Prochasson, Christophe. *Paris 1900: essai d'histoire culturelle.* Paris: Calmann-Lévy, 1999.

Prod'homme, Jacques-Gabriel, and Arthur Dandelot. *Gounod: sa vie et ses œuvres, d'après des documents inédits.* Paris: Charles Delagrave, 1919.

Proust, Dr. Adrien. *Traité d'hygiène publique et privée.* Paris: Masson, 1877.

Proust, Dr. Adrien, and Dr. Gilbert Ballet. *Hygiène de neurasthénie.* Paris: Masson, 1897.

Racine, Jean. *Œuvres complètes: théâtre, poésie.* Edited by Georges Forestier. Paris: Gallimard/Pléïade, 1999.

Raymond, E. Neill. *Victorian Viceroy: The Life of Robert, the First Earl of Lytton.* London and New York: Regency, 1980.

Régnier, Henri de. *Les Cahiers inédits: 1887–1936.* Edited by David J. Niederauer and François Broche. Paris: Pygmalion/Gérard Watelet, 2002.

———. *Nos rencontres.* Paris: Mercure de France, 1931.

Reinach, Joseph. *Les Petites Catilinaires: Bruno-le-fileur.* Paris: Victor-Havard, 1889.

Renard, Georges François. *Les Princes de la jeune critique.* Paris: La Nouvelle Revue, 1890.

Renard, Jules. *Critique de combat.* Paris: E. Dentu, 1894.

———. *Journal inédit.* Paris: Bernouard, 1927.

Retté, Adolphe. *Au pays des lys noirs: souvenirs de jeunesse et d'âge mûr.* Paris: P. Téqui, 1913.

Richardson, Joanna. *Portrait of a Bonaparte: The Life and Times of Joseph-Napoleon Primoli, 1851–1927.* London and New York: Quartet, 1984.

Ridley, Jane. *Bertie: A Life of Edward VII.* London: Vintage, 2003.

Robert, Frédéric. *Bizet: l'homme et son œuvre.* Geneva: Slatkine, 1980.

Rochas d'Aiglun, Albert de. *L'Envoûtement.* Paris: Librairie Générale des Sciences Occultes, 1895.

Röhl, John, and Nicolaus Sombart. *Kaiser Wilhelm II: New Interpretations.* Cambridge and London: Cambridge University Press, 1982.

Ronfort, Jean-Dominique, and Jean-Mérée Ronfort. *A l'ombre de Pauline: la residence de l'ambassadeur de Grande-Bretagne à Paris.* Paris: Éditions du Centre de Recherches Historiques, 2001.

Rothschild, Baron Guy de. *Contre bonne fortune . . .* Paris: Pierre Belfond, 1983.

Rougerie, Jacques. *Paris libre: 1871.* Paris: Seuil, 2004.

Rounding, Virginia. *Grandes Horizontales: The Lives and Legends of Four Nineteenth-Century Courtesans.* New York: Bloomsbury USA, 2003.

Rousset-Charny, Gérard. *Les Palais parisiens de la Belle Époque.* Paris: Action Artistique de la Ville de Paris, 1992.

Rouvillois, Frédéric. *Histoire du snobisme.* Paris: Flammarion, 2008.

Sachs, Maurice. *Au temps du Boeuf sur le toit.* Paris: La Nouvelle Revue Critique, 1948.

———. *Le Sabbat: souvenirs d'une enfance orageuse.* Paris: Gallimard, 1960.

———. *Tableau des mœurs de ce temps.* Paris: Gallimard, 1954.

de Sade, Chevalier Louis. *Extraits du "Lexicon politique."* Paris: A. Barbier, 1831.

———. *Préceptes à l'usage d'une monarchie.* Paris, 1822.

de Sade, Donatien-Alphonse-François, Marquis. *Idée sur les romans.* Preface by Octave Uzanne. Paris: Rouveyre, 1878.

———. *Œuvres choisies.* Edited by Guillaume Apollinaire. Paris: Bibliothèque des Curieux, 1909.

———. *La Philosophie dans le boudoir, ou les instituteurs immoraux.* Québec: Bibliothèque Électronique de Québec, n.d. [1795].

de Sade, Jacques-François-Paul, Abbé. *Mémoires pour la vie de François Pétrarque.* Amsterdam: Arskée & Mercus, 1764.

de Sade, Louis-Marie, Comte. *Histoire de la nation française, première race.* Paris: Delaunay, 1805.

Saint-Simon, Louis de Rouvroy, Duc de. *Mémoires.* 21 vols. Edited by M. Chéruel. Preface by Charles-Augustin Sainte-Beuve. Paris: Hachette, 1858.

Samuels, Maurice. *Inventing the Israelite: Jewish Fiction in Nineteenth-Century France.* Palo Alto, CA: Stanford University Press, 2008.

———. *The Right to Difference: French Universalism and the Jews.* Chicago and London: University of Chicago Press, 2016.

Sanborn, Alvan Francis. *Paris and the Social Revolution.* Boston: Small, Maynard & Co., 1905.

San Filippo, Pietro Amat di. *Gli illustri viaggiatori italiani con una antologia dei loro scritti.* Rome: Stabilimento Tipografico dell'Opinione, 1885.

Sante, Luc. *The Other Paris.* New York: Farrar, Straus & Giroux, 2015.

Sapin, Philippe. *Les Juifs dans toute la presse française, l'armée et la finance.* Lyon: n.p., 1898.

Sartoris, Adelaide. *A Week in a French Country House.* London: Smith, Elder & Company, 1867.

Schlumberger, Gustave. *Mes souvenirs: 1844–1928.* 2 vols. Paris: Plon, 1934.

Schneider, Marcel. *L'Éternité fragile.* Vol. 2: *Innocence et vérité.* Paris: Grasset, 1991.

———. *Moi qui suis né trop tard.* Paris: Grasset & Fasquelle, 2006.

Scholl, Aurélien. *Le Fruit défendu.* Paris: Librairie Universelle, 1888.

Scribe, Eugène. *La Juive (The Jewess): Opera in Five Acts.* Libretto to the opera by Fromental Halévy. New York: Fred Rullman, 1919.

Scribe, Eugène, and Henri de Saint-Georges. *Le Juif-Errant: opéra en cinq actes, musique de Fromental Halévy.* Paris: Brandus, 1852.

Segal, Harold B. *Turn-of-the-Century Cabaret: Paris, Barcelona, Berlin, Munich, Vienna.* New York: Columbia University Press, 1987.

Seigel, Jerrold. *Bohemian Paris: Culture, Politics, and the Boundaries of Bourgeois Life, 1830–1930.* Baltimore and London: The Johns Hopkins University Press, 1986.

Senevas, Bruno-Marie Terrasson, Baron de. *Une famille française du XIVᵉ au XIXᵉ siècles. Étude sur les conditions sociales, la vie et les alliances des Terrasson de Senevas.* 4 vols. Paris: J. Moulin, 1939.

Sert, Misia. *Misa and the Muses: The Memoirs of Misia Sert.* New York: The John Day Company, 1953.

Shapcott, Thomas. *The White Stag of Exile.* Brisbane: A. Lane, 1984.

Sherard, Robert Harborough. *Twenty Years in Paris, Being Some Recollections of a Literary Life.* London: Hutchinson, 1905.

Sheridan, Alan. *Time and Place.* London: Scribner, 2003.

Sillery, J. *Monographie de l'hôtel de Sagan.* Paris: Frazier, 1909.

Skinner, Cornelia Otis. *Elegant Wits and Grand Horizontals: Paris—La Belle Époque.* New York: Houghton Mifflin, 1962.

———. *Madame Sarah.* Boston: Houghton Mifflin, 1967.

———. *Robert de Montesquiou: The Magnificent Dandy.* London: Michael Josephs, 1962.

Smith, Richard Langham, and Caroline Potter. *French Music Since Berlioz.* Aldershot, UK: Ashgate, 2006.

Soderini, Conte Edoardo. *Il Principe Don Marco Antonio Borghese.* Rome: Bafani, 1886.

Somerville, Frankfort. *The Spirit of Paris.* London: Black, 1913.

Sowerwine, Charles. *France Since 1870: Culture, Society, and the Making of the Republic.* New York: Palgrave Macmillan, 2009.

Steele, Valerie. *Paris Fashion: A Cultural History.* New York: Berg, 2001.

Stewart, C. Nelson. *Bulwer-Lytton as Occultist.* New York: Kessinger, 2010.

Straus, Émile. *La Distinction des biens.* Paris: Jouaust, 1867.

Stricker, Rémy. *Georges Bizet.* Paris: Gallimard, 1999.

Syme, Alison. *A Touch of Blossom: John Singer Sargent and the Queer Flora of Fin-de-Siècle Art.* University Park: Penn State University Press, 2010.

Tarnowska, Countess Maria. *The Future Will Tell: A Memoir.* Victoria, BC: Friesen, 2014.

Tassart, François. *Souvenirs sur Guy de Maupassant par François, son valet de chambre, 1883–1893.* Paris: Plon, 1911.

Techener, Léon. *Bulletin du bibliophile et du bibliothécaire.* Paris: L. Techener, 1873.

Tenroc, Charles (pseud. Charles Cornet). *Féminités.* Paris: Imprimeries Techniques, 1902.

Thomas, Louis. *La Maladie et la Mort de Maupassant.* Bruges: Arthur Herbert, 1906.

Ticknor, George. *Life, Letters, and Journals.* Vol. 2. New York: Houghton Mifflin, 1879.

Tiersten, Lisa. *Marianne in the Market: Envisioning Consumer Society in Fin-de-Siècle France.* Berkeley: University of California Press, 2001.

d'Uzès, Anne de Rochechouart de Mortemart, Duchesse. *Souvenirs 1847–1933.* Paris: Lacurne, 2011.

Vasili, Comte Paul (pseud. Juliette Adam). *France from Behind the Veil.* London: Fassell, 1915.

———. *Le Grand Monde.* Paris: La Nouvelle Revue, 1887.

———. *Society in Paris: Letters to a Young French Diplomat.* Translated by Raphael Ledos de Beaufort. London: Chatto & Windus, 1890.

———. *Les Soirées de Paris.* Paris: La Nouvelle Revue, 1887.

Vatout, Jean. *Le Château d'Eu: notices historiques.* 6 vols. Paris: Félix Malteste, 1836.

de Vaux, Baron. *Le Sport en France et à l'étranger.* Paris: J. Rothschild, 1899.

Verne, Suzanne. *Guermantes de Louis XIII à nos jours.* Paris: Ferenczi, 1961.

Viel-Castel, Comte Horace de. *Le Faubourg Saint-Germain.* 6 vols. Paris: L'Advocat, 1837–1838.

———. *Mémoires sur le règne de Napoléon III.* Vol. 3. Paris: Guy Le Part, 1979.

Vigny, Alfred de. *Œuvres complètes.* Vol. 1. Paris: A. Lemerre, 1883.

Villoteau, Pierre. *La Vie parisienne à la Belle Époque.* Paris: Levallois-Perret, 1968.

Vitali, Lamberto. *Un fotografo fin de siècle: il conte Primoli.* Turin: Einaudi, 1968.

Vizetelly, Ernest. *The Court of the Tuileries, 1852–1870.* London: Chatto & Windus, 1907.

———. *Republican France, 1870–1912: Her Presidents, Statesmen, Policy, Vicissitudes, and Social Life.* London: Holden & Hardingham, 1912.

Vogüé, Vicomte Eugène-Melchior de. *Pages choisies.* Preface by Paul Bourget. Paris: Plon-Nourrit, 1912.

———. *Le Roman russe.* 5th ed. Paris: Plon-Nourrit, 1904 [1886].

Vuiller, Gaston. *A History of Dancing.* Translated by Joseph Grego. New York: D. Appleton, 1898.

de Waal, Edmund. *The Hare with Amber Eyes: A Hidden Inheritance*. New York: Picador, 2010.
Waddington, Mary Alsop King. *Letters of a Diplomat's Wife: 1883–1900*. London: Smith, Elder, & Co., 1903.
Wagner, Richard. *Actors and Singers*. Translated by William Ashton Ellis. London: Kegen Paul, Trench, Trübner, & Co., 1896.
Wawra de Fernsee, Heinrich. *Les Broméliacées découvertes pendant les voyages des princes Auguste et Ferdinand de Saxe-Cobourg*. Liège: C. Anoot-Braeckman, 1880.
Weber, Eugen. *France, Fin de Siècle*. Cambridge and London: Harvard University Press/Belknap, 1986.
Weber, William, ed. *The Musician as Entrepreneur 1700–1914*. Bloomington: Indiana University Press, 2004.
Wilde, Oscar. *The Picture of Dorian Gray*. Edited by Robert Mighal. London: Penguin Classics, 2006 [1891].
———. *Salomé, drame en un acte*. Paris: G. Crès, 1922 [1893].
Willy (pseud. Henry Gauthier-Villars). *Soirées perdues*. Paris: Tresse & Stock, 1894.
Wilson, Barbara Lister (Lady Wilson). *The House of Memories*. London: William Heinemann, 1929.
Wolff, Jetta Sophia. *Historic Paris*. Paris: John Lane, 1923.
Wright, Leslie A. *Bizet Before "Carmen."* Ph.D. dissertation. Ann Arbor: University of Michigan, 1985.
X., Dr. Jacobus (pseud.). *Le Marquis de Sade et son œuvre devant la science médicale et la littérature moderne*. Paris: Charles Carrington, 1901.
Zed (pseud. Comte Albert de Maugny). *Le Demi-monde sous le Second Empire: souvenirs d'un sybarite*. Paris: E. Kolb, 1892.
———. *La Grande Vie de Paris*. Paris: E. Kolb, 1889.
———. *Les Inconvenances sociales: fragments du journal d'un vieux garçon*. Paris: E. Kolb, 1891.
———. *Parisiens et Parisiennes en déshabillé*. Paris: E. Kolb, 1889.
———. *La Société parisienne*. Paris: Librairie Illustrée, 1891.

B · *Primary and Secondary Sources—Articles*

1. Attributed Articles

A.B. (pseud.). "Marah." *National Review* 19 (March–August 1892): 200–211.
A. de B. (pseud.). "Par çi, par là." *Le Voleur illustré* (June 11, 1885): 382–83.
Alcanter et Saint-Jean (pseud. Marcel Bernhardt). "Les Vendredis d'Aristide." *Le Nouvel Écho* 3 (February 1, 1892): 78–80.
Allain, Paul. "En Passant: La Place à table." *Le Radical* (November 9, 1922): 1.
An American (pseud.). "To Blow Up a Princess: Dynamite Bombs Explode in the Doorway of the Princesse de Sagan." *Baltimore American* (March 1, 1892): 1.
A.M.M. (pseud.). "Gossip of the French Capital." *New York Dramatic Mirror* (May 2, 1896): 18.
Amodio, Marquis de. "Le Château de Verteuil." *Mémoires de la Société Archéologique et Historique de la Charente* (1958).
Archiduc (pseud.). "La Journée mondaine." *Le Matin* (August 18, 1898): 2.
d'Arenberg, Prince Auguste. "Notice sur le duc d'Aumale." In *Annales de l'Académie des Beaux-Arts*. Paris: Firmin-Didot, 1898.
Asmodée (pseud. Baron de Vaux). "Notes mondaines." *Gil Blas* (June 5, 1885).
Associated Press Dispatches. "Panic-Stricken Paris: Consternation Reigning at the French Capital." *Los Angeles Herald* (April 7, 1892): 2.
Barrès, Maurice. "The Panama Scandal." *Cosmopolitan* 17 (May–October 1894): 203–10.
Bataille, Albert. "Gazette des Tribunaux." *Le Figaro* (April 29, 1880).
———. "Gazette des Tribunaux." *Le Figaro* (March 13, 1884).
Baudouin. "Tribunal de Commerce: Faillites." *Gazette des tribunaux: journal de jurisprudence et de débats judiciaires* (January 24, 1857): 38.
Benjamin, Walter. "Pariser Köpfe." In *Walter Benjamin Passagen: Schriften zur französische Literatur*. Edited by Gérard Raulet. Frankfurt: Suhrkamps, 2007.
Bernard, Alice. "Le Grand Monde parisien à l'épreuve de la guerre." *XXᵉ siècle* 99 (July–September 2008): 13–32.
Beyens, Baron de. "L'Avenir des petits états: la Bulgarie." *La Revue des deux mondes* 44 (April 1918): 874–94.
Bleuzet, Ludivine. "Mystères et code secret au château de Condé." *L'Union* (July 23, 2004): 7.
Blondeau, Amédée. "L'Empoisonneuse d'Aïn-Fezza: Mme Weiss." *Le Rappel* (May 30, 1890): 1.
Blum, Ernest. "Un krach princier." *Le Rappel* (August 10, 1891).

Borel d'Hauterive, A. "Musée de Versailles: Notice sur les cinq salles des Croisades et sur les person-nages dont les noms et les armes y figurent." *Annuaire historique pour la Société de l'Histoire de France* 9 (1845): 127–95.

Bras, Jean-Yves. "Qui était Éraïm Miriam Delaborde?" *Bulletin de la Société Alkan* 4 (March 1987): 3–6.

Brionne (pseud.). "Carnet mondain." *Gil Blas* (June 7, 1897).

Brooks, Peter. "Persons and Optics." *Arcade* (March 16, 2015).

Brunetière, Ferdinand. "La Tragédie de Racine." *La Revue des deux mondes* 62 (1884): 213–24.

Brusquet (pseud.). "Le Régime du sabre." *Le Triboulet* (May 23, 1880): 5.

Calmette, Gaston. "Au jour le jour: le château de Bois-Boudran." *Le Figaro* (November 22, 1891): 1.

———. "Les Compositeurs français joués en France." *Le Figaro* (April 10, 1890): 1–2.

Caraman-Chimay, Princesse Alexandra de Riquet de. "Généalogie de Riquet." Presented by "les Amis de Riquet," June 13–14, 2009.

Cassagnac, Paul de. "Les Élections." *L'Express du Midi* (May 25, 1898): 1.

Castelbajac, Gaston, Marquis de. "La Chasse à tir." In *Le Protocole mondain*. Edited by André de Fouquières. Paris: Levallois-Perret, n.d., 359–64.

Catani, Damian. "Notions of Evil in Baudelaire." *Modern Language Review* 102, no. 4, 990–1007.

Chaline, Jean-Pierre. "La Sociabilité mondaine au XIXᵉ siècle." In *Élites et sociabilité*. Edited by Fumaroli, Broglie, and Chaline, op. cit.

Charle, Christophe. "Noblesses et élites en France au début du XXe siècle." In *Les Noblesses europé-ennes au XIXᵉ siècle: Actes du colloque organisé par l'École Française de Rome et l'Université de Milan, Milan-Rome, 21–23 novembre 1985*. Milan: EFR, 1988.

Chéron, Raoul. "Nécrologie: M. Charles Haas." *Le Gaulois* (July 16, 1902): 2.

Child, Theodore. "Characteristic Parisian Cafés." *Harper's New Monthly Magazine* 77 (April 1889).

———. "Literary Paris." *Harper's New Monthly Magazine* 35 (August 1892): 337–39.

———. "Society in Paris." *The Fortnightly Review* 39 (January–June 1886): 480–99.

Colas, Damien. "Halévy and His Contribution to the Evolution of the Orchestra." In *The Impact of Composers and Works on the Orchestra: Case Studies*. Edited by Niels Martin Jensen and Franco Piperno. Berlin: Berliner Wissenschafts Verlag, 2007, 143–84.

Consuelo (pseud.). "Chronique parisienne." *La Grande Dame* 28 (April 1895).

Corpechot, Lucien. "Les Lettres françaises: Le Comte Robert de Montesquiou." *La Revue de France* 2, no. 23 (February 15, 1922).

Cotta, Laurent. "Paul César Helleu: Représenter l'intime." In *La Mode retrouvée*. Edited by Olivier Saillard and Valerie Steele. Paris: Paris Musées, 2015.

D. (pseud.). "Échos de Paris." *Le Figaro* (March 29, 1884).

Dalq, Louise. "Lord Lytton: Philosophe et poète." *Le Figaro: supplément littéraire* (November 12, 1887): 1–2.

Dame Pluche (pseud.). "Chronique." *La Gazette des Femmes* (June 10, 1884).

Dangeau, Marquise de (pseud.). "Chronique mondaine." *La Mode de style* (February 11, 1891): 51–54; and (July 1, 1891): 208–11.

Dantin (pseud.). "Mondanités: Chronique de l'élégance." *Le Gaulois* (June 12, 1896).

———. "Mondanités: Chronique de l'élégance." *Le Gaulois* (December 17, 1896).

Darcours, Charles (pseud. Charles Réty). "Notes de musique à l'Exposition." *Le Figaro* (October 2, 1889).

Demailly, Charles. "Bizet." *Le Gaulois* (December 11, 1890).

Descaves, Lucien. "Opinions et souvenirs: Fernand Vandérem, *Gens de qualité*." *Le Journal* (February 6, 1938).

Le Diable Boiteux (pseud. Baron de Vaux). "Échos." *Gil Blas* (December 7, 1894).

———. "Nouvelles et échos." *Gil Blas* (January 31, 1880); (April 5, 1881); (May 15, 1883); (Novem-ber 3, 1883); (June 2, 1884); (June 12, 1884); (June 13, 1884); (June 20, 1884); (September 2, 1884); (September 20, 1884); (December 22, 1884); (April 13, 1885); (May 10, 1885); (June 4, 1885); (August 7, 1885); (June 13, 1889); (June 7, 1891); (March 15, 1892); (June 13, 1892); (July 2, 1892); (June 12, 1893); (July 4, 1893); (January 23, 1894); and (May 12, 1894).

Un Diplomate (pseud.). "La Grande-Duchesse Wladimir." *La Grande Dame* 1 (1893): 192–98.

Dives, Auguste (pseud.). "Mondanités. *Le Gaulois* (June 12, 1889).

Dominique, Pierre. "Sous le règne de l'étiquette." *Le Crapouillot: Les Bonnes Manières* 19 (1952): 19–25.

Un Domino (pseud. Arthur Meyer). "Échos de Paris." *Le Gaulois* (May 26, 1880); (May 10, 1885); (May 29, 1885); (June 3, 1885); (April 28, 1888); (April 29, 1888); (February 1, 1889); (April 1, 1889); (March 28, 1890); (May 12, 1890); (July 21, 1890); (December 24, 1890); (February 20, 1891); (March 2, 1892); and (December 17, 1896).

————. "Les Fidèles." *Le Gaulois* (August 24, 1883).

Don Caprice (pseud.). "Nouvelles: Rome." *Gil Blas* (October 31, 1891).

Dubois, Philippe. "L'Affaire Ravachol-Koenigstein." *L'Intransigeant* (April 8, 1892): 1–2.

Durel, Pétrus. "Les Faux-Monnayeurs." *La Nouvelle Revue* 19 (November–December 1902): 410–17.

E. C. (pseud.). *"Les Rimes de François Pétrarque,* traduction nouvelle par Francisque Reynard." *Le Livre* (1883): 504.

Elfenbein, Andrew. "The Shady Side of the Sword: Bulwer-Lytton, Disraeli, and Byron's Homosexuality." In *Byron.* Edited by Jane Stabler. New York and London: Routledge, 2014.

Éluard, Paul. "L'Intelligence révolutionnaire du Marquis de Sade." *Clarté* 6 (February 1927).

Étincelle (pseud. Vicomtesse de Peyronny). "Carnet d'un mondain." *Le Figaro* (April 29, 1881); (May 3, 1881); (June 25, 1883); (May 28, 1885); (June 5, 1885); (June 10, 1885); (June 5, 1891); and (November 22, 1891).

————. "Les Grandes Réceptions: Le Bal Blanc de la Princesse de Léon." *Le Figaro* (April 11, 1891).

————. "Les Maréchales de la mode." *Le Figaro* (September 1, 1884).

————. "Mondains et mondaines." *Le Monde illustré* (January 10, 1891).

————. "Les Parisiennes au Léman." *La Grande Dame* 1 (1893): 5–7.

————. "Tableaux mondains." *Le Figaro* (May 28, 1884).

Feather (pseud.). "Les Adieux." *L'Art et la Mode* 29 (June 19, 1886).

Ferrari, M. "Au jour le jour." *Le Figaro* (May 23, 1895): 1.

————. "Le Monde et la ville." *Le Figaro* (April 25, 1899): 2.

Fidus (pseud. Arthur Meyer). "Le Château de Frohsdorf." *Le Gaulois* (July 5, 1883): 1.

————. "Le Jour de l'An à Göritz." *Le Gaulois* (January 2, 1881): 1–2.

Flament, Albert. "Je débute!" *Le Figaro* (May 13, 1923): 1.

Flers, Robert de. "Théâtre d'amour: Georges de Porto-Riche." *La Presse* (July 13, 1898): 4.

Fouquières, André de. "Une saison de printemps commence." *La Semaine à Paris* (May 8, 1936): 4.

Fourcaud (pseud.). *"Carmen." Le Gaulois* (December 12, 1890): 1.

France, Alphonse. "Courrier des théâtres: Le Dîner de la Société des Auteurs Dramatiques." *Le Figaro* (May 26, 1905): 5.

Friedrichs, Otto. "Desinit in Piscem." *La Légitimité* 19 (May 16, 1886): 289–93.

Frimousse (pseud.). "La Soirée parisienne: article de toilettes." *Le Gaulois* (December 11, 1890).

————. "La Soirée parisienne: *Le Cœur de Paris." Le Gaulois* (May 22, 1887).

————. "La Soirée parisienne: la représentation de gala." *Le Gaulois* (December 12, 1890).

Frivoline (pseud.). "Art et chiffons." *L'Art et la Mode* 29 (June 20, 1885).

Galérant, Germain. "Psychopathologie de Maupassant." *Actes de la Société Française d'Histoire de la Médecine* (February 2, 1991).

Ganderax, Louis. "Les Petits Souliers: conte de Noël." *La Revue des deux mondes* 109 (January 1, 1892).

Gant de Saxe (pseud. M. Ferrari). "Mondanités: A l'hôtel de Sagan." *Le Gaulois* (June 23, 1891).

————. "Mondanités: Bulletin." *Le Gaulois* (May 5, 1894).

————. "Mondanités: Réceptions." *Le Gaulois* (June 7, 1891); (February 2, 1893); (June 22, 1893); (August 30, 1893); and (January 20, 1894).

————. "Mondanités: Tout au papier." *Le Gaulois* (March 2, 1892).

Gay, Robert Coleman, Jr. "Porto-Riche: Pathologist of Love." *Texas Review* 6, no. 4 (July 1921): 337–51.

Gérard, Marc. "Bonheur manqué." *Le Gaulois* (July 14, 1889): 2.

————. "Carnet de mariage." *Le Gaulois* (September 27, 1887); (January 17, 1889); (January 24, 1889); and (July 26, 1889).

————. "Carnet mondain." *Le Gaulois* (November 23, 1880); (May 9, 1888); (June 11, 1889); (May 28, 1890); and (June 7, 1890).

————. "La Journée du Grand-Duc." *Le Gaulois* (April 25, 1888).

Gérault-Richard (pseud.). "Le Scandale Greffulhe: Achat d'une circonscription." *Le Briard* (March 13, 1889).

Gérôme, Le Père (pseud. A. Vernant). "Greffulhe la Sabine." *Le Briard* (November 4, 1903).

————. "Notes sur la Grande Propriété: Chez M. le Comte Greffulhe." *Le Briard* (October 21, 22, and 25, 1892).

Godin, Romaric. "Les Frères Pereire, le salut par le credit." *La Tribune* (December 26, 2011).

Gopnik, Adam. "The Life of the Party." Review of *The Politics of Pleasure: A Portrait of Benjamin Disraeli,* by William Kuhn. *New Yorker* (July 3, 2006).

Goubaut, Christian. "Maupassant et le journalisme." *Précis analytique de l'Académie des Sciences, Belles-Lettres et Arts de Rouen* (February 6, 1993): 187–208.

Goujon, Bertrand. "Un lignage aristocrtique d'envergure internationale dans l'Europe du XIXe siècle: La Maison d'Arenberg." *Revue belge de Philologie et d'Histoire,* 88 (2010): 497–518.

Gourdon de Genouillac (pseud.). "Gazette Héraldique." *L'Art et la mode* 20 (April 15, 1887).

Gratin (pseud.). "Femmes et fleurs." *Le Gaulois* (August 30, 1885).

Le Greffier (pseud.). "Carnet judiciaire." *Gil Blas* (July 30, 1892).

Gregh, Fernand. "Hommage à Porto-Riche." *Les Nouvelles littéraires* (September 13, 1930).

Guimard, René. "Les Borghèse." *Gil Blas* (August 30, 1891): 1–2.

Guiral, Pierre. "Anatole Prévost-Paradol." In *Entre le théâtre et l'histoire*. Edited by Henri Loyrette. Paris: Fayard, 1996.

———. "Les Écrivains français et la notion de la décadence." *Romantisme* 13, no. 32 (1983): 9–22.

Guyot-Daubès. "Les Phoques savants." *La Nature: Revue des sciences et de leurs applications aux arts* 647 (October 24, 1885): 321–23.

H.N. "Les Attentats à la dynamite." *L'Intransigeant* (April 8, 1892): 2.

Halévy, Jean-Pierre. "Ludovic Halévy par lui-même." In *Entre le théâtre et l'histoire: La Famille Halévy, 1760–1960*. Edited by Henri Loyrette. Paris: Fayard, 1996.

Haliou, Bruno. "Comment la syphilis emporta Maupassant." *La Revue du practicien* 53 (2003): 1386–89.

Harding, James S. "Art Notes from Paris." *Art Amateur* 17, no. 2 (July 1887): 31.

Heugel, Jacques. "Hortense Schneider." *Le Ménestrel* (May 14, 1920): 208.

Hubert, Eugène. "La Fête de l'Opéra." *Gil Blas* (April 8, 1883): 3–4.

Hy de Hem (pseud. Henri de Montaut). "Le Bal de Mme la Princesse de Sagan." *L'Art et la Mode* 28 (June 13, 1885): 6–7.

———. "La Fête villageoise de Mme la Princesse de Sagan." *L'Art et la Mode* 30 (June 21, 1884): 8–9.

Irvine, William D. "French Royalists and Boulangism." *French Historical Studies* 15, no. 3 (Spring 1988): 395–406.

Jean-Jacques (pseud.). "Nouvelles." *Gil Blas* (January 25, 1895).

Jung, Sir Salar. "An Indian Mayor of the Palace." *Today* 1 (July 1883): 342–52.

Junior, Jehu (pseud. Thomas Gibson Bowls). "Statesman: Lord Lytton." *Vanity Fair* 219 (March 18, 1876): 223.

Kindleberger, Charles P. "Origins of United States Direct Investment in France." MIT Department of Economics. Working Paper 105 (March 1973).

L.D. (pseud.). "Le Charmant chroniqueur Robert Dreyfus." *La Tribune juive Strasbourg-Paris* 28 (1939): 433–34.

Lacambre, Geneviève. "De la maison au musée" and "Des œuvres pour le musée." In *La Maison-musée de Gustave Moreau*. Edited by Marie-Cécile Forest. Paris: Somogy, 2014, 25–68.

Lambert, Louis. "Autour de la séance." *Le Gaulois* (November 16, 1889): 2.

Landauro, Inti. "Louvre to Restore da Vinci's *John the Baptist*." *Wall Street Journal* (January 13, 2016).

Largillière (pseud.). "La Société de Paris: La Duchesse de Talleyrand et Sagan." *Gil Blas* (May 13, 1903).

Lauzun (pseud.). "Chronique mondaine." *L'Art et la Mode* 8 (1883); 16 (1883); and 24 (1883).

Lavedan, Henri. "Paul Hervieu." *Le Figaro* (September 26, 1895): 1.

———. "Un raffiné: Georges de Porto-Riche." *Le Journal* (May 16, 1894): 1.

Lazarille (pseud. Fernand Bourgeat). "Échos de partout." *La Semaine littéraire* 7 (September 30, 1899): 464.

Lemaître, Jules. "*La Chance de Françoise* de Georges de Porto-Riche." *La Revue illustrée* (January 1, 1889): 1.

———. "Le Théâtre à Paris." *Cosmopolis* 1 (January 1896): 196–208.

Letorière, Vicomte Georges de (pseud.). "Le Bal costumé de la Princesse de Sagan." *Le Monde illustré* (June 19, 1880).

Magali (pseud.). "Le Monde et la mode." *La Vie élégante* 2 (July 15, 1882).

Maizeroy, René. "Guy de Maupassant à Sartrouville." *Le Gaulois* (July 3, 1912): 1.

Marciat, Dr. "Le Marquis de Sade et le sadisme." In *Vacher l'éventreur et les crimes sadiques*. Edited by A. Lacassagne. Paris: Masson, 1899, 185–237.

Masck (pseud.). "En redingote noire." *Le Gaulois* (May 24, 1884).

Le Masque de Fer (pseud. Émile Blavet). "Échos de Paris." *Le Figaro* (March 29, 1884); (September 1, 1884); (September 26, 1884); (November 29, 1884); (May 23, 1887); (September 27, 1887); (January 30, 1891); (November 22, 1891); (May 30, 1894); and (December 12, 1897).

Massard, Émile. "Jeanne Weiss." *La Presse* (May 30, 1891): 1.

Massolleau, Louis. "Henri Meilhac." *Le Rappel* (July 9, 1897).

McCallum, Stephanie. "Alkan: Enigma or Schizophrenia?" *Alkan Society Bulletin* 75 (April 2007): 2–10.

Meyer, Henri. "Les Funérailles de Lord Lytton." *Le Journal illustré* (December 13, 1891).

Monselet, Charles. "Théâtres." *Le Monde illustré* (July 5, 1873): 11.

Un Monsieur de l'Orchestre (pseud. Émile Blavet). "La Soirée théâtrale." *Le Figaro* (December 12, 1890): 2; and (April 26, 1891): 2.

Montesquiou-Fezensac, Comte Robert de. "Japonais d'Europe." *Le Gaulois* (March 9, 1897).

Montferrier, H. G. "Étranger: Le Prince de Saxe-Cobourg en Bulgarie." *Le Journal des débats* (September 21, 1887).

Montjoye (pseud.). "Chronique mondaine." *L'Art et la Mode* 20 (April 12, 1884); 22 (April 26, 1884); 27 (May 30, 1884); 28 (June 7, 1884); 42 (September 13, 1884); 43 (September 20, 1884); 48 (October 25, 1884); 23 (May 9, 1885); 25 (May 23, 1885); 27 (June 6, 1885); 28 (June 13, 1885); 30 (June 27, 1885); 25 (May 22, 1886); 28 (June 13, 1886); 8 (January 7, 1887); 22 (April 29, 1887); 8 (January 20, 1888); 29 (June 15, 1888); and 8 (June 26, 1889).

de Mun, Comte Albert. "Les Dernières Heures du drapeau blanc." *La Revue hebdomadaire* 46 (November 13, 1909): 141–63.

Nekludoff, A. "Auprès de Ferdinand de Bulgarie." *La Revue des deux mondes* 54 (November–December 1919): 547–76.

Nicault, Catherine. "Comment 'en être'? Les Juifs et la haute société dans la seconde moitié du XIXe siècle." *Archives juives: revue d'histoire des Juifs de France* 42 (2009): 8–32.

Notre envoyé spécial (pseud.). "L'Empoisonneuse d'Aïn-Fezza." *Le Petit Parisien* (May 31, 1891): 1–2.

Our Own Reporter (pseud.). "A Visit to Wappingers Falls." *Poughkeepsie Eagle* (June 12, 1891): 1.

The Paris Galignani's Messenger (pseud.). "The Fate of the Hôtel de Chimay." *New York Times* (July 4, 1884).

Parisis (pseud. Émile Blavet). "L'Hôtel de Chimay." *Le Figaro* (June 14, 1884).

———. "La Vie parisienne: chez Arsène Houssaye." *Le Figaro* (March 29, 1884).

———. "La Vie parisienne: la chasse à courre." *Le Figaro* (September 26, 1884).

———. "La Vie parisienne: le bal Sagan." *Le Figaro* (June 5, 1885).

———. "La Vie parisienne: le matin au Bois." *Le Figaro* (October 29, 1884).

Pas Perdus (pseud.). "La Chambre." *Le Figaro* (December 24, 1889).

Le Passant (pseud. Ernst d'Hervilly). "Les On-Dit." *Le Rappel* (June 11, 1884); and (July 9, 1897).

Paulhan, Claire. "*La Revue blanche:* Tout l'esprit d'une époque." *Le Monde: le Monde des livres* (December 6, 2007).

Pharaon, Florian (pseud.). "La Vie en plein air." *Le Figaro* (June 18, 1884).

Ponchon, Raoul. "Gazette rimée: le mot 'chic.'" *Le Journal* (April 16, 1902).

Pringué, Gabriel-Louis. "La Haute Société de la Belle Époque." *Le Crapouillot: La Belle Époque* 29 (1955): 2–7.

Prudent, Louis (pseud.). "A la rue de Sèze: fête de charité." *Le Gaulois* (May 1, 1885).

———. "Ouverture de l'Exposition Canine." *Le Gaulois* (May 29, 1884).

Régamey, Félix de. "La Guerre de demain." *Le Figaro-graphic* (January 25, 1892).

Reinhardt, Rolf. "The French Revolution as a European Media Event." *EGO: European History Online* (August 27, 2012).

Renneville, Vicomtesse de. "Chronique de l'élégance." *La Nouvelle Revue* 28 (May–June 1884); and 34 (May–June 1885).

Rochefort, Henri. "Les Policiers possibilistes." *L'Intransigeant* (August 8, 1892): 1.

Rod, Édouard. "L'Esprit littéraire." *Cosmopolis* 2 (February 1896): 455–56.

Rodays, Fernand de. "Gazette des Tribunaux." *Le Figaro* (March 12, 1877): 2; and (December 29, 1877): 2.

Roma, A. I. "La Question juive." *La Bastille: journal anti-maçonnique* 530 (March 21, 1914): 5–6.

Royer-Saint-Micaud, Vicomte André de. "Avons-nous une noblesse française?" *La Revue des revues* (October 1898): 1–20.

De la Rue (pseud.). "Quelques profils de chasseurs: Le Comte Greffulhe." *Le Figaro: supplément littéraire du dimanche* (September 5, 1880): 2.

Sadinet, Abbé (pseud.). "Le Bal des bêtes." *La Vie moderne* 24 (June 13, 1885): 392–93.

Saint-Cère, Jacques (pseud. Armand Rosenthal). "Une heure chez le Comte Robert de Montesquiou." *La Revue illustrée* (June 15, 1894): 117–24.

———. "Les Nouveaux élus." *Le Figaro* (September 13, 1893).

Saint-Pierre, B. de (pseud.). "Soirée mondaine." *Gil Blas* (June 12, 1893).

Saint-Réal (pseud.). "La détente mondaine." *Le Gaulois* (April 6, 1892).

———. "La mort de Lord Lytton." *Le Gaulois* (November 25, 1891).

Santillane (pseud.). "Courrier de Paris." *Gil Blas* (November 24, 1883).

Sarah-Bernhardt, Lysiane (pseud.). "Les Courses." In *Le Protocole mondain.* Edited by André de Fouquières. Paris: Levallois, n.d.

Scott (pseud.). "Les Obsèques de Lord Lytton." *Le Monde illustré* (December 5, 1891).

Scrutator (pseud.). "Dîners à la Russe." *Truth* (July 31, 1879).

———. "Notes from Paris: Intermarriage and Degeneracy." *Truth* (August 14, 1902).

Smith, Paul. "Théâtre du Grand Opéra: *Le Juif-Errant*." *Revue et gazette musicale de Paris* 17 (April 25, 1852): 137–40.

Stead, Évanghélia. "A Flurry of Images and Its Unfurling through *La Revue illustrée*." *Studi de Memofonte* 13 (2014): 3–28.

Straus, Émile. "Golo s'amuse (Conte chagrin)." *Le Nouvel Écho* 29 (June 15, 1892): 356–60.

———. "Le Petit Pierrot (Conte chagrin)." *Le Nouvel Écho* 8 (April 15, 1892): 230–33.

———. "Villa à vendre (Conte chagrin)." *Le Nouvel Écho* 10 (May 15, 1892): 295–304.

Surmay, A. "Exposition de peinture: Salon de 1878." *Musée des familles: lectures du soir* 45 (September 1878): 258.

Suzuki, Junji. "Le jardinier japonais de Robert de Montesquiou: ses évocations dans les milieux littéraires." *Cahiers Edmond et Jules de Goncourt* 118 (2011): 103–12.

Tom (pseud.). "La Grande Villégiature." *L'Illustration* 92 (July 21, 1888).

Tout-Paris (pseud.).* "A l'épatant." *Le Gaulois* (June 15, 1889).

———. "Feuilles d'hiver." *Le Gaulois* (November 16, 1890).

———. "Le Monde et la ville." *Le Gaulois* (June 13, 1885).

———. "Pour les enfants délaissés." *Le Gaulois* (March 17, 1889).

de Traz, Robert. "Chroniques." *La Revue hebdomadaire* 2, no. 7 (February 12, 1938).

Trégastels, Comtesse de (pseud.). "Chronique de la vie mondaine." *La Diplomatie* 1 (May 5, 1897): 17–19.

de V., A. (pseud.). "Mœurs contemporaines: la société à Paris." *La Revue britannique* (1886): 67–92.

de V . . . (pseud.). "Nos grandes mondaines: la Princesse de Sagan." *La Revue mondaine illustrée* (February 10, 1893).

Vassili, Comte Paul (pseud. Juliette Adam). "La Société étrangère à Paris." *La Nouvelle Revue* 70 (May–June 1891).

de Vaux, Baron. "Concours hippique." *Gil Blas* (April 13, 1885).

Vérissey, Comtesse de. "Chronique mondaine." *La Mode de style* (June 3, 1891) and (July 1, 1891).

A Veteran Diplomat (pseud.). "The Passing of Talleyrand, *le Roi du Chic:* A Chapter in the Fall of Past Grandeur." *New York Times* (February 27, 1910).

Veuillot, Eugène. "La Mort du Comte de Chambord." *L'Univers* 25 (August 1883).

Vicomte Rolph (pseud.). "Échos du High-Life." *Le Triboulet* (February 9, 1879).

———. "Échos du High-Life." *Le Triboulet* (February 16, 1879).

———. "Échos du High-Life." *Le Triboulet* (August 17, 1879).

Victor-Meunier, Lucien. "A la Chambre." *Le Rappel* (December 25, 1889).

Violetta (pseud. Comtesse Alice de Laincel). "Sous le masque." *Le Gaulois* (April 5, 1882); (May 27, 1882); and (June 6, 1882).

Vogüé, Vicomte Eugène-Melchior de. "L'histoire à Versailles." *La Revue des deux mondes* 6 (1901): 193–209.

W. (pseud.). "Mondanités." *Le Gaulois* (June 27, 1891).

Wailly, Georges de. "La Vénérie moderne." *La Nouvelle Revue* 80 (January–February 1893).

X. (pseud.). "Choses et autres." *La Vie parisienne* (February 5, 1870); (November 13, 1875); and (June 7, 1890).

Xau, Bernard. "Derniers Échos de Göritz." *Gil Blas* (September 9, 1883).

Yon, Jean-Claude. "Le Théâtre de Meilhac et Halévy: satire et indulgence." In *Entre le théâtre et l'histoire*. Edited by Henri Loyrette. Paris: Fayard, 1996.

Zola, Émile. "Types de femmes en France." *Le Messager de l'Europe* (June 1878).

2. Unattributed Articles

"Les Abus de la Grande Propriété." *Le Briard* (January 23, 1897): 1–2.

"Appel pour la fondation de la Société des Études Juives." *La Revue des études juives* 1 (1880): 161–62.

"Au Village." *Le Gaulois* (June 11, 1884).

"Avis mondains." *Le Figaro* (April 8, 1883); (April 25, 1883); (May 23, 1883); (August 19, 1884); and (November 19, 1888).

"Bankrupts." *Solicitor's Journal & Reporter* (March 14, 1857): 281.

---

* Before Proust took it as his alias in 1893–1894, "Tout-Paris" designated another columnist for *Le Gaulois*. The reader will note that the earliest of the articles by this "Tout-Paris" listed here appeared in 1885, shortly before Proust's fourteenth birthday.

"Bloc-notes parisien." *Le Gaulois* (May 20, 1884); (May 26, 1884); (June 11, 1884); and (June 14, 1885).

"Les Borghèse." *Le Gaulois* (January 28, 1880).

"Ça manque de pigeons!" *La Lanterne* (August 3, 1878): 1.

"À la Chambre: clôture de la session." *La Lanterne* (December 25, 1889).

"Chambre des Députés: la séance." *Le Temps* (December 25, 1889).

"Chez Greffulhe et cie." *Le Briard* 75 (September 30, 1908).

"Chronique électorale: conscience et liberté." *La Croix* (August 11, 1893).

"Chronique électorale: dans les departments—Melun." *Le Rappel* (August 12, 1893).

"Count Albert de Mun." *Public Opinion* 48 (November 13, 1885).

"Dans les départements." *Le Rappel* (August 12, 1893).

"Deuil: le Comte Robert de Fitz-James." *Le Figaro* (September 26, 1900).

"Les Distractions de Mme Bizet." *Le Temps* (June 10, 1885).

"Échos de l'étranger." *Le Gaulois* (August 29, 1887); and (May 20, 1885).

"L'Election Greffulhe: discours de M. Camille Pelletan." *La Justice* (December 25, 1889): 1–3.

"L'Expédition Borghèse." *L'Exploration.* 17 (1884): 228–29.

"L'Exposition de Marie Antoinette et son temps." *La Chronique des arts et de la curiosité* (April 14, 1894): 117–18.

"Fin de session." *Le Petit Journal* (December 25, 1889).

"France." *Papers Relating to the Foreign Relations of the United States, for the Year 1887.* Washington, DC: Government Printing Office, 1888, 303–55.

"French Topics of the Day: Two Charitable Fêtes." *New York Times* (May 2, 1885).

"Les Funérailles de Lord Lytton." *Le Petit Express* (November 29, 1891).

"G. Aberigh-Mackay's *Twenty-One Days in India.*" In *Essays on Anglo-Indian Literature.* Edited by Sujit Bose. New Delhi: Northern Book Center, 2004.

"Gazette des Tribunaux." *Le Figaro* (January 14, 1900): 3.

"Geographical Notes: Italian Explorers in Africa." *Proceedings of the Royal Geographical Society* (September 1880): 317–18.

"Gossip of the French Capital." *New York Dramatic Mirror* (May 2, 1896): 18.

"Greffulhe-Bischoffsheim." *La Lanterne* (January 24, 1890): 1.

"Historic Residences of Paris Now Occupied by Antiquaries." *New York Herald* (January 2, 1910): 11.

"Hommes et choses." *Le Matin* (July 10, 1884): 3; and (July 16, 1893): 2.

"Informations." *Journal officiel de la République française* 18, no. 72 (March 14, 1886): 1235.

"Le Jockey-Club à l'armée." *Le Figaro* (October 25, 1870): 2.

"La Journée parisienne." *Le Gaulois* (January 21, 1880): 2.

"The Late Lord Lytton an Opium-Smoker." *Friend of China* 16, no. 4 (October 1896): 109.

"A Leader of French Fashion." *Searchlight* 25 (January 21, 1905): 27–28.

"Le Livre d'or du *Figaro.*" *Le Figaro* (December 26, 1877): 2.

"Madame de [*sic*] Récamier." Edited by Oscar Wilde. *A Woman's World* 2 (November 1889): 349–52.

"Maître Émile Straus." *Le Gaulois* (June 22, 1889): 2–3.

"Le Mariage d'Étincelle." *La Revue des grands procès contemporains* 14 (1896): 266–348.

"Married to a Marquis." *New York Times* (March 3, 1891).

"Marx et al. v. Strauss [*sic*] et al." *Southern Reporter* 9 (April 1891): 818–20.

"Meetings for Proof of Debts." *Solicitor's Journal & Reporter* (December 25, 1858): 139.

"Mœurs électorales: l'incident Breton-Greffulhe." *Le Rappel* (March 13, 1898): 1–2.

"Mondanités." *Le Petit Parisien* (September 27, 1887): 1.

"Musical Notes." *Monthly Musical Review* 20 (May 1, 1890): 116–17.

"Nos dépêches." *L'Aurore* (November 9, 1897).

"Nouvelles." *Gil Blas* (July 17, 1892).

"Nouvelles et faits: Seine-et-Marne." *Le Journal du Loiret* (November 24, 1891).

"Obituary: The Earl of Lytton." *Annual Register and Review of Public Events at Home and Abroad* (November 1891): 197–98.

"Opportuno-Réactionnaires." *La Lanterne* (December 28, 1889): 1.

"Owen Meredith." *Illustrated American* (December 12, 1891): 162–65.

"Paul Bourget in New York." *Pittsburgh Press* (August 21, 1893): 2.

"Personal Intelligence." *New York Herald* (March 28, 1887).

"Personalities in Comedies." *New York Times* (May 3, 1896).

"Personals." *Daily Alta California* (June 13, 1887).

"Petites nouvelles." *La Croix* (August 30, 1887).

"Prince de Sagan Suffering from Brain Trouble." *New York Times* (May 26, 1897).

"Propos de coulisses." *Gil Blas* (October 21, 1891).

"Queer Prince de Sagan." *New York Times* (November 3, 1897).
"Report from the Geographical Society of Rome." *Proceedings of the Royal Geographical Society* (December 1881): III–12.
"Rothschild Buys a Raphael." *Chicago Tribune* (October 4, 1891).
"Royalty on Half-Pay." *Switchmen's Journal* 7, no. 8 (December 1892): 597–99.
"La Salle des samedis à l'Opéra-Comique." *Le Figaro* (December 3, 1885): 3.
"Le Salon des Beaux-Arts de 1878." *Gazette des Beaux-Arts* (July 1878).
"Séance du 23 décembre 1889." In *Annales de la Chambre des Députés,* 5e Législature. (Paris: November–December 1889), 649–66.
"La Société Étrangère à Paris: la maison de Caraman-Chimay." *La Nouvelle Revue* (May–June 1891): 692–94.
"Société Médico-Psychologique: le cas du Baron Seillière." *La Petite République française* (June 30, 1887).
"Society." *Lady's Realm* 14 (May–October, 1903): 675–78.
"Le Suicide de Mme Weiss." *L'Avenir de Bel-Abbès* (June 3, 1891): 1–2.
"Suite de la vérification des pouvoirs: l'élection du Comte Greffulhe dans l'arrondissement de Melun (Seine-et-Marne)." *Le Journal officiel de la République française* (December 23, 1889): 520–28.
"Télégrammes et correspondances: Autriche-Hongrie." *Journal officiel de la République française* (February 16, 1896).
"Things in Paris." *Vanity Fair* 25 (March 26, 1881).
Le Tour du monde: nouveau journal des voyages 40–41 (1881).
"La Traversée de l'Afrique." *Bulletin de la Société Royale Belge de Géographie* 7 (1885).
"La Vente de la collection Émile Strauss [*sic*]." *Le Petit Parisien* (June 5, 1929): 2.

C · Selected Reference Works

1. *Mondain* Paris

Annuaire international des cercles et du sport. Paris: Hinrichsen, 1884.
Briat, Pierre de. *Les Grands Cercles de Paris.* Paris: n.p., 1933.
Le Carnet mondain. Paris: Carnet Historique et Littéraire, 1901–1905.
Kerviler, René Pocard de Cosquer de, Sir Humphrey Davy, and Louis-Marie Chauffier, eds. *Répertoire général de bio-bibliographie bretonne.* Vol. 9. Rennes: Plihon & Hervé, 1897.
Saint-Martin, A. de, ed. *Paris mondain: annuaire du grand monde et de la colonie étrangère.* Paris: n.p., 1894.
Septfontaines (pseud. Comte Ducos). *L'Année mondaine 1889.* Paris: Firmin-Didot, 1889.
Tout-Paris: Annuaire de la société parisienne—noms et adresses, dictionnaire des pseudonymes. Paris: A. La Fare, 1893.
Tully, Baron de. *Annuaire des grands cercles de Paris: Cercle de l'Union, Jockey-Club, Cercle Agricole, Cercle de la rue Royale, Cercle des Chemins de fer, Cercle de l'Union Artistique, Sporting-Club.* Paris: A. Lahure, 1897–1930.
Yriarte, Charles. *Les Cercles de Paris: 1828–1864.* Paris: Dupray de la Mahérie, 1864.

2. Royal and Noble Genealogy*

Almanach de Gotha: Annuaire généalogique, diplomatique et statistique
Annuaire de la noblesse de France
Annuaire de la noblesse de France et des maisons souveraines de l'Europe
Annuaire de la pairie et de la noblesse de France et des maisons souveraines de l'Europe
Annuaire général héraldique
Armorial général, ou registres de la noblesse de France
Armorial universel, précédé d'un traité complet de la science du blason
Bulletin héraldique de France, ou revue historique de la noblesse
Dictionnaire des familles françaises, anciennes ou notables
Dictionnaire des figures héraldiques
Dictionnaire universel de la noblesse de France
La France héraldique
Légendaire de la noblesse française: devises, cris de guerre
Nobiliaire universel, ou recueil général des généalogies

* No publication dates are given for these works as they were regularly updated.

3. Other Reference Works

Annuaire de la Société des Auteurs et Compositeurs Dramatiques. Volume 2. Paris: Commission des Auteurs et Compositeurs Dramatiques, 1885.

Annuaire de la Société des Études Juives. Vol. 3. Paris: A. Durlacher, 1884.

Annuaire des artistes, 2nd ed. Paris: E. Risacher, 1903.

Dictionnaire français: argot. Edited by Aristide Bruant. Paris: Flammarion, 1905.

Dizionario Biografico degli Italiani. Vol. 70. Rome: Treccani, 2008.

The Encyclopaedia Britannica. Vol. 6. London and Edinburgh: Charles and Adam Black, 1902.

Galignani's New Paris Guide. London: Simpkin, Marshall & Co., 1863.

A Handbook for Travellers on the Riviera. London: John Murray, 1896.

Liste des membres de la Société de Géographie, avec la date de leur admission. Paris: Hôtel de la Société, 1885.

Manuel de politesse à l'usage de la jeunesse: savoir-vivre, savoir-parler, savoir-écrire. Paris: Librairie Générale, 1922.

Les Pseudonymes du jour. Edited by Charles Joliet. Paris: E. Dentu, 1884.

Staats-und Adress-Handbuch der Freien Stadt Frankfurt. Vol. 114. Frankfurt: G.-F. Krugs Verlag, 1852.

Sténographie Duployé, ou l'art de suivre avec l'écriture la parole la plus rapide. 25th ed. Paris: Duployé, 1907.

4. Catalogues

A. AUCTION CATALOGUES

The Belle Époque: Fashionable Life in Paris, London, and New York 1870–1914. New York: Stair Galleries, November 10–December 4, 1981.

Catalogue de la bibliothèque de S. E. Don Paolo Borghèse, Prince de Sulmona. Rome: Unione Cooperativa Editrice, 1892.

Catalogue des objets d'art et d'ameublement du palais du Prince Borghèse à Rome. Rome: Palazzo Borghese, March 28–April 9, 1892.

Catalogue on a Selected Portion of the Renowned Collection of Pictures and Drawings Formed by the Comte Greffulhe. London: Sotheby's, June 22, 1937.

Collection de livres anciens et modernes provenant de la famille Greffulhe. Monte Carlo: Sotheby's/Sporting d'Hiver, February 10, 1982.

Collection Émile Straus: Tableaux modernes, aquarelles, pastels, dessins, sculptures, tableaux anciens, terre cuites, meubles et sièges anciens, tapisseries Aubusson. Paris: Galerie Georges Petit, June 1–2, 1929.

Collection Greffulhe: Tableaux anciens, mobilier, objets d'art, tapisseries. Paris: Drouot, March 6, 2000.

Manuscrits et autographes. Paris: Ader, June 27, 2013.

Manuscrits, photographies, livres anciens et modernes. Paris: Tajan/Drouot, June 11, 2014.

Précieux livres anciens à figures; Neuf lettres inédites de Marcel Proust à la Comtesse Greffulhe. Paris: Drouot, November 8, 1991.

A Selected Portion of the Renowned Collection of Pictures and Drawings Formed by the Comte Greffulhe. London: Sotheby's, July 22, 1937.

Souvenirs historiques: Archives et collections de la Princesse Marie d'Orléans. Edited by Olivier Coutau-Bégarie. Paris: Drouot, April 26–28, 2014.

B. EXHIBITION CATALOGUES AND CATALOGUES RAISONNÉS

L'Art de notre temps: Gustave Moreau. Edited by Jean Laran. Paris: Librairie Centrale des Beaux-Arts, 1914.

La Belle Époque. Preface by Philippe Julian with illustrations selected by Diana Vreeland. New York: The Metropolitan Museum of Art, 1982.

Catalogue de l'exposition de Marie Antoinette et son temps. Preface by Germain Bapst. Paris: Galerie Sedelmeyer, 1894.

Catalogue des tableaux par Gustave Jacquet. Preface by Comte Robert de Montesquiou-Fezensac. Paris: Galerie Georges-Petit, 1909.

Chantilly: Le Cabinet des livres. Paris: Plon, 1900.

Chantilly: Visite de l'Institut de France. Paris: Plon, 1896.

Degas: A Strange New Beauty. Edited and with an introduction by Jodi Hauptman. New York: MoMA, 2016.

Edgar Degas, Photographer. Edited by Malcolm R. Daniel. New York: Metropolitan Museum of Art, 1998.

Exposition des arts de la femme: Guide-livret illustré. Paris: Warmont, 1892.

Exposition Gustave Moreau. Preface by Comte Robert de Montesquiou-Fezensac. Paris: Galerie Georges-Petit, 1906.

Jewish Women and Their Salons: The Power of Conversation. Edited by Emily D. Bilsky and Emily Braun. New York: The Jewish Museum, 2005.

The Louvre: All the Paintings. Edited by Pomar de Vincent. London: Black Dog & Leventhal, 2011.

Les Lys et la République: Henri, Comte de Chambord (1820–1883). Edited by Luc Forlivesi. Paris: Somogy, 2013.

La Maison-musée de Gustave Moreau. Edited by Marie-Cécile Forest. Paris: Somogy, 2014.

La Mode retrouvée: les robes-trésors de la Comtesse Greffulhe. Edited by Olivier Saillard and Valerie Steele. Paris: Paris Museés, 2015.

Robert de Montesquiou, ou l'art de paraître. Edited by Philippe Thiébaut. Paris: Éditions de la RMN, 1999.

Portraits by Ingres: Images of an Epoch. Edited by Gary Tinterow and Philip Conisbee. New York: Metropolitan Museum of Art/Harry N. Abrams, 1999.

Whistler and Montesquiou: The Butterfly and the Bat. Edited by Edward Munhall. New York and Paris: The Frick Collection and Flammarion, 1995.

D · Selected Periodicals

Annales de la Chambre des Députés: Débats parlementaires
L'Art et la mode
L'Aurore
Le Banquet
Bollettino della Società Geografica Italiana
The Bookman
Le Briard
Bulletin de la Société d'Acclimatation Nationale de France
Bulletin de la Société des Agriculteurs de France
Bulletin de la Société Royale Belge de Géographie
Bulletin de la Société Royale d'Anvers de Géographie
Bulletin des Séances de la Société Nationale d'Agriculture
Bulletin du Ministère de l'Agriculture
Bulletin héraldique de France, ou revue hebdomadaire
Cosmopolis
Le Crapouillot
La Croix
Daily Alta California
L'Express du Midi
Le Figaro
Le Figaro-Modes
Le Gaulois
La Gazette de France
La Gazette des Beaux-Arts
La Gazette des femmes
La Gazette des tribunaux
Gil Blas
La Grande Dame
L'Illustration
L'Intransigeant
Le Journal
Le Journal de l'agriculture
Le Journal des débats
Le Journal illustré
Le Journal officiel de la République
La Légitimité: Organe de la survivance du roi-martyr
La Libre Parole
Le Livre
Le Lundi
Le Matin

Le Ménestrel
Le Mensuel
Le Messager de l'Europe
Il Messaggero
Les Missions catholiques
La Mode de style
Le Monde illustré
Le Monde moderne
Musical Standard
The Nation
National Review
New York Herald
New York Times
Le Nouvel Écho
La Nouvelle Revue
La Nouvelle Revue française
Les Nouvelles littéraires
La Patrie
Le Pays
Le Pèlerin
Le Petit Journal
Le Petit Parisien
La Petite République française
La Presse
Le Progrès agricole et viticole
La Quinzaine: revue littéraire, artistique et scientifique
Le Radical
Le Rappel
Le Recueil général des lois et des arrêts
La Revue blanche
La Revue de l'agriculture et de la viticulture
La Revue de Paris
La Revue des deux mondes
La Revue des revues
La Revue de viticulture
La Revue et gazette musicale de Paris
La Revue illustrée
La Revue lilas
La Revue mondiale
La Revue verte
Le Rire
Le Sans-Culotte
Searchlight
The Standard
Le Temps
Le Triboulet
Truth
L'Union
L'Univers
Vanity Fair
La Vie élégante
La Vie moderne
La Vie parisienne
Woman's World
Le XIXe siècle

ILLUSTRATION CREDITS

The illustrations appearing on the following pages are reproductions of items from the author's personal collection of vintage postcards, chocolate cards, calling cards, press clippings, party programs, original photographs and sketches, family papers, and magic-lantern slides:

IN TEXT: 24, 54, 68 *(top)*, 101, 176, 178, 180, 185, 191, 198, 207, 249, 256, 257, 259, 262, 269, 277, 298, 330, 331, 336, 342, 360, 412, 427, 432, 446, 504, 514, 516, 520, 523 *(left)*, 548.
COLOR INSERT: 3 *(bottom)*, 4 *(bottom right)*, 11 *(bottom)*, 13 *(all 4 images)*.

As far as the author has been able to determine, these images are either in the public domain or, regrettably, cannot be traced to a copyright holder. The same holds true for the images reproduced on the following pages:

IN TEXT: 67, 86, 173, 190, 205, 225, 250, 290, 291, 292, 295, 351, 401, 417, 464, 465, 495, 513, 538 *(right)*, 549.
COLOR INSERT: 4 *(bottom)*, 7 *(top)*.

Copyright holders of images uncredited here are asked to contact the publisher so that this information might be included in future editions.

The remaining illustrations are used by permission and courtesy of the following:

IN TEXT:
Archivio Primoli, Fondazione Primoli, Rome, Italy: 158, 170, 195, 372, 434, 451, 463, 493, 549.
Art Resource, New York, NY, USA: 251.
Bibliothèque Nationale de France, Paris, France: 2, 9, 22, 39, 68 *(bottom)*, 88, 95, 105, 135, 146, 150, 157, 160, 162, 167, 204, 270, 271, 282, 293, 298, 303, 312, 387, 390, 485. 511, 523 *(right)*, 535, 547, 550.
Beinecke Rare Book and Manuscript Library, Yale University, New Haven, CT, USA: 564.
Fine Art Photographic Library/Art Resource, New York, NY, USA: 521.
© Gramont family. Image source: Gramont/Greffulhe private archives. Archives Nationales de France, Paris, France: 235, 253, 296, 358, 369, 490 *(both)*
Harvard University Libraries, Harvard University, Cambridge, MA, USA: 565.
HIP/Art Resource, New York, NY, USA: 197 *(left)*
The Jewish Museum, New York, NY, USA/Art Resource, New York, NY, USA: 538 *(left)*.
La Revue Illustrée (June 15, 1894): 556.
La Vie Moderne (June 1885): 24.
Le Gaulois (December 11, 1890): 168.
Mary Evans Picture Library, London, England: 14, 449.
© The Metropolitan Museum of Art. Image source: Art Resource, New York, NY, USA: 164, 279, 307, 311, 389, 425, 435, 526.
© Ministère de la Culture/Médiathèque du Patrimoine, dist. RMN-Grand Palais, Paris, France/Art Resource, New York, NY, USA: 232 *(left)*, 313 *(both)*, 329, 370.
Musée des Beaux-Arts, Nantes, France: 154
© Musée du Louvre, dist. RMN-Grand Palais, Paris, France/Angèle Dequier/Art Resource, New York, NY, USA: 342.
National Portrait Gallery, London, England: 374
New York Public Library, New York, NY, USA: 197 *(right)*, 222, 226, 471.
Österreichische Nationalbibliothek, Vienna, Austria: 103.
© RMN–Grand Palais, Paris, France/Art Resource, New York, NY, USA: 28, 119, 127, 129, 211, 353, 383, 394, 496, 569.
Roger–Viollet, Paris, France: 29, 47, 52, 57, 70, 85, 97, 130, 183, 188, 220, 232 *(right)*, 247, 498, 534.
Rue des Archives, Paris, France: 433.
© Scala/Art Resource, New York, NY, USA: 25, 115.
© Snark/Art Resource, New York, NY, USA: 35.
State Library of Victoria, Melbourne, Australia: 214, 238, 275, 409, 410.

INDEX

Page numbers in *italics* refer to illustrations.

A NOTE ABOUT THE AUTHOR

Caroline Weber is Professor of French and Comparative Literature at Barnard College, Columbia University; she has also taught at the University of Pennsylvania and Princeton. She is the author of *Queen of Fashion: What Marie Antoinette Wore to the Revolution* (2006) and *Terror and Its Discontents: Suspect Words and the French Revolution* (2003). She has written for *The New York Times, The New York Times Book Review,* the *Financial Times,* the *London Review of Books, The Wall Street Journal, Vogue, Town & Country, W,* and *New York* magazine. She lives in New York City and Litchfield County, Connecticut.

A NOTE ON THE TYPE

This book was set in Adobe Garamond. Designed for the Adobe Corporation by Robert Slimbach, the fonts are based on types first cut by Claude Garamond (c. 1480–1561). Garamond was a pupil of Geoffroy Tory and is believed to have followed the Venetian models, although he introduced a number of important differences, and it is to him that we owe the letter we now know as "old style." He gave to his letters a certain elegance and feeling of movement that won their creator an immediate reputation and the patronage of Francis I of France.

Composed by North Market Street Graphics, Lancaster, Pennsylvania

Printed and bound by Berryville Graphics, Berryville, Virginia

Designed by Iris Weinstein